KEY CORNERSTONE	KEY RATIOS	MANAGERIAL FOCUS
Using the Basic Accounting Equation	Current Ratio	Assessing customer creditworthiness
Applying the Conceptual Framework		Recognizing economic events
Applying the Revenue Recognition Principle and Matching Concept		Investment decisions
Performing a Bank Reconciliation		Cash management
Estimating the Allowance for Doubtful Accounts Using the Aging Method	Accounts Receivable Turnover Gross and Net Profit Margins	Accounts receivable management
Applying the Cost of Goods Sold Model	Inventory Turnover	Inventory management
Measuring and Recording the Cost of Property, Plant, and Equipment	Tangible Capital Asset Turnover Return on Assets	Managing production capacity
Calculating Liquidity Ratios	Quick Ratio Accounts Payable Turnover	Corporate capital structure
Recording the Issuance of Bonds at Face Value, at a Premium, and at a Discount	Debt to Equity Times Interest Earned	Financing with long-term debt
Recording the Issuance of Common and Preferred Shares	Earnings per Share Dividend Yield Return on Equity	Corporation ownership
Calculating Net Cash Flow from Operating Activities: Indirect Method		Cash flow management
Effective Interest Rate Method of Bond Amortization		Investment strategy
Interpreting Cross-sectional and Time Series (or Trend) Analysis	Asset Turnover DuPont Analysis	Ratio summary

SECOND CANADIAN EDITION

CORNERSTONES
OF FINANCIAL ACCOUNTING

Jay S. Rich
Illinois State University

Jefferson P. Jones
Auburn University

Maryanne M. Mowen
Oklahoma State University

Don R. Hansen
Oklahoma State University

Donald Jones
University of Windsor

Ralph Tassone
University of Toronto

NELSON

NELSON

Cornerstones of Financial Accounting, Second Canadian Edition

by Jay S. Rich, Jefferson P. Jones, Maryanne M. Mowen, Don R. Hansen, Donald Jones, Ralph Tassone

VP, Product and Partnership Solutions:
Anne Williams

Publisher, Digital and Print Content:
Anne-Marie Taylor

Marketing Manager:
Dave Stratton

Technical Reviewer:
Jay Perry

Content Development Manager:
Maria Chu

Photo and Permissions Researcher:
Carrie McGregor

Senior Production Project Manager:
Imoinda Romain

Production Service:
Cenveo Publisher Services

Copy Editor:
Marcia Gallego

Proofreader:
Sudhir Babu

Indexer:
Bob Saigh

Design Director:
Ken Phipps

Managing Designer:
Franca Amore

Interior Design:
Mike Stratton

Cover Design:
Trinh Truong

Cover Image:
Mina De La O/Getty Images

Interior Cornerstone Icon:
iStock/Thinkstock

Compositor:
Cenveo Publisher Services

Library and Archives Canada Cataloguing in Publication

Rich, Jay S., author
    Cornerstones of financial accounting / Jay S. Rich, Jefferson P. Jones, Maryanne M. Mowen, Don R. Hansen, Donald Jones, Ralph Tassone.—Second Canadian edition.

Includes index.
Issued in print and electronic formats.
ISBN 978-0-17-670712-5 (hardback).—
ISBN 978-0-17-676783-9 (pdf)

    1. Accounting—Textbooks. I. Jones, Jefferson P., author II. Mowen, Maryanne M., author III. Hansen, Don R., author IV. Jones, Donald, author V. Tassone, Ralph, author VI. Title.

HF5636.R53 2016   657
C2016-903250-7
C2016-903251-5

ISBN-13: 978-0-17-670712-5
ISBN-10: 0-17-670712-3

This book is dedicated to our students—past, present, and future—
who are at the heart of our passion for teaching.

—Jay Rich, Jefferson Jones, Maryanne Mowen, and Don Hansen

This book is dedicated to Linda and to our children, Marc,
Michelle, and Daniel, for their support and patience during the
extensive hours required to write this new Canadian edition.
Also, to my colleagues and students at the University
of Windsor, who provided encouragement and
support for the task.

—Donald Jones

I dedicate this book to my parents, without whose guidance
I would not have been able to achieve success, and to my
colleagues and students for all the inspiration. I would also like to
give a special thank you to my wife, Lorraine, for all her support
and encouragement.

—Ralph Tassone

BRIEF CONTENTS

CONTENTS

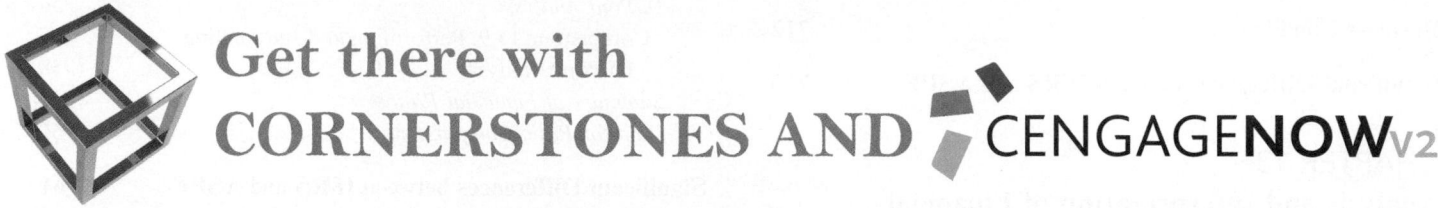

Get there with CORNERSTONES AND CENGAGE**NOW**v2

Cornerstones is a complete text and technology solution that helps you and your students reach course goals and objectives. The Cornerstone pedagogy incorporates step-by-step coverage of important concepts throughout each chapter by utilizing the familiar Cornerstone examples and exercises throughout. The approach provides students with a solid foundation of the core concepts, which allows them to build on that knowledge to get to a higher understanding of financial accounting. The integration of the *Cornerstones* text and unique features in CengageNOWv2™ will get students thinking like managers! The goal of this text is to solidify homework concepts so that students can spend more time learning how to analyze business situations and become good decision makers.

The *Cornerstones* approach focuses on three core needs:

BUILDING A STRONG FOUNDATION

Students simply cannot move forward in this course until they have built and practised the foundational aspects of accounting. With *Cornerstones*, students learn the foundations of financial accounting FASTER, so that they can easily transition into applying and analyzing business information in a conceptual manner.

ANALYZING RELATIONSHIPS

Students also need to be able to analyze and interpret the interrelationships between the numbers and how they affect one another in order to make sound business decisions. Because accounting is an interrelated accounting system, *Cornerstones* incorporates digital technology to allow students to see actual end results.

DECISION MAKING

Cornerstones has a plethora of tools to give students practice in decision making. Armed with the foundational knowledge and interrelationship understanding, students should now feel comfortable analyzing the data in order to make sound business decisions.

BUILDING A STRONG FOUNDATION

Students need to obtain a solid understanding of the foundations of accounting to set the stage for thinking like a manager.

Where other texts bury their examples in blocks of text, **Cornerstone examples** are easy to find, clear, and consistently formatted to help students digest material faster. Students value step-by-step, clear examples more than any other feature in a text.

Preparing a Journal Entry   CORNERSTONE 2.5

Information:
On January 1, Lee Inc. purchases a $3,000 computer from Bay Electronics on credit, with payment due in 60 days.

Required:
Prepare a journal entry to record this transaction.

Why:
A journal entry records the effects of a transaction on accounts using debits and credits. Journal entries must accurately reflect increases or decreases to the general ledger accounts in terms of both amount and classification since the general ledger is the source of data used in the preparation of financial statements.

Solution:
First, analyze the transaction using the procedures described in Cornerstone 2.2:

CORNERSTONE VIDEO

Required:
Prepare journal entries for the transactions.

Cornerstone Exercise 2-27   Journalize Transactions   OBJECTIVE 5
Four transactions that occurred during May are listed below.   CORNERSTONE 2.5
a. May 5: Borrowed cash of $20,000 from CIBC
b. May 10: Made cash sales of $14,500 to customers
c. May 19: Paid salaries of $8,600 to employees for services performed
d. May 22: Purchased and used $4,100 of supplies in operations of the business

Required:
Prepare journal entries for the transactions.

Cornerstone Exercise 2-28   Preparing a Trial Balance   OBJECTIVE 7
Listed below are the ledger accounts for Borges Inc. at December 31, 2018. All accounts have   CORNERSTONE 2.6
normal balances.

Service Revenue	$23,150	Dividends Declared	$ 1,500
Cash	12,850	Salaries Expense	4,300
Accounts Payable	2,825	Equipment	12,725
Common Shares	15,000	Accounts Receivable	5,700
Rent Expense	2,400	Advertising Expense	1,500

Required:
Prepare a trial balance for Borges at December 31, 2018.

Each end-of-chapter **Cornerstone Exercise** references the corresponding Cornerstone example from the text that will aid students in completing that particular exercise. This makes getting started with the homework less intimidating and encourages students to learn independently.

As further reinforcement, newly revised **Cornerstone Videos** are available for every Cornerstone example and are linked to the Cornerstone Exercises in CengageNOWv2. These videos further solidify concepts as they walk through Cornerstone examples in a way that appeals to visual and auditory learners!

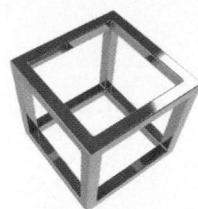

ANALYZING RELATIONSHIPS

Students need to be able to get beyond just understanding the individual pieces of an accounting system and be able to connect concepts and see the relationships between the parts.

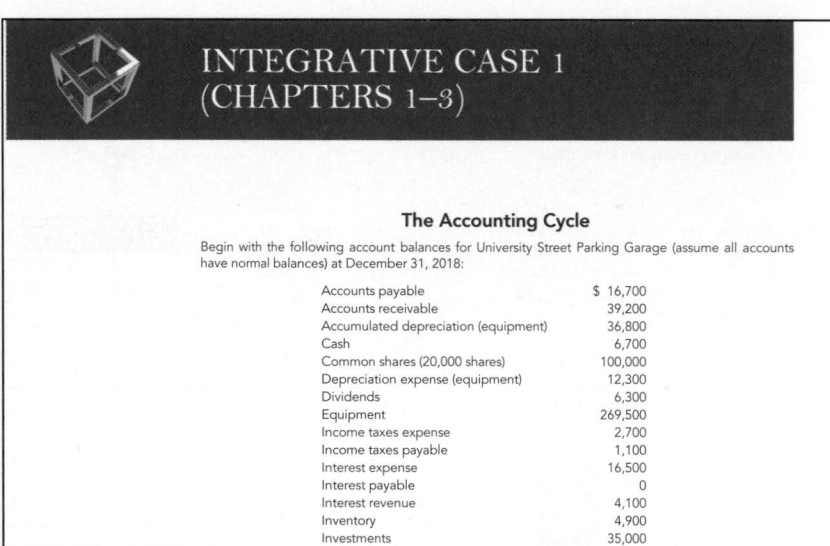

The chapter-spanning **Integrative Cases** present opportunities to integrate concepts from several chapters in order to analyze financial accounting information in a broader context.

Instructors have told us most texts do not explain the interrelationships between the numbers. The *Cornerstones* text explains those relationships where appropriate throughout the text and identifies them as **Illustrating Relationships**.

The end-of-chapter materials also contain exercises and problems that challenge students to think backward, to give students a better understanding of the different accounting interrelationships.

DECISION MAKING

Students need concrete ways to practice how to use accounting information to make sound business decisions.

You Decide takes *Cornerstones'* concepts beyond the foundations. Students must put themselves in the shoes of a manager or business owner and consider the different implications and outcomes of their "company's" decisions. *Cornerstones* gives students a chance to actually *practise* making decisions.

YOU DECIDE Quality of Earnings

Investors and other users often assess the quality of a company's earnings when analyzing companies. The quality of earnings refers to how well a company's reported earnings reflect the company's true earnings. High-quality earnings are generally viewed as permanent or persistent earnings that assist financial statement users in predicting future earnings and cash flows. Low-quality earnings are temporary or transitory earnings from one-time transactions or events that do not aid in predicting future earnings or cash flows. While there is no consensus on how best to measure earnings quality, research suggests that investors recognize differences in earnings quality and that these differences affect a company's share price.

How do adjusting entries influence the quality of earnings?

Because adjusting entries always affect amounts reported on the statement of earnings, the estimates and judgments involved in determining accruals and deferrals (prepayments) of revenues and expenses can have a significant impact on a company's net income. Companies that make relatively pessimistic estimates and judgments are said to follow prudent accounting practices and are generally viewed as having earnings that are of higher quality. In contrast, many companies use relatively optimistic estimates and judgments and employ aggressive accounting practices. These companies are normally viewed as having a lower quality of earnings.

Adjusting entries that lead to better predictors of future earnings or cash flows are viewed as contributing to a higher quality of earnings.

 [*Cornerstones*] is a very good book with a good balance of technical procedures and analysis for critical thinking. It focuses on decision making and concept application. Yes, I would recommend this book to my colleagues.

—LIANG CHEN, University of Toronto

Required:

Calculate the amount of net income that Lauhl should recognize in April under (1) cash-basis accounting and (2) accrual-basis accounting.

OBJECTIVE ❸ **Brief Exercise 3-31   Identification of Adjusting Entries**

Examine the following accounts:

a. Prepaid Insurance
b. Inventory
c. Interest Payable
d. Unearned Service Revenue
e. Accumulated Depreciation

Required:

CONCEPTUAL CONNECTION Identify and explain why each account may or may not require adjustment.

OBJECTIVE ❹ **Brief Exercise 3-32   Adjusting Entries—Accruals**

Nichols Company had the following items that required adjustment at December 31, 2018.

a. Electricity used during December was estimated to be $320. This amount will be paid in January

Conceptual Connection requirements within many end-of-chapter assignments ask students to go beyond the calculations and analyze the conceptual context of the problem. Students will better understand how companies use the calculations to make sound business decisions.

 The quality examples and problems [in *Cornerstones*] are realistic and challenging. They will not only equip students with technical skills but will also develop problem solving and critical thinking.

—KARIN JONSSON, CPA, CA. Director, Corporate Finance, Rio Tinto

KEY FEATURES

- **Experience Financial Accounting** vignettes offer a relational approach to teaching and learning materials through the use of chapter-opening cases that show how real businesses deal with financial accounting issues.
- The **You Decide** feature helps students actively practise decision making. Students play the part of a manager or business owner, then consider the different factors in their decisions and how they will affect outcomes. You Decide helps students prepare for work in the real world.
- **Conceptual Connection** requirements within many end-of-chapter assignments ask students to go beyond the calculations and analyze the conceptual context of the problem. Students will better understand how companies use the calculations to make sound business decisions.
- The **Concept Q&A** boxes throughout the text challenge students to use higher-level reasoning skills. Students are prompted to go beyond the procedures and understand the broader business implications.
- The chapter-spanning **Integrative Cases** present opportunities to integrate concepts from several chapters in order to analyze financial accounting information in a broader context.
- The **Integrated Learning System** (ILS) anchors chapter concepts, provides a framework for study, and links all the instructor resources. Learning objectives with number icons are listed at the start of each chapter. These icons reappear throughout the text and end-of-chapter materials, linking them to the chapter learning objectives. The ILS provides structure for instructors preparing lectures and exams, and helps students learn quickly and study efficiently.

CENGAGE**NOW**v2

- **CengageNOWv2**™ is an online learning resource that provides students with access to the tools that will help them get the most out of their course. Interactive learning resources include the Adaptive Study Plan, Animated Activities, and the Blueprint Problems and Cornerstone Video resources detailed below.
- **Author-Revised Check My Work Feedback:** CengageNOWv2 helps students progress further outside the classroom and keeps them from getting stuck in their studies by providing them with meaningful guidance and tips as they work through their homework assignments. Feedback has been fully revised by the author team and is consistent with material presented in the text.
- **Post-submission Feedback:** Also available in CengageNOWv2 is the ability to show the full solution in addition to newly added source calculations to enhance the learning process. Now students can see where they may have gone wrong so that they can correct their work through further practice.
- **Animated Activities:** Animated Activities in CengageNOWv2 are the perfect pre-lecture assignment to expose students to concepts before class! These cartoon-like illustrations visually guide students through selected core topics. A realistic company example illustrates how the concepts relate to the everyday activities of a business. Animated Activities are assignable or available for self-study and review.
- **Blueprint Connections:** These scenario-based teaching problems solidify concepts and demonstrate their interrelationships as well as promoting critical thinking. Blueprint Connections combine multiple topics, allowing students to explore a larger concept more fully.

NEW TO THIS EDITION

- **Updated and enhanced end-of-chapter assignments.** The end-of-chapter questions have been updated throughout the text to include new data and the most recent developments in accounting. They also to incorporate current company information and the CPA Educational Standards. Integrative Cases have been added following Chapters 3, 7, and 10.
- **New Brief Exercises.** A new section of exercises, with an average of 15 exercises per chapter, has been added to the second Canadian edition.
- **"Why" in Cornerstones.** The "Why" section has been expanded in each Cornerstone example to provide students with additional reasons for covering the topic.
- **New real-company references.** The Experience Financial Accounting opening vignettes have been updated to reflect additional Canadian companies or multinational corporations that have prominent operations in Canada. These companies are then appropriately referenced within the chapters to reinforce the connections between key concepts and their applications in real-world business situations.
- **Highlights of content updates.** Chapter 1 has been amended to focus on the basics of an introductory accounting course. Chapter 3 has been expanded with additional content concerning the reversal of accruals and the closing of accounts. Chapter 4 has been expanded with respect to the application of internal controls and fraud. Chapter 5 has increased discussion on the allowance for doubtful accounts and the use of credit and debit cards. Chapter 7 includes increased discussion of goodwill impairment. Chapter 12 has been updated to reflect recent changes in investment accounting.
- **New IFRS content.** The content in each chapter has been changed or updated to fully reflect IFRS for publicly accountable enterprises in Canada.
- **New summaries of differences between accounting standards.** Each chapter contains an appropriate summary of "Significant Differences between IFRS and ASPE" in Canada.

CENGAGENOWv2

- Newly released **CengageNOWv2™** connects students to assignable content matched to their text. CengageNOWv2 is an interactive learning solution that helps students focus on what they need to learn. It improves academic performance by increasing students' time on task and giving them prompt feedback. With a focus on active learning, concept mastery, and automatic grading, CengageNOWv2 is an easy-to-use digital resource designed to get students involved in their learning progress and be better prepared for class participation and assessment. CengageNOWv2 for *Cornerstones of Financial Accounting* can be used for self-study or assigned as homework. Each student's unique needs are identified with a pre-test that generates an Adaptive Study Plan for each chapter. Platform enhancements in CengageNOWv2 allow for more advanced types of questions, providing students with an even richer learning experience.
- **Blueprint Problems:** These are new to CengageNOWv2 for this edition and are author-written specifically for this text. Blueprint Problems are teaching-type problems that are based on the Cornerstones from within the chapter. Each chapter contains two to four Blueprint Problems written to help students understand the fundamental accounting concepts and their associated building blocks—not just memorize the formulas. They are written in a step-by-step format, from an overview to application of the concepts.
- **Blueprint Problems Using Excel:** These are also new to CengageNOWv2 for this edition and are designed as an alternative to the Blueprint Problems as a way to incorporate Microsoft Excel in greater detail. Students build their own spreadsheets and create their own formulas rather than simply input numbers into a template. The unique Blueprint format starts as a conceptual overview and is followed by application of the chapter concepts using Excel.
- **Cornerstone Videos:** Revised and updated Cornerstone videos provide clear examples. Additional hints and tips have been added to guide students through each Cornerstone problem.

SUPERIOR SUPPLEMENTS

Inspired Instruction at Nelson

The **Nelson Education Teaching Advantage (NETA)** program delivers research-based instructor resources that promote student engagement and higher order thinking to enable the success of Canadian students and educators. Be sure to visit Nelson Education's **Inspired Instruction** website at **www.nelson.com/inspired** to find out more about NETA. Don't miss the testimonials of instructors who have used NETA supplements and seen student engagement increase!

Instructor's Resource

Key instructor ancillaries are provided on the Instructor's Website: **www.nelson.com/instructor**.

- **NETA Test Bank**: This resource was revised by Tamera Ebl of the University of British Columbia. It includes over 1,100 multiple-choice questions written according to NETA guidelines for effective construction and development of higher order questions. Also included are over 400 true/false questions, over 300 problems, over 100 essay questions, over 250 fill-in-the-blank exercises, and over 450 matching questions.

The NETA Test Bank is available in a new cloud-based platform. **Nelson Testing Powered by Cognero®** is a secure online testing system that allows instructors to author, edit, and manage Test Bank content from anywhere Internet access is available. No special installations or downloads are needed, and the desktop-inspired interface, with its drop-down menus and familiar, intuitive tools, allows instructors to create and manage tests with ease. Multiple test versions can be created in an instant, and content can be imported or exported into other systems. Tests can be delivered from a learning management system, the classroom, or wherever an instructor chooses. Nelson Testing Powered by Cognero for *Cornerstones of Financial Accounting* can be accessed through **www.nelson.com/instructor**.

- **NETA Presentation**: Microsoft® PowerPoint® lecture slides for every chapter have been revised by Liang Chen of the University of Toronto, Scarborough Campus. There is an average of 55 slides per chapter, many featuring key concepts, exhibits, and tables from *Cornerstones of Financial Accounting*. NETA principles of clear design and engaging content have been incorporated throughout.
- **Instructor's Manual**: The Instructor's Manual to accompany *Cornerstones of Financial Accounting* has been prepared by Robert Ducharme of the University of Waterloo. This manual contains learning objectives, chapter outlines, suggested Cornerstone exercises, and suggested application exercises.
- **Instructor's Solutions Manual**: This manual, prepared by Ralph Tassone, author of the second Canadian edition textbook, has been independently checked for accuracy by Jay Perry of Niagara College. It contains complete solutions to discussion questions, multiple-choice exercises, Cornerstone exercises, exercises, problem sets, and cases.
- **Spreadsheet Solutions**: The complete solutions to the Excel-based spreadsheet exercises are provided.
- **Image Library**: This resource consists of digital copies of exhibits, Cornerstones, Concept Q&As, and You Decide boxes used in the book. Instructors may use these jpegs to create their own PowerPoint presentations.

CENGAGE**NOW**v2

With its engaging learning and assessment tools, Cengage-NOWv2 supports the entire student workflow, from motivation to mastery. For instructors, CengageNOWv2 provides control and customization with the opportunity to tailor the learning experience to improve outcomes. Class-tested and student-praised, CengageNOWv2 offers a variety of features that support course objectives and interactive learning. These features include:

- Multipanel View
- Adaptive Study Plan
- Animated Activities
- Cornerstones Videos
- Blueprint Problems
- Blueprint Connections

Ask your Nelson Education learning solutions consultant for more information about integrating CengageNOWv2 into your course.

ACKNOWLEDGMENTS AND THANKS

We would like to thank the following authors of the U.S. text whose work provided a foundation for this second Canadian edition:

Jay S. Rich, *Illinois State University*
Jefferson P. Jones, *Auburn University*
Maryanne M. Mowen, *Oklahoma State University*
Don R. Hansen, *Oklahoma State University*

We would also like to thank the following reviewers, whose helpful suggestions were used in the preparation of the second Canadian edition:

Jerry Aubin, *Algonquin College*
Liang Chen, *University of Toronto*
Tamara Ebl, *University of British Columbia*
Sonya von Heyking, *University of Lethbridge*
Karin Jonsson, CPA, CA, *Rio Tinto*
Lauren Kirychuk, *Bow Valley College*
Shiraz Kurji, *Mount Royal University*
Darlene Lowe, *MacEwan University*
Sylvie Monette, CPA, CA, *KPMG*
Dal Pirot, *Grant MacEwan University*
Haiping Wang, *York University*

We are grateful to the experts who worked diligently as technical reviewers on the textbook and solutions manual: Jay Perry, Niagara College, and Tamara Ebl, University of British Columbia.

We would also like to acknowledge the instructors who worked on updating and adapting the rich ancillary package for *Cornerstones of Financial Accounting*:

Robert Ducharme, *University of Waterloo* (Instructor's Manual)
Liang Chen, *University of Toronto, Scarborough Campus* (PowerPoint presentations)
Tamara Ebl, *University of British Columbia* (Computerized Test Bank)
John Love, *Ted Rogers School of Management, Ryerson University*, and Ralph Tassone, *Joseph L. Rotman School of Management, University of Toronto* (Cornerstone videos)

Finally, we would like to thank the faculty and students at the University of Windsor who provided ideas and suggestions as the text was prepared and the staff at Nelson Education and its associates: Publisher Anne-Marie Taylor, Content Development Manager Maria Chu, Senior Production Project Manager Imoinda Romain, Rights Project Manager Lynn McLeod, Copy Editor Marcia Gallego, and Project Manager Rajachitra S.

Donald Jones
Ralph Tassone
June 2016

ABOUT THE AUTHORS

Donald Jones is a tenured lecturer who teaches accounting, auditing, and income tax at the University of Windsor. He received his B.Comm. degree from the University of Windsor and his M.B.A. degree from the University of Toronto. Jones is a Canadian Chartered Professional Accountant (CPA), having qualified as both a Chartered Accountant (CA) and a Certified Management Accountant (CMA) in the Province of Ontario. Jones is a member in good standing of CPA Canada and CPA Ontario. Jones has 36 years of professional public accounting experience, including service as a partner of Deloitte, an international professional accounting firm. In addition to his academic duties at the University of Windsor, Jones has led seminars for both large corporate audiences on accounting and auditing matters, including IFRS, and for private enterprise shareholder-managers on accounting and tax issues. Jones is licensed as an active public accountant (LPA) in the Province of Ontario, where he carries on a professional practice. Jones enjoys watching football and hockey and expanding his Canadian coin and currency collection. He and his wife, Linda, have three children, each of whom is a professionally qualified accountant.

Ralph Tassone Ralph Tassone teaches accounting at the Joseph L. Rotman School of Management (Rotman), University of Toronto. He is a Canadian Chartered Professional Accountant (CPA), having qualified as a Chartered Accountant (CA) in the Province of Ontario, and has over 16 years of public accounting experience. His focus in public accounting is on owner-managed businesses. Tassone advises clients on accounting and tax planning arrangements. At Rotman, his teaching focus is accounting; he has taught several undergraduate courses, including Introductory and Intermediate Financial Accounting, Managerial Accounting, and Management Control. At the graduate level, he has taught Advanced Financial Reporting for the Rotman Graduate Diploma in Professional Accounting program. He graduated from the University of Toronto Commerce program in 2000 and subsequently commenced his articling with KPMG LLP. He completed his Master of Education at OISE, University of Toronto, in 2014. He enjoys watching sports and travelling to new places around the world.

Jay S. Rich is a Professor of Accounting at Illinois State University. He received his B.S., M.S., and Ph.D. from the University of Illinois. Before entering the Ph.D. program, Rich worked as an auditor at Price Waterhouse & Co. and earned his CPA. His primary teaching interest is financial accounting, and he has taught numerous courses at the undergraduate, master's, and doctoral levels. Rich has been awarded both the Outstanding Dissertation Award and Notable Contribution to the Literature Award by the Audit Section of the American Accounting Association. He has published articles in *The Accounting Review*; *Auditing: A Journal of Practice & Theory*; *Accounting Horizons*; *Organizational Behavior and Human Decision Processes*; and *Accounting Organizations and Society*, and has served on the editorial board of *Auditing: A Journal of Practice and Theory*. His outside interests include family, travel, reading, and watching sports, but he spends most of his free time driving his children to various activities. He also repeatedly develops plans to exercise and diet at some point in the future and has not been to a movie in years. By all accounts, he is a master at grilling meat, a mediocre skier, and a shameful golfer.

Jefferson P. Jones is the PricewaterhouseCoopers Associate Professor of Accounting at Auburn University. He received his Bachelor's and Master of Accountancy degrees from Auburn University and his Ph.D. in accounting from Florida State University. While earning his CPA, he worked for Deloitte & Touche. He has received numerous teaching awards, including the Outstanding Master of Accountancy Professor Award, the Beta Alpha Psi Outstanding Teaching Award (six times), the Auburn University College of Business McCartney Teaching Award, and the Auburn University School of Accountancy Teaching Award. In addition to an Intermediate Accounting text, his published articles have appeared in *Advances in Accounting*; *Review of Quantitative Finance and Accounting*; *Issues in Accounting Education*; *International Journal of Forecasting*; *The CPA Journal*; *Managerial Finance*; *Journal of Accounting and Finance Research*; and *The Journal of Corporate Accounting and Finance*. Jones has made numerous presentations around the country on research and pedagogical issues. He is a member of the American Accounting Association (AAA), the American Institute of Certified Public Accountants (AICPA), and the Alabama Society of CPAs (ASCPA). He is married, has two children, and enjoys playing golf.

Maryanne M. Mowen is Associate Professor of Accounting at Oklahoma State University. She received her Ph.D. from Arizona State University. With degrees in economics and history, she brings a unique interdisciplinary perspective to teaching and writing in both cost accounting and management accounting. Her research interests include management accounting, behavioural decision theory, and Sarbanes-Oxley compliance, and she teaches an ethics course about the impact of Sarbanes-Oxley on the accounting profession. Mowen has published articles in journals such as *Decision Science*; *Journal of Economic Psychology*; and *Journal of Management Accounting Research*. She has also served as a consultant to mid-sized and Fortune 100 companies and works with corporate controllers on management accounting issues. Outside the classroom, she enjoys hiking, travelling, reading mysteries, and solving crossword puzzles.

Don R. Hansen is Professor of Accounting at Oklahoma State University. He received his Ph.D. from the University of Arizona and has an undergraduate degree in mathematics from Brigham Young University. His research interests include activity-based costing and mathematical modelling. Hansen's published articles appear in *The Accounting Review*; *Journal of Management Accounting Research*; *Accounting, Organizations, and Society*; *Accounting Horizons*; and *IIE Transactions*, and he served on the editorial board of *The Accounting Review*. His outside interests include taking part in family and church activities, reading, watching movies, watching sports, and studying Spanish.

1

Financial Statements and Decision Making

After studying Chapter 1, you should be able to:

1 Identify who the different users of financial statements are and how they use financial statements.

2 Identify different forms of business organization and business activities.

3 Understand the periods of time covered by the basic four financial statements and the underlying basic accounting equation.

4 Understand how a statement of financial position is prepared and used by different decision makers.

5 Understand how a statement of earnings is prepared and used by different decision makers.

6 Understand how a statement of changes in equity is prepared and used by different decision makers.

7 Identify the components of a statement of cash flows and understand how it is used by different decision makers.

8 Describe the relationships among the four basic financial statements and how management uses financial statements.

9 Describe information contained in the annual report.

10 Understand the role of International Accounting Standards in determining the content of financial statements.

11 Understand the importance of ethics and legal liability in accounting.

goodluz/Shutterstock

NEL

EXPERIENCE FINANCIAL ACCOUNTING
with Canadian Tire

Canadian Tire Corporation, Limited, is a Canadian retail company. Its operations include Canadian Tire (the core retail and automotive service operation), Canadian Tire Petroleum, Canadian Tire Financial Services, Mark's, Forzani Group Ltd., and PartSource. The company's head office is in Toronto.

The business that became Canadian Tire was started in 1922 in Toronto by John William Billes and Alfred Jackson Billes, who invested their combined personal savings of $1,800. The name Canadian Tire Corporation was incorporated in 1927. The first Canadian Tire catalogue was issued in 1928. The first associate store opened in Hamilton, Ontario, in 1934. The company's first gas bar opened in 1958 in Toronto. The company has since grown to a total of 1,700 retail and gas outlets across Canada and is a publicly listed corporation on the Toronto Stock Exchange. It employs around 68,000 people. Canadian Tire has a long history of growth and success.[1]

What type of information can help someone predict the successes of a company like Canadian Tire? A good place to start is with the financial information contained in a company's annual report. This financial information is provided in the form of financial statements—a summary of the results of a company's operations, its cash flows, and its financial position. A study of a company's financial statements will help you determine how successful a company has been in the past as well as its prospects for the future. While this information is easily accessible and free of charge, your final judgment on a company's prospects will be influenced by how well you understand the information contained in its financial statements.

Source: Canadian Tire website, www.canadiantire.ca, accessed July 21, 2012.

[1] www.canadiantire.ca, accessed July 31, 2012.

FINANCIAL STATEMENTS AND DECISION MAKING

Our economy is composed of many different businesses. Some companies, such as Canadian Tire, focus on **providing goods**, which for Canadian Tire, take many forms including automotive products, work apparel, and sporting goods. Other companies are primarily concerned with **providing services**. For example, Walt Disney offers a variety of entertainment services from theme parks to motion pictures. While most entities, like Canadian Tire and Disney, exist in order to earn a profit, some not-for-profit organizations are formed to generate some other benefit to society (e.g., school boards exist to meet the educational needs of a community). Regardless of their objective, all entities use accounting information to make decisions concerning investing, financing, and operating activities.

Financial statements result from an **accounting** process of identifying, measuring, recording, and communicating information about a company's business activities so that decision makers can make informed decisions. Financial statements are useful because they assist different users in answering questions and making better decisions.

The demand for financial statements comes from **users internal and external** to the business. Inside the business, managers use accounting information to help them plan and make decisions about the company's operating, investing, and financing activities. For example, they use financial statements to predict the consequences of their actions and to help decide which actions to take. They also use financial statements to control the operations of the company and to evaluate the effectiveness of past decisions. Employees use financial statements to help them judge the prospects of their company, which should translate into future promotion opportunities. External to the business, investors (shareholders) use financial statements to evaluate the prospects of a company and to decide where to invest their money. Creditors (lenders) use financial statements to evaluate whether to loan money to a company. Governments use financial statements to determine taxes owed by companies, to implement regulatory objectives, and to make policy decisions. The demand for financial statements by various users is summarized in Exhibit 1.1.

Financial statements result from an accounting process that consists of recording information and maintaining accounting records—activities that are frequently called bookkeeping. This accounting information system communicates the results of business activities of a company to interested parties. The focus of this book is on providing information that satisfies the needs of external decision makers (outside demand) and is termed **financial accounting**. Separate accounting courses termed *management accounting* address the production of accounting information for decision making by users internal to a business organization.

The objectives of the accounting information system involve providing decision makers with information that assists them in assessing the amounts, timing, and uncertainties of a company's future cash flows. This information is provided through four basic financial statements: the statement of financial position (balance sheet), the statement of comprehensive income (statement of earnings), the statement of changes in equity (statement of retained earnings), and the statement of cash flows.

In this chapter, we will discuss the functioning of the accounting information system within a business. We will address the following questions:

- What forms do businesses take?
- What are the basic business activities?
- How does the accounting information system summarize and report these business activities?
- How can decision makers use the information provided by the accounting information system?

(EXHIBIT 1.1)

The Demand for Financial Statements by Decision Makers and Their Typical Questions

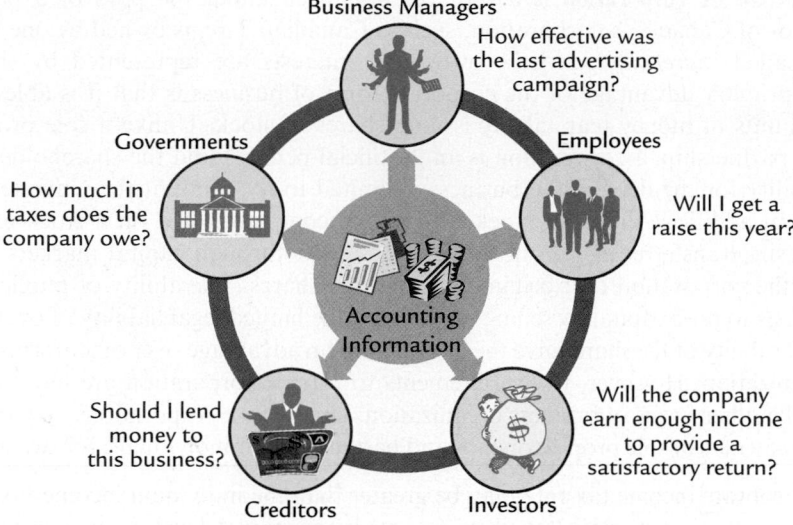

External Decision Makers

- Lenders (banks)
- Suppliers
- Investors
- Governments

Internal Decision Makers

- Board of Directors
- Executive management (CEO, CFO)
- Employees
- Functional managers

© Cengage Learning

Regardless of your major area of study or career plans, knowledge of the accounting information system and the ability to use accounting information will be critical to your success in business.

BUSINESS: FORMS AND ACTIVITIES

The accounting process identifies, measures, records, and communicates financial information about a business entity. A business entity has an identity separate from that of its owners and managers and maintains accounting records.

OBJECTIVE ❷

Identify different forms of business organization and business activities.

Forms of Business Organization

This text emphasizes accounting for business entities that take one of three different forms: sole proprietorship, partnership, or corporation.

Sole Proprietorship A **sole proprietorship** is an unincorporated business owned by one person. Sole proprietorships are usually small, local businesses such as restaurants, photography studios, retail stores, website providers, and professionals. This organizational form is popular because it is simple to set up and gives the (proprietor) owner control over the business. While a sole proprietorship is a business entity separate from its owner, the owner is personally responsible for the debts of the business. Sole proprietorships can be formed or dissolved at the wishes of the owner.

Partnership A **partnership** is a business owned jointly by two or more individuals or corporations, or a combination thereof. Small businesses and many professional practices of physicians, lawyers, and accountants are often organized as partnerships. Relative to sole proprietorships, partnerships provide increased access to financial resources as well as access to the individual skills of each of the partners. Similar to sole proprietorships, partnerships are accounting entities separate from the partners; however, the partners are jointly responsible for all the debt of the partnership.[2] A partnership is automatically dissolved when any partner leaves the partnership; of course, the remaining partners may form a new partnership and continue to operate.

Corporation A **corporation** is a business organized under the laws of a particular province or of Canada. A corporation, such as Canadian Tire, is owned by one or more persons called *shareholders*, whose ownership interests are represented by shares of stock. A primary advantage of the corporate form of business is that it is able to raise large amounts of money (capital) by issuing shares of stock. Unlike a sole proprietorship or a partnership, a corporation is an "artificial person" and the shareholders' legal responsibility for the debt of the business is limited to the amount they invested in the business. In addition, shares of stock of a public company listed on a stock exchange can be easily transferred from one owner to another through capital markets without affecting the corporation that originally issued the shares. The ability of publicly listed corporations to raise capital by selling new shares, the limited legal liability of owners, and the transferability of the shares give the corporation an advantage over other forms of business organization. However, the requirements to form a corporation are more complex than for the other forms of business organization. In addition, corporations may pay more taxes than owners of sole proprietorships and partnerships or individuals, for two reasons:

- The corporate income tax rate may be greater than the individual income tax rate.
- A corporation's income is taxed twice—at the corporate level as income is earned, and at the individual level as earnings are distributed to shareholders. This is known as double taxation, the financial effect of which may be decreased by the existence of the dividend tax credit mechanism in Canada.

Canadian-controlled private corporations benefit from lower corporate income tax rates on certain types of business income compared to publicly listed corporations in Canada. Detailed analysis is required to assess the form of business organization that will minimize the income tax expense for a business in a particular set of circumstances. Such analysis is beyond the scope of this text.

Exhibit 1.2 illustrates the advantages and disadvantages of each form of organization. While many sole proprietorships and partnerships carry on business, the majority of business in Canada is conducted by corporations. Therefore, this book emphasizes the corporate form of organization.

Business Activities

All businesses engage in activities that can be categorized as financing, investing, or operating activities. Examples of these activities are provided in Exhibit 1.3 and are described in the following paragraphs.

(EXHIBIT 1.2)

Forms of Business Organization

Sole Proprietorship

- ⊕ Easily formed
- ⊕ Tax advantages
- ⊕ Controlled by owner
- ⊖ Personal liability
- ⊖ Limited life

Partnership

- ⊕ Access to the resources and skills of partners
- ⊕ Tax advantages
- ⊖ Shared control
- ⊖ Personal liability
- ⊖ Limited life

Corporation

- ⊕ Easier to raise money
- ⊕ Easier to transfer ownership
- ⊕ Limited liability
- ⊖ More complex to organize
- ⊖ Higher taxes

© Cengage Learning

---

[2] Many professional partnerships—including the largest public accounting firms—have been reorganized as *limited liability partnerships* (LLPs), which protect the personal assets of the partners from being used to pay partnership debts.

(EXHIBIT 1.3)

Business Activities

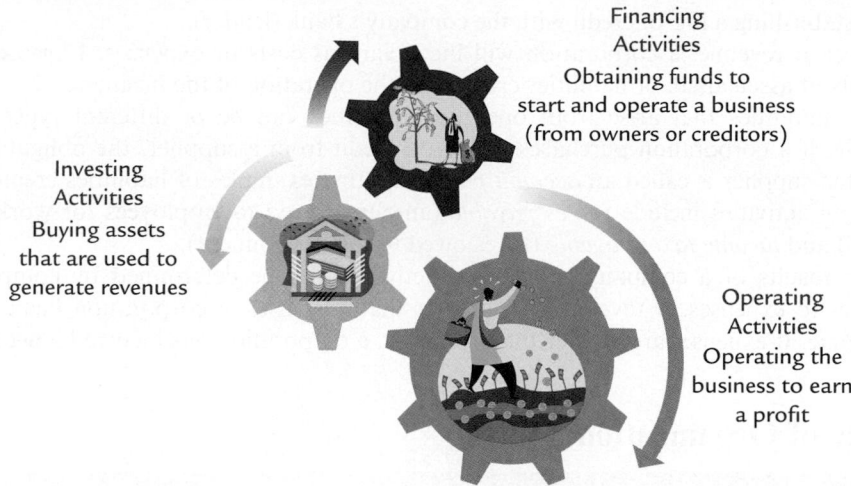

Financing
Activities
Obtaining funds to
start and operate a business
(from owners or creditors)

Investing
Activities
Buying assets
that are used to
generate revenues

Operating
Activities
Operating the
business to earn
a profit

© Cengage Learning

Financing Activities A company's financing activities include obtaining the funds necessary to begin and operate a business. These funds come from either issuing shares or borrowing money (debt). Most companies use both types of financing to obtain funds.

When a corporation borrows money from another entity such as a bank, it must repay the amount borrowed. The person to whom the corporation owes money is called a **creditor**. This obligation to repay a creditor is termed a **liability** and can take many forms. A common way for a corporation to obtain cash is to borrow money with the promise to repay the amount borrowed plus interest at a future date. Such borrowings are commonly referred to as *loans payable*. A special form of loan payable that is used by corporations to obtain large amounts of money is called a *bond payable*.

In addition to borrowing money from creditors, a corporation may issue shares to investors in exchange for cash. The dollar amount paid to a corporation for shares is termed **common stock** and represents the basic ownership interest in a corporation. The corporation is not obligated to repay the shareholder the amount invested; however, many corporations distribute a portion of their earnings to shareholders on a regular basis. These distributions are called *dividends*.

Creditors and shareholders have a claim on the **assets**, or economic resources, of a corporation. However, the claims on these resources differ. In the case of financial difficulty or distress, the claims of the creditors (liabilities) must be paid prior to the claims of the shareholders (called **shareholders' equity**). Shareholders' equity is considered a residual interest in the assets of a corporation that remain after deducting its liabilities.

Investing Activities Once a corporation has obtained funds through its financing activities, it buys assets that enable it to operate. The corporation may also obtain intangible assets that lack physical substance, such as copyrights and patents. The purchase (and sale) of the assets that are used in operations (commonly referred to as property, plant, and equipment) are a corporation's investing activities.

Regardless of their form, assets are future economic benefits that a corporation controls. The assets purchased by a corporation vary depending on the type of business that the corporation engages in, and the composition of these assets is likely to vary across different companies and different industries.

Operating Activities Once a corporation has acquired the assets it needs, it can begin to operate. While different businesses have different purposes, they all want to generate revenue. **Revenue** is the increase in assets that results from the sale of products or services. In addition to revenue, assets such as *cash*, *accounts receivable* (the right to collect an amount due from customers), *supplies*, and *inventory* (products held for resale) often result from operating activities. Short-term cash needs are usually obtained by a company establishing a line of credit with the company's bank (lender).

To earn revenue, a corporation will incur various costs or expenses. **Expenses** are the costs of assets used, or liabilities created, in the operation of the business.

The liabilities that arise from operating activities can be of different types. For example, if a corporation purchases goods on credit from a supplier, the obligation to repay the supplier is called an *account payable*. Other examples of liabilities created by operating activities include *wages payable* (amounts owed to employees for work performed) and *income taxes payable* (taxes owed to the government).

The results of a company's operating activities can be determined by comparing revenues to expenses. If revenues are greater than expenses, a corporation has earned **net income**. If expenses are greater than revenues, a corporation has incurred a **net loss**.

YOUDECIDE Choice of Organizational Form

You are an entrepreneur who has decided to start a campus-area bookstore. In order to start your business, you have to choose among three organizational forms—sole proprietorship, partnership, or corporation. You have enough personal wealth to finance 40% of the business, but you must get the remaining 60% from other sources.

How does the choice of organizational form impact your control of the business and ability to obtain the needed funds?

The choice of organizational form can greatly impact many aspects of a business's operations. Each form has certain advantages and disadvantages that you should carefully consider.

- *Sole Proprietorship*: A sole proprietorship would give you the most control of your business. However, you would be forced to obtain the additional 60% of funds needed from a bank or other creditor. It is often difficult to get banks to support a new business.

- *Partnership*: If you choose to form a partnership, you would still have access to bank loans. In addition, you would also have the ability to obtain the additional funds from your partner or partners. In this situation, the other partners would then want a 60% interest in the business, which may be an unacceptable loss of control.

- *Corporation*: If you choose to form a corporation, you could obtain the needed funds by issuing shares to investors. While a 60% interest may still be transferred to the shareholders, if the shares were widely dispersed among many investors, you might still retain effective control of the business with a 40% interest.

The choice of organizational form involves the consideration of many different factors.

COMMUNICATION OF ACCOUNTING INFORMATION

OBJECTIVE ③
Understand the periods of time covered by the basic four financial statements and the underlying basic accounting equation.

The financing, investing, and operating activities of a company are recorded by accounting systems as detailed transactions. To effectively communicate a company's activities to decision makers, these detailed transactions are summarized and reported in a set of standardized reports called **financial statements**. The role of financial statements is to provide information that will assist investors, creditors, and other users make judgments and predictions that will serve as the basis for the various decisions they make. Financial statements help answer questions such as those shown in Exhibit 1.4.

The Four Basic Financial Statements

Companies prepare four basic financial statements:

- The **statement of financial position** reports the resources (assets) owned by a company and the claims against those resources (liabilities and shareholders' equity) at a

© Cengage Learning

(EXHIBIT 1.4)

Questions Answered by Financial Statements

How much better off is the company at the end of the year than it was at the beginning of the year (disclosed in the statement of comprehensive income)?

What are the economic resources of the company and the claims against those resources (disclosed in the statement of financial position)?

From what sources did a company's cash come and for what did the company use cash during the year (disclosed in the statement of cash flows)?

---

specific point in time. Private companies often name this financial statement a **balance sheet**.

- The **statement of comprehensive income** reports how well a company has performed its operations (revenues, expenses, and income) over a period of time. The statement of comprehensive income may be used by public companies only to report other income or expenses not recognized in the statement of earnings.
- The **statement of changes in equity** reports how much of the company's net earnings was retained in the business, dividend distributions to owners, the dollar amount of shares issued and repurchased, and other changes in equity over a period of time.[3] Private companies prepare a different statement called a **statement of retained earnings**.
- The **statement of cash flows** reports the sources and uses of a company's cash over a period of time.

While financial statements can be prepared at any point or for any period of time, most companies prepare financial statements at the end of each month, quarter, and year. Note that the statement of financial position is prepared at a specific date or point in time, whereas the other financial statements cover a period of time and explain the business activities between statement of financial position dates as shown in Exhibit 1.5.

The basic four financial statements are prepared and issued at the end of an accounting period. While the accounting period can be a year, companies also issue statements monthly or quarterly to satisfy the users' needs for timely information. The financial statements are accompanied by supporting information and explanatory material called the notes to the financial statements.

(EXHIBIT 1.5)

Time Periods Relating to Basic Four Financial Statements

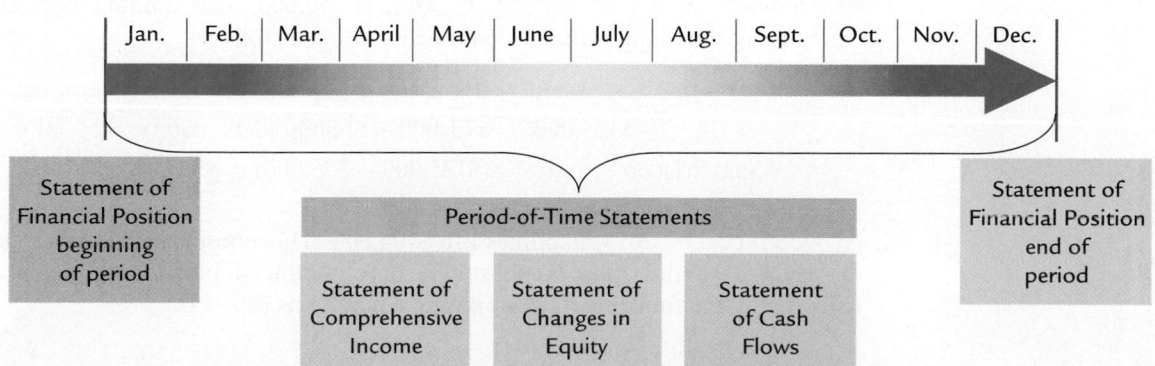

---

[3] The statement of changes in equity, which describes changes in all components of equity, is presented in Chapter 10.

The Basic Accounting Equation

To understand financial statements, it is necessary that you understand how the accounting system records, classifies, and reports information about business activities. The **fundamental accounting equation** illustrates the foundation of the accounting system.

Assets	=	Liabilities + Shareholders' equity
Resources		Sources of Financing

The basic accounting equation captures two basic features of any company. The left side of the accounting equation shows the assets, or economic resources of a company. The right side of the accounting equation indicates who has a claim on the company's assets. These claims may be the claims of creditors (liabilities) or they may be the claims of owners (shareholders' equity). The implication of the basic accounting equation is that what a company owns (its assets) must always be equal to what it owes (its liabilities and shareholders' equity). Cornerstone 1.1 illustrates this key relationship implied by the basic accounting equation.

CORNERSTONE 1.1

CORNERSTONE
VIDEO

Using the Basic Accounting Equation

Information:

On January 1, 2018, Gundrum Company reported assets of $125,000 and liabilities of $75,000. During 2018, assets increased by $44,000 and shareholders' equity increased by $15,000.

Required:

1. What is the amount reported for shareholders' equity on January 1, 2018?

2. What is the amount reported for liabilities on December 31, 2018?

Why:

A company's resources (its assets) must always equal the claims on those resources (its liabilities and shareholders' equity). Also, an understanding of the basic accounting equation is useful is assessing the impact of future business transactions on a company's financial statements.

Solution:

1. Shareholders' equity on January 1, 2018, is $50,000. This amount is calculated by rearranging the fundamental accounting equation as follows:

$$\text{Assets} = \text{Liabilities} + \text{Shareholders' equity}$$
$$\$125,000 = \$75,000 + \text{Shareholders' equity}$$
$$\text{Shareholders' equity} = (\$125,000 - \$75,000) = \underline{\underline{\$50,000}}$$

2. At December 31, 2018, liabilities are $104,000. This amount is computed by adding the change to the appropriate statement of financial position elements and then rearranging the fundamental accounting equation as follows:

(Continued)

CORNERSTONE

1.1

(Continued)

$$\text{Assets} = \text{Liabilities} + \text{Shareholders' equity}$$

$$(\$125{,}000 + \$44{,}000) = \text{Liabilities} + (\$50{,}000 + \$15{,}000)$$

(Assets beginning	(Increase in assets	(Shareholders'	(Increase in
of year)	during the year)	equity beginning	shareholders' equity
		of year)	during the year)

$$\text{Liabilities} = (\$125{,}000 + \$44{,}000) - (\$50{,}000 + \$15{,}000)$$
$$= (\$169{,}000 - \$65{,}000) = \underline{\underline{\$104{,}000}}$$

The basic accounting equation is used to capture all the economic activities recorded by an accounting system.

THE STATEMENT OF FINANCIAL POSITION
Elements

The purpose of the statement of financial position is to report the financial position of a company (its assets, liabilities, and shareholders' equity) at a specific point in time. The relationship between the elements of the statement of financial position is given by the fundamental accounting equation:

$$\text{Assets} = \text{Liabilities} + \text{Shareholders' equity}$$

OBJECTIVE 4

Understand how a statement of financial position is prepared and used by different decision makers.

Note that on the statement of financial position, the economic resources of a company (assets) must always equal, or be in balance with, the claims against those resources (liabilities and shareholders' equity).

Although a company may prepare its statement of financial position on an unclassified basis for management's internal use, accounting standards require that the general-purpose statement of financial position be prepared on a classified basis. Therefore, the statement of financial position is organized, or classified, to help users identify the fundamental economic similarities and differences between the various items within the statement of financial position. These classifications help users answer questions such as these:

- how a company obtained its resources
- whether a company will be able to pay its obligations when they become due

While companies often use different classifications and different levels of detail on their statements of financial position, some common classifications are shown in Exhibit 1.6.

Let's examine the statement of financial position classifications in more detail by looking at Canadian Tire's statement of financial position shown in Exhibit 1.7.

With regard to the heading of the financial statement, several items are of interest:

- *Company name*: The company for which the accounting information is collected and reported is clearly defined.
- *Financial statement type*: The title of the financial statement follows the name of the company.
- *Date*: The specific date of the statement is listed. Canadian Tire operates on a fiscal year that ends in December. A **fiscal year** is an accounting period that runs for one year. While many companies adopt a fiscal year that corresponds to the calendar year, others adopt a fiscal year that more closely corresponds with their business cycle.
- *Unit of Measure*: Canadian Tire reports its financial results rounded to the nearest millions of dollars. Large companies often round the amounts presented to make for a clearer presentation.

EXHIBIT 1.6

Common Statement of Financial Position Classifications

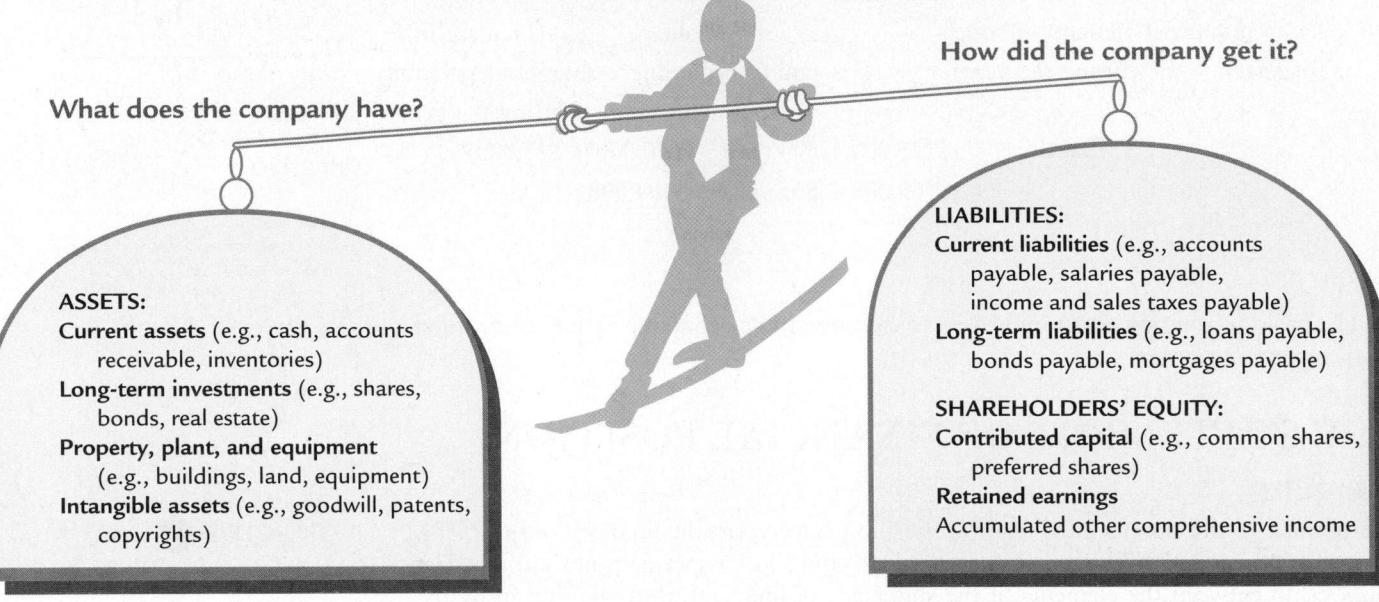

What does the company have?

How did the company get it?

ASSETS:
Current assets (e.g., cash, accounts receivable, inventories)
Long-term investments (e.g., shares, bonds, real estate)
Property, plant, and equipment (e.g., buildings, land, equipment)
Intangible assets (e.g., goodwill, patents, copyrights)

LIABILITIES:
Current liabilities (e.g., accounts payable, salaries payable, income and sales taxes payable)
Long-term liabilities (e.g., loans payable, bonds payable, mortgages payable)

SHAREHOLDERS' EQUITY:
Contributed capital (e.g., common shares, preferred shares)
Retained earnings
Accumulated other comprehensive income

© Cengage Learning

Current Assets

The basic classification of a company's assets is between current and noncurrent items. In a typical company, it is reasonable to designate one year as the dividing line between current and noncurrent items. However, if the operating cycle of a company is longer than one year, it may be necessary to extend this dividing line beyond one year so that it corresponds to the length of the operating cycle. The **operating cycle** of a company is the average time that it takes a company to purchase goods, resell the goods, and collect the cash from customers. In other words, **current assets** consist of cash and other assets that are reasonably expected to be converted into cash within one year or one operating cycle, whichever is longer. Because most companies have operating cycles less than one year, we will use the one-year dividing line to distinguish between current and noncurrent items. Common types of current assets are the following:

- Cash
- Short-term investments or marketable securities—investments in the debt and shares of other companies as well as government securities held for sale in the next fiscal year
- Accounts receivable—the right to collect an amount due from customers
- Inventories—goods or products held for resale to customers
- Other current assets—a "catch-all" category that includes items such as prepaid expenses (advance payments for rent, insurance, and other services) and supplies

Current assets are listed on the statement of financial position by North American companies in order of liquidity or nearness to cash. That is, the items are reported in the order in which the company expects to convert them into cash. However, under IFRS, companies can alternatively list their assets, both current and noncurrent, in order of least liquid (e.g., goodwill) first and most liquid (e.g., cash) last. This latter practice is often adopted by non–North American companies. The current assets for Canadian Tire were reported as $8,510.9 million.

---

concept Q&A

Many classifications on the statement of financial position are essentially subtotals. Is it very important to place accounts within the right category or is it enough to simply understand if they are assets, liabilities, or shareholders' equity?

Answer:

It is critical that you be able to identify specific accounts as assets, liabilities, or shareholders' equity accounts. However, the classifications are also important. Financial accounting is concerned with communicating useful information to decision makers. These classifications provide decision makers with information about the nature and source of assets, liabilities, and shareholders' equity that assists them in understanding a company's financial position.

(EXHIBIT 1.7)

Classified Statement of Financial Position of Canadian Tire Corporation, Limited

Canadian Tire Corporation, Limited
Statement of Financial Position*
January 3, 2015
(in millions of dollars) (Summarized)

ASSETS

Current assets:		
Cash and cash equivalents	$ 662.1	
Short-term investments	289.1	
Accounts receivable	880.2	
Loans receivable	4,905.5	
Merchandise inventories	1,623.8	
Other current assets	149.5	
Total current assets		$ 8,510.2
Long-term receivables and other		684.2
Long-term investments		176.0
Property, plant, and equipment	6,272.5	
Less: Accumulated depreciation	(2,529.4)	
Total property, plant, and equipment		3,743.1
Goodwill and intangible assets		1,251.7
Other assets		188.0
Total assets		$14,553.2

LIABILITIES AND SHAREHOLDERS' EQUITY

Current liabilities:		
Bank indebtedness	$ 14.3	
Deposits	950.7	
Accounts payable	1961.2	
Provisions	206.0	
Short-term borrowings	199.8	
Loans payable	604.4	
Income taxes payable	54.9	
Current portion of long-term debt	587.5	
Total current liabilities		$ 4,578.8
Long-term liabilities		4,769.4
Total liabilities		8,922.4
Shareholders' equity:		
Share capital	695.5	
Contributed surplus	2.9	
Retained earnings	4,075.1	
Other equity**	857.3	
Total shareholders' equity		5,630.8
Total liabilities and shareholders' equity		$14,553.2

*The statement of financial position information was taken from the January 3, 2015, annual report of Canadian Tire
 Corporation and has been summarized and reformatted by the author.
**The other equity reported by Canadian Tire represents $82 million accumulated other comprehensive
 income (discussed in Chapter 10) and $775.3 attributable to noncontrolling interests (discussed in Chapter 12).
 Accumulated other comprehensive income is discussed in Chapter 10.

Source: Canadian Tire Corporation Annual Report 2014, page 63.

Noncurrent Assets

Assets that are not classified as current are classified as long-term or noncurrent assets.
These include long-term investments; property, plant, and equipment; intangible assets;
and other noncurrent assets.

Long-Term Investments **Long-term investments** are similar to short-term invest-ments, except that the company expects to hold the investment for longer than one year. This category also includes land or buildings that a company is not currently using in operations. Canadian Tire reported long-term investments of $176.0 million.

Property, Plant, and Equipment **Property, plant, and equipment** represents the tangible, long-lived, productive assets used by a company in its operations to produce revenue. This category includes land, buildings, machinery, manufacturing equipment, office equipment, and furniture. Canadian Tire reported property, plant, and equipment of $3,743.1 million, representing 25.7% ($3,743.1 ÷ $14,553.2) of its total assets. Prop-erty, plant, and equipment is originally recorded at the cost to obtain the asset. Because property, plant, and equipment helps produce revenue over a number of years, compa-nies assign, or allocate, a portion of the asset's cost as an expense in each period in which the asset is used. This process is called *depreciation*. The *accumulated depreciation* reported in Canadian Tire's statement of financial position of $2,529.4 million represents the total amount of depreciation that the company has expensed over the life of its assets. Because accumulated depreciation is subtracted from the cost of an asset, it is called a *contra-asset account*. The difference between the cost and the accumulated depreciation is the asset's book value (or carrying value).

Intangible Assets **Intangible assets** are similar to property, plant, and equipment in that they provide a benefit to a company over a number of years; however, these assets lack physical substance. Examples of intangible assets include patents, copyrights, trademarks, and goodwill. Canadian Tire reported goodwill and intangible assets of $1,251.7 million.

Other Noncurrent Assets **Other noncurrent assets** is a catch-all category that includes items such as deferred charges (long-term prepaid expenses) and other long-term miscellaneous items.

Current Liabilities

Current liabilities are closely related to current assets. **Current liabilities** consist of obligations that will be satisfied within one year or the operating cycle, whichever is longer. These liabilities can be satisfied through the payment of cash or by providing goods or services. Current liabilities include the following:

- Accounts payable—an obligation to repay a vendor or supplier for merchandise supplied to the company
- Salaries payable—an obligation to pay an employee for services performed
- Unearned revenue—an obligation to deliver goods or perform a service for which a company has already been paid
- Interest payable—an obligation to pay interest on money that a company has borrowed
- Income taxes payable—an obligation to pay taxes on a company's income

Current liabilities are usually listed in increasing order of maturity (due date). Under IFRS, companies can alternatively list current and noncurrent liabilities by decreasing order of their due date (maturity). Current liabilities reported by Canadian Tire were $4,578.8 million.

Long–Term Liabilities and Shareholders' Equity

Long-term liabilities are the obligations of the company that will require payment beyond one year or the operating cycle, whichever is longer. Common examples are:

- Loans or notes payable—an obligation to repay cash borrowed at a future date
- Bonds payable—a form of an interest-bearing note payable issued by corporations in an effort to attract a large amount of investors

Shareholders' equity is the last major classification on a company's statement of financial position. Shareholders' equity arises primarily from two sources:

- Contributed capital—the owners' contributions of cash and other assets to the company (includes the common and preferred shares of a company)
- Retained earnings—the accumulated net income of a company that has not been distributed to owners in the form of dividends

If a company has been profitable for many years, and if its shareholders have been willing to forgo large dividends, retained earnings may be a large portion of equity. Canadian Tire reported approximately $4.1 billion of retained earnings, representing over 72% of its total shareholders' equity.

   Together, a company's liabilities and shareholders' equity make up the **capital** of a business. Canadian Tire has total liabilities of approximately $8.9 billion. Of this, approximately $4.6 billion comes from current creditors, while approximately $4.3 billion comes from long-term creditors. Canadian Tire's equity capital, which is the capital of all shareholders, is approximately $5.6 billion (total shareholders' equity).

Preparing a Statement of Financial Position

Using the fundamental accounting equation and the common classifications of statement of financial position items, a company will prepare its statement of financial position by following five steps:

Step 1. Prepare a heading that includes the name of the company, the title of the financial statement, the date of the statement, and the unit of measure.
Step 2. List the assets of the company in decreasing order of their liquidity or nearness to cash. Use appropriate classifications. Add the assets and double-underline the total.
Step 3. List the liabilities of the company in increasing order of their time to maturity. Use appropriate classifications.
Step 4. List the shareholders' equity balances with appropriate classifications.
Step 5. Add the liabilities and shareholders' equity and double-underline the total.

In general, only the first items in a column as well as the final totals have dollar signs. Also, when multiple items exist within a classification, these items are grouped together in a separate column (to the left of the main column) and their total is placed in the main column. Cornerstone 1.2 illustrates the steps in the preparation of a classified statement of financial position.

Preparing a Classified Statement of Financial Position   CORNERSTONE 1.2

Information:

Hightower Inc. reported the following account balances at December 31, 2018:

Inventories	$ 2,300	Accounts receivable	$ 4,200	Accounts payable	$ 3,750
Land	12,100	Cash	2,500	Common shares	14,450
Salaries payable	1,200	Equipment	21,000	Patents	2,500
Retained earnings	11,300	Accumulated depreciation	5,800	Notes payable	8,100

(*Continued*)

CORNERSTONE
VIDEO

CORNERSTONE

1.2

(Continued)

Required:

Prepare Hightower's statement of financial position at December 31, 2018.

Why:

A statement of financial position reports a company's assets, liabilities, and shareholders' equity position at a point in time. This statement can then be reviewed when future operating and financial improvements are being made.

Solution:

Hightower Inc. **Statement of Financial Position** **December 31, 2018**			Step 1
ASSETS			
Current assets:			
Cash	$ 2,500		
Accounts receivable	4,200		
Inventories	2,300		
Total current assets		$ 9,000	
Property, plant, and equipment:			
Land	12,100		
Equipment	21,000		Step 2
Less: accumulated depreciation	(5,800)		
Total property, plant, and equipment		27,300	
Intangible assets:			
Patents		2,500	
Total assets		$38,800	
LIABILITIES AND SHAREHOLDERS' EQUITY			
Current liabilities:			
Accounts payable	$ 3,750		
Salaries payable	1,200		
Total current liabilities		$ 4,950	Step 3
Long-term liabilities:			
Notes payable		8,100	
Total liabilities		13,050	
Shareholders' equity:			
Common shares	14,450		Step 4
Retained earnings	11,300		
Total shareholders' equity		25,750	
Total liabilities and shareholders' equity		$38,800	Step 5

Using Statement of Financial Position Information

The statement of financial position conveys important information about the structure of assets, liabilities, and shareholders' equity, which is used to judge a company's financial health. For example, the relationship between current assets and current liabilities gives investors and creditors insights into a company's **liquidity**—that is, the ability to pay obligations as they become due. Two useful measures of liquidity are *working capital* and the *current ratio*. Working capital and the current ratio for a company are helpful when they are compared to other companies in the same industry. It is even more helpful to look at the trend of these measures in the same company over several years.

Working Capital   **Working capital** is a measure of liquidity, computed as:

$$\text{Working capital} = \text{Current assets} - \text{Current liabilities}$$

Because current liabilities will be settled with current assets, Canadian Tire's working capital of $3,931.4 million ($8,510.2 million − $4,578.8 million) signals that it has adequate funds with which to pay its current obligations. Because working capital is expressed as a dollar amount, the information it conveys in comparisons between companies is limited.

Current Ratio   The **current ratio** is an alternative measure of liquidity that allows meaningful comparisons to be made between different companies and is computed as:

$$\text{Current ratio} = \frac{\text{Current assets}}{\text{Current liabilities}}$$

For example, Canadian Tire's current ratio of 1.86 ($8,510.2 million ÷ $4,578.8 million) can be compared with that of its competitors. Canadian Tire's current ratio tells us that for every dollar of current liabilities, it has $1.86 of current assets. Canadian Tire is very liquid.

YOUDECIDE   Assessing the Creditworthiness of a Prospective Customer

You are the regional credit manager for Nordic Equipment Company. Thin Inc., a newly organized health club, has offered to purchase $50,000 worth of exercise equipment by paying the full amount plus 9% interest in six months. At your request, Thin provides the following figures from its statement of financial position:

Current Assets		Current Liabilities	
Cash	$10,000	Accounts payable	$25,000
Accounts receivable	50,000	Notes payable	30,000
Supplies	4,000	Current portion of mortgage payable	18,000
Total	$64,000	Total	$73,000

Based on what you know about the company's current assets and liabilities, do you allow Thin to purchase the equipment on credit?

In making your decision, it is important to consider the relationship between a company's current assets and its current liabilities. Observe that Thin's current liabilities exceed current assets by $9,000 ($64,000 − $73,000) resulting in negative working capital. In addition, Thin's current ratio is 0.88 ($64,000 ÷ $73,000). By all indications, Thin is suffering from liquidity issues. Finally, there is no evidence presented that Thin's liquidity problem will improve. If Thin does fail to pay its liabilities, it is possible that the existing creditors could force Thin to sell its assets in order to pay off the debt. In such situations, it is possible that you will not receive the full amount promised. Unless Thin can demonstrate how it will pay its current short-term obligations, short-term credit should not be extended.

Allowing a company to purchase assets on credit requires evaluating the debtor's ability to repay the loan out of current assets.

THE STATEMENT OF COMPREHENSIVE INCOME

The statement of comprehensive income under IFRS is a two-part statement that reports the changes that have occurred in shareholders' equity over a period of time from all business activities other than investments by shareholders and distributions to shareholders.

OBJECTIVE 5

Understand how a statement of earnings is prepared and used by different decision makers.

The first part of this statement reports the excess of revenues over expenses during an accounting period; this excess is referred to as "profit" or "net earnings." The second part of this statement reports comprehensive income, which consists of income and expense components that are not recorded in the statement of earnings under IFRS. Private enterprises that follow ASPE do not have comprehensive income and continue to disclose their profit in a statement of earnings. The statement of earnings terminology continues to be used by publicly accountable enterprises that do not have comprehensive income to report. The statement of comprehensive income is further discussed in Chapter 10. The focus in this chapter is on the statement of earnings. The Comprehensive Income Statement for Canadian Tire is shown in Exhibit 1-8A.

The statement of earnings reports the results of a company's operations—the sale of goods and services and the associated expenses of operating the company—for a given period. The long-term survival of a company depends on its ability to produce net earnings, or net income, by earning revenues in excess of expenses. Net earnings enables a company to pay for the capital it uses (dividends to shareholders and interest to creditors) and attract new capital necessary for continued existence and growth. Investors buy and sell shares and creditors loan money based on their beliefs about a company's future performance. The past net earnings or net income reported on a company's statement of earnings provides investors with information about a company's ability to earn future income.

(EXHIBIT 1.8A)

The Comprehensive Income Statement for Canadian Tire

Consolidated Statements of Comprehensive Income For the Years Ended (CDN$ in millions)		
	January 3, 2015	December 28, 2013
Net income	$639.3	$564.4
Other comprehensive income		
Items that may be reclassified subsequently to net income:		
Cash flow hedges:		
Gains, net of tax of $40.4 (2013—$30.0)	114.0	83.1
Reclassification of gains to nonfinancial assets, net of tax of $27.2 (2013—$12.2)	(77.5)	(33.7)
Reclassification of gains to income, net of tax of $0.6 (2013—$0.1)	(1.5)	(0.4)
Available-for-sale financial assets:		
(Losses) gains, net of tax of $0.1 (2013—$nil)	(0.1)	0.1
Reclassification of gains to income, net of tax of $nil (2013—$nil)	(0.1)	–
Item that will not be reclassified subsequently to net income:		
Actuarial (losses) gains, net of tax of $4.7 (2013—$3.6)	(13.2)	10.0
Other comprehensive income	21.6	59.1
Other comprehensive income attributable to:		
Owners of Canadian Tire Corporation	$ 21.5	$ 59.1
Noncontrolling interests	0.1	–
	$ 21.6	$ 59.1
Comprehensive income	$660.9	$623.5
Comprehensive income attributable to:		
Owners of Canadian Tire Corporation	$625.5	$620.3
Noncontrolling interests	35.4	3.2
	$660.9	$623.5

Source: Canadian Tire Corporation Annual Report 2014, page 65.

Elements

The statement of earnings consists of two major items: revenues and expenses. A statement of earnings for Canadian Tire is presented in Exhibit 1.8B.

Examining the heading of the statement of earnings, you should notice that it follows the same general format as the statement of financial position—it indicates the name of the company, the title of the financial statement, the time period covered by the statement, and the unit of measure. However, the statement of earnings differs from the statement of financial position in that it covers a period of time instead of a specific date.

Revenues Revenues are the increase in assets that result from the sale of products or services. Revenues can arise from different sources and have different names depending on the source of the revenue. *Sales revenue* (or *service revenue* for companies that provide services) arises from the principal activity of the business. For Canadian Tire, its revenue comes from sales of goods, interest income, royalties and licence fees, and service and rental income. Canadian Tire, like most other companies, generally recognizes sales revenue in the period that a sale occurs. Revenues also can be generated from activities other than the company's principal operations (nonoperating activities). For example, in addition to sales of its products, Canadian Tire also earns *finance income* from invested funds.

Expenses Expenses are the cost of resources used to earn revenues during a period. Expenses have different names depending on their function. Canadian Tire's statement of earnings in Exhibit 1.8B reports five different expenses:

- *Cost of goods sold* (often called *cost of sales*)—the cost to the seller of all goods sold during the accounting period.[4]
- *Sales and marketing expenses*—the expenses that a company incurs in selling goods, providing services, or managing the company that are not directly related to production. These expenses include advertising expenses; salaries paid to salespersons or managers; depreciation on buildings; and expenses related to insurance, utilities, property taxes, and repairs.

(EXHIBIT 1.8B)

Statement of Earnings of Canadian Tire Corporation, Limited

Canadian Tire Corporation, Limited Statement of Earnings* For the Year Ended January 3, 2015 (in millions of dollars)		
Revenues:		
Sales	$12,462.9	$12,462.9
Expenses:		
Costs of goods sold	8,033.2	
Sales and marketing expenses	3,052.9	
Administrative expenses	389.7	
Net finance costs	108.9	
Income tax expense	238.9	11,823.6
Net income		$ 639.3

*The statement of earnings information was taken from the January 3, 2015, annual report of Canadian Tire Corporation and has been summarized and reformatted by the author.

Source: Canadian Tire Corporation Annual Report 2014.

---

[4] We will discuss procedures for calculating cost of goods sold in Chapter 6.

- *Administrative expenses*— the cost of administering the company's business.
- *Net finance costs*—the net interest expense incurred by the company.
- *Income tax expense*—the income taxes related to the company's pretax income.

Net Income   Net income, or net earnings, is the difference between total revenues and expenses. Canadian Tire reported net income of $639.3 million ($12,462.9 million – $11,823.6 million). If total expenses are greater than total revenues, the company will report a net loss.

Preparing a Statement of Earnings

The preparation of a statement of earnings involves four steps:

Step 1. Prepare a heading that includes the name of the company, the title of the financial statement, the time period covered, and the unit of measure.

Step 2. List the revenues of the company, starting with sales revenue (or service revenue) and then listing other revenue items. Add the revenues to obtain total revenue.

Step 3. List the expenses of the company, usually starting with cost of goods sold. Add the expenses to obtain total expenses.

Step 4. Subtract the expenses from the revenues to get net income (or net loss if expenses exceed revenues). Double-underline net income.

In general, only the first items in a column as well as the final totals have dollar signs. Also, when multiple items exist within a classification, these items are grouped together in a separate column (to the left of the main column) and their total is placed in the main column. Cornerstone 1.3 shows how to prepare a statement of earnings.

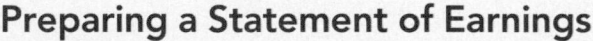

CORNERSTONE 1.3

Preparing a Statement of Earnings

Information:

Hightower Inc. reported the following account balances for the year ended December 31, 2018:

Cost of goods sold	$31,300	Interest expense	$ 540
Salaries expense	8,800	Sales revenue	50,600
Insurance expense	700	Depreciation expense	1,500
Interest income	1,200	Rent expense	2,100
Income tax expense	2,000		

Required:

Prepare Hightower's statement of earnings for the year ended December 31, 2018.

Why:

The statement of earnings reports the results of a company's operations (its revenues less expenses) for a specified period of time. This statement can be reviewed from the perspective of planning how reported profit or loss for a specified period can be improved upon in the future.

(Continued)

Solution:

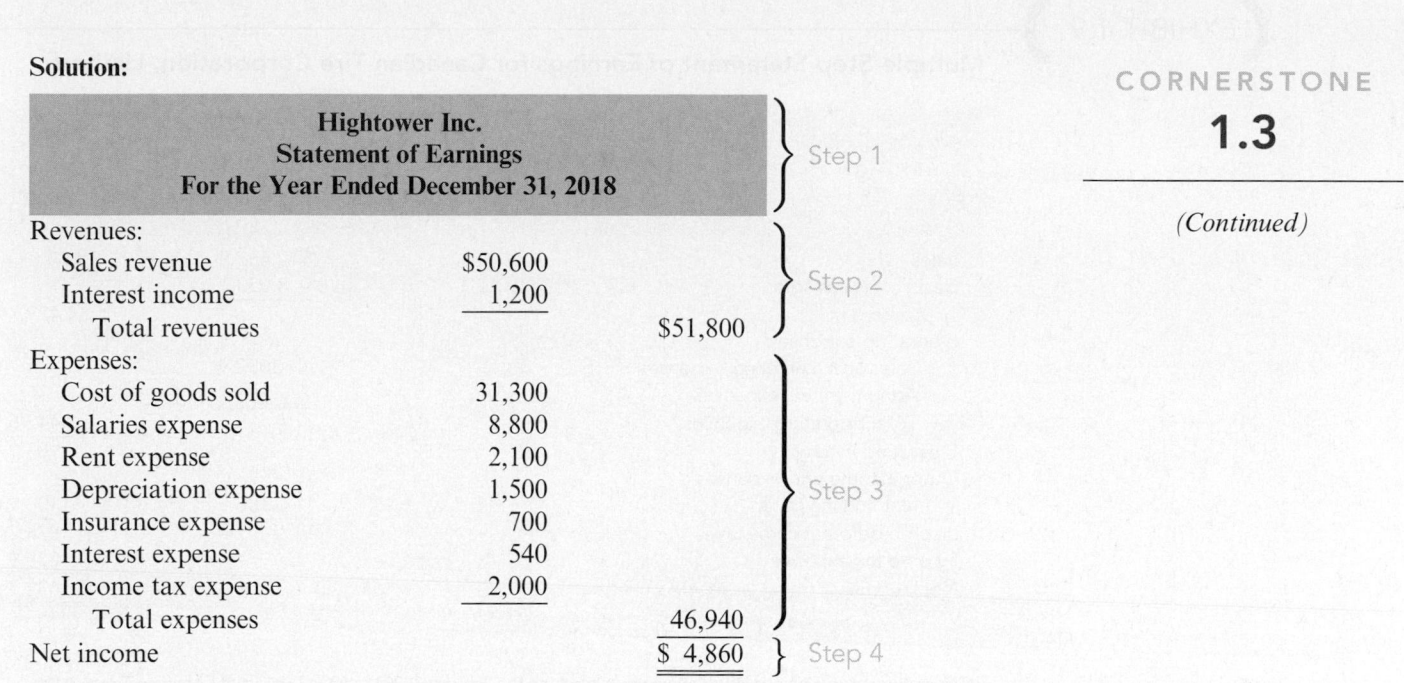

Hightower Inc. Statement of Earnings For the Year Ended December 31, 2018		
Revenues:		
Sales revenue	$50,600	
Interest income	1,200	
Total revenues		$51,800
Expenses:		
Cost of goods sold	31,300	
Salaries expense	8,800	
Rent expense	2,100	
Depreciation expense	1,500	
Insurance expense	700	
Interest expense	540	
Income tax expense	2,000	
Total expenses		46,940
Net income		$ 4,860

Step 1
Step 2
Step 3
Step 4

CORNERSTONE

1.3

(Continued)

Statement of Earnings Formats

Companies prepare their statements of earnings in one of two different formats: single-step or multiple-step.

Single-Step Statement of Earnings The format that we illustrate in Cornerstone 1.3 is called a *single-step statement of earnings*. In a single-step statement of earnings, there are only two categories: total revenues and total expenses. Total expenses are subtracted from total revenues in a *single step* to arrive at net income. The advantage of a single-step statement of earnings is its simplicity.

Multiple-Step Statement of Earnings A second format is the *multiple-step statement of earnings*. The multiple-step statement of earnings provides classifications of revenues and expenses that financial statement users find useful. A multiple-step statement of earnings contains three important subtotals:

- **Gross margin (gross profit)**—the difference between net sales and cost of goods sold (or cost of sales)
- **Income from operations**—the difference between gross margin and operating expenses
- **Net income**—the difference between income from operations and any nonoperating revenues and expenses, less income tax expense.

A multiple-step statement of earnings for Canadian Tire is shown in Exhibit 1.9.

Gross Margin A company's *gross margin* or *gross profit* is calculated as:

> Gross margin = Net sales − Cost of goods sold

Gross margin represents the initial profit made from selling a product, but it is *not* a measure of total profit because other operating expenses have not yet been subtracted. However, gross margin is closely watched by managers and other financial statement users. A change in a company's gross margin can give insights into a company's current pricing and purchasing policies, thereby providing insight into the company's past and future performance.

(EXHIBIT 1.9)

Multiple-Step Statement of Earnings for Canadian Tire Corporation, Limited

Canadian Tire Corporation, Limited Statement of Earnings* For the Year Ended January 3, 2015 (in millions of dollars)		
Sales	$12,462.9	
Costs of goods sold	8,033.2	
Gross margin		$4,429.7
Operating expenses:		
Sales and marketing expenses	3052.9	
Administrative expenses	389.7	
Total operating expenses		3,442.6
Operating income		987.1
Other income and expenses		
Net finance costs	108.9	108.9
Income before income taxes		878.2
Income tax expense		238.9
Net income		$ 639.3

*The statement of earnings information was taken from the January 3, 2015, annual report of Canadian Tire and has been summarized and reformatted by the author.

Source: Canadian Tire Corporation Annual Report 2014.

Income from Operations *Income from operations* is computed as:

$$\text{Income from operations} = \text{Gross margin} - \text{Operating expenses}$$

Operating expenses are the expenses the business incurs in selling goods or providing services and managing the company. Operating expenses typically include research and development expenses, selling expenses, and general and administrative expenses. Income from operations indicates the level of profit produced by the principal activities of the company. Canadian Tire can increase its income from operations by either increasing its gross margin or decreasing its operating expenses.

Nonoperating Activities A multiple-step statement of earnings reports nonoperating activities in a section that is frequently called *other income and expenses. Nonoperating activities* are revenues and expenses from activities other than the company's principal operations. They include gains and losses from the sale of equipment and other assets that were not acquired for resale. For many companies, the most important nonoperating component is interest. Exhibit 1.10 lists some common nonoperating revenues, gains, expenses, and losses.

(EXHIBIT 1.10)

Typical Nonoperating Items

Other Revenues and Gains

Interest revenue on investments
Dividend revenue from investments
 in shares of other companies
Rent revenue
Gains on sale of property, plant,
 and equipment

Other Expenses and Losses

Interest expense from loans
Losses from sale of property,
 plant, and equipment
Losses from accidents or vandalism
Losses from employee strikes
Income tax expense

© Cengage Learning

Net Income Nonoperating items are subtracted from income from operations to obtain income before taxes. Income tax expense is then subtracted to obtain net income. Regardless of the format used, the amount of the revenues and expenses reported is the same. That is, net income is the same under either the single-step or the multiple-step format. The only difference is how the revenues and expenses are classified.

Using Statement of Earnings Information

A company's ability to generate current income is useful in predicting its ability to generate future income. When investors believe that future income will improve, they will buy shares. Similarly, creditors rely on their judgments of a company's future income to make loans. Investors' and creditors' estimates of the future profitability and growth of a company are aided by a careful examination of how a company has earned its revenue and managed its expenses. Users must remember that **a company's profit is not necessarily equal to, and is usually *not* equal to, the company's cash flow from operations!** These two concepts, profit and cash flow, are both critical to a company's financial health but they are seperately determined.

Net Profit Margin A useful measure of a company's ability to generate profit is its **net profit margin** (sometimes called return on sales). Net profit margin shows the percentage of profit in each dollar of sales and is computed as:

$$\text{Net profit margin} = \frac{\text{Net income}}{\text{Sales revenue}}$$

This ratio provides an indication of management's ability to control expenses. Future income depends on maintaining (or increasing) market share while controlling expenses.

YOUDECIDE Assessing Future Profitability

You are looking to invest in one of two companies in the same industry—Growth Inc. or Stagnation Company. Your initial examination revealed that both companies reported the same amount of net income for 2018. Further analysis produced the following five-year summary:

Growth Inc.

	2014	2015	2016	2017	2018
Sales revenue	$625,000	$750,000	$820,000	$920,000	$1,000,000
Net income	$ 30,000	$ 36,000	$ 40,000	$ 45,000	$ 50,000
Net profit margin	4.8%	4.8%	4.9%	4.9%	5.0%

Stagnation Company

	2014	2015	2016	2017	2018
Sales revenue	$1,025,000	$975,000	$940,000	$1,020,000	$1,040,000
Net income	$ 51,000	$ 48,000	$ 46,000	$ 49,000	$ 50,000
Net profit margin	5%	4.9%	4.9%	4.8%	4.8%

Which company is the better investment?

Investors seek those investments that will provide the largest return at the lowest risk. One factor associated with large returns is future profitability. Over the past five years, Growth's sales and net income have steadily increased while Stagnation's sales and net income have remained, on average, stable. Sales growth is an indicator of the possibility of increasing future income. Furthermore, Growth's increasing net profit margin (compared to a decreasing net profit margin for Stagnation) indicates that Growth is doing a better job at controlling its expenses relative to Stagnation, enabling Growth to earn more profit on each dollar of sales. While the future never can be predicted with certainty, the data suggest that, if current trends continue, Growth will grow more rapidly than Stagnation. Therefore, an investment in Growth would probably yield the larger future return.

Financial statement information can help you judge a company's potential for future profitability and growth.

THE STATEMENT OF CHANGES IN EQUITY

OBJECTIVE

Understand how a statement of changes in equity is prepared and used by different decision makers.

Public companies prepare a statement of changes in equity, which reports how profit, dividends, share capital increases (decreases), and other changes in shareholders' equity have affected the company's statement of financial position.

Private companies prepare a statement of retained earnings, which presents only the changes in the retained earnings account during the period. This chapter focuses on the retained earnings component of shareholders' equity. Other components of changes in equity and the statement of changes in equity are discussed in Chapter 10.

The owners of a company contribute capital in one of two ways:

- directly, through purchases of common shares from the company, and
- indirectly, by the company retaining some or all of the net income earned each year rather than paying it out in dividends.

Net income earned by the company but not paid out in the form of dividends is called retained earnings. The beginning balance in retained earnings is increased by net income earned during the year and decreased by any dividends that were declared.

Exhibit 1.11 shows the statement of changes in equity for Canadian Tire. Notice the heading is similar to the heading for the income statement in that it covers a period of time (the fiscal year ended January 3, 2015). In addition, Canadian Tire declared dividends for the year ended January 3, 2015, of $1514.1 million. Companies may choose not to pay dividends in order to reinvest their earnings and support future growth.

(**EXHIBIT 1.11**)

Statement of Changes in Equity for Canadian Tire Corporation, Limited

Canadian Tire Corporation, Limited
Statement of Changes in Equity*
For the Year Ended January 3, 2015
(in millions of dollars)

	Share Capital	Contributed Surplus	Total Accumulated Other Comprehensive Income	Retained Earnings	Equity Attributable to Noncontrolling Interests	Total
Balance, beginning of year	$712.9	$2.4	$47.4	$4,404.6	$282.6	5,449.9
Total comprehensive income						
Net income				604.0	35.3	639.3
Other comprehensive income (loss)	–	–	34.6	(13.1)	.1	21.6
Contributions by and distributions to shareholders						
Class A shares issued	6.9					6.9
Repurchase of Class A shares	(24.3)					(24.3)
Other changes		.5		(766.3)	457.3	
Dividends				(154.1)		(154.1)
Balance, end of year	$695.5	$2.9	$82.0	$4,075.1	775.3	$5,630.8

*The statement of changes in equity was created by the author from information contained in the January 3, 2015, annual report of Canadian Tire Corporation.

Source: Canadian Tire Corporation Annual Report 2014.

The preparation of the statement of changes in equity involves four steps:

Step 1. Prepare a heading that includes the name of the company, the title of the financial statement, the time period covered, and the unit of measure.

Step 2. List the balances for each equity component at the beginning of the period obtained from the previous year's statement of financial position.

Step 3. Add net income obtained from the statement of earnings and other comprehensive income from the statement of comprehensive income.

Step 4. Subtract any dividends declared during the period and add (deduct) any other items affecting the equity components of the business. Double-underline the totals, which should equal the balances of each equity component at the end of the period as reported on the statement of financial position.

The preparation of a retained earnings statement for a private company is detailed in Cornerstone 1.4 using a four-step process similar to that outlined above.

Preparing a Statement of Retained Earnings

CORNERSTONE 1.4

Information:

Hightower Inc. reported the following account balances for the year ended December 31, 2018:

| Net income | $4,860 | Retained earnings, 1/1/2018 | $ 9,440 |
| Dividends | 3,000 | Retained earnings, 12/31/2018 | 11,300 |

Required:

Prepare Hightower's retained earnings statement for the year ended December 31, 2018.

Why:

A statement of retained earnings must be prepared to determine how this account has been impacted by business and certain shareholder transactions during a period of time. This statement can be reviewed from the perspective of planning business and shareholder transactions that will positively impact the company.

► | CORNERSTONE VIDEO

Solution:

Hightower Inc. **Statement of Retained Earnings** **For the Year Ended December 31, 2018**	} Step 1
Balance, January 1, 2018	$ 9,440 } Step 2
Add: Net income	4,860 } Step 3
Less: Dividends	(3,000)
Balance, December 31, 2018	$11,300 } Step 4

Use of the Retained Earnings Statement

The retained earnings balance is used to monitor and evaluate a company's dividend payouts to its shareholders. For example, some older investors seek out companies with high dividend payouts so that they will receive cash during the year. Other investors are more interested in companies that are reinvesting a sufficient amount of earnings that will enable them to pursue profitable growth opportunities. Also, creditors are interested in a company's dividend payouts. If a company pays out too much in dividends, it may not have enough cash on hand to repay its debt when it becomes due.

YOUDECIDE Dividend Policy Decisions

You are the manager of a fast-growing software engineering firm. Over the past five years, your company has doubled the amount of its income every year. This tremendous growth has been financed through funds obtained from shareholders and cash generated from operations. The company has virtually no debt.

How would you respond to shareholders who have recently complained that the company's policy not to pay dividends is preventing them from sharing in the company's success?

Retained earnings can be an important source of financing for many companies. When companies feel that they have profitable growth opportunities, they should reinvest the earnings in the business instead of paying out the amount to shareholders as dividends. The reinvestment of these funds should result in higher share prices (and increased wealth for the shareholders) as the company grows. If the company chose to pay a dividend, it would be forced to either abandon the growth opportunities or finance them through some other, more costly method, such as issuing debt.

When management feels that the company has growth opportunities that will increase the value of the company, the reinvestment of earnings is usually preferable.

STATEMENT OF CASH FLOWS

OBJECTIVE

Identify the components of a statement of cash flows and understand how it is used by different decision makers.

The fourth major financial statement, the statement of cash flows, describes the company's cash receipts (cash inflows) and cash payments (cash outflows) for a period of time. The statement of cash flows for Canadian Tire is shown in Exhibit 1.12.

Elements

Cash flows are classified into one of three categories:

- **Cash flows from operating activities**—any cash flows directly related to earning income. This category includes cash sales and collections of accounts receivable as well as cash payments for goods, services, salaries, and interest.

(EXHIBIT 1.12)

Statement of Cash Flows

Canadian Tire Corporation, Limited Statement of Cash Flows* For the Year Ended January 3, 2015 (in millions of dollars)	
Net cash provided from operating activities	$ 574.8
Net cash used for investing activities	(589.5)
Net cash used for financing activities	(88.6)
Cash generated in the year	(73.9)
Cash at the beginning of the year	573.9
Cash at the end of the year	$ 647.8

*The statement of cash flows information was taken from the January 3, 2015, annual report of Canadian Tire Corporation and has been summarized and reformatted by the author.

Source: Canadian Tire Corporation Annual Report 2014, page 63.

- **Cash flows from investing activities**—any cash flows related to the acquisition or sale of investments and long-term assets such as property, plant, and equipment and long-term share investments.
- **Cash flows from financing activities**—any cash flows related to obtaining capital for the company. This category includes the issuance and repayment of debt, the issuance and repurchase of shares, and the payment of dividends.

The preparation of the statement of cash flows will be discussed in Chapter 11.

Use of the Statement of Cash Flows

Because cash is the lifeblood of any company and is critical to success, the statement of cash flows can be an important source of information as users attempt to answer how a company generated and used cash during a period. Such information is helpful as users assess the company's ability to generate cash in the future. Creditors can use the statement of cash flows to assess the creditworthiness of a company. A company with healthy cash flow—particularly if it comes from operating activities—is in a good position to repay debts as they come due and is usually a low-risk borrower. Shareholders are also interested in the adequacy of cash flows as an indicator of the company's ability to pay dividends and to expand its business.

RELATIONSHIPS AMONG THE FOUR FINANCIAL STATEMENTS

It is important to recognize the natural relationships of the four basic financial statements and the natural progression from one financial statement to another. The accounting period begins with a closing statement of financial position from the previous accounting period. During the year, the company earns net income from operating its business. Net income from the income statement increases retained earnings on the retained earnings statement. Ending retained earnings is then reported in the shareholders' equity section of the statement of financial position at the end of the accounting period. Therefore, the income statement can be viewed as explaining, through the statement of retained earnings, the change in the financial position during the year. Finally, the statement of cash flows explains the change in cash during the year (and reconciles the cash balance at the beginning of the period to the cash balance at the end of the period on the statement of financial position). These relationships are shown in Exhibit 1.13.

OBJECTIVE 8

Describe the relationships among the four basic financial statements and how management uses financial statements.

Use of Financial Statements by Management

Management members make extensive use of the data produced by a company's accounting information system. Financial statement information can impact management decisions concerning credit to be granted to customers, inventory to be purchased to meet a company's sales goals, strategies to be used in negotiating pay adjustments with employees, and tax strategies to be implemented to reduce tax payable on a company's profit. Additional information is also generated by a company's management accounting information system to assist in decisions in areas such as make or buy, expand or subcontract, and product pricing.

It is common business practice for companies to request the financial statement of their customers and suppliers. Management uses this external financial statement information to assist in making customer credit decisions and supplier purchasing decisions.

COMPONENTS IN THE ANNUAL REPORT

The financial statements discussed in the previous sections were reported to users in an *annual report.* For publicly traded companies that are required to file reports with the provincial securities commissions, the annual report includes the audited financial

OBJECTIVE 9

Describe information contained in the annual report.

EXHIBIT 1.13

Relationships among the Four Financial Statements

Beginning of the Period ———→   End of the Period ———→

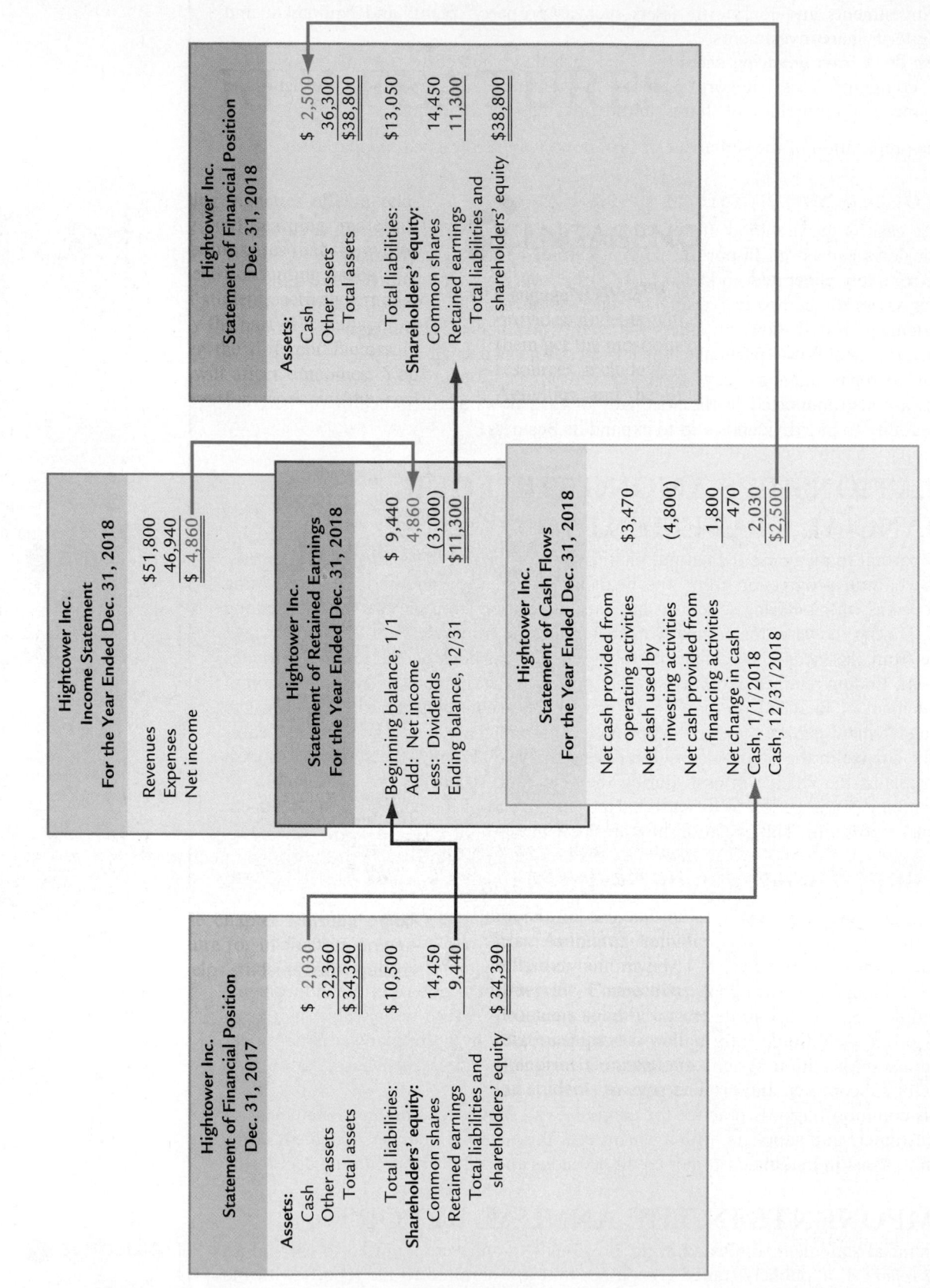

Hightower Inc.
Income Statement
For the Year Ended Dec. 31, 2018

Revenues	$51,800
Expenses	46,940
Net income	$ 4,860

Hightower Inc.
Statement of Retained Earnings
For the Year Ended Dec. 31, 2018

Beginning balance, 1/1	$ 9,440
Add: Net income	4,860
Less: Dividends	(3,000)
Ending balance, 12/31	$11,300

Hightower Inc.
Statement of Cash Flows
For the Year Ended Dec. 31, 2018

Net cash provided from operating activities	$3,470
Net cash used by investing activities	(4,800)
Net cash provided from financing activities	1,800
Net change in cash	470
Cash, 1/1/2018	2,030
Cash, 12/31/2018	$2,500

Hightower Inc.
Statement of Financial Position
Dec. 31, 2017

Assets:	
Cash	$ 2,030
Other assets	32,360
Total assets	$34,390
Total liabilities:	$10,500
Shareholders' equity:	
Common shares	14,450
Retained earnings	9,440
Total liabilities and shareholders' equity	$34,390

Hightower Inc.
Statement of Financial Position
Dec. 31, 2018

Assets:	
Cash	$ 2,500
Other assets	36,300
Total assets	$38,800
Total liabilities:	$13,050
Shareholders' equity:	
Common shares	14,450
Retained earnings	11,300
Total liabilities and shareholders' equity	$38,800

statements of a company and other important information such as the notes to the financial statements, management's discussion and analysis of the condition of the company, and the auditor's report.

Notes to the Financial Statements

The **notes to the financial statements** (or **footnotes**) clarify and expand upon the information presented in the financial statements. The notes are an integral part of the financial statements and help to fulfill the company's responsibility for full disclosure of all relevant information. Without the information contained in the notes, the financial statements would be incomplete and could not be adequately understood by users. The information contained in the notes can be either quantitative (numerical) or qualitative (non-numerical).

Generally, the first note contains a summary of significant accounting policies and rules used in the financial statements. For example, the following is an excerpt from Canadian Tire's notes to the financial statements concerning its accounting for revenues:

Revenue

The company recognizes revenue when the amount can be reliably measured, it is probable that future economic benefits will flow to the entity, and when specific criteria have been met for each of the company's activities.

Other footnotes provide additional detail on line items presented in the financial statements. For example, while Canadian Tire only reports a single number on the statement of financial position for property, plant, and equipment, the company provides a detailed breakdown of the components of property, plant, and equipment (land, buildings, fixtures, and equipment) in the notes. Other notes provide disclosures about items not reported in the financial statements. For instance, Canadian Tire provides detailed explanations of its stock option activity over the past two years—an activity not directly reported on the financial statements yet of significant interest to users.

Management's Discussion and Analysis

The annual report also includes a section titled **Management's Discussion and Analysis**. In this section, management provides a discussion and explanation of various items reported in the financial statements. Additionally, management uses this opportunity to highlight favourable and unfavourable trends and significant risks facing the company.

Report of Independent Auditors

An independent auditor is an accounting professional who conducts an examination of a company's financial statements. The objective of this examination is to gather evidence that will enable the auditor to form an opinion as to whether the financial statements fairly present the financial position and financial performance of the company. The auditor's opinion of the financial statements is presented in the form of an **audit report**.

Because financial statement users cannot directly observe the company's accounting practices, companies hire auditors to give the users of the financial statements assurance or confidence that the financial statements are a fair presentation of the company's financial health. In performing an audit, it is impractical for an auditor to retrace every transaction of the company for the entire accounting period. Instead, the auditor performs procedures (e.g., sampling of transactions) that enable an opinion to be expressed on the financial statements as a whole.

---

concept Q&A

Is there a single equation or financial statement that captures the business activities (operating, investing, and financing) that all companies engage in?

Answer:

The fundamental accounting equation captures the business activities of companies and encompasses all the major financial statements. While certain statements provide more information on certain business activities (e.g., the income statement provides information about a company's operating activities), information is also contained in other statements (e.g., current assets and current liabilities provide insight into a company's operations). Therefore, all financial statements and the notes to the financial statements must be examined as an integrated whole.

YOUDECIDE The Business Need for Accountants and Career Choices

Keep in mind that virtually every organization must have an accounting system. Thus, accountants are employed in a wide range of businesses, including public and private companies, public accounting firms, governments, and banks.

What skills and character traits are required for accountants?

Accountants must have well-developed analytical skills and must be effective communicators, both verbally and in writing. Most accounting assignments—whether in business, government, or public accounting—are team assignments in which team members must be able to communicate effectively and work quickly and cooperatively to a solution.

As a profession, accounting requires a high level of academic study and is subject to professional competence requirements. Most members of public accounting firms, and many management accountants and consultants, are Chartered Professional

Accountants (CPAs). This professional designation is designed to ensure that the accountants who offer their services are properly qualified and maintain a high level of personal integrity and ethical behaviour.

The career opportunities for accountants are virtually boundless and could include careers in auditing, tax, education, financial advisory services, insurance, forensic accounting, and management consulting. Even if you choose a different career path outside of the formal accounting profession, the knowledge and experience that you can gain from accounting will prove invaluable in your career, whether in the profit, not-for-profit, or government sector.

Accountants must possess strong analytical and communication skills, demonstrate professional competency, and behave ethically.

INTERNATIONAL FINANCIAL REPORTING STANDARDS

OBJECTIVE

Understand the role of International Accounting Standards in determining the content of financial statements.

To make it easier to use financial statements over time and across companies, common rules and conventions have been developed to guide the preparation of financial statements. These rules and conventions, referred to as **generally accepted accounting principles (GAAP)**, have been developed by a number of organizations over the years. In Canada, provincial securities commissions (the Ontario Securities Commission [OSC] in Ontario) were formed to establish accounting rules for publicly traded companies. In the United States, the Securities and Exchange Commission (SEC) performs a similar function.

In Canada, the provincial securities commissions work closely with the Accounting Standards Board (AcSB) of CPA Canada (formerly the Canadian Institute of Chartered Accountants (CICA)). CPA Canada has established detailed accounting principles, which it publishes in the *CPA Canada Handbook.* These have become the professional accounting standards. The AcSB in Canada establishes accounting principles for publicly accountable enterprises, private enterprises, government entities, and not-for-profit organizations. In the United States, the SEC has delegated its authority over accounting principles to the Financial Accounting Standards Board (FASB).

Globalization has created the need for a common set of global accounting principles. The International Accounting Standards Board (IASB) has developed a set of **International Financial Reporting Standards (IFRS)**. IFRS is used by more than 100 countries to facilitate business around the world.

The use of IFRS in Canada is now mandatory for all publicly accountable enterprises. Private enterprises in Canada can adopt IFRS but are permitted, as an alternative, to follow a simpler set of accounting principles, referred to as **Accounting Standards for Private Enterprises (ASPE)**. Under these less complex principles, private enterprises prepare a **statement of retained earnings** rather than a **statement of changes in equity**. Also, private enterprises prepare a **statement of earnings** and not a statement of comprehensive income (see Chapter 10).

Not-for-profit organizations and pension plans in Canada follow a different set of accounting principles, contained in the *CPA Handbook.*

This text focuses on the accounting standards for publicly accountable enterprises (IFRS); however, important differences between IFRS and ASPE are highlighted throughout the text.

While financial statements prepared under GAAP provide the kind of information users want and need, the financial statements do not *interpret* this information. The financial statement user must use his or her general knowledge and understanding of business and accounting to interpret the financial statements as a basis for decision making.

ETHICS AND LEGAL LIABILITY IN ACCOUNTING

Confidence that standards of ethical behaviour will be maintained—even when individuals have incentives to violate those standards—is essential to the conduct of any business activity. Owners of businesses must trust their managers, managers must trust one another and their employees, and the investing public must trust accountants to behave according to accepted ethical standards, which may or may not be reflected in formal written codes. The violation of ethical standards may bring clear and direct penalties but more often brings subtle and long-lasting negative consequences for individuals and companies.

For the economy to function effectively and efficiently, users must have faith that the information reported in financial statements is accurate and dependable. This can only be accomplished through ethical behaviour of the accountants involved in the financial reporting process. The various professional accounting bodies in Canada, recognizing that their members have an obligation of self-discipline above and beyond the requirements of generally accepted accounting principles, have each adopted a code of professional conduct, which provides ethical guidelines for accountants in the performance of their duties. These ethical principles require accountants to serve the public interest with integrity. For example, auditors should fulfill their duties with objectivity, independence, and due professional care. In no situation should an auditor yield to pressure from management to report positively on financial statements that overstate the company's performance or prospects. Violation of these ethical standards can result in severe penalties and legal liabilities, including revocation of an accountant's licence to practise as a public accountant.

In recent years, there have been an increasing number of news reports about unethical behaviour involving accounting practices. Acting ethically is not always easy. However, because of the important role of accounting in society, accountants are expected to maintain the highest level of ethical behaviour. Throughout this book, you will be exposed to ethical dilemmas that we urge you to consider. As you analyze these cases, consider the guidelines in Exhibit 1.14, which contains a process that can be used to make ethical decisions.

OBJECTIVE **11**

Understand the importance of ethics and legal liability in accounting.

(EXHIBIT 1.14)

Guidelines in Ethical Decision Making

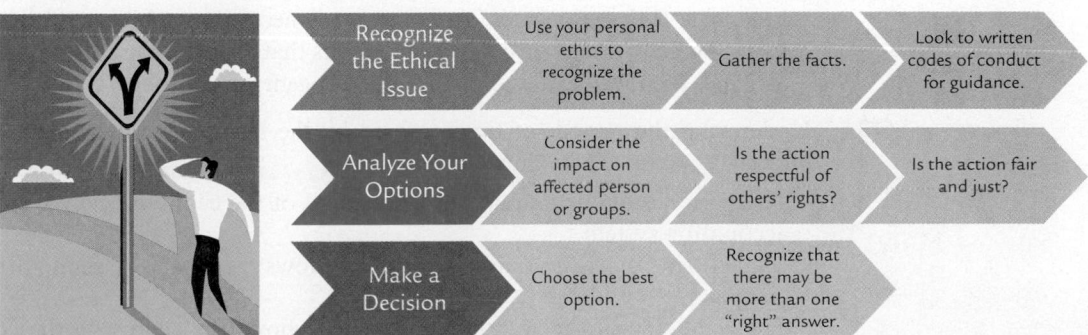

© Cengage Learning

SIGNIFICANT DIFFERENCES BETWEEN IFRS AND ASPE

The following significant differences exist between international financial reporting standards and accounting standards for private enterprises with reference to accounting standards and accounting terminology:

1. Public corporations whose securities trade on a stock exchange must use IFRS. Private corporations can choose to follow IFRS or ASPE, but the choice, once made, must be applied consistently each year.

2. Under IFRS, the statement of financial position title is used by most, but not all, public companies to reflect the assets, liabilities, and shareholders' equity of the corporation. Under ASPE, most private companies, and some public companies, use the title of "balance sheet" to refer to this same financial statement.

3. IFRS requires that a statement of changes in equity be prepared detailing the changes in each component of shareholders' equity for the period. ASPE requires that a statement of retained earnings be prepared detailing only the changes in the retained earnings account for the period. Under ASPE, other changes in shareholders' equity are disclosed in the notes to the financial statements.

4. Public companies prepare a statement of comprehensive income, which contains certain income and expense components not included in calculating net income. Private companies prepare a statement of earnings, which includes all revenues, expenses, gains, and losses for the period. Comprehensive income or loss is not reported by private companies.

SUMMARY OF LEARNING OBJECTIVES

LO1.   Identify who the different users of financial statements are and how they use financial statements.

- Accounting is the process of identifying, measuring, recording, and communicating financial information.
- This information is used both inside and outside of the business to make better decisions.
- Accounting is also called the language of business.
- Financial accounting focuses on the needs of external decision makers. Management accounting focuses on the information needs of internal decision makers.

LO2.   Identify different forms of business organization and business activities.

- The three forms of business organizations are the sole proprietorship (owned by one person), the partnership (jointly owned by two or more persons), and the corporation (separate legal entity organized under the laws of a provincial or federal jurisdiction).
- Regardless of the form of business, all businesses are involved in three activities. Financing activities include obtaining funds necessary to begin and operate a business. Investing activities involve buying the assets that enable a business to operate. Operating activities are the activities of a business that generate a profit.

LO3.   Understand the periods of time covered by the basic four financial statements and the underlying basic accounting equation.

- The basic accounting equation captures all of the economic activities recorded by an accounting system.
- The left side of the accounting equation shows the assets, or economic resources, of a company.
- The right side of the accounting equation shows the claims on the company's assets (liabilities or shareholders' equity).

LO4.   Understand how a statement of financial position is prepared and used by different decision makers.

- A statement of financial position reports the resources (assets) owned by a company and the claims against those resources (liabilities and shareholders' equity) at a specific point in time.
- These elements are related by the fundamental accounting equation: Assets = Liabilities + Shareholders' equity.
- To help users identify the fundamental economic similarities and differences between the various items on the statement of financial position, assets and liabilities are classified as either current or noncurrent (long term). Shareholders' equity is classified as either contributed capital or retained earnings.

LO5.   Understand how a statement of earnings is prepared and used by different decision makers.

- The statement of earnings reports how well a company has performed its operations over a period of time and provides information about the future profitability and growth of a company.
- The statement of earnings includes the revenues and expenses of a company, which can be reported in either a single-step or multiple-step format.

LO6.   Understand how a statement of changes in equity is prepared and used by different decision makers.

- The statement of changes in equity reports how much of a company's income was retained in the business and how much was distributed to owners for a period of time.
- The statement of changes in equity provides users with insights into a company's dividend payouts.

LO7.   Identify the components of a statement of cash flows and understand how it is used by different decision makers.

- The statement of cash flows reports the sources of a company's cash inflow and the uses of a company's cash over time.
- The statement of cash flows can be used to assess the creditworthiness of a company.

LO8.   Describe the relationships among the four basic financial statements and how management uses financial statements.

- There is a natural relationship among the four basic financial statements so that financial statements are prepared in a particular order.
- Starting with the statement of financial position at the beginning of the accounting period, financial statements are generally prepared in the following order: the statement of earnings, the statement of cash flows, the statement of changes in equity, and the statement of financial position at the end of the accounting period.
- The statement of cash flows explains the change in cash on the statements of financial position at the beginning and end of the accounting period.

LO9.   Describe information contained in the annual report.

- The notes to the financial statements clarify and expand upon the information presented in the financial statements and are considered an integral part of a company's financial statements.
- Management's discussion and analysis provides a discussion and explanation of various items reported in the financial statements.
- The auditor's report gives the auditor's opinion as to whether the financial statements fairly present the financial position and financial performance of the company.

LO10. Understand the role of International Accounting Standards in determining the content of financial statements.

- International Financial Reporting Standards (IFRS) are mandatory for publicly accountable enterprises in Canada.
- IFRS are developed by the International Accounting Standards Board (IASB).
- Private companies in Canada can voluntarily choose to report under IFRS or ASPE (Accounting Standards for Private Enterprises).

LO11. Understand the importance of ethics and legal liability in accounting.

- Maintenance of standards of ethical behaviour is essential to the conduct of any business activity. Violation of these standards often brings significant short- and long-term negative professional and legal consequences for individuals and companies.
- The maintenance of a high ethical standard is necessary for users to have faith in the accuracy of the financial statements, which is a key factor in the effective and efficient functioning of the economy.

CORNERSTONES

CORNERSTONE 1.1   Using the basic accounting equation, page 10

CORNERSTONE 1.2   Preparing a classified statement of financial position, page 15

CORNERSTONE 1.3   Preparing a statement of earnings, page 20

CORNERSTONE 1.4   Preparing a statement of retained earnings, page 25

KEY TERMS

Accounting (p. 4)
Accounting Standards for Private Enterprises (ASPE) (p. 30)
Assets (p. 7)
Audit report (p. 29)
Balance sheet (p. 9)
Capital (p. 15)
Cash flows from financing activities (p. 27)
Cash flows from investing activities (p. 27)
Cash flows from operating activities (p. 26)
Corporation (p. 6)
Creditor (p. 7)
Current assets (p. 12)
Current liabilities (p. 14)
Current ratio (p. 17)
Expenses (p. 8)
Financial accounting (p. 4)
Financial statements (p. 8)
Fiscal year (p. 11)

Footnotes (p. 29)
Fundamental Basic Accounting equation (p. 10)
Generally Accepted Accounting Principles (GAAP) (p. 30)
Gross margin (gross profit) (p. 21)
Income from operations (p. 22)
Intangible assets (p. 14)
International Financial Reporting Standards (IFRS) (p. 30)
Liability (p. 7)
Liquidity (p. 17)
Long-term investments (p. 14)
Long-term liabilities (p. 14)
Management's Discussion and Analysis (p. 29)
Net income (p. 8)
Net loss (p. 8)
Net profit margin (p. 23)
Notes to the financial statements (p. 29)
Operating cycle (p. 12)

Partnership (p. 5)
Property, plant, and equipment (p. 14)
Revenue (p. 8)
Shareholders' equity (p. 7)
Sole proprietorship (p. 5)
Statement of cash flows (p. 9)

Statement of changes in equity (p. 9)
Statement of comprehensive income (p. 9)
Statement of earnings (p. 30)
Statement of financial position (p. 8)
Statement of retained earnings (p. 9)
Working capital (p. 17)

REVIEW PROBLEM
Preparing Financial Statements

Concept:

A company's business activities are summarized and reported in its financial statements. The statement of financial position reports the company's financial position (assets, liabilities, and shareholders' equity) at a specific point in time. The statement of earnings reports the results of a company's operations (revenues less expenses) for a given period of time. The statement of retained earnings summarizes and explains the changes in retained earnings during the accounting period.

Information:

Enderle Company reported the following account balances at December 31, 2018:

Equipment	$19,800	Sales revenue	$82,500	Interest expense	$ 1,200
Retained earnings, 12/31/2018	15,450	Accumulated depreciation	5,450	Retained earnings, 1/1/2018	10,300
Copyright	1,200	Cash	2,900	Depreciation expense	3,500
Accounts payable	5,500	Salaries expense	18,100	Cost of goods sold	52,000
Interest income	2,300	Common shares	11,500	Inventory	5,600
Bonds payable	10,000	Land	15,000	Income tax expense	3,000
Dividends declared	1,850	Accounts receivable	3,700	Interest payable	300

Required:

1. Prepare Enderle's single-step statement of earnings for the year ended December 31, 2018.
2. Prepare Enderle's statement of retained earnings for the year ended December 31, 2018.
3. Prepare Enderle's statement of financial position at December 31, 2018.

Solution:

1.

Enderle Company
Statement of Earnings
For the Year Ended December 31, 2018

Revenues:		
Sales revenue	$82,500	
Interest income	2,300	
Total revenues		$84,800
Expenses:		
Cost of goods sold	52,000	
Salaries expense	18,100	
Depreciation expense	3,500	
Interest expense	1,200	
Income tax expense	3,000	
Total expenses		77,800
Net income		$ 7,000

2.

Enderle Company
Statement of Retained Earnings
For the Year Ended December 31, 2018

Balance, January 1, 2018	$10,300
Add: Net income	7,000
Deduct: Dividends	(1,850)
Balance, December 31, 2018	**$15,450**

3.

Enderle Company
Statement of Financial Position
December 31, 2018

ASSETS

Current assets:		
Cash	$ 2,900	
Accounts receivable	3,700	
Inventory	5,600	
Total current assets		$12,200
Property, plant, and equipment:		
Land	15,000	
Equipment	19,800	
Less: accumulated depreciation	(5,450)	
Total property, plant, and equipment		29,350
Intangible assets:		
Copyright		1,200
Total assets		$42,750

LIABILITIES AND SHAREHOLDERS' EQUITY

Current liabilities:		
Accounts payable	$ 5,500	
Interest payable	300	
Total current liabilities		$ 5,800
Long-term liabilities:		
Bonds payable		10,000
Total liabilities		15,800
Shareholders' equity:		
Common shares	11,500	
Retained earnings	15,450	
Total shareholders' equity		26,950
Total liabilities and shareholders' equity		$42,750

DISCUSSION QUESTIONS

1. Define *accounting*. How does accounting differ from *bookkeeping*?
2. Why is there a demand for accounting information? Name five groups that create demand for accounting information about businesses, and describe how each group uses accounting information.
3. What is an accounting entity?
4. Name and describe three different forms of business organization.

5. Name and describe the three main types of business activities.

6. Define the terms *assets*, *liabilities*, and *shareholders' equity*. How are the three terms related?

7. Define the terms *revenue* and *expense*. How are these terms related?

8. Name and briefly describe the purpose of the four financial statements.

9. What types of questions are answered by the financial statements?

10. What is point-in-time measurement? How does it differ from period-of-time measurement?

11. Write the basic accounting equation. Why is it significant?

12. What information is included in the heading of each of the four financial statements?

13. Define current assets and current liabilities. Why are current assets and current liabilities separated from noncurrent assets and long-term liabilities on the statement of financial position?

14. Describe how items are ordered within the current assets and current liabilities sections on a statement of financial position.

15. Name the two main components of shareholders' equity. Describe the main sources of change in each component.

16. What equation describes the statement of earnings?

17. How does the multiple-step statement of earnings differ from the single-step statement of earnings?

18. Explain the items reported on a statement of retained earnings.

19. Name and describe the three categories of the statement of cash flows.

20. How is the statement of retained earnings related to the statement of financial position? How is the statement of earnings related to the statement of retained earnings?

21. Describe the items (other than the financial statements) found in the annual report.

22. Give an example of unethical behaviour by a public accountant and describe its consequences.

MULTIPLE-CHOICE EXERCISES

1-1 Which of the following statements is false concerning forms of business organization?
  a. A corporation always has tax advantages over the other forms of business organization.
  b. It is easier for a corporation to raise large sums of money than it is for a sole proprietorship or partnership.
  c. A sole proprietorship is an easy type of business to form.
  d. Owners of sole proprietorships and partnerships have personal liability for the debts of the business while owners of corporations have limited legal liability.

1-2 Which of the following are *all* considered external decision makers of financial statements?

  a. Board of Directors, employees, investors, lenders (banks)
  b. Lenders (banks), suppliers, functional managers, government
  c. Investors, governments, executive management, employees
  d. Governments, suppliers, investors, lenders (banks)

1-3 Which of the following statements regarding business activities is true?
  a. Operating activities involve buying the long-term assets that enable a company to generate revenue.
  b. Financing activities include obtaining the funds necessary to begin and operate a business.
  c. Investing activities centre around earning interest on a company's investments.

(Continued)

d. Companies spend a relatively small amount of time on operating activities.

1-4 At December 31, Perugia Ltd. has assets of $10,500 and liabilities of $5,800. What is the shareholders' equity for Perugia at December 31?
  a. $4,700
  b. $5,800
  c. $15,200
  d. $16,300

1-5 Which of the following is not one of the four basic financial statements?
  a. Statement of earnings
  b. Auditor's report
  c. Statement of financial position
  d. Statement of cash flows

1-6 What type of questions do the financial statements help answer?
  a. Is the company better off at the end of the year than at the beginning of the year?
  b. What resources does the company have?
  c. For what did a company use its cash during the year?
  d. All of the above.

1-7 Which of the following is not shown in the heading of a financial statement?
  a. The title of the financial statement
  b. The name of the company
  c. The time period covered by the financial statement
  d. The name of the auditor

> Use the following information for Multiple-Choice Exercises 1-8 and 1-9:
> At December 31, Marker reported the following items: cash, $8,200; inventory, $3,700; accounts payable, $6,300; accounts receivable, $3,900; common shares, $5,900; property, plant, and equipment, $10,000; interest payable, $1,400; retained earnings, $12,200.

1-8 Refer to the information for Marker above. What is the total of Marker's current assets?
  a. $10,100
  b. $15,800
  c. $16,000
  d. $25,800

1-9 Refer to the information for Marker above. What is Marker's shareholders' equity?
  a. $5,900
  b. $12,200
  c. $18,100
  d. $25,800

1-10 Which of the following statements regarding the statement of earnings is true?
  a. The statement of earnings provides information about the future profitability and growth of a company.
  b. The statement of earnings shows the results of a company's operations at a specific point in time.
  c. The statement of earnings consists of assets, expenses, liabilities, and revenues.
  d. Typical statement of earnings accounts include sales revenue, unearned revenue, and cost of goods sold.

1-11 For the most recent year, Girand Company reported revenues of $165,500, cost of goods sold of $92,100, inventory of $5,400, salaries expense of $43,850, rent expense of $15,000, and cash of $17,330. What was Girand's net income?
  a. $9,150
  b. $14,550
  c. $19,950
  d. $31,880

1-12 Which of the following statements concerning retained earnings is true?
  a. Retained earnings is the difference between revenues and expenses.
  b. Retained earnings is increased by dividends and decreased by net income.
  c. Retained earnings represents accumulation of the income that has not been distributed as dividends.
  d. Retained earnings is reported as a liability on the statement of financial position.

1-13 Which of the following sentences regarding the statement of cash flows is false?
  a. The statement of cash flows describes the company's cash receipts and cash payments for a period of time.
  b. The statement of cash flows reconciles the beginning and ending cash balances shown on the statement of financial position.

c. The statement of cash flows reports cash flows in three categories: cash flows from business activities, cash flows from investing activities, and cash flows from financing activities.

d. The statement of cash flows may be used by creditors to assess the credit-worthiness of a company.

1-14 Which of the following statements is true?

a. The auditor's opinion is typically included in the notes to the financial statements.

b. The notes to the financial statements are an integral part of the financial statements that clarify and expand on the information presented in the financial statements.

c. The management's discussion and analysis section does not convey any information that cannot be found in the financial statements themselves.

d. The annual report is required to be filed with the Toronto Stock Exchange.

CORNERSTONE EXERCISES

Cornerstone Exercise 1-15   Using the Basic Accounting Equation

Listed below are three independent scenarios.

Scenario	Assets	Liabilities	Equity
1	$ (a)	$33,000	$44,000
2	110,000	(b)	68,000
3	49,000	32,000	(c)

OBJECTIVE ❸

CORNERSTONE 1.1

ILLUSTRATING RELATIONSHIPS

Required:

Use the basic accounting equation to find the missing amounts.

Cornerstone Exercise 1-16   Using the Basic Accounting Equation

At the beginning of the year, Mumbai Company had total assets of $440,000 and total liabilities of $285,000.

OBJECTIVE ❸

CORNERSTONE 1.1

Required:

Use the basic accounting equation to answer the following independent questions:

a. What is total shareholders' equity at the beginning of the year?

b. If, during the year, total assets increased by $85,000 and total liabilities increased by $38,000, what is the amount of total shareholders' equity at the end of the year?

c. If, during the year, total assets decreased by $65,000 and total shareholders' equity increased by $45,000, what is the amount of total liabilities at the end of the year?

d. If, during the year, total liabilities increased by $95,000 and total shareholders' equity decreased by $75,000, what is the amount of total assets at the end of the year?

Cornerstone Exercise 1-17   Financial Statements

Listed below are elements of the financial statements.

a. Liabilities
b. Net change in cash
c. Assets
d. Revenue
e. Cash flow from operating activities
f. Expenses
g. Shareholders' equity
h. Dividends

OBJECTIVE ❹❺❻❼

CORNERSTONE 1.2

CORNERSTONE 1.3

CORNERSTONE 1.4

(Continued)

Required:

Match each financial statement element with its financial statement: statement of financial position (SFP), statement of earnings (SE), statement of retained earnings (RE), or statement of cash flows (CF).

OBJECTIVE ④
CORNERSTONE 1.2

Cornerstone Exercise 1-18   Statement of Financial Position

Listed below are items that may appear on a statement of financial position.

Item	Classification
1. Accounts payable	a. Current assets
2. Machinery	b. Property, plant, and equipment
3. Inventory	c. Intangible assets
4. Common shares	d. Current liabilities
5. Notes payable (due in 5 years)	e. Long-term liabilities
6. Cash	f. Contributed capital
7. Copyright	g. Retained earnings
8. Net income less dividends	
9. Accumulated depreciation	
10. Accounts receivable	

Required:

Match each item with its appropriate classification on the statement of financial position.

OBJECTIVE ④
CORNERSTONE 1.2

Cornerstone Exercise 1-19   Statement of Financial Position

An analysis of the transactions of Cavernous Homes Ltd. yields the following totals at December 31, 2018: cash, $3,200; accounts receivable, $4,500; notes payable, $5,000; supplies, $8,100; common shares, $7,000; retained earnings, $3,800.

Required:

Prepare a statement of financial position for Cavernous Homes Ltd. at December 31, 2018 (Ignore current vs non-current classification).

OBJECTIVE ⑤
CORNERSTONE 1.3

Cornerstone Exercise 1-20   Statement of Earnings

An analysis of the transactions of Canary Cola Inc. for the year 2018 yields the following information: revenue, $78,000; supplies expense, $33,200; rent expense, $20,500; dividends, $7,000.

Required:

What is the amount of net income reported by Canary Cola for 2018?

OBJECTIVE ⑥
CORNERSTONE 1.4

Cornerstone Exercise 1-21   Statement of Retained Earnings

Park Company has a balance of $25,000 in retained earnings on January 1, 2018. During 2018, Park reported revenues of $74,000 and expenses of $57,000. Park also declared and paid a dividend of $8,000.

Required:

What is the balance of retained earnings on December 31, 2018?

BRIEF EXERCISES

OBJECTIVE ①

Brief Exercise 1-22   Decision Makers of Financial Information

Listed below are several decision makers of accounting information and decisions that decision makers may make.

Decision Maker of Accounting Information		Decision
1.	Manager	a. Determines whether the company paid the proper amount of taxes.
2.	Employee	b. Decides if a factory is profitable or should be closed.
3.	Investor	c. Determines if a company will be able to repay its obligations.
4.	Creditor	d. Decides if the reported net income will cause the share price to rise or fall.
5.	Government	e. Estimates the amount of a possible bonus.

Required:

Indicate which decision maker of accounting information is responsible for each of the decisions.

Brief Exercise 1-23   Forms of Business Organization

OBJECTIVE ❷

Listed below are the forms of business organization and several related advantages or disadvantages.

Form of Business Organization		Advantage or Disadvantage
1.	Sole proprietorship	a. Most complex to organize
2.	Partnership	b. Owner(s) have personal responsibility for the debt of the organization
3.	Corporation	c. Access to the individual skills of each of the owners
		d. Limited personal liability for the debt of the organization
		e. Easier to raise large amounts of capital
		f. The greatest percentage of businesses are organized in this manner
		g. Owners might be subject to double taxation

Required:

Match each form of business organization with its respective advantage or disadvantage. (*Hint:* Some advantages or disadvantages may be related to more than one form of business organization.)

Brief Exercise 1-24   Business Activities

OBJECTIVE ❷

Marni Restaurant Company engaged in the following transactions during March, its first month of operations.

a. Received $100,000 cash from the sale of shares
b. Purchased $20,000 of inventory from J&J Wholesale Company
c. Purchased $30,000 of kitchen equipment for its restaurants
d. Obtained a $25,000 loan from First State Bank
e. Sold $18,000 of food to customers
f. Paid employee weekly salaries of $8,500
g. Repaid $10,000 of principal relating to the loan in item *d*

Required:

For each of the above business activities, indicate whether it is an operating, investing, or financing activity.

Brief Exercise 1-25   The Basic Accounting Equation

OBJECTIVE ❸

Financial information for three independent cases is as follows:

a. The liabilities of Dent Company are $82,000, and its shareholders' equity is $120,000. What is the amount of Dent's total assets?
b. The total assets of Wayne Inc. are $55,000, and its shareholders' equity is $22,500. What is the amount of Wayne's total liabilities?
c. Gordon Company's total assets increased by $60,000 during the year, and its liabilities decreased by $35,000. Did Gordon's shareholders' equity increase or decrease? By how much?

Required:

Determine the missing amount for each case.

OBJECTIVE **4**

Brief Exercise 1-26   Statement of Financial Position

Below are items that may appear on the statement of financial position.

Item		Classification	
1.	Buildings	a.	Current assets
2.	Copyright	b.	Property, plant, and equipment
3.	Supplies	c.	Intangible assets
4.	Unearned service revenue	d.	Current liabilities
5.	Prepaid insurance	e.	Long-term liabilities
6.	Common shares	f.	Contributed capital
7.	Rent payable	g.	Retained earnings
8.	Accounts receivable		
9.	Allowance for doubtful accounts		
10.	Bonds payable		

Required:

Match each item with its appropriate classification.

OBJECTIVE **5**

Brief Exercise 1-27   Statement of Earnings

An analysis of the transactions of Rutherford Company for the year ended December 31, 2018, yields the following information: sales revenue, $65,000; insurance expense, $4,300; interest income, $3,900; cost of goods sold, $28,800; and loss on disposal of property, plant, and equipment, $1,200.

Required:

Prepare a single-step statement of earnings.

OBJECTIVE **6**

Brief Exercise 1-28   Statement of Retained Earnings

Listed below are events that affect shareholders' equity.

a. Reported net income of $85,000
b. Paid a cash dividend of $10,000
c. Reported sales revenue of $120,000
d. Issued common shares of $50,000
e. Reported a net loss of $20,000
f. Reported expenses of $35,000

Required:

For each of the events, indicate whether it increases retained earnings (I), decreases retained earnings (D), or has no effect on retained earnings (NE).

OBJECTIVE **7**

Brief Exercise 1-29   Statement of Cash Flows

Listed below are items that would appear on a statement of cash flows.

a. Cash received from customers
b. Cash paid for dividends
c. Cash received from a bank loan
d. Cash paid to suppliers
e. Cash paid to purchase equipment

Required:

Indicate in which part of the statement of cash flows each of the items would appear: operating activities (O), investing activities (I), or financing activities (F).

Brief Exercise 1-30   Relationships among the Financial Statements

OBJECTIVE 8

Listed below are three independent scenarios.

Scenario	Statement of Financial Position: Beginning Retained Earnings	Statement of Earnings: Net Income	Statement of Financial Position: Ending Retained Earnings
1.	$30,000	$25,000	$ (a)
2.	(b)	30,000	94,000
3.	50,000	(c)	70,000

Required:

Compute the missing amount in each row. Assume no withdrawals or dividends.

Brief Exercise 1-31   Annual Report Items

OBJECTIVE 9

Listed below are several descriptions related to other items found in an annual report.

Description	Location in the Annual Report
1. An integral part of the financial statements that helps to fulfill the accountant's responsibility for full disclosure of all relevant information	a. Notes to the financial statements
2. An opinion as to whether the financial statements fairly present the financial position and result of operations of the company	b. Management's discussion and analysis c. Report of independent accountants
3. A discussion and explanation of various items reported in the financial statements	
4. Clarification of or expansion upon the information presented in the financial statements	

Required:

Match each of the descriptions with the location in the annual report in which it may be found.

EXERCISES

Exercise 1-32   Decisions Based on Accounting Information

OBJECTIVE 1

Decision makers use accounting information in a wide variety of decisions, including the following:
1. Deciding whether or not to lend money to a business
2. Deciding whether or not an individual has paid enough in taxes
3. Deciding whether or not to place merchandise on sale in order to reduce inventory
4. Deciding whether or not to invest in a business
5. Deciding whether or not to demand additional benefits for employees

Required:

Match each decision with one of the following decision makers who is primarily responsible for the decision: a government (G), an investor (I), a labour union (U), business managers (M), or a lender (banks) (B).

Exercise 1-33   Forms of Business Organizations

OBJECTIVE 2

Listed below are definitions, examples, or descriptions related to business entities.
1. Owned by one person and personally liable.
2. Can make and sell goods (manufacturing)

(Continued)

3. Owned by more than one person
4. Can sell goods (merchandising)
5. Can provide and sell services
6. Legally, a separate entity from the owner(s)
7. A law firm owned by some of the employees, who are each liable for the financial obligations of the entity
8. Tim Hortons Inc.

Required:

1. For each of the three types of business entities (sole proprietorship, partnership, and corporation), select as many of the definitions, examples, or descriptions as apply to that type of entity.

YOUDECIDE   2. Explain the advantages and disadvantages of each type of business entity.

OBJECTIVE ❷   ### Exercise 1-34   Business Activities

Listed below are various activities that companies engage in during a period.

a. The purchase of equipment
b. The payment of a dividend
c. The purchase of supplies
d. The sale of equipment
e. The sale of goods or services
f. Borrowed money from a bank
g. Contribution of cash by owners

Required:

For each of the activities listed above, classify the activity as operating (O), investing (I), or financing (F).

OBJECTIVE ❷   ### Exercise 1-35   Business Activities

Bill and Steve recently formed a company that manufactures and sells high-end kitchen appliances. The following is a list of activities that occurred during the year.

a. Bill and Steve each contributed cash in exchange for common shares in the company.
b. Land and a building to be used as a factory to make the appliances were purchased for cash.
c. Machines used to make the appliances were purchased for cash.
d. Various materials used in the production of the appliances were purchased for cash.
e. Three employees were paid cash to operate the machines and make the appliances.
f. Running low on money, the company borrowed money from a local bank.
g. The money from the bank loan was used to buy advertising on local radio and television stations.
h. The company sold the appliances to local homeowners for cash.
i. Due to extremely high popularity of its products, Bill and Steve built another factory building on its land for cash.
j. The company paid a cash dividend to Bill and Steve.

Required:

Classify each of the business activities listed as either an operating activity (O), an investing activity (I), or a financing activity (F).

Exercise 1-36 Accounting Concepts

OBJECTIVE

A list of accounting concepts and related definitions is presented below.

Concept	Definition
1. Revenue	a. Owner's claim on the resources of a company
2. Expenses	b. The difference between revenues and expenses
3. Net income (loss)	c. Increase in assets from the sale of goods or services
4. Dividend	d. Economic resources of a company
5. Assets	e. Cost of assets consumed in the operation of a business
6. Liabilities	f. Creditors' claims on the resources of a company
7. Shareholders' equity	g. Distribution of earnings to shareholders

Required:

Match each of the concepts with its corresponding definition.

Exercise 1-37 The Basic Accounting Equation

Financial information for three independent cases is given below.

	Assets	Liabilities	Equity
1.	$275,000	$ (b)	$51,000
2.	75,000	162,500	(c)
3.	(a)	15,000	43,200

Required:

Compute the missing numbers in each case.

Exercise 1-38 Structure of Statement of Financial Position

The following accounts exist in the ledger of Huang Company: accounts payable, accounts receivable, accumulated depreciation, bonds payable, building, common shares, cash, equipment, income taxes payable, inventory, notes payable (due in 5 years), prepaid insurance, retained earnings, trademarks, wages payable.

Required:

1. Organize the above items into a properly prepared classified statement of financial position.   **YOU**DECIDE
2. Which information might be helpful to assess liquidity?

Exercise 1-39 Identifying Current Assets and Liabilities

Dunn Sporting Goods sells athletic clothing and footwear to retail customers. Dunn's accountant indicates that the firm's operating cycle averages six months. At December 31, 2018, Dunn has the following assets and liabilities:

a. Prepaid rent in the amount of $8,500. Dunn's rent is $500 per month.
b. A $9,700 account payable due in 45 days.
c. Inventory in the amount of $46,230. Dunn expects to sell $38,000 of the inventory within three months. The remainder will be placed in storage until September 2019. The items placed in storage should be sold by November 2019.
d. An investment in marketable securities in the amount of $1,900. Dunn expects to sell $700 of the marketable securities in six months. The remainder are not expected to be sold until 2021.
e. Cash in the amount of $1,050.
f. An equipment loan in the amount of $60,000 due in March 2023. Interest of $4,500 is due in March 2019 ($3,750 of the interest relates to 2018, with the remainder relating to the first three months of 2019).

(Continued)

g. An account receivable from a local university in the amount of $2,850. The university has promised to pay the full amount in three months.

h. Store equipment at a cost of $9,200. Accumulated depreciation has been recorded on the store equipment in the amount of $1,250.

Required:

1. Prepare the current asset and current liability portions of Dunn's December 31, 2018, statement of financial position.
2. Compute Dunn's working capital and current ratio at December 31, 2018.
3. As an investor or creditor, what do these ratios tell you about Dunn's liquidity?

YOUDECIDE

OBJECTIVE **4**

Exercise 1-40   Current Assets and Current Liabilities

Hanson Construction has an operating cycle of nine months. On December 31, 2018, Hanson has the following assets and liabilities:

a. A note receivable in the amount of $1,200 to be collected in six months.
b. Cash totalling $475.
c. Accounts payable totalling $1,800, all of which will be paid within two months.
d. Accounts receivable totalling $12,000, including an account for $8,000 that will be paid in two months and an account for $4,000 that will be paid in 18 months.
e. Construction supplies costing $8,800, all of which will be used in construction within the next 12 months.
f. Construction equipment costing $60,000, on which depreciation of $22,400 has accumulated.
g. A note payable to the bank in the amount of $7,600 is to be paid within the next year.

Required:

1. Calculate the amounts of current assets and current liabilities reported on Hanson's statement of financial position at December 31, 2018.
2. Comment on Hanson's liquidity.

OBJECTIVE **4**

Exercise 1-41   Characteristics of Financial Statement Items

Which of the following characteristics of financial statement items are correct?

a. Current assets consist of cash and other assets that are expected to reasonably be converted into cash at any point in time.
b. Common types of current assets include the following: cash, short-term investments, accounts receivable, inventories.
c. Current assets are listed on the statement of financial position in order of liquidity or nearness to cash.
d. Property, plant, and equipment represents all tangible and intangible, long-lived, productive assets used by a company in its operations to produce revenue.
e. Unearned revenue is an unavoidable obligation to deliver goods or perform a service for which a company has already been paid.

YOUDECIDE

f. Liabilities must always be satisfied through the payment of cash.

OBJECTIVE

Exercise 1-42   Depreciation

Shiva Products was organized as a new business on January 1, 2018. On that date, Shiva acquired equipment at a cost of $425,000, which is depreciated at a rate of $40,000 per year.

Required:

Describe how the equipment and its related depreciation will be reported on the statement of financial position at December 31, 2018, and on the 2018 statement of earnings.

Exercise 1-43   Shareholders' Equity

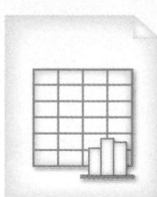

OBJECTIVE **4**

On January 1, 2018, Mulcahy Manufacturing Inc., a newly formed corporation, issued 1,000 common shares in exchange for $135,600 cash. No other shares were issued during 2018, and no shares were repurchased by the corporation. On November 1, 2018, the corporation's major shareholder sold 300 shares to another shareholder for $43,800. The corporation reported net income of $25,300 for 2018.

Required:

Prepare the shareholders' equity section of Mulcahy's statement of financial position at December 31, 2018.

Exercise 1-44   Classified Statement of Financial Position

OBJECTIVE **4**

College Spirit sells sportswear with logos of major universities. At the end of 2018, the following statement of financial position account balances were available.

Accounts payable	$104,700	Income taxes payable	$ 11,400
Accounts receivable	6,700	Inventory	481,400
Accumulated depreciation	23,700	Long-term investment	110,900
Bonds payable	180,000	Note payable, short-term	50,000
Cash	13,300	Prepaid rent (current)	54,000
Common shares	300,000	Retained earnings, 12/31/2018	84,500
Furniture	88,000		

Required:

1. Prepare a classified statement of financial position for College Spirit at December 31, 2018.
2. Compute College Spirit's working capital and current ratio at December 31, 2018.
3. Comment on College Spirit's liquidity as of December 31, 2018.

YOUDECIDE

Exercise 1-45   Classified Statement of Financial Position

OBJECTIVE **4**

Bathsheba Company operates a wholesale hardware business. The following statement of financial position accounts and balances are available for Bathsheba at December 31, 2018.

Accounts payable	$ 65,100	Trucks	$106,100
Accounts receivable	95,500	Income taxes payable	21,600
Accumulated depreciation		Interest payable	12,600
(on data processing equipment)	172,400	Inventory	187,900
Accumulated depreciation		Land	41,000
(on building)	216,800	Investments (long term)	32,700
Accumulated depreciation (on trucks)	31,200	Notes payable (due June 1, 2019)	150,000
Bonds payable (due 2021)	200,000	Prepaid insurance (for 4 months)	5,700
Building (warehouse)	419,900	Retained earnings, 12/31/2018	?
Cash	11,400	Salaries payable	14,400
Common shares	150,000	Investments (short term)	21,000
Equipment, data processing	309,000		

Required:

1. Prepare a classified statement of financial position for Bathsheba at December 31, 2018.
2. Compute Bathsheba's working capital and current ratio at December 31, 2018.
3. If Bathsheba's management is concerned that a large portion of its inventory is obsolete and cannot be sold, how will its liquidity be affected?

YOUDECIDE

Exercise 1-46   Statement of Earnings Structure

OBJECTIVE **5**

The following accounts exist in the ledger of Sayed Company: salaries expense, advertising expense, cost of goods sold, depreciation expense, interest expense, income tax expense, sales revenue, utilities expense.

(Continued)

Required:

1. Organize the above items into a properly prepared single-step statement of earnings.
2. **CONCEPTUAL CONNECTION** What information would be helpful in assessing Sayed's ability to generate future income?

OBJECTIVE **5**   **Exercise 1-47   Statement of Earnings**

ERS Ltd. maintains and repairs office equipment. ERS had an average of 10,000 common shares outstanding for the year. The following statement of earnings account balances are available for ERS at the end of 2018.

Advertising expense	$24,200	Salaries expense	
Depreciation expense		(for administrative personnel)	$195,600
(on service van)	16,250	Service revenue	933,800
Income tax expense	15,150	Supplies expense	66,400
Interest expense	10,100	Utilities expense	26,100
Rent expense	58,400	Wages expense	
Insurance expense	11,900	(for service technicians)	448,300

Required:

1. Prepare a single-step statement of earnings for ERS for 2018.
2. **CONCEPTUAL CONNECTION** Compute net profit margin for ERS. If ERS is able to increase its service revenue by $100,000, what should be the effect on future income?

YOUDECIDE
3. Assume that ERS's net profit margin was 8.5% for 2017. As an investor, what conclusions might you draw about ERS's future profitability?

OBJECTIVE **5**   **Exercise 1-48   Multiple-Step Statement of Earnings**

The following information is available for Bergin Pastry Shop.

Gross margin	$34,700
Income from operations	9,200
Income tax expense (15% of income before taxes)	?
Interest expense	1,800
Net sales	85,300

Required:

Prepare a multiple-step statement of earnings for Bergin.

OBJECTIVE **5**   **Exercise 1-49   Statement of Earnings**

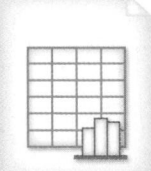

The following information is available for Wang Auto Supply at December 31, 2018.

Cost of goods sold	$277,000	Rent expense	$ 18,000
Depreciation expense	29,000	Salaries (administrative)	32,000
Income tax expense	38,085	Sales revenue	583,900
Interest expense	2,700	Wages expense (salespeople)	98,250

Required:

1. Prepare a single-step statement of earnings for the year ended December 31, 2018.
2. Prepare a multiple-step statement of earnings for the year ended December 31, 2018.
3. **CONCEPTUAL CONNECTION** Comment on the differences between the single-step and the multiple-step statement of earnings.

OBJECTIVE **6**   **Exercise 1-50   Statement of Retained Earnings**

At the end of 2017, Sherwood Company had retained earnings of $18,240. During 2018, Sherwood had revenues of $837,400 and expenses of $792,100, and paid cash dividends of $38,650.

Required:

1. Determine the amount of Sherwood's retained earnings at December 31, 2018.
2. Comment on Sherwood's dividend policy.

YOUDECIDE

Exercise 1-51   Statement of Cash Flows

OBJECTIVE **7**

Walters Ltd. began operations on January 1, 2018. The following information relates to Walters's cash flows during 2018.

Cash received from owners	$201,500	Cash paid to purchase machine	$ 32,000
Cash paid for purchase of land		Cash paid to employees for salaries	46,400
and building	128,700	Cash paid for dividends to shareholders	139,800
Cash paid for advertising	34,200	Cash paid for supplies	28,700
Cash received from customers	139,800		

Required:

1. Calculate the cash provided/used for each cash flow category.
2. Comment on Walters's creditworthiness.

YOUDECIDE

Exercise 1-52   Relationships among the Financial Statements

OBJECTIVE **8**

Zachary Corporation's December 31, 2017, statement of financial position included the following amounts:

Cash	$ 17,400
Retained earnings	103,600

Zachary's accountant provided the following data for 2018:

Revenues	$673,900	Cash inflow from operating activities	$ 857,300
Expenses	587,100	Cash outflow for investing activities	(994,500)
Dividends	34,200	Cash inflow from financing activities	156,600

Required:

Calculate the amount of cash and retained earnings at the end of 2018.

Exercise 1-53   Relationships among the Financial Statements

OBJECTIVE **8**

The following information for Kellman Ltd. is available at the end of 2018:

Total assets on 12/31/2017	$72,400	Common shares on 12/31/2017	$50,000
Total assets on 12/31/2018	78,500	Common shares on 12/31/2018	50,000
Total liabilities on 12/31/2017	12,100	Net income for 2018	14,300
Total liabilities on 12/31/2018	9,800		

Required:

Calculate the amount of dividends reported on the statement of retained earnings for 2018.

Exercise 1-54   Relationships among the Financial Statements

OBJECTIVE **8**

During 2018, Mauro Corporation paid $14,500 of dividends. Mauro's assets, liabilities, and common shares at the end of 2017 and 2018 were as follows:

	12/31/2017	12/31/2018
Total assets	$144,200	$178,100
Total liabilities	52,600	59,700
Common shares	60,000	60,000

Required:

Using the information provided, compute Mauro's net income for 2018.

OBJECTIVE **9**   **Exercise 1-55   Annual Report Items**

DeSalle Company's annual report includes the following items: financial statements, notes to the financial statements, management's discussion and analysis, and a report of independent auditors.

Required:

For each of the following items, where would you most likely find the information in the annual report?

a. A description of the risks associated with operating the company in an international market
b. Detailed information on the outstanding debt of the company, including the interest rate being charged and the maturity date of the debt
c. A description of the accounting methods used by the company
d. The total resources and claims to the resources of the company
e. A discussion of the sales trends of the company's most profitable products
f. The amount of dividends paid to common shareholders
g. An opinion as to whether the financial statements are a fair presentation of the company's financial position and results of operations
h. The cost of operating the company over a period of time

OBJECTIVE **11**   **Exercise 1-56   Professional Ethics**

Ethical behaviour is essential to the conduct of business activity. Consider each of the following business behaviours:

a. A manager prepares financial statements that grossly overstate the performance of the business.
b. An auditor resigns from an audit engagement rather than allow a business client to violate an accounting standard.
c. An internal auditor decides against confronting an employee of the business with minor violations of business policy. The employee is a former university classmate of the auditor.
d. An accountant advises his client on ways to legally minimize tax payments to the government.
e. A manager legally reduces the price of a product to secure a larger share of the market.
f. Managers of several large companies secretly meet to plan price reductions designed to drive up-and-coming competitors out of the market.
g. An accountant keeps confidential details of her employer's legal operations that would be of interest to the public.
h. A recently dismissed accountant tells competitors details about her former employer's operations as she seeks a new job.

Required:

Identify each behaviour as ethical (E) or unethical (U) and explain your rationale.

PROBLEM SET A

OBJECTIVE **3**   **Problem 1-57A   Applying the Basic Accounting Equation**

At the beginning of 2018, Huffer Corporation had total assets of $226,800, total liabilities of $84,200, common shares of $80,000, and retained earnings of $62,600. During 2018, Huffer had net income of $42,750, paid dividends of $11,900, and issued additional common shares for $12,800. Huffer's total assets at the end of 2018 were $278,200.

Required:

Calculate the amount of liabilities that Huffer must have at the end of 2018 in order for the statement of financial position to balance.

Problem 1-58A Accounting Relationships

OBJECTIVE 4 5 6 8

Information for Beethoven Music Company is given below.

Total assets at the beginning of the year	$145,200	Equity at the beginning of the year	$ (b)
Total assets at the end of the year	(a)	Equity at the end of the year	104,100
Total liabilities at the beginning of the year	92,600	Dividends declared and paid during	
Total liabilities at the end of the year	126,900	the year	(c)
		Net income for the year	77,500
		Revenues	554,800
		Expenses	(d)

Required:

Use the relationships in the statement of financial position, statement of earnings, and statement of retained earnings to determine the missing values.

Problem 1-59A Arrangement of the Statement of Earnings

OBJECTIVE 5

Perez Wrecking Service demolishes old buildings and other structures and sells the salvaged materials. During 2018, Perez had $425,000 of revenue from demolition services and $137,000 of revenue from salvage sales. Perez also had $1,575 of interest income from investments. Perez incurred $243,200 of wages expense, $24,150 of depreciation expense, $48,575 of supplies expense, $84,000 of rent expense, $17,300 of miscellaneous expense, and $43,900 of income tax expense.

Required:

Prepare a single-step statement of earnings for Perez for 2018.

Problem 1-60A Statement of Earnings and Statement of Financial Position Relationships

OBJECTIVE 4 5 8

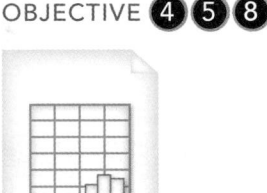

Each column presents financial information taken from one of four different companies, with one or more items of data missing.

	Company			
Financial Statement Item	Floyd	Singh	Wang	O'Bannion
Total revenue	$125	$ 715	$ (e)	$2,475
Total expense	92	(c)	54	(g)
Net income (net loss)	(a)	184	18	(600)
Total assets	905	1,988	(f)	8,140
Total liabilities	412	(d)	117	2,280
Total equity	(b)	823	80	(h)

Required:

Use your understanding of the relationships among financial statements and financial statement items to find the missing values (a–h).

Problem 1-61A Statement of Earnings and Statement of Financial Position

OBJECTIVE 4 5 8

The following information for Roget Enterprises is available at December 31, 2018, and includes all of Roget's financial statement amounts except retained earnings:

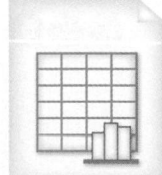

Accounts receivable	$72,920	Property, plant, and equipment	$ 90,000
Cash	13,240	Rent expense	135,000
Common shares (10,000 issued)	70,000	Retained earnings	?
Income tax expense	12,800	Salaries expense	235,200
Income taxes payable	4,150	Salaries payable	14,800
Interest expense	16,000	Service revenue	463,500
Notes payable (due in 10 years)	25,000	Supplies	42,000
Prepaid rent (building)	31,500	Supplies expense	34,400

(Continued)

Required:

Prepare a single-step statement of earnings and a classified statement of financial position for the year ended December 31, 2018, for Roget.

 OBJECTIVE **7 8** **Problem 1-62A   Understanding the Four Financial Statements**

Revenues	$24,000	Total liabilities	$13,500
Common shares	12,500	Dividends paid	3,000
Cash, December 31, 2017	13,000	Cash, December 31, 2018	18,000
Retained earnings	5,500	Cash from operating activities	5,000
Cash from financing activities	2,500	Other assets	1,000
Cash used for investing activities	(2,500)	Common shares	2,500

Required:

Taking into consideration the information above, calculate the cash balance on December 31, 2018.

OBJECTIVE **6** **Problem 1-63A   Statement of Retained Earnings**

Dittman Expositions has the following data available:

Dividends, 2017	$ 8,250	Retained earnings, 12/31/2016	$ 16,900
Dividends, 2018	9,910	Revenues, 2017	419,700
Expenses, 2017	386,500	Revenues, 2018	442,400
Expenses, 2018	412,600		

Required:

Prepare statements of retained earnings for 2017 and 2018.

OBJECTIVE **6** **Problem 1-64A   Statements of Retained Earnings**

The table below presents the statements of retained earnings for Bass Corporation for three successive years. Certain numbers are missing.

	2016	2017	2018
Retained earnings, beginning	$21,500	$ (b)	$33,600
Add: Net income	9,200	10,100	(f)
	30,700	(c)	(g)
Less: Dividends	(a)	(d)	(3,900)
Retained earnings, ending	$27,200	$ (e)	$41,200

Required:

Use your understanding of the relationship between successive statements of retained earnings to calculate the missing values (a–g).

OBJECTIVE **4 5 6** **Problem 1-65A   Statement of Earnings, Statement of Retained Earnings, and Statement of Financial Position**

The following information relates to Ishtar Appliances for 2018.

Accounts payable	$ 16,800	Income tax expense	$ 16,650
Accounts receivable	69,900	Income taxes payable	12,000
Accumulated depreciation (building)	104,800	Insurance expense	36,610
Accumulated depreciation (furniture)	27,600	Interest expense	15,500
Bonds payable (due in 7 years)	192,000	Inventory	59,850
Building	300,000	Other assets	92,800

Cash	41,450	Rent expense (store equipment)	80,800
Common shares	243,610	Retained earnings, 12/31/2017	54,000
Cost of goods sold	511,350	Salaries expense (administrative)	101,000
Depreciation expense (building)	11,050	Salaries payable	7,190
Depreciation expense (furniture)	12,000	Sales revenue	948,670
Furniture	130,000	Wages expense (store staff)	127,710

Required:

1. Prepare a single-step statement of earnings for 2018, a statement of retained earnings for 2018, and a properly classified statement of financial position as at December 31, 2018.
2. **CONCEPTUAL CONNECTION** How would a multiple-step statement of earnings be different from the single-step statement of earnings you prepared for Ishtar?

Problem 1-66A   Shareholders' Equity Relationships

OBJECTIVE 8

Data from the financial statements of four different companies are presented in separate columns in the table below. Each column has one or more data items missing.

	Company			
Financial Statement Item	**Berko**	**Manning**	**Lucas**	**Perlman**
Equity, 12/31/2017				
Common shares	$50,000	$35,000	$ (i)	$15,000
Retained earnings	12,100	(e)	26,400	21,900
Total equity	(a)	44,300	66,400	36,900
Net income (loss) for 2018	7,000	(1,800)	6,000	(m)
Dividends during 2018	2,000	0	(j)	1,400
Equity, 12/31/2018				
Common shares	50,000	35,000	55,000	15,000
Retained earnings	(b)	(f)	(k)	27,600
Total equity	(c)	(g)	84,500	(n)
Total assets, 12/31/2018	92,500	(h)	99,200	(o)
Total liabilities, 12/31/2018	(d)	14,800	(l)	10,700

Required:

Use your understanding of the relationships among the financial statement items to determine the missing values (a–o).

Problem 1-67A   Relationships among Financial Statements

OBJECTIVE 3 8

Carson Corporation reported the following amounts for assets and liabilities at the beginning and end of a recent year.

	Beginning of Year	End of Year
Assets	$392,500	$415,100
Liabilities	148,550	149,600

Required:

Calculate Carson's net income or net loss for the year in each of the following independent situations:

1. Carson declared no dividends, and its common shares remained unchanged.
2. Carson declared no dividends and issued additional common shares for $33,000 cash.
3. Carson declared dividends totalling $11,000, and its common shares remained unchanged.
4. Carson declared dividends totalling $17,000 and issued additional common shares for $29,000.

PROBLEM SET B

OBJECTIVE ❸

Problem 1-68B   Applying the Basic Accounting Equation

At the beginning of 2018, KJ Corporation had total assets of $553,700, total liabilities of $261,800, common shares of $139,000, and retained earnings of $152,900. During 2018, KJ had net income of $225,200, declared and paid dividends of $74,400, and issued additional common shares for $94,000. KJ's total assets at the end of 2018 were $721,800.

Required:

Calculate the amount of liabilities that KJ must have at the end of 2018 in order for the statement of financial position to balance.

OBJECTIVE ❹❺❻❽

ILLUSTRATING
RELATIONSHIPS

Problem 1-69B   Accounting Relationships

Information for TTL Ltd. is given below.

Total assets at the beginning of the year	$ (a)	Equity at the end of the year	$ (c)
Total assets at the end of the year	758,150	Dividends declared and paid	
Total liabilities at the beginning of the year	368,200	during the year	35,500
Total liabilities at the end of the year	(b)	Net income for the year	(d)
Equity at the beginning of the year	272,900	Revenues	929,440
		Expenses	835,320

Required:

Use the relationships in the statement of financial position, statement of earnings, and statement of retained earnings to determine the missing values.

OBJECTIVE ❺

Problem 1-70B   Arrangement of the Statement of Earnings

Kim Renovation Inc. renovates historical buildings for commercial use. During 2018, Kim had $763,400 of revenue from renovation services and $5,475 of interest income from miscellaneous investments. Kim incurred $222,900 of wages expense, $135,000 of depreciation expense, $65,850 of insurance expense, $109,300 of utilities expense, $31,000 of miscellaneous expense, and $61,400 of income tax expense.

Required:

Prepare a single-step statement of earnings for Kim for 2018.

OBJECTIVE ❹❺❽

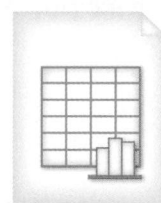

ILLUSTRATING
RELATIONSHIPS

Problem 1-71B   Statement of Earnings and Statement of Financial Position Relationships

Each column presents financial information taken from one of four different companies, with one or more items of data missing.

Financial Statement Item	Company			
	Crick	Pascal	Eiffel	Hilbert
Total revenue	$925	$ 533	$ (e)	$1,125
Total expense	844	(c)	377	(g)
Net income (net loss)	(a)	289	126	(340)
Total assets	709	1,810	(f)	3,150
Total liabilities	332	(d)	454	2,267
Total equity	(b)	950	98	(h)

Required:

Use your understanding of the relationships among financial statements and financial statement items to find the missing values (a–h).

Problem 1-72B   Statement of Earnings and Statement of Financial Position

OBJECTIVE 4 5 8

Ross Airport Auto Service provides parking and minor repair service at the local airport while customers are away on business or pleasure trips. The following account balances (except for retained earnings) are available for Ross Airport Auto Service at December 31, 2018.

Accounts payable	$ 17,200	Interest income	$ 4,100
Accounts receivable	39,200	Inventory (repair parts)	6,100
Accumulated depreciation (equipment)	42,300	Investments (long term)	35,000
Cash	7,700	Notes payable (due May 2, 2025)	160,000
Common shares (20,000 issued)	100,000	Prepaid rent (3 months)	27,300
Depreciation expense (equipment)	12,450	Rent expense	103,500
Dividends	6,300	Retained earnings, 12/31/2018	48,200
Equipment	270,800	Service revenue (parking)	232,600
Income tax expense	2,700	Service revenue (repair)	198,500
Income taxes payable	1,100	Supplies expense (repair parts)	36,900
Interest expense	21,300	Wages expense	246,100
Interest payable	4,800	Wages payable	12,500

Required:

Prepare a single-step statement of earnings and a classified statement of financial position for the year ended December 31, 2018.

Problem 1-73B   Understanding the Four Financial Statements

OBJECTIVE 7 8

Revenues	$27,000	Total liabilities	$13,500
Common shares	12,500	Dividends paid	3,000
Cash, December 31, 2017	13,000	Cash, December 31, 2018	21,500
Retained earnings	5,500	Cash from operating activities	7,500
Cash from financing activities	4,000	Other assets	1,000
Cash used for investing activities	(3,000)	Common shares	2,500

Required:

Taking into consideration the information above, calculate the cash balance on December 31, 2018.

Problem 1-74B   Statement of Retained Earnings

OBJECTIVE 6

Magical Experiences Vacation Company has the following data available:

Dividends, 2017	$ 13,200	Retained earnings, 12/31/2016	$ 47,100
Dividends, 2018	15,900	Revenues, 2017	244,900
Expenses, 2017	185,300	Revenues, 2018	391,400
Expenses, 2018	308,600		

Required:

Prepare statements of retained earnings for 2017 and 2018.

Problem 1-75B   Statements of Retained Earnings

OBJECTIVE 6

The table below presents the statements of retained earnings for Labelle Corporation for three successive years. Certain numbers are missing.

	2016	2017	2018
Retained earnings, beginning	$ (a)	$19,500	$26,700
Add: Net income	11,100	(c)	9,500
	26,900	(d)	(f)
Less: Dividends	(7,400)	(5,200)	(g)
Retained earnings, ending	$ (b)	$ (e)	$34,100

(Continued)

Required:

Use your understanding of the relationship between successive statements of retained earnings to calculate the missing values (a–g).

 OBJECTIVE ④⑤⑥   **Problem 1-76B   Statement of Earnings, Statement of Retained Earnings, and Statement of Financial Position**

McDonald Marina provides docking and cleaning services for pleasure boats at its marina in Vancouver. The following account balances are available for 2018:

Accounts payable	$ 26,400	Interest expense	$ 236,000
Accounts receivable	268,700	Interest payable	18,000
Accumulated depreciation (building)	64,500	Land	875,000
Accumulated depreciation (equipment)	950,400	Rent expense	14,600
Bonds payable (due 2023)	2,000,000	Rent payable	2,400
Building	197,300	Retained earnings, 12/31/2017	128,600
Cash	22,300	Service revenue (cleaning)	472,300
Common shares (40,000 issued)	600,000	Service revenue (docking)	1,460,000
Depreciation expense (building)	21,500	Supplies expense	89,100
Depreciation expense (equipment)	246,300	Supplies	9,800
Dividends	25,300	Utilities expense	239,400
Equipment	2,490,000	Wages expense	987,200
Income tax expense	21,700	Wages payable	21,600

Required:

1. Prepare a single-step statement of earnings, a statement of retained earnings, and a classified statement of financial position for the year ended December 31, 2018.
2. **CONCEPTUAL CONNECTION** How would a multiple-step statement of earnings be different from the single-step statement of earnings you prepared for McDonald Marina?

 OBJECTIVE ⑧   **Problem 1-77B   Shareholders' Equity Relationships**

ILLUSTRATING RELATIONSHIPS

Data from the financial statements of four different companies are presented in separate columns in the table below. Each column has one or more data items missing.

Financial Statement Item	Company			
	Stackhouse	Compton	Bellefleur	Merlotte
Equity, 12/31/2017				
Common shares	$45,000	$39,000	$ 80,000	$25,000
Retained earnings	18,800	15,300	6,900	(k)
Total equity	63,800	(d)	86,900	38,900
Net income (loss) for 2018	(a)	7,100	9,700	(4,500)
Dividends during 2018	2.100	800	(h)	0
Equity, 12/31/2018				
Common shares	45,000	39,000	80,000	25,000
Retained earnings	21,700	(e)	(i)	(l)
Total equity	(b)	(f)	95,300	(m)
Total assets, 12/31/2018	(c)	88,200	113,400	(n)
Total liabilities, 12/31/2018	14,400	(g)	(j)	15,700

Required:

Use your understanding of the relationships among the financial statement items to determine the missing values (a–n).

 OBJECTIVE ③⑧   **Problem 1-78B   Relationships among Financial Statements**

Leno Corporation reported the following amounts for assets and liabilities at the beginning and end of a recent year.

	Beginning of Year	End of Year
Assets	$231,500	$348,100
Liabilities	84,550	125,900

Required:

Calculate Leno's net income or net loss for the year in each of the following independent situations:

1. Leno declared no dividends, and its common shares remained unchanged.
2. Leno declared no dividends and issued additional common shares for $12,000 cash.
3. Leno declared dividends totalling $8,000, and its common shares remained unchanged.
4. Leno declared dividends totalling $11,000 and issued additional common shares for $15,000.

CASES

Case 1-79 Using Accounting Information

Jim Hadden is a freshman at Major Canadian University. His earnings from a summer job, combined with a small scholarship and a fixed amount per term from his parents, are his only sources of income. He has a new MasterCard that was issued to him the week he began classes. It is spring term, and Jim finds that his credit card is "maxed out" and that he does not have enough money to carry him to the end of the term. Jim confesses that irresistible opportunities for spring-term entertainment have caused him to overspend his resources.

Required:

Describe how accounting information could have helped Jim avoid this difficult situation.

Case 1-80 Analysis of Accounting Periodicals

The accounting profession is organized into three major groups: (1) accountants who work in nonbusiness entities, (2) accountants who work in business entities, and (3) accountants in public practice. The periodical literature of accounting includes monthly or quarterly journals that are written primarily for accountants within each of these groups.

Required:

1. Use your library and identify one journal published for each of the three professional groups. Identify the publisher of each journal and describe its primary audience.
2. Choose two of the three audiences you have just described. Briefly explain how members of one audience would benefit by reading a journal published primarily for members of the other audience.

Case 1-81 Career Planning

A successful career requires us to take advantage of opportunities that are difficult to foresee. Success is also aided by having a plan or strategy by which to choose among career alternatives as they arise.

Required:

1. How do you want to be employed in five years, and what must you do to get there?
2. How do you want to be employed in ten years, and what must you do to get there?

Case 1-82 Financial Statement Analysis

Gekas Rent-A-Car Inc. rents cars to customers whose vehicles are unavailable due to accident, theft, or repair ("Wheels while your car heals"). The company has a fleet of more than 40,000 cars located at 700 offices throughout North America. Its statements of financial position at January 31, 2018, and January 31, 2017, contain the following information (all dollar amounts are stated in thousands of dollars):

(Continued)

	1/31/2018	1/31/2017
Assets		
Cash	$ 4,850	$ 3,408
Accounts receivable	27,409	30,989
Supplies	6,864	7,440
Property and equipment	279,189	287,456
Other assets	15,666	14,441
	$333,978	$343,734
Liabilities and Shareholders' Equity		
Accounts payable	$ 18,602	$ 33,384
Other noncurrent liabilities	157,861	163,062
Shareholders' equity	157,515	147,288
	$333,978	$343,734

Required:

1. What is the dollar amount of current assets and current liabilities at January 31, 2018? At January 31, 2017? What does this information tell you about the company's liquidity?
2. Assume that shareholders were paid dividends of $18,100 during 2017 and that there were no other changes in shareholders' equity except for net income. How much net income did the business earn during the year ended January 31, 2018?

Case 1-83   Financial Statement Analysis

Reproduced below are portions of the president's letter to shareholders and selected income statement and statement of financial position data for the Brothers Aviation Company. Brothers is a national airline that provides both passenger service and package delivery service.

To Our Shareholders:

In 2018, the airline industry began to show some life. As fuel prices levelled and travellers showed an increased willingness to fly domestically, it was generally perceived that a gradual recovery was in place. The worldwide increase in the demand for air travel throughout the year translated into improved demand for the Company's services. In fact, revenues for both the passenger and package segments improved in every quarter of 2018. Most importantly, the Company started generating cash from operations in the last half of the year, and the passenger segments returned to generating profits in the third quarter . . .

   With improved operating performance as the basis for negotiating a financial restructuring, the next critical step for the Company is to satisfactorily restructure its obligations in order to ensure that the Company can operate effectively in the future. With that in mind, a strategic decision, albeit a difficult one, was made in February 2018—the Company filed for reorganization under the Companies' Creditors Arrangement Act (Canada).

	2018	2017	2016	2015	2014
Revenues:					
Passenger services	$ 141,343	$ 136,057	$354,246	$ 390,080	$ 337,871
Package services	35,199	60,968	145,940	203,675	202,615
Total revenues	176,542	197,025	500,186	593,755	540,486
Operating income	(54,584)	(92,613)	(16,663)	52,137	39,527
Net income (loss)	(182,647)	(340,516)	(67,269)	(14,553)	(22,461)
Current assets	123,553	134,009	183,268	193,943	209,944
Total assets	542,523	678,846	952,623	1,040,903	1,133,498
Current liabilities	698,583	641,645	542,640	129,369	120,960
Long-term debt	116,572	119,481	144,297	576,446	655,383
Shareholders' equity	(272,632)	(82,280)	265,686	335,088	357,155

Required:

1. What trends do you detect in revenues, operating income, and net income for the period 2014–2018?
2. What happened to working capital over the 2014–2018 period? To what do you attribute this result?
3. The price of Brothers shares declined steadily throughout the 2014–2018 period. Do you consider this decline to be a reasonable reaction to the financial results reported? Why or why not?

Case 1-84   Professional Ethics

Professional ethics guide public accountants in their work with financial statements.

Required:

Why is ethical behaviour by public accountants important to society? Be sure to describe the incentives that public accountants have to behave ethically and unethically.

Case 1-85   Ethical Issues

Lola, the CEO of JB Inc., and Frank, the accountant for JB Inc., were recently having a meeting to discuss the upcoming release of the company's financial statements. Following is an excerpt of their conversation:

Lola: These financial statements don't show the hours of hard work that we've put in to restore this company to financial health. In fact, these results may actually prevent us from obtaining loans that are critical to our future.

Frank: Accounting does allow for judgment. Tell me your primary concerns and let's see if we can work something out.

Lola: My first concern is that the company doesn't appear very liquid. As you can see, our current assets are only slightly more than current liabilities. The company has always paid its bills—even when cash was tight. It's not really fair that the financial statements don't reflect this.

Frank: Well, we could reclassify some of the long-term investments as current assets instead of noncurrent assets. Our expectation is that we will hold these investments for several years, but we could sell them at any time; therefore, it's fair to count these as current assets. We could also reclassify some of the accounts payable as noncurrent. Even though we expect to pay them within the next year, no one will ever look close enough to see what we've done. Together these two changes should make us appear more liquid and properly reflect the hard work we've done.

Lola: I agree. However, if we make these changes, our long-term assets will be smaller and our long-term debt will be larger. Many analysts may view this as a sign of financial trouble. Isn't there something we can do?

Frank: Our long-term assets are undervalued. Many were purchased years ago and recorded at historical cost. However, companies that bought similar assets recently are allowed to record them at an amount closer to their current market values. I've always thought this was misleading. If we increase the value of these long-term assets to their market value, this should provide the users of the financial statements with more relevant information and solve our problem, too.

Lola: Brilliant! Let's implement these actions quickly and get back to work.

Required:

Describe any ethical issues that have arisen as the result of Lola and Frank's conversation.

Case 1-86   Research and Analysis Using the Annual Report

Obtain Canadian Tire Corporation, Limited's 2014 annual report through the "Investor Relations" portion of their website (do a web search for Canadian Tire investor relations). Be sure to get the annual report for the year ended January 3, 2015. Note this is for fiscal year 2014.

Required:

Answer the following questions:

1. On what date did Canadian Tire's fiscal year end? Was this date different from the previous year? If so, why?
2. How many years of statement of financial position and statement of income/statement of earnings does Canadian Tire present?
3. With regard to the statement of financial position:

   a. What amounts did Canadian Tire report as total assets, liabilities, and shareholders' equity for fiscal 2014?
   b. Did the amounts reported as assets, liabilities, and shareholders' equity change over the last year? If so, by how much?
   c. What amounts were reported as current assets and current liabilities for the years presented?
   d. Provide an assessment of Canadian Tire's liquidity based on the information obtained in part *c*.
4. With regard to the statement of earnings / income statement:

   a. What amounts did Canadian Tire report as revenues, expenses, and net income for fiscal 2014?
   b. Do you detect any trends with regard to revenues, expenses, or net income?
5. With regard to the statement of cash flows, what amounts did the company report for cash flow from operating activities, cash flow from investing activities, and cash flow from financing activities for fiscal 2014?
6. With regard to management's discussion and analysis:

   a. What accounting policies and estimates does Canadian Tire consider critical? Where would these policies and estimates be described?
   b. Does management believe that the company performed well during the current year? On what do you base this assessment?
7. Are the financial statements audited? If so, by whom?

Case 1-87   Continuing Problem: Front Row Entertainment

Cam Mosley and Anna Newton met during their freshman year of university as they were standing in line to buy tickets to a concert. Over the next several hours, the two shared various aspects of their lives. Cam, whose father was an executive at a major record label, was raised in Toronto. Some of his favourite memories were meeting popular musical artists—from the Rolling Stones to the Black Eyed Peas—as he accompanied his father on business trips. Anna, on the other hand, was born and raised in a small rural town in southern Ontario. Her fondest childhood memories involved singing with her family, who often performed at county fairs and other small events. Even though they had different backgrounds, they felt an instant bond through their shared passion for music. Over the course of the next couple of years, this friendship strengthened as they attended numerous concerts and other events together.

While on a road trip to see a new band during their senior year, Cam and Anna started discussing their future career plans. Both had an entrepreneurial spirit and were seeking a way to combine their majors in business with their passion for music. Cam had recently overheard his father discussing how many artists were unhappy with the current concert promoters. Anna had heard similar complaints from her cousin, whose band recently had their first top 25 hit. When Cam suggested that he and Anna form a concert promotion business, they both knew they had found the perfect careers.

Concert promoters sign artists, usually through the artists' agents, to contracts in which the promoter is responsible for organizing live concert tours. Typically, this includes booking the venue, pricing the tour, advertising the tour, and negotiating other services from local vendors. In general, the barriers to entry in the concert promotion industry are relatively low, with one of the more important items being forming a relationship with the various artists. Through their industry contacts (Cam's father, Anna's cousin), they felt that they could develop a client list relatively easily. A second major barrier would be to obtain the up-front cash necessary to promote the tour properly.

Since their friendship had started many years ago as they were trying to get front row seats, they decided to name their business Front Row Entertainment. With their first big decision made, it was time to get to work.

Required:

1. Discuss some of the typical business activities (financing, investing, and operating) that a business like Front Row Entertainment is likely to have. (*Hint:* You may want to perform an Internet search for concert promoters to obtain a better understanding of the industry.) Be sure to list some of the specific account names for assets, liabilities, shareholders' equity, revenues, and expenses that may arise from these activities.
2. Explain the advantages and disadvantages of the forms of business organization that Cam and Anna might choose for Front Row Entertainment. Which form would you recommend?
3. Cam and Anna will need to prepare financial statements to report company performance. What type of information does each financial statement provide? Be sure to describe the insights that each financial statement provides to decision makers.

Case 1-88   Professional and Ethical Behaviour

Your friend Lorraine has recently approached you for advice on starting her new business. Her love of baking at home during her spare time has given her the great idea of selling baked goods to students at her local university. Her idea was to bake the goods fresh every morning and start delivering the goods as an afternoon delight for students starting at 2 p.m. She planned to drive around the university and sell these items out of her car. She is excited to start her new venture and cannot wait to start making all kinds of money from this amazing idea. She heard setting up a sole proprietorship is the best way to maximize her profit. Her long-time friend Christina told her that setting up a sole proprietorship is the best way of hiding profits from the government as everything will get reported on her own personal tax return. She said that the government knows that sole proprietorship owners omit some revenue earned from their business, but the government is fine with it and never bothers the owners about this.

Required:

Provide advice to Lorraine on starting her new business and comment on any ethical issues identified.

2

The Accounting Information System and Financial Statements

After studying Chapter 2, you should be able to:

1. Describe the qualitative characteristics, assumptions, principles, and constraints that underlie accounting.
2. Explain the relationships among economic events, transactions, and the expanded basic accounting equation.
3. Analyze the effect of business transactions on the basic accounting equation.
4. Discuss the role of accounts and show how debits and credits are used in the double-entry accounting system using T-accounts.
5. Prepare journal entries for transactions.
6. Explain why transactions are posted to the general ledger.
7. Prepare a trial balance and explain its purpose.

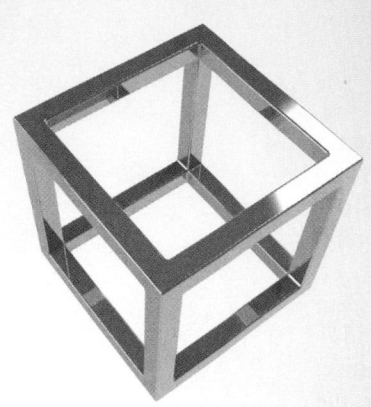

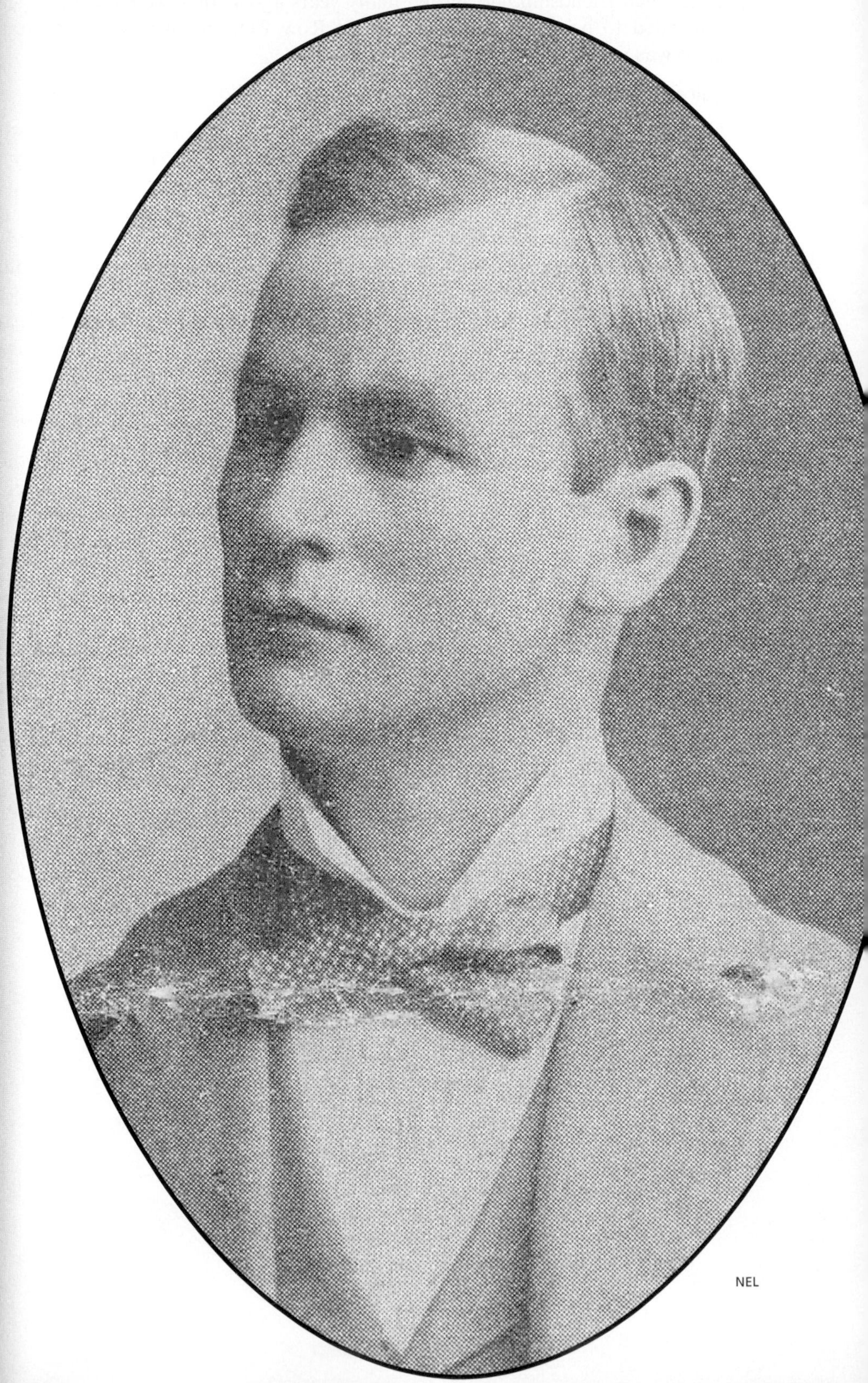

Courtesy of George Weston Limited

EXPERIENCE FINANCIAL ACCOUNTING
with George Weston Limited

In 1882, a young Toronto bread salesman and former baker's apprentice named George Weston went into business for himself when he bought a bread route from his employer. By the turn of the century, Weston's Bread was known throughout the city and George Weston had become Canada's biggest baker. Today, George Weston Limited is a Canadian public company engaged in food processing and distribution. It has two reportable segments—Weston Foods and Loblaw Companies Limited—and holds cash and short-term investments.

Weston Foods is a leader in the North American baking industry, producing a variety of fresh, frozen, and specialty bakery products. Its operations include more than 35 facilities across Canada and employs more than 4,000 workers. Weston Foods' Canadian operations include Weston Bakeries, Ready Bake Foods, and ACE Bakery. Weston Foods' U.S. operations consist of Maplehurst Bakeries and Interbake Foods.

Loblaw Companies Limited is Canada's largest food distributer and a leading provider of general merchandise products, drugs, and financial products and services. Loblaws' brand names include President's Choice, Joe Fresh, No Frills, Shopper's Drug Mart, Fortinos, and Provigo. Loblaws has more than 1,000 corporate and franchised stores across Canada, which employ more than 136,000 full- and part-time employees.

With so many different activities throughout the company, Weston faces a difficult task in measuring and reporting its activities. Companies like Weston rely on comprehensive accounting systems to capture, record, and report their various business activities. The type of system a company uses depends on many factors, such as its size and the volume of transactions it processes; most companies, though, use computerized accounting systems to efficiently provide information that is needed by the users of its financial statements. Weston has invested heavily in its accounting system, but it also recognizes that no system is foolproof. Financial accounting systems should be based on several key principles, including rigorous oversight by management and dedication to a system of internal controls that have been designed to ensure the accuracy and reliability of accounting records. Because Weston so strongly emphasizes its accounting system, users of its financial statements can feel confident that its business activities have been recorded and reported properly.

OBJECTIVE

Describe the qualitative characteristics, assumptions, principles, and constraints that underlie accounting.

FUNDAMENTAL ACCOUNTING CONCEPTS

In Chapter 1, we described the typical business activities in which companies engage and how accounting systems report these activities through the financial statements. It's also important to understand the underlying concepts behind accounting information systems. This chapter will discuss those concepts as well as the procedures that companies use to record information about business activities and how this information ultimately is transformed into financial statements. That is, you will see where the numbers on the financial statements actually come from. An understanding of these procedures is essential if you are to be an effective user of financial statements. As you review the financial statements, you are assessing a company's performance, cash flows, and financial position. To make those assessments, you need to be able to infer the past actions of a company from what you see in the financial statements. That inference depends on your understanding of how companies transform the results of their activities into financial statements.

These transforming procedures are called the **accounting cycle**. The accounting cycle is a simple and orderly process, based on a series of steps and conventions. If the financial statements are to present fairly the effects of the company's activities, proper operation of the accounting cycle is essential. For example, if Weston failed to properly apply accounting procedures, it is likely that many of its business activities would be improperly recorded (if they were even recorded at all) and its financial statements would be seriously misstated.

In this chapter, we will begin the discussion of the accounting cycle and how the completion of each step of the accounting cycle moves the accounting system toward its end product—the financial statements. We will address the following questions in this discussion:

- What concepts and assumptions underlie accounting information?
- How do companies record business activities?
- What procedures are involved in transforming information about business activities into financial statements?
- How do business activities affect the financial statements?

The Conceptual Framework

Accounting standards rest on a conceptual framework of accounting. This framework flows logically from the fundamental objective of financial reporting: to provide information that is useful in making business decisions. The conceptual framework is designed to support the development of a consistent set of accounting standards and provide a consistent body of thought for financial reporting. An understanding of the conceptual framework should help you understand complex accounting standards by providing a logical structure to financial accounting; in other words, the concepts help explain "why" accountants adopt certain practices. Exhibit 2.1 summarizes the characteristics of useful information as well as the underlying assumptions and principles that make up the conceptual framework.

Qualitative Characteristics of Useful Information

Given the overall objective of providing useful information, there are **two fundamental characteristics** that useful information should possess—relevance and faithful representation. The application of these criteria determines which economic events should be shown in the financial statements and how best to record these events.

- **Relevance**: Information is relevant if it is capable of making a difference in a business decision by helping users predict future events (*predictive value*) or providing feedback about prior expectations (*confirmatory value*). If the omission or misstatement of information could influence a decision, the information is said to be *material*. Therefore, materiality is an aspect of relevance.

(EXHIBIT 2.1)

The Conceptual Framework

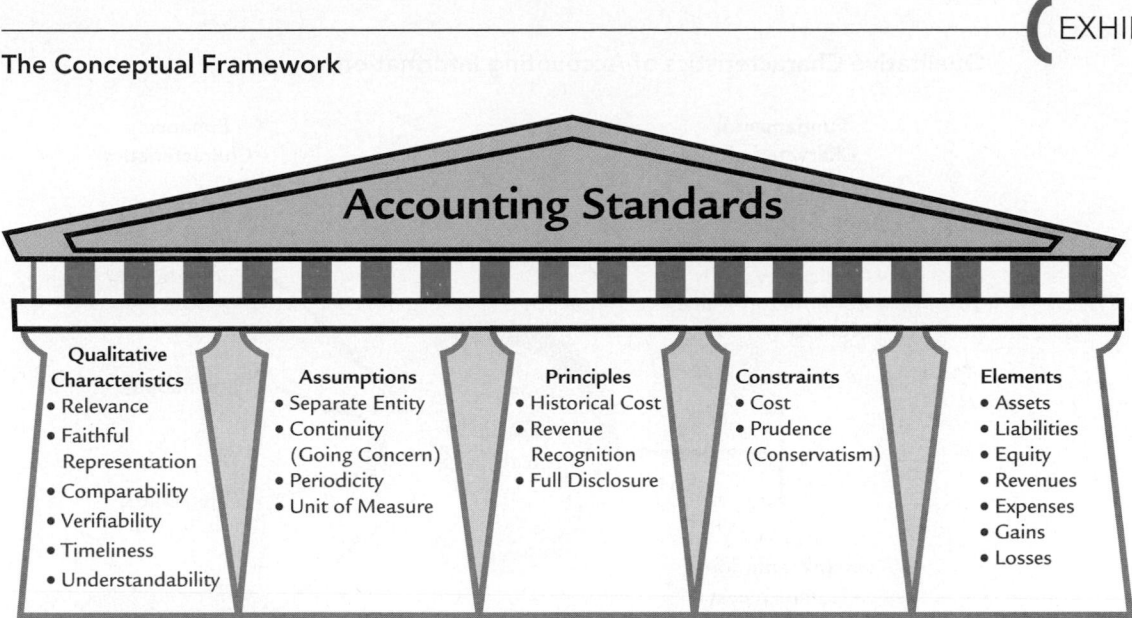

- **Faithful representation**: Accounting information should be a faithful representation of the real-world economic event that it is intending to portray. Faithfully represented information should be complete (includes all necessary information for the user to understand the economic event), neutral (unbiased), and free from error (as accurate as possible).

In applying these fundamental characteristics, the usual process is to identify the most relevant information and then determine whether it can be faithfully represented. If so, the fundamental qualitative characteristics have been satisfied. If not, the process should be repeated with the next most relevant type of information.

In addition to the fundamental characteristics, **four enhancing characteristics**—comparability, verifiability, timeliness, and understandability—have been identified. These enhancing characteristics are considered complementary to the fundamental characteristics, and their presence should help determine the degree of the information's usefulness.

- **Comparability**: Comparable information allows external users to identify similarities and differences between two or more items. Information is useful when it can be compared with similar information about other companies or with similar information about the same company for a different time period. Included within comparability is consistency. **Consistency** can be achieved by a company applying the same accounting principles for the same items over time. Consistency can also be achieved by multiple companies using the same accounting principles in a single time period. Comparability should be viewed as the goal, while consistency helps to achieve that goal.
- **Verifiability**: Information is verifiable when independent parties can reach a consensus on the measurement of the activity. When multiple independent observers can reach a general consensus, there is an implication that the information faithfully represents the economic event being measured.
- **Timeliness**: Information is timely if it is available to users before it loses its ability to influence business decisions.
- **Understandability**: If users who have a reasonable knowledge of accounting and business can, with reasonable effort, comprehend the meaning of the information, it is considered understandable.

(EXHIBIT 2.2)

Qualitative Characteristics of Accounting Information

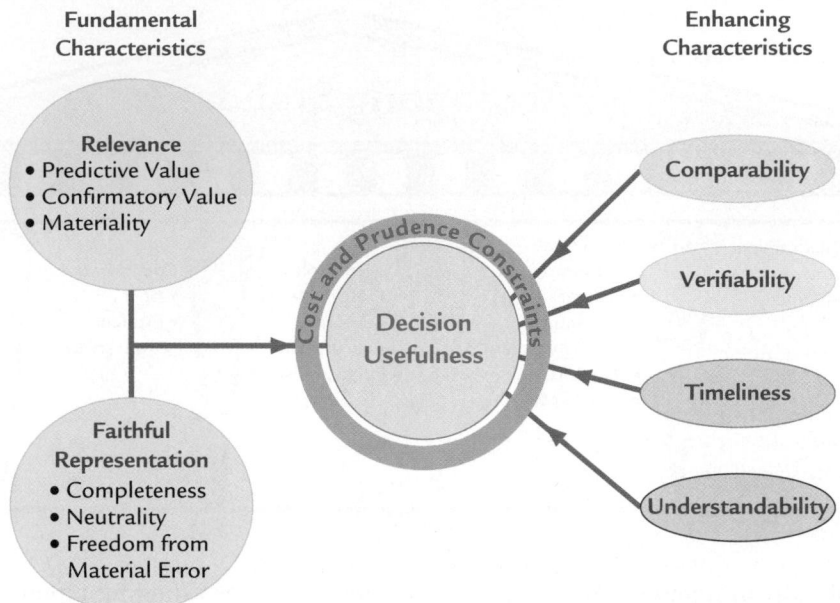

© Cengage Learning

Enhancing characteristics should be maximized to the extent possible.

These qualitative characteristics are bound by two pervasive constraints—the cost and prudence (conservatism) constraints. The **cost constraint** states that the benefit received from accounting information should be greater than the cost of providing that information. If the cost exceeds the benefit, the information is not considered useful. The **prudence constraint** states that extra care should be taken to ensure that assets and revenues are not overstated and that liabilities and expenses are not understated. Exhibit 2.2 illustrates the qualitative characteristics of useful financial information.

Trade-offs are often necessary in evaluating these criteria. For example, the most relevant information may not be able to be faithfully represented. Similarly, changing economic situations may require a change in the accounting principle used. Such a change may decrease the comparability of the information presented. In these situations, the accountant must exercise judgment in determining the accounting principles that will produce the most useful information for the decision maker. In all situations, accountants should follow a **full disclosure** policy. That is, any information that would make a difference to decisions of financial statement users should be revealed.

Assumptions

The following four basic assumptions underlie accounting:

- **Separate entity assumption**: Under this assumption, each company is accounted for separately from its owners. Bill Gates's personal transactions, for instance, are not recorded in Microsoft's financial statements.
- **Continuity (or going-concern) assumption**: This assumption assumes that a company will continue to operate long enough to carry out its existing commitments. Without this assumption, many of our accounting procedures could not be followed. For example, if Weston were expected to go bankrupt in the near future, its assets and liabilities would be

concept Q&A

Companies assume they are going concerns. Wouldn't the valuation of a company's assets be more relevant if this assumption were relaxed and the net assets valued at their current selling values?

Answer:

Current selling values are only relevant if the company intends to sell the assets in the near term. However, many assets (such as machinery, buildings) are used over long periods of time, and in these situations, the use of current selling prices would be of little value to financial statement users. In addition, the cost of obtaining current values for these assets would greatly outweigh the benefits received.

reported on the statement of financial position at an amount the company expects to receive if sold (less any costs of disposal).

- **Periodicity (or time period) assumption**: This assumption allows the life of a company to be divided into artificial time periods so that net income can be measured for a specific period of time (e.g., monthly, quarterly, annually). Without this assumption, a company's income could only be reported at the end of its life.
- **Unit of measure (or monetary unit) assumption**: This assumption requires that a company account for and report its financial results in the national monetary unit, which is assumed to have a constant purchasing power over time (such as Canadian dollar, euro, Japanese yen). While this assumption provides for the efficient production of financial statements over time for multinational companies, it does not recognize that the purchasing power of most currencies changes over time. As a result, we need to recognize that when we prepare a financial statement for a Canadian company using the Canadian dollar to report its business activities, we are adding together Canadian dollars that have a differing purchase power, or economic size, over time. This assumption also implies that certain nonmonetary items (such as brand loyalty, customer satisfaction) are not reported in a company's financial statements since they do not result from transactions that are measured in monetary terms.

Principles

Principles are general approaches that are used in the measurement and recording of business activities. The three basic principles of accounting are as follows: the historical cost principle, the revenue recognition principle, and the full disclosure principle.

- **Historical cost principle**: This principle requires that the activities of a company be initially measured at their cost—the exchange price at the time the activity occurs. For example, when Weston buys equipment used in manufacturing its products, it initially records the equipment at the cost paid to acquire the equipment. Accountants use historical cost because it provides an objective and verifiable basis of measure of the activity. However, the historical cost principle has been criticized because, after the date of acquisition, it does not reflect changes in market value. Accounting standards adopted under IFRS often include asset and liability measures that use market values to measure certain assets and liabilities (such as investments in marketable securities) *after* the date of acquisition. Alternative measurement bases for assets are discussed in Chapters 5, 6, 7, and 9.
- **Revenue recognition principle**: This principle is used to determine when revenue is recorded and reported. Five conditions must be met in order for revenue to be recognized in a company's financial statements. Detailed discussion of this principle is in Chapter 3.
- **Full disclosure principle**: The full disclosure principle requires that financial statements include all information required for the financial statement users to make informed decisions about the company's financial position, operating results, and cash flows. This principle, for example, requires the inclusion of a note to the financial statements that discloses which accounting policies have been adopted by the reporting company.

The application of the conceptual framework is illustrated in Cornerstone 2.1 .

Elements of the Financial Statements

- **Assets**: Assets are economic resources of a business entity that are controlled by a business entity and are expected to provide a future benefit.
- **Liabilities**: Liabilities are existing obligations or debts of a business entity that will be satisfied by payment with assets or the provision of services. The recognition of

CORNERSTONE 2.1

Applying the Conceptual Framework

Information:

Mario is faced with the following questions as he prepares the financial statements of DK Company:

1. Should the purchase of inventory be valued at what DK paid to acquire the inventory or at its estimated selling price?

2. Should information be provided that financial statement users might find helpful in predicting DK's future income?

3. Although DK is profitable, should the financial statements be prepared under the assumption that DK will go bankrupt?

4. Should DK's inventory be reported in terms of the number of units on hand or the dollar value of those units?

5. Should equipment leased on a long-term basis be reported as an asset (the economic substance of the transaction) or should it be reported as a rental (the form of the transaction)?

6. Should DK recognize revenue from the sale of its products when the sale is made or when the cash is received?

7. Should DK record the purchase of a vacation home by one of its shareholders?

8. Should DK report income annually to its shareholders, or should it wait until all transactions are complete?

Required:

Which qualitative characteristic, assumption, or principle should Mario use in resolving the situation?

Why:

The conceptual framework provides a logical structure and direction to financial accounting and reporting and supports the development of a consistent set of accounting standards. An understanding of the conceptual framework is required to analyze complex accounting issues.

Solution:

1. *Historical cost:* The activities of a company (such as purchase of inventory) should be initially measured at the exchange price at the time the activity occurs.

2. *Relevance:* Material information that has predictive or confirmatory value should be provided.

3. *Continuity (going-concern):* In the absence of information to the contrary, it should be assumed that a company will continue to operate indefinitely.

4. *Monetary unit:* A company should account for and report its financial results in its national monetary unit.

(Continued)

5. *Faithful representation:* Information should portray the economic event that it is intending to portray completely, accurately, and without bias.

6. *Revenue recognition:* Revenue must satisfy five conditions (discussed in Chapter 5) before it can be recognized.

7. *Separate entity:* A company's transactions should be accounted for separately from its owners.

8. *Time period:* The life of a company can be divided into artificial time periods so that income can be measured and reported periodically to interested parties.

CORNERSTONE

2.1

(Continued)

environmental liabilities in financial statements has and is continuing to receive increased attention in accounting standards.

- **Equity**: Shareholders' equity in a corporation consists of the capital provided to the company by its shareholders combined with undistributed earnings of the company.

The elements of revenues, expenses, gains, and losses are discussed in Chapters 3 and 4.

Given this conceptual foundation, we will now turn our attention to the process of recording information about business activities in the accounting system.

MEASURING BUSINESS ACTIVITIES: THE ACCOUNTING CYCLE

The sequence of procedures used by companies to transform the effects of business activities into financial statements is called the accounting cycle. The accounting cycle is shown in Exhibit 2.3.

OBJECTIVE

Explain the relationships among economic events, transactions, and the expanded basic accounting equation.

(EXHIBIT 2.3)

The Accounting Cycle

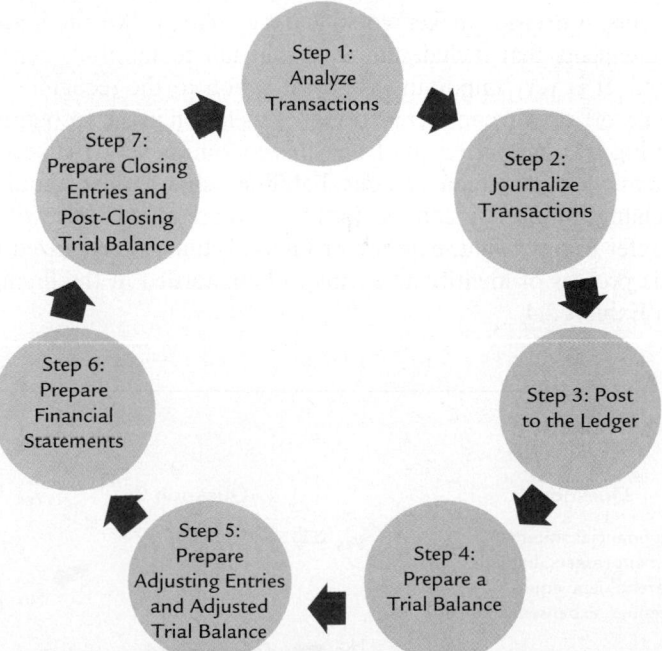

The steps in the accounting cycle are performed each period and then repeated. Steps 1 through 4 are performed regularly each period as business activities occur. We will discuss these four steps in this chapter. Steps 5 through 7 are performed at the end of a period and are discussed in Chapter 3.

Economic Events

As we discussed in Chapter 1, a company engages in numerous activities that can be categorized as financing, investing, or operating activities. Each of these activities consists of different **events** that affect the company. Some of these events are *external* and result from exchanges between the company and another entity outside of the company. For example, when Weston issues common shares to investors, purchases equipment used to increase bakery production, or pays its employees a salary, it is engaging in an exchange with another entity. Other events are *internal* and result from the company's own actions. When Weston uses equipment to make its products, no other entity is involved; however, the event still has an impact on the company.

Accounting measures the effects of events that influence a company and incorporates these events into the accounting system, which, ultimately, produces the financial statements. However, not every event that affects a company is recorded in the accounting records. In order for an event to be recorded, or recognized, in the accounting system, the items making up the event must impact a financial statement element (asset, liability, shareholders' equity, revenue, or expense) and should be a faithful representation of the event.

The first requirement usually is met when at least one party to a contract performs its responsibility according to the contract. For example, assume that a buyer and seller agree upon the delivery of an asset and sign a contract. The signing of the contract usually is not recorded in the accounting system because neither party has performed its responsibility. Instead, recognition typically will occur once the buyer receives the asset or pays the seller, whichever comes first.

Even when the event impacts a financial statement element, a faithful representation of the event must be possible if it is to be recorded. A sudden increase in the price of raw materials, for instance, may have an effect on Weston's ability to sell its bakery and food products. However, the effects of this price increase cannot be faithfully represented, so the event will not be recognized in the financial statements. Providing a measurement that is complete, unbiased, and free from error is important in accounting to avoid misleading users of financial statements. A decision maker would find it extremely difficult, if not impossible, to use financial statements that include amounts that fail to faithfully represent what has actually occurred. It is very important to pay attention to the recognition criteria in the conceptual framework as you consider an event for inclusion in the accounting system.

An accounting transaction results from an economic event that causes one of the elements of the financial statements (assets, liabilities, shareholders' equity, revenues, or expenses) to change and that can be faithfully represented. We will use the term **transaction** to refer to any event, external or internal, that is recognized in the financial statements. The process of identifying events to be recorded in the financial statements is illustrated in Exhibit 2.4.

(**EXHIBIT 2.4**)

Transaction Identification

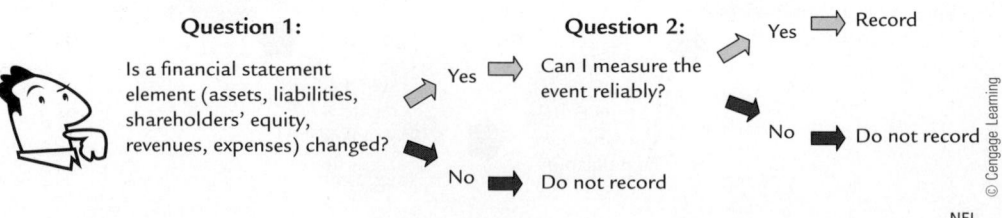

© Cengage Learning

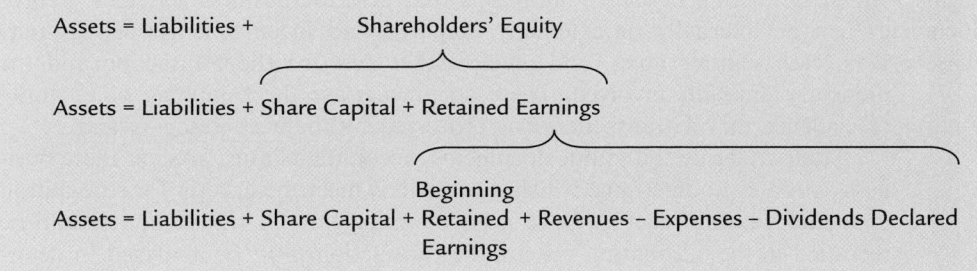

EXHIBIT 2.5

The Expanded Accounting Equation

The Expanded Basic Accounting Equation

Because accounting is concerned with the measurement of transactions and their effect on the financial statements, a starting point in the measurement and recording process is the basic accounting equation:

$$\text{Assets} = \text{Liabilities} + \text{Shareholders' equity}$$

Recall from Chapter 1 that:

- The two sides of the accounting equation must always be equal or "in balance" as a company conducts its business. Accounting systems record these business activities in a way that maintains this equality. As a consequence, every transaction has a two-part, or double-entry, effect on the equation. This is referred to as the *duality* of the basic accounting equation.
- The statement of financial position and the income statement are related through retained earnings. Specifically, net income (revenues minus expenses) increases retained earnings. Given this relationship, the basic accounting equation can be rewritten to show the elements that make up shareholders' equity.

With the expanded basic accounting equation shown in Exhibit 2.5, we are now ready to analyze how transactions affect a company's financial statements.

YOUDECIDE   Recognition of Economic Events

As you are analyzing the most recent financial statements of Essex Oil Company, you question whether the company properly recorded an economic event. You know that Essex owns and operates several offshore oil drilling platforms in the Gulf of Mexico. You also recall from news reports that a hurricane severely damaged two of the platforms, leading to a significant loss in revenue while the platforms were inactive. While you see evidence in the financial statements of the damage and repair to the platforms, you cannot find any evidence of the lost revenue in the financial statements.

Does the loss in revenue from the damaged oil platforms qualify for recognition in the financial statements?

To be recognized in the financial statements, the event must impact a financial statement element and be faithfully represented.

While Essex may have been able to measure the loss in revenue, no financial statement element has been affected. While you may argue that this event affected revenue, revenue is an increase in assets resulting from the sale of products. Because the lost sales did not result in an inflow of assets or reduce liabilities, it is not considered revenue. In addition, expenses are defined as the cost of resources used or liabilities incurred to earn revenues. The lost revenue did not represent a use of resources, nor did it result in a liability being incurred and it is therefore not an expense. Therefore the lost revenue cannot be recognized in the financial statements.

Recognition of events in the financial statements requires analysis of whether the event impacted a financial statement element and can be faithfully represented.

OBJECTIVE ❸

Analyze the effect of business transactions on the basic accounting equation.

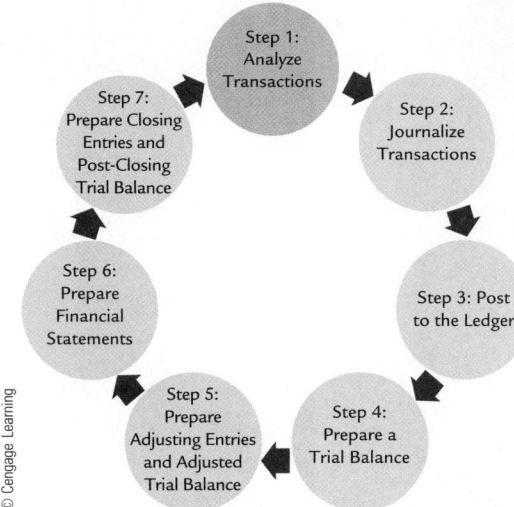

STEP 1: ANALYZE TRANSACTIONS

Transaction analysis is the process of determining the economic effects of a transaction on the elements of the basic accounting equation. Transaction analysis usually begins with the gathering of *source documents* that describe business activities. Source documents can be internally or externally prepared and include items such as purchase orders, cash register tapes, and invoices that describe the transaction and the monetary amounts involved. These documents are the beginning of a "trail" of evidence that a transaction was processed by the accounting system.

After gathering the source documents, accountants must analyze these business activities to determine which transactions meet the criteria for recognition in the accounting records. Once it is determined that a transaction should be recorded in the accounting system, the transaction must be analyzed to determine how it will affect the accounting equation. In performing transaction analysis, it is important to remember that the accounting equation must always remain in balance. Therefore, each transaction will have at least two effects on the accounting equation.

In summary, transaction analysis involves the following three steps:

*   *Step 1: Write down the basic accounting equation.* In this chapter, we often use an expanded version of the basic accounting equation because it provides more information in the analysis. However, the single version of the basic accounting equation could also be used.
*   *Step 2: Identify the financial statement elements that are affected by the transaction.*
*   *Step 3: Determine whether the elements increased or decreased.*

Cornerstone 2.2 illustrates the basic process of transaction analysis.

CORNERSTONE 2.2

Performing Transaction Analysis

CORNERSTONE VIDEO

Information:

Lee Inc. purchases a $3,000 computer from Bay Electronics on credit, with payment due in 60 days.

Required:

Determine the effect of the transaction on the elements of the accounting equation.

Why:

The economic effect of a transaction will have a two-part, or dual, effect on the basic accounting equation that results in the equation always being in balance. The basic accounting equation must remain in balance after each transaction to facilitate the preparation of accurate financial statements.

Solution:

A computer is an economic resource, or asset, that will be used by Lee in its business. The purchase of the computer increased assets and also created an obligation, or

(Continued)

liability, for Lee. Therefore, the effect of the transaction on the accounting equation is as follows:

CORNERSTONE

2.2

(Continued)

Assets	=	Liabilities	+	Shareholders' Equity	
				Share Capital	**Retained Earnings**
+$3,000		+$3,000			

Note that the transaction analysis in Cornerstone 2.2 conforms to the two underlying principles of transaction analysis:

- There is a dual effect on the accounting equation.
- The accounting equation remains in balance after the transaction.

All transactions can be analyzed using a similar process.

To provide a further illustration of the effect of transactions on the accounting equation, consider the case of HighTech Communications Inc. HighTech is a newly formed corporation that operates an advertising agency that specializes in promoting computer-related products in the Winnipeg area. We show the effects of thirteen transactions on HighTech's financial position during its first month of operations, March 2018. These transactions are summarized in Exhibit 2.6.

Transaction 1: Issuing Common Shares

On March 1, HighTech sold 1,000 of its common shares to several investors for cash of $12,000. The effect of this transaction on the basic accounting equation is:

Assets	=	Liabilities	+	Shareholders' Equity	
				Share Capital	**Retained Earnings**
+$12,000				+$12,000	

The sale of shares increases assets, specifically cash, and also increases shareholders' equity (specifically, share capital or common shares). Notice that there is a dual effect, and although both assets and equity change, the equality of the equation is maintained. The issuance of shares would be considered a financing activity.

Transaction 2: Borrowing Cash

On March 2, HighTech raised additional funds by borrowing $3,000 from the Royal Bank in Winnipeg. HighTech promised to pay the amount borrowed plus 8% interest to the Royal Bank in one year. The financial effect of this transaction is:

Assets	=	Liabilities	+	Shareholders' Equity	
				Share Capital	**Retained Earnings**
+$3,000		+$3,000			

concept Q&A

Why must the accounting equation always remain in balance?

Answer:

The accounting equation captures the business activities of a company. Its left-hand side describes the economic resources, or assets, that the company has acquired. Its right-hand side describes the claims on these assets—either from creditors (liabilities) or from shareholders (shareholders' equity). Because all resources belong to either the creditors or the shareholders, the equation must balance.

This borrowing has two effects: the asset cash is increased and a liability is created. High-Tech has an obligation to repay the cash borrowed according to the terms of the borrowing. Such a liability is termed a note payable. Because this transaction is concerned with obtaining funds to begin and operate a business, it is classified as a financing activity.

Transaction 3: Purchase of Equipment for Cash

On March 3, HighTech purchased office equipment (such as computer equipment) from MicroCentre Inc. for $4,500 in cash. The effect of this transaction on the accounting equation is:

Assets	=	Liabilities	+	Shareholders' Equity	
				Share Capital	Retained Earnings
+$4,500					
−$4,500					

There is a reduction in cash (an asset) as it is spent and a corresponding increase in another asset, equipment. The purchased equipment is an asset because HighTech will use it to generate future revenue. Notice that this transaction merely converts one asset (cash) into another (equipment). Total assets remain unchanged and the accounting equation remains in balance. Because transaction 3 is concerned with buying long-term (non-current) assets that enable HighTech to operate, it is considered an investing activity.

Transaction 4: Purchasing Insurance

On March 4, HighTech purchased a six-month insurance policy for $1,200 cash. The effect of this transaction on the accounting equation is:

Assets	=	Liabilities	+	Shareholders' Equity	
				Share Capital	Retained Earnings
+$1,200					
−$1,200					

There is a reduction in cash (an asset) as it is spent and a corresponding increase in another asset, prepaid insurance. The purchased insurance is an asset because the insurance will benefit more than one accounting period. This type of asset is often referred to as a prepaid asset. Notice that like transaction 3, this transaction merely converts one asset (cash) into another (prepaid insurance). Total assets remain unchanged and the accounting equation remains in balance. Because transaction 4 is concerned with the operations of the company, it is classified as an operating activity.

Transaction 5: Purchase of Supplies on Credit

On March 6, HighTech purchased office supplies from Hamilton Office Supply for $6,500. Hamilton Office Supply agreed to accept full payment in 30 days. As a result of this transaction, HighTech received an asset (supplies) but also incurred a liability to pay for these supplies in 30 days. The financial effect of this transaction is:

Assets	=	Liabilities	+	Shareholders' Equity	
				Share Capital	Retained Earnings
+$6,500		+$6,500			

A transaction where goods are purchased on credit is often referred to as a purchase "on account," and the liability that is created is referred to as an account payable. Because transaction 5 is concerned with the operations of the company, it is classified as an operating activity.

Transaction 6: Sale of Services for Cash

On March 10, HighTech sold advertising services to Regina Valley Products in exchange for $8,800 in cash. Remember from Chapter 1 that revenue is defined as an increase in assets resulting from the sale of products or services. Since HighTech is an advertising company, the sale of advertising services is HighTech's primary revenue-producing activity. Therefore, this transaction results in an increase in assets (cash) and an increase in revenue.

Assets	=	Liabilities	+	Shareholders' Equity	
				Share Capital	Retained Earnings (Sales Revenue)
+$8,800					+$8,800

As shown in the expanded accounting equation discussed earlier, *revenues increase retained earnings*. The dual effects (the increase in assets and the increase in retained earnings) maintain the balance of the accounting equation. Because transaction 6 is concerned with the operations of the company, it is classified as an operating activity.

Transaction 7: Sale of Services for Credit

On March 15, HighTech sold advertising services to the *Winnipeg Enquirer* for $3,300. HighTech agreed to accept full payment in 30 days. When a company performs services for which they will be paid at a later date, this is often referred to as a sale "on account." Instead of receiving cash, HighTech received a promise to pay from the *Winnipeg Enquirer*. This right to collect amounts due from customers creates an asset called an account receivable. Similar to the cash sale in transaction 6, the credit sale represents revenue for HighTech because assets (accounts receivable) were increased as a result of the sale of the advertising service. The financial effect of this transaction is:

Assets	=	Liabilities	+	Shareholders' Equity	
				Share Capital	Retained Earnings (Sales Revenue)
+$3,300					+$3,300

Consistent with the revenue recognition principle, *revenue is recorded when earned* (e.g., the service is provided) and the collection of cash is reasonably assured, not when the cash is actually received. Because transaction 7 is concerned with the operations of the company, it is classified as an operating activity.

Transaction 8: Receipt of Cash in Advance

On March 19, HighTech received $9,000 from the *Winnipeg News* for advertising services to be completed in the next three months. Similar to transaction 6, HighTech received cash for services. However, due to the revenue recognition principle, HighTech cannot recognize revenue until it has performed the advertising service. Therefore, the receipt of cash creates a liability for HighTech for the work that is due in the future. The effect of this transaction on the accounting equation is:

Assets	=	Liabilities	+	Shareholders' Equity	
				Share Capital	Retained Earnings
+$9,000		+$9,000			

The liability that is created by the receipt of cash in advance of performing the revenue-generating activities is called an unearned revenue. Because transaction *8* is concerned with the operations of the company, it is classified as an operating activity.

Transaction 9: Payment to a Supplier

On March 23, HighTech paid $6,000 cash for the supplies previously purchased from Hamilton Office Supply on credit (transaction *5*). The payment results in a reduction of an asset (cash) and the partial settlement of HighTech's obligation (liability) to Hamilton Office Supply. The financial effect of this transaction is:

Assets	=	Liabilities	+	Shareholders' Equity	
				Share Capital	Retained Earnings
−$6,000		−$6,000			

As a result of this cash payment, the liability "Accounts Payable" is reduced to $500 ($6,500 − $6,000). This means that HighTech still owes Hamilton Office Supply $500. Notice that the payment of cash did not result in an expense. The expense related to the use of supplies will be recorded as supplies are used. Because transaction *9* is concerned with the operations of the company, it is classified as an operating activity.

Transaction 10: Payment of Salaries

On March 26 (a Friday), HighTech paid weekly employee salaries of $1,800. Remember from Chapter 1 that an expense is the cost of an asset consumed or the amount of a liability created in the operation of the business. Because an asset (cash) is consumed as part of HighTech's normal operations, salaries are an expense. As shown in the expanded accounting equation discussed earlier, *expenses decrease retained earnings*. The effect of this transaction on the accounting equation is:

Assets	=	Liabilities	+	Shareholders' Equity	
				Share Capital	Retained Earnings (Salary Expense)
−$1,800					−$1,800

Because transaction *10* is concerned with the operations of the company, it is classified as an operating activity.

Transaction 11: Collection from a Customer

On March 29, HighTech collected $3,000 cash from the *Winnipeg Enquirer* for services sold earlier on credit (transaction *7*). The collection of cash increases assets. In addition, the accounts receivable (an asset) from the *Winnipeg Enquirer* is also reduced. The financial effect of this transaction is:

Assets	=	Liabilities	+	Shareholders' Equity	
				Share Capital	Retained Earnings
+$3,000					
−$3,000					

As a result of this cash payment, the *Winnipeg Enquirer* still owes HighTech $300. Notice that the cash collection did not result in the recognition of a revenue. The revenue was recognized as the service was performed (transaction 7). Because transaction *11* is concerned with the operations of the company, it is classified as an operating activity.

Transaction 12: Payment of Utilities

On March 30, HighTech paid its utility bill of $5,200 for March. Because an asset (cash) is consumed by HighTech as part of the operations of the business, the cost of utilities used during the month is an expense. The effect of this transaction on the accounting equation is:

Assets	=	Liabilities	+	Shareholders' Equity	
				Share Capital	Retained Earnings (Utilities Expense)
−$5,200					−$5,200

Similar to the payment of salaries, utility expense is recorded as a decrease in retained earnings in the same period that it helped to generate revenue. Because transaction *12* is concerned with the operations of the company, it is classified as an operating activity.

Transaction 13: Declaration and Payment of a Dividend

On March 31, HighTech declared and paid a cash dividend of $500 to its shareholders. Dividends are not an expense. Dividends are a distribution of net income and are recorded as a reduction of retained earnings. The effect of this transaction on the accounting equation is:

Assets	=	Liabilities	+	Shareholders' Equity	
				Share Capital	Retained Earnings
−$500					−$500

IFRS allows dividends paid to be treated as either an operating, investing, or financing activity at management's discretion, but the choice, once made, must be consistently applied in subsequent accounting periods.

The payment of a dividend is classified as a financing activity under ASPE.

Overview of Transactions for HighTech Communications Inc.

Exhibit 2.6 summarizes HighTech's transactions in order to show their cumulative effect on the basic accounting equation. The transaction number is shown in the first

(EXHIBIT 2.6)

Summary of Transactions for HighTech Communications Inc.

	Assets	=	Liabilities +	Share Capital	Retained Earnings
				Shareholders' Equity	
(1)	+ $12,000			+ $12,000	
(2)	+ $3,000		+ $3,000		
(3)	+ $4,500				
	− $4,500				
(4)	+ $1,200				
	− $1,200				
(5)	+ $6,500		+ $6,500		
(6)	+ $8,800				+ $8,800 ⎫
(7)	+ $3,300				+ $3,300 ⎬ Revenue
(8)	+ $9,000		+ $9,000		
(9)	− $6,000		− $6,000		
(10)	− $1,800				− $1,800 ⎫
(11)	+ $3,000				⎪ Expense
	− $3,000				⎬
(12)	− $5,200				− $5,200 ⎭
(13)	− $500				− $500 Dividend
	$29,100		**$12,500**	**$12,000**	**$4,600**

$29,100   = $29,100

column on the left. Revenue and expense items are identified on the right. Notice that this summary reinforces the two key principles discussed earlier:

- Each transaction has a dual effect on the elements of the accounting equation.
- The basic accounting equation always remains in balance—the total change in assets ($29,100) equals the change in liabilities plus shareholders' equity ($29,100).

Transaction analysis can be used to answer many important questions about a company and its activities. Using the information in Exhibit 2.6, we can answer the following questions:

- *What are the amounts of total assets, total liabilities, and total equity at the end of March?* At the end of March, HighTech has total assets of $29,100, total liabilities of $12,500, and total equity of $16,600 ($12,000 of share capital plus $4,600 of retained earnings). These amounts for assets, liabilities, and shareholders' equity at the end of March would be carried over as the beginning amounts for April.
- *What is net income for the month?* Net income is $5,100, which represents the excess of revenues of $12,100 ($8,800 + $3,300) over expenses of $7,000 ($5,200 + $1,800). Notice that dividends are not included on the statement of earnings; instead they are included on the statement of retained earnings.
- *How much cash was received during the month? How much was spent? How much cash does HighTech have at the end of the month?* During March HighTech received a total of $35,800 in cash ($12,000 + $3,000 + $8,800 + $9,000 + $3,000) and spent a total of $19,200 ($4,500 + $1,200 + $6,000 + $1,800 + $5,200 + $500). At the end of the month, HighTech had cash on hand of $16,600 ($35,800 − $19,200).

The summary in Exhibit 2.6 can become quite cumbersome. For example, in order to determine the amount of cash that HighTech has at the end of the month, you may find it necessary to refer back to the actual transactions to determine which ones involved cash and which did not. In addition, what if an investor or creditor wanted to know not only net income but also the *types* of expenses that HighTech incurred? (For example, what was the dollar amount spent for salaries?) To answer these questions, more information is needed than the transaction summary provides. For a company like Weston, a spreadsheet such as the preceding one would prove inadequate to convey its financial information to investors, creditors, and other users. A better way to record and track information that is consistent with the preceding model is necessary. The solution is double-entry accounting.

DOUBLE-ENTRY ACCOUNTING

Double-entry accounting describes the system used by companies to record the effects of transactions on the basic accounting equation. The effects of transactions are recorded in accounts. Under double-entry accounting, each transaction affects at least two accounts. In this section, we explore accounts and the process by which transactions are reflected in specific accounts.

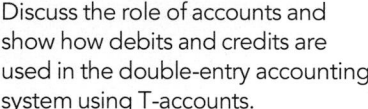

OBJECTIVE 4

Discuss the role of accounts and show how debits and credits are used in the double-entry accounting system using T-accounts.

Accounts

To aid in the recording of transactions, an organizational system consisting of accounts has been developed. An **account** is a record of increases and decreases in each of the basic elements of the financial statements. Each financial statement element is composed of a variety of accounts. All changes in assets, liabilities, shareholders' equity, revenues, and expenses are then recorded in the appropriate account. The list of accounts used by the company is termed a **chart of accounts**.[1] The chart of accounts can be changed over time as the nature of business activities change. A typical list of accounts is shown in Exhibit 2.7. These accounts were all discussed in Chapter 1.

Every company will have a different chart of accounts depending on the nature of its business activities. However, once a company selects which accounts will be used, all transactions must be recorded into these accounts. As the company engages in transactions, the transaction will either increase or decrease an account. The amount in an account at any given time is called the *balance* of the account. For example, the purchase of equipment will increase the balance in the equipment account, whereas the disposal of equipment will decrease the balance of the equipment account. For financial reporting purposes, the balances of related accounts typically are combined and

(EXHIBIT 2.7)

Typical Accounts

Assets	Liabilities	Shareholders' Equity	Revenue	Expense
Cash	Accounts Payable	Common Shares	Sales Revenue	Cost of Goods Sold
Investments	Salaries Payable	Preferred Shares	Interest Income	Salary Expense
Accounts Receivable	Unearned Sales Revenue	Retained Earnings	Dividend Revenue	Rent Expense
Inventory	Interest Payable	Dividends Declared	Rent Revenue	Insurance Expense
Land	Income Tax Payable			Depreciation Expense
Buildings	Notes Payable			Advertising Expense
Equipment	Bonds Payable			Utilities Expense
Patent				Repairs & Maintenance Expense
Copyright				Property Tax Expense
Goodwill				

© Cengage Learning

[1] This textbook uses a simplified and standardized chart of accounts, which can be found on the back endpaper of the book. Account titles for real company financial statements may vary. Common alternative account titles are introduced, as appropriate, when the account is introduced.

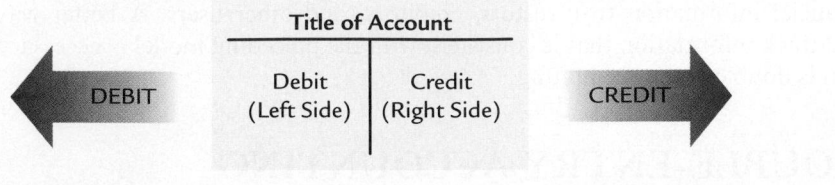

(EXHIBIT 2.8)

Form of a T-Account

© Cengage Learning

reported as a single amount. For example, Weston reports a combined, or net, amount of property, plant, and equipment on its statement of financial position as fixed assets. However, in its footnotes, Weston discloses the amounts of individual accounts such as land, buildings, and equipment.

Although an account can be shown in a variety of ways, transactions are frequently analyzed using a **T-account**. The T-account receives its name because it resembles the capital letter T (see Exhibit 2.8). A T-account is a two-column record that consists of an account title and two sides divided by a vertical line—the left and the right side. The left side is referred to as the **debit** side and the right side is referred to as the **credit** side.

Note that the terms debit and credit simply refer to the left and the right side of an account. The left is always the debit side and the right is always the credit side. *Debit and credit do not represent increases or decreases.* (Increases or decreases to accounts are discussed in the next section.) Instead, debit and credit simply refer to *where* an entry is made in an account. The terms debit and credit will also be used to refer to the act of entering dollar amounts into an account. For example, entering an amount on the left side of an account will be called debiting the account. Entering an amount on the right side of an account will be called crediting the account.

You may be tempted to associate the terms credit and debit with positive or negative events. For example, assume you returned an item that you purchased with a credit card to the local store and the store credited your card. This is generally viewed as a positive event since you now owe less money to the credit card company. Or, if you receive a notice that your bank has debited your account to pay for service charges that you owe, this is viewed negatively because you now have less money in your account. Resist this temptation. In accounting, **debit means the left side of an account and credit means the right side of an account**.

concept Q&A

On a bank statement, a credit to a person's account means the account has increased. Similarly, a debit means the account has decreased. Why don't credit and debit always mean "add" and "subtract"?

Answer:

From the bank's perspective, a person's account is a liability since the bank must pay cash on demand. Because liabilities have normal credit balances, a credit will increase the account and a debit will decrease the account. However, from an individual's perspective, cash is an asset that has a normal debit balance. Therefore, debits increase cash and credits decrease cash. It is critical to always look at the normal balance of an account before determining whether a transaction increases or decreases an account.

Debit and Credit Procedures

Using the basic accounting equation, we can incorporate debits and credits in order to determine how statement of financial position accounts increase or decrease. There are three steps in determining increases or decreases to a statement of financial position account:

- *Step 1: Draw a T-account and label each side of the T-account as either debit (left side) or credit (right side).*
- *Step 2: Determine the normal balance of an account.* All accounts have a **normal balance**. While individual transactions will increase and decrease an account, it would be unusual for an account to have a non-normal balance.
- *Step 3: Increases or decreases to an account are based on the normal balance of the account.*

This procedure is shown in Cornerstone 2.3 .

Determining Increases or Decreases to a Statement of Financial Position Account

Information:

The statement of financial position is composed of three fundamental accounts—assets, liabilities, and shareholders' equity.

CORNERSTONE
VIDEO

Required:

Determine how each of the three statement of financial position accounts increases or decreases.

Why:

Increases or decreases to an account are based on the normal balance of the account. Increases or decreases to assets, liabilities, and shareholders' equity must be determined to prepare an accurate statement of financial position.

Solution:

- Because assets are located on the left side of the accounting equation, their normal balance is a debit. Therefore, debits will increase assets and credits will decrease assets.
- Because liabilities and shareholders' equity are on the right side of the accounting equation, their normal balance is a credit. Therefore, credits will increase liabilities and shareholders' equity while debits will decrease these accounts.

This is illustrated in the following T-accounts:

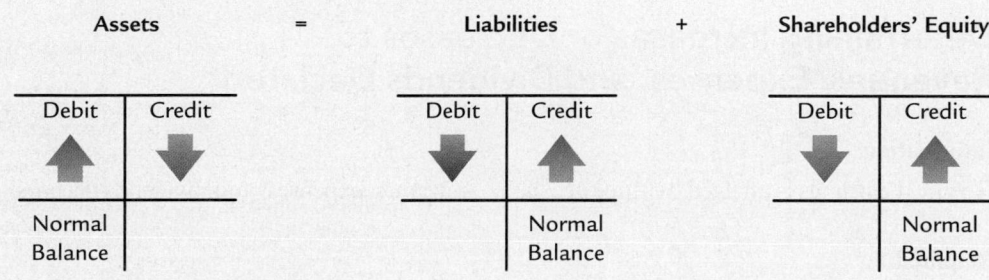

As we illustrated earlier in the chapter, every transaction will increase or decrease the elements of the basic accounting equation—assets, liabilities, and shareholders' equity. The direction of these increases and decreases must be such that the accounting equation stays in balance—the left side must equal the right side. In other words, **debits must equal credits**. This equality of debits and credits provides the foundation of double-entry accounting in which the two-sided effect of a transaction is recorded in the accounting system.

A similar procedure can be used to determine how increases and decreases are recorded for other financial statement elements. From the expanded basic accounting equation shown in Exhibit 2.5, we can see that shareholders' equity consists of both share capital (such as common shares) and retained earnings. As shareholders' equity accounts, both share capital and retained earnings have normal credit balances as shown in Exhibit 2.9. Because these accounts have normal credit balances, they are increased by credits and decreased by debits.

(EXHIBIT 2.9)

Normal Balances of Share Capital and Retained Earnings

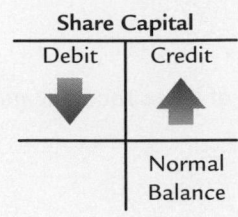

Share Capital	
Debit	Credit
⬇	⬆
	Normal Balance

Retained Earnings	
Debit	Credit
⬇	⬆
	Normal Balance

Retained earnings represent a company's accumulated net income (revenues minus expenses) minus any dividends declared. As we saw from the transaction analysis presented earlier in the chapter:

* Revenues increase retained earnings.
* Expenses decrease retained earnings.
* Dividends declared decrease retained earnings.

In order to determine increases or decreases in revenues, expenses, and dividends declared, we can use the following steps:

* *Step 1: Label each side of the T-account as either debit or credit.*
* *Step 2: Determine the normal balance of an account.*
* *Step 3: Increases or decreases to an account are based on the normal balance of the account.*

Cornerstone 2.4 demonstrates how increases and decreases in these accounts are recorded.

CORNERSTONE 2.4

CORNERSTONE VIDEO

Determining Increases or Decreases to Revenues, Expenses, and Dividends Declared

Information:

Retained earnings is affected by three accounts—revenues, expenses, and dividends declared.

Required:

Determine how each of these three accounts increases or decreases.

Why:

Increases or decreases to an account are based on the normal balance of the account. Increases or decreases to revenues, expenses, and dividends declared must be determined to prepare an accurate income statement and statement of changes in shareholders' equity.

Solution:

* Revenues increase shareholders' equity through retained earnings. Therefore, revenues have a normal credit balance. That means that credits will increase revenues and debits will decrease revenues.
* Expenses decrease shareholders' equity through retained earnings. Therefore, expenses have a normal debit balance. That means that debits will increase expenses and credits will decrease expenses.

(Continued)

- Dividends declared are defined as a distribution of retained earnings. Because dividends declared reduce retained earnings and shareholders' equity, dividends declared have a normal debit balance. That means that debits will increase dividends declared while credits will decrease dividends declared.

These procedures are summarized below.

CORNERSTONE

2.4

(Continued)

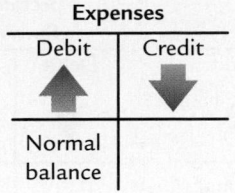

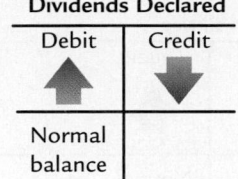

Revenues			Expenses			Dividends Declared	

From Cornerstone 2.4, you should notice several items. First, revenues and expenses have opposite effects on retained earnings; therefore, revenues and expenses have opposite normal balances. Second, any change (increase or decrease) in revenue, expense, or dividends declared affects the balance of shareholders' equity. Specifically,

- an increase in revenue increases shareholders' equity
- a decrease in revenue decreases shareholders' equity
- an increase in expense or dividends declared decreases shareholders' equity
- a decrease in expense or dividends declared increases shareholders' equity

Finally, when revenues exceed expenses, a company has reported net income, which increases shareholders' equity. When revenues are less than expenses, a company has reported a net loss, which reduces shareholders' equity. These debit and credit procedures are summarized in Exhibit 2.10.

The important point from this analysis is that while debits are always on the left and credits are always on the right, the effect of a debit or credit on an account balance depends upon the normal balance of that account.

YOUDECIDE Inferring Activities from T-Accounts

As you examine the accounting records of Weber Inc. you notice that accounts receivable increased from $4,500 to $5,200 during the year and that credit sales were $65,800.

What was the amount of accounts receivable collected?

The primary activities that affect accounts receivable are the sale of goods and services on credit (increases in accounts receivable) and the collection of cash related to these credit sales (decreases in accounts receivable). To help visualize the account activity, prepare a T-account as follows:

Accounts Receivable			
Beginning balance	4,500		
Credit sales	65,800	?	Cash collections
Ending balance	5,200		

Because you know the beginning and ending balances of accounts receivable and the amount of credit sales, you can determine (infer) the cash collections as:

Cash collections = $4,500 + $65,800 − $5,200 = **$65,100**

An understanding of how business activities affect individual accounts can yield valuable insights into the economic events that occurred during a period.

(EXHIBIT 2.10)

Summary of Debit and Credit Procedures

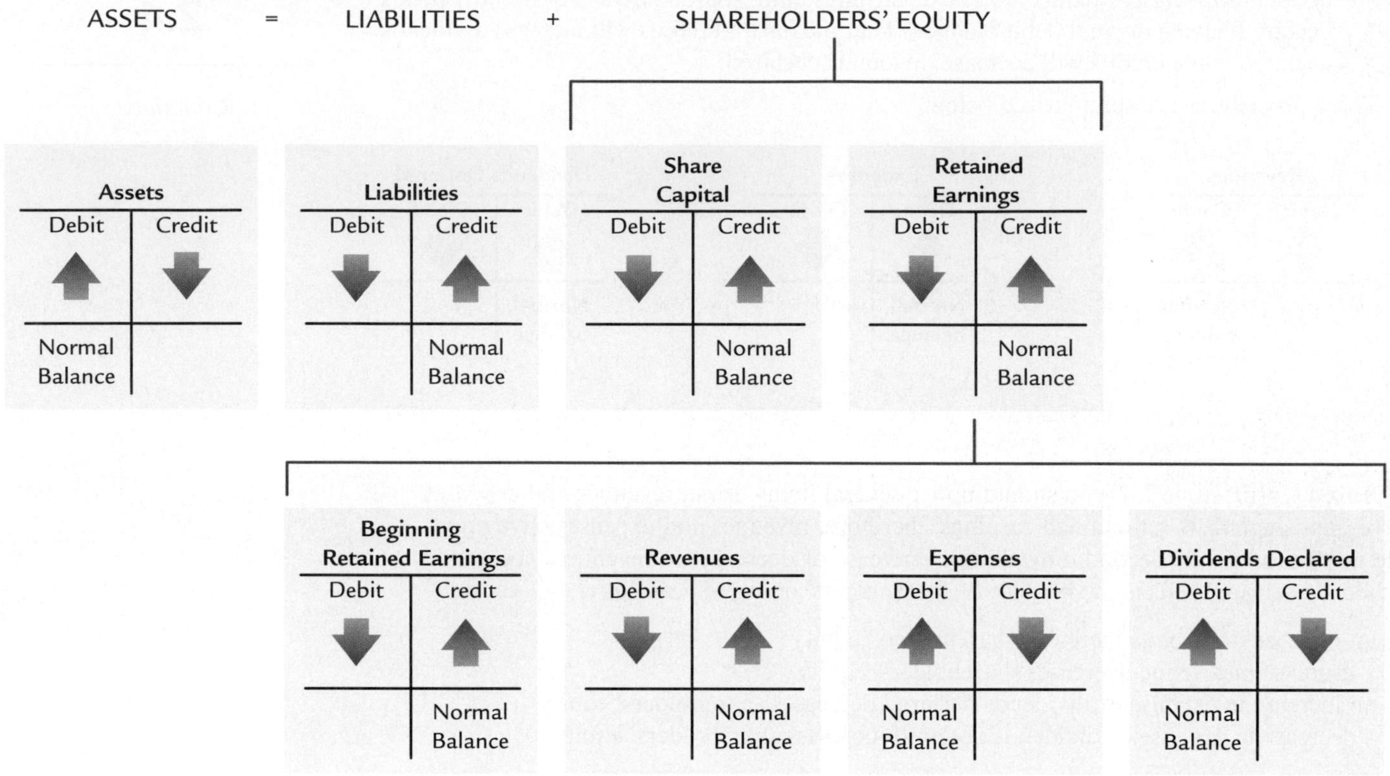

ASSETS   =   LIABILITIES   +   SHAREHOLDERS' EQUITY

Assets	
Debit	Credit
⬆	⬇
Normal Balance	

Liabilities	
Debit	Credit
⬇	⬆
	Normal Balance

Share Capital	
Debit	Credit
⬇	⬆
	Normal Balance

Retained Earnings	
Debit	Credit
⬇	⬆
	Normal Balance

Beginning Retained Earnings	
Debit	Credit
⬇	⬆
	Normal Balance

Revenues	
Debit	Credit
⬇	⬆
	Normal Balance

Expenses	
Debit	Credit
⬆	⬇
Normal Balance	

Dividends Declared	
Debit	Credit
⬆	⬇
Normal Balance	

OBJECTIVE ⑤

Prepare journal entries for transactions.

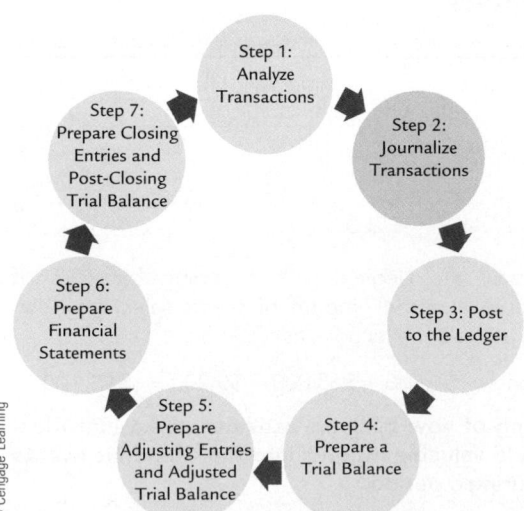

Step 1: Analyze Transactions

Step 2: Journalize Transactions

Step 3: Post to the Ledger

Step 4: Prepare a Trial Balance

Step 5: Prepare Adjusting Entries and Adjusted Trial Balance

Step 6: Prepare Financial Statements

Step 7: Prepare Closing Entries and Post-Closing Trial Balance

STEP 2: JOURNALIZE TRANSACTIONS

While it would be possible to record transactions directly into accounts, most companies enter the effects of the transaction in a journal using the debit and credit procedures described in the previous section. A **journal** is a chronological record showing the debit and credit effects of transactions on a company. Each transaction is represented by a **journal entry** so that the entire effect of a transaction is contained in one place. The process of making a journal entry is often referred to as journalizing a transaction. Because a transaction first enters the accounting records through journal entries, the journal is often referred to as the book of original entry.

A journal entry consists of three parts:

1. the date of the transaction

2. the accounts and amounts to be increased or decreased

3. a brief explanation of the transaction

Each journal entry shows the debit and credit effects of a transaction on specific accounts. In preparing a journal entry, the following steps should be followed:

* *Step 1: Analyze the transaction using the procedures described in Cornerstone 2.2.*
* *Step 2: Determine which accounts are affected.*
* *Step 3: Prepare the journal entry using the debit and credit procedures in Cornerstones 2.3 and 2.4.*

This process is illustrated in Cornerstone 2.5 .

© Cengage Learning

Preparing a Journal Entry

Information:

On January 1, Lee Inc. purchases a $3,000 computer from Bay Electronics on credit, with payment due in 60 days.

CORNERSTONE
VIDEO

Required:

Prepare a journal entry to record this transaction.

Why:

A journal entry records the effects of a transaction on accounts using debits and credits. Journal entries must accurately reflect increases or decreases to the general ledger accounts in terms of both amount and classification since the general ledger is the source of data used in the preparation of financial statements.

Solution:

First, analyze the transaction using the procedures described in Cornerstone 2.2:

Assets	=	Liabilities	+	Shareholders' Equity	
				Share Capital	Retained Earnings
+$3,000		+$3,000			

The purchase of a computer has increased the asset account "Equipment," which is recorded with a debit. In addition, a liability, "Accounts Payable," was created and the increase in this account is recorded with a credit.

Date	Account and Explanation	Debit	Credit
January 1	Equipment	3,000	
	Accounts Payable		3,000
	(Purchased office equipment on credit)		

From the journal entry in Cornerstone 2.5, notice several items:

- The date of the transaction is entered in the date column.
- For each entry in the journal, the debit (the account and amount) is entered first and flush to the left. If there were more than one debit, it would be entered directly underneath the first debit on the next line. The credit (the account and the amount) is written below the debits and indented to the right. The purpose of this standard format is to make it possible for anyone using the journal to identify debits and credits quickly and correctly.
- **Total debits must equal total credits.**
- An explanation should appear beneath the credit.

In some instances, more than two accounts may be affected by an economic event. For example, assume that Lee Inc. purchases a $3,000 computer from Bay Electronics by paying $1,000 cash with the remainder due in 60 days. The purchase of this equipment increased the asset "Equipment," decreased the asset "Cash," and increased the liability "Accounts Payable" as shown in the analysis below:

Assets	=	Liabilities	+	Shareholders' Equity	
				Share Capital	**Retained Earnings**
+$3,000		+$2,000			
−$1,000					

Lee Inc. would make the following journal entry:

Date	Account and Explanation	Debit	Credit
Jan. 1	Equipment	3,000	
	Cash		1,000
	Accounts Payable		2,000
	(Purchased office equipment for cash and on credit)		

This type of entry is called a **compound journal entry** because more than two accounts were affected.

The use of a journal helps prevent the introduction of errors in the recording of business activities. Because all parts of the transaction appear together, it is easy to see whether equal debits and credits have been entered. If debits equal credits for *each* journal entry, then debits equal credits for *all* journal entries. At the end of the period, this fact leads to a useful check on the accuracy of journal entries. However, if the wrong amounts or the wrong accounts are used, debits can still equal credits, yet the journal entries will be incorrect. Additionally, each entry can be examined to see if the accounts that appear together are logically appropriate.

---

concept Q&A

If all journal entries have equal debits and credits, how can mistakes or errors occur?

Answer:

Mistakes or errors can still occur when entire transactions are not recorded, transactions are recorded for the wrong amounts or in the wrong accounts, or transactions are not recorded in the proper accounting period. While journal entries provide a safeguard against errors and mistakes, it will not prevent them all.

ETHICAL DECISIONS   When an error is discovered in a journal entry, the accountant has an ethical responsibility to correct the error (subject to materiality), even if others would never be able to tell that the error had occurred. For example, if an accountant accidentally records a sale of merchandise by crediting Interest Revenue instead of Sales Revenue, total revenue will be unaffected. However, this error could significantly affect summary performance measures such as gross margin (sales minus cost of goods sold) that are important to many financial statement users. When material errors are discovered, they should be corrected, even if this means embarrassment to the accountant.

To provide a further illustration of recording transactions using journal entries, consider the case of HighTech Communications Inc. that was presented earlier in the chapter. For the remainder of the book, we analyze each transaction and report its effects on the basic accounting equation in the margin next to the journal entry. Next, we identify the specific accounts that were affected by incorporating account titles into the transaction analysis model. Finally, we prepare the journal entry based on the analysis. You should always perform these steps as you prepare journal entries.

Transaction 1: Issuing Common Shares

On March 1, HighTech issued 1,000 of its common shares to several investors for cash of $12,000.

Assets	= Liabilities +	Shareholders' Equity
+12,000		+12,000

Date	Account and Explanation	Debit	Credit
March 1	Cash	12,000	
	Common Shares		12,000
	(Issued common shares)		

Transaction 2: Borrowing Cash

On March 2, HighTech raised additional funds by borrowing $3,000 on a one-year, 8% note payable to the Royal Bank.

Date	Account and Explanation	Debit	Credit
March 2	Cash	3,000	
	Notes Payable		3,000
	(Borrowed cash from bank)		

Assets	= Liabilities +	Shareholders' Equity
+3,000	+3,000	

Transaction 3: Purchase of Equipment for Cash

On March 3, HighTech purchased office equipment (computer equipment) from Micro-Centre Inc. for $4,500 in cash.

Date	Account and Explanation	Debit	Credit
March 3	Equipment	4,500	
	Cash		4,500
	(Purchased equipment)		

Assets	= Liabilities +	Shareholders' Equity
+4,500		
−4,500		

Transaction 4: Purchasing Insurance

On March 4, HighTech purchased a six-month insurance policy for $1,200 in cash.

Date	Account and Explanation	Debit	Credit
March 4	Prepaid Insurance	1,200	
	Cash		1,200
	(Purchased insurance in advance)		

Assets	= Liabilities +	Shareholders' Equity
+1,200		
−1,200		

Transaction 5: Purchase of Supplies on Credit

On March 6, HighTech purchased office supplies from Hamilton Office Supply for $6,500. Hamilton Office Supply agreed to accept full payment in 30 days.

Date	Account and Explanation	Debit	Credit
March 6	Supplies	6,500	
	Accounts Payable		6,500
	(Purchased supplies on account)		

Assets	= Liabilities +	Shareholders' Equity
+6,500	+6,500	

Transaction 6: Sale of Services for Cash

On March 10, HighTech sold advertising services to Regina Valley Products in exchange for $8,800 in cash.

Date	Account and Explanation	Debit	Credit
March 10	Cash	8,800	
	Service Revenue		8,800
	(Sold advertising services)		

Assets	= Liabilities +	Shareholders' Equity
+8,800		+8,800

Transaction 7: Sale of Services for Credit

On March 15, HighTech sold advertising services to the *Winnipeg Enquirer* for $3,300. HighTech agreed to accept full payment in 30 days.

Date	Account and Explanation	Debit	Credit
March 15	Accounts Receivable	3,300	
	Service Revenue		3,300
	(Sold advertising services)		

Assets	= Liabilities +	Shareholders' Equity
+3,300		+3,300

Transaction 8: Receipt of Cash in Advance

On March 19, HighTech received $9,000 in advance for advertising services to be completed in the next three months.

Assets	= Liabilities +	Shareholders' Equity
+9,000	+9,000	

Date	Account and Explanation	Debit	Credit
March 19	Cash	9,000	
	Unearned Service Revenue		9,000
	(Sold advertising services in advance)		

Transaction 9: Payment to a Supplier

On March 23, HighTech paid $6,000 cash for the supplies previously purchased from Hamilton Office Supply (transaction 5).

Assets	= Liabilities +	Shareholders' Equity
−6,000	−6,000	

Date	Account and Explanation	Debit	Credit
March 23	Accounts Payable	6,000	
	Cash		6,000
	(Paid accounts payable)		

Transaction 10: Payment of Salaries

On March 26, HighTech paid employees their weekly salary of $1,800 cash.

Assets	= Liabilities +	Shareholders' Equity (Salary Expense)
−1,800		−1,800

Date	Account and Explanation	Debit	Credit
March 26	Salaries Expense	1,800	
	Cash		1,800
	(Paid employee salaries)		

Transaction 11: Collection from a Customer

On March 29, HighTech collected $3,000 cash from the *Winnipeg Enquirer* for services sold earlier on credit (transaction 7).

Assets	= Liabilities +	Shareholders' Equity
+3,000		
−3,000		

Date	Account and Explanation	Debit	Credit
March 29	Cash	3,000	
	Accounts Receivable		3,000
	(Collected accounts receivable)		

Transaction 12: Payment of Utilities

On March 30, HighTech paid its utility bill of $5,200 for March.

Assets	= Liabilities +	Shareholders' Equity (Utilities Expense)
−5,200		−5,200

Date	Account and Explanation	Debit	Credit
March 30	Utilities Expense	5,200	
	Cash		5,200
	(Paid for utilities used)		

Transaction 13: Declaration and Payment of a Dividend

On March 31, HighTech declared and paid a cash dividend of $500 to its shareholders.

Assets	= Liabilities +	Shareholders' Equity
−500		−500

Date	Account and Explanation	Debit	Credit
March 31	Dividends	500	
	Cash		500
	(Declared and paid a cash dividend)		

YOUDECIDE   Detecting Journal Entry Errors

You have been asked to inspect a delivery company's journal. Upon doing so, you find the following entry:

Date	Account and Explanation	Debit	Credit
June 29	Equipment, Delivery Truck	11,000	
	Prepaid Rent		11,000
	(Purchased delivery truck)		

Is this journal entry correct?

Because delivery trucks cannot be exchanged for prepaid rent, you conclude that an error was made in preparing this journal entry. Given the explanation contained in the journal entry, it's likely that the error was in the credit side of the entry. Instead of prepaid rent, the credit could be either to cash (if the purchase of the truck was for cash) or to note payable (if the purchase was on credit). Had the same data been entered directly into the accounts, this error would have been much more difficult to detect and correct. To correct the journal entry, a correcting journal entry should be recorded in June as (Debit) Prepaid Rent $11,000, (Credit) Note Payable $11,000 (assuming the purchase was on credit).

The use of a journal helps prevent the introduction of errors in the recording of business activities.

STEP 3: POST TO THE LEDGER

Because the journal lists each transaction in chronological order, it can be quite difficult to use the journal to determine the balance in any specific account. For example, refer to the journal entries shown earlier for HighTech Communications. What is the balance in cash at the end of the month? This relatively simple question is difficult to answer with the use of the journal.

OBJECTIVE 6

Explain why transactions are posted to the general ledger.

To overcome this difficulty, companies will use a general ledger to keep track of the balances of specific accounts. A **general ledger** is a collection of all the individual financial statement accounts that a company uses.[2] In a manual accounting system, a ledger could be as simple as a notebook with a separate page for each account. Ledger accounts are often shown using the T-account format introduced earlier.

The process of transferring the information from the journalized transaction to the general ledger is called **posting**. Posting is essentially copying the information from the journal into the ledger. Debits in the journal are posted as debits to the specific ledger account, and credits in the journal are posted as credits in the specific ledger account. To facilitate this process, most journals and ledgers have a column titled "Posting Reference." As the information is copied into the ledger, the number assigned to the account is placed in the "Posting Reference" column of the journal and the journal page number is placed in the "Posting Reference" column of the ledger.

This column provides a link between the ledger and journal that

- helps to prevent errors in the posting process, and
- allows you to trace the effects of a transaction through the accounting system.

The posting process is illustrated in Exhibit 2.11, which shows an illustration of a journal page and a ledger page for HighTech Communications.

The ledger for HighTech is shown using T-accounts in Exhibit 2.12. The number in parentheses corresponds to the transaction number.

[2] Most companies supplement the general ledger with subsidiary ledgers that record "subaccounts" that contain the details of the larger general ledger account. For example, a single account such as Accounts Receivable may appear in the general ledger; however, the accounts receivable for individual customers are usually contained in a subsidiary ledger. The general ledger account will equal the total balance of all the accounts in the subsidiary ledger for that account.

(EXHIBIT 2.11)

The Posting Process for HighTech Communications Inc.

	GENERAL JOURNAL				
					Page: 2
Date	Account and Explanation	Post. Ref.	Debit	Credit	
Mar. 31	Dividends declared	3900	500		
	Cash	1000		500	
	(Declared and paid cash dividend)				

	GENERAL LEDGER				
Account: CASH				Account Number: 1000	
Date	Explanation	Post. Ref.	Debit	Credit	Balance
Mar. 1	Issued shares	1	12,000		12,000
2	Borrowed from bank	1	3,000		15,000
3	Purchased equipment	1		4,500	10,500
4	Purchased insurance	1		1,200	9,300
10	Sold advertising services	1	8,800		18,100
19	Sold advertising services in advance	1	9,000		27,100
23	Paid accounts payable	1		6,000	21,100
26	Paid salaries	1		1,800	19,300
29	Collected receivable	2	3,000		22,300
30	Paid utilities	2		5,200	17,100
31	Paid dividend	2		500	16,600

Transactions are analyzed, journalized, and posted in the same manner for both IFRS and private company (ASPE) purposes.

OBJECTIVE 7

Prepare a trial balance and explain its purpose.

STEP 4: PREPARE A TRIAL BALANCE

To aid in the preparation of financial statements, some companies will prepare a trial balance before they prepare financial statements. The **trial balance** is a list of all active accounts and each account's debit or credit balance. The accounts are listed in the order they appear in the ledger—assets first, followed by liabilities, shareholders' equity, revenues, and expenses. By organizing accounts in this manner, the trial balance serves as a useful tool in preparing the financial statements. The preparation of the trial balance for HighTech Communications is shown in Cornerstone 2.6 .

In addition, the trial balance is used to *prove the equality of debits and credits.* If debits did not equal credits, the accountant would quickly know that an error had been made. The error could have been in the journalizing of the transaction, in the posting of the transaction, or in the computation of the balance in the ledger. However, a word of caution is necessary: a trial balance whose debits equal credits does *not* mean that all transactions were recorded correctly. A trial balance will not detect errors of analysis or amounts. Sometimes the incorrect account is selected for a journal entry or an incorrect amount is recorded for a transaction. In other cases, a journal entry is omitted or entered twice. As long as both the debit and credit portions of the journal entry or posting reflect the incorrect information, the debit and credit totals in a trial balance will still be equal.

Preparing a Trial Balance

CORNERSTONE 2.6

CORNERSTONE VIDEO

Information:

Refer to the general ledger for HighTech in Exhibit 2.12.

Required:

Prepare a trial balance for HighTech Communications Inc. at March 31, 2018.

Why:

A trial balance is prepared at the end of each accounting period to provide a source for initial review and potential adjustment prior to the preparation of final financial statements for the period.

Solution:

HighTech Communications Inc. Trial Balance March 31, 2018		
Account	**Debit**	**Credit**
Cash	$16,600	
Accounts Receivable	300	
Supplies	6,500	
Prepaid Insurance	1,200	
Equipment	4,500	
Accounts Payable		$ 500
Unearned Service Revenue		9,000
Notes Payable		3,000
Common Shares		12,000
Dividends Declared	500	
Service Revenue		12,100
Salaries Expense	1,800	
Utilities Expense	5,200	
	$36,600	$36,600

SIGNIFICANT DIFFERENCES BETWEEN IFRS AND ASPE

The following significant differences exist between IFRS and ASPE with respect to the accounting information system:

1. At this writing, the conceptual framework for financial reporting under IFRS by public companies is still being developed. The new IFRS Conceptual Framework is expected to provide additional guidance in areas not covered or covered insufficiently in the existing Conceptual Framework and to provide clarification in the existing Conceptual Framework. Finalization by the International Accounting Standards Board is expected to occur in 2016. Private companies in Canada currently use the existing Canadian Conceptual Framework.

(EXHIBIT 2.12)

General Ledger of HighTech Communications

Assets	Liabilities	Shareholders' Equity

Assets

Cash			
(T1)	12,000	(T3)	4,500
(T2)	3,000	(T4)	1,200
(T6)	8,800	(T9)	6,000
(T8)	9,000	(T10)	1,800
(T11)	3,000	(T12)	5,200
		(T13)	500
16,600			

Accounts Receivable			
(T7)	3,300	(T11)	3,000
300			

Supplies	
(T5) 6,500	
6,500	

Prepaid Insurance	
(T4) 1,200	
1,200	

Equipment	
(T3) 4,500	
4,500	

Liabilities

Accounts Payable			
(T9)	6,000	(T5)	6,500
		500	

Unearned Service Revenue		
	(T8)	9,000
	9,000	

Notes Payable		
	(T2)	3,000
	3,000	

Shareholders' Equity

Common Shares		
	(T1)	12,000
	12,000	

Service Revenue		
	(T6)	8,800
	(T7)	3,300
	12,100	

Salaries Expense	
(T10) 1,800	
1,800	

Utilities Expense	
(T12) 5,200	
5,200	

Dividends Declared	
(T13) 500	
500	

Also, since accounting standards used by Canadian private companies may differ from IFRS, typically in areas of complex transactions and required financial statement note disclosure, significant difference may also arise in the reporting of assets, liabilities, and shareholders' equity. Significant differences in accounting standards between IFRS and ASPE are discussed in subsequent chapters of this text.

2. IFRS terminology can differ from ASPE. IFRS uses the term *depreciation* to refer to the process that allocates the cost of depreciable tangible capital assets, such as buildings and equipment, over their useful lives to the statement of earnings. The term *amortization* is used in IFRS to refer to the process that allocates the costs of certain intangible assets (such as patents and franchises) over their useful lives to the statement of earnings. By contrast, ASPE uses the term *amortization* to refer to the process of allocating the cost of both depreciable tangible and certain intangible assets over their useful lives to the statement of earnings.

SUMMARY OF LEARNING OBJECTIVES

LO1. Describe the qualitative characteristics, assumptions, principles, and constraints that underlie accounting.

- The fundamental qualitative characteristics of accounting information are:
  - Relevance—refers to whether information is capable of making a difference in the decision-making process. Relevant information is material and helps predict the future or provides feedback about prior expectations.
  - Faithful representation—refers to whether information faithfully represents the economic event that it is intending to portray. Faithfully presented information should be complete, neutral, and free from error.
- The enhancing qualitative characteristics are:
  - Comparability—allows external users to identify similarities and differences between two or more items.
  - Verifiability—results when independent parties can reach a consensus on the measurement of an activity.
  - Timeliness—available to users before the information loses its ability to influence decisions.
  - Understandability—able to be comprehended (with reasonable effort) by users who have a reasonable knowledge of accounting and business.
- The four assumptions are:
  - Separate entity—each company is accounted for separately from its owners.
  - Continuity (going-concern)—assumption that a company will continue to operate long enough to carry out its commitments.
  - Periodicity or time period—allows the life of a company to be divided into artificial time periods.
  - Unit-of-measure or monetary unit—requires financial information to be reported in a national monetary unit.
- The three principles are:
  - Historical cost—requires a business activity to be recorded at the exchange price at the time the activity occurs.
  - Revenue recognition—requires revenue to be recognized when it is earned.
  - Full disclosure—all information necessary for users to make informed decisions is disclosed.
- Constraints:
  - Cost—the benefit of users receiving information should exceed the cost of producing the information.
  - Prudence—assets and revenues should not be overstated and liabilities and expenses should not be understated.
- The elements of financial statements are:
  - Assets—economic resources of a business entity that are expected to provide future benefit.
  - Liabilities—existing obligations or debts of a business entity that will be satisfied by payment with assets or the provision of services.
  - Equity—capital provided to the company by its shareholders combined with undistributed earnings of the business entity.

LO2. Explain the relationships among economic events, transactions, and the expanded basic accounting equation.

- A company's business activities (operating, investing, and financing) consist of many different economic events that are both external to the company and internal to the company. Accounting attempts to measure the economic effects of these events. However, not all events are recognized, or recorded, in the basic accounting system.

- A transaction is an economic event that is recognized in the financial statements. An accounting transaction causes the elements of the basic accounting equation (assets, liabilities, share capital, retained earnings, revenues, expenses, or dividends declared) to change in a way that maintains the equality of their relationship.

LO3.   Analyze the effect of business transactions on the basic accounting equation.

- This is Step 1 of the accounting cycle.
- Transaction analysis is the process of determining the economic effects of a transaction on the elements of the basic accounting equation.
- Transaction analysis involves three steps:
  - Step 1: Write down the accounting equation (basic or expanded version).
  - Step 2: Identify the financial statement elements that are affected by the transaction.
  - Step 3: Determine whether the element increased or decreased.
- Each transaction will have a dual effect on the accounting equation, and the accounting equation will remain in balance after the effects of the transaction are recorded.

LO4.   Discuss the role of accounts and show how debits and credits are used in the double-entry accounting system using T-accounts.

- An account is a record of increases and decreases in each of the basic elements of the financial statements.
- Each financial statement element is made up of a number of different accounts.
- All transactions are recorded into accounts.
- The final account balance, after all changes are recorded, is used in the preparation of the financial statements.
- The left side of an account is referred to as a debit. The right side of an account is referred to as a credit.
- All accounts have a normal balance, which is a positive account balance. Assets, expenses, and dividends declared have a normal debit balance. Liabilities, shareholders' equity, and revenues have a normal credit balance.
- Increases or decreases to an account are based on the normal balance of an account. Normal debit balance accounts (assets, expenses, and dividends declared) are increased with debits and decreased with credits. Normal credit balance accounts (liabilities, revenues, and shareholders' equity) are increased with credits and decreased with debits.

LO5.   Prepare journal entries for transactions.

- This is Step 2 of the accounting cycle.
- A journal entry represents the debit and credit effects of a transaction in the accounting records.
- A journal entry is prepared by following three steps:
  - Step 1: Analyzing the transaction.
  - Step 2: Determining which accounts are affected.
  - Step 3: Using the debit and credit procedures to record the effects of the transaction.
- A journal entry is recorded in chronological order and consists of the date of the transaction, the accounts affected, the amount of the transaction, and a brief explanation.

LO6.   Explain why transactions are posted to the general ledger.

- This is Step 3 of the accounting cycle.
- To overcome the difficulty of determining account balances listed chronologically in the journal, information in the journal is transferred to the general ledger in a process called posting.
- As a result of posting, the general ledger accumulates the effects of transactions in individual financial statement accounts.

LO7.   Prepare a trial balance and explain its purpose.

- This is Step 4 of the accounting cycle.
- The trial balance is a list of all active accounts, in the order they appear in the ledger, and each account's debit or credit balance.
- The trial balance is used to prove the equality of debits and credits and helps uncover errors in journalizing or posting transactions.
- The trial balance serves as a useful tool in preparing the financial statements.

CORNERSTONES

CORNERSTONE 2.1	Applying the conceptual framework, page 68
CORNERSTONE 2.2	Performing transaction analysis, page 72
CORNERSTONE 2.3	Determining increases or decreases to a statement of financial position account, page 81
CORNERSTONE 2.4	Determining increases or decreases to revenues, expenses, and dividends declared, page 82
CORNERSTONE 2.5	Preparing a journal entry, page 85
CORNERSTONE 2.6	Preparing a trial balance, page 91

KEY TERMS

Account (p. 79)

Accounting cycle (p. 64)

Assets (p. 67)

Chart of accounts (p. 79)

Comparability (p. 65)

Consistency (p. 65)

Continuity (or going-concern) assumption (p. 66)

Cost constraint (p. 66)

Credit (p. 80)

Debit (p. 80)

Double-entry accounting (p. 79)

Equity (p. 69)

Events (p. 70)

Faithful representation (p. 65)

Full disclosure principle (p. 67)

General ledger (p. 89)

Historical cost principle (p. 67)

Journal (p. 84)

Journal entry (p. 84)

Liabilities (p. 67)

Normal balance (p. 80)

Periodicity (or time period) assumption (p. 67)

Posting (p. 89)

Prudence constraint (p. 66)

Relevance (p. 64)

Revenue recognition principle (p. 67)

Separate entity assumption (p. 66)

T-account (p. 80)

Timeliness (p. 65)

Transaction (p. 70)

Transaction analysis (p. 72)

Trial balance (p. 90)

Understandability (p. 65)

Unit-of-measure (or monetary unit) assumption (p. 67)

Verifiability (p. 65)

REVIEW PROBLEM

I. The Accounting Cycle

Concept:

Economic events are recorded in the accounting system through a process of analyzing transactions, journalizing these transactions in a journal, and posting them to the ledger. These activities are the initial steps in the accounting cycle.

Information:

Deauville Delivery Service was recently formed to fill a need for speedy delivery of small packages. In December 2018, its first month of operations, the following transactions occurred.

a. On December 1, Deauville issue common shares to several investors for $32,000.

b. On December 2, Deauville borrows $20,000 on a one-year note payable from Warrick National Bank, to be repaid with 8% interest on December 2, 2019.

c. On December 2, Deauville pays rent of $8,000 on its package-sorting building for the month of December.

d. On December 6, Deauville purchases $7,000 worth of office furniture by paying $1,400 in cash and signing a one-year, 12% note payable for the balance.

e. On December 20, Deauville completes a delivery contract for Tornado Corporation and bills its customer $15,000.

f. On December 24, Deauville makes a rush delivery for $5,300 cash.

g. On December 28, Tornado pays the $15,000 owed from transaction e.

h. On December 28, Deauville signs an agreement with BigTime Computers to accept and deliver approximately 400 packages per business day during the next 12 months. Deauville expects to receive $400,000 of revenue for this contract, but the exact amount will depend on the number of packages delivered.

i. On December 29, Deauville receives a $1,500 bill from Mac's Catering for miscellaneous services performed at a Christmas party Deauville held for its clients. (No previous entry has been made for this activity.)

j. On December 31, Deauville pays $2,600 cash in salaries to its secretarial staff for work performed in December.

k. On December 31, Deauville declares and pays dividends of $5,000 on its common shares.

Required:

1. Analyze and journalize the transactions *a* through *k*.
2. Post the transactions to the general ledger.
3. Prepare the December 31, 2018, trial balance for Deauville.

Solution:

1. **Analyzing and Journalizing Transactions**
    Transaction a: *Issuing Common Shares.*

Assets	=	Liabilities	+	Shareholders' Equity	
				Share Capital	Retained Earnings
Cash				Common Shares	
+$32,000				+$32,000	

Date	Account and Explanation	Debit	Credit
Dec. 1	Cash	32,000	
	Common Shares		32,000
	(Issued common shares)		

Transaction b: *Borrowing Cash*

Assets	=	Liabilities	+	Shareholders' Equity	
				Share Capital	Retained Earnings
Cash +$20,000		Notes Payable +$20,000			

Date	Account and Explanation	Debit	Credit
Dec. 2	Cash	20,000	
	Notes Payable		20,000
	(*Borrowed cash from bank*)		

Transaction c: *Paying Rent*

Assets	=	Liabilities	+	Shareholders' Equity	
				Share Capital	Retained Earnings
Cash −$8,000					(Rent Expense) −$8,000

Date	Account and Explanation	Debit	Credit
Dec. 2	Rent Expense	8,000	
	Cash		8,000
	(*Paid rent for December*)		

Transaction d: *Purchasing Asset with Cash and Credit*

Assets	=	Liabilities	+	Shareholders' Equity	
				Share Capital	Retained Earnings
Cash −$1,400 Furniture +$7,000		Notes Payable +$5,600			

Date	Account and Explanation	Debit	Credit
Dec. 6	Furniture	7,000	
	Cash		1,400
	Notes Payable		5,600
	(*Purchased office furniture*)		

Transaction e: *Performing Services for Credit*

Assets	=	Liabilities	+	Shareholders' Equity	
				Share Capital	Retained Earnings
Accounts Receivable +$15,000					(Service Revenue) +$15,000

Date	Account and Explanation	Debit	Credit
Dec. 20	Accounts Receivable	15,000	
	Service Revenue		15,000
	(Performed delivery services)		

Transaction f: *Performing Services for Cash*

Assets	=	Liabilities	+	Shareholders' Equity	
				Share Capital	**Retained Earnings**
Cash					(Service Revenue)
+$5,300					+$5,300

Date	Account and Explanation	Debit	Credit
Dec. 24	Cash	5,300	
	Service Revenue		5,300
	(Performed delivery services)		

Transaction g: *Collecting an Account Receivable*

Assets	=	Liabilities	+	Shareholders' Equity	
				Share Capital	**Retained Earnings**
Cash					
+$15,000					
Accounts Receivable					
−$15,000					

Date	Account and Explanation	Debit	Credit
Dec. 28	Cash	15,000	
	Accounts Receivable		15,000
	(Collected accounts receivable)		

Transaction h: *Signing of an Agreement to Provide Service*

This is an example of an important event that does not produce a journal entry at the time it occurs. There will be no recording of the transaction until one of the companies performs on its part of the contract (so, until Deauville provides the delivery service or BigTime Computers makes a payment to Deauville).

Transaction i: *Using Services*

Assets	=	Liabilities	+	Shareholders' Equity	
				Share Capital	**Retained Earnings**
		Accounts Payable			(Miscellaneous Expense)
		+$1,500			−$1,500

Date	Account and Explanation	Debit	Credit
Dec. 29	Miscellaneous Expense	1,500	
	Accounts Payable		1,500
	(Used catering service)		

Transaction j: *Payment of Salaries*

Assets	=	Liabilities	+	Shareholders' Equity	
				Share Capital	Retained Earnings
Cash					(Salaries Expense)
−$2,600					−$2,600

Date	Account and Explanation	Debit	Credit
Dec. 31	Salaries Expense	2,600	
	Cash		2,600
	(Paid secretarial staff salaries)		

Transaction k: *Declaring and Paying a Cash Dividend*

Assets	=	Liabilities	+	Shareholders' Equity	
				Share Capital	Retained Earnings
Cash					(Dividends Declared)
−$5,000					−$5,000

Date	Account and Explanation	Debit	Credit
Dec. 31	Dividends Declared	5,000	
	Cash		5,000
	(Declared and paid a cash dividend)		

2. **Posting of Transactions to the Ledger**

General Ledger of Deauville Delivery Service

Assets

Cash
(a)	32,000	(c)	8,000
(b)	20,000	(d)	1,400
(f)	5,300	(j)	2,600
(g)	15,000	(k)	5,000
55,300			

Accounts Receivable
(e)	15,000	(g)	15,000
0			

Furniture
(d)	7,000	
7,000		

Liabilities

Accounts Payable
	(i)	1,500
	1,500	

Notes Payable
	(b)	20,000
	(d)	5,600
	25,600	

Shareholders' Equity

Common Shares
	(a)	32,000
	32,000	

Dividends Declared
(k)	5,000	
5,000		

Service Revenue
	(e)	15,000
	(f)	5,300
	20,300	

Salaries Expense
(j)	2,600	
2,600		

Miscellaneous Expense
(i)	1,500	
1,500		

Rent Expense
(c)	8,000	
8,000		

3. **Preparing a Trial Balance**

Deauville Delivery Service Trial Balance December 31, 2018		
Account	**Debit**	**Credit**
Cash	$55,300	
Accounts Receivable	0	
Furniture	7,000	
Accounts Payable		$ 1,500
Notes Payable		25,600
Common Shares		32,000
Dividends Declared	5,000	
Service Revenue		20,300
Rent Expense	8,000	
Salaries Expense	2,600	
Miscellaneous Expense	1,500	
	$79,400	$79,400

DISCUSSION QUESTIONS

1. What is the conceptual framework of accounting?

2. Identify the characteristics of useful information.

3. Discuss the trade-offs that may be necessary between the qualitative characteristics.

4. Distinguish between comparability and consistency.

5. Describe the constraints on providing useful information.

6. Identify the four assumptions that underlie accounting.

7. Discuss the three principles that are used to measure and record business transactions.

8. How are the financial statements related to accounting standards?

9. Of all the events that occur each day, how would you describe those that are recorded in a firm's accounting records?

10. In order for a transaction to be recorded in a business's accounting records, the effects of the transaction must be faithfully represented. What is faithful representation, and why is it important?

11. What is the basic process used in transaction analysis?

12. In analyzing a transaction, can a transaction only affect one side of the basic accounting equation? If so, give an example.

13. How do revenues and expenses affect the basic accounting equation?

14. What is a T-account? Describe the basic components of any account.

15. Do you agree with the statement that "debits mean increase and credits mean decrease"? If not, what do debit and credit mean?

16. The words *debit* and *credit* are used in two ways in accounting: "to debit an account" and "a debit balance." Explain both usages of the terms *debit* and *credit*.

17. All accounts have normal balances. What is the normal balance of each of these accounts?

    a. cash
    b. sales
    c. notes payable
    d. inventory

    e. retained earnings
    f. salary expense
    g. equipment
    h. unearned revenue

18. When a journal entry is prepared, what must be equal? Why?

19. Can accounting transactions be directly recorded in the general ledger? If so, why do most companies initially record transactions in the journal?

20. Why is the term *double-entry* an appropriate expression for describing an accounting system?

21. What are the initial steps in the accounting cycle and what happens in each step?

22. What kinds of errors will a trial balance detect? What kinds of errors will not be detectable by a trial balance?

MULTIPLE-CHOICE EXERCISES

2-1 Which of the following is not a benefit derived from the conceptual framework?
   a. Supports the objective of providing information useful for making business and economic decisions
   b. Provides a logical structure to aid in the understanding of complex accounting standards
   c. Provides specific guidance on how transactions should be recorded
   d. Supports the development of a consistent set of accounting standards

2-2 Which of the following is not a characteristic of useful information?
   a. Prudence
   b. Relevance
   c. Faithful representation
   d. Comparability

2-3 Information that provides feedback about prior expectations is:

	Relevant	Faithfully Represented
a.	Yes	Yes
b.	No	Yes
c.	Yes	No
d.	No	No

2-4 Relevant information possesses this quality:

	Freedom from Error	Predictive Value
a.	Yes	Yes
b.	No	Yes
c.	Yes	No
d.	No	No

2-5 Which of the following is not an assumption that underlies accounting?
   a. Separate entity
   b. Historical cost
   c. Periodicity
   d. Continuity (going concern)

2-6 Which principle requires that expenses be recorded and reported in the same period as the revenue that it helped generate?
   a. Historical cost
   b. Revenue recognition
   c. Full disclosure
   d. Matching

2-7 Taylor Company recently purchased a piece of equipment for $2,000 that will be paid for within 30 days after delivery. At what point will the event be recorded in Taylor's accounting system?
   a. When Taylor signs the agreement with the seller
   b. When Taylor receives an invoice (a bill) from the seller
   c. When Taylor receives the asset from the seller
   d. When Taylor pays $2,000 cash to the seller

2-8 The effects of purchasing inventory on credit are to:
   a. increase assets and increase liabilities.
   b. increase assets and increase shareholders' equity.
   c. decrease assets and decrease shareholders' equity.
   d. decrease assets and decrease liabilities.

2-9 The effects of paying salaries for the current period are to:
   a. increase assets and increase shareholders' equity.
   b. increase assets and increase liabilities.
   c. decrease assets and decrease liabilities.
   d. decrease assets and decrease shareholders' equity.

2-10 Which of the following statements is false?
a. Transactions are frequently analyzed using a T-account.
b. All T-accounts have both a debit and a credit side.
c. The left side of a T-account is called the credit side.
d. The amount in an account at any time is called the balance of the account.

2-11 Which of the following statements is/are true?

I.   Debits represent decreases and credits represent increases.
II. Debits must always equal credits.
III. Assets have normal debit balances while liabilities and shareholders' equity have normal credit balances.

a. I
b. I and II
c. II and III
d. All of these are true.

2-12 Debits will:
a. increase assets, liabilities, revenues, expenses, and dividends declared.
b. increase assets, expenses, and dividends declared.
c. decrease assets, liabilities, revenues, expenses, and dividends declared.
d. decrease liabilities, revenues, and dividends declared.

2-13 Which of the following statements are true?

I.   A journal provides a chronological record of a transaction.
II. A journal entry contains the complete effect of a transaction.
III. The first step in preparing a journal entry involves analyzing the transaction.

a. I and II
b. II and III
c. I and III
d. All of these are true.

2-14 Posting:
a. involves transferring the information in journal entries to the general ledger.
b. is an optional step in the accounting cycle.
c. is performed after a trial balance is prepared.
d. involves transferring information to the trial balance.

2-15 A trial balance:
a. lists only revenue and expense accounts.
b. lists all accounts and their balances.
c. will help detect omitted journal entries.
d. detects all errors that could be made during the journalizing or posting steps of the accounting cycle.

2-16 Which of the following corresponds to "when independent parties can reach a consensus on the measurement of the activity."
a. Understandability
b. Comparability
c. Consistency
d. Verifiability

2-17 Which of the following corresponds to "financial statements including all information required for the financial statement decision makers to make informed decisions about the company's financial position, operating results, and cash flows."
a. Historical cost principle
b. Materiality
c. Conservatism
d. Full disclosure principle

CORNERSTONE EXERCISES

OBJECTIVE **1**
CORNERSTONE 2.1

Cornerstone Exercise 2-18   Qualitative Characteristics

Three statements are given below.

a. When financial information is free from error or bias, the information is said to possess this characteristic.
b. Genoa Company uses the same depreciation method from period to period.
c. A trash can that is purchased for $10 is expensed even though it will be used for many years.

Required:

Give the qualitative characteristic or constraint that is most applicable to each of the statements.

Cornerstone Exercise 2-19   Qualitative Characteristics

OBJECTIVE ❶
CORNERSTONE 2.1

Three statements are given below.

a. A financial item that may be useful to investors is not required to be reported because the cost of measuring and reporting this information is judged to be too great.
b. Timely information that is used to predict future events or provide feedback about prior events is said to possess this characteristic.
c. A quality of information that enables an analyst to evaluate the financial performance of two different companies in the same industry.

Required:

Give the qualitative characteristic or constraint that is most applicable to each of the statements.

Cornerstone Exercise 2-20   Accounting Assumptions

OBJECTIVE ❶
CORNERSTONE 2.1

Four statements are given below.

a. Pewterschmidt Company values its inventory reported in the financial statements in terms of dollars instead of units.
b. Property, plant, and equipment is recorded at cost (less any accumulated depreciation) instead of liquidation value.
c. The accounting records of a company are kept separate from its owners.
d. The accountant assigns revenues and expenses to specific years before preparing the financial statements.

Required:

Give the accounting assumption that is most applicable to each of the statements.

Cornerstone Exercise 2-21   Accounting Principles

OBJECTIVE ❶
CORNERSTONE 2.1

Three statements are given below.

a. Quagmire Company recognizes revenue when the goods are delivered to a customer, even though cash will not be collected from the customer for 30 days.
b. Inventory, which was recently damaged by a flood, was considered a significant amount and will impact decision makers' decision about investing in this company.
c. Land, located in a desirable location, is reported at the original acquisition price, even though its value has increased by over 100% since it was purchased.

Required:

Give the accounting principle that is most applicable to each of the statements.

Cornerstone Exercise 2-22   Transaction Analysis

OBJECTIVE ❸
CORNERSTONE 2.2

Four transactions are listed below.

a. Sold goods to customers on credit
b. Collected amounts due from customers
c. Purchased supplies on account
d. Used supplies in operations of the business

(Continued)

Required:

Prepare three columns labelled assets, liabilities, and shareholders' equity. For each of the transactions, indicate whether the transaction increased (+), decreased (–), or had no effect (NE) on assets, liabilities, and shareholders' equity.

OBJECTIVE ❸ ❹
CORNERSTONE 2.2

Cornerstone Exercise 2-23   Transaction Analysis

Stanfield Inc. entered into the following transactions.

a. Issued common shares to investors in exchange for $50,000 cash
b. Borrowed $15,000 cash from Royal Bank
c. Purchased $8,000 of supplies on credit
d. Paid for the purchase in *c*

Required:

Show the effect of each transaction using the following model.

Assets	=	Liabilities	+	Shareholders' Equity	
				Share Capital	Retained Earnings

OBJECTIVE ❸ ❹
CORNERSTONE 2.2

Cornerstone Exercise 2-24   Transaction Analysis

Aziz Company entered into the following transactions:

a. Performed services on account, $18,500
b. Collected $7,200 from client related to services performed in *a*
c. Paid $1,500 dividend to shareholders
d. Paid salaries of $3,500 for the current month

Required:

Show the effect of each transaction using the following model:

Assets	=	Liabilities	+	Shareholders' Equity	
				Share Capital	Retained Earnings

OBJECTIVE ❹
CORNERSTONE 2.3
CORNERSTONE 2.4

Cornerstone Exercise 2-25   Debit and Credit Procedures

Refer to the accounts listed below.

a. Accounts Payable   e. Equipment
b. Accounts Receivable   f. Common Shares
c. Retained Earnings   g. Salary Expense
d. Sales   h. Repair Expense

Required:

For each of the accounts, complete the following table by entering the normal balance of the account (debit or credit) and the word *increase* or *decrease* in the debit and credit columns.

Account	Normal Balance	Debit	Credit

Cornerstone Exercise 2-26 Journalize Transactions

OBJECTIVE ❺

CORNERSTONE 2.5

Four transactions that occurred during June are listed below.

a. June 1: Issued common shares to several investors for $83,000
b. June 8: Purchased equipment for $12,800 cash
c. June 15: Made cash sales of $21,400 to customers
d. June 29: Declared and paid a $6,500 dividend to shareholders

Required:

Prepare journal entries for the transactions.

Cornerstone Exercise 2-27 Journalize Transactions

OBJECTIVE ❺

CORNERSTONE 2.5

Four transactions that occurred during May are listed below.

a. May 5: Borrowed cash of $20,000 from CIBC
b. May 10: Made cash sales of $14,500 to customers
c. May 19: Paid salaries of $8,600 to employees for services performed
d. May 22: Purchased and used $4,100 of supplies in operations of the business

Required:

Prepare journal entries for the transactions.

Cornerstone Exercise 2-28 Preparing a Trial Balance

OBJECTIVE ❼

CORNERSTONE 2.6

Listed below are the ledger accounts for Borges Inc. at December 31, 2018. All accounts have normal balances.

Service Revenue	$23,150	Dividends Declared	$ 1,500
Cash	12,850	Salaries Expense	4,300
Accounts Payable	2,825	Equipment	12,725
Common Shares	15,000	Accounts Receivable	5,700
Rent Expense	2,400	Advertising Expense	1,500

Required:

Prepare a trial balance for Borges at December 31, 2018.

BRIEF EXERCISES

Brief Exercise 2-29 Qualitative Characteristics

OBJECTIVE ❶

Six statements are given below.

a. The two fundamental qualitative characteristics that information should possess are _____ and _____.
b. _____ is the characteristic that allows external decision makers to identify similarities and differences between two or more items.
c. _____ requires accounting information to be comprehensible to decision makers who have a reasonable knowledge of business and economic activities and who are willing to study the information carefully.
d. When accounting information is complete, neutral, and free from error, it is said to be a _____ of the real-world economic event that it is intending to portray.
e. When multiple independent parties can agree on the measurement of an activity, the information is said to be _____.
f. The characteristic of _____ is illustrated by a financial analyst needing information within the next week in order to make an investment decision.

(Continued)

Required:

Complete each of the statements with the appropriate qualitative characteristic.

OBJECTIVE **1**   **Brief Exercise 2-30   Assumptions and Principles**

Four common accounting practices are listed below.

a.   A customer pays $20 to mail a package on December 30. The delivery company recognizes revenue when the package is delivered in January.

b.   Jim Trotter owns C&S Heating Company. In preparing the financial statements, Trotter makes sure that the purchase of a new truck for personal use is not included in C&S's financial statements.

c.   Moseley Inc. recorded land at its purchase price of $50,000. In future periods, the land is reflected in the financial statements at $50,000.

d.   Mueller Inc. prepares quarterly and annual financial statements.

Required:

Identify the accounting principle or assumption that best describes each practice.

OBJECTIVE **2**   **Brief Exercise 2-31   Events and Transactions**

Several events are listed below.

a.   Paid $30,000 for land.

b.   Purchased office supplies for cash.

c.   Performed consulting services for a client with the amount to be collected in 30 days.

d.   Signed a contract to perform consulting services over the next six months.

Required:

For each of the events, identify which ones qualify for recognition in the financial statements. If an event does not qualify for recognition, explain why.

OBJECTIVE **3**   **Brief Exercise 2-32   Transaction Analysis**

Galle Inc. entered into the following transactions during January:

a.   Borrowed $50,000 from First Street Bank by signing a note payable.

b.   Purchased $25,000 of equipment for cash.

c.   Paid $500 to landlord for rent for January.

d.   Performed services for customers on account, $10,000.

e.   Collected $3,000 from customers for services performed in transaction *d*.

f.   Paid salaries of $2,500 for the current month.

Required:

Show the effect of each transaction using the following model:

Assets	=	Liabilities	+	Shareholders' Equity		
				Share Capital	+	**Retained Earnings**

Brief Exercise 2-33   Debit and Credit Procedures   OBJECTIVE 4

Refer to the accounts listed below.

a. Accounts Receivable
b. Accounts Payable
c. Cash
d. Equipment

e. Notes Payable
f. Rent Expense
g. Salaries Expense
h. Service Revenue

Required:

For each of the accounts, indicate the normal balance of the account and the effect of a debit or a credit on the account.

Brief Exercise 2-34   Journalize Transactions   OBJECTIVE 5

Galle Inc. entered into the following transactions during January:

a. January 1: Borrowed $50,000 from First Street Bank by signing a note payable.
b. January 4: Purchased $25,000 of equipment for cash.
c. January 6: Paid $500 to landlord for rent for January.
d. January 15: Performed services for customers on account, $10,000.
e. January 25: Collected $3,000 from customers for services performed in transaction d.
f. January 30: Paid salaries of $2,500 for the current month.

Required:

Prepare journal entries for the transactions.

Brief Exercise 2-35   Posting Journal Entries   OBJECTIVE 6

Listed below are selected T-accounts and their beginning balances for Galle Inc.

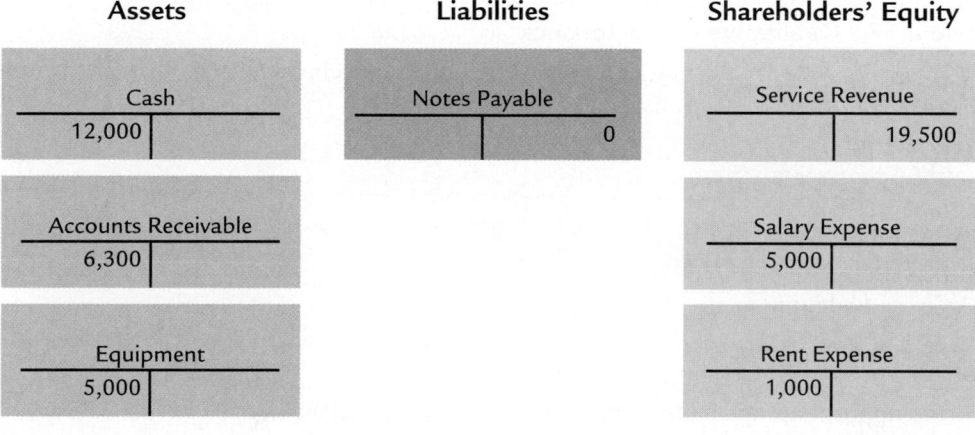

Required:

Post the journal entries from Brief Exercise 2-34 to these accounts and compute the ending balance for each account.

Brief Exercise 2-36   Preparing a Trial Balance   OBJECTIVE 7

The following trial balance, prepared by the bookkeeper of Mason Company, does not balance.

(Continued)

Mason Company Trial Balance December 31, 2018		
	Debit	**Credit**
Cash		$20,000
Accounts Payable	$ 3,000	
Insurance Expense	1,500	
Supplies	1,200	
Accounts Receivable		10,300
Salaries Payable	1,900	
Notes Payable		3,100
Common shares		10,000
Dividends		2,000
Retained Earnings	8,000	
Service Revenue	19,200	
Unearned Service Revenue	2,100	
Prepaid Insurance		1,900
Salaries Expense	9,500	
Supplies Expense		900
	$46,400	$48,200

Required:

Prepare a correct trial balance. Assume all accounts have normal balances.

EXERCISES

OBJECTIVE ❶   **Exercise 2-37   Qualitative Characteristics**

Listed below are the fundamental and enhancing qualitative characteristics that make accounting information useful.

a. Relevance
b. Faithful representation
c. Comparability
d. Verifiability
e. Timeliness
f. Understandability

Required:

Match the appropriate qualitative characteristic with the statements below (items can be used more than once).

1. When information is provided before it loses its ability to influence decisions, it has this characteristic.
2. When several accountants can agree on the measurement of an activity, the information possesses this characteristic.
3. If decision makers can comprehend the meaning of the information, the information is said to have this characteristic.
4. If information confirms prior expectations, it possesses this characteristic.
5. If information helps predict future events, it possesses this characteristic.
6. Freedom from bias is a component of this characteristic.
7. When several companies in the same industry use the same accounting methods, this qualitative characteristic exists.
8. Information that accurately portrays an economic event satisfies this characteristic.

Exercise 2-38   Assumptions and Principles

OBJECTIVE **1**

Presented below are the four assumptions and three principles used in measuring and reporting accounting information.

Assumptions		Principles	
a.	Separate entity	e.	Historical cost
b.	Continuity (going-concern)	f.	Revenue recognition
c.	Periodicity	g.	Full disclosure
d.	Unit-of-measure		

Required:

Identify the assumption or principle that best describes each situation below.

1. Requires that an activity be recorded at the exchange price at the time the activity occurred
2. Allows a company to report financial activities separate from the activities of the owners
3. Implies that items such as customer satisfaction cannot be reported in the financial statements
4. Specifies that revenue should only be recognized when earned and collection reasonably assured
5. Justifies why some assets and liabilities are not reported at their value if sold
6. Allows the life of a company to be divided into artificial time periods so that accounting reports can be provided on a timely basis
7. Requires materially relevant information to be disclosed

Exercise 2-39   Events and Transactions

OBJECTIVE **2**

Several events are listed below.

a. Common shares are issued to investors.
b. An agreement is signed with a janitorial service to provide cleaning services over the next 12 months.
c. Inventory is purchased.
d. Inventory is sold to customers.
e. Two investors sell their common shares to another investor.
f. A two-year insurance policy is purchased.

Required:

1. For each of the events, identify which events qualify for recognition in the financial statements.
2. **CONCEPTUAL CONNECTION** For events that do not qualify for recognition, explain your reasoning.

YOUDECIDE

Exercise 2-40   Events and Transactions

OBJECTIVE **2**

The following economic events that were related to A&P Grocery Store occurred during 2018.

a. On February 7, A&P received a bill from Chatham Power and Light indicating that it had used electric power during January 2018 at a cost of $120; the bill need not be paid until February 25, 2018.
b. On February 15, A&P placed an order for a new cash register with NCR, for which $700 would be paid after delivery.
c. On February 21, the cash register ordered on February 15 was delivered. Payment was not due until March.
d. On February 22, the A&P store manager purchased a new passenger car for $15,000 in cash. The car is entirely for personal use and was paid for from the manager's personal assets.

(Continued)

e.   On February 24, A&P signed a two-year extension of the lease on the building occupied by the store. The new lease is effective April 1, 2018, and requires an increase in the monthly rental from $5,750 to $5,900.

f.   On March 1, A&P paid $120 to Chatham Power and Light.

g.   On March 5, A&P paid $5,750 to its landlord for March rent on the store building.

Required:

YOU**DECIDE**

1.   Using the words "qualify" and "does not qualify," indicate whether each of the above events would qualify as a transaction and be recognized and recorded in the accounting system on the date indicated.

2.   **CONCEPTUAL CONNECTION** For any events that did not qualify as a transaction to be recognized and recorded, explain why it does not qualify.

OBJECTIVE ❸   **Exercise 2-41   Transaction Analysis**

The following events occurred for Erie Company:

a.   Performed consulting services for a client in exchange for $1,200 cash

b.   Performed consulting services for a client on account, $700

c.   Paid $5,000 cash for land

d.   Purchased office supplies on account, $300

e.   Paid a $1,000 cash dividend to shareholders

f.   Paid $250 on account for supplies purchased in transaction *d*

g.   Paid $200 cash for the current month's rent

h.   Collected $500 from client in transaction *b*

i.   Shareholders invested $12,000 cash in the business

Required:

1.   Analyze the effect of each transaction on the basic accounting equation. For example, if salaries of $500 were paid, the answer would be "Decrease in shareholders' equity (expense) $500 and decrease in assets (cash) $500."

2.   **CONCEPTUAL CONNECTION** For *d*, what accounting principle did you use to determine the amount to be recorded for supplies?

OBJECTIVE ❸   **Exercise 2-42   Transaction Analysis**

Amanda Weisman opened a home health care business under the name Home Care Inc. During its first month of operations, the business had the following transactions:

a.   Issued common shares to Ms. Weisman and other shareholders in exchange for $30,000 cash

b.   Paid $18,500 cash for a parcel of land on which the business will eventually build an office building

c.   Purchased supplies for $2,750 on credit

d.   Used the supplies purchased in part *c*.

e.   Paid rent for the month on office space and equipment, $800 cash

f.   Performed services for clients in exchange for $3,910 cash

g.   Paid salaries for the month, $1,100

h.   Purchased and used $650 of supplies

i.   Paid $1,900 on account for supplies purchased in part *c*

j.   Performed services for clients on credit in the amount of $1,050

k.   Declared and paid a $600 dividend to shareholders

Required:

Prepare an analysis of the effects of these transactions on the basic accounting equation of the business. Use the format below.

Assets	=	Liabilities	+	Shareholders' Equity	
				Share Capital	Retained Earnings

Exercise 2-43   Transaction Analysis and Business Activities

OBJECTIVE ③

The accountant for Huron Corporation has collected the following information:

a. Huron purchased a tract of land from Jacobsen Real Estate for $925,000 cash.
b. Huron issued 2,000 common shares to George Micros in exchange for $110,000 cash.
c. Huron purchased a John Deere tractor for $62,000 on credit.
d. Michael Rotunno paid Huron $8,400 cash for services performed. The services had been performed by Huron several months ago for a total price of $10,000, of which Rotunno had previously paid $1,600.
e. Huron paid its monthly payroll by issuing cheques totalling $34,750.
f. Huron declared and paid its annual dividend of $10,000 cash.

Required:

1. Prepare an analysis of the effects of these transactions on the basic accounting equation of the business. Use the format below.

Assets	=	Liabilities	+	Shareholders' Equity	
				Share Capital	Retained Earnings

2. Indicate whether the transaction is a financing, investing, or operating activity.

YOUDECIDE

Exercise 2-44   Inferring Transactions from Statement of Financial Position Changes

OBJECTIVE ③

ILLUSTRATING RELATIONSHIPS

Each of the following statement of financial position changes is associated with a particular transaction:

a. Cash decreases by $22,000 and land increases by $22,000.
b. Cash decreases by $9,000 and retained earnings decreases by $9,000.
c. Cash increases by $100,000 and common shares increase by $100,000.
d. Cash increases by $15,000 and notes payable increases by $15,000.

Required:

Describe the nature of each transaction listed above.

Exercise 2-45   Transaction Analysis

OBJECTIVE ③

Goal Systems, a business consulting firm, engaged in the following transactions:

a. Issued common shares for $50,000 cash
b. Borrowed $20,000 from a bank
c. Purchased equipment for $7,000 cash
d. Prepaid rent on office space for six months in the amount of $6,600
e. Performed consulting services in exchange for $4,300 cash
f. Performed consulting services on credit in the amount of $16,000
g. Incurred and paid wage expense of $7,500
h. Collected $7,200 of the receivable arising from transaction f
i. Purchased supplies for $1,100 on credit

(Continued)

j.   Used $800 of the supplies purchased in transaction *i*
k.   Paid for all the supplies purchased in transaction *i*

Required:

For each transaction described above, indicate the effects on assets, liabilities, and shareholders' equity using the format below.

Assets	=	Liabilities	+	Shareholders' Equity	
				Share Capital	Retained Earnings

Exercise 2-46   Transaction Analysis

During December, Cynthiana Refrigeration Service engaged in the following transactions:

a.   On December 3, Cynthiana sold a one-year service contract to Cub Foods for $12,000 cash.
b.   On December 10, Cynthiana repaired equipment of the A&W Root Beer Drive-In. A&W paid $1,100 in cash for the service call.
c.   On December 10, Cynthiana purchased a new Chevy truck for business use. The truck cost $36,500. Cynthiana paid $5,500 down and signed a one-year note for the balance.
d.   On December 19, Cynthiana received $3,200 worth of repair parts that it had previously ordered from Carrier Corporation. Carrier is expected to bill Cynthiana for $3,200 in early January.
e.   On December 23, Cynthiana purchased 20 turkeys from Cub Foods for $300 cash. Cynthiana gave the turkeys to its employees as a Christmas gift.

Required:

For each transaction described above, indicate the effects on assets, liabilities, and shareholders' equity using the format below.

Assets	=	Liabilities	+	Shareholders' Equity	
				Share Capital	Retained Earnings

Exercise 2-47   Inferring Transactions from Statement of Financial Position Changes

Each of the changes in the statement of financial position below is associated with a particular transaction:

a.   Equipment increases by $5,000 and cash decreases by $5,000.
b.   Cash increases by $4,100 and shareholders' equity increases by $4,100.
c.   Supplies increases by $400 and accounts payable increases by $400.
d.   Supplies decreases by $250 and shareholders' equity decreases by $250.

Required:

YOUDECIDE   Describe the nature of each transaction listed above.

Exercise 2-48   Normal Balances and Financial Statements

The following accounts are available for Haubstadt Shoe Works:

Accounts Payable   Utilities Expense
Accounts Receivable   Interest Expense
Accumulated Depreciation (Equipment)   Inventory
Common Shares   Notes Payable
Cost of Goods Sold   Retained Earnings
Depreciation Expense (Equipment)   Sales Revenue
Equipment   Advertising Expense

Required:

Using a table like the one below, indicate whether each account normally has a debit or credit balance and indicate on which of the financial statements (statement of earnings, statement of retained earnings, or statement of financial position) each account appears.

Account	Debit	Credit	Financial Statement

Exercise 2-49 Debit and Credit Effects of Transactions

OBJECTIVE 4

Mackenzie Corporation was involved in the following transactions during the current year:

a. Mackenzie borrowed cash from the local bank on a note payable.
b. Mackenzie purchased operating assets on credit.
c. Mackenzie declared and paid dividends in cash.
d. Mackenzie purchased supplies on credit.
e. Mackenzie used a portion of the supplies purchased in transaction *d*.
f. Mackenzie provided services in exchange for cash from the customer.
g. A customer received services from Mackenzie on credit.
h. The owners invested cash in the business in exchange for common shares.
i. The payable from transaction *d* was paid in full.
j. The receivable from transaction *g* was collected in full.
k. Mackenzie paid wages in cash.

Required:

Prepare a table like the one shown below and indicate the effect on assets, liabilities, and shareholders' equity. Be sure to enter debits and credits in the appropriate columns for each of the transactions. Transaction *a* is entered as an example:

Assets	=	Liabilities	+	Shareholders' Equity	
				Share Capital	Retained Earnings
(a) Increase (Debit)		Increase (Credit)			

Exercise 2-50 Debit and Credit Effect on Transactions

OBJECTIVE 4

Jiang Framers engaged in the following transactions:

a. Purchased land for $15,200 cash
b. Purchased equipment for $23,600 in exchange for a one-year, 8% note payable
c. Purchased office supplies on credit for $1,200 from Office Depot
d. Paid the $10,000 principal plus $700 interest on a note payable
e. Paid an account payable in the amount of $2,600
f. Provided $62,100 of services on credit
g. Provided $11,400 of services for cash
h. Collected $29,800 of accounts receivable
i. Paid $13,300 of wages in cash
j. Issued common shares for $21,000 cash

Required:

Using a table like the one below, enter the necessary information for each transaction. Enter the debits before the credits. Transaction *a* is entered as an example.

Transaction	Account	Increase/Decrease	Debit/Credit	Amount
(a)	Land	Increase	Debit	$15,200
	Cash	Decrease	Credit	$15,200

OBJECTIVE ❺

Exercise 2-51   Journalizing Transactions

Great Bear Adventures rents and sells snowshoes and dogsledding equipment. During March, Great Bear engaged in the following transactions:

March 2	Received $41,200 cash from customers for rental
3	Purchased on credit five new pairs of snowshoes (which Great Bear classifies as inventory) for $140 each
6	Paid wages to employees in the amount of $8,500
9	Paid office rent for the month in the amount of $1,300
12	Purchased a new Ford truck for $37,800; paid $1,000 down in cash and secured a loan from Scotiabank for the $36,800 balance
13	Collected a $950 account receivable
16	Paid an account payable in the amount of $870
23	Borrowed $15,000 on a six-month, 8% note payable
27	Paid the monthly telephone bill of $145
30	Paid a monthly advertising bill of $1,260

Required:

Prepare a journal entry for each of these transactions.

OBJECTIVE ❺

Exercise 2-52   Journalizing Transactions

King Communications has been providing cellular phone service for several years. During November and December 2018, the following transactions occurred:

Nov. 2	King received $2,400 for November phone service from Hanaman Company.
6	King purchased $4,750 of supplies from Technology Associates on account.
10	King paid $5,250 to its hourly employees for their weekly wages.
15	King paid $4,750 to Technology Associates in full settlement of their account payable.
28	King paid $2,150 for utilities used during November.
30	King received a bill from Stormont Construction for $1,230 for repairs made to King's loading dock on November 15. King plans to pay the bill in early December.
Dec. 10	King paid $1,230 to Stormont Construction to settle the repair bill received on November 30.

Required:

1. Prepare a journal entry for each of these transactions.
2. **CONCEPTUAL CONNECTION** What accounting principle did you apply in recording the November 10 transaction?

OBJECTIVE ❸ ❺

Exercise 2-53   Transaction Analysis and Journal Entries

Pasta House Inc. was organized in January 2018. During the year, the following transactions occurred:

a. On January 14, Pasta House sold Martin Halter, the firm's founder and sole owner, 10,000 of its common shares for $8 per share.
b. On the same day, National Bank loaned Pasta House $45,000 on a 10-year note payable.
c. On February 22, Pasta House purchased a building and the land on which it stands from Frank Jakubek for $34,000 cash and a 5-year, $56,000 note payable. The land and building had appraised values of $30,000 and $60,000, respectively.
d. On March 1, Pasta House signed a $15,000 contract with Crosby Renovations to remodel the inside of the building. Pasta House paid $4,000 down and agreed to pay the remainder when Crosby completed its work.
e. On May 3, Crosby completed its work and submitted a bill to Pasta House for the remaining $11,000.
f. On May 20, Pasta House paid $11,000 to Crosby Renovations.
g. On June 4, Pasta House purchased restaurant supplies from Goa Supply for $650 cash.

Required:

Prepare a journal entry for each of these transactions.

Exercise 2-54 Accounting Cycle

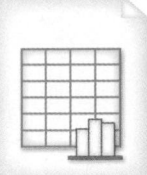

Rosenthal Decorating Inc. is a commercial painting and decorating contractor that began operations in January 2018. The following transactions occurred during the year:

a. On January 15, Rosenthal issued 500 of its common shares to William Hensley for $10,000.

b. On January 24, Rosenthal purchased $720 of painting supplies from Westwood Builders' Supply Company on account.

c. On February 20, Rosenthal paid $720 cash to Westwood Builders' Supply Company for the painting supplies purchased on January 24.

d. On April 25, Rosenthal billed Bultman Condominiums $12,500 for painting and decorating services performed in April.

e. On May 12, Rosenthal received $12,500 from Bultman Condominiums for the painting and decorating work billed in April.

f. On June 5, Rosenthal sent Gatineau Builders a $9,500 bill for a painting job completed on that day.

g. On June 24, Rosenthal paid wages for work performed during the preceding week in the amount of $6,700.

Required:

1. Prepare a journal entry for each of the transactions.
2. Post the transactions to T-accounts.
3. Prepare a trial balance at June 30, 2018.

Exercise 2-55 Preparing a Trial Balance

The following accounts and account balances are available for Badger Auto Parts at December 31, 2018:

Accounts Payable	$ 8,500	Income Tax Payable	$ 3,600
Accounts Receivable	40,800	Interest Expense	6,650
Accumulated Depreciation (Furniture)	47,300	Interest Payable	1,800
Cash	3,200	Inventory	60,500
Common Shares	100,000	Notes Payable (Long-Term)	50,000
Cost of Goods Sold	184,300	Prepaid Rent	15,250
Depreciation Expense (Furniture)	10,400	Retained Earnings, 12/31/2017	15,900
Furniture	128,000	Sales Revenue	264,700
Utilities Expense	9,700	Advertising Expense	29,200
Income Tax Expense	3,800		

Required:

Prepare a trial balance. Assume that all accounts have normal balances.

Exercise 2-56 Effect of Errors on a Trial Balance

The bookkeeper for Rao Ltd. made the following errors:

a. A cash purchase of supplies of $348 was recorded as a debit to Supplies for $384 and a credit to Cash of $384.

b. A cash sale of $3,128 was recorded as a debit to Cash of $3,128 and a credit to Sales of $3,182.

c. A purchase of equipment was recorded once in the journal and posted twice to the ledger.

(Continued)

d. Cash paid for salaries of $5,270 was recorded as a debit to Salaries Expense of $5,270 and a credit to Accounts Payable of $5,270.

e. A credit sale of $7,600 was recorded as a credit to Sales Revenue of $7,600; however, the debit posting to Accounts Receivable was omitted.

Required:

Indicate whether or not the trial balance will balance after the error. If the trial balance will not balance, indicate the direction of the misstatement for any affected account (such as, Cash will be overstated by $50).

PROBLEM SET A

 **OBJECTIVE 2 3**

Problem 2-57A   Events and Transactions

The accountant for Boatsman Products Inc. received the following information:

a. Boatsman sent its customers a new price list. Prices were increased an average of 3% on all items.

b. Boatsman accepted an offer of $150,000 for land that it had purchased two years ago for $130,000. Cash and the deed for the property are to be exchanged in five days.

c. Boatsman accepted $150,000 cash and gave the purchaser the deed for the property described in item *b*.

d. Boatsman's president purchased 600 of the firm's common shares from another shareholder. The president paid $15 per share. The former shareholder had purchased the shares from Boatsman for $4 per share.

e. Boatsman leases its delivery trucks from a local dealer. The dealer also performs maintenance on the trucks for Boatsman. Boatsman received a $1,254 bill for maintenance from the dealer.

Required:

 **YOU**DECIDE

1. Indicate whether or not each item qualifies as a transaction and should be recorded in the accounting information system. Explain your reasoning.

2. **CONCEPTUAL CONNECTION** What accounting concept is illustrated by item *d*?

 **OBJECTIVE 3 7**

Problem 2-58A   Analyzing Transactions

Luis Madero, after working for several years with a large public accounting firm, decided to open his own accounting service. The business is operated as a corporation under the name Madero Accounting Inc. The following captions and amounts summarize Madero's statement of financial position at July 31, 2018:

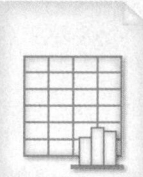

	Assets		=	Liabilities		+	Shareholders' Equity	
Cash	Accounts Receivable	Supplies	=	Accounts Payable	Notes Payable	+	Common Shares	Retained Earnings
8,000	15,900	4,100		2,500	4,000		12,000	9,500

The following events occurred during August 2018:

a. Issued common shares to Ms. Garriz in exchange for $15,000 cash

b. Paid $850 for first month's rent on office space

c. Purchased supplies of $2,250 on credit

d. Borrowed $8,000 from the bank

e. Paid $1,080 on account for supplies purchased earlier on credit

f. Paid secretary's salary for August of $2,150

g. Performed accounting services for clients who paid cash upon completion of the service in the total amount of $4,700

h. Used $3,180 of the supplies on hand
i. Performed accounting services for clients on credit in the total amount of $1,920
j. Purchased $500 in supplies for cash
k. Collected $1,290 cash from clients for whom services were performed on credit
l. Declared and paid $1,000 dividend to shareholders

Required:

1. Record the effects of the transactions listed above on the basic accounting equation. Use the format given in the problem, starting with the totals at July 31, 2018.
2. Prepare the trial balance at August 31, 2018.

Problem 2-59A   Inferring Transactions from T-Accounts

OBJECTIVE ❸❹❼

The following T-accounts summarize the operations of Chen Construction Company for July 2018.

Assets	Liabilities	Shareholders' Equity

Cash

7/1	200		
7/2	1,000	7/5	150
7/7	2,500	7/9	700
7/11	150	7/14	750

Accounts Payable

		7/1	1,100
7/5	150	7/4	250

Common Shares

	7/1	4,000
	7/2	1,000

Accounts Receivable

7/1	1,400	7/11	150

Retained Earnings

		7/1	250
7/14	750	7/7	2,500

Supplies

7/1	750	
7/4	250	

Land

7/1	3,000	
7/9	700	

Required:

YOU DECIDE

1. Assuming that only one transaction occurred on each day (beginning on July 2) and that no dividends were declared or paid, describe the transactions that most likely took place.
2. Prepare a trial balance at July 31, 2018.

Problem 2-60A   Debit and Credit Procedures

OBJECTIVE ❹

A list of accounts for Bennett Inc. appears below.

Accounts Payable	Interest Expense
Accounts Receivable	Land
Accumulated Depreciation (Equipment)	Notes Payable
Cash	Prepaid Rent
Common Shares	Retained Earnings
Depreciation Expense (Equipment)	Salaries Expense
Equipment	Service Revenue
Income Tax Expense	Supplies

(Continued)

Required:

Complete the table below for these accounts. The information for the first account has been entered as an example.

Account	Type of Account	Normal Balance	Increase	Decrease
Accounts Payable	Liability	Credit	Credit	Debit

OBJECTIVE **5**

Problem 2-61A   Journalizing Transactions

Laurent Company rents and sells electronic equipment. During September 2018, Laurent engaged in the transactions described below.

Sept. 5	Purchased a Chevrolet truck for $34,900 cash
8	Purchased inventory for $3,400 on account
10	Purchased $1,450 of office supplies on credit
11	Rented sound equipment to a travelling stage play for $12,800. The producer of the play paid for the service at the time it was provided.
12	Rented sound equipment and lights to a local student organization for a school dance for $3,600. The student organization will pay for services within 30 days.
18	Paid employee wages of $4,170 that have been earned during September
22	Collected the receivable from the September 12 transaction
23	Borrowed $14,100 cash from a bank on a three-year note payable
28	Sold common shares to new shareholders for $40,000
30	Declared and paid a $4,350 cash dividend to shareholders

Required:

Prepare a journal entry for each transaction.

OBJECTIVE **5** **6**

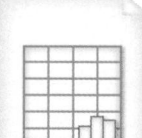

Problem 2-62A   Journalizing and Posting Transactions

London Painting Service Ltd. specializes in painting houses. During June, its first month of operations, London Painting engaged in the following transactions:

June 1	Issued common shares for $10,000
3	Purchased painting supplies from River City Supply for $1,125 on credit
8	Purchased a used truck from London Used Car Sales for $8,700, paying $2,000 down and agreeing to pay the balance in six months
14	Paid $3,960 to hourly employees for work performed in June
22	Billed various customers a total of $9,430 for June painting jobs
26	Received $5,800 cash from James el-Said for a house painting job completed and billed in May
29	Collected $450 from Albert Montgomery on completion of a one-day painting job. This amount is not included in the June 22 bills.

Required:

1. Prepare a journal entry for each transaction.
2. Post the journal entries to London Painting's T-accounts.

OBJECTIVE **2** **3** **4**
5 **6** **7**

Problem 2-63A   The Accounting Cycle

Karleen's Catering Service provides catered meals to individuals and businesses. Karleen's purchases its food ready to serve from Mel's Restaurant. In order to prepare a realistic trial balance, the events described below are aggregations of many individual events during 2018.

a.   Common shares were issued for $22,000.
b.   During the year, Karleen's paid office rent of $13,500.
c.   Utilities expenses incurred and paid were $5,320.
d.   Wages of $58,800 were earned by employees and paid during the year.

e. During the year, Karleen's provided catering services:

On credit	$128,200
For cash	18,650

f. Karleen's paid $59,110 for supplies purchased and used during the year.
g. Karleen's declared and paid dividends in the amount of $3,500.
h. Karleen's collected accounts receivable in the amount of $109,400.

Required:

1. Analyze the events for their effect on the basic accounting equation.
2. Prepare journal entries. (*Note:* Ignore the date because these events are aggregations of individual events.)
3. Post the journal entries to T-accounts.
4. Prepare a trial balance at December 31, 2018. Assume that all beginning account balances at January 1, 2018, are zero.

Problem 2-64A   Comprehensive Problem

OBJECTIVE ❷❸❹ ❺❻❼

Western Sound Studios records and masters audio tapes of popular artists in live concerts. The performers use the tapes to prepare "live" albums, CDs, and MP3s. The following account balances were available at the beginning of 2018:

Accounts Payable	$ 11,900
Accounts Receivable	384,000
Cash	16,300
Common Shares	165,000
Interest Payable	11,200
Notes Payable (Long-Term)	100,000
Rent Payable (Building)	10,000
Insurance Payable	1,000
Retained Earnings, 12/31/2017	101,200

During 2018, the following transactions occurred (the events described below are aggregations of many individual events):

a. Taping services in the amount of $994,000 were billed.
b. The accounts receivable at the beginning of the year were collected.
c. In addition, cash for $983,000 of the services billed in transaction *a* was collected.
d. The rent payable for the building was paid. In addition, $48,000 of building rental costs was paid in cash. There was no rent payable or prepaid rent at year-end.
e. The insurance payable on January 1 was paid. In addition, $4,000 of insurance costs was paid in cash. There was no insurance payable or prepaid insurance at year-end.
f. Utilities expense of $56,000 was incurred and paid in 2018.
g. Salaries expense for the year was $702,000. All $702,000 was paid in 2018.
h. The interest payable at January 1 was paid. During the year, an additional $11,000 of interest was paid. At year-end no interest was payable.
1. Income taxes for 2018 in the amount of $19,700 were incurred and paid.

Required:

1. Establish T-accounts for the accounts listed above and enter the beginning balances. Use a chart of accounts to order the T-accounts.
2. Analyze each transaction. Journalize as appropriate. (*Note:* Ignore the date because these events are aggregations of individual events.)
3. Post your journal entries to the T-accounts. Add additional T-accounts when needed.
4. Use the ending balances in the T-accounts to prepare a trial balance.

PROBLEM SET B

OBJECTIVE

Problem 2-65B   Events and Transactions

The following list contains events that occurred during January 2018 at the local Ford dealer, Malcom Motors:

a. Windsor University (WU) signed a contract to purchase a fleet of Ford Crown Victoria vehicles from Malcom Motors at a total price of $200,000, payable to Malcom in two equal amounts on August 1, 2018, and September 1, 2018. The cars will be delivered to WU during August 2018.

b. The principal shareholder in Malcom Motors sold 10% of her shares in the company to John Lewis, the president of Malcom Motors, in exchange for $100,000 in cash.

c. Malcom Motors issued new shares to John Lewis in exchange for $50,000 in cash.

d. Malcom Motors owns the building it occupies; the company occupied the building during the entire month of January.

e. Malcom Motors owns land used for the storage of cars awaiting sale; the land was used by the company during the entire month of January.

f. Malcom Motors paid its lawyer $1,000 for services rendered in connection with the purchase agreement signed with Windsor University.

g. Maintenance Management Company performed cleaning services for Malcom Motors during January under a contract that does not require payment for those services until March 1, 2018.

Required:

YOU DECIDE

1. Indicate whether each item qualifies as a transaction and should be recorded in the accounting information system. Explain your reasoning.

2. **CONCEPTUAL CONNECTION** What concept is illustrated by the event in item *b*?

OBJECTIVE

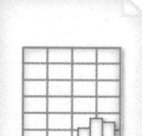

Problem 2-66B   Analyzing Transactions

Several years ago, Mary Leung founded Leung Consulting Inc., a consulting business specializing in financial planning for young professionals. The following captions and amounts summarize Leung Consulting's statement of financial position at December 31, 2018, the beginning of the current year:

	Assets		=	Liabilities		+	Shareholders' Equity	
Cash	Accounts Receivable	Supplies	=	Accounts Payable	Notes Payable	+	Common Shares	Retained Earnings
3,000	6,600	4,800		500	1,000		10,000	2,900

During January 2019, the following transactions occurred:

a. Issued common shares to a new shareholder in exchange for $12,000 cash

b. Performed advisory services for a client for $3,850 and received the full amount in cash

c. Received $925 on account from a client for whom services had been performed on credit

d. Purchased supplies for $1,140 on credit

e. Paid $875 on accounts payable

f. Performed advisory services for $2,980 on credit

g. Paid cash of $1,350 for secretarial services during January

h. Paid cash of $800 for January's office rent

i. Paid utilities used in January 2019 in the amount of $1,340

j. Declared and paid a dividend of $500

Required:

1. Record the effects of the transactions listed above on the basic accounting equation. Use the format given in the problem, starting with the totals at December 31, 2018.

2. Prepare the trial balance at January 31, 2019.

Problem 2-67B Inferring Transactions from T-Accounts

The following T-accounts summarize the operations of Brilliant Minds Ltd., a tutoring service, for April 2018.

Assets	Liabilities	Shareholders' Equity

Assets

Cash
4/1	500	4/8	700
4/3	2,000	4/9	325
4/18	1,500	4/15	150
4/24	375		

Accounts Receivable
| 4/1 | 700 | 4/24 | 375 |

Supplies
| 4/1 | 900 | 4/11 | 140 |
| 4/15 | 150 | | |

Equipment
| 4/1 | 1,200 | | |
| 4/8 | 700 | | |

Liabilities

Accounts Payable
| 4/9 | 325 | 4/1 | 625 |

Notes Payable
| | | 4/3 | 2,000 |

Shareholders' Equity

Common Shares
| | | 4/1 | 2,000 |

Retained Earnings
| 4/11 | 140 | 4/1 | 675 |
| | | 4/18 | 1,500 |

Required:

1. Assuming that only one transaction occurred on each day (beginning on April 3) and that no dividends were declared or paid, describe the transaction that most likely took place.
2. Prepare a trial balance at April 30, 2018.

Problem 2-68B Debit and Credit Procedures

A list of accounts for Bennett Inc. appears below.

Accounts Payable	Copyright
Accounts Receivable	Interest Expense
Bonds Payable	Inventory
Building	Investments
Cash	Retained Earnings
Common Shares	Sales Revenue
Cost of Goods Sold	Unearned Revenue
Depreciation Expense (Building)	Utilities Expense
Income Tax Payable	Income Tax Expense
Insurance Expense	

Required:

Complete the table below for these accounts. The information for the first account has been entered as an example.

Account	Type of Account	Normal Balance	Increase	Decrease
Accounts Payable	Liability	Credit	Credit	Debit

OBJECTIVE **5**

Problem 2-69B   Journalizing Transactions

Monilast Chemicals engaged in the following transactions during December 2018:

Dec. 2   Paid rent on office furniture, $900
       3   Borrowed $20,000 on a nine-month, 8% note
       7   Provided services on credit, $38,600
Dec. 10   Purchased supplies on credit, $3,200
      13   Collected accounts receivable, $18,800
      19   Issued common shares, $55,000
      22   Paid employee wages for December, $11,650
      23   Paid accounts payable, $6,975
      25   Provided services for cash, $15,430
      30   Paid utility bills for December, $2,180

Required:

Prepare a journal entry for each transaction.

OBJECTIVE **5** **6**

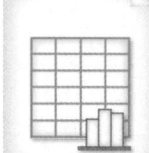

Problem 2-70B   Journalizing and Posting Transactions

Federov Testing Inc. provides water testing and maintenance services for owners of hot tubs and swimming pools. During September the following transactions occurred:

Sept. 1   Issued common shares for $12,000
       2   Purchased chemical supplies for $1,480 cash
       5   Paid office rent for October, November, and December; the rent is $600 per month
       8   Purchased $895 of advertising for September on account
      13   Billed the City of Bell River $4,200 for testing the water in the city's outdoor pools during September
      18   Received $6,850 from Alexander Blanchard upon completion of overhaul of his swimming pool water circulation system. Since the job was completed and collected for on the same day, no bill was sent to Blanchard.
      25   Received $495 from the City of Bell River for water testing that was previously billed
      30   Recorded and paid September salaries of $4,320

Required:

1.   Prepare a journal entry for each transaction.
2.   Post the journal entries to Federov Testing's T-accounts.

OBJECTIVE **2** **3** **4**
          5 **6** **7**

Problem 2-71B   The Accounting Cycle

Sweetwater Temporary Clerical Help Service opened for business in June 2018. From the opening until the end of the year, Sweetwater engaged in the activities described below. So that a realistic trial balance can be prepared, the events described below are aggregations of many individual events.

a.   Issued 10,000 common shares for $4.50 per share
b.   Purchased office equipment from Furniture Max Inc. for $18,710 cash
c.   Received $112,880 from clients for services provided
d.   Paid wages of $87,300
e.   Borrowed $20,000 from the Royal Bank on a three-year note payable
f.   Paid office rent of $10,200
g.   Purchased office supplies on credit for $2,120 from Office Supply Ltd.
h.   Paid $1,200 toward the payable established in transaction g
i.   Paid utility charges incurred during the year of $3,250

Required:

1.   Analyze the events for their effect on the basic accounting equation.
2.   Prepare journal entries. (*Note:* Ignore the date because these events are aggregations of individual events.)

3. Post the journal entries to T-accounts.
4. Prepare a trial balance at December 31, 2018.

Problem 2-72B   Comprehensive Problem

OBJECTIVE ②③④ ⑤⑥⑦

Mulberry Services sells electronic data processing services to firms too small to own their own computing equipment. Mulberry had the following accounts and account balances as of January 1, 2018:

Accounts Payable	$ 14,000
Accounts Receivable	130,000
Common Shares	114,000
Cash	6,000
Interest Payable	8,000
Notes Payable (Long-Term)	80,000
Prepaid Rent (Short-Term)	96,000
Retained Earnings, 12/31/2017	16,000

During 2018, the following transactions occurred (the events described below are aggregations of many individual events):

a. During 2018, Mulberry sold $690,000 of computing services, all on credit.
b. Mulberry collected $570,000 from the credit sales in transaction *a* and an additional $129,000 from the accounts receivable outstanding at the beginning of the year.
c. Mulberry paid the interest payable of $8,000.
d. Wages of $379,000 were paid in cash.
e. Repairs and maintenance of $9,000 were incurred and paid.
f. The prepaid rent at the beginning of the year was used in 2018. In addition, $28,000 of computer rental costs were incurred and paid. There is no prepaid rent or rent payable at year-end.
g. Mulberry purchased computer paper for $13,000 cash in late December. None of the paper was used by year-end.
h. Advertising expense of $26,000 was incurred and paid.
i. Income tax of $10,300 was incurred and paid in 2018.
j. Interest of $5,000 was paid on the long-term loan.

Required:

1. Establish T-accounts for the accounts listed above and enter the beginning balances. Use a chart of accounts to order the T-accounts.
2. Analyze each transaction. Journalize as appropriate. (*Note:* Ignore the date because these events are aggregations of individual events.)
3. Post your journal entries to the T-accounts. Add additional T-accounts when needed.
4. Use the ending balances in the T-accounts to prepare a trial balance.

CASES

Case 2-73   Analysis of the Accounting Cycle

Susan Ehrat wants to sell you her wholesale fish store. She shows you a statement of financial position with total assets of $150,000 and total liabilities of $20,000. According to the income statement, last year's net income was $40,000.

When examining the accounting records, you notice that several accounts receivable in the $10,000 to $15,000 range are not supported by source documents. You also notice that there is no source documentation to support the $30,000 balance in the building account and the $10,000 balance in the equipment account. Susan tells you that she gave the building and refrigeration equipment to the business in exchange for shares. She also says that she has not had time to set up and monitor any paperwork for accounts receivable or accounts payable.

(Continued)

Required:

1. What requirements for transaction recognition appear to have been ignored when the accounts receivable, building, and equipment were recorded?
2. What would be the effect on the financial statements if the values appearing on the statement of financial position for accounts receivable, building, and equipment were overstated? What would be the effect if the accounts payable were understated?
3. Assuming that you want to purchase the company, what would you do to establish a reasonable purchase price?

**ILLUSTRATING
RELATIONSHIPS**

Case 2-74   Analysis of the Effects of Current Asset and Current Liability Changes on Cash Flows

You have the following data for Cawnpore Company's accounts receivable and accounts payable for 2018:

Accounts receivable, 1/1/2018	$ 4,750
2018 sales on credit	97,400
Accounts receivable, 12/31/2018	8,300
Wages payable, 1/1/2018	5,870
2018 wage expense	38,100
Wages payable, 12/31/2018	3,900

Required:

1. How much cash did Cawnpore collect from customers during 2018?
2. How would you classify cash collected from customers on the statement of cash flows?
3. How much cash did Cawnpore pay for wages during 2018?
4. How would you classify the cash paid for wages on the statement of cash flows?

YOUDECIDE

Case 2-75   Ethical Issues

Kathryn Goldsmith is the chief accountant for Clean Sweep, a national carpet-cleaning service with a December fiscal year-end. As Kathryn was preparing the 2018 financial statements for Clean Sweep, she noticed several odd transactions in the general ledger for December. For example, rent for January 2019, which was paid in December 2018, was recorded by debiting rent expense instead of prepaid rent. In another transaction, Kathryn noticed that the use of supplies was recorded with a debit to insurance expense instead of supplies expense. Upon further investigation, Kathryn discovered that the December ledger contained numerous such mistakes. Even with the mistakes, the trial balance still balanced.

Kathryn traced all of the mistakes back to a recently hired bookkeeper, Ben Goldsmith, Kathryn's son. Kathryn had hired Ben to help out in the accounting department over Christmas break so that he could earn some extra money for school. After discussing the situation with Ben, Kathryn determined that Ben's mistakes were all unintentional.

Required:

1. What ethical issues are involved?
2. What are Kathryn's alternatives? Which would be the most ethical alternative to choose?

Case 2-76   Research and Analysis Using the Annual Report

Obtain George Weston Limited's 2014 annual report through the "Investor Relations" portion of its website.

Required:

1. Determine the amounts in the basic accounting equation for the most recent year. Does it balance?
2. What is the normal balance for the following accounts?
   a. Accounts Receivable
   b. Short-Term Debt

    c. Sales/Revenue
    d. Fixed Assets (Net)
    e. Cost of Inventories Sold
    f. Inventories
    g. Retained Earnings

3. Identify the additional account that is most likely involved when:

    a. Accounts payable/trade payable is increased.
    b. Accounts Receivable is increased.
    c. Share capital/common shares is increased.
    d. Wages Payable is increased.

Case 2-77   Accounting for Partly Completed Events: A Prelude to Chapter 3

Ehrlich Smith, the owner of The Shoe Box, has asked you to help him understand the proper way to account for certain accounting items as he prepares his 2018 financial statements. Smith has provided the following information and observations:

a. A three-year fire insurance policy was purchased on January 1, 2018, for $2,400. Smith believes that a part of the cost of the insurance policy should be allocated to each period that benefits from its coverage.

b. The store building was purchased for $80,000 in January 2010. Smith expected then (as he does now) that the building will be serviceable as a shoe store for 20 years from the date of purchase. In 2010, Smith estimated that he could sell the property for $6,000 at the end of its serviceable life. He feels that each period should bear some portion of the cost of this long-lived asset that is slowly being consumed.

c. The Shoe Box borrowed $20,000 on a one-year, 8% note that is due on September 1 next year. Smith notes that $21,600 cash will be required to repay the note at maturity. The $1,600 difference is, he feels, a cost of using the loaned funds and should be spread over the periods that benefit from the use of the loan funds.

Required:

1. Explain what Smith is trying to accomplish with these three items. Are his objectives supported by the concepts that underlie accounting?

2. Describe how each of the three items should be reflected in the 2018 statement of earnings and the December 31, 2018, statement of financial position to accomplish Smith's objectives.

Case 2-78   CONTINUING PROBLEM: FRONT ROW ENTERTAINMENT

After much consideration, Cam and Anna decide to organize their company as a corporation. On January 1, 2018, Front Row Entertainment Inc. begins operations. Due to Cam's family connections in the entertainment industry, Cam assumes the major responsibility for signing artists to a promotion contract. Meanwhile, Anna assumes the financial accounting and reporting responsibilities. The following business activities occurred during January:

Jan. 1   Cam and Anna invested $8,000 each in the company in exchange for common shares.
     1   The company obtained a $25,000 loan from a local bank. Front Row Entertainment agreed to pay annual interest of 9% each January 1, starting in 2019. It will repay the amount borrowed in five years.
     1   The company paid $1,200 in legal fees associated with incorporation.
     1   Office equipment was purchased with $7,000 in cash.
     1   The company paid $800 to rent office space for January.
     3   A one-year insurance policy was purchased for $3,600.
     3   Office supplies of $2,500 were purchased from Equipment Supply Services. Equipment Supply Services agreed to accept $1,000 in 15 days with the remainder due in 30 days.

(Continued)

5   The company signed Charm City, a local band with a growing cult following, to a four-city tour that starts on February 15.

8   Venues for all four Charm City concerts were reserved by paying $10,000 cash.

12   Advertising costs of $4,500 were paid to promote the concert tour.

18   Paid $1,000 to Equipment Supply Services for office supplies purchased on January 3.

25   To aid in the promotion of the upcoming tour, Front Row Entertainment arranged for Charm City to perform a 20-minute set at a local festival. Front Row Entertainment earned $1,000 for Charm City's appearance. Of this total amount, $400 was received immediately with the remainder due in 15 days.

25   Paid Charm City $800 for performing at the festival. Note: Front Row Entertainment recorded the fees paid to the artist in an operating expense account called Artist Fee Expense.

28   Due to the success of the marketing efforts, Front Row Entertainment received $3,800 in advance ticket sales for the upcoming tour.

30   The company collected $200 of the amount due from the January 25 festival.

30   Paid salaries of $1,200 each to Cam and Anna.

Required:

1.   Analyze and journalize the January transactions.
2.   Post the transactions to T-accounts.
3.   Prepare a trial balance at January 31, 2018.

Case 2-79   Professional and Ethical Behaviour

Your close friend Avery was recently hired to work in the accounting department at Ted's Automotive Ltd. You are excited to have your friend working at the same place as you. You were a bit surprised that he got an accounting job given he was in the sciences program when you both attended university.

After one month, you decide to go for lunch with Avery, who tells you he really doesn't understand what he is doing in that Accounting Department, especially when it comes to recording journal entries, but he says, "As long as the debits equal the credits, I should be good. The accounting software we use would have told me if I was doing something wrong, plus by the time anyone reviews any of my work, I will probably be working at another place."

Required:

Identify and discuss any ethical issues.

3

Accrual Accounting and Financial Statements

After studying Chapter 3, you should be able to:

1. Explain the difference between cash-basis and accrual-basis accounting.

2. Explain how the periodicity assumption, revenue recognition principle, and matching concept affect the determination of income.

3. Identify the types of transactions that may require adjustments at the end of an accounting period.

4. Prepare adjusting entries for accruals and prepayments.

5. Prepare financial statements from an adjusted trial balance.

6. Explain why and how companies prepare closing entries and understand the quality of earnings.

7. Understand the steps in the accounting cycle.

Purolator Express™
Box/Boîte

⊿⫴**Purolator**

Extremely Urgent! / Très urge

EXPERIENCE FINANCIAL ACCOUNTING
with Purolator

Purolator Inc., a subsidiary of Canada Post Corporation, is Canada's largest courier company and has been in existence for more than 50 years. Purolator provides customers with services and customized solutions required to deliver their shipments across town or internationally. Purolator has 170 operations locations, 125 shipping centres, over 590 authorized shipping agents, and more than 230 drop boxes. It has a fleet of over 3,600 vehicles and makes more than 365 million deliveries and pickups each year. Purolator has over 5,500 vehicles and support equipment that move 432,000 pounds of air freight each night and 108 million pounds of air freight each year. Purolator serves over 210 countries and territories throughout the world.[1]

The end of the fiscal year, or accounting period, is a busy time as companies like Purolator make adjustments to their accounting information. Adjustments are necessary because a company's business activities often occur over several accounting periods. In its 2014 annual review shown below in Exhibit 3.1, Purolator's segmented financial information includes many expenses, such as salaries and fuel expenses, that would not have been recognized without adjustments.

When Purolator recognizes additional expenses (except for depreciation and amortization), it also records a liability for them. Clearly, the failure to adjust for and record various significant existing but unrecorded expenses at the end of the accounting period would significantly affect Purolator's statement of net earnings and statement of financial position.

(EXHIBIT 3.1)

Excerpt from Purolator's Annual Review

Purolator Inc.* Segmented Income Statement (partial) For the Year Ended December 31, 2014	
(in millions)	
Revenues	$1,687
Operating expenses	1,607
Other income (expense)	(6)
Income before income taxes	74
Income taxes	20
Net income	$ 54

*Information for Purolator Inc. was obtained from Canada Post Corporation's 2014 annual report.

[1] Source: Purolator 2014 Annual Report as amended by the author.

OBJECTIVE

Explain the difference between cash-basis and accrual-basis accounting.

COMPLETING THE ACCOUNTING CYCLE

In Chapter 2, we examined how companies use the double-entry accounting system to record business activities that occur during the accounting period. However, accountants also make numerous adjustments at the end of accounting periods for business activities that occur over several accounting periods—activities such as the performance of services for customers, the renting of office space, and the use of equipment. These end-of-period adjustments can be significant.

Why are so many business activities recognized in the accounts through adjustments rather than through the normal journal entry process described in Chapter 2? The illustrations used in Chapter 2 excluded activities that were still under way at the end of the accounting period. However, the recognition of business activities in financial accounting uses the accrual basis of accounting. Accrual accounting requires that any incomplete activities be recognized in the financial statements. This often requires estimates and judgments about the timing of revenue and the recognition of expenses. The result is that accountants must adjust the accounts to properly reflect these partially completed business activities.

In this chapter, we review the concepts that form the basis for adjustments and then complete the accounting cycle that was introduced in Chapter 2 by exploring the preparation and effects of adjusting journal entries, preparing financial statements from the adjusted accounts, and closing the accounts in order to prepare for the next accounting period. We will address the following questions:

- What is the difference between the cash basis and the accrual basis of accounting?
- What is the purpose of adjusting entries?
- What types of transactions require adjustment, and how are the adjustments recorded in the accounting system?
- Which accounts are closed at the end of the period, and why is this necessary?

Accrual versus Cash Basis of Accounting

If you were asked what your net income (revenues less expenses) for the month was, what would you do? Most likely, you would go online and look at your bank activity for the month. You would then list the total of the deposits as revenue and the total of the withdrawals as expenses. The difference would be your cash basis net income. This method of accounting is called **cash-basis accounting**. Under cash-basis accounting, revenue is recorded when cash is received, regardless of when it is actually earned. Similarly, an expense is recorded when cash is paid, regardless of when it is actually incurred. Therefore, cash-basis accounting does not link recognition of revenues and expenses to the actual business activity as required by generally accepted accounting principles, but rather to the exchange of cash. In addition, because they record only the cash effect of transactions, cash-basis financial statements may not reflect all of the assets and liabilities of a company at a particular date as required by generally accepted accounting principles. For these reasons, most companies do not use cash-basis accounting.

Accrual-basis accounting (also called *accrual accounting*) is an alternative to cash-basis accounting and is required by IFRS and ASPE. Under accrual accounting, transactions are recorded when they occur. Accrual accounting is superior to cash-basis accounting because it links income measurement to the earnings activity of the company. That is, revenue is recognized as it is earned and expenses are recognized when they are incurred. Compared to cash-basis accounting, accrual accounting is a more complex system that records both *cash and noncash* transactions. Net earnings determined on the accrual basis of accounting will usually be substantially different from net earnings determined on a cash basis.

KEY ELEMENTS OF ACCRUAL ACCOUNTING

An accrual accounting system rests principally upon the periodicity assumption, the revenue recognition principle, and the matching concept.

OBJECTIVE 2

Explain how the periodicity assumption, revenue recognition principle, and matching concept affect the determination of income.

Periodicity Assumption

Investors, creditors, and other financial statement users demand timely information from companies. For that reason, companies report their financial results for specific periods of time—a month, a quarter, or a year. The **periodicity assumption** allows companies to artificially divide their operations into time periods so that they can satisfy users' demands for information.

Companies frequently engage in continuing activities that affect more than one time period. For example, Purolator often receives cash from a company to deliver products in one time period, although the actual delivery does not occur until a different time period. In addition, the delivery vehicles used by Purolator are acquired at a single point in time but are used over many years. Purolator is required to assign the revenue by accrual accounting, so that the use of its aircraft is properly recorded. This is quite often a difficult task, which is guided by the revenue recognition principle.

The Revenue Recognition Principle—Current (IAS 18) and Proposed (IAS 15)

International Financial Reporting Standards (IFRS) have significantly expanded the revenue principle from earlier understandings. At the time of writing of this text, International Accounting Standard (IAS) 18 is in effect and sets out *five conditions that must all be met in order to recognize revenue.* These five conditions are as follows:

1. The significant risks and rewards of ownership of the goods must have been transferred to the purchaser by the seller. The transfer of legal title, the delivery of goods to a customer, or the performance of services for a customer usually meets this requirement.

2. The amount of revenue must be reliably measurable. The amount to be collected by the seller must not be uncertain.

3. Continuing managerial involvement to the degree usually associated with ownership should not be retained by the seller, nor should the seller maintain effective control over the goods sold.

4. It must be probable that the economic benefits (usually cash or a promise to pay cash) associated with the transaction will flow to the seller. If the customer is creditworthy, this condition would normally be satisfied.

5. Costs incurred or to be incurred with respect to the transaction must be reliably measurable. If costs cannot be reliably measured, revenue cannot be recognized.

These requirements are usually met when goods have been delivered to a customer or when services have been performed for a customer. At this point, the risks and rewards of ownership usually have been transferred from the seller to the buyer. **Notice that revenue is recorded when these conditions are met, regardless of when cash is received.**

To illustrate the **revenue recognition principle**, assume that on March 31, Purolator picks up a computer from a specified distribution centre and receives a cash payment of $30 to ship the computer to a customer. Purolator delivers the computer on April 2. Even though cash was received on March 31, Purolator will recognize the $30 of revenue on April 2, the date the computer is delivered to the customer. Notice that revenue is not recognized until it is earned by Purolator (delivery of the computer), and that the receipt of cash prior to the delivery does not affect when revenue is recognized. Exhibit 3.2 shows an excerpt of Purolator's revenue recognition policy that is disclosed in the notes to its financial statements.

(EXHIBIT 3.2)

Annual Report Excerpt: Purolator's Revenue Recognition Policy*

Note 1: Basis of Presentation and Significant Accounting Policies (in part)

REVENUE RECOGNITION. Revenue is recognized when the service has been rendered, goods have been delivered, or work has been completed. Payments received in advance are deferred until services are rendered or products are delivered.

* Source: Extracted from Canada Post Corporation 2014 Annual Report note information.

At the time of writing, IFRS 15 Revenue from Contracts with Customers applies to public company annual reporting periods commencing on or after January 1, 2018, although earlier adoption is allowed. This new standard specifies how revenue is to be recognized in financial statements and provides financial statement users with more relevant disclosures about the nature, amount, timing, and uncertainty of revenues and cash flows from customer contracts.

The main principle of IFRS 15 is that revenue will be recognized, which demonstrates the transfer of promised goods or services to customers, in an amount that reflects the consideration to which the entity expects to become entitled in exchange for those goods or services. This main principle is to be applied to all contracts with customers through the following five-step principles-based model:

1. Identify the contract(s) with a customer.

2. Identify the performance obligations in the contract.

3. Determine the transaction price.

4. Allocate the transaction price to the performance obligation in the contract.

5. Recognize revenue as the business entity satisfies the performance obligations.

The application of this standard depends upon the facts and circumstances that exist in a contract with a customer and requires the exercise of professional judgment. Companies need to analyze their revenue sources in light of the requirements of IFRS 15 to determine to what extent, if any, their current revenue recognition accounting policies and disclosures in their financial statements need to change.

concept Q&A

Cash-basis accounting seems straightforward. Why complicate matters by introducing accrual accounting?

Answer:

The objective of financial reporting is to provide information that is useful in making business and economic decisions. Most of these decisions involve predicting a company's future cash flows. The use of accrual accounting through the application of the revenue recognition principle and the matching concept links income recognition to the principal activity of the company, selling goods and services. Therefore, accrual accounting provides a better estimate of future cash flows than cash-basis accounting.

The Matching Concept

Companies incur expenses for a variety of reasons. Sometimes expenses are incurred when an asset is used. In other instances, expenses are incurred when a liability is created. For example, Purolator incurs fuel expense as fuel is used to deliver packages. Purolator also incurs salary expense when employees work but are not paid immediately. The key idea is that **an expense is recorded when it is incurred, regardless of when cash is paid**.

Expense recognition is the process of identifying an expense with a particular time period. Under accrual accounting, expenses are recognized, recorded, and reported in the same period as the revenue that it helped to generate. Expenses for an accounting period should *include* only those costs incurred to earn revenue that was recognized in the accounting period. Expenses for an accounting period should *exclude* those costs used to earn revenue in an earlier period and those costs that will be used to earn revenue in a later period. Thus, the key to expense recognition is matching the expense with revenue.

ETHICAL DECISIONS AND FRAUD The revenue recognition principle and matching concept have been abused in recent years. As members of company senior management strive to meet or exceed the stock market's expectations in order to avoid a reduction in share price, management may be tempted to recognize revenue that has not yet been earned or to hide expenses that should be recognized. In addition, a common method used to remunerate senior management members is through the use of stock options. In order to maximize the increase in their own wealth, management may be driven by greed to overstate accrued revenues and understate accrued expenses in order to maximize profit in the company and their own stock option awards. While fraud is a serious criminal offence, some senior management members continue to indulge in this activity. In recent years, there have been numerous instances involving the abuse of both revenue and expense recognition. Notable cases are listed in Exhibit 3.3.

The actions summarized in Exhibit 3.3 were fraudulent and led to severe fines or jail time; innocent parties were also affected by these unethical actions. Shareholders, many of whom who had bought the shares at inflated prices, saw a significant drop in share value after these actions were made public. In addition, innocent employees lost their jobs as the companies struggled to deal with the fraud that occurred. When faced with an ethical dilemma related to manipulating the recognition of revenue or expenses, make the decision that best portrays the economic reality of your company.

Applying the Revenue Recognition Principle and Matching Concept

When using financial statements, it is important to understand how the revenue recognition principle and matching concept affect the amounts reported. Cornerstone 3.1 discusses further how the application of these principles and concepts results in accrual-basis income that differs from cash-basis income.

(EXHIBIT 3.3)

Instances of Accounting Manipulations

Company	Fraudulent Actions and Results
Nortel	Recognized revenue before it was earned. Numerous accounting executives and staff had their positions terminated.
Madoff Investment Securities	Mr. Bernard Madoff, CEO, implemented a Ponzi scheme, which caused a loss of over $50 billion to investors. Mr. Madoff was sentenced to a prison term of 150 years.
Regina Vacuum	Backdated sales invoices, improperly recorded revenue on consignment sales that had not been earned, and hid unpaid bills in a filing cabinet to reduce expenses.
Livent Inc.	Mr. Garth Drabinsky and Mr. Myron Gottlieb, both senior management members, created false invoices and a kickback scheme to fraudulently obtain $500 million from investors. Both Mr. Drabinsky and Mr. Gottlieb were sentenced to jail terms.
Miniscribe	Improperly recognized revenue through a variety of means, including packaging and shipping bricks as finished products. Chief executive was fined $250 million.
Sunbeam	Used a variety of techniques to improperly recognize revenue (including bill and hold transactions and channel stuffing). CEO fined $500,000 and barred from ever serving as an officer or director of a public company.
WorldCom	Improperly reduced operating expenses, which inflated income, by reversing (releasing) accrued liabilities and improperly classifying certain expenses as assets. Chief executive was sentenced to 25 years in jail.
Bally Total Fitness	Recognized revenue on gym membership contracts before it was earned, and improperly delayed the recognition of expenses. In total, more than two dozen improprieties were discovered that caused shareholders' equity to be overstated by $1.8 billion. Bally's auditor paid $8.5 million to settle charges of improper auditing.

© Cengage Learning

NEL

CORNERSTONE 3.1

Applying the Revenue Recognition Principle and Matching Concept

Information:

The Province of Ontario hired Conservation Ltd., a consulting company specializing in the conservation of natural resources, to explore options for providing water resources to the Toronto metropolitan area. In November 2018, Conservation Ltd. incurred $60,000 of expenditures, on account, while investigating the water shortage facing the city. Conservation Ltd. also delivered its recommendations and billed the province $100,000 for its work. In December 2018, Conservation Ltd. paid the $60,000 of expenses. In January 2019, Conservation Ltd. received the province's cheque for $100,000.

Required:

Calculate net income for November 2018, December 2018, and January 2019 using the following methods: (1) the cash basis of accounting, and (2) the accrual basis of accounting.

Why:

Under accrual accounting, revenue is recognized when it is earned and the collection of cash is reasonably assured. Expenses are recognized in the same period as the revenue they helped generate. Appropriate application of the revenue principle and matching concept is required to prevent a material error from occurring in financial statements.

Solution:

1. Cash-Basis Accounting

November 2018		December 2018		January 2019	
Revenue	$0	Revenue	$ 0	Revenue	$100,000
Expense	0	Expense	60,000	Expense	0
Net income	$0	Net income	$(60,000)	Net income	$100,000

➤ Performed Service   ➤ Paid Expenses   ➤ Received Payment

2. Accrual-Basis Accounting

November 2018		December 2018		January 2019	
Revenue	$100,000	Revenue	$0	Revenue	$0
Expense	60,000	Expense	0	Expense	0
Net income	$ 40,000	Net income	$0	Net income	$0

➤ Performed Service   ➤ Paid Expenses   ➤ Received Payment

Notice that, under accrual accounting, revenue is recognized when it is earned and expenses are matched with revenues. Even though Conservation Ltd. did not receive the payment from the Province of Ontario until January 2019, Conservation Ltd. had performed services in November 2018 and appropriately recognized the revenue as the service was performed. The $60,000 of expenses were matched with revenues and also recognized in November 2018. If cash-basis accounting had been used, $60,000 of expense would have been recognized in December 2018 (when the cash was paid) and $100,000 of revenue would have been recognized in January 2019 (when the cash was received). By following the revenue recognition principle and matching concept, net income was properly recognized in the period that the business activity occurred. **In short, the difference between cash-basis and accrual-basis accounting is a matter of timing.**

YOUDECIDE Recognizing a Security Service Contract

You are the chief financial officer of Secure Entry Ltd., a security company, and it is your responsibility to develop the company's revenue and expense recognition policies. In April 2018, Secure Entry signed a two-year contract with the Metropolis Stadium Authority (MSA) to provide security services at its stadium gates beginning in January 2019. Under the terms of the contract, MSA agrees to make 24 equal monthly payments to Secure Entry beginning in October 2018.

When should Secure Entry Ltd. recognize revenue and expenses associated with the security contract?

To provide investors and creditors with the most useful information and to be consistent with IFRS/ASPE, you decide that Secure Entry should follow accrual accounting principles. Therefore, the contract is initially recognized in October 2018, when MSA makes the first payment. At that time, Secure Entry will record an increase in cash for the payment received and an equal increase in a liability (Unearned Revenue) to recognize that future services are owed. Secure Entry will not record the contract in its accounting system in April 2018 because the event does not meet the recognition criteria discussed in Chapter 2.

Consistent with the revenue recognition principle, Secure Entry will recognize revenue each month, as services are performed, beginning in January 2019. Additionally, expenses related to the performance of security services will be matched against revenue from providing the security services and recognized monthly beginning in January 2019.

The proper recognition of revenue and expenses is critical in properly measuring and reporting income in the period that a business activity occurs.

ADJUSTING ENTRIES AND ACCRUAL ACCOUNTING

Which Transactions Require Adjustment?

Many business activities continue for a period of time—for example, the use of rented facilities or interest incurred on borrowed money. Because entries in the accounting system are made at particular points in time rather than continuously, adjustments are needed at the end of an accounting period to record partially complete activities.[2] **Adjusting entries** are journal entries made at the end of an accounting period to record the completed portion of partially completed transactions. Adjusting entries are necessary to apply the revenue recognition principle and matching concept and to ensure that a company's financial statements include the proper amount for revenues, expenses, assets, liabilities, and shareholders' equity.

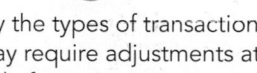

OBJECTIVE **3**

Identify the types of transactions that may require adjustments at the end of an accounting period.

---

[2] The distinction between business activities requiring adjustment and those that do not depends to some extent on our ability and willingness to keep track of activities. Some activities may occur so frequently or are so difficult to measure that no record of individual activities is maintained. In such cases, the sequence of individual activities becomes, for all intents and purposes, a continuous activity. For example, the purchase of office supplies is often treated as a continuous business activity because the benefit of maintaining a record of each time supplies are purchased and used is judged to be less than the related recordkeeping costs.

In Cornerstone 3.2 , three representative transactions are described. The implications of the "length" of these transactions for recognition in the accounting system and for adjustment are discussed.

The preparation of adjusting entries is necessary to get the account balances properly stated and up to date. These end-of-period adjustments can have significant effects on a company's financial statements.

CORNERSTONE 3.2

Determining Which Transactions Require Adjustment

Information:

Computer Town sells computer equipment and provides computer repair service. Sales are typically made in cash or on account. Repairs are provided under service contracts, which customers purchase up front for a specified period of time (two, three, or five years). Customers pay nothing when the computer is brought in for repair.

Required:

1. How should Computer Town account for cash and credit sales of equipment?

2. How should Computer Town account for repair services provided under service contracts?

3. How should Computer Town account for the use of office supplies?

Why:

Adjusting journal entries are required for continuous transactions that are partially complete at the end of an accounting period. Adjusting journal entries ensure that partially completed transactions are accounted for in the proper accounting period.

Solution:

1. Cash sales should be recorded as they occur and the equipment is delivered, often at a cash register that tracks total sales for the day. When orders are received from customers who want to purchase equipment on credit, the sale should be recorded when the equipment is delivered to the customer. In both situations, the sale is complete at a single point in time (the delivery of the equipment) and no adjusting entry is needed.

2. Repair service contracts are continuous activities that require an adjustment at the end of the accounting period. Revenue is earned as time passes under the service contract and should be recorded in proportion to the period of time that has passed since the contract became effective. The unexpired portion of the service contract should be recorded as a liability (unearned revenue) until earned. Any expenses associated with the repair services should be recognized in the same period that service revenue is recognized (the matching concept).

3. The use of supplies can be viewed as a sequence of individual activities. However, the benefit of preparing documents required to keep track of each activity individually would not exceed the related costs. Instead, the use of supplies can be treated as a continuous transaction and recognized as an expense when acquired. Alternatively, if material, office supplies can be recorded as an asset. Periodically the unused portion of office supplies would be determined and an adjusting entry prepared to record office supplies used.

STEP 5: ADJUSTING THE ACCOUNTS AND PREPARING THE ADJUSTED TRIAL BALANCE

Adjustments are often necessary because timing differences exist between when a revenue or expense is recognized and cash is received or paid. These timing differences give rise to two categories of adjusting entries—accruals and deferrals (prepayments). As shown in Exhibit 3.4, each category has two subcategories, resulting in four possible types of adjustments.

The purpose of all adjustments is to ensure that revenues and expenses are recorded in the proper time period. As the revenue and expense balances are adjusted, asset and liability balances will be adjusted also. Therefore, **all adjusting entries will affect at least one income statement account and one statement of financial position account. Note that cash is never affected by adjustments.**

A four-step procedure can be followed in the process of adjusting journal entries.

Step 1: Identify the statement of earnings and statement of financial position accounts that require adjustment.
Step 2: Calculate the amount of the required adjustment based on the amount of revenue that was earned or the amount of expense that was incurred during the accounting period.
Step 3: Record the adjusting journal entry.
Step 4: Prepare the **adjusted trial balance** to ensure that the trial balance remains in balance after the adjusting entries have been posted.

The recording processes used for the four types of adjusting entries are illustrated in the following sections.

Accrued Revenues

Companies often engage in revenue-producing activities but are not paid until after the activities are complete. For example, Purolator has packages in transit at the end of an accounting period, meaning that Purolator has only partially completed its service. These transactions for which Purolator has earned revenue but not received the cash are called **accrued revenues**. Another example of an accrued revenue is interest

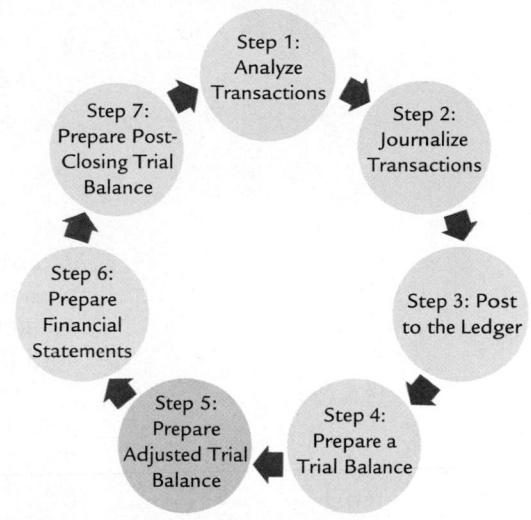

OBJECTIVE **4**

Prepare adjusting entries for accruals and prepayments.

© Cengage Learning

---

concept Q&A

Why don't adjusting entries involve cash?

Answer:

Cash receipts and cash payments are recorded when they occur at a specific point in time. Adjusting entries are concerned with applying the revenue recognition and matching principles to continuous activities. Because revenue and expense recognition does not depend on cash receipts or cash payments, adjusting entries for continuous revenue and expense activities will not involve cash.

(EXHIBIT 3.4)

Types of Adjusting Entries

Accruals:

- **Accrued revenues:** Previously unrecorded revenues that have been earned but for which no cash has yet been received
- **Accrued expenses:** Previously unrecorded expenses that have been incurred but not yet paid in cash

Prepayments:

- **Unearned revenues:** Liabilities arising from the receipt of cash for which revenue has not yet been earned
- **Prepaid expenses:** Assets arising from the payment of cash that have not been used or consumed by the end of the period

(EXHIBIT 3.5)

Accrued Revenues

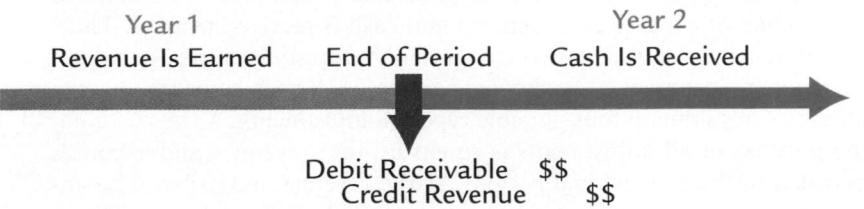

	Year 1		Year 2
	Revenue Is Earned	End of Period	Cash Is Received

Debit Receivable $$
Credit Revenue $$

© Cengage Learning

earned, but not yet received, on a loan receivable. While interest is earned as time passes, the company only receives the cash related to interest periodically (e.g., monthly, semiannually, or annually). Therefore, an adjustment is necessary to record the amount of interest earned but not yet received.

For accrued revenues, an adjustment is necessary to record the revenue and the associated increase in a company's assets, usually a type of receivable. Exhibit 3.5 demonstrates the process necessary to record accrued revenues at the end of a period and to reverse that accrued revenue in the following period. Note that the accrual of revenue is necessary because the revenue was earned prior to the receipt of cash.

The adjusting entry required to record accrued revenues is shown in Cornerstone 3.3 .

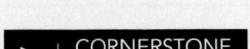

CORNERSTONE 3.3

CORNERSTONE
VIDEO

Recording Accrued Revenues

Information:

Assume that Porter Properties Inc., a calendar-year company, rented office space, to be occupied immediately, to Tiger Travel Agency on November 1, 2018, for $5,000 per month. Porter requires Tiger Travel to make a rental payment at the end of every three months. No payment was made on November 1.

Required:

1. Prepare the adjusting journal entry necessary for Porter on December 31, 2018.

2. Prepare the entry necessary on January 31, 2019, to record the receipt of cash and the reversal of the prior period's accrual.

Why:

Revenue is recognized when it is earned, regardless of when cash is received. The adjusting entry for an accrued revenue will result in an increase to a revenue account and an increase to an asset account.

Solution:

1. **Step 1: Identify the accounts that require adjustment.** Consistent with the revenue recognition principle, Rent Revenue needs to be increased because Porter has earned revenue from providing the office space. Because no payment was received, Porter will need to increase Rent Receivable to reflect its right to receive payment from Tiger Travel.

(Continued)

Step 2: Calculate the amount of the required adjustment. The amount of the adjustment will be calculated as:

$5,000 per month × 2 months (office space occupied) = $10,000

Step 3: Record the adjusting journal entry.

Date	Account and Explanation	Debit	Credit
Dec. 31, 2018	Accrued Rent Receivable	10,000	
	Rent Revenue		10,000
	(Record rent revenue earned in 2018 but not received)		

Assets	= Liabilities +	Shareholders' Equity (Rent Revenue)
+10,000		+10,000

2. The amount of cash received is calculated as:

$5,000 per month × 3 months (office space rented) = $15,000

Date	Account and Explanation	Debit	Credit
Jan. 31, 2019	Cash	15,000	
	Rent Revenue		5,000
	Accrued Rent Receivable		10,000
	(reverses December accrual)		
	(Record revenue earned in 2019 and the receipt of cash and the reversal of the prior period's accrued revenue)		

Assets	= Liabilities +	Shareholders' Equity (Rent Revenue)
+15,000		+5,000
−10,000		

The $5,000 of Rent Revenue represents the one month earned in 2018.

If the adjusting entry on December 31, 2018, were not made, assets, shareholders' equity, revenues, and net income would be understated by $10,000. The adjusting journal entry recognizes two months of revenue (November and December 2018) in the accounting period in which it was earned and updates the corresponding balance in Rent Receivable. The revenue has been earned because Porter has provided a service to Tiger Travel. Later, when cash is received, the remaining portion of the revenue that was earned in January 2019 is recognized and the receivable is reduced to reflect that it was paid. Consistent with the revenue recognition principle, revenue is recorded in the period that it is earned.

Accrued Expenses

Similar to the situation with accrued revenues, many companies incur expenses in the current accounting period but do not pay cash for these expenses until a later period. This situation is quite common for operating costs such as payroll, taxes, utilities, rent, and interest. **Accrued expenses** are previously unrecorded expenses that have been incurred but not yet paid in cash.

For accrued expenses, an adjustment is necessary to record the expense and the associated increase in a company's liabilities, usually a payable. Exhibit 3.6 demonstrates the process necessary to record accrued expenses.

(EXHIBIT 3.6)

Accrued Expenses

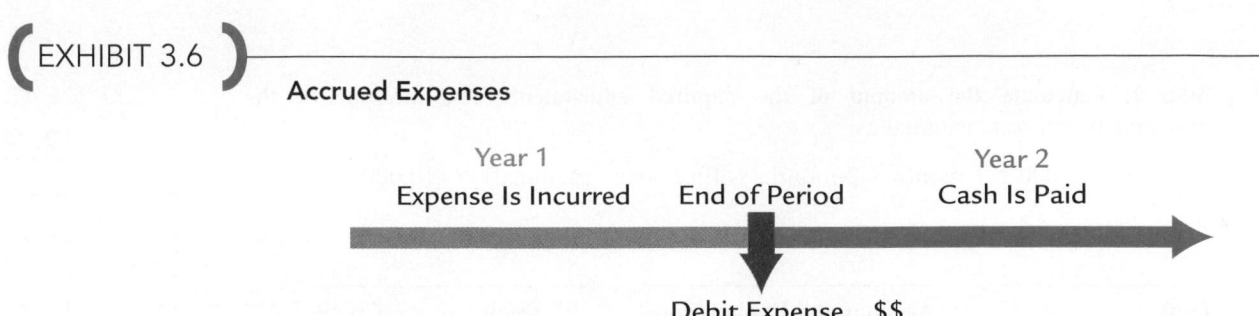

| | Year 1 | | | Year 2 |
| Expense Is Incurred | End of Period | Cash Is Paid |

Debit Expense $$
Credit Payable $$

© Cengage Learning

Note that the accrual of the expense is necessary because the expense was incurred prior to the payment of cash. The adjusting entry required to record accrued expenses at the end of a period and to reverse that accrued expense in the following period is shown in Cornerstone 3.4 .

CORNERSTONE 3.4

Recording Accrued Expenses

▶ | CORNERSTONE VIDEO

Information:

Assume that Porter Properties Inc., a calendar-year company, pays its clerical employees every two weeks. Employees work five days a week for a total of 10 work days every two weeks. Total wages for 10 days is $50,000. Also assume that December 31, 2018, is four days into a 10-day pay period.

Required:

1. Prepare the adjusting journal entry necessary for Porter on December 31, 2018.

2. Prepare the entry necessary on January 10, 2019, to record the payment of salaries.

Why:

Expenses are recorded as they are incurred, regardless of when cash is paid. The adjusting entry for an accrued expense will result in an increase to an expense account and an increase to a liability account.

Solution:

1. **Step 1: Identify the accounts that require adjustment.** Salaries Expense needs to be increased because Porter has incurred an expense related to its employees working for four days in December. This expense needs to be matched against December revenues (an application of the matching concept). Because no payment to the employees was made, Porter will need to increase Salaries Payable to reflect its obligation to pay its employees.

   Step 2: Calculate the amount of the required adjustment. The amount of the adjustment will be calculated as:

   $50,000 bi-weekly salaries × (4 days/10 days) worked in two weeks = $20,000

(Continued)

Step 3: Record the adjusting entry.

Date	Account and Explanation	Debit	Credit
Dec. 31, 2018	Salaries Expense	20,000	
	Accrued Salaries Payable		20,000
	(Record expenses incurred not paid)		

CORNERSTONE

3.4

(Continued)

2. The amount of the salaries expense for the current year will be accrued and calculated as:

$50,000 bi-weekly salaries × (6 days/10 days) worked in two weeks = $30,000

			Shareholders' Equity (Salaries
Assets	= Liabilities +		Expense)
	+20,000		−20,000

Date	Account and Explanation	Debit	Credit
Jan. 10, 2019	Salaries Expense	30,000	
	Accrued Salaries Payable	20,000	
	Cash		50,000
	(Record expense incurred in 2018		
	and the payment of cash and the		
	reversal of the expense accrued at		
	the end of the prior period)		

			Shareholders' Equity (Salaries
Assets	= Liabilities +		Expense)
−50,000	−20,000		−30,000

If the adjusting journal entry on December 31, 2018, were not made, liabilities and expenses would be understated by $20,000, while income and shareholders' equity would be overstated by $20,000. The adjusting journal entry recognizes the expense that was incurred during the accounting period and updates the balance in the corresponding liability. Later, when the cash is paid to the employees, the portion of the expense that was incurred in January 2019 is recognized and the previously created liability is reduced. Consistent with the matching concept, expenses are recorded in the period they were incurred.

Unearned Revenues

A company may collect payment for goods or services that it sells before it delivers those goods or services. For example, Purolator often collects cash for a package delivery prior to the actual performance of the delivery service. When the cash is collected, the revenue recognition is deferred, or delayed, until the service is performed. Transactions for which a company has received cash but has not yet earned the revenue are called **unearned revenues**. Other examples of unearned revenues are rent received in advance, magazine or newspaper subscriptions received in advance, and tickets (e.g., for airlines, sporting events, concerts) sold in advance. In all of these situations, the receipt of cash creates a liability for the company to deliver goods or perform services in the future. The unearned revenue account delays, or defers, the recognition of revenue by recording the revenue as a liability until it is earned.

As the goods are delivered or the service is performed, an adjustment is necessary to reduce the previously recorded liability and to recognize the portion of the revenue that has been earned. The portion of revenue that has not been earned remains in the liability account, unearned revenue, until it is earned. Therefore, revenue recognition is delayed until the revenue is earned. Exhibit 3.7 demonstrates the process necessary to record unearned revenues.

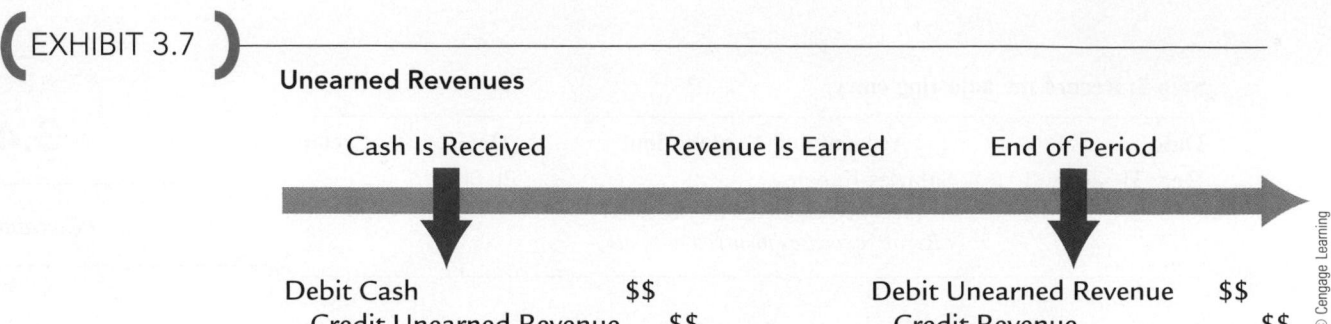

— EXHIBIT 3.7 —

Unearned Revenues

	Cash Is Received	Revenue Is Earned	End of Period

Debit Cash $$ Debit Unearned Revenue $$
    Credit Unearned Revenue $$ Credit Revenue $$

© Cengage Learning

Note that the delay of revenue recognition is necessary because the revenue was not earned at the time of the cash receipt. The adjusting entry recognizes the amount of revenue that has been earned from the time of the cash receipt until the end of the accounting period. The adjusting entry required to adjust unearned revenues is shown in Cornerstone 3.5.

CORNERSTONE 3.5   Adjusting Unearned Revenues

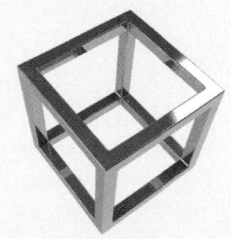

CORNERSTONE
VIDEO

Information:

Assume that Porter Properties Inc., a calendar-year company, rented office space to Tiger Travel Agency on November 1, 2018, for $5,000 per month. Porter requires Tiger Travel to make a rental payment every three months. If Tiger Travel pays its entire three-month rental in advance, Porter has agreed to reduce the monthly rental to $4,500. Tiger Travel agrees and pays Porter $13,500 for three months' rental.

Required:

1. Prepare the entry on November 1, 2018, to record the receipt of cash.

2. Prepare the adjusting journal entry necessary for Porter on December 31, 2018.

Why:

An unearned revenue account balance arises when cash is received from a customer before the related revenue is earned. When the related revenue is subsequently earned, an adjusting entry is required to increase a revenue account and decrease the liability (unearned revenue) account.

Solution:

1.

Date	Account and Explanation	Debit	Credit
Nov. 1, 2018	Cash	13,500	
	Unearned Rent Revenue		13,500
	(Record receipt of cash for three months' rent)		

Assets	=	Liabilities	+	Shareholders' Equity
+13,500		+13,500		

(Continued)

2. **Step 1: Identify the accounts that require adjustment.** Rent Revenue needs to be increased because Porter has earned revenue from providing the office space. Because a liability was previously recorded, Porter will need to decrease the liability, Unearned Rent Revenue, to reflect the decrease in their obligation to perform the service.

Step 2: Calculate the amount of the required adjustment. The amount of the adjustment will be calculated as:

$4,500 per month × 2 months (office space rented) = $9,000

Step 3: Record the adjusting entry.

Date	Account and Explanation	Debit	Credit
Dec. 31, 2018	Unearned Rent Revenue	9,000	
	Rent Revenue		9,000
	(Record rent revenue earned in 2018)		

Assets	=	Liabilities	+	Shareholders' Equity (Rent Revenue)
		−9,000		+9,000

If the adjusting entry on December 31, 2018, were not made, liabilities (Unearned Rent Revenue) would be overstated by $13,500 while shareholders' equity, revenue, and net income would be understated by $13,500. The adjusting journal entry recognizes two months of revenue (November and December 2018) in the accounting period in which it was earned and updates the corresponding balance in the liability, Unearned Rent Revenue. As a result of the adjusting entry, revenue is recorded in the period that it is earned.

Prepaid Expenses

Companies often acquire goods and services before they are used. These prepayments are recorded as assets called **prepaid expenses**. Common prepaid expenses include items such as supplies, prepaid rent, prepaid advertising, and prepaid insurance.

As the prepaid asset is used in business operations to generate revenue, an adjustment is necessary to reduce the previously recorded prepaid asset and recognize the related expense. The portion of the prepaid asset that has not been used represents the unexpired benefits and remains in the asset account until it is used. Therefore, expense recognition is delayed until the expense is incurred. Exhibit 3.8 demonstrates the process necessary to record prepaid expenses.

Note that the delay in the expense recognition was necessary because the initial cash payment did not result in an expense. Instead, an asset that provides future economic benefit was created. The adjusting entry recognizes the amount of expense that has been incurred from the time of the cash payment until the end of the accounting period. The adjusting entry required to adjust prepaid expenses is shown in Cornerstone 3.6 .

(EXHIBIT 3.8)

Prepaid Expenses

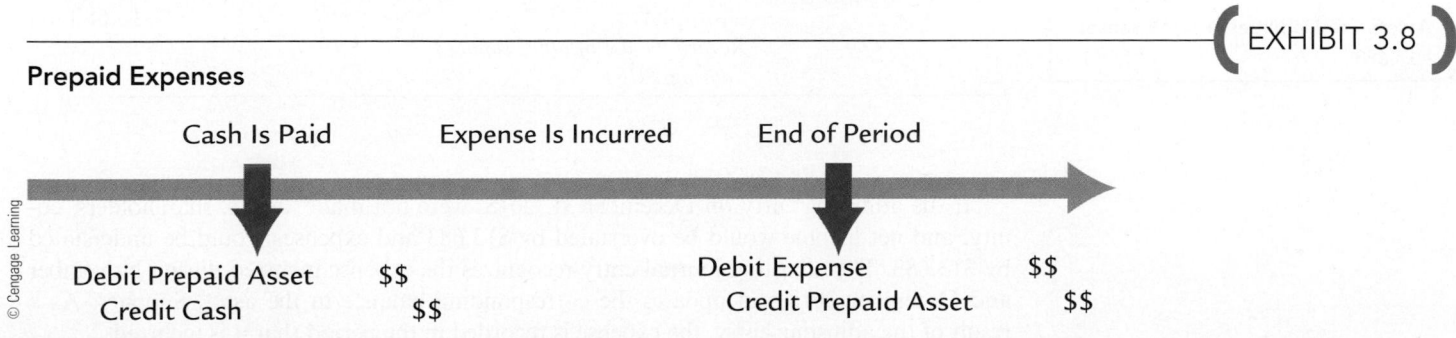

© Cengage Learning

CORNERSTONE 3.6

CORNERSTONE
VIDEO

Adjusting Prepaid Expenses

Information:

Assume that Porter Properties Inc., a calendar-year company, had $4,581 of office supplies on hand at the beginning of November. On November 10, Porter purchased office supplies totalling $12,365. The amount of the purchase was added to the Supplies account. At the end of the year, the balance in Supplies was $16,946 ($4,581 + $12,365). A count of office supplies on hand indicated that $3,263 of supplies remained.

Required:

1. Prepare the entry on November 10, 2018, to record the purchase of supplies.

2. Prepare the adjusting journal entry necessary for Porter on December 31, 2018.

Why:

A prepaid expense balance arises when cash is paid to a supplier (other than inventory) before the related expense is incurred. When the related expense is incurred, an adjusting entry is required to increase an expense account and to decrease an asset (prepaid expense) account.

Solution:

1.

Assets	=	Liabilities	+	Shareholders' Equity
+12,365				
−12,365				

Date	Account and Explanation	Debit	Credit
Nov. 10, 2018	Supplies	12,365	
	Cash		12,365
	(Record purchase of office supplies)		

2. **Step 1: Identify the accounts that require adjustment.** Supplies Expense needs to be increased because Porter has used office supplies during November and December of 2018. The use of the supplies also decreases the asset, Supplies.

3. **Step 2: Calculate the amount of the required adjustment.** The amount of the adjustment will be calculated as:

$16,946 (supplies available to be used) − $3,263 (supplies on hand) = $13,683

This amount represents the cost of supplies used during November and December 2018.

Step 3: Record the adjusting entry.

Assets	=	Liabilities	+	Shareholders' Equity (Supplies Expense)
−13,683				−13,683

Date	Account and Explanation	Debit	Credit
Dec. 31, 2018	Supplies Expense	13,683	
	Supplies		13,683
	(Record the use of office supplies during 2018)		

If the adjusting entry on December 31, 2018, were not made, assets, shareholders' equity, and net income would be overstated by $13,683 and expenses would be understated by $13,683. The adjusting journal entry recognizes the expense incurred during November and December 2018 and updates the corresponding balance in the asset, Supplies. As a result of the adjusting entry, the expense is recorded in the period that it is incurred.

Depreciation While most prepaid expenses are accounted for in a manner similar to that illustrated in Cornerstone 3.6, the purchase of long-lived assets such as buildings and equipment presents a unique situation. Recall from Chapter 1 that these types of assets are classified as property, plant, and equipment on the statement of financial position. Because property, plant, and equipment helps produce revenue over a number of years (instead of just one period), the matching concept requires companies to systematically assign, or allocate, the asset's cost as an expense to each period in which the asset is used. This process is called **depreciation**. This concept and the methods used to compute depreciation expense are discussed in Chapter 7.

The depreciation process requires an adjustment to recognize the expense incurred during the period and to reduce the carrying value of the long-lived asset. The unused portion of the asset is reported as property, plant, and equipment, net of accumulated depreciation, on the statement of financial position. Therefore, the purchase of a long-lived asset is essentially a long-term prepayment for the service the asset will provide.

Assume that Porter Properties purchased an office building on January 1, 2016, for $450,000. The depreciation expense on this building is $15,000 per year. Because depreciation is a continuous activity, Porter will need to make the following adjustment at the end of 2018.

Date	Account and Explanation	Debit	Credit
Dec. 31, 2018	Depreciation Expense	15,000	
	Accumulated Depreciation—Building		15,000
	(Record depreciation for 2018)		

Assets	=	Liabilities +	Shareholders' Equity (Depreciation Expense)
−15,000			−15,000

Depreciation expense represents the portion of the cost of the long-lived asset that is matched against the revenues that the asset helped generate. In addition, the depreciation process reduces the carrying value of the asset. Accountants normally use a contra account called Accumulated Depreciation to reduce the carrying value of a long-lived asset. **Contra accounts** are accounts that have a balance that is opposite of the balance in a related account. In this case, Accumulated Depreciation—Building is a contra account to the building asset account. Therefore, while the building asset account has a normal debit balance, the contra account has a normal credit balance. Contra accounts are deducted from the balance of the related asset account in the financial statements, and the resulting difference is known as the net book value of the asset. Therefore, by increasing the contra account, the above journal entry reduces the net book value of the asset. Exhibit 3.9 shows the financial statement presentation of the accumulated depreciation account.

(EXHIBIT 3.9)

Financial Statement Presentation of Accumulated Depreciation

Porter Properties Inc. Statement of Financial Position December 31, 2018	
Assets:	
Current assets	$ 370,000
Property, plant, and equipment (net)	1,450,000
Other assets	80,000
Total assets	$ 1,900,000
Liabilities	$ 825,000
Equity	1,075,000
Total liabilities and equity	$ 1,900,000

Sample of accumulated depreciation presentation:

Building	$ 450,000
Less: Accumulated depreciation	(45,000)
Building (net)	$ 405,000

Notice that the accumulated depreciation amount includes the total amount of depreciation recorded in all years of the asset's life ($15,000 per year for 2016, 2017, and 2018). Therefore, the balance in the accumulated depreciation account will increase over the asset's life. The use of the contra account provides more information to users of the financial statements because it preserves both the original cost of the asset and the total cost that has expired to date.

Summary of Financial Statement Effects of Adjusting Entries

The effects of the adjustment process are summarized in Exhibit 3.10.

Adjusting entries ensure that revenues and expenses are recorded in the proper time period. As the revenue and expense balances are adjusted, asset and liability balances will be adjusted also. Therefore, *all adjusting entries affect at least one income statement account and one statement of financial position account.* Remember, *the cash account is never used in an adjusting entry.*

Comprehensive Example

To provide a comprehensive example of the adjusting process, consider the unadjusted trial balance of HighTech Communications that was introduced in Chapter 2 (see Exhibit 3.11).

Upon review of the trial balance, the accountant for HighTech noted that certain accounts needed to be adjusted.

Adjustment 1: Accrued Revenue HighTech's accountant noted that HighTech had performed $1,500 of advertising services for which it had not yet billed the customer. Because the services had not yet been billed, no entry was made in the accounting system. However, HighTech must record the revenue that was earned during the accounting period, even though the cash flow will not occur until a later date. The adjusting entry to record this accrued revenue is:

Date	Account and Explanation	Debit	Credit
March 31	Accounts Receivable	1,500	
	Service Revenue		1,500
	(Recognize services earned)		

concept Q&A

What is the relationship between the cash receipt or payment and the recognition of accruals or prepayments?

Answer:

Adjusting entries can be classified as accruals or prepayments depending on the timing of the cash flow relative to when the revenue is earned or the expense is incurred. When the revenue is earned or the expense is incurred **before** the associated cash flow occurs, an accrual adjusting entry is necessary. When the revenue is earned or the expense is incurred **after** the associated cash flow occurs, a prepayment adjusting entry is necessary.

Assets	= Liabilities +	Shareholders' Equity (Service Revenue)
+1,500		+1,500

(EXHIBIT 3.10)

Effects of Adjusting Entries

	Type of Adjustment	Adjusting Entry	Asset	Liability	Revenue	Expense
Accruals	Accrued Revenue	Dr Asset Cr Revenue	↑		↑	
	Accrued Expense	Dr Expense Cr Liability		↑		↑
Prepayments	Unearned Revenue	Dr Liability Cr Revenue	↓		↑	
	Unearned Expense	Dr Expense Cr Asset	↓			↑

(EXHIBIT 3.11)

Trial Balance

Account	Debit	Credit
HighTech Communications Inc. Unadjusted Trial Balance March 31, 2018		
Cash	$16,600	
Accounts Receivable	300	
Supplies	6,500	
Prepaid Insurance	1,200	
Equipment	4,500	
Accounts Payable		$ 500
Unearned Service Revenue		9,000
Notes Payable		3,000
Common Shares		12,000
Dividends Declared	500	
Service Revenue		12,100
Salaries Expense	1,800	
Utilities Expense	5,200	
	$36,600	$36,600

Adjustment 2: Accrual of Interest The note payable for $3,000 that HighTech signed on March 2 required it to pay interest at an annual rate of 8%. The formula for computing interest is:

$$\text{Interest} = \text{Principal} \times \text{Interest rate} \times \text{Time}$$

The principal amount of the loan is usually the face value of the note. The interest rate is stated as an annual rate, and the time period is the fraction of a year that the note is outstanding. For HighTech, interest expense for March 2018 is computed as:

$$\text{Interest} = \$3,000 \times 8\% \times 1/12 = \$20$$

Because interest expense has been incurred but the cash payment for interest will not occur until a later date, interest is an accrued expense that requires an increase to an expense account and an increase to a liability account. The adjusting entry to recognize accrued interest is:

Date	Account and Explanation	Debit	Credit
March 31	Interest Expense	20	
	Interest Payable		20
	(Recognize accrued interest)		

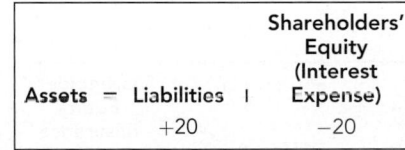

Assets	=	Liabilities	I	Shareholders' Equity (Interest Expense)
		+20		−20

Adjustment 3: Accrual of Salaries HighTech paid its weekly salaries on March 26, a Friday, and properly recorded an expense (Transaction 10 from Chapter 2). Salaries for a five-day work week are $1,800, or $360 per day. HighTech will not pay salaries again until April 2. However, employees worked on March 29, March 30, and March 31. Because employees have worked but will not be paid until a later date, an adjustment is necessary to record the salaries incurred in March. Accrued salaries are $1,080 (3 days × $360 per day). The adjusting entry to recognize accrued salaries is:

	Shareholders' Equity (Salaries
Assets = Liabilities +	Expense)
+1,080	−1,080

Date	Account and Explanation	Debit	Credit
March 31	Salaries Expense	1,080	
	Salaries Payable		1,080
	(Recognize accrued salaries)		

Adjustment 4: Unearned Revenue HighTech's trial balance shows that a customer paid $9,000 in advance for services to be performed at a later date. This amount was originally recorded as a liability, Unearned Service Revenue. As HighTech performs services, the liability will be reduced and revenue will be recognized. Based on HighTech's analysis of work performed during March, it is determined that $3,300 of revenue has been earned. The adjusting entry to record this previously unearned revenue is:

	Shareholders' Equity (Service
Assets = Liabilities +	Revenue)
−3,300	+3,300

Date	Account and Explanation	Debit	Credit
March 31	Unearned Service Revenue	$3,300	
	Service Revenue		$3,300
	(Recognize service revenue earned)		

Adjustment 5: Expense—Supplies HighTech's trial balance shows a balance of $6,500 in the Supplies account. However, an inventory count at the close of business on March 31 determines that supplies on hand are $1,200. Because it is not efficient to record supplies expense during the period, HighTech must make an adjustment at the end of the period to record the supplies used during the period. It is determined that HighTech has used $5,300 ($6,500 available to be used minus $1,200 not used) of supplies. The adjustment necessary to record the supplies used during March is:

	Shareholders' Equity (Supplies
Assets = Liabilities +	Expense)
−5,300	−5,300

Date	Account and Explanation	Debit	Credit
March 31	Supplies Expense	5,300	
	Supplies		5,300
	(Recognize supplies used)		

Adjustment 6: Prepaid Expense—Insurance HighTech's trial balance shows a balance of $1,200 in the Prepaid Insurance account related to a six-month insurance policy purchased at the beginning of March. Because time has passed since the purchase of the insurance policy, the asset, Prepaid Insurance, has partially expired and an expense needs to be recognized. The expired portion of the insurance is $200 ($1,200 × 1/6). The adjustment necessary to record insurance expense is:

	Shareholders' Equity (Insurance
Assets = Liabilities +	Expense)
−200	−200

Date	Account and Explanation	Debit	Credit
March 31	Insurance Expense	200	
	Prepaid Insurance		200
	(Recognize insurance used)		

Adjustment 7: Depreciation HighTech's trial balance shows that $4,500 of equipment was purchased. Because this equipment is used to generate revenue, a portion of the cost of the equipment must be allocated to expense. For HighTech, assume that depreciation expense is $125 per month. The adjustment necessary to record depreciation expense is:

Date	Account and Explanation	Debit	Credit
March 31	Depreciation Expense	125	
	Accumulated Depreciation—		125
	Equipment		
	(Recognize depreciation on equipment)		

Assets	=	Liabilities	+	Shareholders' Equity
−125				−125

The general ledger for HighTech Communications, after posting of the adjusting journal entries, is shown in Exhibit 3.12.

To ensure the integrity of the general ledger after the adjusting journal entries have been posted, an adjusted trial balance is prepared. Exhibit 3.13 contains the adjusted trial balance for HighTech that has been prepared from the general ledger balances in Exhibit 3.12.

(EXHIBIT 3.12)

General Ledger of HighTech Communications

Assets

Cash

16,600	
16,600	

Accounts Receivable

300	
(A1) 1,500	
1,800	

Supplies

6,500	
	5,300 (A5)
1,200	

Prepaid Insurance

1,200	
	200 (A6)
1,000	

Equipment

4,500	
4,500	

Accumulated Depreciation—Equipment

	125 (A7)
	125

Liabilities

Accounts Payable

	500
	500

Notes Payable

	3,000
	3,000

Interest Payable

	20 (A2)
	20

Salaries Payable

	1,080 (A3)
	1,080

Unearned Service Revenue

	9,000
(A4) 3,300	
	5,700

Shareholders' Equity

Common Shares

	12,000
	12,000

Service Revenue

	12,100
	1,500 (A1)
	3,300 (A4)
	16,900

Salaries Expense

1,800	
(A3) 1,080	
2,880	

Utilities Expense

5,200	
5,200	

Depreciation Expense

(A7) 125	
125	

Interest Expense

(A2) 20	
20	

Insurance Expense

(A6) 200	
200	

Supplies Expense

(A5) 5,300	
5,300	

Dividends Declared

500	
500	

(EXHIBIT 3.13)

Adjusted Trial Balance

Account		Debit	Credit
HighTech Communications Inc.			
Adjusted Trial Balance			
March 31, 2018			
Cash		$16,600	
Accounts Receivable		1,800	
Supplies		1,200	
Prepaid Insurance		1,000	
Equipment	Statement of	4,500	
Accumulated Depreciation—Equipment	Financial		$ 125
Accounts Payable	Position		500
Unearned Service Revenue	Accounts		5,700
Interest Payable			20
Salaries Payable			1,080
Notes Payable			3,000
Common Shares			12,000
Dividends Declared		500	
Service Revenue			16,900
Salaries Expense		2,880	
Utilities Expense	Statement of	5,200	
Depreciation Expense	Earnings	125	
Interest Expense	Accounts	20	
Insurance Expense		200	
Supplies Expense		5,300	
		$39,325	$39,325

Two major items should be apparent:

- Adjusting entries affect one statement of financial position account and one statement of earnings account. Without adjusting entries, the balances reported on both the statement of financial position and the statement of earnings would have been incorrect. If the adjustments had not been recorded, HighTech would have understated revenue by $4,800 ($1500 + $3300) and understated expenses by $6,725 ($200 + $5300 + $1080 + $125 + $20).
- Adjusting entries do not affect cash.

YOUDECIDE How Adjusting Entries Affect Financial Statements

You are considering investing in Get Fit Ltd., a chain of gymnasiums and wellness facilities. As you are analyzing the financial statements to determine whether Get Fit is a good investment, three items catch your attention:

- Get Fit requires customers to pay the first six months' membership fees at the time the customer joins one of its facilities. These fees are recorded as revenue at the time of cash receipt since the amount is nonrefundable.
- Get Fit paid for and distributed flyers to advertise its recent membership drive. Because these flyers will circulate and attract customers for approximately one year, Get Fit recorded the expenditures as prepaid advertising that will be expensed over the next year.

- Get Fit provides healthy snacks to its customers by charging their membership accounts. Get Fit records revenue at the end of the month when it bills customers, although customers do not pay until the next month.

Do you think that Get Fit is properly recording the above transactions? If not, what is the effect on the financial statements?

First, the membership fees are a continuous activity that Get Fit is incorrectly treating as a point-in-time activity. Because the revenue has not yet been earned, the membership fees should be initially recorded as unearned revenue. As the customers have use of the facility each month, an adjusting entry should be made to reduce unearned revenue and increase revenue. The fact that the fees are nonrefundable is irrelevant in deciding whether revenue should or should not be recognized.

Second, because it is difficult to measure any future benefits associated with advertising costs, accountants take a conservative position and these costs should not be recorded on the statement of financial position; instead, they should be expensed as incurred.

Finally, Get Fit is appropriately recording an accrued revenue related to providing snacks. The fact that the customers do not pay until a later time period is not relevant in determining when the revenue is recorded.

If the above transactions had been properly recorded, Get Fit would have reported less revenue, higher expenses, and, therefore, lower net income. Financial statement users need to pay close attention to a company's policies with regard to revenue and expense recognition.

Adjusting entries can have a material impact on a company's reported assets, liabilities, revenues, expenses, and net income.

STEP 6: PREPARING THE FINANCIAL STATEMENTS

The financial statements can now be prepared using the balances obtained from the adjusted trial balance. As discussed in Chapter 1, the financial statements are interrelated. That is, there is a natural progression from one financial statement to another as the numbers on one financial statement flow into another financial statement. Because of this natural progression, financial statements are prepared in a particular order.

1. The statement of earnings is prepared from the revenue and expense accounts.

2. Net income is used to prepare the statement of retained earnings.

3. The statement of financial position is prepared using the ending balance of retained earnings from the statement of retained earnings.

The financial statements and their interrelationship are shown in Exhibit 3.14.

STEP 7: CLOSING THE ACCOUNTS AND PREPARING THE POST-CLOSING TRIAL BALANCE

When we introduced the basic accounting equation in Chapter 1, we identified three types of statement of financial position accounts: assets, liabilities, and shareholders' equity. These accounts are **permanent accounts** in that their balances are carried forward from the current accounting period to future accounting periods. We also identified three other accounts: revenues, expenses, and dividends declared. These accounts are used to collect the activities of only one period, so they are considered **temporary accounts**. The final step of the accounting cycle, closing the accounts, is done to:

- Transfer the balances (reduce their balances to zero) in the revenues, expenses, and dividends declared accounts (the temporary accounts) to the permanent shareholders' equity account named Retained Earnings.
- Clear (reduce their balances to zero) the revenue, expenses, and dividends declared accounts in order that those accounts are ready to accumulate the business activities of the next accounting period. Without closing entries, the temporary accounts would accumulate the business activities of *all* accounting periods, not just the current time period.

OBJECTIVE ❺

Prepare financial statements from an adjusted trial balance.

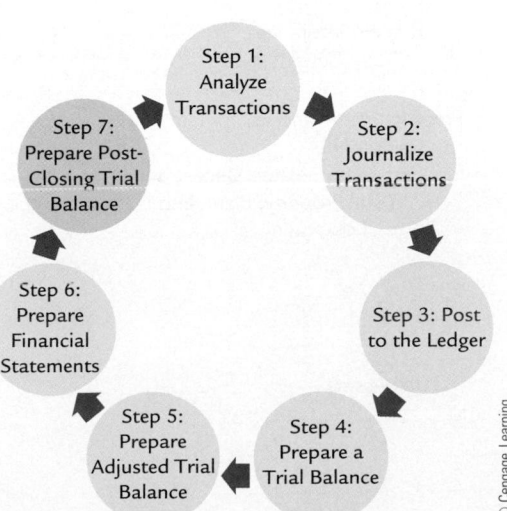

OBJECTIVE ❻

Explain why and how companies prepare closing entries and understand the quality of earnings.

(EXHIBIT 3.14)

Relationships among the Financial Statements

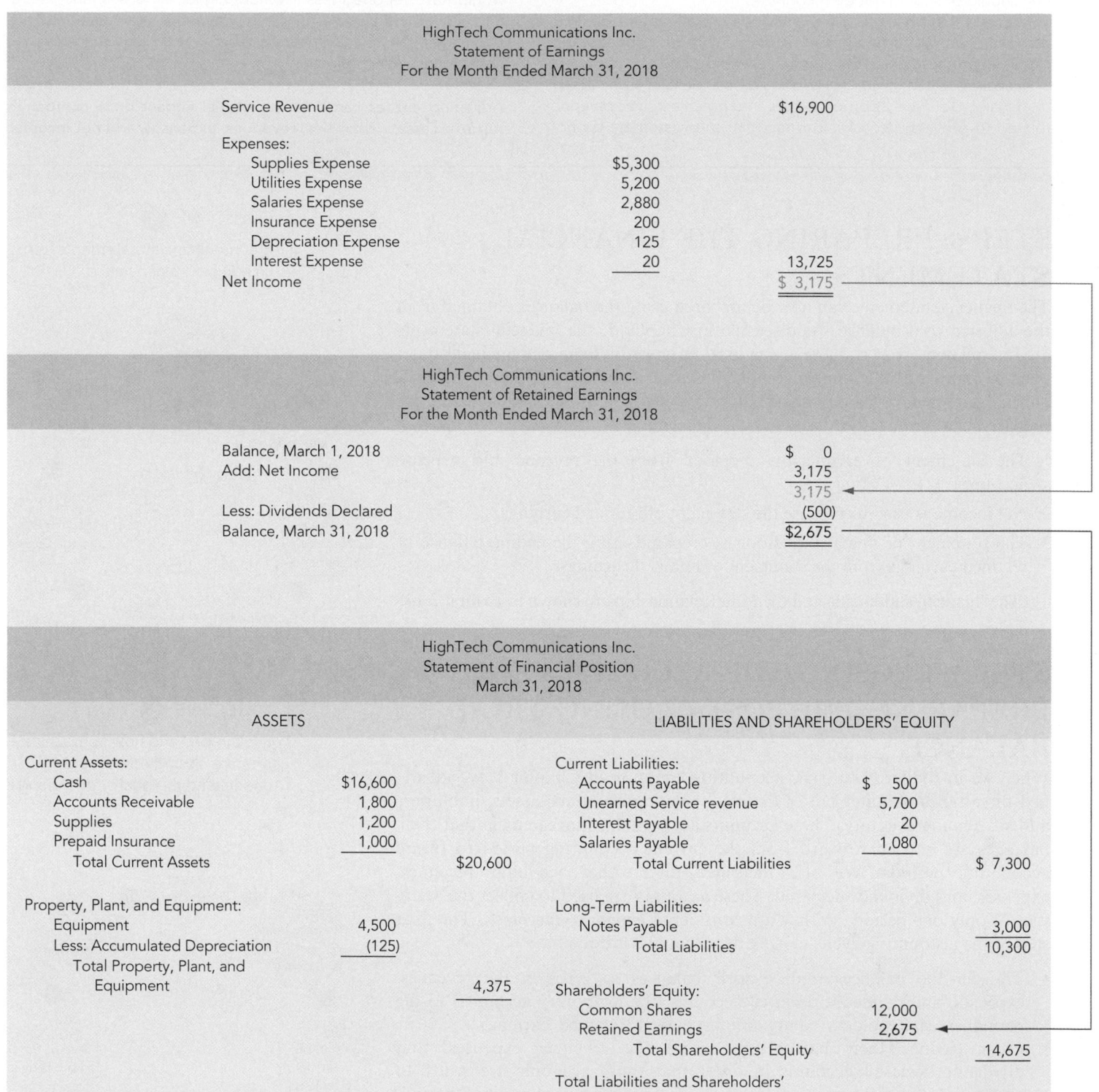

HighTech Communications Inc.
Statement of Earnings
For the Month Ended March 31, 2018

Service Revenue		$16,900
Expenses:		
Supplies Expense	$5,300	
Utilities Expense	5,200	
Salaries Expense	2,880	
Insurance Expense	200	
Depreciation Expense	125	
Interest Expense	20	13,725
Net Income		$ 3,175

HighTech Communications Inc.
Statement of Retained Earnings
For the Month Ended March 31, 2018

Balance, March 1, 2018	$ 0
Add: Net Income	3,175
	3,175
Less: Dividends Declared	(500)
Balance, March 31, 2018	$2,675

HighTech Communications Inc.
Statement of Financial Position
March 31, 2018

ASSETS			LIABILITIES AND SHAREHOLDERS' EQUITY		
Current Assets:			Current Liabilities:		
Cash	$16,600		Accounts Payable	$ 500	
Accounts Receivable	1,800		Unearned Service revenue	5,700	
Supplies	1,200		Interest Payable	20	
Prepaid Insurance	1,000		Salaries Payable	1,080	
Total Current Assets		$20,600	Total Current Liabilities		$ 7,300
Property, Plant, and Equipment:			Long-Term Liabilities:		
Equipment	4,500		Notes Payable		3,000
Less: Accumulated Depreciation	(125)		Total Liabilities		10,300
Total Property, Plant, and Equipment		4,375	Shareholders' Equity:		
			Common Shares	12,000	
			Retained Earnings	2,675	
			Total Shareholders' Equity		14,675
			Total Liabilities and Shareholders'		
Total Assets		$24,975	Equity		$24,975

YOUDECIDE Quality of Earnings

Investors and other users often assess the quality of a company's earnings when analyzing companies. The quality of earnings refers to how well a company's reported earnings reflect the company's true earnings. High-quality earnings are generally viewed as permanent or persistent earnings that assist financial statement users in predicting future earnings and cash flows. Low-quality earnings are temporary or transitory earnings from one-time transactions or events that do not aid in predicting future earnings or cash flows. While there is no consensus on how best to measure earnings quality, research suggests that investors recognize differences in earnings quality and that these differences affect a company's share price.

How do adjusting entries influence the quality of earnings?

Because adjusting entries always affect amounts reported on the statement of earnings, the estimates and judgments involved in determining accruals and deferrals (prepayments) of revenues and expenses can have a significant impact on a company's net income. Companies that make relatively pessimistic estimates and judgments are said to follow prudent accounting practices and are generally viewed as having earnings that are of higher quality. In contrast, many companies use relatively optimistic estimates and judgments and employ aggressive accounting practices. These companies are normally viewed as having a lower quality of earnings.

Adjusting entries that lead to better predictors of future earnings or cash flows are viewed as contributing to a higher quality of earnings.

The closing process is accomplished through a series of journal entries that are dated as of the last day of the accounting period. Occasionally, another temporary account, called income summary, is used to aid the closing process. The use of the income summary account allows the company to easily identify the net income (or net loss) for the period. The closing process can be completed in a four-step procedure:

Step 1: Close (transfer) revenue account balances to the income summary.

Step 2: Close (transfer) balances in expense accounts to the income summary. At this point, the balance in the income summary account should be equal to net income (or net loss).

Step 3: Close (transfer) the income summary account balance to the retained earnings account.

Step 4: Close (transfer) the dividends declared account balance to the retained earnings account.

The closing process is illustrated in Cornerstone 3.7 .

Notice that revenues, which have a normal credit balance, are closed by debiting the revenue account. Similarly, expenses, which normally have a debit balance, are closed by crediting the expense accounts. Also, after the first two journal entries, the balance in the income summary account is $3,175 ($16,900 − $13,725), which is the amount of net income for the period. This amount is then transferred to retained earnings. Finally, the dividends declared account is not closed to income summary (because dividends are not part of net income) but rather is closed directly to retained earnings. The ending retained earnings account will have a balance of $2,675 ($0 + $3,175 − $500). The closing process for High Tech is illustrated in Exhibit 3.15.

The post-closing trial balance for HighTech appears in Exhibit 3.16.

concept Q&A

What would happen if we didn't make closing entries?

Answer:

The closing process transfers temporary account balances (revenues, expenses, and dividends declared) to retained earnings. If the accounts were not closed, these amounts would not be properly reflected in shareholders' equity and the accounting equation wouldn't balance. In addition, the temporary accounts would accumulate amounts from different accounting periods, making it extremely difficult to determine the effect of business activities for a specific accounting period.

CORNERSTONE 3.7

▶| CORNERSTONE
VIDEO

Closing the Accounts

Information:

HighTech decided to have its first year-end occur on March 31, 2018. HighTech's adjusted general ledger at March 31, 2018, shows the balances (see Exhibit 3.13). Retained Earnings at the beginning of the year was zero.

Required:

Prepare the closing entries for HighTech at March 31, 2018.

Why:

The closing process at the end of the company's fiscal period (usually one year) is designed to transfer the balances in the temporary accounts to retained earnings and to reset the temporary accounts to a zero balance to commence the next accounting period.

Solution:

Step 1: Close Revenues to Income Summary.

Date	Account and Explanation	Debit	Credit
Mar. 31	Service Revenue	16,900	
	Income Summary		16,900
	(Close revenue accounts)		

Step 2: Close Expenses to Income Summary.

Date	Account and Explanation	Debit	Credit
Mar. 31	Income Summary	13,725	
	Supplies Expense		5,300
	Utilities Expense		5,200
	Salaries Expense		2,880
	Insurance Expense		200
	Depreciation Expense		125
	Interest Expense		20
	(Close expense accounts)		

Step 3: Close Income Summary to Retained Earnings.

Date	Account and Explanation	Debit	Credit
Mar. 31	Income Summary	3,175	
	Retained Earnings		3,175
	(Close income summary)		

Step 4: Close Dividends Declared to Retained Earnings.

Date	Account and Explanation	Debit	Credit
Mar. 31	Retained Earnings	500	
	Dividends Declared		500
	(Close dividends declared)		

(EXHIBIT 3.15)

The Closing Process

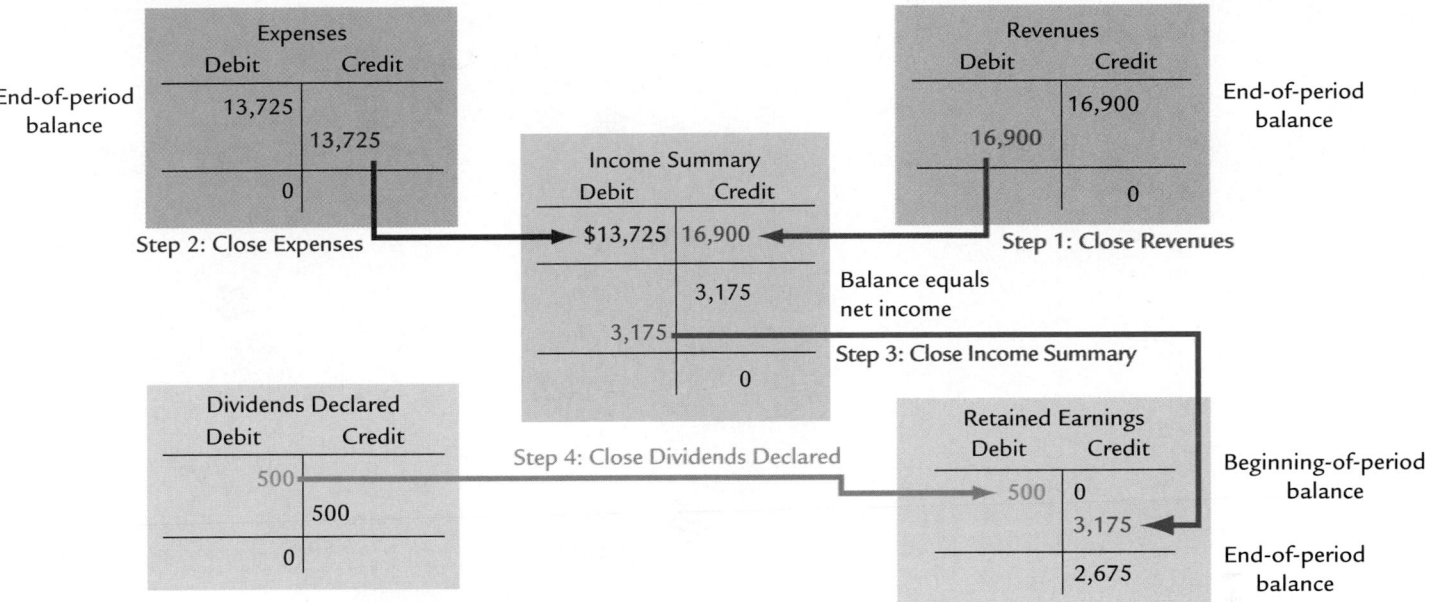

SUMMARY OF THE ACCOUNTING CYCLE

In Chapter 2, we introduced the accounting cycle as a sequence of procedures that transforms business activities into financial statements. The accounting cycle is shown in Exhibit 3.17.

Notice that the accounting cycle begins with the analysis of transactions to determine which business activities are recognized in the accounting records and their effect on the fundamental accounting equation. Those activities that meet the recognition criteria are journalized and posted to the general ledger. Steps 1 to 3 are repeated many times during an accounting period. The remaining steps (4 to 7) of the accounting cycle

OBJECTIVE **7**

Understand the steps in the accounting cycle.

(EXHIBIT 3.16)

Post-closing Trial Balance

	HighTech Communications Inc. Post-Closing Trial Balance March 31, 2018	
Account	**Debit**	**Credit**
Cash	$16,600	
Accounts Receivable	1,800	
Supplies	1,200	
Prepaid Insurance	1,000	
Equipment	4,500	
Accumulated Depreciation—Equipment		$ 125
Accounts Payable		500
Unearned Service Revenue		5,700
Interest Payable		20
Salaries Payable		1,080
Notes Payable		3,000
Common Shares		12,000
Retained Earnings		2,675
	$25,100	$25,100

(EXHIBIT 3.17)

The Accounting Cycle

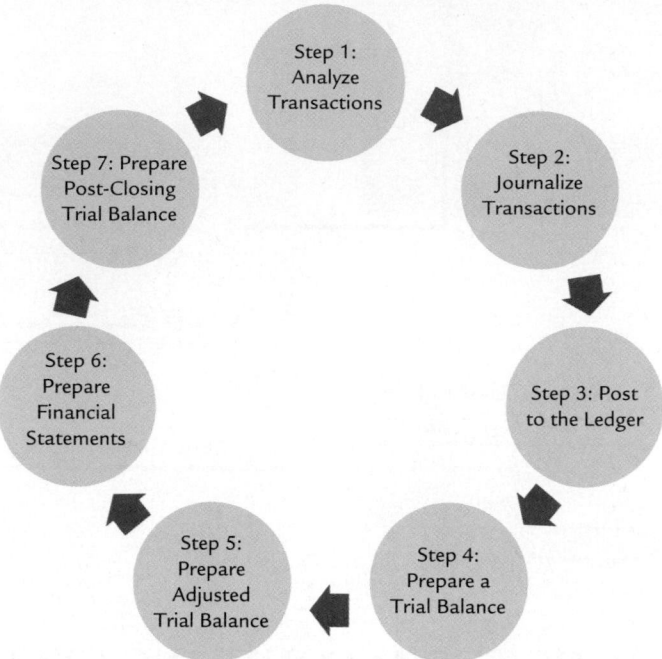

are performed only **at the end** of the accounting period. For those transactions still under way at the end of the accounting period, adjusting entries are prepared followed by an adjusted trial balance. Next, the financial statements are prepared. At year-end, the temporary accounts—revenues, expenses, and dividends declared—are closed and their balances transferred to retained earnings and a post-closing trial balance is prepared to confirm the general ledger is in balance. After year-end closing has occurred, the statement of earnings accounts have zero balances, and the statement of financial position accounts all contain the correct beginning balances for the start of the next accounting period. The accounting cycle can begin again.

SIGNIFICANT DIFFERENCES BETWEEN IFRS AND ASPE

The following significant differences exist between IFRS and ASPE:

1. IFRS 15 will introduce new revenue recognition policies for public companies effective January 1, 2018. Private companies using ASPE will assess their revenue recognition policies at that time.

2. Many public companies have elements of comprehensive income in their business operations. Under IFRS, at the end of the fiscal period, these elements of comprehensive income will be closed, not into retained earnings, but into the accumulated other comprehensive income account, which is a part of shareholders' equity. By contrast, private companies using ASPE do not report comprehensive income. Comprehensive income is discussed in Chapter 10.

3. Public and private companies usually prepare monthly financial statements for review by management. In addition, private companies often provide their bankers with internal financial statements on a monthly basis for review, and public companies must report to their shareholders on a quarterly basis. Therefore, in order

to maintain the accuracy of their accounting records on a current basis for these reasons, both public and private companies will usually record adjusting entries on a monthly basis. As a result, there are no significant differences in the timing of adjusting entry preparation for most public and private companies.

SUMMARY OF LEARNING OBJECTIVES

LO1. **Explain the difference between cash-basis and accrual-basis accounting.**

- Cash-basis and accrual-basis accounting are two alternatives for recording business activities in the accounting records. IFRS and ASPE require the use of accrual-basis accounting.
- Under cash-basis accounting, revenues and expenses are recorded when cash is received or paid, regardless of when the revenues are earned or the expenses are incurred.
- Accrual-basis accounting links income measurement to the earnings activities of a company by recognizing revenues and expenses when they occur.

LO2. **Explain how the periodicity assumption, revenue recognition principle, and matching concept affect the determination of income.**

- The revenue recognition principle under IAS 18 currently specifies five criteria to be met before revenue can be recognized. These conditions are normally met when goods have been delivered or services have been performed and cash collection is reasonably assured.
- The matching concept requires that expenses be recognized in the same period as the revenue it helped generate.
- The application of these principles results in income being measured as the business activity occurs, regardless of when cash is received or paid.

LO3. **Identify the types of transactions that may require adjustments at the end of an accounting period.**

- Many business activities do not occur at a single point in time but rather continuously over time. Because entries in the accounting system are made at particular points in time, adjustments are needed at the end of an accounting period to record the completed portion of any partially completed activities.
- Adjusting entries ensure that a company's financial statements reflect the proper amount for revenues, expenses, assets, liabilities, and shareholders' equity.
- Adjusting entries are categorized as either accruals (accrued revenues and accrued expenses) or prepayments (unearned revenues and prepaid expenses).

LO4. **Prepare adjusting entries for accruals and prepayments.**

- Accruals occur when revenues have been earned or expenses have been incurred but no cash has been received or paid.
- The adjusting entry for an accrued revenue will result in an increase to a revenue account and an increase to an asset account. The adjusting entry for an accrued expense account will result in an increase to an expense account and an increase to a liability account.
- Prepayments occur when cash has been received or paid prior to revenue being earned or the expense being incurred.
- The adjusting entry for an unearned revenue will result in an increase to a revenue account and a decrease to a liability account. The adjusting entry for a prepaid expense will result in an increase to an expense account and a decrease to an asset account.

LO5. **Prepare financial statements from an adjusted trial balance.**

- An adjusted trial balance lists all of the general ledger accounts and updates the trial balance to reflect the adjustments that have been posted.
- The adjusted trial balance is the primary source of information needed to prepare the financial statements.

- Due to the interrelation between the financial statements, the statement of earnings is prepared first, followed by the statement of retained earnings, and finally, the statement of financial position.

LO6. **Explain why and how companies prepare closing entries and understand the quality of earnings.**

- Closing entries transfer the effects of revenues, expenses, and dividends declared to the shareholders' equity account, Retained Earnings, and clear the balances in revenues, expenses, and dividends declared (reduce their balances to zero) so that they are ready to accumulate the business activities of the next accounting period.
- To close the accounts, companies make a series of journal entries, dated as of the last day of the accounting period.

LO7. **Understand the steps in the accounting cycle.**

- During the accounting period, transactions are analyzed to determine their effect on the accounting equation.
- Transactions that meet the recognition criteria are then journalized and posted to the general ledger.
- An unadjusted trial balance is prepared to summarize the effects of these transactions.
- At the end of the accounting period, adjusting entries are prepared to recognize the completed portion of any partially completed business activities and an adjusted trial balance is prepared.
- The financial statements are prepared from the adjusted trial balance and the temporary accounts are closed. A post-closing trial balance is prepared.
- The accounting cycle repeats for the next accounting period.

CORNERSTONES

CORNERSTONE 3.1	Applying the revenue recognition principle and matching concept, page 134
CORNERSTONE 3.2	Determining which transactions require adjustment, page 136
CORNERSTONE 3.3	Recording accrued revenues, page 138
CORNERSTONE 3.4	Recording accrued expenses, page 140
CORNERSTONE 3.5	Adjusting unearned revenues, page 142
CORNERSTONE 3.6	Adjusting prepaid expenses, page 144
CORNERSTONE 3.7	Closing the accounts, page 154

KEY TERMS

Accrual-basis accounting (p. 130)
Accrued expenses (p. 139)
Accrued revenues (p. 137)
Adjusted trial balance (p. 137)
Adjusting entries (p. 135)
Cash-basis accounting (p. 130)
Contra accounts (p. 145)

Depreciation (p. 145)
Periodicity assumption (p. 131)
Permanent accounts (p. 151)
Prepaid expenses (p. 143)
Revenue recognition principle (p. 131)
Temporary accounts (p. 151)
Unearned revenues (p. 141)

Chapter 3   Accrual Accounting and Financial Statements   159

REVIEW PROBLEM
I. The Adjustment Process

Concept:

Adjusting journal entries are required for continuous transactions that are partially complete at the end of an accounting period. This often requires estimates and judgments about the timing of revenue and expense recognition. Once the adjustments are made, financial statements can be prepared and the accounts are closed.

Information:

Madras Laundry has one laundry plant and uses five rented storefronts on the west side of Calgary as its retail locations. At the end of 2018, Madras had the following balances in its accounts before adjustment:

Cash	Accounts Receivable	Supplies
4,800	26,000	128,000

Land	Building	Accumulated Depreciation (Building)
124,400	249,000	36,000

Equipment	Accumulated Depreciation (Equipment)	Other Assets
122,000	24,000	16,000

Accounts Payable	Notes Payable (due 2020)	Unearned Service Revenue
8,000	120,000	12,000

Common Shares	Retained Earnings, 12/31/2017	Service Revenue
240,000	69,000	874,200

Rent Expense	Wages Expense	Insurance Expense
168,000	431,000	14,000

Salaries Expense	Interest Expense	
92,000	8,000	

An examination identified the following items that require adjustment:

a. Madras launders shirts for the service staff of a local car dealer. At the end of 2018, the car dealer owes Madras $1,040 for laundry services that have been performed but will not be billed until early in 2019.
b. Madras's supplies on hand at the end of 2018 was $21,400.
c. Madras launders uniforms for a nearby McDonald's franchise. The franchisee pays Madras in advance for the laundry service once every three months. After examining the records, Madras's accountant determines that the laundry has earned $8,400 of the $12,000 of unearned revenue.
d. Salaries in the amount of $1,500 are owed but unpaid and unrecorded.
e. Two months' interest at 8% on the note payable (due in 2020) is owed but unpaid and unrecorded.
f. Depreciation expense for the building is $12,000.
g. Depreciation expense for the equipment is $24,000.
h. Income tax expense of $5,200 is owed but unpaid and unrecorded.

NEL

Required:

1. Determine and record the adjusting entries at December 31, 2018, for Madras Laundry.
2. Post the effects of the adjustments to the proper accounts, and determine the account balances.
3. Prepare a statement of earnings, a statement of retained earnings, and a statement of financial position for Madras using the adjusted account balances.
4. Close the necessary accounts.

Solution:

1. The adjustments for Madras are as follows:

   a. The adjustment to record accrued revenue for services already provided is:

Date	Account and Explanation	Debit	Credit
Dec. 31	Accounts Receivable	1,040	
	Service Revenue		1,040
	(Recognize revenue for services performed but not billed)		

		Shareholders' Equity (Service	
Assets	= Liabilities +	Revenue)	
+1,040		+1,040	

   b. The before-adjustment balance in supplies is $128,000. Supplies actually on hand are $21,400. Supplies expense (used) is $106,600 ($128,000 − $21,400):

Date	Account and Explanation	Debit	Credit
Dec. 31	Supplies Expense	106,600	
	Supplies		106,600
	(Recognize supplies used)		

		Shareholders' Equity (Supplies	
Assets	= Liabilities +	Expense)	
−106,600		−106,600	

   c. The adjustment to record the amount of unearned revenue earned in 2018 is:

Date	Account and Explanation	Debit	Credit
Dec. 31	Unearned Service Revenue	8,400	
	Service Revenue		8,400
	(Recognize revenue earned)		

		Shareholders' Equity (Service	
Assets	= Liabilities +	Revenue)	
	−8,400	+8,400	

   d. The entry to record the accrual of salaries is:

Date	Account and Explanation	Debit	Credit
Dec. 31	Salaries Expense	1,500	
	Salaries Payable		1,500
	(Recognize salary expense incurred but not paid)		

		Shareholders' Equity (Salaries	
Assets	= Liabilities +	Expense)	
	+1,500	−1,500	

   e. Interest expense is $1,600 ($120,000 × 8% × 2/12. The entry to accrue interest expense is:

Date	Account and Explanation	Debit	Credit
Dec. 31	Interest Expense	1,600	
	Interest Payable		1,600
	(Recognize interest expense incurred but not paid)		

		Shareholders' Equity (Interest	
Assets	= Liabilities +	Expense)	
	+1,600	−1,600	

   f. The entry to record depreciation expense for the building is:

Date	Account and Explanation	Debit	Credit
Dec. 31	Depreciation Expense (Building)	12,000	
	Accumulated Depreciation (Building)		12,000
	(Record depreciation expense)		

		Shareholders' Equity (Depreciation	
Assets	= Liabilities +	Expense)	
−12,000		−12,000	

   g. The entry to record depreciation expense for the equipment is:

Date	Account and Explanation	Debit	Credit
Dec. 31	Depreciation Expense (Equipment)	24,000	
	Accumulated Depreciation (Equipment)		24,000
	(Record depreciation expense)		

		Shareholders' Equity (Depreciation	
Assets	= Liabilities +	Expense)	
−24,000		−24,000	

   h. The adjustment for income tax expense is:

Date	Account and Explanation	Debit	Credit
Dec. 31	Income Tax Expense	5,200	
	Income Tax Payable		5,200
	(Record accrual of income taxes)		

		Shareholders' Equity (Income Tax	
Assets	= Liabilities +	Expense)	
	+5,200	−5,200	

2. The adjusted account balances for Madras Laundry are shown in Exhibit 3.18.

(EXHIBIT 3.18)

Madras Laundry Adjusted Account Balances

Assets

Cash

4,800	

Accounts Receivable

26,000	
(a) 1,040	
27,040	

Supplies

128,000	106,600 (b)
21,400	

Land

124,400	

Building

249,000	

Accumulated Depreciation (Building)

	36,000
	12,000 (f)
	48,000

Equipment

122,000	

Accumulated Depreciation (Equipment)

	24,000
	24,000 (g)
	48,000

Other Assets

16,000	

Liabilities

Accounts Payable

	8,000

Notes Payable (due 2020)

	120,000

Interest Payable

	1,600 (e)
	1,600

Salaries Payable

	1,500 (d)
	1,500

Income Tax Payable

	5,200 (h)
	5,200

Unearned Service Revenue

(c) 8,400	12,000
	3,600

Shareholders' Equity

Common Shares

	240,000

Retained Earnings, 12/31/2017

	69,000

Service Revenue

	874,200
	1,040 (a)
	8,400 (c)
	883,640

Rent Expense

168,000	

Wages Expense

431,000	

Insurance Expense

14,000	

Salaries Expense

92,000	
(d) 1,500	
93,500	

Interest Expense

8,000	
(e) 1,600	
9,600	

Supplies Expense

(b) 106,600	
106,600	

Depreciation Expense (Building)

(f) 12,000	
12,000	

Depreciation Expense (Equipment)

(g) 24,000	
24,000	

Income Tax Expense

(h) 5,200	
5,200	

3. The statement of earnings, statement of retained earnings, and statement of financial position for Madras Laundry are prepared from the adjusted account balances and appear in Exhibit 3.19.

(EXHIBIT 3.19)

Financial Statements for Madras Laundry

Madras Laundry
Statement of Earnings
For the Year Ended December 31, 2018

Service Revenue		$883,640
Less Expenses:		
Wages Expense	$431,000	
Rent Expense	168,000	
Supplies Expense	106,600	
Salaries Expense	93,500	
Depreciation Expense (Equipment)	24,000	
Insurance Expense	14,000	
Depreciation Expense (Building)	12,000	
Interest Expense	9,600	
Income Tax Expense	5,200	863,900
Net Income		$ 19,740

Madras Laundry
Statement of Retained Earnings
For the Year Ended December 31, 2018

Balance, 12/31/2017	$69,000
Add: Net Income	19,740
	88,740
Less: Dividends Declared	0
Balance, 12/31/2018	$88,740

Madras Laundry
Statement of Financial Position
December 31, 2018

ASSETS

Current Assets:			
Cash		$ 4,800	
Accounts Receivable		27,040	
Supplies		21,400	
Total Current Assets			$ 53,240
Property, Plant, and Equipment:			
Land		124,400	
Building	$249,000		
Less: Accumulated Depreciation	(48,000)	201,000	
Equipment	122,000		
Less: Accumulated Depreciation	(48,000)	74,000	
Total Property, Plant, and Equipment			399,400
Other Assets			16,000
Total Assets			$468,640

LIABILITIES AND SHAREHOLDERS' EQUITY		
Current Liabilities:		
Accounts Payable	$ 8,000	
Salaries Payable	1,500	
Interest Payable	1,600	
Income Tax Payable	5,200	
Unearned Service Revenue	3,600	
Total Current Liabilities		$ 19,900
Long-Term Liabilities:		
Notes Payable (due 2020)		120,000
Total Liabilities		139,900
Shareholders' Equity:		
Common Shares	240,000	
Retained Earnings	88,740	
Total Shareholders' Equity		328,740
Total Liabilities and Shareholders' Equity		$468,640

4. The entries to close the accounts are:

Date	Account and Explanation	Debit	Credit
Dec. 31	Service Revenue	883,640	
	Income Summary		883,640
	(Close revenues)		
Dec. 31	Income Summary	863,900	
	Rent Expense		168,000
	Wages Expense		431,000
	Insurance Expense		14,000
	Salaries Expense		93,500
	Supplies Expense		106,600
	Depreciation Expense (Building)		12,000
	Depreciation Expense (Equipment)		24,000
	Interest Expense		9,600
	Income Tax Expense		5,200
	(Close expenses)		
Dec. 31	Income Summary	19,740	
	Retained Earnings		19,740
	(Close income summary)		

DISCUSSION QUESTIONS

1. How does accrual-basis net income differ from cash-basis net income?

2. Explain when revenue may be recognized and give an example.

3. What happens during the accounting cycle?

4. Provide two examples of transactions that begin and end at a particular point in time and two examples of continuous transactions.

5. Why are adjusting entries needed?

6. What accounting concepts require that adjusting entries be employed?

7. Describe the recording of transactions that begin and end at a particular point in time and the recording of continuous transactions.

8. For each of the four categories of adjusting entries, describe the business activity that produces circumstances requiring adjustment.

9. What is the difference between an *accrual* and a *prepayment*?

10. Which type of adjustment will (a) increase both assets and revenues, (b) increase revenues and decrease liabilities, (c) increase expenses and decrease assets, and (d) increase both expenses and liabilities?

11. How is the amount for an interest expense (or interest revenue) adjustment determined?

12. Describe the effect on the financial statements when an adjustment is prepared that records (a) unrecorded revenue and (b) unrecorded expense.

13. On the basis of what you have learned about adjustments, why do you think that adjusting entries are made on the last day of the accounting period rather than at several times during the accounting period?

14. What is the purpose of closing entries?

15. Describe the four steps in the closing process.

16. Identify each of the following categories of accounts as temporary or permanent: assets, liabilities, equity, revenues, expenses, dividends declared. How is the distinction between temporary and permanent accounts related to the closing process?

17. Why are only the statement of financial position accounts permanent?

18. List the seven steps in the accounting cycle in the order in which they occur and explain what occurs at each step of the accounting cycle.

MULTIPLE-CHOICE EXERCISES

3-1 Which of the following statements is true?
  a. Under cash-basis accounting, revenues are recorded when earned and expenses are recorded when incurred.
  b. Accrual-basis accounting records both cash and noncash transactions when they occur.
  c. IFRS/ASPE requires companies to use cash-basis accounting.
  d. The key elements of accrual-basis accounting are the revenue recognition principle, the periodicity assumption, the matching concept, and the historical cost principle.

3-2 In December 2018, Liang Ltd. receives a cash payment of $3,000 for services performed in December 2018 and a cash payment of $4,000 for services to be performed in January 2019. Liang also receives the December utility bill for $500 but does not pay this bill until 2019. For December 2018, under the accrual basis of accounting, Liang would recognize:
  a. $7,000 of revenue and $500 of expense.
  b. $7,000 of revenue and $0 of expense.
  c. $3,000 of revenue and $500 of expense.
  d. $3,000 of revenue and $0 of expense.

3-3 Which transaction would require adjustment at December 31?
  a. The sale of merchandise for cash on December 30
  b. Common shares issued on November 30
  c. Salaries paid to employees on December 31 for work performed in December
  d. A one-year insurance policy (which took effect immediately) purchased on December 1

3-4 Which of the following statements is false?
  a. Adjusting entries are necessary because timing differences exist between when a revenue or expense is recognized and cash is received or paid.
  b. Adjusting entries always affect at least one revenue or expense account and one asset or liability account.

c. The cash account will always be affected by adjusting journal entries.

d. Adjusting entries can be classified as either accruals or prepayments.

3-5 Aylmer Company loaned $10,000 to Pembroke Company on December 1, 2018. Pembroke will pay Aylmer $600 of interest ($50 per month) on November 30, 2019. Aylmer's adjusting entry at December 31, 2018, is:

a. Interest Expense 50
   Cash 50

b. Cash 50
   Interest Revenue 50

c. Interest Receivable 50
   Interest Revenue 50

d. No adjusting entry is required.

3-6 Ivan's Diner received the following bills for December 2018 utilities:

- Electricity: $850 on December 29, 2018
- Telephone: $475 on January 5, 2019

Both bills were paid on January 10, 2019. On the December 31, 2018, statement of financial position, Ivan's Diner will report accrued expenses of:

a. $0
b. $475
c. $850
d. $1,325

3-7 In September 2018, *GolfWorld Magazine* obtained $12,000 of subscriptions for one year of magazines and credited Unearned Sales Revenue. The magazines will begin to be delivered in October 2018. At December 31, 2018, *GolfWorld* should make the following adjustment:

a. Debit Sales Revenue by $3,000 and credit Unearned Sales Revenue by $3,000.

b. Debit Unearned Sales Revenue by $3,000 and credit Sales Revenue by $3,000.

c. Debit Sales Revenue by $9,000 and credit Unearned Sales Revenue by $9,000.

d. Debit Unearned Sales Revenue by $9,000 and credit Sales Revenue by $9,000.

3-8 Hurd Inc. prepays rent every three months on March 1, June 1, September 1, and December 1. Rent for the three

months totals $3,600. On December 31, 2018, Hurd will report Prepaid Rent of:

a. $0
b. $1,200
c. $2,400
d. $3,600

3-9 Which of the following statements is incorrect regarding preparing financial statements?

a. The adjusted trial balance lists only the statement of financial position accounts in a "debit" and "credit" format.

b. The adjusted trial balance is the primary source of information needed to prepare the financial statements.

c. The financial statements are prepared in the following order: (1) the statement of earnings, (2) the statement of retained earnings, (3) the statement of financial position.

d. The statement of earnings and the statement of financial position are related through the retained earnings account.

3-10 Reinhardt Company reported revenues of $122,000 and expenses of $83,000 on its 2018 statement of earnings. In addition, Reinhardt declared $4,000 of dividends during 2018. On December 31, 2018, Reinhardt prepared closing entries. The net effect of the closing entries on retained earnings was a(n):

a. decrease of $4,000.
b. increase of $35,000.
c. increase of $39,000.
d. decrease of $87,000.

3-11 Which of the following is true regarding the accounting cycle?

a. The accounts are adjusted after preparing the financial statements.

b. Journal entries are made prior to the transaction being analyzed.

c. The temporary accounts are closed after the financial statements are prepared.

d. An adjusted trial balance is usually prepared after the accounts are closed.

3-12 It is November 28 and XYZ Ltd. notices that the roof in its warehouse has a major leak. XYZ calls Jim at Jim's All-Purpose Roofing Ltd.(JAPRL) to come out and assess the damage. Jim says it will cost $5,000 to repair the leak, of

which a $1,000 deposit is due today on signing of the work order agreement; the remaining $4,000 is due when the work is complete. Jim says the work will be completed by December 3. JAPRL's year-end is November 30.
Select the correct entry to be recorded by JAPRL below, assuming the company uses accrual accounting:
a. Record nothing until the roof is repaired on December 3.

b. Record the full $5,000 as a credit to roof repair revenue and debit cash for the same amount at the time of signing the agreement on November 28.
c. Record $1,000 on November 28 as a credit to unearned roof repair revenue and debit to cash $1,000.
d. Record $5,000 on November 28 as a credit to unearned roof repair revenue and a debit to cash of $5,000.

CORNERSTONE EXERCISES

Cornerstone Exercise 3-13   Accrual- and Cash-Basis Revenue

Magnani Music sells used CDs for $2.00 each. During the month of April, Magnani sold 8,750 CDs for cash and 15,310 CDs on credit. Magnani's cash collections in April included the $17,500 for the CDs sold for cash, $10,300 for CDs sold on credit during the previous month, and $9,850 for CDs sold on credit during April.

Required:

Calculate the amount of revenue recognized in April under (a) the cash basis of accounting and (b) the accrual basis of accounting.

Cornerstone Exercise 3-14   Accrual- and Cash-Basis Expenses

Speedy Delivery Company provides next-day delivery across Eastern Canada. During May, Speedy incurred $132,600 in fuel costs. Speedy paid $95,450 of the fuel cost in May, with the remainder paid in June. In addition, Speedy paid $15,000 in May to another fuel supplier in an effort to build up its supply of fuel.

Required:

Calculate the amount of expense recognized in May under (a) the cash basis of accounting and (b) the accrual basis of accounting.

Cornerstone Exercise 3-15   Revenue and the Revenue Recognition Principle

Heartstrings Gift Shoppe sells an assortment of gifts for any occasion. During October, Heartstrings started a Gift-of-the-Month program. Under the terms of this program, beginning in the month of the sale, Heartstrings would select and deliver a random gift each month, over the next 12 months, to the person the customer selects as a recipient. During October, Heartstrings sold 25 of these packages for a total of $11,280 in cash.

Required:

For the month of October, calculate the amount of revenue that Heartstrings will recognize.

OBJECTIVE 2
CORNERSTONE 3.1

Cornerstone Exercise 3-16   Expenses and the Matching Concept

The following information describes transactions for Morgenstern Advertising Company during July:

a. On July 5, Morgenstern purchased and received $24,300 of supplies on credit from Drexel Supply Ltd. During July, Morgenstern paid $20,500 cash to Drexel and used $18,450 of the supplies.

b. Morgenstern paid $9,600 to salespeople for salaries earned during July. An additional $1,610 was owed to salespeople at July 31 for salaries earned during the month.

c. Morgenstern paid $2,950 to the local utility company for electric service. Electric service in July was $2,300 of the $2,950 total bill.

Required:

Calculate the amount of expense recognized in July under (a) the cash basis of accounting and (b) the accrual basis of accounting.

Cornerstone Exercise 3-17 Identification of Adjusting Entries

OBJECTIVE ③
CORNERSTONE 3.2

Sayed Inc. uses the accrual basis of accounting and had the following transactions during the year:

a. Sold merchandise to customers on credit.
b. Purchased equipment to be used in the operation of its business.
c. Purchased a two-year insurance contract.
d. Received cash for services to be performed over the next year.
e. Paid monthly employee salaries.
f. Borrowed money from First Bank by signing a note payable due in five years.

Required:

Identify and explain why each transaction may or may not require adjustment.

Cornerstone Exercise 3-18 Accrued Revenue Adjusting Entries

OBJECTIVE ④
CORNERSTONE 3.3

Powers Rental Service had the following items that require adjustment at year-end.

a. Revenue of $9,880 from the rental of equipment was earned but the customer had not yet paid.
b. Interest of $650 on a note receivable has been earned but not yet received.

Required:

1. Prepare the adjusting entries needed at December 31.
2. What is the effect on the financial statements if these adjusting entries are not made?

Cornerstone Exercise 3-19 Accrued Expense Adjusting Entries

OBJECTIVE ④
CORNERSTONE 3.4

Moreau Manufacturing Ltd. had the following items that require adjustment at year-end.

a. Salaries of $4,980 that were earned in December are unrecorded and unpaid.
b. Used $2,430 of utilities in December, which are unrecorded and unpaid.
c. Interest of $1,575 on a note payable has not been recorded or paid.

Required:

1. Prepare the adjusting entries needed at December 31.
2. What is the effect on the financial statements if these adjusting entries are not made?

Cornerstone Exercise 3-20 Unearned Revenue Adjusting Entries

OBJECTIVE ④
CORNERSTONE 3.5

Olney Cleaning Company had the following items that require adjustment at year-end:

a. For one cleaning contract, $10,500 cash was received in advance. The cash was credited to unearned revenue upon receipt. At year-end, $1,250 of the service revenue was still unearned.
b. For another cleaning contract, $8,300 cash was received in advance and credited to unearned revenue upon receipt. At year-end, $2,700 of the services had been provided.

Required:

1. Prepare the adjusting journal entries needed at December 31.

(Continued)

2. What is the effect on the financial statements if these adjusting entries are not made?
3. What is the balance in unearned revenue at December 31 related to the two cleaning contracts?

OBJECTIVE ④
CORNERSTONE 3.6

Cornerstone Exercise 3.21   Prepaid Expense Adjusting Entries

Best Company had the following items that require adjustment at year-end:

a. Cash for equipment rental in the amount of $3,800 was paid in advance. The $3,800 was debited to prepaid rent when paid. At year-end, $2,950 of the prepaid rent had been used.
b. Cash for insurance in the amount of $8,200 was paid in advance. The $8,200 was debited to prepaid insurance when paid. At year-end, $1,850 of the prepaid insurance was still unused.

Required:

1. Prepare the adjusting journal entries needed at December 31.
2. What is the effect on the financial statements if these adjusting entries are not made?
3. What is the balance in prepaid rent and insurance expense at December 31 (assume this is the first insurance policy the company ever took out)?

OBJECTIVE ④
CORNERSTONE 3.6

Cornerstone Exercise 3-22   Adjustment for Supplies

Pain-Free Dental Group Inc. purchased dental supplies of $12,800 during the year. At the end of the year, a physical count of supplies showed $1,475 of supplies on hand.

Required:

1. Prepare the adjusting entry needed at the end of the year.
2. What is the amount of supplies reported on Pain-Free's statement of financial position at the end of the year?

OBJECTIVE ④
CORNERSTONE 3.6

Cornerstone Exercise 3-23   Adjustment for Depreciation

LaGarde Company has a machine that it purchased for $125,000 on January 1. Annual depreciation on the machine is estimated to be $14,500.

Required:

1. Prepare the adjusting entry needed at the end of the year.
2. What is the net book value of the machine reported on LaGarde's statement of financial position at the end of the year?

OBJECTIVE ④
CORNERSTONE 3.3
CORNERSTONE 3.4
CORNERSTONE 3.5
CORNERSTONE 3.6

Cornerstone Exercise 3-24   Financial Statement Effects of Adjusting Entries

When adjusting entries were made at the end of the year, the accountant for Park Company did not make the following adjustments.

a. $2,900 of wages had been earned by employees but were unpaid.
b. $3,750 of revenue had been earned but was uncollected and unrecorded.
c. $2,400 of revenue had been earned. The customer had prepaid for this service and the amount was originally recorded in the Unearned Sales Revenue account.
d. $1,200 of insurance coverage had expired. Insurance had been initially recorded in the Prepaid Insurance account.

Required:

Identify the effect on the financial statements of the adjusting entries that were omitted.

Use the following information for Cornerstone **Exercises 3-25** through **3-28**: Sparrow Company had the following adjusted trial balance at December 31, 2018.

Sparrow Company
Adjusted Trial Balance
December 31, 2018

	Debit	Credit
Cash	$ 3,150	
Accounts Receivable	5,650	
Prepaid Insurance	4,480	
Equipment	42,000	
Accumulated Depreciation, Equipment		$ 24,000
Accounts Payable		2,800
Salaries Payable		4,450
Unearned Service Revenue		3,875
Common Shares		8,000
Retained Earnings		2,255
Dividends Declared	10,500	
Service Revenue		99,600
Salaries Expense	49,400	
Rent Expense	17,250	
Insurance Expense	2,200	
Depreciation Expense	4,950	
Income Tax Expense	5,400	
Total	144,980	144,980

Cornerstone Exercise 3-25 Preparing a Statement of Earnings

Refer to the information for Sparrow Company above.

OBJECTIVE 5
CORNERSTONE 1.3

Required:

Prepare a single-step statement of earnings for Sparrow for 2018.

Cornerstone Exercise 3-26 Preparing a Statement of Retained Earnings

Refer to the information for Sparrow Company above.

OBJECTIVE 5
CORNERSTONE 1.4

Required:

Prepare a statement of retained earnings for Sparrow for 2018.

Cornerstone Exercise 3-27 Preparing a Statement of Financial Position

Refer to the information for Sparrow Company above.

OBJECTIVE 5
CORNERSTONE 1.2

Required:

Prepare a classified statement of financial position for Sparrow at December 31, 2018.

Cornerstone Exercise 3-28 Preparing and Analyzing Closing Entries

Refer to the information for Sparrow Company above.

OBJECTIVE 5
CORNERSTONE 3.7

Required:

1. Prepare the closing entries for Sparrow at December 31, 2018.
2. How does the closing process affect retained earnings?

BRIEF EXERCISES

Brief Exercise 3-29 Accrual- and Cash-Basis Accounting

The following are several transactions for Halpin Advertising Company.

OBJECTIVE 1

(Continued)

a. Purchased $1,000 of supplies.
b. Sold $5,000 of advertising services, on account, to customers.
c. Used $250 of supplies.
d. Collected $3,000 from customers in payment of their accounts.
e. Purchased equipment for $10,000 cash.
f. Recorded $500 depreciation on the equipment for the current period.

Required:

Identify the effect, if any, that each of the above transactions would have on net income under cash-basis accounting and accrual-basis accounting.

OBJECTIVE ❷

Brief Exercise 3-30 Revenue and Expense Recognition

Lauhl Corporation provides janitorial services to several office buildings. During April, Lauhl engaged in the following transactions:

a. On April 1, Lauhl received $24,000 from Metro Corporation to provide cleaning services over the next six months.
b. On April 5, Lauhl purchased and received $8,500 of supplies on credit from Eagle Supply Company. During the month, Lauhl paid $5,000 to Eagle and used $1,300 of the supplies.
c. On April 20, Lauhl performed one-time cleaning services of $2,500 for Jones Company. Jones paid Lauhl the full amount on May 10.
d. On April 30, Lauhl paid employees wages of $3,400. An additional $850 was owed to employees for work performed in April.

Required:

Calculate the amount of net income that Lauhl should recognize in April under (1) cash-basis accounting and (2) accrual-basis accounting.

OBJECTIVE ❸

Brief Exercise 3-31 Identification of Adjusting Entries

Examine the following accounts:

a. Prepaid Insurance
b. Inventory
c. Interest Payable
d. Unearned Service Revenue
e. Accumulated Depreciation

Required:

CONCEPTUAL CONNECTION Identify and explain why each account may or may not require adjustment.

OBJECTIVE ❹

Brief Exercise 3-32 Adjusting Entries—Accruals

Nichols Company had the following items that required adjustment at December 31, 2018.

a. Electricity used during December was estimated to be $320. This amount will be paid in January.
b. Owed wages to employees of $3,250 that were earned in December but unrecorded and unpaid as of the end of the year.
c. Service revenue of $4,900 was earned in December but unbilled and unpaid as of year-end.

Required:

1. Prepare the adjusting entries needed at December 31.
2. **CONCEPTUAL CONNECTION** What is the effect on the financial statements if these adjusting entries were not made?

Brief Exercise 3-33   Adjusting Entries—Prepayments

OBJECTIVE 4

Tyndal Company had the following items that required adjustment at December 31, 2018.

a. Purchased equipment for $40,000 on January 1, 2018. Tyndal estimates annual depreciation expense to be $3,100.

b. Paid $2,400 for a two-year insurance policy on July 1, 2018. The amount was debited to Prepaid Insurance when paid.

c. Collected $1,200 rent for the period December 1, 2018, to March 30, 2019. The amount was credited to Unearned Service Revenue when received.

Required:

1. Prepare the adjusting entries needed at December 31.
2. **CONCEPTUAL CONNECTION** What is the effect on the financial statements if these adjusting entries were not made?

Brief Exercise 3-34   Preparing a Statement of Earnings

OBJECTIVE 5

The adjusted trial balance of Pelton Company at December 31, 2018, includes the following accounts:

- Wages Expense, $22,400
- Service Revenue, $38,400
- Rent Expense, $3,200
- Dividends, $4,000
- Retained Earnings, $12,200
- Prepaid Rent, $1,000

Required:

Prepare a single-step statement of earnings for Pelton for 2018.

Brief Exercise 3-35   Preparing a Statement of Retained Earnings

OBJECTIVE 5

Refer to the information presented in Brief Exercise 3-34 for Pelton Company. The balance in Retained Earnings of $12,200 represents the balance as of January 1, 2018.

Required:

Prepare a statement of retained earnings for Pelton for 2018.

Brief Exercise 3-36   Classifying Statement of Financial Position Items

OBJECTIVE 5

A classified statement of financial position contains the following categories:

- Current assets
- Long-term investments
- Property, plant, and equipment
- Intangible assets
- Other assets
- Current liabilities
- Long-term liabilities
- Shareholders' equity

Required:

For each of the following accounts, list the correct balance sheet category where the item would typically appear.

a. Notes Payable (due in five years)
b. Accounts Receivable

(Continued)

c. Patent
d. Prepaid Rent
e. Accumulated Depreciation
f. Common Shares
g. Accounts Payable
h. Cash
i. Unearned Service Revenue
j. Equipment

OBJECTIVE ⑥   **Brief Exercise 3-37   Preparing and Analyzing Closing Entries**

At December 31, 2018, the ledger of Aulani Company includes the following accounts, all having normal balances:

- Sales Revenue, $59,000
- Cost of Goods Sold, $31,000
- Retained Earnings, $20,000
- Interest Expense, $3,200
- Dividends, $5,000
- Wages Expense $8,000
- Interest Payable, $2,100

Required:

1. Prepare the closing entries for Aulani at December 31, 2018.
2. How does the closing process affect Aulani's retained earnings?

OBJECTIVE ⑦   **Brief Exercise 3-38   The Accounting Cycle**

Below are the steps of the accounting cycle:
    Journalize transaction. Analyze transaction. Close the accounts. Prepare financial statements. Adjust the account. Post to the ledger. Prepare a trial balance. Prepare adjusted trial balance.

Required:

List these steps of the accounting cycle in their proper order.

EXERCISES

OBJECTIVE ①   **Exercise 3-39   Accrual- and Cash-Basis Expense Recognition**

The following information is taken from the accrual accounting records of Kroger Sales Company:

a. During January, Kroger paid $9,150 for supplies to be used in sales to customers during the next two months (February and March). The supplies will be used evenly over the next two months.
b. Kroger pays its employees at the end of each month for salaries earned during that month. Salaries paid at the end of February and March amounted to $4,925 and $5,100, respectively.
c. Kroger placed an advertisement in the local newspaper during March at a cost of $850. The ad promoted the pre-spring sale during the last week in March. Kroger did not pay for the newspaper ad until mid-April.

Required:

1. Under cash-basis accounting, how much expense should Kroger report for February and March?
2. Under accrual-basis accounting, how much expense should Kroger report for February and March?
3. **CONCEPTUAL CONNECTION** Which basis of accounting provides the most useful information for decision makers? Why?

Exercise 3-40 Revenue Recognition

OBJECTIVE 2

Each of the following situations relates to the recognition of revenue:

a. A store sells a gift card in December that will be given as a Christmas present. The card is not redeemed until January.
b. A furniture store sells and delivers furniture to a customer in June with no payments and no interest for six months.
c. An airline sells an airline ticket and collects the fare in February for a flight in March to a spring break destination.
d. A theme park sells a season pass that allows entrance into the park for an entire year, collecting the cash in January.
e. A package delivery service delivers a package in October but doesn't bill the customer and receive payment until November.

Required:

For each situation, indicate when the company should recognize revenue.

YOUDECIDE

Exercise 3-41 Revenue and Expense Recognition

OBJECTIVE 2

Electronic Repair Company repaired a high-definition television for Sarah Markov in December 2018. Sarah paid $80 at the time of the repair and agreed to pay Electronic Repair $80 each month for five months beginning on January 15, 2019. Electronic Repair used $120 of supplies, which were purchased in November 2018, to repair the television.

Required:

1. In what month or months should revenue from this service be recorded by Electronic Repair?
2. In what month or months should the expense related to the repair of the television be recorded by Electronic Repair?
3. **CONCEPTUAL CONNECTION** Describe the accounting principles used to answer the above questions.

Exercise 3-42 Cash-Basis and Accrual-Basis Accounting

OBJECTIVE 2

The records of Summers Building Company reveal the following information for 2018.

a. Cash receipts during 2018 (including $50,000 paid by shareholders in exchange for common shares) were $273,500.
b. Cash payments during 2018 (including $8,000 of dividends declared and paid to shareholders) were $164,850.
c. Total selling price of services billed to customers during 2018 was $201,700.
d. Salaries earned by employees during 2018 were $114,250.
e. Cost of supplies used during 2018 in operation of the business was $47,325.

Required:

1. Calculate Summers Building's net income for 2018 on an accrual basis.
2. Calculate Summers Building's net income for 2018 on a cash basis.
3. **CONCEPTUAL CONNECTION** Explain how the cash basis of accounting allows for the manipulation of income.

Exercise 3-43 Revenue Recognition and Matching

OBJECTIVE 2

Omega Transportation Inc., headquartered in Saint John, New Brunswick, uses the accrual basis of accounting and engaged in the following transactions:

(Continued)

- billed customers $2,415,250 for transportation services
- collected cash from customers in the amount of $1,381,975
- purchased fuel supplies for $1,333,800 cash
- used fuel supplies that cost $1,303,490
- employees earned salaries of $291,500
- paid employees $280,300 cash for salaries

Required:

Determine the amount of sales revenue and total expenses for Omega's statement of earnings.

OBJECTIVE

Exercise 3-44   Recognizing Expenses

Troika Dental Services gives each of its patients a toothbrush with the name and phone number of the dental office and a logo imprinted on the brush. Troika purchased 15,000 of the toothbrushes in October 2018 for $3,130. The toothbrushes were delivered in November and paid for in December 2018. Troika began to give the patients the toothbrushes in February 2019. By the end of 2019, 4,500 of the toothbrushes remained in the supplies account.

Required:

1. How much expense should be recorded for the 15,000 toothbrushes in 2018 and 2019 to properly match expenses with revenues?
2. Describe how the 4,500 toothbrushes that remain in the supplies account will be handled in 2020.

OBJECTIVE

Exercise 3-45   Revenue Recognition and Matching

Carrico Advertising Inc. performs advertising services for several public companies. The following information describes Carrico's activities during 2018.

a. At the beginning of 2018, customers owed Carrico $45,800 for advertising services performed during 2017. During 2018, Carrico performed an additional $695,100 of advertising services on account. Carrico collected $708,700 cash from customers during 2018.

b. At the beginning of 2018, Carrico had $13,350 of supplies on hand for which it owed suppliers $8,150. During 2018, Carrico purchased an additional $14,600 of supplies on account. Carrico also paid $19,300 cash owed to suppliers for goods previously purchased on credit. Carrico had $2,230 of supplies on hand at the end of 2018.

c. Carrico's 2018 operating and interest expenses were $437,600 and $133,400, respectively.

Required:

1. Calculate Carrico's 2018 income before taxes.
2. Calculate the amount of Carrico's accounts receivable, supplies, and accounts payable at December 31, 2018.
3. **CONCEPTUAL CONNECTION** Explain the underlying principles behind why the three accounts computed in part 2 exist.

OBJECTIVE

Exercise 3-46   Identification of Adjusting Entries

Conklin Services prepares financial statements only once per year using an annual accounting period ending on December 31. Each of the following statements describes an entry made by Conklin on December 31 of a recent year.

a. On December 31, Conklin completed a service agreement for Pizza Planet and recorded the related revenue. The job started in August.

b. Conklin provides weekly service visits to the local C.J. Nickel department store to check and maintain various pieces of computer printing equipment. On December 31, Conklin recorded revenue for the visits completed during December. The cash will not be received until January.

c. Conklin's salaried employees are paid on the last day of every month. On December 31, Conklin recorded the payment of December salaries.

d. Conklin's hourly wage employees are paid every Friday. On December 31, Conklin recorded as payable the wages for the first three working days of the week in which the year ended.

e. On December 31, Conklin recorded the receipt of a shipment of office supplies from Office Supplies Inc. to be paid for in January.

f. On December 31, Conklin recorded the estimated use of supplies for the year. The supplies were purchased for cash earlier in the year.

g. Early in December, Conklin was paid in advance by Perez Enterprises for two months of weekly service visits. Conklin recorded the advance payment as a liability. On December 31, Conklin recorded revenue for the service visits to Perez Enterprises that were completed during December.

h. On December 31, Conklin recorded depreciation expense on office equipment for the year.

Required:

Indicate whether each entry is an adjusting entry or a regular journal entry, and if it is an adjusting entry, identify it as one of the following types: (1) revenue recognized before collection, (2) expense recognized before payment, (3) revenue recognized after collection, or (4) expense recognized after payment.

Exercise 3-47   Identification and Analysis of Adjusting Entries

OBJECTIVE 3

Medina Motor Service is preparing adjusting entries for the year ended December 31, 2018. The following items describe Medina's continuous transactions during 2018:

a. Medina's salaried employees are paid on the last day of every month.

b. Medina's hourly employees are paid every other Friday for the preceding two weeks' work. The next payday falls on January 5, 2019.

c. In November 2018, Medina borrowed $600,000 from Bank One, giving a 9% note payable with interest due in January 2019. The note was properly recorded.

d. Medina rents a portion of its parking lot to the neighbouring business under a long-term lease agreement that requires payment of rent six months in advance on April 1 and October 1 of each year. The October 1, 2018 rental payment was received and recorded as prepaid rent.

e. Medina's service department recognizes the entire revenue on every auto service job when the job is complete. At December 31, several service jobs are in process.

f. Medina recognizes depreciation on shop equipment annually at the end of each year.

g. Medina purchases all of its office supplies from Office Supplies Ltd. All purchases are recorded in the supplies account. Supplies expense is calculated and recorded annually at the end of each year.

Required:

Indicate whether or not each item requires an adjusting entry at December 31, 2018. If an item requires an adjusting entry, indicate which accounts are increased by the adjustment and which are decreased.

Exercise 3-48   Revenue Adjustments

OBJECTIVE 4

Sentry Transport Inc. of Regina provides in-town parcel delivery services in addition to a full range of passenger services. Sentry engaged in the following activities during the current year:

a. Sentry received $3,500 cash in advance from Rich's Department Store for an estimated 175 deliveries during December 2018 and January and February of 2019. The entire amount was recorded as unearned revenue when received. During December 2018, 60 deliveries were made for Rich's.

b. Sentry operates several small buses that take commuters from suburban communities to the central downtown area of Regina. The commuters purchase, in advance, tickets for 50 one-way

(Continued)

trips. Each 50-ride ticket costs $500. At the time of purchase, Sentry credits the cash received to unearned revenue. At year-end, Sentry estimates that revenue from 9,750 one-way rides has been earned.

c.   Sentry operates several buses that provide transportation for the clients of a social service agency in Regina. Sentry bills the agency quarterly at the end of January, April, July, and October for the service performed that quarter. The contract price is $9,000 per quarter. Sentry follows the practice of recognizing revenue from this contract in the period in which the service is performed.

d.   On December 23, WestJet Airlines chartered a bus to transport its marketing group to a meeting at a resort in Alberta. The meeting will be held during the last week in January 2019, and WestJet agrees to pay for the entire trip on the day the bus departs. At year-end, none of these arrangements have been recorded by Sentry.

Required:

1.   Prepare adjusting entries at December 31 for these four activities.

YOUDECIDE

2.   What would be the effect on revenue if the adjusting entries were not made?

OBJECTIVE ❹

Exercise 3-49   Expense Adjustments

Faraday Electronic Service repairs stereos and DVD players. During a recent year, Faraday engaged in the following activities:

a.   On September 1, Faraday paid Wausau Insurance $4,860 for its liability insurance for the next 12 months. The full amount of the prepayment was debited to prepaid insurance.

b.   At December 31, Faraday estimates that $1,520 of utility costs are unrecorded and unpaid.

c.   Faraday rents its testing equipment from JVC. Equipment rent in the amount of $1,440 is unpaid and unrecorded at December 31.

d.   In late October, Faraday agreed to become the sponsor for the sports segment of the evening news program on a local television station. The station billed Faraday $4,350 for three months' sponsorship—November 2018, December 2018, and January 2019—in advance. When these payments were made, Faraday debited prepaid advertising. At December 31, two months' advertising has been used and one month remains unused.

Required:

1.   Prepare adjusting entries at December 31 for these four activities.

YOUDECIDE

2.   What would be the effect on expenses if the adjusting entries were not made?

OBJECTIVE ❹

Exercise 3-50   Prepayments, Collections in Advance

Genstar Properties Inc. owns a building in which it leases office space to small businesses and professionals. During 2018, Genstar Properties engaged in the following transactions:

a.   On March 1, Genstar Properties paid $10,500 in advance to Patna Insurance Company for one year of insurance beginning March 1, 2018. The full amount of the prepayment was debited to prepaid insurance.

b.   On May 1, Genstar Properties received $30,000 for one year's rent from Angela Cottrell, a lawyer and new tenant. Genstar Properties credited unearned rent revenue for the full amount collected from Cottrell.

c.   On July 31, Genstar Properties received $240,000 for six months' rent on an office building that is occupied by Newnan and Chang, a regional accounting firm. The rental period begins on August 1, 2018. The full amount received was credited to unearned rent revenue.

d.   On November 1, Genstar Properties paid $4,500 to Abbey Security for three months' security services beginning on that date. The entire amount was debited to prepaid security services.

Required:

1.   Prepare the journal entry to record the receipt or payment of cash for each of the transactions.

2. Prepare the adjusting entries you would make at December 31, 2018, for each of these items.
3. What would be the total effect on the statement of earnings and statement of financial position if these entries were not recorded?

YOUDECIDE

Exercise 3-51   Prepayment of Expenses

OBJECTIVE 4

JDM Inc. made the following prepayments for expense items during 2018:

a. Prepaid building rent for one year on April 1 by paying $6,600. Prepaid rent was debited for the amount paid.
b. Prepaid twelve months' insurance on October 1 by paying $4,200. Prepaid insurance was debited.
c. Purchased $5,250 of office supplies on October 15, debiting supplies for the full amount. Office supplies costing $1,085 remain unused at December 31, 2018.
d. Paid $600 for a 12-month service contract for repairs and maintenance on a computer. The contract begins November 1. The full amount of the payment was debited to prepaid repairs and maintenance.

Required:

1. Prepare journal entries to record the payment of cash for each transaction.
2. Prepare adjusting entries for the prepayments at December 31, 2018.
3. For all of the above items, assume that the accountant failed to make the adjusting entries. What would be the effect on net income?

YOUDECIDE

Exercise 3-52   Adjustment for Supplies

OBJECTIVE 4

The downtown location of Montreal Clothiers purchases large quantities of supplies, including plastic garment bags, paper bags, and boxes. At December 31, 2018, the following information is available concerning these supplies:

ILLUSTRATING
RELATIONSHIPS

Supplies, 1/1/2018	$ 4,150
Supplies, 12/31/2018	5,220
Supplies purchased for cash during 2018	12,690

All purchases of supplies during the year are debited to the supplies account.

Required:

1. What is the expense reported on the statement of earnings associated with the use of supplies during 2018?
2. What is the proper adjusting entry at December 31, 2018?
3. By how much would assets and income be overstated or understated if the adjusting entry were not recorded?

Exercise 3-53   Adjusting Entries

OBJECTIVE 4

Guelon Services Inc. is preparing adjusting entries for the year ended December 31, 2018. The following data are available:

a. Interest is owed at December 31, 2018, on a six-month, 8% note. Guelon borrowed $120,000 from NBD on September 1, 2018.
b. Guelon provides daily building maintenance services to Mack Trucks for a quarterly fee of $2,700, payable on the fifteenth of the month following the end of each quarter. No entries have been made for the services provided to Mack Trucks during the quarter ended December 31, and the related bill will not be sent until January 15, 2019.
c. At the beginning of 2018, the cost of office supplies on hand was $1,220. During 2018, office supplies with a total cost of $6,480 were purchased from Office Depot and debited to office

(Continued)

supplies. On December 31, 2018, Guelon determined the cost of office supplies on hand to be $970.

d.   On September 23, 2018, Guelon received a $7,650 payment from Bethlehem Steel for nine months of maintenance services beginning on October 1, 2018. The entire amount was credited to unearned service revenue when received.

Required:

1.   Prepare the appropriate adjusting entries at December 31, 2018.
2.   What would be the effect on the statement of financial position and the statement of earnings if the accountant failed to make the above adjusting entries?

OBJECTIVE **4**

Exercise 3-54   Adjusting Entries

Reynolds Computer Service offers data processing services to retail clothing stores. The following data have been collected to aid in the preparation of adjusting entries for Reynolds Computer Service for 2018:

a.   Computer equipment was purchased from IBM in 2015 at a cost of $540,000. Annual depreciation is $132,500.
b.   A fire insurance policy for a two-year period beginning September 1, 2018, was purchased from Good Hands Insurance Company for $12,240 cash. The entire amount of the prepayment was debited to prepaid insurance. (Assume that the beginning balance of prepaid insurance was $0 and that there were no other debits or credits to that account during 2018.)
c.   Reynolds has a contract to perform the payroll accounting for Degas's Department Stores. At the end of 2018, $5,450 of services have been performed under this contract but are unbilled.
d.   Reynolds rents 12 computer terminals for $65 per month per terminal from Extreme Terminals Inc. At December 31, 2018, Reynolds owes Extreme Terminals for half a month's rent on each terminal. The amount owed is unrecorded.
e.   Perry's Tax Service prepays rent for time on Reynolds's computer. When payments are received from Perry's Tax Service, Reynolds credits unearned rent revenue. At December 31, 2018, Reynolds has earned $1,810 for computer time used by Perry's Tax Service during December 2018.

Required:

1.   Prepare adjusting entries for each of the transactions.
2.   What would be the effect on the statement of financial position and the statement of earnings if the accountant failed to make the above adjusting entries?

OBJECTIVE **4**

Exercise 3-55   Recreating Adjusting Entries

Selected statement of financial position accounts for Gardner Company are presented below:

Prepaid Insurance		Wages Payable		Unearned Sales Revenue		Interest Receivable	
May 5 4,300		?			May 10 9,500	?	
	?			?			
1,250		5,400			2,250	825	

Required:

Analyze each account and recreate the journal entries that were made. For prepayments, be sure to include the original journal entry as well as the adjusting journal entry. Month-end is May 31, 2018.

OBJECTIVE **4**

Exercise 3-56   Effect of Adjustments on the Financial Statements

Van Brush Enterprises, a painting contractor, prepared the following adjusting entries at year-end:

Wages Expense	2,550	
Wages Payable		2,550
Accounts Receivable	8,110	
Service Revenue		8,110
Unearned Service Revenue	5,245	
Service Revenue		5,245
Rent Expense	3,820	
Prepaid Rent		3,820

Required:

1. Show the effect of these adjustments on (1) assets, liabilities, and shareholders' equity, and (2) revenues, expenses, and net income.
2. If these adjustments were made with estimates that were considered conservative, how would this affect your interpretation of earnings quality?

YOUDECIDE

Exercise 3-57   Preparation of Closing Entries

OBJECTIVE **6**

Erie Rapids Consulting Ltd. began 2018 with a retained earnings balance of $38,100 and has the following accounts and balances at year-end:

Sales Revenue	$162,820	Supplies Expense	$ 4,348
Salaries Expense	91,660	Income Tax Expense	13,800
Rent Expense	11,250	Dividends Declared	8,400
Utilities Expense	8,415		

Required:

1. Prepare the closing entries made by Erie Rapids Consulting at the end of 2018.
2. Prepare Erie Rapids Consulting's statement of retained earnings for 2018.

Exercise 3-58   Preparation of Closing Entries

OBJECTIVE **6**

James and Susan Morley recently converted a large turn-of-the-century house into a hotel and incorporated the business as Nanaimo Enterprises. Their accountant is inexperienced and has made the following closing entries at the end of Nanaimo's first year of operations:

Income Summary	210,000	
Service Revenue		177,000
Accumulated Depreciation		33,000
Depreciation Expense	33,000	
Income Tax Expense	8,200	
Utilities Expense	12,700	
Wages Expense	66,000	
Supplies Expense	31,000	
Accounts Payable	4,500	
Income Summary		155,400
Income Summary	54,600	
Retained Earnings		54,600
Dividends Declared	3,200	
Income Summary		3,200

Required:

1. Indicate what is wrong with the closing entries above.
2. Prepare the correct closing entries. Assume that all necessary accounts are presented above and that the amounts given are correct.
3. **CONCEPTUAL CONNECTION** Explain why closing entries are necessary.

PROBLEM SET A

OBJECTIVE  **Problem 3-59A   Cash-Basis and Accrual-Basis Income**

George Hathaway, an electrician, entered into an agreement with a real estate management company to perform all maintenance of basic electrical systems and air-conditioning equipment in the apartment buildings under the company's management. The agreement, which is subject to annual renewal, provides for the payment of a fixed fee of $6,420 on January 1 of each year plus amounts for parts and materials billed separately at the end of each month. Amounts billed at the end of one month are collected at some point in the future. During the first three months of 2018, George makes the following additional billings and cash collections:

	Billings for Parts and Materials	Cash Collected	Cash Paid for Parts and Materials	Cost of Parts and Materials Used
January	$510	$6,530*	$375	$360
February	0	435	280	270
March	380	0	315	330

*Includes $110 for parts and materials billed in December 2017.

Required:

1. Calculate the amount of cash-basis income reported for each of the first three months.
2. Calculate the amount of accrual-basis income reported for each of the first three months.
3. **CONCEPTUAL CONNECTION** Why do decision makers prefer the accrual basis of accounting?

OBJECTIVE  **Problem 3-60A   Revenue Recognition and Matching**

Securit performs security services for local businesses. During 2018, Securit performed $915,700 of security services and collected $930,000 cash from customers. Securit employees earned salaries of $42,350 per month. During 2018, Securit paid salaries of $491,410 cash for work performed. At the beginning of 2018, Securit had $2,875 of supplies on hand. Supplies of $80,000 were purchased during the year, and $12,150 of supplies were on hand at the end of the year. Other general and administrative expenses incurred during the year were $31,000.

Required:

1. Calculate revenue and expenses for 2018.
2. Prepare the 2018 statement of earnings.
3. **CONCEPTUAL CONNECTION** Describe the accounting principles used to prepare the statement of earnings.

OBJECTIVE **Problem 3-61A   Identification and Preparation of Adjusting Entries**

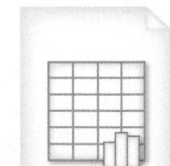

Kuepper's Day Care is a large day care centre in Victoria, British Columbia. The day care centre serves several nearby businesses, as well as a number of individual families. The businesses pay $6,180 per child per year for day care services for their employees' children. The businesses pay in advance on a quarterly basis. For individual families, day care services are provided monthly and billed at the beginning of the next month. The following transactions describe Kuepper's activities during December 2018:

a. On December 1, Kuepper borrowed $60,000 by issuing a five-year, $60,000, 9% note payable.
b. Day care service in the amount of $12,450 was provided to individual families during December. These families will not be billed until January 2019.
c. At December 1, the balance in unearned service revenue was $43,775. At December 31, Kuepper determined that $3,090 of this revenue was still unearned.
d. On December 31, the day care centre collected $131,325 from businesses for services to be provided in 2019.

e. On December 31, the centre recorded depreciation of $2,675 on a bus that it uses for field trips.

f. The day care centre had prepaid insurance at December 1 of $4,200. An examination of the insurance policies indicates that prepaid insurance at December 31 is $2,200.

g. Interest on the $60,000 note payable (see item *a*) is unpaid and unrecorded at December 31.

h. Salaries of $25,320 are owed but unpaid on December 31.

i. Supplies of disposable diapers on December 1 are $4,400. At December 31, the cost of diapers in the supplies account is $890.

Required:

1. Identify whether each entry is an adjusting entry or a regular journal entry. If the entry is an adjusting entry, identify it as an accrued revenue, accrued expense, unearned revenue, or prepaid expense.
2. Prepare the journal entries necessary to record the above transactions.

Problem 3-62A Preparation of Adjusting Entries

OBJECTIVE ④

Balint Photographic Services takes wedding and graduation photographs. At December 31, the end of Balint's accounting period, the following information is available:

a. All wedding photographs are paid for in advance, and all cash collected for them is credited to unearned service revenue. Except for a year-end adjusting entry, no other entries are made for service revenue from wedding photographs. During the year, Balint received $42,600 for wedding photographs. At year-end, $37,400 of the $42,600 had been earned. The beginning-of-the-year balance of unearned service revenue was zero.

b. During December, Balint photographed 225 members of the next year's graduating class of Shaw High School. The school has asked Balint to print one copy of a photograph of each student for the school files. Balint delivered these photographs on December 28 and will bill the school $5.00 per student in January of next year. Revenue from photographs ordered by students will be recorded as the orders are received during the early months of next year.

c. Equipment used for developing and printing was rented for $22,500. The rental term was for one year beginning on August 1 and the entire year of rent was paid on August 1. The payment was debited to prepaid rent.

d. Depreciation on the firm's building for the current year is $9,400.

e. Wages of $4,170 are owed but unpaid and unrecorded at December 31.

f. Supplies at the beginning of the year were $2,400. During the year, supplies costing $19,600 were purchased. When the purchases were made, their cost was debited to supplies. At year-end a physical count indicated that supplies costing $4,100 were on hand.

Required:

1. Prepare the adjusting entries for each of these items.
2. By how much would net income be overstated or understated if the accountant failed to make the adjusting entries?

YOU DECIDE

Problem 3-63A Effects of Adjusting Entries on the Basic Accounting Equation

OBJECTIVE ④

Four adjusting entries are shown below.

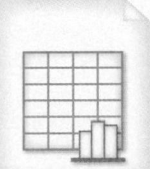

Wages Expense	3,410	
Wages Payable		3,410
Accounts Receivable	8,350	
Service Revenue		8,350
Rent Expense	2,260	
Prepaid Rent		2,260
Unearned Service Revenue	5,510	
Service Revenue		5,510

(Continued)

Required:

CONCEPTUAL CONNECTION Analyze the adjusting entries and identify their effects on the financial statement accounts. (*Note:* Ignore any income tax effects.) Use the following format for your answer:

Transaction	Assets	Liabilities	Beginning Common Shares	Retained Earnings	Revenues	Expenses

OBJECTIVE  **Problem 3-64A   Adjusting Entries and Financial Statements**

You have the following unadjusted trial balance for Rangoon Corporation at December 31, 2018:

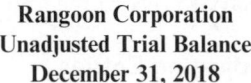

Rangoon Corporation
Unadjusted Trial Balance
December 31, 2018

Account	Debit	Credit
Cash	$ 3,100	
Accounts Receivable	15,900	
Supplies	4,200	
Prepaid Rent	9,500	
Equipment	625,000	
Accumulated Depreciation (Equipment)		$ 104,000
Other Assets	60,900	
Accounts Payable		9,400
Unearned Service Revenue		11,200
Note Payable (due 2021)		50,000
Common Shares		279,500
Retained Earnings, 12/31/2017		37,000
Service Revenue		598,000
Wages Expense	137,000	
Rent Expense	229,000	
Interest Expense	4,500	
Total	$1,089,100	$1,089,100

At year-end, you have the following data for adjustments:

a. An analysis indicates that prepaid rent on December 31 should be $2,300.
b. A physical inventory shows that $650 of office supplies is on hand.
c. Depreciation for 2014 is $35,250.
d. An analysis indicates that unearned service revenue should be $3,120.
e. Wages in the amount of $3,450 are owed but unpaid and unrecorded at year-end.
f. Six months' interest at 8% on the note was paid on September 30. Interest for the period from October 1 to December 31 is unpaid and unrecorded.
g. Income tax of $55,539 is owed but unrecorded and unpaid.

Required:

1. Prepare the adjusting entries.
2. Prepare a statement of earnings, a statement of retained earnings, and a statement of financial position using adjusted account balances.
3. **CONCEPTUAL CONNECTION** Why would you not want to prepare financial statements until after the adjusting entries are made?

Problem 3-65A   Inferring Adjusting Entries from Account Balance Changes

OBJECTIVE ④

The following schedule shows all the accounts of Brandon Travel Agency that received year-end adjusting entries:

Account	Unadjusted Account Balance	Adjusted Account Balance
Prepaid Insurance	$ 23,270	$ 6,150
Prepaid Rent	3,600	2,100
Accumulated Depreciation	156,000	(a)
Wages Payable	0	6,750
Unearned Service Revenue	13,620	(b)
Service Revenue	71,600	78,980
Insurance Expense	0	(c)
Rent Expense	29,700	(d)
Depreciation Expense	0	12,500
Wages Expense	44,200	(e)

Required:

1. Calculate the missing amounts identified by the letters *a* through *e*.
2. Prepare the five adjusting entries that must have been made to cause the account changes as indicated.

Problem 3-66A   Preparation of Closing Entries and a Statement of Earnings

OBJECTIVE ⑤ ⑥

Bell Grove Alarm Company provides security services to homes in northwestern Ontario. At year-end 2018, after adjusting entries have been made, the following list of account balances is prepared:

Accounts Receivable	$ 36,800	Prepaid Rent	$ 4,750
Accounts Payable	23,250	Rent Expense	27,600
Accumulated Depreciation (Equipment)	124,000	Retained Earnings, 12/31/2017	29,400
Common Shares	150,000	Salaries Payable	12,600
Depreciation Expense (Equipment)	45,300	Salaries Expense	148,250
Dividends Declared	6,000	Service Revenue	612,900
Equipment	409,500	Supplies	12,700
Income Tax Expense	30,800	Supplies Expense	51,900
Income Tax Payable	24,300	Utilities Expense	48,800
Interest Expense	4,800	Wages Expense	183,500
Notes Payable (due in 2021)	34,000	Wages Payable	7,950
Other Assets	7,700		

Required:

1. Prepare closing entries for Bell Grove Alarm.
2. Prepare a statement of earnings for Bell Grove Alarm.

Problem 3-67A   Comprehensive Problem: Reviewing the Accounting Cycle

OBJECTIVE ④⑤⑥⑦

Fodor Freight Service provides delivery of merchandise to retail grocery stores in northern Manitoba. At the beginning of 2018, the following account balances were available:

Cash	$ 92,100	Accumulated Depreciation	
Accounts Receivable	361,500	(Equipment)	$ 580,000
Supplies	24,600	Land	304,975
Prepaid Advertising	2,000	Accounts Payable	17,600
Building (Warehouse)	2,190,000	Wages Payable	30,200
Accumulated Depreciation		Notes Payable (due in 2022)	1,000,000
(Warehouse)	280,000	Common Shares	1,400,000
Equipment	795,000	Retained Earnings, 12/31/2017	462,375

(Continued)

During 2018 the following transactions occurred:

a.   Fodor performed deliveries for customers, all on credit, for $2,256,700. Fodor also made cash deliveries for $686,838.
b.   There remains $286,172 of accounts receivable to be collected at December 31, 2018.
c.   Fodor purchased advertising of $138,100 during 2018 and debited the amount to prepaid advertising.
d.   Supplies of $27,200 were purchased on credit and debited to the supplies account.
e.   Accounts payable at the beginning of 2018 were paid early in 2018. There remains $5,600 of accounts payable unpaid at year-end.
f.   Wages payable at the beginning of 2018 were paid early in 2018. Wages were earned and paid during 2018 in the amount of $666,142.
g.   During the year, Trish Hurd, a principal shareholder, purchased an automobile costing $42,000 for her personal use.
h.   One-half year's interest at 6% annual rate was paid on the note payable on July 1, 2018.
i.   Property taxes were paid on the land and buildings in the amount of $170,000
j.   Dividends were declared and paid in the amount of $25,000.

The following data are available for adjusting entries:

- Supplies in the amount of $13,685 remained unused at year-end.
- Annual depreciation on the warehouse building is $70,000.
- Annual depreciation on the warehouse equipment is $145,000.
- Wages of $60,558 were unrecorded and unpaid at year-end.
- Interest for six months at 6% per year on the note is unpaid and unrecorded at year-end.
- Advertising of $14,874 remained unused at the end of 2018.
- Income taxes of $482,549 related to 2018 are unpaid at year-end.

Required:

1.   Post the 2018 beginning balances to T-accounts. Prepare journal entries for transactions *a* through *j* and post the journal entries to T-accounts, adding any new T-accounts you need.
2.   Prepare the adjustments and post the adjustments to the T-accounts, adding any new T-accounts you need.
3.   Prepare a statement of earnings.
4.   Prepare a statement of retained earnings.
5.   Prepare a classified statement of financial position.
6.   Prepare closing entries.
7.   **CONCEPTUAL CONNECTION** Did you include transaction *g* among Fodor's 2018 journal entries? Why or why not?

PROBLEM SET B

 **Problem 3-68B   Cash-Basis and Accrual-Basis Income**

Martin Sharp, who repairs lawn mowers, collects cash from his customers when the repair services are completed. He maintains an inventory of repair parts that are purchased from a wholesale supplier. Martin's records show the following information for the first three months of 2018.

	Cash Collected for Repair Work	Cost of Repair Parts Purchased	Cash Payments to Supplier	Cost of Parts Used in Repairs
January	$2,400	$820	$710	$635
February	1,875	0	440	295
March	1,950	695	0	390

Required:

1. Ignoring expenses other than repair parts, calculate net income for each of the three months on a cash basis.
2. Ignoring expenses other than repair parts, calculate net income for each of the three months on an accrual basis.
3. **CONCEPTUAL CONNECTION** Why do decision makers prefer the accrual basis of accounting?

Problem 3-69B   Revenue Recognition and Matching

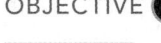

Aunt Bea's Catering Service provides catering service for special occasions. During 2018, Aunt Bea performed $128,300 of catering services and collected $118,500 of cash from customers. Salaries earned by Aunt Bea's employees during 2018 were $38,500. Aunt Bea paid employees $35,000 during 2018. Aunt Bea had $1,200 of supplies on hand at the beginning of the year and purchased an additional $8,000 of supplies during the year. Supplies on hand at the end of 2018 were $1,830. Other selling and administrative expenses incurred during 2018 were $5,800.

Required:

1. Calculate revenue and expenses for 2018.
2. Prepare the 2018 statement of earnings.
3. **CONCEPTUAL CONNECTION** Describe the accounting principles used to prepare the statement of earnings.

Problem 3-70B   Identification and Preparation of Adjusting Entries

OBJECTIVE 3 4

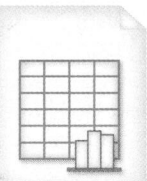

Dance Inc. provides ballet, tap, and jazz dancing instruction to promising young dancers. Dance began operations in January 2019 and is preparing its monthly financial statements. The following items describe Dance's transactions in January 2019:

a. Dance requires that dance instruction be paid in advance—either monthly or quarterly. On January 1, Dance received $3,275 for dance instruction to be provided during 2019.
b. On January 31, Dance noted that $450 of dance instruction revenue is still unearned.
c. On January 20, Dance's hourly employees were paid $1,350 for work performed in January.
d. Dance's insurance policy requires semi-annual premium payments. Dance paid the $4,500 insurance policy, which covered the first half of 2019, in December 2018.
e. When there are no scheduled dance classes, Dance rents its studio for birthday parties for $100 per two-hour party. Three birthday parties were held during January. Dance will not bill the parents until February.
f. Dance purchased $250 of office supplies on January 10.
g. On January 31, Dance determined that office supplies of $75 were unused.
h. Dance received a January utility bill for $685. The bill will not be paid until it is due in February.

Required:

1. Identify whether each entry is an adjusting entry or a regular journal entry. If the entry is an adjusting entry, identify it as an accrued revenue, accrued expense, unearned revenue, or prepaid expense.
2. Prepare the journal entries necessary to record the above transactions.

Problem 3-71B   Preparation of Adjusting Entries

OBJECTIVE 4

Osaga Beach Resort operates a resort complex that specializes in hosting small business and professional meetings. Osaga Beach closes its fiscal year on January 31, a time when it has few meetings under way. At January 31, 2019, the following data are available:

(Continued)

a.   A training meeting is under way for 16 individuals from Fashion Design. Fashion Design paid $4,500 in advance for each person attending the 10-day training session. The meeting began on January 28 and will end on February 6.

b.   Twenty-one people from Northern Publishing are attending a sales meeting. The daily fee for each person attending the meeting is $280 (charged for each night a person stays at the resort). The meeting began on January 29, and guests will depart on February 2. Northern will be billed at the end of the meeting.

c.   Depreciation on the golf carts used to transport the guests' luggage to and from their rooms is $11,250 for the year. Osaga Beach records depreciation yearly.

d.   At January 31, Friedrich Catering is owed $1,795 for food provided for guests through that date. This amount is unrecorded. Osaga Beach classifies the cost of food as an "other expense" on the statement of earnings.

e.   An examination indicates that the cost of office supplies on hand at January 31, 2019, is $189. During the year, $850 of office supplies was purchased from Supply Depot. The cost of supplies purchased was debited to office supplies. No office supplies were on hand on January 31, 2018.

Required:

1.   Prepare adjusting entries at January 31 for each of these items.
2.   By how much would net income be overstated or understated if the accountant failed to make the adjusting entries?

YOUDECIDE

OBJECTIVE **4**

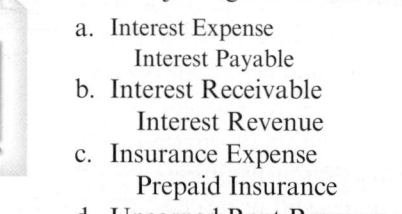

Problem 3-72B   Effects of Adjusting Entries on the Basic Accounting Equation

Four adjusting entries are shown below:

a. Interest Expense	1,875	
Interest Payable		1,875
b. Interest Receivable	1,150	
Interest Revenue		1,150
c. Insurance Expense	2,560	
Prepaid Insurance		2,560
d. Unearned Rent Revenue	4,680	
Rent Revenue		4,680

Required:

CONCEPTUAL CONNECTION Analyze the adjusting entries and identify their effects on the financial statement accounts. (*Note:* Ignore any income tax effects.) Use the following format for your answer:

Transaction	Assets	Liabilities	Beginning Common Shares	Retained Earnings	Revenues	Expenses

OBJECTIVE **4 5**

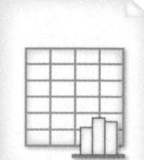

Problem 3-73B   Adjusting Entries and Financial Statements

The unadjusted trial balance for Mitchell Pharmacy appears below.

Mitchell Pharmacy
Unadjusted Trial Balance
December 31, 2018

Account	Debit	Credit
Cash	$ 3,400	
Accounts Receivable	64,820	
Inventory	583,400	
Prepaid Insurance	11,200	

Account	Debit	Credit
Building	230,000	
Accumulated Depreciation (Building)		$ 44,000
Land	31,200	
Other Assets	25,990	
Accounts Payable		47,810
Notes Payable (due 2020)		150,000
Common Shares		600,000
Retained Earnings, 12/31/2017		41,200
Service Revenue		950,420
Wages Expense	871,420	
Interest Expense	12,000	
Total	$1,833,430	$1,833,430

The following information is available at year-end for adjustments:

a. An analysis of insurance policies indicates that $2,180 of the prepaid insurance is coverage for 2019.
b. Depreciation expense for 2018 is $10,130.
c. Four months' interest at 10% is owed but unrecorded and unpaid on the notes payable.
d. Wages of $4,950 are owed but unpaid and unrecorded at December 31.
e. Income taxes of $11,370 are owed but unrecorded and unpaid at December 31.

Required:

1. Prepare the adjusting entries.
2. Prepare a statement of earnings, a statement of retained earnings, and a statement of financial position using adjusted account balances.
3. **CONCEPTUAL CONNECTION** Why would you not want to prepare financial statements until after the adjusting entries are made?

Problem 3-74B   Inferring Adjusting Entries from Account Balance Changes

OBJECTIVE  4

The following schedule shows all the accounts of Eagle Imports that received year-end adjusting entries:

ILLUSTRATING
RELATIONSHIPS

Account	Unadjusted Account Balance	Adjusted Account Balance
Prepaid Insurance	$ 15,390	$ (a)
Accumulated Depreciation	92,500	103,000
Interest Payable	0	(b)
Wages Payable	0	(c)
Unearned Service Revenue	12,250	2,620
Service Revenue	122,500	(d)
Insurance Expense	1,500	12,746
Interest Expense	1,125	5,300
Depreciation Expense	0	(e)
Wages Expense	24,200	41,800

Required:

1. Calculate the missing amounts identified by the letters a through e.
2. Prepare the five adjusting entries that must have been made to cause the account changes as indicated.

Problem 3-75B   Preparation of Closing Entries and a Statement of Earnings

OBJECTIVE  5 6

Clayoquot Boat Repair Ltd. has entered and posted its adjusting entries for 2018. The following are selected account balances after adjustment:

(Continued)

Accounts Payable	$ 8,330	Prepaid Rent	$ 7,200
Accounts Receivable, 12/31/2018	65,000	Rent Expense	28,800
Accumulated Depreciation (Equipment)	75,000	Sales Revenue	692,500
Depreciation Expense (Equipment)	20,000	Supplies Expense	68,350
Dividends Declared	7,800	Supplies	179,000
Income Tax Expense	12,300	Unearned Sales Revenue	12,200
Income Tax Payable	8,300	Utilities Expense	12,300
Insurance Expense	94,300	Wages Expense	405,300
Interest Expense	9,500	Wages Payable	11,700
Interest Revenue	7,600		

Required:

1. Using the accounts and balances above, prepare the closing entries for 2018.
2. Prepare a statement of earnings for Clayoquot Boat Repair.

OBJECTIVE  **Problem 3-76B   Comprehensive Problem: Reviewing the Accounting Cycle**

Talbot Riding Stables provides stables, care for animals, and grounds for riding and showing horses. The account balances at the beginning of 2018 were:

Cash	$ 2,200	Accounts Payable	$ 23,700
Accounts Receivable	4,400	Income Tax Payable	15,100
Supplies (Feed and Straw)	27,800	Interest Payable	2,700
Land	167,000	Wages Payable	14,200
Buildings	115,000	Notes Payable (due in 2022)	60,000
Accumulated Depreciation (Buildings)	36,000	Common Shares	150,000
Equipment	57,000	Retained Earnings, 12/31/2017	55,200
Accumulated Depreciation (Equipment)	16,500		

During 2018, the following transactions occurred:

a. Talbot provided animal care services, all on credit, for $210,300. Talbot rented stables to customers for $20,500 cash. Talbot rented its grounds to individual riders, groups, and show organizations for $41,800 cash.
b. There remains $15,600 of accounts receivable to be collected at December 31, 2018.
c. Feed in the amount of $62,900 was purchased on credit and debited to the supplies account.
d. Straw was purchased for $7,400 cash and debited to the supplies account.
e. Wages payable at the beginning of 2018 were paid early in 2018. Wages were earned and paid during 2018 in the amount of $112,000.
f. The income tax payable at the beginning of 2018 was paid early in 2018.
g. Payments of $73,000 were made to creditors for supplies previously purchased on credit.
h. One year's interest at 9% was paid on the notes payable on July 1, 2018.
i. During 2018, Jon Talbot, a principal shareholder, purchased a horse for his wife, Jennifer, to ride. The horse cost $7,000, and Talbot used his personal credit to purchase it.
j. Property taxes were paid on the land and buildings in the amount of $17,000.
k. Dividends were declared and paid in the amount of $7,200.

The following data are available for adjusting entries:

• Supplies (feed and straw) in the amount of $30,400 remained unused at year-end.
• Annual depreciation on the buildings is $6,000.
• Annual depreciation on the equipment is $5,500.
• Wages of $4,000 were unrecorded and unpaid at year-end.
• Interest for six months at 9% per year on the note is unpaid and unrecorded at year-end.
• Income taxes of $16,500 were unpaid and unrecorded at year-end.

Required:

1. Post the 2018 beginning balances to T-accounts. Prepare journal entries for transactions *a* through *k* and post the journal entries to T-accounts, adding any new T-accounts you need.
2. Prepare the adjustments and post the adjustments to the T-accounts, adding any new T-accounts you need.
3. Prepare a statement of earnings.
4. Prepare a statement of retained earnings.
5. Prepare a classified statement of financial position.
6. Prepare closing entries.
7. **CONCEPTUAL CONNECTION** Did you include transaction *i* among Talbot's 2018 journal entries? Why or why not?

CASES

Case 3-77   Cash- or Accrual-Basis Accounting

Karen Raj owns a business that rents parking spots to students at the local university. Karen's typical rental contract requires the student to pay the year's rent of $450 ($50 per month) on September 1. When Karen prepares financial statements at the end of December, her accountant requires that Karen spread the $450 over the nine months that each parking spot is rented. Therefore, Karen can recognize only $200 of revenue (four months) from each parking spot rental contract in the year the cash is collected and must defer (delay) recognition of the remaining $250 (five months) to the next year. Karen argues that getting students to agree to rent the parking spot is the most difficult part of the activity so she ought to be able to recognize all $450 as revenue when the cash is received from a student.

Required:

Why does IFRS/ASPE require the use of accrual accounting rather than cash-basis accounting for transactions like the one described here?

Case 3-78   Recognition of Service Contract Revenue

Zac Murphy is president of Blooming Colours Inc., which provides landscaping services in Leamington, Ontario. On November 20, 2018, Murphy signed a service contract with Eastern University. Under the contract, Blooming Colours will provide landscaping services for all of Eastern's buildings for a period of two years, beginning on January 1, 2019, and Eastern will pay Blooming Colours on a monthly basis, beginning on January 31, 2019. Although the same amount of landscaping services will be rendered in every month, the contract provides for higher monthly payments in the first year.

Initially, Murphy proposed that the revenue from the contract be recognized in 2018; however, his accountant, Sue Storm, convinced him that this would be inappropriate. Then Murphy proposed that the revenue be recognized in an amount equal to the cash collected under the contract in 2018. Again, Storm argued against his proposal, saying that ASPE requires recognition of an equal amount of contract revenue each month.

Required:

1. Give a reason that might explain Murphy's desire to recognize contract revenue earlier rather than later.
2. Put yourself in Storm's position. How would you convince Murphy that his two proposals are unacceptable and that an equal amount of revenue should be recognized every month?
3. If Storm's proposal is adopted, how would the contract be reflected on the statement of financial position at the end of 2018 and at the end of 2019?

Case 3-79   Revenue Recognition

Melaney Parks purchased HealthPlus Fitness in January 2018. Melaney wanted to increase the size of the business by selling three-year memberships for $3,000, payable at the beginning of the membership period. The normal yearly membership fee is $1,500. Since few prospective members were expected to want to spend $3,000 at the beginning of the membership period, Melaney arranged for a local bank to provide a $3,000 installment loan to prospective members. By the end of 2018, 250 customers had purchased the three-year memberships using the loan provided by the bank.

Melaney prepared her statement of earnings for 2018 and included $750,000 ($3,000 × 250 members) as revenue because the club had collected the entire amount in cash. Melaney's accountant objected to the inclusion of the entire $750,000. The accountant argued that the $750,000 should be recognized as revenue as the club provides services for these members during the membership period. Melaney countered with a quotation from IFRS/ASPE:

Profit is deemed to be realized when a sale in the ordinary course of business is effected, unless the circumstances are such that collection of the sale price is not reasonably assured.

Melaney notes that memberships have been sold and the collection of the selling price has occurred. Therefore, she argues, all $750,000 is revenue in 2018.

Required:

1. Write a short statement supporting either Melaney or the accountant in this dispute.
2. Would your answer change if the $3,000 fee were nonrefundable? Why or why not?

Case 3-80   Applying the Matching Concept

Nevsky Properties Inc. completed construction of a new shopping centre in July 2018. During the first six months of 2018, Nevsky spent $550,000 for salaries, preparation of documents, travel, and other similar activities associated with securing tenants for the centre. Nevsky was successful (Best Buy and Office Depot will be tenants) and the centre will open on August 1 with all its stores rented on four-year leases. The rental revenue that Nevsky expects to receive from the current tenants is $8,500,000 per year for four years. The leases will be renegotiated at the end of the fourth year. The accountant for Nevsky wonders whether the $550,000 should be expensed in 2018 or whether it should be initially recorded as an asset and matched against revenues over the four-year lease term.

Required:

Write a short statement indicating why you support expensing the $550,000 in the current period or spreading the expense over the four-year lease term.

Case 3-81   Adjusting Entries for Refund Coupons

Cal-Lite Products Ltd. manufactures a line of food products that appeals to persons interested in weight loss. To stimulate sales, Cal-Lite includes cash refund coupons in many of its products. Cal-Lite issues the purchaser a cheque when the coupon is returned to the company, which may be many months after the product is sold to stores and distributors. In addition, a significant number of coupons issued to customers are never returned. As cash distributions are made to customers, they are recorded in an expense account.

Required:

1. Explain the conceptual basis for the determination of the expense in each year. Describe the information and calculations required to estimate the amount of expense for each year.
2. Describe the year-end adjusting entry required at the end of the first year of the program's existence.
3. Describe the adjusting entry at the end of the second year of the program's existence.

Case 3-82   Adjusting Entries for Motion Picture Revenues

Link Pictures Inc. sells (licenses) the rights to exhibit motion pictures to theatres. Under the sales contract, the theatre promises to pay a licence fee equal to the larger of a guaranteed minimum or a percentage of the box office receipts. In addition, the contract requires the guaranteed minimum to be paid in advance. Consider the following contracts entered by Link during 2018:

a.   Contract A authorizes a group of theatres in St. John's, Newfoundland, to exhibit a film called *Garage* for two weeks ending January 7, 2019. Box office statistics indicate that first-week attendance has already generated licensing fees well in excess of the guaranteed minimum.

b.   Contract B authorizes a chain of theatres in Winnipeg, Manitoba, to exhibit a film called *Blue Denim* for a period of two weeks ending January 20, 2019. In most first-run cities, the film has attracted large crowds, and the percentage of box office receipts has far exceeded the minimum.

c.   Contract C authorizes a chain of theatres in Vancouver, British Columbia, to exhibit a film called *Toast Points* for a period of two weeks ending on December 12, 2018. The film is a "dog" and the theatres stopped showing it after the first few days. All prints of the film were returned by December 31, 2018.

The guaranteed minimum has been paid on all three contracts and recorded as unearned revenue. No other amounts have been received, and no revenue has been recorded for any of the contracts. Adjusting entries for 2018 are about to be made.

Required:

Describe the adjusting entry you would make at December 31, 2018, to record each contract.

Case 3-83   The Effect of Adjusting Entries on the Financial Statements (A Conceptual Approach)

Don Berthrong, the manager of the local Books-A-Million, is wondering whether adjusting entries will affect his financial statements. Don's business has grown steadily for several years, and Don expects it to continue to grow for the next several years at a rate of 5% to 10% per year. Nearly all of Don's sales are for cash. Other than cost of goods sold, which is not affected by adjusting entries, most of Don's expenses are for items that require cash outflows (e.g., rent on the building, wages, utilities, insurance).

Required:

1.   Would Don's financial statement be affected significantly by adjusting entries?
2.   Consider all businesses. What kinds of transactions would require adjustments that would have a significant effect on the financial statements? What kinds of businesses would be likely to require these kinds of adjustments?

Case 3-84   Interpreting Closing Entries

Cairo Building Systems made the following closing entries at the end of a recent year:

a. Income Summary	129,750	
Retained Earnings		129,750
b. Retained Earnings	25,000	
Dividends Declared		25,000
c. Sales Revenue	495,300	
Income Summary		495,300
d. Income Summary	104,100	
Interest Expense		104,100

Required:

1.   What was Cairo's net income?
2.   By how much did Cairo's retained earnings change?
3.   If the sales revenue identified in entry *c* was Cairo's only revenue, what was the total amount of its expenses?

Case 3-85   Continuing Problem: Front Row Entertainment

Cam and Anna are very satisfied with their first month of operations. Their major effort centred on signing various artists to live performance contracts, and they had more success than they had anticipated. In addition to Charm City, they were able to use their contacts in the music industry to sign 12 other artists. With the tours starting in February, Cam and Anna were eager to hold their first big event. Over the next month, the following transactions occurred.

Feb. 1   Collected advance ticket sales of $28,400 relating to various concerts that were being promoted.

     1   Paid $800 to rent office space in February.

     2   Paid Equipment Supply Services $1,500, the balance remaining from the January 3 purchase of supplies.

     6   Paid $30,150 to secure venues for future concerts.

     9   Received $325 related to the festival held on January 25.

     12   Purchased $475 of supplies on credit from Equipment Supply Services.

     15   Collected $3,400 of ticket sales for the first Charm City concert on the day of the concert.

     15   Paid Charm City $9,000 for performing the Feb. 15 concert. (*Remember:* Front Row Entertainment records the fees paid to the artist in the Artist Fee Expense account.)

     20   Collected advance ticket sales of $10,125 relating to various concerts that were being promoted.

     21   Collected $5,100 of ticket sales for the second Charm City concert on the day of the concert.

     21   Paid Charm City $12,620 for performing the Feb. 21 concert.

At the end of February, Cam and Anna felt that their business was doing well; however, they decided that they needed to prepare financial statements to better understand the operations of the business. Anna gathered the following information relating to the adjusting entries that needed to be prepared at the end of February.

a.   Two months of interest on the note payable is accrued.

b.   A count of the supplies revealed that $1,825 of supplies remained on hand at the end of February.

c.   Two months of insurance has expired.

d.   Depreciation related to the office equipment was $180 per month.

e.   The rental of the venues for all four Charm City concerts was paid in advance on January 8. As of the end of February, Charm City had performed two of the four concerts in the contract.

f.   An analysis of the unearned sales revenue account reveals that $8,175 of the balance relates to concerts that have not yet been performed.

g.   Cam and Anna have not received their salaries of $1,200 each for February.

h.   A utility bill of $435 relating to utility service on Front Row Entertainment's office for January and February was received but not paid by the end of February.

Required:

1. Analyze and journalize the February transactions.
2. Set up T-accounts for each account, and post the transactions to the T-accounts. Be sure to use the balances computed in Chapter 2 as the beginning balances of the T-accounts.
3. Prepare a trial balance at February 28, 2018.
4. Prepare and post the adjusting entries needed at February 28, 2018.
5. By how much would net income be overstated or understated if the adjusting entries were not made?
6. Prepare a statement of earnings and a statement of retained earnings for the two-month period ended February 28, 2018. Prepare a classified statement of financial position as at February 28, 2018.
7. Prepare the necessary closing entries.

Case 3-86   Professional and Ethical Behaviour

Larry was responsible for recording all accounting entries at ABC Inc. He had a good understanding of accrual accounting and had been working at the company for over two years.

Although Larry was a good accountant, he was also very lazy. He hated that every single month on the last day of the month, he had to make sure that all entries, including any accruals that related to that month, were journalized, and draft financial statements had to be on the owner, Tim's, desk, on the first day following that month. Tim liked the fact that he could start the month knowing exactly what his company looked like and could make decisions based on those statements for that month. Larry could be heard on the telephone on November 30 speaking with his wife, saying that he was rushing to get out of the office and would be home shortly. "Don't worry, honey," Larry said, "I normally just book a few accruals to keep Tim happy, but he will never know that I didn't book them all. He never looks at the statements closely. See you soon!"

Required:

Identify and discuss any ethical issues.

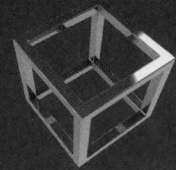

INTEGRATIVE CASE 1 (CHAPTERS 1–3)

The Accounting Cycle

Begin with the following account balances for University Street Parking Garage (assume all accounts have normal balances) at December 31, 2018:

Accounts payable	$ 16,700
Accounts receivable	39,200
Accumulated depreciation (equipment)	36,800
Cash	6,700
Common shares (20,000 shares)	100,000
Depreciation expense (equipment)	12,300
Dividends	6,300
Equipment	269,500
Income taxes expense	2,700
Income taxes payable	1,100
Interest expense	16,500
Interest payable	0
Interest revenue	4,100
Inventory	4,900
Investments	35,000
Notes payable (due May 2, 2024)	160,000
Prepaid rent (4 months)	36,400
Rent expense	94,400
Retained earnings, 12/31/2017	43,000
Service revenue, parking	224,600
Service revenue, repair	208,100
Supplies expense	36,900
Wages expense	233,600
Wages payable	0

Required:

1. For the following transactions, provide the necessary adjusting entries and update the account balances to appropriately reflect these adjusting entries:

   a. The only lease held by University Street Parking required a rental payment of $9,100 per month. University Street Parking has prepaid rent through March 31, 2019.

   b. At December 31, 2018, University Street Parking owes employees wages of $12,500.

   c. University Street Parking should have total depreciation expense on equipment for 2018 of $14,300.

   d. The note payable of $160,000 has an interest rate of 6.75%. University Street Parking has paid interest through October 31, 2018.

2. Prepare a properly classified statement of earnings for 2018, a statement of retained earnings for 2018, and a properly classified statement of financial position as of December 31, 2018, using the post-adjustment account balances.

4

Internal Control and Cash

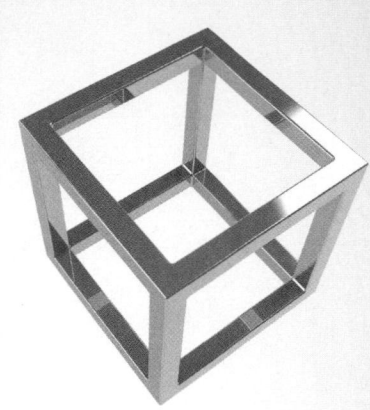

After studying Chapter 4, you should be able to:

1. Discuss the role of internal controls in managing a business.
2. Discuss five elements of a good internal control system.
3. Describe procedures used by businesses to control cash.
4. Describe how businesses account for and report cash.
5. Describe the operating cycle and explain the principles of cash management.

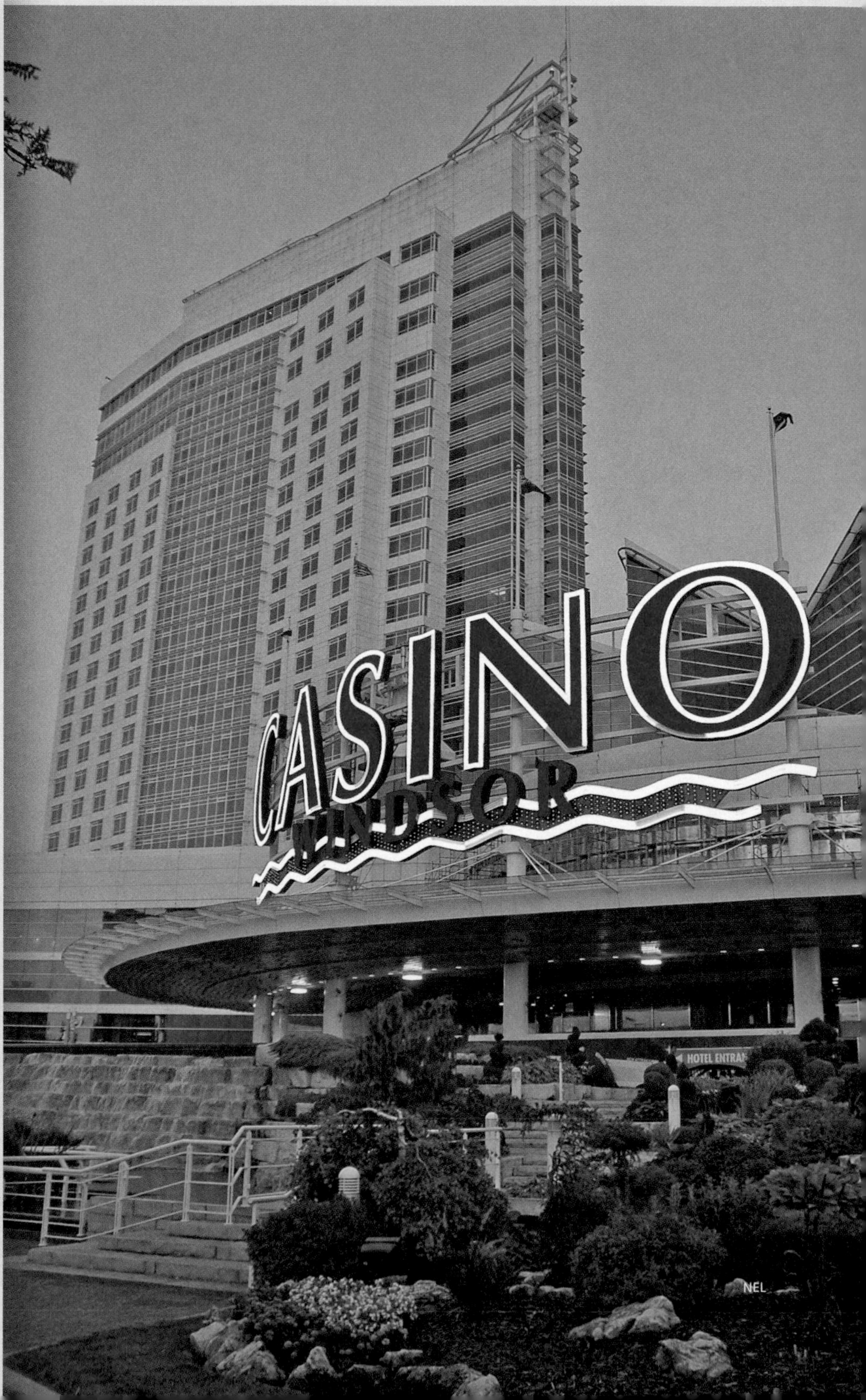

Ivan Cholakov/Shutterstock

EXPERIENCE FINANCIAL ACCOUNTING
with Caesars Windsor

In 1993, the Ontario government moved into the casino industry by selecting a joint venture to build and operate a provincially owned casino in Windsor, Ontario. The original Casino Windsor has expanded from a temporary location in 1994 to become a world-class casino business renamed Caesars Windsor. It has grown from its original facility containing slots and table games to include a convention centre, an entertainment centre, a hotel complex and tower, several restaurants, and a sports book operation.

Caesars Windsor conducts many transactions during a normal day's business that involve the handling of either cash or near-cash financial instruments. The latter include debit cards, credit cards, reward cards, and gift cards. Because Windsor is a border community with the City of Detroit in the United States, business operations at Caesars Windsor are further complicated by transactions being frequently conducted in both Canadian and US dollars. Also, because of the nature and complexity of its business operations and transactions, Caesars Windsor is exposed to significant loss through theft, error, and fraud.

In this chapter, we discuss the policies and procedures that companies put in place to prevent intentional and unintentional losses. These policies and procedures are referred to collectively as an internal control system. A strong internal control system is a necessary line of defence against fraud or theft.

FRAUD—A REASON FOR INTERNAL CONTROL

Fraud causes businesses to lose millions of dollars in revenues each year. Fraud is an intentional act committed to misappropriate assets or to misstate financial statements. Canada has experienced its share of corporate fraud. One well-known case was Livent Inc., where the principals and management recorded nonexistent revenues, recorded assets that were in fact expenses, and decreased depreciation expense by overstating the useful lives of various assets. Another case involved Bre-X Minerals Ltd., where ore samples taken from a mine were "salted" (sprinkled) with real gold to enhance the value of both the samples and the projected gold reserves. Bre-X was valued at $6 billion on the Toronto Stock Exchange around one year before it went bankrupt. In the United States, companies such as Enron Corporation and WorldCom Corporation attempted to conceal debts and record assets that had little or no market value. In a still more recent highly publicized case, Bernard "Bernie" Madoff defrauded many investors of billions of dollars by operating what is known as a Ponzi scheme. Conrad Black, a former Canadian citizen, was convicted of significant fraud against a company he controlled, Hollinger Inc., the publisher of many well-known newspapers around the world.

Bernard "Bernie" Madoff   Conrad Black

In the United States, Congress has taken action against fraud by passing the Sarbanes-Oxley Act ("SOX"), which requires public companies to maintain proper and adequate internal control systems and which also requires the senior corporate officers to sign a certification as to the adequacy of their internal control system over financial reporting.

In Canada, publicly listed companies are regulated by the 13 securities commissions (one for each province and territory). An organization called the Canadian Securities Administrators (CSA) has been formed by the 13 securities commissions in part to issue National Instruments on behalf of those commissions. In order to decrease the opportunity for senior company executives to commit fraud in financial statements, National Instrument 52-109, which is in effect for public companies having a year-end after December 15, 2008, was established and contains many of the SOX rules for Canadian public companies, including certification by the Chief Executive Officer (CEO) and Chief Financial Officer (CFO) of annual financial statements and the systems of internal control necessary to the preparation of the annual financial statements. This National Instrument also requires that any weaknesses in internal control be reported in the company's annual report in Management's Discussion and Analysis (MD&A). Exhibit 4.1 contains an example of the annual certification required by the CEO and CFO of publicly listed companies in Canada under National Instrument 52-109.

Accountants need to be alert for the existence of the three components of the fraud triangle. Fraud may be more likely to occur where an individual is under **pressure** to commit fraud (perhaps because of a personal financial need), has the **opportunity** due to position or circumstances to commit fraud, and can **rationalize** an act of fraud (perhaps due to lack of

(EXHIBIT 4.1)

Management's Responsibility for Financial Statements

The management of Canadian Tire Corporation, Limited is responsible for the accompanying consolidated financial statements. The financial statements have been prepared by management in accordance with International Financial Reporting Standards, which recognize the necessity of relying on some best estimates and informed judgements. All financial information in our Management's Discussion and Analysis is consistent with the consolidated financial statements.

To discharge its responsibilities for financial reporting and safeguarding of assets, management depends on the Company's systems of internal accounting control. These systems are designed to provide reasonable assurance that the financial records are reliable and form a proper basis for the timely and accurate preparation of financial statements. Management meets the objectives of internal accounting control on a cost effective basis through the prudent selection and training of personnel, adoption and communication of appropriate policies, and employment of an internal audit program.

The Board of Directors oversees management's responsibilities for the consolidated financial statements primarily through the activities of its Audit Committee, which is composed solely of directors who are neither officers nor employees of the Company. This Committee meets with management and the Company's independent auditors, Deloitte LLP, to review the consolidated financial statements and recommend approval by the Board of Directors. The Audit Committee is also responsible for making recommendations with respect to the appointment of and for approving remuneration and the terms of engagement of the Company's auditors. The Audit Committee also meets with the auditors, without the presence of management, to discuss the results of their audit, their opinion on internal accounting controls, and the quality of financial reporting.

The consolidated financial statements have been audited by Deloitte LLP, who were appointed by shareholder vote at the annual shareholders' meeting. Their report is presented below.

Michael B. Medline

President and Chief Executive Officer

Dean McCann

Executive Vice-President and Chief Financial Officer

February 26, 2015

Source: Canadian Tire Corporation Annual Report 2014, page 61.

promotion or appropriate pay increase). Strong internal control systems can contribute to significantly reducing the risk of fraud occurring in financial statements.

ROLE OF INTERNAL CONTROL

Except in very small businesses, top management delegates authority and responsibility for engaging in business activities and recording their effects in the accounting system to other managers and employees. Top management wants to make sure that these employees both:

- operate within the scope of their assigned responsibility and
- act for the good of the business.

To ensure that business activities are properly recorded in the accounting system, management implements procedures that collectively are called the **internal control system**.

OBJECTIVE

Discuss the role of internal controls in managing a business.

Internal control systems include all the policies and procedures established by top management and the board of directors to provide reasonable assurance that the company's objectives are being met in the following three areas:[1]

- effectiveness and efficiency of operations
- reliability of internal and external reporting
- compliance with applicable laws and regulations and internal policies

As such, internal control systems include many elements only indirectly related to our primary concern—the accounting system and financial statements. For example, policies and procedures concerning the extent and nature of research and development or advertising activities may have important effects on the achievement of an entity's objectives but only indirectly affect its accounting system and financial statements.

In this chapter, we will examine the elements of internal controls and demonstrate controls over cash, a company's most vulnerable asset. We will address the following questions:

- What are the elements of a good internal control system?
- How are those controls applied to cash?
- How does the operating cycle affect cash?
- Why is cash management so important to a company?

ELEMENTS OF INTERNAL CONTROL

OBJECTIVE 2

Discuss five elements of a good internal control system.

Following are five elements of a good internal control system (see Exhibit 4.2):[2]

- *Control environment.* The "tone at the top" of the organization must be set by management. Management must emphasize through its statements and actions that ethical behaviour, honesty, and integrity are values supported by the organization.
- *Risk assessment.* Management must have a system in place to identify and manage the risks associated with the business being operated.
- *Control activities.* Management must ensure that policies and procedures are in place that support the achievement of the organization's business objectives.

(EXHIBIT 4.2)

Elements of Internal Control

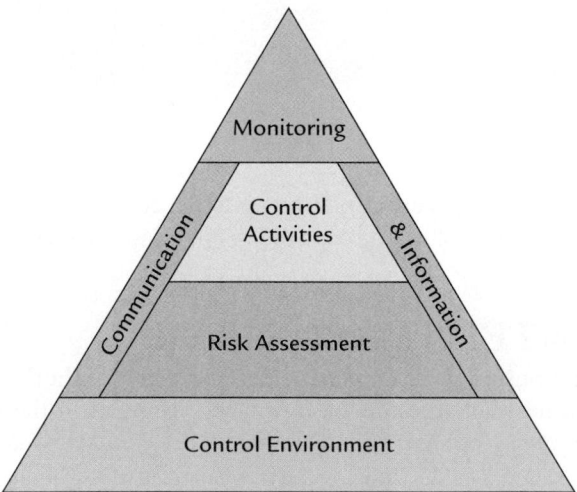

Source: COSO, Internal Control – Integrated Framework, 1992. Used with permission of COSO.

[1] Criteria of Control Committee, Canadian Institute of Chartered Accountants, 1995.

[2] Committee of Sponsoring Organizations of the Treadway Commission (COSO), Internal Control Integrated Framework, 1992.

- *Information and communication.* Management must have a communication system in place that accumulates and disseminates required information throughout the organization.
- *Monitoring.* An internal control system should monitor actual compared to desired performance. Significant internal control deficiencies should be detected and corrected. These deficiencies should be reported to the board of directors and management on a periodic basis.

These five elements are expanded upon in the following discussion.

CONTROL ENVIRONMENT AND ETHICAL BEHAVIOUR

The foundation of the internal control system is the **control environment**—the collection of environmental factors that influence the effectiveness of control procedures. The control environment includes the following:

- the philosophy and operating style of management
- the personnel policies and practices of the business
- the overall integrity, attitude, awareness, and actions of the board of directors and top management of the business concerning the importance of control (commonly called the *tone at the top*)

An important feature of the control environment is recognizing that an individual employee's goals may differ from the goals of other individuals and the goals of the business. For example, when managers receive a bonus based on certain accounting numbers, such as sales, they have been known to ship a large quantity of merchandise to customers right before year-end—even if the merchandise was not ordered. Although much of the merchandise will be returned in the following year, sales targets for the current year have been met and bonuses paid. However, one must ask whether a company's senior executives consider this behaviour ethical and supportable by the organization.

Resolving these conflicting incentives in an ethical manner that promotes organizational objectives is highly dependent on the tone at the top. For example, hiring and firing practices that put zero tolerance on unethical behaviour are increasingly common. Additionally, the law requires publicly traded corporations to establish formal procedures to receive, retain, and address any information that may affect the company's accounting or auditing. To comply with this requirement, companies have created ethics hotlines that allow employees to anonymously report unethical behaviour. While this was an important step in empowering subordinates to report unethical behaviour by their superiors, hotlines only address procedures to receive the information. Companies must also have procedures in place to make sure that such information is never destroyed and that it is communicated to those with the power to resolve any issues, such as the board of directors and top management.

ETHICAL DECISIONS   Donna Jones has just been hired as an accounting clerk. One of her jobs is to summarize invoices presented for payment by various creditors. Once prepared, the summary is first inspected by Carmen Adams, the assistant controller to whom Donna reports, and then presented to Dick Stewart, the controller, for approval. After signing the form, Dick prepares and mails the cheques.

During Donna's second week on the job, Carmen tells her that City Consulting Services Inc. will make trouble for the company unless paid immediately. She says, "Dick is rarely at his desk and never looks at signatures anyway. It would cost us at least another day to get the controller's signature. Just put the unsigned summary on Stewart's desk, and the cheque will be in the mail by the end of the day."

Donna suspects that Carmen will give her a low performance rating if she refuses to follow these instructions, and she wants to do well on her first job. Furthermore, she is quite sure that Dick will not notice the omitted control procedure. On the other hand,

Donna knows that the controller's approval is an important control procedure. Consider two possible endings for this story:

1. *Donna goes along with Carmen.* Every month, Carmen tells Donna that City Consulting Services needs to be paid immediately. Donna places the unauthorized summary on Dick's unoccupied desk. All goes well until the internal auditor runs a routine check on the credit ratings of the entities with which the company does business and discovers that City Consulting is nothing more than a bank account established by Carmen. Carmen is charged with fraud, and Donna's role is exposed in the public trial that follows. Donna is not charged in the case, but she loses her job and has great difficulty finding another comparable position.

2. *Donna refuses to go along with Carmen.* Donna receives a negative review from Carmen and is asked to leave the company. During an exit interview, Donna tells the controller why she believes Carmen gave her a negative review. The controller asks the internal audit department to follow up on City Consulting Services, at which time it is discovered to be a bank account established by Carmen. Carmen is charged with fraud. The controller contacts Donna saying, "After investigating your comments regarding Carmen's request, we have uncovered her scheme to defraud the company, and would like you to return to the company."

Like Donna, most people in business face difficult ethical dilemmas from time to time. The effectiveness of internal control systems depends on the ethical tone set by management and the ethical awareness of all company personnel.

RISK ASSESSMENT

Risk assessment procedures (also called enterprise risk management or ERM) are designed to identify, analyze, and manage **strategic risks** and **business process risks**.

Strategic Risks

Strategic risks are possible threats to the organization's success in accomplishing its objectives and are *external* to the organization. These risks are often classified around industry forces such as competitors, customers, substitute products or services, suppliers, and threat of new competitors (these are known as Porter's Five Forces) or macro factors such as political, economic, social, and technological (also known as PEST factors).

Although entire courses are devoted to management of these strategic risks, the general idea is simple. For example, when Amazon was formed, Barnes & Noble was in the midst of high growth and was opening cafés and music shops within supersized bookstores. Barnes & Noble was so deeply rooted in its "bricks and mortar" that it failed to respond to a technological factor: the Internet's transformation of the industry. By the time Barnesandnoble.com was launched, Amazon had secured the leading Web presence for booksellers—a lead that Barnes & Noble has been unable to erode.

Business Process Risks

Business processes are the *internal* processes of the company—specifically, how the company allocates its resources to meet its objectives. There are many business processes, but some of the more common ones are materials acquisition, production, logistics and distribution, branding and marketing, and human resources. The nature and relative importance of the business processes will vary from company to company based on their specific objectives. For example, Dell has adopted a low-cost provider objective. As such, it has concentrated on achieving operating efficiencies in order processing, production, and distribution. Apple, on the other hand, has adopted a product differentiation objective. This objective has led to an emphasis on product quality and continual research to develop better products with more features. As such, the risk assessment controls for these two companies will differ. Dell will be focused on monitoring inventory levels and production times, while Apple will focus on quality control and product development.

CONTROL ACTIVITIES

Control activities are the policies and procedures that top management establishes to help ensure that its objectives are met. The control activities most directly related to the accounting system and financial statements vary widely from one business to another, but generally can be identified with one of the following six categories.

1. authorization of transactions and other business activities
2. segregation of duties
3. documentation adequacy
4. physical controls
5. independent checks on performance
6. human resource controls

These six categories are discussed below.

Authorization of Transactions and Other Business Activities

The **authorization of transactions** is delegated to specific individuals, and those individuals should be held *responsible* for the performance of those duties in the evaluation of their performance. Among the designated duties of an individual may be the authority to perform specified types of activities for the business or to authorize others to execute such transactions. The clear delegation of authority and responsibility motivates individuals to perform well because they know they are accountable for their actions. For example, at most retailers, cashiers enter a code into the cash register and maintain responsibility for cash entering and leaving the register. At the end of their shift, a supervisor counts the money. Should the register have too much or too little cash, the cashier will be held responsible for the error.

Segregation of Duties

Accounting and administrative duties should be performed by different individuals, so that no one person prepares all the documents and records for an activity. This **segregation of duties** (also called *separation of duties*) reduces the likelihood that records will be used to conceal *irregularities* (intentional misstatements, theft, or fraud) and increases the likelihood that irregularities will be discovered. Segregation of duties also reduces the likelihood that unintentional record-keeping errors will remain undiscovered.

Although segregation of duties cannot eliminate the possibility of fraud, it does require people to work together, which is referred to as *collusion*. For example, movie theatres require one employee to collect the cash and another employee to collect the tickets to admit the customer into the theatre. If one person were responsible for collecting cash and admitting customers, this person could pocket the cash and let the customer in without issuing a ticket. This lack of segregation of duties represents a weakness in internal control related to the handling of cash. In this case, the number of tickets issued would match up with the cash collected because no ticket was issued and the cash was pocketed. Instead, movie theatres have one person collect the cash and issue the ticket and a second person admit customers with tickets. Cash can still be pocketed, but the segregation of duties in this example requires both employees to engage in the fraudulent scheme (an example of collusion) or the cash collected will not match the tickets collected. Segregation of duties is an important control at Caesars Windsor due to the accessibility of actual cash in slots and at gaming tables.

Perhaps the most important aspect of segregation of duties is separating the record-keeping responsibility from the physical control of the assets. For example, if a customer pays $1,000, the employee who collects the $1,000 could easily steal some or all of the money if a weakness in internal control exists and he or she has access to the accounting records. In this case, the employee could record that the money was paid and hide the fact that the money was not in the company or record that some or all of the money was not paid and that the debt was "bad."

Documentation Adequacy

Accounting records are the basis for the financial statements and other reports prepared for managers, owners, and others both inside and outside the business. **Documentation adequacy** requires that records and their underlying documentation must provide information about specific activities and help in the evaluation of individual performance. For example, prenumbered shipping documents provide a basis for monitoring shipments of goods to customers. When warehouse employees receive a shipping document, they ship the goods. If the shipping documents were not prenumbered, a shipping document could be sent to the warehouse and later destroyed. Without the missing number in the sequence to signal a missing document, nobody would realize that the document was missing and employees in the warehouse, due to this weakness in internal control, may seize the opportunity to misappropriate and sell inventory for personal gain.

Physical Controls

Both assets and records must be secured against theft and destruction. **Safeguarding** requires physical protection of the assets through, for example, fireproof vaults, locked storage facilities, keycard access, and anti-theft tags on merchandise. An increasingly important part of safeguarding assets and records is access controls for computers. Safeguards must be provided for computer programs and data files, which are more fragile and susceptible to unauthorized access than manual record-keeping systems. For example, access controls often mandate use of both alpha and numeric characters in passwords and also require password changes every few months. Some examples of **physical controls** are shown below.

Physical Controls

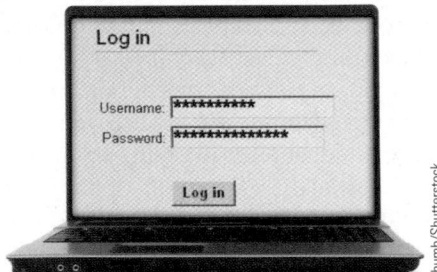

Vaults and safes   Warehouses with locked access   Computer with password protection

Independent Checks on Performance

Recorded amounts should be checked by an independent person to determine that amounts are correct and that they correspond to properly authorized activities. These procedures include clerical checks, reconciliations, comparisons of asset inspection reports with recorded amounts, computer-programmed controls, and management review of reports. For example, accounting records should be checked (or reconciled) to the bank statement by an independent person and any discrepancies should be resolved immediately. Bank reconciliations are illustrated later in this chapter.

Such controls are effective at mitigating unintentional error, theft, and fraud. One of the elements typically cited in discussions of theft and fraud is opportunity. That is, persons committing theft or fraud believe they have the opportunity to "get away with it." Control activities are designed to prevent and detect theft and fraud by reducing employees' opportunity to conceal their actions. Yet, every year billions of dollars are lost to employee theft and fraud because effectively designed control activities are not followed.

In large companies, **independent checks** are often performed by **internal auditors**. Internal auditors are employees of the business who perform tests of the internal control system to assess its effectiveness and contribution to efficient business operations. The Chief Internal Auditor usually reports directly to the Audit Committee of the organization to maintain the independence of work performed by an internal audit function.

All public companies are required by law to have an independent audit performed by **external auditors**. External auditors are independent in that they are not employed by the company being audited. External auditors render an audit opinion on the financial statements of the audited company. An external audit typically includes a review and evaluation of the audited company's system of internal control. Weaknesses in internal control are reported to the Audit Committee of the company being audited for correction as deemed necessary.

Public companies are also required to have an independent Audit Committee chosen from the board of directors. This committee is responsible for reviewing the company's internal control system to ensure that it is adequate for purposes of generating accuracy and completeness in the company's financial reporting.

Human Resource Controls

An internal control system cannot be perfect since it is in part controlled by imperfect human beings. To protect against the actions of its employees, companies usually implement **human resource controls**.

In the recruiting process, references are requested and checked. This provides the company with assurance that it is hiring individuals who are honest and who exhibit integrity.

Companies usually purchase a bond, which is a form of insurance policy, on employees who handle cash. The bond provides insurance protection to the company in case of theft, embezzlement, or other criminal acts. This "fidelity" insurance is provided by insurance companies to customers for a premium depending on a number of factors, including the nature of the activities against which the company desires protection and the level of loss to be insured.

Where employees are in a sensitive position of handling cash or other assets of a company, it is common for the company to rotate employees' duties during times of vacation or other absences. Rotation of duties helps make it difficult if not impossible for employees to conceal theft or fraud for a lengthy period of time.

INFORMATION AND COMMUNICATION

An internal control system will be unable to help a company achieve its objective unless adequate information is identified and accumulated on a timely basis. Furthermore, this information must be communicated to the appropriate employees in the organization. For example, consider a company like Mercedes that has a strategy of providing high-quality products. This company may accumulate information on the percentage of production that is rejected by quality control. If that percentage rises, it signals the possibility of problems in production (such as inferior material being used, poor training of new personnel, etc.). If such information is accumulated and communicated, these problems can be addressed before the company's reputation for high quality is harmed; if, on the other hand, such information is not accumulated and communicated, then management may not become aware of the problem until goods sold are returned and complaints are made by dissatisfied customers. At this time, it may be too late to avoid damage to their reputation.

MONITORING

Monitoring is the process of tracking potential and actual problems in the internal control system. Monitoring is accomplished through normal supervising activities such as when a manager asks a subordinate how things are going. However, best practices for larger organizations suggest that an internal independent audit staff, as discussed above, monitor the effectiveness of the internal control system. Some public companies outsource their internal audit functions. Normally in such cases, the firm providing those internal audit services is precluded from providing the *external* audit services because of the perception that the external audit firm's independence would be impaired.

RELATIONSHIP BETWEEN CONTROL ACTIVITIES AND THE ACCOUNTING SYSTEM

The **accounting system** consists of the methods and records used to identify, measure, record, and communicate financial information about a business. Although we distinguish between the accounting system and the internal control system, the two are really one integrated system designed to meet the needs of a particular business. It is difficult to generalize the relationship between internal control activities and accounting systems because it directly depends on the objectives of a particular business. Consequently, the relationship is best explored through an example.

Consider Hendrickson Theatres Ltd., which operates 10 movie theatres in a single city. All the theatres are rented, as are the projection equipment and concession facilities. Hendrickson's administrative offices, furnishings, and office equipment are also rented. The following chart of accounts indicates the structure of Hendrickson's accounting system:

Chart of Accounts for Hendrickson Theatres Ltd.

Assets	*Revenues*
Cash	Admissions revenue
Concessions inventory	Concessions revenue
Prepaid rent	*Expenses*
Liabilities	Salaries expense
Accounts payable	Wages expense
Salaries payable	Cost of concessions sold
Wages payable	Rent expense, movie
Equity	Rent expense, theatre
Share capital	Rent expense, equipment
Retained earnings	Rent expense, office
	Utilities expense
	Advertising expense
	Office supplies expense

Hendrickson's accountant makes journal entries daily for revenues, bi-weekly for wages, and monthly for the other expenses using general-purpose accounting software. Because Hendrickson has a relatively small number of accounts, its accounting system is quite simple. The portion of Hendrickson's accounting system related to revenues and the associated control activities are described in Exhibit 4.3.

(EXHIBIT 4.3)

Relationship between the Accounting System and Control Procedures

Illustrations from the Internal Control Structure for Revenue and Cash for Hendrickson Theatres Ltd.	
Accounting System	**Control Procedures**
Entries: Admissions and concessions revenues are recorded daily by increasing both cash and the appropriate revenue accounts.	*Authority and responsibility:* Each theatre manager is responsible for the control of cash in his or her theatre, but the central office accountant makes all general ledger entries related to cash.
Documentation: The cash register at each ticket booth and concession stand prepares a detailed list of cash transactions and a daily cash summary report. The daily summary reports from the 10 theatres are electronically transferred to the central office each night and are automatically summarized upon receipt. Each morning, the accountant generates a report and makes revenue entries in the computerized general ledger.	*Segregation of duties:* Maintenance of the general ledger is segregated from responsibility for local cash control. Ticket sellers and concession operators may assist in preparation of daily cash deposits, but the manager must check and sign deposit documents.
	Documentation: Prenumbered admission tickets are dispensed by machine at each theatre. The machine also prepares a report of the tickets issued each day, which is used by the theatre manager to reconcile cash collected with the number of tickets sold.
Reports: A variety of revenue analyses can be prepared on the computer system, including analyses by theatre, movie, day of the week, and month.	*Safeguards:* The cash accumulates in each theatre until the end of each day. When cash drawers reach a specified level, however, the cash register signals that a fixed amount of cash should be removed by the manager and placed in the theatre's safe.
	Checks: On an unannounced schedule, Hendrickson's accountant visits each theatre and verifies cash receipts reported against the number of tickets issued. On these same visits, the accountant checks concession revenues against the amounts reported by inventorying concession supplies.
	Human resources: Employees handling cash are bonded through an insurance policy.

© Cengage Learning

CASH CONTROLS

Internal controls are designed to protect all assets. But the more liquid an asset (the more "liquid" an asset, the more easily it is converted into cash), the more likely it is to be stolen. In fact, a study by the Association of Certified Fraud Examiners suggested that 80% of all workplace frauds involved employee theft of company assets (i.e., embezzlement) and that 90% of these thefts involved cash.[3]

Casinos like Caesars Windsor and bingo operations operate in a particularly difficult environment to control cash, but all companies must use internal control activities. As discussed, the internal controls in Exhibit 4.4 help businesses effectively control cash receipts and disbursements.

Electronic funds transfer (EFT) is a method of transferring cash from one bank account directly to another without human involvement in handling cash or cheques. Interac e-transfer is one example of an EFT mechanism; credit and debit cards are another. While EFT transactions normally increase internal control—because humans do not handle cash or cheques—opportunities for fraud still exist if proper internal controls over electronic processing are not in place.

Although many of the cash controls with which you are most familiar (e.g., cash registers) might appear to be outside the accounting system, we will highlight three important areas where the accounting system interacts with the internal control system to strengthen cash controls:

OBJECTIVE ③

Describe procedures used by businesses to control cash.

---

[3] The other 20% includes such things as fraudulent financial statements.

YOUDECIDE Internal Control over Cash in a Student University Pub

You are the treasurer of your university's pub and have responsibility for collecting sales, depositing cash in the bank, writing all cheques, maintaining accounting records, and preparing bank reconciliations and financial statements. After taking your financial accounting course, you realize that this is a clear violation of segregation of duties and mention this to the pub's president. The president agrees, but says that segregation of duties is not nearly as important as simply finding someone willing to perform the treasurer's tasks.

What steps can you advise your university's pub president to take to strengthen the internal control system?

You can advise the president to look into each of the following areas. A "no" answer to any question indicates a potential internal control weakness.

- *Is supporting documentation obtained from vendors whenever cash is paid or a liability is incurred?*
  The use of appropriate documentation assures the proper payment of bills and facilitates the appropriate accrual of liabilities on the year-end statement of financial position.
- *Is every vendor invoice and all supporting documentation cancelled (e.g., by writing "Paid by cheque number 841 on November 29, 2018") at the time the cheque is written?*
  This action helps ensure that duplicate payments are not made.
- *Does the organization's president co-sign all cheques written for amounts greater than some specified minimum (say $500)?*

This control reduces the possibility of unauthorized payments.
- *Are receipts of sales deposited promptly (at least daily)?*
  Prompt deposits help avoid misplacing receipts.
- *Does the organization have procedures to assist in the collection of accounts receivable?*
  Despite the mutual trust and friendship that are a part of most student organizations, uncollectible accounts can be a serious problem. The treasurer may need the assistance of formal procedures in collecting overdue accounts.
- *Does the organization have an accounting policies and procedures manual?*
  Such a manual may be needed to prepare the year-end financial report in conformity with university and/or national governing body requirements.
- *Are complete minutes of all officers' meetings maintained?*
  The minutes should include (a) a listing of all changes in officers, including the names of new officers, (b) authorization of cheque signers, and (c) approval of all capital expenditures. Including this information, along with descriptions of important decisions of the organization's governing body, documents all the important activities of the organization.

Businesses can control cash effectively with internal controls, which include guidelines for collecting, holding, and paying cash as well as keeping records and assigning individuals different responsibilities.

- bank reconciliations
- cash over and short
- petty cash

concept Q&A

If a debit increases an asset and decreases a liability and a credit decreases an asset and increases a liability, why does the bank "credit" your account when you make a deposit and "debit" your account when you make a withdrawal?

Answer:

Because the "credit" and "debit" are from the bank's point of view. When you make a deposit, it actually increases the bank's liability to you—the bank now owes you more. When you make a withdrawal, it decreases the bank's liability to you.

RECONCILIATION OF ACCOUNTING RECORDS TO BANK STATEMENT

The use of a bank is one of the most important controls over cash. The bank duplicates the company's accounting by keeping its own accounting records of your account. Unfortunately, the bank's accounting records and the company's accounting records often disagree because the transactions are not recorded at the same time (e.g., a company writes a cheque on January 18 and credits cash immediately; however, the bank will not debit your account until the cheque is presented to the bank—typically many days later). Therefore, to ensure that the company's accounting records are consistent with the bank's accounting records, any differences must be "reconciled." This process is called the **bank reconciliation**.

Periodically—usually once a month—the bank returns all cheques processed during the period, together with a detailed record of the activity of the account. This document is a *bank statement*, which shows the beginning and ending account balance and the individual deposits and withdrawals

(EXHIBIT 4.4)

Examples of Control Activities for Cash Receipts and Disbursements

Control Activity	Cash Receipts	Cash Disbursements
Authorization of transactions	Only specifically assigned persons should collect cash.	Only specifically assigned persons should sign cheques.
Segregation of duties	Different persons should handle and record cash.	Different persons should handle cash, make payments, and record cash.
Documentation	Accounting records should include remittance advices, cash register tapes, and bank deposit slips, which should be regularly reconciled by independent persons.	Accounting records should include prenumbered cheques with sequence regularly accounted for. Cheques issued only if attached to a supplier invoice.
Physical controls	Cash on hand should be kept in safes or vaults that have limited access. Encourage customers to send cash by electronic means.	Blank cheques and signing machines should be in safes or vaults with limited access. Use electronic disbursements when possible.
Independent checks	Cash receipts should be counted daily by employee supervisors. An independent person should reconcile cash recorded to bank deposits daily.	Cheque amounts should be agreed to invoice amounts before issuing cheques. Reconcile bank account monthly.
Human resources	Bond employees who have access to cash. Rotate employee duties during vacation periods. Require and check references before hiring.	Bond employees who have access to cash. Rotate employee duties during vacation periods. Require and check references before hiring.

recorded by the bank during the period. Basically, the bank statement is a copy of the bank's accounting records showing customers the increases and decreases in their balances (see Exhibit 4.5). Remember, a chequing account is a liability for the bank (the bank owes you the balance). Therefore, deposits and other events that increase your bank account balance are labelled "credits" on the bank statement (because they increase the bank's liability to you), and withdrawals and other events that decrease your bank account balance are labelled "debits" (because they decrease the bank's liability to you).

Reconciliation of these separately maintained records serves two purposes:

- It serves a control function by identifying errors and providing an inspection of detailed accounting records that deters theft.
- It serves a transaction detection function by identifying transactions performed by the bank, so that the business can make the necessary journal entries in its accounting records.

In general, differences between the company's account balance (see Exhibit 4.6) and the bank statement balance develop from three sources:

- transactions recorded by the business, but not recorded by the bank in time to appear on the current bank statement
- transactions recorded by the bank, but not yet recorded by the business
- errors in recording transactions on either set of records

(EXHIBIT 4.5)

Bank Statement

T N B

THIRD NATIONAL BANK   Account Statement
123 Main Street
La Salle, ON N9J 1X3   Statement Date:
                                        August 31, 2018

ONTARIO ENTERPRISES INC.   Account Number:
519 MAIN STREET   40056
LA SALLE, ON N9J 1X3

Previous Balance	Cheques and Debits	Deposits and Credits	Current Balance
$7,675.20	$10,685.26	$7,175.10	$4,165.04

Cheques and Debits			Deposits and Credits		Daily Balance	
Date	No.	Amount	Date	Amount	Date	Amount
8/3/18	1883	182.00			8/3/18	7,493.20
8/4/18	1884	217.26	8/4/18	2,673.10	8/4/18	9,949.04
8/6/18	1885	1,075.00	EFT Collection from ABC Ltd.		8/6/18	8,874.04
8/7/18	1886	37.50	8/7/18	4,500.00	8/7/18	13,336.54
8/10/18	1887	826.00			8/10/18	12,510.54
8/11/18	1888	50.00			8/11/18	12,460.54
8/12/18	1889	2,670.00				
8/12/18	1890	67.90			8/12/18	9,722.64
8/13/18	1891	890.00			8/13/18	8,832.64
8/14/18	1892	27.50			8/14/18	8,805.14
8/17/18	1893	111.00			8/17/18	8,694.14
8/18/18	DM	380.00			8/18/18	8,314.14
8/19/18	1894	60.00				
8/19/18	1895	510.00			8/19/18	7,744.14
8/20/18	1896	30.00			8/20/18	7,714.14
8/21/18	1897	1,600.00			8/21/18	6,114.14
8/24/18	1898	78.00			8/24/18	6,036.14
8/25/18	NSF	200.00			8/25/18	5,836.14
8/26/18	1899	208.80			8/26/18	5,627.34
8/27/18	EFT	1,250.00			8/27/18	4,377.34
	payment				8/28/18	4,202.34
	of wages					
8/28/18	1900	175.00				
8/31/18	1902	25.30	8/31/18 INT	2.00		
8/31/18	SC	14.00			8/31/18	4,165.04

Symbols:	**CM** Credit Memo	**EC** Error Correction	**NSF** Non-sufficient Funds
	DM Debit Memo	**INT** Interest Earned	**SC** Service Charge

Reconcile your account immediately

Transactions Recorded by the Company, but Not Yet Recorded by the Bank

There are generally two types of transactions recorded by the company, but not recorded by the bank in time to appear on the current statement: outstanding cheques, and deposits in transit.

(EXHIBIT 4.6)

T-Account for Cash, Prior to Reconciliation

Ontario Enterprises Inc.							
		Cash					
Balance, 7/31/18	$6,200.94						
Date	Amount Deposited		Cheque Number	Cheque Amount	Cheque Number	Cheque Amount	
8/1	$2,673.10		1886	$ 37.50	1896	$ 30.00	
8/5	4,500.00		1887	826.00	1897	1,600.00	
8/31	300.00		1888	50.00	1898	87.00	
Total deposits	$7,473.10		1889	2,670.00	1899	208.80	
			1890	67.90	1900	175.00	
			1891	890.00	1901	93.00	
			1892	27.50	1902	25.30	
			1893	111.00	1903	72.50	
			1894	60.00	1904	891.00	
			1895	510.00	EFT	1,250.00	
						$9,682.50	
					Total disbursements		
Balance, 8/31/18	$3,991.54						

Outstanding Cheques An **outstanding cheque** is a cheque issued and recorded by the company that has not been "cashed" by the recipient of the cheque. The company has (properly) recorded the cheque as lowering its cash balance and the bank has (properly) not recorded the cheque as lowering the company's account balance because it has not been cashed. For example, when a cheque is written during December, but not cashed until the following January, the company's December 31 general ledger cash balance will be lower than its account balance on the December 31 bank statement.

Deposits in Transit A **deposit in transit** is an amount that has been received and recorded by the company, but that has not been recorded by the bank in time to appear on the current bank statement. Deposits in transit cause the bank's balance to be smaller than the company's general ledger cash account balance. Deposits in transit arise because many banks post any deposit received after 2 or 3 p.m. into their records on the next business day and because companies often make deposits on weekends or holidays when the bank is not open for business, which could cause the deposit to appear on the next bank statement.

Transactions Recorded by the Bank, but Not Yet Recorded by the Company

Several types of transactions are recorded by the bank but not yet recorded by the company, including service charges, nonsufficient funds cheques, and debit and credit memos. After the reconciliation process, the company must make journal entries to record all the transactions that have been recorded by the bank but not yet recorded in the company's ledger cash account.

Service Charges **Service charges** are fees charged by the bank for chequing account services. The amount of the fee is not known to the company (and therefore cannot be recorded) until the bank statement is received. Bank service charges unrecorded by the company at the end of a month cause the bank balance to be smaller than the company's general ledger cash account balance.

Nonsufficient Funds Cheques A **nonsufficient funds (NSF) cheque** is a cheque that has been returned to the depositor because funds in the issuer's account are not sufficient to pay the cheque (also called a *bounced* or *dishonoured cheque*). The amount of the cheque was added to the depositor's account when the cheque was deposited; however, since the cheque cannot be paid, the bank deducts the amount of the NSF cheque from the account. This deduction is recorded by the bank before it is recorded by the business. NSF cheques cause the bank balance to be smaller than the cash account balance.

Debit and Credit Memos A debit memo might result, for example, if the bank makes a prearranged deduction from the company's account to pay a utility bill. Debit memos recorded by the bank but not yet recorded by the company cause the bank balance to be smaller than the general ledger cash account balance. A credit memo could result if the bank collected a note receivable for the company and deposited the funds in the company's account. Credit memos recorded by the bank but not recorded by the company cause the bank balance to be larger than the general ledger cash account balance.

Errors

The previous differences between the accounting records and the bank's account balances are the result of time lags between the recording of a transaction by the company and the recording by the bank. Errors in recording transactions represent yet another source of difference between a company's general ledger cash account balance and the bank's account balance. Errors are inevitable in any accounting system and should be corrected as soon as discovered. In addition, an effort should be made to determine the cause of any error as a basis for corrective action. Obviously, an intentional error designed to hide a misappropriation of funds calls for quite different corrective action than does an error resulting from human fatigue or machine failure.

Performing a Bank Reconciliation

To begin the reconciliation, start with the "cash balance from the bank statement" and the "cash balance from company records." These two balances are then adjusted as necessary to produce identical "adjusted cash balances" by following these steps:

Step 1. Compare the deposits on the bank statement to the deposits debited to the cash account. Any deposits debited to the cash account but not on the bank statement are likely deposits in transit, so look at a bank-stamped deposit slip to ensure that these amounts were actually deposited. Deposits in transit should be added to the "cash balance from the bank statement."

Step 2. Compare the paid (often called *cancelled*) cheques returned with the bank statement to the amounts credited to the cash account and the list of outstanding cheques from prior months. Any cheques credited to the general ledger cash account but not on the bank statement are likely outstanding cheques. These amounts should be subtracted from the "cash balance from the bank statement."

Step 3. Look for items on the bank statement that have not been debited or credited to the general ledger cash account. These include bank service charges, interest payments, NSF cheques, automatic payments (debit memos), and bank collections on behalf of the company (credit memos). Bank debits should be subtracted from the "cash balance from company records," while bank credits should be added to the "cash balance from company records." Of course, all these amounts should be verified by checking source documents.

Step 4. If the "adjusted cash balances" are still not the same, search for errors. The most common error is a "transposition" error in which, for example, a cheque is written for $823 but recorded as $283 (the 8 and 2 are transposed). In this case, the accounting records will show a $283 credit to the cash account, but the bank will show an $823 debit to the company's account. All errors made by the company must be added or subtracted from the "cash balance from company records." All errors made by the bank must be added or subtracted from the "cash balance from the bank statement."

This process is illustrated in Cornerstone 4.1 .

Performing a Bank Reconciliation

CORNERSTONE 4.1

Information:

Refer to the bank statement in Exhibit 4.5 and the cash account in Exhibit 4.6. Recognize that the beginning balance was reconciled at the end of last month (July). Assume that this was performed correctly and that all outstanding cheques (numbers 1883, 1884, and 1885) and deposits in transit from July cleared during August.

CORNERSTONE
VIDEO

Required:

1. Determine the adjustments needed by comparing the bank statement to the cash account.

2. Complete the bank reconciliation.

Why:

A bank reconciliation is prepared each accounting period to ensure that the cash balance is accurately recorded in the general ledger and to ensure that proper control is maintained over cash. The bank reconciliation procedure compares the accounting records to the bank statement, determines where differences exist, and accounts for the differences.

Solution:

1. Four items in the cash account do not appear on the bank statement: the August 31 deposit (in transit), and cheques 1901, 1903, and 1904 (outstanding). There is also an error. The amount posted to the cash account for cheque 1898 does not equal the amount cleared on the bank statement. The cancelled cheque on record was written for $78.00, not $87.00, so the error is on the company's records.

2.

Cash balance from bank statement		$ 4,165.04	Cash balance from company records		$3,991.54
Add: Deposit in transit (8/31)		300.00	Add:		
Less: Outstanding cheques			Error in recording cheque 1898 (we recorded as $87, should be $78)	$ 9.00	
1901	$ (93.00)		Interest earned	2.00	11.00
1903	(72.50)		Less:		
1904	(891.00)	(1,056.50)	Service charge	14.00	
Adjusted cash balance		**$ 3,408.54**	NSF cheque	200.00	
			Electric bill (Debit Memo)	380.00	(594.00)
			Adjusted cash balance		**$3,408.54**

Adjusted cash balances should equal.

If the person who writes the cheques also performs the reconciliation, it is easier for him or her to cover up theft and fraud. Therefore, there are additional benefits when the bank reconciliation is performed by someone with no other responsibilities related to cash as this lack of segregation of duties represents a weakness in internal control over cash.

Making Journal Entries as a Result of the Bank Reconciliation

Once the bank reconciliation is completed, some adjustments to the accounting records may be necessary. No adjustments are necessary for outstanding cheques or deposits in transit because the accounting records have correctly recorded these amounts. However, as shown in Cornerstone 4.2, adjustments are necessary for any company errors or

---

CORNERSTONE 4.2

Recording Journal Entries as a Result of the Bank Reconciliation

CORNERSTONE VIDEO

Information:

Refer to the bank reconciliation performed in Cornerstone 4.1. Assume that all cheques from this account were written to satisfy accounts payable.

Required:

Prepare the necessary adjusting journal entries.

Why:

Adjusting journal entries are required in order to record transactions processed by the bank but that have not yet been recorded in the accounting records.

Assets	=	Liabilities	+	Shareholders' Equity
+9		+9		

Assets	=	Liabilities	+	Shareholders' Equity (Interest Income)
+2				+2

Assets	=	Liabilities	+	Shareholders' Equity (Bank Charges)
−14				−14

Assets	=	Liabilities	+	Shareholders' Equity
+200				
−200				

Assets	=	Liabilities	+	Shareholders' Equity (Utilities Expense)
−380				−380

Solution:

Account and Explanation	Debit	Credit
Cash	9	
Accounts Payable		9
(Correct error in recording cheque 1898)		
Cash	2	
Interest Income		2
(Record interest)		
Bank Service Charge Expense	14	
Cash		14
(Record bank service charge)		
Accounts Receivable	200	
Cash		200
(Record NSF cheque)		
Utilities Expense	380	
Cash		380
(Record debit memo for payment of electric bill)		

items such as bank charges or interest that the company does not find out about until receiving the bank statement.

CASH OVER AND SHORT

Another important control activity requires that cash receipts be deposited in a bank daily. At the end of each day, the amount of cash received during the day is debited to the general ledger cash account to which it has been deposited. The amount deposited should equal the total of cash register tapes. If it does not (and differences will occasionally occur even when cash-handling procedures are carefully designed and executed), the discrepancy is recorded in an account called **cash over and short**, as illustrated in Cornerstone 4.3 .

CORNERSTONE 4.3

Recording Cash Over and Short

Information:

RSA has $20,671.12 prepared for deposit. However, the total of cash register tapes and other documents supporting the receipt of cash on that day is $20,685.14, including collections of accounts receivable of $6,760.50.

Required:

Prepare the necessary journal entry.

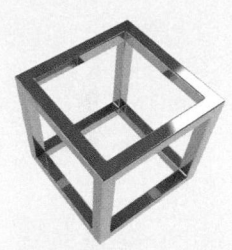

CORNERSTONE VIDEO

Why:

When the cash in the cash register does not agree with the cash register tapes, the difference is recorded in the cash over and short general ledger account. The recording of cash over and short in the general ledger provides a means for management to be aware of and to follow up on why these differences are occurring.

Solution:

Account and Explanation	Debit	Credit
Cash	20,671.12	
Cash Over and Short	14.02	
Sales Revenue*		13,924.64
Accounts Receivable		6,760.50
(*Record cash register collections*)		

* $20,685.14 − $6,760.50

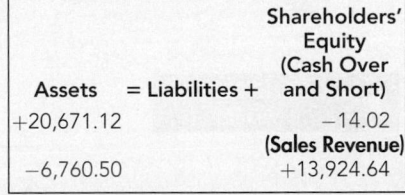

Assets	= Liabilities +	Shareholders' Equity (Cash Over and Short)
+20,671.12		−14.02
		(Sales Revenue)
−6,760.50		+13,924.64

Observe that a cash *shortage* (as in Cornerstone 4.3) requires a debit to cash over and short, whereas a cash *overage* would require a credit.

One common source of cash over and short is errors in making change for cash sales. Significant amounts of cash over and short signal the need for a careful investigation of the causes and appropriate corrective action. Cash over and short is usually treated as an income statement account and is reported as a part of other expenses or other revenues.

PETTY CASH

Cash controls are more effective when companies pay with a cheque for the following reasons:

* Only certain people have the authority to sign the cheque. Those authorized to sign do not keep the accounting records and only sign the cheque with the proper documentation supporting the payment (e.g., evidence that the goods being paid for were properly ordered and received).
* Supporting documents are marked paid to avoid duplicate payment.
* Cheques are prenumbered, which makes it easy to identify any missing cheques.

However, issuing cheques to pay small amounts is usually more costly than paying cash.[4] Therefore, a company may establish a **petty cash** fund to pay for items such as stamps or a cake for an employee birthday party. The petty cash fund is overseen by a petty cash custodian, who both pays for small dollar amounts directly from the fund and reimburses employees who have receipts for items they've bought with their own money. At the end of the month, the custodian submits all receipts (and other supporting documentation) to the company. After company personnel (other than the petty cash custodian) determine that the documents are authentic and that each transaction is supported by appropriate documentation, the custodian is given an amount to replenish the petty cash fund. The company then records the amounts spent in the accounting records. Because the custodian replenishes petty cash at the end of the month, the accounting records are appropriately updated each month. This process is illustrated in Cornerstone 4.4 .

CORNERSTONE 4.4

CORNERSTONE VIDEO

Accounting for Petty Cash

Information:

On January 1, Alberta Industries establishes a petty cash fund of $500. On January 31, the petty cash custodian presents the following records of the month's transactions, together with related documents, and requests reimbursement:

Jan. 12	Hansen's Grocery (coffee)	$ 30
15	Canada Post Office (postage)	70
17	Northwest Messenger (package delivery)	25
19	Office Depot (office supplies)	175
25	Mr. Strand, Controller (food for lunch meeting)	63
	Total	$363

After approving the expenses, the company issues a cheque to the custodian for $363.00 to replenish the fund.

Required:

1. Prepare the journal entry to establish the petty cash fund on January 1.

2. Prepare the journal entry to record the replenishment of the fund on January 31.

(Continued)

---

[4] Cheques cost money to print, mail, and process. Some estimate the cost of processing a cheque to be over $1. Therefore, banks developed ways for companies to transfer money without the use of paper cheques. For example, most employees do not see an actual paycheque; instead, money is automatically deposited into their bank account. Use of EFTs is quite common and has become commonplace at the individual level through the use of debit cards.

3. Assuming the entry from requirement 2 has been made, prepare the journal entry needed to increase the fund balance to $600.

CORNERSTONE

4.4

(Continued)

Why:

Companies use a petty cash fund to pay for small-dollar-amount expenses. The use of a petty cash fund avoids the more costly procedure of preparing cheques to pay small-dollar-amount expenses.

Solution:

	Date	Account and Explanation	Debit	Credit
1.	Jan. 1	Petty Cash	500.00	
		Cash		500.00
		(Establish petty cash fund)		
2.	Jan. 31	Office Supplies	175.00	
		Postage Expense	70.00	
		Delivery Expense	25.00	
		Miscellaneous Expense	93.00	
		Cash*		363.00
		(Replenish petty cash fund and recognize expenses)		
3.		Petty Cash	100.00	
		Cash		100.00
		(Increase the fund balance to $600)		

Assets	=	Liabilities	+	Shareholders' Equity
+500				
−500				

Assets	=	Liabilities	+	Shareholders' Equity (Specified Expense Accounts)
−363				−175
				−70
				−25
				−93

Assets	=	Liabilities	+	Shareholders' Equity
−100				
+100				

* The expenditures of petty cash are not recorded in the accounting records until the fund is replenished. The replenishment does not alter the balance of the petty cash fund on Alberta's records; the balance remains at $500.00.

Replenishment of petty cash may also occur during the month if the amount of petty cash available gets too low. However, to ensure that all expenses are recorded in the appropriate accounting period, replenishment should occur at the end of the month or accounting period. As an additional control measure, a company should periodically verify its petty cash balances by counting the cash in the hands of custodians and comparing it to the custodian's petty cash record.

We have spent considerable time discussing internal controls in general, and over cash in particular, for two reasons. First, internal controls are an integral part of the accounting system and business. Second, the accounting and reporting of cash is not complex. After our next discussion of accounting and reporting cash, we will address the operating cycle and cash management strategies.

ACCOUNTING AND REPORTING CASH

Cash is not only currency and coins, but also savings and chequing accounts and negotiable instruments such as cheques and money orders. When cash is received, a general ledger cash account is increased by a debit; and when cash is paid out, a general ledger cash account is decreased by a credit. Receipt and payment of cash are frequently accomplished by a cheque sent through the mail, a process that may require several days, and additional

OBJECTIVE **4**

Describe how businesses account for and report cash.

(EXHIBIT 4.7)

Statement of Financial Position Reporting of Cash for Canadian Tire

Canadian Tire Corporation, Limited Consolidated Statements of Financial Position (partial) (in millions)		
	Jan. 3, 2015	Dec. 28, 2013
ASSETS		
Current assets:		
Cash and cash equivalents*	$662.1	$643.2
Short-term investments	289.1	416.6

*Cash and cash equivalents are defined as cash plus highly liquid and rated certificates of deposit or commercial paper with an original term to maturity of three months or less.

Source: Canadian Tire Corporation Annual Report 2014.

time may pass between receipt of the cheque and its deposit in the bank by the payee. Even though there may be a time lag between the issuance of a cheque and the actual transfer of funds, the accounting system treats payment by cheque in exactly the same way that it treats the transfer of currency. The receipt of either a cheque or currency is recorded by a debit to cash. Conversely, either the issue of a cheque or the payment of currency is recorded by a credit to cash.

Cash is reported on both the statement of financial position and the statement of cash flows. The statement of financial position typically reports the amount of cash and cash equivalents (highly liquid short-term investments) available at the statement of financial position date, as shown in Exhibit 4.7. The statement of cash flows shows the sources and uses of cash during the year. The statement of cash flows will be discussed in more detail in Chapter 11.

As explained in Exhibit 4.7, for Canadian Tire, the definition of **cash equivalents** is a standard definition in that cash equivalents are noted as being both:

- easily convertible into known amounts of cash and
- close enough to maturity that they are relatively insensitive to changes in interest rates.

But why do companies bother to invest cash in short-term investments rather than holding cash? The answer is that such investments earn a greater rate of return than cash sitting in a bank account. Canadian Tire had $289,100,000 in short-term investments at January 3, 2015. If their investment strategy earns a mere 1% more than a bank account, they will earn an extra $2.891 million in interest income for the year.

OPERATING CYCLE

OBJECTIVE 5

Describe the operating cycle and explain the principles of cash management.

The **operating cycle** is the elapsed time between the purchase of goods for resale (or the purchase of materials to produce saleable goods or services) and the collection of cash from customers (presumably a larger amount of cash than was invested in the goods sold). Although typically a year or less, the operating cycle can be as short as a few days for perishable goods, or as long as many years for the production and sale of products such as timber or wine (see Exhibit 4.8).

Consider the operating cycle for H.H. Gregg, a large appliance retailer that provides long-term financing for customers. Cash is used to purchase appliances that remain in inventory for an average of three months before being sold. Most are sold on credit, and it takes an average of 12 months to collect the full amount of cash that resulted from the sale. Thus, Gregg's operating cycle is 15 months, representing the average purchase-to-collection interval (three months to sell plus 12 months to collect).

(EXHIBIT 4.8)

The Operating Cycle

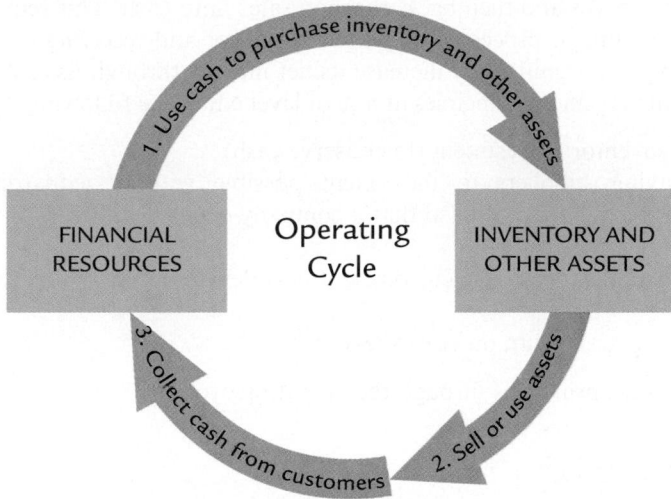

© Cengage Learning

The length of the operating cycle influences the classification of assets and liabilities on statements of financial position. In addition, the operating cycle plays an important role in the measurement of income. The length of the operating cycle also affects the amount of capital a business needs and the policies that govern its sales of goods and services, as the You Decide case demonstrates.

YOU DECIDE Operating Cycle and Capital Requirements

You are the CFO of Tolland Gizmo. You sell, on credit, approximately 1,000 Gizmos per month at $10 per unit. In addition to the accounts receivable, you have an inventory of 200 Gizmos that were purchased at a cost of $6 per unit (a total inventory of $1,200) and $1,000 in cash. Currently, Tolland has one month's sales in accounts receivable and the following statement of financial position:

ASSETS	
Cash	$ 1,000
Inventory	1,200
Accounts receivable	10,000
Total	$12,200

LIABILITIES AND SHAREHOLDERS' EQUITY	
Equity	$12,200
Total	$12,200

The sales force wants to lengthen the collection period of the accounts receivable to three months.

How would lengthening the collection period of the accounts receivable affect Tolland's financing requirements?

Tolland will now need to obtain an operating bank line of credit to fund the longer collection period and will have interest expense. Presumably, the company would not allow its customers to take three months to pay cash out unless compensated for doing so. Thus, Tolland will probably charge a higher price because of the extended payment terms.

Tolland's higher price to cover the interest expense it pays for a longer collection period will result in greater revenues.

CASH MANAGEMENT

With an understanding of the operating cycle, we now turn our attention to cash management strategies. As discussed, the activities of the operating cycle transform cash into goods and services and then back, through sales, into cash. This sequence of activities includes a continual process of paying cash out of and receiving cash in the business. A company can significantly increase its net income through its cash management policies. Cash management principles at a high level entail the following:

- minimizing inventory investment (to conserve cash)
- delaying paying suppliers to the extent possible without jeopardizing supplier relationships or purchase cost (so that a company can earn as much interest on their cash as possible)
- speeding up collection from customers (in order to obtain and invest the cash sooner)
- earning the greatest return on any excess cash

We can follow these principles through the operating cycle.

Buying Inventory

The first stage of the operating cycle is buying inventory. Money that is tied up in inventory sitting on the shelves is not earning any return. As such, an important goal of cash management and cash conservation is to keep inventory levels low. This decreases the need for cash. Companies have made great strides in inventory management over the past few decades by adopting "just in time" inventory delivery policies and procedures. For example, car companies such as Toyota time the delivery of parts such as windows and seats down to the minute.

Paying for Inventory

The second stage of the operating cycle is paying for the inventory. As with all payments, a good cash management principle is to delay payments as long as possible while maintaining a good relationship with the payee. The longer a company keeps cash, the more interest it can collect. This may seem trivial, but consider a company like Microsoft. Its 2015 financial statements reveal approximately US$6.5 billion in accounts payable. If Microsoft can earn 5% on this money, it will earn close to US$890,000 per day in interest income. You may practise this principle in your own lives if you wait to pay your tuition on the last possible day.

Selling Inventory

The third stage is selling the inventory, which usually produces accounts receivable. Good cash management suggests increasing the speed of accounts receivable collections. This is an area that has become increasingly sophisticated over the past 20 years. In fact, many companies sell their accounts receivable rather than wait for their customers to pay. Of course, they sell the accounts receivable for less than they would have received (which represents interest income and return for the buyer), but it also allows the company to receive the cash sooner and to avoid hiring employees to service the accounts receivable.

Short-Term Investments

Beyond delaying payments and speeding up collections, businesses try to keep their bank cash balances to a minimum because most bank accounts earn relatively small amounts of interest income. Accordingly, short-term investments are purchased with temporary cash surpluses. The value and composition of short-term investment portfolios may change continually in response to seasonal factors and other shifts in the business environment.

These investments will usually be liquidated (converted to cash through selling or maturity) before the business undertakes any significant short-term borrowing because the interest expense on short-term borrowings usually exceeds the income that can be earned on short-term investments. Nonetheless, temporary cash needs can result from the day-to-day ups and downs in the inflows and outflows of cash, as well as unforeseen needs for cash. A business with a good credit rating can borrow funds to resolve a temporary cash need. Such borrowings frequently are made under a line of credit, an agreement between the company and its bank in which the bank promises to lend the company funds up to a specified limit and at specified interest rates. The use of short-term investments as part of cash management is illustrated in the following You Decide case.

YOU DECIDE Cash Management

You are the treasurer at Canada Wire, a medium-size manufacturer of cable and wire used in building and bridge construction. Since most construction is seasonal, Canada Wire tends to have far more cash inflows during the summer months. Furthermore, during the winter its cash outflows are often greater than its inflows.

How do you manage the excess cash accumulated during the summer months knowing that cash will be needed during the winter?

Canada Wire will use its excess cash to make short-term investments. It should be possible to liquidate these investments easily by winter when the cash will be needed. Examples of such investments could be certificates of deposit, treasury bills, and short-term equity holdings. Furthermore, most companies will have a line of credit at a bank. This arrangement allows the company to borrow an amount with a prearranged limit on a demand basis.

Investing excess cash in short-term investments allows companies to have immediate access to cash to cover temporary shortfalls, while minimizing borrowing costs.

Cash Flow Projections

The cash flow that a business will generate from its future operations is uncertain. To ensure that an adequate balance of cash is on hand at all times, proactive management teams prepare cash flow projections. A cash flow projection starts with the cash balance at the beginning of the projection period; adds projected cash inflows generated by collections from sales and capital sources such as banks and shareholders; deducts projected cash outflows from disbursements to suppliers, creditors, and shareholders; and calculates the projected cash balance at the end of the projection period. An ongoing cash flow projection system helps ensure that management has an early warning sign of cash balance problems.

Effective cash management ultimately requires some understanding of future cash flows. For example, if the company is planning to expand or pay off a loan, it must make sure it has the necessary cash on hand. If a company receives most of its cash for the year around the holidays, it must effectively manage the excess until the time it is needed. These projections are made as part of the budgeting process and are an integral part of managerial accounting courses.

SIGNIFICANT DIFFERENCES BETWEEN IFRS AND ASPE

There are no significant differences between IFRS and ASPE with respect to cash and cash equivalents.

SUMMARY OF LEARNING OBJECTIVES

LO1.   Discuss the role of internal controls in managing a business.

- Internal control systems provide reasonable assurance that the company's objectives are being met in three areas:
  - effectiveness and efficiency of operations
  - reliability of financial reporting
  - compliance with applicable laws and regulations

LO2.   Discuss five elements of a good internal control system.

- The internal control system includes:
  - the control environment
  - risk assessment
  - control activities
  - information and communication
  - monitoring
- Although we distinguish between the accounting system and the internal control system, the two are really one integrated system designed to meet the needs of a particular business.

LO3.   Describe the procedures used by businesses to control cash.

- Keeping control over cash is extremely difficult.
- It is important to:
  - safeguard cash with physical controls such as vaults
  - adequately segregate the custody of cash from the authorization of payments and the accounting records
- Cash accounts include:
  - cash in bank
  - change funds
  - petty cash
- Controls over these cash accounts include:
  - bank reconciliations
  - daily deposits and recording cash over and short amounts
  - accounting procedures for petty cash funds

LO4.   Describe how businesses account for and report cash.

- A cash account is debited when cash is received and credited when cash is paid out.
- Cash is reported on the statement of financial position as the amount of cash and cash equivalents available on the statement of financial position date.
- The statement of cash flows shows the sources and uses of cash during the accounting period.
- Cash equivalents are amounts that are easily convertible into known amounts of cash and investments that are close to maturity (90 days or less to maturity).

LO5.   Describe the operating cycle and explain the principles of cash management.

- The operating cycle of the business starts when the business uses cash to purchase inventory.
- When a business sells goods on credit, creating accounts receivable, cash is not replenished until the receivables are collected, which completes the operating cycle.
- Cash management is an important function at all companies because business is really a continuous cycle of paying and receiving cash.
- Although aspects of cash management have become extremely sophisticated, basic strategies are:

- keeping inventory levels low
- delaying payment of liabilities as long as possible
- speeding up collection of accounts receivable
- investing idle cash to earn the greatest possible return while still keeping it available when needed

CORNERSTONE 4.1	Performing a bank reconciliation, page 213	**CORNERSTONES**
CORNERSTONE 4.2	Recording journal entries as a result of the bank reconciliation, page 214	
CORNERSTONE 4.3	Recording cash over and short, page 215	
CORNERSTONE 4.4	Accounting for petty cash, page 216	

KEY TERMS

REVIEW PROBLEM

I. Bank Reconciliation

Fugazi Enterprises has the following information in its accounting records for their primary chequing account:

Balance at April 30	$ 18,350
Cheques written during May	114,700
Deposits during May	112,200

Fugazi's May bank statement contained the following information:

Balance per bank at April 30	$ 19,800
Credits during May:	
Deposits	109,600

Debits during May:
    Cheques paid $107,400
    Debit memo (May utilities)   8,000
    Bank service charge   80   115,480
    Balance per bank at May 31 $ 13,920

The April bank reconciliation had deposits in transit of $850 and outstanding cheques of $2,300. All these items cleared during May. These were the only reconciling items in April.

Required:

1. Prepare a bank reconciliation at May 31.
2. Prepare any adjusting entries necessary because of the bank reconciliation.

Solution:

1. Cash balance from bank statement		$13,920
Add: Deposits in transit	$112,200 – ($109,600 – $850)*	3,450
Less: Outstanding cheques	$114,700 – ($107,400 – $2,300)**	(9,600)
Adjusted cash balance		**$ 7,770**
Cash balance from company records	($18,350 + $112,200 – $114,700)	$15,850
Less:		
Debit memo (utilities)	$8,000	
Service charge	80	(8,080)
Adjusted cash balance		**$ 7,770**

* $112,200 was deposited during May, but the account was only credited for $109,600 during May. However, this $109,600 included $850 that was in transit at April 30, so only $108,750 ($109,600 – $850) of the May deposits were credited to the account.

** $114,700 in cheques were written in May and $107,400 in cheques cleared the bank during May. However, this $107,400 included $2,300 in cheques that were outstanding from April, so only $105,100 ($107,400 – $2,300) in cheques cleared that were written in May.

Assets	=	Liabilities	+	Shareholders' Equity (Utilities Expense)
–8,080				–8,000
				(Bank Service Charge Expense)
				–80

2.

Date	Account and Explanation	Debit	Credit
May 31	Utilities Expense	8,000	
	Bank Service Charge Expense	80	
	Cash		8,080
	(To record expenses arising from bank reconciliation)		

DISCUSSION QUESTIONS

1. What is the purpose of an internal control system?
2. Internal control systems include policies and procedures to do what?
3. How did National Instrument 52-109 increase top management's responsibility?
4. What are the elements of a good internal control system?
5. What is meant by "tone at the top"? Why is it so important to an effective system of internal controls?
6. What are strategic risks?
7. What are business process risks?
8. What are the categories of control activities?
9. How do these control activities help protect a company against error, theft, and fraud?
10. How do control activities relate to the accounting system?

11. Why does a company give particular attention to internal controls for cash?

12. Why is it important to segregate the duties for handling cash from the duties for keeping the accounting records for cash?

13. Describe two advantages of performing reconciliations of the cash account to the balances on the bank statements.

14. Describe the potential sources of difference between a cash account and its associated bank statement balance.

15. What types of bank reconciliation items require the firm to make journal entries?

16. Describe how cash over and short can be used for internal control purposes.

17. Why do most companies have petty cash funds?

18. What are cash equivalents?

19. Why do companies invest their cash in short-term investments?

20. What is the operating cycle?

21. Describe the basic cash management principles.

MULTIPLE-CHOICE EXERCISES

4-1 What is the primary role of internal controls in managing a business?
   a. To prevent cash from being stolen
   b. To constrain subordinates' activities in order to prevent employees from deviating from the scope of their responsibilities and encouraging them to act in the best interest of the business
   c. To ensure that the financial statements are presented in such a manner as to provide relevant and reliable information for financial statement decision makers and the company's creditors
   d. To encourage theft and to ensure that segregation of duties does not take place

4-2 Which of the following is not one of the three areas for which internal control systems are intended to provide reasonable assurance?
   a. Certification that the financial statements are without error
   b. Compliance with applicable laws and regulations
   c. Effectiveness and efficiency of operations
   d. Reliability of financial reporting

4-3 Which of the following is not one of the elements of a good system of internal control?
   a. Risk assessment
   b. Information and communication
   c. Control environment
   d. Analysis of control procedures

4-4 Which of the following is not one of the categories of control activities?
   a. Defalcation and financial reporting
   b. Checks on recorded amounts
   c. Clearly defined authority and responsibility
   d. Segregation of duties

4-5 The internal audit function is part of what element of the internal control system?
   a. Control environment
   b. Control activities
   c. Monitoring
   d. Risk assessment

4-6 Which of the following is not generally an internal control activity?
   a. Establishing clear lines of authority to carry out specific tasks
   b. Physically counting inventory in a perpetual inventory system
   c. Limiting access to computerized accounting records
   d. Reducing the cost of hiring seasonal employees

4-7 Allowing only certain employees to order goods and services for the company is an example of what internal control procedure?
   a. Proper authorization
   b. Segregation of duties
   c. Safeguarding of assets and records
   d. Independent verification

4-8 Deposits made by a company but not yet reflected in a bank statement are called:
   a. Credit memoranda
   b. Debit memoranda
   c. Deposits in transit
   d. None of the above

4-9 Which one of the following would not appear on a bank statement for a chequing account?
   a. Interest earned
   b. Deposits
   c. Service charges
   d. Outstanding cheques

4-10 Which one of the following is not a cash equivalent?
   a. 30-day certificate of deposit
   b. 60-day corporate commercial paper
   c. 90-day treasury bill
   d. 180-day note issued by a local or provincial government

4-11 Business activity is best described as:
   a. noncyclical.
   b. cyclical.
   c. lacking deviation.
   d. predictable.

4-12 The five primary activities of a business generally are:
   a. making a profit, issuing financial statements, repaying debts, issuing dividends to shareholders, and complying with laws and regulations.
   b. receiving assets, selling assets, issuing financial statements, collecting cash, and making cash disbursements.
   c. receiving cash, disbursing cash, buying assets, issuing dividends, and paying off liabilities.
   d. receiving assets, purchasing assets, selling goods or services, collecting cash from customers, and repaying owners and creditors.

4-13 Effective cash management and control includes all of the following except:
   a. purchase of shares and bonds.
   b. bank reconciliations.
   c. the use of a petty cash fund.
   d. short-term investment of excess cash.

4-14 Cash management principles do not include:
   a. speeding up collection from customers.
   b. earning the greatest return possible on excess cash.
   c. paying suppliers promptly.
   d. delaying payment of suppliers.

4-15 Which one of the following statements is true?
   a. Sound internal control practice dictates that cash disbursements be made by cheque, unless the disbursement is very small
   b. The person handling the cash should also prepare the bank reconciliation
   c. Good cash management practices dictate that a company should maintain as large a balance as possible in its cash account
   d. Petty cash can be substituted for a chequing account to expedite the payment of all disbursements

CORNERSTONE EXERCISES

OBJECTIVE ❸
CORNERSTONE 4.1

Cornerstone Exercise 4-16   Bank Reconciliation

Firebird Corp. prepares monthly bank reconciliations of its chequing account balance. The bank statement for May 2018 indicated the following:

Balance, May 31, 2018	$42,600
Service charge for May	50
Interest earned during May	650
NSF cheque from Valerie Corp. (deposited by Firebird)	870
Note ($7,000) and interest ($250) collected for Firebird from a customer of Firebird's	7,250

An analysis of cancelled cheques and deposits and the records of Firebird Corp. revealed the following items:

Chequing account balance per Firebird's books	$37,205
Outstanding cheques as of May 31	4,100
Deposit in transit at May 31	5,640
Error in recording cheque #4456 issued by Firebird	45

The correct amount of cheque #4456 is $550. It was recorded as a cash disbursement of $505 by mistake. The cheque was issued to pay for merchandise purchases. The cheque appeared on the bank statement correctly.

Required:

1. Prepare a bank reconciliation schedule at May 31, 2018, in proper form.
2. What is the amount of cash that should be reported on the May 31, 2018, statement of financial position?

Cornerstone Exercise 4-17   Bank Reconciliation

OBJECTIVE ❸
CORNERSTONE 4.1

The accountant for Beaume Corp. was preparing a bank reconciliation as of April 30. The following items were identified:

Beaume's book balance	$28,750
Outstanding cheques	900
Interest earned on chequing account	75
Customer's NSF cheque returned by the bank	380

In addition, Beaume made an error in recording a customer's cheque; the amount was recorded in cash receipts as $370; the bank recorded the amount correctly as $730.

Required:

What amount will Beaume report as its adjusted cash balance at April 30?

Cornerstone Exercise 4-18   Journal Entry from Bank Reconciliation

OBJECTIVE ❸
CORNERSTONE 4.2

A customer of Mutare paid for merchandise originally purchased on account with a cheque that has been erroneously entered into Mutare's cash account for $570 (it actually has been issued and paid for $750).

Required:

Record the appropriate journal entry to correct the error.

Cornerstone Exercise 4-19   Journal Entry from Bank Reconciliation

OBJECTIVE ❸
CORNERSTONE 4.2

Pyramid Corporation is assessed a $20 fee as the result of a $185 NSF cheque received from a customer for services purchased on account. Neither the fee nor the NSF cheque has been accounted for on Pyramid's books.

Required:

Record the appropriate journal entry to update Pyramid's books.

Cornerstone Exercise 4-20   Bank Reconciliation

OBJECTIVE ❸
CORNERSTONE 4.1
CORNERSTONE 4.2

Tiny Corp. prepares monthly bank reconciliations of its chequing account balance. The bank statement for October 2018 indicated the following:

Balance, beginning of the month	$15,640
Service charge for October	65
Interest earned during October	80
NSF cheque from Akbar Corp. (deposited by Tiny) for goods purchased on account	615
Note ($2,500) and interest ($75) collected for Tiny from a customer	2,575

An analysis of cancelled cheques and deposits and the records of Tiny revealed the following items:

(Continued)

Chequing account balance per Tiny's books	$12,951
Outstanding cheques as of October 31	1,410
Deposit in transit at October	$ 750
Error in recording a cheque issued by Tiny (Correct amount of the cheque is $606, but was recorded as a cash disbursement of $660. The cheque was issued to pay for merchandise originally purchased on account.)	54

Required:

1. Prepare a bank reconciliation at October 31, 2018, in proper form.
2. Record any necessary journal entries.
3. What is the amount of cash that should be reported on the October 31, 2018, statement of financial position?

Cornerstone Exercise 4-21 Cash Over and Short

On a recent day, Peshawar Company obtained the following data from its cash registers:

	Cash Sales per Register Tape	Cash in Register after Removing Opening Change
Register 1	$12,675.12	$12,649.81
Register 2	11,429.57	11,432.16
Register 3	11,591.18	11,590.18

Peshawar deposits its cash receipts in its bank account daily.

Required:

Prepare a journal entry to record these cash sales.

Cornerstone Exercise 4-22 Cash Over and Short

Walker Department Store has one cash register. On a recent day, the cash register tape reported sales in the amount of $8,784.17. Actual cash in the register (after deducting and removing the opening change amount of $50) was $8,792.44, which was deposited in the firm's bank account.

Required:

Prepare a journal entry to record these cash collections.

Cornerstone Exercise 4-23 Petty Cash Fund

Minsky Ltd. maintains a balance of $2,500 in its petty cash fund. On December 31, Minsky's petty cash account has a balance of $216. Minsky replenishes the petty cash account to bring it back up to $2,500. Minsky classifies all petty cash transactions as miscellaneous expense.

Required:

What journal entry is made to record the replenishment of the petty cash fund?

Cornerstone Exercise 4-24 Petty Cash with Change in Fund Balance

Basque Ltd. maintains a petty cash fund with a balance of $800. On December 31, Basque's petty cash account has a balance of $60. Basque replenishes the petty cash account, as it does at the end of every month, but also decides to increase the fund balance to $1,000. Basque classifies all petty cash transactions as miscellaneous expense.

Required:

What journal entry is made to record this activity?

BRIEF EXERCISES

Brief Exercise 4-25   Role of Internal Control

OBJECTIVE **1**

Internal controls play a crucial role in a business.

Required:

CONCEPTUAL CONNECTION Discuss why internal controls are important. What are the potential consequences of an internal control failure?

Brief Exercise 4-26   Elements of Internal Control

OBJECTIVE **2**

Discuss five elements of internal control.

Required:

Define and discuss these five elements of internal control.

Brief Exercise 4-27   Bank Reconciliation

OBJECTIVE **3**

Hula Corp. utilizes J.P. Chase in its banking transactions. For the month of August, 2018, J.P. Chase presented Hula with its bank statement as follows:

Balance, August 31, 2018	$64,900
Service charge for August	100
Interest earned during August	875
NSF cheque from Jeffrey Corp. (deposited by Hula)	450
Note ($11,000) and interest ($425) collected for Hula from a customer	11,425

Upon receiving the bank statement, Hula's accountants analyzed its cash transactions for possible reconciling items between its cash balance per books and J.P. Chase's cash balance:

Checking account balance per Hula's books	$53,453
Outstanding cheques as of August 31	3,700
Deposit in transit at August 31, 2018	3,940
Error in recording cheque 9288 issued by Hula	63

The correct amount of cheque 9288 is $770. It was recorded as a cash disbursement of $707 by mistake. The cheque was issued to pay for merchandise purchases. The cheque appeared on the bank statement correctly.

Required:

Prepare a bank reconciliation schedule at August 31, 2018, in proper form.

Brief Exercise 4-28   Journal Entry from bank reconciliation

OBJECTIVE **3**

Eagel, a furniture company, made an error in recording a cheque received from a customer. Last month, Eagel's customer bought a table for $909. Upon receiving the cheque from the customer, Eagel entered the cheque as an increase of cash of $990.

Required:

Record the appropriate journal entry to correct the error.

Brief Exercise 4-29   Journal Entry from bank reconciliation

OBJECTIVE **3**

Samba Corporation operates in an industry with high collectability issues. Recently, one of Samba's customers wrote a cheque for $235 for services performed. Samba's bank later informed Samba that its customer did not have cash available in his account to cover the $235 charge. Samba's bank assesses a $30 fee as the result of the NSF cheque received. Samba has not yet adjusted its books for the bank fee or the NSF cheque.

Required:

Record the appropriate journal entry to update Samba's books.

OBJECTIVE ③   **Brief Exercise 4-30   Bank Reconciliation**

Garrison Corporation was closing its books on May 31, 2018. Garrison's accountant prepared a bank reconciliation as of May 31, 2018, and has found the following possible reconciling items between its book balance and its cash balance per the bank:

Garrison's book balance	$80,760
Outstanding cheques	660
Customer's NSF cheque returned by the bank	190
Interest earned on chequing account	80

In the search for reconciling items, the accountant also discovered that Garrison made an error in recording a customer's cheque: the amount was recorded in cash receipts as $290; the bank recorded the amount correctly as $920.

Required:

What amount will Garrison report as its adjusted cash balance at May 31, 2018?

OBJECTIVE ③   **Brief Exercise 4-31   Bank Reconciliation**

Zing Corp. prepares monthly bank reconciliations as part of its cash controls. Zing's bank provided the following amount about Zing's cash balance at the bank for the month of April 2018:

Balance, April 30, 2018	$74,350
Service charge for April	75
Note ($3,000) and interest ($90) collected for Zing from a customer	3,090
Interest earned during April	140
NSF cheque from Orange Corp. (deposited by Zing) for goods purchased on account	470

Zing then analyzed its cash balance on its own set of books, revealing the following details:

Chequing account balance per Zing's books	$72,329
Deposit in transit at April 30	2,100
Outstanding cheques as of April 30	1,400
Error in recording a cheque issued by Zing (Correct amount of the cheque is $737, but was recorded as a cash disbursement of $773. The cheque was issued to pay for merchandise originally purchased on account.)	36

Required:

1. Prepare a bank reconciliation at April 30, 2018, in proper form.
2. Record any necessary adjusting journal entries.

OBJECTIVE ③   **Brief Exercise 4-32   Cash Over and Short**

At the end of each day, Spangle counts the cash in its cash registers. Spangle then compares the physical amount of cash to the amount of cash that the register tape indicates should be in the cash drawer. On a recent day, Spangle Company obtained the following data from its cash registers:

	Cash Sales per Register Tape	Cash in Register after Removing Opening Change
Register 1	$14,759.62	$14,757.98
Register 2	15,101.59	15,104.06
Register 3	14,802.18	14,798.87

Spangle deposits its cash receipts in its bank account daily.

Required:

Prepare a journal entry to record these cash sales.

Brief Exercise 4-33   Cash Over and Short

OBJECTIVE ③

Milner Department Store has one cash register on which it performs daily cash counts. Recently, the cash count indicated that there was $9,218.47 in the register after deducting and removing the opening change amount of $50. However, the cash register tape reported sales in the amount of $9,217.85. Milner deposited its cash collected in its bank account.

Required:

Prepare a journal entry to record these cash collections.

Brief Exercise 4-34   Petty Cash Fund

OBJECTIVE ③

Kingery Inc. maintains a balance of $3,000 in its petty cash fund for routine purchases such as supplies. During the year, Kingery's employees paid for various office supplies and food purchases for office birthdays. As a result, Kingery's petty cash account has a balance of $374 on December 31, 2018. At the end of each year, Kingery replenishes the petty cash in full. Kingery classifies all petty cash transactions as miscellaneous expense.

Required:

What entry is made to record the replenishment of the petty cash fund?

Brief Exercise 4-35   Petty Cash with Change in Fund Balance

OBJECTIVE ③

Canary Inc. maintains a petty cash fund with a balance of $1,800. During the month of September, Canary's employees made routine expenses using cash from the petty cash fund totalling $1,150. At the end of September, Canary replenishes the petty cash account, but it also decides to increase the fund balance to $2,000. Canary classifies all petty cash transactions as miscellaneous expense.

Required:

What entry is made to record this activity?

Brief Exercise 4-36   Cash Reporting

OBJECTIVE ④

Richter Industries has the following items:

Currency	$27,500
Customer cheques that have not been deposited	850
Canada government bonds that originally mature in 3 months	11,000
Canada government bonds that originally mature in 12 months	14,000
Cash in saving and chequing accounts	50,000
Certificates of deposits that originally mature in 18 months	47,000

Required:

How much should Richter report as cash and equivalents on its balance sheet?

Brief Exercise 4-37   Operating Cycle

OBJECTIVE ⑤

Businesses must decide whether to issue credit to customers.

Required:

CONCEPTUAL CONNECTION Describe how selling to customers on credit affects the operating cycle.

OBJECTIVE ❺   **Brief Exercise 4-38 Cash Management**

Effective cash management is very important to the operating performance of a business.

Required:

CONCEPTUAL CONNECTION Explain the principles of cash management. Why might it be advantageous to delay paying suppliers?

EXERCISES

OBJECTIVE ❶ ❷   **Exercise 4-39 Internal Control System**

Required:

A list of terms and another list of definitions and examples are presented below. Make a list numbered 1 through 5 and match the letter of the most directly related definition or example with the number of each term.

Term	Definition or Example
1. Business process risk 2. Control environment 3. Information and communication 4. Monitoring 5. Strategic risk	a. The internal audit group is testing the operating effectiveness of various internal control activities. b. A member of upper management was fired for violating the company's code of conduct. c. Reports documenting problems with production are forwarded to management. d. Competitors begin offering extended warranty coverage on products. e. Problems with our suppliers have resulted in lost sales because our stores were out of stock.

OBJECTIVE ❶ ❷   **Exercise 4-40 Internal Control Terminology**

Required:

A list of terms and another list of definitions and examples are presented below. Make a list numbered 1 through 7 and match the letter of the most directly related definition or example with the number of each term.

Term	Definition or Example
1. Accounting controls 2. Adequate documents and records 3. Checks on recorded amounts 4. Effective personnel policies 5. Internal control structure 6. Safeguards over assets and records 7. Segregation of duties	a. Company policy prevents accountants from handling cash. b. Company policy requires receiving reports to be made for all deliveries by suppliers. c. Cash deposits are reconciled with cash register records at the end of every day. d. This includes the accounting system, all policies and procedures of the business, and the environment in which they operate. e. Every evening, a jewellery store removes all items of merchandise valued at over $100 from its display. f. These are policies and procedures that govern the identification, measurement, recording, and communication of economic information. g. Every new employee is required to spend two days in training courses to learn company policies.

Exercise 4-41   Classifying Internal Control Procedures

OBJECTIVE **2**

Required:

Match each of the control procedures listed below with the most closely related control procedures type. Your answer should pair each of the numbers 1 through 11 with the appropriate letter.

Control Procedure Types

a. Documentation adequacy
b. Independent checks on performance
c. Authorization of transactions and other business activities
d. Physical controls
e. Segregation of duties
f. Human resource controls

Control Procedures

1. Only the cashier assigned to the cash register is allowed to perform transactions.
2. Division managers are evaluated annually on the basis of their division's profitability.
3. Invoices received from outside suppliers are filed with purchase orders.
4. Employees with access to the accounting records are not permitted to open the mail because it contains many payments by cheque from customers.
5. The extent of access to the many segments of the company's computer system is tightly controlled by individual identification cards and passwords that change at regular intervals.
6. Each shipment to customers from inventory is recorded on a specially printed form bearing a sequential number; these forms are the basis for entries into the computer system, which makes entries to inventory records and produces periodic reports of sales and shipments.
7. At regular intervals, internal audit reviews a sample of expenditure transactions to determine that payment has been made to a bona fide supplier and that the related goods or services were received and appropriately used.
8. A construction company stores large steel girders in an open yard surrounded by a five-foot fence and stores welding supplies in a controlled-access, tightly secured concrete building.
9. Cash registers display the price of each item purchased to the customer as it is recorded and produce a customer receipt that describes each item and gives its price.
10. The person in the controller's office who prepares and mails cheques to suppliers cannot make entries in the general ledger system.
11. Potential new employees are interviewed by two managers before being given an employment offer.

Exercise 4-42   Internal Control of Cash

OBJECTIVE **2** **3**

Edward Tang, a long-time employee of a small grocery wholesaler, is responsible for maintaining the company's cash records and for opening the daily mail, through which the company receives about 40% of its daily cash receipts. Virtually all cash received by mail is in the form of cheques made payable to the company. Tang is also responsible for preparing deposits of currency and cheques for the bank at the end of each day.

Required:

1. **CONCEPTUAL CONNECTION** Explain briefly how Tang might be able to misappropriate some of the company's cash receipts.
2. What internal control procedures would you recommend to prevent this misappropriation?

YOU DECIDE

OBJECTIVE **3**

Exercise 4-43   Cash Over and Short

Miller Enterprises deposits the cash received during each day at the end of the day. Miller deposited $48,287 on October 3 and $50,116 on October 4. Cash register records and other documents supporting the deposits are summarized as follows:

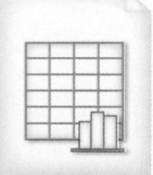

(Continued)

	10/3	10/4
Cash sales	$36,690	$40,310
Collections on account	10,875	9,813
Total receipts	$47,565	$50,123

Required:

1. Calculate the amount of cash over or cash short for each day.
2. Prepare the journal entry to record the receipt and deposit of cash on October 3.
3. Prepare the journal entry to record the receipt and deposit of cash on October 4.
4. **CONCEPTUAL CONNECTION** If you were the manager with responsibility over the cash registers, how would you use this information?

OBJECTIVE ❸   **Exercise 4-44   Bank Reconciliation**

Javinal Corporation's bank statement for October reports an ending balance of $22,381, whereas Javinal's cash account shows a balance of $22,025 on October 31. The following additional information is available:

a. A $855 deposit made on October 31 was not recorded by the bank until November.
b. At the end of October, outstanding cheques total $1,222.
c. The bank statement shows bank service charges of $125 not yet recorded by the company.
d. The company erroneously recorded as $973 a cheque that it had actually written for $379. It was correctly processed by the bank.
e. A $480 cheque from a customer, deposited by the company on October 29, was returned with the bank statement for lack of funds.

Required:

1. Prepare the October bank reconciliation for Javinal Corporation.
2. What amount will be reported as cash on the October 31 statement of financial position?

OBJECTIVE ❸   **Exercise 4-45   Bank Reconciliation (Partial)**

The cash account for Feldman Company contains the following information for April:

Cash balance, 3/31		$14,685
Cash received during April		55,680
		70,365
Cash disbursements during April:		
Cheque 7164	$33,500	
Cheque 7165	11,250	
Cheque 7166	18,750	
Cheque 7167	900	64,400
Cash balance, 4/30		$ 5,965

The bank statement for April contains the following information:

Bank balance, 3/31		$25,285
Add: Deposits during April		55,680
		80,965
Less: Cheques paid during April:		
Cheque 7162	$ 8,900	
Cheque 7163	1,700	
Cheque 7164	33,500	
Cheque 7165	11,250	55,350
Bank balance, 4/30		$25,615

Required:

Assuming there were no deposits in transit at March 31 and that all outstanding cheques at March 31 cleared during April, do the following:
1. Identify the outstanding cheques at April 30.
2. Prepare the reconciliation of the bank and cash account balances at April 30.
3. Identify the outstanding cheques at March 31.
4. Prepare the reconciliation of the bank and cash account balances at March 31.
5. **CONCEPTUAL CONNECTION** Why could you not perform the bank reconciliations without knowing that there were no deposits in transit on March 31 and that all outstanding cheques at March 31 cleared during April?

Exercise 4-46 Bank Reconciliation

OBJECTIVE 3

Valentine Investigations has the following information for its cash account:

Balance, 1/31	$ 7,444
Deposits during February	106,780
Cheques written during February	102,341

Valentine's bank statement for February contained the following information:

Balance per bank, 1/31		$ 8,910
Add: February deposits		104,950
		113,860
Less:		
Cheques paid in February	$(101,400)	
Bank service charge	(50)	
Debit memo (electric bill)	(800)	(102,250)
Balance per bank, 2/28		$ 11,610

A comparison of company records with the bank statement provided the following data:

	At 1/31	At 2/28
Deposits in transit	$2,750	$4,580
Outstanding cheques	4,216	5,157

Required:

1. Prepare a bank reconciliation as of February 28.
2. Prepare journal entries for Valentine based on the information developed in the bank reconciliation.
3. What is the amount of cash that should be reported on the February 28 statement of financial position?

Exercise 4-47 Bank Reconciliation

OBJECTIVE 3

Conway Company reported the following information:

ILLUSTRATING
RELATIONSHIPS

Cash balance on statement of financial position (12/31)	$22,066
Pre-reconciliation cash account balance (12/31)	23,916
Bank statement (12/31)	23,220
Bank service charges	350
Bank debit memos (utility payments)	1,500
Deposits in transit (12/31)	9,160

Required:

1. Calculate the amount of outstanding cheques as of December 31.
2. Prepare the journal entries that Conway must make at December 31.

OBJECTIVE ③

Exercise 4-48 Adjusting Entries from a Bank Reconciliation

Cooper Advisory Services identified the following items on its October reconciliation that may require adjusting entries:

a. A deposit of $670 was recorded in Cooper's accounting records, but not on the October 31 bank statement.
b. A cheque for $5,444 was outstanding at October 31.
c. Included with the bank statement was a cheque for $300 written by Hooper Advertising Services. The bank had, in error, deducted this cheque from Cooper's account.
d. Bank service charges were $250.
e. An NSF cheque written by one of Cooper's customers in the amount of $987 was returned by the bank with Cooper's bank statement. This customer was paying for merchandise originally purchased on account.

Required:

For each of these five items, prepare an adjusting entry for Cooper's journal, if any is required.

OBJECTIVE ③④

Exercise 4-49 Recording Petty Cash Account Transactions

During March, Drapeau Company engaged in the following transactions involving its petty cash fund:

a. On March 1, Drapeau Company established the petty cash fund by issuing a cheque for $1,500 to the fund custodian.
b. On March 4, the custodian paid $85 out of petty cash for freight charges on new equipment. This amount is properly classified as equipment.
c. On March 12, the custodian paid $140 out of petty cash for supplies. Drapeau expenses supplies purchases as supplies expense.
d. On March 22, the custodian paid $25 out of petty cash for express mail services for reports sent to Environment Canada. This is considered a miscellaneous expense.
e. On March 25, the custodian filed a claim for reimbursement of petty cash expenditures during the month totalling $250.
f. On March 31, Drapeau issued a cheque for $250 to the custodian, replenishing the fund for expenditures during the month.

Required:

Prepare the journal entries required to record the petty cash account transactions that occurred during the month of March.

OBJECTIVE ④

Exercise 4-50 Cash Reporting

Brown Industries has the following items:

Currency	$15,500
Customer cheques that have not been deposited	675
Cash in saving and chequing accounts	35,000
Certificates of deposits that mature in 18 months	44,000
Canadian federal government bonds that mature in 2 months	8,000
Canadian federal government bonds that mature in 12 months	10,000

Required:

How much should Brown report as cash and equivalents on its statement of financial position?

OBJECTIVE ④

Exercise 4-51 Components of Cash

The office manager for Rajachitra Products had accumulated the following information at the end of a recent year:

Item	Amount
Accounts receivable	$16,450
Change for cash registers (currency and coin)	2,500
Amount on deposit in chequing account (bank balance)	9,280
Amount on deposit in savings account (bank balance)	25,000
Balance in petty cash	300
Cheques received from customers, but not yet deposited in bank	430
Cheques sent by Rajachitra to suppliers, but not yet presented at bank for payment	670
Deposits in transit	1,420
IOU from Gerry Rajachitra, company president	1,000
Notes receivable	10,000
NSF cheque written by Johnson Company	320
Prepaid postage	250

Required:

Calculate the total cash amount Rajachitra will report on its statement of financial position.

Exercise 4-52   Operating Cycle
OBJECTIVE **5**

Business activity is often described as being cyclical in nature.

Required:

CONCEPTUAL CONNECTION Describe the cyclical nature of business activity.

Exercise 4-53   Operating Cycle
OBJECTIVE **5**

Businesses must decide whether to issue credit to customers.

Required:

CONCEPTUAL CONNECTION Describe how selling to customers on credit affects the operating cycle.

Exercise 4-54   Cash Management
OBJECTIVE **5**

Effective cash management is very important to the operating performance of a business.

Required:

CONCEPTUAL CONNECTION Explain the principles of cash management. Why might it be advantageous to delay paying suppliers?

Exercise 4-55   Operating Cycle
OBJECTIVE **5**

A list of businesses is presented below:

Business	Operating-Cycle Description
1. Tree nursery	a. Very short—customers typically pay cash, and inventory is often held less than one day.
2. Fast-food restaurant	b. A few months —merchandise is typically on hand for several weeks, and some customers may use credit.
3. Appliance store	c. More than one year—merchandise may be in inventory for several months, and most customers will pay for purchases after one or two years.
4. Electric utility	d. Several years—a number of years are required to prepare merchandise for sale. Customers probably pay cash for most items.
5. Clothing store	e. A few months—customers pay monthly. The current assets used to provide customer services are consumed within a few months.

(Continued)

Required:

1. Match each business with a description of the operating cycle for that business.
2. How does a longer operating cycle (such as description *c* or *d*) change a company's financing needs relative to a shorter operating cycle (such as description *a*)?

YOUDECIDE

OBJECTIVE ⑤   **Exercise 4-56   Operating Cycle and Current Receivables**

a. Dither and Sly are lawyers who specialize in income tax law. They complete their typical case in six months or less and collect from the client within one additional month.
b. Mercouri's Market specializes in fresh meat and fish. All merchandise must be sold within one week of purchase. Almost all sales are for cash, and any receivables are generally paid by the end of the following month.
c. Mortondo's is a women's clothing store specializing in high-style merchandise. Merchandise spends an average of seven months on the rack following purchase. Most sales are on credit, and the typical customer pays within one month of sale.
d. Trees Ltd. grows Christmas trees and sells them to various Christmas tree lots. Most sales are for cash. It takes six years to grow a tree.

Required:

For each of the businesses described above, indicate the length of the operating cycle.

PROBLEM SET A

OBJECTIVE ① ②   **Problem 4-57A   Role of Internal Control**

Internal control systems include policies and procedures designed to provide reasonable assurance that the corporation's objectives are being met in three areas: (a) effectiveness and efficiency of operations, (b) reliability of financial reporting, and (c) compliance with applicable laws and regulations. Like any other business, a grocery store uses internal control activities to meet its objectives in these three areas.

Required:

YOUDECIDE   Name an internal control for each area of a grocery store's operations and describe how the internal control helps accomplish the store's objectives in these areas.

OBJECTIVE ② ③   **Problem 4-58A   Internal Control Procedures for Cash Receipts**

Corey and Dee Post are planning to open and operate a 24-hour convenience store near a university campus. Corey and Dee are concerned that part of the cash that customers pay for merchandise might be kept by some of the store's employees.

Required:

Identify some internal control procedures that could help ensure that all cash paid by customers is remitted to the business.

OBJECTIVE ② ③   **Problem 4-59A   Internal Control for Cash**

After comparing cash register tapes with inventory records, the accountant for Ming Convenience Stores is concerned that someone at one of the stores is not recording some of that store's cash sales and is misappropriating the cash from the unreported sales.

Required:

1. **CONCEPTUAL CONNECTION** Explain why a comparison of sales and inventory records would reveal a situation in which cash sales are not being recorded and cash from those sales is being misappropriated.

2. **CONCEPTUAL CONNECTION** Describe how an employee might be able to misappropriate cash from sales.
3. What internal control procedures would you recommend to make the misappropriation you described in requirement 2 more difficult?

YOUDECIDE

Problem 4-60A Bank Reconciliation

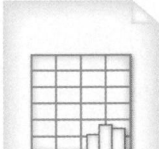
OBJECTIVE 3

Shortly after July 31, Morse Corporation received a bank statement containing the following information:

Date	Cheques			Deposits	Balance
6/30 Beg. balance					$ 7,958
7/1				$ 1,200	9,158
7/2	$ 620	$ 550	$ 344	12,500	20,144
7/3	35	8,100			12,009
7/5	311	97	4,000	9,100	16,701
7/9	4,500	790	286		11,125
7/12	34	7,100			3,991
7/15	634	1,880		7,000	8,477
7/19	3,780	414			4,283
7/24	1,492	649			2,142
7/29	350	677*		4,620	5,735
7/31	575	18**			5,142

* NSF cheque
** Bank service charge

July cash transactions and balances on Morse's records are shown in the following T-account:

Cash

Date	Amount Deposited	Cheque Number	Cheque Amount	Cheque Number	Cheque Amount
Balance, 6/30	**$ 7,609**				
7/1	$12,500	176	$8,100	186	$ 1,880
7/5	9,100	177	97	187	634
7/15	7,000	178	4,000	188	3,780
7/29	4,620	179	311	189	649
7/30	2,050	180	7,100	190	1,492
Total deposits	$35,270	181	4,500	191	37
		182	790	192	350
		183	34	193	575
		184	286	194	227
		185	414	195	1,123
Balance, 7/31	**$ 6,500**		Total disbursements		$36,379

Required:

1. Prepare a bank reconciliation for July.
2. Prepare the journal entries to be made by Morse Corporation as a result of this reconciliation process.
3. What amount is reported as cash on the statement of financial position at July 31?

Problem 4-61A Bank Reconciliation

OBJECTIVE 3

Romain Corporation received the following bank statement for the month of October:

(Continued)

Date		Cheques			Deposits	Balance
9/30	Beg. balance					$ 4,831.50
10/2		$1,204.50			$2,970.18	6,597.18
10/4		43.80	$ 321.70			6,231.68
10/8		905.36				5,326.32
10/10		100.20	60.00	$38.11		5,128.01
10/13					4,000.00	9,128.01
10/14		290.45*				8,837.56
10/17		516.11	309.24			8,012.21
10/19		106.39	431.15	21.72	2,850.63	10,303.58
10/21		3,108.42				7,195.16
10/23		63.89				7,131.27
10/25		290.00**	111.90			6,729.37
10/27		88.90				6,640.47
10/31		20.00***	1,308.77			5,311.70

* NSF cheque
** Debit memo (Rent Expense)
*** Service charge

The cash records of Romain Corporation provide the following information:

Date	Item	Debit	Credit	Balance
10/1	Balance from 9/30			$ 6,553.38
10/2	Cheque #1908		$ 321.70	
10/5	Cheque #1909		905.36	5,326.32
10/6	Cheque #1910		100.20	5,226.12
10/6	Cheque #1911		60.00	5,166.12
10/7	Cheque #1912		38.11	5,128.01
10/12	Deposit #411	$4,000.00		9,128.01
10/15	Cheque #1913		516.11	8,611.90
10/16	Cheque #1914		309.24	8,302.66
10/17	Cheque #1915		431.15	7,871.51
10/17	Cheque #1916		21.72	7,849.79
10/18	Deposit #412	2,850.63		10,700.42
10/18	Cheque #1917		106.39	10,594.03
10/20	Cheque #1918		63.89	10,530.14
10/20	Cheque #1919		3,108.42	7,421.72
10/23	Cheque #1920		111.90	7,309.82
10/25	Cheque #1921		88.90	7,220.92
10/29	Cheque #1922*		1,803.77	5,417.15
10/30	Cheque #1923		284.77	5,132.38
10/31	Cheque #1924		628.32	4,504.06
10/31	Deposit #413	$3,408.20		7,912.26

* Assume that cheque 1922 is paying off accounts payable

The items on the bank statement are correct. The debit memo is for the payment by the bank of Romain's office furniture rent expense for October.

Required:

1. Prepare a bank reconciliation. (*Hint:* There is one transposition error in the cash account.)
2. Prepare journal entries based on the bank reconciliation.
3. What amount is reported for cash in bank on the statement of financial position at October 31?

OBJECTIVE ❸   **Problem 4-62A   Bank Reconciliation**

The cash account of Dixon Products reveals the following information:

Cash

Balance, 4/30	11,800		
Deposits during May	37,600	Cheques written during May	41,620

The bank statement for May contains the following information:

Bank balance, 4/30		$ 11,750
Add: Deposits during May		37,250
		49,000
Less: Cheques paid during May	$(40,230)	
NSF cheque from Frolin Inc.	(190)	
Bank service charges	(40)	(40,460)
Bank balance, 5/31		$ 8,540

A comparison of detailed company records with the bank statement indicates the following information:

	At 4/30	At 5/31
Deposit in transit	$800	$1,150
Outstanding cheques	750	2,140

The bank amounts are determined to be correct.

Required:

1. Prepare a bank reconciliation for May.
2. Prepare the journal entries made by Dixon as a result of the reconciliation process.
3. What amount is reported for cash on the statement of financial position at May 31?

Problem 4-63A Recording Petty Cash Transactions

OBJECTIVE

SCB Inc. had a balance of $400 in cash in its petty cash fund at the beginning of September. The following transactions took place in September:

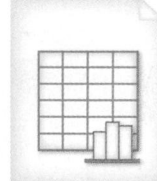

a. On September 4, the custodian paid $43 out of petty cash for new stationery on which the company president's name appeared prominently. This is considered supplies.
b. On September 11, the custodian paid $75 out of petty cash for maintenance manuals for some equipment. This is a maintenance expense.
c. On September 15, the custodian paid $33 out of petty cash for transportation-in.
d. On September 23, the custodian paid $46 out of petty cash to have documents delivered to the lawyers who were defending the firm in a lawsuit. This is considered an other expense.
e. On September 27, the custodian paid $123 out of petty cash to reimburse the president for costs he had incurred when bad weather prevented the company jet from landing to pick him up after a meeting. This is a travel expense.
f. On September 30, the custodian submitted receipts for the above expenditures and a cheque was drawn for the amount to replenish the fund.

Required:

Prepare any journal entries to be made by the corporation to record these transactions.

PROBLEM SET B

Problem 4-64B Role of Internal Control

OBJECTIVE

Internal control systems include policies and procedures designed to provide reasonable assurance that the corporation's objectives are being met in three areas: (1) effectiveness and efficiency of operations, (2) reliability of financial reporting, and (3) compliance with applicable

Chapter 4 Internal Control and Cash

laws and regulations. Like any other business, a bookstore uses internal control activities to meet its objectives in these three areas.

Required:

 **YOU**DECIDE Name an internal control for each of a bookstore's operations and describe how the internal control helps accomplish the store's objectives in these areas.

 OBJECTIVE ② ③ **Problem 4-65B Internal Control Procedures for Cash Receipts**

Sean and Liz Kinsella are planning to open and operate a coffee shop on a university campus. Sean and Liz are concerned that part of the cash that customers pay for food might be kept by some of the store's employees.

Required:

YOUDECIDE Identify internal control procedures that could help ensure that all cash paid by customers is remitted to the business.

OBJECTIVE ② ③ **Problem 4-66B Internal Control for Cash**

After comparing cash register tapes with inventory records, the accountant for Good Times Music store is concerned that someone at one of the stores is not recording some of that store's cash sales and is misappropriating the cash from the unreported sales.

Required:

1. **CONCEPTUAL CONNECTION** Explain why a comparison of sales and inventory records would reveal a situation in which cash sales are not being recorded and cash from those sales is being misappropriated.
2. **CONCEPTUAL CONNECTION** Describe how an employee might be able to misappropriate cash from sales.

YOUDECIDE 3. What internal control procedures would you recommend to make the misappropriation you described in requirement 2 more difficult?

OBJECTIVE ③ **Problem 4-67B Bank Reconciliation**

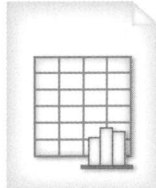

Shortly after July 31, Towanda Corporation received a bank statement containing the following information:

Date		Cheques			Deposits	Balance
6/30 Beg. balance						$ 5,550
7/1					$ 300	5,850
7/2		$ 270	$ 150	$ 330	4,500	9,600
7/3		25	7,025			2,550
7/5		150	450	1,400	10,000	10,550
7/9		1,500	25	325		8,700
7/12		500	100			8,100
7/15		1,600	2,700		3,500	7,300
7/19		75	425			6,800
7/24		650	550			5,600
7/29			525*			5,075
7/31			25**			5,050

* NSF cheque (deposited in previous period but withdrawn this period)
** Bank service charge

July cash transactions and balances on Towanda's records are shown in the following T-account:

Cash

Balance, 6/30	$ 5,550				
Date	Amount Deposited	Cheque Number	Cheque Amount	Cheque Number	Cheque Amount
7/1	$ 300	176	$ 270	186	$ 25
7/2	4,500	177	150	187	100
7/5	10,000	178	330	188	500
7/15	3,500	179	25	189	2,700
7/30	950	180	7,025	190	1,600
Total deposits	$19,250	181	150	191	75
		182	450	192	425
		183	1,400	193	550
		184	1,500	194	650
		185	325	195	275
Balance, 7/31	$ 6,275		Total disbursements		$18,525

Required:

1. Prepare a bank reconciliation for July.
2. Prepare the adjusting journal entries made by Towanda Corporation as a result of this reconciliation process.
3. What amount is reported as cash on the statement of financial position at July 31?

Problem 4-68B Bank Reconciliation

OBJECTIVE ③

Darjeeling Corporation received the bank statement shown below for the month of October:

Date		Cheques			Deposits	Balance
9/30 Beg. balance						$ 5,205
10/2	$1,200				$2,950	6,955
10/4	50	$ 300				6,605
10/8	900					5,705
10/10	100	60	$35		4,000	5,510
10/13						9,510
10/14	300*					9,210
10/17	525	325			2,850	8,360
10/19	105	430	20			10,655
10/21	3,110					7,545
10/23	65					7,480
10/25	250**	110				7,120
10/27	90					7,030
10/31	25***	1,305				5,700

*NSF cheque
**Debit memo (Rent Expense)
***Service charge

The cash records of Darjeeling Corporation provide the following information:

Date	Item	Debit	Credit	Balance
10/1	Balance from 9/30			$ 6,905
10/2	Cheque #1908		$ 300	6,605
10/5	Cheque #1909		900	5,705
10/6	Cheque #1910		100	5,605
10/6	Cheque #1911		60	5,545
10/7	Cheque #1912		35	5,510
10/12	Deposit #411	$4,000		9,510
10/15	Cheque #1913		525	8,985

(Continued)

Date	Item	Debit	Credit	Balance
10/16	Cheque #1914		325	8,660
10/17	Cheque #1915		430	8,230
10/17	Cheque #1916		20	8,210
10/18	Deposit #412	2,850		11,060
10/18	Cheque #1917		105	10,955
10/20	Cheque #1918		65	10,890
10/20	Cheque #1919		3,110	7,780
10/23	Cheque #1920		110	7,670
10/25	Cheque #1921		90	7,580
10/29	Cheque #1922*		1,350	6,230
10/30	Cheque #1923		250	5,980
10/31	Cheque #1924		650	5,330
10/31	Deposit #413	3,300		8,630

* Assume that cheque 1922 is paying off accounts payable

The items on the bank statement are correct. The debit memo is for the payment by the bank of Darjeeling's office furniture rent expense for October.

Required:

1. Prepare a bank reconciliation. (*Hint:* There is one transposition error in the cash account.)
2. Prepare journal entries based on the bank reconciliation.
3. What amount is reported for cash in bank on the statement of financial position at October 31?

OBJECTIVE 3

Problem 4-69B　Bank Reconciliation

The cash account of Mason Products reveals the following information:

Cash

Balance, 4/30	$10,100		
Deposits during May	39,600	Cheques written during May	$40,000

The bank statement for May contains the following information:

Bank balance, 4/30		$ 10,100
Add: Deposits during May		37,400
		47,500
Less: Cheques paid during May	$(38,500)	
NSF cheque from Frolin Inc.	(140)	
Bank service charges	(60)	(38,700)
Bank balance, 5/31		$ 8,800

A comparison of detailed company records with the bank statement indicates the following information:

	At 4/30	At 5/31
Deposit in transit	$900	$2,200
Outstanding cheques	550	1,500

The bank amounts are determined to be correct.

Required:

1. Prepare a bank reconciliation for May.
2. Prepare the journal entries made by Mason Products as a result of the reconciliation process.
3. What amount is reported for cash on the statement of financial position at May 31?

Problem 4-70B   Recording Petty Cash Transactions

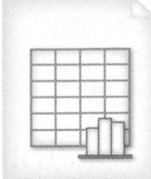

Sudbury Ltd. had a balance of $1,200 in cash in its petty cash fund at the beginning of September. The following transactions took place in September:

a. On September 4, the custodian paid $75 out of petty cash for new stationery on which the company president's name appeared prominently. This is considered supplies expense.

b. On September 11, the custodian paid $350 out of petty cash for maintenance manuals for some equipment. This is a maintenance expense.

c. On September 15, the custodian paid $25 out of petty cash for transportation-in.

d. On September 23, the custodian paid $50 out of petty cash to have documents delivered to the lawyers who were defending the firm in a lawsuit. This is considered an other expense.

e. On September 27, the custodian paid $175 out of petty cash to reimburse the president for costs he had incurred when bad weather prevented the company jet from landing to pick him up after a meeting. This is a travel expense.

f. On September 30, the custodian submitted receipts for the above expenditures and a cheque was drawn for the amount to replenish the fund.

Required:

Prepare any journal entries to be made by the corporation to record these transactions.

CASES

Case 4-71   Ethics and Cash Controls

Suppose that you have just been hired as a part-time clerk in a large department store. Each week you work three evenings and all day Saturday. Without the income provided by this job, you would be unable to stay in university. Charles Christos, the manager in the clothing department to which you are assigned, has worked for the store for many years. Managers receive both a salary and a commission on their sales.

Late one afternoon, just as you begin work, Mr. Christos is ringing up a purchase. You observe that the purchase consists of two expensive suits, a coat, and several pairs of trousers and that the customer declines Mr. Christos's offer to have the store's tailor do the alterations. After the customer departs with his merchandise and as Mr. Christos is departing for the evening, you say, "See you tomorrow." Mr. Christos gives a brief, barely audible response and departs for the evening.

As you return to the sales counter, you glance at the paper tape displayed through a small opening in the cash register that records all sales on an item-by-item basis. You have just completed the store course in register operation, so you are quite familiar with the register and the tape it produces. To your surprise, you note that the last sale consisted of just a single pair of trousers.

Required:

1. What do you conclude about this transaction?
2. What are the possible consequences for the store, for Mr. Christos, and for you personally of reporting your observations to Mr. Christos's superiors?
3. What are the possible consequences for the store, for Mr. Christos, and for you personally of not reporting your observations to Mr. Christos's superiors?
4. What would your decision be?

Case 4-72   The Operating Cycle

There are two retail stores in Millersburgh. One is a full-service store that typically sells on credit to its customers; the other is a smaller discount store that usually sells for cash. Full-service stores typically charge higher prices than do discount stores for identical items.

(Continued)

Required:

1. Does the operating cycle suggest some economic reason for a portion of this price difference? Explain your answer.
2. Can you think of other reasons why a full-service store might charge more than a discount store for the same merchandise?

YOUDECIDE   **Case 4-73   Internal Controls for Cash Disbursements**

Campus Supply Store purchases merchandise on credit from a large number of suppliers. During the past five years, Campus's annual sales have grown from $100,000 to $1,500,000. A recent article in the local newspaper disclosed that an employee of another firm had been arrested for embezzling funds from his employer by diverting payments for purchases to his own bank account. Because of that article, the accountant for Campus has decided to examine Campus's procedures for purchases and payables.

Currently three different employees are authorized to order merchandise for the store. These employees normally complete paperwork provided by the suppliers' sales representatives, keeping a copy for their records. When the ordered merchandise arrives, whomever the delivery person can locate signs for the package. Bills are sent to the store by suppliers and are paid by Campus's accountant when due.

Required:

1. Indicate which general principles of internal control are violated by Campus's procedures for purchases and payables.
2. Recommend procedures that would incorporate the general categories of internal control where possible.

YOUDECIDE   **Case 4-74   Internal Controls for Collection of Receivables**

Carolyn Furniture Galleries sells traditional furniture from two stores in Victoria. Carolyn's credit terms allow customers to pay for purchases over three months with no finance charges. Carolyn's accountant has been responsible for approving customers for credit, recording cash received from customers in the accounting records, depositing cash collections in the bank, and following up on customers who are behind in their payments. Each month the accountant has prepared a report for Carolyn's president, indicating the cash collected, outstanding receivables, and uncollectible accounts.

Carolyn's president has been concerned about a significant increase in uncollectible accounts that began about two years ago, shortly after the current accountant was hired. Recently, a personal friend of Carolyn's president called. The caller had moved from Victoria to Regina about six months ago. A month ago, the caller's new bank had refused a loan because a credit rating bureau in Victoria had indicated that the caller had left bills unpaid at Carolyn Furniture. Carolyn's president knew that the caller had paid his account before leaving the community.

Carolyn's president called a detective agency and arranged for an investigation. Two weeks later, Carolyn's president was informed that the accountant had been spending much more money than his salary would warrant. Carolyn then called its auditor and arranged to have the accounting records for receivables and uncollectible accounts examined. This examination indicated that about $400,000 of cash had been stolen from the firm by the accountant. The accountant had identified customers who had moved and had recorded cash sales to continuing customers as credit sales in the accounts of the relocated customers. Carolyn's accountant had kept the cash received from the cash sales and had eventually written off the fictitious credit sales as uncollectible accounts. Without the accountant's knowledge, one of Carolyn's new employees had sent the names of the customers who had apparently defaulted on their accounts to the credit bureau.

Required:

Identify the internal control weaknesses that permitted the accountant to misappropriate the $400,000. Suggest internal control procedures that would make it difficult for someone else to repeat this misappropriation.

Case 4-75   Cash Management

Hiboux Corporation has the following budgeted schedule for expected cash receipts and cash disbursements.

Month	Expected Cash Receipts	Expected Cash Disbursements
July	$210,000	$200,000
August	280,000	210,000
September	230,000	190,000
October	160,000	180,000

Hiboux begins July with a cash balance of $20,000, $15,000 of short-term debt, and no short-term investments. Hiboux uses the following cash management policy:

a. End-of-month cash should equal $20,000 plus the excess of expected disbursements over receipts for the next month.
b. If receipts are expected to exceed disbursements in the next month, the current month ending cash balance should be $20,000.
c. Excess cash should be invested in short-term investments unless there is short-term debt, in which case excess cash should first be used to reduce the debt.
d. Cash deficiencies are met first by selling short-term investments and second by incurring short-term debt.

Required:

1. Calculate the expected buying and selling of short-term investments and the incurrence and repayment of short-term debt at the end of July, August, and September.
2. Discuss the general considerations that help accountants develop a cash management policy.

Case 4-76   Cash and Internal Controls

Identify a business with which you are familiar.

Required:

1. Describe the ways in which it prevents misappropriation of cash.
2. Can you think of a way in which dishonest employees could circumvent the internal controls and misappropriate cash?

Case 4-77   Continuing Problem: Front Row Entertainment

Over the next two months, Front Row Entertainment continues to enjoy success in signing artists and promoting events. However, the increased business is placing considerable stress on the keeping of timely and up-to-date financial records. In particular, both Cam and Anna are concerned about the accounting and management of the company's cash.

The tour promotion industry is a cash-intensive industry, normally requiring large prepayments to secure venues and arrange advertising. When the number of artists under contract was small, Cam and Anna developed a simple system to manage the company's cash. Normally, any cash received was put in a file cabinet in the company's office. If the amount appeared to be getting large, a deposit was made. Similarly, if a large cheque needed to be written, either Cam or Anna would check the balance in the chequebook. If cash was not sufficient to cover the cheque, they'd get cash from the file cabinet and deposit the amount necessary to cover the cheque. However, with the increasing business, they often forget to make deposits, and this has caused several cheques to be returned for nonsufficient funds. In addition, they are in the process of hiring additional office staff who will start work on May 1. They know that leaving cash in a file cabinet is not a good idea.

In order to obtain a better understanding of their cash position, Anna decides to perform a bank reconciliation—something she has neglected to do since the company was started.

(Continued)

According to the accounting records, the cash balance at April 30 was $7,495. Anna has obtained the following information from Front Row's April bank statement and an analysis of cancelled cheques and deposits:

Balance per bank at April 30	$3,250
Deposits in transit at April 30	4,370
Outstanding cheques as of April 30	1,160
Debit memo for April utilities	845
Bank service charge for April	50
Interest earned during April	450
NSF cheque from customer	590

Required:

1. Discuss the purpose of an internal control system. How would the development of an internal control system benefit Front Row Entertainment? In your answer, be sure to highlight any problems that you noted with Front Row Entertainment's current system of accounting for cash.
2. Prepare a bank reconciliation for Front Row Entertainment for the period ended April 30, 2018.
3. Prepare any journal entries necessary because of the bank reconciliation.
4. How could the failure to prepare a bank reconciliation before April 30 have potentially affected previous monthly financial statements?

Case 4-78   Internal Controls Relating to Inventory

Recall our discussion relating to internal controls and the safeguarding of assets of the organization. Inventory is normally one of the largest balances on the statement of financial position. Identify and discuss internal controls relating to inventory.

Case 4-79   Identification of Controls

Controls are important in any organization. Controls are in place to assist with minimizing the chance of fraud occurring and safeguarding assets of an organization. Controls are around us on a daily basis and at times we don't even realize it. In order to understand how effective controls can be in an organization, it is important to be able to identify those controls.

Think of the following situations and identify the different control activities that are present. Identify the control and explain how the control would work to safeguard the assets of the organization.
a.   Local coffee shop
b.   Sporting event

Case 4-80   Professional and Ethical Behaviour

You have recently been hired to work for a large scaffolding company called PR Scaffolding (PR), which is located in Ontario. The primary customers for PR are contractors in the construction industry who rent scaffolding when working on residential or commercial properties. The company has been around for about five years, but has been growing at a rapid pace as the real estate market has been booming in Ontario. Due to the rapid expansion of PR, PR was looking for a professional accountant to come on board and assist with all accounting-related functions of the organization. You knew you had a good chance of getting the job because your friend Cathy worked at PR as an administrative assistant and she highly recommended you to the owners.

You have been at PR for several weeks now and a few things have caught your eye. Contractors come in on a daily basis for the rental of scaffolding. You notice that they seem to always pay cash for the rental. You ask Larry, who is the manager of the scaffolding rental department, about this and he says, "Contractors are so busy, they don't want to be delayed at all with any paper work.

They want to pay cash and be on their way; they don't need a receipt for anything." Larry goes on to tell you that "we have never had any issues in the past. I make a quick note of the rental, log it into our system, and document the amount of cash paid. I don't think it is a big deal."

Larry tells you, "Depending on the day, we sometimes will have about two thousand dollars sitting here in cash." He goes on to say, "Don't worry. I remember reading something from my accounting course in university about having good controls and to never leave cash lying around, so I make sure to give all the cash I collected for the day to Cathy before I go home each night. She takes care of the rest."

You start thinking a bit more about what Larry told you and you know you should probably recommend a few changes to the process.

One day, you and Cathy are getting ready to go for lunch, when you notice that you forgot your wallet at home. You ask Cathy if she could give you ten dollars for lunch and you'll repay her the next day. She says not to worry about it—she'll just take the money from the cash Larry gave her the other day. Cathy says she uses that cash all the time for small purchases. Once she forgot her wallet and needed to buy a birthday gift at the mall for her children, so she just used the cash available on site. She says that as long as it all goes back before anyone looks, it's all good and no one really cares.

You decide to go have lunch with Cathy. At the same time, you realize you have a lot of work and recommendations to make at PR.

Required:

Identify any internal control weaknesses and discuss any ethical issues. Provide any recommendations, if needed.

5

Reporting and Analyzing Sales Revenue and Receivables

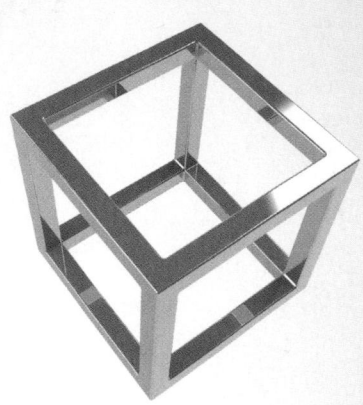

After studying Chapter 5, you should be able to:

1. Apply the criteria for revenue recognition to a retail, service, or manufacturing business.
2. Measure and report net sales revenue.
3. Explain the principal types of receivables.
4. Measure and report bad debt expense and the allowance for doubtful accounts.
5. Explain the cash flow implications of accounts receivable.
6. Account for notes receivable from inception to maturity.
7. Explain internal control procedures for merchandise sales.
8. Calculate profitability and asset management ratios using sales and receivables data.

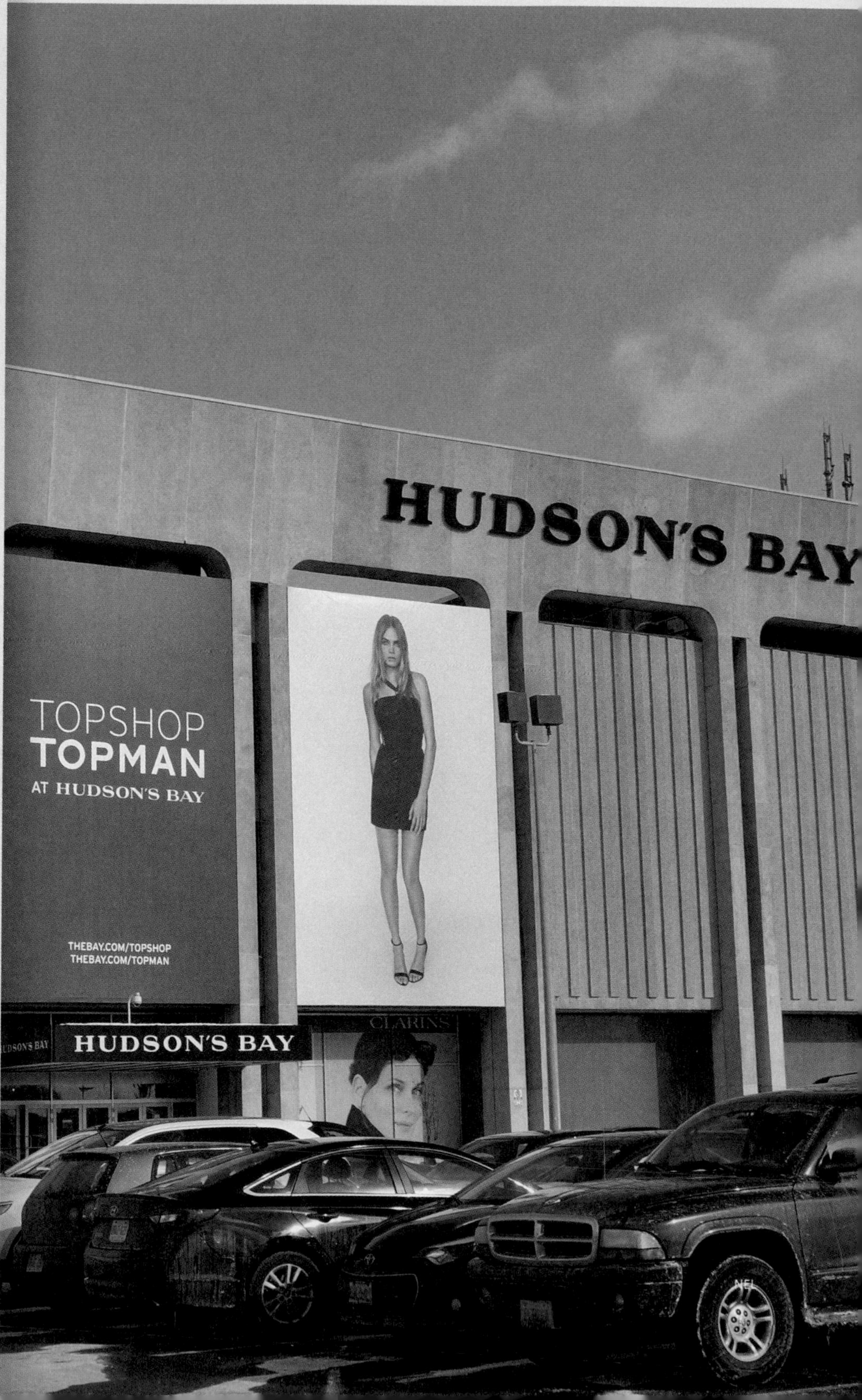

Lester Balajadia/Shutterstock

EXPERIENCE FINANCIAL ACCOUNTING
with Hudson's Bay Company (HBC)

In 1970, coincident with its 300th anniversary, HBC became a Canadian corporation. Retail acquisitions increased with takeovers of Zellers/Fields (1978), Simpsons (1978), and Robinson's (1979). Strategic expansion to strengthen its share of the market continued with the acquisition of Towers/Bonimart (1990), Woodward's (1993), and Kmart Canada (1998).

Since then HBC has explored new shopping channels and ways of doing business. Club Z, the Company's first customer loyalty program, was launched in 1986. In 2001 it was superseded by HBC Rewards. Specialty arrived with the opening of Home Outfitters in 1999. Online shopping was introduced with the launch of hbc.com in 2000. And the off-price segment of the market was covered by Designer Depot / Style Depot, which operated from 2004–2008. In 2003 HBC Signature, a private brand inspired by the Company's unique heritage, was introduced.

Today, Hudson's Bay Company is one of the fastest-growing department store retailers in the world, based on its successful formula of driving the performance of high quality stores and their all-channel offerings, unlocking the value of real estate holdings and growing through acquisitions. With the recent completion of its acquisition of GALERIA Kaufhof Group, HBC's portfolio today includes eight banners, in formats ranging from luxury to better department stores to off price, with more than 460 stores and 65,000 employees around the world.

In North America, HBC's leading banners include Hudson's Bay, Lord & Taylor, Saks Fifth Avenue and Saks OFF 5TH, along with Home Outfitters. In Europe, its banners include GALERIA Kaufhof, the largest department store group in Germany, Belgium's only department store group, Galeria INNO, as well as Sportarena.

HBC has significant investments in real estate joint ventures. It has partnered with Simon Property Group Inc. in HBS Global Properties Joint Venture, which owns properties in the United States and Germany. In Canada, it has partnered with RioCan Real Estate Investment Trust in the RioCan-HBC Joint Venture.

HBC, now in its fourth century of retailing in Canada, proudly proclaims itself as "Canada's Merchants Since 1670."

Source: HBC website, "Our History: Overview," found at http://hbcheritage.ca/hbcheritage/history/overview

OBJECTIVE ❶

Apply the criteria for revenue recognition to a retail, service, or manufacturing business.

TIMING OF REVENUE RECOGNITION

While cash-basis accounting recognizes revenue in the period that payment is received (as on your tax return for wages and salary), accrual-basis accounting recognizes revenue when it is (1) **realized** or **realizable** and (2) **earned**. Since sales transactions can be extremely complicated and businesses frequently attempt to recognize revenue too soon, IFRS applies the revenue recognition principle using specific criteria.

International Financial Reporting Standards (IFRS) in IAS 18 requires that the following five conditions all be met in order for revenue to be recognized:

- The significant risks and rewards of ownership of the goods have been transferred to the purchaser by the seller. This requirement is usually met by the transfer of legal title, the delivery of goods to a customer, or the performance of services for a customer.
- The amount of revenue can be reliably measured. The amount to be collected by the seller must not be uncertain.
- The seller has not retained continuing managerial involvement to the degree usually associated with ownership or effective control over the goods sold.
- It is probable that the economic benefits (usually payment) associated with the transaction will flow to the seller. Normally, if the customer is creditworthy, this condition is satisfied.
- Cost incurred or to be incurred with respect to the transaction can be reliably measured. If costs cannot be reliably measured, revenue cannot be recognized.

Although these criteria are easy to understand, they can be difficult to apply to complicated sales contracts. Such complicated transactions are the subject of advanced accounting courses. For now, recognize that the vast majority of sales transactions are straightforward and simple—service companies (such as airlines, accountants, lawyers, health clubs, lawn services, and so on) recognize revenue in the period they provide the services to the customer, and sellers of goods such as Hudson's Bay Company recognize revenue in the period when title passes (the customer takes possession of the goods).

Title (ownership) can pass at the shipping point or the delivery point.

- **FOB** (free on board) **shipping point**: If the shipping terms are FOB shipping point, ownership of the inventory passes from the seller to the buyer at the shipping point. Under FOB shipping point terms, the buyer normally pays the transportation costs, commonly termed **freight-in**. These costs are considered part of the total cost of purchases and the inventory account is increased. The seller would normally recognize revenue at the time of the shipment.
- **FOB** (free on board) **destination**: When the shipping terms are FOB destination, ownership of the inventory passes when the goods are delivered to the buyer. Under FOB destination shipping terms, the seller is usually responsible for paying the transportation costs, commonly termed **freight-out**. In this case, the transportation costs are not considered part of inventory; instead, the seller will expense these costs as a selling expense on the income statement. Revenue is not normally recognized by the seller until delivery of the goods has occurred.

ETHICAL DECISIONS   Publicly traded corporations are under tremendous pressure to meet analyst targets for key financial statement data, such as sales and earnings per share. Many corporations, when faced with the reality of sales not meeting analysts' targets, have resorted to a variety of practices to avoid such shortfalls. For example, Coca-Cola was accused by regulatory authorities of, among other things, "channel stuffing." In channel stuffing, companies ship more goods to a customer than the customer ordered near the end of a period. However, because sales are recognized at the time of shipment, all of these sales are recorded in the current period. Of course, this practice results in lower sales in the subsequent period when the customer returns the unwanted goods.

AMOUNT OF REVENUE RECOGNIZED

The appropriate amount of revenue to recognize is generally the cash received or the **cash equivalent** of the receivable. However, companies often induce customers to buy by modifying the terms of the sale. In this section, we discuss four changes to sales revenues: sales discounts, credit card discounts, sales returns, and sales allowances.

OBJECTIVE ❷

Measure and report net sales revenue.

Sales Discounts and Credit Card Discounts

To encourage prompt payment, businesses may offer a **sales discount**. This discount is a reduction of the normal selling price and is attractive to both the seller and the buyer. For the buyer, it is a reduction to the cost of the goods and services. For the seller, the cash is more quickly available and collection costs are reduced. For example, when cash is not available quickly, the seller may need to borrow money in order to pay its suppliers, employees, and so on. The interest expense associated with borrowing money has a negative effect on net income.

Sales invoices use a standard notation to state discount and credit terms. For example, the invoice of a seller who expects payment in 30 days and offers a 2% discount if payment is made within 10 days would bear the notation 2/10, n/30 (which is read "2/10, net 30"). The notation n/30 indicates that the gross amount of the invoice (the full pre-discount amount) must be paid in 30 days. The notation 2/10 indicates that if full payment is made within the 10-day discount period, the amount owed is 2% less than the gross (pre-discount) amount of the invoice. Of course, if payment is made within the 20 days following the end of the discount period, then the amount owed is equal to the gross (pre-discount) amount of the invoice.

Most companies record the sale and the associated receivable at the gross (pre-discount) amount of the invoice. If payment is received after the discount period, the cash received equals the associated receivable so no adjustment is needed. But when a discount is taken, the amount of the discount is recorded in a contra-revenue account (i.e., it reduces Gross Sales Revenue to Net Sales Revenue) called *sales discounts,* which balances the entry. This method is illustrated in Cornerstone 5.1 .

Recording Sales Discounts

CORNERSTONE 5.1

Information:

On May 5, 2018, GCD Advisors billed Richardson's Wholesale Hardware $15,000 for consulting services provided during April. GCD offered terms of 2/10, n/30.

Required:

1. Prepare the journal entry to record the sale using the gross method.

2. Prepare the journal entry assuming the payment is received on May 15, 2018 (within the discount period).

3. Prepare the journal entry assuming the payment is received on May 25, 2018 (after the discount period).

4. How would sales revenues be disclosed on the statement of earnings, assuming the payment is made within 10 days?

CORNERSTONE VIDEO

(Continued)

CORNERSTONE

5.1

(Continued)

Why:

Invoices to customers that include the offer of a sales discount are recorded in accounts receivable on a gross (pre-discount) basis. Discounts taken by customers are separately recorded at the time of payment in a Sales Discount account where total discounts taken by customers can be monitored by management to ascertain the effect of credit terms on cash inflow.

Solution:

Shareholders' Equity		
Assets = Liabilities + (Sales Revenue)		
+15,000		+15,000

Shareholders' Equity		
Assets = Liabilities + (Sales Discounts)		
+14,700		−300
−15,000		

Shareholders'		
Assets = Liabilities + Equity		
+15,000		
−15,000		

Date	Account and Explanation	Debit	Credit
1. May 5, 2018	Accounts Receivable	15,000	
	Sales Revenue		15,000
	(Record sale of merchandise)		
2. May 15, 2018	Cash*	14,700	
	Sales Discounts**	300	
	Accounts Receivable		15,000
	(Record collection within the discount period)		
3. May 25, 2018	Cash	15,000	
	Accounts Receivable		15,000
	(Record collection after the discount period)		

* $15,000 × 98%
** $15,000 × 2%

4. Partial statement of earnings:

Sales revenue	$15,000
Less: Sales discounts	(300)
Net sales	$14,700

It is also important to monitor changes in how customers use sales discounts. For example, customers who stop taking sales discounts may be experiencing cash flow problems and therefore are potential credit risks. On the other hand, failure of a large number of customers to take discounts may indicate that an increase in the discount percentage is needed.

Finally, sales discounts must be distinguished from both trade and quantity discounts:

- A *trade discount* is a reduction in the selling price granted by the seller to a particular class of customers, for example, to customers who purchase goods for resale rather than for use.
- A *quantity discount* is a reduction in the selling price granted by the seller because selling costs per unit are less when larger quantities are ordered. This is why, for example, a 750 mL soft drink does not cost double what a 375 mL one costs at a restaurant.

For accounting purposes, the selling or invoice price is usually assumed to be the price after adjustment for the trade or quantity discounts; accordingly, trade and quantity discounts are not recorded separately in the accounting records.

Many individuals purchase goods with a credit card (VISA and MasterCard being examples). The credit card company charges a fee for the use of the card to the seller.

As an example, if a $1,000 sale was made with the customer using a credit card to pay for the goods, and the credit card company charged a fee of 5%, net sales in the financial statements of the seller would show the following:

Sales	$1,000
Less:	
Credit card discounts	(50)
Net sales	$ 950

Alternatively, if a debit card was used by an individual customer to purchase $100 of goods from a seller, the seller would record net sales at $100, not $95, because there is no charge by the debit card companies for the use of debit cards by individuals since funds are being electronically transferred directly from the customer's bank account to the seller.

Sales Returns and Allowances

Occasionally, a customer will return goods as unsatisfactory. In other cases, a customer may agree to keep goods with minor defects if the seller is willing to make an "allowance" by reducing the selling price. The accounting for sales returns and allowances, which is described in the paragraphs that follow, has the effect of reversing all or part of a previously recorded sale.

When goods or services arrive late, or in some other way are rendered less valuable, a customer may be induced to accept the goods/services if a price reduction, called a **sales allowance**, is offered by the seller. A contra-revenue account called *sales returns and allowances* (returns are discussed next) is used to record the price reduction. For example, on November 1, 2018, GCD Advisers completed a consulting project for Bolt Manufacturing for which the agreed-upon price was $11,400. Because GCD had promised Bolt that the project would be completed by September 15, 2018, GCD offered and Bolt accepted a $1,600 reduction as an allowance for the missed deadline. GCD made the following accounting entries to record these events:

Date	Account and Explanation	Debit	Credit
Nov. 1, 2018	Accounts Receivable	11,400	
	Sales Revenue		11,400
	(Record sale of services)		
Nov. 1, 2018	Sales Returns and Allowances	1,600	
	Accounts Receivable		1,600
	(Record allowance for missed deadline)		

Assets	= Liabilities +	Shareholders' Equity (Sales Revenue)
+11,400		+11,400

Assets =	Liabilities +	Shareholders' Equity (Sales Returns and Allowances)
−1,600		−1,600

If the bill has already been paid, the seller can either refund a portion of the purchase price and record a credit to cash or apply the allowance against future purchases by the customer by recording a credit to accounts receivable.

Merchandise or goods returned by the customer to the seller are **sales returns**. Companies also record these returned goods in *sales returns and allowances*. Sales returns will be discussed in Chapter 6 when we introduce inventory.

On the statement of earnings, as indicated in Chapter 2, sales returns and allowances, like sales discounts, are subtracted from gross sales revenue to produce **net sales revenue**, as shown here:

Sales revenue	$752,000
Less: Sales returns and allowances	(1,600)
Net sales	$750,400

Sales returns and allowances is a contra-revenue account. Presenting both gross sales revenue and sales returns and allowances, rather than net sales revenue alone, permits financial statement users to respond to unusual behaviour in either account. Careful users of financial statements look for unusual behaviour in both sales revenue and sales returns and allowances on the statement of earnings. Often, significant changes in these accounts help explain other changes in statement of earnings or statement of financial position accounts, as illustrated in the You Decide below.

YOUDECIDE Sales Returns and Allowances

You are the controller at Interplains Corporation. Data for the past four years for sales revenue, sales returns and allowances, and net income are shown below.

	2015	2016	2017	2018
Sales revenue	$624,000	$653,000	$671,000	$887,000
Sales returns				
and allowances	6,100	6,400	6,300	14,800
Net income	30,000	29,000	31,500	12,200

What concerns are raised by the significant changes in sales revenue, sales returns and allowances, and net income in 2018?

Sales revenue, which had been relatively stable, increased by 32% in 2018. Often, significant growth in output is accompanied by quality assurance problems, as might be indicated by the 135% growth in sales returns and allowances. A check of production data might reveal the use of less highly trained workers or supervisors, or might indicate that the current workforce is being worked heavily on overtime.

Furthermore, notice the significant decrease in net income despite the large increase in sales revenue. When this happens, you must attempt to discover why. For example, when a firm becomes significantly more or less profitable, the attitude of the employees toward their work can change, causing changes in the quality of output. Some key employees may leave a firm with declining profitability, thus causing quality difficulties.

Significant changes in sales revenue, sales returns and allowances, and net income can indicate important changes or trends in the workforce or workflow and should be analyzed so that management can take appropriate action.

TYPES OF RECEIVABLES

OBJECTIVE ❸

Explain the principal types of receivables.

Now that we've addressed the timing of revenue recognition and measurement of net sales revenue, we will shift our attention to the accounting and analysis of the related receivables.

A receivable is money due from another business or individual. Receivables are typically categorized along four different dimensions:

- *Accounts or trade receivable or notes receivable:* A "note" is a legal document given by a borrower to a lender stating the timing of repayment and the amount (principal and/or interest) to be repaid. We discuss notes receivable later in the chapter. **Accounts receivable**, on the other hand, do not have a formal note. For example, while you signed a formal agreement to rent your apartment, you probably did not sign a formal agreement for your utilities. Accounts receivable are occasionally referred to as *trade receivables*.
- *Other receivables* include interest receivable, loans due from directors or company officers, advances to employees, loans to subsidiaries, and sales taxes and income taxes recoverable from government entities.
- *Current or noncurrent receivables:* Although in practice both accounts and notes receivable are typically classified as current, accounts receivable are typically due in 30 to 60 days and do not have interest while notes receivable have interest and typically are due in anywhere from 3 to 12 months. Of course, if the due date is over one year, the note receivable typically will be classified as noncurrent.
- *Trade or nontrade receivables:* **Trade receivables** are due from customers purchasing inventory or receiving services in the ordinary course of business, while **nontrade receivables** arise from transactions not involving the purchasing of inventory or the receiving of services (such as interest receivable or cash advances to employees).

Receivables in Foreign Currencies

Hudson's Bay Company sells goods in countries outside of Canada, which generates receivables in foreign currencies such as the US dollar and Euro. When Hudson's Bay Company prepares its financial statements, foreign currency receivables must be converted to Canadian dollars. For example, if a sale occurred on November 30, 2018, for US$100 when each US dollar was worth Cdn$1.30, then the original receivable and sale would be recorded at Cdn$130. If the exchange rate changed to US$1.00 = Cdn$1.35 at Hudson's Bay Company's year-end date of January 31, 2019, then the receivable would be increased to $135 and an exchange gain recorded of $5. Advanced accounting courses further explore the accounting for foreign exchange transactions.

Interest Revenue

Companies usually charge customers interest each month when their accounts receivable balances are not paid when due (usually 30 days). The use of an accounts receivable sub-ledger facilitates the timely determination of the balance due from each customer at the end of each accounting period. Interest can be calculated and added to the customer's account balance at the end of each accounting period.

Interest revenue is recorded by the seller as an increase (debit) to accounts receivable on the statement of financial position and as an increase (credit) to interest or finance income on the statement of earnings. The interest charge is indicated on the customer's statement of account that the customer receives from the seller, usually each month.

Accounts Receivable Control Account and Subsidiary Ledger

Accounts receivable is a general ledger account. For companies that have a small number of accounts receivable, this general ledger account is normally sufficient. However, businesses that have numerous accounts receivable owing from customers—and that is most of them—maintain an accounts receivable subsidiary ledger. This subsidiary ledger maintains a separate account for each customer. When a total is taken of all accounts in the accounts receivable subsidiary ledger, that total should agree to the accounts receivable account in the general ledger. A normal internal control practice is to regularly ensure that the accounts receivable control account in the general ledger is reconciled to (or agreed to) the total of the accounts receivable subsidiary ledger.

In this system of control and subsidiary accounts, transactions are recorded twice: once to the general ledger and once to the subsidiary ledger. Normally, posting to the subsidiary ledger occurs immediately at the time of the transaction. The posting to the general ledger represents the total of the transactions posted to the subsidiary ledger and normally occurs on at least a daily basis.

Typically, subsidiary ledgers are also maintained for inventory (to facilitate tracking of inventory quantities on hand and balances), accounts payable (to track balances owing to individual suppliers), and payroll (to track individual payroll records). Although it is rarely done, a subsidiary ledger should be maintained for companies that have significant balances of capital assets such as land, equipment, and buildings.

VALUATION OF ACCOUNTS RECEIVABLE AND ACCOUNTING FOR BAD DEBTS

We discussed the recognition of accounts receivable in the revenue section, but an equally important concept is ensuring that the proper amount for accounts receivable is shown on the statement of financial position. IFRS requires accounts receivable to be shown at their "net realizable value," which is the amount of cash the company expects to collect after

OBJECTIVE

Measure and report bad debt expense and the allowance for doubtful accounts.

consideration is given to receivables whose collection is impaired. Unfortunately, the amount of cash collected will almost never equal the total amount recognized in accounts receivable because some customers will not pay (e.g., a customer who declares bankruptcy and ceases operations creates an impairment in any outstanding receivables from this customer). When customers do not pay their accounts receivable, bad debts result (also called uncollectible accounts or impaired accounts). Although efforts are made to control bad debts, it is an expense of providing credit to customers (the hope is that the increased business associated with providing credit more than makes up for the bad debts).

As we saw in the previous section, when sales revenues are reduced to reflect sales returns and allowances, the reductions are accomplished through a contra-revenue account. Although it might seem logical to reduce sales revenues in the same way when customers default on accounts receivable arising from credit sales, this treatment is inappropriate. Reductions in sales revenue should be recorded only for transactions that result from actions of the seller, such as acceptance of returned merchandise (a sales return) or price reductions offered to purchasers (a sales allowance or discount). Since defaults on credit sales arise from actions of the purchaser rather than the seller, bad debts cannot be recorded as revenue reductions. If bad debts are not treated as negative revenues, then they must be treated as expenses. And if they are expenses, the question then arises as to when the expense should be recorded. The timing of recording bad debt expense is important because reported net income for each period will be affected by this decision.

There are two methods to record **bad debt expense**: the direct write-off method and the allowance method.

Direct Write-Off Method

The direct write-off method waits until an account is deemed uncollectible before reducing accounts receivable and recording the bad debt expense. As you recall, the matching concept requires that expenses be matched with the related revenues in the period in which the revenues are recognized on the statement of earnings. Since accounts are often determined to be uncollectible in accounting periods subsequent to the sale period, the direct write-off method is inconsistent with the matching concept and can only be used if bad debts are immaterial under IFRS. For example, if ABX Inc. owed $25,000 to Hawthorne and ABX Inc. became bankrupt on December 31, 2018, with the result that the account receivable was not collectible, the bad debt would be recorded as follows by Hawthorne:

Date	Account	Debit	Credit
Dec. 31, 2018	Bad Debt Expense	$25,000	
	Accounts Receivable		$25,000
	(Write-off bad debt)		

Note that if the bankruptcy had not occurred, this journal entry would not have been made by Hawthorne under the direct write-off method.

Allowance Method

In the allowance method, bad debt expense is recorded in the period of sale, which allows it to be properly matched with revenues according to the matching concept. The result is that bad debt expense is recognized before the actual default. Because defaults for the current period's sales have not actually occurred, the specific accounts receivable are not lowered; instead, an account is established to "store" the estimate until specific accounts are identified as uncollectible. This account is called **Allowance for Doubtful Accounts**.

---

concept Q&A

Why is the direct write-off method not GAAP?

Answer:

Because the direct write-off method fails to "match" the bad debt expense to the sales revenue that it helped generate and does not show accounts receivable at net realizable value on the statement of financial position.

For example, assume at the end of the first year of operations that Hawthorne has an accounts receivable balance of $1,000,000. Although no customers have defaulted, Hawthorne estimates that $25,000 of that balance is uncollectible. At the end of the first year, in 2018, Hawthorne will make the following adjusting entry:

Date	Account and Explanation	Debit	Credit
Dec. 31, 2018	Bad Debt Expense	25,000	
	Allowance for Doubtful Accounts		25,000
	(Record estimate of uncollectible accounts)		

Assets	= Liabilities +	Shareholders' Equity (Bad Debt Expense)
−25,000		−25,000

This entry looks very similar to the entry that would be made under the direct write-off method. The major differences are in the timing of the entry and the use of an allowance account. The direct write-off method makes the entry in the period the customer defaults and records a direct reduction to the accounts receivable account in the general ledger, while the allowance method makes the entry in the period of sale and uses an allowance account with the account receivable account not being affected at that point in time. It is important to recognize that Hawthorne's statement of financial position would report the full $1,000,000 as accounts receivable under the direct write-off method at the end of the first year but only at $975,000 under the allowance method.

When a specific account is ultimately determined to be uncollectible under the allowance method, it is *written off* by a debit to the allowance account and a credit to accounts receivable. Assuming that the doubtful amount of $25,000 owed by ABX Inc. was determined to be uncollectible by Hawthorne at December 31, 2018, the necessary journal entry would be as follows:

Date	Account	Debit	Credit
Dec. 31, 2018	Allowance for Doubtful Accounts	$25,000	
	Accounts Receivable		$25,000
	(Write-off bad debt)		

This write-off removes the defaulted balance from the accounts receivable balance and also removes it from the estimate "storage" account.

Under the allowance procedure, two methods commonly used to estimate bad debt expense are the *percentage of credit sales method* and the *aging method*.

Percentage of Credit Sales Method The simpler of the two methods for determining bad debt expense is the **percentage of credit sales method**. Using past experience and management's views of how the future may differ from the past (e.g., if credit policies change), it is possible to estimate the percentage of the current period's credit sales that will eventually become uncollectible. This percentage is multiplied by the total credit sales for the period to calculate the estimated bad debt expense for the period:

Total credit sales × Percentage of credit sales estimated to default
= Estimated bad debt expense

The adjusting entry is then prepared to recognize the bad debt expense as shown in Cornerstone 5.2.

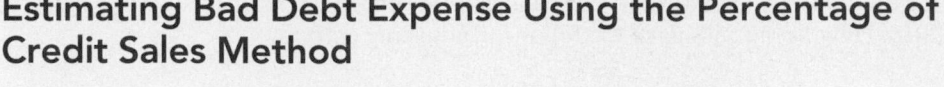

Estimating Bad Debt Expense Using the Percentage of Credit Sales Method

Information:

Crimson Company has credit sales of $620,000 during 2018 and estimates at the end of 2018 that 1.43% of these credit sales will eventually default. Also, during 2018, a customer defaults on a $524 balance related to goods purchased in 2017. Prior to the adjusting entries, Crimson's accounts receivable and allowance for doubtful accounts balances were $304,000 and $134 (credit), respectively.

Required:

1. Estimate the bad debt expense for the period.

2. Prepare the journal entry to record the write-off of the defaulted $524 balance.

3. Prepare the adjusting entry to record the bad debt expense for 2018.

4. What is the net accounts receivable balance at the end of the year? How would this balance have changed if Crimson had not written off the $524 balance during 2018?

Why:

Under the percentage of credit sales method, bad debt expense is calculated as a percentage of credit sales. This method is a statement of earnings approach to determining bad debt expense.

Solution:

1. $620,000 \times 0.0143 = $8,866$

2.

Assets	=	Liabilities	+	Shareholders' Equity
+524				
−524				

Date	Account and Explanation	Debit	Credit
Dec. 31, 2018	Allowance for Doubtful Accounts	524	
	Accounts Receivable		524
	(Record write-off of defaulted account)		

3. *Note*: The calculation in part 1 estimated the *ending* balance of bad debt expense. This amount is also the adjustment because the balance before the adjustment is zero. This is usually the case for statement of earnings accounts because they were closed at the end of the prior year.

Assets	=	Liabilities	+	Shareholders' Equity (Bad Debt Expense)
−8,866				−8,866

Date	Account and Explanation	Debit	Credit
Dec. 31, 2018	Bad Debt Expense	8,866	
	Allowance for Doubtful Accounts		8,866
	(Record adjusting entry for bad debt expense estimate)		

Bad Debt Expense		
Preadjustment balance, 12/31/18	0	
Adjustment	**8,866**	
Ending balance	8,866	

(Continued)

Allowance for Doubtful Accounts

		Beginning balance	134
Write-offs during 2018	524		
Preadjustment balance, 12/31/18	390		
		Adjustment	8,866
		Ending balance	8,476

4.

	Year-End	Assuming No Write-Off
Accounts receivable	$303,476*	$304,000
Less: Allowance for doubtful accounts	(8,476)**	(9,000)***
Net accounts receivable	$295,000	$295,000

* $304,000 − $524 = $303,476
** $134 − $524 + $8,866 = $8,476 (see T-account in part 3).
*** T-account from part 3 without the $524 debit for the write-off.

Note: Under the allowance method the write-off of a specific account does not affect the balance of *net* accounts receivable.

Occasionally, accounts receivable that are written off are later partially or entirely collected. Suppose that on February 5, 2019, Crimson receives $25 of the $524 that was written off at the end of the previous year (see part 2 of Cornerstone 5.2). Crimson would make the following entries:

Date	Account and Explanation	Debit	Credit
Feb. 5, 2019	Accounts Receivable	25	
	Allowance for Doubtful Accounts		25
	(Reverse portion of write-off)		
	Cash	25	
	Accounts Receivable		25
	(Record collection of account receivable)		

Assets	=	Liabilities	+	Shareholders' Equity
+25				
−25				
+25				
−25				

Crimson's first entry reverses the appropriate portion of the write-off by restoring the appropriate portion of the accounts receivable and allowance for doubtful accounts balances. The second entry records the cash collection in the typical manner.

Aging Method Under the **aging method**, bad debt expense is estimated by determining the collectibility of the accounts receivable rather than by taking a percentage of total credit sales. At the end of each accounting period, the individual accounts receivable are categorized by age. Then an estimate is made of the amount expected to default in each age category based on past experience and expectations about how the future may differ from the past. As you may expect, the overdue accounts are more likely to default than the currently due accounts, as shown in the example below:

Accounts Receivable Age	Amount	Proportion Expected to Default	Amount Expected to Default
Less than 16 days	$190,000	0.01	$1,900
16–30 days	40,000	0.04	1,600
31–60 days	10,000	0.10	1,000
Over 60 days	9,000	0.30	2,700
	$249,000		$7,200

The total amount expected to default on year-end accounts receivable, $7,200 in the above example, is the amount that should be the ending balance in the allowance for doubtful accounts. Since the objective of the aging method is to estimate the ending balance in the allowance for doubtful accounts, any existing balance in the allowance account must be considered when determining the amount of the adjusting entry, as shown in Cornerstone 5.3 .

CORNERSTONE 5.3

CORNERSTONE
VIDEO

Estimating the Allowance for Doubtful Accounts Using the Aging Method

Information:

On January 1, 2018, Sullivan Ltd. has the following balances for accounts receivable and allowance for doubtful accounts:

Accounts receivable	$224,000 (debit)
Allowance for doubtful accounts	6,700 (credit)

During 2018, Sullivan had $3,100,000 of credit sales, collected $3,015,000 of accounts receivable, and wrote off $60,000 of accounts receivable as uncollectible.

Required:

1. What is Sullivan's preadjustment balance in accounts receivable on December 31, 2018?

2. What is Sullivan's preadjustment balance in allowance for doubtful accounts on December 31, 2018?

3. Assuming Sullivan's analysis of the accounts receivable balance indicates that $7,200 of the current accounts receivable balance is uncollectible, by what amount will the allowance for doubtful accounts need to be adjusted?

4. What will be the ending balance in bad debt expense?

5. Prepare the necessary adjusting entry for 2018.

Why:

Under the accounts receivable aging method, the ending balance of the allowance for doubtful accounts is determined by aging the accounts receivable invoices outstanding from customers at the end of the accounting period. This method is a statement of financial position approach to determining bad debt expense.

Solution:

1.

Accounts Receivable			
Beginning balance	224,000		
Sales	3,100,000	Collections	3,015,000
		Write-offs	60,000
Preadjustment balance	249,000		

(Continued)

CORNERSTONE

5.3

(Continued)

2.

Allowance for Doubtful Accounts

		Beginning balance	6,700
Write-offs	60,000		
Preadjustment balance	53,300		

3.

Allowance for Doubtful Accounts

Preadjustment balance, 12/31/18	53,300		
		Adjusting entry	**60,500***
		Adjusted balance	7,200**

* Necessary adjustment to end up with an ending balance of $7,200.

** Estimate of ending balance determined by analyzing the receivables aging. This information was given in part 3 of the "Required" section.

4.

Bad Debt Expense

Preadjustment balance, 12/31/18	0
Adjustment	**60,500**
Ending balance	60,500

5.

Date	Account and Explanation	Debit	Credit
Dec. 31, 2018	Bad Debt Expense	60,500	
	Allowance for Doubtful Accounts		60,500
	(Record adjusting entry for bad debt expense estimate)		

Assets	=	Liabilities	+	Shareholders' Equity (Bad Debt Expense)
−60,500				−60,500

Comparison of Percentage of Credit Sales Method and Aging Method The underlying difference between the percentage of credit sales method and the aging method is what is being estimated. The percentage of credit sales method is primarily concerned with appropriately estimating bad debt expense on the statement of earnings. Because of the focus on the expense account, any existing balance in the allowance account is not considered when determining the amount of the adjusting entry. The aging method, on the other hand, is a statement of financial position approach that analyzes the accounts receivable to estimate its net realizable value. This estimate provides the necessary ending allowance for doubtful accounts balance to report net accounts receivable at net realizable value.

Bad Debts from a Management Perspective

Although bad debts result from actions of the purchaser (nonpayment), the amount of bad debt expense is influenced by the credit policies of the seller, as the You Decide below illustrates.

concept Q&A

What are the conceptual and practical differences between the percentage of credit sales and aging methods?

Answer:

The percentage of credit sales method estimates the amount to be shown as bad debt expense on the statement of earnings. The aging method estimates the amount to be shown as the allowance for doubtful accounts on the statement of financial position. The preadjustment balance in these accounts must be adjusted so that the ending balance equals the respective estimates. However, because bad debt expense is a statement of earnings account that is closed to retained earnings at the end of every period, its preadjustment balance should be zero. As such, the adjustment is equal to the estimate of the ending balance. The allowance for doubtful accounts, on the other hand, is a statement of financial position account and will typically have an existing balance.

YOUDECIDE   Are Bad Debts Always Bad? Should Increased Discounts Be Offered to Customers?

You are the owner/operator of Mt. Sterling Drug Company, a pharmaceutical wholesaler. In response to Mt. Sterling's "cash only" sales terms, competitors have attempted to lure business away by offering various incentives. Among these are credit terms whereby a customer typically has 30 to 60 days to pay for a purchase and receives a 1% to 2% discount for prompt payment (usually within 10 days of sale).

Which is worse—the potential bad debts that come with offering credit or the lost business from not offering credit?

There is no question that the inability to collect an account receivable is a serious problem. However, most wholesalers have come to accept bad debts as just another business expense. Certainly, no company would grant credit knowing that the specific customer will not pay for the goods purchased. Nonetheless, granting credit is a "necessary evil"—something that must be done to generate repeat business and maintain a competitive position.

An existing relationship with customers does not guarantee future business, especially if the customers can get a better deal elsewhere. Furthermore, prudent screening of each customer's credit history should enable you to identify some of those who may have difficulty paying their accounts. Placing such restrictions as relatively low credit limits on these risky accounts or, in some cases, denying credit altogether should help keep bad debts to a minimum.

Suppose Mt. Sterling's gross margin is 30% of sales and that, as a result of the more liberal credit policy, sales increase by $100,000 and bad debts are limited to 3% of the new credit sales. Then Mt. Sterling's income from operations should increase by $27,000 (increased gross margin of $30,000 less bad debt expense of $3,000), rather than decreasing.

Alternatively, and even with the more liberal credit policy, if a 2% discount was taken by all customers on the $100,000 sales increase, income from operations would still increase by $28,000 [increased gross margin of $30,000 less cash discounts of $2,000 ($100,000 × 2%)].

When caution is used, most companies agree that the loss of income by not offering credit (either $27,000 or $28,000 above) is more detrimental than the bad debt expenses or cash discount expenses incurred in doing so.

OBJECTIVE **5**

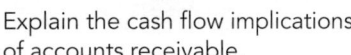

Explain the cash flow implications of accounts receivable.

MANAGING ACCOUNTS RECEIVABLE

We now focus on the cash management principles associated with accounts receivable.

Factoring Receivables

In Chapter 4, we mentioned that a principle of cash management is increasing the speed of cash collection for receivables. An increasingly common practice is to **factor**, or sell, receivables. When receivables are factored, the seller receives an immediate cash payment reduced by the factor's fees. The factor, the buyer of the receivables, acquires the right to collect the receivables and the risk of uncollectibility. In a typical factoring arrangement, the sellers of the receivables have no continuing responsibility for their collection.

Factoring arrangements vary widely, but typically the factor charges a fee ranging from 1% to 3%. This fee compensates the factor for the time value of money (i.e., interest), the risk of uncollectibility, and the tasks of billing and collection. Large businesses and financial institutions frequently package factored receivables as financial instruments or securities and sell them to investors. This process is known as **securitization**.

Credit Cards

Bank **credit cards**, such as Visa and MasterCard, are really just a special form of factoring. The issuer of the credit card (i.e., the bank) pays the seller the amount of each sale less a service charge (on the date of purchase) and then collects the full amount of the sale from the buyer (at some later date).[1] For example, if a retail customer uses a bank's Visa card to pay $100 for a haircut, the salon will make the following entry assuming the bank charges a 1.55% service charge:

---

[1] The bank may also pay the full amount of the sale to the seller and then bill the service charge at the end of the period.

Account and Explanation	Debit	Credit
Cash	98.45	
Sales Revenue		98.45
(Record sales)		

Assets	= Liabilities +	Shareholders' Equity
+98.45		(Sales Revenue) +98.45

Although a 1.55% service charge may seem expensive, credit card sales provide sellers with a number of advantages over supplying credit directly to customers, including the following:

- Sellers receive the money immediately.
- Sellers avoid bad debts because as long as the credit card verification procedures are followed, the credit card company absorbs the cost of customers who do not pay.
- Record-keeping costs lessen because employees are not needed to manage these accounts.
- Sellers believe that by accepting credit cards, their sales will increase. For example, how many of you have ever driven away from a gas station that does not accept credit cards or even one that merely does not allow you to pay at the pump?

Of course, many large retailers are willing to take on these costs to avoid the credit card service charge. For example, Canadian Tire, Hudson's Bay Company, Sears, and most other large retailers have internal credit cards. When such a card is used, the seller records it like any other account receivable and no service charge expense is incurred; however, that seller is accepting the risk of uncollectible accounts and the cost of servicing these accounts.

Nonbank credit cards, such as American Express, also result in a receivable for the seller because the issuer of the credit card (American Express) does not immediately pay the cash to the seller. American Express also charges a higher service charge to the seller. Consequently, sellers find American Express to be more costly than bank cards, such as Visa or MasterCard, which explains why many businesses do not accept American Express.

Debit Cards

A **debit card** authorizes a bank to make an immediate electronic withdrawal (debit) from the holder's bank account. The debit card is used like a credit card except that a bank electronically reduces (debits) the holder's bank account and increases (credits) the merchant's bank account for the amount of a sale made on the card.

Debit cards appear to be somewhat disadvantageous to the card holder as transactions cannot be rescinded by stopping payment. Furthermore, a purchase using a debit card causes an immediate reduction in a bank account balance, while a cheque written at the same time will require at least one or two days to clear, allowing the depositor to benefit from the additional money in the account until the cheque is presented at the bank for payment. However, debit cards offer significant advantages to banks and merchants in reduced transaction-processing costs. Thus, banks and merchants have an incentive to design debit cards that minimize or eliminate the disadvantages and costs to card users.

Extending Credit to Customers

An important part of managing accounts receivable is determining who should receive credit. If credit policy is too loose, bad debts may be incurred as a result of customers not paying their accounts. If credit policy is too tight, the company may lose future sales.

Common methods for managing risk when it is extended to customers is to require security or a down payment, with the balance due in cash on delivery. When possible, companies should verify credit references before advancing credit to a customer.

When a company has a concentration of credit risk as a result of having large amounts of receivables due from a few customers, this risk must be discussed in the financial statement notes. Exhibit 5.1 shows an excerpt from Note 4 of Sears Canada's January 31, 2015, financial statements:

(EXHIBIT 5.1)

Credit Risk

Note 14: Financial Instruments Credit Risk
Credit risk refers to the possibility that the Company can suffer financial losses due to the failure of the Company's counterparties to meet their payment obligations. The Company is exposed to minimal credit risk from customers as a result of ongoing credit evaluations and review of accounts receivable collectability.

Source: 2014 Sears Canada Annual Report, page 32.

Determining the Credit Period

When credit is granted to a customer, the period for which credit is granted should be determined and the customer informed. To maximize sales and collectibility, payment periods generally should be approximately the same length of time as allowed by competitors.

Monitoring Accounts Receivable Collection

The accounts receivable aging schedule should be regularly prepared and reviewed by management. The aging schedule identifies customers that are not paying according to agreed payment terms. These problem customers should be contacted and payment arranged. For customers that refuse to pay, businesses may find it necessary to arrange a special payment schedule with the customer or to pursue legal action for collection.

NOTES RECEIVABLE

OBJECTIVE ❻

Account for notes receivable from inception to maturity.

Notes receivable are receivables that generally specify an interest rate and a maturity date at which any interest and principal must be repaid. Our discussion here is limited to simple notes that specify the repayment of interest and principal in a single payment on a given day (more complicated interest-bearing notes are discussed in the context of notes payable in Chapter 10).

The amount lent is the **principal**. The excess of the total amount of money collected over the amount lent is called **interest**. For example, as shown in Exhibit 5.2, if Toromont, a Caterpillar dealer, lends $500,000 to a customer and is repaid $580,000 at some later date, then $80,000 of interest was collected.

Interest can be considered compensation paid to the lender for giving up the use of resources for the period of a note (the time value of money). The interest rate specified in the note is an annual rate. Therefore, when calculating interest, you must consider the duration of the note using the following formula:

Interest = Principal × Annual interest rate × Fraction of one year

For example, in the example illustrated in Exhibit 5.2, what is the annual interest rate? The answer is that we have no way of knowing because the duration of the loan is not specified. If the duration of the loan is exactly one year, then the annual rate is 16%. If the duration is more (or less) than one year, however, then the annual rate is less (or more) than 16%.

Furthermore, you will recall from Chapter 2 that the matching concept and the revenue recognition principle require that expenses and revenues be identified with specific accounting periods. If only one month of interest has been earned by year-end, an

(EXHIBIT 5.2)

Principal and Interest in Loan Repayments

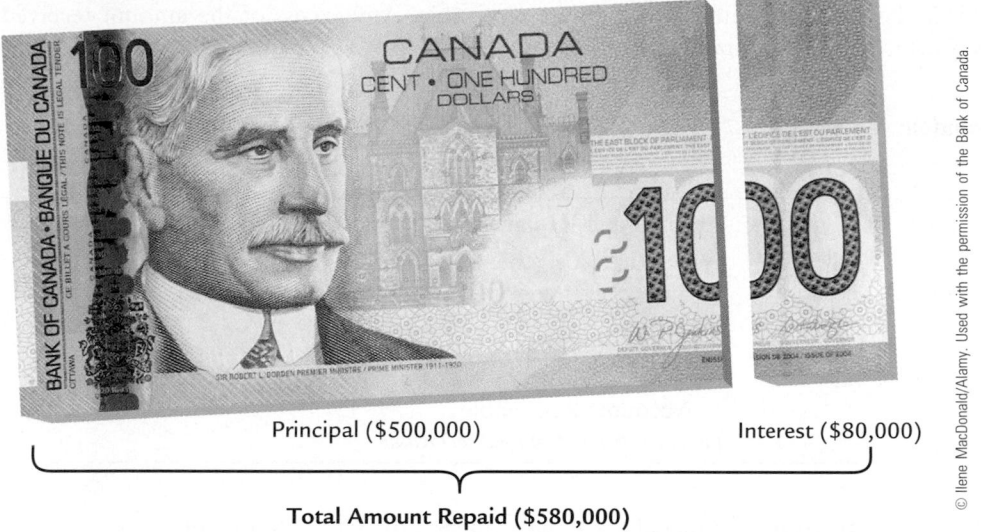

Principal ($500,000)　　　　　Interest ($80,000)

© Ilene MacDonald/Alamy. Used with the permission of the Bank of Canada.

Total Amount Repaid ($580,000)

adjusting entry is required to recognize interest income and a corresponding interest receivable. Any remaining interest is recognized in subsequent periods.[2] The accounting for notes receivable is demonstrated in Cornerstone 5.4 .

Accounting for Notes Receivable

Information:

Dover Electric Company purchased, on account, $50,000 of consulting services from Thomas Ltd. on November 1, 2018. The amount is due in full on January 1, 2019. Dover Electric is unable to pay the account by the due date and negotiates an extension with a 10% note in lieu of the unpaid account receivable.

Required:

1. Prepare Thomas's journal entries to record the sale on November 1, 2018, and the modification of payment terms on January 1, 2019.

2. How much interest will be paid if Dover Electric repays the note on (a) July 1, 2019, (b) December 31, 2019, and (c) March 31, 2020?

3. Prepare Thomas's adjusting entry to accrue interest on December 31, 2019, assuming the note is repaid on March 31, 2020.

4. Prepare Thomas's journal entries to record the cash received to pay off the note and interest on each of the three dates specified in part 2.

CORNERSTONE
VIDEO

(Continued)

[2] Interest is, in fact, often computed in terms of days rather than months. Suppose, for example, that the three-month note runs for 92 days (two 31-day months and one 30-day month). The total interest on a 92-day note for $10,000 would be $302.47 [($10,000)(0.12)(92/365)], and the first 31-day month's interest would be $101.92 [($10,000)(0.12)(31/365)]. Observe that daily interest complicates the arithmetic associated with interest calculations but does not alter the basic form of the calculations. To simplify interest computations, we will use monthly interest throughout this chapter.

CORNERSTONE

5.4

_____

(Continued)

Why:

Notes receivable are recognized for the amount of cash loaned or goods/services sold. This is the principal amount of the note receivable. Any excess of the amount received over principal is recognized as interest income in the period the interest was earned.

Solution:

1.

Assets	= Liabilities +	Shareholders' Equity (Sales Revenue)
+50,000		+50,000

Date	Account and Explanation	Debit	Credit
Nov. 1, 2018	Accounts Receivable	50,000	
	Sales Revenue		50,000
	(Record sale)		

Assets	= Liabilities +	Shareholders' Equity
+50,000		
−50,000		

Date	Account and Explanation	Debit	Credit
Jan. 1, 2019	Notes Receivable	50,000	
	Accounts Receivable		50,000
	(Record issuance of note receivable)		

2.   Interest = Principal × Annual interest rate × Fraction of one year

a) July 1, 2019:
  = $50,000 × 10% × (6/12)
  = $2,500

b) Dec. 31, 2019:
  = $50,000 × 10% × (12/12)
  = $5,000

c) March 31, 2020:
  = $50,000 × 10% × (15/12)
  = $6,250

3.

Assets	= Liabilities +	Shareholders' Equity (Interest Income)
+5,000		+5,000

Date	Account and Explanation	Debit	Credit
Dec. 31, 2019	Interest Receivable	5,000	
	Interest Income		5,000
	(Record accrual of interest)		

4.

Assets	= Liabilities +	Shareholders' Equity (Interest Income)
+52,500		+2,500
−50,000		

Date	Account and Explanation	Debit	Credit
July 1, 2019	Cash	52,500	
	Notes Receivable		50,000
	Interest Income		2,500
	(Record collection of note receivable)		

Assets	= Liabilities +	Shareholders' Equity (Interest Income)
+55,000		+5,000
−50,000		

Date	Account and Explanation	Debit	Credit
Dec. 31, 2019	Cash	55,000	
	Notes Receivable		50,000
	Interest Income		5,000
	(Record collection of note receivable)		

Assets	= Liabilities +	Shareholders' Equity (Interest Income)
+56,250		+1,250
−50,000		
−5,000		

Date	Account and Explanation	Debit	Credit
Mar. 31, 2020	Cash	56,250	
	Notes Receivable		50,000
	Interest Receivable		5,000
	Interest Income		1,250
	(Record collection of note receivable)		

Honouring and Dishonouring Notes Receivable

In Cornerstone 5.4, Dover Electric Company honoured the note receivable by paying it when due at the maturity date. A dishonoured note is one that has not been honoured (paid) at the maturity date of the note.

Normally, on the date of note dishonour the balance of the note and accrued interest is transferred to accounts receivable. Using the data in Cornerstone 5.4, and assuming that the note was dishonoured on March 31, 2020, the following journal entry will be recorded, assuming that it is reasonably expected that the note will be paid:

March 31, 2020	Debit	Credit
Account Receivable	56,250	
Note Receivable		50,000
Interest Receivable		5,000
Interest Income		1,250

If it is determined on March 31, 2020, that the note will *not* be collected, the principal and all accrued interest should be written off. No interest will be accrued from the year 2020 of December 31, 2019, to March 31, 2020, since collection is not expected:

March 31, 2020	Debit	Credit
Allowance for Doubtful Accounts	55,250	
Note Receivable		50,000
Interest Receivable		5,000

Zero Interest Notes

Notes are sometimes issued with an interest rate of zero. This type of note is known as a deep discount note. Such a note is only worth the discounted (present) value of the face amount. Discounts on notes are discussed in Chapter 10 of this text in the context of bonds payable.

INTERNAL CONTROL OVER SALES

Since sales revenues have a significant effect on a company's net income, internal control procedures must be established to ensure that the amounts reported for these items are correct. For sales revenues, these controls normally involve the following documents and procedures:

OBJECTIVE **7**

Explain internal control procedures for merchandise sales.

- Accounting for a sale begins with the receipt of a purchase order or some similar document from a customer. The order document is necessary for the buyer to be obligated to accept and pay for the ordered goods.
- Shipping reports and billing documents are prepared based on the order document. Billing documents are usually called *invoices*.
- A sale and its associated receivable are recorded only when the purchase order, shipping, and billing documents are all present.

As illustrated in Exhibit 5.3, sales revenue should be recorded only when these three control documents are completed. When any of these three documents is not present, it is possible for valid sales to be unrecorded and for invalid sales to be recorded.

For sales returns, allowances, and discounts, internal control procedures must be established that identify the conditions and documentation required before a sales return, allowance, or discount can be recorded. These controls protect the firm from unwarranted reductions in revenues and receivables and ultimately cash.

(EXHIBIT 5.3)

Internal Controls for Recording Sales Revenue

PURCHASE ORDER	No. R450

Richardson's Wholesale Hardware

Date: Sept. 1, 2018

To:
Bolt Manufacturing

QTY.	DESCRIPTION	PRICE	AMOUNT
30	Model No. SB100 snowblower	$500	$15,000

Ordered by: Jim Richardson

Jim Richardson

Purchase order number must appear on all shipments and invoice

SHIPPING REPORT	No. B275

Bolt Manufacturing

Date: Sept. 1, 2018

To:
Richardson's Wholesale Hardware

QTY.	DESCRIPTION
30	Model No. SB100 snowblower

Purchase order: R450

INVOICE	No. B100

Bolt Manufacturing

Date: Sept. 1, 2018

Sold to:
Richardson's Wholesale Hardware
Purchase order: R450

QTY.	DESCRIPTION	PRICE	AMOUNT
30	Model No. SB100 snowblower	$500	$15,000
	SUBTOTAL		$15,000
	SALES TAX		0
	SHIPPING & HANDLING		0
	TOTAL DUE		$15,000

Date	Account and Explanation	Debit	Credit
Sept. 1	Accounts Receivable	15,000	
	Sales Revenue		15,000
	To record sale to customer		

ANALYZING SALES AND RECEIVABLES

OBJECTIVE

Calculate profitability and asset management ratios using sales and receivables data.

Analysts of the financial statements are extremely concerned with both sales and receivables.

Sales

Because sales revenue is such a key component of a company's success, analysts are interested in a large number of ratios that incorporate sales. Many of these ratios attempt to measure the return the company is earning on sales. These are called **profitability ratios**. For example, the ratios of statement of earnings subtotals such as gross margin, operating income, and net income to sales are examined, but really any statement of earnings subtotal can be of interest. The three most common ratios are gross profit margin, operating margin, and net profit margin:

$$\text{Gross profit margin} = \frac{\text{Gross profit}}{\text{Net sales}}$$

$$\text{Operating margin} = \frac{\text{Operating income}}{\text{Net sales}}$$

$$\text{Net profit margin} = \frac{\text{Net income}}{\text{Net sales}}$$

Industry Comparison

Each of the profitability ratios listed above reveals information about a company's strategy and the competition it faces. For example, consider two large players in the retail industry—Walmart and Nordstrom. Information available indicates that these two stores possess the following five-year averages for these ratios:

	Walmart	Nordstrom
Gross profit percentage	24.44%	38.6%
Operating margin percentage	5.86%	10.85%
Net profit margin percentage	3.56%	5.98%

Nordstrom's higher gross profit percentage suggests that Nordstrom is able to charge a premium on its merchandise. That is, Nordstrom follows a product differentiation strategy in which it tries to convince customers that its products are superior, distinctive, and so on. Walmart, on the other hand, is a low-cost provider that attempts to convince customers that it offers the lowest prices.

Analysts also like to look at the operating margin and net profit margin percentages to see how much is left from a sales dollar after paying for the product and all its operations. For these ratios, Nordstrom still retains a larger percentage of each sales dollar than Walmart. How is it, then, that Walmart makes so much money? Walmart has a large sales dollar volume—its net sales revenue of US$485 billion in fiscal 2015 was approximately 36 times greater than Nordstrom's US$13.5 billion.

The availability of industry data allows company managers to compare their own results to industry averages. Differences are usually evident. No two companies are alike; even so, such comparisons are often highly useful.

Receivables

Analysts are also concerned about asset management. Asset management refers to how efficiently a company is using the resources at its disposal. Two of the most widely used asset management ratios are accounts receivable turnover and average collection period:

$$\text{Accounts receivable turnover} = \frac{\text{Net sales}}{\text{Average net accounts receivable}}$$

$$\text{Average collection period} = \frac{\text{Average net accounts receivable}}{\text{Net sales/365}}$$

These ratios provide a measure of how many times average trade receivables are collected during the period and how many days' sales are in the accounts receivable balance. In theory, net credit sales would be a much better numerator, but that figure is not normally disclosed. A higher turnover number and lower collection period are better because these indicate that the company is collecting cash more quickly (through sales) from its inventory. As discussed in Chapter 4's section on cash management, this reduces borrowing costs and allows for greater investment in other areas of the business. Changes in these ratios over time are also very important. For example, a significant reduction in receivables turnover may indicate that management is extending credit to customers who are not paying.

Accounts receivable turnover and average collection period for Walmart and Nordstrom are:

	Walmart	Nordstrom
Accounts receivable turnover	72.2 times	6.0 times
Average collection period	5.1 days	60.6 days

As expected, Walmart is extremely efficient with its asset management because effective cash management is necessary for low-cost providers. Of course, it is difficult to compare Nordstrom to Walmart because they engage in different financing practices. For example, a greater proportion of Walmart sales are made using cash or external credit cards (such as Visa), while Nordstrom has a larger proportion of sales using internal credit cards (a Nordstrom card). The internal credit cards result in lower accounts receivable turnover and greater collection period. Cornerstone 5.5 illustrates the calculation of these ratios for Hudson's Bay Company.

CORNERSTONE 5.5

Calculating the Gross Profit Margin, Operating Margin, Net Profit Margin, Accounts Receivable Turnover, and Average Collection Period Ratios

Information:

The following information (in Canadian millions) is available for Hudson's Bay Company for its fiscal year ended January 31, 2015:

Net sales	$8,169	Accounts receivable, 1/31/14	$137
Gross profit	3,276	Accounts receivable, 1/31/15	212
Operating income	481		
Net income	238		

Required:

Compute the (1) gross profit margin, (2) operating margin, (3) net profit margin, (4) accounts receivable turnover, and (5) average collection period for Hudson's Bay Company for the year ended January 31, 2015.

Why:

The gross profit margin, operating margin, and net profit margin provide measures of the return the company is earning on sales. The accounts receivable turnover ratio and average collection period, respectively, provide a measure of how many times accounts receivable are collected during the period and how many days it takes to collect average accounts receivable.

Solution:

1.   Gross profit margin ratio $= \dfrac{\text{Gross profit}}{\text{Net sales}}$

$$= \dfrac{\$3,276}{\$8,169} = 40.1\%$$

2.   Operating margin ratio $= \dfrac{\text{Operating income}}{\text{Net sales}}$

$$= \dfrac{\$481}{\$8,169} = 5.9\%$$

3.   Net profit margin ratio $= \dfrac{\text{Net income}}{\text{Net sales}}$

$$= \dfrac{\$238}{\$8,169} = 2.91\%$$

(Continued)

4. $\text{Accounts receivable turnover ratio} = \dfrac{\text{Net sales}}{\text{Average net accounts receivable}}$

$$= \dfrac{\$8,169}{(\$137 + \$212) \div 2} = 46.81 \text{ times}$$

CORNERSTONE

5.5

(Continued)

5. $\text{Average collection period} = \dfrac{\text{Average net accounts receivable}}{(\text{Net sales} \div 365)}$

$$= \dfrac{((\$137 + \$212) \div 2)}{\$8,169 \div 365}$$

$$= 7.8 \text{ days}$$

STATEMENT PRESENTATION OF RECEIVABLES

Receivables that are due within the greater of one year or the normal operating cycle of the business from the reporting date are disclosed as current assets. Current receivables are usually listed after cash and short-term investments on the statement of financial position. Although only the net amount of accounts receivable must be disclosed in the financial statements, the allowance for doubtful accounts, because it is useful information, is usually also disclosed on either the face of the statement of financial position or in the notes to the financial statements. Each major type of receivable is reported either on the statement of financial position or in the notes to the financial statements.

The 2014 consolidated financial statements for Domtar Corporation disclosed the following accounts receivable information on the statement of financial position:

Domtar Corporation
Consolidated Statements of Financial Position (partial)
December 31, 2014 (in millions of $)

	Dec. 31, 2014	Dec. 31, 2013
Receivables, less allowances of $6 and $4	$628	$601

SUMMARY OF LEARNING OBJECTIVES

LO1. **Apply the criteria for revenue recognition to a retail, service, or manufacturing business.**

- Revenue is recognized when:
  - significant risks and benefits of ownership have been transferred to the buyer
  - revenue can be reliably measured
  - the seller does not retain control or managerial involvement with the goods sold
  - the economic benefits of the transaction will flow to the seller
  - the costs of the transaction can be reliably measured

LO2. **Measure and report net sales revenue.**

- The appropriate amount of revenue to recognize is generally the cash received or the cash equivalent of accounts receivable.
- However, companies often induce customers to buy by offering:
  - sales discounts
  - sales returns
  - sales allowances

- Sales discounts are reductions of the normal selling price to encourage prompt payment.
- Credit card charges are recorded as a reduction of net sales.
- Sales returns occur when a customer returns goods as unsatisfactory.
- Sales allowances occur when a customer agrees to keep goods with minor defects if the seller reduces the selling price.
- These events are recorded in contra-revenue accounts that reduce gross sales to net sales.

LO3.   Explain the principal types of receivables.

- Receivables are classified along four different dimensions:
  - accounts receivable (or trade receivables) and notes receivable
  - other receivables
  - trade and nontrade receivables
  - current and noncurrent receivables

LO4.   Measure and report bad debt expense and the allowance for doubtful accounts.

- The primary issues in accounting for accounts receivable are when and how to measure bad debts (i.e., accounts that will not be paid).
- IFRS requires receivables to be shown at net realizable value on the statement of financial position.
- Furthermore, the matching concept says that an expense should be recognized in the period in which it helps generate revenues.
- Consequently, we must estimate and recognize bad debt expense in the period the sale is made—even though we do not know which accounts will be uncollectible.
- The bad debts expense estimate is made by using either:
  - the percentage of credit sales method or
  - the aging method
- The percentage of credit sales method estimates the bad debt expense directly (statement of earnings focus).
- The aging method estimates the ending balance needed in the allowance for doubtful accounts, and bad debt expense follows (statement of financial position focus) based on aging of the accounts receivable.

LO5.   Explain the cash flow implications of accounts receivable.

- Companies can increase the speed of cash collection on receivables by factoring, or selling, their receivables.
- The buyer of the receivables will charge a fee to compensate itself for the time value of money, the risk of uncollectibility, and the tasks of billing and collection.
- Receivables may also be packaged as financial instruments or securities and sold to investors. This type of arrangement is referred to as securitization.
- A special case of selling receivables occurs when credit cards like MasterCard and Visa are accepted by vendors.
- Credit decisions include who should be granted credit and the length of the credit period.
- Accounts receivable aging should be regularly prepared and reviewed.

LO6.   Account for notes receivable from inception to maturity.

- Notes receivable are recognized for the amount of cash borrowed or goods/services purchased.
- This is the principal amount of the note receivable.
- Any excess of amount repaid over principal is recognized as interest revenue in the period the interest was earned.

LO7.   Explain internal control procedures for merchandise sales.

- Since sales revenues have a significant effect on a company's net income, internal control procedures must be established to ensure that the amounts reported are correct.
- Typically, sales are not recorded by businesses until a three-way match is performed between:

- the customer purchase order (which indicates that the customer ordered the goods)
- the shipping document (which indicates that the goods ordered have been shipped to the customer)
- the invoice (which indicates that the customer has been billed for the goods shipped at the agreed price.)

LO8. **Calculate profitability and asset management ratios using sales and receivables data.**

- Because sales revenue is such a key component of a company's success, analysts are interested in a large number of ratios that incorporate sales.
- Many of these ratios attempt to measure how much profit the company is making on sales. These ratios are called profitability ratios and include:
  - gross profit margin
  - operating margin
  - net profit margin
- Analysts are also concerned with asset management. Asset management refers to how efficiently a company is using the resources at its disposal.
- Two of the most widely used asset management ratios are accounts receivable turnover and the average collection period ratios.

CORNERSTONES

CORNERSTONE 5.1	Recording sales discounts, page 253
CORNERSTONE 5.2	Estimating bad debt expense using the percentage of credit sales method, page 260
CORNERSTONE 5.3	Estimating the allowance for doubtful accounts using the aging method, page 262
CORNERSTONE 5.4	Accounting for notes receivable, page 267
CORNERSTONE 5.5	Calculating the gross profit margin, operating margin, net profit margin, accounts receivable turnover, and average collection period ratios, page 272

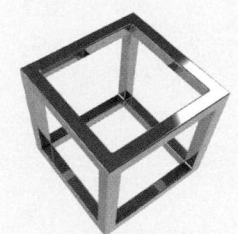

KEY TERMS

Accounts receivable (p. 256)

Aging method (p. 261)

Allowance for Doubtful Accounts (p. 258)

Bad debt expense (p. 258)

Cash equivalent (p. 253)

Credit cards (p. 264)

Debit card (p. 265)

Earned (p. 252)

Factor (p. 264)

FOB destination (p. 252)

FOB shipping point (p. 252)

Freight-in (p. 252)

Freight-out (p. 252)

Interest (p. 266)

Net sales revenue (p. 255)

Nontrade receivables (p. 256)

Notes receivable (p. 266)

Percentage of credit sales method (p. 259)

Principal (p. 266)

Profitability ratios (p. 270)

Realizable (p. 252)

Realized (p. 252)

Sales allowance (p. 255)

Sales discount (p. 253)

Sales returns (p. 255)

Securitization (p. 264)

Trade receivables (p. 256)

REVIEW PROBLEM

I. Recording Sales and Receivables

Qwurk Productions performs graphic design services including designing and maintaining websites. The following activities occurred during 2018 and 2019:

11/1/18	Qwurk delivers a new logo to GCD Advisers and submits a bill for $2,000 with terms 2/10, n/30.
11/15/18	Qwurk delivers an overall Web concept to Mutare, which Mutare approves. Qwurk submits a bill for $1,000 with terms 2/10, n/30.
11/20/18	Qwurk delivers paper and envelopes incorporating the new logo to GCD Advisers and submits a bill for $200.
11/22/18	Mutare pays for the 11/15 bill related to a new overall Web concept.
11/25/18	GCD complains that the printing on much of the paper and envelopes is unacceptable. Qwurk offers to reduce the bill from $200 to $75. GCD accepts.
11/29/18	GCD pays for the 11/1 bill for a new logo and $75 for the 11/20 bill for paper and envelopes.
12/1/18	Qwurk installs a new website incorporating order fulfillment applications for Redbird Enterprises. Redbird signs a note to pay $20,000 plus 6% interest due on 7/1/19.
12/15/18	Qwurk writes off a $600 account receivable.
12/31/18	After performing an aging of its accounts receivable, Qwurk estimates that $2,000 of its accounts receivable will be uncollectible on a total balance of $600,000. The allowance for doubtful accounts has a credit balance of $300 prior to adjustment.
7/1/19	Redbird pays the note and interest in full.
12/31/19	For the year ended December 31, 2019, Qwurk has sales of $6,000,000; sales discounts of $15,000; sales returns and allowances of $20,000.

Required:

1. Provide the journal entry for November 1, 2018, assuming Qwurk uses the gross method of recording receivables.
2. Provide the journal entry for November 15, 2018, assuming Qwurk uses the gross method of recording receivables.
3. Provide the journal entry for November 20, 2018, assuming Qwurk uses the gross method of recording receivables.
4. Calculate how much Mutare paid and provide the journal entry for November 22, 2018.
5. Provide the journal entry for November 25, 2018.
6. Calculate how much GCD paid and provide the journal entry for November 29, 2018.
7. Provide the journal entry for December 1, 2018.
8. Provide the journal entry for December 15, 2018.
9. Provide the necessary adjusting entries for December 31, 2018, to accrue interest on the note and adjust the allowance account.
10. What is the net realizable value of Qwurk's accounts receivable at December 31, 2018?
11. Calculate how much interest Redbird paid and provide the journal entry for July 1, 2019.
12. Provide the statement of earnings presentation of Qwurk's 2019 sales.

Solution:

Date	Account and Explanation	Debit	Credit
2018			
1. Nov. 1	Accounts Receivable	2,000	
	Sales		2,000
	(Record sale)		
2. Nov. 15	Accounts Receivable	1,000	
	Sales		1,000
	(Record sale)		

Assets	=	Liabilities	+	Shareholders' Equity (Sales)
+2,000				+2,000

Assets	=	Liabilities	+	Shareholders' Equity (Sales)
+1,000				+1,000

Date	Account and Explanation	Debit	Credit
2018			

3. Nov. 20   Accounts Receivable   200

         Sales   200

         (Record sale)

		Shareholders'
Assets	= Liabilities +	Equity (Sales)
+200		+200

4. Nov. 22   Cash[a]   980

         Sales Discounts   20

            Accounts Receivable   1,000

         (Record collection within the discount period)

		Shareholders' Equity (Sales
Assets	= Liabilities +	Discounts)
+980		−20
−1,000		

[a] Gross amount $1,000
   Less: Discount ($1,000 × 2%)   (20)
     Total paid $ 980

5. Nov. 25   Sales Returns and Allowances   125

            Accounts Receivable   125

         (Record allowance for unacceptable merchandise)

		Shareholders' Equity (Sales Returns and
Assets	= Liabilities +	Allowances)
−125		−125

6. Nov. 29   Cash[b]   2,075

            Accounts Receivable   2,075

         (Record collection after discount period)

		Shareholders'
Assets	= Liabilities +	Equity
+2,075		
−2,075		

[b] Gross amount $2,000
   Less: Discount (not allowed; paid after 10 days)   (0)
     Total paid $2,000 + 75 = $2,075

7. Dec. 1   Notes Receivable   20,000

         Sales   20,000

         (Record sale)

		Shareholders'
Assets	= Liabilities +	Equity (Sales)
+20,000		+20,000

8. Dec. 15   Allowance for Doubtful Accounts   600

            Accounts Receivable   600

         (Write-off an accounts receivable)

		Shareholders'
Assets	= Liabilities +	Equity
+600		
−600		

9. Dec. 31   Interest Receivable[c]   100

         Interest Income   100

         (Record one month's interest on Dec. 1 note receivable)

         Bad Debt Expense   1,700

            Allowance for Doubtful Accounts[d]   1,700

         (Record adjusting entry for bad debt expense estimate)

		Shareholders' Equity (Interest Income and Bad
Assets	= Liabilities +	Debt Expense)
+100		+100
−1,700		−1,700

[c] 20,000 × 6% × 1/12
[d] Qwurk's estimate warrants a $2,000 credit balance. Because the account already has a $300 credit balance, a $1,700 credit is needed.

10. December 31, 2018:   Accounts receivable accounts $600,000
               Less: Allowance for doubtful accounts   (2,000)
                   Net realizable value $598,000

Net accounts receivable are shown at net realizable value.

11.   July 1, 2019:

$$\text{Interest paid} = \$20{,}000 \times 6\% \times 7/12$$
$$= \$700$$

However, interest income recognized for Qwurk is for the period December 1, 2018, through July 1, 2019. The interest for December 2018 was recognized in 2018 (see journal entry in 9).

	Shareholders' Equity (Interest
Assets = **Liabilities** +	**Income)**
+20,700	+600
−100	
−20,000	

Account and Explanation	Debit	Credit
Cash	20,700	
Interest Income		600
Interest Receivable (from 9)		100
Notes Receivable		20,000
(Record collection of note receivable)		

12.

Gross sales revenue	$6,000,000
Less: Sales discounts	(15,000)
Less: Sales returns and allowances	(20,000)
Net sales revenue	$5,965,000

DISCUSSION QUESTIONS

1. When is revenue recognized?
2. Explain the criteria for revenue recognition.
3. When is revenue generally considered earned?
4. What criteria has the IASB issued as guidance for revenue recognition?
5. How is net sales revenue calculated?
6. Why might users of financial statements prefer the separate disclosure of gross sales revenue and sales returns and allowances to the disclosure of a single net sales revenue amount?
7. Why are sales discounts offered?
8. What are sales returns?
9. What are sales allowances? How do sales allowances differ from sales discounts?
10. What are trade discounts and quantity discounts? From an accounting viewpoint, how does the effect of trade and quantity discounts on selling (or invoice) price differ from the effect of sales discounts?
11. What are the principal types of receivables?
12. Under the allowance method, why do we make an entry to record bad debt expense in the period of sale rather than in the period in which an account is determined to be uncollectible?
13. Why is the direct write-off method not accepted under IFRS?
14. What is the conceptual difference between the (1) percentage of credit sales and (2) aging methods of estimating bad debts?
15. What kind of account is *allowance for doubtful accounts*? What does it represent?
16. Why do companies issue credit when their past experience indicates that some customers will not pay?
17. How much interest will be due at maturity for each of the following interest-bearing notes?

	Principal	Months to Maturity	Annual Interest Rate
a.	$10,000	2	12%
b.	42,000	5	14
c.	18,000	4	13
d.	37,000	6	11

18. A business borrows $1,000, giving a note that requires repayment of the amount borrowed in two payments of $600 each, one at the end of each of the next two six-month periods. Calculate the total interest on the note. What is the principal amount of the note?

19. A business borrows $1,000, giving a note that requires an interest rate of 12% per year and repayment of principal plus interest in a single payment at the end of one year. Calculate the total interest on the note. What is the amount of the single payment?

20. Describe what happens when receivables are factored.

21. Accepting major credit cards requires the seller to pay a service charge. What advantages does the seller obtain by accepting major credit cards?

22. Why is interest typically charged on notes receivable, but not on accounts receivable?

23. What documents must be present to trigger the recording of a sale (and associated receivable) in the accounting records?

24. Describe the documents that underlie the typical accounting system for sales. Give an example of a failure of internal control that might occur if these documents were not properly prepared.

25. How may analyzing sales and receivables provide information about a firm's profitability?

26. How may analyzing sales and receivables provide information about a firm's asset management?

MULTIPLE-CHOICE EXERCISES

5-1 Which of the following is not one of the criteria for revenue recognition?
   a. Significant risks and rewards of ownership have been transferred.
   b. Continuing managerial involvement does not exist.
   c. Economic benefits will probably flow to the seller.
   d. Customers have an excellent credit rating.

5-2 Food To Go is a local catering service. Conceptually, when should Food To Go recognize revenue from its catering service?
   a. At the date the invoice is mailed to the customer
   b. At the date the customer places the order
   c. At the date the customer's payment is received
   d. At the date the meals are served

5-3 When should revenue from the sale of merchandise normally be recognized?
   a. When the customer pays for the merchandise
   b. When the customer takes possession of the merchandise
   c. Either on the date the customer takes possession of the merchandise or on the date on which the customer pays
   d. When the customer takes possession of the merchandise, if sold for cash, or when payment is received, if sold on credit

5-4 What does the phrase "Revenue is recognized at the point of sale" mean?
   a. Revenue is recorded in the accounting records when the cash is received from a customer and reported on the statement of earnings when sold to the customer.
   b. Revenue is recorded in the accounting records and reported on the statement of earnings when the cash is received from the customer.
   c. Revenue is recorded in the accounting records when the goods are sold to a customer and reported on the statement of earnings when the cash payment is received from the customer.
   d. Revenue is recorded in the accounting records and reported on the statement of earnings when goods are sold and delivered to a customer.

5-5 On August 31, 2018, Nova Corporation signed a four-year contract to provide services for Minefield Company at $30,000 per year. Minefield will pay for each year of services on the first day of each service year, starting with

September 1, 2018. Using the accrual basis of accounting, when should Nova recognize revenue?

a. Only at the end of the entire contract

b. Equally throughout the year as services are provided

c. On the first day of each year when the cash is received

d. On the last day of each year after the services have been provided

5-6 Under the gross method, the seller records discounts taken by the buyer:

a. in a contra-revenue account at the date of sale.

b. never; discounts are irrelevant under the gross method.

c. before the receivable is collected.

d. when the payment is made, if applicable.

5-7 On April 20, Legault Company provides lawn care services to Tazwell Corporation for $3,000 with terms 1/10, n/30. On April 28, Tazwell pays for half of the services provided and on May 19 it pays for the other half. What is the total amount of cash Legault received?

a. $2,700

b. $2,970

c. $2,985

d. $3,000

5-8 Which of the following statements concerning internal control procedures for merchandise sales is not correct?

a. A sale and its associated receivable are recorded only when the order, shipping, and billing documents are all present.

b. Shipping and billing documents are prepared based on the order document.

c. The order document is not necessary for the buyer to be obligated to accept and pay for the ordered goods.

d. Accounting for a sale begins with the receipt of a purchase order or some similar document from a customer.

5-9 All of the following are ways in which receivables are commonly classified in financial statements except:

a. accounts or notes receivable.

b. current or noncurrent.

c. collectible or uncollectible.

d. trade or nontrade receivable.

5-10 Which one of the following best describes the allowance for doubtful accounts?

a. Cash flow account

b. Contra account

c. Statement of earnings account

d. Liability account

5-11 If a company uses the direct write-off method of accounting for bad debts,

a. it is applying the matching concept.

b. it will reduce the accounts receivable account at the end of the accounting period for estimated uncollectible accounts.

c. it will report accounts receivable on the statement of financial position at their net realizable value.

d. it will record bad debt expense only when an account is determined to be uncollectible.

5-12 Which of the following best describes the objective of estimating bad debt expense with the percentage of credit sales method?

a. To estimate bad debt expense based on a percentage of credit sales made during the period

b. To estimate the amount of bad debt expense based on an aging of accounts receivable

c. To determine the amount of uncollectible accounts during a given period

d. To facilitate the use of the direct write-off method

5-13 Which of the following best describes the concept of the aging method of receivables?

a. Accounts receivable should be directly written off when the due date arrives and the customers have not paid the bill.

b. An accurate estimate of bad debt expense may be arrived at by multiplying historical bad debt rates by the amount of credit sales made during a period.

c. Estimating the appropriate balance for the allowance for doubtful accounts results in the appropriate value for net accounts receivable on the statement of financial position.

d. The precise amount of bad debt expense may be arrived at by multiplying historical bad debt rates by the amount of credit sales made during a period.

5-14 The aging method is closely related to the:
   a. statement of financial position.
   b. statement of retained earnings.
   c. statement of cash flows.
   d. statement of earnings.

5-15 The percentage of credit sales approach is closely related to the:
   a. statement of financial position.
   b. statement of retained earnings.
   c. statement of cash flows.
   d. statement of earnings.

5-16 The process by which firms package factored receivables as financial instruments or securities and sell them to investors is known as:
   a. credit extension.
   b. aging of accounts receivable.
   c. bundling.
   d. securitization.

5-17 Which one of the following statements is true if a company's collection period for accounts receivable is unacceptably long?
   a. The company should expand operations with its excess cash.
   b. The company may need to borrow to acquire operating cash.
   c. The company may offer trade discounts to lengthen the collection period.

   d. Cash flows from operations may be higher than expected for the company's sales.

5-18 Zenephia Corp. accepted a nine-month note receivable from a customer on October 1, 2018. If Zenephia has an accounting period that ends on December 31, 2018, when would it most likely recognize interest income from the note?
   a. On October 1, 2018
   b. On December 31, 2018, only
   c. On December 31, 2018, and July 1, 2019
   d. On July 1, 2019, only

5-19 The "principal" of a note receivable refers to:
   a. the present value of the note.
   b. the amount of cash borrowed.
   c. the financing company that is lending the money.
   d. the amount of interest due.

5-20 Net profit margin percentage is calculated by:
   a. dividing net income by (net) sales.
   b. dividing operating income by (net) sales.
   c. subtracting operating income from (net) sales.
   d. subtracting net income from (net) sales.

CORNERSTONE EXERCISES

Cornerstone Exercise 5-21   Service Revenue

Kibitz Fitness received $24,000 from customers on August 1, 2018. These payments were advance payments of yearly membership dues.

OBJECTIVE **1** **2**
CORNERSTONE 5.1

Required:

At December 31, 2018, calculate what the balances in the Unearned Service Revenue and Service Revenue accounts will be.

Cornerstone Exercise 5-22   Service Revenue

Hockey Magazine Company received advance payments of $75,000 from customers during 2018. At December 31, 2018, $20,000 of the advance payments still had not been earned.

OBJECTIVE **1** **2**
CORNERSTONE 5.1

Required:

After the adjustments are recorded and posted at December 31, 2018, calculate what the balances will be in the Unearned Magazine Revenue and Magazine Revenue accounts from the 2018 advance payments.

OBJECTIVE **2**
CORNERSTONE 5.1

Cornerstone Exercise 5-23   Sales Discounts Taken

Bolton sold a customer service contract with a price of $37,000 to Sammy's Wholesale Company. Bolton offered terms of 1/10, n/30.

Required:

Prepare the journal entry to record the sale. Then prepare the journal entry to record the payment assuming the payment is made within 10 days. (within the discount period).

OBJECTIVE **2**
CORNERSTONE 5.1

Cornerstone Exercise 5-24   Sales Discounts Not Taken

Bolton sold a customer service contract with a price of $37,000 to Sammy's Wholesale Company. Bolton offered terms of 1/10, n/30.

Required:

Prepare the journal entry to record the sale. Then prepare the journal entry to record the payment assuming the payment is made after 10 days. (after the discount period).

OBJECTIVE **2**
CORNERSTONE 5.1

Cornerstone Exercise 5-25   Sales Discounts

Rama Inc. provided consulting services with a gross price of $40,000 and terms of 2/10, n/30.

Required:

1. Prepare the necessary journal entry to record the net sales to be reported in the financial statements.
2. Prepare the necessary journal entry to record collection of the receivable assuming the customer pays within 10 days.
3. Prepare the necessary journal entry to record collection of the receivable assuming the customer pays after 10 days.

OBJECTIVE **4**
CORNERSTONE 5.2

Cornerstone Exercise 5-26   Percentage of Credit Sales

Shanghai Company has credit sales of $550,000 during 2018 and estimates at the end of 2018 that 2.5% of these credit sales will eventually default. Also, during 2018 a customer defaults on a $775 balance related to goods purchased in 2017. Prior to the write-off for the $775 default, Shanghai's accounts receivable and allowance for doubtful accounts (preadjustment) balances were $402,000 and $129 (credit), respectively.

Required:

1. Prepare the journal entry to record the defaulted account.
2. Prepare the adjusting entry to record the bad debt expense for 2018.

OBJECTIVE **4**
CORNERSTONE 5.2

Cornerstone Exercise 5-27   Write-Off of Uncollectible Accounts

The Rock has credit sales of $500,000 during 2018 and estimates at the end of 2018 that 2% of these credit sales will eventually default. Also, during 2018 a customer defaults on a $1,800 balance related to goods purchased in 2017.

Required:

1. Prepare the journal entry to record the defaulted balance.
2. Prepare the adjusting entry to record the bad debt expense for 2018.

OBJECTIVE **4**
CORNERSTONE 5.3

Cornerstone Exercise 5-28   Aging Method

On January 1, 2018, Khalid Inc. has the following balances for accounts receivable and allowance for doubtful accounts:

| Accounts Receivable | $1,280,000 |
| Allowance for Doubtful Accounts (a credit balance) | 44,000 |

During 2018, Khalid had $18,500,000 of credit sales, collected $17,945,000 of accounts receivable, and wrote off $60,000 of accounts receivable as uncollectible. At year-end, Khalid performs an aging of its accounts receivable balance and estimates that $52,000 will be uncollectible.

Required:

1. Calculate Khalid's preadjustment balance in accounts receivable on December 31, 2018.
2. Calculate Khalid's preadjustment balance in allowance for doubtful accounts on December 31, 2018.
3. Prepare the necessary adjusting entry for 2018.

Cornerstone Exercise 5-29   Aging Method

On January 1, 2018, Smith Inc. has the following balances for accounts receivable and allowance for doubtful accounts:

| Accounts Receivable | $382,000 |
| Allowance for Doubtful Accounts (a credit balance) | 4,200 |

During 2018, Smith had $2,865,000 of credit sales, collected $2,905,000 of accounts receivable, and wrote off $3,850 of accounts receivable as uncollectible. At year-end, Smith performs an aging of its accounts receivable balance and estimates that $3,800 will be uncollectible.

Required:

1. Calculate Smith's preadjustment balance in accounts receivable on December 31, 2018.
2. Calculate Smith's preadjustment balance in allowance for doubtful accounts on December 31, 2018.
3. Prepare the necessary adjusting entry for 2018.

Cornerstone Exercise 5-30   Percentage of Credit Sales Method

At December 31, 2018, Garneau has a $10,000 credit balance in its allowance for doubtful accounts. Garneau estimates that 3% of its 2018 credit sales will eventually default. During 2018, Garneau had credit sales of $1,130,000.

Required:

Estimate the bad debt expense under the percentage of credit sales method.

Cornerstone Exercise 5-31   Accounts Receivable Balance

Beginning accounts receivable were $32,350. All sales were on account and totalled $286,480. Cash collected from customers totalled $276,750.

Required:

Calculate the ending accounts receivable balance.

Cornerstone Exercise 5-32   Accounts Receivable Balance

Beginning accounts receivable were $275,500 and ending accounts receivable were $302,300. Cash amounting to $2,965,000 was collected from customers' credit sales.

Required:

Calculate the amount of sales on account during the period.

OBJECTIVE 4
CORNERSTONE 5.3

OBJECTIVE 4
CORNERSTONE 5.2

OBJECTIVE 5
CORNERSTONE 5.3

OBJECTIVE 4 5
CORNERSTONE 5.3

ILLUSTRATING
RELATIONSHIPS

OBJECTIVE **5**

CORNERSTONE 5.3

Cornerstone Exercise 5-33   Accounts Receivable Balance

Beginning accounts receivable were $135,720 and ending accounts receivable were $128,640. All sales were on credit and totalled $1,682,480.

Required:

Determine how much cash was collected from customers.

OBJECTIVE **5**

CORNERSTONE 5.3

Cornerstone Exercise 5-34   Accounting for Credit Card Sales

Frank's Tattoos and Body Piercing operates near campus. At the end of a recent day, Frank's cash register included credit card documents for the following sales amounts:

MasterCard	$756
Visa	486

The merchant's charges are 1.8% for MasterCard and 2.1% for Visa. Frank's also had cash sales of $375 and $800 of sales on credit to a local business.

Required:

Prepare a journal entry to record these sales.

OBJECTIVE **6**

CORNERSTONE 5.4

Cornerstone Exercise 5-35   Notes Receivable—Honoured and Dishonoured

Metzler Communications designs and programs a website for a local business. Metzler charges $33,000 for the project and the local business signs a 7% note January 1, 2018.

Required:

1. Prepare the journal entry to record the sale on January 1, 2018.
2. Determine how much interest Metzler will receive if the note is repaid on July 1, 2018.
3. Prepare Metzler's journal entry to record the cash received to pay off the note and interest on July 1, 2018.
4. Prepare the journal entry required on July 1, 2018, if the note is then dishonoured (assume the note will not be collected).

OBJECTIVE **6**

CORNERSTONE 5.4

Cornerstone Exercise 5-36   Notes Receivable—Honoured and Dishonoured

Link Communications programs voicemail systems for businesses. For a recent project they charged $135,000. The customer secured this amount by signing a note bearing 9% interest on February 1, 2018.

Required:

1. Prepare the journal entry to record the sale on February 1, 2018.
2. Determine how much interest Link will receive if the note is repaid on December 1, 2018.
3. Prepare Link's journal entry to record the cash received to pay off the note and interest on December 1, 2018.
4. Prepare the journal entry required on December 1, 2018, if the note is then dishonoured. (Assume the note will not be collected).

OBJECTIVE **8**

CORNERSTONE 5.5

Cornerstone Exercise 5-37   Ratio Analysis

The following information pertains to Perle Corporation's financial results for the past year.

Net sales	$135,000
Cost of goods sold	48,000
Other expenses	37,000
Net income	50,000

Required:

Calculate Perle's (1) gross profit margin ratio and (2) net profit margin ratio.

Cornerstone Exercise 5-38   Ratio Analysis

Diviney Corporation's net sales and average net trade accounts receivable were $8,750,000 and $630,000, respectively.

Required:

Calculate Diviney's accounts receivable turnover and average collection period.

OBJECTIVE 8
CORNERSTONE 5.5

Cornerstone Exercise 5-39   Ratio Analysis

Bari Sports' net sales, average net trade accounts receivable, and net income were $7,300,000, $842,000, and $390,000, respectively.

Required:

Calculate Bari's (1) accounts receivable turnover, (2) average collection period, and (3) net profit margin ratio.

OBJECTIVE 8
CORNERSTONE 5.5

BRIEF EXERCISES

Brief Exercise 5-40   Service Revenue

H&R Wholesalers is a retailer providing low-cost, bulk items to small companies. Companies must pay an annual membership fee of $100 to access H&R's warehouses. H&R received yearly membership fees from 320 companies on August 1, 2018.

Required:

At December 31, 2018, calculate the remaining amount of Unearned Revenue and the account balance of the Revenue account. Assume this is their first year of business.

OBJECTIVE 1 2

Brief Exercise 5-41   Service Revenue

Melrose Milk Delivery provides weekly gourmet milk delivery to the residents of Nicetown. Melrose charges each customer $45 per week for its milk delivery, and it received advance payments for 2,000 weeks of milk delivery services in 2018. At December 31, 2018, two-thirds of the advance payments had been earned.

Required:

After the adjustments are recorded and posted at December 31, 2018, calculate what the balances will be in the Unearned Revenue and Revenue accounts. Assume this is their first year of business.

OBJECTIVE 1 2

Brief Exercise 5-42   Sales Discounts Taken

Gordon's Grocers purchases bread from Buddy's Bread Company at $1.45 per loaf. Gordon's recently engaged in a customer service contract with Buddy's to purchase 20,000 loaves of Buddy's bread. Buddy offered credit to Gordon's at terms of 2/10, n/30.

Required:

Prepare the journal entry to record the sale. Then prepare the journal entry to record the payment assuming the payment is made within 10 days.

OBJECTIVE 2

Brief Exercise 5-43   Sales Discounts Not Taken

Assume the same information as in Brief Exercise 5-42: Gordon's Grocers purchases bread from Buddy's Bread Company at $1.45 per loaf. Gordon's engaged in a customer service contract to purchase 20,000 loaves of Buddy's bread. Buddy offered credit at terms of 2/10, n/30 and uses the gross method.

OBJECTIVE 2

(Continued)

Required:

Prepare the journal entry for Buddy to record the payment assuming the payment is made after 10 days (after the discount period).

OBJECTIVE ❷   **Brief Exercise 5-44   Sales Discounts**

Harry Gardner provides tax services for small businesses. This year's tax season has proved especially lucrative for Harry; he earned $45,000 for providing his services. Harry uses terms of 1/10, n/30 in billing his customers.

Required:

1. Prepare the necessary journal entry to record the net sales to be reported on the financial statements.
2. Prepare the necessary journal entry to record collection of the receivable assuming the customer pays within 10 days.
3. Prepare the necessary journal entry to record collection of the receivable assuming the customer pays after 10 days.

OBJECTIVE ❹   **Brief Exercise 5-45   Percentage of Credit Sales**

Roeker Company provides information systems consultation services to large companies in the Chicagoland area. Due to a dip in the economy, Roeker has increased the percentage of credit sales that it believes will be uncollectible from 3.0% to 3.2% for 2018. Roeker's consulting services provided revenues of $700,000 in 2018. During 2018, Roeker has write-offs of $750 related to goods purchased in 2017. Prior to the write-off for the $750 default, Roeker's accounts receivable and allowance for doubtful accounts balances were $480,000 and $232 (credit), respectively.

Required:

1. Prepare the journal entry to record the defaulted account.
2. Prepare the adjusting entry to record the bad debt expense for 2018.

OBJECTIVE ❹   **Brief Exercise 5-46   Write-Off of Uncollectible Accounts**

King Enterprises had 27 customers utilizing its financial planning services in 2018. Each customer paid King $25,000 for receiving King's assistance. King estimates that 2% of its $675,000 credit sales in 2018 will be uncollectible. During 2019, King wrote off $2,700 related to services performed in 2018.

Required:

1. Prepare the journal entry to record the defaulted balance.
2. Prepare the adjusting entry to record the bad debt expense for 2019.

OBJECTIVE ❹   **Brief Exercise 5-47   Aging Method**

Spotted Singer sells karaoke machines to businesses and consumers via the Internet. On January 1, 2018, Spotted Singer Inc. has an accounts receivable balance of $997,000 and a credit balance in its allowance for doubtful accounts of $24,000. During 2018, Spotted Singer had $10,800,000 of credit sales, collected $1,725,000 of accounts receivable, and had customer defaults of $45,000. At year-end, an aging analysis indicates that $28,000 of Spotted Singer's receivables will be uncollectible.

Required:

1. Calculate Spotted Singer's balance in accounts receivable on December 31, 2018, prior to the adjustment.
2. Calculate Spotted Singer's balance in allowance for doubtful accounts on December 31, 2018, prior to the adjustment.
3. Prepare the necessary adjusting entry for 2018.

Brief Exercise 5-48 Aging Method

OBJECTIVE 4

Ingrid Inc. has strict credit policies and only extends credit to customers with outstanding credit history. The company examined its accounts and determined that at January 1, 2018, it had balances in accounts receivable and allowance for doubtful accounts of $478,000 and $7,900 (credit), respectively. During 2018, Ingrid extended credit for $3,075,000 of sales, collected $2,715,000 of accounts receivable, and had customer defaults of $4,280. Ingrid performed an aging analysis on its receivables at year-end and determined that $6,800 of its receivables will be uncollectible.

Required:

1. Calculate Ingrid's balance in accounts receivable on December 31, 2018, prior to the adjustment.
2. Calculate Ingrid's balance in allowance for doubtful accounts on December 31, 2018, prior to the adjustment.
3. Prepare the necessary adjusting entry for 2018.

Brief Exercise 5-49 Percentage of Credit Sales Method

OBJECTIVE 4

Ruby Red manufactures, markets, and distributes citrus-flavoured soft drinks across the globe. Ruby Red hired a collection agency in 2017 to increase collection rates from customers. As a result, Ruby estimates that only 2% of its 2018 credit sales will be written off, compared to the 4% of 2017's credit sales that were estimated to be uncollectible. At December 31, 2018, Ruby Red has a $12,800 credit balance in its allowance for doubtful accounts and credit sales of $1,570,000.

Required:

Use the percentage of credit sales method to calculate the bad debt expense.

Brief Exercise 5-50 Collection of Amounts Previously Written Off

OBJECTIVE 4

Hannah purchased a laptop computer from Perry Corp. for $1,500. Hannah's receivable has been outstanding for over 180 days, and Perry determines that the total amount is uncollectible and writes off all of Hannah's debt. Hannah later receives a windfall and pays the amount of her balance to Perry Corp.

Required:

Make the appropriate journal entries (if any) to record the receipt of $450 by Perry Corp.

Brief Exercise 5-51 Accounts Receivable Balance

OBJECTIVE 5

Hart Inc. began the year with $315,700 of accounts receivable. During the year, Hart sold a considerable amount of merchandise on credit and collected $2,427,000 of its credit sales. At the end of the year, the accounts receivable balance is $16,800 lower than the beginning balance.

Required:

Calculate the amount of credit sales during the period.

Brief Exercise 5-52 Accounts Receivable Balance

OBJECTIVE 5

XYZ Corp sells widgets to consumers for $20 each. Its beginning accounts receivable balance was $24,975, and it sold 12,376 widgets throughout the year. The total cash collections for the year amounted to $217,750.

Required:

Calculate the ending accounts receivable balance.

OBJECTIVE 5

Brief Exercise 5-53   Accounts Receivable Balance

Ray's beginning and ending accounts receivables balances are $147,990 and $142,720, respectively. Ray's sold $3,745,060 of merchandise, of which 50% was on credit.

Required:

Determine the amount of accounts receivable collected in the period.

OBJECTIVE 5

Brief Exercise 5-54   Accounting for Credit Card Sales

Jarrod's Meat Shop doubles as a butcher shop and a sandwich shop that sells to both individuals and a nearby hospital system. On a particular day, Jarrod's had cash sales of $450, credit sales of $600, sales on MasterCard of $657, and sales on Visa of $923. The sales on credit cards incur merchant charges of 1.6% for MasterCard and 1.9% for Visa.

Required:

Prepare a journal entry to record these sales.

OBJECTIVE 6

Brief Exercise 5-55   Notes Receivable

Harrigan Enterprises utilizes Snoopy Systems to design and implement a cash management system. Due to Harrigan's cash management problems, it cannot currently pay for the system out of pocket. Snoopy chooses to extend a 6% note on January 1, 2018, for the $27,000 project cost.

Required:

1. Prepare Snoopy's journal entry to record the service performed on January 1, 2018.
2. Determine how much interest Snoopy will receive if the note is repaid on May 1, 2018.
3. Provide Snoopy's journal entry to record the cash received to pay off the note and interest on May 1, 2018.

OBJECTIVE 6

Brief Exercise 5-56   Notes Receivable

Kelsey's Kleening provides cleaning services for Clinton Inc., a business with four buildings. Kelsey's assigned different cleaning charges for each building based on the amount of square feet to be cleaned. The charges for the four buildings are $35,000, $27,000, $45,000, and $10,000. Clinton secured this amount by signing a note bearing 7% interest on March 1, 2018.

Required:

1. Prepare the journal entry to record the sale on March 1, 2018.
2. Determine how much interest Kelsey will receive if the note is repaid on December 1, 2018.
3. Prepare Kelsey's journal entry to record the cash received to pay off the note and interest on December 1, 2018.

OBJECTIVE 8

Brief Exercise 5-57   Ratio Analysis

Dobby's statement of earnings lists net sales of $179,000 and a gross margin of $111,000. All other expenses not included in the gross margin totalled $46,500.

Required:

1. Calculate Dobby's gross profit ratio.
2. Calculate Dobby's net profit margin ratio.

OBJECTIVE 8

Brief Exercise 5-58   Ratio Analysis

Rose Corporation sells upscale lamps to boutiques across the country. The average net trade accounts receivable for Rose is $540,000. In addition, the company has average net sales of $6,950,000.

Required:

Calculate Rose's accounts receivable turnover.

Brief Exercise 5-59   Ratio Analysis

OBJECTIVE **8**

Watts Inc. specializes in imported goods, focusing particularly on food products. For 2018, the company realized net sales of $9,700,000 and average net trade accounts receivable were $1,057,000. In 2017, Watts had realized a net loss for the year in the amount of $20,000; however, extraordinary efficiency efforts in 2018 increased net income by $445,000.

Required:

1. Calculate Watts' accounts receivable turnover.
2. Calculate Watts' net profit margin ratio.

EXERCISES

Exercise 5-60   Calculation of Revenue

OBJECTIVE **1** **2**

Steven Motors buys and sells used cars. Steven made the following sales during January and February:

a. Three cars were sold to Ruiz Taxi for a total of $75,000; the cars were delivered to Ruiz on January 18. Ruiz paid $20,000 on January 18 and the remaining $55,000 on February 12.
b. One car was sold to Hastings Classics for $28,000. The car was delivered to Hastings on January 25. Hastings paid Steven on February 1.

Required:

Calculate the monthly revenue for Steven for January and February.

Exercise 5-61   Revenue Recognition

OBJECTIVE **1** **2**

Volume Electronics sold a television to Sarah Chang on December 15, 2018. Sarah paid $100 at the time of the purchase and agreed to pay $100 each month for five months beginning January 15, 2019.

Required:

Determine in what month or months revenue from this sale should be recorded by Volume Electronics to ensure proper application of accrual accounting.

Exercise 5-62   Calculation of Revenue from Cash Collection

OBJECTIVE **1** **2**

Anderson Lawn Service provides mowing, weed control, and pest management services for a flat fee of $140 per lawn per month. During July, Anderson collected $6,300 in cash from customers, which included $560 for lawn care provided in June. At the end of July, Anderson had not collected from 11 customers who had promised to pay in August when they returned from vacation.

ILLUSTRATING
RELATIONSHIPS

Required:

Calculate the amount of Anderson's revenue for July.

Exercise 5-63   Effects of Sales Discounts

OBJECTIVE **2**

Citron Mechanical Systems makes all sales on credit, with terms 1/15, n/30. During 2018, the list price (prediscount) of services provided was $687,500. Customers paid $482,000 (list price) of these sales within the discount period and the remaining $205,500 (list price) after the discount period. Citron reports net sales to be reported in the financial statements.

(Continued)

Required:

1. Compute the amount of sales that Citron recorded for 2018.
2. Compute the amount of cash that Citron collected from these sales.
3. Prepare a summary journal entry to record these sales and a second summary entry to record the cash collected.

OBJECTIVE **2** **4**

Exercise 5-64   Sales Discount Recorded

Columbia Company provided services with a list price of $48,500 to Small Enterprises with terms 2/15, n/45. Columbia records sales to be reported in the financial statements.

Required:

1. Prepare the entries to record this sale in Columbia's journal.
2. Prepare the entry for Columbia's journal to record receipt of cash in payment for the sale within the discount period.
3. Prepare the entry for Columbia's journal to record receipt of cash in payment for the sale after the discount period.
4. Assume that Columbia's customer does not have the available cash to pay Columbia within the discount period. How much interest should the customer be willing to pay for a loan to permit them to take advantage of the discount period (assuming no additional costs to the loan)?

OBJECTIVE **2**

Exercise 5-65   Sales and Sales Returns and Allowances

Rubin Enterprises had the following sales-related transactions on a recent day:

a. List price of services provided on credit was $18,150; terms 2/10, n/45.
b. Collected $3,650 in cash for services to be provided in the future.
c. The customer complained about aspects of the services provided in part *a*. To maintain a good relationship with this customer, Rubin granted an allowance of $1,200 off the list price. The customer had not yet paid for the services.
d. Rubin provided the services for the customer in part *b*. Additionally, Rubin granted an allowance of $250 because the services were provided after the promised date. Because the customer had already paid, Rubin paid the $250 allowance in cash.

Required:

1. Prepare the necessary journal entry (or entries) for each of these transactions.
2. What concerns would Rubin have, assuming that its sales allowances for this period were significantly higher than in previous periods both in absolute terms and as a percentage of gross sales?

YOUDECIDE

OBJECTIVE **4**

Exercise 5-66   Average Uncollectible Account Losses and Bad Debt Expense

The accountant for Pirelli Company prepared the following data for sales and losses from uncollectible accounts:

Year	Credit Sales	Losses from Uncollectible Accounts*
2014	$ 883,000	$13,125
2015	952,000	14,840
2016	1,083,000	16,790
2017	1,189,000	16,850

* Losses from uncollectible accounts are the actual losses related to sales of that year (rather than write-offs of that year).

Required:

1. Calculate the average percentage of losses from uncollectible accounts for 2014 through 2017.

2. Assume that the credit sales for 2018 are $1,260,000 and that the weighted average percentage calculated in part 1 is used as an estimate of losses from uncollectible accounts for 2018 credit sales. Determine the bad debt expense for 2018 using the percentage of credit sales method.

3. **CONCEPTUAL CONNECTION** Do you believe this estimate of bad debt expense is reasonable?

4. **CONCEPTUAL CONNECTION** How would you estimate 2018 bad debt expense if losses from uncollectible accounts for 2017 were $30,000? What other action would management consider?

Exercise 5-67 Bad Debt Expense: Percentage of Credit Sales Method

OBJECTIVE 4

Gilmore Electronics had the following data for a recent year:

Cash sales	$135,000
Credit sales	512,000
Accounts receivable determined to be uncollectible	9,650

The firm's estimated rate for bad debts is 2.2% of credit sales.

Required:

1. Prepare the journal entry to write off the uncollectible accounts.
2. Prepare the journal entry to record the estimate of bad debt expense.
3. By how much would bad debt expense reported on the statement of earnings have changed if Gilmore had written off $3,000 of receivables as uncollectible during the year?
4. Assuming that Gilmore's estimate of bad debts is correct (2.2% of credit sales) and that its gross margin is 20%, by how much did Gilmore's income from operations increase, assuming that $150,000 of the sales would have been lost if credit sales had not been offered?

YOUDECIDE

Exercise 5-68 Bad Debt Expense: Percentage of Credit Sales Method

OBJECTIVE 4

Beliveau Plumbing had the following data for a recent year:

Credit sales	$873,600
Allowance for doubtful accounts, 1/1 (a credit balance)	19,430
Accounts receivable, 1/1	67,350
Collections on account receivable	846,000
Accounts receivable written off	16,840

Beliveau estimates that 2.4% of credit sales will eventually default.

Required:

1. Compute bad debt expense for the year (rounding to the nearest whole number).
2. Determine the ending balances in accounts receivable and allowance for doubtful accounts.

Exercise 5-69 Bad Debt Expense: Aging Method

OBJECTIVE 4

Glencoe Supply had the following accounts receivable aging schedule at the end of a recent year.

Accounts Receivable	Age Amount	Proportion Expected to Default	Allowance Required
Current	$310,500	0.005	$ 1,553
1–30 days past due	47,500	0.01	475
31–45 days past due	25,000	0.13	3,250
46–90 days past due	12,800	0.20	2,560
91–135 days past due	6,100	0.25	1,525
Over 135 days past due	4,200	0.60	2,520
			$11,883

The balance in Glencoe's allowance for doubtful accounts at the beginning of the year was $58,620 (credit). During the year, accounts in the total amount of $62,400 were written off.

(Continued)

Required:

1. Determine bad debt expense.
2. Prepare the journal entry to record bad debt expense.
3. By how much would bad debt expense reported on the statement of earnings have changed if Glencoe had written off $90,000 of receivables as uncollectible during the year?

OBJECTIVE ④   **Exercise 5-70   Aging Receivables and Bad Debt Expense**

Kim Corporation sells paper products to a large number of retailers. Kim's accountant has prepared the following aging schedule for its accounts receivable at the end of the year:

Accounts Receivable Category	Amount	Proportion Expected to Default
Within discount period	$384,500	0.004
1–30 days past discount period	187,600	0.015
31–60 days past discount period	41,800	0.085
Over 60 days past discount period	21,400	0.200

Before adjusting entries are entered, the preadjustment balance in the allowance for doubtful accounts is a *debit* of $480.

Required:

1. Calculate the desired postadjustment balance in Kim's allowance for doubtful accounts.
2. Determine bad debt expense for the year.

OBJECTIVE ④   **Exercise 5-71   Allowance for Doubtful Accounts**

ILLUSTRATING
RELATIONSHIPS

At the beginning of the year, Kullerud Manufacturing had a credit balance in its allowance for doubtful accounts of $6,307 and at the end of the year it was a credit balance of $9,000. During the year Kullerud made credit sales of $890,000, collected receivables in the amount of $812,000, and recorded bad debt expense of $33,750.

Required:

Compute the amount of receivables that Kullerud wrote off during the year.

OBJECTIVE ④   **Exercise 5-72   Collection of Amounts Previously Written Off**

Customer Rob Hufnagel owes Kellman Corp. $1,250. Kellman determines that the total amount is uncollectible and writes off all of Hufnagel's debt. Hufnagel later pays $350 to Kellman.

Required:

Make the appropriate journal entries (if any) to record the receipt of $350 by Kellman.

OBJECTIVE ④   **Exercise 5-73   Correcting an Erroneous Write-Off**

ILLUSTRATING
RELATIONSHIPS

The new bookkeeper at Kaolin Construction Company was asked to write off two accounts totalling $1,710 that had been determined to be uncollectible. Accordingly, he debited accounts receivable for $1,710 and credited bad debt expense for the same amount.

Required:

1. Determine what was wrong with the bookkeeper's entry, assuming that Kaolin uses the allowance method.
2. Given the entry required to correct his error.

OBJECTIVE ⑥   **Exercise 5-74   Accounting for Notes Receivable—Honoured and Dishonoured**

On November 30, 2018, Tucker Products performed computer programming services for Damascus Inc. in exchange for a five-month, $75,000, 10% note receivable. Damascus Inc. paid

Tucker the full amount of interest and principal on April 30, 2019. Tucker has a December 31 year-end.

Required:

1. Prepare the necessary entries for Tucker to record the transactions described above.
2. Prepare the journal entry required if the note is dishonoured on April 30, 2019.

Exercise 5-75   Recording Notes Receivable: Issuance, Payment, and Default

OBJECTIVE **6**

Marydale Products permits its customers to defer payment by giving personal notes instead of cash. All the notes bear interest and require the customer to pay the entire note in a single payment six months after issuance. Marydale has a December 31 year-end. Consider the following transactions, which describe Marydale's experience with two such notes:

a. On October 31, 2018, Marydale accepts a six-month, 9% note from customer A in lieu of a $3,600 cash payment for services provided that day.
b. On February 28, 2019, Marydale accepts a six-month, $2,400, 7% note from customer B in lieu of a $2,400 cash payment for services provided on that day.
c. On April 30, 2019, customer A pays the entire note plus interest in cash.
d. On August 31, 2019, customer B pays the entire note plus interest in cash.

Required:

1. Prepare the necessary journal and adjusting entries required to record transactions *a* through *d* in Marydale's records.
2. Prepare the journal entries required if customer A defaults on its note obligation on April 30, 2019, and if Company B defaults on its note obligation on August 31, 2019 (assume that the amount is thought to be collectible).

Exercise 5-76   Internal Control for Sales

OBJECTIVE **7**

Arrow Products is a mail-order computer software sales outlet. Most of Arrow's customers call on its toll-free phone line and order software, paying with a credit card.

Required:

CONCEPTUAL CONNECTION Explain why the shipping and billing documents are important internal controls for Arrow.

Exercise 5-77   Ratio Analysis

OBJECTIVE **8**

The following information was taken from Bash Ltd.'s trial balances as of December 31, 2018, and December 31, 2019.

	12/31/2019	12/31/2018
Accounts receivable	$ 32,000	$ 39,000
Accounts payable	47,000	36,000
Sales	219,000	128,000
Sales returns	4,000	2,300
Retained earnings	47,000	16,000
Dividends declared	5,000	1,000
Net income	36,000	9,000

Required:

1. Calculate the net profit margin and accounts receivable turnover for 2019. (*Note:* Round answers to two decimal places.)
2. How much does Bash make on each sales dollar?
3. How many days does the average receivable take to be paid (assuming all sales are on account)?

OBJECTIVE **8**

Exercise 5-78　Ratio Analysis

The following information was taken from Den Manufacturing's trial balances as of December 31, 2018, and December 31, 2019.

	12/31/2019	12/31/2018
Accounts receivable	$ 13,000	$ 17,000
Accounts payable	22,000	15,000
Cost of goods sold	140,000	119,000
Sales	274,000	239,000
Sales returns	12,000	11,000
Retained earnings	47,000	16,000
Dividends declared	5,000	1,000
Income from operations	25,000	16,000
Net income	21,000	18,000

Required:

1. Calculate the gross profit margin and operating margin percentage for 2019. (*Note:* Round answers to two decimal places.)
2. Assuming that all of the operating expenses are fixed (or won't change as sales increase or decrease), what will be the operating margin percentage if sales increase by 25%?

PROBLEM SET A

OBJECTIVE **1**

Problem 5-79A　Revenue Recognition

Katie Vote owns a small business that rents computers to students at the local university for the nine-month school year. Katie's typical rental contract requires the student to pay the year's rent of $900 ($100 per month) in advance. When Katie prepares financial statements at the end of December, her accountant requires that Katie spread the $900 over the nine months that a computer is rented. Therefore, Katie can recognize only $400 revenue (four months) from each computer rental contract in the year the cash is collected and must defer recognition of the remaining $500 (five months) to next year. Katie argues that getting students to agree to rent the computer is the most difficult part of the activity so she ought to be able to recognize all $900 as revenue when the cash is received from a student.

Required:

CONCEPTUAL CONNECTION Explain why IFRS requires the use of accrual accounting rather than cash-basis accounting for the above, and similar, transactions.

OBJECTIVE **1 2 4**

Problem 5-80A　Recording Revenue, Receivables, and Bad Debt Expense

On January 1, 2019, Import Properties Inc. reported the following balances on its statement of financial position:

Accounts receivable	$2,105,000
Allowance for doubtful accounts	195,000

During 2019, the company conducted the following transactions:

a. Sold goods on account for $6,000,000
b. Processed sales returns of $50,000
c. Processed sales allowances of $40,000
d. Collected $6,950,000 of accounts receivable
e. Added interest to overdue accounts receivable of $150,000
f. Wrote off accounts receivable considered uncollectible of $75,000
g. Recovered accounts receivable previously written off of $45,000

Required:

1. Prepare the journal entries to record the above transactions.
2. Record the journal entry for bad debt expense at December 31, assuming that the allowance for doubtful accounts at December 31 should be $225,000.
3. Post all of the above entries to T-accounts for accounts receivable, allowance for doubtful accounts, and other accounts you deem are required.
4. Prepare the proper statement of financial position presentation of accounts receivable at December 31, 2019.
5. Prepare the proper statement of earnings presentation of the statement of earnings accounts for the year ended December 31.

Problem 5-81A Discount Policy and Gross Profit

OBJECTIVE **2**

Parkdale Audio sells MP3 players. During 2018, Parkdale sold 1,000 units at an average of $250 per unit. Each unit cost Parkdale $100. At present, Parkdale offers no sales discounts. Parkdale's controller suggests that a generous sales discount policy would increase annual sales to 1,400 units and also improve cash flow. She proposes 5/10, n/30 and believes that 80% of the customers would take advantage of the discount.

Required:

1. If the controller is correct, determine how much the new sales discount policy would add to net sales and gross margin.
2. **CONCEPTUAL CONNECTION** Explain why the sales discount policy might improve cash flow.

Problem 5-82A Effects of Discounts on Sales and Purchases

OBJECTIVE **2**

Helm Products sells golf clubs and accessories to pro shops. Gross sales in 2018 were $2,850,700 (Helm's list price) on terms 2/15, n/45. Customers paid for $2,000,000 (Helm's list price) of the merchandise within the discount period and the remaining $850,700 after the end of the discount period.

Required:

1. Compute the amount of sales.
2. Determine how much cash was collected from sales.

Problem 5-83A Sales Discounts

OBJECTIVE **2**

Sims Company regularly provides services to Laurier Supply on terms 1/15, n/30 and records sales at gross. During a recent month, the two firms engaged in the following transactions:

a. Sims provided services with a list price of $85,000.
b. Sims provided services with a list price of $30,000.
c. Laurier paid for the purchase in transaction *a* within the discount period.
d. Laurier paid for the purchase in transaction *b* after the discount period.

Required:

1. Prepare the journal entries for Sims to record the sales in *a* and *b* (make separate entries).
2. Record the journal entry for Sims to record Laurier's payment in *c*.
3. Record the journal entry for Sims to record Laurier's payment in *d*.
4. **CONCEPTUAL CONNECTION** What implied annual interest rate is Laurier incurring by failing to take the sales discount and, instead, paying the gross amount after 30 days?

Problem 5-84A Internal Control for Sales

OBJECTIVE **7**

Yancy's Hardware has three stores. Each store manager is paid a salary plus a bonus on the sales made by his or her store. On January 5, 2019, Bill Soong, manager of one of the stores, resigned. Bill's store had doubled its expected December 2018 sales, producing a bonus for Bill of $8,000 in December alone. Charles Brook, an assistant manager at another store, was assigned as manager of Bill's store. Upon examination of the store's accounting records, Charles reported that the store's records indicated sales returns and allowances of $110,000 in the first four days of January 2019, an amount equal to about half of December 2018 sales.

Required:

1. **CONCEPTUAL CONNECTION** Explain what the large amount of sales returns and allowances suggests that Bill might have done.
2. **CONCEPTUAL CONNECTION** Determine how Yancy could protect itself from a manager who behaved as Bill did.

OBJECTIVE **4**

Problem 5-85A   Bad Debt Expense: Percentage of Credit Sales Method

The Glass House, a glass and china store, sells nearly half its merchandise on credit. During the past four years, the following data have been developed for credit sales and losses from uncollectible accounts:

Year of Sales	Credit Sales	Losses from Uncollectible Accounts*
2015	$197,000	$12,608
2016	202,000	13,299
2017	212,000	13,285
2018	273,000	22,274
Total	$884,000	$61,466

* Losses from uncollectible accounts are the actual losses related to sales of that year (rather than write-offs of that year).

Required:

1. Calculate the loss rate for each year from 2015 through 2018. (*Note:* Round answers to three decimal places.)
2. Determine whether there appears to be a significant change in the loss rate over time.
3. **CONCEPTUAL CONNECTION** If credit sales for 2019 are $400,000, determine what loss rate you would recommend to estimate bad debts. (*Note:* Round answers to three decimal places.)
4. Using the rate you recommend, record bad debt expense for 2019.
5. **CONCEPTUAL CONNECTION** Assume that the increase in The Glass House's sales in 2019 was largely due to granting credit to customers who would have been denied credit in previous years. How would this change your answer to part 4? Describe a legitimate business reason why The Glass House would adopt more lenient credit terms.
6. Use the data from 2015 to 2018 and assume that 50% of the sales would have been lost if no credit had been granted and assume that the average gross margin is 25%. Calculate how much extra income was realized over the four years in total because the store did indeed allow credit sales.

YOUDECIDE

OBJECTIVE **4**

Problem 5-86A   Aging Method Bad Debt Expense

Cindy Bagnal, the manager of Cayce Printing Service, has provided you with the following aging schedule for Cayce's accounts receivable:

Accounts Receivable Category	Amount	Proportion Expected to Default
0–20 days	$ 88,200	0.02
21–40 days	21,500	0.08
41–60 days	11,700	0.15
Over 60 days	5,300	0.30
	$126,700	

Cindy indicates that the $126,700 of accounts receivable identified in the table does not include $8,900 of receivables that should be written off.

Required:

1. Journalize the $8,900 write-off.
2. Determine the desired postadjustment balance in allowance for doubtful accounts.
3. If the preadjustment balance in allowance for doubtful accounts before the $8,900 write-off was a debit of $450, compute bad debt expense. Prepare the adjusting entry to record bad debt expense.

Problem 5-87A   Determining Bad Debt Expense Using the Aging Method

OBJECTIVE **4**

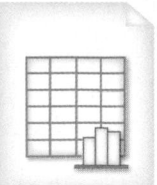

At the beginning of the year, Amherst Auto Parts had an accounts receivable balance of $31,800 and a balance in the allowance for doubtful accounts of $2,980 (credit). During the year, Amherst had credit sales of $624,300, collected accounts receivable in the amount of $602,700, wrote off $18,600 of accounts receivable, and had the following data for accounts receivable at the end of the period:

Accounts Receivable Age	Amount	Proportion Expected to Default
Current	$20,400	0.01
1–15 days past due	5,300	0.02
16–45 days past due	3,100	0.08
46–90 days past due	3,600	0.15
Over 90 days past due	2,400	0.30
	$34,800	

Amherst has a December 31 year-end.

Required:

1. Determine the desired postadjustment balance in allowance for doubtful accounts.
2. Determine the preadjustment balance in allowance for doubtful accounts before the bad debt expense adjusting entry is posted.
3. Compute bad debt expense.
4. Prepare the adjusting entry to record bad debt expense.

Problem 5-88A   Accounting for Notes Receivable—Honoured and Dishonoured

OBJECTIVE **6**

Yarnell Electronics sells computer systems to small businesses and has a December 31 year-end. Yarnell engaged in the following activities involving notes receivable:

a. On November 1, 2018, Yarnell sold a $5,000 system to Rosen Company. Rosen gave Yarnell a six-month, 9% note as payment.
b. On December 1, 2018, Yarnell sold an $8,000 system to Searfoss Inc. Searfoss gave Yarnell a nine-month, 8% note as payment.
c. On May 1, 2019, Rosen paid the amount due on its note.
d. On September 1, 2019, Searfoss paid the amount due on its note.

Required:

1. Prepare the necessary journal and adjusting entries for Yarnell Electronics to record these transactions.
2. Prepare the journal entries to record both a note default by Rosen on May 1, 2019, and a note default by Searfoss on September 1, 2019. Assume the note default is deemed collectible.

Chapter 5 Reporting and Analyzing Sales Revenue and Receivables

OBJECTIVE 8 Problem 5-89A Ratio Analysis

Selected information from Bigg Company's financial statements follows.

	Fiscal Year Ended December 31		
	2018	**2017**	**2016**
		(in thousands)	
Gross sales	$2,004,719	$1,937,021	$1,835,987
Less: Sales discounts	(4,811)	(4,649)	(4,406)
Less: Sales returns and allowances	(2,406)	(2,324)	(2,203)
Net sales	1,997,502	1,930,048	1,829,378
Cost of goods sold	621,463	619,847	660,955
Gross profit	1,376,039	1,310,201	1,168,423
Operating expenses	577,369	595,226	583,555
Operating income	798,670	714,975	584,868
Other income (expenses)	15,973	(5,720)	(8,773)
Net income	$ 814,643	$ 709,255	$ 576,095

	At December 31		
	2018	**2017**	**2016**
		(in thousands)	
Accounts receivable	$201,290	$195,427	$182,642
Less: Allowance for doubtful accounts	(2,516)	(2,736)	(2,192)
Net accounts receivable	$198,774	$192,691	$180,450

Required:

1. Calculate the following ratios for 2017 and 2018: (a) gross profit margin, (b) operating margin, (c) net profit margin, (d) accounts receivable turnover, and (e) average collection period. (*Note:* Round answers to two decimal places.)
2. **CONCEPTUAL CONNECTION** For each of the first three ratios listed above, provide a plausible explanation for the year-over-year changes. For example, why is the net profit margin higher or lower than it was the previous year?
3. **CONCEPTUAL CONNECTION** Explain what each ratio attempts to measure. Make an assessment about Bigg Company based upon the ratios you have calculated. Are operations improving or worsening?

PROBLEM SET B

OBJECTIVE 1 Problem 5-90B Revenue Recognition

Mary Wade owns a small business that rents parking spaces to students at the local university. Mary's typical rental contract requires the student to pay the year's rent of $720 ($60 per month) in advance. When Mary prepares financial statements at the end of December, her accountant requires that Mary spread the $720 over the 12 months that a parking space is rented. Therefore, Mary can recognize only $240 revenue (four months) from each contract in the year the cash is collected and must defer recognition of the remaining $480 (eight months) to next year. Mary argues that getting students to agree to rent the parking space is the most difficult part of the activity so she ought to be able to recognize all $720 as revenue when the cash is received from a student.

Required:

CONCEPTUAL CONNECTION Explain why IFRS requires the use of accrual accounting rather than cash-basis accounting for the above, and similar, transactions.

Problem 5-91B   Recording Revenue, Receivables, and Bad Debt Expense

OBJECTIVE ❶ ❷ ❹

On January 1, 2019, Export Properties Inc. reported the following balances on its statement of financial position:

Accounts receivable	$3,965,000
Allowance for doubtful accounts	292,000

During 2019, the company conducted the following transactions:

a.   Sold goods on account for $4,000,000
b.   Processed sales returns of $30,000
c.   Processed sales allowances of $20,000
d.   Collected $5,360,000 of accounts receivable
e.   Added interest to overdue accounts receivable of $175,000
f.   Wrote off accounts receivable considered uncollectible of $96,000
g.   Recovered accounts receivable previously written off of $57,000

Required:

1.   Prepare the journal entries to record the above transactions.
2.   Record the journal entry for bad debt expense at December 31, assuming that the allowance for doubtful accounts at December 31 should be $345,000.
3.   Post all of the above entries to T-accounts for accounts receivable, allowance for doubtful accounts, and other accounts you deem are required.
4.   Prepare the proper statement of financial position presentation of accounts receivable at December 31, 2019.
5.   Prepare the proper statement of earnings presentation of the statement of earnings accounts for the year ended December 31.

Problem 5-92B   Discount Policy and Net Sales Reported

OBJECTIVE ❷

Park Electronics sells cell phones. During 2018, Park sold 1,500 units at an average of $500 per unit. Each unit cost Park $350. At present, Park offers no sales discounts. Park's controller suggests that a generous sales discount policy would increase annual sales to 2,000 units and also improve cash flow. She proposes 3/15, n/20 and believes that 75% of the customers would take advantage of the discount.

Required:

1.   If the controller is correct, determine how much the new sales discount policy would add to net sales and gross margin.
2.   **CONCEPTUAL CONNECTION** Explain why the sales discount policy might improve cash flow.

Problem 5-93B   Effects of Discounts on Sales and Purchases

OBJECTIVE ❷

Smithson Products sells shoes and accessories to retail stores. Gross sales in 2018 were $1,500,250 (Smithson's list price) on terms 4/10, n/30. Customers paid for $1,200,000 (Smithson's list price) of the merchandise within the discount period and the remaining $300,250 after the end of the discount period.

Required:

1.   Compute the amount of sales.
2.   Determine how much cash was collected from sales.

Problem 5-94B   Sales Discounts

Spartakos Inc. regularly provides services to Grieder Supply on terms 3/10, n/40 and records sales at gross. During a recent month, the two firms engaged in the following transactions:

a.   Spartakos sold merchandise with a list price of $250,000.
b.   Spartakos sold merchandise with a list price of $75,000.
c.   Grieder paid for the purchase in transaction *a* within the discount period.
d.   Grieder paid for the purchase in transaction *b* after the discount period.

Required:

1.   Provide the journal entries for Spartakos to record the sales in *a* and *b* (make separate entries).
2.   Provide the journal entry for Spartakos to record Grieder's payment in *c*.
3.   Provide the journal entry for Spartakos to record Grieder's payment in *d*.
4.   **CONCEPTUAL CONNECTION** What implied annual interest rate is Grieder incurring by failing to take the sales discount and, instead, paying the gross amount after 40 days?

Problem 5-95B   Internal Control for Sales

Johnson Tires has three stores. Each store manager is paid a salary plus a bonus on the sales made by his or her store. On January 5, 2019, Kevin Samuel, manager of one of the stores, resigned. Kevin's store had doubled its expected December 2018 sales, producing a bonus for Kevin of $7,000 in December alone. Jason Jones, an assistant manager at another store, was assigned as manager of Kevin's store. Upon examination of the store's accounting records, Jason reported that the store's records indicated sales returns and allowances of $124,000 in the first four days of January 2019, an amount equal to about half of December 2018 sales.

Required:

1.   **CONCEPTUAL CONNECTION** Explain what the large amount of sales returns and allowances suggest Kevin might have done.
2.   **CONCEPTUAL CONNECTION** Determine how Johnson could protect itself from a manager who behaved as Kevin did.

OBJECTIVE ④   **Problem 5-96B   Bad Debt Expense: Percentage of Credit Sales Method**

Kelly's Collectibles sells nearly half its merchandise on credit. During the past four years, the following data were developed for credit sales and losses from uncollectible accounts:

Year of Sales	Credit Sales	Losses from Uncollectible Accounts*
2015	$205,000	$15,527
2016	185,000	11,692
2017	209,000	14,184
2018	253,000	21,933
Total	$852,000	$63,336

* Losses from uncollectible accounts are the actual losses related to sales of that year (rather than write-offs of that year).

Required:

1.   Calculate the loss rate for each year from 2015 through 2018. (*Note:* Round answers to three decimal places.)
2.   Determine if there appears to be a significant change in the loss rate over time.
3.   **CONCEPTUAL CONNECTION** If credit sales for 2019 are $415,000, explain what loss rate you would recommend to estimate bad debts. (*Note:* Round answers to three decimal places.)
4.   Using the rate you recommend, record bad debt expense for 2019.
5.   **CONCEPTUAL CONNECTION** Assume that the increase in Kelly's sales in 2019 was largely due to granting credit to customers who would have been denied credit in previous

years. How would this change your answer to part 4? Describe a legitimate business reason why Kelly's would adopt more lenient credit terms.

6. Use the data from 2015 to 2018 and assume that 20% of the sales would have been lost if no credit has been granted and assume that the average gross margin is 40%. Calculate how much extra income was realized over the 4 years in total because the store did indeed allow credit sales.

Problem 5-97B   Aging Method Bad Debt Expense

YOUDECIDE

OBJECTIVE **4**

Carol Simone, the manager of Handy Plumbing, has provided you with the following aging schedule for Handy's accounts receivable:

Accounts Receivable Category	Amount	Proportion Expected to Default
0–20 days	$ 92,600	0.03
21–40 days	12,700	0.09
41–60 days	17,800	0.14
Over 60 days	2,100	0.30
	$125,200	

Carol indicates that the $125,200 of accounts receivable identified in the table does not include $9,400 of receivables that should be written off.

Required:

1. Journalize the $9,400 write-off.
2. Determine the desired postadjustment balance in allowance for doubtful accounts.
3. If the preadjustment balance in allowance for doubtful accounts before the $9,400 write-off was a debit of $550, compute bad debt expense. Prepare the adjusting entry to record bad debt expense.

Problem 5-98B   Determining Bad Debt Expense Using the Aging Method

OBJECTIVE **4**

At the beginning of the year, Lennon Electronics had an accounts receivable balance of $29,800 and a balance in the allowance for doubtful accounts of $2,425 (credit). During the year, Lennon had credit sales of $752,693, collected accounts receivable in the amount of $653,800, wrote off $20,400 of accounts receivable, and had the following data for accounts receivable at the end of the period:

Accounts Receivable Category	Amount	Proportion Expected to Default
Current	$22,700	0.01
1–15 days past due	8,600	0.04
16–45 days past due	4,900	0.09
46–90 days days past due	3,200	0.17
Over 60 days	2,100	0.30
	$41,500	

Lennon has a December 31 year-end.

Required:

1. Determine the desired postadjustment balance in allowance for doubtful accounts.
2. Determine the preadjustment balance in allowance for doubtful accounts before the bad debt expense adjusting entry is posted.
3. Compute bad debt expense.
4. Prepare the adjusting entry to record bad debt expense.

OBJECTIVE ❻

Problem 5-99B   Accounting for Notes Receivable—Honoured and Dishonoured

Slav Systems sells voicemail systems to small businesses and has a December 31 year-end. Slav engaged in the following activities involving notes receivable:

a. On October 1, 2018, Slav sold an $8,000 system to Majors Company. Majors gave Slav a seven-month, 10% note as payment.

b. On November 1, 2018, Slav sold a $6,000 system to Hadley Inc. Hadley gave Slav a ten-month, 12% note as payment.

c. On May 1, 2019, Majors paid the amount due on its note.

d. On September 1, 2019, Hadley paid the amount due on its note.

Required:

1. Prepare the necessary journal and adjusting entries for Slav Systems to record these transactions.

2. Prepare the journal entries required if Majors defaults on its note on May 1, 2019, and if Hadley defaults on its note on September 1, 2019. Assume the note default is deemed collectible.

OBJECTIVE ❽

Problem 5-100B   Ratio Analysis

Selected information from Small Company's financial statements follows.

	Fiscal Year Ended December 31		
	2018	**2017**	**2016**
		(in thousands)	
Gross sales	$1,663,917	$1,697,195	$1,714,167
Less: Sales discounts	(2,995)	(3,055)	(3,086)
Less: Sales returns and allowances	(2,496)	(2,546)	(2,571)
Net sales	1,658,426	1,691,594	1,708,510
Cost of goods sold	881,876	891,027	860,512
Gross profit	776,550	800,567	847,998
Operating expenses	482,050	496,958	487,214
Operating income	294,500	303,609	360,784
Other income (expenses)	3,534	(3,036)	(1,804)
Net income	$ 298,034	$ 300,573	$ 358,980

	At December 31		
	2018	**2017**	**2016**
		(in thousands)	
Accounts receivable	$376,062	$365,109	$341,223
Less: Allowance for doubtful accounts	(8,461)	(71,926)	(5,971)
Net accounts receivable	$367,601	$293,183	$335,252

Required:

1. Calculate the following ratios for 2017 and 2018: (a) gross profit margin, (b) operating margin, (c) net profit margin, (d) accounts receivable turnover, and (e) average collection period. (*Note:* Round answers to two decimal places.)

2. **CONCEPTUAL CONNECTION** For each of the first three ratios listed above, provide a plausible explanation for the year-over-year changes. (For example, why is the net profit margin higher or lower than it was the previous year?)

3. **CONCEPTUAL CONNECTION** Explain what each ratio attempts to measure. Make an assessment about Small Company based upon the ratios you have calculated. Are operations improving or worsening?

CASES

Case 5-101   Ethics and Revenue Recognition

Alan Spalding is CEO of a large appliance wholesaler. Alan is under pressure from Wall Street Analysts to meet his aggressive sales revenue growth projections. Unfortunately, near the end of the year he realizes that sales must dramatically improve if his projections are going to be met. To accomplish this objective, he orders his sales force to contact their largest customers and offer them price discounts if they buy by the end of the year. Alan also offered to deliver the merchandise to a third-party warehouse with whom the customers could arrange delivery when the merchandise was needed.

Required:

1. Do you believe that revenue from these sales should be recognized in the current year? Why or why not?
2. What are the probable consequences of this behaviour for the company in future periods?
3. What are the probable consequences of this behaviour for investors analyzing the current-year financial statements?

Case 5-102   Recognition of Service Contract Revenues

Jackson Duclos is president of New Moncton Maintenance Inc., which provides building maintenance services. On October 15, 2018, Jackson signed a service contract with Eastern College and Eastern made a down payment of $12,000. Under the contract, New Moncton will provide maintenance services for all of Eastern's buildings for a period of two years, beginning on January 1, 2019, and Eastern will pay New Moncton $1,000 per month, beginning on January 31, 2019.

Initially, Jackson proposed that some portion of the revenue from the contract should be recognized in 2018; however, his accountant, Rita McGonigle, convinced him that this would be inappropriate. Then Jackson proposed that the revenue be recognized in an amount equal to the cash collected under the contract in 2018. Again, Rita argued against his proposal, saying that IFRS requires recognition of an equal amount of contract revenue each month.

Required:

1. Give a reason that might explain Jackson's desire to recognize contract revenue earlier rather than later.
2. Put yourself in Rita's position. How would you convince Jackson that his two proposals are unacceptable and that an equal amount of revenue should be recognized every month?
3. If Rita's proposal is adopted, how would the contract be reflected on the statements of financial position at the end of 2018 and at the end of 2019?

Case 5-103   Revenue Recognition

Beth Rader purchased North Shore Health Club in June 2018. Beth wanted to increase the size of the business by selling five-year memberships for $2,000, payable at the beginning of the membership period. The normal yearly membership fee is $500. Since few prospective members were expected to have $2,000, Beth arranged for a local bank to provide $2,000 installment loans to prospective members. By the end of 2018, 250 customers had purchased the five-year memberships, using the loans provided by the bank.

Beth prepared her statement of earnings for 2018 and included $500,000 as revenue because the club had collected the entire amount in cash. Beth's accountant objected to the inclusion of the entire $500,000, arguing that the $500,000 should be recognized as revenue as the club provides services for these members during the membership period. Beth notes that the memberships have been sold and that collection of the selling price has occurred. Therefore, she argues, all $500,000 is revenue in 2018.

Required:

Write a short statement supporting either Beth or the accountant in this dispute.

Case 5-104   Sales Discount Policies

Consider three businesses, all of which offer price reductions to their customers. The first is an independently owned gas station located at a busy intersection in Windsor, Ontario, that offers a 3% discount for cash purchases of gasoline. The second is a large home improvement store in suburban London, Ontario, that offers building contractors terms of 3/10, n/45. The third is a clothing manufacturer and catalogue retailer in Lasalle, Ontario. Several times during each year, it distributes a catalogue in which men's dress shirts are heavily discounted if purchased in lots of four or more.

Required:

1. What are the main objectives of the discount policies in each of the three businesses?
2. How does accounting information assist each business in achieving its discount policy objectives?

Case 5-105   Financial Analysis of Receivables

A chain of retail stores located in Ontario and Manitoba has requested a loan from the bank at which you work. The statement of financial position of the retail chain shows significant accounts receivable related to its in-house credit card. You have been assigned to evaluate these receivables.

Required:

1. What questions concerning the quality of these receivables can you answer by analyzing the retailer's financial statements?
2. What additional questions would you raise, and what information would you request from the retailer, to answer these questions?

Case 5-106   Income Effects of Uncollectible Accounts

The credit manager and the accountant for Goldsmith Company are attempting to assess the effect on net income of writing off $100,000 of receivables. Goldsmith uses the aging method of determining bad debt expense and has the following aging schedule for its accounts receivable at December 31, 2018:

Accounts Receivable Category	Amount	Proportion Expected to Default
Current	$2,980,400	0.004
1–30 days past due	722,600	0.035
31–60 days past due	418,500	0.095
Over 60 days past due	322,800	0.250
	$4,444,300	

The receivables being considered for write-off are all over 60 days past due.

Required:

1. Assume that the tax rate is 30%. What will be the effect on net income if the $100,000 is written off?
2. What data would you examine to provide some assurance that a company was not holding uncollectible accounts in its accounts receivable rather than writing them off when they are determined to be uncollectible?

Case 5-107   CONTINUING PROBLEM: FRONT ROW ENTERTAINMENT

While Front Row Entertainment was having considerable success in signing artists and promoting concerts, Cam and Anna still had a few ideas to grow their business that they wanted to implement. One idea that they both agreed on was to start an online fan "community" for each of their artists. Each community would serve as an online fan club that would generate increased interest in and attendance at the artists' concerts. In addition, Front Row Entertainment could sell advertising space on each fan community to companies interested in reaching the particular demographic that the artist attracted. Because the summer concert season is one of the busiest and most lucrative times of the year, Cam and Anna felt it was extremely important to get the fan communities in place before summer. So, they engaged in the following selected transactions for May and June:

May 1	Paid Web Design Inc. $8,500 to develop the fan websites. The fan websites were operational on May 10. Front Row charged this expenditure to other expense.
May 10	Front Row Entertainment sold $550 worth of advertising to Little John's Restaurant with terms 2/10, n/30. The advertising will randomly appear on the artists' websites throughout the month of May.
May 15	Front Row Entertainment sold $475 worth of advertising to Sherwood Media with terms 2/10, n/30. The advertising related to an in-store DVD promotion that Sherwood was holding later in the month.
May 19	Front Row Entertainment received payment from Little John for the May 10 bill.
May 20	Sherwood Media informed Front Row that an error had been made on its advertisement. Sherwood's promotion was supposed to run from May 20 to May 25; however, the advertisement stated that the promotion would run from May 15 to May 25. Because the error was Front Row's fault, Front Row agreed to reduce the amount owed by $150.
June 1	Front Row Entertainment sold $750 worth of advertising to Big House Entertainment Company with terms 2/10, n/30. The advertising will randomly appear on the artists' websites throughout the month of June.
June 10	Sherwood paid Front Row the amount owed for the May 15 bill less the allowance granted on May 20.
June 20	When Front Row learned that Big House Entertainment had filed for bankruptcy, it wrote off the $750 receivable.

Over the next few months, the fan communities continued to grow in popularity, with more and more companies purchasing advertising space. By the end of 2018, Front Row reported the following balances:

Accounts receivable	$17,900
Allowance for doubtful accounts	250 (debit)
Credit sales	45,000

Required:

1. Prepare journal entries for the May and June transactions.
2. Prepare the adjusting entry required at December 31, 2018, with regard to bad debts under each of the following independent assumptions.
a. Front Row performed an aging of its accounts receivable. Front Row estimated that $895 of its accounts receivable would be uncollectible.
b. Front Row, using the percentage of credit sales method, estimated that 2% of credit sales would be uncollectible.

Case 5-108   Professional and Ethical Behaviour

You are so excited to start your new job at Leaf Inc., especially after the long process of on-campus recruiting. You thought you would never get a job. Your goal is to learn as much as possible and make a real contribution to your organization, and at the same time work on getting your professional accounting designation within the next two years. You are assigned to the accounts receivable department. You aren't exactly thrilled about that, as normally nothing exciting happens in the accounts receivable department.

Six months into your job, you are assisting your boss, Jessica, with getting ready for the upcoming external audit of the organization. She mentions that normally these audits are routine. "As long as we tell the auditors what they want to hear, this should go quickly," she says.

You're not sure what to make of your boss's comments, but you think to yourself that you are here to learn and that is what you will do.

(Continued)

Jessica asks you to identify and provide her with a list of all accounts receivable customers that have outstanding balances of greater than 120 days. She mentions, "The auditors will be paying close attention to these balances, as they always do, so we need to make sure our story makes sense. We don't want the auditors to think these are not going to be collected."

You recall from your financial accounting course in university that any accounts receivable balances that are deemed to be uncollectible should be provided for in the financial statements. You can't understand why Jessica wants a story about the balances being collectible, as it appears they most likely are not.

You remember that your goal is to learn as much as possible, so you ask your boss, "What is the reason behind what we are doing here? I learned in my accounting course that we should be providing for these as uncollectible." Jessica is shocked that you are asking her such a question, but feels that she needs to explain now that you have asked. She says Don, the CEO of the company, hates seeing write-offs of any sort in the financial statements, especially when they relate to customers and a potential uncollectible accounts receivable. "He tells us to make up a story to the auditors that they will buy and never provide for or write off any accounts," Jessica says. "We do what the boss tells us, it's that simple. We want to keep him happy. Plus, if we don't have to provide for any accounts, the net income on the statement of earnings will look better and I get a larger bonus, so it really is win-win for me."

You continue on with your work for the day, but cannot focus given what your boss just told you.

Required:

Identify and discuss any ethical issues. Discuss any other issues that are important.

6

Reporting and Analyzing Inventory and Cost of Goods Sold

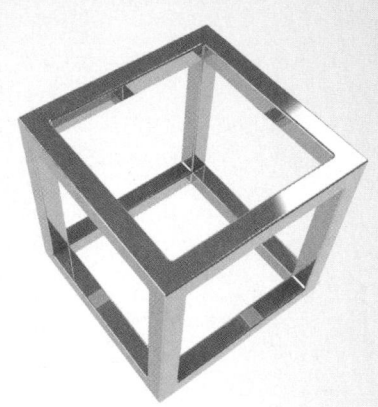

After studying Chapter 6, you should be able to:

1. Explain the types of inventories held by merchandisers and manufacturers, and understand how inventory costs flow through a company.

2. Explain how to record purchases and sales of inventory using a perpetual inventory system.

3. Apply the three inventory costing methods to compute ending inventory and cost of goods sold under a perpetual inventory system.

4. Analyze the financial reporting and tax effects of the various inventory costing methods.

5. Apply the lower of cost and net realizable value rule to the valuation of inventory.

6. Evaluate inventory management using the gross profit and inventory turnover ratios.

7. Explain how errors in ending inventory affect statements of earnings and statements of financial position.

8. Explain how to record purchases of inventory using a periodic inventory system.

9. (Appendix) Compute ending inventory and cost of goods sold under a periodic inventory system.

Barry Winiker/Getty

EXPERIENCE FINANCIAL ACCOUNTING

with Hudson's Bay Company

Hudson's Bay Company, based in Toronto, Ontario, is a major public corporation with $8.1 billion in sales for its January 31, 2015, fiscal year. Hudson's Bay Company serves customers through 333 locations across North America and internationally. Given the large volume of merchandise it sells, its profits depend heavily on the control and management of its inventory. After all, as shown in Exhibit 6.1, inventory makes up 83% of its current assets.

For many companies, inventory is at the heart of the operating cycle and must be carefully managed and controlled. If a company doesn't have enough inventory on its shelves to meet customers' demand, it will lose sales. On the other hand, too much inventory will increase carrying costs such as storage and interest costs, increase the risk of inventory obsoles-

cence, and delay or reduce cash inflows as a result of delayed or reduced sales. Hudson's Bay Company uses technology to manage and control its inventory and distribution.

As you will see in this chapter, even though inventory is an asset, it can have a major impact on net income. That is because all inventory accounting systems allocate the cost of inventory between ending inventory and cost of goods sold. Therefore, the valuation of inventory affects cost of goods sold, which in turn affects net income. By managing and controlling its inventory, Hudson's Bay Company has been able to tie up less of its cash in inventory, resulting in greater profits. This focus on inventory allows the company to sell its merchandise at competitive prices.

(EXHIBIT 6.1)

Composition of Hudson's Bay Company Current Assets

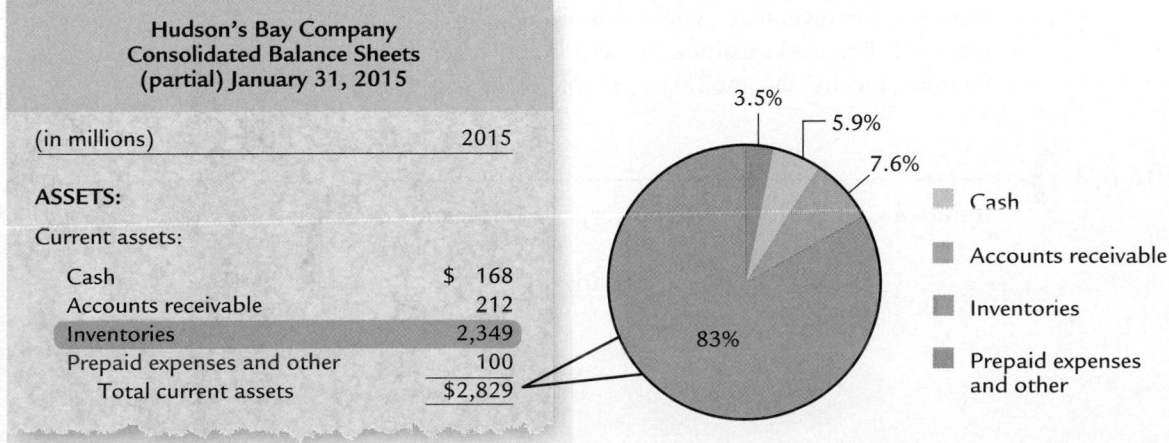

Source: HBC Hudson's Bay Company 2014 Annual Report, page 54.

Hudson's Bay Company Consolidated Balance Sheets (partial) January 31, 2015

(in millions)	2015
ASSETS:	
Current assets:	
Cash	$ 168
Accounts receivable	212
Inventories	2,349
Prepaid expenses and other	100
Total current assets	$2,829

3.5%
5.9%
7.6%
83%

- Cash
- Accounts receivable
- Inventories
- Prepaid expenses and other

NATURE OF INVENTORY AND COST OF GOODS SOLD

Inventory represents products held for resale and is classified as a current asset on the statement of financial position. The inventories of large companies like Hudson's Bay Company (e.g., shoes, dresses, suits, furniture, and appliances) and Canadian Tire (e.g., tires, barbeques, garden tools, and shop tools) are composed of thousands of different products or materials and millions of individual units that are stored in hundreds of different locations. For other companies, inventories are a much less significant portion of total assets. Exhibit 6.2 shows the relative composition of inventory for Hudson's Bay Company and Microsoft.

For companies like Hudson's Bay Company, these vast and varied inventories are at the heart of company operations and profitability and must be carefully controlled and accounted for. For example, one of Hudson's Bay Company's key performance measures is the comparison of inventory growth to sales growth. In the recessionary economy of 2009, Canadian Tire's sales decreased by 4.7%. In response, it was able to limit its inventory growth to 1.7%—an indication that it was effectively managing and controlling its inventory level in response to sales pressures.

When companies like Hudson's Bay Company sell their inventory to customers, the cost of the inventory sold becomes an expense called cost of goods sold. **Cost of goods sold** (or **cost of sales**) represents the outflow of asset resources caused by the sale of inventory and is the most important expense on the statements of earnings of companies that sell goods instead of services. **Gross margin** (also called **gross profit**), a key performance measure, is defined as sales revenue less cost of goods sold. Thus, gross margin indicates the extent to which the asset resources generated by sales can be used to pay operating expenses (selling and administrative expenses) and provide for net income. For January 31, 2015, Hudson's Bay Company reported a gross margin of $3,276,000,000, calculated as:

$$\text{Revenue} - \text{Cost of goods sold} = \text{Gross margin}$$
$$\$8,169,000,000 - \$4,893,000,000 = \$3,276,000,000 \ (40.1\% \text{ of revenue})$$

The cost of inventory has a direct effect on the calculation of cost of goods sold and gross margin. To correctly interpret and analyze financial statements, one must understand inventory accounting. Accounting for inventories requires the application of the matching concept whereby costs are matched with revenues based on an appropriate inventory costing method. Management is allowed considerable latitude in determining the cost of inventory and may choose among several different costing methods. In addition, IFRS and ASPE allow certain departures from the cost principle for inventory. The inventory choices that managers make affect the statement of financial position valuation of inventory, the amount of reported net income, and the income taxes payable from year to year.

(EXHIBIT 6.2)

Relative Composition of Inventory for Different Companies

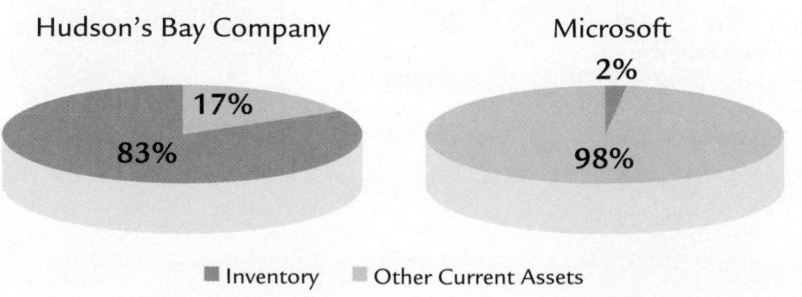

In this chapter, we examine the reporting and analysis of inventory and cost of goods sold. We address the following questions:

- What are the different types of inventory that exist?
- What costs should be included in inventory?
- Which inventory system (perpetual or periodic) should be employed?
- How are inventory transactions recorded?
- How is cost of goods sold computed?
- What are the financial effects of the three alternative inventory costing methods?
- How does application of the lower of cost and net realizable value rule affect inventory valuation?

An understanding of inventory accounting will help in the analysis of financial statements as well as in managing a business.

Types of Inventory and Flow of Costs

In previous chapters, we have generally discussed companies that sell services such as advertising agencies, delivery companies, repair companies, and accounting firms. For these companies, inventory plays a much smaller role. For example, in 2015, Alphabet Inc. didn't even report an amount for inventory! Our focus in this chapter will be on companies that sell inventory. These companies are often referred to as either merchandisers or manufacturers.

Merchandisers are companies (either retailers or wholesalers) that purchase inventory in a finished condition and hold it for resale without further processing. **Retailers** such as Hudson's Bay Company, RONA, and Walmart are merchandisers that sell directly to consumers, while **wholesalers** are merchandisers that sell to other retailers. For example, Shellmo Distributors Inc. is a Canadian wholesaler that supplies pharmaceutical products to health care providers; The Horizon Group is a Canadian wholesaler that distributes natural, organic, and specialty foods to various retailers. The inventory held by merchandisers is termed **merchandise inventory**. Merchandise inventory is an asset. When that asset is sold to a customer, it becomes an expense called cost of goods sold, which appears on the statement of earnings. Hudson's Bay Company's inventory disclosure, shown earlier in Exhibit 6.1, is an example of a typical disclosure made by a merchandising company.

Manufacturers are companies that buy and transform raw materials into finished products, which are then sold. Beaver Machine Corporation (vending machines), Buhler Industries Inc. (augers, mowers), and Magna International Inc. (auto parts) are all manufacturing companies. Manufacturing companies classify inventory into three categories: raw materials, work-in-process, and finished goods.

- **Raw materials inventory** refers to the basic ingredients used to make a product. When these raw materials are purchased, the raw materials inventory account is increased. As raw materials are used to manufacture a product, the related raw material costs are transferred to the work-in-process inventory account.
- **Work-in-process inventory** consists of the raw materials that are used in production as well as other production costs such as labour and utilities. These costs stay in this account until the product is complete. Once the production process is complete, these costs are moved to the finished goods inventory account.
- The **finished goods inventory** account represents the cost of the final product that is available for sale. When the finished goods inventory is sold to a customer, the related costs of producing the finished goods become an expense called cost of goods sold, which appears on the statement of earnings.

The inventory disclosure of Magna International, shown in Exhibit 6.3, is an example of a typical disclosure made by a manufacturing company.

(EXHIBIT 6.3)

Inventory Disclosure of Magna International

(in $US millions)	December 31, 2014	2013
Current Assets		
Cash and cash equivalents	$ 1,253	$1,554
Accounts receivable	5,635	5,246
Inventories	2,757	2,637
Other current assets	362	486
Total current assets	$10,007	$9,923

Note 8: Inventories

(in $US millions)	December 31, 2014	2013
Raw materials and supplies	$ 914	$ 947
Work-in-process	241	273
Finished goods	362	339
Tooling and engineering	1,240	1,078
Total inventories	$2,757	$2,637

Source: Magna International 2014 Annual Report, pages 38 and 48.

The relationship between the various inventory accounts and cost of goods sold is shown in Exhibit 6.4.

The concepts involved in accounting for inventories of manufacturers and merchandisers are similar. However, due to the additional complexities of accounting for manufacturing inventory, the remainder of this chapter will focus on merchandising companies.

Cost of Goods Sold Model

As shown in Exhibit 6.4, cost of goods sold is the cost to the seller of all goods sold during the accounting period. Recall that the *matching concept* requires that any costs used to generate revenue be recognized in the same period that the revenue is recognized. Because revenue is recognized as goods are sold, cost of goods sold is an expense.

(EXHIBIT 6.4)

Flow of Inventory Costs

Merchandiser

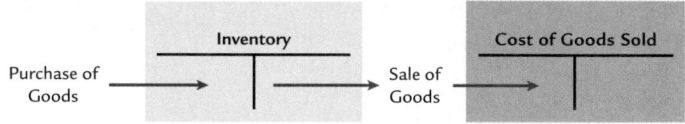

Manufacturer

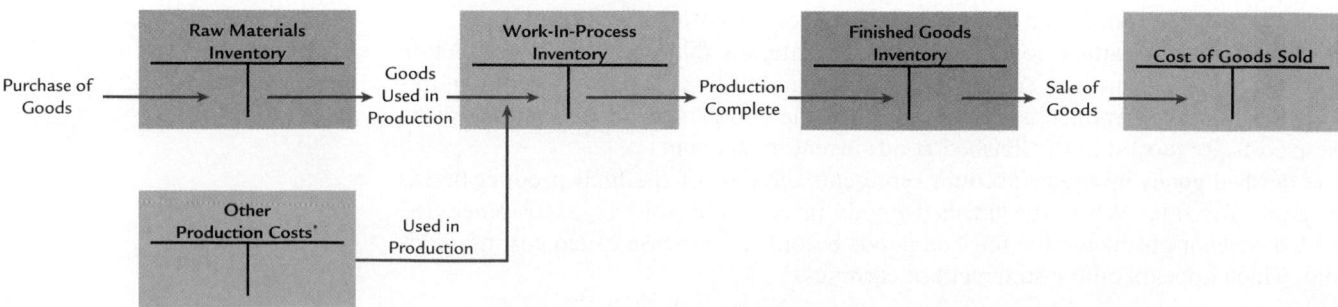

* Work-In-Process Inventory consists of raw materials used in production (also known as direct materials) as well as other production costs. These other production costs are called direct labour and factory overhead. The process by which these costs are converted to a final cost of a product is covered in managerial accounting courses.

The relationship between cost of goods sold and inventory is given by the cost of goods sold model:

	Beginning inventory
+	Purchases
=	Cost of goods available for sale
−	Ending inventory
=	Cost of goods sold

Except in the case of a new company, merchandisers and manufacturers will start the year with an amount of inventory on hand called *beginning inventory*. The sum of beginning inventory and purchases during the period represents the **cost of goods available for sale**. The portion of the cost of goods available for sale that remains unsold at the end of the year is the company's *ending inventory* (the ending inventory for one period becomes the beginning inventory of the next period). The portion of the cost of goods available for sale that is sold becomes *cost of goods sold*. The cost of goods sold model is illustrated in Exhibit 6.5.

The determination of cost of goods sold requires an allocation of the cost of goods available for sale between ending inventory and cost of goods sold. An application of the cost of goods sold model is illustrated in Cornerstone 6.1 .

Applying the Cost of Goods Sold Model

CORNERSTONE 6.1

Information:

Bargain Shops, a retail clothing store, had a beginning inventory of $26,000 on January 1, 2018. During 2018, the company purchased goods from a supplier costing $411,000. At the end of 2018, the cost of the unsold inventory was $38,000.

Required:

Compute cost of goods sold for the year ended December 31, 2018.

Why:

The determination of cost of goods sold requires an allocation of the cost of goods available for sale between ending inventory and cost of goods sold. The calculation of cost of goods sold affects a company's gross margin ratio, which is a key indicator of profitability.

CORNERSTONE VIDEO

Solution:

Beginning inventory	$ 26,000
+ Purchases	411,000
= Cost of goods available for sale	437,000
− Ending inventory	38,000
= Cost of goods sold	$399,000

The general structure of the cost of goods sold model can be rearranged to solve for any missing amount if the other three amounts are known. For example, if Bargain Shops

(Continued)

CORNERSTONE
6.1

(Continued)

did not know the cost of ending inventory but knew the cost of goods sold was $399,000, the company could determine ending inventory by rearranging the model as follows:

	Beginning inventory	$ 26,000
+	Purchases	411,000
=	Cost of goods available for sale	437,000
−	Cost of goods sold	399,000
=	Ending inventory	$ 38,000

concept Q&A

Because all inventories ultimately are expensed as cost of goods sold, why aren't all costs recorded as cost of goods sold when they are incurred?

Answer:

If all inventory-related costs were expensed when incurred, users of financial statements would see a distorted picture of the company's profitability, because costs related to inventory still on hand represent an asset that should be recorded on the statement of financial position.

Cornerstone 6.1 reinforces the concept that the computation of cost of goods sold or ending inventory is simply an allocation of the cost of goods available for sale. An understanding of this cost of goods sold model should enhance your understanding of how the matching concept is applied to cost of goods sold.

Inventory Systems

Because inventory is at the heart of the operating cycle for most wholesalers and retailers, the inventory accounting systems that record purchases and sales and track the level of inventory are particularly important. These systems provide the information needed to determine cost of goods sold and to analyze inventory. In addition, these systems signal the need to purchase additional inventory or the need to make special efforts to sell existing inventory. They also provide information necessary to safeguard the inventory from misappropriation or theft. In short, these systems provide the information that managers need to manage and control inventory.

Companies use one of two types of inventory accounting systems: a perpetual inventory system or a periodic inventory system.

Perpetual Inventory System In a **perpetual inventory system**, balances for inventory and cost of goods sold are continuously (perpetually) updated with each sale or purchase of inventory. This type of system requires that detailed records be

(EXHIBIT 6.5)

Cost of Goods Sold Model

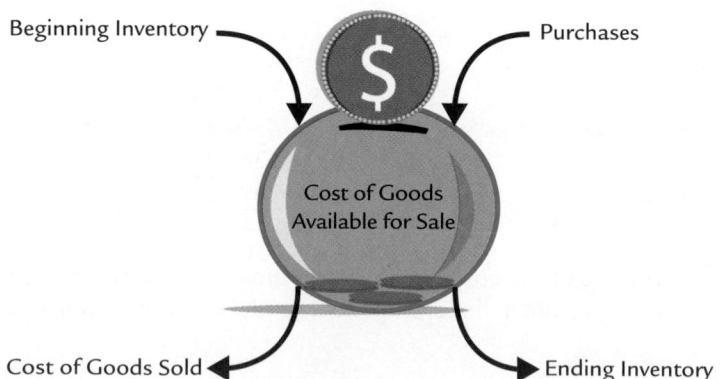

maintained on a transaction-by-transaction basis for each purchase and sale of inventory. For example, every time that Hudson's Bay Company purchases inventory from a supplier, it records this purchase directly in its inventory records. Similarly, when Hudson's Bay Company makes a sale to a customer, it not only records the sale (as illustrated in Chapter 5) but also updates its inventory and cost of goods sold balances by decreasing inventory and increasing cost of goods sold. In other words, a perpetual inventory system records both the *revenue* side of sales transactions and the *cost* side at the same point in time.

With the volume of transactions that Hudson's Bay Company has on a daily basis, this task may appear quite daunting. However, with the advent of "point of sale" cash register systems and optical bar code scanners, the implementation of perpetual inventory systems has become quite common. Some companies, such as Walmart, have taken this idea a step further and are using radio frequency identification (RFID) technology to track inventory. By attaching RFID tags to its inventory, Walmart is able to more easily track inventory from its suppliers to the final customer, dramatically reducing inventory losses.

In a perpetual inventory system, the accounting system keeps an up-to-date record of both ending inventory and cost of goods sold at any point in time. However, a company that uses a perpetual system should still take a physical count of inventory at least once a year to confirm the accuracy of the balance in the inventory account. Any difference between the physical count of inventory and the inventory balance provided by the accounting system could be the result of errors, waste, breakage, or theft.

Periodic Inventory System A **periodic inventory system** does not require companies to keep detailed, up-to-date inventory records. Instead, a periodic system records the cost of purchases as they occur (in a purchases account, which is separate from the inventory account), takes a physical count of inventory at the end of the period, and applies the cost of goods sold model to determine the balances of ending inventory and cost of goods sold Thus, a periodic system only produces balances for ending inventory and cost of goods sold at the end of each accounting period (periodically and typically only at year-end). If a company using the periodic system needs to know the balance of inventory or cost of goods sold during a period, it must do either of the following:

- perform a physical count of inventory, or
- estimate the amount of inventory using an acceptable estimation technique such as the gross profit method of inventory determination.

Comparison of Perpetual and Periodic Inventory Systems Perpetual and periodic systems offer distinct benefits, and any choice between the two inventory systems must weigh each system's advantages against its operating costs. The principal advantage of a periodic system is that it is relatively inexpensive to operate. Because perpetual systems require entering and maintaining more data than periodic systems, the additional costs can be quite substantial for a company with thousands of different items in inventory. However, with technological advances, the periodic system's advantage of being inexpensive to operate is rapidly disappearing. The perpetual system has the advantage of making the balances of inventory and cost of goods sold continuously available for decision-making purposes. This provides management with greater control over inventory than they would have under a periodic inventory system. Providing managers with more timely information can be a significant and extremely valuable advantage in a competitive business environment. For example, much of Walmart's success has been attributed to its sophisticated inventory management and control system.

We will illustrate both perpetual and periodic inventory systems in this chapter. Exhibit 6.6 compares the timing and nature of journal entries normally recorded under both methods assuming that goods costing $1,000 are sold for $1,500.

(EXHIBIT 6.6)

Comparison of Journal Entries Required by Perpetual and Periodic Systems

	Periodic System	Perpetual System
1. Date Goods Received	Dr Purchases $1,000 (Statement of Earnings Account) Cr Accounts Payable/Cash $1,000	Dr Inventory $1,000 (Statement of Financial Position Account) Cr Accounts Payable/Cash $1,000
2. Date Goods Sold	Dr Accounts Receivable/Cash $1,500 Cr Sales $1,500 No entry to adjust inventory	Dr Accounts Receivable/Cash $1,500 Cr Sales $1,500 Dr Cost of Goods Sold $1,000 Cr Inventory $1,000 (Statement of Financial Position Account)
3. Date Inventory Counted	Dr/Cr Cost of Goods Sold $1,000 Dr/Cr Inventory $1,000	No entry (assumes inventory on statement of financial position is accurate)

YOUDECIDE   Just-In-Time Inventory Management

As the inventory manager for Goliath Corp., a large national merchandising company, it is your job to balance the costs of carrying inventory (e.g., finance costs, storage costs) against the costs of not meeting customer demand (e.g., the cost of lost sales). If Goliath can rely on its suppliers to deliver inventory on very short notice and in ready-to-use forms, then very low inventory levels can be maintained. This approach to inventory management is called just in time (JIT) and is consistent with minimizing both inventory carrying costs and "out-of-stock" costs.

What information would you need to maintain a just-in-time inventory policy?

To synchronize the arrival of new inventory with the selling of the old inventory, you need detailed information about order-to-delivery times, receiving-to-ready-for-sale times, and inventory quantities. Delivery and make-ready times are used to control and minimize time lags between shipment of goods by suppliers and delivery to customers. In some retail stores, for example, merchandise arrives tagged, stacked, and ready for placement on the sales floor, while in other retail stores several days may be required to get the merchandise ready for sale. Information on inventory quantities would also be useful as a signal to reorder a particular item of inventory. Perpetual inventory systems, which make inventory balances continuously available, can provide the needed information on inventory quantities in a timely manner.

Inventory management and control can lead to significant cost reductions and improved profitability.

RECORDING INVENTORY TRANSACTIONS— PERPETUAL SYSTEM

OBJECTIVE ②

Explain how to record purchases and sales of inventory using a perpetual inventory system.

The historical cost principle requires that the activities of a company be initially measured at their historical cost—the exchange price at the time the activity occurs. Applied to inventory, this principle implies that *inventory cost includes the purchase price of the merchandise plus any cost of bringing the goods to a saleable condition and location.* Therefore, the cost of inventory includes the purchase price plus other "incidental" costs, such as freight charges to deliver the merchandise to the company's warehouse, insurance cost on the inventory while it is in transit, and various taxes.

In general, a merchandising company should stop accumulating costs as a part of inventory once the inventory is ready for sale. For a manufacturing company, raw material costs should be accumulated as raw materials inventory until the goods are ready for use in the manufacturing process.

Accounting for Purchases of Inventory in a Perpetual System

Let's first take a look at how a merchandising company would account for inventory purchases. In a perpetual inventory system, the inventory account is used to record the costs associated with acquiring merchandise.

Purchases **Purchases** refers to the cost of merchandise acquired for resale during the accounting period. The purchase of inventory is recorded by increasing the inventory account. All purchases should be supported by a source document, such as an *invoice,* that provides written evidence of the transaction as well as the relevant details of the purchase. A typical invoice is shown in Exhibit 6.7. Note the various details on the invoice, such as the names of the seller and the purchaser, the invoice date, the credit

(EXHIBIT 6.7)

Sample Invoice

Shoes Unlimited   INVOICE

We Care About Your Feet

301 College Street   INVOICE #100
Toronto, Ontario M5X 3R2   DATE: Sept. 1, 2017
Phone 800-555-2389 Fax 866-555-2300

TO:

J. Parker Jones, Purchasing Manager
Brandon Shoes
879 University Ave.
Toronto, Ontario M5L 2B5

SALESPERSON	P.O. NUMBER	REQUISITIONER	SHIPPED VIA	FOB POINT	TERMS
E. Higgins	4895721	J. Parker Jones	Purolator	Destination	2/10, n/30

QUANTITY	DESCRIPTION	UNIT PRICE	TOTAL
100	Model No. 754 Athletic Running Shoe	$100	$10,000
	SUBTOTAL		$10,000
	SALES TAX		1,300
	SHIPPING & HANDLING		150
	TOTAL DUE		$11,450

(EXHIBIT 6.8)

Shipping Terms

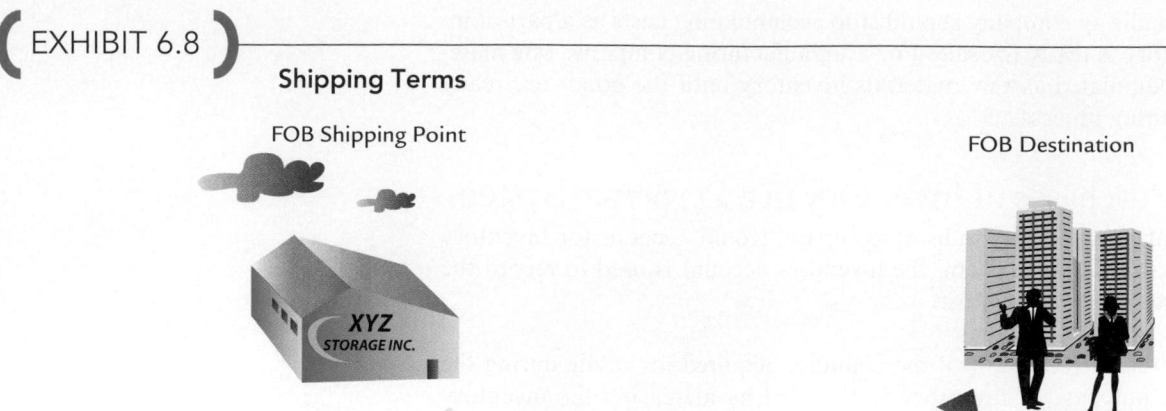

FOB Shipping Point

FOB Destination

➢ Ownership passes from the seller to the buyer when the goods are shipped.

➢ Buyer usually pays freight costs.

➢ Seller recognizes revenue at shipment.

➢ Ownership passes from the seller to the buyer when the goods are received.

➢ Seller usually pays freight costs.

➢ Seller recognizes revenue at delivery.

terms, the freight terms, a description of the goods purchased, and the total invoice amount.

Relying on the cost principle, the cost of purchases must include the effects of purchase discounts, purchase returns, and transportation charges.

Purchase Discounts As noted in Chapter 5, companies that sell goods on credit often offer their customers sales discounts to encourage prompt payment. From the viewpoint of the customer, such price reductions are called **purchase discounts**. The credit terms specify the amount and timing of payments. For example, credit terms of "2/10, n/30" mean that a 2% discount may be taken on the invoice price if payment is made within 10 days of the invoice date. This reduced payment period is known as the **discount period**. Otherwise, full payment is due within 30 days of the invoice date. If a purchase discount is taken, the purchaser reduces the inventory account for the amount of the discount taken, resulting in the inventory account reflecting the net cost of the purchase.

Generally, all available discounts should be taken. Failure to pay within the discount period is equivalent to paying interest for the use of money and can be quite expensive. For example, failure to take advantage of the 2% discount for credit terms of "2/10, n/30" is equivalent to an annual interest rate of 36.5%.[1] Clearly, paying within the discount period is a good cash management policy.

Purchase Returns and Allowances Merchandise is inspected when received and may be tested in various ways before it becomes available for sale. The following issues may result in dissatisfaction with the merchandise:

- The wrong merchandise was delivered.
- The merchandise did not conform to specification.
- The merchandise was damaged or defective.
- The merchandise arrived too late at its destination.

---

[1] This implied interest rate is computed as $[365 \text{ days} \div (30 \text{ days} - 10 \text{ days})] \times 2\%$. Notice that this formula uses a 20-day interest period computed as the days until final payment is due (30 days) less the days in the discount period (10 days). This period can be adjusted to fit the specific credit terms of the transaction.

If the purchaser is dissatisfied with the merchandise, it is frequently returned to the seller for credit or for a cash refund. The cost of merchandise returned to suppliers is called **purchase returns**. In some instances, the purchaser may choose to keep the merchandise if the seller is willing to grant a deduction (allowance) from the purchase price. This situation is called a **purchase allowance**. Increases in purchase returns and allowances may signal deteriorating supplier relationships; thus, purchase returns are monitored very closely by purchasing managers. Because inventory was increased when the purchase was initially made, a purchase return or allowance is recorded by decreasing inventory and, if not yet paid, decreasing the related accounts payable, with the result that the inventory account reflects the accurate cost of goods purchased and not returned prior to sale. If the returned inventory had previously been paid for, a credit or cash refund would be requested by the purchaser.

Transportation Costs Transportation, or freight, costs are expenditures made to move the inventory from the seller's location to the purchaser's location. The proper recording of transportation costs depends upon whether the buyer or the seller pays for the transportation. Effectively, this question is the same as asking at what point the ownership of the inventory transfers from the seller to the buyer. The point at which ownership, or title, of the inventory changes hands depends on the shipping terms of the contract. The shipping terms can be either FOB (free on board) shipping point or FOB destination, as illustrated in Exhibit 6.8.

Consigned Goods In a **consignment** arrangement, goods owned by one party (the *consignor*) are shipped to and offered by sale by another party (the *consignee*). The consignee does not take ownership of the goods, but earns a fee when the goods are sold. Until the goods are sold, the goods are included in the consignor's inventory. Manufacturers often use consignments to encourage large retailers, such as Hudson's Bay and Walmart, to offer their products for sale. Retailers find these arrangements attractive because it enables them to reduce their investment in inventory. In consignment arrangements, the goods are not included in the seller's inventory.

Application of Materiality to Inventory Numerous incidental costs are connected with the acquisition of inventory such as unpacking, inspection, and delivery. These costs are often insignificant when compared to the cost of the inventory item itself. Therefore, many companies record the incidental costs incurred in the acquisition of inventory directly in an expense account instead of adding these immaterial costs to the cost of inventory on the statement of financial position.

ETHICAL DECISIONS The proper determination of whether goods should or should not be considered part of the seller's inventory has created an ethical dilemma for some companies. With shipping terms of FOB shipping point, managers may attempt to encourage customers to take delivery of more goods than are currently needed since such goods would generate revenue when the inventory is shipped. This practice, termed *channel stuffing,* effectively steals sales from the next period and distorts the results of the company's operations. Securities regulators closely examine transactions that are thought to be channel stuffing. For example, Coca-Cola paid $137.5 million as a result of channel stuffing allegations that allowed it to report artificially higher sales volumes to maintain a higher share price. Bristol-Myers Squibb paid $150 million to settle allegations that included channel stuffing.

Recording Purchase Transactions To summarize, the purchase price of inventory includes any cost of bringing the goods to a saleable condition and location. Therefore, the inventory account is increased for the invoice price of a purchase as well as any transportation costs paid for by the buyer. Any purchase discounts, returns, or allowances reduce the inventory account. Cornerstone 6.2 illustrates the journal entries required to record purchases of merchandise inventory.

> ## concept Q&A
>
> The purchase transactions that affect inventory seem complicated. Why go to all that trouble and effort when the periodic inventory system could be used?
>
> **Answer:**
>
> A perpetual inventory system requires a number of entries that directly affect inventory. While this system is certainly more complex than a periodic inventory system, the numerous entries provide management with up-to-date information that allows them to better manage and control their inventory.

CORNERSTONE 6.2

CORNERSTONE
VIDEO

Recording Purchase Transactions in a Perpetual Inventory System

Information:

On September 1, Brandon Shoes purchased 50 pairs of hiking boots for $3,750 cash (or $75 a pair) and paid $150 of transportation costs. Also, on September 1, Brandon purchased 100 pairs of running shoes for $10,000; however, the seller paid the transportation costs of $300. The running shoes were purchased on credit with terms of 2/10, n/30. Brandon paid for one-half ($5,000) of the running shoes on September 10, within the discount period. The remaining shoes were paid for on September 30. After inspection, Brandon determined that 10 pairs of the hiking boots were defective and returned them on September 30 for a cash refund.

Required:

Prepare the journal entries necessary to record the September transactions for Brandon Shoes, assuming a perpetual inventory system.

Why:

The cost of inventory includes the purchase price of the merchandise plus any cost of bringing the goods to a saleable condition and location. The recording of purchases in a perpetual inventory system contributes to management knowing the company's balance of inventory at any point in time.

Solution:

		Shareholders'
Assets	**= Liabilities +**	**Equity**
+3,750		
−3,750		

		Shareholders'
Assets	**= Liabilities +**	**Equity**
+150		
−150		

		Shareholders'
Assets	**= Liabilities +**	**Equity**
+10,000	+10,000	

		Shareholders'
Assets	**= Liabilities +**	**Equity**
−4,900	−5,000	
−100		

		Shareholders'
Assets	**= Liabilities +**	**Equity**
−5,000	−5,000	

		Shareholders'
Assets	**= Liabilities +**	**Equity**
+750		
−750		

Date		Account and Explanation	Debit	Credit
Sept.	1	Inventory	3,750	
		Cash		3,750
		(Purchased inventory for cash)		
	1	Inventory	150	
		Cash		150
		(Recorded payment of freight costs)		
	1	Inventory	10,000	
		Accounts Payable		10,000
		(Purchased inventory on credit)		
	10	Accounts Payable	5,000	
		Cash		4,900
		Inventory ($5,000 × 2%)		100
		(Recorded payment within the discount period)		
	30	Accounts Payable	5,000	
		Cash		5,000
		(Recorded payment outside the discount period)		
	30	Cash	750	
		Inventory (10 pairs × $75/pair)		750
		(Returned defective hiking boots)		

(EXHIBIT 6.9)

Calculation of Net Purchases

Invoice price of purchase	$13,750
Less: Purchase discounts	(100)
Purchase returns and allowances	(750)
Add: Transportation costs (freight-in)	150
Net cost of purchases	$13,050

Note that the purchase of the hiking boots in Cornerstone 6.2 included the $150 of transportation costs (freight-in) because Brandon paid the freight. However, the purchase of the running shoes did not include freight costs because it was paid by the seller.

These journal entries illustrate that, under a perpetual inventory system, inventory is constantly updated with each purchase so that the net effect of purchases is reflected in the inventory account. The computation of net purchases for Brandon Shoes is summarized in Exhibit 6.9. Although the original invoice price was $13,750, the consideration of purchase discounts, returns, and transportation charges resulted in a much different value in the inventory account.

Accounting for Sales of Inventory in a Perpetual System

In addition to purchase transactions, merchandising companies must also account for the inventory effects of sales and sales returns. Because a perpetual inventory system is being used, the merchandise inventory account is also affected in addition to the sales account.

Sales As discussed in Chapter 5, companies generally recognize sales revenue when it is earned and the collection of cash is reasonably assured. The recording of sales revenue involves two journal entries:

- In the first journal entry, sales revenue is recognized.
- The second journal entry recognizes, consistent with the matching concept, the cost of the goods that are sold. It also reduces the inventory account so that the perpetual inventory system will reflect an up-to-date balance for inventory.

Sales Returns and Allowances If a customer returns an item for some reason, the company will make an adjustment to sales as shown in Chapter 5. In addition, the company must make a second entry to decrease cost of goods sold and increase inventory to reflect the return of the merchandise.

Recording Inventory Effects of Sales Transactions The use of a perpetual inventory system requires that two journal entries be made for both sales and sales return transactions. These journal entries are illustrated in Cornerstone 6.3 .

concept Q&A

Instead of making two entries to record a sale under a perpetual system, why not just make one entry for the net amount? Wouldn't gross margin be the same?

Answer:

A system could be developed that combines the two entries necessary to record a sale of inventory under a perpetual system; however, important information would be lost. If an entry were made to an account such as "Gross Margin" for the difference between sales revenue and cost of goods sold, no information would be provided on the gross amount of revenues or cost of goods sold. This loss of information would be inconsistent with the purpose of financial reporting.

CORNERSTONE 6.3

Recording Sales Transactions in a Perpetual Inventory System

Information:

On August 1, Brandon Shoes sold 100 pairs of football cleats to the local university football team for $12,000 cash (each pair of cleats was sold for $120 per pair). Brandon had paid $10,000 (or $100 per pair) for the cleats from its supplier. On August 15, the local university football team returned 10 pairs of cleats for a cash refund of $1,200.

Required:

1. Prepare the journal entries to record the sale of the football cleats.

2. Prepare the journal entries to record the return of the football cleats.

Why:

The sale or return of inventory in a perpetual system requires two journal entries–one to record the revenue portion of the transaction and one to record the expense (inventory) portion of the transaction. The recording of sales in a perpetual inventory system contributes to management knowing the company's balance of inventory and cost of goods sold at a point in time.

Solution:

Assets	= Liabilities +	Shareholders' Equity (Sales Revenue)
+12,000		+12,000

Assets	= Liabilities +	Shareholders' Equity (Cost of Goods Sold)
−10,000		−10,000

Assets	= Liabilities +	Shareholders' Equity (Sales Returns and Allowances)
−1,200		−1,200

Assets	= Liabilities +	Shareholders' Equity (Cost of Goods Sold)
+1,000		+1,000

	Date		Account and Explanation	Debit	Credit
1.	Aug.	1	Cash	12,000	
			Sales Revenue		12,000
			(Recorded sale to customer)		
		1	Cost of Goods Sold	10,000	
			Inventory		10,000
			(Recorded cost of merchandise sold)		
2.		15	Sales Returns and Allowances	1,200	
			Cash		1,200
			(Recorded return of merchandise)		
		15	Inventory	1,000	
			Cost of Goods Sold		1,000
			(Recorded cost of merchandise returned)		

In the sale transaction in Cornerstone 6.3, the external selling price of $120 was recorded as Sales Revenue. The cost of goods sold (or inventory) portion of the transaction was recorded at the cost to Brandon Shoes of $100. Therefore, for each pair of shoes sold, Brandon Shoes made a gross margin of $20 ($120 − $100). The total cost of goods sold recognized by Brandon Shoes is $9,000 ($10,000 − $1,000). *In dealing with sales to customers, it is important to remember to record revenues at the selling price and to record expenses (and inventory reduction) at cost.*

YOUDECIDE   Impact of Shipping Terms on Revenue Recognition

You are a CPA auditing the financial statements of Henderson Electronics, a computer retailer located in Toronto, Ontario. Henderson's policy is to record a sales transaction when the merchandise is shipped to customers (FOB shipping point). During the audit, you notice that 50 computers were sold to the Toronto School Board near the end of the year. Further investigation reveals that these 50 computers are still in Henderson's warehouse. James Henderson, the owner, tells you that the school board wanted to purchase the computers with funds from the board's current fiscal year, but couldn't take delivery because the computer labs at the various schools were under renovation. Therefore, Henderson billed the board and recorded a credit sale in the current year.

Was this transaction accounted for properly?

Because the company has an FOB shipping point policy and the inventory had not been delivered, the computers are not considered sold in the current year. Therefore, the recording of the credit sale should not have been made and the inventory should be included in Henderson's ending inventory. This type of transaction is commonly referred to as a "bill and hold" sale. Although it may be perfectly legal, such transactions have come under scrutiny by securities regulators as a means for companies to improperly inflate sales revenue and should be carefully scrutinized.

The proper determination of whether goods should or should not be included in inventory impacts both the statement of financial position and the statement of earnings.

INVENTORY COSTING METHODS

A key feature of the cost of goods sold model illustrated in Cornerstone 6.1 is that the determination of cost of goods sold requires an allocation of the cost of goods available for sale between ending inventory and cost of goods sold. If the prices paid for goods are constant over time, this allocation is easy to compute—just multiply the cost per unit times the number of units on hand at year-end (to determine the cost of ending inventory) or times the number of units sold (to determine the cost of goods sold). For example, if Windsor Company began operations by purchasing 1,000 units of a single product for $24 each, total goods available for sale would be $24,000, calculated as:

 OBJECTIVE **3**

Apply the three inventory costing methods to compute ending inventory and cost of goods sold under a perpetual inventory system.

$$\text{Inventory available to be sold} \times \text{Cost per unit} = \text{Goods available for sale}$$
$$1{,}000 \text{ units} \times \$24 = \$24{,}000$$

If 800 units were sold during the period, the cost of the remaining 200-unit ending inventory would be $4,800:

$$\text{Ending inventory} \times \text{Cost per unit} = \text{Cost of ending inventory}$$
$$200 \text{ units} \times \$24 = \$4{,}800$$

Cost of goods sold would be $19,200, calculated as:

$$\text{Units sold} \times \text{Cost per unit} = \text{Cost of goods sold}$$
$$800 \text{ units} \times \$24 = \$19{,}200$$

It makes no difference which of the 1,000 units remain in ending inventory because all units have the same cost ($24).

Alternatively, if the price paid for a good changes over time, the cost of goods available for sale may include units with different costs per unit. In such cases, the question arises: Which prices should be assigned to the units sold and which assigned to the units in ending inventory? For example, assume that Windsor Company purchased the same total of 1,000 units during a period at different prices as follows:

Jan. 3	300 units purchased at $22 per unit	=	$ 6,600
Jan. 15	400 units purchased at $24 per unit	=	9,600
Jan. 24	300 units purchased at $26 per unit	=	7,800
	Cost of goods available for sale		$24,000

While the cost of goods available for sale is the same ($24,000), the cost of the 200-unit ending inventory depends on which goods remain in ending inventory. As illustrated by the cost of goods sold model discussed earlier, the cost assigned to ending inventory also affects the calculation of cost of goods sold.

	If ending inventory is made up of $22 per unit goods	If ending inventory is made up of $26 per unit goods
Ending inventory	$4,400	$5,200
	(200 units × $22/unit)	(200 units × $26/unit)
Cost of goods sold	$19,600	$18,800
	($24,000 − $4,400)	($24,000 − $5,200)

The determination of the cost of ending inventory and cost of goods sold depends on management's choice of inventory system (perpetual or periodic) and method of allocating inventory costs.

Gross Profit Method of Inventory Estimation

If a company uses the periodic method of inventory determination and does not maintain a perpetual inventory record, a physical taking of inventory is required to compute inventory and cost of goods sold. To avoid costly inventory counts, companies use the gross profit method to estimate inventory and cost of goods sold when preparing financial statements for internal purposes. The gross profit method uses historical gross profit percentages (the gross profit percentage concept is discussed in Chapter 5) to estimate inventory and cost of goods sold.

For example, assume that XYZ Corporation's historical gross profit percentage is 30%. If sales for the month of June are $1,000,000, the cost of goods sold will be estimated at $1,000,000 \times 70\% (100\% - 30\%)$. The cost of goods sold model will then be used, together with purchase information for the month, to calculate an estimate of the ending inventory. The gross profit method is not an acceptable method under IFRS or ASPE for use in preparing annual external financial statements. Insurance companies generally accept this method to estimate losses.

Inventory Costing Methods

The inventory system (perpetual or periodic) determines *when* cost of goods sold is calculated—after every sales transaction or at the end of the period. An *inventory costing method* determines how costs are allocated to cost of goods sold and ending inventory. Although the assumption about how inventory costs flow could take many different forms, accountants typically use one of three inventory costing methods:

- Specific identification
- First-in, first-out (FIFO)
- Weighted average

Each of these three costing methods represents a different procedure for allocating the cost of goods available for sale between ending inventory and cost of goods sold. Only the specific identification method allocates the cost of purchases according to the *physical flow* of specific units through inventory. That is, specific identification is based on a *flow of goods* principle. In contrast, the other two methods—FIFO and weighted average cost—are based on a *flow of cost* principle. When the FIFO or weighted average cost methods are used, the physical flow of goods into inventory and out to the customers is generally unrelated to the flow of unit costs. We make this point here so that you will not be confused in thinking that a cost flow assumption describes the physical flow of goods in a company. *IFRS and ASPE do not require that the cost flow assumption be consistent with the physical flow of goods.*

Companies disclose their choice of inventory methods in a note to the financial statements. The 2015 annual report of Canadian Tire Corporation includes the following partial statement:

Notes to Consolidated Financial Statements

Merchandise inventories are carried at the lower of cost and net realizable value. The cost of merchandise inventory is determined based on weighted average cost and includes costs incurred in bringing the merchandise inventories to their present location and condition. All inventories are finished goods.

Net realizable value is the estimated selling price of inventory during the normal course of business less estimated selling expenses.

With the exception of specific identification, the inventory costing methods allocate cost of goods available for sale between ending inventory and cost of goods sold using the following process.

Step 1: Calculate the cost of goods available for sale *immediately prior* to any sale transaction.

Step 2: Apply the inventory costing method to determine ending inventory and cost of goods sold.

Step 3: Repeat steps 1 and 2 for all inventory transactions during the period. The sum of the cost of goods sold computed in step 2 is the cost of goods sold for the period. Ending inventory is the amount computed during the final application of step 2 for the period.

To understand how inventory costing systems allocate costs (step 2), it is useful to think of inventory as if it were a stack of separate layers, with each stack distinguished by the purchase price. Each time a purchase is made at a unit cost different from that of a previous purchase, a new layer of inventory cost is added to the stack. As inventory is sold, it is removed from the stack according to the cost flow assumption used. This process is illustrated in Exhibit 6.10 for the FIFO method.

Specific Identification

The **specific identification method** determines the cost of ending inventory and the cost of goods sold based on the identification of the *actual* units sold and in inventory. This method does not require an assumption about the flow of costs but assigns cost based on the specific flow of inventory. It requires that detailed records of each purchase and sale be maintained so that a company knows exactly which items were sold and the cost of those items. Historically, this method was practical only for high-cost items with unique identifiers (e.g., serial numbers) that were sold in low numbers—for example, automobiles and jewellery. With the introduction of bar coding, electronic scanners, and radio frequency identification, this method has become easier to implement, but its application is still relatively rare. The specific identification method is illustrated in Cornerstone 6.4 .

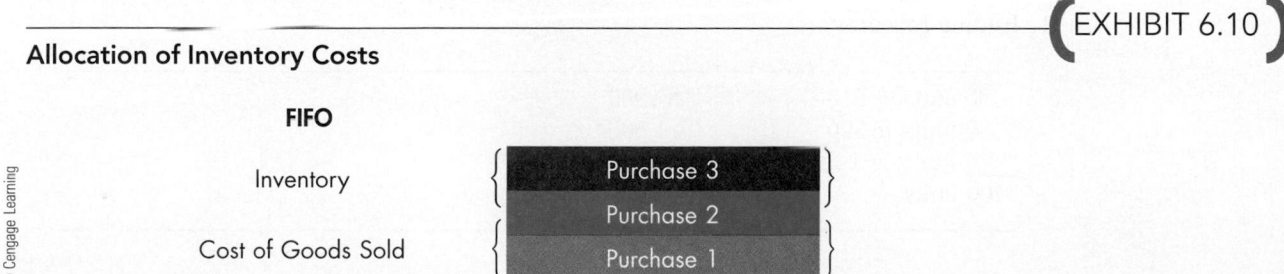

(EXHIBIT 6.10)

Allocation of Inventory Costs

FIFO

© Cengage Learning

CORNERSTONE 6.4

CORNERSTONE
VIDEO

Applying the Specific Identification Method

Information:

Tampico Beachwear, a retail store specializing in beach apparel, has the following information related to purchases and sales of one of its more popular products, Crocs brand shoes. (Each inventory layer is a different colour.)

Date	Description	Units Purchased at Cost	Units Sold at Retail
Oct. 1	Beginning inventory	300 units @ $16 = $4,800	
3	Purchase 1	600 units @ $18 = $10,800	
8	Sale 1		800 units @ $30
Oct. 15	Purchase 2	250 units @ $20 = $5,000	
20	Purchase 3	150 units @ $22 = $3,300	
25	Sale 2		300 units @ $30

Goods available for sale: Sales:
1,300 units = $23,900   1,100 units = $33,000

The following units were sold during the month and remain in ending inventory at the end of the month:

Description	Units Sold	Units in Ending Inventory
Beginning inventory	300	–
Purchase 1	550	50
Purchase 2	170	80
Purchase 3	80	70
Total	1,100	200

Required:

1. Compute the cost of ending inventory at October 31 under the specific identification method.

2. Compute the cost of goods sold at October 31 under the specific identification method.

Why:

Cost of goods sold and ending inventory are determined based on the identification of the actual units sold and in inventory. The specific identification method is typically used when inventory units are not homogeneous.

Solution:

1. Ending Inventory is

50 units @ $18	$ 900
80 units @ $20	1,600
70 units @ $22	1,540
200 units	$4,040

(Continued)

2. Cost of Goods Sold is

300 units @ $16	$ 4,800	
550 units @ $18	9,900	
170 units @ $20	3,400	
80 units @ $22	1,760	
1,100 units	$19,860	

Three items in Cornerstone 6.4 are of interest.

- *Cost of Goods Available for Sale*: The sum of ending inventory ($4,040) and cost of goods sold ($19,860) equals cost of goods available for sale ($23,900). The specific identification method, like all inventory costing methods, allocates the cost of goods available for sale between ending inventory and cost of goods sold.
- *Cost of Goods Sold*: Because there are usually far fewer units in ending inventory than in cost of goods sold, it is often easier to compute the cost of ending inventory and then find the cost of goods sold by subtracting ending inventory from cost of goods available for sale ($23,900 − $4,040 = $19,860).
- *Financial Statement Effects*: The determination of inventory cost affects both the statement of financial position and the statement of earnings. The amount assigned to ending inventory will appear on the statement of financial position. The amount assigned to cost of goods sold appears on the statement of earnings and is used in the calculation of a company's gross margin.

First-In, First-Out (FIFO)

The **first-in, first-out (FIFO) method** is based on the assumption that costs move through inventory in an unbroken stream, with the costs entering and leaving the inventory in the same order. In other words, *the earliest purchases (the first-in) are assumed to be the first sold (the first-out), and the more recent purchases are in ending inventory.* Every time inventory is sold, the cost of the earliest (oldest) purchases that make up cost of goods available for sale is allocated to cost of goods sold, and the cost of the most recent purchases is allocated to ending inventory. In many instances, this cost flow assumption is an accurate representation of the physical flow of goods. Hewlett-Packard and restaurant companies such as Tim Hortons all use FIFO. Cornerstone 6.5 illustrates the application of the FIFO method.

The application of FIFO in Cornerstone 6.5 results in the following:

- Ending inventory reported on the statement of financial position is $4,300.
- Cost of goods sold reported on the statement of earnings is $19,600 ($13,800 + $5,800).

Because the sum of ending inventory and cost of goods sold ($4,300 + $19,600) equals cost of goods available for sale ($23,900), Tampico could have also calculated cost of goods sold as the difference between cost of goods available for sale and ending inventory ($23,900 − $4,300).

Last-In, First-Out (LIFO)—A Divergence from IFRS and ASPE

The **last-in, first-out (LIFO) method** allocates the cost of goods available for sale between ending inventory and cost of goods sold based on the assumption that the most

CORNERSTONE 6.5

CORNERSTONE
VIDEO

Applying the FIFO Inventory Costing Method in a Perpetual Inventory System

Information:

Tampico Beachwear, a retail store specializing in beach apparel, has the following information related to purchases and sales of one of its more popular products, Crocs brand shoes. (Each inventory layer is a different colour.)

Date		Description	Units Purchased at Cost	Units Sold at Retail
Oct.	1	Beginning inventory	300 units @ $16 = $ 4,800	
	3	Purchase 1	600 units @ $18 = $10,800	
	8	Sale 1		800 units @ $30
	15	Purchase 2	250 units @ $20 = $ 5,000	
	20	Purchase 3	150 units @ $22 = $ 3,300	
	25	Sale 2		300 units @ $30
			Goods available for sale:	Sales:
			1,300 units = $23,900	1,100 units = $33,000

Required:

Compute the cost of ending inventory and the cost of goods sold at October 31 using the FIFO method.

Why:

The cost of the earliest purchases that make up cost of goods available for sale is allocated to cost of goods sold, and the cost of the most recent purchases is allocated to ending inventory. During a period of rising prices, the first-in, first-out inventory costing method provides a greater dollar amount for ending inventory compared to the weighted average costing method.

Solution:

Step 1: Compute the cost of goods available for sale immediately prior to the first sale. This produces an inventory balance of $15,600 ($4,800 + $10,800). Notice that this inventory balance is made up of two layers—a $16 layer and an $18 layer.

Step 2: Apply FIFO to determine ending inventory and cost of goods sold. The cost of goods available for sale is allocated between inventory (the most recent purchases) and cost of goods sold (the earliest purchases)

Date		Description	Cost of Goods Sold	Inventory Balance	
Oct.	1	Beginning inventory		300 × $16	= $ 4,800
	3	Purchase 1 (600 @ $18)		300 × $16 = $ 4,800 } 600 × $18 = $10,800 } = $15,600	
	8	Sale 1 (800 @ $30)	300 × $16 = $4,800 } 500 × $18 = $9,000 } = $13,800	100 × $18	= $ 1,800

(Continued)

Step 3: Repeat steps 1 and 2 for the remaining inventory transactions during the period.

CORNERSTONE

6.5

(Continued)

Date		Description	Cost of Goods Sold	Inventory Balance	
Oct.	8	Inventory on hand		$100 \times \$18$	$= \$1,800$
	15	Purchase 2 (250 @ $20)		$\left.\begin{array}{l}100 \times \$18 = \$1,800 \\ 250 \times \$20 = \$5,000\end{array}\right\}$	$= \$6,800$
	20	Purchase 3 (150 @ $22)		$\left.\begin{array}{l}100 \times \$18 = \$1,800 \\ 250 \times \$20 = \$5,000 \\ 150 \times \$22 = \$3,300\end{array}\right\}$	$= \$10,100$
	25	Sale 2 (300 @ $30)	$\left.\begin{array}{l}100 \times \$18 = \$1,800 \\ 200 \times \$20 = \$4,000\end{array}\right\} = \underline{\$\ 5,800}$	$\left.\begin{array}{l}50 \times \$20 = \$1,000 \\ 150 \times \$22 = \$3,300\end{array}\right\}$	$= \$4,300$
			Total \$19,600		

recent purchases (the last-in) are the first to be sold (the first-out). Under the LIFO method, *the most recent purchases (newest costs) are allocated to the cost of goods sold and the earliest purchases (oldest costs) are allocated to inventory.* Except for companies that stockpile inventory (e.g., piles of coal, stacks of hay, stacks of rock), this cost flow assumption rarely coincides with the actual physical flow of inventory. Companies in the United States such as General Mills, Target, and Macy's all use LIFO since it does have income tax advantages over other methods. IAS 2 does not allow the use of LIFO under IFRS and LIFO is also not acceptable under ASPE.

As a result, users of financial statements must be careful when comparing operating results and statements of financial position of companies using IFRS or ASPE with those of US corporations using US GAAP, which allows LIFO. The reason is that the LIFO method can significantly affect the inventory balance on the statement of financial position and the net earnings for the period.

Weighted Average Cost

The **weighted average cost method** allocates the cost of goods available for sale between ending inventory and cost of goods sold based on a weighted average cost per unit. This weighted average cost per unit is calculated after each purchase of inventory as follows:

$$\text{Weighted average cost per unit} = \frac{\text{Cost of goods available for sale}}{\text{Units available for sale}}$$

Because a new average is computed after each purchase, this method is often called the moving weighted average method. This weighted average cost per unit is then used to calculate ending inventory and cost of goods sold as follows:

> Ending inventory = Units on hand × Weighted average cost per unit
>
> Cost of goods sold = Units sold × Weighted average cost per unit

The average cost method is used by companies such as Office Depot and OfficeMax. Cornerstone 6.6 illustrates the application of the average cost method.

CORNERSTONE 6.6

CORNERSTONE VIDEO

Applying the Weighted Average Cost Inventory Costing Method in a Perpetual Inventory System

Information:

Tampico Beachwear, a retail store specializing in beach apparel, has the following information related to purchases and sales of one of its more popular products, Crocs brand shoes. (Each inventory layer is a different colour.)

Required:

Compute the cost of ending inventory and the cost of goods sold at October 31 using the weighted-average cost method. (*Note:* Use four decimal places for per-unit calculations and round all other numbers to the nearest dollar.)

Why:

The cost of goods available for sale is allocated between ending inventory and cost of goods sold based on the weighted average cost of goods available for sale. During a period of rising prices, the weighted average inventory costing method provides a lower dollar amount for inventory compared to the first-in, first-out costing method.

Date		Description	Units Purchased at Cost	Units Sold at Retail
Oct.	1	Beginning inventory	300 units @ $16 = $4,800	
	3	Purchase 1	600 units @ $18 = $10,800	
	8	Sale 1		800 units @ $30
	15	Purchase 2	250 units @ $20 = $5,000	
	20	Purchase 3	150 units @ $22 = $3,300	
	25	Sale 2		300 units @ $30
			Goods available for sale: 1,300 units = $23,900	Sales: 1,100 units = $33,000

Solution:

Step 1: Compute the cost of goods available for sale immediately *prior* to the first sale. This produces an inventory balance of $15,600 ($4,800 + $10,800) and inventory units of 900(300 + 600).

(Continued)

Step 2: Apply the weighted-average cost method to determine ending inventory and cost of goods sold. The cost of goods available for sale is allocated between inventory and cost of goods sold using a weighted average cost per unit calculated as:

$$\text{Weighted average cost per unit} = \frac{\text{Cost of goods available for sale}}{\text{Units available for sale}}$$

$$= \frac{\$15,600}{900 \text{ units}} = \$17.3333 \text{ per unit}$$

CORNERSTONE

6.6

(Continued)

Date	Description	Cost of Goods Sold	Inventory Balance	
Oct. 1	Beginning inventory		$300 \times \$16$	$= \$ \ 4,800 \ (\$16/\text{unit})$
3	Purchase 1 (600 @ $18)		$\left.\begin{array}{l} 300 \times \$16 = \$ \ 4,800 \\ 600 \times \$18 = \$10,800 \end{array}\right\}$	$= \$ 15,600 \ (\$17.3333/\text{unit})^{a}$
8	Sale 1 (800 @ $30)	$800 \times \$17.3333 = \$13,867$	$100 \times \$17.3333$	$= \$ \ 1,733$

$^{a}\ \$15,600 \div 900 \text{ units} = \$17.3333/\text{unit}$

Step 3: Repeat steps 1 and 2 for the remaining inventory transactions during the period.

Date	Description	Cost of Goods Sold	Inventory Balance	
Oct. 8	Inventory on hand		$100 \times \$17.3333$	$= \$ \ 1,733 \ (\$17.3333/\text{unit})^{a}$
15	Purchase 2 (250 @ $20)		$\left.\begin{array}{l} 100 \times \$17.3333 = \$1,733 \\ 250 \times \$20.00 \ \ = \$5,000 \end{array}\right\}$	$= \$ \ 6,733 \ (\$19.2371/\text{unit})^{b}$
20	Purchase 3 (150 @ $22)		$\left.\begin{array}{l} 350 \times \$19.2371 = \$6,733 \\ 150 \times \$22.00 \ \ = \$3,300 \end{array}\right\}$	$= \$10,033 \ (\$20.0660/\text{unit})^{c}$
25	Sale 2 (300 @ $30)	$300 \times \$20.0660 = \underline{\$ \ 6,020}$ **Total** $= \textbf{\$19,887}$	$200 \times \$20.0660$	$= \$ \ 4,013$

$^{b}\ \$6,733 \div 350 \text{ units} = \$19.2371/\text{unit}$
$^{c}\ \$10,033 \div 500 \text{ units} = \$20.0660/\text{unit}$

The application of the weighted average cost method in Cornerstone 6.6 results in the following:

- Ending inventory reported on the statement of financial position is $4,013.
- Cost of goods sold reported on the statement of earnings is $19,887, the sum of cost of goods sold during the period ($13,867 + $6,020).

Because the sum of ending inventory and cost of goods sold ($4,013 + $19,887) equals cost of goods available for sale ($23,900), Tampico could have also calculated cost of goods sold as the difference between cost of goods available for sale and ending inventory ($23,900 − $4,013).

The weighted average cost method results in an allocation to ending inventory and cost of goods sold that is somewhere between the allocations that would be produced by FIFO and LIFO.

ANALYSIS OF INVENTORY COSTING METHODS

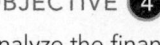

OBJECTIVE ❹

Analyze the financial reporting and tax effects of the various inventory costing methods.

Companies are free to choose among the three inventory costing methods, and the inventory accounting policy decisions that are made can have major effects on the financial statements. Proper management of these decisions, within the bounds of generally accepted accounting principles and good business ethics, can also affect the timing of income tax payments and the judgments of creditors, shareholders, and others. Therefore, it is important to understand the consequences of these accounting choices.

concept Q&A

Why doesn't the IASB simply mandate the most conceptually correct inventory costing method instead of giving companies a choice between alternative methods?

Answer:

All inventory costing methods provide an allocation of the total dollar amount of goods available for sale between ending inventory and cost of goods sold. No one cost method is conceptually superior to any other. In fact, LIFO, which is not allowed under IFRS, actually achieves a better matching of current costs with current revenues on the statement of earnings; however, the resulting statement of financial position valuation can be quite misleading about the current market value of inventory on the statement of financial position. Companies make the choice between inventory methods for a variety of reasons unique to their own situation. Some companies will adopt certain methods for the tax benefits, while others will adopt FIFO because they want to report higher profits.

Illustrating Relationships: Financial Statement Effects of Alternative Costing Methods

Financial statement analysts frequently ask the hypothetical question, "How much would inventory and income have been if a different costing method had been used?" If the prices paid for purchased inventory are stable, all inventory costing methods will yield the same amounts for ending inventory and cost of goods sold. However, when purchase prices vary, the different costing methods will produce different amounts for ending inventory, cost of goods sold, and, therefore, income. To properly analyze financial statements, it is necessary to understand the impact of changing prices on inventories and income.

To illustrate, consider the inventory data for Tampico Beachwear, which had revenues for the period of $33,000 (1,100 units sold × $30 per unit) and operating expenses of $4,000 (assumed amount). This information and the related inventory cost calculations in Cornerstones 6.4 through 6.6 produced the statement of earnings amounts shown in Exhibit 6.11.

Notice that sales, purchases, and cost of goods available for sale are the same for each method. However, the changing purchase prices of each inventory layer result in different amounts for cost of goods sold, gross margin, and net income.

When purchase prices are rising, as they are in our example (remember that shoes went from $16 to $18 to $20 to $22), the FIFO method produces the highest cost for ending inventory, the lowest cost of goods sold, and, therefore, the higher gross margin (and net income) compared to weighted average cost. *When purchase prices are falling,* the situation is reversed. Exhibit 6.12 summarizes these relationships.

Income Tax Effects of Alternative Costing Methods

In the long run, all inventory costs will find their way to cost of goods sold and the statement of earnings. Therefore, choosing a costing method to minimize current taxes does not avoid the payment of taxes; it merely postpones it, temporarily reducing the company's cash and capital requirements for a period of time.

ETHICAL DECISIONS   When managers select an inventory costing method, it may not always be in the best interest of the company. For example, in a period of rising prices, the owners of the company may prefer that a company use a costing method to reduce the taxes that must be paid. However, many management bonus plans are based on net income so that the use of certain methods, such as FIFO, would result in larger bonuses compared to other costing methods. If managers let the choice of inventory costing method be guided solely by its effect on their compensation, the ethics of their behaviour can be questioned.

(EXHIBIT 6.11)

Financial Statement Effects of Alternative Inventory Costing Methods—Perpetual Method

	Tampico Beachwear Condensed Statements of Earnings For the Month Ended October 31					
	FIFO		Specific Identification		Weighted Average Cost	
Sales		$33,000		$33,000		$33,000
Beginning inventory	$ 4,800		$ 4,800		$ 4,800	
Add: Purchases	19,100		19,100		19,100	
Cost of goods available for sale	23,900		23,900		23,900	
Less: Ending inventory	(4,300)		(4,040)		(4,013)	
Cost of goods sold		19,600		19,860		19,887
Gross margin		13,400		13,140		13,113
Operating expenses		4,000		4,000		4,000
Income before taxes		9,400		9,140		9,113
Income tax expense (30%)		2,820		2,742		2,734
Net income		$ 6,580		$ 6,398		$ 6,379

Consistency in Application

Companies are free to choose whichever inventory costing method they prefer, regardless of whether the method matches the physical flow of goods. However, once a company adopts a particular costing method for an item, it must continue to use it consistently over time. The consistent application of an accounting principle over time discourages changes in accounting methods from one period to another, even if acceptable alternative methods exist. This enhances the comparability and usefulness of accounting information. A change in accounting method may still be made; however, the effects of the change must be fully disclosed. The consistent application of accounting methods and the required disclosures of any accounting changes permit readers of financial statements to assume that accounting methods do not change over time unless specifically indicated. A company may use more than one method in determining the cost of inventory.[2]

(EXHIBIT 6.12)

Financial Statement Effects of Alternative Inventory Costing Methods

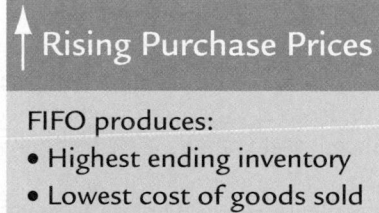

↑ Rising Purchase Prices

FIFO produces:
- Highest ending inventory
- Lowest cost of goods sold
- Highest income

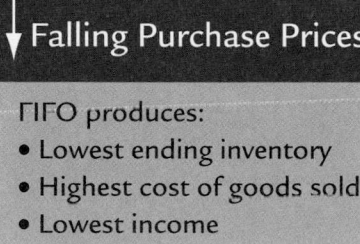

↓ Falling Purchase Prices

FIFO produces:
- Lowest ending inventory
- Highest cost of goods sold
- Lowest income

[2] IAS 2 requires inventory items of a similar nature and use to be valued using the same cost formula. Items in inventory with a different nature or use may be valued using different cost formulas.

YOUDECIDE Choosing among Inventory Costing Methods

You are the owner and manager of Simply Fresh, a supermarket that specializes in selling fresh, organic food. You know that managing inventory is crucial to the company's success and that IFRS gives you the freedom to choose between FIFO, weighted average, and the specific identification cost methods to report inventory and cost of goods sold.

What factors should you consider in selecting among the different inventory costing methods?

Three factors that should be considered are as follows:

- *Actual physical flow of inventory*: Because most companies sell their oldest merchandise first, FIFO will give the closest approximation to the physical flow of inventory. However, IFRS does not require that the choice of inventory costing method be consistent with the physical flow of goods.

- *Financial statement effects*: During periods of rising prices, the use of FIFO will result in the highest cost for ending inventory, the lowest cost of goods sold, and the highest net income. These positive financial results may be desirable to satisfy shareholders who demand higher share prices or to meet lending agreements that are tied to financial performance. In addition, if management's bonus plan is tied to reported income, the use of FIFO may result in higher bonuses for management.
- *Tax benefits*: During periods of rising prices, the use of FIFO will result in higher income and possibly create significant income tax costs for the company.

It is important for financial statement users who wish to make good decisions to understand the differences that result from management's choice of inventory costing method.

LOWER OF COST AND NET REALIZABLE VALUE RULE

OBJECTIVE ⑤

Apply the lower of cost and net realizable value rule to the valuation of inventory.

The inventory accounting procedures described to this point have followed the cost principle—inventory is recorded in the firm's records at its purchase price (or cost). The price for which inventory items can be sold (their market value) may decline because the goods have become obsolete, have been damaged, or have otherwise diminished in value. For example, clothes that have gone out of style due to changing fashions or seasons have declined in value. Similarly, technology companies experience rapid obsolescence due to quickly changing technologies. In cases where the market value of inventory has dropped below its original cost, IFRS and ASPE require a departure from the historical cost principle.

This departure from the cost principle is called the **lower of cost and net realizable value (LCNRV) rule**. Under LCNRV, if the net realizable value of a company's inventory is lower than its cost, the company reduces the amount recorded for inventory to its net realizable value. To apply LCNRV, a company must first determine the cost of its inventory using one of the inventory costing methods discussed earlier in the chapter (specific identification, FIFO, or weighted average cost). Next, the company will establish the net realizable value of the inventory. Net realizable value is the expected selling price less estimated selling costs such as disposal or commission costs. Finally, the net realizable value is compared with cost (usually on an item-by-item basis), and the lower of net realizable value and cost is used as the amount reported for inventory on the financial statements. Cornerstone 6.7 illustrates the application of the LCNRV rule.

Note that, in Cornerstone 6.7, the net realizable value of the LCD HDTVs is greater than its cost; however, for the other two products, cost is greater than net realizable value. Thus, only the plasma HDTVs and the DVD recorders are reduced to net realizable value; the LCD HDTVs remain at cost. The journal entry reduces inventory to its net realizable value, and the loss is recorded as an increase to cost of goods sold in the period that the net realizable value of the item dropped.

Valuing Inventory at Lower of Cost and Net Realizable Value

CORNERSTONE 6.7

Information:

Magli Electronics prepared the following analysis of its inventory at December 31:

Product	Quantity	Historical Cost per Item	Net Realizable Value per Item
42″ LCD HDTV	12	$1,000	$1,100
50″ Plasma HDTV	7	1,300	1,000
DVD Recorders	20	120	100

CORNERSTONE VIDEO

Required:

1. Determine the lower of cost and net realizable value for each item of inventory.

2. Prepare the journal entry needed on December 31 to value the inventory at LCNRV.

Why:

The valuation of inventory at the lower of cost and net realizable value ensures that inventory losses are recognized (written off) as an expense in the period they occur rather than in the period that the particular inventory is sold.

Solution:

1. The LCNRV amounts are shown in the last column of the analysis below.

Product	Cost		Net Realizable Value		Lower of Cost and Net Realizable Value
42″ LCD HDTV	$12,000	(12 × $1,000)	$13,200	(12 × $1,100)	$12,000
50″ Plasma HDTV	9,100	(7 × $1,300)	7,000	(7 × $1,000)	7,000
DVD Recorders	2,400	(20 × $120)	2,000	(20 × $100)	2,000
	$23,500		$22,200		$21,000

2. To apply LCNRV, the inventory must be reduced by $2,500 ($23,500 − $21,000) as follows:

Date	Account and Explanation	Debit	Credit
Dec. 31	Loss Due to Inventory Write-Down	2,500	
	Inventory		2,500
	(*Reduced inventory to net realizable value*)		

			Shareholders' Equity (Loss Due to Inventory
Assets	= Liabilities +		Write-Down)
−2,500			−2,500

The LCNRV rule is an application of the prudence principle. The *prudence principle* leads accountants to select the accounting methods or procedures that produce the lowest (most prudent) net income and net assets in the current period. Thus, accountants tend to recognize expenses and losses as early as possible and to recognize gains and revenues as late as possible. Because it prudently values inventory, the LCNRV rule ensures against overstating the current earnings and financial strength of a company. It does so by recognizing an expense in the period that there is a decline in market value of inventory rather than in the period that the inventory is sold.

YOUDECIDE An Ethical Dilemma Involving Overvalued Inventory

You are the controller for PC Location Ltd., a retailer that operates six computer stores in the Vancouver area. An analysis of year-end inventory reveals a large number of obsolete laptop computers that require a $180,000 write-down to net realizable value. When you inform the CEO of this issue, she reminds you that PC Location is currently negotiating with the bank to increase its long-term loan and that the bank has asked to review PC Location's preliminary financial statements. The CEO asks you to delay recognizing the write-down until the bank has seen the preliminary financial statements. "Let the auditors write down the inventory when they show up in February," she says. "That's what we pay them for."

What should you do in this situation?

If you agree to ignore the required lower of cost and net realizable value adjustment, the bank may decide to grant the loan on the basis of the misleading financial statements. But when they receive the audited financial statements several months later, an investigation will no doubt be launched, and you are likely to take the blame. The ethical course of action is for you to refuse to go along with the CEO. You should be prepared to support your adjustment and to argue the disastrous consequences of trying to mislead the bank. In addition, you should be prepared to present alternatives to proceeding with the new loan at this time. Of course, if you refuse to go along with the CEO, you may find yourself unemployed. However, that is better than having legal action commenced against you as well as possible professional misconduct charges if you are a CPA.

The application of judgment in accounting may lead to ethical dilemmas and legal liability issues.

ANALYZING INVENTORY

OBJECTIVE

Evaluate inventory management using the gross profit and inventory turnover ratios.

Inventories are at the heart of many companies' operations and must be carefully controlled and accounted for. Two measures of how successful a company is at managing and controlling its inventory are the gross profit ratio and the inventory turnover ratio.

concept Q&A

If the IASB allows the value of inventory to be reduced to market value when the net realizable value is less than cost, why can't the value of inventory be increased when the net realizable value is greater than cost?

Answer:

For the same reason that the prudence principle allows inventory to be written down to net realizable value, it prevents inventory from being written up to net realizable value. Given uncertainty as to the actual future selling price of the inventory, a prudent reaction would be to avoid being overly optimistic about the company's future prospects. Overly optimistic projections of the future usually have far more serious negative consequences for people relying on the financial statements than do understatements.

Gross Profit Ratio

The **gross profit ratio** is calculated as:

$$\frac{\text{Gross profit}}{\text{Net sales}} = \text{Gross profit ratio}$$

This ratio is carefully watched by managers, investors, and analysts as a key indicator of a company's ability to sell inventory at a profit. In short, the gross profit ratio tells us how many cents of every dollar are available to cover expenses other than cost of goods sold and to earn a profit. An increasing gross profit ratio could signal that a company is able to charge more for its products due to high demand or that it has effectively controlled the cost of its inventory. A decrease in this ratio could signal trouble. For example, a company may have reduced its selling price due to increased competition or is paying more for its inventory. In these circumstances, management will be expected to develop action plans to increase gross profit, which might include product innovation, product diversification, supplier changes, or outsourcing of work.

Inventory Turnover Ratio

The **inventory turnover ratio** is calculated as:

$$\frac{\text{Cost of goods sold}}{\text{Average inventory}} = \text{Inventory turnover ratio}$$

This ratio describes how quickly inventory is purchased (or produced) and sold. Companies want to satisfy the conflicting goals of having enough inventory on hand to meet customer demand while minimizing the cost of holding inventory (e.g., storage costs, obsolescence). Inventory turnover provides an indicator of how much of the company's funds are tied up in inventory. High inventory turnover ratios indicate that a company is rapidly selling its inventory, thus reducing inventory costs. Low inventory turnover reflects that the company may be holding too much inventory, thereby incurring avoidable costs or signalling that demand for a company's products has fallen, possibly due to inventory obsolescence.

Financial statement users can also compute the **average days to sell inventory** as follows:

$$\frac{365 \text{ days}}{\text{Inventory turnover}} = \text{Average days to sell inventory}$$

An increase in the number of days to sell inventory could indicate that inventory might be overvalued in the financial statements and should be reviewed.

Cornerstone 6.8 illustrates the analysis of these performance measures for Walmart and Target.

Calculating the Gross Profit and Inventory Turnover Ratios

CORNERSTONE 6.8

Information:

The following information is available for two large retailers, Walmart and Target, for the fiscal year ended January 31, 2015 (all amounts in $US millions):

	Walmart	Target
Net sales	$485,651	$72,618
Cost of goods sold	367,638	51,278
Gross profit	118,013	21,340
Inventory, January 31, 2014	44,858	8,278
Inventory, January 31, 2015	45,141	8,790

CORNERSTONE VIDEO

Required:

1. Compute the gross profit ratios for Walmart and Target.

2. Compute the inventory turnover ratios and the average days to sell inventory for Walmart and Target.

Why:

Calculation of the gross profit and inventory turnover ratios indicates the effectiveness of a company's management of inventory, which significantly impacts a company's profit or loss.

Solution:

1. Gross profit ratio $= \dfrac{\text{Gross profit}}{\text{Net sales}}$

Walmart	Target
$\dfrac{\$118,013}{\$485,651} = 24.3\%$	$\dfrac{\$21,340}{\$72,618} = 29.4\%$

(Continued)

CORNERSTONE
6.8

(Continued)

2. Inventory turnover ratio $= \dfrac{\text{Cost of goods sold}}{\text{Average inventory}}$

Walmart	**Target**
$\dfrac{\$367,638}{(\$44,858 + \$45,141) \div 2} = 8.17$ times	$\dfrac{\$51,278}{(\$8,278 + \$8,790) \div 2} = 6.01$ times

Average days to sell inventory $= \dfrac{365 \text{ days}}{\text{Inventory turnover}}$

Walmart	**Target**
$\dfrac{365}{8.17} = 44.7$ days	$\dfrac{365}{6.01} = 60.7$ days

As you can see in Cornerstone 6.8, both Walmart and Target have gross profit ratios below the retail industry average of 31.28%. Target generates a higher gross profit on each dollar of sales (29.4% vs. 24.3%), but Walmart is able to more rapidly sell its inventory (approximately 16 (60.7 − 44.7) days faster than Target). This higher inventory turnover allows Walmart to lower its cost of carrying inventory, which, in addition to greater sales, leads to higher income.

EFFECTS OF INVENTORY ERRORS

OBJECTIVE 7

Explain how errors in ending inventory affect statements of earnings and statements of financial position.

The cost of goods sold model, illustrated in Cornerstone 6.1, describes the relationship between inventory and cost of goods sold. This relationship implies that the measurement of inventory affects both the statement of financial position and the statement of earnings. Even with recent technological advances, it is easy to make errors in determining the cost of the hundreds of items in a typical ending inventory. Incorrect counts, mistakes in costing, and errors in identifying items are common. Because the ending inventory of one period is the beginning inventory of the next period, errors in the measurement of ending inventory affect two accounting periods.

To illustrate the effect of an error in valuing ending inventory on the financial statements, consider the information in Exhibit 6.13. The "Correct" column shows the financial statements for 2017 and 2018 as they would appear if no error were made. The "Erroneous" column shows the financial statements for the two years as they would appear if the firm understated its inventory at December 31, 2017, by $15,000. The "Error" column describes the effect of the error on each line of the statements.

The understatement of the 2017 ending inventory causes an overstatement of 2017 cost of goods sold. Thus, gross margin for 2017 is understated by $15,000. Ignoring income taxes, this error then flows into both net income and retained earnings for 2017. However, the effect is not limited to 2017. Because the ending inventory for 2017 is the beginning inventory for 2018, the beginning inventory for 2018 is understated by $15,000. Assuming that no other errors are made, this leads to an understatement of cost of goods sold and an overstatement of gross margin (and net income) by $15,000 in 2018. However, notice that when this flows into retained earnings, the understatement in 2017 is offset by the overstatement in 2018 so that retained earnings is correctly stated by the end of 2018. This illustrates the self-correcting nature of inventory errors. Cornerstone 6.9 illustrates the analysis of inventory errors.

(EXHIBIT 6.13)

Effect of an Inventory Error

(amounts in thousands)	Correct		Erroneous	Error*
2017 Financial Statements				
Statement of Earnings (partial)				
Sales		$500	$500	
Cost of goods sold:				
Beginning inventory	$ 50		$ 50	
Purchases	250		250	
Cost of goods available for sale	300		300	
Less: Ending inventory	(60)		(45)	−$15
Cost of goods sold		240	255	+$15
Gross margin		$260	$245	−$15
Statement of Financial Position (partial)				
Inventory		$ 60	$ 45	−$15
Retained earnings		100	85	−$15
2018 Financial Statements				
Statement of Earnings (partial)				
Sales		$600	$600	
Cost of goods sold:				
Beginning inventory	$ 60		$ 45	−$15
Purchases	290		290	
Cost of goods available for sale	350		335	−$15
Less: Ending inventory	(50)		(50)	
Cost of goods sold		300	285	−$15
Gross margin		$300	$315	+$15
Statement of Financial Position (partial)				
Inventory		$ 50	$ 50	
Retained earnings		180	180	

*A minus sign (−) indicates an understatement and a plus sign (+) indicates an overstatement.

Analyzing Inventory Errors

CORNERSTONE 6.9

Information:

Dunn Corporation reported net income of $75,000 for 2017. Early in 2018, Dunn discovers that the December 31, 2017, ending inventory was overstated by $6,000.

Required:

Determine the financial statement effects of the inventory errors for 2017 and 2018.

Why:

Errors in the measurement of ending inventory will affect the current period and subsequent period statements of earnings by misstating the cost of goods sold in both periods. They will also affect the current period statement of financial position inventory balance.

CORNERSTONE
VIDEO

(Continued)

CORNERSTONE

6.9

(Continued)

Solution:

For 2017, assets (ending inventory) are overstated by $6,000. The overstatement of ending inventory causes an understatement of cost of goods sold (an expense) by $6,000 in 2017. This error flows through to 2017 income and retained earnings (equity). Because the ending inventory for 2017 is the beginning inventory for 2018, the error has the opposite effects on income for 2018. Assuming no other errors are made, the inventory error self-corrects and the 2018 statement of financial position is correctly stated. These effects are summarized below.

	Assets	Liabilities	Equity	Revenues	Expenses	Income
2017	$6,000 overstated	No effect	$6,000 overstated	No effect	$6,000 understated	$6,000 overstated
2018	No effect	No effect	No effect	No effect	$6,000 overstated	$6,000 understated

Even though inventory errors are self-correcting over two periods, it is still necessary to correct them in order to produce properly stated financial information. If the error is not corrected, both statements of earnings and the 2017 statement of financial position will be incorrect.

INVENTORY TRANSACTIONS IN A PERIODIC SYSTEM

OBJECTIVE **8**

Explain how to record purchases of inventory using a periodic inventory system.

In a periodic inventory system, the inventory records are not maintained continuously or perpetually, up to date. Instead, the inventory account is updated at the end of the period based on a physical count of the inventory on hand. The balance in the inventory account remains unchanged throughout the period. As purchase transactions occur, they are recorded in one of four temporary accounts:

- *Purchases*: The purchases account in the statement of earnings accumulates the cost of the inventory acquired during the period.
- *Purchase Discounts*: The purchase discounts account in the statement of earnings accumulates the amount of discounts on purchases taken during the period.
- *Purchase Returns and Allowances*: The purchase returns and allowances account in the statement of earnings accumulates the cost of any merchandise returned to the supplier or any reductions (allowances) in the purchase price granted by the supplier.
- *Transportation-In*: The transportation-in account in the statement of earnings accumulates the cost paid by the purchaser to transport inventory from suppliers.

The balances in these temporary accounts, along with the beginning and ending inventory balances obtained from the physical count of inventory, are used to compute cost of goods sold using the cost of goods sold model illustrated in Cornerstone 6.1. Cornerstone 6.10 illustrates how to record purchase transactions in a periodic inventory system.

Under either the periodic or the perpetual inventory system, the net cost of purchases (shown below) is the same.

Purchases	$13,750
Less: Purchase discounts	(100)
Purchase returns and allowances	(750)
Add: Transportation costs (freight-in)	150
Net cost of purchases	$13,050

Recording Purchase Transactions in a Periodic Inventory System

CORNERSTONE 6.10

CORNERSTONE VIDEO

Information:

On September 1, Brandon Shoes purchased 50 pairs of hiking boots for $3,750 cash (or $75 a pair) and paid $150 of transportation costs. Also, on September 1, Brandon purchased 100 pairs of running shoes for $10,000; however, the seller paid the transportation costs of $300. The running shoes were purchased on credit with credit terms of 2/10, n/30. Brandon paid for one-half ($5,000) of the running shoes on September 10, within the discount period. The remaining shoes were paid for on September 30. After inspection, Brandon determined that 10 pairs of the hiking boots were defective and returned them on September 30 for a cash refund.

Required:

Prepare the journal entries necessary to record the September transactions for Brandon Shoes, assuming a periodic inventory system.

Why:

The cost of inventory includes the purchase price of the merchandise plus any cost of bringing the goods to a saleable condition and location. The inventory balance on hand at the end of an accounting period for internal reporting purposes can be reasonably estimated using the gross profit method.

Solution:

Date		Account and Explanation	Debit	Credit
Sept.	1	Purchases	3,750	
		Cash		3,750
		(Purchased inventory for cash)		
	1	Transportation-In Expense	150	
		Cash		150
		(Recorded payment of freight costs)		
	1	Purchases	10,000	
		Accounts Payable		10,000
		(Purchased inventory on credit)		
	10	Accounts Payable	5,000	
		Cash		4,900
		Purchase Discounts ($5,000 × 2%)		100
		(Recorded payment within the discount period)		
	30	Accounts Payable	5,000	
		Cash		5,000
		(Recorded payment outside the discount period)		
	30	Cash (10 pairs × $75 per pair)	750	
		Purchase Returns and Allowances		750
		(Returned defective hiking boots)		

Assets = Liabilities + Shareholders' Equity (Purchases)
−3,750   −3,750

Assets = Liabilities + Shareholders' Equity (Transportation-In)
−150   −150

Assets = Liabilities + Equity (Purchases)
+10,000   −10,000

Assets = Liabilities + Shareholders' Equity (Purchase Discounts)
−4,900   −5,000   + 100

Assets = Liabilities + Shareholders' Equity
−5,000   −5,000

Assets = Liabilities + Shareholders' Equity (Purchase Returns and Allowances)
+750   +750

EXHIBIT 6.14

Perpetual vs. Periodic Inventory Systems

Activity	Perpetual System	Periodic System
Purchase	Inventory purchases are recorded in the *inventory account* in the statement of financial position.	The costs of inventory purchases are recorded in the *purchases account* in the statement of earnings.
Sale	When a sale is made, an entry is made to record the amount of sales revenue. *A second entry is made that increases the cost of goods sold account and decreases the inventory account.*	When a sale is made, an entry is made to record the amount of sales revenue only. *No entry is made to cost of goods sold or inventory.*
Costing ending inventory	At the end of the period, the *cost of ending inventory* is the balance in the inventory account (which is verified by a physical count of inventory).	*The amount of ending inventory is determined at the end of the accounting period by taking a physical count of inventory,* a procedure by which all items of inventory on a given date are identified and counted.
Determining cost of goods sold	Cost of goods sold for the period is the balance *in the cost of goods sold account* at the end of the period.	Cost of goods sold is determined only at the end of the period by *applying the cost of goods sold model.*

© Cengage Learning

Additionally, for sales transactions, there is no need to make a second journal entry to record the expense (and inventory) portion of a transaction. Instead, only the revenue portion is recorded, as shown earlier in the text.

The differences between the periodic and perpetual inventory systems are summarized in Exhibit 6.14.

APPENDIX: INVENTORY COSTING METHODS AND THE PERIODIC INVENTORY SYSTEM

OBJECTIVE **9**

(Appendix) Compute ending inventory and cost of goods sold under a periodic inventory system.

Regardless of whether a company uses a perpetual inventory system or a periodic inventory system, inventory costing methods are designed to allocate the cost of goods available for sale between ending inventory and cost of goods sold. Under a periodic inventory system, the inventory costing methods are applied *as if* all purchases during an accounting period take place prior to any sales of the period. While this is not a realistic assumption, it does simplify the computation of the ending inventory and cost of goods sold since only one allocation needs to be made, regardless of the number of purchases and sales. Given this assumption, the following steps can be applied to determine ending inventory and cost of goods sold:

Step 1: Calculate the cost of goods available for sale for the period.
Step 2: Apply the inventory costing method to determine ending inventory and cost of goods sold.

First-In, First-Out (FIFO)

Under the FIFO method, *the earliest purchases (the first-in) are assumed to be the first sold (the first-out) and the more recent purchases are in ending inventory.* Cornerstone 6.11 illustrates the application of the FIFO method. Notice that this is the same information used to illustrate the inventory costing methods applied to a perpetual inventory system (Cornerstones 6.4 through 6.6). However, the information on purchases is listed first and the sales can be combined because all purchases are assumed to occur prior to any sales.

Applying the FIFO Inventory Costing Method in a Periodic Inventory System

CORNERSTONE VIDEO

Information:

Tampico Beachwear, a retail store specializing in beach apparel, has the following information related to purchases and sales of one of its more popular products, Crocs brand shoes. (Each inventory layer is a different colour.)

Date		Description	Units Purchased at Cost	Units Sold at Retail
Oct.	1	Beginning inventory	300 units @ $16 = $ 4,800	
	3	Purchase 1	600 units @ $18 = $10,800	
	8	Sale 1		800 units @ $30
	15	Purchase 2	250 units @ $20 = $ 5,000	
	20	Purchase 3	150 units @ $22 = $ 3,300	
	25	Sale 2		300 units @ $30
			Goods available for sale: 1,300 units = $23,900	Sales: 1,100 units = $33,000

Ending inventory is made up of 200 units (1,300 units available for sale − 1,100 units sold).

Required:

Compute the cost of ending inventory and the cost of goods sold at October 31 using the FIFO method.

Why:

The cost of the earliest purchases that make up cost of goods available for sale is allocated to cost of goods sold, and the cost of the most recent purchases is allocated to ending inventory. During a period of rising prices, the first-in, first-out inventory costing method will provide a greater dollar amount of ending inventory compared to the weighted average method.

Solution:

Step 1: Compute the cost of goods available for sale for the period ($23,900).

Step 2: Apply FIFO to determine ending inventory and cost of goods sold. The cost of goods available for sale is allocated between inventory (the most recent purchases) and cost of goods sold (the earliest purchases) as follows:

Ending Inventory			Cost of Goods Sold		
150 units × $22	=	$3,300	300 units × $16	=	$ 4,800
50 units × $20	=	1,000	600 units × $18	=	10,800
200 units		$4,300	200 units × $20	=	4,000
			1,100 units		$19,600

Weighted Average Cost Method

Under the weighted average cost method, the weighted average cost per unit is multiplied by:

- the number of units in ending inventory to determine the cost of ending inventory
- the number of units sold to determine cost of goods sold

In contrast to the perpetual inventory system, the weighted average cost per unit is not continually calculated. Rather, it is calculated based on the total cost of goods available for sale and the total units available for sale. Cornerstone 6.12 illustrates the application of the weighted average cost method.

CORNERSTONE 6.12

CORNERSTONE VIDEO

Applying the Weighted Average Cost Inventory Costing Method in a Periodic Inventory System

Information:

Tampico Beachwear, a retail store specializing in beach apparel, has the following information related to purchases and sales of one of its more popular products, Crocs brand shoes. (Each inventory layer is a different colour.)

Date		Description	Units Purchased at Cost	Units Sold at Retail
Oct.	1	Beginning inventory	300 units @ $16 = $ 4,800	
	3	Purchase 1	600 units @ $18 = $10,800	
	8	Sale 1		800 units @ $30
	15	Purchase 2	250 units @ $20 = $ 5,000	
	20	Purchase 3	150 units @ $22 = $ 3,300	
	25	Sale 2		300 units @ $30
			Goods available for sale: 1,300 units = $23,900	Sales: 1,100 units = $33,000

Ending inventory is made up of 200 units (1,300 units available for sale − 1,100 units sold).

Required:

Compute the cost of ending inventory and the cost of goods sold at October 31 using the weighted average cost method.

(*Note*: Use four decimal places for per-unit calculations and round all other numbers to the nearest dollar.)

Why:

The cost of goods available for sale is allocated between ending inventory and cost of goods sold based on a weighted average cost of goods available for sale. During a period of rising prices, the weighted average inventory costing method will provide a lower dollar amount of ending inventory compared to the first-in, first-out method.

(Continued)

Solution:

Step 1: Compute the cost of goods available for sale for the period ($23,900).

Step 2: Apply the weighted-average cost method to determine ending inventory and cost of goods sold. This method requires you to compute a weighted average cost of the goods available for sale:

$$\text{Weighted average cost per unit} = \frac{\text{Cost of goods available for sale}}{\text{Units available for sale}}$$

$$= \$23,900 \div 1,300 \text{ units} = \$18.3846 \text{ per unit}$$

The cost of goods available for sale ($23,900) is allocated between inventory and cost of goods sold weighted average cost of the inventory as follows:

Ending Inventory	Cost of Goods Sold
200 units × $18.3846 = $3,677	1,100 units × $18.3846 = **$20,223**

CORNERSTONE
6.12

(Continued)

Under all inventory costing methods, periodic inventory systems allocate the cost of purchased goods between cost of goods sold and ending inventory only at the end of the period. In contrast, the perpetual inventory system performs this allocation each time a sale is made. Due to this difference in the timing of cost allocations, the two systems usually yield different amounts for the cost of goods sold and ending inventory under the weighted average assumption. However, cost of goods sold and ending inventory using FIFO are always the same under both periodic and perpetual inventory systems.[3]

SIGNIFICANT DIFFERENCES BETWEEN IFRS AND ASPE

At the current time, there are no significant differences between IFRS and ASPE with respect to inventory.

[3] This occurs because FIFO always allocates the earliest items purchased to cost of goods sold, resulting in ending inventory being the latest items purchased. Under both the perpetual and periodic inventory systems, these are the same units of inventory at the same cost. Therefore, the timing of the cost allocation is irrelevant under FIFO.

SUMMARY OF LEARNING OBJECTIVES

LO1.   **Explain the types of inventories held by merchandisers and manufacturers, and understand how inventory costs flow through a company.**

- Merchandising companies hold one type of inventory.
- Manufacturing companies have three types of inventory—raw materials, work-in-process, and finished goods.
- When goods are purchased, the cost of the purchase is recorded in inventory (for merchandisers) or raw materials inventory (for manufacturers). During the production process, manufacturers record the cost (raw materials, labour, and overhead) in work-in-process and then transfer the cost to finished goods inventory when the product is complete.

- Once the product is sold, the cost is transferred out of the inventory account (either Inventory or Finished Goods) and into Cost of Goods Sold to match it with Sales Revenue.
- The relationship between inventory and cost of goods sold is described by the cost of goods sold model.

LO2. Explain how to record purchases and sales of inventory using a perpetual inventory system.

- In a perpetual inventory system, purchases of inventory are recorded by increasing the inventory account.
- If a purchase discount exists, inventory is reduced by the amount of the discount taken.
- When a purchased item is returned (purchase return) or a price reduction is granted by the seller (purchase allowance), the inventory item is reduced by the amount of the purchase return or allowance given.
- If transportation costs exist and the shipping terms are FOB shipping point, the transportation costs are considered part of the total cost of purchases and the inventory account is increased.
- If transportation costs exist and the shipping terms are FOB destination, the seller pays these costs and records them as a selling expense on the statement of earnings.
- In a perpetual inventory system, sales require two entries that (1) record the sales revenue and (2) recognize the expense (cost of goods sold) associated with the decrease in inventory.
- If an item is later returned, two entries must also be made: (1) increase Sales Returns and Allowances (a contra-revenue account) and (2) increase the inventory account and decrease Cost of Goods Sold.

LO3. Apply the three inventory costing methods to compute ending inventory and cost of goods sold under a perpetual inventory system.

- The three inventory costing methods are specific identification; first-in, first-out (FIFO); and weighted average cost.
- The specific identification method determines the cost of ending inventory and the cost of goods sold based on the identification of the actual units sold and the units remaining in inventory.
- The other two inventory costing methods allocate cost of goods available for sale between ending inventory and cost of goods sold using the following process.
  - Step 1: Calculate the cost of goods available for sale *immediately prior* to any sales transaction.
  - Step 2: Apply the inventory costing method to determine ending inventory and cost of goods sold.
  - Step 3: Repeat steps 1 and 2 for all inventory transactions during the period. The sum of the cost of goods sold computed in step 2 is the cost of goods sold for the period. Ending inventory is the amount computed during the final application of step 2 for the period.

LO4. Analyze the financial reporting and tax effects of the various inventory costing methods.

- If the prices paid for purchased inventory are stable, all inventory costing methods will yield the same amounts for ending inventory and cost of goods sold.
- When purchase prices vary, FIFO and the weighted average cost methods will produce different amounts for ending inventory, cost of goods sold, and, therefore, income.

- When prices are rising, the FIFO method produces the highest cost for ending inventory, the lowest cost of goods sold, and the highest gross margin (and net income).
- When purchase prices are *falling,* the situation is reversed.

LO5.   Apply the lower of cost and net realizable value rule to the valuation of inventory.

- If the market value of inventory has dropped below its original cost, IFRS and ASPE require a departure from the cost principle.
- A company reduces the amount recorded for inventory to its net realizable value, where net realizable value is defined as expected selling price less estimated selling costs.
- This lower of cost and net realizable value rule is an application of the prudence principle.

LO6.   Evaluate inventory management using the gross profit and inventory turnover ratios.

- Two useful measures of how successful a company is at managing and controlling its inventory are the gross profit ratio (gross profit ÷ net sales) and the inventory turnover ratio (cost of goods sold ÷ average inventory).
- The gross profit ratio indicates how many cents of every dollar are available to cover expenses other than cost of goods sold and to earn a profit. The inventory turnover ratio describes how quickly inventory is purchased (or produced) and sold.

LO7.   Explain how errors in ending inventory affect statements of earnings and statements of financial position.

- Inventory errors can arise for a number of reasons, including incorrect counts of inventory, mistakes in costing, and errors in identifying items.
- Because the ending inventory of one period is the beginning inventory of the next period, an error in the measurement of ending inventory will affect the cost of goods sold and net income of two consecutive periods.
- Inventory errors are self-correcting; therefore, the assets and shareholders' equity of only the first period are misstated (assuming no other errors are made).

LO8.   Explain how to record purchases of inventory using a periodic inventory system.

- In a periodic inventory system, purchases of inventory are recorded by increasing the purchases account.
- If a purchase discount exists, the purchases discount account is increased by the amount of the discount taken.
- When a purchased item is returned (purchase return) or a price reduction is granted by the seller (purchase allowance), the purchase returns and allowances account is increased by the amount of the purchase return or allowance given.
- If transportation costs exist and are paid by the purchaser, the transportation costs are considered part of the total cost of purchases and the transportation or freight-in expense account is increased.

LO9.   *(Appendix)* Compute ending inventory and cost of goods sold under a periodic inventory system.

- Under a periodic inventory system, the inventory costing methods are applied as if all purchases during an accounting period take place prior to any sales of the period. Given this assumption, you will then apply the following steps:
  - Step 1: Calculate the cost of goods available for sale for the period.
  - Step 2: Apply the inventory costing method to determine ending inventory and cost of goods sold.

CORNERSTONES

KEY TERMS

REVIEW PROBLEM

Accounting for Inventory

Concept:

The cost of goods available for sale is allocated between ending inventory and cost of goods sold based on the inventory costing method chosen by management. Under a perpetual inventory system, the accounting records are continuously (perpetually) updated for each sale or purchase of inventory.

Information:

Calgary Supplies, an office supply wholesale store, uses a perpetual inventory system. Calgary recorded the following activity for one of its inventory accounts:

Date		Activity	Number of Units	Cost per Unit
Oct.	1	Beginning inventory	2,500	$16
	15	Purchase	5,100	$17
Nov.	3	Sale	5,900	
	20	Purchase	4,800	$18
Dec.	10	Sale	5,300	

Additional information on the purchases and sales is as follows:

- All purchases were cash purchases.
- All sales were cash sales and all inventory items were sold for $25 per unit.

Required:

1. Compute the cost of ending inventory and the cost of goods sold using the following methods: (a) FIFO and (b) weighted average cost.
2. Assume that Calgary uses the FIFO inventory costing method. Prepare the journal entries to record the purchases and sales of inventory.

Solution:

1.

a. Under FIFO, the cost of ending inventory is $21,600 and cost of goods sold is $191,500 ($97,800 + $93,700).

Date		Description	Cost of Goods Sold	Inventory Balance	
Oct.	1	Beginning inventory		$2,500 \times \$16$	$= \$40,000$
	15	Purchase (5,100 @ $17)		$\left.\begin{array}{l}2{,}500 \times \$16 = \$40{,}000 \\ 5{,}100 \times \$17 = \$86{,}700\end{array}\right\}$	$= \$126{,}700$
Nov.	3	Sale (5,900 @ $25)	$\left.\begin{array}{l}2{,}500 \times \$16 = \$40{,}000 \\ 3{,}400 \times \$17 = \$57{,}800\end{array}\right\} = \$\,\mathbf{97{,}800}$	$1{,}700 \times \$17$	$= \$28{,}900$

This is an interim calculation. Because the period is not over, these steps need to be repeated until the end of the accounting period.

Date		Description	Cost of Goods Sold	Inventory Balance	
Nov.	3	Inventory on hand		$1{,}700 \times \$17$	$= \$28{,}900$
	20	Purchase (4,800 @ $18)		$\left.\begin{array}{l}1{,}700 \times \$17 = \$28{,}900 \\ 4{,}800 \times \$18 = \$86{,}400\end{array}\right\}$	$= \$115{,}300$
Dec.	10	Sale (5,300 @ $25)	$\left.\begin{array}{l}1{,}700 \times \$17 = \$28{,}900 \\ 3{,}600 \times \$18 = \$64{,}800\end{array}\right\} = \$\,\mathbf{93{,}700}$	$1{,}200 \times \$18$	$= \$21{,}600$

(Continued)

b. Under weighted average cost, the cost of ending inventory is $21,183 and cost of goods sold is $191,917 ($98,359 + $93,558).

Date		Description	Cost of Goods Sold	Inventory Balance	
Oct.	1	Beginning inventory		$2,500 \times \$16$	$= \$40,000$ ($16/unit)
	15	Purchase (5,100 @ $17)		$\left.\begin{array}{l} 2{,}500 \times \$16 = \$40{,}000 \\ 5{,}100 \times \$17 = \$86{,}700 \end{array}\right\}$	$= \$126{,}700$ ($16.6711/unit)[a]
Nov.	3	Sale (5,900 @ $25)	$5{,}900 \times \$16.6711 = \mathbf{\$98{,}359}$	$1{,}700 \times \$16.6711$	$= \$28{,}341$

[a] $\$126{,}700 \div 7{,}600 \text{ units} = \$16.6711/\text{unit}$

This is an interim calculation. Because the period is not over, these steps need to be repeated until the end of the accounting period.

Date		Description	Cost of Goods Sold	Inventory Balance	
Nov.	3	Inventory on hand		$1{,}700 \times \$16.6711$	$= \$28{,}341$
	20	Purchase (4,800 @ $18)		$\left.\begin{array}{l} 1{,}700 \times \$16.6711 = \$28{,}341 \\ 4{,}800 \times \$18 \quad = \$86{,}400 \end{array}\right\}$	$= \$114{,}741$ ($17.6525/unit)[b]
Dec.	10	Sale 2 (5,300 @ $25)	$5{,}300 \times \$17.6525 = \mathbf{\$93{,}558}$	$1{,}200 \times \$17.6525$	$= \$21{,}183$

[a] $\$114{,}741 \div 6{,}500 \text{ units} = \$17.6525/\text{unit}$

2.

Assets	= Liabilities +	Shareholders' Equity
+86,700		
−86,700		

Assets	= Liabilities +	Shareholders' Equity (Sales Revenue)
+147,500		+147,500

Assets	= Liabilities +	Shareholders' Equity (Cost of Goods Sold)
−97,800		−97,800

Assets	= Liabilities +	Shareholders' Equity
+86,400		
−86,400		

Assets	= Liabilities +	Shareholders' Equity (Sales Revenue)
+132,500		+132,500

Assets	= Liabilities +	Shareholders' Equity (Cost of Goods Sold)
−93,700		−93,700

Date		Account and Explanation	Debit	Credit
Oct.	15	Inventory	86,700	
		Cash		86,700
		(Purchased inventory for cash)		
Nov.	3	Cash	147,500	
		Sales Revenue		147,500
		(Sold 5,900 units @ $25 per unit)		
	3	Cost of Goods Sold	97,800	
		Inventory		97,800
		(Recorded cost of sale of 5,900 units)		
	20	Inventory	86,400	
		Cash		86,400
		(Purchased inventory for cash)		
Dec.	10	Cash	132,500	
		Sales Revenue		132,500
		(Sold 5,300 units @ $25 per unit)		
	10	Cost of Goods Sold	93,700	
		Inventory		93,700
		(Recorded cost of sale of 5,300 units)		

DISCUSSION QUESTIONS

1. What are the differences between merchandisers and manufacturers?

2. Describe the types of inventories used by manufacturers and merchandisers.

3. Compare the flow of inventory costs between merchandisers and manufacturers.

4. What are components of cost of goods available for sale and cost of goods sold?

5. How is cost of goods sold determined?

6. How do the perpetual and periodic inventory accounting systems differ from each other?

7. Why are perpetual inventory systems more expensive to operate than periodic inventory systems? What conditions justify the additional cost of a perpetual inventory system?

8. Why are adjustments made to the invoice price of goods when determining the cost of inventory?

9. Identify the accounting items for which adjustments are made to the invoice price of goods when determining the net cost of purchases.

10. Describe the difference between FOB shipping point and FOB destination.

11. Why do sales transactions under a perpetual inventory system require two journal entries?

12. Why do the three inventory costing methods produce different amounts for the cost of ending inventory and cost of goods sold?

13. The costs of which units of inventory (oldest or newest) are allocated to ending inventory or cost of goods sold using the FIFO and weighted average cost methods?

14. If inventory prices are rising, which inventory costing method should produce the smallest payment for taxes?

15. How would reported income differ if weighted average rather than FIFO were used when purchase prices were rising? When purchase prices were falling?

16. How would the statement of financial position accounts be affected if weighted average rather than FIFO were used when purchase prices were rising? When purchase prices were falling?

17. Why are inventories written down to the lower of cost and net realizable value?

18. What is the effect on the current period statement of earnings and the statement of financial position when inventories are written down using the lower of cost and net realizable value method? What is the effect on future-period statements of earnings and statements of financial position?

19. What do the gross profit and inventory turnover ratios tell company management about inventory?

20. How does an error in the determination of ending inventory affect the financial statements of two periods?

21. What accounts are used to record inventory purchase transactions under the periodic inventory system? Why aren't these accounts used in a perpetual inventory system?

22. *(Appendix)* "For each inventory costing method, perpetual and periodic systems yield the same amounts for ending inventory and cost of goods sold." Do you agree or disagree with this statement? Explain.

MULTIPLE-CHOICE EXERCISES

6-1 If beginning inventory is $40,000, purchases is $215,000, and ending inventory is $35,000, what is cost of goods sold as determined by the cost of goods sold model?
   a. $140,000
   b. $210,000
   c. $220,000
   d. $290,000

6-2 Which of the following transactions would not result in an entry to the inventory account in the buyer's accounting records under a perpetual inventory system?
   a. The purchase of merchandise on credit
   b. The return of merchandise to the supplier

(Continued)

c. The payment of a credit purchase of merchandise within the discount period

d. The payment of freight by the supplier for goods received by the buyer.

6-3 Razor Company purchased $15,000 of inventory on credit with credit terms of 2/10, n/30. Razor paid for the purchase within the discount period. How much did Razor pay for the inventory?

a. $14,700

b. $14,850

c. $15,000

d. $15,300

6-4 Which of the following transactions would not result in an adjustment to the inventory account under a perpetual inventory system?

a. The sale of merchandise for cash

b. The sale of merchandise on credit

c. The receipt of payment from a customer within the discount period

d. The return of merchandise by a customer

6-5 U-Save Automotive Group purchased 10 vehicles during the current month. Two trucks were purchased for $20,000 each, two SUVs were purchased for $31,000 each, and six hybrid cars were purchased for $27,000 each. A review of the sales invoices revealed that five of the hybrid cars were sold and that both trucks were sold. What is the cost of U-Save's ending inventory if it uses the specific identification method?

a. $89,000

b. $129,000

c. $135,000

d. $175,000

6-6 Morgenstern Ltd. has the following units and costs for the month of April.

1. Beginning inventory, April 1, 1,000 units at $20 (Cost)

2. Purchase (1) April 9, 1,200 units at $23 (cost)

3. Sold, April 12 2,100 units at $40 (Retail)

4. Purchase (2), April 22 800 units at $25 (Cost)

If Morgenstern uses a perpetual inventory system, what is the cost of ending inventory under FIFO at April 30?

a. $18,000

b. $22,300

c. $45,300

d. $49,600

6-7 Refer to the information in Multiple-Choice Exercise 6.6 above. If Morgenstern uses a perpetual inventory system, what is the cost of ending inventory under weighted average cost at April 30? (*Note:* Use four decimal places for per-unit calculations and round to the nearest dollar.)

a. $20,280

b. $22,164

c. $45,436

d. $47,320

6-8 When purchase prices are rising, which of the following statements is true?

a. LIFO produces a higher cost of goods sold than FIFO.

b. LIFO produces a higher cost for ending inventory than FIFO.

c. FIFO produces a lower amount for net income than LIFO.

d. Weighted average cost produces a higher net income than FIFO or LIFO.

6-9 Which method results in a more realistic amount for income because it matches the most current costs against revenue?

a. FIFO

b. Weighted average cost

c. Specific identification

d. LIFO

6-10 Which of the following statements regarding the lower of cost and net realizable value (LCNRV) rule is true?

a. The LCNRV rule is an application of the cost principle.

b. When the replacement cost of inventory drops below the cost of inventory, an adjustment is made to decrease inventory to its net realizable value and decrease income.

c. If a company uses the LCNRV rule, there is no need to use a cost flow assumption such as FIFO, or weighted average cost.

d. When the net realizable value of inventory is above the cost of inventory, an adjustment is made to increase inventory to its net realizable value and increase income.

6-11 Which of the following statements is true with regard to the gross profit ratio?

1. An increase in cost of goods sold would increase the gross profit ratio (assuming sales remain constant).
2. An increase in the gross profit ratio may indicate that a company is efficiently managing its inventory.
3. An increase in selling expenses would lower the gross profit ratio.

   a. 1
   b. 2
   c. 1 and 2
   d. 2 and 3

6-12 An increasing inventory turnover ratio indicates that:

a. a company has reduced the time it takes to purchase and sell inventory.
b. a company is having trouble selling its inventory.
c. a company may be holding too much inventory.
d. a company has sold inventory at a higher profit.

6-13 Ignoring taxes, if a company understates its ending inventory by $10,000 in the current year,

a. assets for the current year will be overstated by $10,000.
b. net income for the subsequent year will be overstated by $10,000.
c. cost of goods sold for the current year will be understated by $10,000.
d. retained earnings for the current year will be unaffected.

6-14 Which of the following statements is true for a company that uses a periodic inventory system?

a. The purchase of inventory requires a debit to Inventory.
b. The return of defective inventory requires a debit to Purchase Returns and Allowances.
c. The payment of a purchase within the discount period requires a credit to Purchase Discounts.
d. Any amounts paid for freight are debited to Inventory.

6-15 Lee Ltd. has the following units and costs for the month of April.

1. Beginning inventory, April 1, 1,000 units at $20 (Cost)
2. Purchase (1) April 9, 1,200 units at $23 (cost)
3. Sold 1, April 12, 2,100 units at $40 (Retail)
4. Purchase 2, April 22, 800 units at $25 (Cost)

If Lee uses a periodic inventory system, what is the cost of goods sold under FIFO at April 30?

a. $18,000
b. $22,300
c. $45,300
d. $49,600

6-16 Refer to the information for Multiple-Choice Exercise 6.15 above. If Lee uses a periodic inventory system, what is the cost of ending inventory under weighted average cost at April 30? (*Note:* Use four decimal places for per-unit calculations and round all other numbers to the nearest dollar.)

a. $20,280
b. $22,164
c. $45,436
d. $47,320

CORNERSTONE EXERCISES

Cornerstone Exercise 6-17   Applying the Cost of Goods Sold Model

Charest Company has the following data for 2018.

OBJECTIVE

CORNERSTONE 6.1

Item	Units	Cost
Inventory, 12/31/2017	980	$10,780
Purchases	4,480	49,280
Inventory, 12/31/2018	750	8,250

(Continued)

Required:

1. How many units were sold?
2. Using the cost of goods sold model, determine the cost of goods sold.

Cornerstone Exercise 6-18   Recording Purchase Transactions

Jeet Company and Reece Company use the perpetual inventory system. The following transactions occurred during the month of April.

a. On April 1, Jeet purchased merchandise on account from Reece with credit terms of 2/10, n/30. The selling price of the merchandise was $3,100, and the cost of the merchandise sold was $2,225.
b. On April 1, Jeet paid freight charges of $250 cash to have the goods delivered to its warehouse.
c. On April 8, Jeet returned $800 of the merchandise. The cost of the merchandise returned was $500.
d. On April 10, Jeet paid Reece the balance due.

Required:

1. Prepare the journal entries to record the April 1 purchase of merchandise and payment of freight by Jeet.
2. Prepare the journal entry to record the April 8 return of merchandise by Jeet.
3. Prepare the journal entry to record the April 10 payment to Reece by Jeet.

OBJECTIVE ❷
CORNERSTONE 6.3

Cornerstone Exercise 6-19   Recording Sales Transactions

Refer to the information for Cornerstone Exercise 6-18 above.

Required:

Prepare the journal entries to record these transactions on the books of Reece Company.

OBJECTIVE ❸
CORNERSTONE 6.5

Cornerstone Exercise 6-20   Inventory Costing: FIFO

Filimonov Inc. has the following information related to purchases and sales of one of its inventory items.

Date		Description	Units Purchased at Cost	Units Sold at Retail
June	1	Beginning inventory	200 units @ $10 = $2,000	
	9	Purchase 1	300 units @ $12 = $3,600	
	14	Sale 1		400 units @ $25
	22	Purchase 2	250 units @ $14 = $3,500	
	29	Sale 2		225 units @ $25

The company uses a perpetual inventory system.

Required:

Calculate the cost of goods sold and the cost of ending inventory using the FIFO inventory costing method.

Cornerstone Exercise 6-21   Inventory Costing: Weighted Average Cost

Refer to the information for Cornerstone Exercise 6-20 above. The company uses a perpetual inventory system.

Required:

Calculate the cost of goods sold and the cost of ending inventory using the weighted average cost method. (*Note:* Use four decimal places for per-unit calculations and round all other numbers to the nearest dollar.)

Cornerstone Exercise 6-22   Effects of Inventory Costing Methods

OBJECTIVE ❹
CORNERSTONE 6.6
CORNERSTONE 6.7

Refer to your answers for Filimonov Inc. in Cornerstone **Exercises 6-20 and 6-21 above**.

Required:

1. In a period of rising prices, which inventory costing method produces the highest amount for ending inventory?
2. In a period of rising prices, which inventory costing method produces the highest net income?
3. In a period of rising prices, which inventory costing method produces the lowest payment for income taxes?
4. In a period of rising prices, which inventory method generally produces the most realistic amount for cost of goods sold? For inventory? Would your answer change if inventory prices were decreasing during the period?

Cornerstone Exercise 6-23   Lower of Cost and Net Realizable Value

OBJECTIVE ❺
CORNERSTONE 6.7

The accountant for Lahore Company prepared the following analysis of its inventory at year-end.

Item	Units	Cost per Unit	Net Realizable Value
RSK-89013	500	$36	$44
LKW-91247	329	49	41
QEC-57429	462	29	33

Required:

1. Compute the carrying value of the ending inventory using the lower of cost and net realizable value method applied on an item-by-item basis.
2. Prepare the journal entry required to value the inventory at lower of cost and net realizable value.

Cornerstone Exercise 6-24   Inventory Analysis

OBJECTIVE ❻
CORNERSTONE 6.8

Singleton Ltd. reported the following information for the current year.

Net sales	$650,000	Inventory, 1/1	$21,250
Cost of goods sold	495,000	Inventory, 12/31	24,850
Gross profit	$155,000		

Required:

Compute Singleton's (a) gross profit ratio, (b) inventory turnover ratio, and (c) average days to sell inventory. (*Note:* Round all answers to two decimal places.)

Cornerstone Exercise 6-25   Inventory Errors

OBJECTIVE ❼
CORNERSTONE 6.9

Lhasa Corp. reported net income of $150,000 for 2018 and $165,000 for 2019. Early in 2019, McLelland discovers that the December 31, 2018, ending inventory was overstated by $15,000. For simplicity, ignore taxes.

Required:

1. What is the correct net income for 2018? For 2019?
2. Assuming the error was not corrected, what is the effect on the statement of financial position at December 31, 2018? At December 31, 2019?

Cornerstone Exercise 6-26   (*Appendix*) Recording Purchase Transactions

OBJECTIVE ❽
CORNERSTONE 6.10

Refer to the information for Jeet Company in Cornerstone Exercise 6-18 above and assume that Jeet uses a periodic inventory system.

(Continued)

Required:

1. Prepare the journal entry to record the April 1 purchase of merchandise and payment of freight by Jeet.
2. Prepare the journal entry to record the April 8 return of merchandise.
3. Prepare the journal entry to record the April 10 payment to Reece.

OBJECTIVE **9**
CORNERSTONE 6.11

Cornerstone Exercise 6-27   *(Appendix)* Inventory Costing Methods: Periodic FIFO

Refer to the information for Filimonov Inc. in Cornerstone Exercise 6-20 above and assume that the company uses a periodic inventory system.

Required:

Calculate the cost of goods sold and the cost of ending inventory using the FIFO inventory costing method.

OBJECTIVE **9**
CORNERSTONE 6.12

Cornerstone Exercise 6-28   *(Appendix)* Inventory Costing Methods: Periodic Weighted Average Cost

Refer to the information for Filimonov Inc. in Cornerstone Exercise 6-20 above and assume that the company uses a periodic inventory system.

Required:

Calculate the cost of goods sold and the cost of ending inventory using the weighted average cost method. (*Note:* Use four decimal places for per-unit calculations and round all other numbers to the nearest dollar.)

BRIEF EXERCISES

OBJECTIVE **1**

Brief Exercise 6-29   Applying the Cost of Goods Sold Model

Milton Company reported inventory of $60,000 at the beginning of 2018. During the year, it purchased inventory of $625,000 and sold inventory for $950,000. A count of inventory at the end of the year determined that the cost of inventory on hand was $50,000.

Required:

1. What was Milton's cost of goods sold for 2018?
2. What is Milton's gross margin for the year?

OBJECTIVE **2**

Brief Exercise 6-30   Recording Purchase and Sales Transactions

Raymond Company and Geeslin Company both use a perpetual inventory system. The following transactions occurred during the month of January:

Jan. 1   Raymond purchased $5,000 of merchandise on account from Geeslin with credit terms of 2/10, n/30. The cost of the merchandise was $3,750.
  8   Raymond returned $500 of the merchandise to Geeslin. The cost of the merchandise returned was $375.
  10   Raymond paid invoices totalling $3,000 to Geeslin for the merchandise purchased on January 1.
  30   Raymond paid Geeslin the balance due.

Required:

Prepare the journal entries to record these transactions on the books of Raymond and Geeslin.

Use the following information for Brief Exercises 6.31 and 6.32.

Tyler Company has the following information related to purchases and sales of one of its inventory items.

Date		Description	Units Purchased at Cost	Units Sold at Retail
Sept.	1	Beginning inventory	20 units @ $5	
	9	Purchase	30 units @ $8	
	14	Sale		40 units @ $15
	22	Purchase	25 units @ $10	

Brief Exercise 6-31   Inventory Costing Methods

OBJECTIVE **3**

Refer to the information for Tyler Company above and assume the company uses a perpetual inventory system.

Required:

Calculate ending inventory and cost of goods sold using the FIFO and weighted average methods.

Brief Exercise 6-32   Effects of Inventory Costing Methods

OBJECTIVE **4**

Refer to the information for Tyler Company above.

Required:

1. Which inventory costing method produces the highest amount for net income?
2. Which inventory costing method produces the highest amount for ending inventory?
3. How would your answers to Requirements 1 and 2 change if inventory prices declined during the period?

Brief Exercise 6-33   Lower of Cost and Net Realizable Value

OBJECTIVE **5**

Garcia Company's inventory at the end of the year was recorded in its accounting records at $17,800. Due to technological changes in the market, Garcia would be able to replace its inventory for $16,500.

Required:

1. Using the lower of cost and net realizable value, what amount should Garcia report for inventory on its statement of financial position at the end of the year?
2. Prepare the journal entry required to value the inventory at the lower of cost and net realizable value.

Brief Exercise 6-34   Inventory Analysis

OBJECTIVE **6**

Callahan Company reported the following information for the current year:

Net sales revenue	$280,000
Cost of goods sold	120,000
Beginning inventory	5,000
Ending inventory	10,000

Required:

1. Compute Callahan's (a) gross profit ratio, (b) inventory turnover ratio, and (c) average days to sell inventory. (*Note:* Round all answers to two decimal places.)
2. Explain the meaning of each number.

Brief Exercise 6-35   Inventory Errors

OBJECTIVE **7**

Haywood Inc. reported the following information for 2018:

Beginning inventory	$ 25,000
Ending inventory	50,000
Sales revenue	1,000,000
Cost of goods sold	620,000

(Continued)

A physical count of inventory at the end of the year showed that ending inventory was actually $65,000.

Required:

1. What is the correct cost of goods sold and gross profit for 2018?
2. Assuming the error was not corrected, what is the effect on the statement of financial position at December 31, 2018? At December 31, 2019?

OBJECTIVE ⑨

Brief Exercise 6-36   *(Appendix)* Recording Purchase and Sales Transactions

Refer to the information for Raymond Company in Brief Exercise 6-30 and assume that the company uses the periodic inventory system.

Required:

Prepare the journal entries to record these transactions on the books of Raymond Company.

OBJECTIVE ⑨

Brief Exercise 6-37   *(Appendix)* Inventory Costing Methods: Periodic Inventory Systems.

Refer to the information for Tyler Company in Brief Exercise 6-31 and assume that the company uses the periodic inventory system.

Required:

Calculate the cost of goods sold and the cost of ending inventory using the FIFO and weighted average cost methods. (*Note:* Use four decimal places for per-unit calculations and round all other numbers to the nearest whole dollar.)

EXERCISES

OBJECTIVE ①

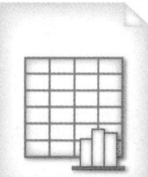

Exercise 6-38   Applying the Cost of Goods Sold Model

Wong Company sells a single product. At the beginning of the year, Wong had 150 units in stock at a cost of $8 each. During the year, Wong purchased 825 more units at a cost of $8 each and sold 240 units at $13 each, 210 units at $15 each, and 335 units at $14 each.

Required:

1. Using the cost of goods sold model, what is the amount of ending inventory and cost of goods sold?
2. What is Wong's gross margin for the year?

OBJECTIVE ①

ILLUSTRATING
RELATIONSHIPS

Exercise 6-39   Applying the Cost of Goods Sold Model

The following amounts were obtained from the accounting records of Steed Company.

	2016	2017	2018
Beginning inventory	$10,400	(b)	(d)
Net purchases	(a)	$52,100	$54,600
Ending inventory	9,800	(c)	12,350
Cost of goods sold	46,200	48,700	(e)

Required:

Compute the missing amounts.

Exercise 6-40 Perpetual and Periodic Inventory Systems

OBJECTIVE 2 8

Below is a list of inventory systems options.

a. Perpetual inventory system
b. Periodic inventory system
c. Both perpetual and periodic inventory systems

Required:

Match each option with one of the following:

1. Only revenue is recorded as sales are made during the period; the cost of goods sold is recorded at the end of the period.
2. Cost of goods sold is determined as each sale is made.
3. Inventory purchases are recorded in an inventory account.
4. Inventory purchases are recorded in a purchases account.
5. Cost of goods sold is determined only at the end of the period by subtracting the cost of ending inventory from the cost of goods available for sale.
6. Both revenue and cost of goods sold are recorded during the period as sales are made.
7. The inventory is verified by a physical count.

Exercise 6-41 Recording Purchases

OBJECTIVE 2

Compass Inc. purchased 1,250 bags of insulation from Glassco Corp. The bags of insulation cost $5.50 each. Compass paid Tremblay Trucking $320 to have the bags of insulation shipped to its warehouse. Compass returned 50 bags that were defective and paid for the remainder. Assume that Compass uses the perpetual inventory system and that Glassco did not offer a purchase discount. (Note: You are doing the accounting for Compass Inc.)

Required:

1. Prepare the journal entry to record the purchase of the bags of insulation.
2. Prepare the entry to record the payment for shipping.
3. Prepare the entry for the return of the defective bags.
4. Prepare the entry to record the payment for the bags kept by Compass.
5. What is the total cost of this purchase?

Exercise 6-42 Recording Purchases

OBJECTIVE 2

Doha Enterprises uses the perpetual system to record inventory transactions. In a recent month, Doha engaged in the following transactions.

a. On April 1, Doha purchased merchandise on credit for $25,150 with terms 2/10, n/30.
b. On April 2, Doha purchased merchandise on credit for $28,200 with terms 3/15, n/25.
c. On April 9, Doha paid for the purchase made on April 1.
d. On April 25, Doha paid for the merchandise purchased on April 2.

Required:

Prepare journal entries for these four transactions.

Exercise 6-43 Recording Purchases and Shipping Terms

OBJECTIVE 2

On May 12, Digital Distributors received three shipments of merchandise. The first was shipped FOB shipping point, had a total invoice price of $142,500, and was delivered by a trucking company that charged an additional $8,300 for transportation charges. The second was shipped FOB shipping point and had a total invoice price of $87,250, including transportation charges of $5,700 that were prepaid by the seller. The third shipment was shipped FOB destination and had an invoice price of $21,650, excluding transportation charges of $1,125 paid by the seller. Digital uses a perpetual inventory system. Digital has not paid any of the invoices.

(Continued)

Required:

Prepare journal entries to record these purchases.

OBJECTIVE **2**

Exercise 6-44   Recording Sales and Shipping Terms

Milano Company shipped the following merchandise during the last week of December 2018. All sales were on credit.

Sales Price	Shipping Terms	Date Goods Shipped	Date Goods Received
$5,460	FOB shipping point	December 27	January 3
$3,800	FOB destination	December 29	January 5
$4,250	FOB destination	December 29	December 31

Required:

YOU**DECIDE**

1. Compute the total amount of sales revenue recognized by Milano from these transactions.
2. If Milano included all of the above shipments as revenue, what would be the effect on the financial statements?

OBJECTIVE **2**

Exercise 6-45   Recording Purchases and Sales

Printer Supply Company sells computer printers and printer supplies. One of its products is a toner cartridge for laser printers. At the beginning of 2018, there were 225 cartridges on hand that cost $62 each. During 2018, Printer Supply purchased 1,475 cartridges at $62 each. After inspection, Printer Supply determined that 15 cartridges were defective and returned them to the supplier. Printer Supply also sold 830 cartridges at $95 each and sold an additional 710 cartridges at $102 each after a mid-year selling price increase. Customers returned 20 of the cartridges that were purchased at $102 to Printer Supply for various reasons. Assume that Printer Supply uses a perpetual inventory system.

Required:

1. Prepare summary journal entries to record the purchases, sales, and return of inventory. Assume that all purchases and sales are on credit but that no discounts were offered.
2. What is the cost of ending inventory, cost of goods sold, and gross profit for 2018?

OBJECTIVE **3** **4**

Exercise 6-46   Inventory Costing Methods

Crandall Distributors uses a perpetual inventory system and has the following data available for inventory, purchases, and sales for a recent year.

Activity	Units	Purchase Price (per unit)	Sale Price (per unit)
Beginning inventory	110	$5.90	
Purchase 1, Jan. 18	575	6.00	
Sale 1	380		$8.80
Sale 2	225		9.00
Purchase 2, Mar. 10	680	6.20	
Sale 3	270		9.00
Sale 4	290		9.50
Purchase 3, Sept. 30	230	6.30	
Sale 5	240		9.90

Required:

1. Compute the cost of ending inventory and the cost of goods sold using the specific identification method. Assume the ending inventory is made up of 40 units from beginning inventory, 30 units from purchase 1, 80 units from purchase 2, and 40 units from purchase 3.
2. Compute the cost of ending inventory and cost of goods sold using the FIFO inventory costing method.

3. Compute the cost of ending inventory and cost of goods sold using the weighted average cost method. (*Note:* Use four decimal places for per-unit calculations and round all other numbers to the nearest dollar.)
4. **CONCEPTUAL CONNECTION** Compare the ending inventory and cost of goods sold computed under all three methods. What can you conclude about the effects of the inventory costing methods on the statement of financial position and the statement of earnings?

Exercise 6-47   Inventory Costing Methods

OBJECTIVE 3 4 6

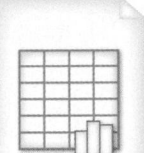

On June 1, Welding Products Company had a beginning inventory of 210 cases of welding rods that had been purchased for $88 per case. Welding Products purchased 1,150 cases at a cost of $95 per case on June 3. On June 19, the company purchased another 950 cases at a cost of $112 per case. Sales data for the welding rods are as follows:

Date	Cases Sold
June 9	990
June 29	975

Welding Products uses a perpetual inventory system, and the sales price of the welding rods was $130 per case.

Required:

1. Compute the cost of ending inventory and cost of goods sold using the FIFO method.
2. Compute the cost of ending inventory and cost of goods sold using the weighted average cost method. (*Note:* Use four decimal places for per-unit calculations and round all other numbers to the nearest dollar.)
3. **CONCEPTUAL CONNECTION** Assume that operating expenses are $21,600 and that Welding Products has a 30% tax rate. How much will the cash paid for income taxes differ between the two inventory methods?
4. **CONCEPTUAL CONNECTION** Compute Welding Products' gross profit ratio (rounded to two decimal places) and inventory turnover ratio (rounded to three decimal places) under both inventory costing methods. How would the choice of inventory costing method affect these ratios?

Exercise 6-48   Financial Statement Effects of FIFO and Weighted Average

OBJECTIVE 3 4

The chart below lists financial statement items that may be affected by the use of either the FIFO or weighted average inventory costing methods.

	FIFO	Weighted Average
Ending inventory		
Cost of goods sold		
Gross margin		
Income before taxes		
Payments for income taxes		
Net income		

Required:

Assuming that prices are rising, complete the chart by indicating whether the specified item is (a) higher or (b) lower under FIFO and weighted average.

YOUDECIDE

Exercise 6-49   Effects of Inventory Costing Methods

OBJECTIVE 4

Borgia Enterprises has the following statement of earnings data available for 2018:

Sales revenue	$737,200
Operating expenses	243,700
Interest expense	39,500
Income tax rate	34%

(Continued)

Borgia uses a perpetual inventory accounting system and the weighted average cost method. Borgia is considering adopting the FIFO method for costing inventory. Borgia's accountant prepared the following data:

	If Weighted Average Cost Used	If FIFO Used
Ending inventory	$ 61,850	$ 80,200
Cost of goods sold	403,150	384,800

Required:

1. Compute income before taxes, income tax expense, and net income for both of the inventory costing methods (rounded to the nearest dollar).
2. **CONCEPTUAL CONNECTION** Why are the cost of goods sold and ending inventory amounts different for each of the two methods? What do these amounts tell us about the purchase price of inventory during the year?
3. **CONCEPTUAL CONNECTION** Which method produces the most realistic amount for net income? For inventory? Explain your answer.

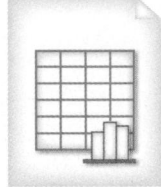

Exercise 6-50   Inventory Costing Methods

Neyman Ltd. has the following data for purchases and sales of inventory:

Date	Units	Cost per Unit
Beginning inventory	22	$400
Purchase 1, Feb. 24	130	370
Sale 1	145	
Purchase 2, July 2	180	330
Purchase 3, Oct. 31	90	250
Sale 2	265	

All sales were made at a sales price of $450 per unit. Assume that Neyman uses a perpetual inventory system.

Required:

1. Compute the cost of goods sold and the cost of ending inventory using the FIFO and weighted average cost methods. (*Note:* Use four decimal places for per-unit calculations and round all other numbers to the nearest dollar.)
2. **CONCEPTUAL CONNECTION** Why is the cost of goods sold lower with weighted average than with FIFO?

Exercise 6-51   Effects of FIFO and Weighted Average

Sheepskin Company sells to colleges and universities a special paper that is used for diplomas. Sheepskin typically makes one purchase of the special paper each year on January 1. Assume that Sheepskin uses a perpetual inventory system. You have the following data for the three years ended in 2018:

2016	
Beginning inventory	0 pages
Purchases	10,000 pages at $1.60 per page
Sales	8,500 pages
2017	
Beginning inventory	1,500 pages
Purchases	16,200 pages at $2.00 per page
Sales	15,000 pages
2018	
Beginning inventory	2,700 pages
Purchases	18,000 pages at $2.50 per page
Sales	20,100 pages

Required:

1. What would the ending inventory and cost of goods sold be for each year if FIFO is used?
2. What would the ending inventory and cost of goods sold be for each year if weighted average is used?
3. **CONCEPTUAL CONNECTION** For each year, explain the cause of the differences in cost of goods sold under FIFO and weighted average.

Exercise 6-52   Lower of Cost and Net Realizable Value

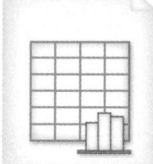

OBJECTIVE 5

Meredith's Appliance Store has the following data for the items in its inventory at the end of the accounting period:

Item	Number of Units	Historical Cost per Unit	Net Realizable Value per Unit
Window air conditioner	18	$194	$110
Dishwasher	30	240	380
Refrigerator	27	415	405
Microwave	19	215	180
Washer (clothing)	32	195	248
Dryer (clothing)	21	197	245

Required:

1. Compute the carrying value of Meredith's ending inventory using the lower of cost and net realizable value (LCNRV) rule applied on an item-by-item basis.
2. Prepare the journal entry required to value the inventory at LCNRV.
3. **CONCEPTUAL CONNECTION** What is the conceptual justification for valuing inventory at LCNRV?

Exercise 6-53   Lower of Cost and Net Realizable Value

OBJECTIVE 5

Silk Road Systems sells a limited line of specially made products, using television advertising campaigns in large cities. At year-end, Silk Road has the following data for its inventory:

Item	Number of Units	Historical Cost per Unit	Net Realizable Value per Unit
Phone	625	$ 24	$ 20
Stereo	180	177	190
Electric shaver	215	30	28
MP3 alarm clock	450	26	25
Handheld game system	570	40	42

Required:

1. Compute the carrying value of the ending inventory using the LCNRV rule applied on an item-by-item basis.
2. Prepare the journal entry required to value the inventory at LCNRV.
3. **CONCEPTUAL CONNECTION** What is the impact of applying the LCNRV rule on the financial statements of the current period? What is the impact on the financial statements of a subsequent period in which the inventory is sold?

Exercise 6-54   Analyzing Inventory

OBJECTIVE 6

The recent financial statements of Tunis Clothing Ltd. include the following data.

Sales	$754,690
Cost of goods sold:	
Computed under FIFO	528,600
Computed under weighted average	555,000
Average inventory:	
Computed under FIFO	72,200
Computed under weighted average	45,800

(Continued)

Required:

1. Calculate Tunis's gross profit ratio (rounded to two decimal places), inventory turnover ratio (rounded to three decimal places), and the average days to sell inventory (assume a 365-day year and round to two decimal places) using the FIFO inventory costing method. Be sure to explain what each ratio means.
2. Calculate Tunis's gross profit ratio (rounded to two decimal places), inventory turnover ratio (rounded to three decimal places), and the average days to sell inventory (assume a 365-day year and round to two decimal places) using the weighted average inventory costing method. Be sure to explain what each ratio means.
3. **CONCEPTUAL CONNECTION** Which ratios—the ones computed using FIFO or weighted average inventory values—provide the better indicator of how successful Tunis was at managing and controlling its inventory?

OBJECTIVE 7  **Exercise 6-55   Effects of an Error in Ending Inventory**

Waymire Company prepared the partial statements of earnings presented below for 2018 and 2017.

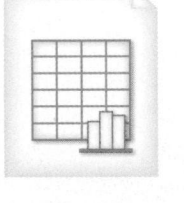

	2018		2017	
Sales revenue		$ 538,200		$ 483,700
Cost of goods sold:				
Beginning inventory	$ 39,300		$ 32,100	
Purchases	343,200		292,700	
Cost of goods available for sale	382,500		324,800	
Ending inventory	(46,800)	335,700	(39,300)	285,500
Gross margin		202,500		198,200
Operating expenses		(167,200)		(151,600)
Income before taxes		$ 35,300		$ 46,600

During 2019, Waymire's accountant discovered that ending inventory for 2017 had been overstated by $8,200.

Required:

1. Prepare corrected statements of earnings for 2018 and 2017.
2. Prepare a schedule showing each financial statement item affected by the error and the amount of the error for that item. Indicate whether each error is an overstatement (+) or an understatement (–).

OBJECTIVE 8  **Exercise 6-56   Recording Purchases**

Compass Inc. purchased 1,250 bags of insulation from Glassco Corporation on account. The bags of insulation cost $5.50 each. Compass paid Tremblay Trucking $320 to have the bags of insulation shipped to its warehouse. Compass returned 50 bags that were defective and paid for the remainder. Assume that Compass uses the periodic inventory system.

Required:

1. Prepare the journal entry to record the purchase of the bags of insulation.
2. Prepare the entry to record the payment for shipping.
3. Prepare the entry for the return of the defective bags.
4. Prepare the entry to record the payment for the bags kept by Compass.
5. What is the total cost of this purchase?
6. **CONCEPTUAL CONNECTION** If you have previously worked Exercise 6-41, compare your answers. What are the differences? Be sure to explain why the differences occurred.

Exercise 6-57 (Appendix) Recording Purchases and Sales

OBJECTIVE 8 9

Printer Supply Company sells computer printers and printer supplies. One of its products is a toner cartridge for laser printers. At the beginning of 2018, there were 225 cartridges on hand that cost $62 each. During 2018, Printer Supply purchased 1,475 cartridges at $62 each, sold 830 cartridges at $95 each, and sold an additional 710 cartridges at $102 each after a mid-year selling price increase. Printer Supply returned 15 defective cartridges to the supplier. In addition, customers returned 20 cartridges that were purchased at $102 to Printer Supply for various reasons. Assume that Printer Supply uses a periodic inventory system.

Required:

1. Prepare journal entries to record the purchases, sales, and return of inventory. Assume that all purchases and sales are on credit but no discounts were offered.
2. What is the cost of inventory, cost of goods sold, and gross profit for 2018?
3. **CONCEPTUAL CONNECTION** If you have previously worked Exercise 6-45, compare your answers. What are the differences? Be sure to explain why the differences occurred.

Exercise 6-58 (Appendix) Inventory Costing Methods: Periodic Inventory System

OBJECTIVE 9

Maidstone Company had 400 units in beginning inventory at a cost of $24 each. Maidstone's 2018 purchases were as follows:

Date	Purchases
Feb. 21	6,100 units at $28 each
July 15	5,700 units at $32 each
Sept. 30	7,800 units at $34 each

Maidstone uses a periodic inventory system and sold 19,300 units at $45 each during 2018.

Required:

1. Calculate the cost of ending inventory and the cost of goods sold using the FIFO and weighted average cost methods (*Note:* Use four decimal places for per-unit calculations and round all other numbers to the nearest dollar).
2. Prepare a statement of earnings through gross margin using both of the costing methods in part 1.
3. **CONCEPTUAL CONNECTION** What is the effect of both inventory costing methods on income?

Exercise 6-59 (Appendix) Inventory Costing Methods: Periodic Inventory System

OBJECTIVE 9

The inventory accounting records for Langer Enterprises contained the following data:

Beginning inventory	1,400 units at $12 each
Purchase 1, Feb. 26	2,400 units at $16 each
Sale 1, March 9	2,300 units at $27 each
Purchase 2, June 14	2,200 units at $20 each
Sale 2, Sept. 22	1,900 units at $29 each

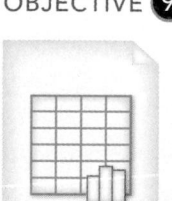

Required:

1. Calculate the cost of ending inventory and the cost of goods sold using the FIFO and weighted average cost methods (*Note:* Use four decimal places for per-unit calculations and round all other numbers to the nearest dollar).
2. **CONCEPTUAL CONNECTION** Compare the ending inventory and cost of goods sold computed under both methods. What can you conclude about the effects of the inventory costing methods on the statement of financial position and the statement of earnings?

(Continued)

OBJECTIVE **9**

Exercise 6-60   *(Appendix)* Inventory Costing Methods: Periodic System

Harrington Company had the following data for inventory during a recent year:

	Units	Cost per Unit	Total Cost
Beginning inventory	500	$ 9.00	$ 4,500
Purchase 1, Jan. 28	1,600	9.40	$15,040
Purchase 2, May 2	1,200	10.20	12,240
Purchase 3, Aug. 13	1,400	10.80	15,120
Purchase 4, Nov. 9	1,100	11.30	12,430
Total purchases	5,300		54,830
Goods available for sale	5,800		$59,330
Less: Sales	(5,240)		
Ending inventory	560		

Assume that Harrington uses a periodic inventory accounting system.

Required:

1. Using the FIFO and weighted average cost methods, compute the ending inventory and cost of goods sold. (*Note:* Use four decimal places for per-unit calculations and round all other numbers to the nearest dollar.)
2. **CONCEPTUAL CONNECTION** Which method will produce the most realistic amount for income? For inventory?
3. **CONCEPTUAL CONNECTION** Which method will produce the lowest amount paid for taxes?

PROBLEM SET A

OBJECTIVE **1**

Problem 6-61A   Applying the Cost of Goods Sold Model

The following amounts were obtained from the accounting records of Rabren Supply Company.

	2017		2018	
Net sales		$359,620		$423,150
Cost of goods sold:				
Beginning inventory	$36,800		(d)	
Purchases	(a)		301,600	
Goods available for sale	(b)		(e)	
Ending inventory	42,780		(f)	
Cost of goods sold		(c)		289,700
Gross margin		$116,450		(g)

Required:

Compute the missing amounts.

OBJECTIVE **2**

Problem 6-62A   Recording Sale and Purchase Transactions

Alpharack Company sells a line of tennis equipment to retailers. Alpharack uses the perpetual inventory system and engaged in the following transactions during April 2018, its first month of operations:

a. On April 2, Alpharack purchased, on credit, 360 Wilbur T-100 tennis racquets with credit terms of 2/10, n/30. The racquets were purchased at a cost of $30 each. Alpharack paid Santiago Trucking $195 to transport the tennis racquets from the manufacturer to Alpharack's warehouse, shipping terms were FOB shipping point, and the items were shipped on April 2.

b. On April 3, Alpharack purchased, for cash, 115 packs of tennis balls for $10 per pack.

c. On April 4, Alpharack purchased tennis clothing, on credit, from Designer Tennis Wear. The cost of the clothing was $8,250. Credit terms were 2/10, n/25.

d. On April 10, Alpharack paid for the purchase of the tennis racquets in transaction *a*.

e. On April 15, Alpharack determined that $325 of the tennis clothing was defective. Alpharack returned the defective merchandise to Designer Tennis Wear.

f. On April 20, Alpharack sold 118 tennis racquets at $90 each, 92 packs of tennis balls at $12 per pack, and $5,380 of tennis clothing. All sales were for cash. The cost of the merchandise sold was $7,580.

g. On April 23, customers returned $860 of the merchandise purchased on April 20. The cost of the merchandise returned was $450.

h. On April 25, Alpharack sold another 55 tennis racquets, on credit, for $90 each and 15 packs of tennis balls at $12 per pack, for cash. The cost of the merchandise sold was $1,800.

i. On April 29, Alpharack paid Designer Tennis Wear for the clothing purchased on April 4 less the return on April 15.

j. On April 30, Alpharack purchased 20 tennis bags, on credit, from Bag Designs for $320. The bags were shipped FOB destination and arrived at Alpharack on May 3.

Required:

1. Prepare the journal entries to record the sale and purchase transactions for Alpharack during April 2018.

2. Assuming operating expenses of $8,500 and income taxes of $1,180, prepare Alpharack's statement of earnings for April 2018.

Problem 6-63A   Inventory Costing Methods

OBJECTIVE ❷❸❹

Anderson's Department Store has the following data for inventory, purchases, and sales of merchandise for December for one of the items the company sells:

Activity	Units	Purchase Price (per unit)	Sale Price (per unit)
Beginning inventory	10	$6.00	
Purchase 1, Dec. 2	22	6.80	
Purchase 2, Dec. 5	26	7.50	
Sale 1, Dec. 7	19		$12.00
Sale 2, Dec. 10	25		12.00
Purchase 3, Dec. 12	12	8.00	
Sale 3, Dec. 14	20		12.00

Anderson's uses a perpetual inventory system. All purchases and sales were for cash.

Required:

1. Compute cost of goods sold and the cost of ending inventory using FIFO.

2. Compute cost of goods sold and the cost of ending inventory using the weighted average cost method. (*Note:* Use four decimal places for per-unit calculations and round all other numbers to the nearest penny.)

3. Prepare the journal entries to record these transactions, assuming Anderson's chooses to use the FIFO method.

4. **CONCEPTUAL CONNECTION** Which method would result in the lowest amount paid for taxes?

Problem 6-64A   Inventory Costing Methods

OBJECTIVE ❷❸❹❻

Gavotte Products uses a perpetual inventory system. For 2017 and 2018, Gavotte has the following data:

(Continued)

Activity	Units	Purchase Price (per unit)	Sale Price (per unit)
2017			
Beginning inventory	200	$ 9	
Purchase 1, Feb. 15	300	11	
Sale 1, Mar. 10	320		$25
Purchase 2, Sept. 15	500	12	
Sale 2, Nov. 3	550		25
Purchase 3, Dec. 20	150	13	
2018			
Sale 3, Apr. 4	200		25
Purchase 4, June 25	200	14	
Sale 4, Dec. 18	150		25

Required:

1. For each year, compute cost of goods sold, the cost of ending inventory, and gross margin using FIFO.
2. For each year, compute cost of goods sold, the cost of ending inventory, and gross margin using the weighted average cost method. (*Note:* Use four decimal places for per-unit calculations and round all other numbers to the nearest dollar.)
3. **CONCEPTUAL CONNECTION** Which method would result in the lowest amount paid for taxes?
4. **CONCEPTUAL CONNECTION** Which method produces the most realistic amount for income? For inventory? Explain your answer.
5. **CONCEPTUAL CONNECTION** Compute Gavotte's gross profit ratio and inventory turnover ratio under both inventory costing methods. (*Note:* Round answers to two decimal places.) How would the choice of inventory costing method affect these ratios?

OBJECTIVE **5**

Problem 6-65A   Lower of Cost and Net Realizable Value

Sue Stone, the president of Canoe Home Products, has prepared the following information for the company's television inventory at the end of 2018:

Model	Quantity	Cost per Unit	NRV per Unit
T-260	15	$250	$445
S-256	28	325	300
R-193	20	210	230
Z-376	15	285	250

Required:

1. Determine the carrying amount of the inventory using LCNRV applied on an item-by-item basis.
2. Prepare the journal entry required to value the inventory at LCNRV.
3. **CONCEPTUAL CONNECTION** What is the impact of applying the LCNRV rule on the financial statements of the current period? What is the impact on the financial statements of a subsequent period in which the inventory is sold?

OBJECTIVE **3** **5**

Problem 6-66A   Inventory Costing and LCNRV

Ortman Enterprises sells a chemical used in various manufacturing processes. On January 1, 2018, Ortman had 5,000,000 litres on hand, for which it had paid $0.50 per litre. During 2018, Ortman made the following purchases.

Date	Litres	Cost per Litre	Total Cost
Feb. 20	10,000,000	$0.52	$ 5,200,000
May 15	25,000,000	0.56	14,000,000
Sept. 12	32,000,000	0.60	19,200,000

During 2018, Ortman sold 65,000,000 litres at $0.75 per litre (35,000,000 litres were sold on June 29 and 30,000,000 litres were sold on Nov. 22), leaving an ending inventory of 7,000,000 litres. Assume that Ortman uses a perpetual inventory system. Ortman uses LCNRV for its inventories.

Required:

1. Assume that the net realizable value of the chemical is $0.76 per litre on December 31, 2018. Compute the cost of ending inventory using the FIFO and weighted average cost methods and then apply LCNRV. (*Note:* Use four decimal places for per-unit calculations and round all other numbers to the nearest dollar.)
2. Assume that the NRV of the chemical is $0.58 per litre on December 31, 2018. Compute the cost of ending inventory using the FIFO and weighted average cost methods and then apply LCNRV. (*Note:* Use four decimal places for per-unit calculations and round all other numbers to the nearest dollar.)

Problem 6-67A   Effects of an Inventory Error

 OBJECTIVE 7

The statements of earnings for Graul Corporation for the three years ended in 2018 appear below.

	2018	2017	2016
Sales revenue	$ 4,643,200	$ 4,287,500	$ 3,647,900
Cost of goods sold	(2,475,100)	(2,181,600)	(2,006,100)
Gross margin	2,168,100	2,105,900	1,641,800
Operating expense	(1,548,600)	(1,428,400)	(1,152,800)
Income from operations	619,500	677,500	489,000
Other expenses	(137,300)	(123,600)	(112,900)
Income before taxes	482,200	553,900	376,100
Income tax expense (34%)	(163,948)	(188,326)	(127,874)
Net income	$ 318,252	$ 365,574	$ 248,226

During 2018, Graul discovered that the 2016 ending inventory had been misstated due to the following two transactions being recorded incorrectly.

a. A purchase return of inventory costing $42,000 was recorded twice.
b. A credit purchase of inventory made on December 20 for $28,500 was not recorded. The goods were shipped FOB shipping point and were shipped on December 22, 2016.

Required:

1. Was ending inventory for 2016 overstated or understated? By how much?
2. Prepare correct statements of earnings for all three years.
3. **CONCEPTUAL CONNECTION** Did the error in 2016 affect cumulative net income for the three-year period? Explain your response.
4. **CONCEPTUAL CONNECTION** Why was the 2018 net income unaffected?

Problem 6-68A   *(Appendix)* Inventory Costing Methods

 OBJECTIVE 8 9

Anderson's Department Store has the following data for inventory, purchases, and sales of merchandise for December for one of the items the company sells:

Activity	Units	Purchase Price (per unit)	Sale Price (per unit)
Beginning inventory	10	$6.00	
Purchase 1, Dec. 2	22	6.80	
Purchase 2, Dec. 5	26	7.50	
Sale 1, Dec. 7	19		$12.00
Sale 2, Dec. 10	25		12.00
Purchase 3, Dec. 12	12	8.00	
Sale 3, Dec. 14	20		12.00

(Continued)

Anderson's uses a periodic inventory system. All purchases and sales were for cash.

Required:

1. Compute cost of goods sold and the cost of ending inventory using FIFO.
2. Compute cost of goods sold and the cost of ending inventory using the weighted average cost method. (*Note:* Use four decimal places for per-unit calculations and round all other numbers to the nearest penny.)
3. Prepare the journal entries to record these transactions, assuming Anderson's chooses to use the FIFO method.
4. **CONCEPTUAL CONNECTION** Which method would result in the lowest amount paid for taxes?
5. **CONCEPTUAL CONNECTION** If you worked Problem 6-63A, compare your results. What are the differences? Be sure to explain why the differences occurred.

OBJECTIVE ⑨ **Problem 6-69A   (*Appendix*) Inventory Costing Methods**

Jet Black Products uses a periodic inventory system. For 2017 and 2018, Jet Black has the following data:

Activity	Units	Purchase Price (per unit)	Sale Price (per unit)
2017			
Beginning inventory	200	$ 9	
Purchase 1, Feb. 15	300	11	
Sale 1, Mar. 10	320		$25.00
Purchase 2, Sept. 15	500	12	
Sale 2, Nov. 3	550		25.00
Purchase 3, Dec. 20	150	13	
2018			
Sale 3, Apr. 4	200		25.00
Purchase 4, June 25	200	14	
Sale 4, Dec. 18	150		25.00

All purchases and sales are for cash.

Required:

1. Compute cost of goods sold, the cost of ending inventory, and gross margin for each year using FIFO.
2. Compute cost of goods sold, the cost of ending inventory, and gross margin for each year using the weighted average cost method. (*Note:* Use four decimal places for per-unit calculations and round all other numbers to the nearest dollar).
3. **CONCEPTUAL CONNECTION** Which method would result in the lowest amount paid for taxes?
4. **CONCEPTUAL CONNECTION** Which method produces the most realistic amount for income? For inventory? Explain your answer.
YOUDECIDE 5. What is the effect of purchases made later in the year on the gross margin when the weighted average method is employed? When FIFO is employed? Be sure to explain why any differences occur.
6. **CONCEPTUAL CONNECTION** If you worked Problem 6-64A, compare your answers. What are the differences? Be sure to explain why any differences occurred.

PROBLEM SET B

Problem 6-70B   Applying the Cost of Goods Sold Model

OBJECTIVE **1**

The following amounts were obtained from the accounting records of Wachter Sports Products.

	2017		2018	
Net sales		(a)	$154,810	
Cost of goods sold:				
Beginning inventory	$ (b)		(d)	
Purchases	104,250		(e)	
Goods available for sale	(c)		$127,500	
Ending inventory	6,940		(f)	
Cost of goods sold		104,730		(g)
Gross margin		$ 28,600		$ 38,980

Required:

Compute the missing amounts.

Problem 6-71B   Recording Sale and Purchase Transactions

OBJECTIVE **2**

Jordan Footwear sells athletic shoes and uses the perpetual inventory system. During June 2018 (its first month of operations), Jordan engaged in the following transactions:

a. On June 1, Jordan purchased, on credit, 100 pairs of basketball shoes and 210 pairs of running shoes with credit terms of 2/10, n/30. The basketball shoes were purchased at a cost of $85 per pair, and the running shoes were purchased at a cost of $60 per pair. Jordan paid Mole Trucking $310 cash to transport the shoes from the manufacturer to Jordan's warehouse, shipping terms were FOB shipping point, and the items were shipped on June 1 and arrived on June 4.

b. On June 2, Jordan purchased 88 pairs of cross-training shoes for cash. The shoes cost Jordan $65 per pair.

c. On June 6, Jordan purchased 125 pairs of tennis shoes on credit. Credit terms were 2/10, n/25. The shoes were purchased at a cost of $45 per pair.

d. On June 10, Jordan paid for the purchase of the basketball shoes and the running shoes in transaction *a*.

e. On June 12, Jordan determined that $585 of the tennis shoes were defective. Jordan returned the defective merchandise to the manufacturer.

f. On June 18, Jordan sold 50 pairs of basketball shoes at $116 per pair, 92 pairs of running shoes for $85 per pair, 21 pairs of cross-training shoes for $100 per pair, and 48 pairs of tennis shoes for $68 per pair. All sales were for cash. The cost of the merchandise sold was $13,295.

g. On June 21, customers returned 10 pairs of the basketball shoes purchased on June 18. The cost of the merchandise returned was $850.

h. On June 23, Jordan sold another 20 pairs of basketball shoes, on credit, for $116 per pair and 15 pairs of cross-training shoes for $100 cash per pair. The cost of the merchandise sold was $2,675.

i. On June 30, Jordan paid for the June 6 purchase of tennis shoes less the return on June 12.

j. On June 30, Jordan purchased 60 pairs of basketball shoes, on credit, for $85 each. The shoes were shipped FOB destination and arrived at Jordan on July 3.

Required:

1. Prepare the journal entries to record the sale and purchase transactions for Jordan during June 2018.
2. Assuming operating expenses of $5,300 and income taxes of $365, prepare Jordan's statement of earnings for June 2018.

(Continued)

OBJECTIVE  **Problem 6-72B   Inventory Costing Methods**

Fayed Company began operations in February 2018. Fayed's accounting records provide the following data for the remainder of 2018 for one of the items the company sells:

Activity	Units	Purchase Price (per unit)	Sale Price (per unit)
Beginning inventory	9	$ 88	
Purchase 1, Feb. 15	6	102	
Purchase 2, Mar. 22	8	110	
Sale 1, Apr. 9	10		$180
Purchase 3, May 29	9	123	
Sale 2, July 10	15		180
Purchase 4, Sept. 10	8	135	
Sale 3, Oct. 15	12		180

Fayed uses a perpetual inventory system. All purchases and sales were for cash.

Required:

1. Compute cost of goods sold and the cost of ending inventory using FIFO.
2. Compute cost of goods sold and the cost of ending inventory using the weighted average cost method. (*Note:* Use four decimal places for per-unit calculations and round all other numbers to the nearest penny.)
3. Prepare the journal entries to record these transactions, assuming Fayed chooses to use the FIFO method.
4. **CONCEPTUAL CONNECTION** Which method would result in the lowest amount paid for taxes?

OBJECTIVE  **Problem 6-73B   Inventory Costing Methods**

Terpsichore Company uses a perpetual inventory system. For 2017 and 2018, Terpsichore has the following data:

Activity	Units	Purchase Price (per unit)	Sale Price (per unit)
2017			
Beginning inventory	100	$45	
Purchase 1, Feb. 25	700	52	
Sale 1, Apr. 15	600		$90
Purchase 2, Aug. 30	500	56	
Sale 2, Nov. 13	600		90
Purchase 3, Dec. 20	400	58	
2018			
Sale 3, Mar. 8	400		90
Purchase 4, June 28	900	62	
Sale 4, Dec. 18	800		90

Required:

1. For each year, compute cost of goods sold, the cost of ending inventory, and gross margin using FIFO.
2. For each year, compute cost of goods sold, the cost of ending inventory, and gross margin using the weighted average cost method. (*Note:* Use four decimal places for per-unit calculations and round all other numbers to the nearest dollar.)
3. **CONCEPTUAL CONNECTION** Which method would result in the lowest amount paid for taxes?
4. **CONCEPTUAL CONNECTION** Which method produces the most realistic amount for income? For inventory? Explain your answer.

5. **CONCEPTUAL CONNECTION** Compute Terpsichore's gross profit ratio and inventory turnover ratio under both inventory costing methods. (*Note:* Round answers to two decimal places.) How would the choice of inventory costing method affect these ratios?

Problem 6-74B   Lower of Cost and Net Realizable Value

OBJECTIVE 5

Kevin Spears, the accountant of Tyler Electronics Corp., has prepared the following information for the company's inventory at the end of 2018:

Model	Quantity	Cost per Unit	NRV per Unit
RSQ535	30	$100	$120
JKY942	52	140	125
LLM112	84	85	80
KZG428	63	105	128

Required:

1. Determine the carrying amount of the inventory using LCNRV applied on an item-by-item basis.
2. Prepare the journal entry required to value the inventory at LCNRV.
3. **CONCEPTUAL CONNECTION** What is the impact of applying the LCNRV rule on the financial statements of the current period? What is the impact on the financial statements of a subsequent period in which the inventory is sold?

Problem 6-75B   Inventory Costing and LCNRV

OBJECTIVE 3 5

J&J Enterprises sells paper cups to fast-food franchises. On January 1, 2018, J&J had 5,000 cups on hand, for which it had paid $0.10 per cup. During 2018, J&J made the following purchases and sales:

Date	Units	Cost per Unit	Total Cost
Feb. 20	100,000	$0.12	$12,000
May 15	57,000	0.14	7,980
Sept. 12	85,000	0.15	12,750

During 2018, J&J sold 240,000 cups at $0.35 per cup (80,000 cups were sold on April 2 and 160,000 cups were sold on October 20), leaving an ending inventory of 7,000 cups. Assume that J&J uses a perpetual inventory system. J&J uses the lower of cost or net realizable for its inventories, as required by GAAP and IFRS.

Required:

1. Assume that the net realizable value of the cups is $0.38 per cup on December 31, 2018. Compute the cost of ending inventory using the FIFO and weighted average cost methods and then apply LCNRV. (*Note:* Use four decimal places for per-unit calculations and round all other numbers to the nearest dollar.)
2. Assume that the net realizable value of the cups is $0.12 per cup on December 31, 2018. Compute the cost of ending inventory using the FIFO and weighted average cost methods and then apply LCNRV. (*Note:* Use four decimal places for per-unit calculations and round all other numbers to the nearest dollar.)

Problem 6-76B   Effects of an Inventory Error

OBJECTIVE 7

The statements of earnings for Picard Company for the three years ended in 2018 appear below.

(Continued)

	2018	2017	2016
Sales revenue	$1,168,500	$ 998,400	$ 975,300
Cost of goods sold	(785,800)	(675,450)	(659,800)
Gross margin	382,700	322,950	315,500
Operating expense	(162,500)	(142,800)	(155,300)
Income from operations	220,200	180,150	160,200
Other expenses	(73,500)	(58,150)	(54,500)
Income before taxes	146,700	122,000	105,700
Income tax expense (34%)	(49,878)	(41,480)	(35,938)
Net income	$ 96,822	$ 80,520	$ 69,762

During 2018, Picard discovered that the 2016 ending inventory had been misstated due to the following two transactions being recorded incorrectly.

a. Inventory costing $37,000 that was returned to the manufacturer (a purchase return) was not recorded. The items were included in ending inventory.

b. A credit purchase of inventory made on August 30, 2016, for $12,800 was recorded twice. The goods were shipped FOB shipping point and were shipped on September 5, 2016.

Required:

1. Was ending inventory for 2016 overstated or understated? By how much?
2. Prepare correct statements of earnings for all three years.
3. **CONCEPTUAL CONNECTION** Did the error in 2016 affect cumulative net income for the three-year period? Explain your response.
4. **CONCEPTUAL CONNECTION** Why was the 2018 net income unaffected?

OBJECTIVE  **Problem 6-77B**   *(Appendix)* **Inventory Costing Methods**

Fayed Company began operations in February 2018. Fayed's accounting records provide the following data for the remainder of 2018 for one of the items the company sells.

Activity	Units	Purchase Price (per unit)	Sale Price (per unit)
Beginning inventory	9	$ 88	
Purchase 1, Feb. 15	6	102	
Purchase 2, Mar. 22	8	110	
Sale 1, Apr. 9	10		$180
Purchase 3, May 29	9	123	
Sale 2, July 10	15		180
Purchase 4, Sept. 10	8	135	
Sale 3, Oct. 15	12		180

Fayed uses a periodic inventory system. All purchases and sales were for cash.

Required:

1. Compute cost of goods sold and the cost of ending inventory using FIFO.
2. Compute cost of goods sold and the cost of ending inventory using the weighted average cost method. (*Note:* Use four decimal places for per-unit calculations and round all other numbers to the nearest dollar.)
3. Prepare the journal entries to record these transactions, assuming Fayed chooses to use the FIFO method.
4. **CONCEPTUAL CONNECTION** Which method would result in the lowest amount paid for taxes?
5. **CONCEPTUAL CONNECTION** If you worked Problem 6-72B, compare your results. What are the differences? Be sure to explain why the differences occurred.

Problem 6-78B   *(Appendix)* Inventory Costing Methods

OBJECTIVE **9**

Grencia Company uses a periodic inventory system. For 2013 and 2014, Grencia has the following data (assume all purchases and sales are for cash):

Activity	Units	Purchase Price (per unit)	Sale Price (per unit)
2017			
Beginning inventory	100	$45	
Purchase 1, Feb. 25	700	52	
Sale 1, Apr. 15	600		$90
Purchase 2, Aug. 30	500	56	
Sale 2, Nov. 13	600		90
Purchase 3, Dec. 20	400	58	
2018			
Sale 3, Mar. 8	400		90
Purchase 4, June 28	900	62	
Sale 4, Dec. 18	800		90

Required:

1. Compute cost of goods sold, the cost of ending inventory, and gross margin for each year using FIFO.
2. Compute cost of goods sold, the cost of ending inventory, and gross margin for each year using the weighted average cost method. (*Note:* Use four decimal places for per-unit calculations and round all other numbers to the nearest dollar.)
3. **CONCEPTUAL CONNECTION** Which method would result in the lowest amount paid for taxes?
4. **CONCEPTUAL CONNECTION** Which method produces the most realistic amount for income? For inventory? Explain your answer.
5. What is the effect of purchases made later in the year on the gross margin when weighted average is employed? When FIFO is employed? Be sure to explain why any differences occur.
6. **CONCEPTUAL CONNECTION** If you worked **Problem 6-73B**, compare your answers. What are the differences? Be sure to explain why any differences occurred.

YOUDECIDE

CASES

Case 6-79   Inventory Valuation and Ethics

Mary Cravens is an accountant for City Appliance Corporation. One of Mary's responsibilities is developing the ending inventory amount for the calculation of cost of goods sold each month. At the end of September, Mary noticed that the ending inventory for a new brand of televisions was much larger than she had expected. In fact, there had been hardly any change since the end of the previous month when the shipments of televisions arrived. Mary knew that the firm's advertising had featured the new brand's products, so she had expected that a substantial portion of the televisions would have been sold.

Because of these concerns, Mary went to the warehouse to make sure the numbers were correct. While at the warehouse, Mary noticed that 30 of the televisions in question were on the loading dock for delivery to customers and another, larger group, perhaps 200 sets, was in an area set aside for sales returns. Mary asked Barry Tompkins, the returns supervisor, why so many of the televisions had been returned. Barry said that the manufacturer had used a cheap circuit board, which failed on many of the sets after they had been in service for a week or two. Mary then asked how the defective televisions had been treated when the inventory was taken at the end of September. Barry said that the warehouse staff had been told to include in the ending inventory any item in the warehouse that was not marked for shipment to customers. Therefore, all returned merchandise was considered part of ending inventory.

(Continued)

Mary asked Barry what would be done with the defective sets. Barry said that they would probably have to be sold to a liquidator for a few cents on the dollar. Mary knew from her examination of the inventory data that all the returned sets had been included in the September inventory at their original cost.

Mary returned to the office and prepared a revised estimate of ending inventory using the information Barry Tompkins had given her to revalue the ending inventory of the television sets. She submitted the revision along with an explanatory note to her boss, Susan Gee. A few days later, Susan stopped by Mary's office to report on a conversation with the chief financial officer, Herb Cobb. Herb told Susan that the original ending inventory amount would not be revised. Herb said that the television sets in question had been purchased by his brother and that adequate documentation existed to support the sale.

Required:

1. What would happen to cost of goods sold, gross margin, income from operations, and net income if the cost of the returned inventory had been reduced to its liquidation price as Mary had proposed?
2. What should Mary do now?

Case 6-80   Inventory Costing When Inventory Quantities Are Small

A number of companies have adopted a just-in-time procedure for acquiring inventory. These companies have arrangements with their suppliers that require the supplier to deliver inventory just as the company needs the goods. As a result, just-in-time companies keep very little inventory on hand.

Required:

1. Should the inventory costing method (FIFO or weighted average) have a material effect on cost of goods sold when a company adopts the just-in-time procedure and reduces inventory significantly?
2. Once a company has switched to the just-in-time procedure and has little inventory, should the inventory costing method (FIFO or weighted average) affect cost of goods sold?

Case 6-81   Inventory Purchase Price Volatility

In 2018, Steel Technologies Inc. changed from the weighted average to the FIFO method for its inventory costing. Steel Technologies' annual report indicated that this change had been instituted because the price at which the firm purchased steel was highly volatile.

Required:

Explain how FIFO cost of goods sold and ending inventory would be different from weighted average when prices are volatile.

Case 6-82   The Effect of Reductions in Inventory Quantities

Hanna Motor Company, one of the country's largest automobile manufacturers, disclosed the following information about its inventory in the notes to its financial statements.

Inventories are stated generally at cost, which is not in excess of net realizable value. The cost of inventory is determined by the weighted average method. If the first-in, first-out (FIFO) method of inventory valuation had been used, inventory would have been about $2,519 million higher at December 31, 2018, and $2,668 million higher at December 31, 2017. As a result of decreases in the purchase price of inventory over time, inventory quantities carried at lower weighted average costs prevailing in prior years, as compared with costs of current purchases, were liquidated in 2018 and 2017. These inventory adjustments improved pre-tax operating results by approximately $134 million in 2018 and $294 million in 2017.

Required:

1. Explain why the reduction in inventory quantities increased Hanna Motor Company's net income.
2. If Hanna Motor Company had used the FIFO inventory costing method, would the reduction in ending inventory quantities have increased net income?

YOU DECIDE

Case 6-83   Errors in Ending Inventory

From time to time, business news will report that the management of a company has misstated its profits by knowingly establishing an incorrect amount for its ending inventory.

Required:

1. Explain how a misstatement of ending inventory can affect profit.
2. Why would a manager intent on misstating profits choose ending inventory to achieve the desired effect?

Case 6-84   Ethics and Inventory

An electronics store has a large number of computers in its inventory that use outdated technology. These computers are reported at their cost. Shortly after the December 31 year-end, the store manager insists that the computers can be sold for well over their cost. But the store's accountant has been told by the sales staff that it will be difficult to sell these computers for more than half of their inventory cost.

Required:

1. Why is the store manager reluctant to admit that these computers have little sales value?
2. What are the consequences for the business of failing to recognize the decline in value?
3. What are the consequences for the accountant of participating in a misrepresentation of the inventory's value?

Case 6-85   Continuing Problem: Front Row Entertainment

In addition to developing online fan communities, Cam and Anna believe that they could increase Front Row Entertainment's revenue by selling live-performance DVDs at the concert. Front Row records the following activity between May and August 2018 for one of its artists.

Date		Activity	Number of Units	Cost per Unit
May	10	Purchase inventory	240	$8.25
	25	Sale	180	
June	5	Purchase inventory	300	8.75
	12	Sale	150	
July	5	Sale	135	
Aug.	8	Purchase inventory	190	9.25
	20	Sale	110	

Front Row sells all of its DVDs for $15 each and uses a perpetual inventory system.

Required:

1. Compute ending inventory and cost of goods sold using the FIFO and weighted average cost methods. (*Note:* Use four decimal places for per-unit calculations and round all other numbers to the nearest penny.)
2. Discuss the advantages and disadvantages of each method.
3. Assume that Front Row decides to use FIFO. Prepare the journal entries necessary to record the above transactions. Assume that all purchases and sales were for cash.

(Continued)

Case 6-86   Professional and Ethical Behaviour

You have been working at Better Buy Ltd. for the last year. Better Buy is a large Canada-wide electronics company, with its head office in Ontario. Better Buy has been in business for over 10 years and is growing. The company has a reputation for having good-quality products with great customer service.

You are responsible for all financial accounting functions related to inventory costing. All inventory is located in Vancouver, and customer orders are handled out of the Vancouver location.

You've never had the opportunity to go to Vancouver to see the warehouse. You think it's a bit strange that whenever you ask if you can fly out to see the warehouse, management says that it's not a good time. You still feel that since you are the main person responsible for costing the inventory, it's important for you to have a clear understanding of the process in Vancouver and the types of inventory in the warehouse.

You were recently invited to your friend's wedding, which happens to be in Vancouver. You feel that this would be a perfect opportunity to see the warehouse and put a name to the faces of the people you've been speaking with on the telephone for the last two years. You decide not to mention to anyone that you plan to visit the location. You think it will be a great surprise.

When you arrive in Vancouver, you ask for a tour of the warehouse. Tom, who is the supervisor of the warehouse, is happy to see you and offers to give you the tour. You are amazed at how large the warehouse is and the amount of inventory on the premises.

During the tour, you notice several areas of inventory in old boxes, in some cases very dirty and ripped boxes. You ask Tom about this inventory and he says that those boxes have been there for years, and he's not even sure what's in them anymore. "Whenever a customer returns an item or we find a box that is ripped, we just toss the inventory in the corner and pull from the new inventory, which looks much nicer to ship to the customers," he says.

You take a closer look at the boxes and items and you identify that they are expensive. You ask Tom for a listing of all the inventory that has been segregated and deemed not suitable for customers. "Clearly this inventory now looks old and out of date, and we should have attempted to return all of this to the manufacturer for a refund," Tom tells you. Some of the items are over two years old, perhaps three. Your concern is that you have all this inventory that really cannot be sold to anyone, and the chances that the manufacturer will take it back are slim.

You identify that the total cost of the segregated inventory is over one million dollars.

You thank Tom for the tour and tell him that it was a pleasure meeting him. You will be in touch.

Required:

Identify and discuss any accounting-related and potential ethical issues.

7

Reporting and Analyzing Property, Plant, and Equipment; Intangibles; and Natural Resources

After studying Chapter 7, you should be able to:

1. Define, classify, and explain the accounting for property, plant, and equipment; intangibles; and natural resources.

2. Explain how the cost principle applies to recording the cost of property, plant, and equipment.

3. Explain the concept of depreciation.

4. Compute depreciation expense using various depreciation methods.

5. Distinguish between capital and revenue expenditures.

6. Explain and account for revisions in depreciation.

7. Explain the concept and recording of asset impairment.

8. Explain the process of recording the disposal of property, plant, and equipment.

9. Evaluate the use of property, plant, and equipment.

10. Explain the measurement and reporting of intangible assets.

11. Explain the measurement and reporting of natural resources.

The Canadian Press/Lee Brown

NEL

EXPERIENCE FINANCIAL ACCOUNTING

with Rogers Communications

With revenues exceeding $12.8 billion, Rogers Communications Inc. is a diversified Canadian telecommunications and media company. Rogers Wireless is Canada's largest provider of wireless communications services. Rogers Communications boasts over 14.6 million subscribers to all the services offered by the company. Rogers Cable is a leading Canadian cable services provider, offering cable TV, high-speed Internet access, and telephony products for residential and business customers. Rogers Media has broadcast, specialty, sports, print, and online media assets; its activities encompass radio and TV broadcasting, televised shopping, sports, entertainment, and magazines and trade journals. In 2014, Rogers's statement of financial position reflected an investment of $10.6 billion in property, plant, and equipment (up from $10.2 billion in 2013). By closely analyzing a company's expenditures on productive assets, you will be able to better assess its long-term productivity, profitability, and ability to generate cash flow.

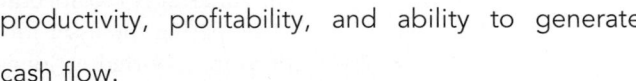

Total Rogers Subscribers
(in millions)

2010	2011	2012	2013	2014
14.0	14.5	14.6	14.7	14.6

Rogers Communications Inc. 2011 Annual Report

Source: Originally published on the Rogers website in 2015. Used with permission of Rogers Communications Inc. All rights reserved.

OBJECTIVE

Define, classify, and explain the accounting for property, plant, and equipment; intangibles; and natural resources.

UNDERSTANDING CAPITAL ASSETS

In this chapter, we examine the measurement and reporting issues related to long-lived assets that are used by the company in the normal course of operations. Unlike inventory, these long-lived assets (which we will call capital assets) are not sold to customers. Instead, capital assets are used by a company in the normal course of operations to generate revenue. They are usually held by a company until they are no longer of service to the company. In other words, capital assets are held until their *service potential* has been exhausted. The typical capital asset is used for a period of 4 to 10 years, although some are held for only 2 or 3 years and others for as long as 30 or 40 years. Capital assets are divided into four categories:

- *Tangible assets*, often called *property, plant, and equipment; fixed assets*; or *plant assets*, are capital assets that can be seen and physically touched. They include, among other things, land, buildings, furniture and fixtures, machinery equipment, office equipment, computer equipment, and automotive equipment. Biological assets, including living animals and plants, are also included in this category.
- *Intangible assets*, which generally result from legal and contractual rights arising from intellectual property, do not have physical substance. They include patents, copyrights, trademarks, licences, and goodwill.
- *Natural resources* are naturally occurring materials in the earth that have economic value. They include timberlands and deposits such as coal, oil, gravel, silver, and gold.

Capital assets represent future economic benefits, or service potential, that will be used in the normal course of operations. At acquisition, based on the cost principle, a capital asset is recorded at its cost, including the cost of acquiring the asset and the cost of preparing the asset for use. These costs are said to be *capitalized*, which means that they are reported as long-term assets with a service potential of greater than one year on the statement of financial position. As the service potential of a capital asset declines, the matching concept applies and requires that the cost of the asset be allocated as an expense among the accounting periods in which the asset is used and benefits are received. This allocation is called *depreciation* for property, plant, and equipment assets; *amortization* for intangible assets; and *depletion* for natural resources.

Capital assets are often the most costly of the various types of assets acquired by an entity. For manufacturing companies, property, plant, and equipment frequently represents a major percentage of a manufacturing company's total assets. However, in other industries, such as computer software, capital assets may be a relatively insignificant portion of a company's assets. For many companies, depreciation, amortization, and depletion are also among the largest items of periodic expense. Exhibit 7.1 shows the percentages of property, plant, and equipment in relation to total assets for various companies.

For Rogers, capital assets (property, plant, and equipment plus intangible assets) compose approximately 65% of total assets. Its capital assets include the expenditures required to build, upgrade, and expand its wireless network. However, Rogers has significant investments in intangible capital assets, primarily licences, roaming agreements, and goodwill. In contrast, companies such as Suncor have relatively more natural resources (oil properties), while Air Canada's capital assets are made up primarily of its airplanes. Information about a company's capital assets gives financial statement users insights into a company's ability to satisfy customer demands (productive capacity) and the effectiveness of management in using the company's assets to generate revenue. While the relative mix of capital assets may vary among companies, it is clear that the management of capital assets is critical to a company's long-term success.

In this chapter, we discuss the measurement and reporting issues related to the initial acquisition, use, and disposition of capital assets. We address the following questions:

- What is included in the cost of a capital asset?
- How should a capital asset's cost be allocated to expense?

Source: Figure has been updated to include Rogers, Suncor, and Air Canada data.

(EXHIBIT 7.1)

Percentages of Property, Plant, and Equipment; Intangible; and Natural Resource Assets in Relation to Total Assets

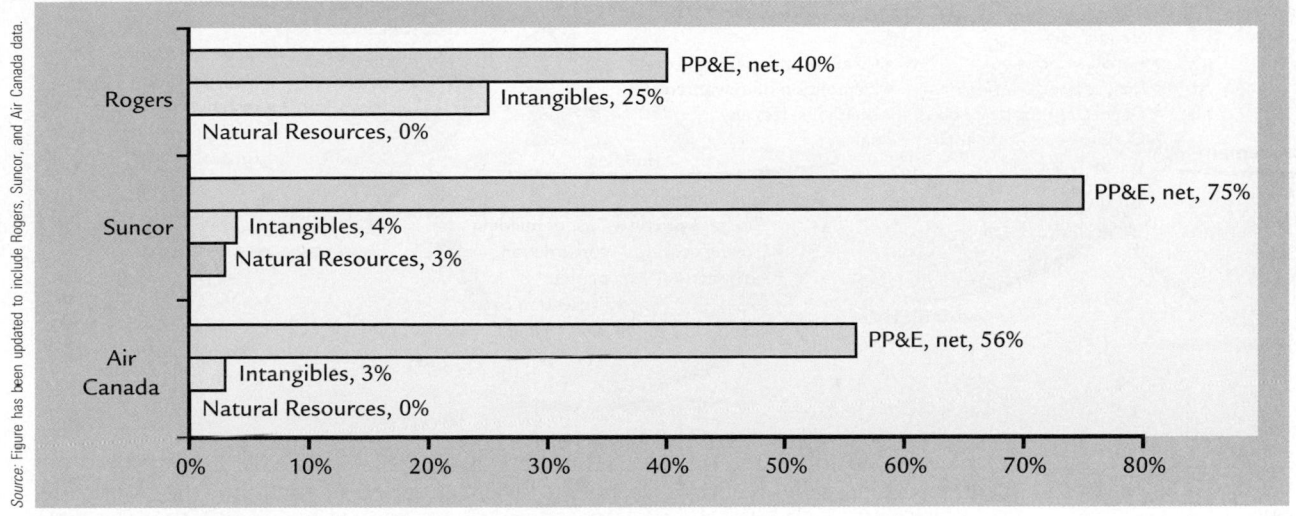

- How should expenditures after acquisition be treated?
- How is the disposition of a capital asset recorded?

ACQUISITION OF PROPERTY, PLANT, AND EQUIPMENT

Property, plant, and equipment are the tangible capital assets used in the normal operations of a company. These assets are tangible in the sense that they have a visible, physical presence in the company. Property, plant, and equipment includes:

- *Land*: The site of a manufacturing facility or office building used in operations[1]
- *Land Improvements*: Structural additions or improvements to land (such as driveways, parking lots, fences, landscaping, lighting)
- *Buildings*: Structures used in operations (factory, office, warehouse)
- *Equipment*: Assets used in operations (machinery, furniture, computers, automobiles)

It is important to note that land has an unlimited life and service potential and is not subject to depreciation. However, land improvements, buildings, and equipment have limited lives and limited service potential. Therefore, the costs of these depreciable assets are recorded in separate accounts and depreciated over the periods in which they are used to generate revenue.

OBJECTIVE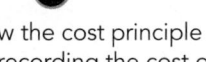

Explain how the cost principle applies to recording the cost of property, plant, and equipment.

Measuring the Cost of Property, Plant, and Equipment

The cost of property, plant, and equipment is any expenditure necessary to acquire the asset and to prepare the asset for use. For example, the cost of a machine would be its purchase price (less any discount offered) plus sales taxes, freight, installation costs, and the cost of labour and materials for trial runs that check its performance before the commencement of normal production activities. Expenditures that are included as part of the cost of the asset are said to be *capitalized*. Exhibit 7.2 shows expenditures that are typically included as part of the cost of various types of property, plant, and equipment.

---

[1] Land purchased for future use or as an investment is not considered part of property, plant, and equipment.

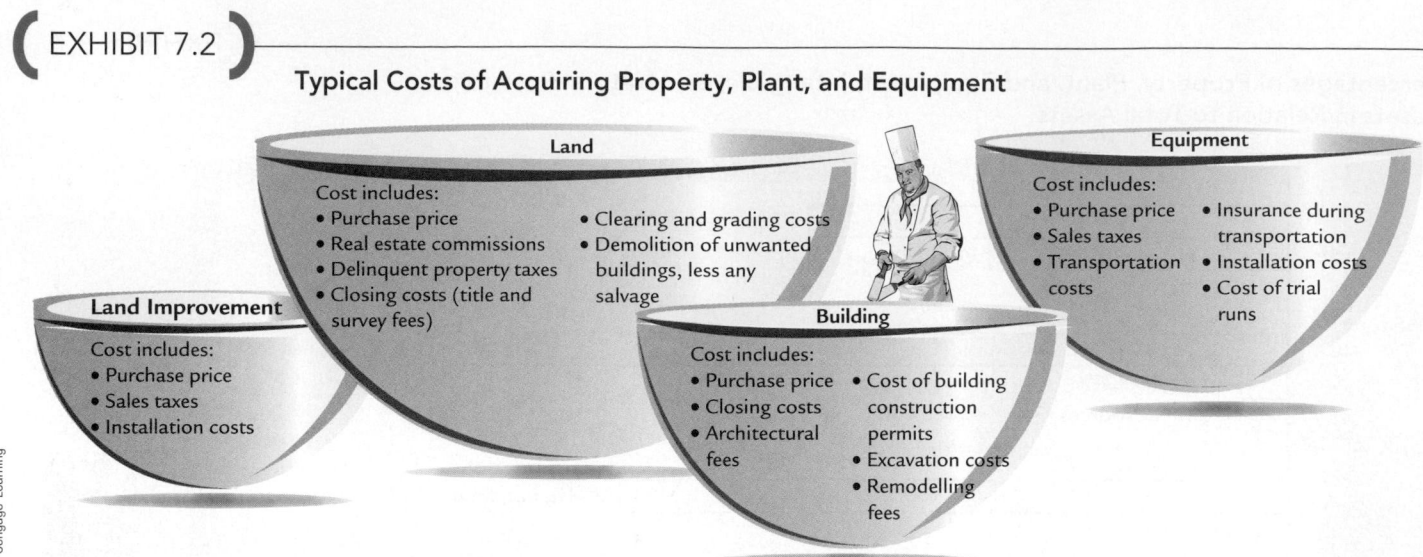

© Cengage Learning

EXHIBIT 7.2

Typical Costs of Acquiring Property, Plant, and Equipment

Expenditures that are *not* included as part of the cost of the asset are expensed immediately. Generally, recurring costs that benefit a period of time, not the asset's life, are expensed instead of capitalized. Careful judgment should be exercised in determining which costs should be capitalized and which costs should be expensed.

ETHICAL DECISION   The distinction between whether an expenditure should be capitalized or expensed can have dramatic consequences for a company's financial statements. A Canadian case occurred when a company known as Livent improperly capitalized certain expenditures as capital assets rather than properly recording the expenditures as operating expenses, resulting in a material and fraudulent overstatement of both net income and assets in several years. In the United States, WorldCom's handling of this issue triggered one of the largest financial restatements in U.S. history. When WorldCom used the telecommunications lines of another company, it paid a fee that should have been expensed in the current period. By improperly capitalizing these fees as assets, WorldCom understated expenses and was thereby able to increase its income and its operating cash flow, and conceal large losses.

concept Q&A

If a company did not record all the costs necessary to acquire an asset and prepare it for use, what would be the effect on the financial statements?

Answer:

If costs were not recorded as an asset, these costs would be immediately expensed, which would lower income in the current period. By recording these costs as assets, the company delays the recognition of expense until the service potential of the asset is used.

Recording the Cost of Property, Plant, and Equipment Acquired by Cash, Debt, Equity (or Other Noncash Consideration), or Construction

The cost principle requires that a company record its property, plant, and equipment at the exchange price at the time the asset is purchased. When cash is paid in exchange for an asset, the amount of cash given becomes the cost of the acquired asset. For example, if equipment was acquired in return for a cash payment of $50,000, the journal entry would be as follows:

	Debit	Credit
Equipment	$50,000	
Cash		$50,000

In addition to cash purchases, companies often purchase property, plant, and equipment by issuing debt. In this situation, the asset is valued at the fair value of the debt (a liability) on the date the asset is acquired. Interest paid on the debt is generally viewed as resulting from a financing decision rather than from the decision to acquire the asset. For example, if equipment is acquired by a cash payment of $10,000 and the issuance of a note payable for $40,000, the acquisition would be recorded as follows:

	Debit	Credit
Equipment	$50,000	
Cash		$10,000
Note payable		40,000

Companies occasionally construct assets for their own use. The costs that can be capitalized in these circumstances include direct material, direct labour, and incremental indirect expenses (such as extra supervision or extra utility costs) used in the construction process. For self-constructed assets that require a long period of preparation for use, such as large plants or buildings, IFRS does permit the addition of interest, known as capitalized interest, to the cost of the asset where the interest is on borrowed funds that are directly attributable to the construction of the asset. For example, assume a company constructed a new piece of equipment for its own use for which it incurred direct labour costs of $100,000, direct material costs of $500,000, and interest costs on incremental borrowings of $150,000. The acquisition would be recorded as follows:

	Debit	Credit
Equipment	$750,000	
Cash		$750,000

This topic is further covered in advanced accounting courses.

When noncash consideration is issued in exchange for an asset, the purchase price of the acquired asset is the fair value of the asset received. If not determinable, the fair value of the asset given up or consideration issued, the cash equivalent consideration, should be used. The fair value of an asset is the estimated amount of cash that would be required to acquire the asset. For example, assume equipment was acquired by payment of cash of $10,000 and the issuance of common shares with a fair market value of $40,000. The acquisition would be recorded as follows:

	Debit	Credit
Equipment	$50,000	
Cash		$10,000
Common shares		40,000

Interest on borrowed funds normally is not added to the purchase price of an asset. Cornerstone 7.1 illustrates the accounting procedures for the measurement and recording of the cost of property, plant, and equipment. It shows that all costs necessary to acquire the machine and prepare it for use—freight ($2,900) and installation costs ($5,300 + $800 + $1,500)—are included in the machine's cost. Interest on the note payable, however, is excluded from the machine's cost and is added to interest expense as it accrues. Finally, note that the cost is capitalized (recorded as an asset) and that there is no immediate effect on the statement of earnings.

CORNERSTONE 7.1

Measuring and Recording the Cost of Property, Plant, and Equipment

CORNERSTONE
VIDEO

Information:

On June 29, 2018, Drew Company acquired a new automatic milling machine from Dayton Inc. Drew paid $20,000 in cash and signed a one-year, 10% note for $80,000. Following the purchase, Drew incurred freight charges, on account, of $2,900 to ship the machine from Dayton's factory to Drew's plant. After the machine arrived, Drew paid J.B. Contractors $5,300 for installation. Drew also used $800 of prepaid supplies and $1,500 of labour on trial runs.

Required:

1. Determine the cost of the machine.

2. Prepare the journal entry necessary to record the purchase of the machine.

Why:

The cost of property, plant, and equipment includes any expenditure to acquire the asset and prepare it for use. The cost of property, plant, and equipment must be measured and recorded accurately to fully and properly reflect the assets of a company and to provide a proper basis on which to calculate depreciation for depreciable assets.

Solution:

1. $20,000 + $80,000 + $2,900 + $5,300 + $800 + $1,500 = $110,500

2.

Assets	= Liabilities +	Shareholders' Equity
+110,500	+80,000	
−25,300	+2,900	
−800	+1,500	

Date	Account and Explanation	Debit	Credit
June 29, 2018	Equipment	110,500	
	Cash ($20,000 + $5,300)		25,300
	Notes Payable		80,000
	Accounts Payable (for freight charges)		2,900
	Supplies (trial runs)		800
	Wages Payable (trial runs)		1,500
	(Record purchase of equipment)		

Had Drew issued 1,600 shares of its own stock, which was selling for $50 per share, instead of the 10% note, the acquisition would have been recorded as follows:

Assets	= Liabilities +	Shareholders' Equity (Common Shares)
+110,500	+2,900	+80,000
−25,300	+1,500	
−800		

Date	Account and Explanation	Debit	Credit
June 29, 2018	Equipment	110,500	
	Cash ($20,000 + $5,300)		25,300
	Common Shares		80,000
	Accounts Payable		2,900
	Supplies (trial runs)		800
	Wages Payable (trial runs)		1,500
	(Record purchase of equipment)		

Since the fair value of the shares [$50 × 1,600 = $80,000] equals the amount of the note, the cost of the asset is the same in both entries.

Basket Purchases

Quite often, several assets—such as land and building—are acquired in a single transaction for a single lump sum. In this situation, known as a basket purchase, the cost of each asset must be measured and recorded separately. The cost for each asset is determined by allocating the purchase cost of the total basket of assets on the basis of the relative fair market values of each asset in the basket. To ensure an appropriate cost allocation, it may be necessary to obtain a formal appraisal of the items in the basket purchase.

Say, for example, that Markel Inc. has acquired a parcel of land and a building for a total cost of $1,000,000 paid with cash. An independent appraisal supports the land value at $400,000 and the building value at $800,000. Given these data, the cost of the land will be recorded by Markel as $400,000/$1,200,000 × $1,000,000 = $333,333. The cost allocated to the building will be $800,000/$1,200,000 × $1,000,000 = $666,667. The journal entry to record the acquisition would be as follows:

	Debit	Credit
Land	$333,333	
Building	666,667	
Cash		$1,000,000

YOUDECIDE The Purchase Decision

You are the controller of Stanley Inc., a struggling manufacturing company that is experiencing cash flow problems. You are reviewing two proposals that would enable the company to obtain a piece of equipment that is critical to its operations. The first proposal would allow the company to purchase the equipment by signing a long-term note payable. The second proposal involves having the company rent the equipment.

What factors should you consider in making the decision whether to purchase or rent the equipment?

Given the company's financial situation, renting (or leasing) the equipment may provide several advantages.

- Renting often requires little or no down payment, allowing a company with cash flow problems access to property, plant, and equipment that it would otherwise not be able to afford while freeing up cash for more immediate needs.
- Renting may allow the company to keep assets and, more importantly, liabilities off the statement of financial position, which increases the perceived borrowing ability of the company. For example, the purchase of the equipment would

increase both property, plant, and equipment and liabilities at the time of the purchase. In contrast, the rental of the equipment would require no entry at the time the agreement is signed. Therefore, the purchase of the asset on credit would cause an immediate increase in the company's debt-to-equity ratio.

- Renting the equipment may protect the renter against obsolescence since the rented asset can be exchanged for a newer model at the end of the rental agreement.
- Rental agreements may provide the renter with an increased tax benefit.

However, renting also has disadvantages, such as interest rates that may be higher than normal long-term borrowing rates. In short, the decision to purchase or rent is a strategic decision that must be carefully considered.

Managers are often confronted with the decision to purchase or rent property, plant, and equipment. In fact, renting assets through leasing arrangements has become one of the more frequently used strategies for acquiring property, plant, and equipment.[2]

DEPRECIATION

We observed earlier that the cost of property, plant, and equipment represents the cost of future benefits or service potential to a company. With the exception of land, this service potential declines over the life of each asset as the asset is used in the operations of the company. **Depreciation** is the process of allocating, in a systematic and rational manner, the cost

OBJECTIVE ❸

Explain the concept of depreciation.

[2] Lease arrangements and their effects are discussed more fully in Chapter 9.

(EXHIBIT 7.3)

Q ROGERS.

Excerpt from Rogers's 2014 Annual Report

Notes to Consolidated Financial Statements	
NOTE 7 Plant, Property, and Equipment (at cost):	
	(millions)
Land and buildings	$ 942
Cable and wireless network	19,588
Computer equipment and software	4,960
Customer premise equipment	1,543
Leasehold improvements	383
Equipment and vehicles	1,236
	28,652
Less: Accumulated depreciation	17,997
Property, plant, and equipment, net	$10,655

of a tangible capital asset (other than land) to expense over the asset's useful life. The matching concept provides the basis for measuring and recognizing depreciation and requires that the cost of a depreciable asset be allocated as an expense among the accounting periods in which the asset is used and revenues are generated by its use.

The amount of depreciation expense is recorded each period by making the following adjusting journal entry:

Depreciation Expense	xxx	
Accumulated Depreciation		xxx

The amount of depreciation recorded each period, or **depreciation expense**, is reported on the statement of earnings. **Accumulated depreciation**, which represents the total amount of depreciation expense that has been recorded for an asset since the asset was acquired, is reported on the statement of financial position as a contra-asset. That is, accumulated depreciation is deducted from the cost of the asset to get the asset's **book value** (or **carrying value**). Exhibit 7.3 shows the disclosures relating to property, plant, and equipment and depreciation made by Rogers in its 2014 annual report.

Before continuing, it is critical to understand the following points:

- Depreciation is a *cost allocation process*. It is *not* an attempt to measure the fair value of the asset or to obtain some other measure of the asset's value. In fact, the book value (cost less accumulated depreciation) of an asset that is reported on a company's statement of financial position is often quite different from the market value of the asset.
- Depreciation is *not* an attempt to accumulate cash for the replacement of an asset.
- Depreciation is a cost allocation process that does not involve cash.

Information Required for Measuring Depreciation

The following information is necessary in order to measure depreciation for a depreciable tangible asset:

- acquisition cost of the asset to the business
- estimated useful life (or expected economic life) of the asset to the business
- estimated residual value (salvage value) of the asset at the end of its useful life to the business

Cost As discussed earlier in the chapter, the **cost** of a capital asset is any expenditure necessary to acquire the asset and to prepare the asset for use. In addition to cost, we

© Cengage Learning

(EXHIBIT 7.4)

Components of Depreciation Expense

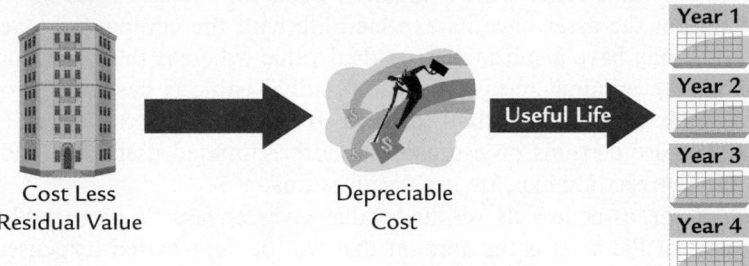

Cost Less Residual Value → Depreciable Cost → Useful Life → Year 1, Year 2, Year 3, Year 4

also need to examine two other items—estimated useful life and estimated residual value—to measure depreciation. Exhibit 7.4 shows the relationships among the factors used to compute depreciation expense.

Estimated Useful Life The estimated **useful life** of an asset is the period of time over which the company anticipates deriving benefit from the use of the asset.[3] The useful life of any depreciable capital asset reflects both the physical capacities of the asset and the company's plans for its use. Many companies plan to dispose of assets before their entire service potential is exhausted. For example, major automobile rental companies typically use an automobile for only a part of its entire economic life before disposing of it. The useful life also is influenced by technological change. Many assets lose their service potential through obsolescence long before the assets are physically inoperable. As shown in Exhibit 7.5, Rogers uses an estimated useful life of 3 to 30 years for most of its depreciable capital assets.

(EXHIBIT 7.5)

Excerpt from Rogers's 2014 Annual Report

◎ ROGERS™

Notes to Consolidated Financial Statements

NOTE 1 Description of Business and Summary of Significant Accounting Policies:

Items of property, plant, and equipment at initial acquisition are measured at cost.... Depreciation is charged to the consolidated statements of income over their estimated useful lives as follows:

Asset	Basis	Rate
Buildings	Diminishing balance	5 to 40 years
Cable and wireless network	Straight-line	3 to 30 years
Computer equipment and software	Straight-line	4 to 10 years
Customer premise equipment	Straight-line	3 to 5 years
Leasehold improvements	Straight-line	Over shorter of estimated useful life or lease term
Equipment and vehicles	Diminishing balance	3 to 20 years

Source: Originally published on the Rogers website in 2015. Used with permission of Rogers Communications Inc. All rights reserved.

[3] The useful life can be estimated in *service units* as well as in *units of time*. For example, an airline may choose to measure the useful life of its aircraft in hours of use rather than years.

Estimated Residual Value The estimated **residual value** (also called **salvage value**) is the amount of cash or trade-in consideration that the company expects to receive when an asset is removed from service at the end of its economic useful life. Accordingly, the residual value reflects the company's plans for the asset and its expectations about the value of the asset once its expected life with the company is over. A truck used for 5 years may have a substantial residual value, whereas the same truck used for 10 years may have minimal residual value. Residual value is based on projections of some of the same future events that are used to estimate an asset's useful life. Since depreciation expense depends on estimates of both estimated useful life and estimated residual value, depreciation expense itself is an estimate.

The cost of the asset less its residual value gives an asset's **depreciable cost**. The depreciable cost of the asset is the amount that will be depreciated (expensed) over the asset's useful life.

DEPRECIATION METHODS

OBJECTIVE ④

Compute depreciation expense using various depreciation methods.

The service potential of a capital asset is assumed to decline with each period of use, but the pattern of decline is not the same for all assets. Some assets decline at a constant rate each year, while others decline sharply in the early years of use and then more gradually as time goes on. For other assets, the pattern of decline depends on how much the asset is used each period. *Depreciation methods* are the standardized calculations required to determine periodic depreciation expense. The most common depreciation methods are:

- straight-line
- declining balance
- units-of-production

For any of these depreciation methods, the total amount of depreciation expense that has been recorded (accumulated depreciation) over the life of the asset will never exceed the depreciable cost (cost less residual value) of the asset.

Straight-Line Method

As its name implies, the **straight-line depreciation** method allocates an equal amount of an asset's cost to depreciation expense for each year of the asset's useful life. It is appropriate to apply this method to those assets for which an equal amount of service potential is considered to be used each period. The straight-line method is the most widely used method because it is simple to apply and is based on a pattern of service potential decline that is reasonable for many depreciable capital assets.

The computation of straight-line depreciation expense is based on an asset's depreciable cost, which is the excess of the asset's cost over its residual value. Straight-line depreciation expense for each period is calculated by dividing the depreciable cost of an asset by the asset's useful life:

$$\text{Straight-line depreciation} = (\text{Cost} - \text{Residual value}) \times \frac{1}{\text{Estimated useful life}}$$

The fraction, (1 ÷ Useful Life), is called the *straight-line rate*. Using the straight-line rate, a company would compute depreciation expense by multiplying the straight-line rate by the asset's depreciable cost. Cornerstone 7.2 illustrates the computation of depreciation expense using the straight-line method.

---

concept Q&A

Why does IFRS allow companies to use different depreciation methods instead of requiring the use of a single depreciation method that would improve comparability?

Answer:

The depreciation method chosen by a company should capture the declining service potential of a capital asset. Because assets are used differently, alternative methods are allowed so that the use of the asset can be better matched with the revenue it helped generate.

Computing Depreciation Expense Using the Straight-Line Method

CORNERSTONE 7.2

▶| CORNERSTONE
VIDEO

Information:

On January 1, 2018, Logan Inc. acquired a machine for $50,000. Logan expects the machine to be worth $5,000 at the end of its five-year useful life. Logan uses the straight-line method of depreciation.

Required:

1. Compute the straight-line rate of depreciation for the machine.

2. Compute the annual amount of depreciation expense.

3. Prepare a depreciation schedule that shows the amount of depreciation expense for each year of the machine's life.

4. Prepare the journal entry required to record depreciation expense in 2018.

Why:

Depreciation is a process that allocates the cost of a depreciable asset over those periods that benefit from the use of the asset (the matching concept).

Depreciation on a straight-line basis provides a cost-efficient method to allocate asset cost when each time period benefits equally from the use of the asset.

Solution:

1. Straight-line rate $= \dfrac{1}{\text{Useful life}} = \dfrac{1}{5 \text{ years}} = 20\%$

2. Straight-line depreciation expense $= (\$50,000 - \$5,000) \times \dfrac{1}{5}$

$$= \$9,000 \text{ per year}$$

3.

End of Year	Depreciation Expense	Accumulated Depreciation	Book Value
			$50,000
2018	$ 9,000	$ 9,000	41,000
2019	9,000	18,000	32,000
2020	9,000	27,000	23,000
2021	9,000	36,000	14,000
2022	9,000	45,000	5,000
	$45,000		

4.

Date	Account and Explanation	Debit	Credit
Dec. 31, 2018	Depreciation Expense	9,000	
	Accumulated Depreciation— Machinery		9,000
	(Record straight-line depreciation expense)		

Assets	=	Liabilities	+	Shareholders' Equity (Depreciation Expense)
−9,000				−9,000

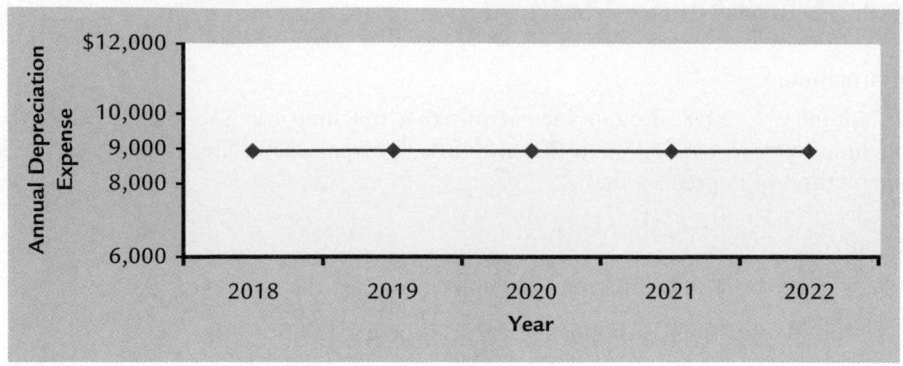

EXHIBIT 7.6

Straight-Line Pattern of Depreciation (Depreciation Amount Is Equal Each Year)

© Cengage Learning

Cornerstone 7.2 illustrates three important points:

- The straight-line depreciation method results in the recording of the same amount of depreciation expense ($9,000) each year, as shown in Exhibit 7.6.
- The contra-asset account, accumulated depreciation, increases at a constant rate of $9,000 per year until it equals the depreciable cost ($45,000).
- The book value of the machine (cost less accumulated depreciation) decreases by $9,000 per year until it equals the residual value ($5,000) at the end of the asset's useful life.

YOUDECIDE   Impact of Depreciation Estimates

You are a loan officer of the Prairie Provincial Bank. The president of a ready-mix concrete company, Concrete Transit Company, has applied for a five-year, $150,000 loan to finance his company's expansion. You have examined Concrete Transit's financial statements for the past three years and found the following:

	2019	2018	2017
Depreciation expense (calculated using the straight-line method)	$ 15,000	$ 15,000	$ 15,000
Income before taxes	$ 15,000	$ 17,000	$ 21,000
Depreciable assets (cost)	$470,000	$470,000	$470,000

Based on other customers in the same business that use the same depreciation method as Concrete Transit, you expected depreciation expense to be approximately 15% of the cost of the depreciable assets.

Should you make the loan?

Since Concrete Transit has similar assets and is using a similar depreciation method to its competitors, the most obvious reason for reporting a lower percentage of depreciation expense is that Concrete Transit is using different estimates of residual value and/or useful life than its competitors. If higher estimates of residual value or useful life are used, depreciation expense will be lower and income will be higher. If you adjust Concrete Transit's depreciation expense to 15% of the cost of its depreciable assets, depreciation expense will increase from $15,000 to $70,500 ($470,000 × 0.15) for each year. This would cause a decrease in income before taxes of $55,500 each year. These adjusted amounts suggest that Concrete Transit has been increasingly unprofitable. Given the difficulties it would likely have in making the required loan payments, the loan should not be made.

While most companies establish policies for depreciable assets that specify the estimation of useful lives and residual values, the measurement of depreciation expense (and income) ultimately relies on judgment.

Declining Balance Method

The **declining balance depreciation method** is an accelerated depreciation method that produces a declining amount of depreciation expense each period by multiplying the declining book value of an asset by a constant depreciation rate. It is called an accelerated method because it results in a larger amount of depreciation expense in the early years of an asset's life relative to the straight-line method. However, because the total amount of depreciation expense (the depreciable cost) must be the same under any depreciation method, accelerated methods result in a smaller amount of depreciation expense in the later years of an asset's life. The declining balance method is appropriate for assets that are subject to a rapid decline in service potential due to factors such as rapid obsolescence.

The declining balance depreciation rate is some multiple (m) of the straight-line rate:

$$\text{Declining balance rate} = (m) \times \frac{1}{\text{Estimated useful life}}$$

The multiple (m) is often 2, in which case the declining balance method is called the *double-declining-balance method*.[4]

Depreciation expense for each period of an asset's useful life under the declining balance method equals the declining balance rate times the asset's carrying or book value (cost less accumulated depreciation) at the beginning of the period as shown by the following equation:

$$\frac{\text{Declining balance depreciation}}{\text{expense}} = \frac{\text{Carrying value of asset}}{\text{beginning of year}} \times \frac{2}{\text{Estimated useful life}}$$

The calculation of declining balance depreciation expense differs from the calculation of straight-line depreciation expense in two important ways:

- The straight-line method multiplies a depreciation rate by the *depreciable cost* (cost less residual value) of the asset. However, the declining balance method multiplies a depreciation rate by the *book value* of the asset. Because the book value declines as depreciation expense is recorded, this calculation produces a declining pattern of depreciation expense over time.
- The straight-line method records an equal amount of depreciation expense *each period* of the asset's life. However, it is likely that the computation of depreciation expense under the declining balance method would cause the asset's book value to fall below its residual value. Because an asset's book value cannot be depreciated below its residual value, a lower amount of depreciation expense (relative to what is calculated under the declining balance method) must be recorded in the last year of the asset's life so that depreciation stops once the residual value is reached.

Cornerstone 7.3 illustrates the computation of depreciation expense using the declining balance method.

Relative to the straight-line method, the double-declining-balance method results in the recognition of higher depreciation expense in the early years of the asset's life and lower depreciation expense in the later years of the asset's life, as shown in Exhibit 7.7.

This pattern of expense is consistent with an asset whose service potential is used more rapidly (and whose contribution to revenue is greater) in the early years of the asset's life. For this reason, the declining balance method is often used by companies in industries that experience rapid obsolescence.

Units–of–Production Method

The two previous depreciation methods resulted in a pattern of expense that was related to the passage of time. However, when the decline in an asset's service potential is

---

[4] In this text, a multiple of 2 is used for the declining balance method unless otherwise noted.

CORNERSTONE 7.3

Computing Depreciation Expense Using the Declining Balance Method

Information:

On January 1, 2018, Logan Inc. acquired a machine for $50,000. Logan expects the machine to be worth $5,000 at the end of its five-year useful life. Logan uses the double-declining-balance method of depreciation.

Required:

1. Compute the double-declining-balance rate of depreciation for the machine.

2. Prepare a depreciation schedule that shows the amount of depreciation expense for each year of the machine's life.

3. Prepare the journal entry required to record depreciation expense in 2018.

Why:

Depreciation is a process that allocates the cost of a depreciable asset over those periods that benefit from the use of the asset (the matching concept).

Depreciation on a declining balance basis is an asset cost allocation method which recognizes that earlier time periods benefit to a greater degree than later periods from the use of an asset.

Solution:

1. $\dfrac{1}{\text{Useful life}} \times 2 = \dfrac{1}{5} \times 2 = \dfrac{2}{5}$ or 40%

2.

End of Year	Depreciation Expense (Rate × Book Value)		Accumulated Depreciation	Book Value
				$50,000
2018	40% × $50,000 =	$20,000	$20,000	30,000
2019	40% × $30,000 =	12,000	32,000	18,000
2020	40% × $18,000 =	7,200	39,200	10,800
2021	40% × $10,800 =	4,320	43,520	6,480
2022		1,480*	45,000	5,000
		$45,000		

*The computed amount of $2,592 (40% × $6,480) would cause book value to be lower than residual value. Therefore, depreciation expense of $1,480 is taken in 2022 so that the book value equals the residual value.

3.

Date	Account and Explanation	Debit	Credit
Dec. 31, 2018	Depreciation Expense	20,000	
	Accumulated Depreciation—Machinery		20,000
	(*Record declining balance depreciation*		
	expense)		

Assets	=	Liabilities	+	Shareholders' Equity (Depreciation Expense)
−20,000				−20,000

© Cengage Learning

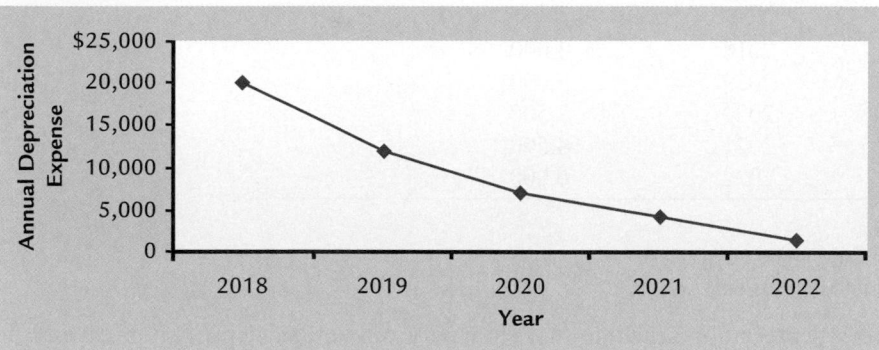

EXHIBIT 7.7

Declining Balance Pattern of Depreciation (Annual Depreciation Expense Decreases)

proportional to the usage of the asset and asset usage can be measured, depreciation expense can be computed using the **units-of-production method**. Usage is typically gauged by a measure of productive capacity (such as units produced, hours worked, or kilometres driven). An automobile is an example of an asset whose service potential usually declines with use, where usage is measured by the number of kilometres travelled.

To compute depreciation expense under the units-of-production method, the depreciation cost per unit is determined as shown in the following equation:

$$\text{Depreciation cost per unit} = \frac{(\text{Cost} - \text{Residual value})}{\text{Expected usage of the asset over useful life}}$$

Next, the depreciation cost per unit is multiplied by the actual usage of the asset in the period:

$$\begin{array}{l}\text{Units-of-production} \\ \text{depreciation expense}\end{array} = \text{Depreciation cost per unit} \times \text{Actual usage of the asset}$$

An example of depreciation expense computed by the units-of-production method is shown in Cornerstone 7.4. Depending on the use of the asset during the year, the units-of-production depreciation method can result in a pattern of depreciation expense that may appear accelerated, straight-line, decelerated, or erratic.

Computing Depreciation Expense Using the Units-of-Production Method

CORNERSTONE 7.4

Information:

On January 1, 2018, Logan Inc. acquired a machine for $50,000. Logan expects the machine to be worth $5,000 at the end of its five-year useful life. Logan expects the machine to run for 30,000 machine hours. Logan uses the units-of-production method of depreciation. The actual machine hours follow:

(Continued)

CORNERSTONE
VIDEO

CORNERSTONE

7.4

(Continued)

	Actual Usage
Year	(in machine hours)
2018	3,000
2019	9,000
2020	7,500
2021	4,500
2022	6,000

Required:

1. Compute the depreciation cost per machine hour.

2. Prepare a depreciation schedule that shows the amount of depreciation expense for each year of the machine's life.

3. Prepare the journal entry required to record depreciation expense in 2018.

Why:

Depreciation is a process that allocates the cost of a depreciable asset over those periods that benefit from the use of the asset (the matching concept).

Depreciation on a unit-of-production basis is an asset cost allocation method that recognizes that the time periods which benefit from the use of an asset are the time periods in which the asset is physically used in business operations.

Solution:

1. $\dfrac{\text{Depreciable cost}}{\text{Estimated usage}} = \dfrac{(\$50,000 - \$5,000)}{30,000 \text{ machine hours}} = \$1.50 \text{ per machine hour}$

2.

End of Year	Cost per Machine Hour	× Actual Usage	= Depreciation Expense	Accumulated Depreciation	Book Value
					$50,000
2018	$1.50	3,000	$ 4,500	$ 4,500	45,500
2019	1.50	9,000	13,500	18,000	32,000
2020	1.50	7,500	11,250	29,250	20,750
2021	1.50	4,500	6,750	36,000	14,000
2022	1.50	6,000	9,000	45,000	5,000
			$45,000		

3.

Date	Account and Explanation	Debit	Credit
Dec. 31, 2018	Depreciation Expense	4,500	
	Accumulated Depreciation— Machinery		4,500
	(Record units-of-production depreciation expense)		

Assets	=	Liabilities	+	Shareholders' Equity (Depreciation Expense)
−4,500				−4,500

Note that when production varies widely and irregularly from period to period, the units-of-production method will result in an erratic pattern of depreciation expense, as shown in Exhibit 7.8.

Relative to the prior year, Logan reported an increase in depreciation expense in 2018 and 2021; depreciation expense decreased in all other years. Thus, the units-of-production method does not produce a predictable pattern of depreciation expense. While this method does an excellent job of matching depreciation expense to usage of the asset, it is difficult to apply because it requires estimation of expected usage (which is a more difficult task than simply estimating useful life in years) and is used less widely than the other two depreciation methods.

Choosing Between Depreciation Methods by Management

The three depreciation methods can be summarized as follows:

- The straight-line depreciation method produces a constant amount of depreciation expense in each period of the asset's life and is consistent with a constant rate of decline in service potential.
- The declining balance depreciation method accelerates the assignment of an asset's cost to depreciation expense by allocating a larger amount of cost to the early years of an asset's life and a smaller amount of cost to the later years of an asset's life. This allocation is consistent with a decline in annual service potential.
- The units-of-production depreciation method is based on a measure of the asset's use in each period, and the periodic depreciation expense increases and decreases with the asset's use. In this sense, the units-of-production depreciation method is based not on a standardized pattern of declining service potential but on a pattern tailored to the individual asset and its use.

Exhibit 7.9 compares the depreciation expense recorded by Logan Inc. under each of the depreciation methods discussed. Note that the total amount of depreciation expense ($45,000) recognized by Logan Inc. was the same under all three methods. This resulted in the asset having a book value of $5,000 at the end of 2022. At this point, book value is equal to residual value. While the total depreciation expense for each method was the same, the yearly amounts of depreciation expense recognized were different.

Because each method is acceptable under IFRS, what factors does management use in selecting a depreciation method? Ideally, management should select the method that best matches the pattern of decline in service potential of the asset. This would result in the best matching of depreciation expense to the period in which the asset helped to

(EXHIBIT 7.8)

Units-of-Production Pattern of Depreciation (Annual Expense Changes with Extent of Asset Use)

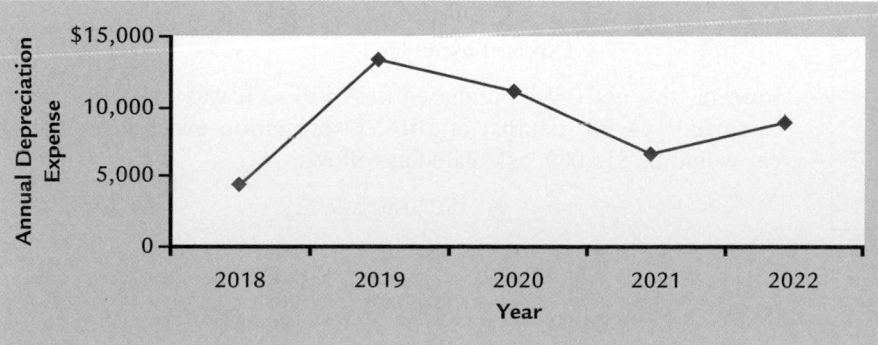

© Cengage Learning

(EXHIBIT 7.9)

Depreciation Patterns over Time

Year	Straight-Line	Double-Declining-Balance	Units-of-Production
2018	$ 9,000	$20,000	$ 4,500
2019	9,000	12,000	13,500
2020	9,000	7,200	11,250
2021	9,000	4,320	6,750
2022	9,000	1,480	9,000
Total	$45,000	$45,000	$45,000

© Cengage Learning

generate revenue. However, in reality, other factors also help motivate this decision. For example, the simplicity and ease of application of the straight-line method is very appealing to management. In addition, the use of the straight-line method produces a higher reported income in the early years of an asset's life. This higher income may increase management bonuses (which are often based on the level of net income achieved) and create a favourable impression to outside users that could result in higher share prices. For these reasons, the straight-line method is the most popular depreciation method. Once a depreciation method is chosen, that method should be consistently applied over time to enhance the comparability of the financial information.

ETHICAL DECISION   The use of estimates in depreciation calculations presents an ethical issue for accountants. If an estimate is biased upward or downward, it can have significant financial statement impacts. For example, accountants may face pressures to increase the useful life of an asset beyond what is reasonable. This upwardly biased estimate of useful life decreases the amount of depreciation expense recorded and increases the company's net income. Accountants must resist these pressures and provide an unbiased estimate that faithfully portrays the service potential of the asset.

Depreciation for Partial Years

Capital assets are purchased (or disposed of) at various times throughout the year. If an asset is purchased at the beginning of the year or disposed of at the end of the year, a full year of depreciation is recorded. If, however, the asset is purchased (or disposed of) during the accounting period, the matching concept requires that depreciation be recorded only for the portion of the year that the asset was used to generate revenue.

To illustrate, consider an asset purchased on April 1, 2018, for $100,000, which is being depreciated using the straight-line method over five years with no residual value. For a full year (12 months), depreciation expense would be $20,000, calculated as follows:[5]

$$\frac{(\text{Cost} - \text{Residual value})}{\text{Expected useful life}} = \frac{(\$100,000 - \$0)}{5 \text{ years}}$$

However, this asset was purchased in April, so it was only depreciated for the partial year (9 months) of 2018. Depreciation expense for the partial year would be $15,000, calculated as follows:

$$\$20,000 \times (9/12)$$

---

concept Q&A

If all depreciation methods result in the same amount being recorded as an expense over the life of the fixed asset, why would a financial statement user be concerned with the depreciation method chosen?

Answer:

The choice of depreciation method affects the amount recognized as an expense during each year of the capital asset's life. Therefore, the company's reported income each year would be different based on the depreciation method chosen.

---

[5] Although acquisitions may occur *during* a month, for purposes of simplifying depreciation calculations, many companies follow the policy of substituting the date of the nearer first of the month for the actual transaction date. Thus, acquisitions on March 25 or April 9 would be treated as acquisitions on April 1 for purposes of calculating depreciation expense.

A full year of depreciation expense, $20,000, would be recorded for the next four years. Because a full year of depreciation was not taken in 2018, a partial year of depreciation (3 months) of $5,000 would need to be recorded in 2023 to fully depreciate the asset, calculated as follows:

$$\$20,000 \times (3/12)$$

At this point, the asset would be fully depreciated.[6]

Depreciation and Income Tax Reporting

A company can choose between the three depreciation methods discussed earlier as it prepares its financial statements, but the depreciation method used in preparing its tax return is usually not the same. The Income Tax Act of Canada specifies which rates and methods a company must use to prepare tax returns. Tax depreciation rules are designed to stimulate investment in capital assets and, therefore, are not guided by the matching concept. Tax depreciation rules provide for the rapid (accelerated) expensing of depreciable assets, which lowers income tax payable. By bringing forward the bulk of depreciation expense, tax depreciation rules enable companies to save cash by delaying the payment of taxes. Depreciation rates and methods under the Income Tax Act of Canada are generally not acceptable for financial reporting purposes. The financial statement effects of different depreciation rules for accounting and tax purposes are discussed in later accounting courses.

YOUDECIDE Impact of Depreciation Method on Income

You are a financial analyst trying to assess the earnings performance and profitability of two companies, Cobine Corp. and Sayed Ltd., which both began operations within the past year. Both companies report the same amount of income and are comparable in almost every respect. However, one item catches your attention. While both companies report the same amount of property, plant, and equipment, Cobine reports a much smaller amount for depreciation expense. In the notes to the financial statements, Cobine indicates that it uses the straight-line depreciation method while Sayed uses the double-declining-balance depreciation method.

How does the difference in depreciation methods affect your assessment of the two companies?

When companies use different depreciation methods, significant variations may result in income although no real economic differences exist. As shown in Exhibit 7.9, all depreciation methods result in the same amount being expensed over the life of the asset; however, the amount expensed each year will differ.

Because its assets are relatively new, Cobine's use of the straight-line depreciation method will result in less expense and higher income compared to Sayed, which uses the double-declining-balance method. However, if the company's depreciable capital assets were relatively older, the situation would be reversed—the use of the accelerated depreciation method would result in lower expense and higher income relative to the straight-line method. In both cases, the differences in expense and income are merely the result of an accounting choice and reflect no real underlying economic differences between the two firms.

Financial statement users must be able to "see through" the financial statement effects of accounting choices and base their decision on the underlying economics of the business.

Components and the Depreciation Process

IFRS requires that when items of property, plant, and equipment contain separate significant components for which different depreciation methods and rates are appropriate, the costs of those components should be determined and depreciated separately. The typical example would be an airplane, where the cost of the airplane body itself

---

[6] For the sake of simplicity, most examples, exercises, and problems in this book assume that asset purchases (and disposals) occur at the beginning of the accounting period.

may need to be segregated from the cost of the engines and the seats and each of the assets depreciated separately if they have different useful lives. This topic is addressed in advanced accounting courses. In this text, it is assumed that all components of an asset have the same useful life.

Revaluation Model Alternative

IFRS allows companies to choose to account for property, plant, and equipment under the cost or revaluation model. Very few companies use the revaluation model. It is most relevant in countries where a high inflation rate exists or in industries where fair values may be more relevant to users than cost, such as in the real estate industry. Under this model the carrying value of property, plant, and equipment is adjusted to fair market value where those values can be reliably measured. Revaluation losses are recorded on the statement of earnings, as are reversals of those losses. Revaluation gains are recorded in Other Comprehensive Income, as are reversals of such gains. At the end of each accounting period, Other Comprehensive Income is closed out to Accumulated Other Comprehensive Income, and hence, revaluation gains form a separate part of shareholders' equity, typically referred to as revaluation surplus. The accounting under the revaluation model is complex and is covered in advanced accounting courses.

Valuation Model—Investment Properties (Rental Real Estate)

IFRS allows companies that own investment properties to record these properties at cost or at fair value under the valuation model. Investment properties are generally properties held for rental purposes and are not occupied by the owner. Under the valuation model, gains and losses are recorded on the statement of earnings but do not affect Other Comprehensive Income. If investment properties are carried at fair value, no depreciation is recorded on these properties. This topic is covered in depth in advanced accounting courses.

EXPENDITURES AFTER ACQUISITION

OBJECTIVE **5**

Distinguish between capital and revenue expenditures.

In addition to expenditures made when property, plant, and equipment is purchased, companies incur costs over the life of the asset that range from ordinary repairs and maintenance to major overhauls, additions, and improvements. Companies must decide whether these expenditures should be capitalized (added to an asset account) or expensed (reported in total on the statement of earnings).

Exhibit 7.10 summarizes different expenditures and how they would be accounted for.

Because it is often difficult to distinguish capital and revenue expenditures, managers must exercise professional judgment in deciding to capitalize or expense these costs. Many companies develop simple policies to aid them in making this decision. For example, a company may decide to expense all costs under $1,000.

Revenue Expenditures

Expenditures that do not increase the future economic benefits of the asset are called **revenue expenditures** and are expensed in the same period the expenditure is made. These expenditures maintain the level of benefits provided by the asset, relate only to the current period, occur frequently, and typically involve relatively small dollar amounts. An example of a revenue expenditure is the ordinary repair and maintenance of an asset.

(EXHIBIT 7.10)

Types of Expenditures

Type of Expenditure	Description	Examples	Accounting Treatment
Ordinary Repairs and Maintenance	Expenditures that keep an asset in normal operating condition	• Oil change for a truck • Painting of a building • Replacement of a minor part • Normal cleaning costs	*Expense* in the current period
Extraordinary or Major Repairs	Expenditures that extend the asset's useful life	• Overhaul or rebuilding of an engine • Fixing structural damage to a building	*Capitalize and depreciate* over the asset's useful life
Additions	Adding a new or major component to an existing asset	• Adding a new wing to a building • Installing a pollution control device on a machine	*Capitalize and depreciate* over the shorter of the life of the asset and the addition
Improvements (or Betterments)	The replacement of a component of an asset with a better one that increases efficiency or productivity	• Replacing an old air conditioning unit with a more efficient one • Replacing a manual machine control with computer-controlled controls	*Capitalize and depreciate* over the improved asset's useful life

© Cengage Learning

Capital Expenditures

Expenditures that extend the life of the asset, expand the productive capacity, or increase efficiency are called **capital expenditures**. Because these expenditures provide benefits to the company in both current and future periods, they are added to an asset account and are subject to depreciation. These expenditures typically involve relatively large dollar amounts. Examples of capital expenditures include extraordinary or major repairs, additions, remodelling of buildings, and improvements (sometimes called betterments).

REVISION OF DEPRECIATION

Depreciation expense is based on estimates of useful life and residual value. As new or additional information becomes available, a company will often find it necessary to revise its estimates of useful life, residual value, or both. The change of these estimates will result in a recalculation of depreciation expense. In addition, when a capital expenditure is made, it is also necessary for a company to recalculate its depreciation expense. In such situations, the company does not change previously recorded amounts related to depreciation. Instead, any revision of depreciation expense is accounted for in current and future periods.

OBJECTIVE ⑥

Explain and account for revisions in depreciation.

To revise depreciation expense, the following steps are performed:

Step 1: Obtain the carrying or book value of the asset at the date of the revision of depreciation.

Step 2: Compute depreciation expense using the revised amounts for carrying or book value, useful life, and/or residual value.

Cornerstone 7.5 illustrates the accounting for a revision in depreciation.

Note that only the current and future years are affected by this revision. Parker does not need to adjust the prior years' financial statements based on this new information. However, if the change in estimate is a material amount, it should be disclosed in the notes to the financial statements.

CORNERSTONE 7.5

CORNERSTONE VIDEO

Revising Depreciation Expense

Information:

On January 1, 2010, Parker Publishing Company bought a printing press for $300,000. Parker estimated that the printing press would have a residual value of $50,000 and a useful life of 10 years. Parker uses the straight-line depreciation method and the book value of the asset on December 31, 2017, was $100,000. On January 1, 2018, Parker paid $90,000 to add a digital typesetting component to the printing press. After the addition, the printing press is expected to have a remaining useful life of six years and a residual value of $10,000.

Required:

1. What is the book value of the printing press on January 1, 2018?

2. What amount should Parker record for depreciation expense for 2018?

Why:

Depreciation expense is occasionally revised to recognize that the estimated residual value and useful life of an asset may change over time. A revision in depreciation estimates is accounted for prospectively in the current and future periods.

Solution:

1. Because the digital typesetting component is a capital expenditure, the cost of the addition is added to the book value of the asset, resulting in a revised book value of $190,000 ($90,000 + $100,000).

2. Using the revised book value, the revised estimate of residual value, and the revised estimate of useful life, Parker would recognize depreciation expense in 2018 of $30,000, calculated as:

$$\text{Depreciation expense} = \frac{\$190,000 - \$10,000}{6 \text{ years}} = \$30,000 \text{ per year}$$

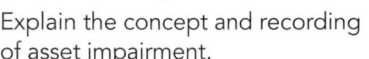

OBJECTIVE 7

Explain the concept and recording of asset impairment.

MEASURING AND RECORDING OF IMPAIRMENT OF PROPERTY, PLANT, AND EQUIPMENT

An **impairment** is a permanent decline in the future benefit or service potential of an asset. The impairment may be due to numerous factors, including too little depreciation expense being recorded in previous years or obsolescence of the asset. A company is required to review an asset for impairment if events or circumstances lead the company to believe that an asset may be impaired. If a depreciable capital asset is impaired, a company should reduce the asset's book value in the year the impairment occurs. In later years, impairment losses can be reversed, but the resulting asset write-ups cannot result in the asset being recorded at an amount that exceeds the asset's original cost.

The impairment test consists of two steps:

Step 1. Existence: An impairment exists if the asset's carrying value exceeds its **recoverable amount**. An asset's recoverable amount is the greater of its value in use or its fair value less costs to sell.

Step 2. Measurement: If an impairment exists, the impairment loss is measured as the difference between the carrying value and the recoverable amount.

Details of the complexities of impairment accounting are covered in advanced accounting courses.

Cornerstone 7.6 illustrates the accounting for an impairment.

Recording an Impairment of Property, Plant, and Equipment

CORNERSTONE 7.6

Information:

Tabor Company acquired a machine on January 1, 2010, for $150,000. On January 1, 2018, when the machine has a carrying value of $60,000, Tabor believes that recent technological innovations may have led to an impairment in the value of the machine. Tabor estimates the machine will generate future cash flows of $50,000 and its current fair value is $42,000. Costs to sell would be $5,000

CORNERSTONE
VIDEO

Required:

1. Determine whether the machine is impaired as of January 2018.

2. If the machine is impaired, compute the loss from impairment.

3. Prepare the journal entry to record the impairment.

Why:

Recording the impairment of property, plant, and equipment results in properly recording the carrying value of an asset that can be recovered from future business operations or from a future sale.

Solution:

1. The machine is impaired because the carrying value of $60,000 exceeds the recoverable amount of $50,000 (the greater value in use of $50,000 and fair value less costs to sell of $37,000).

2. Recoverable amount − Carrying value = Loss from impairment

   $50,000 − $60,000 = $10,000

3. _____

Date	Account and Explanation	Debit	Credit
Jan. 1, 2018	Loss from Impairment	10,000	
	Equipment—		10,000
	Accumulated Impairment		
	(Record impairment of asset)		

	Shareholders' Equity (Loss from
Assets = Liabilities +	Impairment)
−10,000	−10,000

DISPOSAL OF PROPERTY, PLANT, AND EQUIPMENT

Although companies usually dispose of property, plant, and equipment voluntarily, disposition may also be forced.

- **Voluntary disposal** occurs when the company determines that the asset is no longer useful. The disposal may occur at the end of the asset's useful life or at some other

OBJECTIVE ⑧

Explain the process of recording the disposal of property, plant, and equipment.

time. For example, obsolescence due to unforeseen technological developments may lead to an earlier than expected disposition of the asset.

• **Involuntary disposal** occurs when assets are lost or destroyed through theft, acts of nature, or by accident.

In either case, disposals rarely occur on the first or last day of an accounting period. Therefore, the disposal of property, plant, and equipment usually requires two journal entries:

1. An entry to record depreciation expense up to the date of disposal.
2. An entry to:
   • Remove the asset's carrying value (the cost of the asset *and* the related accumulated depreciation).
   • Record a gain or loss on disposal of the asset, which is computed as the difference between the proceeds from the sale and the carrying value of the asset.

Gains and losses on the disposal of property, plant, and equipment are normally reported as "other revenues or gains" or "other expenses and losses," respectively, and appear immediately after income from operations on a multiple-step statement of earnings.

Rogers's policy for recording disposals, as shown in the notes to its 2014 financial statements, is shown below.

> Gains and losses on disposal of an item of PP&E are determined by comparing the proceeds from disposal with the carrying amount of PP&E, and are recognized within other income in the Consolidated Statement of Income.

Cornerstone 7.7 illustrates the accounting for the disposal of property, plant, and equipment.

CORNERSTONE 7.7

Recording the Disposition of Property, Plant, and Equipment

Information:

Dwan Corporation sold a machine on July 1, 2018, for $22,000. The machine had originally cost $100,000. Accumulated depreciation on January 1, 2018, was $80,000. Depreciation expense for the first six months of 2018 was $5,000.

Required:

1. Prepare the journal entry to record depreciation expense up to the date of disposal.
2. Compute the gain or loss on disposal of the machine.
3. Prepare the journal entry to record the disposal of the machine.

CORNERSTONE VIDEO

Why:

When a company disposes of an asset, the carrying value of the asset at the date of disposition is determined and removed from the accounting records, and any related gain or loss is recognized.

(Continued)

Solution:

1.

Date	Account and Explanation	Debit	Credit
July 1, 2018	Depreciation Expense	5,000	
	Accumulated Depreciation—Equipment		5,000
	(Record depreciation expense)		

Assets	= Liabilities +	Shareholders' Equity (Depreciation Expense)
−5,000		−5,000

2.

Proceeds from Sale		$22,000
Less: Carrying Value of Asset Sold		
Cost	$100,000	
Accumulated Depreciation ($80,000 + $5,000)	(85,000)	15,000
Gain on Disposal		$ 7,000

3.

Date	Account and Explanation	Debit	Credit
July 1, 2018	Cash	22,000	
	Accumulated Depreciation—Equipment	85,000	
	Equipment		100,000
	Gain on Disposal of Property, Plant, and Equipment		7,000
	(Record disposal of machine)		

Assets	= Liabilities +	Shareholders' Equity (Gain on Disposal)
+22,000		+7,000
+85,000		
−100,000		

Note that Dwan recorded depreciation expense up to the date of disposal. Once this journal entry is made, the carrying value is updated to reflect the increased accumulated depreciation. This revised carrying value is then used to compute the Gain on Disposal of Property, Plant, and Equipment, which appears in the "other revenues and gains" section of the statement of earnings.

If Dwan had received $12,000 for the asset in Cornerstone 7.7, the following computation would have been made:

Proceeds from sale		$12,000
Less: Carrying value of asset sold		
Cost	$100,000	
Accumulated depreciation ($80,000 + $5,000)	(85,000)	15,000
Loss on disposal of property, plant, and equipment		$ (3,000)

Because the proceeds from the sale were less than the carrying value, Dwan recorded a loss as follows:

Date	Account and Explanation	Debit	Credit
July 1, 2018	Cash	12,000	
	Accumulated Depreciation	85,000	
	Loss on Disposal of Property, Plant, and Equipment	3,000	
	Equipment		100,000
	(Record disposal of machine)		

Assets	= Liabilities +	Shareholders' Equity (Loss on Disposal)
+12,000		−3,000
+85,000		
−100,000		

Dwan would report the loss in the "other expenses and losses" section of the statement of earnings.

YOUDECIDE Future Asset Replacement

You are considering a major investment in one of two long-haul trucking companies. Both companies are about the same size, travel competitive routes, and have similar net incomes. However, the statements of financial position reveal significant differences in the accumulated depreciation for the trucks as shown below:

	Stanley Company	Lucknow Company
Trucks	$ 600,000	$ 550,000
Less: Accumulated depreciation	(138,000)	(477,000)
Carrying value	$ 462,000	$ 73,000

What conclusions can you make regarding the future cash outflows each company will have to make for future asset replacements?

Assuming that the assets' estimates of useful life are consistent with their economic lives, the closer that accumulated depreciation is to

original cost, the older the assets and the more likely that they will have to be replaced. Lucknow Company's assets are closer to being fully depreciated than those of Stanley Company. Therefore, Lucknow is more likely to make cash outflows for the replacement of its assets. Although more information would be needed about Lucknow in order to know the precise impact of the impending replacement, the comparison of the two accumulated depreciation amounts does provide you with valuable insights. While the recording of depreciation expense does not alter cash flow, accumulated depreciation signals the approaching future replacement of depreciable capital assets, which usually requires cash.

A comparison of accumulated depreciation to cost can provide financial statement users with an approximation of the remaining useful life of the assets.

ANALYZING PROPERTY, PLANT, AND EQUIPMENT

OBJECTIVE 9

Evaluate the use of property, plant, and equipment.

Because property, plant, and equipment are major productive assets of most companies, it is useful to understand whether the company is using these assets efficiently. In other words, how well is the company using its property, plant, and equipment to generate revenue? One measure of how efficiently a company is using its capital assets is the **tangible capital asset turnover ratio**. It is calculated as follows:

$$\text{Tangible capital asset turnover ratio} = \frac{\text{Net sales}}{\text{Average tangible capital assets}}$$

Generally, the more efficiently a company uses its capital tangible assets, the greater the ratio will be.

In addition to the tangible capital asset turnover ratio, investors are also concerned with the condition of a company's depreciable capital assets. Because older assets tend to be less efficient than newer assets, the age of a company's depreciable capital assets can provide useful insights into the company's efficiency. The age of a company's depreciable capital assets also can provide an indication of a company's capital replacement policy and assist managers in estimating future capital expenditures. A rough estimate of the **average age of depreciable capital assets** can be computed as follows:

$$\text{Average age of depreciable capital assets} = \frac{\text{Accumulated depreciation}}{\text{Depreciation expense}}$$

A third measure of the efficiency of use of a company's total assets is the **return on assets (ROA)** ratio. A greater ratio generally indicates more efficient use of total assets when one company is being compared to another. This ratio is calculated as follows:

$$\text{Return on assets (ROA)} = \frac{\text{Net profit} + \text{Interest expense (net of tax effect)}}{\text{Average total assets}}$$

Average total assets is calculated as total assets at beginning of year plus total assets at end of year, divided by 2.

Cornerstone 7.8 illustrates the calculation of the tangible capital asset turnover ratio, the average age of tangible capital assets, and the return on total assets.

Analyzing Property, Plant, and Equipment and Total Asset Ratios

Information:

The following information was obtained from the financial statements of Rogers and Shaw Communications (all amounts in millions):

CORNERSTONE
VIDEO

Account	Rogers (Dec. 31)	Shaw (Aug. 31)
Total assets, 2014	$26,522	$13,250
Total assets, 2013	23,601	12,732
Property, plant, and equipment, net, 2013	10,255	3,370
Property, plant, and equipment, net, 2014	10,655	3,652
Accumulated depreciation, 2014	17,997	3,343
Net sales	12,580	5,241
Depreciation expense, 2014	2,144	768
Interest expense, 2014	817	266
Net income, 2014	1,341	887
Income tax rate	27%	26%

Required:

1. Compute the tangible capital asset turnover ratio for Rogers and Shaw for 2014.

2. Compute the average age of Rogers's and Shaw's tangible depreciable capital assets at the end of 2014.

3. Compare the two companies' ROA ratios.

Why:

Calculation of ratios related to property, plant, and equipment assists users in assessing the extent to which such assets are being efficiently used by the company as well as their condition.

(Continued)

CORNERSTONE

7.8

(Continued)

Solution:

1.

$$\text{Tangible capital asset turnover ratio} = \frac{\text{Net sales}}{\text{Average tangible capital assets}}$$

Rogers	Shaw
$\dfrac{\$12{,}580}{\dfrac{(\$10{,}255 + \$10{,}655)}{2}} = 1.20 \text{ times}$	$\dfrac{\$5{,}241}{\dfrac{(\$3{,}370 + \$3{,}652)}{2}} = 1.49 \text{ times}$

2.

$$\text{Average age of tangible depreciable capital assets} = \frac{\text{Accumulated depreciation}}{\text{Depreciation expense}}$$

Rogers	Shaw
$\dfrac{\$17{,}997}{\$2{,}144} = 8.39 \text{ years}$	$\dfrac{\$3{,}343}{\$768} = 4.35 \text{ years}$

3.

$$\text{Return on asset ratio} = \frac{\text{Profit} + \text{interest expense (net of tax)}}{\text{Average total assets}}$$

Rogers	Shaw
$\dfrac{\$1{,}341 + (817 \times (100\% - 26\%))}{\dfrac{\$(26{,}522 + 23{,}601)}{2}} = 7.7\%$	$\dfrac{\$887 + 266 \times (100\% - 27\%)}{\dfrac{\$(13{,}520 + 12{,}732)}{2}} - 8.2\%$

Sources: Rogers Communications Inc. Annual Reports and Shaw Communications Annual Reports.

In Cornerstone 7.8, the capital asset turnover ratio tells us that for each dollar invested in tangible depreciable capital, Rogers generated sales of $1.20 while Shaw generated sales of $1.49. It appears that both Rogers and Shaw are efficiently using their tangible depreciable capital assets to generate sales. In addition, Rogers's assets are, on average, 8.39 years old, while Shaw's assets are approximately 4.39 years old. This signals that Rogers will most likely be making significant capital expenditures before Shaw in terms of increasing or maintaining its productive capacity.

In addition to comparing a company's capital asset turnover ratio with that of prior years and its competitors, it is necessary to gain an understanding of a company's operations to appropriately assess how efficiently a company is using its capital assets. For example, a company's capital asset turnover may be lower than some of its competitors because it is currently spending large amounts to expand its plant capacity in anticipation of future sales. These expansion activities (which are capitalized in the current period) could depress a company's capital turnover ratio.

In fact, this exact rationale is the reason why Rogers's return on total assets is lower than Shaw's for 2014. Rogers is significantly increasing its asset base, which has temporarily decreased its return on assets ratio compared to Shaw. As future earnings accrue to Rogers based on its increased asset base, the difference in the return on assets ratio of .5% (8.2% − 7.7%) should decrease and may increase in favour of Rogers.

INTANGIBLE ASSETS

Intangible capital assets, like tangible assets, represent future economic benefit to the company, but unlike tangible assets, they lack physical substance. Patents, copyrights, trademarks, leaseholds, organization costs, franchises, and goodwill are all examples of intangible assets. The economic benefits associated with most intangible assets are in the form of legal rights and privileges resulting from intellectual property that are conferred on the owner of the asset. The economic value of a patent, for example, is the legal right to restrict, control, or charge for the use of the idea or process covered by the patent.

Because intangible assets lack physical substance, it is often easy to overlook their importance to the overall value of a company. Recent research suggests that between 60% and 80% of a company's market value may be tied to intangible assets. For many companies, intangible assets may be the most important assets they have. A technology company like BlackBerry could easily argue that the true value of the company lies with its intellectual capital and patents, not its tangible property, plant, and equipment. However, due to unique issues with intangibles (such as the highly uncertain nature of future benefits and the possibility of wide fluctuations in value), the economic value of many intangible assets is not generally captured in financial statements by current accounting standards.

OBJECTIVE 10

Explain the measurement and reporting of intangible assets.

Accounting for Intangible Assets

Intangible assets are recorded at cost, consistent with the cost principle. Similar to tangible capital assets, the cost of an intangible asset is any expenditure necessary to acquire the asset and to prepare the asset for use. For intangible assets purchased from outside the company, the primary element of the cost is the purchase price. Costs such as registration, filing, and legal fees are considered necessary costs and are capitalized as part of the intangible asset.

For internally developed intangible assets, the cost of developing the asset is expensed as incurred and normally recorded as **research and development (R&D) expense**. While expenditures for R&D may lead to intangible assets such as patents and copyrights, R&D is not generally an intangible asset. IFRS does allow certain R&D expenditures to be capitalized if it is probable that future benefits will be received and provided that specified criteria are met. Exhibit 7.11 provides a listing of some typical intangible assets.

Companies also incur significant costs such as legal fees, share issue costs, accounting fees, and promotional fees when they are formed. It can be argued that these **organizational costs** are an intangible asset that provides a benefit to a company indefinitely. However, current accounting standards treat organizational costs as an expense in the period the cost is incurred.

Once an intangible asset is recorded, companies must determine whether the asset has a finite life or an indefinite life. The cost of an intangible asset with a *finite life*, like the cost of a tangible asset, is allocated to accounting periods over the life of the asset to reflect the decline in service potential. This process is referred to as **amortization**. Most companies will amortize the cost of an intangible asset on a straight-line basis over the shorter of the economic and legal life of the asset. For example, a patent has a legal life of 20 years from the date it is granted. However, the economic advantage offered by a patent

concept Q&A

If intangible assets represent a major amount of many companies' value, wouldn't any estimate of the intangible asset's value be better than not recording the asset at all?

Answer:

While intangible assets are certainly relevant to financial statement users, information must be reliably measured to be recorded in the financial statements. For many intangibles, the inability to measure the intangible asset reliably results in the inability to record the intangible asset. This trade-off between the relevance and reliability of information is often a matter of judgment.

(EXHIBIT 7.11)

Common Types of Intangible Assets

Intangible Asset	Description	Cost Includes	Amortization
Leasehold Improvements	Physical improvements made to leased premises under terms agreed to in a lease. Length of lease may vary.	Cost of improvements; includes materials and labour, permits, legal costs	Shorter of economic life and legal life of lease term
Patent	Right to manufacture, sell, or use product. The legal life is 20 years from the date of grant of patent.	Purchase price, registration fees, legal costs	Shorter of the economic life and legal life
Copyright	Right to publish, sell, or control a literary or artistic work. The legal life is life of author plus 50 years.	Purchase price, registration fees, legal costs	Shorter of the economic life and legal life
Trademark	Right to the exclusive use of a distinctive name, phrase, or symbol (e.g., the iPod name or the Nike "swoosh"). The legal life is 15 years but it can be renewed indefinitely.	Purchase price, registration fees, legal costs	Not amortized since it has an indefinite life; reviewed at least annually for impairment
Franchise	Exclusive right to conduct a certain type of business in some particular geographic area. Life of the franchise depends on specific terms of the franchise contract.	Initial cost paid to acquire the franchise	Shorter of the economic life and legal life

© Cengage Learning

often expires before the end of its legal life as a result of other technological developments. Therefore, the shorter economic life should be used to amortize the cost of the patent.

If an intangible asset is determined to have an *indefinite life*, it is *not* amortized but is reviewed at least annually for impairment.

Goodwill is the most significant intangible asset reported by most companies. Goodwill in a business arises from such factors as customer satisfaction, quality products, skilled employees who provide excellent service based on their knowledge, and business location. Goodwill is internally generated in a business and is not recorded in financial statements unless it is purchased from an external party.

Goodwill, as an intangible asset, is recognized for accounting purposes as the excess of the purchase price for a business, which is in excess of the fair market value of that business's identifiable assets less identifiable liabilities.

Purchased goodwill is recorded at cost. Since goodwill has an indefinite life, goodwill is reviewed annually for impairment. Impairment losses are recognized in the statement of earnings in the year they occur. Accounting for purchased goodwill and impairments is studied in advanced accounting courses.

Cornerstone 7.9 illustrates the accounting for the acquisition and amortization of intangible assets.

In Cornerstone 7.9, several items are of note:

- Most intangible assets do not have a residual value. Therefore, the cost that is being amortized is usually the entire cost of the intangible asset.
- King amortized the patent over the shorter of its remaining legal life (13 years) and its economic life (10 years). This is consistent with recognizing amortization expense over the period that the intangible asset is expected to provide benefits.
- King recorded the amortization expense by directly crediting the intangible asset, Patent. After the amortization expense is recorded, the book value of the patent is $36,000 ($40,000 − $4,000).

Accounting for Intangible Assets

CORNERSTONE 7.9

Information:

On January 1, 2018, King Company acquired a patent from Queen Corporation for $40,000. The patent was originally granted on January 1, 2011, and has 13 years of its legal life remaining. However, due to technological advancements, King estimates that the patent will only provide benefits for 10 years. In addition, King purchased a trademark from Queen for $60,000.

► | CORNERSTONE VIDEO

Required:

1. Prepare any journal entries necessary to record the acquisition of the patent and the trademark.

2. Compute the amortization expense for the patent.

3. Compute the amortization expense for the trademark.

4. Prepare any adjusting journal entries necessary to record the amortization expense for 2018.

Why:

Intangible assets are recorded at the cost necessary to acquire the asset and to prepare the asset for use. The cost of the asset (excluding goodwill, which is tested for impairment) is allocated as an expense among the accounting periods in which the asset is used and benefits are received (the matching concept).

Solution:

1.

Date	Account and Explanation	Debit	Credit
Jan. 1, 2018	Patent	40,000	
	Trademark	60,000	
	Cash		100,000
	(To purchase patent and trademark)		

		Shareholders'
Assets	**= Liabilities +**	**Equity**
+40,000		
+60,000		
−100,000		

2.

$$\frac{\text{Cost} - \text{Residual value}}{\text{Useful life}} = \frac{\$40,000 - \$0}{10 \text{ years}} = \$4,000$$

3. Because the trademark has an indefinite life, no amortization is necessary.

4.

Date	Account and Explanation	Debit	Credit
Dec. 31, 2018	Amortization Expense	4,000	
	Patent		4,000
	(To record amortization of patent)		

		Shareholders' Equity (Amortization
Assets	**= Liabilities +**	**Expense)**
−4,000		−4,000

- Amortization expense is reported as operating expense on the statement of earnings.
- It is assumed that an impairment of the trademark has not occurred as of December 31, 2018.

YOU DECIDE   Measuring and Estimating the Dimensions of a Patent

You are the controller for Estevan Corporation, a research-intensive company engaged in the design and sale of ceramic products. For the past year, half of Estevan's research staff has been engaged in designing a process for coating iron and steel with a ceramic material for use in high-temperature areas of automobile engines. The company has secured a patent for its process and is about to begin marketing equipment that uses the patented process. The assistant controller has argued that half of the year's cost of research activities should be assigned to the patent, including the salaries paid to researchers. Additionally, while Estevan expects the patented equipment to be a viable product for only five years, the assistant controller recommends that the patent be amortized over its legal life of 20 years.

What is the impact of the assistant controller's recommendation, and how should you account for the patent?

If these costs were capitalized as part of the patent as the assistant controller recommended, current period assets and income would be overstated. In future periods, the higher recorded value of the intangible asset would result in an increase in amortization expense. While many analysts agree with the assistant controller that some research and development expenditures create an intangible asset, current accounting standards require that all research activities be expensed when incurred.

If the patent were amortized over its legal life, the cost of the patent would be spread over 20 years, resulting in lower yearly amounts of amortization expense and higher income. However, accounting standards require that intangible assets be amortized over the shorter of their legal lives or their economic lives. Therefore, a relatively higher amortization expense should be recognized over the five-year useful life of the patent.

Current accounting standards should be followed to avoid misstating the financial statements.

NATURAL RESOURCES

OBJECTIVE 11

Explain the measurement and reporting of natural resources.

Natural resources, such as coal deposits, oil reserves, and mineral deposits, make up an important part of the total assets for many natural resource companies. For example, Suncor Energy recorded oil sand properties of $40.1 billion at December 31, 2014, which represents 50% of its total assets. Like intangible assets, natural resources present difficult estimation and measurement problems. However, natural resources differ from other capital assets in two important ways:

- Unlike depreciable capital assets, natural resources are physically consumed as they are used by a company.
- Natural resources can generally be replaced or restored only by an act of nature. (Timberlands are renewed by replanting and growth, but coal deposits and most mineral deposits are not subject to renewal.)

The accounting for natural resources is quite complex; generally, though, it is similar to the accounting for intangible assets and depreciable capital assets. At acquisition, all the costs necessary to ready the natural resource for separation from the earth are capitalized. At the time a company acquires the property on which a natural resource is located (or the property rights to the natural resource itself), only a small portion of the costs necessary to ready the asset for removal are likely to have been incurred. Costs such as sinking a shaft to an underground coal deposit, drilling a well to an oil reserve, or removing the earth over a mineral deposit can be several times greater than the cost of acquiring the property. Costs to bring natural resources to market often include property or property rights acquisition, exploration costs, development costs, and decommissioning and site restoration costs.

As a natural resource is removed from the earth, its cost is allocated to each unit of natural resource removed. This process of allocating the cost of the natural resource to each period in which the resource is used is called **depletion**. Depletion is computed by using a procedure similar to that for the units-of-production method of depreciation. First, a depletion rate per unit is computed as follows:

$$\text{Unit depletion rate} = \frac{\text{Cost} - \text{Residual value}}{\text{Recoverable units}}$$

Second, depletion is calculated by multiplying the unit depletion rate by the number of units of the natural resource recovered during the period:

$$\text{Depletion} = \text{Unit depletion rate} \times \text{Units recovered}$$

As the natural resource is extracted, the natural resource is reduced and the amount of depletion computed is added to inventory. As the inventory is sold, the company will recognize an expense (cost of goods sold) related to the natural resource. Cornerstone 7.10 illustrates how to account for depletion of a natural resource.

Accounting for Depletion of a Natural Resource

CORNERSTONE 7.10

CORNERSTONE VIDEO

Information:

In 2018, Miller Mining Company purchased rights to coal reserves in northern Canada for $12,000,000, on which it developed an underground coal mine. Miller spent $26,000,000 to sink shafts to the coal seams and otherwise prepare the mine for operation. Miller estimates that there are 10,000,000 tonnes of recoverable coal and that the mine will be fully depleted eight years after mining begins in early 2019. The land has a residual value of $500,000. During 2019, 800,000 tonnes of coal were mined and 400,000 tonnes were sold for $2,000,000 cash.

Required:

1. Compute the cost of the natural resource.

2. Compute the unit depletion rate.

3. How much depletion is to be recorded in 2019?

4. Prepare the journal entries necessary to record depletion, sales revenue, and the cost of goods sold.

Why:

All costs necessary to acquire the natural resource and prepare it for use are capitalized as part of the natural resource. The depletion of the natural resource is added to inventory as the natural resource is depleted (used).

(Continued)

CORNERSTONE

7.10

(Continued)

Solution:

1. The cost of the natural resource includes all costs necessary to get the mine ready for use:

Cost	$12,000,000
Development/preparation costs	26,000,000
Cost	$38,000,000

2. Unit depletion rate $= \dfrac{(\$38,000,000 - \$500,000)}{10,000,000 \text{ tonnes}} = \$3.75$ per tonne

3. Depletion $= \$3.75 \times 800,000 = \$3,000,000$

4.

	Shareholders'
Assets = Liabilities +	**Equity**
+3,000,000	
−3,000,000	

Date	Account and Explanation	Debit	Credit
Dec. 31, 2019	Inventory	3,000,000	
	Accumulated Depletion		3,000,000
	(Record depletion of coal mine)		

	Shareholders' Equity (Sales
Assets = Liabilities +	**Revenue)**
+2,000,000	+2,000,000

Date	Account and Explanation	Debit	Credit
Dec. 31, 2019	Cash	2,000,000	
	Sales		2,000,000
	(Record sales revenue)		

	Shareholders' Equity (Cost of
Assets = Liabilities +	**Goods Sold)**
−1,500,000	−1,500,000

Date	Account and Explanation	Debit	Credit
Dec. 31, 2019	Cost of Goods Sold	1,500,000	
	Inventory		1,500,000
	(Record cost of goods sold)		

In Cornerstone 7.10, the following items are of particular importance:

- Miller records depletion by initially increasing an inventory account. As the coal is sold, inventory will be reduced and cost of goods sold will be recognized. Thus, the expense related to depletion will be matched with the revenue that is generated from the sale of the natural resource.
- Depletion increases the accumulated depletion account.

Companies often incur costs for tangible capital assets in connection with the use of a natural resource (such as buildings, equipment, roads to access the resource). Because the useful life of these assets is often limited by the life of the natural resource, these tangible assets should be depreciated using the units-of-production method on the same basis as the natural resource. However, if the assets have a life shorter than the expected life of the natural resource or a longer life because they will be used for the extraction of other natural resources, the assets should be depreciated over their own useful lives.

Miller could present the coal mine among its additional assets on the statement of financial position as shown in Exhibit 7.12.

EXHIBIT 7.12

Disclosure of Natural Resource

Property, plant, and equipment:	
Land	$ 2,200,000
Equipment and machinery, net of accumulated depreciation of $120,000	19,800,000
Coal mine, net of accumulated depletion of $3,000,000	35,000,000
Total property, plant, and equipment	$57,000,000

SIGNIFICANT DIFFERENCES BETWEEN IFRS AND ASPE

The number of significant differences between IFRS and ASPE has been decreasing over time. There are currently three significant areas of difference between IFRS and ASPE:

1. IFRS allows publicly accountable enterprises to use either the cost model or the revaluation (adjustment to fair value) model to record property, plant, and equipment subsequent to acquisition. The revaluation model allows increases in fair values to be recorded.

    ASPE requires the cost model to be used, which does not recognize increases in fair values.

2. IFRS requires publicly accountable enterprises to perform an impairment test at each annual reporting date on intangible assets with indefinite lives. Impairment losses must be recorded when an asset's carrying value exceeds its recoverable amount (which is the greater of the asset's value in use or fair value less costs of disposition). Impairment losses recorded in previous years may be reversed if there is an increase in the recoverable amount in a subsequent year.

    ASPE requires that an impairment test be performed if it is suspected that an impairment of an asset may have occurred. An impairment loss must be recorded if an asset's carrying value is less than its fair value less costs of disposition. Impairment losses cannot be reversed in subsequent reporting periods. The same approach is used for goodwill and intangible assets with indefinite lives as for property, plant, and equipment and intangible assets with finite lives (see above).

3(a). IFRS uses the term *depreciation* for the cost allocation process for property, plant, and equipment; ASPE allows the term *amortization* to also be used.

3(b). IFRS uses the term *finance leases* to apply to long-term leases that are reported as asset purchases. ASPE uses the term *capital leases* where long-term leases are reported as asset purchases.

SUMMARY OF LEARNING OBJECTIVES

LO1. Define, classify, and explain the accounting for property, plant, and equipment; intangibles; and natural resources.

- Property, plant, and equipment (along with intangibles and natural resources) are long-lived assets used by the company in the normal course of operations to generate revenue.
- These assets are generally recorded at cost.
- As the service potential of the asset is used, the asset's cost is allocated as an expense (called depreciation, amortization, or depletion).

LO2.   **Explain how the cost principle applies to recording the cost of property, plant, and equipment.**

- The cost of an asset is any expenditure necessary to acquire the asset and to prepare the asset for use.
- This amount is generally the cash paid.
- If noncash consideration is involved, cost is the fair value of the asset received or the fair value of the asset given up or consideration issued, whichever is more clearly determinable.

LO3.   **Explain the concept of depreciation.**

- Depreciation is the process of allocating the cost of a tangible depreciable capital asset to expense over the asset's useful life.
- Depreciation is not an attempt to measure fair value.
- Depreciation is designed to capture the declining service potential of a tangible depreciable capital asset.
- Three factors are necessary to compute depreciation expense: cost, useful life, and residual value.

LO4.   **Compute depreciation expense using various depreciation methods.**

- The straight-line method allocates an equal amount of the asset's cost to each year of the asset's useful life by dividing the asset's depreciable cost (cost less residual value) by the asset's useful life.
- The declining balance method is an accelerated method of depreciation that produces a declining amount of depreciation expense each period by multiplying the declining carrying value of an asset by a constant depreciation rate (computed as a multiple of the straight-line rate of depreciation).
- The units-of-production method recognizes depreciation expense based on the actual usage of the asset.

LO5.   **Distinguish between capital and revenue expenditures.**

- Revenue expenditures are expenditures that do not increase the future benefit of an asset and are expensed as incurred.
- Capital expenditures extend the life of the asset, expand productive capacity, or increase efficiency. Capital expenditures are added to the asset account and are subject to depreciation.

LO6.   **Explain and account for revisions in depreciation.**

- When new or additional information becomes available, a company will revise its calculation of depreciation expense.
- A revision in depreciation will be recorded in current and future periods.

LO7.   **Explain the concept and recording of asset impairment.**

- Impairment exists when the recoverable amount of an asset is less than the carrying value of the asset.
- An impairment loss, the excess of the carrying value over the recoverable amount of the asset, is recognized and the asset is reduced.
- The recoverable amount of an asset is the greater of the asset's value in use and fair market value, less disposal costs, of the asset if sold.

LO8.   **Explain the process of recording the disposal of property, plant, and equipment.**

- When a tangible depreciable capital asset is disposed of (either voluntarily or involuntarily), a gain or loss is recognized.
- The gain or loss is the difference between the proceeds from the sale and the carrying value of the asset.
- The gain or loss is reported on the statement of earnings as "other revenues or gains" or "other expenses and losses," respectively.

LO9.   Evaluate the use of property, plant, and equipment.

- The efficiency with which a company uses its property, plant, and equipment can be analyzed by using the tangible capital asset turnover ratio (net sales divided by average tangible capital assets).
- The condition of a company's assets and insights into the company's capital replacement policy can be examined by computing the average age of property, plant, and equipment (accumulated depreciation divided by depreciation expense).

LO10.   Explain the measurement and reporting of intangible assets.

- Intangible assets are recorded at cost, which is any expenditure necessary to acquire the asset and prepare it for use.
- If the intangible asset has a finite life, it is amortized over the shorter of the economic and legal life of the asset.
- If the intangible asset has an indefinite life, it is not amortized but is reviewed at least annually for impairment.

LO11.   Explain the measurement and reporting of natural resources.

- The cost of natural resources is any cost necessary to acquire and prepare the resource for separation from the earth.
- As the natural resource is removed, the cost is allocated to each unit of the natural resource that is removed and recorded in an inventory account. This process is called depletion.
- Depletion is calculated using a procedure similar to the units-of-production depreciation method.

CORNERSTONES

CORNERSTONE 7.1	Measuring and recording the cost of property, plant, and equipment, page 386
CORNERSTONE 7.2	Computing depreciation expense using the straight-line method, page 391
CORNERSTONE 7.3	Computing depreciation expense using the declining balance method, page 394
CORNERSTONE 7.4	Computing depreciation expense using the units-of-production method, page 395
CORNERSTONE 7.5	Revising depreciation expense, page 402
CORNERSTONE 7.6	Recording an impairment of property, plant, and equipment, page 403
CORNERSTONE 7.7	Recording the disposition of property, plant, and equipment, page 404
CORNERSTONE 7.8	Analyzing property, plant, and equipment and total asset ratios, page 407
CORNERSTONE 7.9	Accounting for intangible assets, page 411
CORNERSTONE 7.10	Accounting for depletion of a natural resource, page 413

KEY TERMS

Accumulated depreciation (p. 388)

Amortization (p. 409)

Average age of depreciable capital assets (p. 406)

Book value (p. 388)

Capital expenditures (p. 401)

Carrying value (p. 388)

Copyright (p. 410)

Cost (p. 388)

Declining balance depreciation method (p. 392)

Depletion (p. 413)

Depreciable cost (p. 390)

Depreciation (p. 387)

Depreciation expense (p. 388)

Goodwill (p. 410)

Impairment (p. 402)

Intangible capital assets (p. 409)

Involuntary disposal (p. 404)

Leasehold improvements (p. 410)

Natural resources (p. 412)

Organizational costs (p. 409)

Patent (p. 410)

Property, plant, and equipment (p. 383)

Recoverable amount (p. 402)

Research and development (R&D) expense (p. 409)

Residual value (p. 390)

Return on assets (ROA) (p. 407)

Revenue expenditures (p. 400)

Salvage value (p. 390)

Straight-line depreciation (p. 390)

Tangible capital asset turnover ratio (p. 406)

Trademark (p. 410)

Units-of-production method (p. 395)

Useful life (p. 389)

Voluntary disposal (p. 403)

REVIEW PROBLEM

I. Accounting for Property, Plant, and Equipment; Intangibles; and Natural Resources

Concept:

At acquisition, capital assets are capitalized at their cost. As the service potential of a capital asset declines, the cost of the asset is allocated as an expense among the accounting periods in which the asset is used and benefits are received.

Information:

Carroll Company manufactures a line of cranes, shovels, and hoists, all of which are electronically controlled. During 2017, the following transactions occurred:

a.   On January 2, Carroll purchased a building by signing a note payable for $702,900. The building is expected to have a useful life of 30 years and a residual value of $3,900.

b.   On January 3, Carroll purchased a delivery truck for $34,650 cash. The delivery truck is expected to have a useful life of five years and a $5,000 residual value.

c.   Immediately after the acquisition, Carroll spent $5,350 on a new engine for the truck. After installing the engine, Carroll estimated that this expenditure increased the useful life of the truck to eight years. The residual value is still expected to be $5,000.

d.   In order to ensure a coal supply for its heating plant, Carroll acquired a small operating coal mine for $1,980,000. Carroll estimated that the recoverable coal reserves at acquisition were 495,000 tonnes. Carroll's mine produced 40,000 tonnes of coal during 2017.

e.   Carroll purchased a patent on January 3 for $100,000. The patent has 12 years remaining on its legal life, but Carroll estimated its economic life to be 8 years. Carroll uses the straight-line amortization method.

Required:

1.   Record the acquisition of the building and the delivery truck.

2.   Prepare a depreciation schedule and record a full year's depreciation expense for 2017 on the building (use the straight-line depreciation method) and on the truck (use the double-declining-balance depreciation method).

3. Compute and record 2017 depletion for the coal mine.
4. Compute and record the amortization expense on the patent for 2017 on a straight-line basis.
5. Assume Carroll had sales of $8,800,000, depreciable tangible capital assets with an average net book value of $3,200,000, depreciation expense of $375,000, accumulated depreciation of $2,062,500, net income of $1,500,000, interest expense of $100,000, average annual total assets of $10,000,000, and an income tax rate of 25%. Compute the capital asset turnover ratio, the average age of the tangible capital assets, and the return on total assets. Comment on what the ratios mean.

Solution:

1. The cost of the building is $702,900 and is recorded as:

Date	Account and Explanation	Debit	Credit
Jan. 2, 2017	Buildings	702,900	
	Notes Payable		702,900
	(Purchased building by issuing note payable)		

	Shareholders'
Assets = Liabilities +	Equity
+702,900 +702,900	

The cost of the truck is $40,000 ($34,650 acquisition price + $5,350 from the overhaul of the engine). The purchase of the truck is recorded as:

Date	Account and Explanation	Debit	Credit
Jan. 3, 2017	Truck	40,000	
	Cash		40,000
	(Purchase of truck for cash)		

	Shareholders'
Assets = Liabilities +	Equity
−40,000	
+40,000	

2. Depreciation on the items of property, plant, and equipment:

STRAIGHT-LINE DEPRECIATION ON THE BUILDING

$$\text{Straight-line depreciation expense} = \frac{\text{Cost} - \text{Residual value}}{\text{Expected life}}$$

$$= \frac{\$702,900 - \$3,900}{30 \text{ years}} = \$23,300 \text{ per year}$$

Date	Account and Explanation	Debit	Credit
Dec. 31, 2017	Depreciation Expense	23,300	
	Accumulated Depreciation-Building		23,300
	(To record depreciation on building)		

	Shareholders' Equity (Depreciation
Assets = Liabilities +	Expense)
−23,300	−23,300

DOUBLE-DECLINING-BALANCE DEPRECIATION FOR THE TRUCK

Declining balance depreciation expense = Declining balance rate × Book value

Declining balance rate = (1/Useful life) × 2 = (1/8) × 2 = 2/8, or 25%

Cost = $34,650 (from transaction *b*) + $5,350 overhaul (from transaction *c*)
= $40,000

End of Year	Depreciation Expense			Accumulated Depreciation	Book Value
					$40,000
2017	25% × $40,000	=	$10,000	$10,000	30,000
2018	25% × 30,000	=	7,500	17,500	22,500
2019	25% × 22,500	=	5,625	23,125	16,875
2020	25% × 16,875	=	4,219	27,344	12,656
2021	25% × 12,656	=	3,164	30,508	9,492
2022	25% × 9,492	=	2,373	32,881	7,119
2023	25% × 7,119	=	1,780	34,661	5,339
2024			339*	35,000	5,000
			$35,000		

*The amount needed to achieve a $5,000 book value.

Assets	=	Liabilities	+	Shareholders' Equity (Depreciation Expense)
−10,000				−10,000

Date	Account and Explanation	Debit	Credit
Dec. 31, 2017	Depreciation Expense	10,000	
	Accumulated Depreciation—Truck		10,000
	(To record depreciation on truck)		

3. Depletion on the coal mine:

$$\text{Unit depletion rate} = \frac{\text{Cost} - \text{Residual value}}{\text{Recoverable units}}$$

$$= \frac{\$1,980,000}{495,000} = \$4.00 \text{ per tonne}$$

$$\text{Depletion} = \text{Unit depletion rate} \times \text{Units recovered}$$

$$= \$4.00 \times 40,000 = \$160,000$$

Assets	=	Liabilities	+	Shareholders' Equity
+160,000				
−160,000				

Date	Account and Explanation	Debit	Credit
Dec. 31, 2017	Inventory	160,000	
	Accumulated Depletion		160,000
	(To record depletion)		

4. Amortization of the patent:

$$\text{Straight-line amortization expense} = \frac{\text{Cost} - \text{Residual value}}{\text{Expected life}}$$

$$= \frac{\$100,000 - \$0}{8 \text{ years}}$$

$$= \$12,500 \text{ per year}$$

Assets	=	Liabilities	+	Shareholders' Equity (Amortization Expense)
−12,500				−12,500

Date	Account and Explanation	Debit	Credit
Dec. 31, 2017	Amortization Expense	12,500	
	Patent		12,500
	(To record amortization of patent)		

5. The tangible capital asset turnover ratio is computed as the net sales divided by the average of the tangible capital assets. Carroll Company's tangible capital asset turnover ratio is 2.75 ($8,800,000/$3,200,000). This ratio describes how efficiently Carroll is using its tangible capital assets to generate revenue. For every dollar of tangible capital assets, Carroll is generating $2.75 of sales. The average age of tangible capital assets is computed as accumulated depreciation divided by depreciation expense. Carroll's tangible capital assets are approximately $5\frac{1}{2}$ years old ($2,062,500/$375,000).

The return on total assets (ROA) is computed as the total of net income plus interest expense (net of tax), divided by average annual total assets. Carroll's return on total assets is $[(\$1,500,000 + 100,000)(1 - 25\%)]/10,000,000 = 15.75\%$. This ratio describes how efficiently Carroll is using its total assets.

DISCUSSION QUESTIONS

1. How do capital assets differ from other assets? What benefits do capital assets provide to the company?

2. What are the different types of capital assets? How do they differ from one another?

3. How does the cost concept affect accounting for capital assets? Under this concept, what is included in the cost of a tangible capital asset?

4. How is the cost of a tangible capital asset measured in a cash transaction? In a noncash transaction?

5. What is the effect on the financial statements if a company incorrectly records an expense as an asset?

6. How does the matching concept affect accounting for capital assets?

7. What factors must be known or estimated in order to compute depreciation expense?

8. How do the accelerated and straight-line depreciation methods differ?

9. What objective should guide the selection of a depreciation method for financial reporting purposes?

10. What objective should be of primary importance in the selection of a depreciation method for income tax reporting?

11. What accounting concepts should be considered when evaluating the accounting for expenditures that are made for tangible capital assets after acquisition? Be sure to distinguish between revenue and capital expenditures.

12. What is the proper accounting for depreciation when new or additional information becomes available that causes a company to change its estimates of useful life or residual value?

13. What is an impairment of a tangible capital asset? How is a depreciable capital asset impairment recorded in the financial statements?

14. How is the sale of equipment at an amount greater than its book value recorded? How would your answer change if the equipment is sold at an amount less than its book value?

15. What information do the tangible capital asset turnover ratio, the average age of tangible capital assets, and the return on total assets provide users of financial statements?

16. Describe the benefits that intangible assets provide to a company.

17. What factors should be considered when selecting the amortization period for an intangible asset?

18. What basis underlies the computation of depletion?

MULTIPLE-CHOICE EXERCISES

7-1 Anniston Company purchased equipment and incurred the following costs:

Purchase price	$52,000
Cost of trial runs	750
Installation costs	250
Sales tax	2,600

What is the cost of the equipment?
a. $52,000
b. $54,600
c. $54,850
d. $55,600

7-2 The cost principle requires that companies record tangible capital assets at:
a. fair value
b. book value
c. historical cost
d. market value

7-3 When depreciation expense is recorded each period, what account is debited?
a. Depreciation Expense
b. Cash
c. Accumulated Depreciation
d. The tangible capital asset account involved

7-4 Fontaine Inc. acquired a machine for $600,000 on January 1, 2018. The machine has a salvage value of $10,000 and a five-year useful life. Fontaine expects the machine to run for 15,000 machine hours. The machine was actually used for 4,800 hours in 2018 and 3,150 hours in 2019. What would be the balance in the accumulated depreciation account at December 31, 2019, if the straight-line method were used?
a. $216,000
b. $236,000
c. $240,000
d. $250,000

7-5 Refer to the information in Exercise 7-4. What amount would Fontaine record as depreciation expense for the year ending December 31, 2019, if the double-declining-balance method were used?
a. $144,000
b. $145,600
c. $236,000
d. $240,000

7-6 Refer to the information in Exercise 7-4. What amount would Fontaine record as depreciation expense for 2018 if the units-of-production method were used? (*Note:* Round your answer to the nearest hundred dollars.)
a. $123,900
b. $188,800
c. $192,000
d. $195,200

7-7 Which of the following statements is true regarding depreciation methods?
a. The use of a declining balance method of depreciation will produce lower depreciation charges in the early years of an asset's life compared to the straight-line depreciation method.
b. Over the life of an asset, a declining balance depreciation method will recognize more depreciation expense relative to the straight-line method.
c. The use of a declining-balance method instead of the straight-line method will produce higher book values for an asset in the early years of the asset's life.
d. The use of a longer estimated life and a higher residual value will lower the annual amount of depreciation expense recognized on the statement of earnings.

7-8 Normal repair and maintenance of an asset is an example of what?
a. Revenue expenditure
b. Capital expenditure
c. An expenditure that will be depreciated
d. An expenditure that should be avoided

7-9 Chang Ltd. purchased a piece of equipment in 2018. Chang depreciated the equipment on a straight-line basis over a useful life of 10 years and used a residual value of $12,000. Chang's depreciation expense for 2019 was $11,000. What was the original cost of the equipment?
a. $98,000
b. $110,000
c. $122,000
d. $134,000

7-10 Bradley Company purchased a machine for $34,000 on January 1, 2017. It depreciates the machine using the straight-line method over a useful life of eight years and a $2,000 residual value. On January 1, 2019, Bradley revised its estimate of residual value to $1,000 and shortened the machine's useful life to four more years. Depreciation expense for 2019 is:
a. $4,000
b. $5,750
c. $6,000
d. $6,250

7-11 Murnane Company purchased a machine on February 1, 2013, for $100,000. In January 2018, when the book value of the machine is $70,000, Murnane believes the machine is impaired due to recent technological advances. Murnane expects the machine to generate future cash flow of $10,000 and has estimated the fair value of the machine to be $55,000. What is the loss from impairment?
a. $5,000
b. $15,000
c. $30,000
d. $45,000

7-12 Jerabek Inc. decided to sell one of its tangible capital assets that had a cost of $55,000 and accumulated depreciation of $35,000 on July 1, 2018. On that date, Jerabek sold the asset for $15,000. What was the resulting gain or loss from the sale?
a. $5,000 loss
b. $5,000 gain
c. $15,000 loss
d. $15,000 gain

7-13 Which of the following statements is true?
a. The tangible capital asset turnover ratio assists managers in determining the estimated future capital expenditures that are needed.
b. The average age of the tangible capital assets is computed by dividing accumulated depreciation by depreciation expense.
c. If net sales increases, the tangible capital asset turnover ratio will decrease.
d. A relatively low tangible capital asset turnover ratio signals that a company is efficiently using its assets.

7-14 Which of the following is not an intangible asset?
a. Patent
b. Trademark

c. Research and development
d. Goodwill

7-15 Mysore Company acquired a patent on January 1, 2018, for $75,000. The patent has a remaining legal life of 15 years, but Mysore expects to receive benefits from the patent for only five years. What amount of amortization expense does Mysore record in 2018 related to the patent?
   a. $5,000
   b. $7,500
   c. $15,000
   d. $0—patents are not amortized

7-16 Howton Paper Company purchased $1,400,000 of timberland in 2017 for its paper operations. Howton estimates

that there are 10,000 hectares of timberland and it cut 2,000 hectares in 2018. The land is expected to have a residual value of $200,000 once all the timber is cut. Which of the following is true with regard to depletion?
   a. Depletion will cause Howton's timber inventory to increase.
   b. Howton will record depletion expense of $280,000 in 2018.
   c. Howton's depletion rate is $140 per hectare of timber.
   d. Howton should deplete the timber at a rate of 20% (2,000 hectares ÷ 10,000 hectares) per year.

CORNERSTONE EXERCISES

Cornerstone Exercise 7-17   Cost of a Tangible Capital Asset

OBJECTIVE ❷
CORNERSTONE 7.1

Borges Ltd. recently purchased land to use for the construction of its new manufacturing facility and incurred the following costs: purchase price, $85,000; real estate commissions, $5,100; delinquent property taxes, $1,500; closing costs, $3,500; clearing and grading of the land, $8,100.

Required:

Determine the cost of the land.

Cornerstone Exercise 7-18   Acquisition Cost

OBJECTIVE ❷
CORNERSTONE 7.1

Cox Company recently purchased a machine by paying $8,500 cash and signing a six-month, 10% note for $10,000. In addition to the purchase price, Cox incurred the following costs related to the machine: freight charges, $800; interest charges, $500; special foundation for machine, $400; installation costs, $1,100.

Required:

Determine the cost of the machine.

Cornerstone Exercise 7-19   Straight-Line Depreciation

OBJECTIVE ❸ ❹
CORNERSTONE 7.2

Irons Delivery Inc. purchased a new delivery truck for $45,000 on January 1, 2018. The truck is expected to have a $3,000 residual value at the end of its five-year useful life. Irons uses the straight-line method of depreciation.

Required:

Prepare the journal entry to record depreciation expense for 2018 and 2019.

Cornerstone Exercise 7-20   Declining Balance Depreciation

OBJECTIVE ❸ ❹
CORNERSTONE 7.3

Refer to the information in Exercise 7-19. Irons uses the double-declining-balance method of depreciation.

Required:

Prepare the journal entry to record depreciation expense for 2018 and 2019.

OBJECTIVE ③ ④
CORNERSTONE 7.4

Cornerstone Exercise 7-21   Units-of-Production Depreciation

Refer to the information in Exercise 7-19. Irons uses the units-of-production method of depreciation. Irons expects the truck to run for 160,000 kilometres. The actual kilometres driven in 2018 and 2019 were 40,000 and 36,000, respectively.

Required:

Prepare the journal entry to record depreciation expense for 2018 and 2019.

OBJECTIVE ⑥
CORNERSTONE 7.5

Cornerstone Exercise 7-22   Revision of Depreciation

On January 1, 2016, Shapiro Inc. purchased a machine for $115,000. Shapiro depreciated the machine with the straight-line depreciation method over a useful life of 10 years, using a residual value of $5,000. At the beginning of 2018, a major overhaul, costing $30,000, was made. After the overhaul, the machine's residual value is estimated to be $7,500, and the machine is expected to have a remaining useful life of 11 years.

Required:

Determine the depreciation expense for 2018.

OBJECTIVE ⑦
CORNERSTONE 7.6

Cornerstone Exercise 7-23   Impairment

Brown Industries has two machines that it believes may be impaired. Information on the machines is shown below.

	Book Value	Estimated Future Cash Flows	Fair Value
Machine 1	$42,000	$50,000	$40,000
Machine 2	50,000	40,000	32,000

Required:

For each machine, determine if the machine is impaired. If so, calculate the amount of the impairment loss.

OBJECTIVE ⑧
CORNERSTONE 7.7

Cornerstone Exercise 7-24   Disposal of a Tangible Capital Asset

On August 30, Lhasa Manufacturing Company decided to sell one of its fabricating machines, which was 15 years old, for $6,000. The machine, which originally cost $105,000, had accumulated depreciation of $102,500.

Required:

Prepare the journal entry to record the disposal of the machine.

OBJECTIVE ⑨
CORNERSTONE 7.8

Cornerstone Exercise 7-25   Analyze Property, Plant, and Equipment

At December 31, 2018, Clark Corporation reported beginning net property, plant, and equipment of $94,150; ending net property, plant, and equipment of $103,626; accumulated depreciation of $49,133; net sales of $212,722; and depreciation expense of $12,315.

Required:

Compute Clark Corporation's tangible capital asset turnover ratio and the average age of its tangible capital assets. (*Note:* Round answers to two decimal places.)

OBJECTIVE ⑩
CORNERSTONE 7.9

Cornerstone Exercise 7-26   Cost of Intangible Assets

Advanced Technological Devices Inc. acquired a patent for $120,000. It spent an additional $24,744 defending the patent in legal proceedings.

Required:

Determine the cost of the patent.

Cornerstone Exercise 7-27   Amortization of Intangible Assets

Micro Systems Corp. acquired a patent for $180,000. Micro Systems amortizes the patent on a straight-line basis over its remaining economic life of 12 years.

OBJECTIVE 10
CORNERSTONE 7.9

Required:

Prepare the journal entry to record the amortization expense related to the patent.

Cornerstone Exercise 7-28   Depletion of Natural Resources

Brandon Oil Company recently purchased oil and natural gas reserves in northern Manitoba for $1,850,000. Brandon spent $10,000,000 preparing the oil for extraction from the ground. Brandon estimates that 108,000,000 barrels of oil will be extracted from the ground. The land has a residual value of $20,000. During 2018, 15,000,000 barrels are extracted from the ground.

OBJECTIVE 11
CORNERSTONE 7.10

Required:

Calculate the amount of depletion taken in 2018. (*Note:* Use two decimal points for calculations.)

BRIEF EXERCISES

Brief Exercise 7-29   Understanding Capital Assets

Descriptions of capital assets are listed below.

OBJECTIVE 1

a.   Naturally occurring materials that have economic value
b.   Tangible assets that can be seen and touched
c.   Do not have physical substance
d.   Depreciated over the accounting periods in which the asset is used and benefits are received
e.   Generally result from legal and contractual rights

Required:

Identify the category of capital asset associated with each description as property, plant, and equipment; intangible assets; or natural resources.

Brief Exercise 7-30   Acquisition Cost

Desert State University installed an HD video board with an invoice price of $5,000,000 in its football stadium. Desert State paid an additional $100,000 of delivery and installation costs relating to this board. Because this is one of the largest boards in the world, Desert State also installed 10 five-tonne air-conditioning units at a total cost of $120,000 to keep the board cool in the desert heat.

OBJECTIVE 2

Required:

Determine the cost of the video board.

Brief Exercise 7-31   Depreciation Concepts

Listed below are concepts and terminology related to depreciation.

OBJECTIVE 3

Concepts	Terminology
1. The period of time over which the company anticipates deriving benefit from the use of the asset	a. Depreciation
2. The cost of the asset minus its accumulated depreciation	b. Accumulated depreciation

(Continued)

Concepts	Terminology
3. The total amount of depreciation expense that has been recorded for an asset since the asset was acquired	c. Book value
4. The amount of cash or trade-in consideration that the company expects to receive when an asset is retired from service	d. Estimated useful life
5. A process of cost allocation, not an attempt to measure the fair value of an asset	e. Residual value

Required:

Match each concept with the related terminology.

OBJECTIVE **4**

Brief Exercise 7-32   Depreciation Methods

On January 1, 2017, Loeffler Company acquired a machine at a cost of $200,000. Loeffler estimates that it will use the machine for four years or 8,000 machine hours. It estimates that after four years the machine can be sold for $20,000. Loeffler uses the machine for 2,100 and 1,800 machine hours in 2017 and 2018, respectively.

Required:

Compute depreciation expense for 2017 and 2018 using the (1) straight-line, (2) double-declining-balance, and (3) units-of-production methods of depreciation.

OBJECTIVE **5**

Brief Exercise 7-33   Expenditures after Acquisition

Listed below are several transactions:

a. Paid $80 cash to replace a minor part of an air-conditioning system
b. Paid $40,000 to fix structural damage to a building
c. Paid $8,000 for monthly salaries
d. Paid $12,000 to replace a manual cutting machine with a computer-controlled machine
e. Paid $1,000 related to the annual painting of a building

Required:

Classify each transaction as a revenue expenditure, a capital expenditure, or neither.

OBJECTIVE **6**

Brief Exercise 7-34   Revision of Depreciation

On January 1, 2017, the Kelley Company ledger showed a building with a cost of $250,000 and related accumulated depreciation of $96,000. The depreciation resulted from using straight-line depreciation with a useful life of 20 years and no residual value. On this date, Kelley determined that the building had an estimated remaining useful life of 16 years and a residual value of $14,000.

Required:

Determine the depreciation expense for 2017.

OBJECTIVE **8**

Brief Exercise 7-35   Disposal of a Capital Asset

Jolie Company owns equipment with a cost of $85,500 and accumulated depreciation of 76,200.

Required:

Prepare the journal entry to record the disposal of the equipment on April 9, assuming:
1. Jolie sold the equipment for $11,200 cash.
2. Jolie sold the equipment for $7,900 cash.

Brief Exercise 7-36   Analyzing Fixed Assets

OBJECTIVE 9

Pitt reported the following information for 2017 and 2018:

	2017	2018
Property, plant, and equipment, cost	$550,000	$ 550,000
Accumulated depreciation	170,000	220,000
Net sales		4,600,000
Depreciation expense		50,000

Required:

Compute Pitt's tangible capital asset turnover ratio and the average age of tangible depreciable capital assets. (*Note:* Round all answers to two decimal places.)

Brief Exercise 7-37   Cost and Amortization of Intangible Assets

OBJECTIVE 10

On January 2, 2018, Frazier Company purchased a restaurant franchise for $85,000. The terms of the franchise agreement allowed Frazier to have exclusive rights to operate a restaurant under the "Simply Fried" brand name for the next 10 years.

Required:

Prepare any journal entries related to the franchise that Frazier should make during 2018.

Brief Exercise 7-38   Depletion of Natural Resources

OBJECTIVE 11

Luper Company acquired a tract of land that contained iron deposits for $2,500,000. Luper spent $120,000 to access the iron ore. Luper estimates that 2,000,000 tonnes of ore will be extracted. The estimated value of the land after the ore is extracted is $100,000. During the current year, Luper extracts 150,000 tonnes of iron ore.

Required:

Compute the cost of the natural resource and the amount of depletion taken during the year.

EXERCISES

Exercise 7-39   Statement of Financial Position Presentation

OBJECTIVE 1

Listed below are items that may appear on a classified statement of financial position.
1. Land
2. Amounts due from customers
3. Office building
4. Truck
5. Goods held for resale
6. Amounts owed to suppliers
7. Patent
8. Timberland
9. Land held as investment
10. Goodwill

Required:

Indicate whether each item is included as a capital asset on a classified statement of financial position. If the item is a capital asset, indicate whether the item is property, plant, and equipment; an intangible asset; or a natural resource, as well as the cost allocation process used (depreciation, amortization, or depletion). If the item is not a capital asset, indicate the proper statement of financial position classification.

OBJECTIVE ❶

Exercise 7-40   Statement of Financial Position Classification

Micro-Technologies Inc., a computer manufacturer, has the following items on its statement of financial position—office furniture, delivery truck, patent, computer assembly machine, building, memory chips.

Required:

Indicate the proper statement of financial position classification of each item and the cost allocation process used (depreciation, amortization, depletion).

OBJECTIVE ❷

Exercise 7-41   Acquisition Cost

Items that may relate to property, plant, and equipment follow:
1. Purchase price of a machine
2. Delinquent property taxes at the time of purchase
3. Interest on debt used to purchase equipment
4. Sales taxes paid on purchase of equipment
5. Costs to install a machine
6. Ordinary repairs to equipment
7. Cost to remodel a building
8. Architectural fees paid for design of a building
9. Cost of training employees to run equipment
10. Transportation costs to have furniture delivered

Required:

CONCEPTUAL CONNECTION Determine whether each item is included as part of the cost of property, plant, and equipment. For any item excluded from the cost of property, plant, and equipment, explain why the item was excluded.

OBJECTIVE ❷

Exercise 7-42   Cost of a Tangible Capital Asset

Lauro Cleaners purchased an automatic dry cleaning machine for $145,000 from TGF Corporation on April 1, 2018. Lauro paid $45,000 in cash and signed a five-year, 10% note for $100,000. Lauro will pay interest on the note each year on March 31, beginning in 2019. Transportation charges of $3,815 for the machine were paid by Lauro. Lauro also paid $2,400 for the living expenses of the TGF installation crew. Solvent, necessary to operate the machine, was acquired for $1,000. Of this amount, $600 of the solvent was used to test and adjust the machine.

Required:

1. Compute the cost of the new dry cleaning machine.
2. **CONCEPTUAL CONNECTION** Explain why you excluded any expenditures from the cost of the dry cleaning machine.

OBJECTIVE ❷

Exercise 7-43   Cost of a Tangible Capital Asset

Colson Photography Service purchased a new digital imaging machine on April 15 for $11,200. During installation Colson incurred and paid in cash the following costs:

Rental of drill	$ 150
Electrical contractor	1,300
Plumbing contractor	785

Colson also paid $160 to replace a bracket on the digital imager that was damaged when one of Colson's employees dropped a box on it while it was being installed.

Required:

1. Determine the cost of the digital imaging machine.
2. **CONCEPTUAL CONNECTION** Explain why you included or excluded the $160 bracket replacement cost.

Exercise 7-44   Cost of Tangible Capital Assets

OBJECTIVE ❷

Mooney Sounds, a local stereo retailer, needed a new store because it had outgrown the leased space it had used for several years. Mooney acquired and remodelled a former grocery store. As a part of the acquisition, Mooney incurred the following costs:

Cost of grocery store	$277,400	Wire and electrical supplies	$ 4,290
Cost of land (on which the		New doors	6,400
grocery store is located)	83,580	New windows	3,850
New roof for building	74,000	Wages paid to workers for remodelling	12,500
Lumber used for remodelling	23,200	Additional inventory purchased for grand	
Paint	515	opening sale	45,300

Required:

1. Determine the cost of the land and the building.
2. **CONCEPTUAL CONNECTION** If management misclassified a portion of the building's cost as part of the cost of the land, what would be the effect on the financial statements?

Exercise 7-45   Cost and Depreciation

OBJECTIVE ❷ ❹

On January 1, 2018, Quick Stop, a convenience store, purchased a new soft-drink cooler. Quick Stop paid $25,780 cash for the cooler. Quick Stop also paid $1,090 to have the cooler shipped to its location. After the new cooler arrived, Quick Stop paid $1,810 to have the old cooler dismantled and removed. Quick Stop also paid $820 to a contractor to have new wiring and drains installed for the new cooler. Quick Stop estimated that the cooler would have a useful life of six years and a residual value of $700. Quick Stop uses the straight-line method of depreciation.

Required:

1. Prepare any necessary journal entries to record the cost of the cooler.
2. Prepare the adjusting entry to record 2018 depreciation expense on the new cooler.
3. What is the book value of the cooler at the end of 2018?
4. If Quick Stop had used a useful life of 10 years and a residual value of $1,500, how would this affect depreciation expense for 2018 and the book value of the cooler at the end of 2018?

YOUDECIDE

Exercise 7-46   Characteristics of Depreciation Methods

OBJECTIVE ❸

Below is a common list of depreciation methods and characteristics related to depreciation.

Depreciation Methods
a. Straight-line depreciation method
b. Declining balance depreciation method
c. Units-of-production depreciation method when actual units produced increases over the life of the asset

Characteristics
1. Results in depreciation expense that decreases over the life of the asset
2. Results in depreciation expense that increases over the life of the asset
3. Allocates the same amount of cost to each period of a depreciable asset's life

(Continued)

4. Calculated by multiplying a constant depreciation rate by depreciable cost
5. Calculated by applying a constant depreciation rate to the asset's book value at the beginning of the period
6. Results in lowest income tax expense in early years of the asset's life
7. Consistent with the matching concept

Required:

Match one or more of the depreciation methods with each characteristic.

 **OBJECTIVE 3 4**

Exercise 7-47   Depreciation Methods

Muskoko Corporation purchased a copying machine for $8,700 on January 1, 2018. The machine's residual value was $425 and its estimated life was five years or 2,000,000 copies. Actual usage was 480,000 copies the first year and 400,000 the second year.

Required:

1. Compute depreciation expense for 2018 and 2019 using the (a) straight-line method, (b) double-declining-balance method, and (c) units-of-production method.
2. For each depreciation method, what is the book value of the machine at the end 2018? At the end of the 2019?
3. Assume that Muskoko uses the double-declining-balance method of depreciation. What is the effect on assets and income relative to if Muskoko had used the straight-line method of depreciation instead of the double-declining-balance method of depreciation?

YOUDECIDE

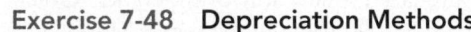 **OBJECTIVE 3 4**

Exercise 7-48   Depreciation Methods

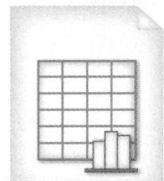

Clearcopy, a printing company, acquired a new press on January 1, 2018. The press cost $173,400 and had an estimated life of eight years or 4,500,000 pages and an estimated residual value of $15,000. Clearcopy printed 675,000 pages in 2018.

Required:

1. Compute 2018 depreciation expense using the (a) straight-line method, (b) double-declining-balance method, and (c) units-of-production method.
2. What is the book value of the machine at the end of 2018 under each method?

 **OBJECTIVE 3 4**

Exercise 7-49   Depreciation Methods

Quick-as-Lightning, a delivery service, purchased a new delivery truck for $45,000 on January 1, 2018. The truck is expected to have an estimated useful life of 10 years or 150,000 kilometres and an expected residual value of $3,000. The truck was driven 15,000 kilometres in 2018 and 13,000 kilometres in 2019.

Required:

1. Compute depreciation expense for 2018 and 2019 using the (a) straight-line method, (b) double-declining-balance method, and (c) units-of-production method.
2. For each method, what is the book value of the machine at the end 2018? At the end of 2019?
3. If Quick-as-Lightning used an estimated eight-year useful life or 100,000 kilometres and an estimated residual value of $1,000, what would be the effect on (a) depreciation expense and (b) book value under each of the depreciation methods?

YOUDECIDE

 **OBJECTIVE 3 4**

Exercise 7-50   Inferring Original Cost

ILLUSTRATING RELATIONSHIPS

Bengal Construction Company purchased a piece of heavy equipment on January 1, 2018, which it is depreciating using the straight-line method. The equipment's estimated useful life is five years and its estimated residual value is $5,000. Bengal recorded depreciation expense of $44,000 in 2019.

Required:

Determine the original cost of the equipment.

Exercise 7-51   Choice among Depreciation Methods

OBJECTIVE

Walnut Ridge Production Ltd. purchased a new computerized video editing machine at a cost of $450,000. The system has an estimated residual value of $64,000 and an estimated life of five years.

Required:

1. Compute depreciation expense, accumulated depreciation, and book value for the first three years of the machine's life using the (a) straight-line method and (b) double-declining-balance method.
2. Which method would produce the largest income in the first, second, and third years of the asset's life?
3. Why might the controller of Walnut Ridge Production be interested in the effect of choosing a depreciation method? Evaluate the legitimacy of these interests.

YOUDECIDE

Exercise 7-52   Revision of Depreciation

OBJECTIVE

On January 1, 2016, Blizzards-R-Us purchased a snow-blowing machine for $73,000. The machine was expected to have an estimated residual value of $5,000 at the end of its five-year estimated useful life. On January 1, 2018, Blizzards-R-Us concluded that the machine would have a remaining useful life of six years with an estimated residual value of $3,800.

Required:

1. Determine the revised annual depreciation expense for 2018 using the straight-line method.
2. **CONCEPTUAL CONNECTION** How does the revision in depreciation affect Blizzards-R-Us's financial statements?

Exercise 7-53   Capital versus Revenue Expenditure

OBJECTIVE ⑤

Waleed Company, a privately owned business, supplies water to several communities. Waleed has just performed an extensive overhaul on one of its water pumps. The overhaul is estimated to extend the life of the pump by 10 years. The residual value of the pump is unchanged. You have been asked to determine which of the following costs should be capitalized as a part of this overhaul. Those costs not capitalized should be expensed.

Element of Cost	Classification Explanation
New pump motor	
Repacking of bearings (performed monthly)	
New impeller	
Painting of pump housing (performed annually)	
Replacement of Pump Foundation	
New wiring (needed every five years)	
Installation labour, motor	
Installation labour, impeller	
Installation labour, wiring	
Paint labour (performed annually)	
Placement of fence around pump*	

*A legal requirement that will add to maintenance costs over the remaining life of the pump.

Required:

CONCEPTUAL CONNECTION Classify each cost as part of the overhaul or as an expense. Be sure to explain your reasoning for each classification

OBJECTIVE **5**

Exercise 7-54   Expenditures after Acquisition

The following expenditures were incurred during the year:

a. Paid $4,000 for an overhaul of an automobile engine
b. Paid $20,000 to add capacity to a cellular phone company's wireless network
c. Paid $200 for routine maintenance of a manufacturing machine
d. Paid $10,000 to remodel an office building
e. Paid $300 for ordinary repairs

Required:

1. Classify the expenditures as either capital or revenue expenditures.
2. **CONCEPTUAL CONNECTION** If management improperly classified these expenditures, what would be the impact on the financial statements?

OBJECTIVE **5**

Exercise 7-55   Expenditures after Acquisition

Rimouski Manufacturing placed a robotic arm on a large assembly machine on January 1, 2018. At the time, the assembly machine, which was acquired on January 1, 2011, was estimated to last another three years. The following information is available concerning the assembly machine.

Cost, assembly machine	$750,000
Accumulated depreciation, 1/1/2018	480,000

The robotic arm cost $225,000 and was estimated to extend the useful life of the machine by three years. Therefore, the useful life of the assembly machine, after the arm replacement, is six years. The assembly machine is estimated to have a residual value of $120,000 at the end of its useful life.

Required:

1. Prepare the journal entry necessary to record the addition of the robotic arm.
2. Compute 2018 depreciation expense for the machine using the straight-line method, and prepare the necessary journal entry.
3. What is the book value of the machine at the end of 2018?
4. **CONCEPTUAL CONNECTION** What would have been the effect on the financial statements if Rimouski had expensed the addition of the robotic arm?

OBJECTIVE **5**

Exercise 7-56   Expenditures after Acquisition and Depreciation

National Bank installed a wireless encryption device in January 2014. The device cost $180,000. At the time the device was installed, National Bank estimated that it would have an estimated life of eight years and an estimated residual value of $10,000. By 2017, the bank's business had expanded and modifications to the device were necessary. At the beginning of 2018, National Bank spent $45,000 on modifications for the device. National Bank estimates that the new estimated life of the device (from January 2018) is six years and that the new residual value is $5,000. National Bank uses the straight-line method of depreciation. Had National Bank not modified the device, processing delays would have caused it to lose at least $100,000 of business per year.

Required:

1. Compute the accumulated depreciation for the device at the time the modifications were made (four years after acquisition).
2. What is the book value of the device before and after the modification?
3. What will be the annual straight-line depreciation expense for the device after the modification?
4. **CONCEPTUAL CONNECTION** The bank's president notes, "Since the after-modification depreciation expense exceeds the before-modification depreciation expense, this modification was a poor idea." Comment on the president's assertion.

Exercise 7-57   Impairment

On January 1, 2011, Tofino Company acquired a pie-making machine for $75,000. The machine was estimated to have a useful life of 10 years with no residual value. Tofino uses the straight-line depreciation method. On January 1, 2018, due to technological changes in the bakery industry, Tofino believed that the asset might be impaired. Tofino estimates that the machine will generate net cash flows of $12,000 and that it has a current fair value of $10,000.

OBJECTIVE 7

Required:

1. What is the book value of the machine on January 1, 2018?
2. Compute the loss related to the impairment.
3. Prepare the journal entry necessary to record the impairment of the machine.

Exercise 7-58   Disposal of Tangible Capital Asset

OBJECTIVE 8

Perfect Auto Rentals sold one of its cars on January 1, 2018. Perfect had acquired the car on January 1, 2016, for $23,400. At acquisition Perfect assumed that the car would have an estimated life of three years and an estimated residual value of $3,000. Assume that Perfect has recorded straight-line depreciation expense for 2016 and 2017.

Required:

1. Prepare the journal entry to record the sale of the car, assuming the car sold for (a) $9,800 cash, (b) $7,500 cash, and (c) $11,500 cash.
2. How should the gain or loss on the disposition (if any) be reported on the statement of earnings?

Exercise 7-59   Disposal of Tangible Capital Asset

OBJECTIVE 8

Pacifica Manufacturing retired a computerized metal stamping machine on December 31, 2018. Pacifica sold the machine to another company and did not replace it. The following data are available for the machine:

Cost (installed), 1/1/2013	$ 920,000
Residual value estimated on 1/1/2013	160,000
Estimated life as of 1/1/2013	10 years

The machine was sold for $188,000 cash. Pacifica uses the straight-line method of depreciation.

Required:

1. Prepare the journal entry to record depreciation expense for 2018.
2. Compute accumulated depreciation at December 31, 2018.
3. Prepare the journal entry to record the sale of the machine.
4. **CONCEPTUAL CONNECTION** Explain how the disposal of the tangible capital asset will affect the 2018 financial statements.

Exercise 7-60   Depreciation and Disposal of Tangible Capital Assets

OBJECTIVE 3 4 5 8

Slavko Company reported the following information regarding its equipment:

Account	Amount
Equipment, Jan. 1, 2018	$745,120
Equipment, Dec. 31, 2018	831,410
Accumulated depreciation, Jan. 1, 2018	224,350
Accumulated depreciation, Dec. 31, 2018	257,690
Capital expenditures	148,735
Accumulated depreciation on equipment sold	50,320
Cash received for equipment sold	14,150

(Continued)

Required:

1. What journal entry did Slavko make to record depreciation expense for 2018?
2. What journal entry did Slavko make to record the disposal of the equipment?

OBJECTIVE ❾

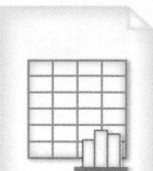

Exercise 7-61   Analyze Tangible Capital Assets

Lanka Industries is a technology company that operates in a highly competitive environment. In 2015, management had significantly curtailed its capital expenditures due to cash flow problems. Lanka reported the following information for 2018:

- Net tangible capital assets (beginning of year), $489,000
- Net tangible capital assets (end of year), $505,000
- Net sales, $1,025,000
- Accumulated depreciation (end of year), $543,000
- Depreciation expense, $126,000

An analyst reviewing Lanka's financial history noted that Lanka had previously reported tangible capital asset turnover ratios and average age of its assets as follows:

	2013	2014	2015	2016	2017
Tangible capital asset turnover	2.48	2.45	2.74	2.57	2.33
Average age of assets (years)	1.81	1.79	1.94	2.81	3.74

During this time frame, the industry average tangible capital asset turnover ratio is 2.46 and the industry average age of assets is 1.79 years.

Required:

1. Compute Lanka's tangible capital asset turnover ratio for 2018.
2. Compute the average age of Lanka's tangible capital assets for 2018.
3. **CONCEPTUAL CONNECTION** Comment on Lanka's tangible capital asset turnover ratios and the average age of the tangible capital assets.

OBJECTIVE ❿

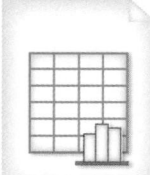

Exercise 7-62   Acquisition and Amortization of Intangible Assets

TLM Technologies had these transactions related to intangible assets during 2018:

Jan. 2	Purchased a patent from Luna Industries for $175,000. The estimated remaining legal life of the patent is 15 years and TLM estimated the patent to be useful for 8 years.
Jan. 5	Paid legal fees in a successful legal defence of the patent of $90,000.
June 29	Registered a trademark with the federal government. Registration costs were $4,000. TLM expects to use the trademark indefinitely.
Sept. 2	Paid research and development costs of $478,200.

Required:

1. Prepare the journal entries necessary to record the transactions.
2. Prepare the entries necessary to record amortization expense for the intangible assets.
3. What is the balance of the intangible assets at the end of 2018?

OBJECTIVE ❶❸❹
❾❿

Exercise 7-63   Statement of Financial Position Presentation

The following information relates to the assets of Westfield Semiconductors as of December 31, 2018. Westfield uses the straight-line method for depreciation and amortization for all assets except for the truck, which they use the units of production method.

Asset	Acquisition Cost	Estimated Expected Life	Estimated Residual Value	Time Used
Land	$104,300	Infinite	$100,000	10 years
Building	430,000	25 years	30,000	10 years

Asset	Acquisition Cost	Estimated Expected Life	Estimated Residual Value	Time Used
Machine	285,000	5 years	10,000	2 years
Patent	80,000	10 years	0	3 years
Truck	21,000	100,000 kilometres	3,000	44,000 kilometres

Required:

Use the information above to prepare the property, plant, and equipment and intangible assets portions of a classified statement of financial position for Westfield.

Exercise 7-64 Amortization of Intangibles

OBJECTIVE 10

On January 1, 2018, Birnbaum Investments Ltd. acquired a franchise to operate a Burger Doodle restaurant. Birnbaum paid $275,000 for a 10-year franchise and incurred organization costs of $8,000.

Required:

1. Prepare the journal entry to record the cash payment for the franchise fee and the organization costs.
2. Prepare the journal entry to record the annual amortization expense at the end of the first year.

Exercise 7-65 Depletion Rate

OBJECTIVE 11

Oxford Quarries purchased 45 hectares of land for $185,000. The land contained stone that Oxford will remove from the ground, finish, and then sell as facing material for buildings. Oxford spent $435,000 preparing the quarry for operation. Oxford estimates that the quarry contains 55,000 tonnes of usable stone and that it will require six years to remove all the usable stone once quarrying begins. Oxford estimates that upon completion of quarrying, the land will have a residual value of $11,150. During the current year, Oxford extracted 8,500 tonnes of stone.

Required:

1. Compute the depletion rate per tonne.
2. Prepare the journal entry to record the extraction of the stone.

Exercise 7-66 Depletion of Timber

OBJECTIVE 11

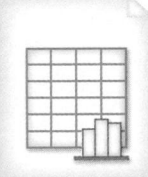

Oldman Development has purchased a 5,000-hectare tract of forested land in northern British Columbia. The tract contains about 1,440,000 pine trees that, when mature, can be used for utility poles. Bedford paid $900 per hectare for the timberland. The land will have a residual value of $180 per hectare when all the trees are harvested. During 2018, Oldman harvested 150,000 trees.

Required:

1. Compute the depletion per tree.
2. Prepare the journal entry to record the harvesting of the trees for 2018.

PROBLEM SET A

Problem 7-67A Financial Statement Presentation of Capital Assets

 OBJECTIVE 1

Olympic Acquisitions Corp. prepared the following post-closing trial balance at December 31, 2018:

(Continued)

	Debit	Credit
Cash	$ 5,400	
Accounts Receivable	16,200	
Supplies	25,800	
Land	42,350	
Buildings	155,900	
Equipment	278,650	
Truck	31,100	
Franchise	49,600	
Goodwill	313,500	
Natural Resources	94,600	
Accounts Payable		$ 4,250
Accumulated Depreciation, Buildings		112,000
Accumulated Depreciation, Equipment		153,000
Accumulated Depreciation, Truck		16,300
Wages Payable		6,850
Interest Payable		7,125
Income Tax Payable		12,125
Notes Payable (due in 8 years)		185,550
Common Shares		304,500
Retained Earnings		211,400
Totals	$1,013,100	$1,013,100

Required:

Prepare a classified statement of financial position for Olympic at December 31, 2018. (*Note:* Olympic reports the four categories of capital assets in separate subsections of assets.)

OBJECTIVE ❷

Problem 7-68A   Cost of a Tangible Capital Asset

Mist City Car Wash purchased a new brushless car-washing machine for one of its bays. The machine cost $32,300. Mist City borrowed the purchase price from its bank on a one-year, 8% note payable. Mist City paid $1,250 to have the machine transported to its place of business and an additional $275 in shipping insurance. Mist City incurred the following costs as a part of the installation:

Plumbing	$2,700
Electrical	1,640
Water (for testing the machine)	35
Soap (for testing the machine)	18

During the testing process, one of the motors became defective when soap and water entered the motor because its cover had not been installed properly by Mist City's employees. The motor was replaced at a cost of $450.

Required:

1. Compute the cost of the car-washing machine.
2. **CONCEPTUAL CONNECTION** Explain why any costs were excluded from the cost of the machine.

OBJECTIVE ❸ ❹

Problem 7-69A   Depreciation Methods

Hansen Supermarkets purchased a radio frequency identification (RFID) system for one of its stores at a cost of $130,000. Hansen determined that the system had an estimated life of eight years (or 50,000,000 items scanned) and an estimated residual value of $6,000.

Required:

1. Determine the amount of depreciation expense for the first and second years of the system's life using the (a) straight-line and (b) double-declining-balance depreciation methods.
2. If the number of items scanned the first and second years were 7,200,000 and 8,150,000, respectively, compute the amount of depreciation expense for the first and second years of the system's life using the units-of-production depreciation method.
3. Compute the book values for all three depreciation methods as of the end of the first and second years of the system's life.
4. **CONCEPTUAL CONNECTION** What factors might management consider when selecting among depreciation methods?

Problem 7-70A Depreciation Schedules

OBJECTIVE ❸ ❹

Wendt Corporation acquired a new depreciable asset for $94,000. The asset has a four-year estimated life and a residual value of zero.

Required:

1. Prepare a depreciation schedule for all four years of the asset's estimated life using the straight-line depreciation method.
2. Prepare a depreciation schedule for all four years of the asset's expected life using the double-declining-balance depreciation method.
3. **CONCEPTUAL CONNECTION** What questions should be asked about this asset to decide which depreciation method to use?

Problem 7-71A Expenditures after Acquisition

OBJECTIVE ❸ ❹ ❺

Pasta, a restaurant specializing in fresh pasta, installed a pasta cooker in early 2016 at a cost of $12,400. The cooker had an estimated life of five years and an estimated residual value of $900 when installed. As the restaurant's business increased, it became apparent that renovations would be necessary so that the cooker's output could be increased. In January 2019, Pasta spent $8,200 to install new heating equipment and $4,100 to add pressure-cooking capability. After these renovations, Pasta estimated that the remaining useful life of the cooker was 10 years and that the residual value was now $1,500.

Required:

1. Compute one year's straight-line depreciation expense on the cooker before the renovations.
2. Assume that three full years of straight-line depreciation expense had been recorded on the cooker before the renovations were made. Compute the book value of the cooker immediately after the renovations were made.
3. Compute one year's straight-line depreciation expense on the renovated cooker.

Problem 7-72A Repair Decision

OBJECTIVE ❺

Kingston Transit operates a summer ferry service to islands in the St. Lawrence River. Farmers use the ferry to move farming equipment to and from the islands. Kingston's ferry is in need of repair. A new engine and steering assembly must be installed, or the Coast Guard will not permit the ferry to be used. Because of competition, Kingston will not be able to raise its rates for ferry service if these repairs are made. Costs of providing the ferry service will not be decreased if the repairs are made.

Required:

1. Identify the factors that Kingston should consider when evaluating whether or not to make the repairs.
2. **CONCEPTUAL CONNECTION** Since the revenue rate cannot be increased and costs will not be decreased if the repairs are made, can the cost of the repairs be capitalized? Why or why not?

Problem 7-73A Disposition of Tangible Capital Assets

In order to provide capital for new hotel construction in other locations, Wilton Hotel Corporation has decided to sell its hotel in Digby, Nova Scotia. Wilton auctions the hotel and its contents on October 1, 2018, with the following results:

Land	$600,000
Building	225,000
Furniture	120,000

Wilton's accounting records reveal the following information about the assets sold:

Asset	Acquisition Cost	Accumulated Depreciation
Land	$ 55,000	
Building	350,000	$155,000
Furniture	285,500	133,000

Required:

1. Prepare a separate journal entry to record the disposition of each of these assets.
2. **CONCEPTUAL CONNECTION** Explain how the disposals of these tangible capital assets would affect the current period financial statements.

Problem 7-74A Natural Resource and Intangible Accounting

McLeansboro Oil Company acquired a small oil company with only three assets during a recent year. The assets were acquired for $1,350,000 cash.

Asset	Fair Value	Estimated Life
Oil	$1,125,000	55,000 barrels
Land	78,000	Indefinite
Equipment	62,000	550,000 barrels

Required:

1. Record the entry to record this acquisition in McLeansboro's journal. (*Hint:* Record the cost in excess of fair value as goodwill.)
2. If McLeansboro pumps and sells 11,000 barrels of oil in one year, compute the amount of depletion.
3. Prepare journal entries to record depletion for the 11,000 barrels of oil pumped and sold.
4. **CONCEPTUAL CONNECTION** Is the goodwill amortized? Explain your reasoning.
5. **CONCEPTUAL CONNECTION** Why are the land and the equipment capitalized separately from the oil well?

OBJECTIVE 10

Problem 7-75A Accounting for Intangible Assets

On January 1, 2011, Technocraft Inc. acquired a patent that was used for manufacturing semiconductor-based electronic circuitry. The patent was originally recorded in Technocraft's ledger at its cost of $1,596,000. Technocraft has been amortizing the patent using the straight-line method over an estimated economic life of 10 years. Residual value was assumed to be zero. Technocraft sued another company for infringing on its patent. As of January 1, 2018, Technocraft spent $122,500 on this suit and won a judgment to recover the $122,500 plus damages of $500,000. The company that was sued paid the $622,500.

Required:

1. Compute and record amortization expense on the patent for 2017 (prior to the lawsuit).
2. Prepare the necessary journal entry on January 1, 2018, to record the expenditure of $122,500 to defend the patent.

3. Prepare the journal entry to record the award of $622,500 on January 1, 2018.
4. Indicate the entry you would have made had Technocraft lost the suit. (*Note:* Assume that the patent would be valueless if Technocraft had lost the suit.)
5. What are the financial statement effects of capitalizing or expensing the cost of defending the patent?

PROBLEM SET B

YOUDECIDE

Problem 7-76B   Financial Statement Presentation of Capital Assets

OBJECTIVE **1**

Athena Inc. prepared the following post-closing trial balance at December 31, 2018:

	Debit	Credit
Cash	$ 3,325	
Accounts Receivable	27,975	
Prepaid Insurance	8,350	
Land	21,150	
Buildings	305,520	
Equipment	126,310	
Patent	9,970	
Goodwill	42,400	
Natural Resources	134,800	
Accounts Payable		$ 7,775
Accumulated Depreciation, Buildings		101,950
Accumulated Depreciation, Equipment		47,875
Unearned Revenue		9,825
Interest Payable		3,625
Income Tax Payable		17,150
Notes Payable (due in 10 years)		170,000
Common Shares		125,000
Retained Earnings		196,600
Totals	$679,800	$679,800

Required:

Prepare a classified statement of financial position for Athena at December 31, 2018. (*Note:* Athena reports the four categories of capital assets in separate subsections of assets.)

Problem 7-77B   Cost of a Tangible Capital Asset

OBJECTIVE **2**

Essex Country Club purchased a new tractor to be used for golf course maintenance. The tractor cost $53,800. Essex borrowed the purchase price from its bank on a one-year, 7% note payable. Essex incurred the following costs:

Shipping costs	$875
Shipping insurance	150
Calibration of cutting height	83

Required:

1. Compute the cost of the tractor.
2. **CONCEPTUAL CONNECTION** Explain why any costs were excluded from the cost of the tractor.

Problem 7-78B   Depreciation Methods

OBJECTIVE **3** **4**

Graphic Design Inc. purchased a state-of-the-art laser engraving machine for $94,500. Graphic determined that the system had an estimated life of 10 years (or 2,000,000 items engraved) and an estimated residual value of $5,400.

(Continued)

Required:

1. Determine the amount of depreciation expense for the first and second years of the machine's life using the (a) straight-line and (b) double-declining-balance depreciation methods.
2. If the number of items engraved the first and second years was 220,000 and 180,000, respectively, compute the amount of depreciation expense for the first and second years of the machine's life using the units-of-production depreciation method.
3. Compute the book values for all three depreciation methods as of the end of the first and second years of the system's life.
4. **CONCEPTUAL CONNECTION** What factors might management consider when selecting among depreciation methods?

OBJECTIVE ❸ ❹   ## Problem 7-79B   Depreciation Schedules

Quito Corporation acquired a new depreciable asset for $135,000. The asset has a five-year estimated life and a residual value of zero.

Required:

1. Prepare a depreciation schedule for all five years of the asset's estimated life using the straight-line depreciation method.
2. Prepare a depreciation schedule for all five years of the asset's estimated life using the double-declining-balance depreciation method.
3. **CONCEPTUAL CONNECTION** What questions should be asked about this asset to decide which depreciation method to use?

OBJECTIVE ❸ ❹ ❺   ## Problem 7-80B   Expenditures after Acquisition

Murray's Fish Market, a store that specializes in providing fresh fish to the Halifax, Nova Scotia, area, installed a new refrigeration unit in early 2015 at a cost of $27,500. The refrigeration unit had an estimated life of eight years and a residual value of $500 when installed. As the fish market's business increased, it became apparent that renovations were necessary so that the capacity of the refrigeration unit could be increased. In January 2018, Murray's spent $18,785 to install an additional refrigerated display unit (that was connected to the original unit) and replace the refrigeration coils. After this addition and renovation, Murray's Fish Market estimated that the remaining useful life of the original refrigeration unit was 12 years and that the residual value was now $1,000.

Required:

1. Compute one year's straight-line depreciation expense on the refrigeration unit before the addition and renovations.
2. Assume that three full years of straight-line depreciation expense were recorded on the refrigeration unit before the addition and renovations were made. Compute the book value of the refrigeration unit immediately after the renovations were made.
3. Compute one year's straight-line depreciation expense on the renovated refrigeration unit.

OBJECTIVE ❺   ## Problem 7-81B   Remodelling Decision

Ferinni Company operates a travel agency out of a historic building in Smalltown. Ferinni's CEO believes that the building needs to be remodelled in order to reach a wider customer base. The CEO proposes building a new entry that would be adjacent to Main Street in order to attract more foot traffic. The current entry faces a parking deck at the rear of the building and is easily overlooked by customers. The new entry will require the rearrangement of several offices inside the building. Because of competition from Internet travel sites, Ferinni will not be able to raise rates for its travel service after the remodelling is made.

Required:

1. Identify the factors that Ferinni should consider when evaluating whether to remodel the building.
2. **CONCEPTUAL CONNECTION** Since the revenue rate cannot be increased, can the cost of the remodelling be capitalized? Why or why not?

Problem 7-82B   Disposition of Tangible Capital Assets

OBJECTIVE **8**

Salva Pest Control disposed of four assets recently. Salva's accounting records provided the following information about the assets at the time of their disposal:

Asset	Cost	Accumulated Depreciation
Pump	$ 6,200	$ 4,800
Truck	18,600	17,500
Furniture	4,200	3,850
Chemical testing apparatus	6,800	4,000

The truck was sold for $2,450 cash, and the chemical testing apparatus was donated to the local high school. Because the pump was contaminated with pesticides, $500 in cash was paid to a chemical disposal company to decontaminate the pump and dispose of it safely. The furniture was taken to the local landfill.

Required:

1. Prepare a separate journal entry to record the disposition of each of these assets.
2. **CONCEPTUAL CONNECTION** Explain how the disposals of the tangible capital assets would affect the current period financial statements.

Problem 7-83B   Natural Resource and Intangible Accounting

OBJECTIVE **10** **11**

In 2010, Mudcat Gas Company purchased a small natural gas company with two assets—land and natural gas reserves—for $158,000,000. The fair value of the land was $1,500,000 and the fair value of the natural gas reserves was $155,250,000. At that time, estimated recoverable gas was 105,000,000 cubic metres.

Required:

1. Record the entry to record this acquisition in Mudcat's journal. (*Hint:* Record any cost in excess of fair value as goodwill.)
2. If Mudcat recovers and sells 2,500,000 cubic metres in one year, compute the depletion.
3. Prepare journal entries to record depletion for the 2,500,000 cubic metres of natural gas recovered and sold.
4. **CONCEPTUAL CONNECTION** Is the goodwill amortized? Explain your reasoning.
5. **CONCEPTUAL CONNECTION** Why is the land capitalized separately from the natural gas reserves?

Problem 7-84B   Accounting for Intangible Assets

OBJECTIVE **10**

Blackford and Medford Publishing Company own the copyrights on many top authors. In 2018, Blackford and Medford acquired the copyright on the literary works of Susan Monroe, an underground novelist in the 1960s, for $725,000 cash. Due to a recent resurgence of interest in the 1960s, the copyright has an estimated economic life of eight years. The residual value is estimated to be zero.

Required:

1. Prepare a journal entry to record the acquisition of the copyright.
2. Compute and record the 2018 amortization expense for the copyright.

CASES

Case 7-85   Ethics, Internal Controls, and the Capitalization Decision

James Sage, an assistant controller in a large company, has a friend and former classmate, Henry Basil, who sells computers. Sage agrees to help Basil get part of the business that has been going to a large national computer manufacturer for many years. Sage knows that the controller would not approve a shift away from the national supplier but believes that he can authorize a number of small orders for equipment that will escape the controller's notice. Company policy requires that all capital expenditures be approved by a management committee; however, expenditures under $2,000 are considered expenses and are subject to much less scrutiny. The assistant controller orders four computers, to be used in a distant branch office. In order to keep the size of the order down, he makes four separate orders over a period of several months.

Required:

1. What are the probable consequences of this behaviour for the company? For the assistant controller?
2. Describe internal control procedures that would be effective in discouraging and detecting this kind of behaviour.

Case 7-86   Management's Depreciation Decision

Great Lakes Enterprises, a large holding company, acquired North Spruce Manufacturing, a medium-sized manufacturing business, from its founder, who wishes to retire. Despite great potential for development, North Spruce's income has been dropping in recent years. Great Lakes has installed a new management group (including a new controller, Christie Horvath) at North Spruce and has given the group six years to expand and revitalize the operations. Management compensation includes a bonus based on net income generated by the North Spruce operations. If North Spruce does not show considerable improvement by the end of the sixth year, Great Lakes will consider selling it. The new management immediately makes significant investments in new equipment but finds that new revenues develop slowly. Most of the new equipment will be replaced in 8 to 10 years. In preparing financial statements, Ms. Horvath uses the straight-line method with maximum residual values and expected lives that average 12 years for the new equipment.

Required:

1. Why did the controller compute depreciation expense on the financial statements as she did?
2. What are the possible consequences of the controller's decision about the amount of depreciation expense shown on the financial statements if this decision goes unchallenged?

Case 7-87   The Effect of Estimates of Life and Residual Value on Depreciation Expense

Summerside Manufacturing purchased a new computer-integrated system to manufacture a group of fabricated metal and plastic products. The equipment was purchased from Bessemer Systems at a cost of $550,000. As a basis for determining annual depreciation expense, Summerside's controller requests estimates of the expected life and residual value for the new equipment. The engineering and production departments submit the following divergent estimates:

	Engineering Department Estimates	Production Department Estimates
Expected life	10 years	8 years
Residual value	$90,000	0

Before considering depreciation expense for the new equipment, Summerside Manufacturing has net income in the amount of $250,000. Summerside uses the straight-line method of depreciation.

Required:

1. Compute a full year's depreciation expense for the new equipment, using each of the two sets of estimates.
2. Ignoring income taxes, what will be the effect on net income of including a full year's depreciation expense based on the engineering estimates? Based on the production estimates?
3. If a business has a significant investment in depreciable assets, the expected life and residual value estimates can materially affect depreciation expense and therefore net income. What might motivate management to use the highest or lowest estimates?

Case 7-88   Continuing Problem: Front Row Entertainment

After a successful first year, Cam and Anna decide to expand Front Row Entertainment's operations by becoming a venue operator as well as a tour promoter. A venue operator contracts with promoters to rent the venue (which can range from amphitheatres to indoor arenas to night-clubs) for specific events on specific dates. In addition to receiving revenue from renting the venue, venue operators also provide services such as concessions, parking, security, and ushering services. By vertically integrating their business, Cam and Anna can reduce the expense that they pay to rent venues. In addition, they will generate additional revenue by providing services to other tour promoters.

After a little investigation, Cam and Anna locate a small venue operator that owns Toronto Music House, a small indoor arena with a rich history in the music industry. The current owner has experienced severe health issues and has let the arena fall into a state of disrepair. However, he would like the arena to be preserved and its musical legacy to continue. After a short negotiation, on January 1, 2018, Front Row Entertainment purchased the venue by paying $10,000 in cash and signing a 15-year 10% note for $390,000. The land on which the arena sits is worth $100,000. In addition, Front Row Entertainment purchased the right to use the "Toronto Music House" name for $25,000.

During the month of January 2018, Front Row Entertainment incurred the following expenditures as they renovated the arena and prepared it for the first major event scheduled for February:

Jan. 5   Paid $21,530 to repair damage to the roof of the arena.
    10   Paid $45,720 to remodel the stage area.
    21   Purchased concessions equipment (e.g., popcorn poppers, soda machines) for $12,350.

Renovations were completed on January 28, and the first concert was held in the arena on February 1. The arena is expected to have a useful life of 30 years and a residual value of $35,000. The concessions equipment will have an estimated useful life of 5 years and a residual value of $250.

Required:

1. Prepare the journal entries to record the acquisition of the arena, the concessions equipment, and the trademark.
2. Prepare the journal entries to record the expenditures made in January.
3. Compute and record the depreciation for 2018 (11 months) on the arena (use the straight-line method) and on the concessions equipment (use the double-declining-balance method). Round all answers to the nearest dollar.
4. Would amortization expense be recorded for the trademark? Why or why not?

Case 7-89   Professional and Ethical Behaviour—Controls Relating to Property, Plant, and Equipment

Recall your knowledge of internal controls from Chapter 4. Identify and explain controls that should be in place when purchasing and recording any property, plant, and equipment. Explain what can go wrong if the control is weak.

Case 7-90   Professional and Ethical Behaviour—Ethics Relating to the Recording of Property, Plant, and Equipment and Weaknesses in Internal Controls

You have just accepted a job working in the accounts payable department at IEM Limited. IEM is one of Canada's largest IT and consulting companies. IEM sells computer-related products, such as computers, printers, and tablets, and other business-related items, but also offers consulting services to assist smaller companies looking to start a new business. Recently there has been a decline in the growth of business at IEM. In fact, sales have been declining by a considerable amount over the last three years. Pressure has mounted on IEM to show a better bottom line as investors have been worried about the decreasing sales and lower net income.

During your first month at IEM, you make it a point to get to know everyone in your department. Four people work in accounts payable. You were hired to take over Joe's position. Joe worked for the company for 20 years and has recently retired. You report directly to Pat, supervisor of the accounts payable department.

You have been working under Pat's supervision since you started. Pat recently told you that he was looking forward to finally taking his two-week holiday with his family. He was worried at first that he wouldn't get his bonus to pay for the trip, given that it looked as though the net income on the statement of earnings wouldn't meet the targets required for a bonus payout. He was happy when it actually did.

Pat told you not to worry about anything while he was away, as he'd take care of everything when he returned. In fact, he told you to take a week's vacation if you liked. You thought that was strange as you had only started a month ago. He told you that you were doing a great job and he liked how motivated you were.

One month later, with Pat away, you decide to impress your boss by attempting to do as much as possible in the department. As you start to review all available documentation, you realize that several invoices for equipment bought by IEM were all recorded as capital items on the statement of financial position; however, no depreciation has been taken on these items all year, despite the items being used in the business. You recall from your accounting courses that if a capital item is used in the business, it should be depreciated.

You start to dig deeper and notice that documents for the items that were recorded in the financial statements, such as invoices and cheques showing payment of the items purchased, have only one signature on them, and the signature is Pat's. You recall from the policy manual provided to you on your first day at IEM that it's company policy to have two signatures for all items that are purchased and paid in the accounts payable department, especially if the item costs over $10,000. Clearly this is not being followed. After further research, you realize that some of the equipment recorded on the statement of financial position is very old, and you are wondering why it was never written off.

You cannot wait for Pat to return from his trip to question him on the discrepancies you have noticed.

Required:

Identify and discuss any accounting issues and potential ethical issues.

Case 7-91   Professional and Ethical Behaviour

Jim was excited to receive his bonus for the current year. He knew that the company didn't have the best year and the company was watching how much money was spent on expense-related items. Jim knew that if net income was below the estimated net income, employees wouldn't receive their bonus. The CEO recently communicated this to all staff members.

Jim was responsible for recording all journal entries relating to property, plant, and equipment, including all depreciation. He had the great idea to use the depreciation method that would result in the lowest depreciation taken for the year, which would make the bottom line look better and hence result in the company employees receiving their bonuses. He knew everyone would think he was a hero for making sure the staff received their bonuses.

Required:

Identify and discuss any potential issues with Jim's actions.

INTEGRATIVE CASE 2 (CHAPTERS 4–7)

Integrating Asset Accounting

Obtain **Rogers Communications Inc.**'s fiscal 2014 annual report dated February 13, 2015, through the "Investor Relations" portion of its website (do a web search for "Rogers Communications Inc., Investor Relations").

Required:

Using Rogers Communications Inc.'s annual report, answer the following questions:

1. Looking at Note 2: Significant Accounting Policies, identify the basis of presentation of the financial statements for Rogers Communications Inc.

2. Looking at the Independent Auditors' Report supplying an opinion on Rogers's consolidated financial statements, what was the auditor's opinion regarding the financial statements? Who was responsible for the consolidated financial statements?

3. What was Rogers's accounts receivable turnover (rounded to two decimal places) in 2014? (Assuming the industry average for 2014 was 5.00, describe Rogers's relative efficiency with its accounts receivable. Also, assume the sales provided in the financial statements equal net sales).

4. Describe the trend in Rogers's accounts receivable.

5. How many days' sales does Rogers have in receivables? (*Note:* Round answer to two decimal places.)

6. What were Rogers's operating margin, and net profit ratios in 2014? (*Note:* Round answers to two decimal places.) Assuming industry averages for 2014 were 10.00%, describe Rogers's profitability respectively for all three.

7. Looking at Note 2: Significant Accounting Policies, what method of depreciation does Rogers use? What is the range of estimated useful life for customer premise equipment? Do you think this useful life is appropriate?

8

Reporting and Analyzing Current Liabilities

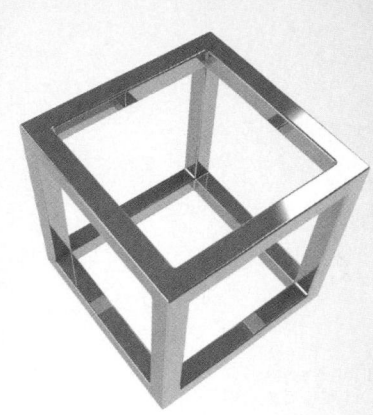

After studying Chapter 8, you should be able to:

1 Explain, measure, and report current liabilities.

2 Identify and record the types of activities that produce current liabilities.

3 Explain, measure, and report contingent liabilities.

4 Explain the nature, measurement, and reporting of provisions such as warranty liabilities.

5 Calculate and analyze the current, quick, cash, and operating cash flow and trade payable ratios.

6 (Appendix 8A) Explain the measurement and reporting for deferred income taxes.

The Canadian Press/Mario Beauregard

EXPERIENCE FINANCIAL ACCOUNTING
with Boston Pizza

Boston Pizza was founded in 1964 when Gus Agioritis opened "Boston House." In 1983, Tim Trevliving, a former RCMP officer, and George Melville, CA, acquired the Boston Pizza chain. There are now more than 365 Boston Pizza restaurants in Canada. Today, this brand is considered one of the top restaurants in Canada, with revenues of over $1 billion in 2014.

Gift cards have become a popular holiday gift among the public generally. As you will learn in this chapter, restaurants such as Boston Pizza

El Nariz/Shutterstock

have a liability (unearned revenues) related to the sale of gift cards until the meal is provided. That is, gift card revenue should not be recognized until the services (in this case, a meal) are provided. Gift card revenue should not be recognized until the card is redeemed (for goods or services), and therefore, Boston Pizza does not expect to see the revenue benefit from this transaction immediately. Generally, this occurs weeks or months after the gift card was purchased.

CURRENT LIABILITIES

Chapters 4, 5, 6, and 7 explained accounting and reporting for assets. Now we will move to the other side of the statement of financial position and discuss liabilities and equity, which are the sources of cash and other financial resources used to acquire assets. We begin by examining liabilities.

Finding potential creditors, arranging attractive credit terms, structuring borrowings with lenders, and arranging to have enough cash coming in to pay the liabilities as they come due are among the most important managerial functions. The results of liability management and the associated accounting recognition, measurement, and reporting appear on the liabilities portion of the statement of financial position. The information provided by Hudson's Bay Company in its 2014 (January 31, 2015) balance sheet is typical:

Hudson's Bay Company Consolidated Balance Sheet (Partial) (in millions C$) January 31, 2015	
LIABILITIES	
Current liabilities	
Loans and borrowings	$ 265
Accounts payable and accrued liabilities	$1,548
Deferred revenue	130
Provisions	115
Income taxes payable	8
Other	78
	2,144
Noncurrent liabilities	
Long-term borrowings	2,859
Other noncurrent liabilities	1,577

Source: HBC Hudson's Bay Company 2014 Annual Report.

Naturally, existing and potential creditors find this information useful as they want to know about the obligations management has assumed.

In this chapter and the next we discuss the three kinds of business obligations: current liabilities, contingent liabilities, and long-term debt. Current liabilities are those obligations that are (1) expected to be retired with existing current assets or creation of new current liabilities, and (2) due within one year or one operating cycle, whichever is longer. All other liabilities are considered long-term. Contingent liabilities can be either current or long-term, but they are "iffy" in two ways. They may or may not turn into actual obligations and, for those contingencies that do become obligations, the timing and amount of the required payment is uncertain. In this chapter we focus on current liabilities and contingent liabilities and address the following questions:

- When are current and contingent liabilities recognized?
- How are current and contingent liabilities measured?
- How are current and contingent liabilities reported?
- What kinds of activities produce current liabilities and how are they recorded in the accounting records?
- What kinds of activities result in contingent liabilities and how are they recorded or disclosed in the financial statements?
- How are warranty liabilities measured and recorded?

RECOGNITION, MEASUREMENT, AND REPORTING OF LIABILITIES

OBJECTIVE **1**

Explain, measure, and report current liabilities.

Liabilities are probable future sacrifices of economic benefits. These commitments, which arise from activities that have occurred in the past, require the business to

© Cengage Learning

EXHIBIT 8.1

Characteristics of Liabilities

Payment of cash:
Although liabilities frequently require the payment of cash, some may require the transfer of assets other than cash, or the future performance of services.

Certainty:
Although the exact amount and timing of future payments are usually known, for some liabilities they may not be.

Legal enforceability:
Although many liabilities are legally enforceable claims, some may represent merely *probable* claims.

Payment recipient:
Although liabilities usually identify the entity to be paid, the definition does not exclude payment to unknown recipients.

transfer assets or provide services to another entity sometime in the future. For example, an account payable liability arises from a transaction in which the business receives goods or services in return for a cash payment at some future time.

Within this general definition, liabilities have a wide variety of characteristics, as shown in Exhibit 8.1.

Thus, the future outflow associated with a liability may or may not involve the payment of cash; may or may not be known with certainty; may or may not be legally enforceable; and may or may not be payable to a known recipient.

Recognition of Liabilities

Most liabilities are recognized when goods or services are received or money is borrowed (see Exhibit 8.2). However, when the existence of a liability depends on the occurrence of a future event (i.e., a **contingent liability**), such as the outcome of a lawsuit, recognition depends on how likely the occurrence of the future event is and whether a reasonable estimate of the payment amount can be made. If the future payment is judged to be less than probable or the payment is not reasonably estimable, the obligation should not be recognized. Such obligations may require disclosure in footnotes to the financial statements, as explained later in this chapter.

EXHIBIT 8.2

Recognition of Wages Owing to Employees as Current Liabilities

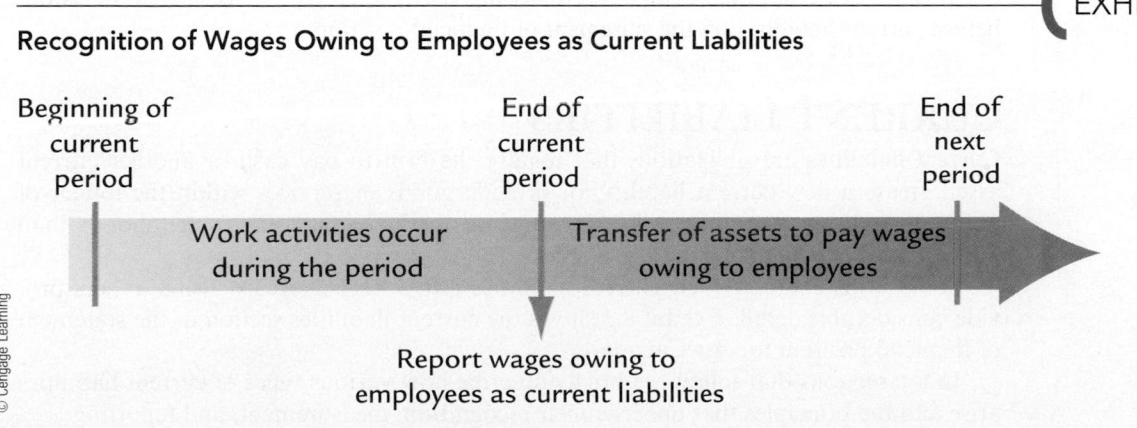

© Cengage Learning

Measurement of Liabilities

We know that when you owe money you typically pay interest. That is, if you borrow $100 at 10% interest, then when you pay it back one year later you must repay $110:

$$\text{Total payment} = \text{Principal} + (\text{Principal} \times \text{Interest rate} \times \text{Period})$$
$$= \$100 + (\$100 \times 10\% \times 12/12)$$

Sometimes companies will appear to give you a zero percent interest loan. For example, furniture and electronics retailers frequently advertise "no interest, no money down for 12 months" or some such terms. Of course, we know this really means that the "interest" is included in the sales price because no business is going to truly provide zero percent interest.

In theory, the amount of the liability reported on the statement of financial position should not include any interest that has not yet occurred. For example, on a statement of financial position prepared six months after borrowing the $100 at 10% interest described above, you should report a liability of $105:

$$\$100 + (\$100 \times 10\% \times 6/12)$$

However, many liabilities are more like your credit card or utilities bill. For example, you might owe your power company $150 for the use of electricity during September. You likely do not receive this bill until sometime during October and you do not have to pay it until near the end of November. Furthermore, there appears to be no interest because you owe $150 whether you pay the bill when you receive it in October or wait until the November due date.

Despite the apparent lack of interest, theoretically interest exists. Consequently, in theory we should calculate the interest on such liabilities. For example, if we prepared a statement of financial position at the end of September, then a liability for the power company should be calculated to exclude the theoretical interest included in the $150 payment at the end of November (i.e., two months' interest at the market rate). Fortunately, we ignore the interest for most current liabilities because the amount of interest is relatively small. So most current liabilities are simply recorded and reported at the total amount owed, as we will see in the next section.

Reporting of Current Liabilities

Current liabilities for North American companies are traditionally listed in order of their liquidity—meaning by their due date—on the statement of financial position. International companies sometimes list their current liabilities in reverse order of liquidity.

In addition to the above difference, North American companies following IFRS generally report current liabilities before noncurrent liabilities on the statement of financial position. International companies following IFRS often report noncurrent liabilities before current liabilities on the statement of financial position.

CURRENT LIABILITIES

OBJECTIVE 2

Identify and record the types of activities that produce current liabilities.

Current liabilities are obligations that require the firm to pay cash or another current asset, create a new current liability, or provide goods or services within the longer of one year and one operating cycle. Since most firms have operating cycles shorter than one year, the one-year rule usually applies.

Some firms combine their current liabilities into a very short list, while others provide considerable detail. Exhibit 8.3 shows the current liabilities section of the statement of financial position for Air Canada.

In the sections that follow we briefly describe how various types of current liabilities arise and the principles that underlie their recognition, measurement, and reporting.

Air Canada Annual Report 2014, page 88. Used with permission of Air Canada.

(EXHIBIT 8.3)

Current Liability Section from Air Canada

Air Canada Consolidated Statement of Financial Position (in millions)	December 31, 2014	December 31, 2013
Current liabilities:		
Accounts payable and accrued liabilities	$1,259	$1,129
Advance ticket sales	1,794	1,687
Current portion of long-term debt and finance leases	484	374
Total current liabilities	$3,537	$3,190

Operating Line of Credit

To better manage the cash available for operating purposes, many companies arrange a line of credit with a financial institution. A company's line of credit represents a preapproved maximum amount of funds that the financial institution will make available for operating purposes. Funds advanced to a company under the terms of a line of credit are normally secured by collectible accounts receivable and by inventory. Financial institutions charge interest to the company on borrowed funds. The interest rate charged depends on the company's creditworthiness. An operating line of credit is typically disclosed in the statement of financial position as bank indebtedness. Note disclosure is required in the financial statements with respect to pertinent details of the line of credit arrangement and the security pledged as collateral for the outstanding line of credit.

Accounts Payable

An **account payable** arises when a business purchases goods or services on credit. It is really just the flip side of an account receivable—when you have a payable, the business you owe has a receivable. Credit terms generally require that the purchaser pay the amount due within 30 to 60 days and seldom require the payment of interest. Accounts payable do not require a formal agreement or contract. For example, your account with the power company usually does not require you to sign a formal contract.

You may recall from Chapter 5 that accounts receivable have some valuation issues related to estimating bad debts. Accounts payable, on the other hand, have no such issues. They are measured and reported at the total amount required to satisfy the account, which is the cost of the goods or services acquired. For example, if Game Time Sporting Goods buys and receives running shoes on May 15, 2018, for which it pays its supplier $2,000 on June 15, 2018, it will need to make the following journal entries:

Date	Account and Explanation	Debit	Credit
May 15	Inventory	2,000	
	Accounts Payable		2,000
	(Record purchase of inventory)		
June 15	Accounts Payable	2,000	
	Cash		2,000
	(Record payment to supplier)		

Assets	= Liabilities +	Shareholders' Equity
+2,000	+2,000	

Assets	= Liabilities +	Shareholders' Equity
−2,000	−2,000	

Accrued Liabilities

Unlike accounts payable, which are recognized when goods or services change hands, **accrued liabilities** are recognized by adjusting entries. They usually represent expenses incurred but not paid at the end of an accounting period. For example, Green's Landscaping pays wages of $10,000 (or $1,000 per work day) to its employees every other Friday. The standard entry to record a payment on December 20 is:

Shareholders' Equity
Assets = Liabilities + (Wages Expense)
−10,000   −10,000

Date	Account and Explanation	Debit	Credit
Dec. 20	Wages Expense	10,000	
	Cash		10,000
	(Record payment of wages)		

What happens, however, when December 31 (the company's year-end date) falls on the Tuesday before the Friday payday? In this case, the expense for the seven days that have already been worked (five days from last week and Monday and Tuesday of this week) must be matched to the proper period. Additionally, because the work has been performed but the employees have not yet been paid, Green's Landscaping has an unpaid liability to its employees as at December 31. As such, on December 31 Green's will record the following adjusting entry:

Shareholders' Equity
Assets = Liabilities + (Wages Expense)
+7,000   −7,000

Date	Account and Explanation	Debit	Credit
Dec. 31	Wages Expense	7,000	
	Wages Payable		7,000
	(Record accrual of wages expense)		

Furthermore, when Green's pays $10,000 to its employees on January 3, three days' pay is an expense of the current year (Wednesday, January 1 through Friday, January 3) and seven days' pay retires the Wages Payable from December 31:

Shareholders' Equity
Assets = Liabilities + (Wages Expense)
−10,000   −7,000   −3,000

Date	Account and Explanation	Debit	Credit
Jan. 3	Wages Expense	3,000	
	Wages Payable	7,000	
	Cash		10,000
	(Record payment of wages)		

This sort of process is used for a wide variety of activities that are completed over time. For example, taxes are paid based on the previous year's net income. As such, on December 31 an adjusting entry will match the appropriate income tax expense to the current year and set up a liability (income tax payable) that will be paid off in the new year. The same logic applies to similar situations, such as property tax and interest expense.

Income Tax Payable

Corporations carrying on business in Canada pay income tax on their taxable income; the amount is calculated under the provisions of the Income Tax Act. Income tax rates depend on several factors, including the type of income earned by the corporation (business income, property income, or taxable capital gains) and the type of corporation it is (e.g., whether it is public or private).

The income tax expense reported on the statement of earnings usually consists of both a current and a deferred (or future) portion. The current portion reflects the actual current tax payable by the corporation for the particular fiscal year and must be paid within limits prescribed under the Income Tax Act. The deferred portion represents the difference that arises between the accounting rules under IFRS and the tax rules used by corporations to calculate their taxable income and results in recording a deferred income tax liability due to the deferring of the payment of income tax to a future year.

Source: Canadian Tire 2014 Annual Report, page 94.

(EXHIBIT 8.4)

Notes to the Consolidated Financial Statements, Canadian Tire

Note 18.2 Income Tax Expense		
The following are the major components of the income tax expense:		
(C$ in millions)	2014	2013
Current tax expense		
Current period	**$248.5**	$216.8
Adjustments in respect of prior years	**7.2**	(2.6)
	255.7	214.2
Deferred tax expense	**(16.8)**	6
Income tax expense	**$238.5**	$220.2

Exhibit 8.4 discloses the current and deferred income tax expense for Canadian Tire for 2014 (January 3, 2015). Exhibit 8.5 discloses the current and deferred income tax payable balances on the statement of financial position for Canadian Tire for 2014 (January 3, 2015). The Appendix at the end of this chapter explores further the relationship between current and deferred income taxes payable and, on occasion, current and deferred tax assets.

Short-Term Notes Payable

A **note payable** typically arises when a business borrows money or purchases goods or services from a company that requires a formal agreement or contract (e.g., when you sign a contract to lease an apartment or buy a car). This formal agreement or contract is what distinguishes a note payable from an account payable. The agreement typically states the timing of repayment and the amount (principal and/or interest) to be repaid. Notes payable typically mature in 3 to 12 months, but it can be longer (if it does not mature for over 12 months, it will be classified as a long-term liability). These longer maturities explain why creditors are more likely to impose interest on notes payable than on accounts payable.

(EXHIBIT 8.5)

Consolidated Statements of Financial Position (Partial)

As at (C$ in millions)	January 3, 2015	December 28, 2013
LIABILITIES		
Bank indebtedness	$ 14.3	$ 69.0
Deposits	950.7	1,178.4
Trade and other payables	1,961.2	1,817.4
Provisions	206.0	196.1
Short-term borrowings	199.8	120.3
Loans payable	604.4	611.2
Income taxes payable	54.9	57.5
Current portion of long-term debt	587.5	272.2
Total current liabilities	**4,578.8**	**4,322.1**
Long-term provisions	44.1	38.2
Long-term debt	2,131.6	2,339.1
Long-term deposits	1,286.2	1,152.0
Deferred income taxes	93.9	100.4
Other long-term liabilities	787.8	228.3
Total liabilities	**8,922.4**	**8,180.1**

Source: Canadian Tire 2014 Annual Report, page 63.

Notes Payable from Borrowing from a Bank Notes payable normally specify the amount to be repaid indirectly, by stating the amount borrowed (the principal) and an interest rate. These notes are called *interest-bearing notes* because they explicitly state an **interest rate** that is charged for the use of money over time, called the **time value of money**. The maturity amount of an interest-bearing note is not stated explicitly but is determined from the interest rate, the principal amount, and the maturity date.

When a business borrows using a short-term, interest-bearing note, the transaction is recorded at the amount borrowed. This is illustrated in Cornerstone 8.1 .

CORNERSTONE 8.1

Recording Notes Payable and Accrued Interest

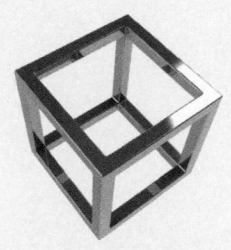

CORNERSTONE
VIDEO

Information:

Feldman Auto Parts borrowed $100,000 from a bank on October 1, 2018, at 10% interest. The interest and principal are due on October 1, 2019. The company's year-end date is December 31.

Required:

1. Prepare the required journal entry on October 1, 2018.

2. Prepare the adjusting journal entry on December 31, 2018.

3. Prepare the journal entry (or entries) on October 1, 2019.

Why:

A note payable may be issued by a company in return for goods or services received. Interest on notes payable must be matched in the same period as the revenues it helped to generate.

Solution:

Date	Account and Explanation	Debit	Credit
1. Oct. 1, 2018	Cash	100,000	
	Note Payable		100,000
	(Record issuance of note payable)		
2. Dec. 31, 2018	Interest Expense	2,500*	
	Interest Payable		2,500
	(Record accrual of interest expense)		
3. Oct. 1, 2019	Note Payable	100,000	
	Interest Expense	7,500**	
	Interest Payable	2,500	
	Cash		110,000
	(Record payment of note and interest)		

*$100,000 × 10% × 3/12
**$100,000 × 10% × 9/12

		Shareholders'
Assets	= Liabilities +	Equity
+100,000	+100,000	

		Shareholders' Equity
Assets	= Liabilities +	(Interest Expense)
	+2,500	−2,500

		Shareholders' Equity
Assets	= Liabilities +	(Interest Expense)
−110,000	−2,500	−7,500
	−100,000	

Exhibit 8.6 illustrates the financial statement effects of the transactions recorded in Cornerstone 8.1. Notice that the interest payment of $10,000 is recorded as interest expense of $2,500 in 2018 and $7,500 in 2019.

Notes Payable from a Payment Extension In addition to short-term borrowings, notes payable are often created when a borrower is unable to pay an account payable in a timely manner. In this case, the borrower is typically granted a payment extension, but the creditor requires a formal note be signed to impose interest. As discussed, a current liability can be retired through the creation of a new current liability. Rolling an account payable into a short-term note payable would be an example of this.

Assume that on March 8, 2018, Gibson Shipping orders $25,000 of packing materials from Ironman Enterprises on account. This amount is due on May 15, 2018. Gibson would need to make the following journal entry:

Date	Account and Explanation	Debit	Credit
Mar. 8	Supplies Inventory	25,000	
	Accounts Payable		25,000
	(Record purchase of packing materials)		

Assets	= Liabilities +	Shareholders' Equity
+25,000	+25,000	

On May 15, Gibson cannot make the $25,000 payment and asks Ironman for a payment extension. If Ironman grants the extension on the condition that Gibson sign a note that specifies 7% interest beginning on May 15, 2018, with a due date of November 15, 2018, Gibson will make the following journal entry:

Date	Account and Explanation	Debit	Credit
May 15	Accounts Payable	25,000	
	Notes Payable		25,000
	(Record issuance of note payable)		

Assets	= Liabilities +	Shareholders' Equity
	+25,000	
	−25,000	

Finally, on November 15, 2018, when Gibson pays the amount in full, the journal entry will be as follows:

(EXHIBIT 8.6)

Effect of Borrowing Money on the Annual Statement of Earnings and Statement of Financial Position

10/1/18 12/31/18   9/30/19 12/31/19

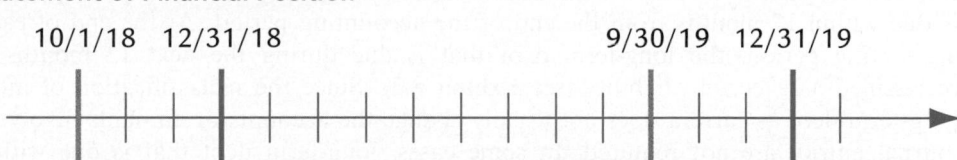

	2018	2019
Annual statement of earnings:		
Interest expense	$ 2,500	$ 7,500
Annual statement of financial position:		
Note payable	$100,000	$ 0
Interest payable	2,500	0
Transactions:		
Cash borrowed	$100,000	
Principal payment		$100,000
Interest payment		10,000

	Shareholders' Equity	
Assets = Liabilities + (Interest Expense)		
−25,875 −25,000	−875	

Date	Account and Explanation	Debit	Credit
Nov. 15	Notes Payable	25,000	
	Interest Expense	875*	
	Cash		25,875
	(Record payment of note and interest)		

*$25,000 × 7% × 6/12

YOUDECIDE Making a Short-Term Loan

You are a commercial loan officer at the Royal Bank of Canada. Hydraulic Controls, a local manufacturer of hydraulic clutch assemblies for compact automobiles, would like to borrow money using a short-term note. The following data are available on Hydraulic's current liabilities, current assets, sales revenue, and net income (loss) for the past three years:

Item	2018	2017	2016
Accounts payable	$ 174,000	$ 146,000	$ 104,000
Short-term notes payable	332,000	291,000	291,000
Income tax payable	-0-	43,000	50,000
Total current liabilities	506,000	480,000	445,000
Total current assets	485,000	546,000	611,000
Sales revenue	5,047,000	5,293,000	5,538,000
Net income (loss)	(10,000)	89,000	130,000

Hydraulic Controls has asked its bank to increase its short-term notes payable by $100,000.

Should you approve a short-term note payable for Hydraulic?

To determine whether to extend additional credit to Hydraulic, you should consider the following:

- *How will the short-term notes be repaid?* The short-term notes would be repaid from current assets. But the decline in the amount of current assets relative to current liabilities suggests that even the present amount of current liabilities may not be repayable with the resources currently available.
- *What might be causing the recent increases in current liabilities and decreases in current assets?* Because profitability is declining, the firm may not be able to borrow from outside sources or secure cash from operations. Therefore, it may be drawing down current assets and increasing current liabilities to provide capital.

The decline in profitability, the trend in the ratio of current assets to current liabilities, and the present excess of current liabilities over current assets suggest that it would be unwise to extend additional credit at this time.

Current Portion of Long-Term Debt

The current portion of long-term debt is the amount of long-term debt principal that is due within 12 months from the end of the accounting period. At the end of each accounting period, the long-term debt that is due during the next 12 months is reclassified as a current liability (see Exhibit 8.3). Since the reclassification of most long-term debt as current does not usually change the accounts or amounts involved, journal entries are not required. In some cases, long-term debt that is due within 12 months will be paid with the proceeds of a new long-term debt issue. Remember that current liabilities must be retired with existing current assets or the creation of new current liabilities—a new long-term debt issue is creation of a new *long-term*, not current, liability.[1]

Other Current Liabilities

So far we have discussed accounts payable, accrued liabilities, and notes payable. However, businesses will have other current liabilities that do not fall into these categories. There are many situations that can give rise to these other payables, but we will restrict our discussion to some of the most common.

[1] We discuss long-term liabilities in more detail in Chapter 9.

Sales Taxes **Sales taxes** are normally charged as a percentage of the sales price of the goods or services sold. The tax charged to the customer may consist of provincial sales tax (PST), federal goods and services tax (GST), or harmonized sales tax (HST); the latter represents a combination in certain provinces of the specific province's PST rate and the federal GST rate. The federal GST rate is currently 5% in Canada. Provincial sales tax rates in Canada vary but are currently in the range of 0% to 10%. In all provinces except Quebec and Prince Edward Island, GST is not charged on PST.

At the time of a sale, the sales tax is collected as part of the total selling price. It is not, however, an increase in revenue for the seller; rather, it is collected from the customer on behalf of the particular government that has levied the tax. These sales tax collections represent liabilities until they are paid (usually each month) to the relevant provincial or federal taxation authority. Companies that are GST/HST registrants are allowed to offset sales taxes collected with sales tax payments made on the company's own eligible purchases; the net amount is payable by or refundable to the company.

Accounting for sales taxes is complex because of the various tax rates that apply to different goods and services. Point-of-sale computer software helps ease the detailed accounting required for sales taxes. Cornerstone 8.2 illustrates the accounting for sales taxes.

Recording Liabilities at the Point of Sale

CORNERSTONE 8.2

Information:
a. During the first quarter of 2018, McLean County Tire sold, on credit, 3,000 truck tires at $75 each plus harmonized sales tax of 13%. This tax is usually paid to the federal government each month.
b. Assume the same sales data as in (a) except that GST of 5% and PST of 6% is charged on sales.

Required:
Prepare the journal entries to record (1) first quarter sales and (2) payment of taxes to the federal government.

CORNERSTONE VIDEO

Why:
Legislation requires that companies must typically collect sales taxes (for example, HST, GST, PST) when goods or services are sold to customers. These taxes are subsequently paid monthly to the appropriate taxation authority.

Solution:
a.

Date	Account and Explanation	Debit	Credit
1. Mar. 31	Accounts Receivable	254,250	
	Sales Revenue		225,000*
	Sales Taxes (HST) Payable (Federal)		29,250**
	(Record sale of truck tires)		

	Assets	= Liabilities +	Shareholders' Equity (Sales Revenue)
	+254,250	+29,250	+225,000

(Continued)

2. Apr. 30   Sales Taxes (HST) Payable (Federal)   29,250
                        Cash   29,250
                        (Record payment of first quarter sales taxes)

*3,000 tires × $75
**3,000 tires × $75 × 13%

(Continued)

	Shareholders'
Assets = Liabilities +	Equity
−29,250 −29,250	

Note: The receivable is larger than the sales revenue because of the amount of taxes McLean collects for the government—liabilities of McLean until the government is paid.

b.

Date	Account and Explanation	Debit	Credit
Mar. 31	Accounts Receivable	249,750	
1.	Sales Revenue		225,000
	PST Payable—Province		13,500*
	GST Payable—Federal		11,250**
	(Record sale of truck tires)		
2. Apr. 30	PST Payable—Province	13,500	
	GST Payable—Federal	11,250	
	Cash		24,750
	(Record sales tax payments to federal and provincial governments)		

*$225,000 × 6%
**$225,000 × 5%

Withholding and Payroll Taxes Businesses are required to withhold certain taxes from employees' earnings and to pay certain additional taxes based on wages and salaries paid to employees. These **withholding** and **payroll taxes** are liabilities until they are paid to the taxing authority. Note that there are really two sources for these taxes: employees and businesses.

Employees Employees must pay certain taxes that are "withheld" from their paycheques. This is the difference between gross pay and net pay. The business does not have any rights to this money; instead, as with sales tax, it must pay these amounts to the proper tax authority. The standard withholdings are federal and provincial income taxes, as well as Canada Pension Plan (CPP) and Employment Insurance (EI). Employees may also have amounts withheld for such things as pension plan, parking, health insurance, union dues, and charitable donations, but these are not taxes.

Businesses The business itself must pay certain taxes based on employee payrolls. These amounts are not withheld from employee pay; rather, they are additional amounts that must be paid over and above gross pay. For example, employers generally match your contributions to the Canada Pension Plan and Employment Insurance. That is, if you have $400 withheld from your paycheque for the Canada Pension Plan (CPP) and $100 for Employment Insurance (EI), your employer generally pays the federal government $1,040 ($400 (employee portion of CPP) + $400 (employer matches employee's CPP contribution) + $100 (employee EI contribution) + $140 (employer matches at 140% of employee's EI contribution)) related to your employment. There are annual maximum amounts that employers must pay for Canada Pension and Employment Insurance; these amounts depend on the amount of an employee's annual earnings. Finally, employers do have other costs—typically called fringe benefits—associated with employees, but these are not taxes. Examples of fringe benefits include employer contributions to retirement accounts (pension plan) and health insurance. Employers in certain industries must also pay prescribed premiums to a provincially legislated worker safety board authority (formal names differ by province and territory) for workers who are injured while on the job. Cornerstone 8.3 illustrates the accounting for payroll obligations.

Recording Payroll Taxes

CORNERSTONE 8.3

CORNERSTONE
VIDEO

Information:

McLean County Tire's hourly employees earned gross pay of $50,000 in the pay period ended March 31. Income taxes withheld at source from gross pay were $11,000. In addition, CPP premiums of $2,000 and EI premiums of $1,000 were withheld from gross pay.

The employer's cost of employee benefits is determined to be as follows: CPP $2,000, EI $1,400, Worker Safety Board $1,500.

Required:

1. Prepare the journal entry to record the gross pay earned by and paid to employees in March.

2. Prepare the journal entry to record the employer's payroll taxes and Worker Safety Board liabilities.

3. Prepare the journal entry to record payment of the tax withholdings, payroll taxes, and Worker Safety Board premium on April 15.

Why:

Companies must accrue a liability for employment-related taxes (CPP/EI/Worker Safety Board, for example) in each period that employees work. These taxes are subsequently paid to the appropriate taxation authority.

Solution:

Date	Account and Explanation	Debit	Credit
1. Mar. 31	Wages expense	50,000	
	CPP Payable—Employees		2,000
	EI Payable—Employees		1,000
	Income Tax Payable—Employees		11,000
	Cash		36,000
	(Record wages earned and paid and *employee tax withholdings)*		
2. Mar. 31	CPP expense	2,000	
	EI expense	1,400	
	Worker Safety Board expense	1,500	
	CPP Payable—Employer		2,000
	EI Payable—Employer		1,400
	Worker Safety Board Payable		1,500
	(Record employer payroll taxes)		

(Continued)

CORNERSTONE
8.3

(Continued)

3. Apr. 15	CPP Payable—Employees	2,000	
	CPP Payable—Employer	2,000	
	EI Payable—Employees	1,000	
	EI Payable—Employer	1,400	
	Worker Safety Board Payable	1,500	
	Income Tax Payable—Employees	11,000	
	Cash—Canada Revenue Agency		17,400
	Cash—Worker Safety Board		1,500
	(provincial authority)		

(Record payment of payroll withholdings, payroll taxes, and Worker Safety Board premium)

YOUDECIDE Full-Time Employee or Consultant?

You are the HR manager of Berndt Chocolates. The marketing department wants to hire a full-time employee at an annual salary of approximately $40,000. They argue that this will save the company money because Berndt will no longer have to pay an outside marketing consultant approximately $48,000 per year to do the same job.

Employer Payroll Taxes	Cost
Canada Pension Plan ($40,000 × 6%)	$2,400
Employment Insurance ($40,000 × 3%)	1,200
Total employer payroll taxes	$3,600

What factors should you consider in deciding whether to hire the full-time employee?

Businesses often must make the decision of whether to hire a full-time employee or pay a self-employed consultant. Of course, of primary concern is which person will perform the function better, but there are other factors to consider. Hiring a consultant can provide several advantages. First, a full-time employee will incur costs in addition to salary. For example, assuming Canada Pension Plan contributions are 6% of salary and Employment Insurance contributions are 3% of salary, for a full-time employee earning $40,000, Berndt's payroll taxes will increase as follows:

Furthermore, most companies have some fringe benefits such as medical insurance, life insurance, pension plans, and bonuses. Assuming these fringe benefits are 30% of the employee's annual salary, this employee would cost $55,600 [$40,000 + $3,600 + $12,000($40,000 × 30%)] per year. Second, it is much easier and less costly to dramatically decrease or eliminate consultants than full-time employees.

Aside from qualifications, the costs of payroll taxes and fringe benefits should be considered when deciding whether to hire full-time employees.

Property Taxes Companies that own real property (land and buildings) incur property taxes each year. Property taxes are charged by municipal governments. Property taxes payable are calculated by multiplying the municipal mill rate per $100 of assessed value. (See Cornerstone 8.4.) Assessed value is based on the use being made of the property. Property taxes are incurred each calendar year, but municipalities differ in terms of when they actually bill their taxpayers for the property taxes.

Unearned (Deferred) Revenues Unearned revenue is the liability created when customers pay for goods or services in advance. In such instances, the amount of the

Recording Property Taxes

CORNERSTONE 8.4

CORNERSTONE VIDEO

Information:

Marc's Manufacturing Ltd. expects to incur $9,000 of property taxes in 2018. The local municipality renders two property tax bills to Marc's of $4,500 each on April 1 and September 1, 2018. Marc's pays the property tax bills as received.

Required:

1. Prepare the journal entry to record the property tax expense January 1 to March 31, 2018.

2. Prepare the journal entry to record the payment of property tax on April 1, 2018.

3. Prepare the journal entry to record the property tax expense from April 1, 2018, to August 31, 2018.

4. Prepare the journal entry to record the payment of property tax on September 1, 2018.

5. Prepare the journal entry to record the property tax expense from September 1 to December 31, 2018.

Why:

Property taxes assessed by municipalities must be accrued as a liability in the period in which they are incurred.

Solution:

	Date	Account and Explanation	Debit	Credit
1.	Mar. 31	Property Tax Expense (9,000 × 3/12)	2,250	
		Accrued Property Tax Payable		2,250
		(Record property tax for 3 months to March 31)		
2.	Apr. 1	Prepaid Property Tax	2,250	
		Accrued Property Tax Payable	2,250	
		Cash		4,500
		(Record property tax payment)		
3.	Aug. 31	Property Tax Expense (9,000 × 5/12)	3,750	
		Prepaid Property Tax		2,250
		Accrued Property Tax Payable		1,500
		(Record property tax expense for 5 months to August 31)		
4.	Sept. 1	Prepaid Property Tax	3,000	
		Accrued Property Tax Payable	1,500	
		Cash		4,500
		(Record property tax payment)		
5.	Dec. 31	Property Tax Expense	3,000	
		Prepaid Property Tax		3,000
		(Record property tax expense for 4 months to December 31)		

prepayment is a liability for the seller. This liability is discharged either by providing the goods or services purchased (at which time revenue is recognized) or by refunding the amount of the prepayment.[2] Cornerstone 8.5 illustrates the accounting for unearned revenues.

CORNERSTONE 8.5

Recording Unearned Revenues

Information:

Luigi's Steakhouse sells $100,000 of gift cards in December 2018. These gift cards may be redeemed at any time; however, they expire on December 31, 2019. During 2019, $98,875 of gift cards is redeemed.

Required:

1. Prepare the journal entry related to the sale of gift cards in 2018.

2. Prepare the journal entry related to redemption of the gift cards in 2019.

3. Prepare the journal entry related to the expiration of the remaining gift cards in 2019.

Why:

Funds received by a business from a customer before goods or services are provided are recorded as an unearned revenue (a liability). Revenue is subsequently recognized when goods or services are provided to the customer.

Solution:

		Shareholders'
Assets	= Liabilities +	Equity
+100,000	+100,000	

		Shareholders' Equity
Assets	= Liabilities +	(Sales Revenue)
	−98,875	+98,875

		Shareholders' Equity
Assets	= Liabilities +	(Sales Revenue)
	−1,125	+1,125

	Date	Account and Explanation	Debit	Credit
1.	Dec. 2018	Cash	100,000	
		Unearned Sales Revenue		100,000
		(Record sale of gift cards)		
2.*	Dec. 31, 2019	Unearned Sales Revenue	98,875	
		Sales Revenue		98,875
		(Record redemption of gift cards)		
3.**	Dec. 31, 2019	Unearned Sales Revenue	1,125	
		Sales Revenue		1,125
		(Record expiration of gift cards)		

* These entries are made individually as each gift card is redeemed.

** When gift cards expire, the sales revenue is recognized because the business does not need to provide any additional goods or services for which cash was previously received.

A similar *long-term* liability, called *customer deposits*, is recorded when customers make advance payments or security deposits that are not expected to be earned or returned soon enough to qualify as current liabilities.

---

[2] If the goods or services are not provided, the seller may also be liable for legal damages. The amount of such damages would be recorded as an expense.

Cornerstone 8.5 demonstrates that revenue will not be recognized until it is realized (or realizable) and earned. Here, revenue is realized because the cash has been collected, so the first criterion is met; however, it is not earned until the goods or services are provided. Recall the chapter opener discussion of Boston Pizza. This same accounting method is used by Boston Pizza to account for gift cards.

CONTINGENT LIABILITIES

Measurement of the liabilities described so far was not affected by uncertainties about the amount, timing, or recipient of future asset outflows. However, such uncertainties exist. In financial accounting, a contingency is an "existing condition, situation, or set of circumstances involving uncertainty" as to possible gain or loss. Contingent liabilities may result, for example, from lawsuit allegations, alleged breaches of environmental laws passed by governments, or potential income tax reassessments by taxing authorities.

A contingent liability is not recognized in the accounts unless

- the event on which it is contingent is probable (meaning more likely than not under IFRS), and
- a reasonable estimate of the loss can be made by management.

If the contingent event is likely to occur, reliable measurement of the liability is usually possible, so recognition is appropriate. For example, contingent liabilities arising from product warranties and pensions are recognized because previous experience allows for reliable measurements to be made. On the other hand, if occurrence of the contingent event is not probable or reliable measurement of the obligation is impossible, the potential obligation is not recorded as a liability. Instead, as shown in Exhibit 8.7, it may be disclosed in footnotes to the financial statements. Contingent liabilities that are remote are not recorded or disclosed in the financial statements.

Lawsuits filed against a business are a classic example of contingent liabilities. Most large companies are party to multiple lawsuits at any point in time. Estimating when a loss is probable and determining a reasonable estimate requires information from the lawyers, but businesses rarely record a contingent liability prior to the jury deciding against them. We've probably all heard of lawsuits such as when Stella Liebeck sued McDonald's. Liebeck spilled coffee while removing the lid to add sugar, burning her legs. She suffered third-degree burns over 6% of her body. McDonald's could have settled the

concept Q&A

Why is a liability recognized when a customer prepays for a good or service (i.e., an unearned revenue)?

Answer:

Liabilities are probable future sacrifices of economic benefits which arise from activities that have already occurred. Because the business here will provide the goods or services purchased by the customer at a future point, the prepayment is a liability.

OBJECTIVE

Explain, measure, and report contingent liabilities.

(EXHIBIT 8.7)

Recognition and Disclosure of Contingent Liabilities

	A Reasonable Estimate Can Be Made	No Reasonable Estimate Can Be Made
Probable	Make a journal entry to record the liability. Disclosure of provision is required in financial statements.	No journal entry is made: disclose information in the financial statements about the contingency.
Not Probable	No journal entry is made: disclosure of contingency in financial statements is required.	No journal entry is made: disclosure of contingency in financial statements is required.
Remote	Neither record as a liability nor disclose in the financial statements.	Neither record as a liability nor disclose in the financial statements.

concept Q&A

Accounts receivable have a contingent loss related to bad debts. A group of customers owes money (the accounts receivable); however, there is uncertainty about whether the customers will pay. How do we account for this contingency and why do we account for it in this way?

Answer:

As discussed in Chapter 5, companies typically use an estimate of uncollectible receivables to recognize "bad debt expense" and reduce the accounts receivable valuation through a credit to the "allowance for doubtful accounts." This is done because it is probable that amounts will be uncollectible and this amount is reasonably estimated (generally based on past experience). So, although bad debt expense does not produce a liability (instead, it reduces an asset), the accounting for this contingency is consistent with contingent liabilities.

case for $20,000, but they refused. Liebeck ultimately was awarded $200,000 in compensatory damages and $2.7 million in punitive damages.[3]

The accounting question becomes: When is a liability (and corresponding expense) recorded? The matching concept suggests that the expense would have been recorded at the time Liebeck spilled the coffee. However, at this time, the loss was contingent. Since the liability and expense were not recorded until it was deemed probable that McDonald's would lose the lawsuit and a reasonable estimate could be made, McDonald's did not record a liability for this amount until they lost the lawsuit many years later.

Of course, the likelihood that a contingent event will occur may change over time. A contingent liability that should not be recorded or disclosed at one time may need to be recorded or disclosed later because the facts and circumstances change. This frequently happens to contingent liabilities arising from litigation.

While contingent assets may arise, those circumstances are extremely rare. Exhibit 8.8 offers an excerpt from the 2014 financial statements of BP with respect to the Gulf of Mexico oil spill and the resulting contingent liabilities related thereto.

ETHICAL DECISIONS   The contingent liability rules create an interesting ethical dilemma in lawsuits. Consider the fictional case of a class-action lawsuit being filed against Giant Pharmaceuticals by patients who used one of Giant's best-selling drugs. Furthermore, company lawyers believe it is probable that Giant will settle the lawsuit for approximately $3 billion. However, if Giant were to recognize a $3 billion liability and expense, the plaintiff lawyers would likely refuse to settle for less. After all, what would you think if you were sitting on a jury and the defendants' lawyer showed you Giant's financial statements, explained the contingency rule, and said, "See, even Giant thinks it's probable that they will lose this lawsuit and pay damages of $3 billion." As you might expect, companies are extremely reluctant to record expenses and liabilities related to lawsuits for this reason or to even disclose that a loss is probable. Is this ethical? It probably isn't ethical, but it is an area that many parties have seemed to allow. As such, users of the financial statements cannot place too much reliance on the lack of expenses and liabilities related to lawsuits.

Commitments

Companies enter into **commitments** during their normal business activities. For accounting purposes, they usually entail contractual commitments to conduct transactions with specified parties in the future. Commitments are not recorded in the financial statements

(**EXHIBIT 8.8**)
_____

Contingent Liabilities (Partial)

Contingent liabilities relating to the Gulf of Mexico oil spill
Note 2. Significant event—Gulf of Mexico oil spill
As a consequence of the Gulf of Mexico oil spill in April 2010, BP continues to incur costs and has also recognized liabilities for certain future costs. Liabilities of uncertain timing or amount, for which no provision has been made, have been disclosed as contingent liabilities.

The total amounts that will ultimately be paid by BP in relation to all the obligations relating to the incident are subject to significant uncertainty and the ultimate exposure and cost to BP will be dependent on many factors, as discussed under Provisions and contingent liabilities below, including in relation to any new information or future developments. These could have a material impact on our consolidated financial position, results of operations and cash flows.

BP has provided for its best estimate of amounts expected to be paid that can be measured reliably. It is not possible, at this time, to measure reliably other obligations arising from the incident, nor is it practicable to estimate their magnitude or possible timing of payment. Therefore, no amounts have been provided for these obligations as at 31 December 2014.

Source: BP 2014 Annual Report, page 111.

_____

[3] Liebeck's compensatory damages were reduced to $160,000 because she was found to be 20% at fault.

because an exchange has not occurred. However, information about commitments to receive or spend cash in the future is meaningful to financial statement users. For that reason, commitments are disclosed in the notes to the financial statements. Common examples of commitments disclosed in the financial statement notes are commitments related to operating leases, raw material purchases, and loan guarantees.

An excerpt from the commitment note in the 2014 (January 3, 2015) financial statements of Canadian Tire is offered in Exhibit 8.9.

PROVISIONS

A liability that is uncertain in amount or timing is referred to as a **provision**. A provision must be recorded when a company has a present obligation that exists because of a past event, a reliable estimate of the amount of the obligation can be made, and it is probable that cash or other assets will be required to settle the obligation. A common example of a provision is a warranty liability.

When goods are sold, the customer is often provided with a warranty against certain defects. A **warranty** usually guarantees the repair or replacement of defective goods during a period (ranging from a few days to several years) following the sale.

The use of parts and labour to satisfy warranty claims may occur in the accounting period in which the sale is made, but it is also likely to occur in some subsequent accounting period. The matching concept requires that all expenses required to produce sales revenue for a given period be recorded in that period. Since warranty costs are sales-related, they

OBJECTIVE 4

Explain the nature, measurement, and reporting of provisions such as warranty liabilities.

(EXHIBIT 8.9)

Guarantees and Commitments (Partial)

Note 37. Guarantees and commitments

Guarantees
In the normal course of business, the Company enters into numerous agreements that may contain features that meet the definition of a guarantee. A guarantee is defined to be a contract (including an indemnity) that contingently requires the Company to make payments to the guaranteed party based on (i) changes in an underlying interest rate, foreign exchange rate, equity or commodity instrument, index or other variable that is related to an asset, a liability or an equity security of the counterparty; (ii) failure of another party to perform under an obligating agreement; or (iii) failure of a third party to pay its indebtedness when due.

The Company has provided the following significant guarantees and other commitments to third parties:

Standby letters of credit
Franchise Trust, a legal entity sponsored by a third-party bank, originates loans to Dealers for their purchase of inventory and fixed assets. While Franchise Trust is consolidated as part of these financial statements, the Company has arranged for several major Canadian banks to provide standby LCs to Franchise Trust to support the credit quality of the Dealer loan portfolio. The banks may also draw against the LCs to cover any shortfalls in certain related fees owing to it. In any case where a draw is made against the LCs, the Company has agreed to reimburse the banks issuing the standby LCs for the amount so drawn. The Company has not recorded any liability for these amounts due to the credit quality of the Dealer Loans and to the nature of the underlying collateral represented by the inventory and fixed assets of the borrowing Dealers. In the unlikely event that all the LCs had been fully drawn simultaneously, the maximum payment by the Company under this reimbursement obligation would have been $144.6 million at January 3, 2015 (2013—$170.4 million).

Lease agreements
The Company has entered into agreements with certain of its lessors that guarantee the lease payments of certain sublessees of its facilities to lessors. Generally, these lease agreements relate to facilities the Company has vacated prior to the end of the term of its lease. These lease agreements require the Company to make lease payments throughout the lease term if the sublessee fails to make the scheduled payments. These lease agreements have expiration dates through March 2016. The Company has also guaranteed leases on certain franchise stores in the event the franchisees are unable to meet their remaining lease commitments. These lease agreements have expiration dates through March 2016. The maximum amount that the Company may be required to pay under these agreements was $6.4 million (2013—$9.4 million). In addition, the Company could be required to make payments for percentage rents, realty taxes and common area costs. No amount has been accrued in the consolidated financial statements with respect to these lease agreements.

Capital commitments
During the year ended January 3, 2015, the Company had capital commitments for the acquisition of property and equipment, investment property and intangible assets for an aggregate cost of approximately $164.6 million (2013—$17.1 million).

Source: Canadian Tire 2014 Annual Report, page 108.

must be recorded in the sales period. And since all warranty costs probably have not been incurred by the end of the sales period, they must be estimated. Businesses are likely able to make reasonable estimates of their warranty costs based on past experience.

The recognition of warranty expense and (estimated) warranty liability is normally recorded by an adjustment at the end of the accounting period. As warranty claims are paid to customers or related expenditures are made, the liability is reduced. Cornerstone 8.6 illustrates the accounting for warranties.

CORNERSTONE 8.6

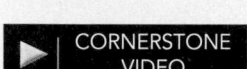

Recording Warranty Liabilities

Information:

Nolan Electronics offers a 12-month warranty on all its computers. Nolan estimates that one computer of each 2,000 sold will require warranty service and that the average warranty claim will cost Nolan $155.

Required:

1. Prepare the journal entry to recognize warranty expense and associated liability, assuming Nolan sells 3,000,000 computers during 2018, for which no warranty work has yet been performed.

2. Prepare the journal entry for warranty repairs, assuming that in January 2019, Nolan sends $10,400 cash and parts costing $8,300 to its dealers for warranty repairs.

Why:

Warranty liabilities are recorded in the same period that the related sale of goods or services occurs (the matching concept).

Solution:

1. $$(3,000,000 \text{ computers sold}) \times \left(\frac{1 \text{ failure}}{2,000 \text{ sold}}\right) \times \left(\frac{\$155}{1 \text{ failure}}\right) = \$232,500$$

	Shareholders' Equity	
Assets = Liabilities +	(Warranty Expense)	
+232,500	−232,500	

Date	Account and Explanation	Debit	Credit
Dec. 31, 2018	Warranty Expense	232,500	
	Warranty Liability		232,500
	(Record warranty expense for 2018)		

Source: Canadian Tire 2014 Annual Report, pages 108–109.

2.

		Shareholders'	
Assets	= Liabilities +	Equity	
−10,400	−18,700		
−8,300			

Date	Account and Explanation	Debit	Credit
Jan. 2019	Warranty Liability	18,700	
	Cash		10,400
	Inventory		8,300
	(Record payment for warranty repairs for Jan. 2019)		

Note: The statement of earnings effect of warranties (activity in the equity column) occurs when goods are sold. Payments or other asset outflows associated with the satisfaction of warranty claims do not normally affect the statement of earnings.

Actual warranty claims are unlikely to exactly equal the business's estimate. Any small overestimate or underestimate is usually combined with the next warranty estimate. However, large overestimates or underestimates must be recognized in the accounts and reported on the statement of earnings as other income or other expenses as soon as they become apparent.

concept Q&A

Why are warranties expensed at the point of sale when a company often does not incur warranty costs until later periods?

Answer:

Remember, the matching concept says that expenses will be recognized in the periods they helped generate revenues. The presence of the warranty "helped" sell the item. Additionally, warranties are contingencies—if the product fails, then the company will experience a loss. When loss contingencies are probable and a reasonable estimate can be made, a journal entry is made to record the expense and recognize a liability.

CALCULATING AND ANALYZING CURRENT LIABILITIES

Both investors and creditors are interested in a company's liquidity— that is, its ability to meet its short-term obligations. Failure to pay current liabilities can lead to suppliers refusing to sell to the company and employees leaving. Even companies with good business models can be forced into bankruptcy by their inability to pay current liabilities.

The following ratios are often used to analyze a company's ability to meet its current obligations:

$$\text{Current ratio} = \frac{\text{Current assets}}{\text{Current liabilities}}$$

$$\text{Quick ratio} = \frac{(\text{Cash} + \text{Marketable securities} + \text{Accounts receivable})}{\text{Current liabilities}}$$

$$\text{Cash ratio} = \frac{(\text{Cash} + \text{Marketable securities})}{\text{Current liabilities}}$$

$$\text{Operating cash flow ratio} = \frac{\text{Cash flows from operating activities}}{\text{Current liabilities}}$$

$$\text{Trades payable turnover ratio} = \frac{\text{Cost of goods sold}}{\text{Average net trade accounts payable}}$$

OBJECTIVE **5**

Calculate and analyze the current, quick, cash, and operating cash flow and trade payable ratios.

The first three ratios compare all or parts of current assets to current liabilities. The logic is that current liabilities need to be paid over approximately the same time frame that current assets are turned into cash. "Acceptable" current ratios vary from industry to industry, but the thought is that current assets must exceed current liabilities (which implies a current ratio > 1) to be able to meet current obligations. In fact, the general rule of thumb appears to be that a current ratio greater than two is often appropriate.

However, the second and third ratios recognize that some current assets are harder to liquidate. The quick and cash ratios exclude inventories because including inventories assumes that sales will be made. The quick ratio measures the ability of a company to pay its current liabilities without selling inventory. The quick ratio also assumes that accounts receivable are liquid. This is true when customers have low credit risk and pay in relatively short amounts of time. Of course, such an assumption is not true for all industries. Consequently, the use of the cash ratio may be more appropriate in these cases, as this ratio measures the ability of a company to pay its current liabilities without selling inventory or collecting accounts receivable.

Operating cash flow, by contrast, looks at the ability of cash generated from operating activities to meet current obligations. As with the current ratio, the operating cash flow ratio assumes that sales will continue into the future.

The trades payable ratio directly addresses the issue as to the number of times that trade creditors are paid in a year. Since most companies purchase their inventory on credit and carry a fairly constant inventory balance from year to year, the cost of goods sold figure is used in this calculation as the net purchase figure, which would be more accurate, is not usually disclosed in a company's financial statements. Cornerstone 8.7 illustrates the analysis of current liabilities.

CORNERSTONE 8.7

CORNERSTONE VIDEO

Calculating Liquidity Ratios

Information:

Consider the following information from Ontario Homes, a large builder of single-family homes, as of December 31, 2018 (in thousands):

Current liabilities	$473,498	Receivables	$ 77,725
Cash and equivalents	17,376	Inventories	3,472,285
Marketable securities	0	Cash flows from operating activities	(360,651)

Cost of goods sold	$1,802,764
Net trade payables, Jan. 1, 2018	323,465
Net trade payables, Dec. 31, 2018	321,384

Required:

Calculate the following: (1) current ratio, (2) quick ratio, (3) cash ratio, (4) operating cash flow ratio, and (5) trade payables ratio.

Why:

Calculation of liquidity ratios will help the user of a financial statement determine whether a company can meet its current financial obligations.

Solution:

1. current ratio: $\dfrac{(\$17{,}376 + 0 + \$77{,}725 + \$3{,}472{,}285)}{\$473{,}498} = 7.53$

2. quick ratio: $\dfrac{(\$17{,}376 + 0 + \$77{,}725)}{\$473{,}498} = 0.20$

3. cash ratio: $\dfrac{(\$17{,}376 + 0)}{\$473{,}498} = 0.04$

4. operating cash flow ratio: $\dfrac{-\$360{,}651}{\$473{,}498} = -0.76$

5. trade payables ratio: $\dfrac{\$1{,}802{,}764}{((\$323{,}265 + 321{,}384)/2)} = 5.59$

Note: Most of the information to calculate these ratios can be found on the statement of financial position (except for cash flows from operating activities, which is on the statement of cash flows).

In isolation, the current ratio in Cornerstone 8.7 appears very strong. For most industries, a current ratio greater than seven is rare. However, a vast majority of the current assets is inventory (unsold homes). In a strong real estate market, new homes can sell quite fast, but when a real estate slump hits, such homes can remain unsold for long periods of time. During a real estate market slump, home builders experience much slower sales. In these circumstances, home builders may resort to selling homes at a loss to generate needed cash.

The quick ratio and cash ratio in Cornerstone 8.7 show that Ontario Homes must sell homes to generate the necessary cash to meet its current obligations. The highly negative cash flows from operations were due to growing inventory in 2018. Although a growing inventory could be interpreted as expanding operations, it could also signal slowing sales. Finally, the trade payables ratio indicates that the company may be paying its creditors much more quickly than can be sustained and may run out of cash.

SIGNIFICANT DIFFERENCES BETWEEN IFRS AND ASPE

There are two main differences between IFRS and ASPE:

1. IFRS defines a contingent liability as being probable when it is more likely than not. ASPE defines a contingent liability as being probable when it is likely. Put another way, the ASPE test is more stringent than the IFRS test regarding the definition of what is probable and results in the recognition of fewer contingent liabilities compared to IFRS.

2. IFRS requires companies to record income tax expense by considering both components (i.e., current and deferred), as explained earlier in this chapter. Under ASPE, Canadian private enterprises are allowed to record income tax expense on the basis of income tax that is actually payable for the reporting period without reference to deferred income taxes.

APPENDIX: DEFERRED (FUTURE) INCOME TAXES: MEASUREMENT AND REPORTING

The calculation and reporting of deferred income taxes in accounting is one of the most complex topics, but we will study an introductory example to demonstrate the theory and mechanics. Deferred income tax accounting is studied further in advanced accounting courses.

We must first recognize that important differences exist between IFRS rules used to prepare general purpose financial statements for publicly accountable enterprises and the rules under the Canadian Income Tax Act, which is a statute of law. Specifically, certain amounts of income under IFRS are never included in income for tax purposes. Also, certain amounts of expense under IFRS are never allowed as deductions for income tax purposes. Such amounts of non-taxable income or non-deductible expense are referred to as *permanent differences*. An example of a permanent income difference is certain dividend income between two corporations, such as a dividend received by a Canadian parent company from its Canadian subsidiary corporation. An example of a permanent expense difference would be 50% of most meal and entertainment expenses. Permanent differences generally do not increase the complexity of deferred income tax accounting, although they must be identified for calculation purposes.

The complicating factor in deferred income tax accounting relates to what are called *timing differences*, whereby certain expenses are deducted for IFRS purposes in

OBJECTIVE **6**

(Appendix 8A) Explain the measurement and reporting for deferred income taxes.

accounting periods that differ from the accounting periods in which those same expenses are deducted for income tax purposes. The largest timing difference that occurs for most companies is that between depreciation for IFRS purposes and its tax equivalent, called *capital cost allowance* (CCA), for capital assets. For example, if a building costing $100,000 is acquired, then over the lifetime of the asset, the total amount of depreciation claimed on the building will be equal to the total CCA claimed on that asset. However, for any particular accounting period, the depreciation expense for IFRS purposes for that building will normally differ from the CCA on that same building asset. These "timing differences" create a difference between tax expense determined based on income reported under IFRS rules in the financial statements and the current income tax actually payable for a particular accounting period based on a separate and differing calculation of taxable income when the company's tax return is prepared.

Deferred income tax is the difference between tax expense calculated based on a company's IFRS income, after adjusting for permanent differences, and the income tax actually payable based on the company's taxable income as recorded in its corporate income tax return. Deferred income tax on the statement of financial position may result in a deferred tax asset (for example, when income is received and subject to tax when received, but not included in income for IFRS purposes until a later accounting period) or a deferred tax credit (for example, when CCA claimed for tax purposes exceeds the depreciation recorded for IFRS purposes).

As an example of deferred income tax accounting, assume Marmidan Inc., a Canadian corporation, purchased a piece of equipment costing $100,000 with no residual value and an economic useful life of five years. Depreciation is calculated on a straight-line basis over five years, while CCA is claimed on a declining balance basis in the amounts indicated below. The company's income tax rate is 40%.

(EXHIBIT 8.10)

		Year				
Income Reconciliation ($000s)		**2017**	**2018**	**2019**	**2020**	**2021**
Income for IFRS purposes	(a)	100	100	100	100	100
Add: Recorded depreciation	(b)	20	20	20	20	20
Deduct: CCA	(c)	−40	−40	−20	−0	−0
Taxable income	(d)	80	80	100	120	120
Statement of Earnings (Partial)						
Statement of earnings expense (recovery)						
Current	((d) × 40%)	32	32	40	48	48
Deferred		8	8	0	(8)	(8)
Total	((a) × 40%)	40	40	40	40	40
Statement of Financial Position (Partial)						
Current liabilities						
Current income taxes payable		32	32	40	48	48
Long-term liabilities						
Deferred income taxes payable		8	16	16	8	0

A few important points should be noted based on Exhibit 8.10:

1. Total income tax expense in the statement of earnings, where no permanent differences exist, is based on the reported IFRS income multiplied by the company's income tax rate.

2. The current income tax expense in the statement of earnings is based on the company's taxable income multiplied by the company's income tax rate.

3. The company's deferred income tax expense (recovery) in the statement of earnings is equal to the difference between the total income tax expense and the current income tax expense.

4. In 2020 and 2021 the accumulating deferred income tax payable balance of $16 at the end of 2019 "reverses" and is reduced as a deferred income tax recovery of $8 in each of 2020 and 2021, bringing the balance of deferred income tax payable to zero at the end of 2021.

Contrary to this simplified example, deferred income tax payable balances generally accumulate over time as companies replace their capital assets and may, as a result, never become actually payable to a taxing authority. This potential result has led to an argument in accounting theory for "present value" deferred income tax liabilities, but this argument has been rejected to date on the grounds of prudence and certain related but significant implementation issues.

In addition to deferred income tax accounting, substantial disclosure is required in financial statements for publicly accountable enterprises under IFRS with respect to their accounting policies for income taxes and to disclosures required concerning the calculation of income tax expense and the balance of deferred income taxes payable in the statement of financial position. Exhibit 8.11 contains examples of the required disclosure for the 2014 fiscal year (January 3, 2015) for Canadian Tire Corporation under IFRS.

(EXHIBIT 8.11)

Note 2: Accounting Policies—Income taxes

Income taxes

The income tax expense for the year comprises current and deferred income tax. Income tax expense is recognized in net income except to the extent that it relates to items recognized either in OCI or directly in equity. In this case, the income tax expense is recognized in OCI or in equity, respectively.

The income tax expense is calculated on the basis of the tax laws enacted or substantively enacted at the date of the consolidated balance sheets in the countries where the Company operates and generates taxable income.

Deferred income taxes is recognized using the liability method on unused tax losses, unused tax benefits and temporary differences arising between the tax bases of assets and liabilities and their carrying amounts in these consolidated financial statements. However, deferred income taxes is not accounted for if it arises from initial recognition of goodwill or initial recognition of an asset or liability in a transaction other than a business combination that at the time of the transaction affects neither accounting nor taxable income. Deferred income taxes is determined using tax rates (and laws) that have been enacted or substantively enacted at the date of the consolidated balance sheets and are expected to apply when the related deferred income tax asset is realized or the deferred income tax liability is settled.

Deferred income tax assets are recognized only to the extent that it is probable that future taxable income will be available against which the temporary differences can be utilized. Deferred income tax liabilities are provided on temporary differences arising on investments in subsidiaries and associates, except where the timing of the reversal of the temporary difference is controlled by the Company and it is probable that the temporary difference will not reverse in the foreseeable future.

18.2 Income tax expense

The following are the major components of the income tax expense:

(C$ in millions)	2014	2013
Current tax expense		
Current period	$248.5	$216.8
Adjustments in respect of prior years	7.2	(2.6)
	$255.7	$214.2
Deferred tax (benefit) expense		
Deferred income tax (benefit) expense relating to the origination and reversal of temporary differences	$ (7.9)	$ 6.0
Deferred income tax (benefit) adjustments in respect of prior years	(8.9)	–
	(16.8)	6.0
Total Income tax expense	$238.9	$220.2

Reconciliation of income tax expense

Income taxes in the consolidated statements of income vary from amounts that would be computed by applying the statutory income tax rate for the following reasons:

(C$ in millions)	2014	2013
Income before tax	$878.2	$784.6
Income taxes based on the applicable statutory tax rate of 26.50% (2013–26.49%)	$232.7	$207.8
Adjustment to income taxes resulting from:		
Non-deductibility of stock option expense	10.5	15.0
Prior years' tax settlements	(7.6)	–
Income attributable to non-controlling interest in flow-through entities	(6.6)	(0.9)
Adjustments of prior years' tax estimates	5.9	(2.6)
Non-deductibility of change in fair value of redeemable financial instrument	4.5	–
Lower income tax rates on earnings of foreign subsidiaries	(0.5)	(0.8)
Other	–	1.7
Income tax expense	$238.9	$220.2

The applicable statutory tax rate is the aggregate of the Canadian federal income tax rate of 15 per cent (2013—15 per cent) and Canadian provincial income tax rate of 11.50 per cent (2013—11.49 per cent).

In the ordinary course of business, the Company is subject to ongoing audits by tax authorities. While the Company has determined that its tax filing positions are appropriate and supportable, from time to time certain matters are reviewed and challenged by the tax authorities.

As a result of the Company's investment in and development of certain information technology Scientific Research and Experimental Development (SR&ED) projects, claims have been filed with the Canada Revenue Agency (CRA) for SR&ED tax credits relating to prior periods (which are currently under audit by the CRA).

No amounts were accrued during the year in the Company's financial statements with respect to the claim for SR&ED tax credits. The 2014 tax expense has been reduced by $7.6 million (2013—$nil) due to prior years' tax settlements and increased by $5.9 million (2013—decreased by $2.6 million) due to adjustments to prior years' tax estimates.

The Company regularly reviews the potential for adverse outcomes with respect to tax matters. The Company believes that the ultimate disposition of these will not have a material adverse effect on its liquidity, consolidated financial position or net income because the Company has determined that it has adequate provision for these tax matters. Should the ultimate tax liability materially differ from the provision, the Company's effective tax rate and its earnings could be affected positively or negatively in the period in which the matters are resolved.

Source: Canadian Tire 2014 Annual Report.

SUMMARY OF LEARNING OBJECTIVES

LO1. Explain, measure, and report current liabilities.

- Most liabilities are recognized in exchange for goods and services or the borrowing of money.
- In theory, the amount reported on the statement of financial position should not include interest that has not yet accrued.
- However, for nearly all current liabilities, unaccrued interest is deemed immaterial, so most current liabilities are simply recorded and reported at the total amount due.

LO2. Identify and record the types of activities that produce current liabilities.

- Current liabilities are obligations to outsiders that require the firm to pay cash or another current asset or provide goods or services within the longer of one year and one operating cycle.
- Such obligations are the result of many common transactions such as:
  - purchasing goods or services on credit (i.e., accounts payable)
  - the completed portion of activities that are in process at the end of the period such as wages, interest, or property taxes (i.e., accrued liabilities)
  - sales taxes collected from customers
  - payroll taxes such as CPP, EI, and income taxes withheld from employees and other payroll-related costs including worker safety board premiums
  - corporation income tax payable
  - notes payable
  - goods or services paid for in advance by customers (i.e., unearned or deferred revenues)
  - the portion of long-term debt due within the year

LO3. Explain, measure, and report contingent liabilities.

- A contingent liability is an obligation whose amount or timing depends on future events.
- A contingent liability is not recognized in the accounts unless the event on which it is contingent is probable (more likely than not to occur) and a reasonable estimate of the liability can be made.
- If occurrence of the contingent event is not probable or reliable measurement of the obligation is impossible, the potential obligation is not recorded as a liability, but must be disclosed in the footnotes.
- If occurrence of the contingent event is remote, the potential obligation is not recorded or disclosed.

LO4. Explain the nature, measurement, and reporting of provisions such as warranty liabilities.

- Provisions are future liabilities that are uncertain in timing or amount such as warranty liabilities.
- Since warranties help generate sales, the estimated future cost of servicing the warranty must be recorded in the sales period (this is an example of the matching concept).
- This is done by expensing the estimate of the future cost of servicing the warranty and creating a liability.
- As warranty claims are paid to customers or related expenditures are made, the estimated liability is reduced.

LO5. Calculate and analyze the current, quick, cash, and operating cash flow and trade payable ratios.

- Both investors and creditors are interested in a company's liquidity—that is, its ability to meet its short-term obligations.
- Failure to pay current liabilities can lead to suppliers refusing to sell needed inventory and employees leaving.
- As such, even companies with good business models can be forced into bankruptcy by their inability to pay current liabilities.

• Common ratios used to analyze a company's ability to meet its current obligations are:
  • current ratio
  • quick ratio
  • cash ratio
  • operating cash flow ratio
  • net trade payable ratio

LO6. *(Appendix 8A)* **Explain the measurement and reporting for deferred income taxes.**

CORNERSTONES		
CORNERSTONE 8.1	Recording notes payable and accrued interest, page 454	
CORNERSTONE 8.2	Recording liabilities at the point of sale, page 457	
CORNERSTONE 8.3	Recording payroll taxes, page 459	
CORNERSTONE 8.4	Recording property taxes, page 461	
CORNERSTONE 8.5	Recording unearned revenues, page 462	
CORNERSTONE 8.6	Recording warranty liabilities, page 466	
CORNERSTONE 8.7	Calculating liquidity ratios, page 468	

KEY TERMS

Account payable (p. 451)
Accrued liabilities (p. 452)
Commitments (p. 464)
Contingent liability (p. 449)
Current liabilities (p. 450)
Interest rate (p. 454)
Liabilities (p. 448)
Note payable (p. 453)

Payroll taxes (p. 458)
Provision (p. 465)
Sales taxes (p. 457)
Time value of money (p. 454)
Unearned revenue (p. 460)
Warranty (p. 465)
Withholding (p. 458)

REVIEW PROBLEM

I. Recording Current Liabilities and Calculating the Current Ratio

ABC Co. has the following balances in its accounts as of the beginning of the day on December 31 (this is not all of the accounts):

Account	Debit	Credit
Accounts payable		$ 100,000
Accounts receivable	$150,000	
Cash	75,000	
Interest payable		0
Inventory	270,000	
Long-term notes payable		1,000,000
Other current assets	60,000	
Other current liabilities		45,000
Sales tax payable		10,000
Short-term notes payable		0
Unearned revenues		30,000

The following information is *not* reflected in these balances:

a. On December 1, ABC bought some equipment for $200,000 with a short-term note payable bearing 12% interest. ABC has not made any journal entries related to this transaction.

b. On December 31, ABC accepted delivery of $30,000 of inventory. ABC has not yet paid its suppliers.

c. Customers prepaid $10,600 related to services ABC will perform next year. This price included 13% HST.

d. Gross salaries and wages in the amount of $20,000 are paid. Canada Pension Plan contributions of $1,200, Employment Insurance contributions of $600, and income taxes of $2,500 are withheld from employees.

Required:

1. Prepare the necessary journal entries for a–d.
2. Determine the current ratio before accounting for the additional information.
3. Determine the current ratio after accounting for the additional information.
4. Explain why ABC's current ratio deteriorated so badly.

Solution:

1. The necessary journal entries for each part are as follows:

	Date	Account and Explanation	Debit	Credit
a.	Dec. 1	Equipment	200,000	
		Short-term Notes Payable		200,000
		(*Record issue of note for equipment purchase*)		
b.	Dec. 31	Inventory	30,000	
		Accounts Payable		30,000
		(*Record purchase of inventory*)		

ABC must also accrue interest on December 31.

	Date	Account and Explanation	Debit	Credit
	31	Interest Expense[a]	2,000	
		Interest Payable		2,000
		(*Record interest accrued on short-term note*)		
c.	31	Cash	11,300	
		Unearned Revenue		10,000
		HST Payable		1,300
		(*Record unearned revenue and sales tax*)		
d.	31	Wages Expense	20,000	
		Canada Pension Plan Payable (Employee)		1,200
		Employment Insurance Payable (Employee)		600
		Income Taxes Payable		2,500
		Cash		15,700
		(*Record wages expense and related liabilities*)		
	Dec. 31	Canada Pension Plan Expense	1,200	
		Employment Insurance Expense	840	
		Canada Pension Plan Payable (Employer)		1,200
		Employment Insurance Payable (Employer)		840
		(*Record employer payroll taxes*)		

a.

Assets	=	Liabilities	+	Shareholders' Equity
+200,000		+200,000		

b.

Assets	=	Liabilities	+	Shareholders' Equity
+30,000		+30,000		

Assets	=	Liabilities	+	Shareholders' Equity (Interest Expense)
		+2,000		−2,000

c.

Assets	=	Liabilities	+	Shareholders' Equity
+11,300		+11,300		

d.

Assets	=	Liabilities	+	Shareholders' Equity (Wages Expense)
−15,700		+1,200		−20,000
		+600		
		+2,500		

Assets	=	Liabilities	+	Shareholders' Equity
		+1,200		−1,200
		+840		−840

[a] $200,000 \times 12\% \times 1/12$

2. Before accounting for the additional information:

Current assets:	
Cash	$ 75,000
Accounts receivable	150,000
Inventory	270,000
Other current assets	60,000
Total current assets	$555,000

Current liabilities:	
Accounts payable	$100,000
Interest payable	—
Sales tax payable	10,000
Short-term notes payable	—
Unearned revenues	30,000
Other current liabilities	45,000
Total current liabilities	$185,000

Current ratio = $555,000/$185,000 = 3.0

3. After accounting for the additional information:

		Debit	Credit	
Current assets:				
Cash	$ 75,000	$11,300 (c)	$ 15,700 (d)	$ 70,600
Accounts receivable	150,000			150,000
Inventory	270,000	30,000 (a)		300,000
Other current assets	60,000			60,000
Total current assets				$580,600
Current liabilities:				
Accounts payable	100,000		30,000 (a)	$130,000
Interest payable	0		2,000 (b)	2,000
Sales tax payable	10,000		1,300 (c)	11,300
Short-term notes payable	0		200,000 (b)	200,000
Unearned revenues	30,000		10,000 (c)	40,000
Other current liabilities	45,000		6,340 (d)*	51,340
Total current liabilities				$434,640

*$1,200 + $600 + $2,500 + $1,200 + $840 = $6,340

Current ratio = $580,600/$434,640 = 1.34

4. The primary cause of the deterioration of ABC's current ratio is the addition of the short-term note payable related to the equipment. This transaction almost doubled the current liabilities, but current assets were unaffected by the addition of equipment. Another way to think about this is that ABC financed long-term operational assets with short-term financing, which business should not generally do.

DISCUSSION QUESTIONS

1. What are liabilities?
2. How is the amount of a liability measured?
3. When are most liabilities recognized?
4. What are current liabilities? Provide some common examples.
5. Describe two ways in which current liabilities are frequently ordered on the statement of financial position.

6. What is the difference between an account payable and a note payable?

7. What sort of transaction typically creates an account payable?

8. What do we mean by accrued liabilities? Provide some common examples.

9. What type of transaction typically creates a note payable?

10. Why is interest ignored when valuing accounts payable?

11. How is interest computed on an interest-bearing short-term note?

12. When would debt that must be repaid within the next year be classified as long-term instead of current?

13. Provide examples of payroll taxes that are paid by the employee through reduction of their gross pay. Provide some examples of payroll taxes that are paid by the employer.

14. Why do unearned revenues and customers' deposits qualify as liabilities?

15. What are contingent liabilities? Provide an example.

16. When is a contingency recognized as a liability?

17. What is a provision? Why is the liability for warranties recognized when products are sold rather than when the warranty services are performed?

18. Describe the circumstances under which the current, quick, and cash ratios, respectively, are more appropriate measures of short-term liquidity than the other ratios.

19. Describe the differences between the current, quick, cash, and trade payables ratios. Which ratio is the most conservative measure of short-term liquidity? Why?

20. How does the rationale for the operating cash flow ratio differ from the rationale for the current, quick, cash, and trade payables ratios?

MULTIPLE-CHOICE EXERCISES

8-1 Liabilities are recognized:
  a. in exchange for goods
  b. in exchange for services
  c. in exchange for borrowing money
  d. all of these

8-2 When reporting liabilities on a statement of financial position, in theory, what measurement should be used?
  a. Future value of the future outflow
  b. Future value of the present outflow
  c. Present value of the future outflow
  d. Present value of the present outflow

8-3 Kinsella Seed borrowed $200,000 on October 1, 2018, at 10% interest. The interest and principal are due on October 1, 2019. What journal entry should be recorded on December 31, 2018?
  a. Debit Interest Expense 5,000; credit Interest Payable 5,000.
  b. Debit Interest Receivable 20,000; credit Interest Expense 20,000.
  c. Debit Interest Payable 5,000; credit Interest Expense 5,000.
  d. No entry is necessary.

8-4 Refer to the information in Exercise 8-3. What journal entry should be made with respect to the interest payment on October 1, 2019?
  a. Debit Cash 20,000; credit Interest Expense 15,000; credit Interest Payable 5,000.
  b. Debit Interest Expense 15,000; credit Cash 15,000.
  c. Debit Interest Expense 20,000; credit Cash 20,000.
  d. Debit Interest Expense 15,000; debit Interest Payable 5,000; credit Cash 20,000.

8-5 Which of the following is not a current liability?
  a. Sales tax payable
  b. Bonds payable due in five years
  c. Accounts payable
  d. Unearned revenue

8-6 Which of the following is not an example of an accrued liability?
  a. Wages payable
  b. Interest payable

(Continued)

c. Accounts payable
d. Property taxes payable

8-7 Labrador Inc. sold 350 oil drums to Tesla Manufacturing for $75 each. In addition to the $75 sale price per drum, there is a $1 per drum federal tax and a 7% provincial sales tax. What journal entry should be made to record this sale?
  a. Debit Accounts Receivable 28,438; credit Sales Revenue 28,438.
  b. Debit Accounts Receivable 26,250; credit Sales Revenue 26,250.
  c. Debit Accounts Receivable 28,438; credit Federal Sales Taxes Payable 350; credit Provincial Sales Taxes Payable 1,838; credit Sales Revenue 26,250.
  d. Debit Accounts Receivable 26,250; debit Taxes Expense 2,188; credit Federal Sales Taxes Payable 350; credit Provincial Sales Taxes Payable 1,838; credit Sales Revenue 26,250.

8-8 All of the following represent taxes commonly collected by businesses except:
  a. Employment Insurance taxes
  b. Federal sales taxes
  c. Provincial sales taxes
  d. Harmonized sales taxes

8-9 Payroll taxes typically include all of the following except:
  a. Health care plan deductions
  b. Employment Insurance contributions
  c. Canada Pension Plan contributions
  d. Federal excise taxes

8-10 When a credit is made to the income taxes payable account related to taxes withheld from an employee, the corresponding debit is made to:
  a. Cash
  b. Taxes Expense
  c. Taxes Payable
  d. Wages Expense

8-11 When should a contingent liability be recognized?
  a. When the contingent liability is probable
  b. When a reasonable estimation can be made
  c. Neither A nor B
  d. A and B

8-12 Which of the following is true?
  a. A contingent liability should always be disclosed in the financial statements.

b. A contingent liability should always be recorded within the financial statements.
  c. A company can choose to record a contingent liability either within its financial statements or disclose the liability in the financial statements.
  d. No journal entries or disclosure is necessary if the possibility of a contingent liability is remote.

8-13 Arcand Advisers is being sued by a former customer. Arcand's lawyers say that it is possible, but not probable, that the company will lose the lawsuit and that the trial should last approximately 18 more months. Should Arcand lose, they will most likely have to pay approximately $750,000. How should this lawsuit be reported on the financial statements?
  a. Current liability of $750,000 and expense of $750,000
  b. Long-term liability of $750,000 and expense of $750,000
  c. No effect on the statement of financial position or statement of earnings, but disclosed in the notes to the financial statements
  d. No disclosure is required

8-14 Warranty expense is:
  a. recorded as it is incurred
  b. capitalized as a warranty asset
  c. recorded in the period of sale
  d. none of these

8-15 To record warranties, the adjusting journal entry would be:
  a. a debit to Warranty Liability and a credit to Cash
  b. a debit to Warranty Expense and a credit to Warranty Liability
  c. a debit to Warranty Expense and a debit to Cash
  d. a debit to Warranty Liability and a credit to Warranty Expense

8-16 How is the current ratio calculated?
  a. Cash flows from operating activities/ Current liabilities
  b. Current assets/Current liabilities
  c. (Cash + Marketable securities)/Current liabilities
  d. (Cash + Marketable securities + Accounts receivable)/Current liabilities

8-17 How is the cash ratio calculated?
   a. (Cash + Marketable securities)/ Current liabilities
   b. Current assets/Current liabilities
   c. Cash flows from operating activities/ Current liabilities
   d. (Cash + Marketable securities + Accounts receivable)/Current liabilities

8-18 Which of the following transactions would cause the current ratio to increase (assuming the current ratio is currently greater than 1)?
   a. Receiving money from a customer related to an account receivable
   b. Paying off a payable for cash
   c. Purchasing inventory on credit
   d. Purchasing property, plant, and equipment

CORNERSTONE EXERCISES

Cornerstone Exercise 8-19 Issuing Notes Payable

On June 30, Carmean Corp. borrows $250,000 from CIBC with an 8-month, 7% note.

OBJECTIVE 2
CORNERSTONE 8.1

Required:

What journal entry is made on June 30?

Cornerstone Exercise 8-20 Notes Payable

Raja Machinery Company borrowed $400,000 on June 1, with a three-month, 7%, interest-bearing note.

OBJECTIVE 2
CORNERSTONE 8.1

Required:

1. Record the borrowing transaction.
2. Record the repayment transaction.

Cornerstone Exercise 8-21 Accrued Interest

On August 1, Wilshire Company borrowed $150,000 from National Bank on a one-year, 8% note.

OBJECTIVE 2
CORNERSTONE 8.1

Required:

What adjusting entry should Wilshire make at December 31?

Cornerstone Exercise 8-22 Accrued Interest

On March 1, Gamal Corporation borrowed $75,000 from TD Bank on a one-year, 5% note.

OBJECTIVE 2
CORNERSTONE 8.1

Required:

If the company keeps its records on a calendar year, what adjusting entry should Gamal make on December 31?

Cornerstone Exercise 8-23 Accrued Wages

Skiles Company's weekly payroll amounts to $10,000 and payday is every Friday. Employees work five days per week, Monday through Friday. The appropriate journal entry was recorded at the end of the accounting period, Wednesday, March 31, 2018.

OBJECTIVE 2
CORNERSTONE 8.2

Required:

What journal entry is made on Friday, April 2, 2018?

Cornerstone Exercise 8-24 Sales Tax

Trudeau's Antique Hot Rods recently sold a 1957 Chevy for $75,000 on account. The provincial sales tax is 6%, and there is a $500-per-car federal tax.

OBJECTIVE 2
CORNERSTONE 8.2

(Continued)

Required:

Prepare the journal entry to record the sale.

OBJECTIVE **2**
CORNERSTONE 8.2

Cornerstone Exercise 8-25   Sales Tax

Cobb Baseball Bats sold 60 bats for $70 each, plus an additional harmonized sales tax of 13%. The customer paid cash.

Required:

Prepare the journal entry to record the sale.

OBJECTIVE **2**
CORNERSTONE 8.3

Cornerstone Exercise 8-26   Payroll Taxes

Hernandez Builders has a gross payroll for January amounting to $500,000. The following amounts have been withheld:

Income taxes	$63,000
Canada Pension Plan contributions	31,000
Employment Insurance contributions	5,000
Pension plan contributions	7,250
Charitable contributions	1% of gross pay
Union dues	2% of gross pay

Required:

1. What is the amount of net pay recorded by Hernandez?
2. Prepare the journal entries to record the payroll (employer pays additional 100% of employees' CPP and 140% of employees' EI).

OBJECTIVE **2**
CORNERSTONE 8.3

Cornerstone Exercise 8-27   Payroll Taxes

Kinsella Inc. has a gross payroll of $10,000 for the pay period. Kinsella must also withhold $1,200 in income taxes from the employees, Employment Insurance premiums of $30, and CPP premiums of $100.

Required:

Prepare the necessary journal entries for Kinsella to record both the gross pay earned by employees and the employer portion of these payroll taxes. The employer pays 1.4 times the employee EI premium and additional 100% of the employees' CPP.

OBJECTIVE **2**
CORNERSTONE 8.3

Cornerstone Exercise 8-28   Payroll Taxes

During October, Seger Insurance employees earned $100,000 in wages. The employer's share of Canada Pension Plan contributions was $3,000 and employer Employment Insurance premiums were $1,400.

Required:

Prepare the necessary journal entry for Seger to record the employer portion of these payroll taxes.

OBJECTIVE **2**
CORNERSTONE 8.4

Cornerstone Exercise 8-29   Property Taxes

Lassoo Engineering Inc. has a December 31 year-end. The company incurred property taxes of $10,000 for 2018. At year-end the company paid $7,500 to the municipal government for 2018 property taxes.

Required:

Prepare the journal entries at December 31 to record property tax expense for 2018 and the payment of 2018 property taxes.

Cornerstone Exercise 8-30   Property Taxes

OBJECTIVE ❷
CORNERSTONE 8.4

Kellman Jerkirer Inc. has a December 31 year-end. The local municipality billed the entire 2018 property taxes of $20,000 on April 1, 2018. Kellman paid $4,000 of the 2018 property taxes on May 31, 2018.

Required:

Calculate the balance of the property tax payable or prepaid property tax account as at May 31, 2018.

Cornerstone Exercise 8-31   Unearned Sales Revenue

OBJECTIVE ❷
CORNERSTONE 8.5

Brodsky Landscaping offers a promotion where they will mow your lawn 20 times if you pay $700 in advance.

Required:

Prepare the journal entry of Brodsky to record (1) your prepayment of $700 and (2) Brodsky's mowing of the lawn one time.

Cornerstone Exercise 8-32   Unearned Rent Revenue

OBJECTIVE ❷
CORNERSTONE 8.5

EWO Property Management leases commercial properties. A new client signs a five-year lease and agrees to pay the first six months in advance. The monthly rent is $50,000.

Required:

Prepare the journal entry to record (1) the customers' prepayment of six months' rent and (2) the necessary adjusting entry after one month has passed.

Cornerstone Exercise 8-33   Warranties

OBJECTIVE ❹
CORNERSTONE 8.6

In 2018, BMJ Plumbing Company sold 300 water heaters for $850 each. The water heaters carry a two-year warranty for repairs. BMJ Plumbing estimates that repair costs will average 1% of the total selling price.

Required:

1. How much is recorded in the warranty liability account as a result of selling the water heaters during 2018, assuming no warranty service has yet been performed?
2. Prepare the necessary adjusting entry at December 31, 2018.

Cornerstone Exercise 8-34   Warranties

OBJECTIVE ❹
CORNERSTONE 8.6

In 2018, Wang Balloons sold 50 hot air balloons at $25,000 each. The balloons carry a five-year warranty for defects. Wang estimates that repair costs will average 3% of the total selling price. The estimated warranty liability at the beginning of the year was $40,000. Claims of $15,000 were actually incurred during the year to honour warranties.

Required:

What was the balance in the warranty liability at the end of 2018?

Cornerstone Exercise 8-35   Liquidity Ratios

OBJECTIVE ❺
CORNERSTONE 8.7

GWA's financial statements contain the following information:

Cash	$300,000	Accounts payable	$ 500,000
Accounts receivable	650,000	Accrued expenses	150,000
Inventory	800,000	Long-term debt	1,000,000
Marketable securities	100,000	Cost of goods sold	2,000,000

(Continued)

Assume the accounts payable balance is all trade payables and opening and closing balances are the same. *Note:* Round answers to two decimal places.

Required:

1. What is the current ratio?
2. What is the quick ratio?
3. What is the cash ratio?
4. What is the trade payable ratio?
5. Discuss GWA's liquidity using these ratios.

OBJECTIVE 5
CORNERSTONE 8.7

Cornerstone Exercise 8-36   Liquidity Ratios

DER's financial statements contain the following information:

Cash	$3,125,000	Accounts payable	$ 3,500,000
Accounts receivable	3,150,000	Accrued expenses	1,800,000
Inventory	4,200,000	Long-term debt	10,000,000
Marketable securities	1,850,000	Cost of goods sold	5,000,000

Assume the accounts payable balance is all trade payables and opening and closing balances are the same. *Note:* Round answers to two decimal places.

Required:

1. What is the current ratio?
2. What is the quick ratio?
3. What is the cash ratio?
4. What is the trades payable ratio?
5. Discuss DER's liquidity using these ratios.

BRIEF EXERCISES

OBJECTIVE 2

Brief Exercise 8-37   Accounts Payable

On May 18, Stanton Electronics purchased, on credit, 1,000 TV sets for $400 each. Stanton plans to resell these TVs in its store. Stanton paid the supplier on June 30.

Required:

Prepare the necessary journal entry (or entries) on May 18 and June 30.

OBJECTIVE 2

Brief Exercise 8-38   Accounts and Notes Payable

On February 15, Barbour Industries buys $800,000 of inventory on credit. On March 31, Barbour approaches its supplier because it cannot pay the $800,000. The supplier agrees to roll the amount into a note due on September 30 with 10% interest.

Required:

Prepare the necessary journal entries from February 15 through payment on September 30.

OBJECTIVE 2

Brief Exercise 8-39   Issuing Notes Payable

On September 30, Bello International borrows $320,000 from Chase Bank with a 9-month, 8% note.

Required:

What journal entry is made at Bello's year-end, December 31?

Brief Exercise 8-40   Notes Payable   OBJECTIVE ❷

Renchen Company, which manufactures steel tubing and casing for automobile production, borrowed $500,000 on January 1 to finance the purchase of a new piece of machinery with new heating technology. The terms of Renchen's note dictate that it is a four-month, 9%, interest-bearing note.

Required:

1. Record the borrowing transaction.
2. Record the repayment transaction.

Brief Exercise 8-41   Accrued Interest   OBJECTIVE ❷

On July 1, Brimley Company issued a note with First National Bank with terms of two years and 10% interest to finance its inventory purchase of 1,000 plasma televisions with a list price of $2,750 each.

Required:

What adjusting entry should Brimley make at December 31?

Brief Exercise 8-42   Accrued Interest   OBJECTIVE ❷

On May 1, the Garnett Corporation wanted to purchase a $200,000 piece of equipment, but Garnett was only able to furnish $75,000 of its own cash to purchase the equipment. Garnett borrowed the remainder of the $200,000 from the People's National Bank on a three-year, 4% note.

Required:

If the company keeps its records on a calendar year, what adjusting entry should Garnett make on December 31?

Brief Exercise 8-43   Accrued Property Taxes   OBJECTIVE ❷

Annual property taxes covering the preceding 12 months are always paid on July 1. Lou Inc. is always assessed $11,000 property taxes.

Required:

Given this information, determine the adjusting journal entry that Lou must make on December 31.

Brief Exercise 8-44   Accrued Income Taxes   OBJECTIVE ❷

Nolan Inc. had taxable income of $400,000 in 2017. Its effective tax rate is 35%. Nolan pays its 2017 income taxes on April 30, 2018.

Required:

1. Given this information, determine the adjusting journal entry that Nolan must make on December 31, 2017.
2. Prepare the journal entry to record the tax payment.

Brief Exercise 8-45   Accrued Wages   OBJECTIVE ❷

Natalie's Bakery pays its 20 hourly employees every Friday. Each of Natalie's employees earns a wage of $10 per hour and works 35 hours per week, spread evenly from Monday through Sunday. During the current year December 31 falls on a Tuesday.

Required:

Given this information, determine the adjusting journal entry that Natalie's Bakery must make on December 31.

OBJECTIVE **2**   **Brief Exercise 8-46   Accrued Wages**

A company employs a part-time staff of 50 employees, each earning $10 per hour and working 30 hours per week. Employees work five days per week, Monday through Friday, and are paid weekly on Fridays. The appropriate journal entry was recorded at the end of the accounting period, Tuesday, April 30, 2017.

Required:

What journal entries are made on Tuesday, April 30, and Friday, May 3, 2017?

OBJECTIVE **2**   **Brief Exercise 8-47   Accrued Wages**

Employees earn $2,500 per day, work five days per week, Monday through Friday, and get paid every Friday. The previous payday was Friday, March 29, and the accounting period ends on Monday, March 31.

Required:

What is the ending balance in the wages payable account on March 31?

OBJECTIVE **2**   **Brief Exercise 8-48   Accrued Wages and Payment of Payroll**

Hansen Legal offices are open Monday through Friday, and Hansen pays employees salaries of $35,000 every other Friday. During the current year December 31 falls on a Wednesday, and the next payday is January 2.

Required:

Given this information, determine the adjusting journal entry that Hansen must make on December 31 as well as the journal entry to record the payment of the payroll on January 2.

OBJECTIVE **2**   **Brief Exercise 8-49   Sales and Excise Tax**

Betty's Antique Shop, a shop specializing in antiques from the 19th century, recently sold a chair from the Civil War era for $60,000 on account. The harmonized sales tax is 13%.

Required:

Provide the journal entry to record the sale.

OBJECTIVE **2**   **Brief Exercise 8-50   Sales Tax**

Farrah's Furniture sold 35 couches to Angel's Inc. for $850 each plus an additional harmonized sales tax of 13%. Angel's Inc. purchased on credit.

Required:

Provide the journal entry to record the sale (round to nearest penny).

OBJECTIVE **2**   **Brief Exercise 8-51   Unearned Sales Revenue**

Curtis's Carpet Cleaning normally charges $90 to clean one room of carpeting. During the holiday season, Curtis offers a promotion to clean the customer's carpet 10 times at a discounted rate if the customer pays $600 in advance.

Required:

Make the journal entry to record the following transactions.
1. A customer's prepayment of $600
2. Curtis's cleaning of the carpet one time

Brief Exercise 8-52   Unearned Rent Revenue

OBJECTIVE 2

Mannion Property Management leases commercial properties and expects its clients to pay rent on a monthly basis. A new client signs a four-year lease with a yearly rent of $420,000 and agrees to pay the first six months in advance.

Required:

Make the journal entry to record the following transactions.
1.   The customer's prepayment of six months' rent
2.   The necessary adjusting entry after one month has passed

Brief Exercise 8-53   Contingent Liabilities

OBJECTIVE 3

Many companies provide warranties with their products. Such warranties typically guarantee the repair or replacement of defective goods for some specified period of time following the sale.

Required:

Why do most warranties require companies to make a journal entry to record a liability for future warranty costs?

Brief Exercise 8-54   Contingent Liabilities

OBJECTIVE 3

SLC Electronics is the plaintiff in a class-action lawsuit. Their attorney has written a letter that it is now extremely likely that SLC will lose the lawsuit and be forced to pay $3,000,000 in damages.

Required:

Prepare the necessary journal entry. If no entry is required state "none." Any recognition will be to Other Expense and Lawsuit Payable.

Brief Exercise 8-55   Warranties

OBJECTIVE 4

In 2018, Lee Electronics, a franchise of electronics stores located in small towns throughout Canada, sold 450 32-inch televisions for $575 each. The televisions carry an attached three-year warranty for repairs. Lee Electronics estimates that repair costs will average 2% of the total selling price.

Required:

1.   How much is recorded in the Warranty Liability account as a result of selling the televisions during 2018, assuming no warranty service has yet been performed?
2.   Provide the necessary adjusting entry at December 31, 2018.

Brief Exercise 8-56   Warranties

OBJECTIVE 4

Wally's Party Warehouse provides wholesale party equipment and materials to Party Shops. In 2018, Wally's Party sold 30 bounce houses at $30,000 each. The bounce houses carry a three-year warranty for defects. Wally estimates that repair costs will average 2% of the total selling price. The estimated warranty liability at the beginning of the year was $26,000. Claims of $19,000 were actually incurred during the year to honour warranties.

Required:

What was the balance in the Estimated Warranty Liability account at the end of the year?

Brief Exercise 8-57   Liquidity Ratios

OBJECTIVE 5

JRL's financial statements contain the following information:

Cash	$400,000	Accounts payable	$ 575,000
Accounts receivable	800,000	Accrued expenses	180,000
Inventory	950,000	Long-term debt	900,000
Marketable securities	115,000	Cost of goods sold	1,000,000

Assume the accounts payable balance is all trade payables and opening and closing balances are the same.

Required:

1. What is its current ratio?
2. What is its quick ratio?
3. What is its cash ratio?
4. What is the trade payable ratio?
5. Discuss JRL's liquidity using these ratios.

OBJECTIVE **5**   **Brief Exercise 8-58   Liquidity Ratios**

SJM's financial statements contain the following information:

Cash	$2,725,000	Accounts payable	$3,275,000
Accounts receivable	3,050,000	Accrued expenses	1,700,000
Inventory	3,950,000	Long-term debt	9,100,000
Marketable securities	1,725,000	Cost of goods sold	4,250,000

Assume the accounts payable balance is all trade payables and opening and closing balances are the same.

Required:

1. What is the current ratio?
2. What is the quick ratio?
3. What is the cash ratio?
4. What is the trade payable ratio?
5. Discuss SJM's liquidity using these ratios.

EXERCISES

OBJECTIVE **2**   **Exercise 8-59   Accrued Wages**

Rising Stars Hockey pays its hourly employees every Saturday. The weekly payroll for hourly employees is $5,000 and the employees' hours are spread evenly from Monday through Saturday. During the current year December 31 falls on a Wednesday.

Required:

Given this information, determine the adjusting journal entry that Rising Stars must make on December 31.

OBJECTIVE **2**   **Exercise 8-60   Recording Various Liabilities**

Glenview Hardware had the following transactions that produced liabilities during 2018:

a. Purchased merchandise on credit for $30,000 (*Note:* Assume a periodic inventory system).
b. Year-end wages of $10,000 incurred, but not paid. Related income taxes of $1,200, Canada Pension Plan of $620 (employee portion), and Employment Insurance premiums (employee portion) of $145 are withheld.
c. Year-end estimated corporation income tax payable, but unpaid, for the year in the amount of $42,850.
d. Sold merchandise on account for $1,262, including provincial sales taxes of $48. (*Note:* Assume a periodic inventory system.)
e. Employer's share of Canada Pension and Employment Insurance premiums for the period were $620 and $203, respectively.
f. Borrowed cash under a 90-day, 9%, $25,000 note.

Required:

Prepare the entries to record these transactions (treat each transaction independently).

Exercise 8-61 Recording Various Liabilities

OBJECTIVE

Yarmouth Electronics had the following transactions that produced liabilities during 2018:

a. Purchased merchandise on credit for $80,000. (*Note:* Assume a periodic inventory system.)
b. Year-end wages of $40,000 incurred, but not paid. Related income taxes of $13,000 and Canada Pension Plan premiums of $580 were withheld.
c. Year-end estimated corporation income tax payable, but unpaid, for the year in the amount of $113,615.
d. Sold merchandise on account for $3,636, including provincial sales taxes of $180. (*Note:* Assume a periodic inventory system.)
e. Employer's share of Canada Pension Plan premiums for the period was $580. The premiums will be paid at a later date.
f. Borrowed cash under a 180-day, 8%, $155,000 note.

Required:

Prepare the entries to record these transactions (treat each transaction independently).

Exercise 8-62 Reporting Liabilities

OBJECTIVE

Mumbai Electronics had the following obligations:

a. A legally enforceable claim against the business to be paid in three months.
b. A guarantee given by a seller to a purchaser to repair or replace defective goods during the first six months following a sale.
c. An amount payable to Royal Bank in 10 years.
d. An amount to be paid next year to National Bank on a long-term note payable.

Required:

CONCEPTUAL CONNECTION Describe how each of these items should be reported on the statement of financial position.

Exercise 8-63 Accounts Payable

OBJECTIVE

Hammerton Autos, a used-car dealer, has a December 31 year-end. For Hammerton, the following transactions occurred during the first 10 days of August:

a. Hammerton purchased, on credit, space for classified advertisements in *The Globe and Mail* for $2,680. The advertising was run the day the space was purchased.
b. Hammerton purchased office supplies from Office Depot on credit in the amount of $250.
c. One of Hammerton's sales staff sold a car. The salesperson's commission is $1,100. The commission will be paid September 10. (*Note:* Concern yourself only with the commission.)
d. The electric bill for July was received. The bill is $6,500 and is due August 15.
e. A $420 bill from Caro Alignment services was received. Caro had repaired 10 cars for Hammerton in late July. The payment is due August 20.

Required:

Prepare journal entries for the above transactions.

OBJECTIVE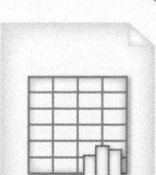

Exercise 8-64 Accrued Liabilities

Charger Inc. had the following items that require adjusting entries at the end of the year.

a. Charger pays its employees $5,000 every Friday for a five-day work week. This year December 31 falls on a Wednesday.

(Continued)

b. Charger earned income of $800,000 for the year for tax purposes. Its effective tax rate is 35%. These taxes must be paid by February 28 of next year.

c. Charger borrowed $280,000 with a note payable dated August 1. This note specifies 6%. The interest and principal are due on March 31 of the following year.

d. Charger's president earns a bonus equal to 10% of income in excess of $650,000. Income for the year was $800,000. This bonus is paid in May of the following year and any expense is charged to wages expense. (Assume the bonus paid is based on his/her pre-tax income.)

Required:

Prepare the adjusting journal entries to record these transactions at the end of the current year.

OBJECTIVE **2**   ### Exercise 8-65   Accrued Liabilities

Thornwood Tile had the following items that require adjusting entries at the end of the year.

a. Thornwood pays payroll of $180,000 every other Friday for a two-week period. This year the last payday is Friday, December 26. (*Note:* The work week is Monday through Friday.)

b. Thornwood purchased $350,000 of tile on June 1 with a note payable requiring 12% interest. The interest and principal on this note are due within one year. As of December 31, Thornwood had not made any principal or interest payments.

c. Thornwood's earned income is $900,000 for the year for tax purposes. Its effective tax rate is 30%. These taxes must be paid by February 28 of next year.

Required:

Prepare the adjusting journal entries to record these transactions at the end of the current year.

OBJECTIVE **2**   ### Exercise 8-66   Sales Tax

Weinstein Cellular provides wireless phone service. During April 2018, it billed a customer a total of $135,000 before taxes. Weinstein also must pay the harmonized sales tax of 13% on these charges.

Required:

Assuming Weinstein collects this tax from the customer, what journal entry would Weinstein make when the customer pays the bill? Assume that the customer paid their bill on the same day they received the bill from Weinstein Cellular.

OBJECTIVE **2**   ### Exercise 8-67   Payroll Accounting and Discussion of Labour Costs

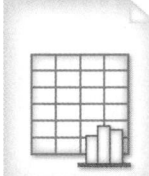

Bas Marketing Research paid its weekly and monthly payroll on January 31. The following information is available about the payroll:

Item	Amount
Monthly salaries	$237,480
Hourly wages	585,000
Canada Pension Plan (employer)	100% of employee contributions
Employment Insurance (employer)	140% of employee contributions
Withholding for income taxes	$108,500
CPP (employee)	24,800
Employment Insurance premiums (employee)	15,800

Bas will pay both the employer's taxes and the taxes withheld on February 15.

Required:

1. Prepare the journal entries to record the payroll payment and the incurrence of the associated expenses and liabilities. (*Note:* Round to nearest penny.)

2. What is the employees' gross pay? What amount does Bas pay in excess of gross pay as a result of taxes and benefits? (*Note:* Provide both an absolute dollar amount and as a percentage of gross pay, rounding to two decimal places.)
3. How much is the employees' net pay as a percentage of total payroll-related expenses? (*Note:* Round answer to two decimal places.)

Exercise 8-68 Unearned Revenue

 OBJECTIVE 2

Irvine Pest Control signed a $1,500-per-month contract on December 1, 2018, to provide pest control services to rental units owned by Garden Grove Properties. Irvine received six months' service fees in advance on signing the contract.

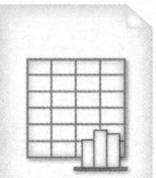

Required:

1. Prepare Irvine's journal entry to record the cash receipt for the first six months.
2. Prepare Irvine's adjusting entry at December 31, 2018.
3. **CONCEPTUAL CONNECTION** How would the advance payment be reported in Irvine Pest Control's December 31, 2018, statement of financial position? How would the advance payment be reported in Garden Grove Properties' December 31, 2018, statement of financial position?

Exercise 8-69 Recognition and Reporting of Contingent Liabilities

 OBJECTIVE 3

A list of alternative accounting treatments is followed by a list of potential contingent liabilities.

Alternative Accounting Treatments

a. Estimate the amount of liability and record.
b. Do not record as a liability but disclose in the notes to the financial statements.
c. Neither record as a liability nor disclose in the notes to the financial statements.

Potential Contingent Liabilities

1. Income taxes related to revenue included in net income this year but payable in a future year.
2. Potential costs in future periods associated with performing warranty services on products sold this period.
3. Estimated cost of future services under a product warranty related to past sales.
4. Estimated cost of future services under a product warranty related to future sales.
5. Estimated cost of pension benefits related to past employee services that has yet to be funded.
6. Potential loss on environmental cleanup suit against company; a court judgment against the company is considered less than probable but more than remotely likely.
7. Potential loss under class-action suit by a group of customers; during the current year, the likelihood of a judgment against the company has increased from remote to possible but less than probable.
8. Potential loss under an affirmative action suit by a former employee; the likelihood of a judgment against the company is considered to be remote.
9. Potential loss from a downturn in future economic activity.
10. Loss from out-of-court settlement of lawsuit that is likely to occur toward the end of next year.

Required:

Match the appropriate accounting treatment with each of the potential liabilities listed above. Your answer should list the numbers 1 through 10 and, opposite each number, the letter of the appropriate accounting treatment.

Exercise 8-70 Warranties

OBJECTIVE 4

Merleau Entertainment sells televisions and other sound and video equipment. Sales and expected warranty claims for the year are as follows:

(Continued)

Item	Unit Sales	Expected Warranty Claims for Warranty Period	Cost per Claim
Televisions	2,500	2 claims per 100 sold	$45
DVDs	360	5 claims per 100 sold	15
Speakers	700	1 claim per 100 sold	25

Required:

1. Prepare the entry to record warranty expense for Merleau Entertainment for the year.
2. **CONCEPTUAL CONNECTION** Why does Merleau have to record a liability for future warranty claims?

OBJECTIVE **5**

Exercise 8-71   Ratio Analysis

Intel Corporation provided the following information on its statement of financial position and statement of cash flows:

Current liabilities	$8,514,000,000	Inventories	$ 4,314,000,000
Cash and equivalents	6,598,000,000	Other current assets	2,146,000,000
Marketable securities	3,404,000,000	Cash flows from operating activities	10,620,000,000
Receivables	2,709,000,000		

Required:

1. Calculate the following: (a) current ratio, (b) quick ratio, (c) cash ratio, and (d) operating cash flow ratio. (*Note:* Round answers to two decimal places.)
2. **CONCEPTUAL CONNECTION** Interpret these results.
3. **CONCEPTUAL CONNECTION** Assume that Intel, as a requirement of one of its loans, must maintain a current ratio of at least 2.3. Given Intel's large amount of cash, how could it accomplish this on December 31 (be specific as to dollar amounts)?

OBJECTIVE **6**

Exercise 8-72   (*Appendix 8A*): Deferred (Future) Income Tax: Timing Differences

Required:

Identify and explain which of the following would be considered a timing difference for deferred income tax accounting purposes:

a. Product warranty liabilities
b. Litigation accruals
c. A regular office supply expense
d. Accounting bookkeeping fees
e. Royalties and rentals received in advance

OBJECTIVE **6**

Exercise 8-73   (*Appendix 8A*): Deferred (Future) Income Tax: Temporary Differences

	2018	2017
Pretax accounting income	$350,000	$250,000

The average income tax rate used for 2017 and 2018 is 40% and for the foreseeable future. Temporary differences of $50,000 and $25,000 were noted for 2017 and 2018, respectively. Permanent differences of $10,000 and $5,000 were noted for 2017 and 2018, respectively. Assume that the permanent differences are deductible for tax purposes from pretax accounting income.

Required:

For 2017 and 2018, calculate (a) the income taxes payable to Canada Revenue Agency and (b) the deferred income tax. Is the deferred income tax a liability or an asset? Explain. *Note:* temporary differences are not deductible for tax purposes in the current year.

Exercise 8-74   (*Appendix 8A*): Deferred (Future) Income Tax: Depreciation

OBJECTIVE ❻

	2018	2017
Pretax accounting income	$350,000	$250,000

Assume the company calculates depreciation using the straight-line method.

The company recently purchased one piece of equipment for the business at $50,000 on January 1, 2017. The equipment has a four-year estimated life and no residual value. The company calculated and recorded capital cost allowance for tax purposes for 2017 of $6,000 and for 2018 of $10,000. The average income tax rate is 30% for 2017 and 2018 and for the foreseeable future.

Required:

For 2017 and 2018, calculate (a) the income taxes payable to Canada Revenue Agency and (b) the deferred income tax. Is the deferred income tax a liability or an asset? Explain.

PROBLEM SET A

Problem 8-75A   Payable Transactions

OBJECTIVE ❷

Richmond Company engaged in the following transactions during 2018:

a. Purchased $16,000 of supplies from ABC Supplies on February 16. Amount due in full on March 31.

b. Paid for 25% of the purchased supplies (transaction *a*) on February 26.

c. On March 31 negotiated a payment extension with ABC for the remainder of the balance from the February 16 purchase by signing a one-year, 10% note.

d. Borrowed $300,000 on a 10-month, 8% interest-bearing note on April 30.

e. Purchased $78,000 of merchandise on June 4. Amount due in full on June 30.

f. Paid for the purchased merchandise (transaction *e*) on June 24.

g. Received from Haywood Inc. on August 19, a $22,000 deposit against a total selling price of $220,000 for services to be performed for Haywood.

h. On December 15, Richmond completed the services ordered by Haywood on August 19. Haywood's remaining balance of $198,000 is due on January 31.

Required:

1. Prepare journal entries for these transactions.
2. Prepare any adjusting entries necessary at December 31, 2018.

Problem 8-76A   Payroll Accounting

OBJECTIVE ❷

Stadium Manufacturing has the following data available for its September 30, 2018, payroll:

Wages earned	$315,000*
Income taxes withheld	79,900

*All subject to matching and withholding of 6.2% for CPP (funded 50% each by employer and employee) and 2.40% for EI (shared on basis of 58% employer and 42% employee).

Required:

1. Compute the amounts of taxes payable and the amount of wages that will be paid to employees. Then prepare the journal entries to record the wages earned and the payroll taxes. (*Note:* Round to the nearest penny.)
2. Stadium Manufacturing would like to hire a new employee at a salary of $50,000. Assuming the payroll taxes are as described above and fringe benefits (e.g., health insurance, retirement, etc.) are 30% of gross pay, what will be the total cost of this employee for Stadium?

Problem 8-77A   Note Payable and Accrued Interest

Farsi Company borrowed $600,000 on an 8%, interest-bearing note on October 1, 2018. Farsi ends its fiscal year on December 31. The note was paid with interest on May 1, 2019.

Required:

1. Prepare the entry for this note on October 1, 2018.
2. Prepare the adjusting entry for this note on December 31, 2018.
3. Indicate how the note and the accrued interest would appear on the statement of financial position at December 31, 2018.
4. Prepare the entry to record the repayment of the note on May 1, 2019.

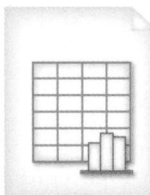

Problem 8-78A   Interest-Bearing Note Replacing an Unpaid Account Payable

Conti Products owed $80,000 on account for inventory purchased on December 1, 2018. Conti uses a perpetual inventory system and has a fiscal year that ends on December 31. Conti was unable to pay the amount owed by the March 1, 2019, due date because of financial difficulties. On March 1, 2019, Conti signed a four-month, $80,000, 6% interest-bearing note. This note was repaid with interest on July 1, 2019.

Required:

1. Prepare the entry recorded on December 1, 2018.
2. Prepare the adjusting entry recorded on December 31, 2018.
3. Prepare the entry recorded on March 1, 2019.
4. Prepare the entry recorded on July 1, 2019.

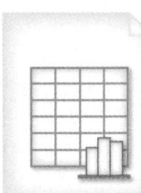

Problem 8-79A   Excise Taxes

Essex Power provides electricity to a wide area of western Ontario. During October 2018 it billed 20,000 of its residential customers located in the town of Heyworth a total of $2,435,000 for electricity (this is considered revenue). In addition, Essex is required to collect the following taxes:

a. Ontario Provincial Excise Tax: A tax of $3.00 per customer plus 2% of billing used to fund the Ontario Energy Commission
b. Federal Excise Tax: A tax of $0.50 per customer plus 0.1% of billing used to fund the Federal Energy Commission

Required:

1. Determine how much Essex will bill these customers in total for the month of October 2018.
2. Prepare the entry to record the billing of these amounts.
3. Prepare the entry to record the collection of these amounts.
4. Prepare the entry to record the payment of the federal and provincial excise taxes to the appropriate governmental unit.

Problem 8-80A   Unearned Revenue and Customer Deposits

On November 20, 2017, Manitoba Electronics agreed to manufacture and supply 750 electronic control units used by Wausau Heating Systems in large commercial and industrial installments. On that date, Wausau deposited $250 per unit upon signing the three-year purchase agreement, which set the selling price of each control unit at $1,000. Manitoba's inventory cost is $225 per unit. No units were delivered during 2017. The first 200 units will be delivered in 2018, 300 units will be delivered during 2019, and the remaining units will be delivered during 2020. Assume Manitoba uses a perpetual inventory system.

Required:

1. **CONCEPTUAL CONNECTION** Prepare the entry by Manitoba to record receipt of the deposit during 2017. How would the deposit be reported in the financial statements at the end of 2017?

2. **CONCEPTUAL CONNECTION** Prepare the entry by Manitoba to record the delivery of 200 units during 2018. How would the deposit be reported in the financial statements at the end of 2018? Wausau pays in cash upon delivery for the excess of the selling price over the applicable deposit.
3. Prepare the entry by Manitoba to record the delivery of 300 units during 2019.

Problem 8-81A   Warranties

OBJECTIVE 4

Mason Auto Repair specializes in the repair of foreign car transmissions. To encourage business, Mason offers a six-month warranty on all repairs. The following data are available for 2018:

Transmissions repaired, 2018	6,350
Expected frequency of warranty claims	0.03 per repair
Actual warranty claims, 2018	$63,000
Estimated warranty liability, 1/1/18	$50,000
Estimated cost of each warranty claim	$ 300

Assume that warranty claims are paid in cash.

Required:

1. Compute the warranty expense for 2018. (Round the number of warranty claims to the nearest whole claim).
2. Prepare the entry to record the payment of the 2018 warranty claims.
3. **CONCEPTUAL CONNECTION** What is the December 31, 2018, balance in the estimated warranty liability account? Why has the balance in the warranty liability account changed from January 1, 2018?
   Note: Round all answers to two decimal places.

OBJECTIVE 5

Problem 8-82A   Ratio Analysis

Consider the following information taken from DER's financial statements:

	September 30 (in thousands)	
	2018	**2017**
Current assets:		
Cash and cash equivalents	$ 1,274	$ 6,450
Receivables	30,071	16,548
Inventories	31,796	14,072
Other current assets	4,818	2,620
Total current assets	$67,959	$39,690
Current liabilities:		
Current portion of long-term debt	$ 97	$ 3,530
Accounts payable	23,124	11,228
Accrued compensation costs	5,606	1,929
Accrued expenses	9,108	5,054
Other current liabilities	874	777
Total current liabilities	$38,809	$22,518

Also, DER's operating cash flows were $12,829 and $14,874 in 2018 and 2017, respectively.
Note: Round all answers to two decimal places.

Required:

1. Calculate DER's current ratio for 2018 and 2017.
2. Calculate DER's quick ratio for 2018 and 2017.
3. Calculate DER's cash ratio for 2018 and 2017.

(Continued)

4. Calculate DER's operating cash flow ratio for 2018 and 2017.
5. Calculate DER's trade payable turnover ratio for 2018. Assume cost of good sold is $100,000.
6. **CONCEPTUAL CONNECTION** Provide some reasons why DER's liquidity may be considered to be improving and some reasons why it may be worsening.

PROBLEM SET B

OBJECTIVE **2**

Problem 8-83B   Payable Transactions

Daniels Company engaged in the following transactions during 2018:

a. Purchased $25,000 of supplies from XYZ Supplies on January 26. Amount due in full on February 28.
b. Paid for 40% of the purchased supplies (transaction *a*) on February 26.
c. On February 28 negotiated a payment extension with XYZ for the remainder of the balance from the January 26 purchase by signing a one-year, 8% note.
d. Borrowed $300,000 on an eight-month, 9% interest-bearing note on July 31.
e. Purchased $150,000 of merchandise on August 2. Amount due in full on September 30.
f. Paid for the purchased merchandise (transaction *e*) on September 28.
g. Received from Martel Inc. on October 4, a $40,000 deposit against a total selling price of $400,000 for services to be performed for Martel.
h. On December 15, Daniels completed the services ordered by Martel on October 4. Martel's remaining balance of $360,000 is due on January 31.

Required:

1. Prepare journal entries for these transactions.
2. Prepare any adjusting entries necessary at December 31, 2018.

OBJECTIVE **2**

Problem 8-84B   Payroll Accounting

Baghdad Manufacturing has the following data available for its March 31, 2018, payroll:

Wages earned	$1,250,000*
Income taxes withheld	180,600

*All subject to matching and withholding of 6.2% for CPP (funded 50% each by employer and employee) and 2.40% for EI (shared on basis of 58% employer and 42% employee).

Required:

1. Compute the taxes payable and wages that will be paid to employees. Then prepare the journal entries to record the wages earned and the payroll taxes. (*Note:* Round to the nearest penny.)
2. Baghdad Manufacturing would like to hire a new employee at a salary of $80,000. Assuming the payroll taxes are as described above and fringe benefits (e.g., health insurance, retirement, etc.) are 28% of gross pay, what will be the total cost of this employee for Baghdad?

OBJECTIVE **2**

Problem 8-85B   Note Payable and Accrued Interest

Bordewick Company borrowed $275,000 on a 6%, interest-bearing note on November 1, 2018. Bordewick ends its fiscal year on December 31. The note was paid with interest on May 31, 2019.

Required:

1. Prepare the entry for this note on November 1, 2018.
2. Prepare the adjusting entry for this note on December 31, 2018.

3. Indicate how the note and the accrued interest would appear on the statement of financial position at December 31, 2018.
4. Prepare the entry to record the repayment of the note on May 31, 2019.

Problem 8-86B   Interest-Bearing Note Replacing an Unpaid Account Payable

OBJECTIVE

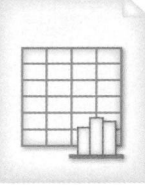

Monte Cristo Products, which uses a perpetual inventory system, owed $770,000 on account for inventory purchased on November 1, 2018. Monte Cristo's fiscal year ends on December 31. Monte Cristo was unable to pay the amount owed by the February 1 due date because of financial difficulties. On February 1, 2019, Monte Cristo signed a $770,000, 12% interest-bearing note. This note was repaid with interest on September 1, 2019.

Required:

1. Prepare the entry recorded on November 1, 2018.
2. Prepare the adjusting entry recorded on December 31, 2018.
3. Prepare the entry recorded on February 1, 2019.
4. Prepare the entry recorded on September 1, 2019.

Problem 8-87B   Excise Taxes

OBJECTIVE

Yossarian Power Corporation provides electricity to a wide area of eastern Alberta. During March 2018, it billed 3,000 of its residential customers located in the town of Maryville a total of $393,000 for electricity. In addition, Yossarian Power is required to collect the following taxes:

a. Alberta Excise Tax: A tax of $3.50 per customer plus 2% of billing used to fund the Alberta Energy Commission
b. Federal Excise Tax: A tax of $0.50 per customer plus 0.15% of billing used to fund the Federal Energy Commission

Required:

1. Determine how much Yossarian Power will bill these 3,000 customers in total for the month of March 2018.
2. Prepare the entry to record the billing of these amounts.
3. Prepare the entry to record the collection of these amounts.
4. Prepare the entry to record the payment of the federal and provincial excise tax to the appropriate government unit.

Problem 8-88B   Unearned Revenue and Customer Deposits

OBJECTIVE

On November 20, 2017, Billy Gramm Technology agreed to manufacture and supply 1,000 centrifuges used by Cathcart Systems to produce chemicals. Cathcart deposited $260 per unit upon signing the three-year purchase agreement, which set the selling price of each centrifuge at $1,300. Billy Gramm will record these units at $500 per unit in inventory. No units were delivered during 2017. During 2018, 350 units will be delivered, 400 units will be delivered during 2019, and the remaining units will be delivered during 2020. Assume Billy Gramm uses a perpetual inventory system.

Required:

1. **CONCEPTUAL CONNECTION** Prepare the entry by Billy Gramm to record receipt of the deposit during 2017. How would the deposit be reported in the financial statements at the end of 2017?
2. **CONCEPTUAL CONNECTION** Prepare the entry by Billy Gramm to record the delivery of 350 units during 2018. How would the deposit be reported in the financial statements at the end of 2018?
3. Prepare the entry by Billy Gramm to record the delivery of 400 units during 2019. Cathcart pays in cash upon delivery for the excess of the selling price over the applicable deposit.

OBJECTIVE

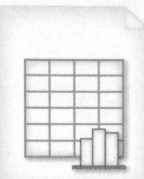

Problem 8-89B   Warranties

Montague Auto Repair specializes in the repair of foreign car transmissions. To encourage business, Montague offers a six-month warranty on all repairs. The following data are available for 2018:

Transmissions repaired, 2018	4,500
Expected frequency of warranty claims	0.09 per repair
Actual warranty claims, 2018	$110,000
Estimated warranty liability, 1/1/18	$ 25,000
Estimated cost of each warranty claim	$ 250

Assume that warranty claims are paid in cash.

Required:

1. Compute the warranty expense for 2018.
2. Prepare the entry to record the payment of the 2018 warranty claims.
3. **CONCEPTUAL CONNECTION** What is the December 31, 2018, balance in the warranty liability account? Why has the balance in the warranty liability account changed from January 1, 2018?
   Note: Round all answers to two decimal places.

OBJECTIVE

Problem 8-90B   Ratio Analysis

Consider the following information taken from Niagara Water Slide's (NWS's) financial statements:

	September 30 (in thousands)	
	2018	**2017**
Current assets:		
Cash and cash equivalents	$ 2,548	$12,900
Receivables	60,142	33,096
Inventories	63,592	28,144
Other current assets	9,636	5,240
Total current assets	$135,918	$79,380
Current liabilities:		
Current portion of long-term debt	$ 194	$ 7,060
Accounts payable	46,248	22,456
Accrued compensation costs	11,212	3,858
Accrued expenses	18,216	10,108
Other current liabilities	1,748	1,554
Total current liabilities	$77,618	$45,036

Also, NWS's operating cash flows were $25,658 and $29,748 in 2018 and 2017, respectively.
Note: Round all answers to two decimal places.

Required:

1. Calculate NWS's current ratio for 2018 and 2017.
2. Calculate NWS's quick ratio for 2018 and 2017.
3. Calculate NWS's cash ratio for 2018 and 2017.
4. Calculate NWS's operating cash flow ratio for 2018 and 2017.
5. Calculate NWS's trade payable turnover ratio for 2018. Assume cost of goods sold is $75,000.
6. **CONCEPTUAL CONNECTION** Provide some reasons why NWS's liquidity may be considered to be improving and some reasons why it may be worsening.

CASES

Case 8-91   Ethics and Current Liabilities

Many long-term loans have contractual restrictions designed to protect the lender from deterioration of the borrower's liquidity or solvency. These restrictions (typically called loan covenants) often take the form of financial-statement ratio values. For example, a lending agreement may state that the loan principal is immediately due and payable if the current ratio falls below 1.2. When borrowers are in danger of violating one or more of these loan covenants, pressure is put on management and the financial accountants to avoid such violations.

Jim is a second-year accountant at a large publicly traded corporation. His boss approaches him and says, "Jim, I know why we increased our warranty liability, but it puts our current ratio in violation of a loan covenant with our bank loan. I know the bank will pass on it this time, but it's a big hassle to get the waiver. I just don't want to deal with it. I need you to reduce our estimate of warranty liability as far as possible."

Required:

1. How would lowering the estimate of warranty liability affect the current ratio?
2. How should Jim respond to his boss?
3. Given that Jim's employer is a publicly traded corporation, what safeguards should be at Jim's disposal?

Case 8-92   Short-Term Borrowing with Restrictions

Rocky Mountain Products has a line-of-credit agreement with the Royal Bank that allows it to borrow up to $100,000 at any given time provided that Rocky Mountain's current assets always exceed its current liabilities by the principal amount of the outstanding loan. If this requirement is violated, the entire loan is payable immediately; thus Rocky Mountain is very careful to fulfill the requirement at all times. All loans under this line of credit are due in one month and bear interest at a rate of 1% per month. On January 1, 2018, Rocky Mountain has current assets of $150,000 and current liabilities of $92,000; hence, the excess of current assets over current liabilities is $58,000. Rocky Mountain's current liabilities at January 1, 2018, include a short-term loan under the line of credit of $35,000 due on February 1, 2018.

Required:

1. Prepare the journal entry to record the borrowing of $35,000 on January 1, 2018. By how much did this transaction increase or decrease the excess of current assets over current liabilities?
2. Assume that Rocky Mountain used the entire amount of the loan to purchase inventory. Prepare the journal entry to record the purchase. (*Note:* The company uses a perpetual inventory system.) By how much did this purchase increase or decrease the excess of current assets over current liabilities?
3. Without violating the loan restriction, how much more could Rocky Mountain borrow under its line of credit on January 1, 2018, to invest in inventory? To invest in new equipment? Explain.

Case 8-93   Continuing Problem: Front Row Entertainment

Front Row has the following selected balances at February 28, 2018:

Account	Debit	Credit
Cash	$12,480	
Accounts receivable	3,900	
Inventory	20,380	
Other current assets	31,000	

(Continued)

Account	Debit	Credit
Accounts payable		$ 8,640
Interest payable		375
Sales taxes payable		1,200
Unearned sales revenue		26,100
Other current liabilities		8,300

The following information is not reflected in these balances:

a. On February 28, 2018, Front Row Entertainment accepted delivery of $5,325 of live-performance DVDs from its supplier. Front Row has not yet paid the supplier.

b. On February 1, Front Row Entertainment purchased $8,000 of equipment for its Toronto Music House venue by issuing a one-year note payable bearing 10% interest. Front Row has not made any journal entries related to this transaction and should accrue for this at month's end. (*Note:* Round any calculations to the nearest dollar.)

c. Front Row Entertainment collected $3,745 of advance ticket sales related to an upcoming concert. This price included 7% provincial sales tax.

In addition, several individuals were injured during a concert in February when they pushed past security and rushed the stage. A personal injury lawsuit has been filed against Front Row Entertainment in the amount of $250,000. After investigating the incident and consulting with legal counsel, it has been determined that the likelihood of a judgment against Front Row is remote.

Required:

1. Prepare the necessary journal entries for *a* through *c*. (*Note:* Round all calculations to the nearest dollar.)
2. Determine the current ratio before and after the additional information.
3. How should this lawsuit be recorded? Disclosed?

Case 8-94   Professional and Ethical Behaviour

Ryan is the owner of Northjet Inc., a regional airline company that has been operating out of Ontario for the last eight years. During those eight years, he has taken the company from three employees to a staff of over 40, including pilots, baggage handlers, and other administrative employees. Revenues also have increased significantly during this time. The airline industry is a competitive one, and he has always known that he doesn't want to stay in this business forever. Once the company establishes itself, he wants to sell it for top dollar and move on to his next business venture.

Ryan was recently talking with his friends David and Bruno, who are entrepreneurs at heart. They have been looking for a new business opportunity and mention that they would be interested in taking over Northjet Inc., if Ryan is looking to sell.

Ryan enters into negotiations with David and Bruno and settles on a price. It is agreed that they will pay five times multiple of earnings. They all agree that they don't need to involve the lawyers and accountants, as that would just delay the purchase and cost everyone more money. Ryan mentions that they have all been friends for years and can trust one another with the deal.

David and Bruno say they expect up-to-date financial statements by next week so they can finalize the deal. Ryan promises them that they will have them by next Friday.

Sam, a Chartered Professional Accountant, an employee of Northjet Inc., comes into Ryan's office during the week and mentions that he heard that Northjet Inc. might be sold in the next week or so. Sam asks him to let him know if anything has to be done. Sam says he's assuming that the purchasers' accountants will contact him directly, but he has heard nothing yet. Two days after this initial discussion, Sam comes back into the office and starts asking a few questions regarding the liabilities account. He recalls the $100,000 roof expense that was incurred two weeks ago on the apron, the area where the airplanes are parked when they're not in use. The roof collapsed and had to be repaired on an emergency basis.

Sam can't understand why this expense wasn't recorded in the financial statements even though it hasn't been paid yet. Clearly, it is an expense and under accrual accounting should appear on the financial statements as a liability owing. Ryan quickly tells Sam not to worry about it, and says that he already notified the purchasers that the large expense would not be in the financial statements.

Ryan tells Sam to have those final statements on his desk by tomorrow morning.

Required:

Identify and discuss any accounting issues and potential ethical issues.

9

Reporting and Analyzing Noncurrent Liabilities

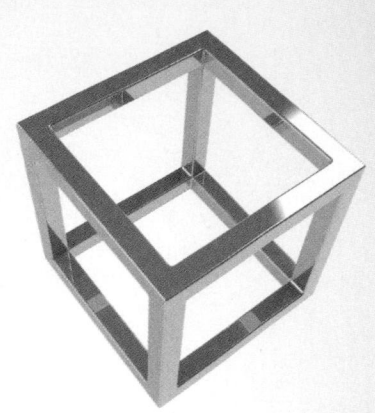

After studying Chapter 9, you should be able to:

1. Explain the nature of debt securities and the markets in which they are issued.
2. Account for the issuance of notes payable and bonds payable.
3. Use the effective interest rate method to account for premium/discount amortization on bonds payable.
4. Use the straight-line method to account for premium/discount amortization on bonds payable.
5. Calculate the after-tax cost of financing with debt and explain financial leverage.
6. Compare and contrast operating and finance leases.
7. Analyze a company's long-term liabilities using the times interest earned, debt to equity, and other debt ratios.
8. Understand the nature of provisions and employee benefit obligations.
9. Calculate the market price of bonds payable using present value techniques.

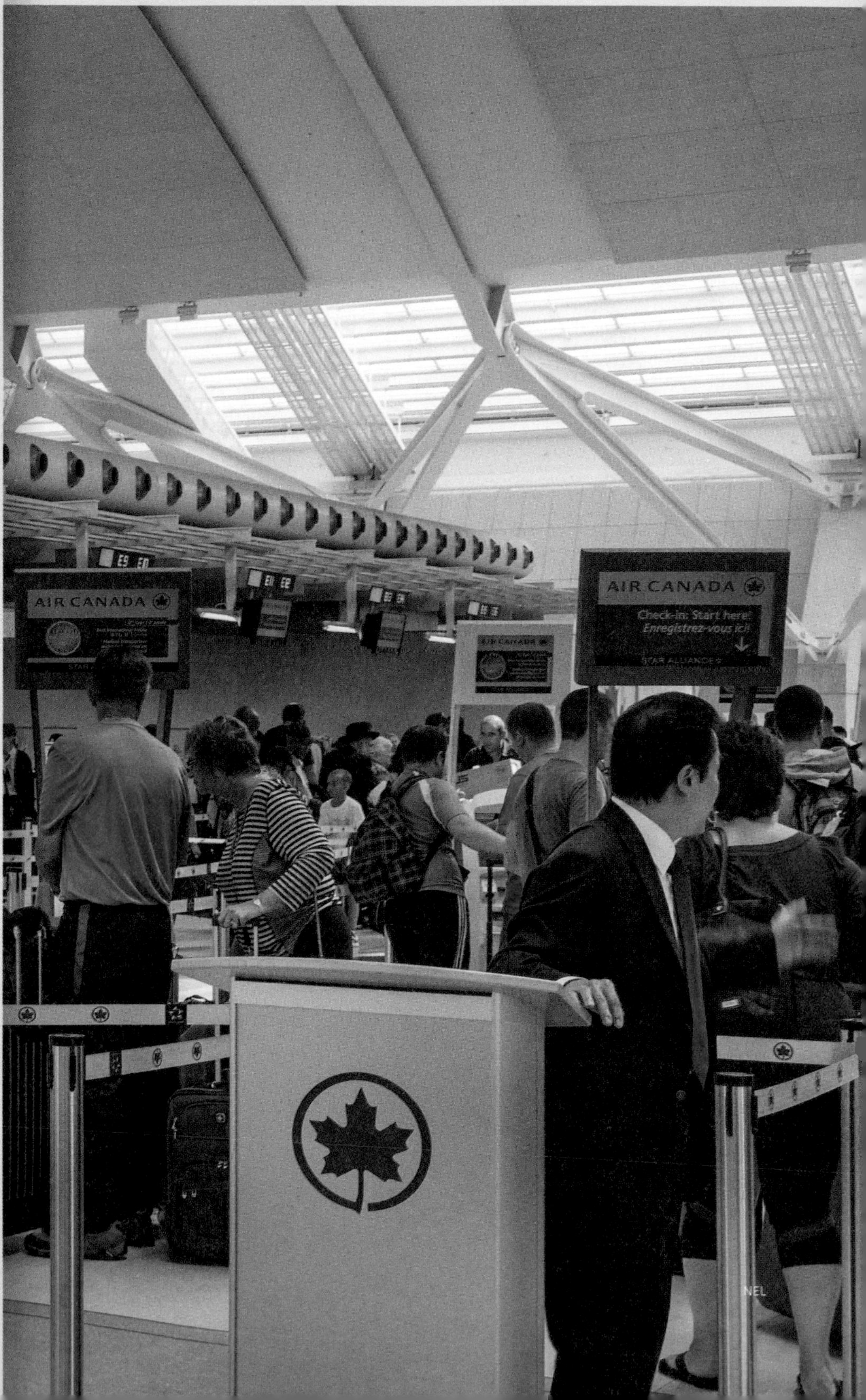

rmnoa357/Shutterstock

EXPERIENCE FINANCIAL ACCOUNTING
with Air Canada

Air Canada, together with regional airlines operating under commercial agreements with Air Canada, flies on average 1,500 flights per day with a mainline fleet of 205 airplanes. In 2014, Air Canada had operating revenues of $13,272,000,000 and total assets of $10,648,000. However, Air Canada also has long-term debt and lease obligations (including current portions) of $8,728,000,000 and total shareholders' equity of −$4,000,000,000.

Companies use long-term debt, along with issuing shares (see Chapter 10), as a way to finance and expand their operations. One measure used to evaluate the mix of debt and equity financing is the long-term debt-to-equity ratio. A ratio above 1.0 indicates that liabilities are greater than shareholders' equity.

Industries that use property, plant, and equipment (PP&E) to generate revenues (such as airlines and hotels) typically have higher debt than industries that use intangible assets (such as pharmaceuticals and software). There are a number of reasons for this, but one is that PP&E is readily transferable to creditors in the event of financial distress, so creditors are more receptive to lending at lower rates.

There is a long history of finance research investigating the optimal mix of debt and equity financing because there are advantages and disadvantages to both. Factors affecting the optimal mix are difficult to quantify.

monticello/Shutterstock

Used with permission of Air Canada

AIR CANADA

Noncurrent liabilities on the statement of financial position typically consists of various types of notes and bonds payable, lease obligations, and employee benefit plan obligations. This chapter explores the accounting and reporting for these types of liabilities.

Relatively large amounts of long-term debt are not necessarily bad. Although more long-term debt means more interest expense, interest expense has the advantage of being tax deductible, unlike dividends paid to shareholders, which are not deductible for income tax purposes. Another advantage of long-term debt is that creditors do not share in the profits of the company, while shareholders do. Thus, if the borrowed money creates a return that is greater than the interest expense on the debt, the shareholders benefit. This is the concept of financial leverage. We will discuss this concept more in Chapter 13.

Long-term debt generally refers to obligations that extend beyond one year from the end of the reporting period. Bonds, long-term notes, debentures, and capital leases belong in this category of liabilities. Exhibit 9.1 shows Air Canada's long-term debt obligations.

(EXHIBIT 9.1)

Excerpt from Air Canada's 2014 Annual Report, Long-Term Debt and Finance Leases

	Final Maturity	Weighted Average Interest Rate (%)	2014	2013
Aircraft financing (a)				
Fixed rate US dollar financing	2015–2026	5.92	$2,029	$1,706
Floating rate US dollar financing	2015–2026	1.79	582	609
Floating rate Japanese yen financing	2020	.24	94	116
Floating rate CDN dollar financing	2026	1.93	310	–
Senior secured notes—US dollar (b)	2019–2020	.61	812	745
Senior secured notes—CDN dollar (b)	2019	7.63	300	300
Other secured financing—US dollar (c)	2016–2019	5.63	433	467
Other secured financing—CDN dollar (d)	2016	–	–	126
Long-term debt			**5,024**	**4,069**
Finance lease obligations (e)	2015–2033	10.01	283	328
Total debt and finance leases			**5,307**	**4,397**
Unamortized debt issuance costs			(91)	(64)
Current portion			(484)	(374)
Long-term debt and finance leases			**$4,732**	**$3,959**

Source: Air Canada Annual Report 2014, page 105. Used with permission of Air Canada.

On the statement of financial position, long-term debt is typically reported as a single number. The more detailed list, like this one for Air Canada, is usually included in the notes to the financial statements.

Notice that Air Canada subtracted current maturities and unamortized debt issuance costs (just before the bottom line) from the rest of its long-term debt. The difference ($4,732 for 2014) is the amount included as long-term debt on the statement of financial position. As we noted in Chapter 8, long-term debt that is due to mature during the year following the end of the reporting period is reported as a current liability. For simplification, we will disregard the reclassification of long-term debt as current liabilities throughout this chapter.

BONDS PAYABLE AND NOTES PAYABLE

OBJECTIVE ❶

Explain the nature of debt securities and the markets in which they are issued.

When a company borrows money from a bank, it typically signs a formal agreement or contract called a "note," in which the borrower agrees to repay the original principal plus interest at one or more points in time specified in the note. Frequently, notes are issued in exchange for a noncash asset such as equipment. Notes payable generally have a relatively short repayment period of five years or less. Collectively, we refer to notes issued in these circumstances as **notes payable**. Larger corporations typically elect to issue bonds instead of notes because they must borrow from more than one lender due to the amount of capital being borrowed. A **bond** is a type of note that requires the issuing entity to pay the face value of the bond to the holder when it matures and usually to pay interest periodically at a specified rate.[1] A bond issue essentially breaks down a large debt (large corporations frequently borrow hundreds of millions of dollars) into smaller portions (usually $1,000) because the total amount borrowed is usually too large for a single lender. For example, rather than try to find a single bank willing (and able) to lend $800,000,000 at a reasonable interest rate, corporations typically find it easier and more economical to issue 800,000 bonds with a $1,000 face value to either a private bank consortium or to the public generally. Bonds issued in public markets can be and are traded by investors based on the market value of the bonds. However, the concept behind the way we account for notes and bonds is identical. As such, the terms have come to be used somewhat interchangeably.

Notes and bonds payable require the borrower to repay the **face value** (also called **par value** or **principal**). Typically the face value is repaid at **maturity**, which is a specified date in the future. However, some contracts require the principal to be repaid in, for example, monthly installments. These contracts, referred to as installment loans, typically require equal payments to be made each period. A portion of each payment is interest and a portion is principal. Car, student, and home loans are examples of installment loans.

Most debt contracts require that the borrower make regular interest payments. Historically, interest payments were made when a bondholder detached a coupon from the debt contract and mailed it to the company on the interest payment date. These obligations are called *coupon notes*, *coupon debentures*, or *coupon bonds*, and the required interest payments are *coupon payments*. The terminology for coupons is still used today, but now the payments are automatically sent to the registered bondholder.

The amount of each interest payment can be calculated from the face amount, the interest rate, and the number of payments per year, which are all stated in the debt contract. (The **interest rate** identified in the contract is referred to as the **stated rate**, **coupon rate**, and **contract rate**.) Recall the formula for calculating interest:

$$\text{Face value} \times \text{Interest rate} \times \text{Time (in number of years)}$$

To illustrate, consider a contract with a face amount of $1,000, a stated interest rate of 8%, and semiannual interest payments. For this $1,000 note, the amount of each semiannual interest payment is $40:

$$\$1{,}000 \times 8\% \times 6/12 = \$40$$

Selling New Debt Securities

Borrowing, through the use of notes or bonds, is attractive to businesses as a source of money because the relative cost of issuing debt (such as the interest payments) is often lower than the cost of issuing equity (such as the cost of giving up ownership shares or paying dividends.). Businesses may sell bonds directly to institutions such as insurance companies or pension funds. However, bonds are frequently sold to the public through an underwriter. Underwriters generate a profit either by offering a price that is slightly less than the expected market price (thereby producing a profit on resale) or by charging the borrower a fee.

Underwriters examine the provisions of the bond instrument (secured or unsecured, callable or not callable, convertible or not convertible), the credit standing of the borrowing business, and the current conditions in the credit markets and the economy as a whole to determine the **market rate** of interest (or **yield**) for the bond. The yield

---

[1] Interest is generally paid semiannually. We use both semiannual and annual interest payments in the text to better illustrate interest amortization.

may differ from the stated rate because the underwriter disagrees with the borrower as to the correct yield or because of changes in the economy or creditworthiness of the borrower between the setting of the stated rate and the date of issue of the bond.

As shown in Exhibit 9.2, there are three possible relationships between the stated interest rate and yield: (1) they can be equal, (2) the yield can be less than the stated rate, or (3) the yield can be greater than the stated rate. If the required yield is equal to the stated rate, the bonds sell for the face value, or at par. If the yield is less than the stated rate, the bonds represent particularly good investments because the interest payments to be made are greater than required by the market. In this case, the demand for such bonds will bid the selling price up above face value. When this happens, bonds are said to sell at a **premium**. On the other hand, if the required yield is greater than the stated rate of interest, the below-market interest payments will drive the selling price of the bond below the face value, in which case, the bond would sell at a **discount**.

Types of Bonds

In practice, bonds differ along a number of other dimensions, as illustrated in Exhibit 9.3.

Secured Bonds A **secured bond** has some collateral pledged to support the corporation's ability to pay. For example, **mortgage bonds** are secured by real estate. In this case, should the borrower fail to make the payments required by the bond, the lender can take possession of (repossess) the real estate that secures the bond. The real estate provides "security" for the lender in case the debt is not paid. Bonds are also frequently secured by the shares or bonds of other corporations and, in theory, can be secured by any asset of value.

Unsecured Bonds Some bonds, however, are **unsecured**. These are typically called **debenture bonds**. In this case, there is no collateral; instead, the lender is relying on the general credit of the corporation. What this really means is that, should the borrower go bankrupt, any secured bondholders will get their collateral before the unsecured bondholders receive a single penny. That is, unsecured bondholders are the last lenders to be paid in bankruptcy (only the shareholders follow).

You may have heard of the term **junk bonds**. These are unsecured bonds where the risk of the borrower failing to make the interest and/or principal payments is relatively high. Why would anyone lend money under such circumstances? Because they receive a high enough rate of interest to compensate them for the risk.

Callable Bonds **Callable bonds** give the borrower the right to pay off (or call) the bonds prior to their due date. The borrower typically "calls" debt when the interest rate being paid is much higher than the current market conditions. This is similar to homeowners "refinancing" to obtain a lower interest rate on their home mortgage.

(EXHIBIT 9.2)

The Relationships between Stated Interest Rate, Yield Rate, and Interest Expense

Bonds Sold At	Required Market Yield Compared to Stated Rate	Interest Over the Life of the Bonds
Premium (above par)	Yield < Stated rate	Interest expense < Interest paid
Par	Yield = Stated rate	Interest expense = Interest paid
Discount (below par)	Yield > Stated rate	Interest expense > Interest paid

© Cengage Learning

(EXHIBIT 9.3)

Long-Term Debt Terms

Notes/Bonds	Different names for debt instruments that require borrowers to pay the lender the face value and usually to make periodic interest payments.
Face Value/Par Value/Principal	The amount of money the borrower agrees to repay at maturity.
Maturity Date	The date on which the borrower agrees to pay the creditor the face (or par) value.
Stated/Coupon/Contract Rate	The rate of interest paid on the face (or par) value. The borrower pays the interest to the creditor each period until maturity.
Market/Yield Rate	The market rate of interest demanded by creditors. This is a function of economic factors and the creditworthiness of the borrower. It may differ from the stated rate.
Secured Bonds	Secured debt provides collateral (such as real estate or another asset) for the lender. That is, if the borrower fails to make the payments required by the debt, the lender can "repossess" the collateral.
Unsecured/Debenture Bonds	Debt that does not have collateral is unsecured. Unsecured bonds typically are called debenture bonds.
Junk Bonds	Junk bonds are unsecured bonds that are also very risky, and, therefore, pay a high rate of interest to compensate the lender for the added risk.
Callable Bonds	Callable bonds give the borrower the option to pay off the debt prior to maturity. Borrowers will typically exercise this option when the interest being paid on the debt is substantially greater than the current market rate of interest.
Convertible Bonds	Convertible bonds give the lender the option to convert the bond into other securities—typically common shares. Lenders will typically exercise this option when the value of the common shares is more attractive than the interest and principal payments supplied by the debt instrument.
Retractable Bonds	Bonds where the bondholders have the option of demanding early repayment.
Zero Coupon Bond	A bond with a coupon rate of zero.

Convertible Bonds **Convertible bonds** allow the bondholder to convert the bond into another security—typically common shares. Convertible bonds will specify the conversion ratio. For example, each $1,000 bond may be convertible into 20 common shares. In this case, bondholders will convert when the value of the 20 shares becomes more attractive than the interest payments and repayment of the $1,000 principal.

Foreign Currency Denominated Bonds In order to reduce (but not necessarily eliminate) the risks attached to foreign exchange risk, large companies carrying on business in foreign jurisdictions may issue bonds payable in a foreign currency to finance the foreign business operations. These bonds are referred to as foreign currency denominated bonds. These foreign currency bonds payable must be converted to Canadian dollars at the reporting date. If exchange rates between the Canadian dollar and foreign currency have changed since the foreign currency bond was issued, the conversion of the foreign bond to Canadian dollars could result in a foreign currency exchange gain or loss. Advanced accounting courses cover the accounting procedures related to foreign currency denominated debt.

ACCOUNTING FOR BONDS AND NOTES PAYABLE

OBJECTIVE ❷

Account for the issuance of notes payable and bonds payable.

The accounting for notes and bonds is conceptually identical, so keep in mind that, in the bond and note examples that follow, everything would stay the same if we substituted the word *note* for *bond* or vice versa.

YOU DECIDE Fixed versus Variable-Rate Debt

You are the CFO of Ajax Corp. Ajax has decided to borrow $100,000,000 to finance expansion plans. One option is to issue 20-year bonds with a fixed rate of 8%. Ajax's investment bankers believe these will sell for par. Another option is to issue 20-year bonds with a variable rate of one-year LIBOR (London Interbank Offered Rate) plus 5%. For the first year, this will result in a 6.2% rate, but the rate will be adjusted annually.

What types of things should you consider in making the decision about which borrowing option is best for Ajax?

Borrowers must trade off the potential benefit of short-term lower rates with the risk of the rate increasing in the future. In fact, risk is what the difference in rates is all about. With a fixed rate, the lender bears all the risk of changing rates. Specifically, if fixed

rates increase dramatically, the lender is stuck with a below-market return. Admittedly, if rates drop, the lender will have an above-market return, but this uncertainty is the definition of risk. With a variable rate, on the other hand, the borrower bears the risk (and rewards) of changing rates. The shift of risk from the lender to the borrower is why the lender is willing to accept a lower rate initially.

Borrowers must consider terms of the contract, such as how frequently the rate is adjusted, the length of the loan, limits on how much the rate can increase each year or how high the rate can go, and so on. Additionally, the borrower must consider its ability to handle increased interest payments should the rate adjust up.

In this case, Ajax should opt for the lower variable rate only if it can absorb the higher interest payments should its rate adjusts up.

There are three basic cash flows for which the issuing corporation must account:

- *Issuance:* the cash received when the bonds are issued (the issue or selling price)
- *Interest:* the interest payments
- *Repayment:* the repayment of the principal (or face value)

Assume that a corporation issues bonds with a total face value of $500,000, with a stated rate of 6.5% payable annually, and that the principal is due in five years. Exhibit 9.4 depicts all three cash flows.

(EXHIBIT 9.4)

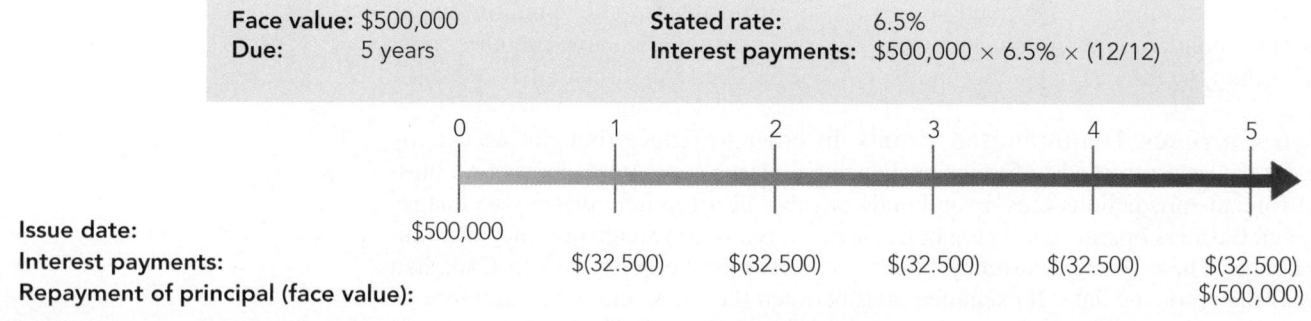

Cash Inflows (Outflows) for a Bond

Face value: $500,000   Stated rate: 6.5%
Due: 5 years   Interest payments: $500,000 × 6.5% × (12/12)

Issue date: $500,000
Interest payments: $(32.500) $(32.500) $(32.500) $(32.500) $(32.500)
Repayment of principal (face value): $(500,000)

Recording Issuance

The market price for bonds is typically quoted as a percentage of face value. For example, if $100,000 face value bonds are issued at 103, their selling price is 103% of face value, or $103,000. Any amount paid above the face value is called a *premium*. In this case, a $3,000 premium will be paid. If the bond is issued below face value, this difference is called a *discount*. For example, if these $100,000 face value bonds were issued at 96, there would be a $4,000 discount.

At the time of issue, the borrower records the face value of the bonds in a bond payable account and records any premium or discount in a separate account called Premium on Bonds Payable or Discount on Bonds Payable. The premium and discount accounts are called "valuation" accounts because they affect the value at which the liability is shown on the statement of financial position. That is, as shown in Exhibit 9.5, both the premium and discount accounts are netted with bonds payable to disclose only one amount on the statement of financial position, so on the date of issue the book value of the bonds payable is equal to the market value.

Cornerstone 9.1 illustrates recording the issuance of bonds at face value (par), at a premium, and at a discount.

(EXHIBIT 9.5)

Statement of Financial Position Presentation

Bond Premium of $3,000			Bond Discount of $4,000	
Long-term liabilities:			Long-term liabilities:	
Bonds payable	$103,000	**OR**	Bonds payable	$96,000

Recording the Issuance of Bonds at Face Value, at a Premium, and at a Discount

CORNERSTONE 9.1

Information:

On December 31, 2018, Laurier Co. issued $100,000 face value of bonds, with a stated rate of 8%, due in five years with interest payable annually on December 31.

Required:

Prepare the journal entries, assuming the bonds sell (1) for par, (2) for 103, and (3) for 96.

Why:

When bonds are issued, any premium or discount should be recorded in a separate general ledger account. Issued bonds must be accurately recorded in order to account properly for both bond principal and bond interest expense.

(Continued)

CORNERSTONE VIDEO

CORNERSTONE

9.1

(Continued)

Assets	= Liabilities +	Shareholders' Equity
+100,000	+100,000	

Assets	= Liabilities +	Shareholders' Equity
+103,000	+100,000	
	+3,000	

Assets	= Liabilities +	Shareholders' Equity
+96,000	+100,000	
	−4,000	

Solution:

Date	Account and Explanation	Debit	Credit
1. Dec. 31, 2018	Cash	100,000	
	Bonds Payable		100,000
	(Record issuance of bonds at par)		
2. Dec. 31, 2018	Cash (100,000 × 103%)	103,000	
	Bonds Payable		100,000
	Premium on Bonds Payable		3,000
	(Record issuance of bonds at premium)		
3. Dec. 31, 2018	Cash (100,000 × 96%)	96,000	
	Discount on Bonds Payable	4,000	
	Bonds Payable		100,000
	(Record issuance of bonds at discount)		

concept Q&A

Why are premiums and discounts on bonds payable amortized to Interest Expense?

Answer:

Discounts occur when the stated rate of interest is below the market rate of interest. In this case, lenders lend less than the face value to the borrower, but are repaid the entire face value at maturity. This difference between the amount lent and the amount repaid conceptually represents an additional interest payment to compensate the lender for accepting a below-market interest rate. Similarly, premiums occur when the stated rate of interest is above the market rate of interest. In this case, lenders lend more than the face value to the borrower but are only repaid the face value at maturity. This difference represents a prepayment of interest by the lender to compensate the borrower for providing above-market interest payments.

RECOGNIZING INTEREST EXPENSE AND REPAYMENT OF PRINCIPAL

Repayment of the principal at maturity is straightforward. Recall that the principal amount repaid is equal to the face value of the note. This is also the amount that was originally credited to the note or bond payable. As such, at maturity you merely need to debit the note or bond payable and credit the cash.

Recognizing the interest expense, on the other hand, is a bit more challenging because any amount paid to the lender in excess of the amount borrowed (face value less any discount or plus any premium) represents interest. In our examples above, when the bonds were issued at par (face value) the amount of cash received when issued was equal to the amount to be repaid at maturity. When the bonds were issued at a premium, the amount of cash received when issued was $103,000 ($3,000 greater than the face value), but only the face value ($100,000) is repaid at maturity. The $3,000 difference represents an effective reduction of the amount of interest paid to the borrower over the life of the bond. In contrast, when the bonds were issued at a discount, the amount of cash received was $96,000 ($4,000 less than the face value), but the entire face value ($100,000) must be repaid at maturity. The additional $4,000 effectively represents additional interest over the life of the bond. The discount or premium that may occur when a bond is issued must be amortized over the life of the bond in order to accurately reflect interest expense, which is the cost of borrowing money.

When an obligation extends over several interest periods, the amount of interest associated with each period also must be determined.

Interest amortization is the process used to determine the amount of interest expense to be recorded in each of the periods that the liability is outstanding.[2]

This allocation has two parts:

- the actual interest payment made to the lender during the period
- amortizing any premium or discount on the bond

Interest Amortization Methods

Although the interest payment made to the lender during the period is always a component of the period's interest expense, there are two methods for amortizing any premium or discount:

- The **effective interest rate method** is based on compound interest calculations. Interest expense for the period is always the yield (the effective interest rate) times the carrying (or book) value of the bonds at the beginning of the period. IFRS requires the use of the effective interest rate method.
- The **straight-line method**, on the other hand, represents a simple approximation of effective interest amortization. Equal amounts of premium or discount are amortized to interest expense each period. ASPE allows either the effective interest rate or the straight-line method.

THE EFFECTIVE INTEREST RATE METHOD: RECOGNIZING INTEREST EXPENSE AND REPAYMENT OF PRINCIPAL

The straight-line and effective interest rate methods are identical when a bond is issued at par because there are no premiums or discounts to amortize. Furthermore, even when premiums or discounts exist, the *total* interest expense over the life of the bonds is identical under both methods. However, the interest expense allocated to the individual accounting periods differs between the two methods because premiums and discounts are amortized in different manners.

Under the effective interest rate method, the amortization of premiums and discounts results in the interest expense for each accounting period being equal to a constant percentage of the bond book value (also called *carrying value*). That is, the interest expense changes every period, but the effective interest rate on the bond carrying value is constant. The straight-line method, on the other hand, has a constant interest expense each period, but the effective interest rate on the bond carrying value changes every period.

To use the effective interest rate method, you must distinguish between interest payments, which are calculated as follows:

> Bond face value × Stated rate × Time (in number of years)

and effective interest expense, which is calculated as follows:

> Bond carrying value × Yield rate × Time (in number of years)

This difference is so important it bears emphasis. Interest payments are calculated with bond face value and the stated rate of interest. These payments are the same each period. Interest expense, under the effective

OBJECTIVE **3**

Use the effective interest rate method to account for premium/discount amortization on bonds payable.

---

concept Q&A

Is the total amount of interest expense over the life of the bond higher when we use straight-line amortization or the effective interest rate method?

Answer:

Neither; the total amount of interest expense is identical under both methods. What changes is the interest expense allocated to each period because the amortization allocated to each period is different between the straight line and effective interest rate methods (see Exhibit 9.6).

---

[2] The same interest amortization procedures used by borrowers to account for liabilities are also used by lenders to account for the corresponding assets.

rate method, is calculated by using the bond carrying value (face value – discount balance or face value + premium balance) and the yield, or market rate, of interest.

Bonds with Regular Interest Payments Sold at Par

When bonds are sold at par there is no premium or discount to amortize. In this case, the interest expense reported on the statement of earnings is equal to the interest payment(s) made to the creditor during the period. This situation typically happens when a business borrows from a single creditor. In this case, the two parties can easily agree on a stated rate that equals the market yield. Cornerstone 9.2 illustrates how interest expense is recorded in this case.

CORNERSTONE 9.2

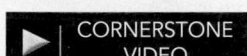
CORNERSTONE VIDEO

Recording Interest Expense for Bonds Sold at Face Value

Information:

On December 31, 2018, Brannigan Co. issued $100,000 of 8% bonds at par. These bonds are due in five years with interest payable annually on December 31.

Required:

1. Calculate the interest payment made on December 31 of each year.

2. Prepare the journal entries necessary to recognize (a) the interest expense on December 31, 2019–2023, and (b) the repayment of the loan principal on December 31, 2023.

Why:

Bonds sold at face value (par) will have interest expense equal to interest paid since the coupon rate of interest on the bond equals the interest rate required by the market when the bond was issued. There is no premium or discount to account for when bonds are issued at face value.

Solution:

1. The interest payment on December 31 of each year will be:

$$\$100,000 \times 8\% = \$8,000$$

2.

	Date	Account and Explanation	Debit	Credit
a.	Dec. 31, 2019–2023	Interest Expense	8,000	
		Cash		8,000
		(Record interest expense)		
b.	Dec. 31, 2023	Bonds Payable	100,000	
		Cash		100,000
		(Record repayment of bond principal)		

Assets	= Liabilities +	Shareholders' Equity (Interest Expense)
−8,000		−8,000

Assets	= Liabilities +	Shareholders' Equity
−100,000	−100,000	

Note, from Cornerstone 9.2, that the interest expense recorded is equal to the cash paid to the lender when the bond is issued at face value (par).

Cornerstone 9.3 illustrates how discounts are amortized under the effective interest rate method.

Recording Interest Expense for Bonds Sold at a Discount Using the Effective Interest Rate Method

CORNERSTONE 9.3

Information:

On December 31, 2018, Brannigan Co. issued $1,000,000 of 8% bonds, due in five years with interest payable annually on December 31. The market rate of interest is 9%. Assume the bond was issued at $961,103. This was calculated using time value of money concepts (see Cornerstone 9.8 for the calculation).

Required:

1. Complete an amortization table for each of the five annual periods.

2. Prepare the journal entry necessary to (a) recognize the interest expense on December 31, 2019 and 2020 and (b) record the repayment of the loan principal on December 31, 2023.

► | CORNERSTONE
VIDEO

Why:

When interest-bearing bonds are issued at a discount, the interest expense for the period is the amount of interest payment for the period plus the discount amortization for the period. Under the effective interest rate method, a constant (or effective) rate of interest on the bond's book (or carrying) value is allocated to the period. Interest expense for bonds sold at a discount will be greater than the interest actually paid since the interest rate required by the market is greater than the coupon rate of interest on the bond when issued.

Solution:

1.

Annual Period	Cash Payment[a] (Credit)	Interest Expense[b] (Debit)	Discount on Bonds Payable[c] (Credit)	Discount on Bonds Payable Balance (Debit)	Bond Payable Carrying Value[d] (Credit)
At issue				$38,897	$ 961,103
12/31/19	$80,000	$86,499	$6,499	32,398	967,602
12/31/20	80,000	87,084	7,084	25,314	974,686
12/31/21	80,000	87,722	7,722	17,592	982,408
12/31/22	80,000	88,417	8,417	9,175	990,825
12/31/23	80,000	89,175	9,175	0	1,000,000

[a] Cash payment = Face value of $1,000,000 × 8% × 12/12 = $80,000
[b] Interest expense = Carrying value × 9% × 12/12
[c] Change in discount balance = Interest expense − Cash payment
[d] New carrying value = Previous carrying value + Change in discount on bonds payable balance

(Continued)

CORNERSTONE 9.3

(Continued)

Assets	= Liabilities +	Shareholders' Equity (Interest Expense)
−80,000	+6,499	−86,499

Assets	= Liabilities +	Shareholders' Equity (Interest Expense)
−80,000	+7,084	−87,084

Assets	= Liabilities +	Shareholders' Equity
−1,000,000	−1,000,000	

2.

Date	Account and Explanation	Debit	Credit
a. Dec. 31, 2019	Interest Expense	86,499	
	Cash		80,000
	Discount on Bonds Payable		6,499
	(Record interest expense)		
Dec. 31, 2020	Interest Expense	87,084	
	Cash		80,000
	Discount on Bonds Payable		7,084
	(Record interest expense)		
b. Dec. 31, 2023	Bonds Payable	1,000,000	
	Cash		1,000,000
	(Record repayment of principal)		

The recording of interest expense for bonds issued at a premium is the mirror image of bonds issued at a discount. Cornerstone 9.4 illustrates how premiums are amortized under the effective interest rate method.

CORNERSTONE 9.4

CORNERSTONE VIDEO

Recording Interest Expense for Bonds Sold at a Premium Using the Effective Interest Rate Method

Information:

On December 31, 2018, Brannigan Co. issued $1,000,000 of 8% bonds, due in five years with interest payable annually on December 31. The market rate of interest is 7%. Assume the bond was issued at $1,041,002 (see Cornerstone 9.8 for the calculation).

Required:

1. Complete an amortization table for each of the five periods.

2. Prepare the journal entry necessary to (a) recognize the interest expense on December 31, 2019 and 2020, and (b) record the repayment of the loan principal on December 31, 2023.

Why:

When interest-bearing bonds are issued at a premium, the interest expense for the period is the amount of interest payment for the period minus the premium amortization for the period. Under the effective interest rate method, a constant (or effective) rate of interest on

(Continued)

the bond's book (or carrying) value is allocated to the period. Interest expense for bonds sold at a premium will be less than the actual amount of interest paid since the interest rate required by the market is less than the coupon rate of interest on the bond when issued.

Solution:

(Continued)

1.

Annual Period	Cash Payment[a] (Credit)	Interest Expense[b] (Debit)	Premium on Bonds Payable[c] (Debit)	Premium on Bonds Payable Balance (Credit)	Bond Payable Carrying Value[d] (Credit)
At issue				$41,002	$1,041,002
1	$80,000	$72,870	$7,130	33,872	1,033,872
2	80,000	72,371	7,629	26,243	1,026,243
3	80,000	71,837	8,163	18,080	1,018,080
4	80,000	71,266	8,734	9,346	1,009,346
5	80,000	70,654	9,346	0	1,000,000

[a] Cash payment = Face value of $1,000,000 × 8% × 12/12 = $80,000
[b] Interest expense = Carrying value × 7% × 12/12
[c] Change in premium balance = Cash payment − Interest expense
[d] New carrying value = Previous carrying value − Change in premium on bonds payable balance

2.

Date	Account and Explanation	Debit	Credit
a. Dec. 31, 2019	Interest Expense	72,870	
	Premium on Bonds Payable	7,130	
	Cash		80,000
	(Record interest expense)		
Dec. 31, 2020	Interest Expense	72,371	
	Premium on Bonds Payable	7,629	
	Cash		80,000
	(Record interest expense)		
b. Dec. 31, 2023	Bonds Payable	1,000,000	
	Cash		1,000,000
	(Record repayment of principal)		

Assets	=	Liabilities	+	Shareholders' Equity (Interest Expense)
−80,000		−7,130		−72,870

Assets	=	Liabilities	+	Shareholders' Equity (Interest Expense)
−80,000		−7,629		−72,371

Assets	=	Liabilities	+	Shareholders' Equity
−1,000,000		−1,000,000		

Note that the interest expense using the straight-line method is the same each period. In contrast, the interest expense using the effective interest method results in a different amount of interest expense each period. This occurs under the effective interest rate method because the interest expense is based on a constant *rate*. This rate is applied to the remaining carrying value of the bonds each period. Exhibit 9.6 illustrates how the carrying value of the bonds is different between the straight-line and effective interest methods for both a premium and a discount.

THE STRAIGHT-LINE METHOD

We will now discuss how interest expense is allocated to the various accounting periods using the straight-line method for debt with regular interest payments sold for more (a premium) or less (a discount) than the face or par value.

OBJECTIVE

Use the straight-line method to account for premium/discount amortization on bonds payable.

concept Q&A

Why is the effective interest rate method recommended?

Answer:

The effective interest rate method does a better job allocating, or matching, the time value of money to the proper period. Under the effective interest rate method, the interest expense is equal to market rate of interest (or yield) at issue on the bond's carrying value. This makes sense because market forces will ensure that the creditor receives the market rate of return on the investment.

Bonds with Regular Interest Payments Sold at a Premium or Discount

As mentioned previously, the sale of a bond at a discount or premium affects the borrower's interest expense. This is because total interest expense is the difference between the payments to the lenders and the amount received by the borrowing business. Let us compare a $1,000,000, 10%, five-year bond contract with semiannual interest payments that is sold at a $10,000 discount (99% of par) with the same issue sold at a $20,000 premium (102% of par).

	Bond Sold at a Discount	Bond Sold at a Premium
Face amount payment at maturity	$1,000,000	$1,000,000
Interest payments (10 at $50,000 each)	500,000	500,000
Total payments to lenders	1,500,000	1,500,000
Less: Proceeds at issue	(990,000)	(1,020,000)
Total interest expense over life of bond	$ 510,000	$ 480,000

For the discounted bond, total interest expense ($510,000) exceeds interest payments ($500,000) by $10,000. For the bond issued at a premium, total interest expense ($480,000) is $20,000 less than the cash interest payments ($500,000).

(EXHIBIT 9.6)

Bond Carrying Value Balance Using Straight-Line and Effective Interest Methods to Amortize Premium and Discount

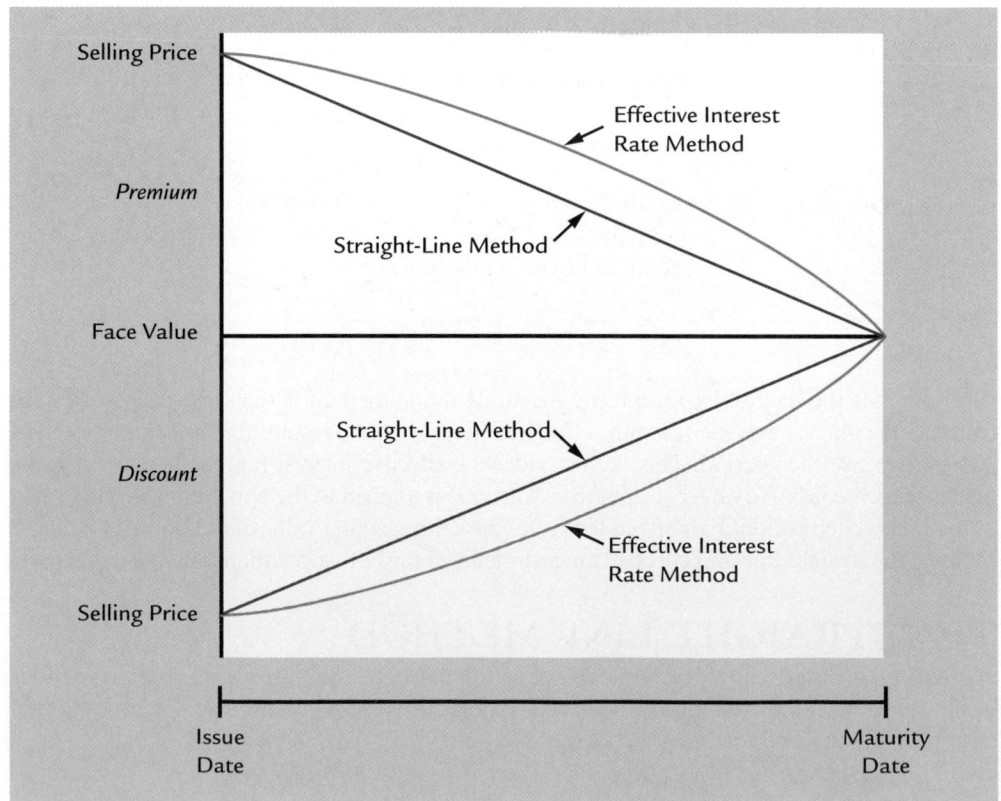

© Cengage Learning

This total interest expense is spread over the life of the bond. For the 10%, $1,000,000 bond sold at 99, interest expense would be $51,000 per six-month interest period:

$$\frac{\$510,000}{10} = \$51,000 \text{ per six-month interest period}$$

Another way of calculating this would be as follows:

Interest paid	$50,000
Amortization of discount (10,000/10 periods)	1,000
Total interest expense per period	$51,000

In business, amortization tables like you see in Cornerstones 9.5 and 9.6 are used to help calculate these amounts. Although such tables aren't really necessary when using the straight-line method for amortizing bond discount or premium, they are extremely helpful when the effective interest rate method is used as is shown earlier in this chapter.

Cornerstone 9.5 shows how to record interest expense when the bond is issued at a discount.

Recording Interest Expense for Bonds Sold at a Discount Using the Straight-Line Method

CORNERSTONE 9.5

Information:

On December 31, 2018, Branningan Co. issued five-year, $100,000,000, 8% bonds at 99 ($99,000,000). The discount at the time of the sale was $1,000,000. Interest is paid semi-annually on June 30 and December 31.

Required:

1. Prepare the journal entry to record the issuance of the bonds on December 31, 2018.

2. Calculate the amount of discount that will be amortized each semiannual period.

3. Calculate the amount of interest expense for each semiannual period.

4. Complete an amortization table for each of the 10 semiannual periods.

5. Prepare the journal entries necessary to (a) recognize the interest expense on June 30 and December 31, 2019–2023 and (b) record the repayment of the loan principal on December 31, 2023.

Why:

When interest-bearing bonds are issued at a discount, the interest expense for the period is the amount of interest payment for the period plus the discount amortization for the period. Under the straight-line method, an equal amount of discount is amortized each period. Interest expense for bonds sold at a discount will be greater than the interest actually paid since the interest rate required by the market is greater than the coupon rate of interest on the bond when issued.

(Continued)

CORNERSTONE

9.5

(Continued)

Assets	=	Liabilities	+	Shareholders' Equity
+99,000,000		−1,000,000 +100,000,000		

Solution:

1.

Date	Account and Explanation	Debit	Credit
Dec. 31, 2018	Cash	99,000,000	
	Discount on Bonds Payable	1,000,000	
	Bonds Payable		100,000,000
	(Record issuance of bonds at a discount)		

2. Discount amortization $= \dfrac{\text{Total discount}}{\text{Number of interest periods}} = \dfrac{\$1,000,000}{10 \text{ periods}}$

$\qquad\qquad\qquad\qquad\quad = \$100,000$ per period

3. Interest expense = Interest payment + Discount amortization

$\qquad\qquad\qquad = (\$100,000,000 \times 8\% \times 6/12) + \$100,000$

$\qquad\qquad\qquad = \$4,000,000 + \$100,000$

$\qquad\qquad\qquad = \$4,100,000$

4.

Semiannual Period	Cash Payment (Credit)	Interest Expense (Debit)	Discount on Bonds Payable (Credit)	Discount on Bonds Payable Balance (Debit)	Bond Payable Carrying Value (Credit)
At issue				$1,000,000	$ 99,000,000
1	$4,000,000	$4,100,000	$100,000	900,000	99,100,000
2	4,000,000	4,100,000	100,000	800,000	99,200,000
3	4,000,000	4,100,000	100,000	700,000	99,300,000
4	4,000,000	4,100,000	100,000	600,000	99,400,000
5	4,000,000	4,100,000	100,000	500,000	99,500,000
6	4,000,000	4,100,000	100,000	400,000	99,600,000
7	4,000,000	4,100,000	100,000	300,000	99,700,000
8	4,000,000	4,100,000	100,000	200,000	99,800,000
9	4,000,000	4,100,000	100,000	100,000	99,900,000
10	4,000,000	4,100,000	100,000	0	100,000,000

Note: The discount on bonds payable is amortized to $0 at maturity.

5.

Date	Account and Explanation	Debit	Credit
a. June 30/Dec. 31	Interest Expense	4,100,000	
	Cash		4,000,000
	Discount on Bonds Payable		100,000
	(Record interest payment on bonds)		
b. Dec. 31, 2023	Bonds Payable	100,000,000	
	Cash		100,000,000
	(Record repayment of bond principal)		

Assets	=	Liabilities	+	Shareholders' Equity (Interest Expense)
−4,000,000		+100,000		−4,100,000

Assets	=	Liabilities	+	Shareholders' Equity
−100,000,000		−100,000,000		

Exhibit 9.7 illustrates how the carrying value of the bond shown in Cornerstone 9.5 grows over time due to the discount amortization. Notice that the beginning carrying value is 99% of the face value. This indicates that although the 8% stated rate is below market yield, it is only slightly below. (In fact, the yield would be approximately 8.25%.) The bond payable discount amortization process increases the bond payable carrying value over the term of the bond payable.

(EXHIBIT 9.7)

Bond Payable Carrying Value over the Life of a Bond Issued at a Discount

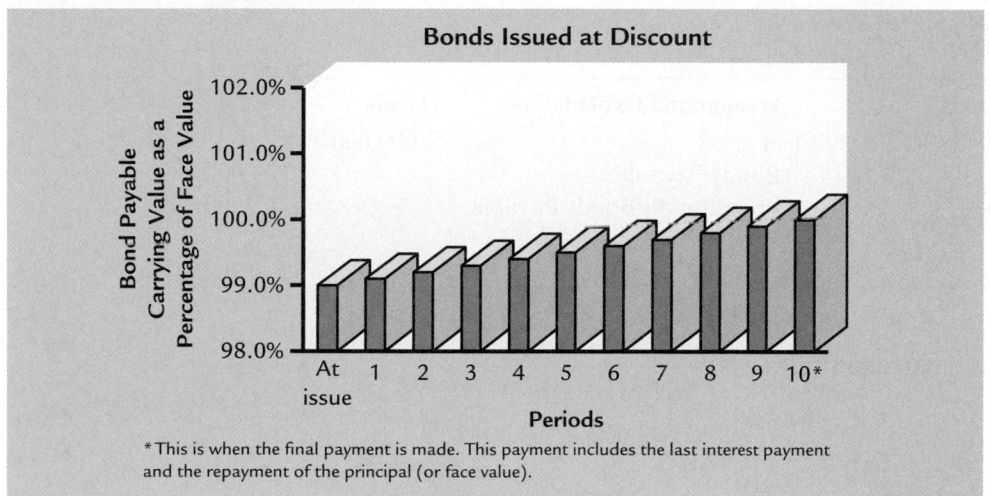

© Cengage Learning

Cornerstone 9.6 shows how calculations change when the bond is issued at a premium.

Recording Interest Expense for Bonds Sold at a Premium Using the Straight-Line Method

CORNERSTONE 9.6

CORNERSTONE VIDEO

Information:

On December 31, 2018, Brannigan Co. issued five-year, $100,000,000, 8% bonds at 102 ($102,000,000). The premium at the time of the sale was $2,000,000. Interest is paid semiannually on June 30 and December 31.

Required:

1. Prepare the journal entry to record the issuance of the bonds on December 31, 2018.

2. Calculate the amount of premium that will be amortized each semiannual period.

3. Calculate the amount of interest expense for each semiannual period.

4. Complete an amortization table for the 10 semiannual periods.

5. Prepare the journal entry necessary to (a) recognize the interest expense on June 30 and December 31, 2019–2023, and (b) record the repayment of the loan principal on December 31, 2023.

(Continued)

CORNERSTONE

9.6

—————

(Continued)

Why:

When interest-bearing bonds are issued at a premium, the interest expense for the period is the amount of interest payment for the period minus the premium amortization for the period. Under the straight-line method, an equal amount of premium is amortized each period. Interest expense for bonds sold at a premium will be less than the actual amount of interest paid since the interest rate required by the market is less than the coupon rate of interest on the bond when issued.

Solution:

1.

Date	Account and Explanation	Debit	Credit
Dec. 31, 2018	Cash	102,000,000	
	Bonds Payable		100,000,000
	Premium on Bonds Payable		2,000,000
	(Record issuance of bonds at a premium)		

Assets	=	Liabilities	+	Shareholders' Equity
+102,000,000		+2,000,000 +100,000,000		

2. Premium amortization $= \dfrac{\text{Total premium}}{\text{Number of interest periods}}$

$$= \frac{\$2,000,000}{10 \text{ periods}}$$

$$= \$200,000$$

3. Interest expense = Interest payment − Premium amortization

$$= (\$100,000,000 \times 8\% \times 6/12) - \$200,000$$

$$= \$4,000,000 - \$200,000$$

$$= \$3,800,000$$

4.

Semiannual Period	Cash Payment (Credit)	Interest Expense (Debit)	Premium on Bonds Payable (Debit)	Premium on Bonds Payable Balance (Credit)	Bond Payable Carrying Value (Credit)
At issue				$2,000,000	$102,000,000
1	$4,000,000	$3,800,000	$200,000	1,800,000	101,800,000
2	4,000,000	3,800,000	200,000	1,600,000	101,600,000
3	4,000,000	3,800,000	200,000	1,400,000	101,400,000
4	4,000,000	3,800,000	200,000	1,200,000	101,200,000
5	4,000,000	3,800,000	200,000	1,000,000	101,000,000
6	4,000,000	3,800,000	200,000	800,000	100,800,000
7	4,000,000	3,800,000	200,000	600,000	100,600,000
8	4,000,000	3,800,000	200,000	400,000	100,400,000
9	4,000,000	3,800,000	200,000	200,000	100,200,000
10	4,000,000	3,800,000	200,000	0	100,000,000

Note: The premium on bonds payable is amortized to $0 at maturity.

(Continued)

5. _____

Date	Account and Explanation	Debit	Credit
a. June 30/ Dec. 31	Interest Expense	3,800,000	
	Premium on Bonds Payable	200,000	
	Cash		4,000,000
	(Record interest payment on bonds)		
b. Dec. 31, 2023	Bonds Payable	100,000,000	
	Cash		100,000,000
	(Record repayment of principal)		

CORNERSTONE

9.6

(Continued)

			Shareholders' Equity (Interest
Assets	=	Liabilities +	Expense)
−4,000,000		−200,000	−3,800,000

			Shareholders'
Assets	=	Liabilities +	Equity
−100,000,000		−100,000,000	

Exhibit 9.8 illustrates how the carrying value of the bond shown in Cornerstone 9.6 declines over time due to the premium amortization. Notice that the beginning carrying value is 102% of the face value. This indicates that the 8% stated rate is slightly above market yield. (In fact, the yield would be approximately 7.51%.) Notice that in this case, the carrying value is the face value of the bond plus the premium because both the bond payable and the premium have credit balances. Furthermore, as the premium is amortized, the premium balance declines and the bond payable carrying value moves closer to face value over the term of the bond payable.

―― (EXHIBIT 9.8)

Bond Payable Carrying Value over the Life of a Bond Issued at a Premium

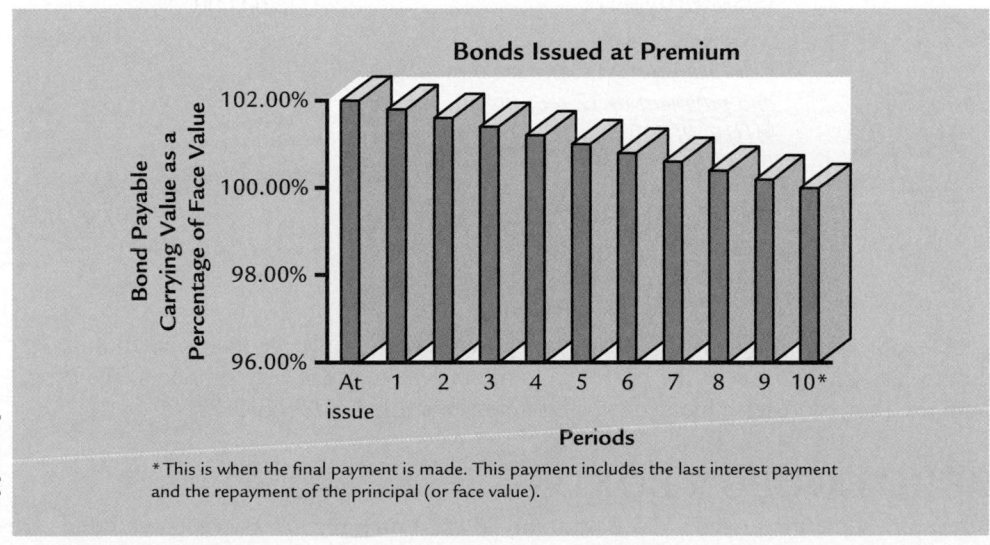

© Cengage Learning

Accruing Interest on Bonds Payable

In the previous discussion, interest payments were made on the last day of the period—December 31. This is frequently not the case in the real world. Assume that on September 1, 2018, Brannigan, which has a year-end of December 31, borrows $120,000,000 on a three-year, 7% note. The note requires annual interest payments (each equal to 7% of

$120,000,000) and repayment of the principal plus the final year's interest at the end of the third year. This borrowing would be recognized in Brannigan's accounts as follows:

	Shareholders'
Assets = Liabilities +	Equity
+120,000,000 +120,000,000	

Date	Account and Explanation	Debit	Credit
Sept. 1, 2018	Cash	120,000,000	
	Notes Payable		120,000,000
	(Record issuance of note)		

Since no interest payment is made at Brannigan's year-end of December 31, interest must be accrued for the period. Interest expense for the four-month period from September through December is $2,800,000 [$120,000,000 × 0.07 × 4/12]. That means interest expense for the eight-month period from January through August is $5,600,000 [$120,000,000 × 0.07 × 8/12]. Brannigan would recognize interest expense and the payment of interest on this note during 2017 through 2020 as follows:

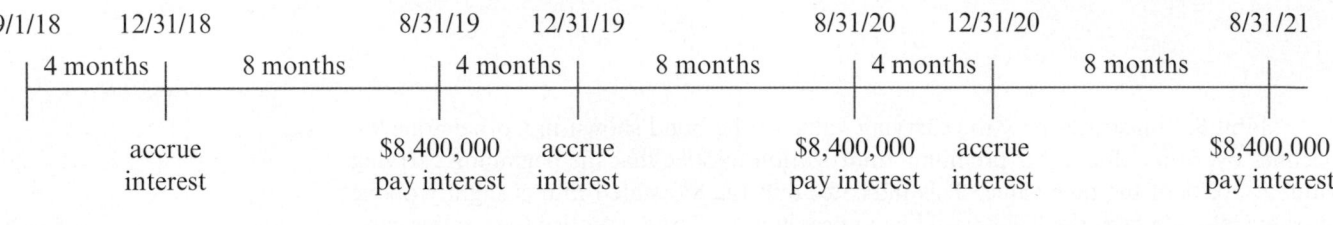

Date	Account and Explanation	Debit	Credit
Dec. 31	Interest Expense	2,800,000	
	Interest Payable		2,800,000
	(Record interest expense and interest payable on 12/31/18, 12/31/19, and 12/31/20)		
Sept. 1	Interest Expense	5,600,000	
	Interest Payable	2,800,000	
	Cash		8,400,000
	(Record interest expense (8 months) and payment of 12 months interest on 9/1/19, 9/1/20 and 9/1/21)		
Sept. 1, 2020	Notes Payable	120,000,000	
	Cash		120,000,000
	(Record repayment of principal on note)		

	Shareholders'
	Equity (Interest
Assets = Liabilities +	Expense)
+2,800,000	−2,800,000

	Shareholders'
	Equity (Interest
Assets = Liabilities +	Expense)
−8,400,000 −2,800,000	−5,600,000

	Shareholders'
Assets = Liabilities +	Equity
−120,000,000 −120,000,000	

Observe that although Brannigan's note involves multiple payments extending over three years, recognition of the borrowing and its repayment is very similar to the procedure used for short-term interest-bearing notes illustrated in Chapter 8.

ZERO COUPON BONDS

Bonds are sometimes issued that do not pay interest on a regular basis. These bonds are referred to as **zero coupon bonds**. Although the stated rate of interest on the bond is zero, the market will adjust the bond value to some amount less than the face value of the bond to reflect the required market yield. A bond with a zero coupon interest rate will sell for a deep discount compared to its maturity value. The Government of Canada issues treasury bills payable for various periods of time. Treasury bills are sold at a discount because they are non-interest bearing. For example, a $100,000 treasury bill issued for five years on January 1, 2018, would result in proceeds to the government of $88,390. These amounts are calculated using present value tables, which are discussed at the end of this chapter.

RETIREMENT OF BONDS PAYABLE

A company may retire (pay off) a bond either at maturity or by purchasing the bond in the open market before maturity. A company may decide to purchase a bond in the open market to decrease financing costs when interest rates have decreased from when the purchased bond was originally issued. Alternatively, a company may have generated excess cash from operations and be in a position to reduce its debt level.

Redeeming a Bond At Maturity

At maturity the carrying value of a bond will be equal to its face value. All discount or premium on the bond will have been amortized as of the bond maturity date. Assuming that Brannigan Co. redeems a $10,000,000 bond at the maturity date of June 30, 2018, and that all interest expense up to the maturity date has previously been recorded, the following journal entry is required to record the redemption:

| June 30, 2018 | Bond payable | $10,000,000 | |
| | Cash | | $10,000,000 |

Redeeming a Bond Before Maturity

When a bond is redeemed before maturity, the company must first record interest expense, including any amortization of bond discount or premium, up to the date of redemption. The second step is to record the payment for the bond and any gain or loss that arises on the redemption. Assuming that Brannigan Co. has a bond payable outstanding on the redemption date of December 31, 2018, of $9,800,000, and that the purchase price of the bond was $9,940,000, the following journal entry is required, assuming that interest expense, including required amortization of bond discount, has been previously recorded:

December 31, 2018	Bond Payable	$9,800,000	
	Loss on redemption	140,000	
	Cash		$9,940,000

Any loss or gain arising on a bond redemption is recorded in the financial statements as "other revenues and gains" or "other expenses and losses."

YOUDECIDE Financial Statement Effects of Refinancing

You are the CFO of Global Industries. Eight years ago, Global issued $100,000,000 of bonds that yielded 11%. Global's borrowing costs are currently 9%. If Global were to refinance the debt, interest payments would drop by $2,000,000 per year.

Should Global refinance? How would the refinancing affect net income?

Unlike debt at a bank (such as a car loan or home mortgage), bonds are not paid off by merely repaying the principal; instead, bonds must be repurchased in the market at their fair market value. To illustrate, assume these bonds were issued at par. This means that their fair value was $100,000,000 on the date of issue. However, the fair value is $100,000,000 only when the market rate of interest is 11% yield (such as at issue) and on the maturity date (because no interest payments remain). If market rates fall below the 11% yield, the fair value of the debt will increase because the lenders will demand a premium to sell the above-market interest payments of 11%. Accordingly, to refinance, Global must pay more than $100,000,000. This purchase premium, coupled with the additional costs of refinancing, may more than offset the decrease in interest payments.

As for the effect on net income, because the carrying value of the existing debt is its amortized cost, not its fair market value, refinancing typically results in a gain or loss on refinancing being recognized. In this case, Global will pay more than the $100,000,000 carrying value of the bonds. The amount of this premium payment will be a loss on Global's statement of earnings, thus lowering net income.

In this case, Global should only consider the cash flow implications. Specifically, Global should refinance if the present value of the interest saved exceeds the costs of refinancing, including the purchase premium. In reality, however, management also considers the financial statement effects of the transaction.

---

concept Q&A

How do credit cards calculate interest?

Answer:

Although terms vary from card to card, they all charge some percentage of our average balance for the period. If your card charges 1.5% of the average balance for the month and you have a $5,000 average balance, then the interest charge will be $75. Interest of 1.5% may not sound that bad, but remember that this is per month. That equates to 18% per year (1.5% × 12 months), without considering the effect of compounding. If all you do is pay the interest, you are not lowering your outstanding balance at all.

INSTALLMENT DEBT

Instead of paying off the principal at maturity, some debt requires a portion of the principal to be paid off each period (usually monthly), along with some interest. Common examples of installment debt are home mortgages and car loans. Payments on this type of debt may be structured as either a fixed amount of principal each month plus interest or as a blended payment of principal and interest. Examples of each type of loan follow.

Installment Debt Payment as Fixed Principal Amount Plus Interest

Assume that on January 1, 2018, John James purchased a Corvette for $70,000. The purchase is financed by an installment loan requiring monthly principal payments of $1,000 plus 12% interest on the outstanding principal balance. An installment payment schedule for the first four months of the loan follows in Exhibit 9.9.

On the date the car is acquired, the following journal entry is required:

Jan. 1	Car	70,000	
	Installment loan payable		70,000

On the first payment date, the following journal entry is required:

Feb. 1	Installment loan payable	1,000	
	Interest expense	700	
	Cash		1,700

(EXHIBIT 9.9)

Monthly Installment Payment Schedule

Date Balance	(1) Payment (2) + (3)	(2) Interest Expense (4) × 12% × 1/12	(3) Principal Repayment	(4) Outstanding Principal (4) – (3)
Jan. 1				$70,000
Feb. 1	$1,700	$700	$1,000	69,000
Mar. 1	1,690	690	1,000	68,000
Apr. 1	1,680	680	1,000	67,000

Under this type of arrangement, the monthly payment required decreases because the interest expense decreases each month as the outstanding principal balance decreases.

Installment Debt Payment as Blended Principal and Interest

Most mortgages and car loans are structured as installment loans that require a blended payment of interest and principal, with the total amount paid each period (usually monthly) remaining constant.

Assume that John James purchased a Corvette on January 1, 2018, and that the purchase is financed by a $70,000 installment loan at 12% that requires monthly payments of $1,900. An installment schedule for the first four months of the loan follows in Exhibit 9.10.

(EXHIBIT 9.10)

Monthly Installment Payment Schedule

Date Balance	(1) Payment	(2) Interest Expense (4) × 12% × 1/12	(3) Principal Repayment (1) – (2)	(4) Outstanding Principal (4) – (3)
Jan. 1				$70,000
Feb. 1	$1,900	$700	$1,200	68,200
Mar. 1	1,900	682	1,218	66,982
Apr. 1	1,900	670	1,230	65,752

© Cengage Learning

The journal entry to record the acquisition of the vehicle is identical to the previous fixed principal payment example. The journal entry required to record the first loan payment is as follows:

Feb. 1	Interest expense	700	
	Installment loan payable	1,200	
	Cash		1,900

Under this type of arrangement, where the monthly payment amount is blended but fixed, the interest expense decreases each month since the outstanding principal amount is decreasing each month. Also, the monthly repayment of principal increases each month since the portion of the blended principal and interest payment that represents interest decreases each month.

PROS AND CONS OF DEBT FINANCING

A business must weigh both the negative and positive aspects of debt financing in deciding whether or not to take the risk. This extremely complex decision is treated more fully in finance courses, but some general points follow.[3]

OBJECTIVE **5**

Calculate the after-tax cost of financing with debt and explain financial leverage.

Tax Deductible Interest Expense

A significant advantage of financing with debt rather than shares is the fact that the interest expense on debt is deductible for income tax purposes. Consider the case of Carmel Company, which issued $1,000,000 of 8% bonds that resulted in interest expense of $80,000 per year. The net cash outflow for Carmel's bonds is significantly less than $80,000, however, because of the effect of interest deductibility for income tax purposes.

---

[3] The following discussion explains the accounting concepts and procedures for debt used by borrowers. Although the concepts and procedures used by investors in debt securities are based on the same measurements and calculations, the reporting conventions are somewhat different. The most fundamental difference is that investors record debt acquired as assets rather than liabilities and record the interest as revenue rather than expense.

Since interest expense is deductible for tax purposes, taxable income is $80,000 less than it is without the bond issue. At a tax rate of 30%($80,000 × 30%), income taxes were reduced by $24,000, resulting in a net cash outflow for the bonds of $56,000($80,000 − $24,000). In other words, the cost of financing with bonds (or any other form of debt with tax-deductible interest payments) is the interest *net of income taxes*, which is determined using the following formula:

$$\text{Net interest cost of bond financing} = \text{Interest net of income taxes} = (1 - \text{Tax rate})(\text{Interest})$$
$$= (1 - 0.30)(\$80,000)$$
$$= \$56,000$$

Financial Leverage

Another potential advantage of debt is that it fixes the amount of compensation to the lender. No matter how successful the firm is in using borrowed capital, its creditors receive only the return specified in the debt agreement (interest plus the face amount). Thus, if the borrowed capital generates income in excess of the interest on the debt, the firm's shareholders benefit. The use of borrowed capital to produce more income than needed to pay the interest on the debt is called **financial leverage**.

Under the right conditions, financial leverage has significant advantages. However, conditions also exist under which the use of financial leverage is disadvantageous. Exhibit 9.11 illustrates both conditions in which two companies—Carmel Company and Noblesville Inc.—have identical financial circumstances except that Carmel finances its operations with debt as well as shares; Noblesville carries no debt.

In 2017, favourable economic conditions allow Carmel to make the most of its financial leverage. Carmel's shareholders earn $3.64 per share, which includes an amount attributable to earnings in excess of the cost of borrowing. In contrast, Noblesville's shareholders earn only $2.80 per share in 2017. However, income from operations falls sharply in 2018. As a result, Carmel's shareholders earn only $0.84 (a decrease of $2.80, or 77%) per share compared to $0.93 (a decrease of $1.87, or 67%) per share for Noblesville's shareholders. The leverage will increase returns to shareholders relative to

(EXHIBIT 9.11)

Effects of Financing with Debt

	2017		2018	
	Carmel Company	Noblesville Inc.	Carmel Company	Noblesville Inc.
Statement of financial position:*				
Assets	$3,000,000	$3,000,000	$3,000,000	$3,000,000
Bonds payable	$1,000,000	—	$1,000,000	—
Shareholders' equity	$2,000,000	$3,000,000	$2,000,000	$3,000,000
Number of outstanding common shares	100,000	150,000	100,000	150,000
Statement of earnings:				
Income from operations	$ 600,000	$ 600,000	$ 200,000	$ 200,000
Interest expense (8%)	80,000	—	80,000	—
Income before tax	520,000	600,000	120,000	200,000
Income tax expense (30%)	156,000	180,000	36,000	60,000
Net income	$ 364,000	$ 420,000	$ 84,000	$ 140,000
Earnings per share	$ 3.64	$ 2.80	$ 0.84	$ 0.93

*Annual averages (assume that current liabilities are negligible).

debtholders during a period of increasing profits. Similarly, the use of leverage will decrease returns to shareholders relative to debtholders during a period of decreasing profits.

Inflation

A third advantage of financing with debt is that in periods of inflation, debt permits the borrower to repay the lender in dollars that have declined in purchasing power. For instance, based on changes in the consumer price index (CPI), $1,000,000 borrowed in 1990 and repaid in 2015 provided the lender with only 59% of the purchasing power of the amount loaned in 1990.

Payment Schedule

The primary negative attribute of debt is the inflexibility of a payment schedule. Debt requires specified payments to creditors on specified dates. If a payment is not made as scheduled, the borrower may be forced into bankruptcy. This attribute of debt makes it a riskier source of capital than equity. The larger the proportion of debt an entity uses to finance its capital needs, the greater the risk of default. As risk increases (because of a higher proportion of debt to equity), the cost of the debt increases. At a certain point, the risk associated with increasing debt becomes so great that additional debt cannot be issued at any cost. For firms whose operational and competitive circumstances produce substantial fluctuations in earnings, even low levels of debt may be considered too risky.

Occasionally, a business finds that it is unable to make the interest or principal payments required by its long-term notes and bonds payable. If there is reason to expect that the firm will eventually be able to secure enough cash to make part of or all the required payments, creditors may permit a restructuring of the cash payment schedule. The amount at which the firm's liabilities are measured may or may not be changed by such a restructuring. In such cases, creditors must analyze the situation to ensure that they are better off than they would be if they forced a bankruptcy.

OPERATING AND FINANCE LEASES

Many companies choose to **lease**, instead of purchase, some of their assets. For example,   Air Canada reported in 2014 that 17 of its airplanes were under finance leases.

OBJECTIVE **6**

Compare and contrast operating and finance leases.

Operating Leases

In an **operating lease**, the **lessor** (the legal owner of the asset) retains substantially all of the risks and obligations of ownership, while the **lessee** uses the asset during the term of the lease. Automobiles, apartments, retail space, office space, and office equipment are usually rented with operating leases.

Under an operating lease, the leased asset does not appear in the records of the lessee because the legal owner of the asset retains the risks and obligations of ownership. Rent paid in advance of the use of the asset is reported as prepaid rent, and rent expense is recognized in the period in which the leased asset is used. However, because many financial statement users view leases as liabilities, the sum of all payments required by noncancellable operating leases for the next five years must be disclosed in a footnote to the lessee's financial statements. Exhibit 9.12 is taken from Air Canada's 2014 financial statements to demonstrate the required financial statement note disclosure for leases.

To further illustrate, although Air Canada reports the present value of the net minimum lease payments ($283,000,000) of its finance leases as a liability, no liability is recorded for the $1,633,000,000 in future operating lease obligations. For this reason, many companies will intentionally structure the lease to qualify as an operating lease in order to minimize recorded liabilities.

AIR CANADA

(EXHIBIT 9.12)

Excerpt from Air Canada 2014 Financial Statements

Note 16
Leases
Minimum future rental payments under finance and operating lease obligations as of December 31, 2014, are as follows *(in millions)*:

Year Ending December 31	Finance leases	Operating leases
2015	$ 91	$ 359
2016	48	300
2017	46	266
2018	46	227
2019	46	185
2020 and thereafter	120	296
	397	$1,633
Less amount representing interest	114	
Present value of net minimum lease payments	$283	

Finance Leases

A **finance lease**, on the other hand, is a noncancellable agreement that is in substance a purchase of the leased asset. Therefore, if a finance lease contains specified criteria, the lease is treated for accounting purposes as an asset purchase. For example, if Marmidan Inc. signs a 20 year equipment lease that meets the requirements of being a finance lease and has a cash equivalent value of $10,000,000, the required accounting entry follows:

	Debit	Credit
Leased equipment	$10,000,000	
Obligation under equipment finance leases		$10,000,000

IFRS 17 requires a finance lease to be capitalized if one or more of the following criteria are met:

- The ownership of the asset is transferred to the lessee at the end of the lease term.
- The lessee is allowed to purchase the asset under the lease terms at an amount that is expected to be lower than its fair market value at the time of acquisition.
- The term of the lease is a major part of the economic life of the asset.
- The present value of the future minimum lease payments represents substantially all of the fair market value of the asset at the time the lease is signed.
- The asset leased is of such a specialized nature that only the lessee can use the asset without major modifications.

Although the lessor remains the legal owner of the leased asset under this lease arrangement, a finance lease transfers virtually all the benefits of ownership to the lessee. Therefore, a finance lease is appropriately shown among the lessee's assets and liabilities. At the beginning of such a lease, a finance lease liability, as shown above, is recorded at the present value of the future lease payments. At this time, an asset is recorded in the same amount. Over the life of the lease the asset is depreciated, using an appropriate depreciation method. The lease liability is reduced and interest expense recorded as lease payments are made under the lease.

IFRS 16 is effective starting January 2019. This new standard will generally not affect lessors but will generally require lessees to capitalize most leases. Lease accounting is studied in intermediate accounting courses.

ANALYZE LONG-TERM LIABILITIES

The debt structure of Air Canada is shown in Exhibit 9.13.

Although long-term creditors are concerned with a company's short-term liquidity, they are primarily concerned with its long-term solvency. As such, long-term creditors focus on ratios that incorporate (1) long-term debt and (2) interest expense/payments.

The following ratios are often used to analyze a company's debt load:

OBJECTIVE 7

Analyze a company's long-term liabilities using the times interest earned, debt to equity, and other debt ratios.

$$\text{Total debt to equity} = \frac{\text{Total liabilities}}{\text{Total equity}}$$

$$\text{Total debt to total assets} = \frac{\text{Total liabilities}}{\text{Total assets}}$$

$$\text{Total long-term debt to total equity} = \frac{\text{Long-term debt}}{\text{Total equity}}$$

The total debt-to-equity ratio is designed to look at the mix of debt and equity financing. For example, if the ratio is 1.00, then 50% of the company's financing comes from shareholders while the other 50% comes from creditors. However, over the past few decades borrowing arrangements have become much more varied. That is, historically when companies borrowed they locked themselves into long-term debt contracts. Now many companies use short-term borrowing, such as revolving credit, as part of their financing plan. This has the advantage of allowing companies to more frequently adjust their levels of borrowing based on current conditions. The downside is that short-term credit exposes them to greater risk of interest rate changes. For example, when interest rates increase, short-term borrowers may be forced to refinance at these higher rates while long-term borrowers will be locked in at the lower rates. Of course, short-term borrowers can, and do, hedge these interest rate risks, but that is a topic for advanced accounting and finance courses.

(EXHIBIT 9.13)

Air Canada Current and Long-Term Liabilities

	December 31, 2014	December 31, 2013
Air Canada Consolidated Statement of Financial Position (Partial) (Canadian dollars in millions)		
LIABILITIES		
Current		
Accounts payable and accrued liabilities	$ 1,259	$ 1,129
Advance ticket sales	1,794	1,687
Current portion of long-term debt and finance leases	484	374
Total current liabilities	3,537	3,190
Long-term debt and finance leases	4,732	3,959
Pension and other benefit liabilities	2,403	2,687
Maintenance provisions	796	656
Other long-term liabilities	313	375
Total liabilities	11,781	10,867

AIR CANADA

concept Q&A

Is it always better to have lower total debt to equity, total debt to total assets, and total long-term debt to equity ratios?

Answer:

No. Debt provides opportunities for leverage. Think about it in this way—if you're guaranteed a return greater than your interest payments, it would not make sense to avoid borrowing. Of course, the reality is that while no returns are guaranteed, interest payments are unavoidable.

Because it is increasingly common to use short-term debt financing, the total debt to equity and total debt to total asset ratios contain all debt. Although the denominators for these two ratios differ, they both give a sense of the extent to which a company is financed with debt. You can see this more clearly by remembering that total assets = total liabilities + total equity. Both ratios therefore measure the relative size of total liabilities in the accounting equation.

Other ratios focus on a company's ability to make interest payments. These ratios are often called coverage ratios because they provide information on the company's ability to meet or cover its interest payments. The most common ratios focus on either accrual basis interest expense or the cash basis interest payment and are typically measured on a pretax basis because interest expense is tax deductible. Generally, these ratios indicate whether a company has sufficient earnings and cash flow to pay interest obligations.

$$\text{Times interest earned (accrual basis)} = \frac{\text{Operating income}}{\text{Interest expense}}$$

$$\text{Times interest earned (cash basis)} = \frac{(\text{Cash flows from operations} + \text{Taxes paid} + \text{Interest paid})}{\text{Interest payments}}$$

Cornerstone 9.7 demonstrates the calculation and analysis of the ratios related to long-term debt and interest.

CORNERSTONE 9.7

CORNERSTONE VIDEO

Calculating and Analyzing Long-Term Debt and Interest Coverage Ratios

Information:

Consider the following information for Northern Airlines and Southern Airlines (in millions).

Northern Airlines

Long-term debt	$15,665	Interest expense	$1,278
Total liabilities	43,294	Operating income	(324)
Total assets	43,539	Interest payments	867
Total equity	245	Cash flows from operations	1,379
		Income tax expense	(344)
		Income tax paid	(15)

Southern Airlines

Long-term debt	$ 3,515	Interest expense	$186
Total liabilities	8,803	Operating income	262
Total assets	14,269	Interest payments	152
Total equity	5,466	Cash flows from operations	985
		Income tax expense	65
		Income tax paid	15

(Continued)

Required:

1. Calculate the following ratios for both companies: (a) total debt to equity, (b) total debt to total assets, (c) total long-term debt to equity, (d) times interest earned (accrual basis), and (e) times interest earned (cash basis).

2. Interpret these results.

Why:

Calculation of ratios related to long-term debt and interest coverage help financial statement users assess the ability of a company to meet its long-term principal and interest payment obligations.

Solution:

1.

	Northern Airlines	Southern Airlines
a. total debt to total equity	$43,294 ÷ $245 = 176.71	$8,803 ÷ $5,466 = 1.61
b. total debt to total assets	$43,294 ÷ $43,539 = 0.99	$8,803 ÷ $14,269 = 0.62
c. total long-term debt to total equity	$15,665 ÷ $245 = 63.94	$3,515 ÷ $5,466 = 0.64
d. times interest earned (accrual basis)	($324) ÷ $1,278 = −0.25	$262 ÷ $186 = 1.41
e. times interest earned (cash basis)	[$1,379 + ($15) + $867] ÷ $867 = 2.57	($985 + $15 + $152) ÷ $152 = 7.58

2. Southern's solvency risk is clearly far lower than Northern's. Not only does Northern have an extremely high debt burden, but it has a net operating loss and all of its operating cash flows are needed to make interest payments. Southern, on the other hand, has a relatively low debt load and can more easily make its interest payments.

   Not surprisingly, Northern may be well below actual industry averages on most ratios while Southern may be above actual industry averages.

ETHICAL DECISIONS   When evaluating a company's solvency, a major concern is whether all debt was properly recorded. Companies have long engaged in transactions designed to hide debt. Such transactions are typically called *off-balance-sheet financing*. Interestingly, many such transactions are legal and considered to be ethical by most. For example, as discussed previously, many companies structure their lease agreements to avoid meeting the criteria for finance leases that require recording an asset and liability related to the future lease obligation. Because these leases are then treated as operating leases, no asset or liability is recorded on the books.

Because many financial statement users view operating leases as unavoidable obligations, IFRS, as noted above, currently requires disclosure of operating lease obligations for each of the subsequent five years and in total. This disclosure allows users to adjust financial ratios to include operating lease commitments.

Some companies also create other legal entities (called "special purpose entities" or SPEs) to "hide" debt. As with leases, such transactions are legal when certain rules are met involving outside investors. Enron, however, created some SPEs in which the documentation appeared to meet the outside investor rules to keep the debt off Enron's statement of financial position. In hindsight, however, either unwritten side agreements or complicated aspects of some of the contracts indicated that the debt should have been included on Enron's statement of financial position. Keeping this debt off its statement of financial position was important in order for Enron to maintain its credit rating; however, these unwritten side agreements and complicated aspects of the contracts were necessary to attract the outside investors. While almost nobody considers structuring a lease to allow treatment as an operating lease to be unethical, the side agreements and subterfuges used by Enron not only were unethical but also, in many cases, were proven to be both illegal and criminal.

OTHER LONG-TERM LIABILITES

Provisions

OBJECTIVE 8

Understand the nature of provisions and employee benefit obligations.

In Chapter 8, we noted that companies record provisions when the amount or timing of a liability is uncertain. Provisions are discussed again in this chapter because some provisions may be of a long-term nature and therefore be reported as long-term liabilities. Companies often make business decisions concerning investments that result in future obligations that may not be determinable with accuracy because those obligations depend on future events. Examples include the restoration of property involving mining or forestry operations, the cost of dismantling and removing equipment, and estimates of future restructuring costs or long-standing lawsuits. Some companies have entered bankruptcy because they had not considered the future costs of these obligations in their investment or operating decisions.

Due to increasing concerns over the environment, accounting standards have been changed to require the recording of asset retirement obligations (AROs) in specified situations. The recording of these obligations affects a company's reported earnings and its statement of financial position. The amount of the ARO liability is calculated using present value concepts. Because of the high level of uncertainty in measuring this obligation due to changing government regulations, interest rates, and technologies, the estimate of the ARO can change over time. Financial statement users should be cautious when analyzing the financial position and profitability of companies involved in business activities where the recording of an ARO is required.

Employee Retirement and Post-employment Benefit Plans

Many companies help fund pension plans for their employees.

A defined contribution pension plan generally requires a company to contribute a fixed amount per year per employee to an investment fund held by a third party. When the employee retires, his or her pension is determined by the fund's earnings during the working years. In this case, the employee bears the risk of the investments made within the pension fund because the amount of the ultimate available pension is not guaranteed by the employer.

A defined benefit pension plan generally requires a company to contribute an amount each year per employee to an investment fund held by a third party that is sufficient in amount to provide for a specified pension for the employee at retirement. The annual contribution required by the employer can change due to fund performance, changes in employee life expectancies, changes in interest rates, and many other factors. In this type of plan, the employer bears the risk of the investments made within the pension fund because the employer essentially guarantees a fixed pension amount to the employee. Due to the high level of uncertainty in funding these types of plans, many employers are currently attempting to change from defined benefit plans to defined contribution plans. The future cost of providing for the required pensions must be estimated and matched with the revenue being generated by the employees currently performing the related work.

Some companies also provide for post-retirement medical and insurance benefits. The future cost of these benefits must be estimated and matched with the revenue generated by the employees performing the related work. These significant liabilities must be estimated and recorded.

The accounting issues related to pension plans and **post-employment benefit plans** are complex. Actuarial assumptions must be made with respect to how long employees will work for an employer, how long employees will live, how ill employees will be in retirement, future investment returns on pension assets, and future medical costs, to list only a few matters. As the population of the country continues to age, and people generally live longer, the cost of these future benefits has already increased and may continue to increase significantly in the future. As a result, many companies are in the process of reducing future benefits and future obligations for new and even existing employees where possible.

It is important to accurately reflect the full cost of an employee's services in the proper accounting period in which those services are rendered. If future benefit costs were not recorded currently, executives and managers could have an incentive to increase current profit by adopting policies to remunerate employees with more future benefits (whose cost would not be recorded until a much later year) as compared with higher current salaries or wages (which would be recorded currently and decrease current profit).

The detailed accounting procedures for these future obligations are included in advanced accounting courses.

PRICING BONDS PAYABLE

Bond agreements create contractually defined cash flows for the lender. Specifically, lenders typically receive

- periodic interest payments and
- repayment of the loan principal at some future date (loan maturity).

To receive these cash flows, the lender must decide how much to lend. When you borrow from a bank or car dealer, this single lender will set the interest rate to reflect the desired market, or yield, rate. However, there are notable exceptions. For example, if you buy a car for $25,000 at 0.9% interest, does that mean the car dealer's yield is 0.9%? No, it really means that they would have been happy to sell you the car for something below $25,000, such as $24,250. In this case, the "extra" principal you repay ($750 = $25,000 − $24,250) represents interest.

Of course, similar situations happen to businesses, but by far the most common situation occurs with bonds because the stated rate of interest (e.g., 8%) on the bond does not provide the desired yield. As previously discussed, if the required or market yield is above the stated rate, the bond will sell at a discount (e.g., 98) and if the required or market yield is below the stated rate, it will sell at a premium (e.g., 103). But how are these prices determined?

Bonds are priced at the present value of the two future cash flows—the periodic interest payments provide an annuity, while the repayment of the principal is a lump sum. This calculation is shown in Cornerstone 9.8 .

SIGNIFICANT DIFFERENCES BETWEEN IFRS AND ASPE

ASPE is different from IFRS reporting standards in the following key areas:

1. Canadian private enterprises are allowed to use either the straight-line amortization for bond discount or premium or the effective interest rate method, whereas under

OBJECTIVE 9

Calculate the market price of bonds payable using present value techniques.

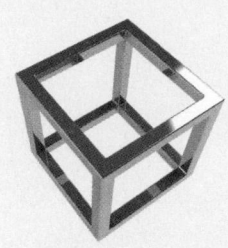

CORNERSTONE 9.8

Determining the Market Value of a Bond

Information:

On December 31, 2018, Brannigan Co. issued $1,000,000 of 8% bonds, due in five years with interest payable annually on December 31.

Required:

1. Draw the cash flow diagram.

2. What is the market value of these bonds if sold to yield (a) 8%, (b) 9%, and (c) 7%?

Why:

Bonds are issued at the present value of the future cash flows. The future cash flows are the future interest payments and the bond principal repayment. These amounts must be discounted at the market rate of interest (or yield rate). The calculation of the market value of a bond at a point in time can inform management of financial opportunities that may exist to repay a bond before maturity.

Solution:

1.

PV = ?   Year 1—2019   Year 2—2020   Year 3—2021   Year 4—2022   Year 5—2023

Year or Time 0

$80,000 $80,000 $80,000 $80,000 $80,000
$1,000,000

2.   a.   PV of interest payments   = Interest payment × PV of an annuity for
            5 periods at 8% per period
            = $80,000 × 3.992710* = $319,417

PV of principal payments = Principal payment × PV of a single sum due in
            5 periods at 8% per period
            = $1,000,000 × 0.680583* = $680,583

Market price of bonds = $319,417 + $680,583 = $1,000,000

*Although present and future value tables provided at the end of Appendix 1 (Exhibits A1-7, A1-8, A1-9, and A1-10) only show five decimal places, we have used factors to six decimal places in these calculations (and those that follow). Use of six decimal places allows the market price of the bond when issued at par to be calculated with no rounding error.

b.   PV of interest payments   = Interest payment × PV of an annuity for
            5 periods at 9% per period
            = $80,000 × 3.889651 = $311,172

PV of principal payments = Principal payment × PV of a single sum due in
            5 periods at 9% per period
            = $1,000,000 × 0.649931 = $649,931

Market price of bonds = $311,172 + $649,931 = $961,103

(Continued)

c.   PV of interest payments   = Interest payment × PV of an annuity for
      5 periods at 7% per period
      = $80,000 × 4.100197 = $328,016

PV of principal payments = Principal payment × PV of a single sum due in
      5 periods at 7% per period
      = $1,000,000 × 0.712986 = $712,986

Market price of bonds = $328,016 + $712,986 = $1,041,002

IFRS, Canadian publicly accountable enterprises are required to use the effective interest rate method of amortization for bond discount or premium.

2. The accounting standards for Canadian private enterprises with respect to finance and operating leases provide specific quantitative guidelines for applying the standards, whereas IFRS provides guidelines that are less specific as they are not quantitative in nature. Therefore, IFRS provides for a broader application of professional judgment (which is studied in advanced accounting courses).

3. Accounting for asset retirement obligations is more rigorous under IFRS compared to the accounting standards for Canadian private enterprises. These differences are studied in advanced accounting courses.

4. A Canadian private corporation can classify in noncurrent liabilities a debt on which a violation of debt covenant occurred as at the year-end date, if that debt agreement was renegotiated with the lender on agreed terms prior to the release of the company's financial statements. Under IFRS, publicly accountable enterprises must classify such a debt as a current liability.

5. The IFRS standards for pension and post-retirement obligations are different from the accounting standards for Canadian private enterprises. These differences are the subject material of advanced accounting courses.

SUMMARY OF LEARNING OBJECTIVES

LO1.   Explain the nature of debt securities and the markets in which they are issued.

- Debt securities are issued in exchange for borrowed cash.
- In return for the borrowed cash, the borrower typically makes periodic interest payments and repays the face, or par, value at maturity.
- These securities may be placed directly with a creditor such as a bank or pension fund or they may be more widely distributed with the help of an underwriter.

LO2.   Account for the issuance of notes payable and bonds payable.

- The issue price of long-term debt is typically quoted as a percentage of face value.
- At the time of issuance the borrower records the face value of the debt in bonds payable (or notes payable).
  - Any amount of cash received over the face value is credited to a premium account.
  - Any amount of cash received under the face value is debited to a discount account.
- The bonds payable (or notes payable) is netted with the premium or discount when reported on the statement of financial position.

LO3. Use the effective interest rate method to account for premium/discount amortization on bonds payable.

- IFRS requires the effective interest rate method to be used to amortize any premium or discount.
- Under this method, premiums and discounts are amortized in a manner that results in the interest expense for each accounting period being equal to a constant percentage of the bond's book, or carrying, value.
- That is, the interest expense changes every period, but the effective interest rate on the bond's book value is constant.
- This constant percentage is called the "yield" and represents the market rate of interest at the date of issue.

LO4. Use the straight-line method to account for premium/discount amortization on bonds payable.

- In the straight-line method, equal amounts of premium or discount are amortized to interest expense each period.
- ASPE allows either the straight-line or the effective interest rate method.

LO5. Calculate the after-tax cost of financing with debt and explain financial leverage.

- Since interest expense is deductible for tax purposes, the presence of interest expense lowers the taxes owed.
- The formula for the after-tax effect of interest expense is $(1 - \text{tax rate}) \times$ interest expense.

LO6. Compare and contrast operating and finance leases.

- A finance lease is a noncancellable agreement that is, in substance, a purchase of the leased asset.
- If a lease includes one of the following requirements it is considered a capital lease:
  - The ownership of the asset is transferred to the lessee at the end of the lease term.
  - The lessee is allowed to purchase the asset under the lease terms at an amount that is expected to be lower than its fair market value at the time of acquisition.
  - The term of the lease covers most of the economic life of the asset.
  - The present value of the future minimum lease payments represents substantially all of the fair market value of the asset at the time the lease is signed.
  - The asset leased is of such a specialized nature that only the lessee can use the asset without major modifications.
- If a lease qualifies as a finance lease, an asset and a liability must be recorded.
- If the lease does not meet requirements to be treated as a finance lease, then it is treated as an operating lease.
- Under an operating lease, the leased asset does not appear in the records of the lessee because the legal owner of the asset retains the risks and obligations of ownership.

LO7. Analyze a company's long-term liabilities using the times interest earned, debt-to-equity, and other debt ratios.

- Although long-term creditors are concerned with a company's short-term liquidity, they are primarily concerned with its long-term solvency.
- As such, long-term creditors focus on ratios that incorporate
  - long-term debt and
  - interest expense/payments.

LO8. Understand the nature of provisions and employee benefit obligations.

- Provisions are recorded for future obligations using estimates and present value concepts.
- Costs of employee benefit plans must be accrued and matched with revenue from employee services.

LO9. Calculate the market price of bonds payable using present value techniques.
- Bonds are issued at the present value of future cash flows.
- The interest payments and repayment of the bond principal (or face value) are the future cash flows.
- These amounts must be discounted at the market rate of interest (or yield).

CORNERSTONES

CORNERSTONE 9.1	Recording the issuance of bonds at face value, at a premium, and at a discount, page 507
CORNERSTONE 9.2	Recording interest expense for bonds sold at face value, page 510
CORNERSTONE 9.3	Recording interest expense for bonds sold at a discount using the effective interest rate method, page 511
CORNERSTONE 9.4	Recording interest expense for bonds sold at a premium using the effective interest rate method, page 512
CORNERSTONE 9.5	Recording interest expense for bonds sold at a discount using the straight-line method, page 515
CORNERSTONE 9.6	Recording interest expense for bonds sold at a premium using the straight-line method, page 517
CORNERSTONE 9.7	Calculating and analyzing long-term debt and interest coverage ratios, page 528
CORNERSTONE 9.8	Determining the market value of a bond, page 532

KEY TERMS

Bond (p. 503)
Callable bonds (p. 504)
Contract rate (p. 503)
Convertible bonds (p. 505)
Coupon rate (p. 503)
Debenture bonds (p. 504)
Discount (p. 504)
Effective interest rate method (p. 509)
Face value (p. 503)
Finance lease (p. 526)
Financial leverage (p. 524)
Installment debt (p. 522)
Interest amortization (p. 509)
Interest rate (p. 503)
Junk bonds (p. 504)
Lease (p. 525)
Lessee (p. 525)
Lessor (p. 525)

Long-term debt (p. 502)
Market rate (p. 503)
Maturity (p. 503)
Mortgage bonds (p. 504)
Notes payable (p. 503)
Operating lease (p. 525)
Par value (p. 503)
Post-employment benefit plans (p. 531)
Premium (p. 504)
Principal (p. 503)
Provisions (p. 530)
Secured bond (p. 504)
Stated rate (p. 503)
Straight-line method (p. 509)
Unsecured (p. 504)
Yield (p. 503)
Zero coupon bonds (p. 520)

REVIEW PROBLEM

I. Straight-Line Method

To finance a new hydroelectric plant, Manitoba Electric issues $100,000,000 of 9%, 15-year bonds on December 31, 2017. The bonds pay interest semiannually on June 30 and December 31. Assume the market rate of interest on December 31, 2017, was above 9%.

Required:

1. Will the bonds be issued at face value, a premium, or a discount? Why?
2. Describe the cash payments made by Manitoba Electric.
3. Prepare the journal entry to record the bond issue assuming the bonds were issued at 91.
4. What is the amount of discount amortization per six-month interest period, assuming the bonds were issued at 91?
5. Complete an amortization table through June 30, 2020.
6. Prepare the journal entries for December 31, 2019, and June 30, 2020.
7. How will the bonds be shown on the December 31, 2019, statement of financial position?
8. Prepare the journal entry to record the repayment of principal at maturity.

Solution:

1. The bonds will be issued at a discount (below face value) because the stated rate is below the market rate. Thus, Manitoba Electric will have to lower the price below face value to compensate creditors for accepting a below-market interest payment.
2. The interest payments are made semiannually, so the interest payments are:

$$\$100,000,000 \times 9\% \times 6/12 = \$4,500,000$$

There are 30 interest payments over the 15-year life of the bonds, so total interest payments are:

$$\$4,500,000 \times 30 = \$135,000,000$$

At maturity, the face value of $100,000,000 is also repaid. Thus, total payments (interest plus principal) of $235,000,000 are made.

3.

Date	Account and Explanation	Debit	Credit
Dec. 31, 2017	Cash	91,000,000	
	Discount on Bonds Payable	9,000,000	
	Bonds Payable		100,000,000
	(Record issuance of bonds)		

Assets	= Liabilities +	Shareholders' Equity
+91,000,000	−9,000,000	
	+100,000,000	

4. $\text{Discount Amortization} = \dfrac{\text{Total discount}}{\text{Number of interest periods}}$

$$= \dfrac{\$9,000,000}{30 \text{ periods}}$$

$$= \$300,000$$

5.

Semiannual Period	Cash Payment (Credit)	Interest Expense (Debit)	Discount on Bonds Payable (Credit)	Discount on Bonds Payable Balance (Debit)	Bond Payable Carrying Value (Credit)
At issue				$9,000,000	$91,000,000
06/30/18	$4,500,000	$4,800,000	$300,000	8,700,000	91,300,000
12/31/18	4,500,000	4,800,000	300,000	8,400,000	91,600,000
06/30/19	4,500,000	4,800,000	300,000	8,100,000	91,900,000
12/31/19	4,500,000	4,800,000	300,000	7,800,000	92,200,000
06/30/20	4,500,000	4,800,000	300,000	7,500,000	92,500,000

6.

Account and Explanation	12/31/19 Debit	12/31/19 Credit	6/30/20 Debit	6/30/20 Credit
Interest Expense	4,800,000		4,800,000	
Cash		4,500,000		4,500,000
Discount on Bonds Payable		300,000		300,00
(Record interest payment on bonds)				

12/31/19

Assets	=	Liabilities	+	Shareholders' Equity (Interest Expense)
−4,500,000		+300,000		−4,800,000

7. Long-term Liabilities:

Bonds Payable	$100,000,000	
Less: Discount on Bonds Payable	(7,800,000)	92,200,000

6/30/20

Assets	=	Liabilities	+	Shareholders' Equity (Interest Expense)
−4,500,000		+300,000		−4,800,000

8.

Date	Account and Explanation	Debit	Credit
Dec. 31, 2032	Bonds Payable	100,000,000	
	Cash		100,000,000
	(Record repayment of bonds)		

Assets	=	Liabilities	+	Shareholders' Equity
−100,000,000		−100,000,000		

II. Effective Interest Rate Method

To finance a new hydroelectric plant, Manitoba Electric issues $100,000,000 of 9%, 15-year bonds on December 31, 2017. The bonds pay interest semiannually on June 30 and December 31. Assume the market rate of interest on December 31, 2017, was 10%.

Required:

1. Will the bonds be issued at face value, a premium, or a discount? Why?
2. Describe the cash payments made by Manitoba Electric.
3. Using present value techniques, verify the bond issue price of $92,314,025.
4. Prepare the journal entry to record the bond issue.
5. Complete an amortization table through June 30, 2020 (round to the nearest dollar).
6. Prepare the journal entries for December 31, 2019, and June 30, 2020.
7. How will the bonds be shown on the December 31, 2019, statement of financial position?
8. Prepare the journal entry to record the repayment of principal at maturity.

Solution:

1. The bonds will be issued at a discount (below face value) because the stated rate is below the market rate. Thus, Manitoba Electric will have to lower the price below face value to compensate creditors for accepting a below-market interest payment.
2. The interest payments are made semiannually, so the interest payments are:

$$\$100,000,000 \times 9\% \times 6/12 = \$4,500,000$$

There are 30 interest payments over the 15-year life of the bonds, so total interest payments are:

$$\$4,500,000 \times 30 = \$135,000,000$$

At maturity the face value of $100,000,000 is also repaid. Thus, total payments (interest plus principal) of $235,000,000 are made.

3. The issue price is the present value of the cash flows:

PV of interest payments $\quad$ = Interest payment × PV of an annuity, 30 semiannual periods, 5%
$$= \$4,500,000 \times 15.37245 = \$69,176,025$$

PV of principal payments = Principal payment × PV of a single sum, 30 semiannual periods, 5%
$$= \$100,000,000 \times 0.23138 = \$23,138,000$$

Market price of bonds = $69,176,025 + $23,138,000 = $92,314,025

4.

Date	Account and Explanation	Debit	Credit
Dec. 31, 2017	Cash	92,314,025	
	Discount on Bonds Payable	7,685,975	
	Bonds Payable		100,000,000
	(Record issuance of bonds)		

Assets	=	Liabilities	+	Shareholders' Equity
+92,314,025		−7,685,975		
		+ 100,000,000		

5.

Annual Period	Cash Payment (Credit)	Interest Expense (Debit)	Discount on Bonds Payable (Credit)	Discount on Bonds Payable Balance (Debit)	Bond Payable Carrying Value (Credit)
At issue				$7,685,975	$92,314,025
06/30/18	$4,500,000	$4,615,701	$115,701	7,570,274	92,429,726
12/31/18	4,500,000	4,621,486	121,486	7,448,788	92,551,212
06/30/19	4,500,000	4,627,561	127,561	7,321,227	92,678,773
12/31/19	4,500,000	4,633,939	133,939	7,187,288	92,812,712
06/30/20	4,500,000	4,640,636	140,636	7,046,652	92,953,348

6.

	12/31/19		6/30/20	
Account and Explanation	Debit	Credit	Debit	Credit
Interest Expense	4,633,939		4,640,636	
Cash		4,500,000		4,500,000
Discount on Bonds Payable		133,939		140,636
(Record interest payment on bonds)				

12/31/19

Assets	=	Liabilities	+	Shareholders' Equity (Interest Expense)
−4,500,000		+133,939		−4,633,939

6/30/20

Assets	=	Liabilities	+	Shareholders' Equity (Interest Expense)
−4,500,000		+140,636		−4,640,636

7.

Long-term Liabilities:

Bonds Payable	$100,000,000	
Less: Discount on Bonds Payable	(7,187,288)	92,812,712

8.

Date	Account and Explanation	Debit	Credit
Dec. 31, 2032	Bonds Payable	100,000,000	
	Cash		100,000,000
	(Record repayment of bonds)		

Assets	=	Liabilities	+	Shareholders' Equity
−100,000,000		−100,000,000		

DISCUSSION QUESTIONS

1. What is a bond payable or note payable?
2. What is the difference between a bond and a note? How do the accounting treatments differ?
3. What does the face value of a bond represent?
4. What is the maturity date of a bond?
5. What is the stated or coupon rate of a bond?
6. How does a bond's stated rate differ from its yield rate? Which one is used to calculate the interest payment?
7. How does a secured bond differ from an unsecured bond?
8. What does it mean if a bond is "callable"?
9. What does it mean if a bond is "convertible"?
10. What is a junk bond?
11. How is total interest for long-term debt calculated?
12. Describe the process that businesses follow to sell new issues of long-term debt.
13. Describe how the relationship between the stated rate and yield rate affect the price at which bonds are sold.

14. How are premiums and discounts presented on the statement of financial position?

15. How do premiums and discounts on long-term debt securities affect interest expense?

16. What is the difference between the straight-line and effective interest rate methods of amortizing premiums and discounts?

17. How can there be interest expense each period for non-interest bearing bonds if there are no interest payments?

18. Under the effective interest rate method, describe the difference in calculating the (a) interest payment and (b) interest expense for the period.

19. How does a firm "leverage" its capital structure? When is leverage advantageous? When is it disadvantageous? Who receives the advantage or bears the disadvantage of leverage?

20. Name and describe two kinds of leases.

21. Which type of lease requires that a long-term debt and an asset be recorded at the inception of the lease?

22. Describe why provisions are recorded.

23. Describe how bond issue price is calculated.

MULTIPLE-CHOICE EXERCISES

9-1 Which of the following statements regarding bonds payable is true?
   a. When an issuing company's bonds are traded in the "secondary" market, the company will receive part of the proceeds when the bonds are sold from the first purchaser to the second purchaser.
   b. The entire principal amount of most bonds matures on a single date.
   c. Generally, bonds are issued in denominations of $100.
   d. A debenture bond is backed by specific assets of the issuing company.

9-2 Bonds are sold at a premium if the
   a. issuing company has a better reputation than other companies in the same business.
   b. market rate of interest was more than the stated rate at the time of issue.
   c. company will have to pay a premium to retire the bonds.
   d. market rate of interest was less than the stated rate at the time of issue.

9-3 If bonds are issued at 101.25, this means that
   a. a $1,000 bond sold for $101.25
   b. a $1,000 bond sold for $1,012.50
   c. the bonds sold at a discount
   d. the bond rate of interest is 10.125% of the market rate of interest

9-4 What best describes the discount on bonds payable account?
   a. A liability
   b. A contra liability
   c. An asset
   d. An expense

9-5 The premium on bonds payable account is shown on the statement of financial position as
   a. an addition to a long-term liability
   b. a subtraction from a long-term liability
   c. a contra asset
   d. a reduction of an expense

9-6 When bonds are issued by a company, the accounting entry typically shows an
   a. increase in assets and an increase in liabilities.
   b. increase in assets and an increase in shareholders' equity.
   c. increase in liabilities and an increase in shareholders' equity.
   d. increase in liabilities and a decrease in shareholders' equity.

9-7 Bower Company sold $100,000 of 20-year bonds for $95,000. The stated rate on the bonds was 7%, and interest is paid annually on December 31. What entry would be made on December 31 when the interest is paid? (Numbers are omitted.)
   a. Interest Expense
      Cash

(Continued)

b. Interest Expense
   Bonds Payable
   Cash
c. Interest Expense
   Discount on Bonds Payable
   Cash
d. Interest Expense
   Discount on Bonds Payable
   Cash

9-8 Bonds in the amount of $100,000 with a life of 10 years were issued by Roundy Company. If the stated rate is 6% and interest is paid semiannually, what will be the total amount of interest paid over the life of the bonds?
a. $6,000
b. $30,000
c. $60,000
d. $120,000

9-9 Sean Corp. issued a $40,000, 10-year bond, with a stated rate of 8%, paid semiannually. How much cash will the bond investors receive at the end of the first interest period?
a. $4,000
b. $3,200
c. $1,600
d. $800

9-10 When bonds are issued at a discount, the interest expense for the period is
a. the amount of interest payment for the period plus the premium amortization for the period.
b. the amount of interest payment for the period minus the premium amortization for the period.
c. the amount of interest payment for the period minus the discount amortization for the period.
d. the amount of interest payment for the period plus the discount amortization for the period.

9-11 When bonds are issued at a premium, the interest expense for the period is
a. the amount of interest payment for the period plus the premium amortization for the period.
b. the amount of interest payment for the period minus the premium amortization for the period.
c. the amount of interest payment for the period minus the discount amortization for the period.

d. the amount of interest payment for the period plus the discount amortization for the period.

9-12 Installment bonds differ from typical bonds in what way?
a. Essentially they are the same.
b. Installment bonds do not have a stated rate.
c. A portion of each installment bond payment pays down the principal balance.
d. The entire principal balance is paid off at maturity for installment bonds.

9-13 In 2018, Dvorak Company issued $200,000 of bonds for $189,640. If the stated rate of interest was 6% and the yield was 6.73%, how would Dvorak calculate the interest expense for the first year on the bonds using the effective interest method?
a. $189,640 × 6.73%
b. $189,640 × 6%
c. $200,000 × 6.73%
d. $200,000 × 6%

9-14 The result of using the effective interest rate method of amortization of the discount on bonds is that
a. a constant interest rate is charged against the debt carrying value.
b. the amount of interest expense decreases each period.
c. the interest expense for each amortization period is constant.
d. the cash interest payment is greater than the interest expense.

9-15 Serenity Company issued $100,000 of 6%, 10-year bonds when the market rate of interest was 5%. The proceeds from this bond issue were $107,732. Using the effective interest rate method of amortization, which of the following statements is true? Assume that interest is paid annually.
a. Interest payments to bondholders each period will be $6,464.
b. Interest payments to bondholders each period will be $5,000.
c. Amortization of the premium for the first interest period will be $613.
d. Amortization of the premium for the first interest period will be $1,464.

9-16 Bonds are a popular source of financing because
a. a company having cash flow problems can postpone payment of interest to bondholders.
b. bond interest expense is deductible for tax purposes, while dividends paid on shares are not.
c. financial analysts tend to downgrade a company that has raised large amounts of cash by frequent issues of shares.
d. the bondholders can always convert their bonds into shares if they choose.

9-17 Which of the following statements regarding leases is false?
a. Lease agreements are a popular form of financing the purchase of assets because leases do not require a large initial outlay of cash.
b. Accounting recognizes two types of leases—operating and finance leases.
c. If a lease is classified as a finance lease, the lessee records a lease liability on its statement of financial position.
d. If a lease is classified as an operating lease, the lessee records a lease liability on its statement of financial position.

9-18 Which of the following lease conditions would result in a finance lease to the lessee?
a. The lessee can purchase the property for $1 at the end of the lease term.
b. The lease term is 70% of the property's economic life.
c. The fair market value of the property at the inception of the lease is $18,000; the present value of the minimum lease payments is $16,000.
d. The lessee will return the property to the lessor at the end of the lease term.

9-19 On January 2, 2018, Sylvester Metals Co. leased a mining machine from EDH Leasing Corp. The lease qualifies as an operating lease. The annual payments are $4,000 paid at the end of each year, and the life of the lease is 10 years. What entry would Sylvester make when the machine is delivered by EDH?
a. Leased Assets   40,000
      Lease Liability   40,000

b. Prepaid Rent   40,000
      Lease Liability   40,000

c. Prepaid Rent   4,000
      Lease Liability   4,000

d. No entry is necessary.

9-20 Willow Corporation's statement of financial position showed the following amounts: current liabilities, $5,000; bonds payable, $1,500; lease obligations, $2,300. Total shareholders' equity was $6,000. The total debt to total equity ratio is
a. 0.63
b. 0.83
c. 1.42
d. 1.47

9-21 Kinsella Corporation's statement of financial position showed the following amounts: current liabilities, $75,000; total liabilities, $100,000; total assets, $200,000. What is the total long-term debt to total equity ratio?
a. 0.125
b. 0.25
c. 0.375
d. 0.75

9-22 McLaughlin Corporation's statement of financial position showed the following amounts: current liabilities, $75,000; total liabilities, $100,000; total assets, $200,000. What is the total debt to total assets ratio?
a. 0.50
b. 0.875
c. 1
d. 2

9-23 The bond issue price is determined by calculating the
a. present value of the stream of interest payments and the future value of the maturity amount.
b. future value of the stream of interest payments and the future value of the maturity amount.
c. future value of the stream of interest payments and the present value of the maturity amount.
d. present value of the stream of interest payments and the present value of the maturity amount.

CORNERSTONE EXERCISES

OBJECTIVE **1** **2**
CORNERSTONE 9.1

Cornerstone Exercise 9-24   Reporting Long-Term Debt on the Statement of Financial Position

Twan Corp. has the following bonds:

a. $1,000,000 in bonds that have $30,000 of unamortized discount associated with them.
b. $2,500,000 in bonds that have $75,000 of unamortized premium associated with them.

Required:

Prepare the statement of financial position presentation for these two bonds.

OBJECTIVE **2**
CORNERSTONE 9.1

Cornerstone Exercise 9-25   Issuance of Bonds

Anne Corp. issued $600,000, 5% bonds.

Required:

Prepare the necessary journal entries to record the issuance of these bonds, assuming the bonds were issued (a) at face value, (b) at 102, and (c) at 92.

OBJECTIVE **2**
CORNERSTONE 9.1

Cornerstone Exercise 9-26   Issuance of Bonds

EWO Enterprises issues $4,500,000 of bonds payable.

Required:

Prepare the necessary journal entries to record the issuance of the bonds, assuming the bonds were issued (a) at face value, (b) at 104.5, and (c) at 99.

OBJECTIVE **2**
CORNERSTONE 9.1

Cornerstone Exercise 9-27   Issuance of Bonds

M. Nicolae Company issued $700,000 of bonds for $684,780. Interest is paid semiannually.

Required:

1.   Prepare the necessary journal entry to record the issuance of the bonds.
2.   Is the yield greater or less than the stated rate? How do you know?

OBJECTIVE **2**
CORNERSTONE 9.2

Cornerstone Exercise 9-28   Debt Issued at Face Value

On December 31, 2018, Brock & Co. issued $800,000 of bonds payable at face value. The bonds have a 7% stated rate, pay interest on June 30 and December 31, and mature on December 31, 2019.

Required:

Prepare the journal entry to record the interest payment on June 30, 2019.

OBJECTIVE **3**
CORNERSTONE 9.3

Cornerstone Exercise 9-29   Bonds Issued at a Discount (Effective Interest)

Sicily Corporation issued $500,000 in 6% bonds (payable on December 31, 2028) on December 31, 2018, for $402,440. Interest is paid on June 30 and December 31. The market rate of interest is 9%.

Required:

Prepare the amortization table using the effective interest rate method. (*Note:* Round to the nearest dollar.)

OBJECTIVE **3**
CORNERSTONE 9.3

Cornerstone Exercise 9-30   Bonds Issued at a Discount (Effective Interest)

Refer to the information in Exercise 9-29.

Required:

Prepare the journal entries for December 31, 2020 and 2021.

Cornerstone Exercise 9-31   Bonds Issued at a Discount (Effective Interest)

Crafty Corporation issued $475,000 of 5%, seven-year bonds on December 31, 2018, for $448,484. Interest is paid annually on December 31. The market rate of interest is 6%.

OBJECTIVE ❸
CORNERSTONE 9.3

Required:

Prepare the amortization table using the effective interest rate method. (*Note:* Round to the nearest dollar.)

Cornerstone Exercise 9-32   Bonds Issued at a Discount (Effective Interest)

Refer to the information in Exercise 9-31.

OBJECTIVE ❸
CORNERSTONE 9.3

Required:

Prepare the journal entries for December 31, 2019 and 2020.

Cornerstone Exercise 9-33   Bonds Issued at a Premium (Effective Interest)

Cookie Dough Corporation issued $850,000 in 9%, 10-year bonds (payable on December 31, 2028) on December 31, 2018, for $907,759. Interest is paid on June 30 and December 31. The market rate of interest is 8%.

OBJECTIVE ❸
CORNERSTONE 9.4

Required:

Prepare the amortization table using the effective interest rate method. (*Note:* Round to the nearest dollar.)

Cornerstone Exercise 9-34   Bonds Issued at a Premium (Effective Interest)

Refer to the information in Exercise 9-33.

OBJECTIVE ❸
CORNERSTONE 9.4

Required:

Prepare the journal entries for December 31, 2020 and 2021.

Cornerstone Exercise 9-35   Bonds Issued at a Premium (Effective Interest)

Charger Battery issued $100,000 of 11%, seven-year bonds on December 31, 2018, for $104,868. Interest is paid annually on December 31. The market rate of interest is 10%.

OBJECTIVE ❸
CORNERSTONE 9.4

Required:

Prepare the amortization table using the effective interest rate method. (*Note:* Round to the nearest dollar.)

Cornerstone Exercise 9-36   Bonds Issued at a Premium (Effective Interest)

Refer to the information in Exercise 9-35.

OBJECTIVE ❸
CORNERSTONE 9.4

Required:

Prepare the journal entries for December 31, 2020 and 2021.

Cornerstone Exercise 9-37   Debt Issued at a Discount (Straight Line)

On December 31, 2018, Dubois Company issued $350,000, five-year bonds for $320,000. The stated rate of interest was 7% and interest is paid annually on December 31.

OBJECTIVE ❹
CORNERSTONE 9.5

(Continued)

Required:

Prepare the necessary journal entry on December 31, 2020, assuming the straight-line method is followed.

OBJECTIVE 4
CORNERSTONE 9.5

Cornerstone Exercise 9-38   Debt Issued at a Discount (Straight Line)

Refer to the information in Exercise 9-37.

Required:

Prepare the amortization table for Dubois Company's bonds.

OBJECTIVE 4
CORNERSTONE 9.6

Cornerstone Exercise 9-39   Debt Issued at a Premium (Straight Line)

On December 31, 2018, Ironman Steel issued $800,000, eight-year bonds for $880,000. The stated rate of interest was 6% and interest is paid annually on December 31.

Required:

Prepare the necessary journal entry on December 31, 2022, assuming the straight-line method is followed.

OBJECTIVE 4
CORNERSTONE 9.6

Cornerstone Exercise 9-40   Debt Issued at a Premium (Straight Line)

Refer to the information in Exercise 9-39.

Required:

Prepare the amortization table for Ironman Steel's bonds.

OBJECTIVE 7
CORNERSTONE 9.7

Cornerstone Exercise 9-41   Ratio Analysis

Waleed Corporation's statement of financial position showed the following amounts: current liabilities, $70,000; bonds payable, $150,000; and lease obligations, $20,000. Total shareholders' equity was $90,000.

Required:

Calculate the total debt to total equity ratio. (*Note:* Round answer to three decimal places.)

OBJECTIVE 7
CORNERSTONE 9.7

Cornerstone Exercise 9-42   Ratio Analysis

Blue Corporation has $2,000,000 in total liabilities and $3,500,000 in total assets.

Required:

Calculate Blue's total debt to total equity ratio. (*Note:* Round answer to three decimal places.)

OBJECTIVE 7
CORNERSTONE 9.7

Cornerstone Exercise 9-43   Ratio Analysis

Red Corporation had $2,000,000 in total liabilities and $3,500,000 in total assets as of December 31, 2018. Of Red's total liabilities, $350,000 is long-term.

Required:

Calculate Red's total debt to total assets ratio and its total long-term debt to total equity ratio. (*Note:* Round answers to four decimal places.)

OBJECTIVE 9
CORNERSTONE 9.8

Cornerstone Exercise 9-44   Bond Issue Price

On December 31, 2018, Goa Hot Rods issued $2,000,000 of 6%, 10-year bonds. Interest is payable semiannually on June 30 and December 31.

Required:

What is the issue price if the bonds are sold to yield 8%? (*Note:* Round to the nearest dollar.)

Cornerstone Exercise 9-45   Bond Issue Price

On December 31, 2018, Callahan Auto issued $1,500,000 of 8%, 10-year bonds. Interest is payable semiannually on June 30 and December 31.

OBJECTIVE ⑨
CORNERSTONE 9.8

Required:

What is the issue price if the bonds are sold to yield 6%? (*Note:* Round to the nearest dollar.)

BRIEF EXERCISES

Brief Exercise 9-46   Reporting Long-Term Debt on the Statement of Financial Position

OBJECTIVE ① ②

Scott Corp. provides contracted home staging services to real estate agencies and their clients. Scott issued the following bonds in the current year:

a.   1,500 bonds with $1,000 face value, which the market has valued at $45,000 below its face value
b.   2,700 bonds with $1,000 face value, which the market has valued at $85,000 above its face value

Required:

Prepare the statement of financial position presentation for these two bonds. Assume the bonds are issued at the end of the year.

Brief Exercise 9-47   Issuance of Bonds

OBJECTIVE ②

Natalie Corp. provides medical supplies to hospitals located in western Washington and Oregon. This year, Natalie Corp. issued 8,000 bonds with a $1,000 face value. The nominal rate for each bond is 7%.

Required:

Prepare the necessary journal entries to record the issuance of these bonds, assuming the bonds were issued (a) at face value, (b) at 103, and (c) at 96.

Brief Exercise 9-48   Issuance of Bonds

OBJECTIVE ②

APL Enterprises required an infusion of cash in order to purchase a large piece of equipment. To finance its equipment purchase, APL issued $3,600,000 of 8% bonds payable.

Required:

Prepare the necessary journal entries to record the issuance of the bonds, assuming the bonds were issued (a) at face value, (b) at 102, and (c) at 97.

Brief Exercise 9-49   Issuance of Bonds

OBJECTIVE ②

H. Simpson Company is an entertainment company located in Springfield, Illinois. H. Simpson recently issued $200,000 of bonds to finance large expenditures for an upcoming television production. H. Simpson received cash of $194,620 upon the issuance of the bonds and plans to pay interest semiannually.

Required:

1.   Prepare the necessary journal entry to record the issuance of the bonds.
2.   Is the stated rate greater or less than the yield? How do you know?

OBJECTIVE **2** **Brief Exercise 9-50   Bonds Issued at Face Value**

On December 31, 2017, Desmond & Co. issued 5,000 bonds with a $1,000 par value at 100. The bonds have an 8% stated rate, pay interest on June 30 and December 31, and mature on December 31, 2018.

Required:

Prepare the journal entries to record the interest payment on June 30, 2018.

OBJECTIVE **4** **Brief Exercise 9-51   Bonds Issued at a Discount (Straight Line)**

On December 31, 2017, Mayor Company issued 40,000 five-year bonds with a $1,000 par value each. The market values the bonds at $30,000 less than the face value of the bonds. The stated rate of interest is 6%, and interest is paid annually on December 31.

Required:

Prepare the necessary journal entry on December 31, 2018, assuming the straight-line method is followed.

OBJECTIVE **4** **Brief Exercise 9-52   Bonds Issued at a Discount (Straight Line)**

Use the information from Brief Exercise 9-51.

Required:

Prepare the amortization table for Mayor Company's bonds.

OBJECTIVE **4** **Brief Exercise 9-53   Bonds Issued at a Premium (Straight Line)**

On December 31, 2017, Solomon Crafts issued 60,000 eight-year bonds with $1,000 face value. External markets value the bonds at $630,000 more than face value. The stated rate of interest on Solomon's bonds is 5%, and interest is paid annually on December 31.

Required:

Prepare the necessary journal entry on December 31, 2019, assuming the straight-line method is followed.

OBJECTIVE **4** **Brief Exercise 9-54   Bonds Issued at a Premium (Straight Line)**

Use the information from Brief Exercise 9-53.

Required:

Prepare the amortization table for Solomon's bonds.

Use the following information for Brief Exercises 9-55 and 9-56:
Roman Corporation decided to issue long-term debt in order to pay off its short-term obligations. On December 31, 2018, Roman issued $900,000 in 7% bonds (payable on December 31, 2028) at 87. Interest is paid on June 30 and December 31. The market rate of interest is 9%.

OBJECTIVE **3** **Brief Exercise 9-55   Bonds Issued at a Discount (Effective Interest)**

Refer to the information for Roman Corporation above.

Required:

Prepare the amortization table through December 31, 2020, using the effective interest rate method.

OBJECTIVE **3** **Brief Exercise 9-56   Bonds Issued at a Discount (Effective Interest)**

Refer to the information for Roman Corporation above.

Required:

Prepare the journal entries for December 31, 2019 and 2020.

> *Use the following information for Brief Exercises 9-57 and 9-58:*
> Crafty Corporation received $472,088 of cash upon issuance of 500 $1,000 par value bonds. Each bond has a stated rate of 5% and will mature on December 31, 2024, seven years after the issuance of the bonds. Interest is paid annually on December 31. The market rate of interest is 6%.

Brief Exercise 9-57   Bonds Issued at a Discount (Effective Interest)   OBJECTIVE **3**

Refer to the information for Crafty Corporation above.

Required:

Prepare the amortization table using the effective interest rate method.

Brief Exercise 9-58   Bonds Issued at a Discount (Effective Interest)   OBJECTIVE **3**

Refer to the information for Crafty Corporation above.

Required:

Prepare the journal entry for December 31, 2020 and 2021.

> *Use the following information for Brief Exercises 9-59 and 9-60:*
> Haley Industries issued $120,000 of 11%, seven-year bonds on December 31, 2017, with a $5,842 premium. Interest is paid annually on December 31. The market rate of interest is 10%.

Brief Exercise 9-59   Bonds Issued at a Premium (Effective Interest)   OBJECTIVE **3**

Refer to the information for Haley Industries above.

Required:

Prepare the amortization table using the effective interest rate method.

Brief Exercise 9-60   Bonds Issued at a Premium (Effective Interest)   OBJECTIVE **3**

Refer to the information for Haley Industries above.

Required:

Record the journal entries for December 31, 2019 and 2020.

Brief Exercise 9-61   Cost of Debt Financing   OBJECTIVE **5**

Topple Corporation leases skyscrapers in cities throughout the world to large corporations. Topple's cost of debt financing is 9%, its cost of equity is 12%, and its tax rate is 35%.

Required:

Calculate the after-tax interest rate to two decimal places.

Brief Exercise 9-62   Cost of Debt Financing   OBJECTIVE **5**

Crackle Company instituted an aggressive plan to lower its cost of financing over the next decade. Currently, Crackle's cost of debt financing is 8%, its cost of equity financing is 14%, and its tax rate is 35%. Crackle currently has $2,500,000 of debt.

(Continued)

Required:

1. Calculate the after-tax cost amount of interest expense.
2. How does the tax effect of interest expense affect financial leverage?

OBJECTIVE 6   **Brief Exercise 9-63   Leases**

Overland Airlines leased an aircraft from JRL Aircraft Company. Overland believes it may have been able to purchase an aircraft at a cost lower than the cost of leasing the aircraft; however, Overland does not want the obligation of including an aircraft as an asset in its financial statements. The annual payments of the lease are $1,250,000, and the life of the lease is 15 years. It is estimated that the useful life of the aircraft is 18 years. The present value of the future lease payments is $9,235,730.

Required:

CONCEPTUAL CONNECTION Would Overland Aircraft record the lease as an operating or finance lease? Why?

OBJECTIVE 7   **Brief Exercise 9-64   Ratio Analysis**

Whitten Corporation's statement of earnings shows the following amounts: current assets, $200,000; current liabilities, $80,000; bonds payable, $155,000; and lease obligations, $25,000. Total stockholders' equity is $120,000.

Required:

Calculate the debt to equity ratio. (*Note:* Round to two decimal places.)

OBJECTIVE 7   **Brief Exercise 9-65   Ratio Analysis**

Valiant Corporation has $1,800,000 in total liabilities, $800,000 of which are current. Valiant has $400,000 of cash and cash equivalents; $300,000 of other current assets; and $2,000,000 in property, plant, and equipment.

Required:

Calculate Valiant's debt to equity ratio.

OBJECTIVE 7   **Brief Exercise 9-66   Ratio Analysis**

Trevor Corporation had $2,900,000 in total liabilities and $4,300,000 in total assets as of December 31, 2017. Trevor calculates that 40% of assets are designated as current, while $500,000 of Trevor's total liabilities are long-term.

Required:

Calculate Trevor's debt to assets ratio and its long-term debt to equity ratio. (*Note:* Round to two decimal places.)

OBJECTIVE 9   **Brief Exercise 9-67   Bond Issue Price**

On December 31, 2017, Ruby Inc. issued 3,000 $1,000 face value bonds with a stated rate of 6% and a 10-year maturity. Interest is payable semiannually on June 30 and December 31.

Required:

What is the issue price if the bonds are sold to yield 8%? (*Note:* Round to the nearest dollar.)

OBJECTIVE 9   **Brief Exercise 9-68   Bond Issue Price**

On December 31, 2017, Nelson Construction issued 3,500 of $1,000 face value bonds with a stated rate of 8%, maturing in 10 years. Interest is payable semiannually on June 30 and December 31.

Required:

What is the issue price if the bonds are sold to yield 6%? (*Note:* Round to the nearest dollar.)

EXERCISES

Exercise 9-69   Issuing at Face Value, a Premium, or a Discount

OBJECTIVE ❶ ❷

Kartel Company is planning to issue 2,000 bonds, each having a face amount of $1,000.

Required:

1. Prepare the journal entry to record the sale of the bonds at face value.
2. Prepare the journal entry to record the sale of the bonds at a premium of $34,000.
3. Prepare the journal entry to record the sale of the bonds at a discount of $41,000.
4. **CONCEPTUAL CONNECTION** In which of the previous three scenarios is the market rate of interest (yield) highest? How do you know?

Exercise 9-70   Bond Premium and Discount

OBJECTIVE ❶ ❷

Moscow Ltd. is contemplating selling bonds. The issue is to be composed of 750 bonds, each with a face amount of $1,000.

Required:

1. Calculate how much Moscow is able to borrow if each bond is sold at a premium of $30.
2. Calculate how much Moscow is able to borrow if each bond is sold at a discount of $10.
3. Calculate how much Moscow is able to borrow if each bond is sold at 92% of face value.
4. Calculate how much Moscow is able to borrow if each bond is sold at 103% of face value.
5. Assume that the bonds are sold for $975 each. Prepare the entry to recognize the sale of the 750 bonds.
6. Assume that the bonds are sold for $1,015 each. Prepare the entry to recognize the sale of the 750 bonds.

Exercise 9-71   Bonds with Annual Interest Payments

OBJECTIVE ❷

Kiwi Corporation issued at face value $350,000 9% bonds on December 31, 2018. Interest is paid annually on December 31. The principal and the final interest payment are due on December 31, 2020.

Required:

1. Prepare the entry to recognize the issuance of the bonds.
2. Prepare the journal entry for December 31, 2019.
3. Prepare the journal entry to record repayment of the principal on December 31, 2020.
4. **CONCEPTUAL CONNECTION** How would the interest expense for 2019 change if the bonds had been issued at a premium?

Exercise 9-72   Issuance and Interest Amortization for Zero Coupon Note (Straight Line)

OBJECTIVE ❷ ❹

Kerala Company borrowed $10,000 on a two-year, zero coupon note. The note was issued on December 31, 2018. The face amount of the note, $12,544, is to be paid at maturity on December 31, 2020. This company uses the straight line method of amortization.

Required:

1. Allocate the interest of $2,544 to the two one-year interest periods, using straight-line interest amortization.
2. Prepare the entries to recognize the borrowing, the first year's interest expense, and the second year's interest expense plus redemption of the note at maturity.

OBJECTIVE ② ④

Exercise 9-73   Interest Payments and Interest Expense for Bonds (Straight Line)

Robson Manufacturing sold 20-year bonds with a total face amount of $1,000,000 and a stated rate of 7.5%. The bonds sold for $1,080,000 on December 31, 2018, and pay interest semiannually on June 30 and December 31. Robson Manufacturing uses the straight-line method of amortization.

Required:

1. Prepare the entry to recognize the sale of the bonds.
2. Determine the amount of the semiannual interest payment required by the bonds.
3. Prepare the journal entry made by Robson at June 30, 2019, to recognize the interest expense and an interest payment, using straight line interest amortization.
4. Determine the amount of interest expense for 2019.
5. **CONCEPTUAL CONNECTION** If Robson issued bonds with a variable interest rate, would you expect the rate to increase, decrease, or stay the same? Why?
6. **CONCEPTUAL CONNECTION** What should Robson consider in deciding whether to use a fixed or variable rate?

YOUDECIDE

OBJECTIVE ③

Exercise 9-74   Note Interest Payment and Interest Expense (Effective Interest Rate)

Cardinal Company sold $600,000 of 15-year, 6% notes for $544,824. The notes were sold on December 31, 2018, and pay interest semiannually on June 30 and December 31. The effective interest rate was 7%. Assume that Cardinal uses the effective interest rate method.

Required:

1. Prepare the entry to record the sale of the notes.
2. Determine the amount of the semiannual interest payments for the notes.
3. Prepare the amortization table through 2020. (*Note:* Round to the nearest dollar.)
4. Prepare the entry for Cardinal's journal at June 30, 2019, to record the payment of six months' interest and the related interest expense.
5. Determine interest expense for 2020.

OBJECTIVE ③

Exercise 9-75   Bond Interest Payments and Interest Expense (Effective Interest Rate)

On December 31, 2018, Huang Corporation issued for $155,989 five-year bonds with a face amount of $150,000 and a stated (or coupon) rate of 9%. The bonds pay interest annually and have an effective interest rate of 8%. Assume that Huang uses the effective interest rate method.

Required:

1. Prepare the entry to record the sale of the bonds.
2. Calculate the amount of the interest payments for the bonds.
3. Prepare the amortization table through 2020. (*Note:* Round to the nearest dollar.)
4. Prepare the journal entry for December 31, 2019, to record the payment of interest and the related interest expense.
5. Calculate the annual interest expense for 2019 and 2020.

OBJECTIVE ③

Exercise 9-76   Completing a Bond Amortization Table (Effective Interest Rate)

Cagney Company sold $200,000 of bonds on June 30, 2018. A portion of the amortization table appears below.

Period	Cash Payment (Credit)	Interest Expense (Debit)	Discount on Bonds Payable (Credit)	Discount on Bonds Payable Balance (Debit)	Bond Payable Carrying Value (Credit)
12/31/19	$9,000	$9,277	$277	$2,340	$197,660
06/30/20	9,000	9,290	290	2,050	197,950
12/31/20	?	?	?	?	?

Required:

1. Indicate the stated interest rate on these bonds.
2. Calculate the effective annual interest rate on these bonds. (*Note:* Round to the nearest 0.1%.)
3. Determine the interest expense and discount amortization for the interest period ending December 31, 2020. (*Note:* Round to the nearest dollar.)
4. Determine the liability balance after the interest payment is recorded on December 31, 2020.

Exercise 9-77   Completing a Bond Amortization Table (Effective Interest Rate)

OBJECTIVE **3**

MacBride Enterprises sold $200,000 of bonds on December 31, 2018. A portion of the amortization table appears below.

Period	Cash Payment (Credit)	Interest Expense (Debit)	Premium on Bonds Payable (Debit)	Premium on Bonds Payable Balance (Credit)	Bond Payable Carrying Value (Credit)
At issue				$6,457	$206,457
06/30/19	$9,000	$8,465	$535	5,922	205,922
12/31/19	9,000	8,443	557	5,365	205,365
06/30/20	9,000	8,420	580	4,785	204,785
12/31/20	?	?	?	?	?

Required:

1. Indicate the stated annual interest rate on these bonds.
2. Calculate the effective annual interest rate on these bonds. (*Note:* Round to the nearest 0.1%.)
3. Determine the interest expense and premium amortization for the interest period ending December 31, 2020. (*Note:* Round to the nearest dollar.)
4. Determine the year in which the bonds will be repaid in full based on the above terms.

Exercise 9-78   Installment Notes

OBJECTIVE **4**

Thornwood Lanes bought a service vehicle for $25,000 by issuing a 6% installment note on December 31, 2018. Thornwood will make 12 monthly payments of $2,151.66 at the end of each month.

Required:

Prepare the amortization table using the effective interest rate method. (*Note:* Round to the nearest cent.)

Exercise 9-79   Installment Notes

OBJECTIVE **4**

Refer to the information in Exercise 9-78.

Required:

Prepare the journal entries for the end of March and the end of April.

Exercise 9-80   Installment Notes

OBJECTIVE **4**

ABC Bank loans $250,000 to Yossarian to purchase a new home. Yossarian will repay the note in equal monthly payments over a period of 30 years. The interest rate is 12%.

Required:

If the monthly payment is $2,571.53, how much of the first payment is interest expense and how much is principal repayment? (*Note:* Round to the nearest cent.)

Exercise 9-81   Interest Payments and Interest Expense for Bonds (Straight Line)

OBJECTIVE **2** **4**

On December 31, 2018, Harrington Corporation sold $425,000 of 15-year, 11% bonds. The bonds sold for $395,000 and pay interest semiannually on June 30 and December 31. The company uses the straight-line method of amortization.

(Continued)

Required:

1. Prepare the journal entry to record the sale of the bonds.
2. Calculate the amount of the semiannual interest payment.
3. Prepare the entry at June 30, 2019, to recognize the payment of interest and interest expense.
4. Calculate the annual interest expense for 2019.

OBJECTIVE **4**

Exercise 9-82   Interest Payments and Interest Expense for Bonds (Straight Line)

On December 31, 2018, Perlman Corporation issued bonds with a total face amount of $1,000,000 and a stated rate of 7%.

Required:

1. Calculate the interest expense for 2019 if the bonds were sold at face value.
2. Calculate the interest expense for 2019 if the bonds were sold at a premium and the straight-line premium amortization for 2019 is $8,000.
3. Calculate the interest expense for 2019 if the bonds were sold at a discount and the straight-line discount amortization for 2019 is $6,000.

OBJECTIVE **4**

Exercise 9-83   Completing a Debt Amortization Table (Straight Line)

ILLUSTRATING RELATIONSHIPS

Chekhov Company sold $200,000 of bonds on December 31, 2018. A portion of the amortization table appears below.

Period	Cash Payment (Credit)	Interest Expense (Debit)	Discount on Bonds Payable (Credit)	Discount on Bonds Payable Balance (Debit)	Bond Payable Carrying Value (Credit)
At issue				$8,000	$192,000
06/30/19	$12,000	$12,800	$800	7,200	192,800
12/31/19	12,000	12,800	800	6,400	193,600
06/30/20	?	?	?	?	?

Required:

1. Determine the stated interest rate on these bonds.
2. Calculate the interest expense and the discount amortization for the interest period ending June 30, 2020.
3. Calculate the liability balance shown on a statement of financial position after the interest payment is recorded on June 30, 2020.

OBJECTIVE **4**

Exercise 9-84   Using a Premium Amortization Table (Straight Line)

For Dingle Corporation, the following amortization table was prepared when $400,000 of five-year, 7% bonds were sold on December 31, 2018, for $420,000.

Period	Cash Payment (Credit)	Interest Expense (Debit)	Premium on Bonds Payable (Debit)	Premium on Bonds Payable Balance (Credit)	Bond Payable Carrying Value (Credit)
At issue				$20,000	$420,000
06/30/19	$14,000	$12,000	$2,000	18,000	418,000
12/31/19	14,000	12,000	2,000	16,000	416,000
06/30/20	14,000	12,000	2,000	14,000	414,000
12/31/20	14,000	12,000	2,000	12,000	412,000
06/30/21	14,000	12,000	2,000	10,000	410,000
12/31/21	14,000	12,000	2,000	8,000	408,000
06/30/22	14,000	12,000	2,000	6,000	406,000
12/31/22	14,000	12,000	2,000	4,000	404,000
06/30/23	14,000	12,000	2,000	2,000	402,000
12/31/23	14,000	12,000	2,000	0	400,000

Required:

1. Prepare the entry to recognize the issuance of the bonds on December 31, 2018.
2. Prepare the entry to recognize the first interest payment on June 30, 2019.
3. Determine what interest expense for this bond issue Dingle will report in its 2020 statement of comprehensive income.
4. Indicate how these bonds will appear in Dingle's December 31, 2020, statement of financial position.

Exercise 9-85 Using a Discount Amortization Table (Straight Line)

OBJECTIVE 4

Panamint Candy Company prepared the following amortization table for $300,000 of five-year, 9% bonds issued and sold by Panamint on December 31, 2018, for $285,000:

Period	Cash Payment (Credit)	Interest Expense (Debit)	Discount on Bonds Payable (Credit)	Discount on Bonds Payable Balance (Debit)	Bond Payable Carrying Value (Credit)
				$15,000	$285,000
06/30/19	$13,500	$15,000	$1,500	13,500	286,500
12/31/19	13,500	15,000	1,500	12,000	288,000
06/30/20	13,500	15,000	1,500	10,500	289,500
12/31/20	13,500	15,000	1,500	9,000	291,000
06/30/21	13,500	15,000	1,500	7,500	292,500
12/31/21	13,500	15,000	1,500	6,000	294,000
06/30/22	13,500	15,000	1,500	4,500	295,500
12/31/22	13,500	15,000	1,500	3,000	297,000
06/30/23	13,500	15,000	1,500	1,500	298,500
12/31/23	13,500	15,000	1,500	0	300,000

Required:

1. Prepare the entry to recognize the sale of the bonds on December 31, 2018.
2. Prepare the entry to recognize the first interest payment on June 30, 2019.
3. Determine the interest expense for these bonds that Panamint will report on its 2021 statement of comprehensive income.
4. Indicate how these bonds will appear in Panamint's December 31, 2022, statement of financial position.

Exercise 9-86 Completing an Amortization Table (Straight Line)

OBJECTIVE 4

Sondrini Corporation sold $1,500,000 face value of bonds at 103 on December 31, 2018. These bonds have an 8% stated rate and mature in four years. Interest is payable on June 30 and December 31 of each year.

Required:

1. Prepare a bond amortization table assuming straight-line amortization.
2. Prepare the journal entry for December 31, 2020.
3. Indicate how these bonds will appear in Sondrini's statement of financial position at December 31, 2020.

Exercise 9-87 Zero Coupon Bond (Straight Line)

OBJECTIVE 4

Johnson Company sold for $90,000 a $102,400, two-year zero coupon bond on December 31, 2018. The bond matures on December 31, 2020.

Required:

1. Prepare the entry to record the issuance of the bond.
2. Prepare the adjustment to recognize 2019 interest expense.
3. Prepare the entry to recognize the 2020 interest expense and the repayment of the bond on December 31, 2020.

OBJECTIVE ❹   **Exercise 9-88   Zero Coupon Note (Straight Line)**

Labrador City Products borrowed $100,000 cash by issuing a 36-month, $120,880 zero coupon note on December 31, 2018. The note matures on December 31, 2021.

Required:

1. Prepare the entry to recognize issuance of the note.
2. Prepare the adjustments to recognize 2019 and 2020 interest.
3. Prepare the entry to recognize 2021 interest and repayment of the note at maturity.

OBJECTIVE ❹   **Exercise 9-89   Non-interest Bearing Bonds (Straight Line)**

Dean Plumbing issues $1,000,000 face value, non-interest bearing bonds on December 31, 2018. The bonds are issued at 65 and mature on December 31, 2022.

Required:

Assuming the straight-line amortization method is followed, prepare the journal entry on December 31, 2021.

OBJECTIVE ❺   **Exercise 9-90   Cost of Debt Financing**

Luis Corporation's cost of debt financing is 7%. Its tax rate is 35%.

Required:

Calculate the after-tax interest rate.

OBJECTIVE ❺   **Exercise 9-91   Cost of Debt Financing**

Diamond Company's cost of debt financing is 10%. Its tax rate is 35%. Diamond has $3,000,000 of debt.

Required:

1. Calculate the after-tax cost amount of interest expense.
2. **CONCEPTUAL CONNECTION** How does the tax effect of interest expense affect financial leverage?

OBJECTIVE ❻   **Exercise 9-92   Leases**

Fort Smith Airlines has leased an aircraft from BAL Aircraft Company. The annual payments are $1,000,000, and the life of the lease is 19 years. It is estimated that the useful life of the aircraft is 20 years. The present value of the future lease payments is $8,755,630.

Required:

CONCEPTUAL CONNECTION Would Fort Smith Airlines record the lease as an operating or finance lease? Why?

OBJECTIVE ❼   **Exercise 9-93   Ratio Analysis**

Rising Stars Academy provided the following information on its 2018 financial statements:

Long-term debt	$ 4,400	Interest expense	$ 398
Total liabilities	8,972	Net income	559
Total assets	38,775	Interest payments	432
Total equity	29,803	Cash flows from operations	1,015
Operating income	1,223	Income tax expense	266
		Income tax paid	150

Required:

1. Calculate the following ratios for Rising Stars: (a) total debt to total equity, (b) total debt to total assets, (c) total long-term debt to total equity, (d) times interest earned (accrual basis), and (e) times interest earned (cash basis). (*Note:* Round answers to three decimal places.)
2. **CONCEPTUAL CONNECTION** Interpret these results.

Exercise 9-94   Calculating Bond Issue Price

OBJECTIVE 9

On December 31, 2018, University Theatres issued $500,000 face value of bonds. The stated rate is 8%, and interest is paid semiannually on June 30 and December 31. The bonds mature in 15 years.

Required:

Calculate at what price the bonds are issued, assuming the market rate of interest is (a) 6% and (b) 10%.

PROBLEM SET A

Problem 9-95A   Reporting Long-Term Debt

OBJECTIVE  1 2

Fridley Manufacturing's accounting records reveal the following account balances after adjusting entries are made on December 31, 2018:

Accounts payable	$ 62,500	Interest payable	$ 38,700
Bonds payable (9.4%, due in 2025)	800,000	Installment note payable (8%, equal	
Lease liability*	41,500	installments due 2019 to 2022)	120,000
Bonds payable (8.7%, due in 2021)	50,000	Notes payable (7.8%, due in 2023)	400,000
Deferred tax liability*	133,400	Premium on notes payable (7.8%, due in	
Discount on bonds payable (9.4%,		2023)	6,100
due in 2025)	12,600	Note payable, 4% $50,000 face amount,	
Income tax payable	26,900	due in 2024 (net of discount)	31,900

*Long-term liability

Required:

Prepare the current liabilities and long-term debt portions of Fridley's statement of financial position at December 31, 2018. Provide a separate line item for each issue (do not combine separate bonds or notes payable), but some items may need to be split into more than one item.

Problem 9-96A   Entries for and Financial Statement Presentation of a Note

OBJECTIVE 2

Perez Company borrowed $100,000 from the National Bank on April 1, 2018, on a three-year, 7.8% note. Interest is paid annually on April 1.

Required:

1. Record the borrowing transaction in Perez's journal.
2. Prepare the adjusting entries made at December 31, 2018 and 2019.
3. Prepare the necessary journal entry to recognize the first interest payment on April 1, 2019.
4. Indicate how the note and associated interest would be presented on Perez's December 31, 2019, statement of financial position.
5. Prepare the necessary journal entries to record the repayment of the note and the last year's interest payment on April 1, 2021.

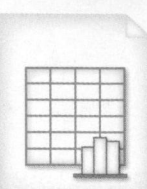

Problem 9-97A　Preparing a Bond Amortization Table (Straight Line)

On December 31, 2018, Distel Company borrowed $102,700 by issuing three-year, 9% bonds with a face amount of $100,000. Interest is paid annually on December 31. Distel uses the straight-line amortization method.

Required:

Prepare an amortization table using the following column headings:

Period	Cash Payment (Credit)	Interest Expense (Debit)	Premium on Bonds Payable (Debit)	Premium on Bonds Payable Balance (Credit)	Bond Payable Carrying Value (Credit)

Problem 9-98A　Note Computations and Entries (Straight Line)

On December 31, 2018, Sisek Company borrowed $800,000 with a 10-year, 9.75% note, interest payable semiannually on June 30 and December 31. Cash in the amount of $792,800 was received when the note was issued. Sisek Company uses the straight-line amortization method.

Required:

1. Prepare the necessary journal entry at December 31, 2018.
2. Prepare the necessary journal entry at June 30, 2019.
3. Prepare the necessary journal entry at December 31, 2019.
4. Determine the carrying amount of these notes at the end of the fifth year (December 31, 2023).

Problem 9-99A　Preparing a Bond Amortization Table (Straight Line)

Edmonton-Alston Corporation issued five-year, 9.5% bonds with a total face value of $700,000 on December 31, 2018, for $726,000. The bonds pay interest on June 30 and December 31 of each year. The company uses the straight-line method of amortization.

Required:

1. Prepare an amortization table (use straight line method).
2. Prepare the entries to recognize the interest payments made on June 30, 2019, and December 31, 2019.

Problem 9-100A　Preparing a Bond Amortization Table (Straight Line)

St. Cloud Manufacturing Inc. issued five-year, 9.2% bonds with a total face value of $500,000 on December 31, 2018, for $484,000. The bonds pay interest on June 30 and December 31 of each year.

Required:

1. Prepare an amortization table (use straight line method).
2. Prepare the entries to recognize the bond issuance and the interest payments made on June 30, 2019, and December 31, 2019.

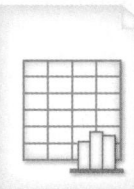

Problem 9-101A　Preparing and Using an Amortization Table (Straight Line)

Girves Development Corporation has agreed to construct a plant in a new industrial park. To finance the construction, the municipal government issued $5,000,000 of 10-year, 4.75% bonds for $5,125,000 on December 31, 2018. Girves will pay the interest and principal on the bonds. When the bonds are repaid, Girves will receive title to the plant. In the interim, Girves will pay property taxes as if it owned the plant. This financing arrangement is attractive to Girves, as municipal government bonds carry a low interest rate. The bonds are attractive to investors, as both Girves and the municipal government are issuers. The bonds pay interest semiannually on June 30 and December 31.

Required:

1. Prepare an amortization table through December 31, 2020, for these bonds, assuming straight-line amortization.
2. **CONCEPTUAL CONNECTION** Discuss whether or not Girves should record the plant as an asset after it is constructed.
3. **CONCEPTUAL CONNECTION** Discuss whether or not Girves should record the liability for these bonds.

Problem 9-102A   Non-interest Bearing Note (Straight Line)

OBJECTIVE 4

On December 31, 2018, Felix Products borrowed $80,000 cash on a $105,800, 24-month zero percent note. Felix uses the straight-line method of amortization.

Required:

1. Record the borrowing in Felix's journal.
2. Prepare the adjusting entry for December 31, 2019.
3. Prepare the entries to recognize the 2020 interest expense and repayment of the note on December 31, 2020.

Problem 9-103A   Preparing an Amortization Table for Non-interest Bearing Bonds (Straight Line)

OBJECTIVE 4

On December 31, 2018, Georgetown Distributors borrowed $2,180,000 by issuing four-year, zero coupon bonds. The face value of the bonds is $3,000,000. Georgetown uses the straight-line method to amortize any premium or discount.

Required:

Prepare an amortization table for these bonds, using the following column headings:

Period	Cash Payment (Credit)	Interest Expense (Debit)	Discount on Bonds Payable (Credit)	Discount on Bonds Payable Balance (Debit)	Bond Payable Carrying Value (Credit)

Problem 9-104A   Finance and Operating Leases

OBJECTIVE 6

Trimurti Company has decided to lease its new office building. The following information is available for the lease:

Payments	$100,000 per year*
Length of lease	15 years
Economic life of building	16 years
Appropriate interest rate	8.4%
Cost of building if purchased	$875,000

* The first payment is due at the end of the first year of the lease.

Required:

1. Determine whether this is a finance lease or an operating lease.
2. Regardless of your answer to the preceding question, assume that this is a finance lease and that the present value of the lease payments is $829,500. Record the liability and corresponding asset for this acquisition.
3. Record the interest expense on the finance lease at the end of the first year. Also assume no residual value and a 15-year lease for the building. Record the first year's straight-line depreciation of the cost of the leased asset.

PROBLEM SET B

OBJECTIVE ① ②

Problem 9-105B   Reporting Long-Term Debt

Craig Corporation's accounting records reveal the following account balances after adjusting entries are made on December 31, 2018:

Accounts payable	$ 73,000	Interest payable	$ 33,400
Bonds payable (9.4%, due in 2023)	900,000	Installment note payable (9%, equal	
Lease liability*	30,000	installments due 2019 to 2029)	110,000
Bonds payable (8.3% due in 2022)	60,000	Notes payable (7.8%, due in 2027)	350,000
Deferred tax liability*	127,600	Premium on notes payable (7.8%,	
Discount on bonds payable (9.4%,		due in 2027)	5,000
due in 2023)	11,900	3% note payable, $50,000 face	
Income tax payable	28,100	amount, due in 2029	29,800

*Long-term liability

Required:

Prepare the current liabilities and long-term debt portions of Craig's statement of financial position at December 31, 2018. Provide a separate line item for each issue (do not combine separate bonds or notes payable), but some items may need to be split into more than one item.

OBJECTIVE ②

Problem 9-106B   Entries for and Financial Statement Presentation of a Note

Gekas Company borrowed $200,000 from the Royal Bank on February 1, 2018, on a three-year, 8.6% note. Interest is paid annually on February 1.

Required:

1. Record the borrowing transaction in Gekas's journal.
2. Prepare the adjusting entries made at December 31, 2018 and 2019.
3. Prepare the necessary journal entry to recognize the first interest payment on February 1, 2019 (round to the nearest dollar).
4. Indicate how the note and associated interest would be presented in Gekas's December 31, 2019, statement of financial position.
5. Prepare the necessary journal entries to record the repayment of the note and the last year's interest payment on February 1, 2021.

OBJECTIVE ② ③

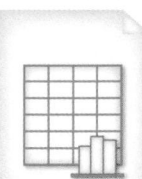

Problem 9-107B   Preparing a Bond Amortization Table (Effective Interest Rate)

On December 31, 2018, The Rock Restaurant borrowed $254,500 by issuing three-year, 7% bonds with a face amount of $250,000. Interest is payable annually on December 31. The company uses the effective interest rate method of amortization.

Required:

Prepare an amortization table using the following column headings:

Period	Cash Payment (Credit)	Interest Expense (Debit)	Premium on Bonds Payable (Debit)	Premium on Bonds Payable Balance (Credit)	Bond Payable Carrying Value (Credit)

OBJECTIVE ③

Problem 9-108B   Note Computations and Entries (Effective Interest Rate)

On December 31, 2018, Benton Corporation borrowed $1,000,000 with 10-year, 8.75% notes, interest payable semiannually on June 30 and December 31. Cash in the amount of $985,500 was received when the note was issued. The company uses the effective interest rate method of amortization.

Required:

1. Prepare the necessary journal entry at December 31, 2018.
2. Prepare the necessary journal entry at June 30, 2019.
3. Prepare the necessary journal entry at December 31, 2019.
4. Determine the carrying amount of these notes at the end of the fifth year (December 31, 2023).

Problem 9-109B Preparing a Bond Amortization Table (Effective Interest Rate)

OBJECTIVE ❸

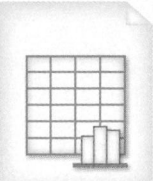

Babur Company issued five-year, 7.5% bonds with a total face value of $900,000 on December 31, 2018, for $950,000. The bonds pay interest on June 30 and December 31 of each year. The company uses the effective interest rate method of amortization.

Required:

1. Prepare an amortization table using the effective interest rate method.
2. Prepare the entries to recognize the interest payments made on June 30, 2019, and December 31, 2019.

Problem 9-110B Preparing a Bond Amortization Table (Effective Interest Rate)

OBJECTIVE ❸

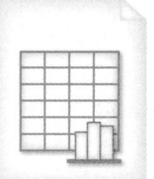

Pennington Corporation issued five-year, 8.6% bonds with a total face value of $700,000 on December 31, 2018, for $680,000. The bonds pay interest on June 30 and December 31 of each year. The company uses the effective interest rate method of amortization.

Required:

1. Prepare an amortization table using the effective interest rate method.
2. Prepare the entries to recognize the bond issuance and the interest payments made on June 30, 2019, and December 31, 2019.

Problem 9-111B Preparing a Bond Amortization Table (Effective Interest Rate)

OBJECTIVE ❸

Dunn-Whitaker Construction has agreed to construct a plant in a new industrial park. To finance the construction, the municipal government issued $4,000,000 of 10-year, 5.25% bonds for $4,100,000 on December 31, 2018. Dunn-Whitaker will pay the interest and principal on the bonds. When the bonds are repaid, Dunn-Whitaker will receive title to the plant. In the interim, Dunn-Whitaker will pay property taxes as if it owned the plant. This financing arrangement is attractive to Dunn-Whitaker, as municipal government bonds carry a low interest rate. The bonds are attractive to investors, as both Dunn-Whitaker and the municipal government are issuers. The bonds pay interest semiannually on June 30 and December 31.

Required:

1. Prepare an amortization table through December 31, 2020, for these revenue bonds assuming effective interest rate method amortization.
2. **CONCEPTUAL CONNECTION** Discuss whether or not Dunn-Whitaker should record the plant as an asset after it is constructed.
3. **CONCEPTUAL CONNECTION** Discuss whether or not Dunn-Whitaker should record the liability for these bonds.

Problem 9-112B Non-interest Bearing Note (Straight Line)

OBJECTIVE ❹

On December 31, 2018, Sorenson Financing Corporation borrowed $90,000 cash on a $110,300, 24-month zero coupon note. Sorenson uses the straight-line method of amortization.

Required:

1. Record the borrowing in Sorenson's journal.
2. Prepare the adjusting entry for December 31, 2019.
3. Prepare the entries to recognize the 2020 interest expense and repayment of the note on December 31, 2020.

OBJECTIVE ④   **Problem 9-113B   Preparing an Amortization Table for Non-interest Bearing Bonds (Straight Line)**

On December 31, 2018, Beauty Box Company borrowed $3,000,000 by issuing three-year, zero coupon bonds. The face value of the bonds is $3,240,000. Beauty Box uses the straight-line method to amortize any premium or discount.

Required:

Prepare an amortization table for these bonds using the following column headings:

Period	Cash Payment (Credit)	Interest Expense (Debit)	Discount on Bonds Payable (Credit)	Discount on Bonds Payable Balance (Debit)	Bond Payable Carrying Value (Credit)

OBJECTIVE ⑥   **Problem 9-114B   Finance and Operating Leases**

Kleinfelder Company has decided to lease its new office building. The following information is available for the lease:

Lease:	
Payments	$75,000 per year*
Length of lease	15 years
Economic life of building	16 years
Appropriate interest rate	7.3%
Cost of building if purchased	$750,000

*The first payment is due at the end of the first year of the lease.

Required:

1. Determine whether this is a finance lease or an operating lease.
2. Regardless of your answer to the preceding question, assume that this is a finance lease and that the present value of the lease payments is $670,300. Record the liability and corresponding asset for this acquisition.
3. Record the interest expense on the finance lease at the end of the first year. Also assume no residual value and a 15-year lease for the building. Record the first year's straight-line depreciation of the cost of the leased asset. (*Note:* Round to the nearest dollar.)

CASES

Case 9-115   Long-Term Debt and Ethics

You are the CFO of Diversified Industries. Diversified has suffered through several tough years. This has deteriorated its financial condition to the point that Diversified is in danger of violating two loan covenants related to its largest loan, which is not due for 12 more years. The loan contract says that if Diversified violates any of these covenants, the loan principal will become immediately due and payable. Diversified will be unable to make this payment, and any additional loans taken to repay this loan will likely be at sufficiently higher rates that Diversified will be forced into bankruptcy. An investment banker suggests forming another entity (called a "special purpose entity" or SPE) and transferring some debt to this SPE. Structuring the SPE very carefully will have the effect of moving enough debt off Diversified's statement of financial position to keep the company in compliance with all its loan covenants. The investment banker assures you that accounting rules permit such accounting treatment.

Required:

How do you react to the investment banker?

Case 9-116   Debt Covenants and Financial Reporting Standards

Debtholders receive note contracts, one for each note, that describe the payments promised by the issuer of the debt. In addition, the issuing corporation frequently enters into a supplementary agreement, called a *note indenture*, with a trustee who represents the debt holders. The provisions or covenants of the indenture may place restrictions on the issuer for the benefit of the debtholders. For example, an indenture may require that the issuer's ratio of total liabilities to total shareholders' equity never rise above a specified level or that periodic payments be made to the trustee, who administers a "sinking fund" to provide for the retirement of debt.

Consider Roswell Manufacturing's debt indenture, which requires Roswell's ratio of total liabilities to total shareholders' equity never to exceed 2:1. If Roswell violates this requirement, the debt indenture specifies very costly penalties, and if the violation continues, the entire debt issue must be retired at a disadvantageous price and refinanced. In recent years, Roswell's ratio has averaged about 1.5:1 ($15 million in total liabilities and $10 million in total shareholders' equity). However, Roswell has an opportunity to purchase one of its major competitors, Ashland Products. The acquisition will require $4.5 million in additional liabilities, but it will double Roswell's net income. Roswell does not believe that a share issue is feasible in the current environment. A new accounting standard requires accounting for post-employment benefits. Implementation of the new standard will add about $2 million to Roswell's long-term liabilities. Roswell's CEO, Martha Cooper, has written a strong letter of objection to the accounting standard-setting organization, which has received similar letters from over 300 companies.

Required:

1. Write a paragraph presenting an analysis of the impact of the new standard on Roswell Manufacturing.
2. If you were a member of the accounting-standard-setting organization and met Martha Cooper at a professional meeting, how would you respond to her objection?

Case 9-117   Evaluating Leverage

Gearing Manufacturing Inc. is planning a $1,000,000 expansion of its production facilities. The expansion could be financed by the sale of $1,250,000 in 8% notes or by the sale of $1,250,000 in common shares, which would raise the number of shares outstanding from 50,000 to 75,000. Gearing pays income taxes at a rate of 30%.

Required:

1. Suppose that income from operations is expected to be $550,000 per year for the duration of the proposed debt issue. Should Gearing finance with notes or shares? Explain your answer.
2. Suppose that income from operations is expected to be $275,000 per year for the duration of the proposed debt issue. Should Gearing finance with notes or shares? Explain your answer.
3. Suppose that income from operations is to be $300,000 40% of the time, and below $300,000, 60% of the time. Should Gearing finance with notes or shares? Explain your answer.
4. As an investor, how would you use accounting information to evaluate the risk of excessive use of leverage? What additional information would be useful? Explain.

Case 9-118   Leverage

Kochlin Corporation issued financial statements at December 31, 2018, that include the following information:

Statement of financial position at December 31, 2018:

Assets	$8,000,000
Liabilities	$1,200,000
Shareholders' equity (300,000 shares)	$6,800,000

(Continued)

Statement of Earnings for 2018:

Income from operations	$1,200,000
Less: Interest expense	(100,000)
Income before tax	1,100,000
Less: Income tax expense (30%)	(330,000)
Net income	$ 770,000

The levels of assets, liabilities, shareholders' equity, and operating income have been stable in recent years; however, Kochlin Corporation is planning a $1,800,000 expansion program that will increase income from operations by $350,000 to $1,550,000. Kochlin is planning to sell 8.5% notes at face value to finance the expansion.

Required:

1. What earnings per share does Kochlin report before the expansion?
2. What earnings per share will Kochlin report if the proposed expansion is undertaken? Would this use of leverage be advantageous to Kochlin's shareholders? Explain.
3. Suppose income from operations will increase by only $150,000. Would this use of leverage be advantageous to Kochlin's shareholders? Explain.
4. Suppose that income from operations will increase by $200,000 and that Kochlin could also raise the required $1,800,000 by issuing an additional 100,000 common shares (assume the additional shares were outstanding for the entire year). Which means of financing would shareholders prefer? Explain.

Case 9-119   Continuing Problem: Front Row Entertainment

In June 2018, Front Row Entertainment had the opportunity to expand its venue operations by purchasing five different venues. To finance this purchase, they issued $1,500,000 of 6%, 5-year bonds on July 1, 2018. The bonds were issued for $1,378,300 and pay interest semiannually on June 30 and December 31.

Required:

1. Prepare the journal entry to record the bond issue at July 1, 2018.
2. Assume that Front Row uses the straight-line method of amortization.

   a. Prepare an amortization table through December 31, 2019.
   b. Prepare the journal entry required at December 31, 2018.
   c. How will the bonds be shown on the December 31, 2018, statement of financial position?

3. Assume that Front Row uses the effective interest rate method of amortization and the annual market rate of interest was 8%.

   a. Prepare an amortization table through December 31, 2019. (*Note:* Round to the nearest dollar.)
   b. Prepare the journal entry required at December 31, 2018.
   c. How will the bonds be shown on the December 31, 2018, statement of financial position?

Case 9-120   Professional and Ethical Behaviour

Recall the Northjet Inc. case from Chapter 8. The deal with Bruno and David didn't go through. In the end, they felt it wasn't the right investment for them. The owner, Ryan, is starting to feel the pressure of selling Northjet Inc. Ryan would have been happy to cash out and move on to his next project, and he feels disappointed now that he has to find another buyer. He's not sure when that next buyer will come, and if the buyer will be serious about the purchase.

Six months later, another investor, Neal, is looking at investing in a project. Neal is very wealthy, having made millions in the IT industry. He has heard that Northjet Inc. is for sale and contacts Ryan about obtaining financial information for his review.

Ryan quickly asks Laura, the new chartered professional accountant, to give him a hand in putting together the financial statements. Laura is a recent CPA graduate and is ready to show off her accounting skills. Sam, whom you may recall was the previous CPA, quit abruptly.

For six months Ryan hired a bookkeeper, who recently quit as well. Ryan is happy to have Laura on board. Laura is still trying to get up-to-speed on all the financial accounting–related information at Northjet and is working hard to try to make sense of the financial accounting mess that the recently departed bookkeeper left behind. Laura finds it weird that the previous CPA left. Ryan explains to Laura that Sam left because he was offered an exciting new opportunity.

As Laura is putting together the financial statements, she realizes that Northjet Inc. has several leases that have been misclassified on the financial statements. The leases are all shown as operating-type leases, when in fact, based on Laura's analysis and review of the criteria under IFRS 17, they should have been classified as finance leases. This will have a significant impact on the financial statements. Laura starts reviewing the impact of this misclassification prior to meeting with the owner of Northjet and discovers that the banking agreement has a debt to total equity covenant ratio, which allows the bank to call the loan at any time if the ratio is breached. Laura does a quick calculation and sees that by showing the leases as finance leases, the ratio would in fact be breached and the bank most likely would call the loan. If Northjet Inc. doesn't have the money to pay back the loan, the company will be in big trouble. Laura doesn't like what she's seeing, but she doesn't want to jump to any conclusions until she discusses this issue with the owner.

Two days later, Laura meets with the owner and tells him what she found. He says that he is well aware of the leasing options available (operating vs. finance) and tells Laura, "These leases will remain as operating as they have been reviewed by Sam, who was also a CPA and had more experience than you, and the recent bookkeeper. Both of them agreed that they were operating." Ryan instructs Laura to leave the leases as they are and finalize the statements to send to Neal, as he doesn't want this deal to fall through because of a delay in getting him the financial statements.

He tells Laura to have the final statements on his desk by tomorrow morning.

Required:

Identify and discuss any accounting issues and potential ethical issues.

10

Reporting and Analyzing Shareholders' Equity

After studying Chapter 10, you should be able to:

1. Distinguish between common and preferred shares and explain their use in raising capital.

2. Explain and report transactions affecting common and preferred shares.

3. Account for share repurchases, dividends, and stock splits.

4. Explain and report changes to retained earnings and accumulated other comprehensive income.

5. Calculate and analyze earnings per share, the dividend yield, and other equity ratios.

6. Explain and report equity accounts in unincorporated businesses.

EXPERIENCE FINANCIAL ACCOUNTING
with Google

In 1998, Sergey Brin and Larry Page, two Ph.D. students at Stanford University, founded Google. The incredible growth of Google is evidenced by the fact that, by 2014, Google had revenues in excess of $66.0 billion (U.S.) and net income of over $14.4 billion (U.S.). These figures are drastically larger than just four years ago. From 2010, revenue was up over 125%, while net income was up over 70%.

One way that shareholders earn a return on their investment is by receiving dividends, yet despite their profitability, Google has never paid a dividend to shareholders. Instead, Google has chosen to invest in growth opportunities.

You are likely aware of some of these growth opportunities, which include Google's purchases of YouTube, DoubleClick, and AdMob, as well as its roll-out of features such as Google Earth and Google Chrome. However, Google's investments do not stop there. In fact, Google's 2014 statement of cash flows shows that it spent more than $21 billion (U.S.) on investing activities. Since past investment is responsible for Google's large growth in revenues and net income, the hope is that the 2014 investments will fuel profitable growth in the coming years. Review the chart at left and notice that Google's investing and operating activities over the past five years have resulted in a large increase in assets with a very small increase in total debt. It is apparent that the asset growth has resulted from profitable operations and wise investing activities rather than a strategy to grow the asset base through large increases in debt.

Legend:
- Total Long-Term Debt
- Cash Used in Investing Activities
- Cash Provided by Operations

Chart years: 2014, 2013, 2012, 2011. Horizontal axis: 0, 5, 10, 15, 20, 25.

Source: Based on data found at www.google.ca/finance.

OWNERSHIP AND GOVERNANCE OF A CORPORATION

A corporation is a separate legal entity under the law. As a separate entity, it has an unlimited life, so it can potentially continue forever. This is in contrast to proprietorships, which end with the death of an individual, and to partnerships, which are owned by individuals and which are usually changed after the death of a partner. A corporation may own assets, incur liabilities, grow or contract in size, and enter into contracts. Corporations may be organized federally (under the Canada Business Corporations Act [CBCA]) or provincially (e.g., in Ontario, under the Ontario Business Corporations Act [OBCA]). Since corporations are separate legal entities, shareholders have limited liability; thus, normally a shareholder's maximum loss would be the amount of that shareholder's investment in the corporation's shares. In private corporations the shareholder/manager may need to sign a bank guarantee that gives the bank access to the shareholder/manager's personal assets if necessary to settle debts with the bank. In this latter case, the limited liability advantage of incorporation is reduced.

For-profit corporations are liable for income tax on their net profits as determined by the tax legislation in the country in which the company is incorporated. Corporations can raise capital by issuing shares and can also borrow capital.

A corporation is formed by the government issuing articles of incorporation. For articles of incorporation to be obtained, an application must be submitted to the appropriate government authority. The application must contain the corporation's name, its business purpose, the number of shares it wants authorized, and the type of shares. The application specifies who the initial directors of the corporation will be as well as the shares (and their assigned values) that the company will issue at the time of incorporation.

A corporation is governed by a Board of Directors, which is elected by the corporation's shareholders. The Board of Directors appoints a President of the company to manage operations and carry out business strategy. The President will normally employ other key executives (Chief Financial Officer, Vice-President Human Resources, etc.) to assist in the management of the corporation.

Public corporations are those that have issued shares on a public stock exchange. A public corporation usually has many shareholders. A private corporation usually has not issued any shares on a public stock exchange and usually consists of only a few shareholders, often less than four.

(EXHIBIT 10.1)

Elements of Shareholders' Equity

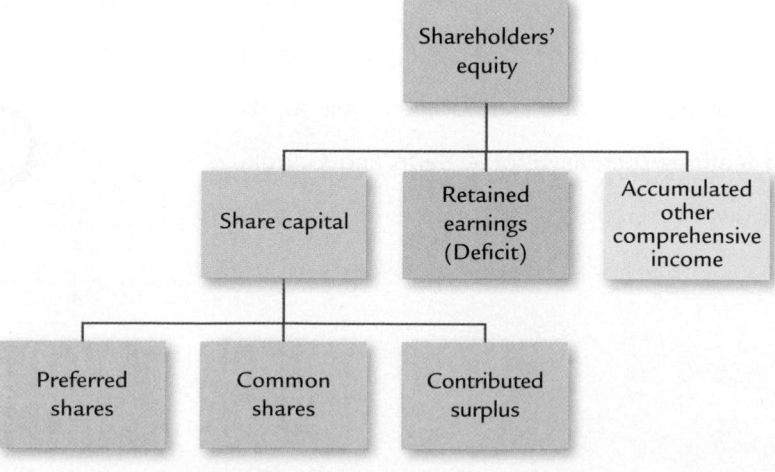

© Cengage Learning

Shareholders' equity represents the owners' (known as shareholders') residual claims against the assets of a corporation after all liabilities have been deducted. The shareholders' equity section of the statement of financial position clearly identifies various elements of equity according to their source. As illustrated in Exhibit 10.1, the most common sources are:

- share capital—split between (1) preferred and (2) common shares
- retained earnings (referred to as a deficit when the balance of this account is negative)
- accumulated other comprehensive income
- contributed surplus

In this chapter, we explain how common and preferred shares are used to raise capital for the corporation, explain how corporations account for the various transactions that affect shareholders' equity, and calculate and analyze shareholder payout and shareholder profitability ratios using information contained in shareholders' equity.

ISSUING SHARE CAPITAL WITHIN A CORPORATION

Recall from Chapter 1 that most large businesses are organized as corporations because incorporation increases the company's ability to raise cash (or capital) by easing the transfer of ownership and limiting the liability of shareholders. Ownership of a corporation is divided into a large number of equal parts or *shares*. Shares are owned in varying numbers by the owners of the corporation called **shareholders**.

OBJECTIVE **1**

Distinguish between common and preferred shares and explain their use in raising capital.

Authorization and Issuance of Shares

Corporations are authorized, or *chartered*, in accordance with the provisions of federal or provincial laws that govern the structure and operation of corporations.

Shares (usually unlimited in number) are sold, or issued, when a corporation is formed. Additional shares may be issued later. The maximum number of shares the business may issue in each class of shares is referred to as the number of **authorized shares**. This number of authorized shares must be distinguished from the number of **issued shares**, which is the number of shares actually sold to shareholders.

Corporations can buy back their own shares for reasons explained later in this chapter. Thus, the number of shares issued is further distinguished from the number of **outstanding shares**—which is the number of issued shares actually in the hands of shareholders. When firms reacquire their own shares, the reacquired shares are not considered to be outstanding. Shares repurchased but not yet cancelled are called treasury

$$\left(\text{EXHIBIT 10.2}\right)$$

Determination of Share Quantities

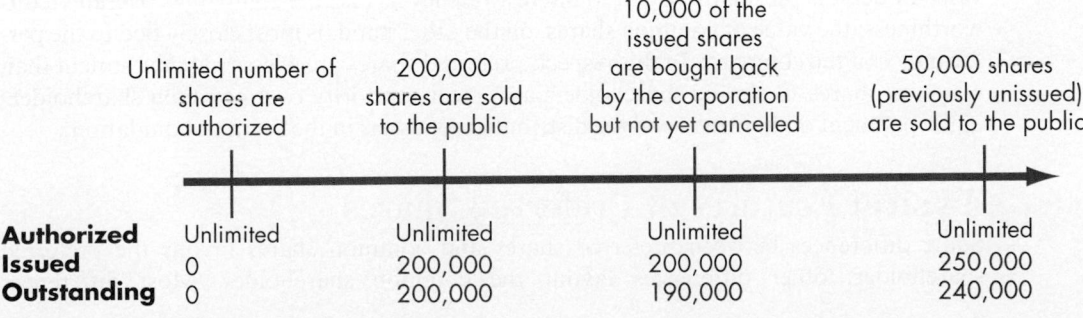

| | | 10,000 of the issued shares | |
Unlimited number of shares are authorized	200,000 shares are sold to the public	are bought back by the corporation but not yet cancelled	50,000 shares (previously unissued) are sold to the public
Authorized Unlimited	Unlimited	Unlimited	Unlimited
Issued 0	200,000	200,000	250,000
Outstanding 0	200,000	190,000	240,000

shares. Exhibit 10.2 illustrates how the share quantities are determined. In Canada, corporations must generally cancel repurchased shares and are not allowed to have treasury shares.

These three share quantities—the number of shares authorized, issued, and outstanding—are reported for each class of shares on the statement of financial position or in the accompanying notes.

Common Shareholders and Their Rights

All classes of shares are designated as either common shares or preferred shares. These shares each come with different financial benefits and provide different rights regarding the governance of the corporation. The primary rights for owners of **common shares** are:

- Voting in the election of the Board of Directors. You will recall that the board controls the operating, investing, and financial policies of the company.
- Sharing in the profits and dividends of the company. We will talk more about this below.
- Keeping the same percentage of ownership if new shares are issued (preemptive right).
- Sharing in the assets in liquidation in proportion to their holdings. This is referred to as the "residual claim" because common shareholders are only paid after all creditors and preferred shareholders are paid in full (which is very rare in liquidation).

When you hear of someone who "made money by investing in stock," it is almost invariably through an investment in common shares. This is because, although the "residual claim" means that common shareholders are paid only after the creditors and preferred shareholders are paid in full based on their entitlements, it also means that common shareholders get *everything* that is left over after the creditors and preferred shareholders are paid in full. As such, the common shareholders receive the bulk of the financial gain from a profitable company through share appreciation and dividends:

- *Share appreciation*: The value of the shares increases above the price initially paid (of course, it is also possible that the shares' value will decrease if the company is unprofitable—this is a risk of owning shares).
- *Dividends*: **Dividends** are payments to a company's shareholders from earnings. These payments are usually in the form of cash, but noncash assets and shares can also be given as dividends. Payment of dividends to common shareholders, however, depends on a company's alternatives. The company may elect to pay down debt or, if the company has growth opportunities, it may elect to keep (or retain) earnings to fund these investment options rather than pay dividends. In fact, many companies do not pay dividends to common shareholders for those reasons.

Preferred Shareholders and Their Rights

Preferred shares generally pay a regular dividend usually determined as a stated amount per share. In this regard, preferred shares are similar to debt, with the preferred share dividend equating to interest payments. Additionally, the value of preferred shares, like the value of debt, is most closely tied to interest rate levels and the company's overall creditworthiness; the value of common shares, on the other hand, is most closely tied to the performance of the company. In this respect, preferred shares are a less risky investment than common shares. Preferred shareholders also receive priority over common shareholders in the payment of dividends and the distribution of assets in the event of liquidation.

Typical Features of Preferred Shares

Some differences between preferred shares and common shares favour the preferred shareholder; other differences favour the common shareholder. Most differences between preferred and common shares are designated in the company's corporate charter and take one or more of the following forms:

- *Dividend preferences*: Preferred shares frequently require that the issuing corporation pay dividends to preferred shareholders before paying dividends to common shareholders. Preferred dividends may be cumulative. Cumulative unpaid dividends accumulate and must be paid before dividends can be paid to common shareholders. Preferred Share Dividend Preferences, later in this chapter, contains a discussion of such shares.
- *Participating preferences*: Preferred shares may participate in dividend payments in excess of a stated, fixed amount per share. Participating Dividend Preference on Preferred Shares, later in this chapter, contains a discussion of such shares.
- *Conversion privileges*: Preferred shares may be convertible into common shares if the preferred shareholder elects to do so and certain conditions are satisfied. For example, each preferred share might be convertible into, say, 10 common shares after a certain date.
- *Liquidation preferences*: If and when a corporation is dissolved, liquidating distributions are made to shareholders. Corporate charters and legislation frequently require the claims of preferred shareholders to be satisfied before those of common shareholders.
- *Call provisions (redeemable)*: The corporate charter may authorize or even require the corporation to repurchase (or redeem) any preferred shares that are sold. In such cases, the charter usually fixes the *call price* (the amount to be paid to the preferred shareholders) and specifies a date on or after which the shares may or must be repurchased. Note that this feature is similar to the repaying of the principal on a loan at the maturity date—particularly when the charter requires redemption at a specific date.
- *A retraction provision* is common in privately owned companies whose controlling shareholders have undertaken an estate freeze. When preferred shares are "retractable," the preferred shareholder can demand payment for the full amount of the preferred shares.
- *Denial of voting rights*: Most preferred shares do not confer voting rights, which means that preferred shareholders, unlike common shareholders, cannot vote at shareholders' meetings.

The first four features of preferred shares are advantageous for preferred shareholders. Call provisions and denial of voting rights usually work in the interest of common shareholders.

Because of the relative advantages of different forms of shares, corporations are typically authorized by their charters to issue several classes of preferred shares, each with a different set of terms and provisions. This excerpt from Procter & Gamble's 2015 audited financial statements illustrates how the different classes of shares are included:

Classes of Shares for Procter & Gamble (amounts in millions) (partial)	2015	2014
Convertible Class A preferred shares, stated value $1 per share (600 shares authorized)	$1,077	$1,111
Nonvoting Class B preferred shares, stated value $1 per share (200 shares authorized)	–	–
Common shares, stated value $1 per share (10,000 shares authorized; shares issued: 2015–4,009.2, 2014–4,009.2)	4,009	4,009

Source: Procter and Gamble 2015 Annual Report, page 47.

YOUDECIDE Issuing Debt or Preferred Shares

You are the CFO of Hamilton Manufacturing. Your company needs to raise capital to pursue an expansion project, but the company does not want to sell additional common shares.

What factors should you consider in deciding whether to issue debt or preferred shares?

In making your decision, it would be helpful to consider the following differences between debt and preferred shares.

Advantage of debt:
• Interest payments are tax deductible, while preferred dividends are not.

Advantages of preferred shares:
• Preferred shares are historically classified as equity, rather than debt, on the statement of financial position. If Hamilton prefers to, or must, show lower debt totals, preferred shares are advantageous. For example, provisions of existing debt contracts may not allow Hamilton to issue additional debt.

• Preferred shares are less risky than debt because, unlike interest payments, missing a preferred dividend payment does not trigger bankruptcy. If Hamilton fears cash flow problems, this will be important.
• Companies with a history of operating losses typically do not pay income taxes. If Hamilton has these so-called net operating loss carryforwards, then debt no longer has the tax advantage.
• Preferred shares are generally sold to other corporations because these corporations do not pay taxes on the full amount of the dividends (i.e., there is a big tax advantage relative to receiving dividend payments as opposed to interest payments).

Although preferred shares and debt have many similarities, they have some important differences.

ACCOUNTING FOR AND REPORTING THE ISSUANCE OF COMMON AND PREFERRED SHARES FOR CASH

OBJECTIVE 2

Explain and report transactions affecting common and preferred shares.

In examples in previous chapters, we recorded the contributions of shareholders in exchange for shares in a single account. In Canada, **stated value** is a monetary amount assigned by companies to each share for legal, accounting, and tax purposes. Stated value usually, but not always, represents the share's market value when issued.

Par value shares and treasury shares are common in the United States. In Canada, the CBCA (Canada Business Corporations Act) and most provincial corporations acts do not allow the issuance of par value shares. The small number of Canadian companies that have par value shares issued and outstanding issued those shares before the CBCA was amended in 1985. In Canada, the shares now issued are no par value shares, which means that the amount initially received from shareholders for those shares is the legal capital of the corporation. The legal capital of a corporation cannot be withdrawn by shareholders before an anticipated corporate bankruptcy. This chapter focuses on no par value shares in light of the past legislative changes.

Cornerstone 10.1 illustrates the accounting procedures for recording the sale of shares, which for public companies follows an IPO (initial public offering) process. Share offerings made by a public company subsequent to an IPO process are known as secondary or seasoned offerings.

Issuance of Shares for Services or Non–cash Assets

Executives working for start-up companies will often work for small salaries plus equity shares of the company rather than for large salaries, which a start-up company

Recording the Issuance of Common and Preferred Shares

CORNERSTONE 10.1

Information:

Spectator Corporation is authorized to issue an unlimited number of preferred and common shares. The preferred shares have a 9% dividend rate. On January 2, 2018, Spectator issued 200 preferred shares at $22 per share and 20,000 common shares at $2.50 per share.

▶ | CORNERSTONE VIDEO

Required:

1. How much cash did Spectator raise through its shares issuance?

2. Prepare the journal entries necessary to record the sale of common and preferred shares separately.

3. Provide the shareholders' equity section of Spectator's statement of financial position. (*Note:* Assume that Spectator has yet to engage in any operations.)

Why:

When companies issue common or preferred shares to raise capital, the resulting ownership claims are recorded in the capital stock section of shareholders' equity.

Solution:

1.

Preferred shares ($22 × 200 shares)	$ 4,400
Common shares ($2.50 × 20,000 shares)	50,000
Total proceeds	**$54,400**

2.

Date	Account and Explanation	Debit	Credit
Jan. 2	Cash	4,400	
	Preferred Shares		4,400
	(*Record sale of preferred shares at $22 per share*)		
Jan. 2	Cash	50,000	
	Common Shares		50,000
	(*Record sale of common shares at $2.50 per share*)		

Assets	=	Liabilities	+	Shareholders' Equity
+4,400				+4,400

Assets	=	Liabilities	+	Shareholders' Equity
+50,000				+50,000

3.

Shareholders' Equity

Authorized
  Unlimited number of 9% preferred shares
  Unlimited number of common shares
Issued

200 preferred shares	$ 4,400	
20,000 common shares	50,000	
Total capital stock		$54,400
Retained earnings*		0
Total shareholders' equity		$54,400

*Note that retained earnings displays a zero balance because Spectator is a newly formed corporation.

cannot pay. Also, suppliers to a business may agree to be paid with equity shares in the company when cash is not available. For example, a law firm that provides legal services to a start-up corporation may agree to be paid with equity shares of the company rather than cash. Assuming that a law firm rendered $200,000 of services to a corporate client, and the corporate client's common shares were trading for $10 per share, the law firm would receive 20,000 common shares for its services. The journal entry that the corporation would record to reflect this transaction is as follows:

	Debit	Credit
Legal fees expense	$200,000	
Common shares		$200,000

The accounting rule that applies to this transaction states that where non-cash assets or services are received in return for shares issued as consideration, the transaction is recorded at the fair market value of the consideration issued. If the fair market value of the consideration issued was unknown, the fair market value of the services or non-cash assets received would be determined and used to record the transaction.

Stated Capital and Contributed Surplus

Stated capital, sometimes referred to as legal capital, is the amount of capital that the law provides cannot be returned to the corporation's owners unless that corporation is liquidated. For corporations issuing no par value shares, the Board of Directors is required to establish the stated or legal capital associated with the shares issued. Funds received for shares in excess of their stated capital are recorded as a credit to contributed surplus.

If shares are issued for an amount in excess of their stated value, the excess amount received is recorded as a credit to the contributed surplus account. Therefore, if Company XYZ issues 100 common shares having a stated value of $1.00 per share for $150, the journal entry to record the transaction is:

	Debit	Credit
Cash	$150	
Common shares		$100
Contributed surplus		$ 50

Shares Issued under Stock Warrants

A **stock warrant** is the right granted by a corporation to purchase a specified number of its common shares at a stated price within a stated time period. Corporations issue stock warrants in the following two situations:

- First, they may issue warrants along with bonds or preferred shares as an "equity kicker," to make the bonds or preferred shares more attractive. Such warrants often have a duration of five or more years.
- Second, they may issue warrants to existing shareholders, who then have a legal right to purchase a specified portion of a new share issue, in order to maintain their relative level of ownership in the corporation. Such warrants usually have a duration of less than six months.

The accounting for the issuance of stock warrants is covered in advanced accounting courses.

Shares Issued under Employee Stock Options

Corporations also grant employees and executives the right to buy shares at a set price as compensation for their services. These "rights" are called *stock options*. Stock options are frequently given to employees and executives as compensation for their services. For example, the employer may give the executive the right to purchase in two years 5,000 of the company's shares at $50 per share, today's market price. If in two years the market price of the shares is higher than $50—say, $62—the executive will purchase the 5,000 shares for $50 each and receive effective compensation of $60,000 [($62 − $50) × 5,000 shares]. Of course, if the price is lower than $50, the executive will not exercise the option.

Corporations elect to grant stock options for two primary reasons:

- First, stock options allow cash-poor companies to compete for top talent in the employee market. For example, market salary for a manager of systems quality and assurance may be $200,000 per year—well beyond the means of many start-up companies. However, such a person may agree to work for $100,000 per year and a significant number of stock options.
- Second, stock options are believed to better align the incentives of the employee with those of the owners. This concept is easy to understand with a bit of exaggeration. Employees would like to be paid millions of dollars a year to do nothing, while owners would like the employees to work hundreds of hours a week for free. Stock options help align these incentives because now an employee's personal wealth is tied to the success of the company's share price—just like the owners.

The use of stock options by public corporations to reward executives has sometimes encouraged those executives to manipulate financial information in order to increase share prices. This enables those executives to buy shares at a low price and sell them later at a price that has been manipulated far higher. To prevent such abuses, corporations are now required to establish adequate internal controls and appropriately balanced compensation plans.

The cost of issuing stock options to executives and employees has been the subject of much controversy over the years. That controversy concerns whether the cost of stock option benefits should be measured and reported, and if so, how. Public companies in Canada are required to measure and report the estimated compensation cost of stock options issued to executives and employees. The detailed procedure for recording this expense is covered in advanced accounting courses.

IFRS requires substantial note disclosure with respect to stock options and other types of share-based compensation plans. Exhibit 10.3 details Canadian Tire's 2014 disclosure on stock options.

ETHICAL DECISIONS   The compensation expense recorded by a company when it grants stock options depends on many factors, including the price at which employees can buy the shares (called the **exercise or strike price**) and the market value of the shares on the date of grant. As discussed, the strike price of the options and the market value of the shares are generally the same on the date of grant. However, in past years, many companies were under investigation for "backdating" stock options. That is, companies have waited to announce the granting of options and then picked the date in the past when the share price was lowest. This maximized the value of each individual option to the employee. This practice has been curtailed by legislation.

(EXHIBIT 10.3)

29. Share-based payments (partial)

The fair value of employee stock options and performance share units is measured using the Black-Scholes formula. Measurement inputs include the share price on the measurement date, exercise price of the instrument, expected volatility (based on weighted average historical volatility adjusted for changes expected based on publicly available information), weighted average expected life of the instruments (based on historical experience and general option holder behaviour), expected dividends, and the risk-free interest rate (based on government bonds). Service and non-market performance conditions attached to the transactions are not taken into account in determining fair value.

The Company's share-based payment plans are described below. There were no cancellations or significant modifications to any of the plans during 2014.

Stock options

The Company has granted stock options to certain employees that enable such employees to exercise their stock options and subscribe for Class A Non-Voting Shares or receive a cash payment equal to the difference between the daily weighted average share price of the Company's Class A Non-Voting Shares on the exercise date and the exercise price of the stock option. The exercise price of each option equals the weighted average closing price of Class A Non-Voting Shares on the Toronto Stock Exchange for the 10-day period preceding the date of grant. Stock options granted from 2008 to 2011 generally vested on the third anniversary of their grant and were exercisable over a term of seven years. Stock options granted from 2012 to 2014 generally vest on a graduated basis over a three-year period and are exercisable over a term of seven years. At January 3, 2015, the aggregate number of Class A Non-Voting Shares that were authorized for issuance under the stock option plan was 3.4 million.

Compensation expense, net of hedging arrangements, recorded for stock options for the year ended January 3, 2015, was $10.7 million (2013—15.4 million).

The following table summarizes information about stock options outstanding and exercisable at January 3, 2015:

			Options outstanding		Options exercisable	
Range of exercise prices	Number of Outstanding Options	Weighted average remaining contractual life[1]	Weighted average exercise price	Number exercisable at January 3, 2015	Weighted average exercise price
$84.53 to 103.61	325,321	6.18	$99.64	–	–
66.73 to 69.01	562,105	5.17	68.99	106,004	69.01
63.67 to 66.04	378,788	4.16	63.68	172,534	63.69
62.30 to 63.42	152,551	2.61	62.50	152,551	62.50
40.04 to 53.67	107,578	1.84	49.92	107,578	49.92
$40.04 to 103.61	1,526,343	4.64	$72.21	538,667	$61.65

[1]Weighted average remaining contractual life is expressed in years.

Source: Canadian Tire 2014 Annual Report.

YOUDECIDE Going Public

You are CEO of Dirko Corp., a successful manufacturer of electronic components for computer hardware. Dirko wishes to double its scale of operations in order to meet both existing and expected demand for its products. Dirko is a *privately held corporation*. High interest rates preclude Dirko from borrowing the necessary expansion capital, and its current owners are unable to invest significantly more capital at this time.

What effect will going public have on corporate control and expenses?

Raising enough capital to double the scale of operations will likely require giving away a substantial ownership interest. If the new owners are sufficiently well organized and cohesive, they could elect a majority of directors and control the company. On the other hand, if the new shares were purchased by a large number of investors with no organized interest in controlling Dirko, then effective control would remain in the hands of the original owners. Of course, the risk of losing control at some future time would still exist. Going public will also substantially increase the costs of financial reporting and corporate governance to comply with legal requirements.

Going public will most likely require giving up control of the company and will also increase expenses in order to comply with financial reporting standards.

ACCOUNTING FOR SHARE REPURCHASES, DIVIDENDS, AND STOCK SPLITS

As discussed, owners invest in corporations through the purchase of shares. Corporations can distribute cash to shareholders in the following ways:

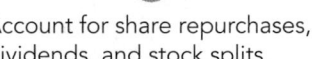

OBJECTIVE **3**

Account for share repurchases, dividends, and stock splits.

- The corporation can repurchase the shares from owners.
- The corporation can issue dividends.

Historically, dividends were the most common method of distributing cash. Over recent years, however, repurchasing shares has become a more frequent method of cash distribution in order to increase the market price per share and earnings per share since fewer shares will remain outstanding after the repurchase.

Share Repurchases

When a corporation purchases its own previously issued shares, the shares that it buys are called **treasury shares**. Corporations purchase treasury shares for many reasons:

- to buy out the ownership of one or more shareholders
- to reduce the size of corporate operations
- to reduce the number of outstanding shares in an attempt to increase earnings per share and market value per share
- to reduce vulnerability to an unfriendly takeover

As noted previously, in most provinces in Canada, repurchased shares must be cancelled and not held in treasury. Therefore, in Canada, repurchased shares are usually immediately cancelled and are no longer issued or outstanding.

At first thought, one might consider recording the acquisition of a corporation's own shares as an exchange of cash for an investment in shares (an exchange of one asset for another). However, that approach fails to recognize that the purchased shares are already represented by amounts in the corporation's equity accounts. Although the shares would represent an asset to another entity if it acquired them, they cannot represent an asset to the entity that issued them. Thus, the purchase of shares is a reduction of equity rather than the acquisition of an investment. Instead of requiring a debit to an investment account, the acquisition by a company of its own shares requires a debit to equity accounts.

Cornerstone 10.2 illustrates how to account for a share repurchase.

---

concept Q&A

If a corporation buys the shares of another corporation and later sells those shares for a different price, a gain or loss is recorded on the statement of comprehensive income. However, when a corporation buys its own shares and later sells them for a different price, the statement of comprehensive income is not affected. Why is this?

Answer:

Transactions with a corporation's owners cannot be included on the statement of comprehensive income, because the purchase is a capital, not an operating, transaction.

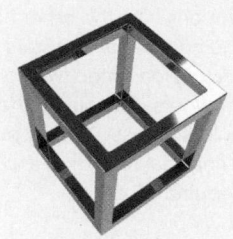

CORNERSTONE 10.2   Accounting for Share Repurchases

CORNERSTONE
VIDEO

Information:

On July 1, 2018, Spectator Corporation repurchases 1,000 shares of its outstanding common shares for $15 per share.

Required (3 independent situations):

Prepare the journal entries to record (1) the purchase of common shares where the average cost of previously issued common shares was $10 per share; (2) the purchase of common shares where the average cost of common shares previously issued was $20 per share; and (3) the purchase of common shares where the average cost of common shares previously issued was $10 per share and where contributed surplus of $2,000 existed with respect to earlier transactions involving common shares.

Why:

The repurchase of previously issued shares will result in a reduction of shareholders' equity. The repurchase of shares previously issued must be accurately recorded in order to properly reflect the shareholder equity accounts relating to each ownership group.

Solution:

				Date	Account and Explanation	Debit	Credit
Assets	**= Liabilities +**		**Shareholders' Equity**	1. July 1, 2018	Common Shares[a]	10,000	
−15,000			−10,000		Retained Earnings	5,000	
			−5,000		Cash		15,000
					(*Record purchase of shares for $15*)		
Assets	**= Liabilities +**		**Shareholders' Equity**	2. July 1, 2018	Common Shares[b]	20,000	
−15,000			−20,000		Contributed Surplus		5,000
			+5,000		Cash		15,000
					(*Record purchase of common shares for $20*)		
Assets	**= Liabilities +**		**Shareholders' Equity**	3. July 1, 2018	Common Shares[c]	10,000	
−15,000			−10,000		Contributed	2,000	
			−2,000		Retained Earnings	3,000	
			−3,000		Cash[d]		15,000
					(*Record purchase of common shares*)		

[a] 1,000 × $15
[b] 1,000 × $20
[c] 1,000 × $10
[d] Average cost of common shares is calculated by dividing total issued share capital by the number of issued common shares on date of purchase.

     In the above transactions, the "gain" or "loss" on repurchase does not affect the statement of comprehensive income because these are capital, not operating, transactions. Further, the contributed surplus account for one class of shares can only be used for transactions involving that same class of share. Contributed surplus accounts usually occur as the result of gains and losses on share repurchases, but can also result from other capital contributions made by shareholders. A separate contributed surplus account must be maintained for each type of transaction class.

Transfers among Shareholders We have been considering the effects on the equity accounts when a corporation buys or sells its own shares. In general, the purchase or sale of shares on a public stock exchange after they are first issued does *not* alter the equity accounts of the issuing corporation, unless that corporation is itself the purchaser or seller. Although the issuing corporation's accounts do not change when shares are sold by one shareholder to another, the corporation's shareholder list must be updated. Large corporations usually retain an independent *stock transfer agent* to maintain their shareholder lists, which include the quantity and serial numbers of the shares held. Stock transfer agents also arrange for the transfer of certificates among shareholders and the issuance of new certificates to shareholders.

Dividends

A dividend is an amount paid periodically by a corporation to a shareholder as a return on invested capital. Dividends represent distributions of accumulated net profit. They are usually paid in cash but may also be paid in the form of noncash assets or even additional shares of the corporation. All dividends, whatever their form, reduce retained earnings (see Exhibit 10.4).

Cash Dividends Cash dividends are by far the most common form of dividend. The payment of a cash dividend is preceded by an official announcement or declaration by the Board of Directors of the company's intention to pay a dividend. The dividend declaration specifies:

- the **declaration date**—the date on which a corporation announces its intention to pay a dividend on common or preferred shares
- the dollar amount of the dividend—usually stated as the number of dollars per share

concept Q&A

Why are dividends not an expense on the statement of comprehensive income?

Answer:

Dividends paid to owners are not included on the statement of comprehensive income because dividends are a distribution of earnings and are not part of the earnings process. Dividends are recorded in the statement of changes in shareholders' equity.

(EXHIBIT 10.4)

Dividends

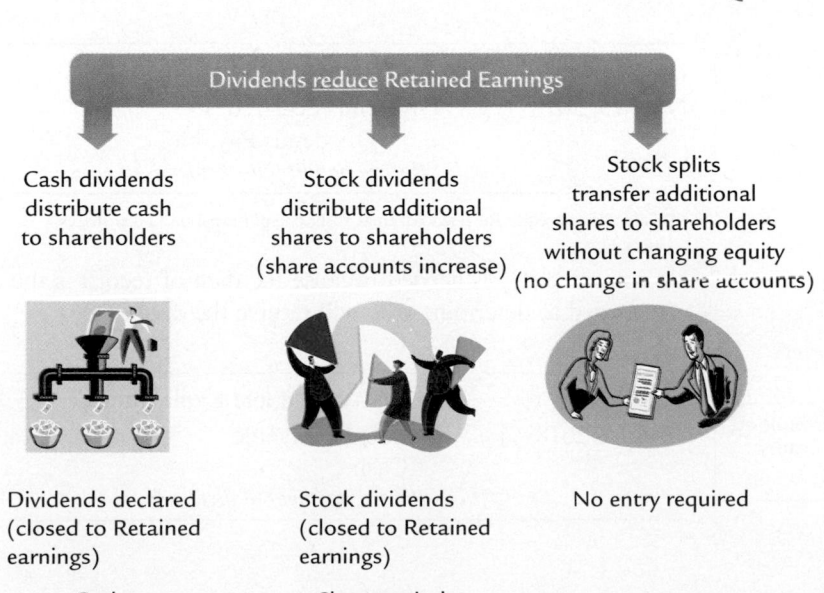

	Dividends reduce Retained Earnings	
Cash dividends distribute cash to shareholders	Stock dividends distribute additional shares to shareholders (share accounts increase)	Stock splits transfer additional shares to shareholders without changing equity (no change in share accounts)

Journal Entry Required	Debit	Dividends declared (closed to Retained earnings)	Stock dividends (closed to Retained earnings)	No entry required
	Credit	Cash	Share capital	

- the **date of record**—the date on which a shareholder must own one or more shares in order to receive the dividend
- the **payment date**—the date on which the dividend will actually be paid

Since the shares of most corporations are continually changing hands, it is necessary to set a date on which the ownership of shares is established as a basis for the payment of dividends. If a share is sold between the date of record and the dividend payment date, the former owner of the share, rather than the new owner, receives the dividend. On the other hand, if a share is sold between the declaration date and the date of record, the new owner, rather than the former owner, receives the dividend. The accounting for cash dividends is illustrated in Cornerstone 10.3 .

CORNERSTONE 10.3 Recording Cash Dividends

Information:

Kingsmill Corporation has 3,000 common shares issued and outstanding. On November 15, 2018, Kingsmill's Board of Directors declares a cash dividend of $2.00 per share payable on December 15, 2018, to shareholders of record on December 1, 2018.

Required:

Prepare the journal entries at (1) the date of declaration, (2) the date of record, and (3) the payment.

Why:

Dividends are generally paid by corporations in the form of cash based on the company's dividend policy.

Solution:

1. A liability is incurred on the date of declaration because the corporation has the legal obligation to pay after declaring the dividend.

	Shareholders' Equity (Retained
Assets = Liabilities +	Earnings)
+6,000	−6,000

Date	Account and Explanation	Debit	Credit
Nov. 15, 2018	Dividends declared*)	6,000	
	Dividends Payable		6,000
	(Record liability for dividends)		

*Dividends is closed to Retained Earnings at the end of the period (3,000 shares × $2 = $6,000)

2. No journal entry is needed because the date of record is the date at which ownership is recorded to determine who will receive the dividend.

3.

	Shareholders'
Assets = Liabilities +	Equity
−6,000 −6,000	

Date	Account and Explanation	Debit	Credit
Dec. 15, 2018	Dividends Payable	6,000	
	Cash		6,000
	(Record payment of dividends)		

Dividend Policy The corporation's record of dividends and retained earnings provides useful information to:

- boards of directors and managers who must formulate a dividend policy
- shareholders and potential investors who wish to evaluate past dividend policies and assess prospects for future dividends

Historical records and long-term future projections of earnings and dividends are of particular interest to shareholders because the dividend policies of most large corporations are characterized by long-term stability. In other words, they are designed to produce a smooth pattern of dividends over time. For this reason, directors approach increases in the per-share dividend very cautiously and avoid decreases at all costs.

Sufficiency of Retained Earnings A corporation must have sufficient retained earnings to pay a dividend. Most corporation laws prohibit dividends if the balance of retained earnings is negative. However, the CBCA states that dividends may be declared and paid if the dividend payment does not prevent the company from paying its liabilities as they become due. The Board of Directors needs to be sensitive to these legal requirements if a dividend is to be declared and paid when the company's retained earnings are negative (i.e., in deficit).

Stock Dividends A cash dividend transfers cash from the corporation to its shareholders. In contrast, a **stock dividend** transfers shares from the corporation to its shareholders—that is, additional shares of the corporation. For each share outstanding, a fixed number of new shares is issued, and an amount of retained earnings is transferred to share capital accounts in a process known as *capitalization of retained earnings.* While a cash dividend reduces both total assets and total equity, a stock dividend alters *neither total assets nor total equity.* A stock dividend merely notifies investors that the equity section of the statement of financial position has been rearranged.

The amount of retained earnings capitalized for each new share depends on the size of the stock dividend.

- *Small stock dividends* increase the number of outstanding shares by less than 25%; they are capitalized using the shares' market value on the dividend declaration date.
- *Large stock dividends* increase the number of outstanding shares by 25% or more and are capitalized based on the average market price for the shares after the dividend announcement. This amount is appropriate because the market price per share typically decreases significantly when a large stock dividend is announced, as a significant increase in the number of outstanding shares will occur after the stock dividend is actually issued.

This accounting process is illustrated in Cornerstone 10.4 .

Note that the stock dividend merely transfers dollars from retained earnings to the share capital accounts.

Although a stock dividend increases the *number* of shares held by each shareholder, it does not alter the *proportion* of shares held by each shareholder. For example, if an investor held 100,000 out of 2,000,000 outstanding shares before a 10% stock dividend, that investor would hold 110,000 out of 2,200,000 outstanding shares after the dividend. Thus the investor would hold 5% of the outstanding shares both before and after the share dividend and would have a 5% claim on earnings and shareholders' equity both before and after:

$$\frac{100,000}{2,000,000} = \frac{110,000}{2,200,000} = 0.05$$

Furthermore, despite the popular belief to the contrary among shareholders and even some financial managers, research shows that neither stock dividends nor stock

CORNERSTONE
VIDEO

CORNERSTONE 10.4   Recording Small and Large Stock Dividends

Information:

On May 18, 2018, Kingsville Corporation has 6,000,000 outstanding common shares previously issued for $10 per share.

Required:

1. Determine how many new shares are issued and prepare the necessary journal entry, assuming that Kingsville declares and pays a 5% stock dividend. These shares trade currently at $12 per share on the date of dividend declaration.

2. Determine how many new shares are issued and prepare the necessary journal entry, assuming that Kingsville declares and pays a 30% stock dividend. The share price on the market decreases from $12 to $10 per share when the stock dividend is announced.

Why:

Large and small stock dividends are recorded differently due to the effect on the market price of the shares when the dividend is announced. Small stock dividends do not usually significantly affect market price of a share whereas large stock dividends will usually significantly affect the market price of a share. Stock dividends must be accurately recorded in order to properly reflect the share capital accounts relating to each ownership group.

Solution:

1. $6,000,000 \times 0.05 = 300,000$ shares

Assets = Liabilities +	Shareholders' Equity
	−3,600,000
	+3,600,000

Account and Explanation	Debit	Credit
Stock dividends (closed to retained earnings)*	3,600,000	
Common Shares		3,600,000
(Record small stock dividend)		

* 300,000 shares × $12 = $3,600,000

2. $6,000,000 \times 0.30 = 1,800,000$ shares

Assets = Liabilities +	Shareholders' Equity
	−18,000,000
	+18,000,000

Account and Explanation	Debit	Credit
Stock dividends (closed to retained earnings)**	18,000,000	
Common Shares		18,000,000
(Record large stock dividend)		

** 1,800,000 shares × $10 = $18,000,000

splits, which we will consider next, enhance the total market value of a corporation's outstanding common shares. Stock dividends should be distinguished from dividend plans that allow shareholders to choose between receiving a cash dividend or shares with equivalent current value. Such plans (known as dividend reinvestment plans) may enhance a shareholder's proportionate ownership and also avoid brokerage fees.

Stock Splits While a stock split is not a dividend, it is often confused with being a stock dividend. A stock split, is similar to a stock dividend because it increases the number of outstanding shares without altering the proportionate ownership of a corporation. However, a stock split is different from a stock dividend in that a stock dividend requires a journal entry to shareholder equity accounts, whereas a stock split does not. In other words, a **stock split** is a share issue that increases the number of outstanding shares of a corporation without changing the balances of its shareholder equity accounts.

Consider a corporation that has 10,000 common shares outstanding, previously issued for $30 per share, which is also the market value. In a two-for-one stock split, shareholders will exchange each of their 10,000 original shares for two new shares; the number of shares will rise from 10,000 to 20,000. The *total* recorded common share capital will remain at $300,000, although the market value per share will decrease from $30 to $15 per share. The stock split has the effect of distributing the company's share value over a larger number of shares.

Stock splits are used to reduce the per-share price of a share. If nothing else changes, a two-for-one split as shown should reduce the market price of a share in half. A corporation may wish to reduce the per-share price to encourage trading of its shares. The assumption is that a higher per-share price is an obstacle to purchases and sales of shares, particularly for small investors.

No journal entry is required to record a stock split because no account balances change. The change in the number of outstanding shares is merely noted in the corporation's records.

The following table compares the effect of a 50% stock dividend with a 50% stock split.

Shareholders' Equity	Initial Position	50% Stock Dividend	1.5 for 1 Stock Split
Number of common shares outstanding	100,000	150,000	150,000
Issue price per share	12	8	8
Common share capital	1,200,000	1,600,000	1,200,000
Retained earnings	6,000,000	5,600,000	6,000,000
Total shareholders' equity	7,200,000	7,200,000	7,200,000

Preferred Share Dividend Preferences While dividends on common shares are set by the corporation's Board of Directors, dividends on preferred shares are usually established as one of the terms of the issue. Most preferred shares fix their dividend rate as a percentage of the stated value assigned to the share when issued. For example, an 8% preferred share with a $100 stated value has an annual dividend of $8 ($100 × 8%). Of course, both preferred and common dividends are subject to various restrictions imposed by statute, by corporate charter, by the terms of preferred share issues, and by contracts with bondholders and others.

Although preferred shareholders usually have no voting rights, they are "preferred" in the sense that corporations are required to pay dividends to them before paying dividends to common shareholders. Such dividend preferences can take three forms:

- current dividend preference
- cumulative dividend preference
- participating dividend preference

Most preferred share issues grant a current dividend preference, and some also grant one or both of the other preferences, thereby further enhancing the likelihood of dividend payments.

Current Dividend Preference on Preferred Shares Preferred shares always have a **current dividend preference**, which provides that current dividends must be paid to preferred shareholders before any dividends are paid to common shareholders. However, the current dividend preference does not guarantee payment of preferred dividends. In lean years, both common and preferred shareholders may fail to receive dividends.

The following illustration demonstrates the impact of the current dividend preference. During the period 2017 through 2020, Harper Corporation maintained the following capital structure:

Preferred shares, unlimited authorized, 8%, $10 stated value, 4,000 shares issued and outstanding	$ 40,000
Common shares, unlimited authorized, 30,000 shares issued and outstanding	210,000
Total issued and outstanding shares	$250,000

Harper's Board of Directors determined the total dollar amount available for preferred and common dividends in each year from 2017 through 2020 as shown in the second column of the following schedule:

Year	Amount Available for Dividends	Dividends to Preferred	Dividends to Common
2017	$12,200	$3,200*	$9,000**
2018	7,000	3,200	3,800
2019	2,000	2,000	0
2020	0	0	0

* 0.08 × $40,000 = $3,200
** $12,200 − $3,200 = $9,000

This schedule shows that the common dividend is any positive amount remaining after the full preferred dividend has been paid. If the total amount available for dividends is less than the full preferred dividend, the entire amount is paid to preferred shareholders.

Cumulative Dividend Preference on Preferred Shares Most preferred shares are cumulative. The **cumulative dividend preference** requires the eventual payment of all preferred dividends—both **dividends in arrears** and current dividends—before any dividends are paid to common shareholders. (Preferred share dividends remaining undeclared for one or more years are considered to be in arrears.) In other words, no dividends can be paid to common shareholders until all prior and current preferred dividends have been declared and paid. The cumulative dividend preference thus includes the current dividend preference. This is illustrated in Cornerstone 10.5 .

Dividends do not become a liability of a corporation until they have been declared by the Board of Directors. If preferred dividends in arrears have not been declared, they are not recorded as liabilities but are disclosed in a footnote to the financial statements.

Participating Dividend Preference on Preferred Shares For some classes of preferred shares, dividends are not restricted to a fixed rate. Preferred shares that pay dividends in excess of their stated dividend rate are called *participating preferred shares*. Preferred shares that cannot pay dividends in excess of the current dividend preference plus cumulative dividends in arrears, if any, are called *nonparticipating preferred shares.*

Calculating Cumulative Preferred Dividends

CORNERSTONE 10.5

Information:

Laurier Manufacturing has a single class of common shares and a single class of cumulative preferred shares. The cumulative preferred shares require the corporation to pay an annual dividend of $6,500 to preferred shareholders. On January 1, 2018, Laurier's preferred dividends were one year in arrears, which means that Laurier declared neither preferred nor common dividends in 2017. From 2018 to 2020, Laurier's Board of Directors determined they would be able to pay dividends at $9,000, $12,000, and $15,000, respectively.

▶| CORNERSTONE
VIDEO

Required:

Show how these anticipated dividend payments will be split between preferred and common shareholders.

Why:

The cumulative feature of preferred shares requires corporations to declare and pay all current and prior-period dividends to preferred shareholders before paying any dividends to common shareholders.

Solution:

Year	Amount Available for Dividends	Dividends to Preferred	Dividends to Common
2018	$ 9,000	$ 9,000*	$ 0
2019	12,000	10,500**	1,500**
2020	15,000	6,500***	8,500

* The $9,000 dividend paid to preferred shareholders in 2018 removes the $6,500 in arrears from 2017, but leaves dividends in arrears at January 1, 2019, of $4,000—the excess of preferred dividends for 2017 and 2018 over the amount paid in 2018 [(2 × $6,500) − $9,000 = $4,000].

** The $10,500 dividend to preferred shareholders in 2019 pays the current preferred dividend ($6,500), removes the $4,000 in arrears from 2018, and leaves $1,500 to be paid to common shareholders [$12,000 − $6,500 − $4,000 = $1,500].

*** annual required dividend.

The **participating dividend preference** provides that shareholders of participating preferred shares receive, in addition to the stated dividend, a share of amounts available for distribution as dividends to other classes of shares. Participating preferred shares may be either fully participating or partially participating:

- Fully participating preferred shares receive a share of *all* amounts available for dividends. Common shares are allocated a dividend at the same rate as the current dividend on preferred shares, and any remainder is divided between preferred and common shareholders—usually in proportion to the total capital accounts of the two classes of shares.
- Partially participating preferred shares also receive a share of all amounts available for dividends, but the share is limited to a specified percentage of preferred stated value.

REPORT AND ANALYZE RETAINED EARNINGS AND ACCUMULATED OTHER COMPREHENSIVE INCOME

OBJECTIVE ④

Explain and report changes to retained earnings and accumulated other comprehensive income.

Retained earnings (or **deficit**) is the accumulated earnings (or losses) over the entire life of the corporation that have not been paid out to shareholders. Generally, ending retained earnings is calculated with a simple formula:

> Beginning retained earnings
> + Net income
> − Dividends declared
> = Ending retained earnings

Restrictions on Retained Earnings

Under most corporate charters, the balance of a corporation's retained earnings represents an upper limit on the entity's ability to pay dividends. (Dividends cannot normally be declared if retained earnings is in a negative balance.) A corporation's capacity to pay dividends may be limited by the amount of cash on hand but may also be restricted by agreements with lenders, by the corporation's Board of Directors, and by various provisions of federal or provincial law, as follows:

- An agreement between the corporation and bondholders may require that retained earnings never fall below a specified level as long as the bonds are outstanding.
- The firm's Board of Directors may set aside a portion of retained earnings and declare it unavailable for the payment of dividends. Such an action may be used to communicate to shareholders changes in dividend policy made necessary by expansion programs or other decisions of the Board.

Restrictions of this sort are usually disclosed in footnotes to the financial statements to signify that the restricted amount is unavailable for dividends. In rare cases, a separate "reserve" account is established for the restricted portion of retained earnings. The reserve account is called either *restricted earnings* or *appropriation of retained earnings*. The account title frequently indicates, quite specifically, the nature of the restriction or the appropriation, as, for example, "restricted retained earnings under agreements with bondholders" or "appropriation of retained earnings for plant expansion." When reserve accounts are used, retained earnings is reported on two or more lines in the equity section of the statement of financial position. One line is devoted to each restriction, and to "unrestricted retained earnings" or "unappropriated retained earnings."

Error Corrections and Retained Earnings Errors in recording transactions can distort the financial statements. If errors are discovered and corrected before the closing process, then no great harm is done. However, if errors go undetected, then flawed financial statements are issued. No matter when they are discovered, errors should be corrected.

If an error has resulted in a misstatement of earnings, then correction may require a direct adjustment to retained earnings, called a **prior period adjustment**. To illustrate, suppose that Byrnes Corporation, a private corporation, uses a computer program to calculate depreciation expense. In 2017, a programming error caused the 2017 depreciation expense to be understated by $16,000. The error was not discovered until August 2018; consequently, 2017 net income after income taxes (which are paid at a rate of 25%) was overstated by $12,000 [$16,000 × (1 − 0.25)]. The error correction would be recorded in 2018 as follows, assuming an additional $16,000 of tax depreciation could be claimed on the company's tax return and a 25% corporate tax rate.

Date	Account and Explanation	Debit	Credit
Aug. 31, 2018	Retained Earnings	12,000	
	Tax Refund Receivable	4,000	
	Accumulated Depreciation		16,000
	(Record prior period adjustment)		

Assets = Liabilities +	Shareholders' Equity (Retained Earnings)
+4,000	−12,000
−16,000	

Byrnes's statement of retained earnings (required under ASPE for private corporations) for 2018 incorporates the $12,000 prior period adjustment as follows:

Byrnes Corporation Statement of Retained Earnings For the Year Ended December 31, 2018		
Retained earnings, January 1, 2018		$157,000
Less: Prior period adjustment:		
Correction of error in calculation of 2017		
depreciation expense (net of tax)		(12,000)
Retained earnings as adjusted, January 1, 2018		145,000
Add: Net income for 2018		65,000
Less: Dividends declared in 2018:		
Cash dividend, preferred shares	$ (4,000)	
Stock dividend, common shares	(20,000)	(24,000)
Retained earnings, December 31, 2018		$186,000

Notice that the adjustment is deducted from the beginning balance of retained earnings to produce an *adjusted* beginning balance.

Financial accounting standards define prior period adjustments in a way that specifically excludes adjustments arising from estimation errors. Estimation errors are to be accounted for on a prospective basis and are corrected by adjusting the related income accounts for the period in which they are discovered.

Adjustments necessary due to a change in accounting policy that materially affects financial statements issued in previous years are to be accounted for on a retrospective basis in the same manner as above for accounting errors. Accounting errors and changes in accounting policies are discussed further in intermediate accounting courses.

Reporting and Analyzing Accumulated Other Comprehensive Income

IFRS requires companies with comprehensive income to prepare a statement of comprehensive income. In addition, accumulated other comprehensive income must be reported as a component of the statement of changes in equity and in the shareholders' equity section of the statement of financial position.

Comprehensive income (loss) includes two components: first, net income as otherwise calculated; and second, other comprehensive income (loss), which includes certain unrealized gains and losses mentioned below. At year-end, net income is closed to retained earnings and other comprehensive income is closed to accumulated other comprehensive income.

IFRS requires public companies to report accumulated other comprehensive income (loss). Normally, revenues, expenses, gains, and losses are included in the calculation of net income. However, certain gains and losses that are unrelated to investments by shareholders or distributions to shareholders bypass the net income calculation and are included in other comprehensive income. Examples include revaluation gains on property, plant, and equipment where the revaluation model is being used; unrealized gains and losses on derivatives that are designated as cash flow hedges; actuarial gains on defined benefit pension plans; and certain unrealized foreign currency translation gains and losses. The measurement and reporting of these unrealized gains and losses is a complex matter and is covered in intermediate and advanced accounting courses.

Exhibit 10.5 is an excerpt from the 2014 (January 3, 2015) audited financial statements of Canadian Tire Corporation. It indicates the required disclosure for comprehensive income. Exhibit 10.6 and Exhibit 10.7 respectively indicate the required disclosure for accumulated other comprehensive income in the balance sheet and in the statement of changes in equity.

(EXHIBIT 10.5)

Consolidated Statements of Comprehensive Income

For the years ended (C$ in millions)	January 3, 2015	December 28, 2013
Net income	$639.3	$564.4
Other comprehensive income		
Items that may be reclassified subsequently to net income:		
Cash flow hedges:		
Gains, net of tax of $40.4 (2013—$30.0)	114.0	83.1
Reclassification of gains to non-financial assets, net of tax of $27.2 (2013—$12.2)	(77.5)	(33.7)
Reclassification of gains to income, net of tax of $0.6 (2013—$0.1)	(1.5)	(0.4)
Available-for-sale financial assets:		
(Losses) gains, net of tax of $0.1 (2013—$nil)	(0.1)	0.1
Reclassification of gains to income, net of tax of $nil (2013—$nil)	(0.1)	–
Item that will not be reclassified subsequently to net income:		
Actuarial (losses) gains, net of tax of $4.7 (2013—$3.6)	(13.2)	10.0
Other comprehensive income	21.6	59.1
Other comprehensive income attributable to:		
Owners of Canadian Tire Corporation	$ 21.5	$ 59.1
Non-controlling interests	0.1	–
	$ 21.6	$ 59.1
Comprehensive income	$660.9	$623.5
Comprehensive income attributable to:		
Owners of Canadian Tire Corporation	$625.5	$620.3
Non-controlling interests	35.4	3.2
	$660.9	$623.5

The related notes form an integral part of these consolidated financial statements.

Source: Canadian Tire 2014 Annual Report, page 65.

(EXHIBIT 10.6)

Excerpts from Canadian Tire Coporation Financial Statement

Canadian Tire Corporation Consolidated Balance Sheet		
(in $ millions)	January 3, 2015	December 28, 2013
Shareholders' Equity:		
Share capital	695.5	712.9
Contributed surplus	2.9	2.4
Retained earnings	4,075.1	4,404.6
Accumulated other comprehensive income (loss)	82.0	(47.3)
	4,855.5	5,167.3

Source: Canadian Tire 2014 Annual Report.

Under ASPE, private companies do not report comprehensive income. These companies continue to prepare a statement of retained earnings.

ANALYZE SHAREHOLDERS' EQUITY

Shareholders want to understand the following:

- how the value of their shares will change
- how the company will distribute any excess cash to shareholders

We all know that investors buy shares to increase their personal wealth. But how do shareholders use the financial statements to better understand these two dimensions?

OBJECTIVE **5**

Calculate and analyze earnings per share, the dividend yield, and other equity ratios.

Shareholder Profitability Ratios

A primary driver of an increase in share price is profitability. Profitability refers to the return that the company earns (in other words, its net income). However, the magnitude of the net income also matters because it shows how much had to be invested to earn the return. That is, would you rather earn $10 on a $100 investment or $20 on a $500 investment? Although the latter return is twice as large as the former, it also took an investment that was five times bigger. Assuming equal risk, and so on, most investors would prefer to invest $100 to earn $10 because they then could use the extra $400 to invest somewhere else.

The two most common ratios used to evaluate shareholder profitability for common shareholders are earnings per share (EPS) and return on common equity.

Earnings per Share (EPS) **Earnings per share (EPS)** measures the net income earned by each common share. It is calculated as follows:

$$\text{EPS} = \frac{\text{Net income} - \text{Preferred dividends}}{\text{Avg. common shares outstanding}}$$

concept Q&A

Assume that a standard condition in a loan contract (called a "loan covenant") requires a borrower to maintain retained earnings of $3,000,000 on a $500,000 loan. The borrower does not like this covenant and asks why it has to be there. What would you say?

Answer:

Loan covenants such as these are there to protect the lender from the borrower removing money from the company, then declaring bankruptcy and never repaying the loan. For example, in the absence of this covenant, an unscrupulous borrower could borrow $500,000 from the bank, then pay out all this cash to shareholders as dividends, leaving little (or at least far less) collateral within the company.

Return on Common Equity **Return on common equity** shows the growth in equity from operating activities. It is calculated as follows:

EXHIBIT 10.7 — Consolidated Statements of Changes in Equity

(C$ in millions)	Share capital	Contributed surplus	Total accumulated other comprehensive income (loss)		Total accumulated other comprehensive income (loss)	Retained earnings	Equity attributable to owners of Canadian Tire Corporation	Equity attributable to non-controlling interests	Total equity
			Cashflow hedges	Fair value changes in available-for-sale financial assets					
Balance at December 28, 2013	(Note 3) $712.9	(Note 3) $2.4	$47.0	$0.4	$47.4	(Note 3) $4,404.6	$5,167.3	$282.6	$5,449.9
Net income						604.0	604.0	35.3	639.3
Other comprehensive income (loss)	–	–	34.8	(0.2)	34.6	(13.1)	21.5	0.1	21.6
Total comprehensive income (loss)	–	–	34.8	(0.2)	34.6	590.9	625.5	35.4	660.9
Contributions by and distributions to owners of Canadian Tire Corporation									
Issuance of Class A Non-Voting Shares (Note 28)	6.9						6.9		6.9
Repurchase of Class A Non-Voting Shares (Note 28)	(290.6)						(290.6)		(290.6)
Excess of repurchase price over average cost (Note 28)	266.3					(266.3)	–		–
Dividends						(154.1)	(154.1)		(154.1)
Issuance of redeemable financial instrument (Note 35)						(500.0)	(500.0)		(500.0)
Contributed surplus arising on sale of property to CT REIT		0.5					0.5		0.5
Contributions by and distributions to non-controlling interests									
Sale of ownership interests in the Financial Services business, net of transaction costs								476.8	476.8
Issuance of trust units to non-controlling interests, net of transaction costs								1.8	1.8
Distributions								(21.3)	(21.3)
Total contributions and distributions	(17.4)	0.5				(920.4)	(937.3)	457.3	(480.0)
Balance at January 3, 2015	$695.5	$2.9	$81.8	$0.2	$82.0	$4,075.1	$4,855.5	$775.3	$5,530.8
Balance at December 29, 2012	$718.5	$ –	$(2.0)	$0.3	$(1.7)	$4,047.5	$4,764.3	$ –	$4,764.3
Net income						561.2	561.2	3.2	564.4
Other comprehensive income	–	–	49.0	0.1	49.1	10.0	59.1	–	59.1
Total comprehensive income	–	–	49.0	0.1	49.1	571.2	620.3	3.2	623.5
Contributions by and distributions to owners of Canadian Tire Corporation									
Issuance of Class A Non-Voting Shares (Note 28)	5.8						5.8		5.8
Repurchase of Class A Non-Voting Shares (Note 28)	(105.9)						(105.9)		(105.9)
Excess of repurchase price over average cost (Note 28)	94.5					(94.5)	–		–
Dividends						(119.6)	(119.6)		(119.6)
Contributed surplus arising on sale of property to CT REIT		2.4					2.4		2.4
Contributions by and distributions to non-controlling interests									
Issuance of trust units to non-controlling interests, net of transaction costs								283.0	283.0
Distributions								(3.6)	(3.6)
Total contributions and distributions	(5.6)	2.4				(214.1)	(217.3)	279.4	62.1
Balance at December 28, 2013	$712.9	$2.4	$47.0	$0.4	$47.4	$4,404.6	$5,167.3	$282.6	$5,449.9

The related notes form an integral part of these condensed consolidated financial statements.
Source: Canadian Tire 2014 Annual Report.

$$\text{Return on common equity} = \frac{\text{Net income} - \text{Preferred dividends}}{\text{Avg. common shareholders' equity}}$$

Common shareholders' equity is calculated by taking total shareholders' equity and subtracting preferred shares.

Cornerstone 10.6 illustrates how to calculate shareholder profitability.

Calculating Shareholder Profitability Ratios

CORNERSTONE 10.6

CORNERSTONE VIDEO

Information:

Consider the following information from My Bank's 2018 financial statements (all numbers in thousands other than per-share amounts).

Common share price (12/31/18)	$40.00/share	2018 Avg. common shares outstanding	429,000
2018 Common dividends	$214,000	2018 Dividends per common share	$0.50/share
2018 Preferred dividends	$564,000	2018 Net income	$884,000
2018 Preferred shares	$0	2017 Preferred shares	$3,100,000
2018 Total shareholders' equity	$27,800,000	2017 Total shareholders' equity	$27,000,000

Required:

Calculate the following shareholder profitability ratios: (1) return on common equity and (2) EPS.

Why:

The calculation of shareholder profitability ratios indicates to investors the rate of return that can be expected on their investment.

Solution:

1.
$$\text{Return on common equity} = \frac{\text{Net income} - \text{Preferred dividends}}{\text{Avg. common shareholders' equity}}$$
$$= \frac{(\$884,000 - \$564,000)}{[(\$27,800,000 - \$0) + (\$27,000,000 - \$3,100,000)] \div 2} = 1.24\%$$

2.
$$\text{EPS} = \frac{\text{Net income} - \text{Preferred dividends}}{\text{Avg. common shares outstanding}} = \frac{(\$884,000 - \$564,000)}{429,000} = \$0.75$$

Shareholder Payout Ratios

Shareholders not only experience an increase in wealth through an increasing share price, but may also receive cash, or a payout, from the company. The most common shareholder payout ratios relate to dividends. Dividend yield considers the ratio of dividends paid to share price. This ratio is conceptually similar to an interest rate for debt:

$$\text{Dividend yield} = \frac{\text{Dividends per common share}}{\text{Common share price}}$$

Another common dividend ratio calculates the proportion of dividends to earnings:

$$\text{Dividend payout} = \frac{\text{Common dividends}}{\text{Net income}}$$

However, as discussed earlier, payouts to shareholders can also take the form of share repurchases. As such, the share repurchase payout ratio is:

$$\text{Share repurchase payout} = \frac{\text{Common share repurchases}}{\text{Net income}}$$

By using these two ratios, shareholders can easily calculate the total payout:

$$\text{Total payout} = \text{Dividend payout} + \text{Share repurchase payout}$$

Or, it can be calculated directly as:

$$\text{Total payout} = \frac{\text{Common dividends} + \text{Common share repurchases}}{\text{Net income}}$$

Total payout should be considered by investors before they invest in a company. Cornerstone 10.7 illustrates how to calculate payout ratios.

CORNERSTONE 10.7   ## Calculating Shareholder Payout Ratios

Information:

Consider the following information from My Bank's 2018 financial statements (all numbers in thousands other than per-share amounts).

CORNERSTONE
VIDEO

Common share price (12/31/18)	$40.00/share	2018 Avg. common shares outstanding	429,000
2018 Common dividends	$214,000	2018 Dividends per common share	$0.50/share
2018 Preferred dividends	$564,000	2018 Net income	$884,000
2018 Preferred shares	$0	2017 Preferred shares	$3,100,000
2018 Total shareholders' equity	$27,800,000	2017 Total shareholders' equity	$27,000,000
2018 Common shares repurchased	$10,000		

(Continued)

Required:

Calculate the following shareholder payout ratios: (1) dividend yield, (2) dividend payout, (3) share repurchase payout, and (4) total payout.

Why:

The calculation of shareholder payout ratios indicates to investors the total cash payout that can be expected on their investment.

Solution:

1. Common share dividend yield $= \dfrac{\text{Dividends per common share}}{\text{Common share price}} = \dfrac{\$0.50}{\$40.00} = 1.25\%$

2. Dividend payout $= \dfrac{\text{Common dividends}}{\text{Net income}} = \dfrac{\$214,000}{\$884,000} = 24.2\%$

3. Share repurchase payout $= \dfrac{\text{Common share repurchases}}{\text{Net income}} = \dfrac{\$10,000}{\$884,000} = 1.13\%$

4. Total payout = Dividend payout + Share repurchase payout = 24.2% + 1.1% = 25.3%

CORNERSTONE

10.7

(Continued)

Interpreting Ratios

What do these shareholder profitability and payout ratios mean? The results of these ratios are usually compared by shareholders and stock analysts to results for other companies in the same industry and are also compared to those of the same company over time. Both comparisons reveal trends that shareholders and stock analysts as investment advisers must evaluate.

UNINCORPORATED BUSINESSES— PROPRIETORSHIPS AND PARTNERSHIPS

This text concentrates on the corporate form of business organization since it is the dominant business form in the economy. However, it is possible to carry on business in an unincorporated form as either a proprietorship (one owner) or partnership (multiple owners).

A proprietorship is the simplest form of business organization. No legal documents are required to form a proprietorship. Similarly, no legal documents are required to form a partnership, though it is always prudent for partners to have a written partnership agreement.

Proprietorships and partnerships of individuals, unlike corporations, are not separate legal entities. Therefore, proprietorships and partners who are individuals can be sued personally and their personal assets are at risk.

For income tax purposes, proprietors and partners who are individuals are taxed personally on their business earnings. As a result, the financial statements for proprietorships and for partnerships do not record income tax expenses or income taxes payable.

Financial statements for proprietorships do not record salary expense to the owner since the owner cannot be an employee and employer simultaneously. Similarly,

OBJECTIVE 6

Explain and report equity accounts in unincorporated businesses.

partnership financial statements do not record salary expense to the partners. If salary expense is recorded in a proprietorship or partnership financial statement, it is considered to be an allocation of profit to the proprietor or partners and not a business expense for tax purposes. The statement of earnings for a partnership will usually present the allocation of each partner's share of profit on the face of the statement itself. In larger partnerships, a separate schedule, indicating the allocation of partnership income to the partners, may be attached to the partnership financial statements.

The accounting and reporting of revenues, expenses, assets, and liabilities for proprietorships and partnerships are generally the same as for corporations. However, the shareholders' equity section of a corporation's statement of financial position is very different in terminology and format from "proprietor's equity" or "partners' equity." The terms "share capital" and "contributed surplus" used by corporations are replaced by the term "capital" in proprietorships and partnerships. Also, the term "dividends" used by corporations is replaced by the word "drawings" in proprietorships and partnerships.

Accounting for Owner's (Proprietor's) Equity in a Proprietorship

Two owner's equity accounts exist in a proprietorship. A capital account records funds invested by the owner and the profit (loss) from operating the business. The drawing account records the funds withdrawn by the owner from the business. At the end of the fiscal period for the business, the statement of earnings accounts and drawing account are closed to the capital account. Exhibit 10.8 demonstrates typical journal entries required in a proprietorship.

Accounting for Partners' Equity in a Partnership

Two or more persons who enter into an agreement to earn a profit in an unincorporated business can form a partnership. A partnership may consist of two or more individuals or a combination of individuals and corporations. The partnership agreement should be in writing. A written partnership agreement is an enforceable contract, and it should specify all pertinent details that may affect the partnership and its partners, including how profits and losses will be shared, how partnership interests may be transferred, how the partnership is to be managed, and how capital will be contributed to and withdrawn from the partnership, as well as the consequences of the death of a partner. Provincial laws apply where a partnership agreement is silent on these or other matters. Since a partnership is easy to form, many professionals, including accountants, lawyers, and medical practitioners, have adopted this form of business.

The accounting entries for the business operated by a partnership are similar to those for a corporation and proprietorship except for the journal entries that affect partners' equity. In a partnership, capital contributions are recorded in the respective partners' capital accounts. Drawings (withdrawals) by each partner are recorded in the respective partners' drawings accounts. Profits and losses of a partnership are divided among the partners according to the partnership agreement. At the end of the fiscal year, the profit or loss of the partnership is closed to the partner capital accounts and the partner drawings accounts are closed to the partner capital accounts. Therefore, after the closing process is complete, a partner's capital account consists of his or her capital contributions, share of the partnership profit or loss, and partner drawings. Exhibit 10.9 presents the typical journal entries that are required in a partnership.

(EXHIBIT 10.8)

2018 Transactions for M. Joliet Proprietorship

Marc Joliet conducted the following transactions in 2018 during the operation of his electrical supply business, which commenced business on January 1, 2018.

1. The proprietor invested $100,000 of capital into his business. The required journal entry for the business is as follows:

	Debit	Credit
Cash	100,000	
Capital, M. Joliet		100,000

2. The owner withdrew $2,000 per month ($24,000 for the year) for his personal use. The required journal entry for the business for each month is as follows:

	Debit	Credit
Drawing, M. Joliet	2,000	
Cash		2,000

3. The business earned revenues of $950,000 and incurred expenses of $775,000 for the fiscal year ended December 31, 2018. The revenue and expense accounts are closed to the proprietor's capital account in the following journal entry:

	Debit	Credit
Each revenue account	950,000	
Each expense account		775,000
Capital, M. Joliet		175,000

4. The owner's drawing account is closed to the capital account at the end of the fiscal year in the following journal entry:

	Debit	Credit
Capital, M. Joliet	24,000	
Drawing, M. Joliet		24,000

A statement of proprietor's equity is normally prepared at the end of the fiscal year as follows:

M. Joliet Electrical
Statement of Proprietor's Equity
For the Year Ended December 31, 2018

Capital, beginning of the year	$ –
Add: Capital contributions	100,000
Profit of the year	175,000
	275,000
Deduct: Drawings for the year	–24,000
Capital, end of the year	$ 251,000

(EXHIBIT 10.9)

2018 Transactions for Zhang and Johnson, a Partnership

The following transactions were conducted by Zhang and Johnson, two lawyers, in 2018 during the operation of their law practice, which commenced business on January 1, 2018.

1. Zhang invested $100,000 of capital into the business. Johnson invested $50,000 of capital into the business. The required journal entry to reflect this transaction is as follows:

	Debit	Credit
Cash	150,000	
Capital, Zhang		100,000
Capital, Johnson		50,000

2. Zhang withdrew $2,000 cash per month ($24,000 for the year) and Johnson withdrew $1,000 cash per month ($12,000 for the year). The following journal entry is required each month to record the cash drawings:

	Debit	Credit
Drawings, Zhang	2,000	
Drawings, Johnson	1,000	
Cash		3,000

3. The law practice earned $850,000 in revenues and incurred $460,000 in expenses in 2018. The partners have agreed to share profits on a 60% (Zhang) and 40% (Johnson) basis. The following journal entry is required to close the statement of earnings accounts for the year and to allocate profits to the partners:

	Debit	Credit
Each revenue account	850,000	
Each expense account		460,000
Capital, Zhang ($390,000 × 60%)		234,000
Capital, Johnson ($390,000 × 40%)		156,000

4. The partner drawing accounts are closed to the partner capital accounts at the end of the fiscal year:

	Debit	Credit
Capital, Zhang	24,000	
Capital, Johnson	12,000	
Drawings, Zhang		24,000
Drawings, Johnson		12,000

A statement of partners' equity is usually prepared at the end of the fiscal year, as follows:

Zhang and Johnson
Statement of Partners' Equity
For the Year Ended December 31, 2018

	Zhang	Johnson	Total
Balance, beginning of the year	$ –	$ –	$ –
Add: Capital contributions	100,000	50,000	150,000
Profit of the year	234,000	156,000	390,000
	334,000	206,000	540,000
Deduct: Drawings for the year	−24,000	−12,000	−36,000
Balance, end of year	$ 310,000	$ 194,000	$ 504,000

SIGNIFICANT DIFFERENCES BETWEEN IFRS AND ASPE

The following differences exist between IFRS and ASPE with respect to the shareholders' equity section of the statement of financial position:

1. Public companies must report earnings per share in the statement of earnings (or comprehensive income if it applies); private companies are not required to report earnings per share on the statement of earnings.

2. Public companies must present accumulated other comprehensive income on the statement of financial position and on the statement of changes in equity. Private companies do not report comprehensive income and do not prepare a statement of changes in equity. Private companies report changes in retained earnings in a statement of retained earnings. Private companies report changes in share capital accounts in the notes to the financial statements.

3. Public companies must measure share-based compensation with specific valuation models. Private companies are permitted to use a simpler valuation model for share-based compensation expense since the market value of private company shares is difficult to determine as they are not publicly traded.

SUMMARY OF LEARNING OBJECTIVES

LO1. **Distinguish between common and preferred shares and explain their use in raising capital.**

- Corporations sell both common shares and preferred shares to raise capital.
- Preferred shares generally guarantee a regular dividend and receive priority over common shares in the payment of dividends and distribution of assets in liquidation.
- Common shares have voting rights and receive all benefits not assigned to the preferred shareholders or creditors.
- Selling different classes of shares (with different features) attracts shareholders with diverse risk preferences and tax situations.

LO2. **Explain and report transactions affecting common and preferred shares.**

- Both preferred and common shares are no par value shares in Canada but are assigned a stated value by the Board when issued.
- Shares issued should be recorded first based on their fair market value. If fair market value cannot be determined, shares should be recorded based on consideration received.

LO3. **Account for share repurchases, dividends, and stock splits.**

- Assets are distributed to shareholders by:
  - repurchasing their shares, or
  - paying dividends.
- Generally the cost of share repurchases is recorded as a reduction in shareholders' equity.
- Typically the corporation pays dividends with cash.
- Stock dividends and stock splits do not represent a payout to shareholders. These transactions have no effect on total shareholders' equity.
- Preferred shares generally have dividend preferences such as being cumulative or participating.

LO4. **Explain and report changes to retained earnings and accumulated other comprehensive income.**

- Retained earnings represents the earnings that the corporation elects not to pay out in dividends.

- Ending retained earnings is calculated by adding net income to beginning retained earnings and subtracting dividends declared.
- Retained earnings can be restricted, which communicates to shareholders that this portion of retained earnings is not eligible for dividend payout.
- Certain nonowner transactions are included in the accumulated other comprehensive income account in the shareholders' equity section of the statement of financial position.

LO5.   Calculate and analyze earnings per share, the dividend yield, and other equity ratios.
- Shareholders are primarily interested in two things:
  - the creation of value, and
  - the distribution of value.
- Analysis of the shareholders' equity section of the statement of financial position in conjunction with the statement of shareholders' equity allows shareholders to separate these concepts.

LO6.   Explain and report equity accounts in unincorporated businesses.
- Proprietorships and partnerships are unincorporated forms of business organization.
- Legal and income tax laws that apply to proprietorships and partnerships differ from the laws that apply to corporations.
- The format and terminology of the proprietor equity and partnership equity section of the statement of financial position differ significantly from those used for shareholder equity.
- The determination of assets, liabilities, revenues, and expenses are similar for proprietorships, partnerships, and corporations.

CORNERSTONES

CORNERSTONE 10.1	Recording the issuance of common and preferred shares, page 571
CORNERSTONE 10.2	Accounting for share repurchases, page 576
CORNERSTONE 10.3	Recording cash dividends, page 578
CORNERSTONE 10.4	Recording small and large stock dividends, page 580
CORNERSTONE 10.5	Calculating cumulative preferred dividends, page 583
CORNERSTONE 10.6	Calculating shareholder profitability ratios, page 589
CORNERSTONE 10.7	Calculating shareholder payout ratios, page 590

KEY TERMS

REVIEW PROBLEM

Shareholders' Equity

Grace Industries Inc., a privately held corporation, has decided to go public. The current ownership group has 10,000,000 common shares (purchased at an average price of $0.50 per share) and the articles of incorporation authorize unlimited, no par value, common shares and unlimited, 10%, $30 stated value, cumulative preferred shares. On January 1, 2017, the public offering issues 8,000,000 common shares at $14 per share and 100,000 preferred shares at $33 per share.

On October 3, 2018, Grace Industries repurchases and cancels 750,000 common shares at $12 per share. After the repurchase, Grace's Board of Directors decides to declare dividends totalling $4,050,000 (no dividends were declared or paid in 2017). This dividend will be declared on November 15, 2018, to all shareholders of record on December 8, 2018. This dividend will be paid on December 23, 2018. On December 28, 2018, 100,000 common shares are issued for $15 per share.

At December 31, 2018, Grace Industries has $12,000,000 of retained earnings before any adjustment for share repurchases and accumulated other comprehensive income (loss) of ($250,000).

Required:

1. Prepare the journal entry to record the January 1, 2017, issuance of the common and preferred shares.
2. Prepare the journal entry to record the October 3, 2018, share repurchase.
3. Determine how much of the dividend will go to preferred shareholders.
4. Calculate what the dividends per common share will be.
5. Prepare the journal entry for the dividend declaration on November 15, 2018.
6. Prepare the journal entry on the date of record (December 8, 2018).
7. Prepare the journal entry on the dividend payment date (December 23, 2018).
8. Prepare the journal entry for the issuance of common shares on December 28, 2018.
9. Prepare the shareholders' equity section of the statement of financial position at December 31, 2018.

Solution:

1.

Date	Account and Explanation	Debit	Credit
Jan. 1, 2017	Cash^a	3,300,000	
	Preferred Shares^b		3,000,000
	Contributed Surplus—Preferred		
	Shares^c		300,000
	(Record issuance of preferred shares)		
	Cash^d	112,000,000	
	Common Shares		112,000,000
	(Record issuance of common shares)		

Assets	= Liabilities +	Shareholders' Equity
+3,300,000		+3,000,000
+112,000,000		+300,000
		+112,000,000

^{a} 100,000 shares × $33 = $3,300,000
^{b} 100,000 shares × $30 stated value = $3,000,000
^{c} 100,000 shares × ($33 − $30) = $300,000
^{d} 8,000,000 shares × $14 = $112,000,000

2.

Date	Account and Explanation	Debit	Credit
Oct. 3, 2018	Retained Earnings	4,125,000	
	Common Shares*	4,875,000	
	Cash**		9,000,000

Assets	= Liabilities +	Shareholders' Equity
−9,000,000		−4,125,000
		−4,875,000

* 750,000 shares × $6.50 (6.50 = (112,000,000 + 5,000,000)/18,000,000 common shares)
** 750,000 shares × $12

3. The preferred shares are cumulative, so the preferred shareholders must be paid their annual dividend for 2018 (the current year) and for 2017 (dividends in arrears).

Preferred Dividends* $600,000

* 100,000 shares × ($30 stated value × 10% × 2 years) = $600,000

4. The common shareholders receive any dividend remaining after the preferred dividend has been paid (because the preferred is not participating). Remember that the ownership group owned 10,000,000 shares, then issued 8,000,000 shares in the initial public offering.

$$\text{Common Dividends} \frac{\$4,050,000 - \$600,000}{18,000,000 \text{ issued shares} - 750,000 \text{ repurchased and cancelled shares}} = \$0.20 \text{ per share}$$

5.

Date	Account and Explanation	Debit	Credit
Nov. 15, 2018	Dividends*	4,050,000	
	Cash Dividends Payable		4,050,000
	(Record declaration of cash dividends)		

Assets	=	Liabilities	+	Shareholders' Equity
+4,050,000				−4,050,000

* Dividends is closed to retained earnings

6. No entry is necessary on the date of record.

7.

Date	Account and Explanation	Debit	Credit
Dec. 23, 2018	Cash Dividends Payable	4,050,000	
	Cash		4,050,000
	(Record payment of cash dividends)		

Assets	=	Liabilities	+	Shareholders' Equity
−4,050,000		−4,050,000		

8.

Date	Account and Explanation	Debit	Credit
Dec. 28, 2018	Cash*	1,500,000	
	Common Shares		1,500,000
	(Record issuance of common shares)		

Assets	=	Liabilities	+	Shareholders' Equity
+1,500,000				+1,500,000

* 100,000 shares × $15 = $1,500,000

9. **Shareholders' Equity:**

Issued and outstanding shares

Preferred shares, 10%, $30 stated value, cumulative, unlimited shares authorized, 100,000 shares issued and outstanding	$ 3,000,000[a]
Common shares, no par, unlimited shares authorized, 17,350,000 shares issued and outstanding	113,625,000[b]
Contributed surplus:	
Preferred shares	300,000[c]
Total issued and outstanding shares	116,925,000
Retained earnings	7,875,000[d]
Less:	
Accumulated other comprehensive income (loss)	(250,000)[e]
Total shareholders' equity	$ 124,550,000

[a] 100,000 shares issued at $30 stated value (see journal entry from part 1).
[b] (10,000,000 shares × $.50) + (8,000,000 shares × $14) + (100,000 shares × $15) − (750,000 shares × $6.50)
[c] 100,000 shares issued at $3 more than stated value ($33 selling price less $30 stated value). See journal entry from part 1.
[d] $12,000,000 (given information) − $4,125,000. See journal entry from part 2.
[e] Given information.

DISCUSSION QUESTIONS

1. What does shareholders' equity represent?
2. What does a share represent?
3. Why do corporations issue shares?
4. What is the difference between a privately and publicly held corporation?
5. What are authorized shares?
6. Why would the number of shares issued be different from the number of shares outstanding?
7. What are the benefits that common shareholders may receive?
8. How do common shares and preferred shares differ?
9. Discuss the similarities between preferred shares and debt.
10. Why do corporations utilize different forms of equity?
11. Describe how cumulative preferred shares differ from non-cumulative preferred shares.
12. How is a preferred share dividend calculated?
13. What statement of financial position accounts are affected by the issuance of shares?
14. Why might a corporation grant stock options to employees in lieu of a higher salary?
15. What is a stock warrant? How are they used by corporations?
16. Describe two ways corporations make payouts to shareholders.
17. What are treasury shares?
18. Give four reasons why a company might repurchase its own shares.
19. What entries are made (if any) at the declaration date, date of record, and date of payment for cash dividends?
20. Describe the effect of a cash versus a stock dividend on a company's shareholders' equity.
21. What is a stock dividend? How does it differ from a stock split?
22. What is the effect of a stock split on shareholders' equity account balances?
23. Explain each of the following preferred share dividend preferences: (1) current dividend preference, (2) cumulative dividend preference, and (3) participating dividend preference.
24. Are dividends in arrears reported among the liabilities of the dividend-paying firm? If not, how are they reported, and why?
25. What are retained earnings?
26. How may a corporation's retained earnings be restricted?
27. When are prior period adjustments used?
28. Distinguish between retained earnings and accumulated other comprehensive income.
29. Describe the statement of changes in shareholders' equity.
30. How are dividend payout and profitability ratios useful to investors?
31. Explain how a proprietorship differs from a partnership.
32. Explain the accounting matters that should be addressed in a written partnership agreement.
33. Discuss how partnership equity would differ in format and terminology from shareholder equity in a statement of financial position.
34. Why are unincorporated forms of business used?
35. Explain the differences and similarities between dividends paid by a corporation and drawings paid to a proprietor.
36. How is profit allocation among partners in a partnership determined?

MULTIPLE-CHOICE EXERCISES

10-1 Which of the following is not a component of shareholders' equity?
a. Loss on sale of equipment
b. Dividends payable
c. Retained earnings
d. Net income

10-2 Which of the following statements is true?
a. The shares that are in the hands of the shareholders are said to be outstanding.
b. It is very unlikely that corporations will have more than one class of shares outstanding.
c. Preferred shares are shares that have been retired.
d. The outstanding number of shares is the maximum number of shares that can be issued by a corporation.

10-3 Authorized shares represent the:
a. number of shares that have been sold.
b. number of shares that are currently held by shareholders.
c. number of shares that have been repurchased by the corporation.
d. maximum number of shares that can be issued.

10-4 McKean Corporation authorized 500,000 common shares in its articles of incorporation. On May 1, 2018, 100,000 shares were sold to the company's founders. However, on October 15, 2018, McKean repurchased and cancelled 20,000 shares to settle a dispute among the founders. On October 15, 2018, how many shares were outstanding?
a. 500,000 and 100,000
b. 100,000 and 100,000
c. 100,000 and 80,000
d. 80,000 and 80,000

10-5 Harvey Corporation shows the following in the shareholders' equity section of its statement of financial position: The stated value of its common shares is $0.25 and the total balance in the common shares account is $50,000. Also noted is that 15,000 shares are currently designated as being repurchased but not yet cancelled. The number of shares outstanding is:
a. 215,000
b. 200,000

c. 196,250
d. 185,000

10-6 Assad Corporation repurchases 10,000 of its shares for $12 per share. The shares were originally issued at an average price of $10 per share. How much gain or loss should Assad report on its statement of comprehensive income as a result of this transaction?
a. $0
b. $20,000 loss
c. $100,000 gain
d. $20,000 loss and $100,000 gain

10-7 With regard to preferred shares,
a. their issuance provides no flexibility to the issuing company because their terms always require mandatory dividend payments.
b. their shareholders may have the right to participate, along with common shareholders, if a dividend is declared.
c. no dividends are expected by the shareholders.
d. there is a legal requirement for a corporation to declare a dividend on preferred shares.

10-8 DAE Parts Shop began business on January 1, 2018. The corporate charter authorized issuance of 20,000 no par value common shares and 5,000 $10 stated value, 5% cumulative preferred shares. DAE issued 12,000 common shares at $25 per share on January 2, 2018. What effect does the entry to record the issuance of shares have on total shareholders' equity?
a. increase of $120,000
b. increase of $150,000
c. increase of $300,000
d. increase of $340,000

10-9 Thornwood Partners began business on January 1, 2018. The corporate charter authorized issuance of unlimited no par value common shares, and 8,000 $3 stated value, 10% cumulative preferred shares. On July 1, Thornwood issued 20,000 common shares in exchange for two years' rent on a retail location. The cash rental price is $3,000 per month and the rental period begins on July 1. What is the correct entry to record the July 1 transaction?

a. Debit to Cash, $72,000; Credit to Prepaid Rent, $57,600

b. Debit to Prepaid Rent, $72,000; Credit to Common Shares, $72,000

c. Debit to Prepaid Rent, $72,000; Credit to Common Shares, $60,000; Credit to Contributed Surplus—Common Shares, $12,000

d. Debit to Prepaid Rent, $72,000; Credit to Common Shares, $20,000; Credit to Contributed Surplus—Common Shares, $52,000

10-10 A company would repurchase its own shares for all of the following reasons except:

a. it believes the shares are overvalued.

b. it wishes to increase the earnings per share.

c. it wishes to prevent unwanted takeover attempts.

d. it needs the shares for employee bonuses.

10-11 When a company purchases treasury shares, which of the following statements is true?

a. Dividends continue to be paid on the treasury shares.

b. They are no longer considered to be issued.

c. Treasury shares are considered to be an asset because cash is paid for the shares.

d. The cost of the treasury shares reduces shareholders' equity.

10-12 When a company retires its own common shares, the company must:

a. decrease the common share account balances by the original issue price.

b. record a gain or loss depending on the difference between original selling price and repurchase cost.

c. get the approval of the government to do so.

d. issue a different class of shares to the former shareholders.

10-13 Which of the following should be considered when a company decides to declare a cash dividend on common shares?

a. The retained earnings balance only

b. The number of authorized common shares

c. The book value of the company's shares

d. The cash available and the retained earnings balance

10-14 When a company declares a cash dividend, which of the following is true?

a. Assets are decreased.

b. Assets are increased.

c. Liabilities are increased.

d. Shareholders' equity is increased.

10-15 What is the effect of a stock dividend on shareholders' equity?

a. Shareholders' equity is decreased.

b. Total shareholders' equity stays the same.

c. Contributed surplus is decreased.

d. Retained earnings is increased.

10-16 As a result of a stock split,

a. shareholders' equity is increased.

b. the stated value of each share recorded in share capital is changed in the reverse proportion as the stock split.

c. the shareholders have a higher proportionate ownership of the company.

d. the market price of the outstanding shares is increasing because a split is evidence of a profitable company.

10-17 The balance of the no par value common share account for Patrice Company was $240,000,000 before its recent 2-for-1 stock split. The market price of the shares was $50 per share before the stock split. What occurred as a result of the stock split?

a. The market price of the shares was not affected.

b. The balance in the common share account was increased.

c. The market price of the shares dropped to approximately $25 per share.

d. The balance in the retained earnings account decreased.

10-18 When a company declares a 3-for-1 stock split, the number of outstanding shares:

a. triples.

b. stays the same, but the number of issued shares triples.

c. is reduced by one-third.

d. is reduced by one-third, and the number of issued shares is tripled.

10-19 Shea Company Ltd. has issued 100,000 6%, $50 stated value, cumulative preferred shares. In 2017, no dividends were declared on preferred shares. In 2018, Shea had a profitable year and decided to pay dividends to shareholders of both preferred and common shares. If Shea has $750,000 available for dividends in 2018, how much can it pay to the common shareholders?
a. $0
b. $150,000
c. $450,000
d. $750,000

10-20 RVR Enterprises shows net income of $100,000 for 2018 and retained earnings of $500,000 on its December 31, 2018, statement of financial position. During the year, RVR declared and paid $60,000 in dividends. What was RVR's retained earnings balance at December 31, 2017?
a. $540,000
b. $460,000
c. $440,000
d. $400,000

10-21 Comprehensive income:
a. is considered an appropriation of retained earnings.
b. includes transactions that affect shareholders' equity with the exception of those transactions that involve owners.
c. includes all transactions that are under management's control.
d. is the result of all events and transactions reported on the statement of earnings.

10-22 Garnean Inc. issued $50,000 in common share dividends. Its net income for the year was $250,000. What is Garnean's dividend payout ratio?
a. 0.2
b. 0.5
c. 2.5
d. 5

CORNERSTONE EXERCISES

OBJECTIVE ②
CORNERSTONE 10.1

Cornerstone Exercise 10-23   Recording the Issuance of Common and Preferred Shares

Delhi Corporation Ltd. is authorized by its charter from the Province of Alberta to issue 2,000 7% preferred shares with a stated value of $30 per share and 125,000 common shares of no par value. On January 1, 2018, Delhi issues 1,300 preferred shares at $35 per share and 84,000 common shares at $12.50 per share.

Required:

Prepare the journal entry to record the issuance of the shares.

OBJECTIVE ②
CORNERSTONE 10.1

Cornerstone Exercise 10-24   Recording the Issuance of Common Shares

Dartmouth Company Ltd. issues 300,000 no par value common shares for $27 per share on June 30, 2018.

Required:

Prepare the journal entry to record this transaction.

OBJECTIVE ②
CORNERSTONE 10.1

Cornerstone Exercise 10-25   Calculating the Number of Shares Issued

Castalia Inc. issued no par value common shares on September 4, 2018, for $8 per share. The Common Shares account was credited for $612,000 in the journal entry to record this transaction.

Required:

How many shares were issued on September 4, 2018?

OBJECTIVE ③
CORNERSTONE 10.2

Cornerstone Exercise 10-26   Accounting for Share Repurchase and Cancellation

On February 15, 2018, Spring Hope Ltd. repurchases and cancels 1,200 of its outstanding common shares for $7 per share. These shares were originally issued for $5 per share.

Required:

Prepare the journal entry to record the share repurchase and cancellation.

Cornerstone Exercise 10-27 Accounting for Share Repurchase and Cancellation

OBJECTIVE ③
CORNERSTONE 10.2

On January 3, 2018, Tommyboy Corporation repurchases and cancels 250,000 of its outstanding common shares for $18 per share. These shares were originally issued for $20 per share.

Required:

1. Prepare the journal entry to record this transaction.
2. How will this transaction affect Tommyboy's 2018 statement of earnings?

Cornerstone Exercise 10-28 Share Repurchases and Cancellation

OBJECTIVE ③
CORNERSTONE 10.2

Kellman Company Inc. repurchases 110,000 of its own shares for $8 per share on September 4, 2018. The shares were originally issued for $6 per share.

Required:

1. How will this transaction affect shareholders' equity?
2. How will this transaction affect net income?

Cornerstone Exercise 10-29 Share Repurchases

OBJECTIVE ③
CORNERSTONE 10.2

Refer to the information in Exercise 10-28.

Required:

What is the appropriate journal entry to record the transaction?

Cornerstone Exercise 10-30 Cash Dividends

OBJECTIVE ③
CORNERSTONE 10.3

King Tut Corporation has issued 25,000 common shares, all of the same class. On December 1, 2018, King Tut's Board of Directors declares a cash dividend of $0.75 per share payable on December 15, 2018, to shareholders of record on December 10, 2018.

Required:

Prepare the appropriate journal entries for the date of declaration, date of record, and date of payment.

Cornerstone Exercise 10-31 Declaration of Cash Dividend

OBJECTIVE ③
CORNERSTONE 10.3

Wilson Corporation declared a cash dividend of $80,000 on December 31, 2018.

Required:

What is the appropriate journal entry to record this declaration?

Cornerstone Exercise 10-32 Stock Dividend

OBJECTIVE ③
CORNERSTONE 10.4

Boyer Corporation reported the following information: common shares, no par value; unlimited shares authorized; 35,000 shares issued and outstanding.

Required:

1. What is the appropriate journal entry to record a 10% stock dividend if the market price of the common shares is $30 per share when the dividend is declared and paid?
2. What is the appropriate journal entry to record a 30% stock dividend if the market price of the common shares is $30 per share when the dividend is declared and paid? The share price on the market decreases from $30 to $28 per share when the stock dividend is announced.
3. How do these transactions affect Boyer's total shareholders' equity?

OBJECTIVE ③
CORNERSTONE 10.5

Cornerstone Exercise 10-33   Preferred and Common Share Dividends

Barstow Corporation has a single class of common shares and a single class of cumulative preferred shares. The cumulative preferred shares require the corporation to pay an annual dividend of $8,000 to preferred shareholders. On January 1, 2018, Barstow's preferred dividends were one year in arrears, which means that Barstow declared neither preferred nor common dividends in 2017. During the three years (2018–2020), Barstow's Board of Directors determined they would be able to pay $9,500, $17,000, and $20,000, respectively.

Required:

Show how these anticipated payments will be split between preferred and common shareholders.

OBJECTIVE ③
CORNERSTONE 10.5

Cornerstone Exercise 10-34   Preferred Share Dividends

Seashell Corporation Inc. has 25,000 8%, $10 stated value, cumulative preferred shares outstanding. In 2016 and 2017, no dividends were declared on preferred shares. In 2018, Seashell had a profitable year and decided to pay dividends to both preferred and common shareholders.

Required:

If Seashell has $200,000 available for dividends in 2018, how much could it pay to the common shareholders?

OBJECTIVE ⑤
CORNERSTONE 10.6

Cornerstone Exercise 10-35   Shareholder Profitability Ratios

The following information pertains to Shanghai Corporation:

Net income	$ 1,420,000
Average common equity	$18,650,000
Preferred dividends	$ 245,500
Average common shares outstanding	625,000

Required:

Calculate the return on common equity and the earnings per share. (*Note:* Round answers to two decimal places.)

OBJECTIVE ⑤
CORNERSTONE 10.7

Cornerstone Exercise 10-36   Shareholder Payout Ratios

The following information pertains to Milo Mindbender Corporation:

Net income	$123,000
Dividends per common share	$ 2.00
Common shares outstanding	12,000
Common share repurchases	$ 85,000
Common share price	$ 20

Required:

Calculate the dividend yield, dividend payout, and total payout. (*Note:* Round answers to two decimal places.)

BRIEF EXERCISES

OBJECTIVE ①

Brief Exercise 10-37   Common Shares versus Preferred Shares

Corporations issue two general types of shares—common and preferred.

Required:

Describe the major differences between common and preferred shares.

Brief Exercise 10-38   Recording the Sale of Common and Preferred Shares   OBJECTIVE ➋

At the end of its first year of operations, Mulligan Corporation has outstanding shares of 96,000 common shares and 1,900 preferred shares. The Province of Ontario authorized Mulligan to issue 3,000 shares of 6% preferred shares with a par value of $40 per share and 110,000 shares of common shares with a par value of $0.01 per share. Any common shares sold during the year had a selling price of $17.50 per share. Mulligan's preferred shares were issued at $47.

Required:

Prepare the journal entry to record the issuance of shares during the first year.

Brief Exercise 10-39   Recording the Sale of Common Shares   OBJECTIVE ➋

Green Company, a food colouring manufacturer that provides its products to large processed food corporations, issues 450,000 shares of common shares (par value $0.10) for $22 per share on September 30, 2018.

Required:

Prepare the necessary journal entry to record this transaction.

Brief Exercise 10-40   Calculating the Number of Shares Issued   OBJECTIVE ➋

Castanet Inc. issued shares of its $1.50 par value common shares on November 9, 2018, for $13 per share. In recording the issuance of the shares, Castanet credited the Common Shares account for $416,300.

Required:

How many shares were issued on November 9, 2018?

Brief Exercise 10-41   Declaration of Cash Dividend   OBJECTIVE ➌

Travis Corporation expected to pay its shareholders a dividend in January 2018. The cash dividend of $75,000 was declared on December 31, 2017.

Required:

What is the appropriate journal entry to record this declaration?

Brief Exercise 10-42   Preferred and Common Shares Dividends   OBJECTIVE ➌

Brookshed Corporation has a single class of common shares and a single class of cumulative preferred shares. The cumulative preferred shares require the corporation to pay an annual dividend of $11,000 to preferred shareholders. On January 1, 2018, Brookshed's preferred dividends were one year in arrears, which means that Brookshed declared neither preferred nor common dividends in 2017. During the three years (2018–2020), Brookshed's Board of Directors determined they would be able to pay $17,000, $18,000, and $21,000, respectively.

Required:

Show how these anticipated payments will be split between preferred and common shareholders.

Brief Exercise 10-43   Preferred Stock Dividends   OBJECTIVE ➌

Eugene Corporation issued 25,000 shares outstanding of 6%, $5 par value, cumulative preferred shares. Eugene purchased 5,000 shares of its preferred shares to remain in its treasury. In 2016 and 2017, no dividends were declared on preferred shares. In 2018, Eugene had a profitable year and decided to pay dividends to shareholders of both preferred and common shares.

(Continued)

Required:

If Eugene has $75,000 available for dividends in 2018, how much could it pay to the common shareholders?

Use the following information for Brief Exercises 10-44 and 10-45:

Titanic Corporation's net income for the year ended December 31, 2018, is $380,000. On June 30, 2018, a $0.75 per-share cash dividend was declared for all common shareholders. Common shares in the amount of 38,000 common shares were outstanding at the time. The market price of Titanic's shares at year-end (12/31/18) is $18 per share. Titanic had a $1,100,000 credit balance in retained earnings at December 31, 2017.

OBJECTIVE ❹   **Brief Exercise 10-44   Retained Earnings**

Refer to the information for Titanic Corporation above.

Required:

Calculate the ending balance (12/31/18) of retained earnings.

OBJECTIVE ❹   **Brief Exercise 10-45   Retained Earnings**

Refer to the information for Titanic Corporation above. Assume that on July 31, 2018, Titanic discovered that 2017 depreciation was overstated by $75,000.

Required:

Prepare Titanic's retained earnings statement for the year ended December 31, 2018, assuming the 2017 tax rate was 30%.

OBJECTIVE ❺   **Brief Exercise 10-46   Shareholder Profitability Ratios**

The following information pertains to Capital Corporation:

Net income	$ 1,005,000
Average common equity	$16,500,000
Preferred shares, $10 par, 230,000 issued, 10% cumulative	$ 2,300,000
Average common shares outstanding	525,000

Required:

Calculate the return on common equity and the earnings per share.

EXERCISES

OBJECTIVE ❶   **Exercise 10-47   Accounting for Shares**

Kress Products Ltd.'s corporate charter authorizes the firm to issue 800,000 no par common shares. At the beginning of 2018, Kress issued 318,000 shares and had reacquired and cancelled 4,500 of those shares. During 2018, Kress issued an additional 24,350 shares and repurchased 8,200 more, which were cancelled.

Required:

Determine the number of issued and outstanding shares at December 31, 2018.

OBJECTIVE ❶   **Exercise 10-48   Outstanding Shares**

Rao Corporation shows the following information in the shareholders' equity section of its statement of financial position: The recorded value of common shares in the common share account is $175,000. Shares were initially issued for $2.50 per share. There were 10,000 shares purchased and cancelled at a cost of $2.50 per share that has not been recorded yet.

Required:

What is the number of shares outstanding?

Exercise 10-49   Outstanding Shares

OBJECTIVE **1**

Stahl Company Ltd. was incorporated as a new business on January 1, 2018. The company is authorized to issue 600,000 no par value common shares and 80,000 6%, $20 stated value, cumulative preferred shares. On January 1, 2018, the company issued 75,000 common shares for $15 per share and 5,000 preferred shares for $25 per share. Net income for the year ended December 31, 2018, was $500,000.

Required:

What is the amount of Stahl's total share capital at December 31, 2018?

Exercise 10-50   Preparation of Shareholders' Equity Section

OBJECTIVE **1**

Refer to the information in Exercise 10-49.

Required:

Prepare the shareholders' equity section of the statement of financial position for Stahl Company.

Exercise 10-51   Issuing Common Shares

OBJECTIVE **2**

Carmean Products Inc. issued 49,750 no par value common shares to shareholders at the time of its incorporation. Carmean received $23 per share.

Required:

Prepare the journal entry to record the issue of the shares.

Exercise 10-52   Issuing and Repurchasing Shares

OBJECTIVE **2**

Radko Inc. had the following transactions related to its common and preferred shares:

January 15	Issued 350,000 no par common shares for $15 per share.
	Issued 5,000 $20 stated value preferred shares at $23 per share.
November 29	Repurchased and cancelled 30,000 common shares at $21 per share.

Required:

Prepare the journal entries for these transactions.

Exercise 10-53   Prepare the Shareholders' Equity Section

OBJECTIVE **2**

Renee Corporation has the following shareholders' equity information:

	No Par Common	$10 Stated Value Preferred
Share capital – Common	$3,750,000	
– Preferred		$130,000
Shares:		
Authorized	unlimited	unlimited
Issued and outstanding	250,000	8,000

Retained earnings is $1,837,000.

Required:

Prepare the shareholders' equity portion of Renee's statement of financial position.

OBJECTIVE ❷

Exercise 10-54   Prepare the Shareholders' Equity Section

Wildcat Drilling Ltd. has the following accounts on its trial balance.

	Debit	Credit
Retained Earnings		600,000
Cash	825,000	
Contributed Surplus—Preferred		400,000
Accounts Payable		345,000
Accounts Receivable	410,000	
Common Shares, no par		3,318,000
Preferred Shares, $10 stated value		340,000
Inventory	1,300,000	
Accumulated Other Comprehensive Income		70,000

Required:

Prepare the shareholders' equity portion of Wildcat's statement of financial position.

OBJECTIVE ❷

Exercise 10-55   Interpret the Shareholders' Equity Section

Medici Inc. has the following shareholders' equity section of the statement of financial position:

Medici Inc.

Statement of Financial Position (Partial)

Shareholders' equity:	
Preferred shares, unlimited authorized; 30,000 issued and outstanding	$ 300,000
Common shares, unlimited shares authorized; 550,000 issued and outstanding	5,200,000
Contributed surplus:	
Preferred shares	90,000
Total share capital	5,590,000
Retained earnings	450,000
Accumulated other comprehensive income	22,000
Total shareholders' equity	$6,062,000

Required:

1. How many preferred shares are authorized?
2. How many common shares are outstanding?
3. What was the average selling price for the common shares when issued?
4. If the annual dividends on the preferred shares are $0.80 per share, what is the dividend rate on the preferred shares?

OBJECTIVE ❸

Exercise 10-56   Cash Dividends on Common Shares

Bergman Company Inc. is authorized to issue an unlimited number of common shares. At the beginning of 2018, Bergman had 248,000 issued and outstanding shares. On July 2, 2018, Bergman repurchased and cancelled 4,610 common shares at $28 per share. On March 1 and September 1, Bergman declared a cash dividend of $1.10 per share. The dividends were paid on April 1 and October 1.

Required:

1. Prepare the journal entries to record the declaration of the two cash dividends.
2. Prepare the journal entries to record the payment of the two dividends.
3. **CONCEPTUAL CONNECTION** Explain why the amounts of the two dividends are different.

Exercise 10-57   Cash Dividends on Common and Preferred Shares

OBJECTIVE 3

ILLUSTRATING
RELATIONSHIPS

Metzler Design Ltd. has the following information regarding its preferred and common shares:

Preferred shares, $50 stated value, 10% cumulative; unlimited shares authorized; 100,000
   shares issued and outstanding
Common shares, no par; unlimited shares authorized; 800,000 shares issued and outstanding

As of December 31, 2018, Metzler was two years in arrears on its dividends. During 2019, Metzler declared and paid dividends. As a result, the common shareholders received dividends of
$0.60 per share.

Required:

1.   What was the total amount of dividends declared and paid?
2.   What journal entry was made at the date of declaration?

YOUDECIDE

Exercise 10-58   Distribution to Shareholders

OBJECTIVE 3

Owners invest in corporations through the purchase of shares.

Required:

Describe two ways that corporations distribute assets to shareholders (without liquidating the
company). Discuss their relative advantages and disadvantages.

Exercise 10-59   Stock Dividends

OBJECTIVE 3

Crystal Corporation has the following information regarding its common shares:

No par, with unlimited shares authorized, 183,700 shares issued and outstanding
On August 22, 2018, Crystal declared and paid a 15% stock dividend when the market price
of the common shares was $30 per share.

Required:

1.   Prepare the journal entry to record the declaration and payment of this stock dividend.
2.   Prepare the journal entry to record the declaration and payment, assuming it was a 30%
     stock dividend. Assume the share price on the market decreases from $30 to $28 per share
     when the stock dividend is announced.

Exercise 10-60   Stock Dividend

OBJECTIVE 3

ILLUSTRATING
RELATIONSHIPS

The statement of financial position of Cohen Enterprises Ltd. includes the following shareholders' equity section (Assume the date of the financial statements is before the stock dividend):

Common shares, no par, unlimited shares	
authorized, 150,000 shares issued and outstanding	$491,800
Retained earnings	173,000
Total equity	$664,800

Required:

1.   On April 15, 2018, when its shares were selling for $18 per share, Cohen Enterprises issued
     a stock dividend. After making the journal entry to recognize the stock dividend, Cohen's
     total share capital increased by $270,000. In percentage terms, what was the size of the stock
     dividend?
2.   Ignoring the stock dividend discussed in (1), assume that on June 1, 2018, when its shares
     were selling for $2 per share, Cohen Enterprises issued a stock dividend. After making the
     journal entry to recognize the stock dividend, Cohen's retained earnings decreased by
     $166,000. In percentage terms, what was the size of the stock dividend?

OBJECTIVE ③

Exercise 10-61   Stock Split

Toy World Inc. reported the following information: common shares, no par; unlimited shares authorized; 200,000 shares issued and outstanding.

Required:

What is the typical effect of a 3-for-1 stock split on the information Toy World reports above? If the market value of the common shares is $30 per share when the stock split is declared, what would you expect the approximate market value per share to be immediately after the split?

OBJECTIVE ③

Exercise 10-62   Stock Dividends and Stock Splits

The statement of financial position of Chungking Corporation includes the following shareholders' equity section:

Common shares, no par, unlimited shares authorized, 60,000 shares issued and outstanding	$491,800
Retained earnings	173,000
Total equity	$664,800

Required:

1. Assume that Chungking issued 60,000 shares for cash at the inception of the corporation and that no new shares have been issued since. Determine how much cash was received for the shares issued at inception.
2. Assume that Chungking issued 30,000 shares for cash at the inception of the corporation and subsequently declared a 2-for-1 stock split. Determine how much cash was received for the shares issued at inception.
3. Assume that Chungking issued 57,000 shares for cash at the inception of the corporation and that the remaining 3,000 shares were issued as the result of stock dividends when the shares were selling for $53 per share. Determine how much cash was received for the shares issued at inception.

OBJECTIVE ③

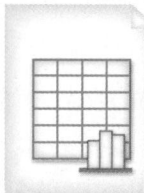

Exercise 10-63   Preferred Dividends

Nathan Product Ltd.'s equity includes 6.5%, $150 stated value preferred shares. There are unlimited shares authorized and 30,000 shares issued and outstanding. Assume that Nathan Products declares and pays preferred dividends quarterly.

Required:

1. Prepare the journal entry to record declaration of one quarterly dividend.
2. Prepare the journal entry to record payment of one quarterly dividend.

OBJECTIVE ③

Exercise 10-64   Cumulative Preferred Dividends

Share capital of Barr Company Ltd. includes:

Common shares, no par, 650,000 shares issued and outstanding	$3,250,000
Preferred shares, 15% cumulative, $60 stated value, 10,000 shares issued and outstanding	600,000

As of December 31, 2017, two years' dividends are in arrears on the preferred shares. During 2018, Barr plans to pay dividends that total $360,000.

Required:

1. Determine the amount of dividends that will be paid to Barr's common and preferred shareholders in 2018.
2. If Barr paid $280,000 of dividends, determine how much each group of shareholders would receive.

Exercise 10-65   Retained Earnings

OBJECTIVE **4**

Titania Corporation's net income for the year ended December 31, 2018, is $380,000. On June 30, 2018, a $0.75 per share cash dividend was declared for all common shareholders. Common shares in the amount of 38,000 were outstanding at the time. The market price of Titania's shares at year-end (12/31/18) is $18 per share. Titania had a $1,100,000 credit balance in retained earnings at December 31, 2017.

Required:

Calculate the ending balance (12/31/18) of retained earnings.

Exercise 10-66   Retained Earnings

OBJECTIVE **4**

Refer to the information in Exercise 10-65. Assume that on July 31, 2018, Titania discovered that 2017 depreciation was overstated by $90,000.

Required:

Provide Titania's retained earnings statement for the year ended December 31, 2018, assuming the 2017 tax rate was 30%.

Exercise 10-67   Retained Earnings

OBJECTIVE **4**

Gibson Products Ltd. had beginning retained earnings of $2,000,000. During the year, Gibson paid cash dividends of $120,000 to preferred shareholders and $25,000 to common shareholders. Net income for the year was $600,000.

Required:

1. Reproduce the retained earnings T-account for the year starting with the beginning balance.
2. Determine what Gibson's ending retained earnings is, assuming that during the year the company discovers that net income was overstated by $28,000 in prior years due to an error. The error was corrected and the current year's net income is correct.

Exercise 10-68   Retained Earnings

OBJECTIVE **4**

ILLUSTRATING RELATIONSHIPS

The December 31, 2018, comparative statement of financial position of Savard Industries Ltd. includes the following shareholders' equity section:

	2018	2017
Common shares, no par, unlimited shares authorized,		
60,000 shares issued and outstanding	$491,800	$491,800
Retained earnings	173,000	116,000
Total equity	$664,800	$607,800

(Continued)

Required:

During 2018, Savard paid dividends of $0.50 per share. What was Savard's net income for 2018?

 OBJECTIVE **2 4**

Exercise 10-69   Restrictions on Retained Earnings

At December 31, 2017, Birney Clothing Ltd. had $226,700 of retained earnings, all unrestricted. During 2018, Birney earned net income of $92,000 and declared and paid cash dividends on common shares of $21,800. During 2018, Birney sold a bond issue with a covenant that required Birney to transfer from retained earnings to restricted retained earnings an amount equal to the principal of the bond issue, $50,000. At December 31, 2018, Birney has 30,000 no par common shares issued and outstanding. Common shares were originally issued for $236,500.

Required:

Prepare the shareholders' equity portion of Birney's December 31, 2018, statement of financial position.

OBJECTIVE **5**

Exercise 10-70   Ratio Analysis

Consider the following information.

Share price	$24.30	Avg. common shares outstanding	28,310,000
Common dividends	$5,662,000	Dividends per common share	$0.20
Preferred dividends	$1,444,000	Net income	$69,385,000
2018 preferred shares	$11,464,000	2017 preferred shares	$11,464,000
2018 total shareholders' equity	$954,846,000	2017 total shareholders' equity	$892,567,000
Purchases of common shares	$85,840,000		

Required:

1. Calculate the following shareholder payout ratios: (1) dividend yield, (2) dividend payout, (3) share repurchase payout, and (4) total payout. (*Note*: Round answers to two decimal places.)
2. Calculate the following shareholder profitability ratios: (1) return on common equity and (2) EPS. (*Note:* Round answers to two decimal places.)

OBJECTIVE **5**

Exercise 10-71   Ratio Analysis

Mojo Inc. has the following shareholders' equity section of the statement of financial position:

Mojo Inc.
Statement of Financial Position (Partial)

Shareholders' equity:	
Preferred shares, unlimited shares authorized; 30,000	
issued and outstanding	$ 300,000
Common shares, unlimited shares authorized; 550,000	
issued and outstanding	5,200,000
Contributed surplus:	
Preferred shares	90,000
Total share capital	5,590,000
Retained earnings	450,000
Accumulated other comprehensive income	22,000
Total shareholders' equity	$6,062,000

On this date Mojo's shares were selling for $25 per share.

Required:

1. Assuming Mojo's dividend yield is 1%, what are the dividends per common share?
2. Assuming Mojo's dividend yield is 1% and its dividend payout is 20%, what is Mojo's net income?

Exercise 10-72   Shareholders' Equity Terminology

OBJECTIVE ❶❷❸❹

A list of terms and a list of definitions or examples are presented below. Make a list of the numbers 1 through 12 and match the letter of the most directly related definition or example with each number.

Terms

1. stock warrant
2. date of record
3. stated value
4. stock split
5. treasury shares
6. stock dividend
7. preferred shares
8. outstanding shares
9. authorized shares
10. declaration date
11. comprehensive income
12. retained earnings

Definitions and Examples

a. Capitalizes retained earnings.
b. Shares issued minus shares repurchased.
c. Emerson Electric will pay a dividend to all persons holding its common shares on December 15, 2018, even if they just bought the shares and sell them a few days later.
d. The accumulated earnings over the entire life of the corporation that have not been paid out in dividends.
e. Preferred share account balance divided by the number of shares issued.
f. The Province of Nova Scotia set an upper limit of 1,000,000 on the number of shares that Gump's Catch Inc. can issue.
g. Any changes to shareholders' equity from transactions with nonowners.
h. A right to purchase shares at a specified future time and specified price.
i. A share issue that requires no journal entry.
j. Shares that may earn guaranteed dividends.
k. On October 15, 2018, BCE announced its intention to pay a dividend on common shares.
l. A corporation purchases its own previously issued shares, the shares that it buys are.

PROBLEM SET A

Problem 10-73A   Presentation of Shareholders' Equity

OBJECTIVE ❶❷

Yeager Corporation was organized in January 2018. During 2018, Yeager engaged in the following shareholders' equity activities:

a. Secured approval for a corporate charter that authorizes Yeager to sell 600,000, no par common shares and 30,000, $50 stated value preferred shares
b. Issued 80,000 of the common shares for $13 per share
c. Issued 2,500 of the preferred shares for $57 per share
d. Repurchased and cancelled 500 of the common shares at a cost of $15 per share
e. Earned net income of $48,000
f. Paid dividends of $5,000

Required:

Prepare the shareholders' equity portion of Yeager's statement of financial position as of December 31, 2018.

Problem 10-74A   Issuing Common and Preferred Shares

OBJECTIVE ❶❷

Klaus Herrmann, a biochemistry professor, organized Bioproducts Inc. early this year. The firm will manufacture antibiotics using gene-splicing technology. Bioproducts' charter authorizes the firm to issue 10,000 7%, $70 stated value preferred shares and an unlimited number of no par value common shares. During the year, the firm engaged in the following transactions.

a. Issued 50,000 common shares to Klaus Herrmann in exchange for $550,000 cash.

(Continued)

b.   Issued 8,000 common shares to a potential customer for $12 per share.
c.   Issued 4,000 preferred shares to a venture capital firm for $85 per share.
d.   Issued 100 common shares to Margaret Robb, a local lawyer, in exchange for Margaret's work in arranging for the firm's incorporation. Margaret usually charges $1,200 for comparable work.

Required:

Prepare a journal entry for each of these transactions.

Problem 10-75A   Statement of Shareholders' Equity

At the end of 2017, Jeffco Inc. had the following equity accounts and balances:

Common shares, no par (175,000 shares issued and outstanding)	$1,926,400
Retained earnings	310,000

During 2018, Jeffco engaged in the following transactions involving its equity accounts:

a.   Issued 8,000 common shares for $35 per share.
b.   Issued 1,000 shares of 9%, $120 stated value preferred shares at $125 per share.
c.   Declared and paid cash dividends of $15,000.
d.   Repurchased and cancelled 500 common shares for $52 per share.

Required:

1.   Prepare the journal entries for *a* through *d*.
2.   Assume that 2018 net income was $89,600. Prepare a partial statement of financial position showing only the shareholders' equity section at December 31, 2018.

Problem 10-76A   Common Dividends

Fusion Payroll Service Ltd. began 2018 with unlimited authorized and 375,000 issued and outstanding no par common shares. During 2018, Fusion entered into the following transactions:

a.   Declared a $0.30 per share cash dividend on March 10.
b.   Paid the $0.30 per share dividend on April 10.
c.   Issued 1,500 common shares for $23 per share on June 9.
d.   Declared a $0.45 per share cash dividend on August 10.
e.   Paid the $0.45 per share dividend on September 10.
f.   Declared and paid a 5% stock dividend on October 15 when the market price of the common shares was $25 per share.
g.   Declared a $0.50 per share cash dividend on November 10.
h.   Paid the $0.50 per share dividend on December 10.

Required:

1.   Prepare journal entries for each of these transactions. (*Note:* Round to the nearest dollar.)
2.   Determine the total dollar amount of dividends (cash and shares) for the year.
3.   **CONCEPTUAL CONNECTION** Determine the effect on total assets and total shareholders' equity of these dividend transactions.

Problem 10-77A   Stock Dividends and Stock Splits

Lopez Products Ltd.'s statement of financial position includes total assets of $587,000 and the following equity account balances at December 31, 2018:

Common shares, no par, 80,000 shares issued and outstanding	$184,000
Retained earnings	217,000
Total shareholders' equity	$401,000

Lopez's common shares are selling for $12 per share on December 31, 2018.

Required:

1. How much would Lopez Products have reported for total assets and retained earnings on December 31, 2018, if the firm had declared and paid a $15,000 cash dividend on December 31, 2018? Prepare the journal entry for this cash dividend.
2. How much would Lopez have reported for total assets and retained earnings on December 31, 2018, if the firm had issued a 15% stock dividend on December 31, 2018? Prepare the journal entry for this stock dividend.
3. **CONCEPTUAL CONNECTION** How much would Lopez have reported for total assets and retained earnings on December 31, 2018, if the firm had effected a 2-for-1 stock split on December 31, 2018? Is a journal entry needed to record the stock split? Why or why not?

Problem 10-78A   Preferred Dividends

OBJECTIVE ❸

Magic Conglomerates Ltd. had the following preferred shares outstanding at the end of a recent year:

$25 stated value, 8%, non-cumulative	10,000 shares
$30 stated value, 8%, cumulative	8,000 shares
$50 stated value, 9%, cumulative, convertible	5,000 shares
$75 stated value, 10%, nonparticipating	15,000 shares

Required:

1. Determine the amount of annual dividends on each issue of preferred shares and the total annual dividend on all four issues.
2. Calculate what the amount of dividends in arrears would be if the dividends were omitted for one year.

Problem 10-79A   Ratio Analysis

OBJECTIVE ❺

Consider the following information taken from the shareholders' equity section:

	(dollar amounts in thousands)	
	2018	**2017**
Preferred shares	$ 1,000	$ 1,000
Common shares, 258,052,356 and 274,001,656 shares issued		
and outstanding in 2018 and 2017, respectively	3,343	3,310
Contributed surplus—common shares	766,382	596,239
Retained earnings	2,192,674	2,424,403
Accumulated other comprehensive (loss) income	(206,662)	58,653
Total shareholders' equity	$2,756,737	$3,083,605

Additional Information (all numbers in thousands other than per share information):	2018
Weighted average common shares outstanding	260,000
Price per share at year-end	$105.45
Net income	$1,358,950
Preferred dividends	$100,000
Common dividends	$213,440
Common dividends per share	$.82
Share repurchases	$834,975

(Continued)

Required:

1. Calculate the following for 2018 (*Note:* Round answers to two decimal places):

Shareholder Payout	Shareholder Profitability
Dividend yield	Return on common equity
Dividend payout	EPS
Total payout	
Share repurchase payout	

2. **CONCEPTUAL CONNECTION** Assume 2017 ratios were:

Shareholder Payout	Shareholder Profitability
Dividend yield: 0.85%	Return on common equity: 34.26%
Dividend payout: 9.80%	EPS: $3.51
Total payout: 70.00%	
Share repurchase payout: 60.20%	

and the current year industry averages are:

Shareholder Payout	Shareholder Profitability
Dividend yield: 0.76%	Return on common equity: 23.81%
Dividend payout: 12.35%	EPS: $1.23
Total payout: 48.37%	
Share repurchase payout: 36.02%	

How do you interpret the company's payout and profitability performance?

OBJECTIVE 6

Problem 10-80A   Proprietorship Accounting

Dan Hawalchuk, proprietor, operated a financial counselling business that generated a profit of $90,000 for the year ended December 31, 2018. The proprietor's capital balance at December 31, 2017, was $25,000 and his drawings in 2018 were $60,000.

Required:

Prepare a statement of proprietor's equity for the year ended December 31, 2018.

OBJECTIVE 6

Problem 10-81A   Partnership Accounting

Michelle Maw and Marc Joness, partners, opened a new consulting business starting January 1, 2018. Profit for the year ended December 31, 2018, was $100,000. Michelle and Marc share profit on a 60% and 40% basis, respectively. During 2018, Michelle's drawings were $36,000 and Marc's drawings were $30,000.

Required:

Prepare a statement of partners' equity for the year ended December 31, 2018.

PROBLEM SET B

OBJECTIVE 1 2

Problem 10-82B   Presentation of Shareholders' Equity

Steven's Restorations Ltd. was organized in January 2018. During 2018, Steven's engaged in the following shareholders' equity activities:

a. Secured approval for a corporate charter that authorizes Steven's to sell unlimited, no par common shares and 75,000, $100 stated value preferred shares.
b. Sold 480,000 of the common shares for $15 per share.

c. Sold 25,000 of the preferred shares for $105 per share.
d. Repurchased and cancelled 2,000 of the common shares at a cost of $18 per share.
e. Earned net income of $107,000.
f. Paid dividends of $13,000.

Required:

Prepare the shareholders' equity portion of Steven's statement of financial position as of December 31, 2018.

Problem 10-83B   Issuing Common and Preferred Shares

Tom Soong, a biochemistry professor, organized Biointernational Inc. earlier this year. The firm will manufacture antibiotics using gene-splicing technology. Biointernational's charter authorizes the firm to issue 20,000 10%, $50 stated value preferred shares and 100,000 no par common shares. During the year, the firm engaged in the following transactions:

a. Issued 12,000 common shares to Tom Soong in exchange for $170,000 cash.
b. Issued 3,000 common shares to a potential customer for $17 per share.
c. Issued 1,000 preferred shares to a venture capital firm for $60 per share.
d. Issued 65 common shares to Susie Thomas, a local lawyer, in exchange for Susie's work in arranging for the firm's incorporation. Susie usually charges $1,000 for comparable work.

Required:

Prepare a journal entry for each of these transactions.

Problem 10-84B   Statement of Shareholders' Equity

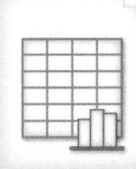

At the end of 2017, Stanley Utilities Inc. had the following equity accounts and balances:

Common shares, no par (4,500,000 shares issued and outstanding)	$5,875,000
Retained earnings	188,000

During 2018, Stanley Utilities engaged in the following transactions involving its equity accounts:

a. Issued 3,300 common shares for $15 per share.
b. Issued 1,000 12%, $100 stated value preferred shares at $105 per share.
c. Declared and paid cash dividends of $8,000.
d. Repurchased and cancelled 1,000 common shares for $38 per share.

Required:

1. Prepare the journal entries for *a* through *d*.
2. Assume that 2018 net income was $87,000. Prepare a partial statement of financial position showing only the shareholders' equity section at December 31, 2018.

Problem 10-85B   Common Dividends

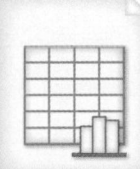

Thompson Payroll Service Ltd. began in 2018 with unlimited authorized and 820,000 issued and outstanding no par common shares. During 2018, Thompson entered into the following transactions:

a. Declared a $0.20 per share cash dividend on March 24.
b. Paid the $0.20 per share dividend on April 6.
c. Issued 2,500 common shares for $15 per share on June 19.
d. Declared a $0.40 per share cash dividend on August 1.
e. Paid the $0.40 per share dividend on September 14.

(Continued)

f.   Declared and paid a 10% stock dividend on October 25 when the market price of the common shares was $15 per share.

g.   Declared a $0.45 per share cash dividend on November 20.

h.   Paid the $0.45 per share dividend on December 20.

Required:

1.   Prepare journal entries for each of these transactions. (*Note:* Round to the nearest dollar.)
2.   What is the total dollar amount of dividends (cash and shares) for the year?
3.   **CONCEPTUAL CONNECTION** Determine the effect on total assets and total shareholders' equity of these dividend transactions.

OBJECTIVE ③   **Problem 10-86B   Stock Dividends and Stock Splits**

Murphy Products Ltd.'s statement of financial position includes total assets of $1,326,000 and the following equity account balances at December 31, 2018:

Common shares, no par, 10,000	
shares issued and outstanding	$298,000
Retained earnings	206,000
Total shareholders' equity	$504,000

Murphy's common shares are selling for $17 per share on December 31, 2018.

Required:

1.   Determine how much Murphy Products would have reported for total assets and retained earnings on December 31, 2018, if the firm had declared and paid a $5,000 cash dividend on December 31, 2018. Prepare the journal entry for this cash dividend.
2.   Determine how much Murphy would have reported for total assets and retained earnings on December 31, 2018, if the firm had issued a 5% stock dividend on December 31, 2018. Prepare the journal entry for this stock dividend.
3.   **CONCEPTUAL CONNECTION** How much would Murphy have reported for total assets and retained earnings on December 31, 2018, if the firm had effected a 3-for-1 stock split on December 31, 2018? Is a journal entry needed to record the stock split? Why or why not?

OBJECTIVE ③   **Problem 10-87B   Preferred Dividends**

Saleem Corporation had the following preferred shares outstanding at the end of a recent year:

$20 stated value, 9%, non-cumulative	30,000 shares
$25 stated value, 10%, cumulative	15,000 shares
$100 stated value, 6%, cumulative, convertible	20,000 shares
$100 stated value, 8%, nonparticipating	8,000 shares

Required:

1.   Determine the amount of annual dividends on each issue of preferred shares and the total annual dividend on all four issues.
2.   Calculate what the amount of dividends in arrears would be if the dividends were omitted for one year.

Problem 10-88B   Ratio Analysis

OBJECTIVE  5

Consider the following information taken from the shareholders' equity section:

	(dollar amounts in thousands)	
	2018	2017
Preferred shares	$ 1,000	$ 2,000
Common shares, 230,000,000 and 176,000,000 shares		
issued in 2018 and 2017, respectively	2,300	1,760
Contributed surplus—common shares	567,000	432,000
Retained earnings	2,854,600	2,725,000
Accumulated other comprehensive (loss) income	(454,600)	147,000
Total shareholders' equity	$2,970,300	$3,307,760

Additional Information (all numbers in thousands other than per share information):	2018
Weighted average common shares outstanding	200,000
Price per share at year-end	$58.30
Net income	$1,584,000
Preferred dividends	$50,000
Common dividends	$300,000
Common dividends per share	$1.50
Share repurchases	$850,000

Required:

1. Calculate the following (*Note:* Round answers to two decimal places):

Shareholder Payout	Shareholder Profitability
Dividend yield	Return on common equity
Dividend payout	EPS
Total payout	
Share repurchase payout	

2. **CONCEPTUAL CONNECTION** Assume last year's ratios were:

Shareholder Payout	Shareholder Profitability
Dividend yield: 2.31%	Return on common equity: 37.41%
Dividend payout: 13.65%	EPS: $6.12
Total payout: 78.59%	
Share repurchase payout: 64.94%	

and the current year industry averages are:

Shareholder Payout	Shareholder Profitability
Dividend yield: 2.50%	Return on common equity: 44.44%
Dividend payout: 15.10%	EPS: $6.48
Total payout: 55.10%	
Share repurchase payout: 40.00%	

How do you interpret the company's payout and profitability performance?

Problem 10-89B   Proprietorship Accounting

OBJECTIVE 6

Dan Hawalchuk, proprietor, opened a financial counselling business on January 1, 2018. The business generated a profit of $70,000 for the year ended December 31, 2018. The proprietor's drawings for 2018 were $80,000. The owner contributed $25,000 of capital in 2018.

(Continued)

Required:

Prepare a statement of proprietorship's equity for the year ended December 31, 2018.

OBJECTIVE 6

Problem 10-90B Partnership Accounting

Michelle Maw and Marc Joness, partners, opened a new consulting business starting January 1, 2018. Profit for the year ended December 31, 2018, was $60,000. Michelle and Marc share profit on a 60% and 40% basis, respectively. During 2018, Michelle's drawings were $40,000 and Marc's drawings were $30,000.

Required:

Prepare a statement of partners' equity for the year ended December 31, 2018.

CASES

Case 10-91 Ethics and Equity

Ivan and Gordon are middle managers at a large, publicly traded corporation. Ivan tells Gordon that the company is about to sign an exclusive product distribution agreement with a small, publicly traded manufacturer. This contract will quadruple the manufacturer's revenue. Ivan mentions to Gordon that the manufacturer's share price will likely go "through the roof." Gordon says, "Maybe we should buy some shares."

Required:

Are Ivan and Gordon being smart, being unethical but not breaking the law, or breaking the law?

Case 10-92 Share Transactions and Ethics

Marilyn Cox is the office manager for DTR Inc. DTR constructs, owns, and manages apartment complexes. Marilyn has been involved in negotiations between DTR and prospective lenders as DTR attempts to raise $425 million to build apartments in a growing area of Vancouver. Based on her experience with past negotiations, Marilyn knows that lenders are concerned about DTR's debt-to-equity ratio. When the negotiations began, DTR had debt of $80 million and equity of $50 million. Marilyn believes that DTR's debt-to-equity ratio of 1.6 is probably the maximum that lenders will accept.

Marilyn is also aware that DTR issued $10 million of common shares to a long-time friend of the corporation's president in exchange for some land just before the negotiations with lenders began. The president's friend constructs and sells single-family homes. The land is in an area zoned only for single-family housing and would be an attractive site for single-family homes. Thus, the land is worth at least $10 million. However, DTR does not intend to build any single-family homes.

Required:

1. What would have been DTR's debt-to-equity ratio if the $10 million of shares had not been issued for the land?
2. If Marilyn believes that the $10 million share issue was undertaken only to improve DTR's debt-to-equity ratio and that it will be reversed whenever the president's friend wants the land back or when DTR's debt-to-equity position improves, what should she do?

Case 10-93 Common and Preferred Shares

Expansion Company Ltd. now has $2,500,000 of equity (100,000 common shares). Current income is $400,000 and Expansion Company needs $500,000 of additional capital. The firm's bankers insist that this capital be acquired by selling either common or preferred shares. If Expansion sells common shares, the ownership share of the current shareholders will be diluted by 16.7% (20,000 more shares will be sold). If preferred shares are sold, the dividend rate will be 15% of the $500,000. Furthermore, the preferred shares will have to be cumulative, participating, and convertible into 20,000 common shares.

Required:

Indicate whether Expansion should sell additional common or preferred shares, and explain the reasons for your choice.

Case 10-94 Leverage

Enrietto Aquatic Products Ltd.'s offer to acquire Fibreglass Products for $2,000,000 cash has been accepted. Enrietto has $1,000,000 of liquid assets that can be converted into cash and plans to either sell common shares or issue bonds to raise the remaining $1,000,000. Before this acquisition, Enrietto's condensed statement of financial position and condensed statement of earnings were as follows:

Enrietto Aquatic Products Ltd.
Preacquisition Condensed Statement of Financial Position

Assets		Liabilities and Equity	
Assets	$20,000,000	Liabilities and Equity	
		Liabilities	$ 8,000,000
		Common shares, $10 stated value	6,000,000
		Retained earnings	6,000,000
		Total liabilities and shareholders' equity	$20,000,000

Enrietto Aquatic Products Ltd.
Preacquisition Condensed Statement of Earnings

Income from operations	$ 6,000,000
Less: Interest expense	(1,000,000)
Income before taxes	5,000,000
Less: Income tax expense (34%)	(1,700,000)
Net income	$ 3,300,000

Enrietto's policy is to pay 60% of net income to shareholders as dividends. Enrietto expects to be able to raise the $1,000,000 it needs for the acquisition by selling 50,000 common shares at $20 each or by issuing $1,000,000 of 20-year, 12% bonds. Enrietto expects income from operations to grow by $700,000 after Fibreglass Products has been acquired. (Interest expense will increase if debt is used to finance the acquisition.)

Required:

1. Determine the return on equity (net income/total equity) before the acquisition and for both financing alternatives.
2. If Enrietto sells additional shares, what will be the cash outflow for dividends?
3. If Enrietto sells bonds, what will be the net cash outflows for new interest and for all dividends? (Remember that interest is tax-deductible.)
4. Assume that Enrietto sells shares and that none of the preacquisition shareholders buy any of the 50,000 new shares. What total amount of dividends will the preacquisition shareholders receive after the acquisition? How does this amount compare with the dividends they receive before the acquisition?
5. Based only on Return on Equity, which alternative is better for Enrietto's preacquisition shareholders?

Case 10-95 Continuing Problem: Front Row Entertainment

After purchasing the five venues in June 2018, Front Row Entertainment needed additional cash to renovate and operate these venues. While the company had successfully borrowed money before (from bank loans as well as from the issuance of bonds), it could not find a lender willing to invest in the business due to the large amount of debt that the company currently has on its statement of financial position.

With debt financing out of the question, Front Row Entertainment considers its other options. The name of an old university friend, Steve Trotter, immediately came to Cam and Anna's mind. Steve had previous work experience in the retail industry and had expressed a desire to manage Front Row Entertainment's current merchandising operations (the sale of DVDs). His vision was to expand the operations to include apparel (T-shirts, hats, etc.) and other items (such as bobble-head dolls of the artists). In addition, several other family members had expressed an interest in investing in the company.

Front Row was authorized to issue an unlimited number of its no par common shares. On January 1, 2018, it had previously issued Cam and Anna 8,000 shares each for $1 per share. Front Row Entertainment was also authorized to issue 20,000 8%, $50 stated value preferred shares. The following transactions occurred during the remainder of 2018.

June 15	Issued 2,000 common shares to Steve for $20 per share.
July 1	Issued 3,000 $50 stated value preferred shares to family members for $75 per share.
July 10	Repurchased and cancelled 700 common shares at $16 per share.
Aug. 5	The Board of Directors declared a $25,000 dividend to all shareholders of record on August 31, 2014. The dividend will be paid on Sept. 15, 2014.
Sept. 15	The $25,000 dividend was paid.
Dec. 15	Issued 300 common shares at $22 per share.

Front Row Entertainment had $53,250 of retained earnings at December 31, 2018, without considering the possible effect of any of the above transactions.

Required:

1. Prepare the journal entries to record the above transactions.
2. Prepare the shareholders' equity section of the statement of financial position at December 31, 2018.

Case 10-96   Professional and Ethical Behaviour

You are the accounting manager who reports directly to the CFO of a large multinational private manufacturing company. The goal of the company's management has been to grow the business to a large enough size that the company will be taken public in the next year or so. Existing shareholders have been putting pressure on management to speed up the process of going public and therefore have put considerable pressure on you to make sure earnings are strong in anticipation of going public. The higher the earnings, the more the market will be willing to pay for a share of the company. Existing shareholders stand to make millions.

Given the economy in the last two years and the difficult times the company has faced, the net income could have been better. You have felt pressure from upper management and existing shareholders to show stronger earnings. You recall the CFO telling you earlier in the year to "make sure profits are strong or start looking for another job." You have been feeling under duress all year long.

As it gets closer to the end of the year, you review all transactions to make sure that anything that can increase net income is recorded. You ask your staff to make sure all sales, no matter what they look like, are recorded. You also tell them to make sure that any items that can be capitalized are capitalized.

The CFO has called you and asked for the financial statements for the year, as the company is planning to go public as soon as possible and management needs to take immediate steps to ensure this happens.

Required:

Comment on any possible ethical issues.

INTEGRATIVE CASE 3 (CHAPTERS 8–10)

Integrating Accounting for Liabilities and Equity

Obtain **Rogers** Communications Inc.'s fiscal 2014 annual report dated February 13, 2015, through the "Investor Relations" portion of its website (do a web search for "Rogers Communications Inc., Investor Relations").

Required:

1. Using Rogers Communications Inc.'s annual report, answer the following questions (*Hint:* It may be easier to use the Word or PDF file and use the search feature within the program):

   a. Calculate Rogers's current and quick ratios for 2013 and 2014. Assume the industry averages for these ratios for 2014 were .50 and .35, respectively. Comment on Rogers's short-term liquidity.

   b. Calculate Rogers's debt to equity ratio for 2013 and 2014. The industry averages for these ratios were 3.5 for 2014 and 3.2 for 2013. Comment on Rogers's mix of debt and equity and long-term solvency.

   c. Calculate Rogers's return on equity ratio for 2014. Assume the industry average for 2014 was 10%. Comment on Rogers's profitability.

   d. Rogers increased the payment of its dividend during 2014 compared to 2013. Where can you find this information? What does this say about Rogers's dividend payment? Why might Rogers elect not to make any payouts to shareholders? Why might the company increase the payout?

11

Reporting and Analyzing the Statement of Cash Flows

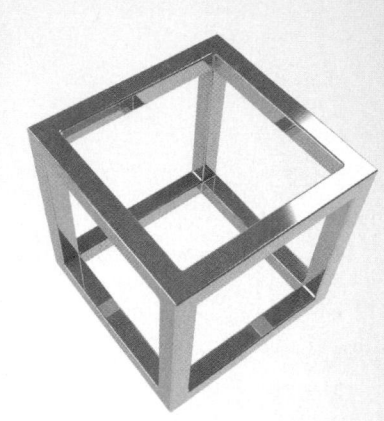

After studying Chapter 11, you should be able to:

1. Explain the purpose of a statement of cash flows.
2. Classify cash inflows and outflows as operating, investing, and financing activities.
3. Explain the relationship between changes in cash and the changes in the statement of financial position accounts.
4. Report and analyze the cash flows from operating activities using the indirect method.
5. Report and analyze cash flows from investing activities.
6. Report and analyze cash flows from financing activities.
7. Analyze information contained in the statement of cash flows.
8. *(Appendix 11A)* Prepare the cash flows from operating activities using the direct method.
9. *(Appendix 11B)* Use a spreadsheet to prepare the statement of cash flows.

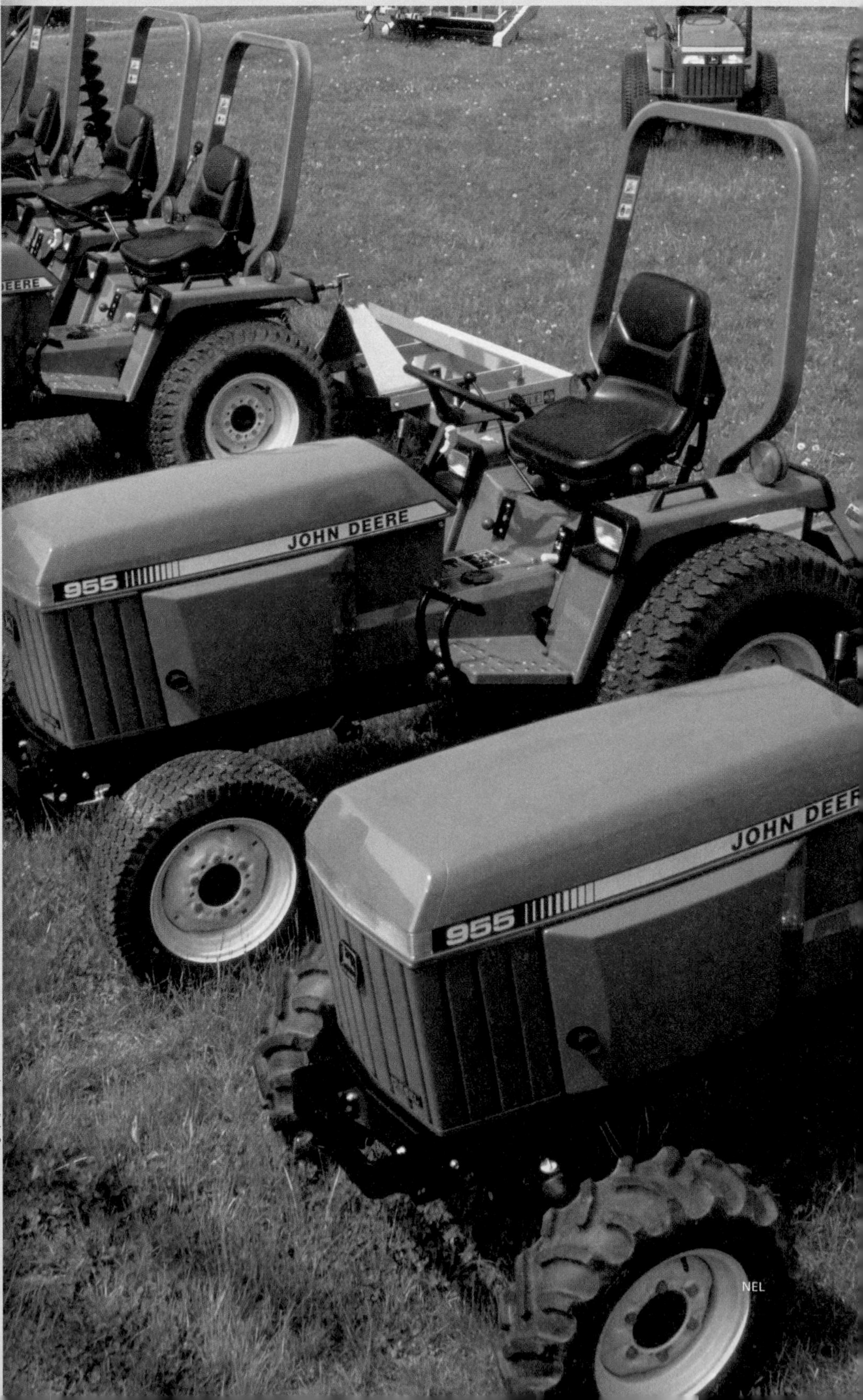

H. Mark Weidman Photography/Alamy Stock Photo

EXPERIENCE FINANCIAL ACCOUNTING
with Deere & Company

Founded in 1837, Deere & Company (collectively known as John Deere), is a business success story. From humble beginnings as a blacksmith shop, John Deere has grown into one of the world's largest corporations.

Not only is John Deere the world's leading manufacturer of farm and forestry equipment, it also sells a broad line of lawn tractors and other outdoor consumer products. John Deere is one of the world's largest equipment finance companies with a managed portfolio of almost $30 billion.

In addition to the statement of earnings, the statement of financial position, and the statement of changes in equity, companies are also required to provide a statement of cash flows. The statement of cash flows measures a company's inflows (sources) and outflows (uses) of cash during a period of time.

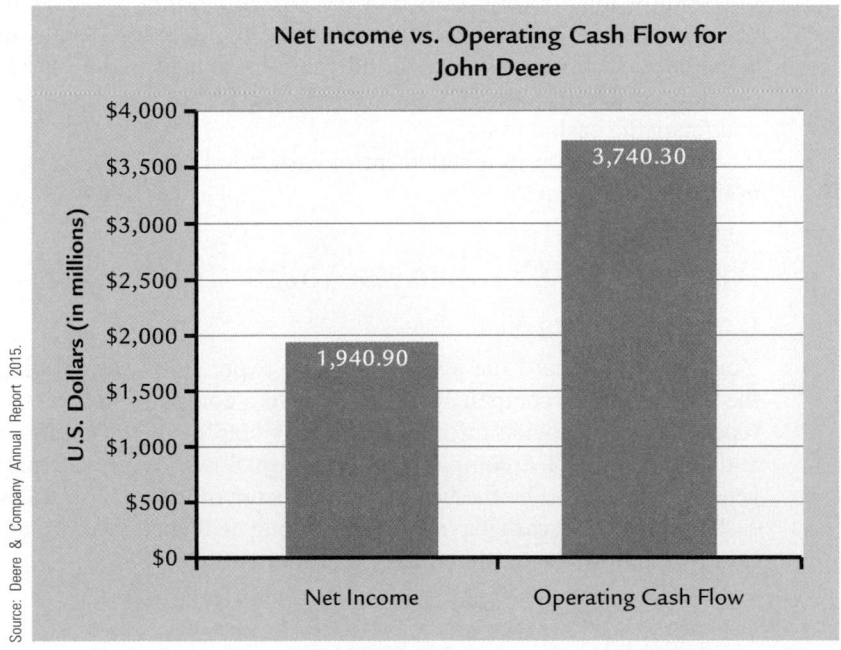

While net income provides important information, the recognition of revenues and expenses can occur at different times than the related cash inflow or outflow. Therefore, a company's net income does not always equal the amount of cash that it received and spent. Because cash is the life-blood of any business, proper cash management is essential for success.

Many financial statement users examine the difference between net income and cash generated from operations to gain valuable insights into a company's operations. Since operating cash flow increased from 92% of net income in 2013 to 193% of net income in 2015, John Deere generated substantial cash flow from operations. From the perspective of generating $3,740.3 million in 2015 operating cash flow, it is easy to see why some think the colour of money is John Deere green.

OBJECTIVE

Explain the purpose of a
statement of cash flows.

ROLE OF THE STATEMENT OF CASH FLOWS

In addition to being interested in the information in the accrual-basis financial statements, most financial statement users also want to know how a company obtained and used its cash. The purpose of the **statement of cash flows** is to provide relevant information to financial statement users about a company's cash receipts (inflows of cash) and cash payments (outflows of cash) during an accounting period.

The statement of cash flows is one of the primary financial statements. Because the other financial statements provide only limited information about a company's cash flows, the statement of cash flows can be viewed as a complement to these other financial statements. That is, while the statement of earnings provides information about the company's performance on an accrual basis, it does not tell how cash was generated or used as a result of the company's operations. Similarly, the statement of financial position provides information on the changes in net assets, but it doesn't provide information on how much cash was used or received in relation to these changes. The statement of cash flows fills this void by explaining the sources from which a company has acquired cash (inflows of cash) and the uses to which the business has applied cash (outflows of cash). Exhibit 11.1 gives an overview of a company's operating, investing, and financing cash flows.

The information in a statement of cash flows helps investors, creditors, and others in the following ways.

Assessing a Company's Ability to Produce Future Net Cash Inflows

You may have heard the age-old business expression "cash is king." Cash is certainly the life-blood of a company and is critical to a company's success. One goal of financial reporting is to provide information that is helpful in predicting the amounts, timing, and uncertainty of a company's future cash flows. While accrual-basis net income is generally viewed to be the best single predictor of future cash flows, information about cash receipts and cash payments can, along with net income, allow users to predict future cash flows better than net income alone.

(EXHIBIT 11.1)

Business Activities

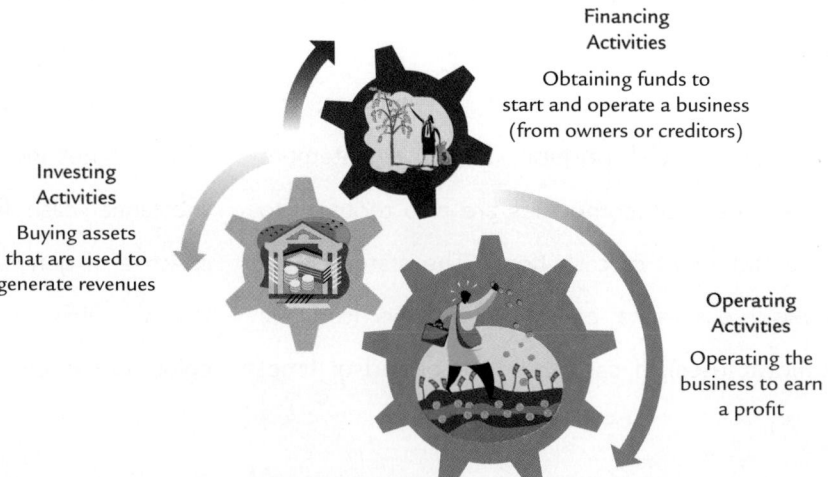

Financing
Activities

Obtaining funds to
start and operate a business
(from owners or creditors)

Investing
Activities

Buying assets
that are used to
generate revenues

Operating
Activities

Operating the
business to earn
a profit

© Cengage Learning

Judging a Company's Ability to Meet Its Obligations and Pay Dividends

As a company performs its business activities, it will incur various obligations. For example, suppliers want to know if the company can pay for the goods purchased on credit. Employees want to assess the company's ability to pay larger salaries and fringe benefits. Lenders are interested in the company's ability to repay the principal and interest on amounts borrowed. Similarly, investors often wish to know if a company is generating enough cash to be able to pay dividends and expand its productive capacity. In addition, success or failure in business often depends on whether a company has enough cash to meet unexpected obligations and take advantage of unexpected opportunities. Information about cash receipts and cash payments helps financial statement users make these important judgments.

Estimating the Company's Needs for External Financing

As companies operate, various expenditures can be financed through either internally generated funds or by external financing (debt or equity). Knowing the amount of cash that a company generates internally helps financial statement users assess whether a company will have to borrow additional funds from creditors or seek additional cash from investors.

Understanding the Reasons for the Differences between Net Income and Related Cash Receipts and Cash Payments

As you have already noticed, the amount of a company's net income and the amount of cash generated from operations are often different amounts. Because of the judgments and estimates involved in accrual accounting, many financial statement users question the usefulness of reported income because net income does not always indicate the amount of cash generated by a business from its operations. However, when provided with cash flow information, these users can gain insights into the quality and reliability of the reported income amounts.

Evaluating the Statement of Financial Position Effects of Both Cash and Noncash Investing and Financing Transactions

Not all changes in cash are directly related to a company's operations (such as manufacturing a product or selling a good or service). Instead, a company may make investments in productive assets as it expands its operations or upgrades its facilities. In addition, a company may seek sources of cash by issuing debt or equity. These activities can be just as crucial to a company's long-term success as its current operations.

In summary, information about a company's cash receipts and cash payments, along with information contained in the statement of financial position and the statement of earnings, is critical to understanding and analyzing a company's operations.

In this chapter, we will explain how a statement of cash flows is prepared from the information contained on the statement of financial position and the statement of earnings. We will explore the measurement, presentation, and analysis of cash flow information and address the following questions:

- What are the principal sources and uses of cash?
- How is the statement of cash flows prepared and reported to external users?
- How is the statement of cash flows used by investors, creditors, and others?

concept Q&A

If we already have the statement of financial position and statement of earnings, why is a statement of cash flows so important?

Answer:

The statement of cash flows provides information about a company's sources and uses of cash. Knowing how companies obtain and use cash provides users with a good idea of a company's financial strength and its long-term viability. The decision to invest in a company is much safer if a potential investor—be it a bank or shareholder—knows how much cash is being produced and where it is coming from.

CLASSIFICATION OF CASH INFLOWS AND CASH OUTFLOWS

OBJECTIVE 2

Classify cash inflows and outflows as operating, investing, and financing activities.

Because our focus is on cash flows, it is important to have a clear understanding of what is included in the term *cash*. For purposes of the statement of cash flows, cash includes both funds on hand (coins and currency) and **cash equivalents**. Recall from Chapter 4 that cash equivalents are short-term, highly liquid investments that are readily convertible to cash and have original maturities of three months or less. Examples of cash equivalents include money market funds and investments in Canadian government securities (for example, treasury bills). Because of their high liquidity or nearness to cash, cash equivalents are treated as cash in the statement of cash flows.

During an accounting period, a company engages in the three fundamental business activities discussed in Chapter 1 and as shown in Exhibit 11.1—operating activities, investing activities, and financing activities. Each of these activities can contribute to (a cash inflow) or reduce (a cash outflow) a company's cash balance. Therefore, the statement of cash flows reconciles the beginning and ending balances of cash by describing the effects of business activities on a company's cash balance. This relationship is shown in Exhibit 11.2.

Reporting and Analyzing Cash Flows from Operating Activities

Cash flows from operating activities (or operating cash flows) are the cash inflows and outflows that relate to acquiring (purchasing or manufacturing), selling, and delivering goods or services. Cash inflows from operating activities include:

- cash sales to customers
- collection of accounts receivable arising from credit sales
- cash dividends received
- interest received on investments in equity and debt securities

Cash outflows from operating activities include payments:

- to suppliers for goods and services
- to employees for wages and salaries
- to governments for taxes
- to lenders for interest on debt

(**EXHIBIT 11.2**)

How the Statement of Cash Flows Links the Two Statements of Financial Position

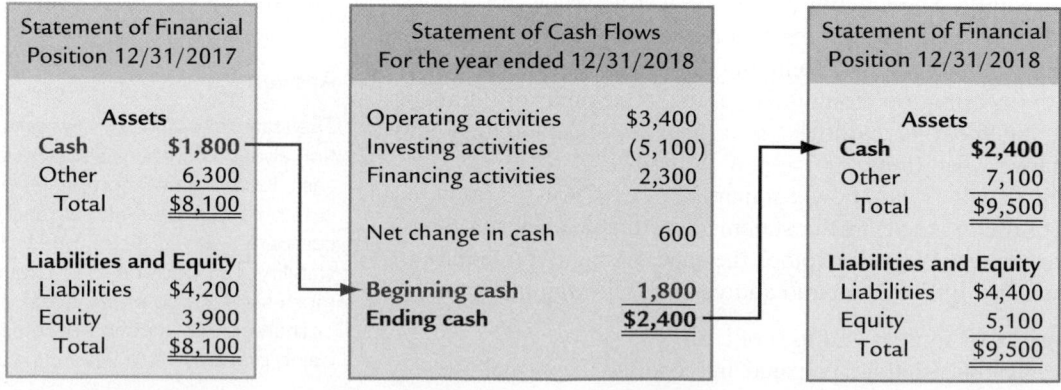

Statement of Financial Position 12/31/2017		Statement of Cash Flows For the year ended 12/31/2018		Statement of Financial Position 12/31/2018	
Assets		Operating activities	$3,400	**Assets**	
Cash	$1,800	Investing activities	(5,100)	Cash	$2,400
Other	6,300	Financing activities	2,300	Other	7,100
Total	$8,100			Total	$9,500
		Net change in cash	600		
Liabilities and Equity				**Liabilities and Equity**	
Liabilities	$4,200	Beginning cash	1,800	Liabilities	$4,400
Equity	3,900	**Ending cash**	$2,400	Equity	5,100
Total	$8,100			Total	$9,500

© Cengage Learning

Operating cash flows correspond to the *types* of items that determine net income (revenues and expenses). However, the *amounts* are different because the statement of earnings is accrual-based while the statement of cash flows is cash-based. Therefore, to isolate the current period operating cash flow, companies must adjust the current period statement of earnings items for any related noncash items, which can be determined by examining the changes in the related current assets and current liabilities.

John Deere in 2015 reported operating cash flow of US$3,740.3 million compared to net income of US$1,940.9 million (see Exhibit 11.7). While various reasons exist for this difference, two major factors include adjustments for noncash items (such as depreciation and amortization) and accrual accounting adjustments of current assets and liabilities. The adjustments needed to reconcile net income with operating cash flow are discussed later in the chapter.

The **quality of earnings** ratio is used by analysts to calculate the amount of cash that is generated by each dollar of earnings. This ratio is calculated as follows:

$$\text{Quality of Earnings Ratio} = \frac{\text{Cash Flow from Operating Activities}}{\text{Net Earnings}}$$

John Deere's quality of earnings ratio in 2015 was $239,033,000/$314,449,000 or $.76. This ratio means that each dollar of net earnings in 2015 generated $0.76 of cash. Generally, the higher the ratio the better. However, a lower ratio in itself is not indicative of a problem as a lower ratio may simply indicate that a business is expanding quickly with increased sales and profitability planned to be realized in the following months or years. Nonetheless, when this ratio is not equal to one, analysis should be performed to determine why a variance exists. Possible explanations for variances in this ratio could include recognizing revenue too early, failing to record liabilities correctly, failing to collect accounts receivable in a timely manner, paying creditors too early, inventory obsolescence, business seasonality, and general corporate expansion or decline. In order to properly analyze this ratio, a sound knowledge of the company's operations and business strategy is required.

Reporting and Analyzing Cash Flows from Investing Activities

Cash flows from investing activities (or investing cash flows) are the cash inflows and outflows that relate to acquiring and disposing of capital assets and investments in other companies (current and long-term), lending money, and collecting loans. Cash inflows from investing activities include cash received from:

- the sale of property, plant, and equipment
- the collection of the principal amount of a loan (a note receivable)
- the sale of investments in other companies
- the sale of a patent

Cash outflows from investing activities include payments made to:

- acquire property, plant, and equipment
- purchase debt or equity securities of other companies as an investment
- loan money to others (notes receivable)
- purchase a patent

In general, investing cash flows relate to increases or decreases of long-term assets and investments.

John Deere in 2015 reported a US$1,058.7 million cash outflow related to investing activities. Its major investing activities were related to the purchase and sale of receivables (its equipment financing business) and purchases of property, plant, and equipment.

Reporting and Analyzing Cash Flows from Financing Activities

Cash flows from financing activities (or financing cash flows) include obtaining resources from creditors and owners. Cash inflows from financing activities include cash received from the:

- issuance of shares
- issuance of debt (bonds or notes payable)

Cash outflows from financing activities include cash payments to:

- repay the principal amount borrowed (bonds or notes payable)
- repurchase a company's own shares (treasury shares)
- pay dividends

In general, financing cash flows involve cash receipts and payments that affect long-term liabilities and shareholders' equity.

John Deere in 2015 reported a cash outflow of US$2,119.1 million related to financing activities. Its major source of funds was from the issuance of long-term debt. Its major use of funds was the repayment of long-term debt and the repurchase of common shares.

Reporting and Analyzing Noncash Investing and Financing Activities

Occasionally, investing and financing activities take place without affecting cash. For example, a company may choose to acquire a capital asset (such as a building) by issuing long-term debt. Alternatively, a company may acquire one asset by exchanging it for another. These types of activities are referred to as **noncash investing and financing activities**. Because these activities do not involve cash, they are *not reported* on the statement of cash flows. However, these transactions still provide useful information about a company's overall investing and financing activities. Any significant noncash investing and financing activities are required to be reported on a supplementary schedule, which is shown either at the bottom of the statement of cash flows or in the notes to the financial statements. This requirement to disclose any significant noncash investing and financing activities is consistent with the full-disclosure principle—any information that would make a difference to financial statement users should be made known.

Exhibit 11.3 summarizes the classification of business activities as either operating, investing, or financing activities. Two particular activities—interest and dividends—are often misclassified by students. IFRS requires interest paid to be reported as either an operating or financing activity, whereas ASPE requires interest paid to be reported as an operating activity where the related interest expense is reported in the statement of earnings. IFRS allows companies to report dividends and interest received as either operating or investing activities, whereas ASPE requires dividend and interest income received to be recorded as operating activities. Both IFRS and ASPE require consistent application of accounting classifications each year to ensure financial results are comparable.

Exhibit 11.4 is the statement of cash flows for Assemblers Inc. for 2018, which discloses how amounts relating to operating, investing, and financing activities are classified.

Reporting and Analyzing Foreign Exchange

Unrealized exchange differences with respect to cash and cash equivalents at year-end are not classified as an operating, investing, or financing activity. Instead, unrealized exchange

(EXHIBIT 11.3)

Classification of Cash Flows

Cash Inflows

Operating Activities
Cash received from:
- Customers for cash sales
- Collections of accounts receivable
- Dividends
- Interest

Investing Activities
Cash received from:
- The sale of property, plant, and equipment
- The collection of principal on a loan
- The sale or maturity of investments
- The sale of a patent

Financing Activities
Cash received from:
- Issuing shares to owners
- Issuing notes or bonds (debt) to creditors

Cash Outflows

Operating Activities
Cash paid to:
- Suppliers of goods and services
- Employees for salaries and wages
- Governments for taxes
- Lenders for interest

Investing Activities
Cash paid to:
- Purchase property, plant, and equipment
- Make loans to other companies
- Purchase investments
- Purchase a patent

Financing Activities
Cash paid to:
- Repayment of principal of long-term debt
- Dividends to owners
- Purchase of shares from shareholders

differences on ending cash and cash equivalent balances must be presented as a separate reconciling item, between the opening and closing balances of cash and cash equivalents in the statement of cash flows. The required disclosure can be seen in Exhibit 11.7.

Cornerstone 11.1 shows how business activities can be classified as either operating, investing, financing, or noncash activities.

Classifying Business Activities

CORNERSTONE 11.1

Information:

Moore Inc. engaged in the following activities during the current year:

a. Payment of wages to employees
b. Issuance of common shares
c. Purchase of property, plant, and equipment
d. Collection of cash from customers
e. Issuance of bonds for cash

f. Retirement of debt by issuing shares
g. Purchase of inventory
h. Sale of property, plant, and equipment
i. Payment of cash dividends
j. Payment of interest

(Continued)

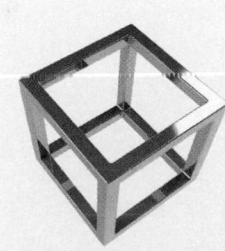

CORNERSTONE VIDEO

Required:

Classify each of the above activities as an operating, investing, or financing activity and indicate whether the activity involved a cash receipt or cash payment. If the transaction does not involve cash, classify it as a noncash investing and financing activity.

Why:

Cash flows from operating activities correspond to the cash effects of the components that determine net income. Cash flows from investing activities relate to increases or decreases in long-term assets and investments. Cash flows from financing activities involve cash receipts and payments that affect long-term liabilities and shareholders' equity. Business activities must be classified so as to correctly reflect each component of the statement of cash flow.

Solution:

a. Because wages are an expense on the statement of earnings, the payment of wages is classified as a cash payment for an operating activity.
b. The issuance of common shares results in an increase of shareholders' equity and cash. Therefore, it is classified as a cash receipt from a financing activity.
c. The purchase of property, plant, and equipment results in an increase to a long-term asset and a decrease of cash. Therefore, it is classified as a cash payment for an investing activity.
d. The collection of cash from customers relates to sales revenue on the statement of earnings and is classified as a cash receipt from an operating activity.
e. Issuing bonds results in an increase to long-term liabilities and cash. Therefore, it is classified as a cash receipt from a financing activity.
f. The retirement of debt by issuing shares is a financing activity that does not involve cash. It is classified as a noncash investing and financing activity.
g. Because inventory is a component of cost of goods sold on the statement of earnings, the purchase of inventory is classified as a cash payment for an operating activity.
h. The sale of property, plant, and equipment results in a decrease in a long-term asset and an increase in cash. Therefore, it is classified as a cash receipt from an investing activity.
i. The payment of cash dividends is a reduction in retained earnings, which is a part of shareholders' equity. Therefore, the payment of dividends is classified typically as a cash payment for a financing activity.
j. Interest is an expense on the statement of earnings. Therefore, the payment of interest is typically classified as a cash payment for an operating activity.

Format of the Statement of Cash Flows

Once a company has properly classified its cash inflows and outflows as operating, investing, or financing activities, it reports each of these three categories as shown in Exhibit 11.5. Note that the three cash flow categories are summed to obtain the net increase or decrease in cash. This change in cash reconciles the beginning and ending balances of cash as noted in Exhibit 11.2.

(EXHIBIT 11.4)

Assemblers Inc.
Consolidated Statements of Cash Flows ($000s)
For the year ended December 31, 2018
(with comparative figures for the year ended December 31, 2017)

	2018	2017
Cash flows from operating activities:		
Net income	$2,500	$2,100
Adjustments to reconcile net income to net cash from operating activities		
Depreciation and amortization	900	850
Changes in operating assets and liabilities		
Decrease in accounts receivable	250	100
Increase in inventories	(100)	(150)
Increase in accounts payable	800	600
Other operating assets and liabilities, net	100	40
Net cash provided by operating activities	4,450	3,540
Cash flows from investing activities:		
Purchase of property and equipment	(450)	(350)
Sale of property and equipment	100	50
Net cash used in investing activities	(350)	(300)
Cash flows from financing activities:		
Proceeds from issuance of long-term debt	700	200
Repurchase of common shares	(50)	(100)
Cash dividends paid	(300)	(200)
Net cash provided by (used in) financing activities	350	(100)
Net increase in cash and cash equivalents	4,450	3,140
Cash and cash equivalents, beginning of year	5,290	2,150
Cash and cash equivalents, end of year	$9,740	$5,290

YOUDECIDE Statement of Cash Flow Classifications

You are preparing the statement of cash flows for Sienna Corporation and consult the CFO about how to properly classify the cash paid for interest. The CFO states that the company chose to finance its recent expansion activities with large amounts of debt. Because the interest payments resulted from this financing decision, he believes that the cash paid for interest should be classified as a financing activity. In addition, the CFO points out that you shouldn't waste any more time on this since it's simply a classification issue. No matter where the interest payment is reported, the total change in cash will be the same and no one will care.

How should you classify the cash paid for interest?

The CFO certainly makes a good argument to classify interest payments as a financing cash flow. Similar to dividend payments (which

are paid for the use of equity capital), interest is paid for the use of debt capital. However, IFRS allows companies to treat interest paid as an operating or financing activity, provided the adopted treatment is consistently applied. While this is a classification issue, the CFO's assertion that the proper classification makes no difference is incorrect. The various classifications on a statement of cash flows provide insights into how a company generated and used its cash.

The proper classification of items in the statement of cash flows is critical for financial statement users as their decisions may be affected.

Format of the Statement of Cash Flows

Superior Sportswear Inc. Statement of Cash Flows For the Year Ended December 31, 2017		
Cash flows from operating activities		
Cash inflows	$xxx	
Cash outflows	(xxx)	
Net cash provided (used) by operating activities		xxx
Cash flows from investing activities		
Cash inflows	xxx	
Cash outflows	(xxx)	
Net cash provided (used) by investing activities		xxx
Cash flows from financing activities		
Cash inflows	xxx	
Cash outflows	(xxx)	
Net cash provided (used) by financing activities		xxx
Net increase (decrease) in cash and cash equivalents		xxx
Cash and cash equivalents at beginning of year		xxx
Cash and cash equivalents at end of year		$xxx
Note disclosure of noncash investing and financing activities		

ANALYZING THE ACCOUNTS FOR CASH FLOW DATA

OBJECTIVE ❸

Explain the relationship between changes in cash and the changes in the statement of financial position accounts.

Unlike the statement of financial position and the statement of earnings, the statement of cash flows cannot be prepared by simply using information obtained from an adjusted trial balance prepared using the accrual basis of accounting. Instead, each item on the statement of financial position and the statement of earnings must be analyzed to *explain* why cash changed by the amount that it did. In other words, the accrual-basis numbers in the statement of financial position and the statement of earnings must be adjusted to a cash basis. Notice that our goal is not with determining the change in cash but the *reasons why* cash changed.

The recording of any business activity creates two types of financial measures— *balances* and *changes*. Balances measure the dollar amount of an account at a given time. Changes measure the increases or decreases in account balances over a period of time. For example, consider the following T-account:

Accounts Receivable			
Balance, 12/31/2018	11,000		
2017 credit sales	90,000	92,000	Cash collections for 2018
Balance, 12/31/2019	9,000		

This T-account shows two balances and two changes. The beginning and ending balances ($11,000 and $9,000) measure accounts receivable at December 31, 2018 and 2019, respectively. The credit sales ($90,000) and cash collections ($92,000) are changes that measure the effects of selling goods and collecting cash. Like accounts receivable, every statement of financial position account can be described in terms of balances and changes.

To understand a company's cash flows, the relationships between the *changes* in statement of financial position accounts and the company's cash flows need to be analyzed. We will begin our analysis with the fundamental accounting equation:

$$\text{Assets} = \text{Liabilities} + \text{Shareholders' Equity}$$

Next, we will restate this equation in terms of changes (Δ):

$$\Delta \text{ Assets} = \Delta \text{ Liabilities} + \Delta \text{ Shareholders' Equity}$$

Separating assets into cash and noncash accounts:

$$\Delta \text{ Cash} + \Delta \text{ Noncash Assets} = \Delta \text{ Liabilities} + \Delta \text{ Shareholders' Equity}$$

Finally, moving the changes in noncash assets to the right-hand side:

$$\Delta \text{ Cash} = \Delta \text{ Liabilities} + \Delta \text{ Shareholders' Equity} - \Delta \text{ Noncash Assets}$$

Where:

Increases in cash = Increases in liabilities + Increases in shareholders' equity + Decreases in noncash assets

Decreases in cash = Decreases in liabilities + Decreases in shareholders' equity + Increases in noncash assets

This analysis reveals that **all cash receipts or cash payments are associated with changes in other statement of financial position accounts.** Cornerstone 11.2 illustrates how to classify specific statement of financial position accounts as increases in cash or decreases in cash.

concept Q&A

Why do we analyze changes in the statement of financial position accounts to determine the inflows and outflows of cash? Wouldn't it be easier to simply look at the cash account in the general ledger?

Answer:

It is correct that the cash account in the general ledger will contain all cash inflows and cash outflows and a statement of cash flows could be prepared by analyzing this account. However, this would require individuals to identify, understand, and classify every single cash receipt or cash payment throughout the accounting period. With the large volume of cash transactions, this would be an extremely time-consuming and inefficient task. It is much easier to determine cash flows by analyzing the changes in the statement of financial position accounts.

Classifying Changes in Statement of Financial Position Accounts

CORNERSTONE 11.2

Information:

The following changes in the statement of financial position accounts have been observed for the current period:

Account	12/31/2018	12/31/2019	Change
a. Accounts receivable	$ 25,000	$ 18,000	$ (7,000)
b. Bonds payable	400,000	300,000	(100,000)
c. Equipment	$145,000	$175,000	$ 30,000
d. Inventory	15,000	18,000	3,000
e. Common shares	150,000	175,000	25,000
f. Retained earnings	75,000	95,000	20,000
g. Accounts payable	12,000	10,000	(2,000)
h. Unearned revenue	17,000	19,000	2,000

(Continued)

CORNERSTONE
11.2

(Continued)

Required:

Classify each change as either an increase in cash or a decrease in cash.

Why:

Increases in cash result from increases in liabilities, increases in shareholders' equity, and decreases in noncash assets. Decreases in cash result from decreases in liabilities, decreases in shareholders' equity, and increases in noncash assets.

Solution:

a. Increase in cash   e. Increase in cash
b. Decrease in cash   f. Increase in cash
c. Decrease in cash   g. Decrease in cash
d. Decrease in cash   h. Increase in cash

Exhibit 11.6 integrates the analysis of the relationships between the *changes* in statement of financial position accounts and the company's cash flows with the cash flow classifications discussed in the previous section. Examining Exhibit 11.6, several items are of interest:

- Cash flows from operating activities generally involve statement of earnings items (which are reflected in retained earnings) and changes in current assets or liabilities.
- Investing activities are related to changes in long-term assets.
- Financing activities are related to changes in long-term liabilities and shareholders' equity.

(EXHIBIT 11.6)

Cash Flow Classifications and Changes in Statement of Financial Position Accounts

Classification	Cash Effect	Statement of Financial Position Items Affected	Example
Operating	Inflow (+)	Decreases in current assets Increases in current liabilities Increases in retained earnings	Collecting an accounts receivable Receipt of revenue in advance Making a cash sale
	Outflow (−)	Increases in current assets Decreases in current liabilities Decreases in retained earnings	Purchasing inventory Paying an accounts payable Paying interest
Investing	Inflow (+)	Decreases in long-term assets	Selling equipment
	Outflow (−)	Increases in long-term assets	Buying equipment
Financing	Inflow (+)	Increases in long-term liabilities Increases in shareholders' equity	Issuing long-term debt Issuing shares
	Outflow (−)	Decreases in long-term liabilities Decreases in shareholders' equity	Repaying long-term debt Paying dividends

- Retained earnings affects both cash flows from operating activities (e.g., revenues, expenses, net income or loss) and cash flows from financing activities (e.g., payment of dividends).
- Each item on the statement of financial position and the statement of earnings is analyzed to explain the change in cash.

PREPARING A STATEMENT OF CASH FLOWS

After the accounts have been analyzed to identify cash inflows and outflows, a statement of cash flows can be prepared. To prepare a statement of cash flows, you need:

- *Comparative statements of financial position*: Used to determine the changes in assets, liabilities, and shareholders' equity during a period
- *A current statement of earnings*: Used to determine cash flows from operating activities
- *Additional information about selected accounts*: Used to determine the reason why cash was received or paid

   Using this information, there are five basic steps in preparing the statement of cash flows.

Step 1: Compute the net cash flow from operating activities. This involves adjusting the amounts on the statement of earnings for noncash changes reflected in the statement of financial position. Two methods, the indirect or direct method (explained in the next section), may be used to determine this amount.

Step 2: Compute the net cash flow from investing activities. Information from the statement of financial position as well as any additional information provided will need to be analyzed to identify the cash inflows and outflows associated with long-term assets.

Step 3: Compute the net cash flow from financing activities. Information from the statement of financial position as well as any additional information provided will need to be analyzed to identify the cash inflows and outflows associated with long-term liabilities and shareholders' equity.

Step 4: Combine the net cash flows from operating, investing, and financing activities to obtain the net increase (decrease) in cash for the period.

Step 5: Compute the change in cash for the period using the amounts reported in the statement of financial position and compare this with the change in cash from Step 4. The change in cash, computed from the beginning balance of cash and the ending balance of cash as shown on the statement of financial position, should be the same amount as the net cash flow computed in Step 4.

   The statement of cash flows for John Deere prepared using the indirect method is shown in Exhibit 11.7.

PREPARING CASH FLOWS FROM OPERATING ACTIVITIES

The cash flows from operating activities section of the statement of cash flows may be prepared using either of two methods: the direct method or the indirect method. Both methods arrive at an identical amount—the net cash provided (used) by operating activities. The two methods differ only in how this amount is computed.

OBJECTIVE

Report and analyze the cash flows from operating activities using the indirect method.

The Direct Method

In the **direct method**, cash inflows and cash outflows are listed for each type of operating activity that a company performs. These cash flows are generally computed by

(EXHIBIT 11.7)

Statement of Cash Flows for John Deere

Deere & Company Statement of Consolidated Cash Flows* For the Year Ended October 31, 2015 (in millions of U.S. dollars)		
Cash flows from operating activities		
Net income	$ 1,940.9	
Adjustments to reconcile net income to net cash provided by operating activities:		
Provision for credit losses	55.4	
Depreciation and amortization	1,382.4	
Other noncash items	81.5	
Changes in assets and liabilities:		
Decrease in receivables related to sales	811.6	
Decrease in insurance receivables	333.4	
Increase in inventories	(691.4)	
Decrease in accounts payable and accrued expenses	(503.6)	
Decrease in accrued income taxes payable/receivable	(137.6)	
Increase in retirement benefit accruals	427.5	
Other	40.2	
Net cash provided by operating activities		$ 3,740.3
Cash flows from investing activities		
Collections of notes receivable	14,919.7	
Proceeds from sales of businesses	149.2	
Proceeds from maturities and sales of marketable securities	860.7	
Proceeds from sales of equipment on operating leases	1,049.4	
Cost of receivable acquired	(14,996.5)	
Purchases of marketable securities	(154.9)	
Purchases of property, plant, and equipment	(694.0)	
Cost of equipment on operating leases acquired	(2,132.1)	
Other	(60.2)	
Net cash used for investing activities		(1,058.7)
Cash flows from financing activities		
Increase in short-term borrowings	501.6	
Proceeds from long-term borrowings	5,711.0	
Payments of long-term borrowings	(4,863.2)	
Proceeds from issuance of common shares	172.1	
Repurchases of common shares	(2,770.7)	
Dividends paid	(816.3)	
Other	(53.6)	
Net cash provided by financing activities		2,119.1
Effect of exchange rate changes on cash and cash equivalents		(187.3)
Net increase in cash and cash equivalents		375.2
Cash and cash equivalents at beginning of year		3,787.0
Cash and cash equivalents at end of year		$ 4,162.2

Source: Deere & Company Annual Report 2015.

*The statement of cash flows information was taken from the annual report of Deere & Company and has been summarized and reformatted by the authors.

adjusting *each item* on the statement of earnings by the changes in the related current asset or liability accounts. Cash flow categories reported under this method are cash collected from customers, cash paid to suppliers, cash paid to employees, cash paid for interest, and cash paid for taxes. The cash outflows are subtracted from the cash inflows to determine the net cash flow from operating activities. If the direct method is used, companies must also provide a supplementary schedule that shows the reconciliation of net income with operating cash flow. While the IFRS prefers the use of the direct method because it is more consistent with the purpose of the statement of cash flows, it is not widely used in practice.

The Indirect Method

The indirect method does not report individual cash inflow and outflows for each type of operating activity that a company performs. Instead, it focuses on the *differences* between net income and operating cash flow. The **indirect method** begins with net income and then adjusts it for noncash items to produce net cash flow from operating activities. These adjustments to net income are necessary for two reasons:

- to eliminate statement of earnings items that do not affect cash (such as depreciation and gains/losses on sales of assets) and
- to adjust accrual-basis revenues and expenses to gross cash receipts and gross cash payments.

The changes in the related current asset and current liability accounts contain the information necessary to make the adjustments to revenue and expense accounts.

Generally, companies prefer the indirect method because it is easier and less costly to prepare. Companies that use the indirect method must disclose interest and dividends paid and received during the period, as well as cash paid for income taxes, either in the appropriate section of the cash flow statement or in the financial statement notes.

ETHICAL DECISIONS By highlighting the differences between operating cash flows and net income, financial statement users may be able to more easily see attempts at earnings management. If managers try to manage earnings by manipulating the accrual accounting process (e.g., if they increase revenues or decrease expenses on the statement of earnings to increase income), these actions will often have no cash flow effect but will instead reveal themselves through changes in the accrual-basis accounts. When there are growing differences between operating cash flow and net income, the indirect method highlights the changes in the accrual accounts and allows users to judge the cause of these differences. ●

Applying the Indirect Method

We will illustrate the preparation of cash flows from operating activities for Superior Sportswear using the more popular indirect method. The direct method is illustrated in Appendix 11A. However, remember two important points.

- Cash flow from operating activities is *the same amount* under either method.
- The indirect and direct methods are only different as they relate to the operating activities section of the statement of cash flows. The investing and financing sections will be prepared *the same way* regardless of which method is used to prepare the operating activities section.

The statement of earnings and comparative statements of financial position for Superior Sportswear are shown in Exhibit 11.8.

Because statements of earnings are prepared on an accrual basis, the revenues and expenses recognized on the statement of earnings are not necessarily the same as the cash receipts and cash payments for a period. For example, revenues may include credit sales for which the company has not collected cash and exclude collections of cash from credit sales made in a previous period. Similarly, expenses may have been incurred for which no cash has been paid, or cash may have been paid related to expenses incurred in a previous period. Therefore, net income must be adjusted for these timing differences between the recognition of net income and the receipt or payment of cash.

(EXHIBIT 11.8)

Financial Statements for Superior Sportswear

Superior Sportswear
Statements of Financial Position
December 31, 2018 and 2017

	2018	2017
ASSETS		
Current assets:		
Cash	$ 15,000	$ 13,000
Accounts receivable	53,000	46,000
Inventory	63,000	51,000
Prepaid insurance	1,000	2,000
Total current assets	132,000	112,000
Long-term investments	53,000	41,000
Property, plant, and equipment:		
Land	325,000	325,000
Equipment	243,000	210,000
Accumulated depreciation	(178,000)	(150,000)
Total assets	$ 575,000	$ 538,000

LIABILITIES AND EQUITY		
Current liabilities:		
Accounts payable	$ 13,000	$ 17,000
Wages payable	3,500	2,000
Interest payable	1,500	1,000
Income tax payable	3,000	6,000
Total current liabilities	21,000	26,000
Long-term liabilities:		
Notes payable	109,000	115,000
Total liabilities	130,000	141,000
Equity:		
Common shares	165,000	151,000
Retained earnings	280,000	246,000
Total equity	445,000	397,000
Total liabilities and equity	$575,000	$538,000

Superior Sportswear
Statement of Earnings
For the Year Ended December 31, 2018

Sales revenue	$ 472,000
Less: Cost of goods sold	(232,000)
Gross margin	240,000
Less operating expenses:	
Wages expense	(142,000)
Insurance expense	(15,000)
Depreciation expense	(40,000)
Income from operations	43,000
Other income and expenses:	
Loss on disposal of property, plant, and equipment	(6,000)
Gain on sale of investments	15,000
Interest expense	(5,000)
Income before income tax	47,000
Less: Income tax expense	(8,000)
Net income	$ 39,000

Additional Information:

1. Equipment with a cost of $20,000 and accumulated depreciation of $12,000 was sold for $2,000 cash. Equipment was purchased for $53,000 cash.

2. Long-term investments with a cost of $16,000 were sold for $31,000 cash. Additional investments were purchased for $28,000 cash.

3. Notes payable in the amount of $35,000 were repaid, and new notes payable in the amount of $29,000 were issued for cash.

4. Common shares were issued for $14,000 cash.

5. Cash dividends of $5,000 were paid (obtained from the retained earnings account analysis).

---

concept Q&A

Why are there differences between net income and net cash flow from operating activities?

Answer:

Net income is prepared under the accrual basis of accounting, which records business activities when they occur instead of when cash is received or paid. Therefore, all of the adjustments that are made to net income reflect timing differences between the reporting of revenues and expenses and the related inflow or outflow of cash.

Under the indirect method, four types of adjustments must be made to net income to adjust it to net cash flow from operating activities:

1. Add to net income any noncash expenses (expenses that did not generate a cash outflow) and subtract from net income any noncash revenues (revenues that did not generate a cash inflow).

2. Add to net income any accounting (or book) losses and subtract from net income any accounting (or book) gains.

3. Add to net income any decreases in current assets or increases in current liabilities that are related to operating activities.

4. Subtract from net income any increases in current assets and decreases in current liabilities that are related to operating activities.

These adjustments and the computation of net cash flow from operating activities are illustrated in Cornerstone 11.3.

Calculating Net Cash Flow from Operating Activities: Indirect Method

CORNERSTONE 11.3

CORNERSTONE
VIDEO

Information:

Refer to the statement of earnings and the current assets and current liabilities sections of Superior Sportswear's statements of financial position found in Exhibit 11.8.

Required:

Compute the net cash flow from operating activities using the indirect method.

Why:

The calculation of net cash flow from operating activities requires adjustments to net income for noncash items, accounting gains and accounting losses, and changes in current assets and current liabilities that affected operating activities.

Solution:

Net income		$39,000
Adjustments to reconcile net income to net cash flow from operating activities:*		
Depreciation expense	$ 40,000	
Loss on disposal of equipment	6,000	
Gain on sale of long-term investments	(15,000)	
Increase in accounts receivable	(7,000)	
Decrease in prepaid insurance	1,000	
Increase in inventory	(12,000)	
Decrease in accounts payable	(4,000)	
Increase in wages payable	1,500	
Increase in interest payable	500	
Decrease in income tax payable	(3,000)	8,000
Net cash provided by operating activities		$47,000

* The explanation of these adjustments is given in the text of this section.

The adjustments made in Cornerstone 11.3 are explained below.

Adjustment of Noncash Revenues and Expenses The statement of earnings often includes various noncash items such as depreciation expense, amortization expense, and bad debt expense.

- Noncash expenses reduce net income but do not reduce cash. Under the indirect method **noncash expenses are added back to net income**.
- Noncash revenues increase income but do not increase cash. Under the indirect method, **noncash revenues are subtracted from net income**.

Adjustment of Accounting Gains and Losses The sale of a long-term asset or the extinguishment of a long-term liability often produces either a gain or loss that is reported on the statement of earnings. However, the gain or loss does not affect cash flow and should, therefore, not be included as an operating activity. Furthermore, the gain or loss does not reveal the total amount of cash received or paid. Instead, it only gives the amount received or paid in excess of the book value of the asset or liability. The correct procedure is to eliminate the gain or loss from net income and record the full amount of the cash flow as either an investing activity or a financing activity.

- Because gains increase net income, under the indirect method, **gains are subtracted from net income**.
- Because losses decrease net income, under the indirect method, **losses are added back to net income**.

Adjustments for Changes in Current Assets and Current Liabilities As discussed earlier in the chapter, all cash receipts or cash payments are associated with changes in one or more statement of financial position accounts. Generally, current assets and liabilities are related to the operating activities of a company, and changes in these accounts cause a difference between net income and cash flows from operating activities. Based on the earlier analysis of the statement of financial position accounts, two general rules emerge.

- **Increases in current assets and decreases in current liabilities are subtracted from net income.**
- **Decreases in current assets and increases in current liabilities are added to net income.**

The adjustments to net income required to calculate cash flow from operating activities are summarized in Exhibit 11.9.

The explanations of these adjustments for Superior Sportswear are shown below.

Accounts Receivable The accounts receivable account increases when credit sales are recorded and decreases when cash is collected from customers.

Accounts Receivable			
Balance, 1/1/2018	46,000		
Credit sales	xxx	Cash collections	xxx
Balance, 12/31/2018	53,000		

The increase of accounts receivable implies that credit sales were $7,000 greater than the cash collected from customers. This is consistent with the results of our earlier analysis indicating that increases in noncash assets are related to decreases in cash. Because cash collections were less than the sales reported in the statement of earnings, the company would need to subtract the increase in accounts receivable from net income when computing net cash flow from operating activities. (A decrease in accounts receivable would be added to net income when computing net cash flow from operating activities.)

Prepaid Insurance The prepaid insurance account increases when cash prepayments are made and decreases as insurance expense is incurred.

Adjustments Required to Calculate Cash Flow from Operating Activities

⊕ Add to Net Income	⊖ Subtract from Net Income
• Noncash expenses	• Noncash revenues
• Accounting losses	• Accounting gains
• Decreases in current assets	• Increases in current assets
• Increases in current liabilities	• Decreases in current liabilities

© Cengage Learning

Prepaid Insurance

Balance, 1/1/2018	2,000		
Cash prepayments	XXX	Expense incurred	XXX
Balance, 12/31/2018	1,000		

The decrease in prepaid insurance indicates that expenses recorded on the statement of earnings were $1,000 higher than the cash payments. Because more expense was incurred than was paid in cash, the company actually has more cash available at the end of the period than at the beginning of the period (because less cash was paid). This is consistent with the results of our earlier analysis indicating that decreases in noncash assets are related to increases in cash. The decrease in the prepaid insurance account needs to be added to net income when computing net cash flow from operating activities. (Increases in prepaid insurance would be subtracted from net income.)

Inventory The inventory account increases when inventory is purchased and decreases as inventory is sold.

Inventory

Balance, 1/1/2018	51,000		
Purchases	XXX	Cost of goods sold	XXX
Balance, 12/31/2018	63,000		

The increase in inventory implies that purchases of inventory exceeded the cost of the inventory sold reported on the statement of earnings by $12,000. Therefore, the company made "extra" cash purchases that were not included in cost of goods sold. To adjust net income to net cash flow from operating activities, the increase in the inventory account, which represents the extra cash purchases, needs to be subtracted from net income. (Decreases in inventory would be added to net income.)

Accounts Payable The accounts payable account increases when credit purchases are made and decreases when cash payments are made to suppliers.

Accounts Payable

Cash payments	XXX	Balance, 1/1/2018	17,000
		Credit purchases	XXX
		Balance, 12/31/2018	13,000

The decrease in accounts payable indicates that the cash payments to suppliers exceeded the purchases of inventory by $4,000. Because the purchase of inventory is part of cost of goods sold, this implies that more cash was paid than was reflected in expenses. This is consistent with the results of our earlier analysis indicating that decreases in liabilities are related to decreases in cash. Therefore, the decrease in accounts payable needs to be subtracted from net income when computing the net cash flow from operating activities. (Increases of accounts payable are added to net income.)

Wages Payable The wages payable account increases when wages are accrued (incurred but not yet paid) and decreases when wages are paid.

Wages Payable

Cash payments	XXX	Balance, 1/1/2018	2,000
		Wages expense	XXX
		Balance, 12/31/2018	3,500

The increase in wages payable indicates that wages expense recorded on the statement of earnings was greater than the cash paid for wages by $1,500. Because less cash was paid than expensed, the company actually has more cash available. This is consistent with the results of our earlier analysis indicating that increases in liabilities are related to increases in cash. Therefore, the increase in wages payable is added to net income when computing the net cash flow from operating activities. (Decreases in wages payable are subtracted from net income.)

Interest Payable Interest payable increases when interest expense is recorded and decreases when interest is paid.

Interest Payable

		Balance, 1/1/2018	1,000
Cash payments	xxx	Interest expense	xxx
		Balance, 12/31/2018	1,500

The increase in interest payable implies that interest expense recorded on the statement of earnings was $500 greater than the cash paid for interest. This is consistent with the results of our earlier analysis indicating that increases in liabilities are related to increases in cash. Therefore, the increase in interest payable is added to net income when computing the net cash flow from operating activities. (Decreases in interest payable are subtracted from net income.)

Income Tax Payable The income tax payable account increases when income tax expense is incurred and decreases when income taxes are paid.

Income Tax Payable

		Balance, 1/1/2018	6,000
Cash payments	xxx	Income tax expense	xxx
		Balance, 12/31/2018	3,000

The decrease in income tax payable implies that the cash payments for income taxes were $3,000 greater than the income tax expense reported on the statement of earnings. This is consistent with the results of our earlier analysis indicating that decreases in liabilities are related to decreases in cash. Therefore, less cash is available at the end of the period and the decrease in income tax payable is subtracted from net income when computing the net cash flow from operating activities. (Increases in income tax payable are added to net income.)

YOU DECIDE Operating Cash Flow and the Quality of Earnings

You are analyzing the financial statements of Glater Ltd., a retail company that operates primarily in eastern Ontario. While Glater has reported increasing net income, you notice that its operating cash flow has been declining. Further investigation reveals increasing accounts receivable and inventory balances.

What inferences can you make about the quality of Glater's earnings?

Many analysts will compare net income to operating cash flow as a means of assessing the quality of a company's earnings. All other things equal, the higher a company's operating cash flow relative to its net income, the greater the quality of the company's earnings. In Glater's situation, increasing income with declining operating cash flow is a warning sign that requires closer scrutiny. The increasing accounts receivable balances could simply signal rapidly growing operations. However, it may also signal that a company is attempting to boost sales by allowing customers to take longer to pay or lending to riskier customers. Similarly, increasing inventory balances may be due to seasonal factors (e.g., the normal inventory growth during a "slow" quarter), or it could signal that the company was not able to sell its merchandise as it had planned. When differences between net income and operating cash flow are noted, it is critical to fully understand their implications for the company's prospects.

Understanding the differences between net income and operating cash flow can provide useful insights into the quality of a company's earnings.

PREPARING CASH FLOWS FROM INVESTING ACTIVITIES

The second major section of the statement of cash flows reports the net cash flow from investing activities. Information for preparing the investing activities portion of the statement of cash flows is obtained from the investment and long-term asset accounts. Because all of these accounts are assets, increases that were financed by cash would be treated as outflows of cash. Decreases in the assets that produced cash receipts would be treated as inflows of cash.

Although the beginning and ending statements of financial position are useful sources for identifying changes in these accounts, you must also refer to any additional data provided to determine the actual amount of investing cash inflows and outflows. For example, a company might purchase land at a cost of $200,000 and, during the same accounting period, sell land that had a cost of $145,000. If only the beginning and ending amounts for land were examined, one would erroneously conclude that there had been a single cash outflow of $55,000 for land, instead of two separate cash flows—a cash outflow for the purchase of land and a cash inflow related to the sale of land.

OBJECTIVE 5

Report and analyze cash flows from investing activities.

Analyzing Investing Activities

To analyze investing activities, follow the three basic steps outlined in Exhibit 11.10.

To illustrate the analysis of the relevant accounts and the recreation of the journal entries, consider the information in Superior Sportswear's financial statements in Exhibit 11.8.

Land Notice that no change occurred in the land account, nor was any additional information given concerning this account. Therefore, there was no cash flow associated with land for the year.

Property, Plant, and Equipment To obtain a complete picture of the equipment account you must examine both the equipment and the related accumulated depreciation account. (For any operating asset that depreciates, you will need to analyze the two related accounts together.) Using the information from the financial statements and the additional information in Exhibit 11.8, you can recreate the activity in these accounts by making the following journal entries:

(EXHIBIT 11.10)

Analyzing Investing Activities

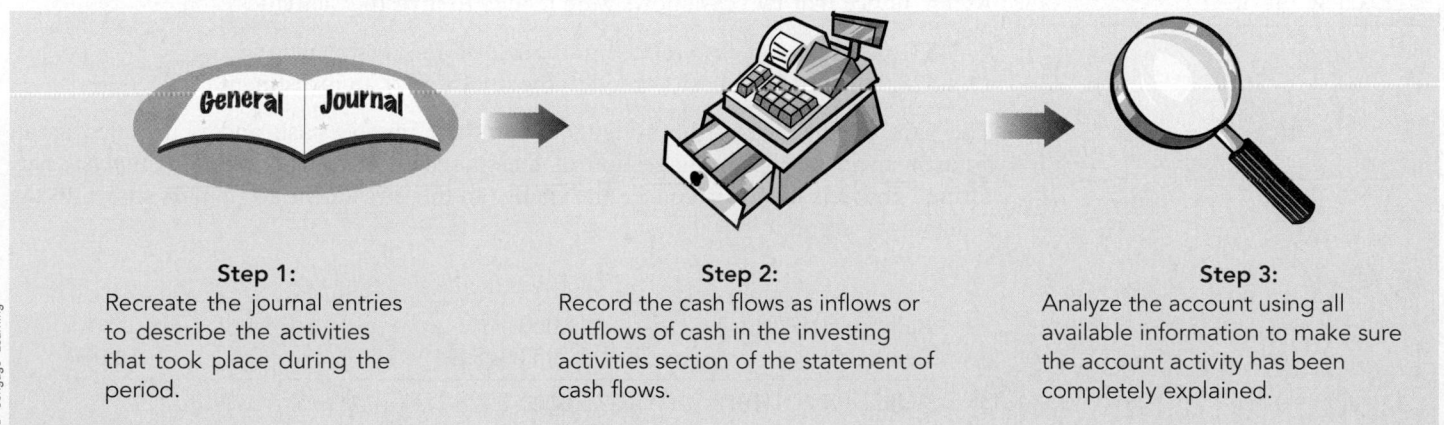

Step 1:
Recreate the journal entries to describe the activities that took place during the period.

Step 2:
Record the cash flows as inflows or outflows of cash in the investing activities section of the statement of cash flows.

Step 3:
Analyze the account using all available information to make sure the account activity has been completely explained.

Assets	= Liabilities +	Shareholders' Equity (Loss on Disposal)
+2,000		−6,000
+12,000		
−20,000		

Assets	= Liabilities +	Shareholders' Equity
+53,000		
−53,000		

Sale of Equipment	Cash	2,000	
	Accumulated Depreciation	12,000	
	Loss on Disposal of Property, Plant, and Equipment	6,000	
	Equipment		20,000

Purchase of Equipment	Equipment	53,000	
	Cash		53,000

Notice that there are only two cash flows related to investing activities:

- a $2,000 cash inflow associated with the disposal of equipment, and
- a $53,000 cash outflow associated with the purchase of equipment.

The loss on the disposal of equipment does not involve cash and is included as an adjustment in the operating section of the statement of cash flows. The analysis performed above is used to reconcile the change in the equipment and accumulated depreciation accounts as shown in the following T-accounts:

Equipment

Balance, 1/1/2018	210,000		
Purchase	53,000	Disposal	20,000
Balance, 12/31/2018	243,000		

Accumulated Depreciation

		Balance, 1/1/2018	150,000
Disposal	12,000	Dep. exp.	40,000
		Balance, 12/31/2018	178,000

Investments Using the information in Exhibit 11.8, you can recreate the activity in the investment account by making the following journal entries:

Assets	= Liabilities +	Shareholders' Equity (Gain on Sale)
+31,000		+15,000
−16,000		

Sale of Investment	Cash	31,000	
	Investments		16,000
	Gain on Sale of Investments		15,000

Assets	= Liabilities +	Shareholders' Equity
+28,000		
−28,000		

Purchase of Investment	Investments	28,000	
	Cash		28,000

Again, notice that two cash flows were related to investing activities:

- a $31,000 inflow of cash related to the sale of an investment, and
- a $28,000 outflow of cash related to the purchase of an investment.

The gain on the sale of the investment does not involve cash and is included as an adjustment in the operating section of the statement of cash flows. The analysis performed above is used to reconcile the change in the investment account as shown in the following T-account.

Investments

Balance, 1/1/2018	41,000		
Purchase	28,000	Sale	16,000
Balance, 12/31/2018	53,000		

Cornerstone 11.4 shows how to compute the investing activities section of the statement of cash flows for Superior Sportswear.

Reporting Net Cash Flow from Investing Activities

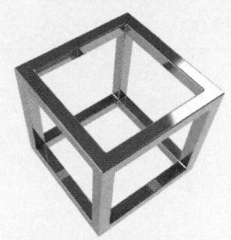

CORNERSTONE 11.4

Information:

Refer to the statement of earnings, the long-term assets sections of Superior Sportswear's statements of financial position, and the first two items of additional information in Exhibit 11.8.

Required:

Compute the net cash flow from investing activities.

Why:

The cash flow effects of changes in long-term assets and investments are reported as investing cash flows.

CORNERSTONE
VIDEO

Solution:

Cash flows from investing activities:	
Cash received from sale of equipment	$ 2,000
Purchase of equipment	(53,000)
Cash received from sale of investments	31,000
Purchase of investments	(28,000)
Net cash used for investing activities	$(48,000)

PREPARING CASH FLOWS FROM FINANCING ACTIVITIES

The intent of the financing activities section of the statement of cash flows is to identify inflows and outflows of cash arising from business activities that either produced capital (long-term debt or shareholders' equity) for the company or repaid capital supplied to the company. Information for preparing the financing activities portion of the statement of cash flows is obtained from the long-term debt and shareholders' equity accounts. Increases in these accounts suggest that cash has been received and decreases suggest that cash has been paid.

 OBJECTIVE 6

Report and analyze cash flows from financing activities.

Analyzing Financing Activities

To analyze financing activities, the same basic steps used to analyze investing activities (see Exhibit 11.10) are followed:

Step 1: Recreate the journal entries to describe the activities that took place during the period.

Step 2: Record the cash flows as inflows or outflows of cash in the financing activities section of the statement of cash flows.

Step 3: Analyze the account to make sure the account activity has been completely explained.

To illustrate the analysis of the relevant accounts and the recreation of the journal entries, consider the information in Superior Sportswear's statement of financial position.

Notes Payable Using information in Exhibit 11.8, you can recreate the activity in the notes payable account by making the following journal entries:

	Assets	=	Liabilities	+	Shareholders' Equity
	−35,000		−35,000		

	Assets	=	Liabilities	+	Shareholders' Equity
	+29,000		+29,000		

Repayment of Principal	Notes Payable	35,000	
	Cash		35,000
Issuance of Note	Cash	29,000	
	Notes Payable		29,000

Notice that there are two cash flows related to financing activities:

- a $35,000 cash outflow associated with the repayment of principal, and
- a $29,000 cash inflow associated with issuing the note.

The payment of interest is usually considered an operating activity and is not relevant to this analysis. The analysis performed above is used to reconcile the change in the notes payable account as shown in the following T-account:

Notes Payable

		Balance, 1/1/2018	115,000
Repaid principal	35,000	Issued note	29,000
		Balance, 12/31/2018	109,000

Common Shares Using information in Exhibit 11.8, you can recreate activity in the common share account by making the following journal entry:

	Assets	=	Liabilities	+	Shareholders' Equity
	+14,000				+14,000

Issuance of Shares	Cash	14,000	
	Common Shares		14,000

One cash inflow ($14,000) has caused the change in common shares. The credit entry to the common share account is used to reconcile the change in the common share account, as shown in the following T-account:

Common Shares

		Balance, 1/1/2018	151,000
Repurchased shares	0	Issued shares	14,000
		Balance, 12/31/2018	165,000

Retained Earnings Using information in Exhibit 11.8, you can recreate the activity in the retained earnings account by making the following journal entry:

	Assets	=	Liabilities	+	Shareholders' Equity
	−5,000				−5,000

Declaration and Payment of Dividends	Dividends	5,000	
	Cash		5,000

The only cash flow, the payment of dividends, is usually a financing activity. The following T-account summarizes the activity in the retained earnings account:

Retained Earnings

		Balance, 1/1/2018	246,000
Dividends	5,000	Net income	39,000
		Balance, 12/31/2018	280,000

Note that retained earnings is increased by net income and decreased by the payment of dividends.[1] Net income does not affect cash flow from financing activities but is considered an operating activity.

Cornerstone 11.5 shows how to compute the financing activities section of the statement of cash flows for Superior Sportswear.

Reporting Net Cash Flow from Financing Activities

CORNERSTONE 11.5

CORNERSTONE VIDEO

Information:

Refer to the statement of earnings, long-term assets, liabilities, and equity sections of Superior Sportswear's statement of financial position, and items 3–5 of additional information in Exhibit 11.8.

Required:

Compute the net cash flow from financing activities.

Why:

The cash flow effects of changes in long-term liabilities and shareholders' equity are reported as financing cash flows.

Solution:

Cash flows from financing activities:	
Cash paid to repay principal on notes payable	$(35,000)
Cash received from issuing notes payable	29,000
Cash received from issuance of common shares	14,000
Cash paid for dividends	(5,000)
Net cash provided by financing activities	$ 3,000

Combining Cornerstones 11.3 through 11-5, a complete statement of cash flows is presented in Exhibit 11.11. This exhibit presents cash flows from operating activities using the indirect method. Notice that the statement of cash flows explains the change in cash shown on the statement of financial position of Superior Sportswear in Exhibit 11.8.

YOUDECIDE   Understanding Patterns in the Statement of Cash Flows

During a recent conference call with analysts, the CEO of Maggones Inc. said that the company expects future sales growth as it expands into several new geographical markets. To corroborate the CEO's statements, you examine the statement of cash flows and find that the company reported negative operating cash flows, positive investing cash flows, and positive financing cash flows.

Does the statement of cash flows support the CEO's statements?

It does not appear that the CEO's statements are supported by the company's cash flows. An expanding company should exhibit negative investing cash flows as it invests in the long-term assets necessary for expansion. The positive investing cash flows shown

---

[1] Dividends declared but not paid also reduce retained earnings but are usually classified as a noncash activity.

by Maggones indicate that it is a net seller of its capital assets—not a purchaser. In addition, one would like to see any expansion supported by positive operating cash flows. Instead of being an expanding company, the pattern of cash flows exhibited by Maggones suggests a company that is experiencing problems in generating operating cash flows. Furthermore, it appears the company may be selling its capital assets and obtaining capital through borrowing or shareholder contributions in order to cover the operating cash flow shortfall.

Careful analysis of the patterns and interrelationships of a company's cash flows can provide users with insights into a company's operations.

Statement of Cash Flows for Superior Sportswear

Superior Sportswear Statement of Cash Flows For the Year Ended December 31, 2018		
Cash flows from operating activities		
Net income		$ 39,000
Adjustments to reconcile net income to net cash flow from operating activities:		
Depreciation expense	$ 40,000	
Loss on disposal of equipment	6,000	
Gain on sale of long-term investments	(15,000)	
Increase in accounts receivable	(7,000)	
Decrease in prepaid insurance	1,000	
Increase in inventory	(12,000)	
Decrease in accounts payable	(4,000)	
Increase in wages payable	1,500	
Increase in interest payable	500	
Decrease in income tax payable	(3,000)	
Net cash provided by operating activities		47,000
Cash flows from investing activities		
Cash received from sale of equipment	2,000	
Purchase of equipment	(53,000)	
Cash received from sale of investments	31,000	
Purchase of investments	(28,000)	
Net cash used for investing activities		(48,000)
Cash flows from financing activities		
Cash paid to repay principal on notes payable	(35,000)	
Cash received from issuing notes payable	29,000	
Cash received from issuance of common shares	14,000	
Cash paid for dividends	(5,000)	
Net cash provided by financing activities		3,000
Net increase in cash		2,000
Cash and cash equivalents, 1/1/2018		13,000
Cash and cash equivalents, 12/31/2018		$ 15,000

OBJECTIVE 7

Analyze information contained in the statement of cash flows.

ANALYZING THE STATEMENT OF CASH FLOWS

Effective analysis of the statement of cash flows requires the following:

- an examination of the statement of cash flows itself,
- a comparison of the information on the current statement of cash flows with earlier statements, and
- a comparison of the information in the current statement of cash flows with information from other companies' statements of cash flow.

Examining the Statement of Cash Flows

One of the most important insights that can be gained by inspecting the current period's statement of cash flows is an estimate of how long it will take to recover the cash outflow associated with long-term uses of cash (such as purchase of property, plant, and equipment or payment of dividends). Investments in property, plant, and equipment are likely to require several profitable years before the investment is completely recovered through the sale of goods or services. Therefore, prudent managers will seek long-term sources of cash, such as long-term debt or equity, which will not need to be repaid before the original investment has been recovered through profitable operations.

The sources most frequently used to provide long-term cash inflows are operations, the sale of long-term debt, and the sale of shares. Of these three, operations is generally considered the least risky, or the most controllable. The sale of debt or equity requires that investors or creditors make sizable commitments to the company. Although cash inflows from operations also require that an outsider (the customer) make a commitment, the size and timing of a customer's cash commitments are more flexible. Thus, it is more likely that the company can produce cash inflows from customers on a regular basis. For this reason, most companies attempt to secure a sizable portion of their total cash inflows from operations. Generally, analysts view cash flows from operations as the most important section of the statement of cash flows because, in the long run, this will be the company's source of cash used to provide a return to investors and creditors.

Because the cost of selling large debt or equity issues in the public capital markets is high, most large companies sell debt or equity in relatively large amounts. They also make smaller long-term or short-term borrowings directly from banks, insurance companies, and other financial intermediaries. Many businesses arrange a "pre-approved" line of credit that can be used, up to some limit, for borrowing whenever cash is needed. Sales of small amounts of shares to employees through stock option and stock bonus plans also help increase cash inflows.

Comparing Statements of Cash Flows from Several Periods and Assessing Financial Statement Interrelationships

An analysis of the statement of cash flows also requires a comparison of the company's current statement of cash flows with earlier statements of cash flow. Typically, several consecutive years should be analyzed in order to determine trends in cash inflows and cash outflows. The following questions may be helpful in beginning the analysis of a series of cash flow statements:

- What proportions of cash have come from operating, financing, and investing activities?
- Are there discernible trends in these proportions?
- What proportions of long-term uses of cash are financed by long-term sources of cash?
- How has the company financed any permanent increases in current assets?
- Has the company begun any investment programs that are likely to require significant cash outflows in the future?
- What are the probable sources for the cash inflows the company will need in the near future?
- Are these sources likely to be both able and willing to provide the cash that is needed?
- If the company is unable to secure all the cash it needs, could cash outflows be restricted to the available supply of cash without seriously affecting operations?
- Do cash flows from operating activities and investing activities in the statement of cash flow over a number of years indicate that a potential fraud may be occurring in the statement of financial position and statement of earnings?

The analysis of cash flow from operations, investing, and financing activities can disclose potential fraud in financial reporting practices. For example, if investors in

Lehman Brothers had fully analyzed cash flows from operations in light of corresponding changes to the company's statements of earnings and statements of financial position over the three years before bankruptcy, the aggressive accounting practices in use by management may have been discovered by investors several years before the bankruptcy of that company.

Financial statement users will rely on summary cash flow measures to help them make these assessments. Two such measures, in addition to the quality of earnings ratio mentioned earlier in this chapter, are a company's free cash flow and its cash flow adequacy ratio.

Free Cash Flow A company's **free cash flow** represents the cash flow that a company is able to generate after considering the maintenance or expansion of its assets (capital expenditures) and the payment of dividends. Free cash flow is computed as:

$$\text{Free cash flow} = \text{Net cash flow from operating activities} - \text{Capital expenditures} - \text{Cash dividends}$$

Having positive free cash flow allows a company to pursue profit-generating opportunities as they arise. However, negative free cash flow is not necessarily a bad thing. For example, a company making large investments in productive assets (large capital expenditures) may show negative free cash flow. If these investments provide a high rate of return, this strategy will be good for the company in the long run.

Cash Flow Adequacy Ratio A second useful measure is the **cash flow adequacy ratio**. The cash flow adequacy ratio provides a measure of the company's ability to meet its maturing debt obligations and is calculated as:

$$\text{Cash flow adequacy} = \frac{\text{Free cash flow}}{\text{Average amount of debt maturing over the next five years}}$$

The cash flow adequacy ratio is also an indicator of whether the company has the capacity to borrow additional debt.

Cornerstone 11.6 illustrates the computation and analysis of these ratios for John Deere and Caterpillar.

CORNERSTONE 11.6   Analyzing Free Cash Flow and Cash Flow Adequacy

CORNERSTONE VIDEO

Information:

The following information was obtained from the 2014 annual reports of John Deere and Caterpillar.

(amounts in millions)	John Deere (U.S.$)	Caterpillar (U.S.$)
Operating cash flows	$3,526	$8,057
Capital expenditures	2,659	3,379
Dividends	786	1,620
Average maturities of long-term debt on equipment over the next five years	4,876.1	5,556.8

(Continued)

Required:

Compute John Deere's and Caterpillar's free cash flow and cash flow adequacy ratios.

Why:

Free cash flow and cash flow adequacy are calculated as measures of the future financial flexibility that a company possesses to expand capacity, meet its obligations, obtain financing, and pay dividends.

Solution:

Free cash flow = Net cash from operating activities − Capital expenditures − Cash dividends

John Deere	Caterpillar
$3,526 $2,659 $786 = **$81**	$8,057 − $3,379 − $1,620 = **$3,058**

$$\text{Cash flow adequacy} = \frac{\text{Free cash flow}}{\text{Average amount of debt maturing over the next five years}}$$

John Deere	Caterpillar
$\dfrac{\$81}{\$4,876.1} = \textbf{1.7\%}$	$\dfrac{\$3,058}{\$5,556.8} = \textbf{55.0\%}$

As you can see in Cornerstone 11.6 , with approximately 3.1 billion in free cash flow, Caterpillar certainly has the financial flexibility to take advantage of profit-generating opportunities and internally finance its expansion needs. Furthermore, Caterpillar is generating almost enough free cash flow in two years to repay its average debt obligations. John Deere, with approximately $81 million of free cash flow, also appears to have a significant amount of free cash flow; however, its cash flow adequacy ratio of 1.7% implies that it may experience difficulty in seizing new business opportunities as they arise unless additional capital is raised. Overall, John Deere will also have a relatively more difficult time in meeting its debt obligations than Caterpillar.

Comparing the Statement of Cash Flows to Similar Companies

Finally, the analysis of the statement of cash flows requires comparing information from similar companies. Such comparisons provide good reference points because similar companies generally secure cash from similar sources and are likely to spend cash for similar activities. Comparative analysis can reveal significant deviations in

- the amounts of cash inflows,
- the source of those inflows, and
- the types of activities to which cash is applied.

When significant differences are found among similar companies, an explanation should be sought in the other financial statements, in the notes accompanying the statements, or from management. Variances in cash flows from similar companies may be an indicator of fraudulent financial reporting.

SIGNIFICANT DIFFERENCES BETWEEN IFRS AND ASPE

The following significant differences exist between IFRS and ASPE with reference to accounting standards and accounting terminology:

1. Interest and dividends received are classified as operating activities under ASPE but may be classified as either operating or investing activities under IFRS. Once a choice is made under IFRS, that choice must be applied consistently.

2. ASPE requires interest paid to be classified as an operating activity and dividends paid as a financing activity. IFRS allows interest and dividends paid to be treated as operating or financing activities. Once a choice is made under IFRS, that choice must be applied consistently.

APPENDIX 11A: THE DIRECT METHOD

In the direct method of computing net cash flow from operating activities, inflows and outflows of cash are listed for *each type of operating activity* that a company performs. This involves adjusting *each item* on the statement of earnings by the changes in the related current asset or liability accounts. Typical operating cash flows and the adjustments necessary to compute them are given below. All numbers are taken from the financial statements for Superior Sportswear given in Exhibit 11.8.

Cash Collected from Customers

Sales revenue includes both cash sales and credit sales. When all sales are for cash, the cash collected from customers equals sales. However, when credit sales are made, the amount of cash that was collected during a period must be determined by analyzing the sales and accounts receivable accounts. The accounts receivable account increases when credit sales are recorded and decreases when cash is collected from customers.

Accounts Receivable			
Balance, 1/1/2018	46,000		
Credit sales	xxx	Cash collections	xxx
Balance, 12/31/2018	53,000		

The increase of accounts receivable implies that credit sales were $7,000 greater than the cash collected from customers. This is consistent with increases in noncash assets reflecting decreases in cash. Because cash collections were less than reported sales ($472,000), Superior Sportswear would subtract the increase in accounts receivable from sales when computing cash collected from customers. A general formula to compute cash collections from customers is:

$$\text{Cash collected from customers} = \text{Sales} \begin{cases} + \text{ Decrease in accounts receivable} \\ - \text{ Increase in accounts receivable} \end{cases}$$

Other Cash Collections

If other revenues exist (such as interest or rent), similar adjustments are made to determine the cash collections. For example, interest revenue is adjusted for any change in interest receivable as follows:

$$\text{Cash collected for interest} = \text{Interest revenue} \begin{cases} + \text{ Decrease in interest receivable} \\ - \text{ Increase in interest receivable} \end{cases}$$

Cash Paid to Suppliers

A company pays its suppliers for inventory, which it later sells to customers, as represented by cost of goods sold. These purchases of inventory from suppliers may be either cash purchases or credit purchases, reflected as accounts payable. To compute cash paid to suppliers, it is necessary to analyze two accounts—inventory and accounts payable—and make two adjustments.

Inventory				Accounts Payable		
Balance, 1/1/2018	51,000				Balance, 1/1/2018	17,000
Purchases	xxx	Cost of goods sold	xxx	Cash payments xxx	Credit purchases	xxx
Balance, 12/31/2018	63,000				Balance, 12/31/2018	13,000

The increase in inventory implies that purchases of inventory exceeded the cost of goods sold by $12,000. (A decrease in inventory would imply that purchases of inventory were less than cost of goods sold.) Therefore, cost of goods sold needs to be increased to reflect the "extra" cash purchases that were not included as an expense. A general formula to capture this relationship is:

$$\text{Cost of purchases} = \text{Cost of goods sold} \begin{cases} + \text{ Increases in inventory} \\ - \text{ Decreases in inventory} \end{cases}$$

Next, the cost of purchases must be adjusted by the change in accounts payable to compute the cash paid to suppliers. The decrease in accounts payable implies that the cash payments to suppliers exceeded the purchases of inventory by $4,000. (An increase in accounts payable would imply that cash payments were less than the cost of purchases.) Therefore, Superior Sportswear would add the increase in accounts payable to the cost of purchases to compute the cash paid to suppliers. A general formula that captures this relationship is:

$$\text{Cash paid to suppliers} = \text{Cost of purchases} \begin{cases} + \text{ Decreases in accounts payable} \\ - \text{ Increases in accounts payable} \end{cases}$$

Combining this adjustment with the first adjustment, the cash paid to suppliers is computed as follows:

$$\begin{matrix} \text{Cash paid to} \\ \text{suppliers} \end{matrix} = \text{Cost of goods sold} \begin{cases} + \text{ Increases in inventory} \\ - \text{ Decreases in inventory} \\ + \text{ Decrease in accounts payable} \\ - \text{ Increase in accounts payable} \end{cases}$$

Cash Paid for Operating Expenses

Recall that operating expenses are the expenses the business incurs in selling goods or providing services and managing the company. These are usually divided into selling and administrative expenses and include items such as advertising expense, salaries and wages, insurance expense, utilities expense and property tax expense. These expenses are recognized when goods and services are used, not when cash is paid. Therefore, the expense amounts reported on the statement of earnings will probably not equal the amount of cash actually paid during the period. Some expenses are paid before they are actually recognized (such as prepaid insurance); other expenses are paid for after they are recognized, where a payable account exists at the time of the cash payment (such as salaries payable).

To determine the amount of cash payments for operating expenses, it is necessary to analyze the changes in the statement of financial position accounts that are related to operating expenses—prepaid expenses and accrued liabilities. A prepaid expense increases when cash prepayments are made and decreases when expenses are incurred. An accrued liability increases when expenses are accrued (incurred but not yet paid) and decreases when cash payments are made. Superior Sportswear has two balances that need to be analyzed—prepaid insurance and wages payable.

Prepaid Insurance					Wages Payable	
Balance, 1/1/2018	2,000				Balance, 1/1/2018	2,000
Cash prepayments	XXX	Expense incurred XXX	Cash payments XXX		Wages expense	XXX
Balance, 12/31/2018	1,000				Balance, 12/31/2018	3,500

The decrease in prepaid insurance indicates that expenses recorded on the statement of earnings were $1,000 higher than the cash payments. Because more expenses were incurred than were paid in cash, the company actually has more cash available at the end of the period than at the beginning of the period. (An increase in prepaid expenses means that cash payments were higher than the expenses recognized on the statement of earnings and a company would have less cash available at the end of the period.) Therefore, Superior Sportswear should add the increase in prepaid insurance ($1,000) to insurance expense ($15,000) to compute the cash paid for insurance.

The increase in wages payable indicates that wages expense recorded on the statement of earnings was greater than the cash paid for wages by $1,500. Because less cash was paid than expensed, the company actually has more cash available. (A decrease in wages payable would imply that cash payments were greater than the expense recorded on the statement of earnings.) Therefore, Superior Sportswear should subtract the increase in wages payable ($1,500) from wages expense to compute cash paid for wages.

Combining these two adjustments, a general formula to compute cash paid for operating expenses is:

$$\text{Cash paid for operating expenses} = \text{Operating expenses} \begin{cases} + \text{ Increases in prepaid expenses} \\ - \text{ Decreases in prepaid expenses} \\ + \text{ Decrease in accrued liabilities} \\ - \text{ Increase in accrued liabilities} \end{cases}$$

Cash Paid for Interest and Income Taxes

Computing cash paid for interest and income taxes is similar to that for operating expenses. Interest payable increases when interest expense is recorded and decreases when interest is paid.

Interest Payable			
		Balance, 1/1/2018	1,000
Cash payments	XXX	Interest expense	XXX
		Balance, 12/31/2018	1,500

The increase in interest payable implies that interest expense recorded on the statement of earnings was $500 greater than the cash paid for interest. (A decrease in interest expense indicates that the cash paid for interest is greater than the interest expense recorded on the statement of earnings.) Therefore, Superior Sportswear would subtract the $500 increase in interest payable from interest expense ($5,000) to compute the cash paid for interest. A general formula to capture this relationship is:

$$\text{Cash paid for interest} = \text{Interest expense} \begin{cases} + \text{ Decreases in interest payable} \\ - \text{ Increases in interest payable} \end{cases}$$

The income tax payable account increases when income tax expense is incurred and decreases when income taxes are paid.

Income Tax Payable			
		Balance, 1/1/2018	6,000
Cash payments	xxx	Income tax expense	xxx
		Balance, 12/31/2018	3,000

The decrease in income tax payable implies that the cash payments for income tax were $3,000 greater than the income tax expense reported on the statement of earnings. (An increase in income tax payable implies that income tax expense reported on the statement of earnings is greater than the cash paid for income tax.) Therefore, Superior Sportswear would add the increase in income taxes payable ($3,000) to income tax expense ($8,000) to compute cash paid for income taxes. A general formula to capture this relationship is:

$$\text{Cash paid for income taxes} = \text{Income tax expense} \begin{cases} + \text{ Decrease in income tax payable} \\ - \text{ Increase in income tax payable} \end{cases}$$

Other Items

Noncash Revenues and Expenses The statement of earnings often includes various noncash items such as depreciation expense, amortization expense, and bad debt expense. Noncash items do not affect cash flow. Therefore, under the direct method, **noncash items are not reported on the statement of cash flows**. Sometimes, depreciation expense (or some other noncash expense) is included as part of operating expenses. In this case, depreciation expense must be subtracted from operating expenses to compute the cash paid for operating expenses.

Accounting Gains and Losses The sale of a long-term asset or the extinguishment of a long-term liability often produces either a gain or loss that is reported on the statement of earnings. However, the gain or loss does not affect cash flow and should not be included as an operating activity. Furthermore, the gain or loss does not reveal the total amount of cash received or paid. Instead, it only gives the amount received or paid in excess of the book value of the asset or liability. Therefore, **gains and losses are not reported on the statement of cash flows under the direct method.**

Applying the Direct Method

Cornerstone 11.7 illustrates and summarizes the computation of the net cash flow from operating activities using the direct method. Because each item on the statement of earnings is adjusted under the direct method, it is common to begin the analysis with the first item on the statement of earnings (sales) and to proceed down the statement of earnings in the order that the accounts are listed.

It is important to note that both the indirect and direct methods arrive at the identical amount for the net cash provided (used) by operating activities. Therefore, the net cash provided by operating activities of $47,000 computed on the previous page is the same as the net cash flow from operating activities computed under the indirect method shown in Cornerstone 11.3. The two methods differ only in how this amount is computed and the presentation of the details on the statement of cash flows. In addition, if the direct method is used, companies must also provide a supplementary schedule that shows the reconciliation of net income with net cash flow from operating activities. This supplementary schedule is, in effect, the presentation shown under the indirect method in Cornerstone 11.3.

CORNERSTONE 11.7

Calculating Net Cash Flows from Operating Activities: Direct Method

Information:
Refer to the financial statements for Superior Sportswear in Exhibit 11.8.

Required:
Compute the net cash flow from operating activities using the direct method.

Why:
To compute net cash flow from operating activities under the direct method, each item on the statement of earnings must be adjusted for changes in the related asset and liability accounts. The calculation of net cash flow from operating activities under the direct method is preferred under IFRS.

Solution:

Cash flows from operating activities		
Cash collected from customers[a]		$ 465,000
Cash paid:		
To suppliers of merchandise[b]	$(248,000)	
For wages[c]	(140,500)	
For insurance[d]	(14,000)	
For interest[e]	(4,500)	
For income taxes[f]	(11,000)	(418,000)
Net cash provided by operating activities		$ 47,000

[a] $472,000 sales − $7,000 change in accounts receivable = $465,000
[b] $232,000 cost of goods sold + $12,000 change in inventory + $4,000 change in accounts payable = $248,000
[c] $142,000 wages expense − $1,500 change in wages payable = $140,500
[d] $15,000 insurance expense − $1,000 change in prepaid insurance = $14,000
[e] $5,000 interest expense − $500 change in interest payable = $4,500
[f] $8,000 income tax expense + $3,000 change in income taxes payable = $11,000

OBJECTIVE 9

Use a spreadsheet to prepare the statement of cash flows.

APPENDIX 11B: USING A SPREADSHEET TO PREPARE THE STATEMENT OF CASH FLOWS

The use of a spreadsheet provides a means of systematically analyzing changes in the statement of financial position amounts, along with the information from the statement of earnings and any additional information, to produce a statement of cash flows. This approach produces spreadsheet entries (made only on the spreadsheet and not in the general ledger) that simultaneously reconstruct and explain the changes in the statement of financial position account balances and identify the cash inflows and outflows. The spreadsheet is based on the same underlying principles as discussed in the chapter. Its primary advantage is that it provides a systematic approach to analyze the data, which is helpful in complex situations.

To construct the spreadsheet, follow these steps:

Step 1: Construct five columns. The first column will contain the statement of financial position account titles. Immediately beneath the statement of financial position accounts, set up the three sections of the statement of cash flows. The second column will contain the beginning balances of the statement of financial position accounts (enter the amounts at this time). The third and fourth columns will contain the debit and credit adjustments, respectively. The fifth column will contain the ending balances of the statement of financial position accounts (enter the amounts at this time).

Step 2: Analyze each change in the statement of financial position accounts in terms of debits and credits. Enter the effects in the adjustments column. Note that each entry will adjust both the statement of financial position account being considered and either a statement of cash flows section of the spreadsheet or another statement of financial position account (other than cash). Note that all inflows of cash are recorded as debits and all outflows of cash are recorded as credits.

Step 3: Prepare the statement of cash flows from the information contained in the statement of cash flows section of the spreadsheet.

Exhibit 11.12 illustrates how to use a spreadsheet to prepare the statement of cash flows for Superior Sportswear. Refer to the information given earlier in the chapter regarding the logic behind the analysis of the changes in the spreadsheet accounts.

Net Income

a. Net income is listed as a cash inflow in the operating activities section. Because net income flows into retained earnings during the closing process, a credit to retained earnings reflects the effect of the closing entry.

Adjusting for Noncash Items

b. For Superior Sportswear, the only noncash item was depreciation expense, which is added back to net income in the operating activities section and is reflected as a credit to accumulated depreciation.

Adjusting for Gains and/or Losses Due to Investing and Financing Activities

c. The actual proceeds from the sale of equipment are shown as a cash inflow in the investing activities section. The loss on the disposal of equipment is added back to net income in the operating activities section. In addition, both equipment and accumulated depreciation should be adjusted to reflect the sale.

d. The cash paid to purchase equipment is shown as a cash outflow in the investing activities section. At this point, note that the beginning and ending balances of the equipment and accumulated depreciation accounts are reconciled.

e. The actual proceeds from the sale of the investment are shown as a cash inflow in the investing activities section. The gain on the sale of the investment is subtracted from net income in the operating activities section. In addition, the investment account should be adjusted to reflect the sale.

f. The cash paid to purchase the investment is shown as a cash outflow in the investing activities section. At this point, note that the beginning and ending balances of the investment account are reconciled.

(EXHIBIT 11.12)

Spreadsheet to Prepare Statement of Cash Flows

	A	B	C	D	E	F	G
1		Superior Sportswear					
2		Spreadsheet to Prepare the Statement of Cash Flows					
3		For the Year Ended December 31, 2018					
4							
5		Beginning		Adjustments			Ending
6		Balance		Debit	Credit		Balance
7	**Statement of Financial Position Accounts**						
8	Cash	13,000	(r)	2,000			15,000
9	Accounts receivable	46,000	(g)	7,000			53,000
10	Prepaid insurance	2,000			1,000	(h)	1,000
11	Inventory	51,000	(i)	12,000			63,000
12	Land	325,000					325,000
13	Equipment	210,000	(d)	53,000	20,000	(c)	243,000
14	Accumulated depreciation	150,000	(c)	12,000	40,000	(b)	178,000
15	Investments	41,000	(f)	28,000	16,000	(e)	53,000
16							
17	Accounts payable	17,000	(j)	4,000			13,000
18	Wages payable	2,000			1,500	(k)	3,500
19	Interest payable	1,000			500	(l)	1,500
20	Income tax payable	6,000	(m)	3,000			3,000
21	Notes payable	115,000	(n)	35,000	29,000	(o)	109,000
22	Common shares	151,000			14,000	(p)	165,000
23	Retained earnings	246,000	(q)	5,000	39,000	(a)	280,000
24							
25	**Statement of Cash Flows**						
26	Cash flow from operating activities						
27	Net income		(a)	39,000			
28	Adjustments to reconcile net						
29	income to net cash flow from						
30	operating activities						
31	Depreciation expense		(b)	40,000			
32	Loss on disposal of equipment		(c)	6,000			
33	Gain on sale of investments				15,000	(e)	
34	Increase in accounts receivable				7,000	(g)	
35	Decrease in prepaid insurance		(h)	1,000			
36	Increase in inventory				12,000	(i)	
37	Decrease in accounts payable				4,000	(j)	
38	Increase in wages payable		(k)	1,500			
39	Increase in interest payable		(l)	500			
40	Decrease in income tax payable				3,000	(m)	
41							
42	Cash flows from investing activities						
43	Sale of equipment		(c)	2,000			
44	Purchase of equipment				53,000	(d)	
45	Sale of investments		(e)	31,000			
46	Purchase of investment				28,000	(f)	
47							
48	Cash flows from financing activities						
49	Repaid note payable				35,000	(n)	
50	Issued note payable		(o)	29,000			
51	Issued common shares		(p)	14,000			
52	Paid dividend				5,000	(q)	
53							
54	Net change in cash				2,000	(r)	
55							
56				325,000	325,000		

Adjusting for Changes in Current Assets and Current Liabilities

g. The increase in accounts receivable is subtracted from net income and reconciles the change in the accounts receivable account.

h. The decrease in prepaid insurance is added to net income and reconciles the change in the prepaid insurance account.

i. The increase in inventory is subtracted from net income and reconciles the change in the inventory account.

j. The decrease in accounts payable is subtracted from net income and reconciles the change in the accounts payable account.

k. The increase in wages payable is added to net income and reconciles the change in the wages payable account.

l. The increase in interest payable is added to net income and reconciles the change in the interest payable account.

m. The decrease in income tax payable is subtracted from net income and reconciles the change in the income tax payable account.

Adjusting for Cash Inflows and Outflows Associated with Financing Activities

n. The repayment of the notes payable is a cash outflow from a financing activity and adjusts the notes payable account.

o. The issuance of a notes payable is a cash inflow from a financing activity and reconciles the change in the notes payable account.

p. The issuance of common shares is a cash inflow from a financing activity and reconciles the change in the common share account.

q. The payment of dividends is a cash outflow from a financing activity and, together with the first entry, item (a), reconciles the change in retained earnings. The final entry reconciles the cash balance.

r. The summation of the three sections of the statement of cash flows equals the change in cash for the period. This amount can be checked by summing the net cash flows from operating, investing, and financing activities computed in the previous steps.

Completing the Statement of Cash Flows

The statement of cash flows can now be prepared from the information developed in the statement of cash flows portion of the spreadsheet. The statement of cash flows for Superior Sportswear is shown in Exhibit 11.11.

SUMMARY OF LEARNING OBJECTIVES

LO1.   Explain the purpose of a statement of cash flows.

- The statement of cash flows is one of the primary financial statements whose purpose is to provide information about a company's cash receipts (inflows of cash) and cash payments (outflows of cash) during an accounting period.

- The statement of cash flows is complementary to the information contained in the statement of earnings and the statement of financial position and is critical to understanding and analyzing a company's operations.

LO2.   **Classify cash inflows and outflows as operating, investing, and financing activities.**

- The statement of cash flows is divided into three main sections based on the fundamental business activities that a company engages in during a period:
  - cash flows from operating activities, which encompass the cash inflows and outflows that relate to the determination of net income;
  - cash flows from investing activities, which are related to acquisitions and disposals of long-term assets and investments; and
  - cash flows from financing activities, which are related to the external financing of the company (debt or shareholders' equity).
- Some business activities take place without affecting cash and are referred to as noncash investing and financing activities.

LO3.   **Explain the relationship between changes in cash and the changes in the statement of financial position accounts.**

- Because of timing issues between the recognition of revenues and expenses and the inflows and outflows of cash, information about a company's cash flows can be obtained by examining the changes in the statement of financial position account balances over a period.
- Increases in cash result from increases in liabilities, increases in shareholders' equity, and decreases in noncash assets.
- Decreases in cash result from decreases in liabilities, decreases in shareholders' equity, and increases in noncash assets.

LO4.   **Report and analyze the cash flows from operating activities using the indirect method.**

- The indirect method for reporting cash flows from operating activities begins with net income and adjusts it for noncash items to produce net cash flow from operating activities.
- The adjustments to net income are necessary to eliminate statement of earnings items that do not affect cash and to adjust accrual-basis revenues and expenses to cash receipts and cash payments.
- Four types of adjustments are necessary:
  - add to net income any noncash expenses and subtract from net income any noncash revenues;
  - add to net income any losses and subtract from net income any gains;
  - add to net income any decreases in current assets or increases in current liabilities that are related to operating activities; and
  - subtract from net income any increases in current assets and decreases in current liabilities that are related to operating activities.

LO5.   **Report and analyze cash flows from investing activities.**

- The cash flows from the investing activities section reports the net cash flow related to buying and selling property, plant, and equipment; purchasing and selling investments in other companies; and lending and collecting the principal amount of loans from borrowers.
- The preparation of the investing activities section of a statement of cash flows involves a careful analysis of the information in the financial statements as well as a recreation of the journal entries that describe the activities that took place during a period.

LO6.   **Report and analyze cash flows from financing activities.**

- The cash flows from the financing activities section reports the net cash flow related to the borrowing and repayment of the principal amount of long-term debt, the sale of common or preferred shares, and the payment of dividends.
- The preparation of the financing activities section of a statement of cash flows involves a careful analysis of the information in the financial statements as well as a recreation of the journal entries that describe the activities that took place during a period.

LO7.   **Analyze information contained in the statement of cash flows.**

- Effective analysis of the statement of cash flows requires an examination of the statement of cash flows itself; a comparison of the information on the current statement of cash flows with earlier statements, as well as with the related statements of financial position and statement of earnings; and a comparison of the information in the current statement of cash flows with information from other companies' statements of cash flow.

- Financial statement users may also rely on summary cash flow measures such as free cash flow (the cash flow that a company is able to generate after considering the maintenance or expansion of its assets) and the cash flow adequacy ratio (a measure of a company's ability to meet its debt obligations).
- Financial statement fraud may be uncovered by a thorough analysis of cash flows over several years.

LO8. *(Appendix 11A)* **Prepare the cash flows from operating activities using the direct method.**

- The direct method for reporting cash flows from operating activities lists cash inflows and cash outflows for each type of operating activity that a company performs.
- Cash flows from operating activities are generally computed by adjusting each item on the statement of earnings by the changes in the related current asset or current liability accounts.
- Cash flow categories reported under the direct method include cash collected from customers, cash paid to suppliers, cash paid to employees, cash paid for interest, and cash paid for taxes.

LO9. *(Appendix 11B)* **Use a spreadsheet to prepare the statement of cash flows.**

- A spreadsheet provides a means of systematically analyzing changes in the statement of financial position amounts, along with the information from the statement of earnings and any additional information, to produce a statement of cash flows.

CORNERSTONES

CORNERSTONE 11.1	Classifying business activities, page 631
CORNERSTONE 11.2	Classifying changes in statement of financial position accounts, page 635
CORNERSTONE 11.3	Calculating net cash flow from operating activities: indirect method, page 641
CORNERSTONE 11.4	Reporting net cash flow from investing activities, page 647
CORNERSTONE 11.5	Reporting net cash flow from financing activities, page 649
CORNERSTONE 11.6	Analyzing free cash flow and cash flow adequacy, page 652
CORNERSTONE 11.7	Calculating net cash flows from operating activities: direct method, page 658

KEY TERMS

Cash equivalents (p. 628)
Cash flow adequacy ratio (p. 652)
Cash flows from financing activities (p. 630)
Cash flows from investing activities (p. 629)
Cash flows from operating activities (p. 628)
Direct method (p. 637)

Free cash flow (p. 652)
Indirect method (p. 639)
Noncash investing and financing activities (p. 630)
Quality of earnings (p. 629)
Statement of cash flows (p. 626)

REVIEW PROBLEM
The Statement of Cash Flows

Concept:

The statement of cash flows measures a company's inflows (sources) and outflows (uses) of cash during a period of time. These cash inflows and cash outflows are classified as operating, investing, and financing activities.

Information:

The statement of earnings and comparative statement of financial position for Solar Systems Company are shown below.

Solar Systems Company Statements of Financial Position December 31, 2017 and 2016	2017	2016
ASSETS		
Current assets:		
Cash	$ 56,000	$ 47,000
Accounts receivable	123,000	107,000
Inventory	52,000	46,000
Prepaid expenses	10,000	9,000
Total current assets	241,000	209,000
Property, plant, and equipment:		
Equipment	270,000	262,000
Accumulated depreciation	(118,000)	(109,000)
Total assets	$ 393,000	$ 362,000
LIABILITIES AND EQUITY		
Current liabilities:		
Accounts payable	$ 18,000	$ 11,000
Salaries payable	5,000	9,000
Income tax payable	7,000	5,000
Total current liabilities	30,000	25,000
Long-term liabilities:		
Notes payable	120,000	130,000
Total liabilities	150,000	155,000
Equity:		
Common shares	213,000	200,000
Retained earnings	30,000	7,000
Total equity	243,000	207,000
Total liabilities and equity	$393,000	$362,000

Solar Systems Company Income Statement For the Year Ended December 31, 2017	
Sales revenue	$1,339,000
Less: Cost of goods sold	(908,000)
Gross margin	431,000
Less operating expenses:	
Salaries expense	(230,000)
Depreciation	(24,000)
Other operating expenses	(116,000)
Income from operations	61,000
Other income and expenses:	
Gain on disposal of equipment	3,000
Interest expense	(14,000)
Income before tax	50,000
Less: Income tax expense	(12,000)
Net income	$ 38,000

Additional Information:

1. Equipment with a cost of $24,000 and accumulated depreciation of $15,000 was sold for $12,000 cash. Equipment was purchased for $32,000 cash.
2. Notes payable in the amount of $10,000 were repaid.
3. Common shares were issued for $13,000 cash during 2017.
4. Cash dividends of $15,000 were paid during 2017.

Required:

Prepare a statement of cash flows for Solar Systems Company using the indirect method.

Solution:

1.

Solar Systems Company Statement of Cash Flows For the Year Ended December 31, 2017		
Cash flows from operating activities		
Net income		$ 38,000
Adjustments to reconcile net income to net cash flow from operating activities:		
Depreciation expense	$ 24,000	
Gain on disposal of equipment	(3,000)	
Increase in accounts receivable	(16,000)	
Increase in prepaid expenses	(1,000)	
Increase in inventory	(6,000)	
Increase in accounts payable	7,000	
Decrease in salaries payable	(4,000)	
Increase in income tax payable	2,000	3,000
Net cash provided by operating activities		41,000
Cash flows from investing activities		
Cash received from sale of equipment	12,000	
Purchase of equipment	(32,000)	
Net cash used by investing activities		(20,000)
Cash flows from financing activities		
Cash paid to retire notes payable	$(10,000)	
Cash received from issuance of common shares	13,000	
Cash paid for dividends	(15,000)	
Net cash used by financing activities		(12,000)
Net increase in cash		9,000
Cash and cash equivalents, 1/1/2017		47,000
Cash and cash equivalents, 12/31/2017		$ 56,000

DISCUSSION QUESTIONS

1. What is a statement of cash flows?

2. How do investors, creditors, and others typically use the information in the statement of cash flows?

3. How is a statement of cash flows different from a statement of earnings?

4. What are cash equivalents? How are cash equivalents reported on the statement of cash flows?

5. What are the three categories into which inflows and outflows of cash are divided? Describe what is included in each of these three categories.

6. Why are companies required to report noncash investing and financing activities? How are these activities reported?

7. Why are direct exchanges of long-term debt for items of property, plant, and equipment included in supplementary information for the statement of cash flows even though the exchanges do not affect cash?

8. Describe the relationship between changes in cash and changes in noncash assets, liabilities, and shareholders' equity.

9. What are two ways to report a company's net cash flow from operating activities? Briefly describe each method.

10. Why are depreciation, depletion, and amortization added to net income when the indirect method is used to report net cash flows from operating activities?

11. Where do the components of the changes in retained earnings appear on the statement of cash flows? Assume the indirect method is used to prepare the statement of cash flows.

12. How is the sale of equipment at a loss reported on the statement of cash flows? Assume the indirect method is used to prepare the statement of cash flows.

13. What does an increase in inventory imply? How would this increase in inventory be reported under the indirect method?

14. What does an increase in accounts payable imply? How would this increase in accounts payable be reported under the indirect method?

15. Does the fact that the cash flow from operating activities is normally positive imply that cash and cash equivalents usually increase each year?

16. What are the most common sources of cash inflows from financing and investing activities?

17. What are the most common cash outflows related to investing and financing activities?

18. What statement of financial position account changes might you expect to find for a company that must rely on sources other than operations to fund its cash outflows?

19. From what source(s) should most companies secure the majority of cash inflows? Why?

20. Why should companies attempt to secure cash for investment in property, plant, and equipment from long-term or permanent sources?

21. *(Appendix 11A)* When using the direct method, which items usually constitute the largest components of cash inflows from operating activities?

22. *(Appendix 11A)* Describe how to compute each of the cash inflows and cash outflows from operating activities under the direct method.

23. *(Appendix 11A)* Why is depreciation expense not generally reported on the statement of cash flows when using the direct method?

24. *(Appendix 11B)* Why do companies often use a spreadsheet to prepare the statement of cash flows?

MULTIPLE-CHOICE EXERCISES

11-1 Which of the following is not a use of the statement of cash flows?
   a. Aids in the prediction of future cash flow
   b. Provides a measure of the future obligations of the company
   c. Helps estimate the amount of funds that will be needed from creditors or shareholders
   d. Provides insights into the quality and reliability of reported income

11-2 Which of the following would be classified as a cash outflow from an operating activity?
   a. Purchase of an investment
   b. Payment of dividends
   c. Purchase of equipment

   d. Payment of goods purchased from suppliers

11-3 Which of the following is an example of a cash inflow from an operating activity?
   a. Collection of cash relating to a note
   b. Sale of property, plant, and equipment
   c. Collection of an account receivable from a receivable credit sale
   d. None of these

11-4 Which of the following is an example of a cash outflow from a financing activity?
   a. Payment of cash dividends to shareholders
   b. Payment of interest on a note payable
   c. Payment of wages to employees
   d. Issuance of common shares for cash

11-5 Which of the following is true?

a. An increase in cash may result from an increase in liabilities.

b. An increase in cash may result from a decrease in shareholders' equity.

c. An increase in cash may result from an increase in noncash assets.

d. A decrease in cash may result from an increase in liabilities.

11-6 Which of the following is true?

a. Cash flow from operating activities must be prepared using the indirect method.

b. The indirect method adjusts sales for changes in noncash items to produce net cash flow from operating activities.

c. Many companies prefer the indirect method because it is easier and less costly to prepare.

d. IFRS prefers the indirect method.

11-7 Mullinix Inc. reported the following information: net income, $40,000; decrease in accounts receivable, $10,000; decrease in accounts payable, $8,000; and depreciation expense, $6,000. What amount did Mullinix report as cash flow from operating activities on its statement of cash flows?

a. $16,000

b. $36,000

c. $48,000

d. $64,000

11-8 Which item is added to net income when computing cash flows from operating activities?

a. Gain on the disposal of property, plant, and equipment

b. Increase in wages payable

c. Increase in inventory

d. Increase in prepaid rent

11-9 Cornett Company reported the following information: cash received from the issuance of common shares, $125,400; cash received from the sale of equipment, $26,500; cash paid to purchase an investment, $12,800; cash paid to retire a note payable, $30,000; cash collected from sales to customers, $248,000. What amount should Cornett report on its statement of cash flows as net cash flows provided by investing activities?

a. $13,700

b. $39,300

c. $86,100

d. None of these

11-10 Refer to the information in Exercise 11-9. What amount should Cornett report on its statement of cash flows as net cash flows from financing activities?

a. $82,600

b. $95,400

c. $108,200

d. None of these

11-11 Chausseur Building Supply Inc. reported net cash provided by operating activities of $243,000, capital expenditures of $112,900, cash dividends of $35,800, and average maturities of long-term debt over the next five years of $122,300. What is Chausseur's free cash flow and cash flow adequacy ratio?

a. $94,300 and 0.77, respectively

b. $94,300 and 0.82, respectively

c. $130,100 and 1.06, respectively

d. $165,900 and 1.36, respectively

11-12 Smoltz Company reported the following information for the current year: cost of goods sold, $315,100; increase in inventory, $14,700; and increase in accounts payable, $8,200. What is the amount of cash paid to suppliers that Smoltz would report on its statement of cash flows under the direct method?

a. $292,200

b. $308,600

c. $321,600

d. $338,000

11-13 Roma Inc. reported the following information for the current year: operating expenses, $210,000; increase in prepaid expenses, $4,900; and decrease in accrued liabilities, $6,100. What is the amount of cash paid for operating expenses that Roma would report on its statement of cash flows under the direct method?

a. $199,000

b. $208,800

c. $211,200

d. $221,000

11-14 Refer to the information in Exercise 11-7. Calculate the quality of earnings ratio.

a. 1.1

b. 1.2

(Continued)

c. 1.3
d. 1.4

11-15 ABC Inc. reported the following information for the current year: net income $100,000; $5,000 in accounts receivable; $5,000 in inventory; $6,000 in accounts payable. Cash flow from operating activities $25,000; cash flow from investing activities $50,000. What is the quality of earnings ratio?

a. 2
b. 4
c. 3
d. 1

CORNERSTONE EXERCISES

OBJECTIVE ②
CORNERSTONE 11-1

Cornerstone Exercise 11-16   Classification of Cash Flows

Stanfield Inc. reported the following items in its statement of cash flows presented using the indirect method.

a. Decrease in inventory
b. Paid a cash dividend to shareholders
c. Purchased equipment for cash
d. Issued long-term debt
e. Depreciation expense
f. Sold a building for cash

Required:

Indicate whether each item should be classified as a cash flow from operating activities, a cash flow from investing activities, or a cash flow from financing activities.

OBJECTIVE ②
CORNERSTONE 11-1

Cornerstone Exercise 11-17   Classification of Cash Flows

Patel Company reported the following items on its statement of cash flows presented using the indirect method.

a. Issuance of common shares
b. Cash paid for interest debt
c. Sold equipment for cash
d. Receipt of cash dividend on investment
e. Repayment of principal on long-term debt
f. Loss on disposal of equipment

Required:

Indicate whether each item should be classified as a cash flow from operating activities, a cash flow from investing activities, or a cash flow from financing activities.

OBJECTIVE ②
CORNERSTONE 11-1

Cornerstone Exercise 11-18   Classification of Cash Flows

A review of the statement of financial position of Petarch Company Ltd. revealed the following changes in the account balances:

a. Increase in long-term investment
b. Increase in accounts receivable
c. Increase in common shares
d. Increase in long-term debt
e. Decrease in accounts payable
f. Decrease in supplies inventory
g. Increase in prepaid insurance

Required:

Classify each change in the statement of financial position account as a cash flow from operating activities (indirect method), a cash flow from investing activities, a cash flow from financing activities, or a noncash investing and financing activity.

Cornerstone Exercise 11-19   Analyzing the Accounts

Refer to the information in Exercise 11-18.

OBJECTIVE ③
CORNERSTONE 11-2

Required:

Indicate whether each of the changes above produces a cash inflow or a cash outflow, or is a noncash activity.

Cornerstone Exercise 11-20   Computing Net Cash Flow from Operating Activities

An analysis of the statement of financial position and statement of earnings of Sanchez Company revealed the following: net income, $12,750; depreciation expense, $32,600; decrease in accounts receivable, $21,500; increase in inventory, $18,300; increase in accounts payable, $19,800; and decrease in interest payable, $1,200.

OBJECTIVE ② ④
CORNERSTONE 11-3

Required:

1. Compute the net cash flows from operating activities using the indirect method.
2. Calculate the quality of earnings ratio.

Cornerstone Exercise 11-21   Computing Net Cash Flow from Operating Activities

Brandon Inc. reported the following items in its statement of financial position and statement of earnings: net income, $92,600; gain on disposal of equipment, $15,800; increase in accounts receivable, $17,400; decrease in accounts payable, $27,900; and increase in common shares, $50,000.

OBJECTIVE ④
CORNERSTONE 11-3

Required:

Compute the net cash flows from operating activities using the indirect method.

Cornerstone Exercise 11-22   Computing Net Cash Flow from Investing Activities

Deng Inc. reported the following information for equipment and investments:

OBJECTIVE ⑤
CORNERSTONE 11-4

	12/31/2018	12/31/2017
Equipment	$160,000	$115,000
Accumulated depreciation	(85,000)	(59,000)
Long-term investment	18,610	10,000

In addition, Deng sold equipment costing $12,500 with accumulated depreciation of $8,150 for $3,800 cash, producing a $550 loss. Deng reported net income for 2018 of $122,350.

Required:

Compute net cash flow from investing activities.

Cornerstone Exercise 11-23   Computing Net Cash Flow from Financing Activities

Hibou Company reported the following information for 2018:

OBJECTIVE ⑥
CORNERSTONE 11-5

Repaid long-term debt	$50,000
Paid interest on note payable	1,320
Issued common shares	25,000
Paid dividends	12,000

(Continued)

Required:

Compute net cash flow from financing activities.

OBJECTIVE **7**
CORNERSTONE 11-6

Cornerstone Exercise 11-24   Analyzing the Statement of Cash Flows

Rollins Inc. is considering expanding its operations into different provinces; however, this expansion will require significant cash flow as well as additional financing. Rollins reported the following information for 2018: cash provided by operating activities, $387,200; cash provided by investing activities, $108,700; average debt maturing over the next five years, $345,500; capital expenditures, $261,430; dividends, $40,000.

Required:

Compute free cash flow and the cash flow adequacy ratio. (*Note:* Round ratio to two decimal places.) Comment on Rollins's ability to expand its operations.

OBJECTIVE **8**
CORNERSTONE 11-7

Cornerstone Exercise 11-25   (Appendix 11A) Cash Receipts from Customers

Sayed Ltd. had accounts receivable of $391,400 at January 1, 2018, and $418,650 at December 31, 2018. Net income for 2018 was $550,000 and sales revenue was $925,000.

Required:

Compute the amount of cash collected from customers in 2018 using the direct method.

OBJECTIVE **8**
CORNERSTONE 11-7

Cornerstone Exercise 11-26   (Appendix 11A) Cash Payments to Suppliers

Blackmon Company reported net income of $805,000 and cost of goods sold of $1,525,000 on its 2018 statement of earnings. In addition, Blackmon reported an increase in inventory of $65,410, a decrease in prepaid insurance of $12,800, and a decrease in accounts payable of $43,190.

Required:

Compute the amount of cash payments to suppliers using the direct method.

OBJECTIVE **8**
CORNERSTONE 11-7

Cornerstone Exercise 11-27   (Appendix 11A) Cash Payments for Operating Expenses

Luna Inc. reported operating expenses of $174,500, excluding depreciation expense of $36,200 for 2018. During 2018, Luna reported a decrease in prepaid expenses of $8,500 and a decrease in accrued liabilities of $18,200.

Required:

Compute the amount of cash payments for operating expenses using the direct method.

BRIEF EXERCISES

OBJECTIVE **1**

Brief Exercise 11-28   Uses of the Statement of Cash Flows

Listed below are the three major financial statements and some of the ways in which they are used by investors, creditors, and others.

Use	Financial Statement
a. Aids in understanding the differences between net income and cash flow.	1. Statement of financial position
b. Helps to assess a company's ability to produce future cash flows.	2. Statement of earnings
c. Assists in judging a company's ability to meets its obligations.	3. Statement of cash flows
d. Helps in estimating the need for external financing.	

Required:

Match each financial statement with its use. (*Note:* Each use may be related to more than one financial statement, and financial statements may be used more than one time.)

Brief Exercise 11-29   Classification of Cash Flows

OBJECTIVE ❷

Foster Company reported the following items in its statement of cash flows presented using the indirect method.

a.   Interest paid on long-term note payable
b.   Proceeds from sale of building
c.   Increase in accounts payable
d.   Increase in retained earnings
e.   Cash dividend paid to shareholders
f.   Taxes paid to the federal government

Required:

Indicate whether each item should be classified as a cash flow from operating activities, a cash flow from investing activities, or a cash flow from financing activities.

Brief Exercise 11-30   Analyzing Statement of Financial Position Accounts

OBJECTIVE ❷ ❸

A review of the statement of financial position of Dixon Company revealed the following changes in the account balances:

a.   Increase in retained earnings
b.   Increase in equipment
c.   Increase in interest receivable
d.   Decrease in bonds payable
e.   Increase in unearned rent revenue
f.   Decrease in prepaid insurance
g.   Decrease in long-term investment
h.   Increase in accounts payable

Required:

1.   Classify each change in the statement of financial position account as a cash flow from operating activities, a cash flow from investing activities, a cash flow from financing activities, or a noncash investing and financing activity.
2.   Indicate whether each of the changes in the statement of financial position accounts produces an increase in cash, produces a decrease in cash, or is a noncash activity.

Brief Exercise 11-31   Determining Net Cash Flow from Operating Activities

OBJECTIVE ❹

Presented below are selected statement of financial position information and the statement of earnings information for Burch Company.

Selected Statement of Financial Position Information

	Dec. 31, 2018	Dec. 31, 2017
Cash	$20,000	$17,500
Accounts receivable	10,500	8,000
Inventory	18,000	21,000
Accounts payable	15,000	10,000
Income taxes payable	1,000	2,500

(Continued)

Burch Company
Statement of Earnings
For the year ended December 31, 2018

Sales	$ 250,000
Cost of goods sold	(160,000)
Depreciation expense	(15,000)
Other expenses	(35,000)
Income tax expense	(12,000)
Net income	$ 28,000

Required:

Compute the net cash flows from operating activities using the indirect method.

OBJECTIVE **5**   **Brief Exercise 11-32   Determining Net Cash Flow from Investing Activities**

Orlando Inc. reported the following information:

	12/31/2018	12/31/2017
Furniture	$46,000	$32,000
Accumulated depreciation	15,900	12,500
Investment (long-term)	38,000	50,000

In addition, Orlando sold furniture costing $8,000 with accumulated depreciation of $5,000 for $3,500. Orlando also reported a $3,000 gain on the sale of long-term investments.

Required:

Compute net cash flow from investing activities.

OBJECTIVE **6**   **Brief Exercise 11-33   Determining Net Cash Flow from Financing Activities**

Madison Company reported the following information:

	12/31/2018	12/31/2017
Notes payable	$ 95,000	$75,000
Common shares	120,000	80,000
Retained earnings	20,000	36,000

Madison reported net income of $26,000 for the year ended December 31, 2018. In addition, Madison repaid $35,000 of the notes payable during 2018.

Required:

Compute net cash flow from financing activities assume that no common shares were retired during the year and assume that no share dividends were paid during the year.

OBJECTIVE **7**   **Brief Exercise 11-34   Analyzing the Statement of Cash Flows**

Manning Company reported the following information for 2018: cash provided by operating activities, $425,000; cash used by investing activities, $200,000; average debt maturing over the next five years, $80,000; capital expenditures, $275,000; cash dividends, $60,000.

Required:

Compute free cash flow and the cash flow adequacy ratio. (*Note:* Round ratios to two decimal places.) Comment on each answer calculated.

Brief Exercise 11-35   *(Appendix 11A)* **Determining Net Cash Flow from Operating Activities—Direct Method**

OBJECTIVE 8

Presented below are selected statement of financial position information and the statement of earnings information for Burch Company.

Selected Statement of Financial Position Information

	Dec. 31, 2018	Dec. 31, 2017
Cash	$20,000	$17,500
Accounts receivable	10,500	8,000
Inventory	18,000	21,000
Accounts payable	15,000	10,000
Income taxes payable	1,000	2,500

Burch Company
Statement of Earnings
For the year ended December 31, 2018

Sales	$ 250,000
Cost of goods sold	(160,000)
Depreciation expense	(15,000)
Other expenses	(35,000)
Income tax expense	(12,000)
Net income	$ 28,000

Required:

Compute the net cash flows from operating activities using the direct method.

EXERCISES

Exercise 11-36   Classification of Cash Flows

OBJECTIVE 2

A review of the financial records for Roget Ltd. uncovered the following items:

a. Collected accounts receivable
b. Paid cash to purchase equipment
c. Received cash from the issuance of bonds
d. Paid interest on long-term debt
e. Sold equipment at book value
f. Depreciation on equipment debt
g. Issued common shares for land
h. Paid rent on building for the current period
i. Paid cash to settle an account payable
j. Declared and paid dividends to shareholders
k. Received cash dividend on investment
l. Repaid the principal amount of long-term debt
m. Amortization of a copyright
n. Sold a long-term investment at a gain

Roget uses the indirect method to prepare the operating activities of its statement of cash flows.

Required:

Indicate whether each item should be classified as a cash flow from operating activities, a cash flow from investing activities, a cash flow from financing activities, or a noncash investing and financing activity.

OBJECTIVE **2**

Exercise 11-37   Classification of Cash Flows

The following are several items that might be disclosed on a company's statement of cash flows presented using the indirect method.

a.   Net income
b.   Depreciation expense
c.   Issuance of common shares
d.   Loss on disposal of equipment
e.   Purchase of a building
f.   Decrease in accounts payable
g.   Converted bonds into common shares
h.   Sale of long-term investment
i.   Payment of interest
j.   Increase in inventory

Required:

1.   Indicate whether each item should be classified as a cash flow from operating activities, a cash flow from investing activities, a cash flow from financing activities, or a noncash investing and financing activity.

2.   Why is the proper classification of cash flows important?

OBJECTIVE **3**

Exercise 11-38   Analyzing the Accounts

A review of the statement of financial position of Matvei Company revealed the following changes in the account balances:

a.   Increase in accounts receivable
b.   Increase in retained earnings
c.   Decrease in salaries payable
d.   Increase in common shares
e.   Decrease in inventory
f.   Increase in accounts payable
g.   Decrease in long-term debt
h.   Increase in property, plant, and equipment

Required:

1.   For each of the above items, indicate whether it produces a cash inflow or a cash outflow.
2.   Classify each change as a cash flow from operating activities (indirect method), a cash flow from investing activities, or a cash flow from financing activities.

OBJECTIVE **3**

Exercise 11-39   Analyzing the Accounts

Casey Company engaged in the following transactions:

a.   Made credit sales of $615,000. The cost of the merchandise sold was $417,500
b.   Collected accounts receivable in the amount of $592,800
c.   Purchased goods on credit in the amount of $445,150
d.   Paid accounts payable in the amount of $403,200

Required:

Prepare the journal entries necessary to record the transactions. Indicate whether each transaction increased cash, decreased cash, or had no effect on cash.

Exercise 11-40 Analyzing the Accounts

OBJECTIVE 3

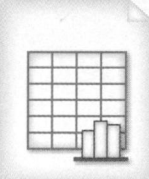

The controller for Kim Sales Inc. provides the following information on transactions that occurred during the year:

a. Purchased supplies on credit, $28,400
b. Paid $24,600 cash toward the purchase in transaction *a*
c. Provided services to customers on credit, $41,800
d. Collected $33,650 cash from accounts receivable
e. Recorded depreciation expense, $10,350
f. Employee salaries accrued, $16,200
g. Paid $16,200 cash to employees for salaries earned
h. Accrued interest expense of $1,400 on long-term debt.
i. Paid a total of $15,000 on long-term debt, which includes $1,400 interest from transaction *h*
j. Paid $1,850 cash for one year's insurance coverage in advance
k. Recognized insurance expense, $1,125, that was paid in a previous period
l. Sold equipment with a book value of $5,700 for $5,700 cash
m. Declared cash dividend, $10,000
n. Paid cash dividend declared in transaction *m*
o. Purchased new equipment for $24,300
p. Issued common shares for $50,000 cash
q. Used $18,100 of supplies to produce revenues

Kim Sales uses the indirect method to prepare its statement of cash flows.

Required:

1. Construct a table similar to the one shown below. Analyze each transaction and indicate its effect on the basic accounting equation. If the transaction increases a financial statement element, write the amount of the increase preceded by a plus sign (+) in the appropriate column. If the transaction decreases a financial statement element, write the amount of the decrease preceded by a minus sign (−) in the appropriate column.
2. Indicate whether each transaction results in a cash inflow or a cash outflow in the "Effect on Cash Flows" column. If the transaction has no effect on cash flow, indicate this by placing "none" in the "Effect on Cash Flows" column.
3. For each transaction that affected cash flows, indicate whether the cash flow would be classified as a cash flow from operating activities, a cash flow from investing activities, or a cash flow from financing activities. If there is no effect on cash flows, indicate this as a noncash activity.

Effects on the Basic According Equation

	Assets		Liabilities Equity			Effects on Cash Flows
Transactions	Current	Noncurrent	Current Liabilities	Noncurrent Liabilities	Equity	

Exercise 11-41 Reporting Net Cash Flow from Operating Activities

OBJECTIVE 4

The following information is available for Cornelius Corp.:

Selected Statement of Earnings Information	Amount
Net income	$41,000
Depreciation expense	9,200

(Continued)

Selected Statement of Financial Position Information	Beginning Balance	Ending Balance
Accounts receivable	$21,200	$27,950
Inventory	45,800	40,125
Accounts payable	23,700	32,600

Required:

1. Compute the net cash flows from operating activities using the indirect method.
2. **CONCEPTUAL CONNECTION** Explain why Cornelius was able to report net cash flow from operating activities that was higher than net income.

3. What could the difference between net income and cash flow from operating activities signal to financial statement decision makers?

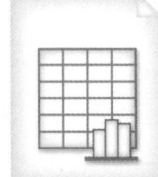

OBJECTIVE 4

Exercise 11-42   Reporting Net Cash Flow from Operating Activities

The following information is available for Bernadetti Corporation for 2018:

Net income	$179,200	Decrease in income tax payable	$ 4,270
Decrease in accounts receivable	7,900	Increase in notes payable (due 2022)	50,000
Increase in inventory	18,300	Depreciation expense	44,700
Decrease in prepaid rent	2,100	Loss on disposal of equipment	11,000
Increase in salaries payable	4,410		

Required:

1. Compute the net cash flows from operating activities using the indirect method.
2. **CONCEPTUAL CONNECTION**: What are the causes of the major differences between net income and net cash flow from operating activities?

OBJECTIVE 5

Exercise 11-43   Determining Cash Flows from Investing Activities

Burns Company's 2018 and 2017 statements of financial position presented the following data for equipment:

	12/31/2018	12/31/2017
Equipment	$275,000	$225,000
Accumulated depreciation	128,300	92,700
Book value	$146,700	$132,300

During 2018, equipment costing $35,000 with accumulated depreciation of $31,275 was sold for cash, producing a $4,400 gain.

Required:

1. Calculate the amount of depreciation expense for 2018.
2. Calculate the amount of cash spent for equipment during 2018.
3. Calculate the amount that should be included as a cash inflow from the disposal of equipment.

OBJECTIVE 5

Exercise 11-44   Determining Cash Flows from Investing Activities

Airco owns several aircraft and its statement of financial position indicated the following amounts for its aircraft accounts at the end of 2018 and 2017:

	12/31/2018	12/31/2017
Equipment, aircraft	$32,700,000	$22,250,000
Accumulated depreciation	13,900,000	13,125,000
Book value	$18,800,000	$ 9,125,000

Required:

1. Assume that Airco did not sell any aircraft during 2018. Determine the amount of depreciation expense for 2018 and the cash spent for aircraft purchases in 2018.
2. If Airco sold for cash aircraft that cost $4,100,000 with accumulated depreciation of $3,825,000, producing a gain of $193,000, determine (a) the amount of depreciation expense, (b) the cash paid for aircraft purchases in 2018, and (c) the cash inflow from the disposal of aircraft.

Exercise 11-45 Determining Cash Flows from Financing Activities

Solomon Construction Company reported the following amounts on its statement of financial position at the end of 2018 and 2017 for notes payable:

	12/31/2018	12/31/2017
Notes Payable	$180,00	$115,000

Required:

1. If Solomon did not repay any notes payable during 2018, determine how much cash Solomon received from the issuance of notes payable.
2. If Solomon repaid $60,000 of notes payable during 2018, determine what amounts Solomon would report in the financing activities section of the statement of cash flows.

Exercise 11-46 Determining Cash Flows from Financing Activities

Nichols Inc. reported the following amounts on its statement of financial position at the end of 2018 and 2017 for equity:

	12/31/2018	12/31/2017
Common shares	$164,000	$105,000
Retained earnings	455,490	376,750

Required:

Assume that Nichols did not repurchase any shares during 2018, that it reported $92,630 of net income for 2018, and that any dividends declared were paid in cash. Determine the amounts Nichols would report in the financing section of the statement of cash flows.

Exercise 11-47 Partial Statement of Cash Flows

Service Company had net income during the current year of $115,500. The following information was obtained from Service's statement of financial position:

Accounts receivable	$22,300 increase
Inventory	28,700 increase
Accounts payable	14,240 decrease
Interest payable	3,180 increase
Accumulated depreciation (equipment)	27,800 increase
Accumulated depreciation (building)	12,340 increase

Additional Information:

1. Equipment with accumulated depreciation of $15,000 was sold during the year.
2. Cash dividends of $36,000 were paid during the year.

Required:

1. Prepare the net cash flows from operating activities using the indirect method.
2. **CONCEPTUAL CONNECTION** How would the cash proceeds from the sale of equipment be reported on the statement of cash flows?

(Continued)

3. **CONCEPTUAL CONNECTION** How would the cash dividends typically be reported on the statement of cash flows?

4. What could the difference between net income and cash flow from operating activities signal to financial statement users?

OBJECTIVE ⑦

Exercise 11-48   Analyzing the Statement of Cash Flows

Information for Jackson Inc. and Fleury Company is given below:

	Jackson Inc.	Fleury Company
Cash provided by operating activities	$2,475,000	$1,639,000
Capital expenditures	1,157,000	748,000
Dividends	285,000	189,000
Average debt maturity over next 5 years	1,988,000	1,212,000

Required:

1. Compute Jackson's and Fleury's free cash flow and cash flow adequacy ratio. (*Note:* Round ratio to two decimal places.)
2. **CONCEPTUAL CONNECTION** What information do these cash-based performance measures provide with regard to the two companies?

OBJECTIVE ④⑤⑥⑦

Exercise 11-49   Preparing the Statement of Cash Flows

The comparative statements of financial position for Bihar Products Company are presented below.

	2018	2017
Assets:		
Cash	$ 36,950	$ 25,000
Accounts receivable	75,100	78,000
Inventory	45,300	36,000
Property, plant, and equipment	256,400	153,000
Accumulated depreciation	(38,650)	(20,000)
Total assets	$375,100	$272,000
Liabilities and Equity:		
Accounts payable	$ 13,100	$ 11,000
Interest payable	11,500	8,000
Wages payable	8,100	9,000
Notes payable	105,000	90,000
Common shares	100,000	50,000
Retained earnings	137,400	104,000
Total liabilities and equity	$375,100	$272,000

Additional Information:
1. Net income for 2018 was $58,400.
2. Cash dividends of $25,000 were declared and paid during 2018.
3. During 2018, Bihar issued $50,000 of notes payable and repaid $35,000 principal relating to notes payable.
4. Common shares were issued for $50,000 cash.
5. Depreciation expense was $18,650, and there were no disposals of equipment.

Required:

1. Prepare a statement of cash flows (indirect method) for Bihar Products for 2018.
2. Compute the following cash-based performance measures: (a) free cash flow, (b) cash flow adequacy, and (c) quality of earnings ratio. (*Note:* Assume that the average amount of debt maturing over the next five years is $85,000. Round ratio to two decimal places.)
3. What can you conclude by examining the patterns in Bihar's cash flows?

YOUDECIDE

Exercise 11-50   *(Appendix 11A)* Preparing Net Cash Flows from Operating Activities— Direct Method

OBJECTIVE ❽

Colassard Industries has the following data available for preparation of its statement of cash flows:

Sales revenue	$356,200	Inventory, increase	$ 5,710
Cost of goods sold	182,500	Prepaid insurance, increase	2,100
Wages expense	58,400	Accounts payable, increase	5,680
Insurance expense	8,300	Notes payable, increase	32,000
Interest expense	20,800	Interest payable, increase	3,125
Income tax expense	16,200	Wages payable, decrease	5,400
Accounts receivable, decrease	14,300		

Required:

Prepare the cash flows from operating activities section of the statement of cash flows, using the direct method.

Exercise 11-51   *(Appendix 11A)* Preparing a Statement of Cash Flows—Direct Method

OBJECTIVE ❽

The controller of Norstrom Software Corp. provides the following information as the basis for a statement of cash flows:

Cash collected from customers	$785,400	Income tax paid	$ 58,300
Cash paid for interest	22,100	Payment of dividends	35,000
Cash paid to employees and other		Principal payments on mortgage	
suppliers of goods and services	221,750	payable	60,000
Cash paid to suppliers of merchandise	395,540	Principal payments on long-term debt	22,000
Cash received from the issuance of		Proceeds from the issuance of	
long-term debt	40,000	common shares	85,000
Cash received from disposal of		Purchase of equipment	120,000
equipment	42,500	Purchase of long-term investments	75,800
Cash received from sale of long-term			
investments	71,400		

Required:

1. Calculate the net cash provided (used) by operating activities.
2. Calculate the net cash provided (used) by investing activities.
3. Calculate the net cash provided (used) by financing activities.

OBJECTIVE **8**   **Exercise 11-52**   *(Appendix 11A)* **Preparing a Statement of Cash Flows—Direct Method**

Financial statements for Rowe Publishing Company are presented below.

Rowe Publishing Company
Statements of Financial Position
December 31, 2018 and 2017

	2018		2017
ASSETS			
Current assets:			
Cash		$ 85,000	$ 66,000
Accounts receivable		240,000	231,000
Inventory		190,000	170,000
Total current assets		515,000	467,000
Property, plant, and equipment:			
Building	$ 400,000		$ 400,000
Equipment	155,000		130,000
	555,000		530,000
Accumulated depreciation	(375,000)		(350,000)
Net property, plant, and equipment		180,000	180,000
Total assets		$695,000	$647,000
LIABILITIES AND EQUITY			
Current liabilities:			
Accounts payable	$ 133,000		$ 121,000
Salaries payable	15,000		11,000
Income tax payable	10,000		17,000
Total current liabilities		$158,000	$149,000
Long-term liabilities:			
Notes payable	115,000		150,000
Bonds payable	50,000		—
Total long-term liabilities		165,000	150,000
Total liabilities		323,000	299,000
Equity:			
Common shares	300,000		300,000
Retained earnings	72,000		48,000
Total equity		372,000	348,000
Total liabilities and equity		$695,000	$647,000

Rowe Publishing Company
Statement of Earnings
for the Year Ended
December 31, 2018

Sales		$1,051,000
Less: Cost of goods sold		(578,000)
Gross margin		473,000
Less operating expenses:		
Salaries	$(351,000)	
Depreciation	(25,000)	(376,000)
Income from operations		97,000
Less: Interest expense		(16,000)
Income before tax		81,000
Less: Income tax expense		(22,000)
Net income		$ 59,000

Additional Information:

1. No buildings nor equipment were sold during 2018. Equipment was purchased for $25,000 cash.
2. Notes payable in the amount of $35,000 were repaid during 2018.
3. Bonds payable of $50,000 were issued for cash during 2018.
4. Rowe Publishing declared and paid dividends of $35,000 during 2018.

Required:

Prepare a statement of cash flows for 2018, using the direct method to determine net cash flow from operating activities.

Exercise 11-53   *(Appendix 11B)* Using a Spreadsheet to Prepare a Statement of Cash Flows

OBJECTIVE 9

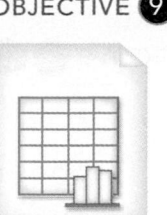

Comparative statements of financial position for Vancouver Health Club are presented below.

Vancouver Health Club
Statements of Financial Position
December 31, 2018 and 2017

	2018	2017
ASSETS		
Current assets:		
Cash	$ 5,300	$ 9,200
Accounts receivable	10,500	8,900
Inventory	19,800	18,600
Total current assets	35,600	36,700
Property, plant, and equipment:		
Building	$ 490,000	$ 490,000
Equipment	280,000	270,000
	770,000	760,000
Accumulated depreciation	(148,000)	(120,000)
Net property, plant, and equipment	622,000	640,000
Total assets	$657,600	$676,700
LIABILITIES AND EQUITY		
Current liabilities:		
Accounts payable	$ 55,300	$ 36,100
Salaries payable	9,500	11,700
Income tax payable	1,100	9,900
Total current liabilities	$ 65,900	$ 57,700
Long-term liabilities:		
Bonds payable	350,000	400,000
Total liabilities	415,900	457,700
Equity:		
Common shares	180,000	150,000
Retained earnings	61,700	69,000
Total equity	241,700	219,000
Total liabilities and equity	$657,600	$676,700

Additional Information:

1. Vancouver Health Club reported net income of $2,700 for 2018.
2. No buildings nor equipment was sold during 2018. Equipment was purchased for $10,000 cash.
3. Depreciation expense for 2018 was $28,000.
4. Bonds payable of $50,000 were issued for cash during 2018.
5. Common shares were issued for $30,000 during 2018.
6. Cash dividends of $10,000 were declared and paid during 2018.

Required:

Using a spreadsheet, prepare a statement of cash flows for 2018. Assume Vancouver Health Club uses the indirect method.

PROBLEM SET A

OBJECTIVE ❷ ❸

Problem 11-54A   Classifying and Analyzing Business Activities

CTT Ltd. reported the following business activities during 2018:

a. Purchased property, plant, and equipment for cash
b. Purchased merchandise inventory for cash
c. Recorded depreciation on property, plant, and equipment
d. Issued common shares
e. Purchased merchandise inventory on credit
f. Collected cash sales from customers
g. Paid cash dividends
h. Purchased a two-year insurance policy
i. Paid salaries of employees
j. Borrowed cash by issuing a note payable
k. Sold property, plant, and equipment for cash
l. Paid cash for principal amount of mortgage
m. Paid interest on mortgage

Required:

1. Indicate whether each activity should be classified as a cash flow from operating activities, a cash flow from investing activities, a cash flow from financing activities, or a noncash investing and financing activity. Assume that CTT uses the indirect method.
2. For each activity that is reported on the statement of cash flows, indicate whether it produces a cash inflow, produces a cash outflow, or has no cash effect.

OBJECTIVE ❹

Problem 11-55A   Reporting Net Cash Flow from Operating Activities

The statement of earnings for Colombo Manufacturing Company is presented below.

Colombo Manufacturing Company Statement of Earnings For the Year Ended December 31, 2018		
Sales		$4,199,830
Cost of goods sold		2,787,210
Gross margin		1,412,620
Operating expenses:		
Salaries expense	$831,800	
Depreciation expense	246,100	
Administrative expense	131,000	
Bad debt expense	51,700	
Other expenses	43,900	1,304,500
Net income		$ 108,120

The following statement of financial position changes occurred during the year:

• Accounts receivable increased by $182,400.
• Inventory increased by $98,725.
• Prepaid expenses decreased by $64,100.
• Accounts payable increased by $43,850.
• Salaries payable increased by $54,900.

Required:

1. Prepare the net cash flows from operating activities using the indirect method.
2. **CONCEPTUAL CONNECTION** What are the causes of the major differences between net income and net cash flow from operating activities?

Problem 11-56A Classification of Cash Flows

OBJECTIVE ② ③ ④

Rolling Meadows Country Club Limited is a privately owned corporation that operates a golf club. Rolling Meadows reported the following inflows and outflows of cash during 2018:

Net income	$115,300	Cash received from sale of used golf carts	$ 9,200
Decrease in accounts receivable	5,125	Depreciation expense, buildings	49,100
Increase in pro shop inventory	28,600	Depreciation expense, golf carts	23,700
Increase in prepaid insurance	15,800	Proceeds from issuance of note payable	45,000
Increase in accounts payable	11,400	Payment on mortgage payable	28,000
Decrease in wages payable	9,210	Cash received from issuance of	
Increase in income tax payable	7,500	common shares	38,500
Cash paid for new golf carts	115,000	Payment of cash dividends	45,000

Rolling Meadows had cash on hand at 1/1/18 of $10,300.

Required:

1. Prepare a properly formatted statement of cash flows using the indirect method.
2. What can you conclude by examining the patterns in Rolling Meadows' cash flows?

YOUDECIDE

Problem 11-57A Preparing a Statement of Cash Flows

OBJECTIVE ④ ⑤ ⑥ ⑦

Hellas Company reported the following comparative statements of financial position:

	2018	2017
Assets:		
Cash	$ 33,200	$ 12,750
Accounts receivable	53,000	44,800
Inventory	29,500	27,500
Prepaid rent	2,200	6,200
Investments (long-term)	17,600	31,800
Property, plant, and equipment	162,000	149,450
Accumulated depreciation	(61,600)	(56,200)
Total assets	$235,900	$216,300
Liabilities and Equity:		
Accounts payable	$ 16,900	$ 19,500
Interest payable	3,500	4,800
Wages payable	9,600	7,100
Income tax payable	5,500	3,600
Notes payable	28,000	53,000
Common shares	100,000	68,500
Retained earnings	72,400	59,800
Total liabilities and equity	$235,900	$216,300

Additional information:

1. Net income for 2018 was $20,500.
2. Cash dividends of $7,900 were declared and paid during 2018.
3. Long-term investments with a cost of $28,600 were sold for cash at a gain of $4,100. Additional long-term investments were purchased for $14,400 cash.
4. Equipment with a cost of $14,800 and accumulated depreciation of $13,500 was sold for $3,800 cash. New equipment was purchased for $27,350 cash.
5. Depreciation expense was $18,900.
6. A principal payment of $25,000 was made on long-term notes.
7. Common shares were sold for $31,500 cash.

(Continued)

Required:

Prepare a statement of cash flows for Hellas, using the indirect method to compute net cash flow from operating activities.

OBJECTIVE ④⑤⑥⑦   Problem 11-58A   **Preparing a Statement of Cash Flows**

Monon Cable Television Company reported the following financial statements for 2018:

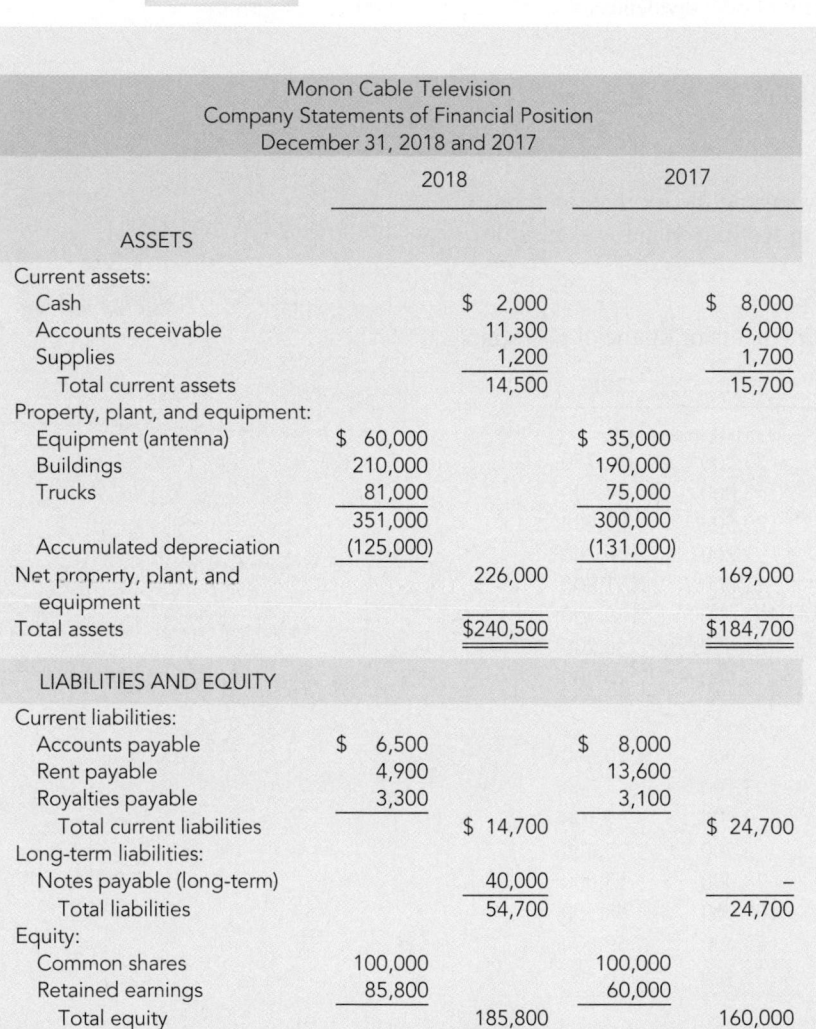

Monon Cable Television Company Statements of Financial Position December 31, 2018 and 2017			
	2018		**2017**
ASSETS			
Current assets:			
Cash	$ 2,000		$ 8,000
Accounts receivable	11,300		6,000
Supplies	1,200		1,700
Total current assets	14,500		15,700
Property, plant, and equipment:			
Equipment (antenna)	$ 60,000		$ 35,000
Buildings	210,000		190,000
Trucks	81,000		75,000
	351,000		300,000
Accumulated depreciation	(125,000)		(131,000)
Net property, plant, and equipment	226,000		169,000
Total assets	$240,500		$184,700
LIABILITIES AND EQUITY			
Current liabilities:			
Accounts payable	$ 6,500		$ 8,000
Rent payable	4,900		13,600
Royalties payable	3,300		3,100
Total current liabilities	$ 14,700		$ 24,700
Long-term liabilities:			
Notes payable (long-term)	40,000		–
Total liabilities	54,700		24,700
Equity:			
Common shares	100,000		100,000
Retained earnings	85,800		60,000
Total equity	185,800		160,000
Total liabilities and equity	$240,500		$184,700

Monon Cable Television Company Statement of Earnings For the Year Ended December 31, 2018		
Sales		$ 519,000
Less operating expenses:		
Royalties expense	$(240,000)	
Salaries expense	(26,000)	
Utilities expense	(83,000)	
Supplies expense	(13,000)	
Rent expense	(79,000)	
Depreciation expense	(28,000)	(469,000)
Income from operations		50,000
Other income (expenses):		
Gain on disposal of property, plant, and equipment	800	
Interest expense	(1,800)	(1,000)
Income before taxes		49,000
Less: Income tax expense		(9,000)
Net income		$ 40,000

Additional Information:

1. Equipment (an old antenna) with a cost of $35,000 and accumulated depreciation of $34,000 was taken down and sold as scrap for $1,800 cash during 2018. A new antenna was purchased for cash at an installed cost of $60,000.
2. A building was purchased for $20,000 cash.
3. Trucks were purchased for $6,000 cash.
4. Depreciation expense for 2018 was $28,000.
5. A long-term note payable was issued for $40,000 cash.
6. Dividends of $14,200 were paid during 2018.

Required:

1. Prepare a statement of cash flows, using the indirect method to compute net cash flow from operating activities.
2. **CONCEPTUAL CONNECTION** Explain what has been responsible for the decrease in cash.

Problem 11-59A   (Appendix 11A) Preparing Net Cash Flows from Operating Activities—Direct Method

OBJECTIVE **8**

Yogurt Plus, a restaurant, collected the following information on inflows and outflows for 2018:

Inflows		Outflows	
Sales (all for cash)	$334,500	Cash payments made for merchandise	
Cash received from sale of common shares	72,000	sold	$176,450
Proceeds from issuance of long-term notes		Cash payments for operating expenses	115,210
payable	50,000	Cash payments for interest	24,600
Proceeds from sale of used restaurant		Cash payments for income taxes	9,475
furniture	11,300	Purchase of restaurant furniture for cash	108,800
Proceeds from issuance of short-term note		Principal payment on mortgage	35,000
payable	15,000	Payment of dividends	10,000
Notes payable issued in exchange for		Cost of kitchen equipment acquired in	
kitchen equipment	30,000	exchange for notes payable	30,000

Yogurt Plus had a cash balance of $21,800 at 1/1/18.

Required:

1. Prepare a statement of cash flows, using the direct method to determine net cash flow from operating activities.
2. What can you conclude by examining the patterns in Yogurt Plus's cash flows?

YOUDECIDE

Problem 11-60A   (Appendix 11A) Preparing Net Cash Flows from Operating Activities—Direct Method

OBJECTIVE **8**

Refer to the information for Colombo Manufacturing Company in Problem 11-55A.

Required:

Prepare the cash flows from operating activities section of the statement of cash flows, using the direct method.

Problem 11-61A   (Appendix 11B) Using a Spreadsheet to Prepare a Statement of Cash Flows

OBJECTIVE **9**

Jane Bahr, the controller of Endicott & Ko, prepared the following statements of financial position at the end of 2018 and 2017:

Endicott & Ko Associates
Statements of Financial Position
December 31, 2018 and 2017

	2018		2017
ASSETS			
Current assets:			
Cash		$ 2,000	$ 17,000
Accounts receivable		78,000	219,000
Prepaid rent		29,000	104,000
Total current assets		109,000	340,000
Long-term investments		51,000	40,000
Property, plant, and equipment:			
Equipment, computing	$ 488,000		$ 362,000
Furniture	400,000		365,000
	888,000		727,000
Accumulated depreciation	(366,000)		(554,000)
Net property, plant, and equipment		522,000	173,000
Total assets		$682,000	$553,000

Additional Information:

1. Computing equipment with a cost of $250,000 and accumulated depreciation of $230,000 was sold for $5,000. New computing equipment was purchased for $376,000.
2. New office furniture was purchased at a cost of $35,000.
3. Depreciation expense for 2018 was $42,000.
4. Investments costing $20,000 were sold for cash at a loss of $2,000. Additional investments were purchased for $31,000 cash.
5. A $25,000 principal payment on the long-term note was made during 2018.
6. A portion of the cash needed to purchase computing equipment was secured by issuing bonds payable for $140,000 cash.
7. Net income was $70,000 and dividends were $38,000.

(Continued)

LIABILITIES AND EQUITY

Current liabilities:				
Accounts payable	$ 56,000		$ 58,000	
Salaries payable	89,000		105,000	
Total current liabilities		$145,000		$163,000
Long-term liabilities:				
Notes payable, long-term		80,000		105,000
Bonds payable		140,000		–
Total liabilities		365,000		268,000
Equity:				
Common shares	225,000		225,000	
Retained earnings	92,000		60,000	
Total equity		317,000		285,000
Total liabilities and equity		$682,000		$553,000

Required:

1.   Using a spreadsheet, prepare a statement of cash flows for 2018. Assume that Endicott & Ko uses the indirect method.
2.   **CONCEPTUAL CONNECTION** Discuss whether Endicott & Ko appears to have matched the timing of inflows and outflows of cash.

PROBLEM SET B

Problem 11-62B   Classifying and Analyzing Business Activities

Cowell Company had the following business activities during 2018:

a.   Paid cash dividend to shareholders
b.   Paid cash for inventory
c.   Purchased equipment for cash
d.   Paid interest on long-term debt
e.   Acquired land in exchange for common shares
f.   Issued common shares for cash
g.   Paid salaries to employees

h.   Received cash from the sale of merchandise
i.   Recorded amortization related to an intangible asset
j.   Issued bonds payable in exchange for cash
k.   Sold equipment for cash
l.   Purchased inventory on account

Cowell Company uses the indirect method to prepare its statement of cash flows.

Required:

1.   Indicate whether each activity should be classified as a cash flow from operating activities, a cash flow from investing activities, a cash flow from financing activities, or a noncash investing and financing activity.
2.   For each activity that is reported on the statement of cash flows, indicate whether each activity produces a cash inflow or a cash outflow, or has no cash effect.

Problem 11-63B Reporting Net Cash Flow from Operating Activities

OBJECTIVE 4

The statement of earnings for Morsi Products is presented below.

Morsi Products Statement of Earnings For the Year Ended December 31, 2018		
Sales		$3,584,600
Cost of goods sold		2,557,500
Gross margin		1,027,100
Other expenses:		
Salaries expense	$455,100	
Administrative expense	247,000	
Depreciation expense	214,500	
Bad debt expense	37,000	
Income tax expense	28,200	981,800
Net income		$ 45,300

The following statement of financial position changes occurred during the year:

- Accounts receivable decreased by $85,150
- Inventory decreased by $138,620
- Prepaid expenses increased by $112,400
- Accounts payable decreased by $67,225
- Salaries payable increased by $18,300

Required:

1. Prepare the net cash flows from operating activities using the indirect method.
2. **CONCEPTUAL CONNECTION** What are the causes of the major differences between net income and net cash flow from operating activities?

YOUDECIDE

Problem 11-64B Classification of Cash Flows

OBJECTIVE

Fannin Company is a manufacturer of premium athletic equipment. Fannin reported the following inflows and outflows of cash during 2018.

Net income	$574,250	Cash received from sale of investment	$ 12,350
Increase in accounts receivable	34,600	Cash paid for property, plant, and	
Decrease in inventory	59,400	equipment	114,410
Decrease in prepaid insurance	45,800	Depreciation expense	103,300
Decrease in accounts payable	39,600	Proceeds from issuance of note payable	25,000
Decrease in income tax payable	11,200	Payment on bonds payable	182,000
Increase in wages payable	28,800	Cash received from issuance of common	
		shares	25,000
		Payment of cash dividends	21,000

Fannin had cash on hand at 1/1/18 of $218,500.

Required:

1. Prepare a properly formatted statement of cash flows using the indirect method.
2. What can you conclude by examining the patterns in Fannin's cash flows?

Problem 11-65B   Preparing a Statement of Cash Flows

Volusia Company reported the following comparative statements of financial position for 2018:

Volusia Company Statement of Financial Position December 31, 2018 and 2017		
	2018	2017
ASSETS		
Cash	$ 28,100	$ 16,300
Accounts receivable	26,500	32,725
Inventory	24,100	28,200
Prepaid rent	3,900	1,800
Investments, long-term	37,200	25,500
Property, plant, and equipment	115,000	102,975
Accumulated depreciation	(47,100)	(38,600)
Total assets	$187,700	$168,900
LIABILITIES AND EQUITY		
Accounts payable	$ 24,900	$ 21,200
Interest payable	4,700	3,300
Wages payable	4,600	6,900
Income tax payable	3,500	5,200
Notes payable	35,000	30,000
Common shares	72,900	65,000
Retained earnings	42,100	37,300
Total liabilities and equity	$187,700	$168,900

Additional Information:

1. Net income for 2018 was $18,300.
2. Cash dividends of $13,500 were declared and paid during 2018.
3. Long-term investments with a cost of $21,200 were sold for cash at a loss of $1,500. Additional long-term investments were purchased for $32,900 cash.
4. Equipment with a cost of $25,000 and accumulated depreciation of $16,300 was sold for $4,500 cash. New equipment was purchased for $37,025 cash.
5. Depreciation expense was $24,800.
6. A principal payment of $15,000 was made on long-term notes. Volusia issued notes payable for $20,000 cash.
7. Common shares were sold for $7,900 cash.

Required:

Prepare a statement of cash flows for Volusia, using the indirect method to compute net cash flow from operating activities.

Problem 11-66B   Preparing a Statement of Cash Flows

SDPS Inc. provides airport transportation services in northern Quebec. A statement of earnings for 2018 and statements of financial position for 2018 and 2017 appear below.

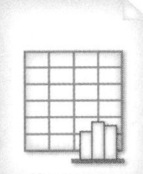

SDPS Inc. Statements of Financial Position December 31, 2018 and 2017				
		2018		2017
ASSETS				
Current assets:				
Cash		$ 40,000		$ 82,000
Accounts receivable		126,000		109,000
Supplies, fuel		11,000		25,000
Total current assets		177,000		216,000
Property, plant, and equipment:				
Equipment, vehicles	$ 524,000		409,000	
Accumulated depreciation	(174,000)		(136,000)	
Net property, plant, and equipment		350,000		273,000
Total assets		$527,000		$489,000

LIABILITIES AND EQUITY				Additional Information:

Current liabilities:				
Accounts payable	$103,000		$ 58,000	
Wages payable	22,000		29,000	
Repair and maintenance				
Payable	41,000		34,000	
Rent payable	92,000		51,000	
Total current liabilities		$258,000	$172,000	
Long-term liabilities:				
Notes payable, long-term		100,000	125,000	
Total liabilities		358,000	297,000	
Equity:				
Common shares	150,000		150,000	
Retained earnings	19,000		42,000	
Total equity		169,000	192,000	
Total liabilities and equity		$527,000	$489,000	

Additional Information:

1. Vehicles with a cost of $310,000 and accumulated depreciation of $177,000 were sold for $130,000 cash. New vehicles were purchased for $425,000 cash.
2. A $25,000 principal payment on the long-term note was made during 2018.
3. No dividends were paid during 2018.

SDPS Inc.
Statement of Earnings
For the Year Ended December 31, 2018

Sales		$ 937,000
Less operating expenses:		
Wages expense	$(278,000)	
Rent expense	(229,000)	
Supplies expense	(83,000)	
Maintenance expense	(138,000)	
Depreciation expense	(215,000)	(943,000)
Income (loss) from operations		(6,000)
Other income (expenses):		
Loss on disposal of property, plant, and equipment	(3,000)	
Interest expense	(14,000)	(17,000)
Net loss		$ (23,000)

Required:

1. Prepare a statement of cash flows, using the indirect method to compute net cash flow from operating activities.
2. **CONCEPTUAL CONNECTION** Explain what has been responsible for the decrease in cash.
3. **CONCEPTUAL CONNECTION** Determine how SDPS financed its increase in net property, plant, and equipment during a period in which it had a net loss.

Problem 11-67B *(Appendix 11A)* **Preparing Net Cash Flows from Operating Activities—Direct Method**   OBJECTIVE 8

Befuddled Corporation collected the following information on inflows and outflows for 2018:

Inflows		Outflows	
Cash collections from sales	$956,500	Cash payments for cost of goods sold	$534,900
Proceeds from disposal of equipment	11,250	Cash payments for operating expenses	193,200
Proceeds received from issuance of		Cash payments for interest	36,400
notes payable	30,000	Cash payments for income taxes	21,300
		Cash payments for purchases of equipment	217,150
		Repayment of short-term notes payable	20,000
		Payment of cash dividends	38,000

Befuddled had a cash balance of $89,200 on 1/1/18.

(Continued)

Required:

1. Prepare a statement of cash flows, using the direct method to determine net cash flow from operating activities.

YOUDECIDE   2. What can you conclude by examining the patterns in Befuddled's cash flows?

OBJECTIVE ❽   **Problem 11-68B   (Appendix 11A) Preparing Net Cash Flows from Operating Activities—Direct Method**

Refer to the information for Morsi Products in Problem 11-63B.

Required:

Prepare the cash flows from operating activities section of the statement of cash flows, using the direct method.

OBJECTIVE ❾   **Problem 11-69B   (Appendix 11B) Using a Spreadsheet to Prepare a Statement of Cash Flows**

Flit Limousine Service Inc. began operations in late March 2018. At the end of 2018, the following statement of financial position was prepared for Flit.

Flit Limousine Service Inc.
Statements of Financial Position
December 31, 2018

ASSETS		
Current assets:		
Cash	$ 7,200	
Accounts receivable	15,900	
Supplies	3,100	
Total current assets		$ 26,200
Long-term investments		15,000
Property, plant, and equipment:		
Land	$ 11,000	
Building	175,000	
Equipment	233,400	
	419,400	
Accumulated depreciation	(35,500)	
Net property, plant, and equipment		383,900
Total assets		$425,100

LIABILITIES AND EQUITY		
Current liabilities:		
Accounts payable	$ 12,700	
Unearned service revenue	21,800	
Salaries payable	4,600	
Rent payable	8,200	
Total current liabilities		$ 47,300
Long-term liabilities:		
Notes payable		95,000
Total liabilities		142,300
Equity:		
Common shares	300,000	
Retained earnings (deficit)	(17,200)	
Total equity		282,800
Total liabilities and equity		$425,100

Additional Information:

1. During 2018, land was purchased for $11,000, a building was purchased for $175,000, and equipment was purchased for $233,400.

2. Depreciation expense for 2018 was $35,500.

3. The long-term note was issued for $100,000, and a principal payment of $5,000 was made during 2018.

4. Common shares were issued for $300,000 cash during 2018.

5. During 2018, there was a net loss of $17,200 and no dividends were paid.

Required:

1. Using a spreadsheet, prepare a statement of cash flows for 2018. Assume Flit Limousine uses the indirect method.
2. **CONCEPTUAL CONNECTION** Discuss whether Flit Limousine appears to have matched the timing of inflows and outflows of cash.

CASES

Case 11-70   The Statement of Cash Flows and Credit Analysis

June's Camera Shop sells cameras and photographic supplies of all types to retail customers. June's also repairs cameras and provides colour prints. To compete with other camera departments, June's offers fast, efficient, and effective repairs and photographic processing. For fiscal 2018 and 2017, June's accountant prepared the following statements of cash flows:

	June's Camera Shop Statements of Cash Flows For the Years Ended January 31, 2018 and 2017			
	2018		2017	
Cash flows from operating activities				
Net income		$ 87,000		$ 63,000
Adjustments to reconcile net income to net cash provided by operating activities:				
Depreciation expense	$ 41,000		$ 37,000	
Increase in accounts receivable	(17,000)		(12,000)	
Increase in inventory	(19,000)		(11,000)	
Increase in accounts payable	15,000		14,000	
Increase in wages payable	11,000		5,000	
Increase in income tax payable	6,000		3,000	
Total adjustments		37,000		36,000
Net cash provided by operating activities		124,000		99,000
Cash flows from investing activities				
Purchase of long-term investments	(15,000)		(10,000)	
Purchase of equipment	(45,000)		(40,000)	
Net cash used by investing activities		(60,000)		(50,000)
Cash flows from financing activities				
Principal payments on mortgage	(15,000)		(15,000)	
Payment of dividends	(12,000)		(10,000)	
Net cash used by financing activities		(27,000)		(25,000)
Net increase in cash and cash equivalents		37,000		24,000
Cash and cash equivalents at beginning of year		158,000		134,000
Cash and cash equivalents at end of year		$195,000		$158,000

Required:

1. Does June's Camera Shop appear to have grown (in terms of property, plant, and equipment) during the past two years?
2. June's president, June Smith, would like to open a second store. Smith believes that $225,000 is needed to equip the facility properly. The business has $100,000 of cash and liquid investments to apply toward the $225,000 required. Do the data in the 2018 and 2017 statements of cash flow suggest whether or not June's Camera Shop is likely to be able to secure a loan for the remaining $125,000 needed for the expansion?
3. How long should it take June's Camera Shop to pay back the $125,000?

Case 11-71 Profitability Declines and the Statement of Cash Flows

The Audio Barn Ltd. is a retail seller of audio equipment in a moderate-sized city. Although initially very successful, The Audio Barn's sales volume has declined since the opening of two competing audio stores two years ago. The accountant for The Audio Barn prepared the following statement of cash flows at the end of the current year:

The Audio Barn Ltd. Statement of Cash Flows For the Year Ended December 31, 2018		
Cash flows from operating activities		
Net income		$ 26,500
Adjustments to reconcile net income to net cash provided by operating activities:		
Depreciation expense	$ 38,500	
Loss on disposal of property, plant, and equipment	2,100	
Increase in accounts receivable	(1,200)	
Increase in inventory	(3,800)	
Increase in accounts payable	6,700	
Decrease in wages payable	(1,200)	
Total adjustments		41,100
Net cash provided by operating activities		67,600
Cash flows from investing activities		
Purchase of equipment	(12,000)	
Proceeds from disposal of equipment	2,300	
Net cash used by investing activities		(9,700)
Cash flows from financing activities		
Payment of dividends	(4,000)	
Repayment of mortgage	(10,000)	
Net cash used by financing activities		(14,000)
Net increase in cash		$ 43,900

Your analysis suggests that The Audio Barn's net income will continue to decline by $8,000 per year to $18,500 as sales continue to fall. Thereafter, you expect sales to stabilize.

Required:

1. What will happen to the amount of cash provided by operations as net income decreases?
2. Assume that equipment is nearly fully depreciated but that it will be fully serviceable for several years. What will happen to cash flows from operations as depreciation declines?
3. Do the operations of businesses experiencing declining sales volumes always consume cash? Explain your answer.
4. Can current assets and current liabilities buffer operating cash flows against the impact of declines in sales volume in the short run? In the long run? Explain your answer.

Case 11-72 Preparing a Prospective Statement of Cash Flows

Jane and Harvey Zucker have decided to open a retail athletic supply store, Fitness Outfitters Inc. They will stock clothing, shoes, and supplies used in running, swimming, bicycling, weight lifting, and other exercise and athletic activities. During their first year of operations, 2018, they expect the following results. (Subsequent years are expected to be more successful.)

Sales revenue	$ 629,000
Less: Cost of goods sold	(291,000)
Gross margin	338,000
Less: Operating expenses	(355,000)
Net loss	$ (17,000)

By the end of 2018, Fitness Outfitters needs to have a cash balance of $5,000 and is expected to have the following partial statement of financial position:

ASSETS		
Inventory		$ 53,000
Equipment	$97,000	
Accumulated depreciation, equipment	15,000	82,000
LIABILITIES AND EQUITY		
Accounts payable		37,000
Common shares		100,000
Retained earnings		(17,000)

Assume that all sales will be for cash and that equipment will be acquired for cash.

Required:

1. Prepare as much of the statement of cash flows for 2018 as you can. Use the direct method to determine cash flows from operations.
2. In the statement that you prepared for requirement 1, by how much does the prospective cash balance exceed or fall short of the desired cash balance? If a shortfall occurs, where would you suggest that Jane and Harvey seek additional cash?
3. Does the preparation of a prospective statement of cash flows seem worthwhile for an ongoing business? Why?

Case 11-73   Income, Cash Flow, and Future Losses

On January 1, 2018, National Bank loaned $5,000,000 under a two-year, zero coupon note to a real estate developer. The bank recognized interest revenue on this note of approximately $400,000 per year. Due to an economic downturn, the developer was unable to pay the $5,800,000 maturity amount on December 31, 2019. The bank convinced the developer to pay $800,000 on December 31, 2019, and agreed to extend $5,000,000 credit to the developer despite the gloomy economic outlook for the next several years. Thus, on December 31, 2019, the bank issued a new two-year, zero coupon note to the developer to mature on December 31, 2021, for $6,000,000. The bank recognized interest revenue on this note of approximately $500,000 per year.

The bank's external auditor insisted that the riskiness of the new loan be recognized by increasing the allowance for uncollectible notes by $1,500,000 on December 31, 2019, and $2,000,000 on December 31, 2020. On December 31, 2021, the bank received $1,200,000 from the developer and learned that the developer was in bankruptcy and that no additional amounts would be recovered.

Required:

1. Prepare a schedule showing annual cash flows for the two notes in each of the four years.
2. Prepare a schedule showing the effect of the notes on net income in each of the four years.
3. Which figure, net income or net cash flow, does the better job of telling the bank's shareholders about the effect of these notes on the bank? Explain by reference to the schedules prepared in requirements 1 and 2.
4. A commonly used method for predicting future cash flows is to predict future income and adjust it for anticipated differences between net income and net cash flow. Does the National Bank case shed any light on the justification for using net income in this way rather than simply predicting future cash flows by reference to past cash flows?

Case 11-74   Continuing Problem: Front Row Entertainment

The statement of earnings and comparative statement of financial position for Front Row Entertainment are shown below:

Front Row Entertainment Inc.
Statements of Financial Position
December 31, 2018 and 2017

	2018	2017
ASSETS		
Current assets:		
Cash	$ 30,322	$ 9,005
Accounts receivable, net	98,250	17,000
Prepaid expenses	133,400	57,200
Supplies	2,200	3,700
Inventory	61,380	2,850
Total current assets	325,552	89,755
Property, plant, and equipment:		
Building	1,857,250	–
Equipment	27,350	7,000
Accumulated depreciation	(53,835)	(2,160)
Trademark	25,000	–
Total assets	$2,181,317	$94,595
LIABILITIES AND EQUITY		
Current liabilities:		
Accounts payable	$ 2,450	$12,240
Salaries payable	2,500	3,690
Interest payable	40,917	2,250
Unearned sales revenue	1,780	28,650
Income tax payable	550	2,180
Notes payable (short-term)	8,000	–
Total current liabilities	56,197	49,010
Long-term liabilities:		
Notes payable	405,000	25,000
Bonds payable, net	1,500,000	–
Less: Discount on bonds payable	(109,530)	–
Total long-term liabilities	1,795,470	25,000
Equity:		
Preferred shares	220,400	–
Common shares	56,000	16,000
Retained earnings	53,250	4,585
Total equity	329,650	20,585
Total liabilities and equity	$2,181,317	$94,595

Front Row Entertainment Inc.
Statement of Earnings
For the Year Ended December 31, 2018

Revenues:	
Sales revenue	$3,142,800
Service revenue	636,000
Total revenues	3,778,800
Expenses:	
Artist fee expense	2,134,260
Rent expense	952,663
Cost of goods sold	74,800
Salaries and wages expense	345,100
Depreciation expense	51,675
Interest expense	98,087
Income tax expense	22,000
Other expenses	26,550
Total expenses	3,705,135
Net income	$ 73,665

Additional Information:

1. Bonds payable of $1,500,000 were issued for $1,378,300 on July 1, 2018. During 2018, $12,170 of the discount on the bonds payable was amortized.
2. In January 2018, a $380,000 long-term note payable was issued in exchange for a building. No buildings were sold during the year.
3. On February 28, an $8,000 short-term note payable was issued in exchange for equipment. No equipment was sold during the year.
4. Cash dividends of $25,000 were declared and paid during 2018.
5. Common shares were issued for $40,000 cash during 2018.
6. Preferred shares were issued for $220,400 cash during 2018.

Required:

1. Prepare a statement of cash flows using the indirect method.
2. What conclusions can you draw about Front Row Entertainment from the observed pattern of cash flows?

Case 11-75   Professional and Ethical Behaviour

You have recently been recruited for a summer intern position at Orangeberry Ltd. (OBL). OBL is a private company that specializes in selling home electronics for personal use. OBL also has a division that focuses on providing installation and repair services. OBL has been in business for six years and has expanded quickly to keep up with demand.

You were hired by Mathew, the head HR recruiter. You're excited to get this summer position, as it will provide you with much-needed work experience.

You work in the accounting department and report directly to Rosanne, who has been with the company since day one and is responsible for all accounting-related functions.

You overhear Rosanne telling Joe in accounting that she doesn't understand why cash flow is down when net income per the statement of earnings is positive. She says she could understand that this would happen if the company were showing a loss, but the net income is positive and has been for the last two years. Yet it seems as if OBL is struggling to pay its bills.

You recall from your accounting course in university that your professor always said, "Don't forget about the statement of cash flow, as it's one of the most important statements you can look at." You quickly go into Rosanne's office to tell her that you overheard her discussion with Joe and heard her concern about the business relating to cash flows. You ask if you can see the financial statements to help out with her issue. Rosanne has a smile on her face, thinking it unlikely that the summer intern would be able to solve the problem, but she thinks that this could be a good learning opportunity for you and provides you with the statement of financial position and statement of earnings for your review.

You ask her where the statement of cash flow is. She quickly replies, "We are a private company and therefore do not need one. The tax authorities don't really care about the statement of cash flow, so we never bothered to prepare one."

Required:

Comment on any professional behaviour issues.

12

Reporting and Analyzing Investments

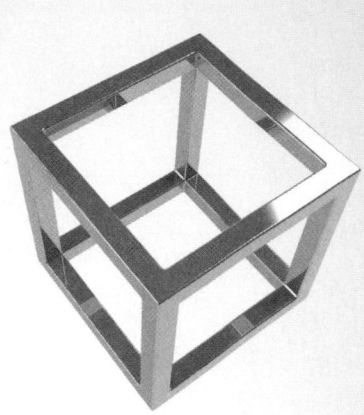

After studying Chapter 12, you should be able to:

1. Classify investments as strategic or nonstrategic.
2. Account for and report nonstrategic investments.
3. Account for and report strategic investments.
4. Describe the consolidated statement of financial position and statement of earnings.
5. Describe accounting for business combinations.

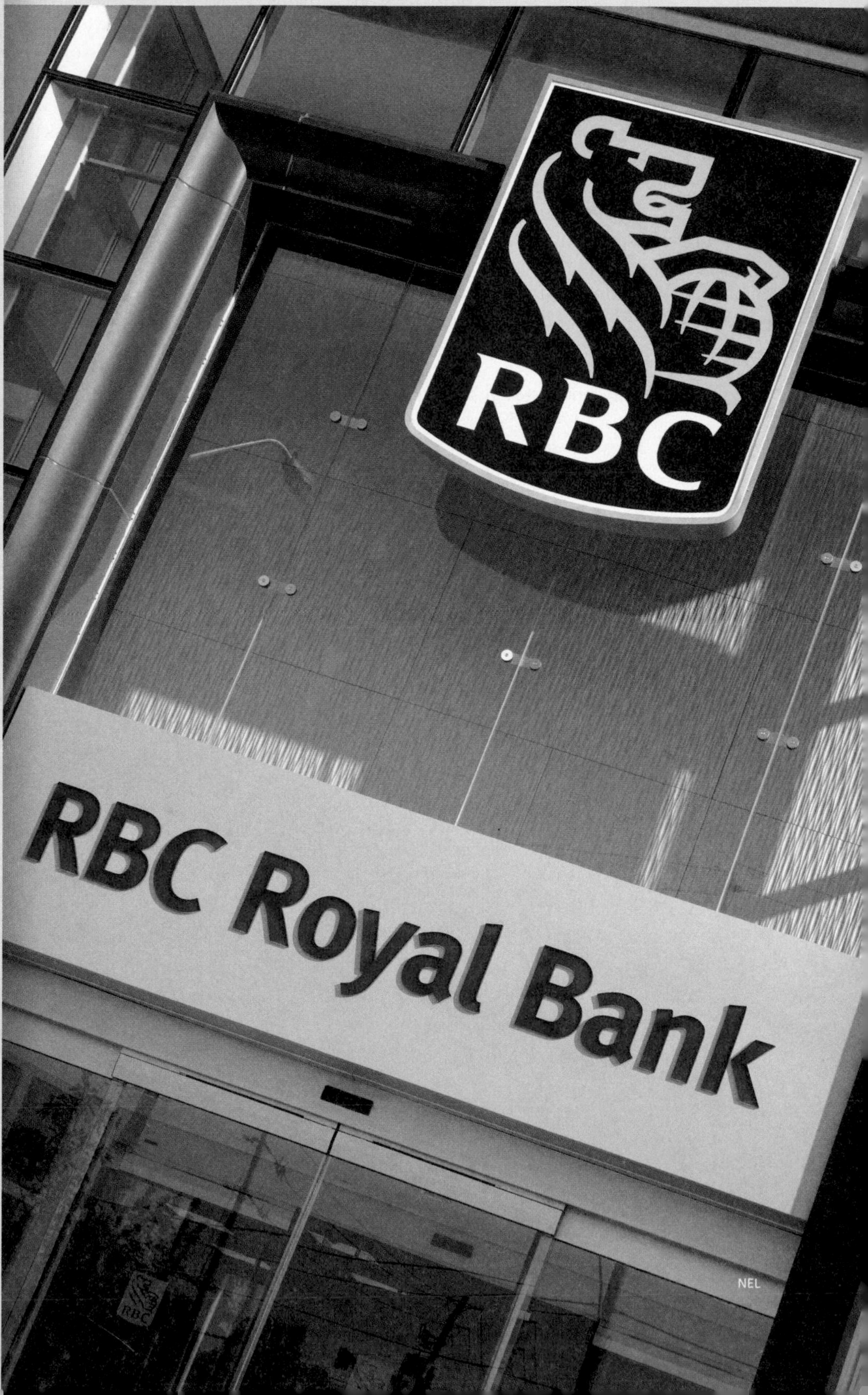

Helen Sessions/Alamy

EXPERIENCE FINANCIAL ACCOUNTING
with Royal Bank of Canada

The Royal Bank of Canada (RY on TSX and NYSE) and its subsidiaries operate under the master brand name RBC.

- RBC is one of Canada's largest banks as measured by assets and market capitalization and is among the largest banks in the world based on market capitalization.

- RBC is one of North America's leading diversified financial services companies and provides personal and commercial banking, wealth management services, insurance, corporate and investment banking, and investor services on a global basis.

- RBC has around 80,000 full- and part-time employees, who serve more than 16 million personal, business, public sector, and institutional clients through offices in Canada, the United States, and 37 other countries.

RBC operates through the following five business segments, which offer a variety of investments to their customers:

1. *Wealth Management* serves high-net-worth and ultra-high-net-worth clients in Canada, the United States, and selected regions outside North America through a full suite of investment, trust, and other

Courtesy Royal Bank of Canada

wealth management solutions and businesses that provide asset management products and services.

2. *Investor & Treasury Services* serves the needs of institutional investing clients and provides custodial, advisory, financing, and other services for clients to safeguard assets, maximize liquidity, and manage risk in multiple jurisdictions around the world.

3. *Capital Markets* comprises certain of RBC's global wholesale banking businesses, which provide corporate and investment banking, sales and trading, and research and related products and services to public and private companies, institutional investors, governments, and central banks.

4. *Insurance* offers life, health, property, and casualty insurance products to individual and group clients across Canada.

5. *Personal & Commercial Banking* comprises RBC's personal banking operations and certain retail investment businesses in Canada, the Caribbean, and the United States as well as RBC's commercial and corporate banking operations in Canada and the Caribbean.

WHY INVESTMENTS ARE MADE

A company's investments may be broadly classified as strategic or nonstrategic. When a company has temporary excess cash that is not required for short-term operations, it may make a nonstrategic investment in order to earn investment income that provides a greater rate of return on those funds than a regular bank account. Companies with seasonal business operations typically find that they have excess cash available for investment. Most financial institutions in Canada provide investment services for their clients.

Alternatively, companies may make longer-term strategic investments in order to be able to control another company's net assets. Companies may acquire influence or control over another company's net assets in order to increase sales (by eliminating a competitor), to secure a raw material source (by acquiring a supplier), or to grow revenues (by acquiring a company's net assets whose services may be leveraged and sold to an existing customer base). Influence or control over another company is usually obtained by purchasing that company's voting common shares, since preferred shares outstanding, if any, are typically nonvoting. The accounting for investments is determined by various factors, including whether the investment is strategic or nonstrategic.

Although companies can invest in virtually any asset (such as land or commodities), here we will concentrate on the most common investments—buying debt or equity securities.

- *Debt Securities*: A **debt security** exists when another entity owes the security holder some combination of interest and principal. Debt securities include bonds, term deposits, guaranteed investment certificates, commercial paper, and other varieties of debt securities.
- *Equity Securities*: An **equity security** represents an ownership interest in a corporation. Equity securities are common and preferred shares. Equity securities bear more risk than debt securities since original investment and ongoing investment returns are not assured. Investors in equity securities expect to earn dividend income and capital appreciation over time.

CLASSIFICATION OF INVESTMENTS

Nonstrategic investments may be in the form of debt or equity. A company that invests in debt usually earns interest income. A company that invests in preferred shares typically earns dividend income. The classification of nonstrategic investments as short- or long-term on the statement of financial position depends on the length of time that management intends to own the investment and the degree of liquidity of that investment.

Strategic investments usually only consist of common shares. The ownership of such shares allows the owner to exercise the voting rights attached to those shares. Since preferred shares are typically nonvoting, they are not generally useful in obtaining influence or control over another company. Strategic investments, due to their nature, are classified as long-term investments on the statement of financial position. The accounting method used for long-term investments depends on the extent of the ownership. These methods are discussed later in this chapter.

IFRS 9, as currently proposed, requires that debt and equity instruments be accounted for under one of two accounting models—fair value through profit or loss and fair value through other comprehensive income (OCI).

ACCOUNTING AND REPORTING FOR NONSTRATEGIC INVESTMENTS

The accounting profession has been thinking for some time about how nonstrategic investments should be accounted for in financial statements. In this regard, IFRS is continuously evolving. IFRS 9—Financial Instruments was scheduled for implementation effective January 1, 2013, with early adoption encouraged, but this date was initially extended to January 1, 2015, and most recently to January 1, 2018, with early adoption permitted. IFRS 9 replaces IAS 39. The material in this text is based on the version of IFRS 9 approved as of the writing of this text due to its imminent implementation.

Accounting Models

Several models exist for accounting for nonstrategic investments subsequent to acquisition. A review of four models follows below.

1. Amortized Cost Model Investments are recorded at cost when acquired. Realized gains and losses on disposition, as well as interest income, together with appropriate amortization of premiums and discounts, are recognized in the statement of earnings. Due to the amortization of discounts and premiums, the **amortized cost method** closely parallels the accounting for long-term liabilities described in Chapter 9. The investment's carrying value is not adjusted to fair market value unless it is impaired, as discussed previously in relation to impairment on property. Unrealized gains and losses are not recognized under this method. Cornerstone 12.1 shows the effective interest rate method of discount amortization for a bond investment.

Effective Interest Rate Method of Bond Amortization

CORNERSTONE 12.1

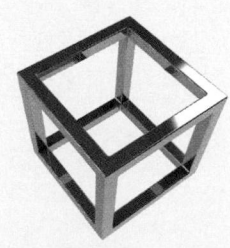

Information:

On January 1, 2018, ABC Corporation purchased a $100,000, 5% bond from XYZ Corporation for $97,291 due December 31, 2020. Interest is paid semiannually. This bond investment will yield 6%.

Required:

1. Record the purchase of the bond on January 1, 2018.

2. Record interest received and bond amortization on June 30, 2020.

3. Record interest received and bond amortization on December 31, 2020.

CORNERSTONE
VIDEO

Why:

The effective interest rate method of bond amortization is required under IFRS.

Solution:

The carrying value of the bond purchased by ABC Corporation is calculated below.

Date	Cash Received	Interest Income	Bond Discount Amortized	Bond Carrying Value
1/1/2018				$ 97,291
6/30/2018	$ 2,500[1]	$ 2,919[2]	$ 419[3]	97,710[4]
12/31/2018	2,500	2,931	431	98,141
6/30/2019	2,500	2,944	444	98,585
12/31/2019	2,500	2,958	458	99,043
6/30/2020	2,500	2,971	471	99,514
12/31/2020	2,500	2,986	486	100,000
	$15,000	$17,709	$2,709	

(Continued)

Date	Transaction	Debit	Credit
Jan. 1, 2018	Investment in XYZ Corporation Bonds	97,291	
	Cash		97,291
	(To record purchase of bonds)		
Jun. 30, 2018	Cash	2,500	
	Bond receivable	419	
	Interest income		2,919
	(To record cash payment received, interest income, and bond amortization)		
Dec. 31, 2018	Cash	2,500	
	Bond receivable	431	
	Interest income		2,931
	(To record cash payment received, interest income, and bond amortization)		

Notes:
1. $\$100,000 \times 5\% \times 6/12$
2. $\$97,291 \times 3\%$
3. $\$2,919 - \$2,500 = \$419$
4. $\$97,291 + \$419 = \$97,710$

2. Fair Value through Profit or Loss Investments are recorded at cost when acquired. Subsequent to acquisition, the carrying values of these investments are adjusted to fair market value at each reporting date, with unrealized gains and losses, together with any interest and dividend income, being recognized in the statement of earnings. Realized gains and losses upon investment disposition are recognized in the statement of earnings. Fair market value means the price for which the investor could sell the asset in an orderly transaction between market participants. For most securities, this price is a quoted price on an active market; however, if no active market exists, other techniques are used to estimate the fair market value.

3. Fair Value through Other Comprehensive Income (OCI) Model This model is very similar to the fair value through profit or loss model. The major difference is that, under this model, unrealized gains and losses are not recognized in net income but are recorded directly on the statement of earnings as components of other comprehensive income. The use of this method of recording unrealized gains and losses means that management's evaluation is not affected by these items because they are not a part of recognized net income in the current period. Ultimately, when these investments are sold, the unrealized gains and losses are reversed from comprehensive income and are recycled directly to retained earnings, thereby entirely passing by the statement of earnings. This model does not exist under ASPE, since those standards do not contain an "other comprehensive income" component. Intermediate accounting courses address this topic in more detail.

4. Cost The cost model is also known as the cost method. Investments are recorded at cost at acquisition. This model is similar to the amortized cost model except that there are no adjustments for premiums or discounts because this model is used only for equity investments. Dividend income and realized gains and losses are recognized in the statement of earnings. A major change under the IFRS 9 standard is that the cost model for equity securities, where there is not an active market, is not allowed. ASPE does allow the cost model in these circumstances.

While the accounting models to be used for non-strategic investments have been in transition for some time, the fair value through profit or loss model generally is to be used to account for nonstrategic investments, although IFRS 9 does allow an election to use fair value through other comprehensive income in specific circumstances. Intermediate accounting courses discuss the various accounting implications of IFRS 9.

The amortized cost and fair value through profit or loss methods are explained below, using Redbird Corporation. A summary of these two accounting models for nonstrategic investments follows in Exhibit 12.1.

Purchase of Bonds On December 31, 2018, Redbird Corporation purchases 10-year, 5% bonds with a face value of $100,000 for $96,000 cash, which reflects a bond discount of $4,000. Bond discount is a contra account, which offsets bond receivable in the statement of financial position. Redbird records the purchase with the following journal entry:

Dec. 31, 2018	Long-term Investments—Bonds	100,000	
	Cash		96,000
	Bond discount		4,000
	(Record purchase of bonds at discount)		

Assets	= Liabilities +	Shareholders' Equity
+96,000		
−96,000		

Receipt of Interest Payment These bonds pay interest of $2,500 ($100,000 × 5% × 6/12) every six months. Additionally, you will recall from Chapter 9 that any premium or discount must be amortized over the life of the bond. For simplicity, we will amortize the discount on a straight-line basis. This results in discount amortization of $200 {[($100,000 − $96,000)/10 years] × 6/12} every six months. The following entries are therefore necessary to record receipt of the interest payments during 2019:

June 30, 2019	Cash	2,500	
	Bond discount	200	
	Interest Income		2,700
	(Record receipt of interest payment and bond discount amortization)		

Assets	= Liabilities +	Shareholders' Equity
+2,500		+2,700
+200		

Dec. 31, 2019	Cash	2,500	
	Bond discount	200	
	Interest Income		2,700
	(Record receipt of interest payment and bond discount amortization)		

Assets	= Liabilities +	Shareholders' Equity
+2,500		
+200		+2,700

The same entries will be made each year to record receipt of the interest payments.

(EXHIBIT 12.1)

Accounting Models for Nonstrategic Investments

Investment Type	Valuation Model	Accounting Method after Acquisition	Reporting of Dividends, Interest Income, Realized Gains and Losses	Reporting of Unrealized Gains and Losses
1. Debt and Equity	Fair Value through Profit or Loss	Fair Value through Profit or Loss	Report in statement of earnings as other revenues, expenses, gains, or losses as appropriate*	Report in statement of earnings as other revenues, expenses, gains, or losses as appropriate*
2. Debt	Amortized cost	Amortized cost	Report in statement of earnings as other revenues, expenses, gains, or losses as appropriate	Not recognized

*IFRS 9 allows an election whereby gains and losses on specified securities can be reported in other comprehensive income (OCI). Otherwise IFRS generally only allows the use the the fair value through profit and loss model for non-strategic investments and prohibits the use of the amortized cost model.

Reporting in the Financial Statements As shown in the preceding entries, at December 31, 2019, $400 of the discount has been amortized to the investment account. This means the carrying value of the long-term bond investment is $96,400 ($96,000 + $400). However, assume that the fair market value of these bonds is $98,000 at December 31, 2019. The 2019 financial statements will report this investment as follows:

Redbird Corporation Partial Statement of Financial Position At December 31, 2019	
Noncurrent assets:	
Investments, net of unamortized discount	$96,400

Redbird Corporation Partial Statement of Earnings For the Year Ended December 31, 2019	
Interest income	$5,400

Because the market value of Redbird's investment is $1,600 ($98,000 − $96,400) more than its carrying value, there is an unrealized gain of $1,600. The rationale for not recognizing unrealized gains or losses on debt investments that earn interest to maturity is that changes in market value do not affect the amount that is realized from such investments. If securities are held to maturity, the amount that is realized is the face value—as determined by the debt agreement.

Receipt of Principal Payment At Maturity When the bonds mature on December 31, 2028, the following journal entry is made:

Assets	= Liabilities +	Shareholders' Equity
+100,000		
−100,000		

Dec. 31, 2028   Cash   100,000
                          Long-term Investments—Bonds   100,000
                          (*Record receipt of principal payment*)

Note that this entry zeros out the investment account because, at maturity, the discount has been fully amortized, which makes the balance in the investment account equal to the face value of the bonds.

Investments Sold Before Maturity If the above bond is sold for $105,000 on January 1, 2020, the following journal entry will be recorded:

Assets	= Liabilities +	Shareholders' Equity (Gain on Sale)
+105,000		+8,600
−96,400		

Date	Account and Explanation	Debit	Credit
Jan. 1, 2020	Cash	105,000	
	Long-term Investments—Bonds		96,400
	Gain realized on sale		8,600

The realized gain will be reported as other revenues and gains on the statement of earnings.

Fair Value through Profit or Loss Method

Nonstrategic investments (debt and equity) generally are to be accounted for by the fair value through profit or loss method under IFRS 9. The fair value through profit or loss method means the investment is valued at the price for which the investor could sell the asset in an orderly transaction between market participants.

Purchase of Securities Investments acquired are recorded at cost, which is also fair value on the date of purchase. To illustrate, on August 1, 2018, Redbird Corporation made the following purchases of securities:

Security	Type	Amount
MMD Enterprises	Equity	$10,000
Marcel Design	Debt	6,000
IMG	Equity	4,100
Total Trading Securities		**$20,100**

These acquisitions are recorded by the following journal entry:

Date	Account and Explanation	Debit	Credit
Aug. 1, 2018	Investments—MMD Enterprises	10,000	
	Investments—Marcel Design	6,000	
	Investments—IMG	4,100	
	Cash		20,100
	(*Record purchase of investments*)		

			Shareholders'
Assets	= Liabilities +		Equity
+20,100			
−20,100			

Receipt of Dividend Payment On September 30, 2018, Redbird received cash dividends of $500 from IMG which were recorded by the following journal entry:[1]

Date	Account and Explanation	Debit	Credit
Sept. 30, 2018	Cash	500	
	Dividend Income		500
	(*Record receipt of dividend*)		

			Shareholders' Equity (Dividend
Assets	= Liabilities +		Income)
+500			+500

Selling Securities On December 20, 2018, the market price of IMG shares had climbed to $4,900, and Redbird decided to sell its entire holding. The following journal entry records the sale:

Date	Account and Explanation	Debit	Credit
Dec. 20, 2018	Cash	4,900	
	Investments—IMG		4,100
	Securities—IMG		
	Gain on Sale of Investments		800
	(*Record sale of security*)		

			Shareholders' Equity (Gain on Sale of
Assets	= Liabilities +		Investments)
+4,900			+800
−4,100			

The $800 gain will be included in Redbird's year-end net income, as will the $500 of dividends received on September 30.

In summary, this investment yielded two forms of income—a dividend ($500) and a gain on sale ($800)—increasing Redbird's net income by $1,300.

Receipt of Interest Payments In addition, Marcel Design paid interest totalling $600 on December 31, 2018. This is recorded with the following journal entry:

Date	Account and Explanation	Debit	Credit
Dec. 31, 2018	Cash	600	
	Interest Income		600
	(*Record receipt of interest payment*)		

			Shareholders' Equity (Interest
Assets	= Liabilities +		Income)
+600			+600

[1] Dividend income should be recognized by investors at the dividend declaration date rather than the dividend payment date. When a cash dividend is declared in one year and paid in the following year, the investor should record the dividend declaration at year-end by a debit to dividends receivable and a credit to dividend income. In the following year, when the related cash is received, the investor should debit cash and credit dividends receivable.

Reporting on the Financial Statements On the statement of financial position, the securities are recorded at fair value. Use of the fair value through profit or loss method results in **unrealized gains** and/or **unrealized losses** because the value of the securities must be written up or down to fair market value at the statement of financial position date (this is often called "marking to market"). For example, consider the securities shown in Exhibit 12.2.

On December 31, Redbird Corporation will make the following entries to "mark the investments to market":

	Shareholders' Equity
Assets = Liabilities +	(Unrealized Loss)
+400	−800
−1,200	

Date	Account and Explanation	Debit	Credit
Dec. 31, 2018	Unrealized Gain (Loss) on Securities*	800	
	Investments—Marcel Design	400	
	Investments—MMD Enterprises		1,200
	(Record trading securities at fair value)		

*Unrealized gains or losses go to the statement of earnings.

At each statement of financial position date, the carrying amounts of each investment are adjusted to reflect the current amount of unrealized gain or loss on each investment. On the statement of financial position, the investment account reports the investments at fair value as follows:

Redbird Corporation
Partial Statement of Financial Position
December 31, 2018

Current assets:	
Securities, at market	$15,200
Shareholders' equity:	
Retained earnings	$ (800)

Redbird Corporation
Partial Statement of Earnings
For the Year Ended December 31, 2018

Other income:	
Interest income	$ 600
Dividend income	500
Gain on sale of investments	800
Other loss:	
Unrealized gain (loss) on securities	(800)

(EXHIBIT 12.2)

Investment Portfolio Data

	Redbird Corporation Investment Portfolio December 31, 2018	
Security	Acquisition Cost	Market Value at 12/31
MMD Enterprises	$ 10,000	$ 8,800
Marcel Design	6,000	6,400
Total Trading Securities	**$16,000**	**$15,200**

Fair Value through Other Comprehensive Income (OCI) Model for Nonstrategic Debt and Equity Investments

A company may own a nonstrategic equity investment that was not acquired for trading. In this situation, instead of using the fair value model, a company can irrevocably elect at the time the security is acquired to account and report for these equity investments using the fair value through OCI model. Intermediate accounting courses review the IFRS 9 accounting implications for non-strategic investments.

ACCOUNT FOR AND REPORT STRATEGIC INVESTMENTS

Three forms of business combinations generally occur. One company may obtain control over the net assets of another company by purchasing its net assets, by acquiring enough of its voting shares to control the use of its net assets, or by obtaining control through a contractual agreement. This text will focus on the situation where control over net assets of another company is acquired through the acquisition of sufficient voting shares of the acquired corporation. Business combinations generally are discussed later in this chapter.

The accounting method to be used for an investment in equity securities depends on the number of common shares owned. The difference in accounting method arises from the nature of influence that the investor (the company that purchased and owns the common shares) has over the investee (the company that issued the common shares).

The guidelines for accounting for strategic investments are set out in Exhibit 12.3.

It is important to note that the presumption of influence may not be valid if other evidence exists to deny it. In addition to the level of voting share ownership, other factors that should be considered in determining the level of influence that in fact exists would include the following:

1. The composition of the investee's Board of Directors, including the extent to which the investor has any representation thereon.
2. The composition of the senior management team, including whether the investor and investee are sharing or otherwise exchanging such personnel.
3. The extent to which material transactions are occurring between the investor and the investee.
4. The extent to which the investor participates in the operating, investing, and financing activities of the investee.
5. The extent to which there is an exchange of scientific, technical, and special knowledge between the investor and the investee.

(EXHIBIT 12.3)

Accounting Guidelines for Strategic Investments

Percentage of Investee Common Shares Owned by Investor	Presumed Level of Influence of Investor	Accounting Method to be Used
Less than 20%	Not significant	Fair value
20 to 50%	Significant	Equity method
More than 50%	Control	Consolidation

Companies are required to use their judgment in determining the appropriate method of accounting for investees in light of all the available information and are not to simply apply the common share ownership criteria in reaching their decision.

Under IFRS, a company whose common shares are owned 20% to 50% by an investor is referred to as an associate. Where an investor owns more than 50% of the common shares in the investee, the investor is referred to as the **parent** company and the investee as the **subsidiary** company. Where one company controls one or more companies, the parent company is required to prepare consolidated financial statements to reflect, for the benefit of the parent company shareholders, all the assets, liabilities, revenues, and expenses over which management has control. In summary, the consolidation process results in replacing the investment in subsidiary account with the subsidiary's assets and liabilities. Consolidated financial statements are discussed later in this chapter and are studied in detail in advanced financial accounting courses.

THE COST METHOD OF ACCOUNTING

The fair value model must be used to account for strategic equity securities where the common share ownership percentage is under 20%, *even if an active market for these shares does not exist.* In this situation, other methods must be used to value the securities. The cost model (also known as the cost method) cannot be used for this type of strategic equity investment under IFRS, but the cost model can be used under ASPE for this type of investment where shares are not quoted in an active market.

The equity method of accounting is required to be used for strategic investments when significant influence exists under IFRS. The consolidation method of accounting is required to be used for strategic investments where control exists over those investments under IFRS.

Investors have a choice under ASPE to use either the cost or equity method of accounting for investments where significant influence exists and where the investments are not actively traded. For many private companies this choice is a reasonable one since in those situations the investors typically prepare the financial statements mainly for income tax purposes. Since the profit under the equity method is not taxable, use of the equity method by investors would usually not make sense. One should note that if the shares of the investee are actively traded, the investor then has the option under ASPE of accounting for the investment using either the equity method or fair value model.

Under the cost method of accounting, the investment is recorded at cost at the date of acquisition and is not adjusted until the investment is ultimately sold. Dividends declared by the investee are recorded by the investor as dividend income. The balance of the investment account is recorded at historical cost in the statement of financial position. Examples of the required journal entries for the typical transactions under the cost method of accounting follow.

Date of Acquisition of Shares

On January 1, 2018, Bluejay Inc. (a private company) purchased 10% of the common shares of Lassoo Inc. for $800,000 cash. We will assume that Bluejay does not intend to trade the shares in Lassoo and that the shares of Lassoo are not actively traded. As a result, the cost method should be used to account for this investment.

This investment would be recorded by Bluejay Inc. as follows:

	Shareholders'
Assets = Liabilities +	Equity
+800,000	
−800,000	

Date	Account and Explanation	Debit	Credit
Jan. 1, 2018	Investment in Lassoo at cost	800,000	
	Cash		800,000
	(Record purchase of Lassoo shares)		

This investment is initially recorded at cost, similar to the amortized cost and fair value methods.

Investee Income and Dividends

In 2018 and during the period of ownership, Lassoo Inc. earned $1,000,000 in net income. On January 1, 2019, Lassoo Inc. declared a total common share dividend of $400,000 payable on February 15, 2019. The journal entries that Bluejay would record are as follows:

Date	Account and Explanation	Debit	Credit
Jan. 1, 2019	Dividend Receivable	40,000	
	Dividend Income		40,000
	(*Record dividend income*)		

Assets	= Liabilities +	Shareholders' Equity (Dividend Income)
+40,000		
		+40,000

Dividend income is recognized to the extent of ownership on the date of declaration, being $400,000 \times 10\% = \$40,000$.

Date	Account and Explanation	Debit	Credit
Feb. 15, 2019	Cash	40,000	
	Dividend Receivable		40,000
	(*Record receipt of dividend*)		

Assets	= Liabilities +	Shareholders' Equity
+40,000		
−40,000		

Sale of Investment in Shares

Assume that Bluejay sells its investment in Lassoo on January 1, 2020, for $950,000. Bluejay will record the following journal entry:

Date	Account and Explanation	Debit	Credit
Jan. 1, 2020	Cash	950,000	
	Investment in Lassoo		800,000
	Realized Gain on Sale		150,000
	(*Record sale of investment*)		

Assets	= Liabilities +	Shareholders' Equity (Gain on Sale)
+950,000		
−800,000		
		+150,000

The sale of an investment in shares will result in a realized gain or loss. A realized gain would be recorded in the other revenues and gains section of the statement of earnings. A realized loss would be recorded in the other expenses and losses section of the statement of earnings.

Reporting on the Financial Statements during the Period of Ownership

Net earnings of the investee are not recognized by Bluejay as they are earned. Dividend income is recognized by Bluejay on the accrual basis. Dividend income from Lassoo would be reported as other revenue on the statement of earnings. The investment in Lassoo is recorded in an investment account separate from securities that are held for trading purposes and which are actively quoted. The investment account would be reported as a noncurrent asset on the statement of financial position of Bluejay.

If Bluejay eventually increased its ownership in Lassoo from 10% to between 20% and 50%, then Bluejay under ASPE could elect to report its investment in Lassoo using either the cost or equity methods.

The Equity Method of Accounting

When the investor possesses significant influence over the operating and financial policies of the investee (e.g., 20% to 50% common share ownership), the investor must use the *equity method* to account for the investment under IFRS. The **equity method** requires an investor to recognize income when it is reported as earned by the investee, rather than when dividends accrue. The earlier recognition of investment income and loss under the equity method is consistent with the close relationship between the investor and investee.

An investment in the common shares of an investee (called an "Associate") under the equity method is recorded at cost in an account called Investment in Associates. The balance of the Investment in Associates account is adjusted annually for the investor's share of changes in the equity of the associate. If the associate earns a profit, the Investment in Associates account is debited for its share of the profit earned by the associate and a revenue account is credited. If the associate incurs a loss, the Investment in Associates account is credited for its share of the loss incurred by the associate and a loss account is debited. If the associate declares a dividend, then the Investment in Associates account is decreased to recognize its share of the dividend declared by the associate. Note that unlike the cost method, dividends declared by an associate are not recorded as income under the equity method. This difference arises because under the equity method of accounting, the underlying income that forms the basis of the dividend has been previously recognized by the investor as part of the accrual-of-earnings process. Therefore, to record the dividend in income under the equity method in addition to the underlying earnings that had been previously recognized would represent an error in that a double-counting of the same income would occur.

Cornerstone 12.2 shows how the equity method of accounting is applied.

CORNERSTONE 12.2   Using the Equity Method of Accounting

CORNERSTONE VIDEO

Information:

Bass Corporation purchased 35% of the common shares of Perch Corporation for $10,000,000 on January 1, 2018. During 2018, Perch Corporation earned net income of $3,000,000; Perch paid a total common share dividend of $600,000 on December 31, 2018.

Required:

Calculate the carrying value of the investment in Perch at December 31, 2018.

Why:

The equity method of accounting for associates under IFRS is a one-line consolidation methodology.

Solution:

The carrying value of Bass Corporation's investment in Perch Corporation at December 31, 2018, would be calculated as follows:

Transactions		Journal Entries	
Purchase cost of investment December 1, 2018	$10,000,000	Debit Investment in Perch	10,000,000
Add:		Credit Cash	10,000,000
Share of 2018 net income of Perch		Debit Investment in Perch	1,050,000
$3,000,000 × 35% =	1,050,000	Credit Investment income	1,050,000
Deduct:		Debit Cash	210,000
Share of 2018 dividend declared and paid by Perch		Credit Investment in Perch	210,000
$600,000 × 35% =	(210,000)		
Bass Corporation carrying value of investment in Perch Corporation at December 31, 2018	$10,840,000		

Date of Acquisition of Shares On January 1, 2018, Redbird purchases 25% of the common shares of one of its major suppliers—Korsgard Mining, a newly formed corporation—for $4,000,000 cash. Redbird will record the purchase with the following journal entry:

Date	Account and Explanation	Debit	Credit
Jan. 1, 2018	Investment in Korsgard—Equity Method	4,000,000	
	Cash		4,000,000
	(Record purchase of Korsgard shares)		

Assets	= Liabilities +	Shareholders' Equity
+4,000,000		
−4,000,000		

Note that the investment is initially recorded at cost, just as it is in the amortized cost and fair value methods. In addition, the investment is recorded in a separate account and not with securities held for trading purposes.

Investee Income and Dividends On November 1, 2018, Korsgard declared and paid a cash dividend of $60,000. Furthermore, for the year ended December 31, 2018, Korsgard reported net income of $440,000. Under the equity method, these events will have the following effect on Redbird's accounts:

Date	Account and Explanation	Debit	Credit
Nov. 1, 2018	Cash*	15,000	
	Investment in Korsgard—Equity Method		15,000
	(Record receipt of dividends)		

Assets	= Liabilities +	Shareholders' Equity
+15,000		
−15,000		

*25% × $60,000 = $15,000

Date	Account and Explanation	Debit	Credit
Dec. 31, 2018	Investment in Korsgard—Equity Method**	110,000	
	Investment Income—Equity Method		110,000
	(Record Redbird's share of Korsgard net income)		

Assets	= Liabilities +	Shareholders' Equity
+110,000		+110,000

**25% × $440,000 = $110,000

Unlike the fair value method, the equity method recognizes income when income is earned by the investee, not when a dividend is declared and paid. Instead, the dividend paid by Korsgard is a distribution to owners and therefore reduces the amount of Redbird's investment.

Reporting on the Financial Statements Equity method investments are carried on the statement of financial position as follows:

Acquisition cost + Investor's share of the investee's income (loss)
− Investor's share of the investee's dividends

This means the investment account is not adjusted for changes in the fair market value of the common shares. Redbird will account for its investment in Korsgard as follows:

Investments—Equity Method (Korsgard Mining)

Purchase of Korsgard shares, 1/1/18	4,000,000	Receipt of Korsgard dividends, 11/1/18	15,000
Redbird's share of Korsgard net income, 12/31/18	110,000		
	4,095,000		

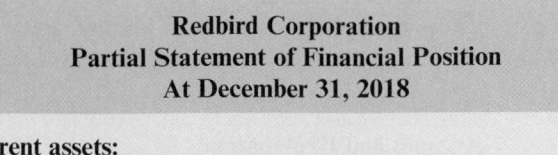

Redbird Corporation Partial Statement of Financial Position At December 31, 2018	
Noncurrent assets:	
Investments—Equity Method (Korsgard Mining)	$4,095,000

Redbird Corporation Partial Statement of Earnings For the Year Ended December 31, 2018	
Investment Income—Equity Method (Korsgard)	$110,000

One advantage of the equity method over the cost method is that it prevents an investor from manipulating its own income by exerting influence over the amount and timing of investee dividends.

The choice of accounting methods for investments can influence the amounts that a company reports as profit and as the carrying value of its assets. Therefore the decision as to whether investments are strategic or nonstrategic is important, as is the decision as to whether a company has significant influence over an investee.

CONSOLIDATED FINANCIAL STATEMENTS

OBJECTIVE 4

Describe the consolidated statement of financial position and statement of earnings.

If the investor holds enough common shares to control the investee (more than 50% common share ownership), then the two corporations are no longer considered separate accounting entities. In such cases the investor must prepare **consolidated financial statements**, which combine information about the two corporations as if they were a single economic entity. In this case the investor is referred to as the parent and the investee is called the subsidiary. Of course, the parent and subsidiary continue to maintain separate accounting records for legal and tax purposes.

Preparing Consolidated Statements

Consolidated financial statements are prepared from information contained in the separate financial statements of the parent and subsidiary using the acquisition method:

- The consolidated statement of financial position is essentially the same as the parent's statement of financial position, except the parent's "investment in subsidiary" account is replaced by the subsidiary's assets and liabilities.
- The consolidated statement of earnings is essentially the parent's statement of earnings, except the parent's "income from subsidiary" is replaced by the subsidiary's revenues and expenses.

Consolidated Statement of Financial Position To illustrate the preparation of consolidated statements of financial position, consider the following situation in which a parent owns 100% of the outstanding shares of its subsidiary.[2]

On January 1, 2018, Parent Inc. purchases all the outstanding common shares of Sub Corporation for $2,750,000 cash, which represents the fair value of Sub Corporation's identifiable assets and liabilities. In this case, since Parent has control over Sub, a consolidated statement of financial position needs to be prepared from the individual statements of financial position of both companies. To do so, a **consolidation worksheet** is usually

---

[2] Many large corporations have a complex network of many subsidiaries. However, for the sake of simplicity, the examples here discuss a two-corporation structure involving one parent and one subsidiary.

prepared. Exhibit 12.4 presents the worksheet that is used to prepare the consolidated statement of financial position for Parent and Sub at acquisition. The corporate statements of financial position for Parent and Sub are listed in the two left-hand columns of the worksheet. Consolidation adjustments are entered into the third column. The amounts in the fourth column can be computed by adding the first two columns and the adjustments.

As you can see in Exhibit 12.4, the consolidation of these two statements of financial position requires a credit adjustment that eliminates Parent's Investment in Sub account. This is offset by debits to the Common Shares and Retained Earnings accounts, which eliminate the related shareholders' equity of Sub. These worksheet adjustments are not recorded in the accounting records of either Parent or Sub.

Consolidated Statement of Earnings Just as a consolidation worksheet was used to prepare the consolidated statement of financial position for Parent and Sub, a similar worksheet must be prepared for the consolidated statement of earnings. Exhibit 12.5 presents the worksheet that is used to prepare the consolidated statement of earnings for Parent and Sub one year after acquisition.

Notice that where the parent company is using the equity method that the consolidated net income is exactly the same as Parent's net income. From Parent's viewpoint, the consolidation procedure does not change net income, only the revenues and expenses on which net income is based. The credit needed to offset the $600,000 debit adjustment (and keep everything in balance) occurs on the statement of financial position—against the Investment in Sub account. Preparation of the consolidated statement of financial position on December 31, 2018, one year after the acquisition, follows the same principles. However, it is complicated by Parent's equity method journal entries. Furthermore, adjustments are required to eliminate any transactions between Parent and Sub (such as the sale or other transfer of assets). Because you cannot make a sale to yourself, such transactions between the two corporations must be eliminated to present the two corporations as a single accounting entity.

Reporting a Minority or Noncontrolling Interest

Consolidation accounting is a complex matter when it involves accounting for noncontrolling (or minority) interests, intercompany profits and losses, and goodwill. Noncontrolling (or minority) interest must be disclosed where the parent owns more than 50% but less than 100% of the common shares of the investee.

(EXHIBIT 12.4)

Worksheet for Preparing the Consolidated Statement of Financial Position on January 1, 2018

	Parent	Sub	Adjustments		Consolidated
			Debit	Credit	
Assets:					
Current assets	$ 9,250,000	$ 700,000			$ 9,950,000
Investment—equity method	2,750,000			2,750,000	—
Property, plant, and equipment	68,000,000	2,300,000			70,300,000
Total assets	$80,000,000	$3,000,000			$80,250,000
Liabilities	$10,000,000	$ 250,000			$10,250,000
Shareholders' equity					
Common shares	40,000,000	1,000,000	1,000,000		40,000,000
Retained earnings	30,000,000	1,750,000	1,750,000		30,000,000
Total liabilities and shareholders' equity	$80,000,000	$3,000,000			$80,250,000

EXHIBIT 12.5

Worksheet for Preparing the Consolidated Statement of Earnings on December 31, 2018

	Parent	Sub	Adjustments Debit	Adjustments Credit	Consolidated
Revenue	$9,000,000	$2,000,000			$11,000,000
Cost of goods sold	3,200,000	950,000			4,150,000
Depreciation expense	2,100,000	220,000			2,320,000
Other expenses	1,600,000	230,000			1,830,000
Investment income—equity method	600,000		600,000		
Net income	$2,700,000	$ 600,000			$ 2,700,000

Consolidation is required when a parent acquires between 50% and 100% of the subsidiary's shares. Any voting shares not held by the parent are called the **minority interest** or **noncontrolling interest**, and the holders of such shares are called minority or noncontrolling interest shareholders. However, even when the parent owns less than 100% of the subsidiary's shares, 100% of the subsidiary's assets and liabilities are included on the consolidated statement of financial position. In other words, if the parent controls the subsidiary, it controls *all* of the subsidiary's assets and liabilities.

For example, assume Parent had acquired only 80% of Sub. The consolidated total assets would still be $80,250,000 because Parent controls all of the assets of Sub. However, the minority interest would be $550,000 [20% × ($1,000,000 + $1,750,000)] and this amount must be shown as a component of shareholders' equity on the consolidated statement of financial position. Furthermore, the consolidated statement of earnings will show 100% of Sub's revenues and expenses, but 20% of net income will be disclosed as belonging to the noncontrolling interest.

BUSINESS COMBINATIONS

Any transaction or set of transactions that brings together two or more previously separate entities to form a single accounting entity is called a **business combination**. Business combinations take many forms. Some, like Parent–Sub described in the previous section, involve the acquisition of another corporation's shares in exchange for cash. Others involve the acquisition of another corporation's shares with the parent's own common shares. In either case, these are called **share acquisitions** because the shares of the other corporation are being acquired. The parent could also purchase some or all of the assets of the other corporation. This is referred to as an **asset acquisition**. Both types of transactions are referred to as business combinations.

Business combinations usually, but not always, transfer ownership of the acquired business entity from one shareholder group to another. In general, purchased assets are recorded at current cost, which is measured as the fair value of the cash and other consideration given up to acquire the asset. Thus, a purchased asset is recorded at its current value to the purchaser, without regard to its recorded value to the seller. Applying this logic to a business combination, a purchased company must be recorded at the value of the cash and other consideration given by the acquiring company.

To illustrate, consider the acquisition of all the assets and liabilities (i.e., an asset acquisition) of Landron Bottling Works by CactusCo for $12,000,000. With the approval of Landron's shareholders and creditors, Landron transfers all of its assets and liabilities to CactusCo and distributes the cash to Landron's shareholders. On the acquisition date, Landron's shareholders' equity was $6,500,000. CactusCo determines that Landron's liabilities of $1,000,000 are correctly valued, but its identifiable assets have a fair value of $3,800,000 more than their book value of $7,500,000. Thus, the acquisition cost exceeds the fair value of the net assets (assets minus liabilities) acquired by $1,700,000:

Acquisition cost			$12,000,000
Current value of identifiable net assets acquired:			
Book value of assets acquired	$7,500,000		
Adjustment to current value	3,800,000	$11,300,000	
Less:			
Book value of liabilities acquired	(1,000,000)		
Adjustment to current value	0	(1,000,000)	(10,300,000)
Excess of acquisition cost over current value (goodwill)			$ 1,700,000

The excess of acquisition cost over the fair value of Landron's identifiable net assets is recorded as goodwill. **Goodwill** is an intangible asset arising from attributes that are not separable from the business—such as customer satisfaction, product quality, skilled employees, and business location. CactusCo's recording of the acquisition will be recorded with the following journal entry:

Account and Explanation	Debit	Credit
Assets (various accounts)	11,300,000	
Goodwill	1,700,000	
Liabilities (various accounts)		1,000,000
Cash		12,000,000
(Record the acquisition of Landron's net assets)		

Assets	= Liabilities +	Shareholders' Equity
+11,300,000	+1,000,000	
+1,700,000		
−12,000,000		

This entry assumes that Landron goes out of existence as a corporation. If, instead of selling its net assets to CactusCo, Landron shareholders sell all their shares (as in a share acquisition) to CactusCo, Landron will continue as a legal entity and the journal entry will be as follows:

Account and Explanation	Debit	Credit
Investment in Landron—Equity Method	12,000,000	
Cash		12,000,000
(Record the acquisition of Landron's shares)		

Assets	= Liabilities +	Shareholders' Equity
+12,000,000		
−12,000,000		

In this case, CactusCo must also consolidate Landron's financial statements, substituting the detailed assets (including goodwill) and liabilities for the investment account in Landron. The financial statements for a 100% asset acquisition will be identical to the consolidated financial statements for a 100% share acquisition.

SIGNIFICANT DIFFERENCES BETWEEN IFRS AND ASPE

The main differences between IFRS and ASPE are as follows:

1. IFRS requires bond premium and discount to be amortized using the effective interest method. ASPE allows alternative methods of amortization of bond premium and discount, including the straight-line method, to be used if the resulting difference in amortization is not materially different from the effective interest method.

2. IFRS requires investments in associates to be recorded using the equity method. ASPE allows a choice between the equity and cost methods if shares for associate companies do not have quoted market prices. If shares do have quoted market prices, ASPE allows a choice between the equity and fair value methods for investments in associate companies.

3. IFRS requires consolidation of financial statements where an investor controls an investee. Under ASPE, where control exists, accounting alternatives generally allowed include the consolidation, equity and cost methods.

4. IFRS allows fair value accounting through other comprehensive income in specified circumstances whereas ASPE prohibits this accounting since ASPE does not recognize other comprehensive income.

SUMMARY OF LEARNING OBJECTIVES

LO1.   Classify investments as strategic or nonstrategic.

- There are four possible methods of accounting for nonstrategic investments.
  - The fair value through profit and loss method must generally be used for both debt and equity securities under IFRS 9.
  - The cost model under ASPE can be used when an investment was not acquired to trade and an active market does not exist for the security. IFRS does not allow the cost method in these circumstances.
- There are three methods of accounting for strategic investments using IFRS:
  - Consolidation is required when the investor owns more than 50% of the voting common shares of the investee.
  - The fair value method is to be used when the investor owns less than 20% of the investee's voting common shares.
  - The equity method is used for equity securities in which 20% to 50% of the outstanding common shares are owned.

LO2.   Account for and report nonstrategic investments.

- Nonstrategic investments are often made to earn investment income on excess cash balances.
- Nonstrategic investments may consist of debt or equity investments.
- Nonstrategic investments may be short-term or long-term in nature.
- Accounting models for nonstrategic investments include amortized cost, fair value through profit or loss, fair value through other comprehensive income, and cost.

LO3.   Account for and report strategic investments.

- Strategic investments are usually made to influence or control another company.
- Strategic investments are classified as long-term investments in the statement of financial position of the investor.
- Accounting models for strategic investments include the fair value, equity, and consolidation methods.
- The extent of ownership typically determines the accounting model to use to account for a strategic investment.

LO4.   Describe the consolidated statement of financial position and statement of earnings.

- When a corporation owns more than 50% of the outstanding common shares of another corporation, the investor (parent) is deemed to control the other corporation (subsidiary).
- In this case, the parent is required to issue consolidated financial statements in which the parent's and subsidiary's financial statements are combined.
- Noncontrolling (or minority) interest is disclosed when the parent owns more than 50%, but less than 100% of the outstanding common shares.

LO5.   Describe accounting for business combinations.

- Business combinations can occur through either an asset or share acquisition.
- The business combination is recorded at the cost of acquisition, without regard to the seller's book value of assets or liabilities.
- The excess of acquisition cost over the fair value of identifiable net assets is recorded as goodwill.

CORNERSTONES

CORNERSTONE 12.1   Effective interest rate method of bond amortization, page 699

CORNERSTONE 12.2   Using the equity method of accounting, page 708

KEY TERMS

DISCUSSION QUESTIONS

1. How do long-term investments differ from short-term investments?
2. Describe two classifications that are possible for nonstrategic investments under IFRS 9?.
3. Describe the amortized cost method of accounting for investments.
4. Describe the fair value through profit and loss method of accounting for investments. Under which circumstances should it be used?

5. Describe the equity method of accounting for investments. Under which circumstances should it be used?

6. What event triggers the recognition of investment income under the amortized cost method? Under the fair value method? Under the equity method?

7. How does the equity method discourage the manipulation of net income by investors?

8. Define the terms *parent* and *subsidiary*.

9. How does the consolidated statement of financial position differ from the statement of financial position of the parent?

10. Why is it necessary to eliminate transactions between the parent and subsidiary in consolidation?

11. What is the difference between an asset acquisition and a share acquisition?

12. What is goodwill, and how is it calculated?

13. What is a business combination?

14. Describe the nature of a subsidiary.

15. Describe the ASPE accounting alternatives for a parent company that owns 100% of a subsidiary.

MULTIPLE-CHOICE EXERCISES

12-1 Equity and debt investments that management intends to sell in the near future are called:
a. trading securities.
b. deferred securities.
c. debt securities.
d. stock securities.

12-2 Which of the following is a reason businesses purchase securities?
a. To profit from changes in day-to-day security prices
b. To diversify risk
c. To save (and earn returns on) money from uneven cash flows
d. All of the above are reasons to purchase securities

12-3 IFRS requires which method to amortize bond premiums/discounts?
a. Straight-line
b. Effective interest
c. Present value
d. Average

12-4 Which method cannot be used to account for nonstrategic investments?
a. Cost
b. Fair value
c. Consolidation
d. Amortized cost

12-5 The equity method requires dividend income to be recorded as:
a. an investment account increase.
b. an investment account decrease.

c. statement of earnings revenue.
d. an increase in retained earnings.

12-6 EMK Corp. is holding two bonds to maturity, both of which have a carrying value of $132,000. At the end of the fiscal year, the fair market value of bond A is $118,000, and the fair market value of bond B is $136,000. What is the unrealized gain or loss recorded by EMK on these two bonds?
a. Unrealized loss of $14,000
b. Unrealized loss of $10,000
c. Unrealized gain of $4,000
d. No unrealized gain or loss

12-7 Shackley Ltd. owns three equity securities held for trading, which have yielded the following fiscal year-end results:
A. Dividend income: $350
B. Gain on sale: $2,000
C. Unrealized loss: $600
Which of these are reported on Shackley's statement of earnings?
a. A and B
b. B only
c. A, B, and C
d. B and C

12-8 Refer to the information in Exercise 12-7. Assume that one of the securities was solely responsible for the $600 unrealized loss and was responsible for $150 of the dividend income. If

Shackley bought that security for $3,500, what is the value of the security on the year-end statement of financial position?

a. $3,500
b. $3,050
c. $3,650
d. $2,900

12-9 PET Inc. buys 30% of the outstanding shares of KLN Company. What account will PET debit?

a. Trading Securities
b. Investments—Consolidation Method
c. Investments—Equity Method
d. Investments—Cost Method

12-10 Whopper Corporation owns a 40% interest in BigMac Corporation, which it purchased for $2.5 million. During fiscal year 2018, BigMac paid cash dividends of $50,000 and reported net income of $700,000. What is the value of Whopper's investment in BigMac reported on its 2018 statement of financial position?

a. $3,150,000
b. $2,500,000
c. $2,760,000
d. $2,450,000

12-11 When the market value of a company's trading securities is lower than its cost, the difference should be:

a. shown as a liability.
b. subtracted from the historical cost of the investments.
c. added to the historical cost of the investments.
d. No entry is made; the securities are shown at historical cost.

12-12 What account title will not appear on consolidated financial statements?

a. Inventory
b. Investment in EBL Corporation (80% ownership)
c. Investment in MJK Corporation (35% ownership)
d. Common shares

12-13 Consolidated financial statements are required:

a. whenever the common shares of another corporation are owned.
b. only when significant influence can be exerted over another company.
c. when over 50% of the common shares of another corporation are owned.
d. only when 100% of the common shares of another corporation are owned.

12-14 Assume a parent has total assets of $6,000,000 and a subsidiary incorporated by the parent company has total assets of $4,000,000. If the parent owns 100% of the subsidiary's common shares, what amount of assets will be reported on the consolidated statement of financial position? Assume the investment in the subsidiary is showing on the parent company books is $2,000,000.

a. $0, consolidation is not necessary
b. $6,000,000
c. $8,000,000
d. $10,000,000

12-15 Goodwill is calculated as the excess of the cost of an acquired company over the:

a. carrying value of net assets acquired.
b. fair value of assets acquired.
c. fair value of identifiable net assets acquired.
d. book value of identifiable net assets acquired.

EXERCISES

Exercise 12-16   Matching Accounting Methods and Investments   OBJECTIVE

Consider the following accounting methods for long-term investments.

a. Amortized cost method
b. Fair value method
c. Equity method
d. Consolidation of parent and sub

(Continued)

Required:

Match one or more of these methods with each of the investments described below.
1.   Mueller Inc. owns 75% of Johnston Corporation's outstanding common shares.
2.   Anderson Inc. owns 25% of Peterson Corporation's outstanding common shares.
3.   Wixon Corporation owns 12% of the outstanding common shares of Gilman Inc., which were acquired to be sold in the near term.
4.   Kohler Corporation holds a $40,000 long-term note receivable from Bennett Inc., a major customer. Kohler expects to sell the note within the next two or three years.
5.   Janis Products Inc. holds $200,000 in Gibson Manufacturing bonds. Janis plans to hold these until they mature.

OBJECTIVE **Exercise 12-17   Trading Securities**

Fehr Finance began operations in 2018 and invests in securities held for trading. During 2018, it entered into the following trading security transactions:

Purchased 20,000 shares of ABC common shares at $38 per share
Purchased 32,000 shares of XYZ common shares at $17 per share

At December 31, 2018, ABC's common shares were trading at $39.50 per share and XYZ's common shares were trading at $16.50 per share.

Required:

1.   Prepare the necessary adjusting entry to value the trading securities at fair market value.
2.   **CONCEPTUAL CONNECTION** What is the statement of earnings effect of this adjusting entry?

OBJECTIVE  **Exercise 12-18   Trading Securities**

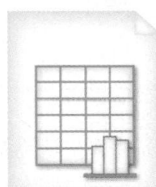

Tolland Financial began operations in 2018 and invests in securities classified as trading securities. During 2018, it entered into the following trading security transactions:

Purchased 10,000 common shares of DTR at $50 per share
Purchased 44,000 common shares of MJO at $22 per share

At December 31, 2018, DTR's common shares were trading at $62 per share and MJO's common shares were trading at $21 per share.

Required:

1.   Prepare the necessary adjusting entry to value the trading securities at fair market value.
2.   **CONCEPTUAL CONNECTION** What is the statement of earnings effect of this adjusting entry?

OBJECTIVE **Exercise 12-19   Trading Securities**

Marco Financial began operations in 2018 and invests in securities held for trading. During 2018, it entered into the following transactions:

Purchased 20,000 common shares of MNO for $40 per share
Purchased 10,000 common shares of BKL for $30 per share
Purchased 5,000 common shares of ABA for $10 per share

At December 31, 2018, MNO was trading for $38 per share, BKL was trading for $22 per share, and ABA was trading for $13 per share.

Required:

1.   Prepare the journal entry to value the trading securities at fair market value.
2.   **CONCEPTUAL CONNECTION** What is the statement of earnings effect of this journal entry?

Exercise 12-20   Amortized Cost Model

OBJECTIVE ❶ ❷

Mahco Financial began operations in 2018 and invests in bonds to be held to maturity. On January 1, 2018, Mahco acquired a $1,000,000 8% bond (yield 7.6%) due December 31, 2037, issued by JJK for $1,040,000. Interest is paid semiannually on June 30 and December 31. On July 1, 2018, Mahco acquired a $2,000,000 6% bond (6.27% yield) due July 1, 2028, issued by MMM for $1,960,000. Interest is paid semiannually on June 30 and December 31.

Required:

1. Prepare the journal entries to record the carrying value of the bonds at December 31, 2018, using the effective interest rate method for bond discount and premium. Include all other entries that are required for 2018.
2. Prepare the journal entries to record the carrying value for the bonds at December 31, 2018, using the straight-line method of amortization for bond discount and premium. Include all other entries that are required for 2018.
3. How would your journal entries change if the market value of the bonds on December 31, 2018, were $1,035,000 (JJK bond) and $1,972,000 (MMM bond)?

Exercise 12-21   Amortized Cost Model

OBJECTIVE ❶ ❷

Mayco Financial began operations in 2018 and invests in bonds held to maturity. On January 1, 2018, Mayco acquired a $5,000,000 6% bond (6.16% yield) due December 31, 2028, issued by BAA for $4,940,000. Interest is paid semiannually on June 30 and December 31. On July 1, 2018, Mayco acquired a $4,000,000 7% bond (6.4% yield) due June 30, 2048, issued by KLM for $4,080,000. Interest is paid semiannually on June 30 and December 31.

Required:

1. Prepare the journal entries to record the carrying value of the bonds on December 31, 2018, using the effective rate interest method for bond discount and premium. Include all other entries that are required for 2018.
2. Prepare the journal entries to record the carrying value of the bonds at December 31, 2018, using the straight-line method of amortization for bond discount and premium. Include all other entries that are required for 2018.
3. How would your journal entries change if the bonds were acquired for trading and the market value of the bonds on December 31, 2018, were $4,985,000 (BAA bond) and $4,090,000 (KLM bond)?

Exercise 12-22   Trading Securities

OBJECTIVE ❶ ❷

Osaka Corporation had a portfolio of trading securities as of December 31, 2018. The original cost of the securities purchase on January 1st of the current year was $117,000. The fair value of the securities at December 31, 2018 is $120,000.

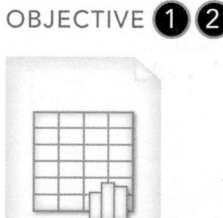

Required:

Prepare the journal entry, if any, to adjust the value of the securities at fair market value.

Exercise 12-23   Trading Securities

OBJECTIVE ❶ ❷

Perry Corporation has the following information for its portfolio of trading securities at the end of the year.

Date	Cost (purchased January 1st 2018)	Fair Market Value, December 31, 2018
12/31/18	$162,300	$153,800
12/31/18	109,600	106,200

(Continued)

Required:

1. Prepare the journal entries, if necessary, to adjust the trading securities at fair market value.
2. **CONCEPTUAL CONNECTION** What is the statement of earnings effect of the 2018 entry?

 OBJECTIVE ❶ ❷

Exercise 12-24   Investments in Trading Securities

Wong Corporation acquired the following equity securities during 2018:

200 shares of Northern Company	$14,600
500 shares of Montgomery Products	14,500

Wong classifies these securities as trading securities. During 2018, Northern paid a dividend of $1.20 per share, and Montgomery paid a dividend of $1.80 per share. At December 31, 2018, the Northern shares have a market value of $75 per share, and the Montgomery shares have a market value of $25 per share.

Required:

1. Prepare entries for Wong's journal to record these two investments and the receipt of the dividends.
2. Calculate the market value of Wong's short-term investment portfolio at December 31, 2018.
3. Prepare the necessary journal entry at December 31, 2018.
4. How would these securities be disclosed on the December 31, 2018, statement of financial position?

 OBJECTIVE ❶ ❷ ❸

Exercise 12-25   Fair Value and Equity Methods

Nadal Corporation purchased 10,000 common shares of Beck Inc., on January 1, 2018, for $100,000. During 2018, Beck declared and paid cash dividends to Nadal in the amount of $8,000. Nadal's share of Beck's net income for 2018 was $12,400. At December 31, 2018, the fair value of the 10,000 shares was $120,000. This is Nadal's only investment.

Required:

1. Assume that Beck has 75,000 common shares outstanding. What journal entries will Nadal make during 2018 relative to this investment?
2. Assume that Beck has 40,000 common shares outstanding. What journal entries will Nadal make during 2018 relative to this investment?

 OBJECTIVE ❶ ❷

Exercise 12-26   Fair Value Method

On January 1, 2018, Reduction Products Inc. acquired 1,500 common shares of Tupper Corp. for $24,000. On that date, Tupper had 10,000 common shares outstanding. On October 1, 2018, Tupper declared and paid a cash dividend of $2 per share. On November 13, 2018, Reduction sold 300 shares of Tupper for $5,000. Tupper reported 2018 net income of $36,000. Tupper's fair market value is $15 per share at December 31, 2018. This is Reduction's only investment and they plan on disposing of the shares in Tupper in the next year.

Required:

1. Prepare Reduction's journal entries to record the transactions related to its investment in Tupper.
2. Give the title and amount of each item (except cash) on the December 31, 2018, statement of financial position related to this investment. Name the statement of financial position section in which each item appears.

 OBJECTIVE ❶ ❸

Exercise 12-27   Equity Method

On January 1, 2018, Hannah Corporation acquired 40% of the outstanding common shares (400 of 1,000 outstanding shares) of Valley Manufacturing Ltd. for $60,000, which equals the book value of Valley. On December 31, 2018, Valley reported net income of $30,000 and declared and paid a cash dividend of $11,500.

Required:

1. Prepare the journal entries made by Hannah to record the transactions related to its investment in Valley.
2. Give the title and amount of each item (except cash) on the December 31, 2018, statement of financial position related to the investment. Name the statement of financial position section in which each item appears.

Exercise 12-28 Accounting for Investments in Equity Securities

OBJECTIVE 1 3

On January 1, 2018, Stern Corporation purchased 100 common shares issued by Milstein Inc. (representing 12% of the total shares outstanding) for $6,000 and 500 shares of Heifetz Inc. (representing 25% of the total shares outstanding) for $20,000. Assume that the acquisition cost of each investment equals the book value of the related shareholders' equity on the records of the investee. During 2018, Milstein declared and paid cash dividends to Stern of $500 and Heifetz declared and paid cash dividends to Stern of $1,700. Milstein reported 2018 net income of $12,000 and Heifetz reported 2018 net income of $15,000. On December 31, 2018, the market value of 100 shares of Milstein was $6,450 and the market value of 500 shares of Heifetz was $19,720.

Required:

Answer the following questions for both investments.

	Milstein	Heifetz

1. Which accounting method is applicable?
2. What amount is recorded in the investment account on the date of acquisition?
3. What amount is recorded in Stern's net income from the investments?
4. What amount is reported for the investments on the statement of financial position of Stern at December 31, 2018?

Exercise 12-29 Equity Method

OBJECTIVE 1 3

On January 1, 2018, Core Corporation acquired 30% of the 10,000 outstanding common shares of Prima Foods Inc. for $2,000,000, which equals the book value of Prima. On December 31, 2018, Prima reported a net profit of $400,000 and declared and paid a total dividend to shareholders of $200,000.

Required:

1. Prepare the journal entries made by Core to record the transactions related to its investment in Prima for 2018.
2. Give the title and amount of each item (except cash) on the December 31, 2018, statement of financial position and statement of earnings of Core related to its investments in Prima. Name the section of each financial statement in which each item appears.

Exercise 12-30 Equity Method

OBJECTIVE  1 3

On January 1, 2018, Copper Corporation acquired 25% of the 5,000 outstanding common shares of Burgess Inc. for $4,000,000, which equals the book value of Burgess. On December 31, 2018, Burgess declared and paid a dividend of $600,000. On December 31, 2018, the carrying value of the Burgess investment in the statement of financial position of Copper was $4,250,000.

Required:

1. Calculate the net income of Burgess for the year ended December 31, 2018.
2. How would Copper record income from Burgess on its 2018 statement of earnings?

OBJECTIVE **1** **2**

Exercise 12-31   Investments in Trading Securities

Maxwell Company engaged in the following transactions involving short-term investments:

a. Purchased 200 shares of Bartco for $12,800.
b. Received a $1.60-per-share dividend on the Bartco investment.
c. Sold 40 shares of Bartco for $61 per share.
d. Purchased 380 shares of Newton for $20,900.
e. Received a dividend of $1.00 per share on the Newton investment.

At December 31, the Bartco shares have a market value of $60 per share, and the Newton shares have a market value of $59 per share.

Required:

1. Prepare entries for Maxwell's journal to record these transactions assuming they are trading securities.
2. Calculate the market value of Maxwell's short-term investment portfolio at December 31.
3. Prepare the necessary journal entry at December 31.
4. **CONCEPTUAL CONNECTION** What is the statement of earnings effect of the adjusting entry?
5. How would these investments be reported on the December 31 statement of financial position?

OBJECTIVE **4**

Exercise 12-32   Consolidated Statement of Financial Position

Maple Corporation acquired 100% of the outstanding common shares of Suncore Company in a business combination. Immediately before the business combination, the two businesses had the following statements of financial position:

Maple		Suncore	
Cash	$ 3,100	Cash	$ 180
Equipment (net)	9,500	Equipment (net)	930
Total assets	$12,600	Total assets	$1,110
Common shares	9,100	Common shares	700
Retained earnings	3,500	Retained earnings	410
Total liabilities & equity	$12,600	Total liabilities & equity	$1,110

Maple agreed to give Suncore's shareholders $1,500 cash in exchange for all their Suncore common shares. Suncore's equipment has a fair value of $1,100.

Required:

1. Prepare the entries for Maple and Suncore to record the business combination.
2. Prepare the statement of financial position of Maple immediately after the business combination.
3. Prepare the statement of financial position of Suncore immediately after the business combination.
4. Calculate the amount of any goodwill.
5. Prepare a consolidated statement of financial position immediately after the combination.

OBJECTIVE **4**

Exercise 12-33   Consolidated Statement of Earnings

Laurier Ltd. is the wholly owned subsidiary of Stuart Corporation. The December 31, 2018, statement of earnings for the two corporations are as follows:

Stuart			Laurier		
Sales revenue		$3,200	Sales revenue		$500
Income from investment in Laurier		?			
Total revenue		?	Total revenue		500
Cost of goods sold	$920		Cost of goods sold	$160	
Depreciation expense	410		Depreciation expense	95	
Other expenses	680	2,010	Other expenses	135	390
Net income		$?	Net income		$110

The acquisition cost of Stuart's 100% ownership interest in Laurier equalled its book value on Laurier's records. During 2018, Laurier paid a cash dividend of $25 to Stuart.

Required:

1. Calculate the income from investment in Laurier as reported on Stuart's statement of earnings.
2. Calculate the 2018 net income reported by the parent company (Stuart) on its statement of earnings.
3. Prepare the 2018 consolidated statement of earnings for Stuart.

Exercise 12-34   Goodwill

OBJECTIVE **3 5**

Pindar Corporation acquired all the outstanding shares of Strauss Company for $23,000,000 on January 1, 2018. On the date of acquisition, Strauss had the following statement of financial position:

Strauss Company
Statement of Financial Position
January 1, 2018

Assets		Liabilities	
Accounts receivable	$ 6,800,000	Accounts payable	$ 2,000,000
Inventory	4,700,000	Notes payable	8,000,000
Property, plant, & equipment		Total liabilities	10,000,000
(net)	16,300,000		
		Shareholders' Equity	
		Common shares	2,000,000
		Contributed surplus–common	
		shares	8,000,000
		Retained earnings	7,800,000
		Total shareholders' equity	17,800,000
Total assets	$27,800,000	Total liabilities & shareholders' equity	$27,800,000

All Strauss's assets and liabilities have book values equal to their fair values except for equipment, which has a fair value of $20,700,000.

Required:

1. Calculate the amount of goodwill.
2. Prepare the journal entry by Pindar to record the acquisition.
3. Assume that instead of acquiring all the outstanding common shares of Strauss, Pindar acquired 100% of Strauss's net assets. What would Pindar's journal entry be in this case to record the acquisition?

13

Analysis and Interpretation of Financial Statements

After studying Chapter 13, you should be able to:

1 Explain how creditors, investors, and others use financial statements in their decisions.

2 Explain the difference between cross-sectional and time series analysis.

3 Analyze and interpret financial statements using horizontal and vertical analysis.

4 Calculate and interpret profitability, liquidity, solvency, and shareholder ratios to evaluate a company's financial position and business operations.

EXPERIENCE FINANCIAL ACCOUNTING

with Canadian Tire Corporation, Limited

Since 1922, Canadian Tire Corporation, Limited, has expanded and now includes Mark's and FGL Sports. Certainly most of us have seen these brands in our communities. But, how do we know whether Canadian Tire would be a good company in which to invest? In this chapter, you will learn about a number of tools used by investors and creditors to analyze the financial status of Canadian Tire Corporation and other companies.

Canadian Tire Corporation, Limited Consolidated Statements of Earnings (Partial)		
(C$ in millions)	January 3, 2015	December 31, 2013
Revenue	$12,462.9	$11,785.6
Cost of producing revenue	(8,416.9)	(8,063.3)
Gross margin	4,046.0	3,722.3
Other income (expense)	11.0	(3.0)
Operating expenses		
Net finance costs	(108.9)	(105.8)
Selling, general and administrative expenses	(3,052.9)	(2,828.9)
Other expenses	(17.0)	–
Income before income taxes	878.2	784.6

Source: Canadian Tire Corporation Annual Report 2014.

Financial Highlights (C$ in millions)			
Consolidated	January 3, 2015	December 31, 2013	% Change
Revenue	$12,462.9	$11,785.6	5.8%
EBITDA	1,376.4	1,235.7	11.4%
Income before income taxes	878.2	784.6	11.9%
Net income	639.3	564.4	13.2%
Cash generated from operating activities	574.8	893.0	(35.7)%
Cash expenditures on property, plant, and equipment	538.6	404.3	33.2%

Source: Canadian Tire Corporation Annual Report 2014.

Throughout this book, you have learned how to record many of the most common transactions in which a company engages using journal entries containing debits and credits. You have also studied how these debits and credits are summarized in the financial statements and how this information is useful to those interested in the company. In this chapter, we review, extend, and summarize the role of financial statements in business decision making. The types of decisions facing customers, suppliers, employees, creditors, and investors are discussed. However, we concentrate primarily on investment and credit decisions and the techniques used for comparing results to those of other companies or to previous years.

Reading this chapter will help you answer the following questions:

- What decision-making groups use financial statements and what questions are they able to answer by analyzing the financial statements?
- What key ratios are used to analyze financial statements?
- How are financial statements analyzed over time?

USE OF FINANCIAL STATEMENTS IN DECISIONS

OBJECTIVE 1

Explain how creditors, investors, and others use financial statements in their decisions.

As we discussed in Chapter 1, the role of financial statements is to provide information that will help creditors, investors, and others make judgments that serve as the foundation for various decisions. While customers, suppliers, employees, creditors, and investors all use financial statement data to make decisions, as shown in Exhibit 13.1, each group uses the accounting information to answer different questions.

Customer Decisions

Customers want to buy from companies that will

- continue to produce goods or provide services in the future
- provide repair or warranty service if required

The financial statements contain data describing the profitability and efficiency of a company's operations, which customers can use to estimate the likelihood that a supplier will be able to deliver goods or services now and in the future.

(EXHIBIT 13.1)

Users of Financial Statements and Typical Questions

Supplier Decisions

A company that is considering selling goods or providing services to another company wants to know whether its customer will

- pay for the purchase as agreed
- be able to continue to purchase and pay for goods and services

Suppliers can use statement of financial position data to estimate the likelihood that a customer will be able to pay for current purchases. They can use statement of earnings data to analyze whether a customer will be able to continue purchasing and paying for goods or services in the future.

Employment Decisions

When you select an employer, you want to be sure that the company will provide

- competitive salary and benefits
- experiences that will prepare you to assume increased responsibility
- a secure position for the foreseeable future

Statement of earnings data can help a prospective employee assess the likelihood that a company will provide the growth and profits necessary to support a successful career. For example, examining a company's current assets over the claims against those assets can help prospective employees determine a company's profitability and growth.

In related decisions, unions representing employees use the financial statements. For example, when the employer's statement of earnings suggests the employer is performing very well, the union will seek greater wages and benefits. Conversely, when the statement of earnings suggests the employer is performing poorly (such as in the automotive industry), unions may accept lower wages and benefits to help the employer stay in operation.

Credit Decisions

An individual or an organization that is considering making a loan needs to know whether the borrower will be able to repay the loan and its interest. For short-term loans (those of one year or less), the principal and interest will be repaid from current assets—cash on hand and cash that can be secured by selling inventory and collecting accounts receivable. A short-term lender, then, is most interested in the composition and amounts of a borrowing company's current assets and current liabilities. The excess of the current assets over current liabilities, an amount called *working capital*, is particularly important.

For a long-term loan, the principal and interest will be repaid from cash provided by profits earned over the period of the loan. A long-term lender, then, is most interested in estimating

- the future profits of the enterprise
- the amount of other claims against those profits, such as dividends to shareholders, payments to other lenders, and future investments by the firm

Information from three different statements is useful in making credit decisions:

- An analysis of the statement of financial position can provide information about the borrower's current liquidity.
- Profitability data developed from current and previous statements of earnings are often helpful in forecasting future profitability.
- Sources and uses of cash presented in the statement of cash flows are helpful in forecasting the amount and timing of future claims against profits.

Investment Decisions

Investors who buy shares in a corporation expect to earn returns on their investment from

- dividends
- an increase in the value of the shares (a capital gain)

Both dividends and increases in the value of the shares depend on the future profitability of the company. The larger the profits, the more resources the company has available for payment of dividends and for investment in new assets to use in creating additional profits.

Although detailed analysis of the corporation is where you find the best information for predicting (or forecasting) future profits, this cannot be done in a vacuum. You must also understand economic and industry factors. For example, if you ignore how economic factors such as rising interest rates affect home construction (it slows it down), then forecasts of corporations whose performances are tied to this industry, such as Lowe's or Home Depot, may be overly optimistic. As such, most analysts take a top-down approach when trying to predict future profits. This approach starts with gathering economic and industry data. In fact, professional analysts typically specialize in certain industries so that their knowledge of how the economy and industry interact will be applicable to all the corporations they analyze (or "follow"). Yet, at some point, you must begin to analyze the corporation itself.

More Than Quantitative Analysis Is Required

This chapter introduces financial statement analysis from a quantitative perspective. Ratios often point out concerns for management as well as operations that have improved. Yet further qualitative analysis is almost always required in order to thoroughly understand the reasons for ratios as well as for their trends, whatever they may be.

Understanding the Company's Business

Before starting your quantitative analysis on a public company, you should orient yourself by obtaining knowledge of the company's business. You can acquire that knowledge by reading the company's annual report, which will tell you about the company's business strategy, the risks it is facing, and the external and internal factors that affected the company during the previous year. Once you understand what management is trying to do in the company, and the environment in which the company operates, you will better understand the ratios that have resulted from the transactions in which the company has engaged.

Understanding Financial Statements (and Notes)

You should read the company's financial statements *before* starting your quantitative work. Most readers begin by checking to confirm that the auditors have issued an unqualified audit opinion on the financial statements. The audit opinion does not guarantee accuracy; however, an unqualified opinion does tell you that the auditors have determined that the financial statements are in accordance with IFRS (or ASPE for private companies). An audit report that is not unqualified amounts to a warning that certain balances in the financial statements may be suspect.

You should also read the notes to the financial statements, for they offer a substantial amount of detail regarding many financial statement elements. In particular, the first note is usually the accounting policy note. If competitors are using different accounting policies, then you should expect that at least some of the ratios then calculated will reflect those differences. Since IFRS allows management to use judgment when selecting accounting policies, a financial statement analyst needs to be familiar with the choices that management has adopted when recording the company's transactions. The ratios calculated will be affected by these decisions.

ANALYZING FINANCIAL STATEMENTS WITH CROSS-SECTIONAL AND TIME SERIES ANALYSIS

As with many things in life, context is all important in financial statement analysis. For example, how well do you believe a corporation with $3.3 billion in net sales is performing? Your answer should be that it depends. That is, if net sales for the previous two years were $4.5 billion and $3.9 billion, respectively, you would say the trend is negative. However, if net sales for the previous two years were $2.0 billion and $2.8 billion, respectively, then you would conclude the trend is positive. Or, you could see how this corporation's sales growth stacks up against a major competitor's sales growth.

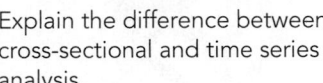

OBJECTIVE ❷

Explain the difference between cross-sectional and time series analysis.

The context with which we placed our hypothetical corporation's net sales and sales growth demonstrates the two general comparisons we make when analyzing financial statements—cross-sectional analysis and time series (or trend) analysis.

Cross-sectional Analysis

Cross-sectional analysis compares one corporation to another corporation and to industry averages. Although this method is useful, it is often difficult to find a good comparison corporation, and even corporations classified in the same industry frequently have different aspects to their operations. Nonetheless, it is useful to highlight similarities, differences, strengths, and weaknesses of the corporation as compared to the competition and the industry as a whole. For example,

- Canadian Tire's gross profit margin percentage was 32.5% (year ended January 3, 2015).
- Sears Canada's gross profit margin percentage was 32.6% (year ended January 31, 2015).
- The retail trade industry had a gross profit margin percentage of 25.9% in 2012.

Along this dimension, Sears Canada and Canadian Tire achieved approximately the same level of profitability on sales and both companies outperformed the industry.

Time Series Analysis

Time series (or trend) analysis compares a single corporation across time. For example, if you look at Canadian Tire's statement of earnings in Appendix 2 and on the company's website (www.canadiantire.ca), you will see that its net sales were:

- $11.4 billion in fiscal 2012 (December 29, 2012)
- $11.8 billion in fiscal 2013 (December 31, 2013)
- $12.4 billion in fiscal 2014 (January 3, 2015)

Net sales indicates a positive trend.

Year-to-year comparisons of important accounts and account groups help identify the causes of changes in a company's income or financial position. Knowing the causes of these changes is helpful in forecasting a company's future profitability and financial position.

Cross–sectional and Time Series Analysis Illustrated

Cross-sectional and time series analyses are demonstrated in Cornerstone 13.1 .

CORNERSTONE 13.1

CORNERSTONE
VIDEO

Interpreting Cross-sectional and Time Series (or Trend) Analysis

Information:

Information from Canadian Tire's and Sears Canada's financial statements follows.

Canadian Tire (in millions)

	Fiscal Year Ended		
	1/3/2015 (2014)	12/31/2013 (2013)	12/29/2012 (2012)
Net sales	$12,462.9	$11,785.6	$11,427.2
Cost of goods sold	8,416.9	8,063.3	7,929.3
Gross profit	$ 4,046.0	$ 3,722.3	$ 3,497.9

Sears Canada (in millions)

	Fiscal Year Ended		
	1/31/2015 (2014)	2/1/2014 (2013)	2/2/2013 (2012)
Net sales	$3,424.5	$3,991.8	$4,346.5
Cost of goods sold	2,308.0	2,548.1	2,749.2
Gross profit	$1,116.5	$1,443.7	$1,597.3

Required:

1. Using time series analysis, comment on the trend of Canadian Tire's cost of goods sold and gross profit.

2. What is the primary weakness of using raw financial statement numbers in cross-sectional and time series analysis? What can you do about it?

3. Using cross-sectional analysis, compare Canadian Tire's gross profit to Sears Canada's gross profit.

Why:

Cross-sectional analysis compares a corporation's financial statements to a competitor or to the industry in which it operates. Time series analysis compares specific line items of the financial statements over multiple years.

Solution:

1. Canadian Tire's cost of goods sold increased by $353.6 ($8,416.9 − $8,063.3) from 2013 to 2014. In isolation this may seem bad, but the primary reason for this increase is that sales were also increasing. In fact, Canadian Tire has a positive trend in gross profit, which increased from $3,497.9 in 2012 to $4,046.0 in 2014.

(Continued)

CORNERSTONE

13.1

(Continued)

2. The primary weakness is that raw financial statement numbers can be difficult to compare. For example, Canadian Tire's net sales increased by $1.04 billion from 2012 to 2014, while their gross profit only increased by about $548.1 million. However, if you look at the percentage change, both net sales and gross profit increased by 15.7% and 8.3% respectively. Furthermore, when comparing two competitors—like Canadian Tire and Sears Canada—making comparisons with raw financial statement numbers is difficult because they are often vastly different in size. Using percentage changes from year to year or between two financial statement line items helps overcome the differences in the relative sizes of items of interest.

3. When we look at the percentage change in gross margin from year to year we discover the following:

Growth in Gross Profit:	2013 to 2014*	2012 to 2013**
Canadian Tire	8.7%	6.4%
Sears Canada	−22.7%	−9.6%

*(2014 Gross profit − 2013 Gross profit) ÷ 2013 Gross profit
**(2013 Gross profit − 2012 Gross profit) ÷ 2012 Gross profit

This analysis suggests that Canadian Tire had a far better year (in both 2014 and 2013) than Sears Canada.

ANALYZING THE FINANCIAL STATEMENTS WITH HORIZONTAL AND VERTICAL ANALYSIS

Comparative financial statements report financial results in dollar amounts. This makes it easy to detect large changes between years in accounts or groups of accounts. These changes may indicate that the corporation is changing or that the conditions under which the corporation operates are changing. However, while comparative financial statements show changes in the amounts of financial statement items, analysts often prefer to restate the financial statements in percentages using common size statements. **Common size statements** express each financial statement line item in percentage terms, which highlights differences. Typically, this conversion from dollar amounts to percentages is done with horizontal or vertical analysis.

OBJECTIVE

Analyze and interpret financial statements using horizontal and vertical analysis.

Horizontal Analysis

In **horizontal analysis**, each financial statement line item is expressed as a percentage of the base year (typically the first year shown). Cornerstone 13.2 shows how to prepare a common size statement of earnings for horizontal analysis.

Horizontal analysis is good for highlighting the growth (or shrinkage) in financial statement line items from year to year and is particularly useful for trend analysis. For example, looking at Canadian Tire's common size statement of earnings in Cornerstone 13.2, we see that sales has grown faster than cost of goods sold when comparing 2014 to 2012. This has resulted in the gross profit growing more quickly than sales.

CORNERSTONE 13.2

CORNERSTONE
VIDEO

Preparing Common Size Statements for Horizontal Analysis

Information:

Canadian Tire's statements of earnings for 2014, 2013, and 2012 follow.

Canadian Tire Corporation, Limited Consolidated Statements of Earnings			
	Fiscal Year Ended		
	January 3, 2015	**December 31, 2013**	**December 29, 2012**
		(in millions)	
Net sales	$12,462.9	$11,785.6	$11,427.2
Cost of sales	8,416.9	8,063.3	7,929.3
Gross profit	4,046.0	3,722.3	3,497.9
Operating expenses	3,058.9	2,831.9	2,700.2
Income from operations	987.1	890.4	803.4
Net finance expense	108.9	105.8	126.2
Income before income taxes	878.2	784.6	677.2
Income taxes	238.9	220.2	178.0
Net income	$ 639.3	$ 564.4	$ 499.2

Required:

Prepare a common size statement of earnings to be used for horizontal analysis for Canadian Tire Corporation, Limited using 2012 as the base year.

Why:

Horizontal analysis using common size statements can assist users and management in identifying areas of past problems and opportunities for future improvement.

Solution:

Canadian Tire Corporation, Limited Consolidated Statements of Earnings						
	Fiscal Year Ended					
	January 3, 2015		**December 31, 2013**		**December 29, 2012**	
			(in millions)			
Net sales	$12,462.9	109.06%	$11,785.6	103.14%	$11,427.2	100.00%
Cost of sales	8,416.9	106.15%	8,063.3	101.69%	7,929.3	100.00%
Gross profit	4,046.0	115.67%	3,722.3	106.42%	3,497.9	100.00%
Operating expenses	3,058.9	113.28%	2,831.9	104.88%	2,700.2	100.00%
Income from operations	987.1	122.87%	890.4	110.83%	803.4	100.00%
Net finance expense	108.9	86.29%	105.8	83.84%	126.2	100.00%

(Continued)

	Fiscal Year Ended		
	January 3, 2015	December 31, 2013	December 29, 2012
	(in millions)		
Income before income taxes	878.2 129.68%	784.6 115.86%	677.2 100.00%
Income taxes	238.9 134.21%	220.2 123.71%	178.0 100.00%
Net income	$ 639.3 128.07%	$ 564.4 113.06%	$ 499.2 100.00%

Source: Canadian Tire 2013 Annual Report and Canadian Tire 2014 Annual Report.

CORNERSTONE

13.2

(Continued)

Vertical Analysis

Vertical analysis, on the other hand, expresses each financial statement line item as a percentage of the largest amount on the statement. On the statement of earnings, this is net sales and on the statement of financial position it is total assets. Vertical analysis helps distinguish between changes in account balances that result from growth and changes that are likely to have arisen from other causes. Cornerstone 13.3 shows how to prepare common size statements of earnings and statements of financial position for vertical analysis.

Preparing Common Size Statements for Vertical Analysis

CORNERSTONE 13.3

Information:

Canadian Tire's statements of earnings and statements of financial position follow.

Canadian Tire Corporation, Limited Consolidated Statements of Earnings			
	Fiscal Year Ended		
	January 3, 2015	December 31, 2014	December 29, 2012
	(in millions)		
Net sales	$12,462.9	$11,785.9	$11,427.2
Cost of sales	8,416.9	8,063.3	7,929.3
Gross profit	4,046.0	3,722.3	3,497.9
Operating expenses	3,058.9	2,831.9	2,694.5
Income from operations	987.1	890.4	803.4
Net finance expense	108.9	105.8	126.2
Income before income taxes	878.2	784.6	677.2
Income taxes	238.9	220.2	178.0
Net income	$ 639.3	$ 564.4	$ 499.2

CORNERSTONE
VIDEO

(Continued)

(Continued)

Canadian Tire Corporation, Limited Consolidated Statements of Financial Position	January 3, 2015	December 31, 2013
	(in millions)	
ASSETS		
Cash and cash equivalents	$ 662.1	$ 643.2
Short-term investments	289.1	416.6
Trade and other receivables	880.2	758.5
Loans receivable	4,905.5	4,569.7
Merchandise inventories	1,623.8	1,481.0
Income taxes recoverable	31.9	31.5
Prepaid expenses and deposits	104.5	68.2
Assets classified as held for sale	13.1	9.1
Total current assets	8,510.2	7,977.8
Long-term receivables and other assets	684.2	686.0
Long-term investments	176.0	134.7
Goodwill and intangible assets	1,251.7	1,185.5
Investment property	148.6	93.5
Property and equipment	3,743.1	3,516.1
Deferred income taxes	39.4	36.4
Total assets	$14,553.2	$13,630.0
LIABILITIES		
Bank indebtedness	$ 14.3	$ 69.0
Deposits	950.7	1,178.4
Trade and other payables	1,961.2	1,817.4
Provisions	206.0	196.1
Short-term borrowings	199.8	120.3
Loans payable	604.4	611.2
Income taxes payable	54.9	57.5
Current portion of long-term debt	587.5	272.2
Total current liabilities	4,578.8	4,322.1
Long-term provisions	44.1	38.2
Long-term debt	2,131.6	2,339.1
Long-term deposits	1,286.2	1,152.0
Deferred income taxes	93.9	100.4
Other long-term liabilities	787.8	228.3
Total liabilities	8,922.4	8,180.1
EQUITY		
Share capital	695.5	712.9
Contributed surplus	2.9	2.4
Accumulated other comprehensive income	82.0	87.4
Retained earnings	4,075.1	4,404.6
Equity attributable to owners of Canadian Tire Corporation	4,855.5	5,167.3
Noncontrolling interest	775.3	282.6
Total equity	5,630.8	5,449.9
Total liabilities and equity	$14,553.2	$13,630.0

(Continued)

Required:

Prepare common size statements of earnings and statements of financial position to be used in vertical analysis for Canadian Tire beginning with the year 2012.

Why:

Vertical analysis expresses each financial statement line item as a percentage of the largest amount on the statement. Vertical analysis using common size statements can help users and management identify areas of past problems and opportunities for future improvement.

Solution:

Canadian Tire Corporation, Limited Consolidated Statements of Earnings			
	Fiscal Year Ended		
	Jan. 3, 2015	**Dec. 31, 2013**	**Dec. 29, 2012**
Net sales	100.00%	100.00%	100.00%
Cost of sales	67.53%	68.41%	69.39%
Gross profit	32.47%	31.59%	30.61%
Operating expenses	24.54%	24.03%	23.58%
Income from operations	7.93%	7.56%	7.03%
Net finance expense	.88%	.90%	1.10%
Income before income taxes	7.05%	6.66%	5.93%
Income taxes	1.92%	1.87%	5.93%
Net income	5.13%	4.79%	4.37%

Canadian Tire Corporation, Limited Consolidated Statements of Financial Position		
	Jan. 3, 2015	**Dec. 31, 2013**
ASSETS		
Cash and cash equivalents	4.55%	4.72%
Short-term investments	1.99%	3.06%
Trade and other receivables	6.05%	5.56%
Loans receivable	33.70%	33.52%
Merchandise inventories	11.16%	10.87%
Income taxes recoverable	.22%	.23%
Prepaid expenses and deposits	.72%	.50%
Assets classified as held for sale	.09%	.07%
Total current assets	58.48%	58.53%
Long-term receivables and other assets	4.70%	5.02%
Long-term investments	1.21%	.99%
Goodwill and intangible assets	8.60%	8.70%
Investment property	1.02%	.69%

(Continued)

CORNERSTONE
13.3
_____

(Continued)

	Jan. 3, 2015	Dec. 31, 2013
Property and equipment	25.72%	25.80%
Deferred income taxes	.27%	.27%
Total assets	100.00%	100.00%
LIABILITIES		
Bank indebtedness	.09%	.51%
Deposits	6.53%	8.65%
Trade and other payables	13.48%	13.33%
Provisions	1.42%	1.44%
Short-term borrowings	1.37%	.88%
Loans payable	4.15%	4.48%
Income taxes payable	.38%	.42%
Current portion of long-term debt	4.04%	2.00%
Total current liabilities	31.46%	31.71%
Long-term provisions	.30%	.27%
Long-term debt	14.65%	17.16%
Long-term deposits	8.84%	8.46%
Deferred income taxes	.65%	.74%
Other long-term liabilities	5.41%	1.68%
Total liabilities	61.31%	60.02%
EQUITY		
Share capital	4.78%	5.23%
Contributed surplus	.02%	.02%
Accumulated other comprehensive income	.56%	.35%
Retained earnings	28.00%	32.32%
Equity attributable to owners of Canadian Tire Corporation	33.36%	37.91%
Noncontrolling interest	5.33%	2.07%
Total equity	38.69%	39.98%
Total liabilities and equity	100.00%	100.00%

Source: Canadian Tire 2013 Annual Report and Canadian Tire 2014 Annual Report.

Identifying nongrowth changes and their causes can help forecast a company's future profitability or its future financial position. For example, in Cornerstone 13.3, Canadian Tire's cost of sales decreased from approximately 69.39% of net sales in 2012 to 67.53% in 2014. This may not seem like much of a change, but if cost of sales had remained at 69.39% of net sales in 2014, then gross profit would have been about $232 million lower in 2014. Determining whether the improvement in cost of sales percentage from 2012 to 2014 is permanent may have a large effect on forecasting future profitability. In addition, vertical analysis of the 2014 statement of financial position reveals a very stable condition, because all of the large dollar amounts are similar in terms of the percentage of total assets each year.

Of course, you can, and should, get much more in-depth with such analysis. A careful horizontal and vertical analysis serves as a starting point for an inquiry into the causes of these changes, with the objective of forecasting the corporation's future financial statements.

ANALYZING THE FINANCIAL STATEMENTS WITH RATIO ANALYSIS

Ratio analysis is an examination of financial statements conducted by preparing and evaluating a series of ratios. **Ratios** (or **financial ratios**), like other financial analysis data, normally provide meaningful information only when compared with ratios from previous periods for the same firm (i.e., time series, or trend, analysis) or similar firms (i.e., cross-sectional analysis). Ratios help by removing most of the effects of size differences. When dollar amounts are used, size differences between firms may make a meaningful comparison impossible. However, properly constructed financial ratios permit the comparison of firms regardless of size.

We discuss five categories of ratio analysis:

- *Short-term liquidity ratios* are particularly helpful to short-term creditors, but all investors and creditors have an interest in these ratios.
- *Debt management (solvency) ratios* and *profitability ratios* provide information for long-term creditors and shareholders.
- *Asset efficiency (or operating) ratios* help management operate the firm and indicate to outsiders the efficiency with which certain of the company's activities are performed.
- *Shareholder ratios* are of interest to a corporation's shareholders.
- *DuPont analysis* decomposes return on equity into margin, turnover, and leverage.

All these ratios are shown and defined in Exhibit 13.3 at the conclusion of this section. We will use data from Canadian Tire's and Telus Corporation's financial statements in Appendices 2 and 3 to illustrate these financial statement ratios.

OBJECTIVE **4**

Calculate and interpret profitability, liquidity, solvency, and shareholder ratios to evaluate a company's financial position and business operations.

Short-Term Liquidity Ratios

Analysts want to know the likelihood that a company will be able to pay its current obligations as they come due. Failure to pay current liabilities can lead to suppliers refusing to sell needed inventory and employees leaving. Even companies with good business models can be forced into bankruptcy by their inability to pay current liabilities.

The cash necessary to pay current liabilities will come from existing cash or from receivables and inventory, which should turn into cash approximately at the same time the current liabilities become due. Property, plant, and equipment and other long-lived assets are much more difficult to turn into cash in time to meet current obligations without harming future operations. Accordingly, the **short-term liquidity ratios** compare some combination of current assets or operations to current liabilities.

Current Ratio Since a company must meet its current obligations primarily by using its current assets, the current ratio is especially useful to short-term creditors. The **current ratio** is expressed as follows:

$$\text{Current ratio} = \frac{\text{Current assets}}{\text{Current liabilities}}$$

Using information from Telus Corporation's Fiscal 2014 statement of financial position, the current ratio for Telus Corporation is calculated as follows:

	Fiscal 2014	Fiscal 2013
	(in millions)	
Total current assets	$2,186.0	$2,329.0
Total current liabilities	3,499.0	3,299.0
Current ratio	**.62**	**.71**

Telus Corporation's current ratio decreased slightly from 2013 to 2014 due to cash being used for capital expenditures.

There are no absolute standards for ratios, so a company's ratios are typically compared to the industry averages and/or competitors. The average for Telus Corporation's sector is .88. By this standard, Telus Corporation's current ratio is slightly below the industry average.

Quick Ratio Some analysts believe that the current ratio overstates short-term liquidity. They argue that prepaid expenses (expenses for which payments are made before consumption) cannot be converted into cash. Furthermore, inventories must be sold and receivables collected from sales before cash is obtained to pay maturing current liabilities. Both the sale of inventory and the collection of receivables can require a lengthy period. Conservative analysts argue that only those current assets that can be turned into cash almost immediately should be used to measure short-term liquidity.

A more conservative measure of short-term liquidity is based on *quick assets* (usually cash, receivables, and short-term investments) and current liabilities. The **quick ratio** (or *acid test ratio*) is expressed as follows:

$$\text{Quick ratio} = \frac{\text{Cash} + \text{Short-term investments} + \text{Receivables}}{\text{Current liabilities}}$$

Looking at the detail of Telus Corporation's current assets, the quick ratio is calculated as follows:

	Fiscal 2014	Fiscal 2013
	(in millions)	
Current Assets:		
Cash and equivalents	$ 60.0	$ 336.0
Receivables	1,483.0	1,461.0
Inventories	320.0	326.0
Prepaid expenses	199.0	168.0
Other current assets	124.0	38.0
Total current assets	$2,186.0	$2,329.0
Quick assets	1,863.0	2,123.0
Total current liabilities	$3,499.0	$3,299.0
Quick ratio	**.53**	**.64**

The industry average quick ratio in the telecom industry is .27. Using this guideline, we see that Telus Corporation exceeds the industry average and should have sufficient "quick assets" to pay its short-term liabilities as they come due.

Cash Ratio An even more conservative short-term liquidity ratio is the cash ratio. Specifically, while the current and quick ratios assume that receivables will be collected, the cash ratio does not make this assumption. This ratio may be more appropriate for industries in which collectability is uncertain or for corporations with high credit risk receivables. The **cash ratio** is expressed as follows:

$$\text{Cash ratio} = \frac{\text{Cash} + \text{Short-term investments}}{\text{Current liabilities}}$$

Although Telus Corporation does not have high credit risk receivables, the cash ratio is calculated as follows:

	Fiscal 2014	Fiscal 2013
	(in millions)	
Current assets:		
Cash and short-term investments	$ 60.0	$ 336.0
Receivables	1,483.0	1,461.0
Inventories	320.0	326.0
Prepaid expenses	199.0	168.0
Other current assets	124.0	38.0
Total current assets	$2,186.0	$2,329.0
Cash and STIs	60.0	336.0
Total current liabilities	$3,499.0	$3,299.0
Cash ratio	**.02**	**.10**

The cash ratio for both years indicates that Telus Corporation, without the collection of accounts receivable, did not have sufficient cash to pay its current liabilities as they became due in 2013 and 2014.

Operating Cash Flow Ratio The operating cash flow ratio takes a slightly different approach. This ratio looks at the ability of operations to generate cash, which recognizes the more general concept that current obligations will be paid through operations (after all, selling inventory and collecting receivables is a big part of operations). The **operating cash flow ratio** is expressed as:

$$\text{Operating cash flow ratio} = \frac{\text{Cash flows from operating activities}}{\text{Current liabilities}}$$

Looking at Telus Corporation's statement of cash flows and statement of financial position, the operating cash flow ratio is calculated as follows:

	Fiscal 2014	Fiscal 2013
Cash flows from operating activities	$3,407.0	$3,246.0
Total current liabilities	3,499.0	3,299.0
Operating cash flow ratio	**.97**	**.98**

In both years, Telus Corporation's operations generated enough cash to almost meet the entire balance of current obligations due at the end of the year without relying on other cash sources. That means that Telus Corporation will not be required to sell assets, borrow, or issue shares to generate cash to be used for operations.

Overview of Short-Term Liquidity Ratios The short-term liquidity ratios for Telus Corporation indicate a generally strong liquidity position at the end of each fiscal year based on industry standards. For creditors, this is clearly good news. Creditors typically prefer all these measures of short-term liquidity be as high as possible. However, because investments in current assets (especially cash, receivables, and inventory) earn very small returns compared to the returns on investments in noncurrent assets, management must minimize the proportion of capital invested in current assets if it is to maximize profit. Using the statement of earnings and statement of financial position shown in Exhibit 13.2, Cornerstone 13.4 illustrates how to calculate and interpret short-term liquidity ratios for Canadian Tire.

CORNERSTONE 13.4   Calculating and Interpreting Short-Term Liquidity Ratios

Information:

Refer to the information in Canadian Tire's statements of earnings and statements of financial position in Exhibit 13.2. Canadian Tire's cash flows from operations were (in millions) $574.8 and $893.0 in 2014 and 2013, respectively.

Required:

Calculate the following short-term liquidity ratios for Canadian Tire for 2014 and 2013: (1) current ratio, (2) quick ratio, (3) cash ratio, and (4) operating cash flow ratio (operating cash flows are provided in the Information section above).

Why:

The calculation of short-term liquidity ratios indicates whether a company will be able to meet its current obligations.

Solution:

	2014	**2013**
1. Current Ratio $= \dfrac{\text{Current Assets}}{\text{Current Liabilities}}$	$\dfrac{\$8,510.2}{\$4,578.8} = 1.86$	$\dfrac{\$7,977.8}{\$4,322.1} = 1.85$

Source: Canadian Tire Corporation 2014 Annual Report.

2. Quick Ratio $= \dfrac{\text{Cash + Short-Term Investments + Receivables}}{\text{Current Liabilities}}$

2014	**2013**
$\dfrac{(\$662.1 + \$289.1 + \$880.2 + \$4,905.5)}{\$4,578.8} = 1.47$	$\dfrac{(\$643.2 + \$416.6 + \$758.5 + \$4,569.7)}{\$4,322.1} = 1.48$

	2014	**2013**
3. Cash Ratio $= \dfrac{\text{Cash + Short-Term Investments}}{\text{Current Liabilities}}$	$\dfrac{(\$662.1 + \$289.1)}{\$4,578.8} = 0.21$	$\dfrac{(\$643.2 + \$416.6)}{\$4,322.1} = .25$

	2014	**2013**
4. Operating Cash Flow Ratio $= \dfrac{\text{Cash Flows from Operating Activities}}{\text{Current Liabilities}}$	$\dfrac{\$574.8^*}{\$4,578.8} = .13$	$\dfrac{\$893.0^*}{\$4,322.1} = .21$

*Taken from the statement of cash flows. The numbers were provided in the information section of this Cornerstone.

From Cornerstone 13.4, you can see that Canadian Tire's current ratio is above that of Telus Corporation of .62, which reflects the difference in industries between the two companies. Furthermore, its ratio is above the 1.5 threshold generally considered adequate. Its cash ratio is stronger than Telus Corporation and is adequate in its circumstances.

EXHIBIT 13.2

Canadian Tire Corporation, Limited, Statements of Earnings and Statements of Financial Position

Canadian Tire Corporation, Limited, Consolidated Statements of Earnings			
	Fiscal Year Ended		
	Jan. 3, 2015	Dec. 31, 2013	Dec. 29, 2012
	(in millions)		
Net sales	$12,462.9	$11,785.6	$11,427.2
Cost of sales	8,416.9	8,063.3	7,929.3
Gross profit	4,046.0	3,722.3	3,497.9
Operating expenses	3,058.9	2,831.9	2,694.9
Income from operations	987.1	890.4	803.0
Net finance expense	108.9	105.8	126.2
Income before income taxes	878.2	784.6	676.8
Income taxes	238.9	220.2	177.9
Net income	$ 639.3	$ 564.4	$ 498.9

Source: Canadian Tire Corporation Annual Report 2014.

Canadian Tire Corporation, Limited Consolidated Statements of Financial Position		
	Jan. 3, 2015	Dec. 31, 2013
	(in millions)	
ASSETS		
Cash and cash equivalents	$ 662.1	$ 643.2
Short-term investments	289.1	416.6
Trade and other receivables	880.2	758.5
Loans receivable	4,905.5	4,569.7
Merchandise inventories	1,623.8	1,481.0
Income taxes recoverable	31.9	31.5
Prepaid expenses and deposits	104.5	68.2
Assets classified as held for sale	13.1	9.1
Total current assets	8,510.2	7,977.8
Long-term receivables and other assets	684.2	686.0
Long-term investments	176.0	134.7
Goodwill and intangible assets	1,251.7	1,185.5
Investment property	148.6	93.5
Property and equipment	3,743.1	3,516.1
Deferred income taxes	39.4	36.4
Total assets	$14,553.2	$13,630.0
LIABILITIES		
Bank indebtedness	$ 14.3	$ 69.0
Deposits	950.7	1,178.4
Trade and other payables	1,961.2	1,817.4
Provisions	206.0	196.1
Short-term borrowings	199.8	120.3
Loans payable	604.4	611.2
Income taxes payable	54.9	57.5
Current portion of long-term debt	587.5	272.2
Total current liabilities	4,578.8	4,322.1
Long-term provisions	44.1	38.2
Long-term debt	2,131.6	2,339.1

(Continued)

Canadian Tire Corporation, Limited, Statements of Earnings and Statements of Financial Position (*Continued*)

	Jan. 3, 2015	Dec. 31, 2013
	(in millions)	
Long-term deposits	1,286.2	1,152.0
Deferred income taxes	93.9	100.4
Other long-term liabilities	787.8	228.3
Total liabilities	8,922.4	8,180.1
EQUITY		
Share capital	695.5	712.9
Contributed surplus	2.9	2.4
Accumulated other comprehensive income	82.0	47.4
Retained earnings	4,075.1	4,404.6
Equity attributable to owners of Canadian Tire Corporation	4,855.5	5,157.3
Noncontrolling interests	775.3	282.6
Total equity	5,630.8	5,449.9
Total liabilities and equity	$14,553.2	$13,630.0

Source: Canadian Tire 2014 Annual Report

Compared to Telus Corporation's short-term liquidity ratios shown above in the body of the text, Canadian Tire's are generally stronger. This suggests that while Canadian Tire's short-term solvency is greater than that of Telus Corporation, both companies have short-term liquidity ratios that are comparable for their industry and neither corporation is in danger of short-term insolvency.

Debt Management (Solvency) Ratios

Debt management ratios provide information on two aspects of debt. First, they provide information on the relative mix of debt and equity financing (often referred to as its capital structure). The primary advantages of debt over equity are as follows:

- Interest payments are tax deductible.
- Creditors do not share in profits.

Debt, however, is riskier than equity, because unless the interest and principal payments are made when due, the firm may fall into bankruptcy. In most corporations, management attempts to achieve an appropriate balance between the cost advantage of debt and its extra risk.

Second, debt management ratios also try to show the corporation's ability to meet, or cover, its debt obligations through operations because interest and principal payments must be made as scheduled or a company can be declared bankrupt. The times interest earned ratio is an example of the latter type of measurement.

Times Interest Earned Ratio Some liabilities, like accounts payable, have flexible payment schedules that can be modified when necessary. Other liabilities—primarily short-term and long-term debt—have specific payment schedules that must be met. The cash used to make these payments must come from operations. Analysts use the times interest earned ratio to gauge a firm's ability to repay its debt from recurring operations. This ratio is measured pre-tax because interest expense is tax deductible. The **times interest earned ratio** is expressed as follows:

$$\text{Times interest earned} = \frac{\text{Earnings before income tax and interest expense}}{\text{Interest expense}}$$

The times interest earned ratios for Canadian Tire are calculated as follows:

	2014	2013
	(in millions)	
Income before tax	$878.2	$784.6
Interest expense	139.0	129.7
Times interest earned	**7.32**	**7.05**

Note that interest expense is often included in the financial statement footnotes because many corporations net interest income with interest expense on the face of the statement of earnings. Also, income before tax used in this calculation should be adjusted to remove the effect, if any, of non-recurring income/gains and expenses/losses to ensure that only earnings that are expected to repeat in future years is used in the calculation. Canadian Tire appears to have an easy time covering its interest expense/payments based on the times interest earned ratio.

While the times interest earned ratio provides information on the relative mix of debt and equity financing, other debt management ratios assess a company's ability to meet, or cover, its debt obligations. We will consider two different ways of measuring the proportion of debt within a corporation's capital structure.

Debt-to-Equity Ratio Debt is also occasionally defined as all liabilities. This is a more inclusive view of debt for it recognizes that if corporations did not have current liabilities such as accounts payable, they would have to take out other borrowings or issue shares to finance their assets. The **debt-to-equity ratio** is expressed as follows:

$$\text{Debt-to-equity ratio} = \frac{\text{Total liabilities}}{\text{Total equity}}$$

Canadian Tire's debt-to-equity ratio was 1.59 in 2014 and 1.50 in 2013, which is conservative given general lending requirements that this ratio not exceed 3.0.

Debt to Total Assets The proportion of total capital provided by creditors is also shown by the **debt-to-total-assets ratio**. This measure is more useful when equity is small or subject to substantial changes. This ratio is expressed as follows:

$$\text{Debt-to-total-assets ratio} = \frac{\text{Total liabilities}}{\text{Total assets}}$$

Overview of Debt Management Ratios Cornerstone 13.5 demonstrates how to calculate and interpret debt management ratios.

From the times interest earned ratios in Cornerstone 13.5, you can see that WestJet Airlines produced more than sufficient income to meet interest expense in both years. Risk decreased in 2015 compared to 2014 as the times interest earned ratio in 2015 indicates an improved ability to cover interest payments. The debt-to-total-assets ratio was virtually unchanged in 2015 from 2014, which indicates that management is closely watching the company's debt levels to ensure it is manageable.

CORNERSTONE 13.5

Calculating and Interpreting Debt Management Ratios

Information:

Information from WestJet Airlines Ltd. 2015 audited financial statements follows.

WestJet Airlines Consolidated Statements of Financial Position (Partial)		
	2015	**2014**
	(in thousands)	
Current Liabilities:		
Accounts payable and accrued liabilities	$ 545,438	$ 415,562
Advance ticket sales	620,216	575,781
Deferred rewards program	117,959	86,870
Nonrefundable guest credits	40,921	45,434
Current position of maintenance provisions	85,819	54,811
Current portion of long-term debt	141,572	159,843
Total current liabilities	1,551,925	1,338,301
Noncurrent Liabilities:		
Maintenance provisions	243,214	191,768
Long-term debt	1,033,261	1,028,820
Other liabilities	13,603	13,150
Deferred income tax	327,028	296,892
Total noncurrent liabilities	1,617,106	1,530,630
Total shareholders' equity	1,959,993	1,777,502
Total assets	5,129,024	4,646,433
Interest expense	53,655	51,838
Earnings before income tax	520,258	390,307

Source: WestJet Airlines 2015 Annual Report.

Required:

Calculate the following debt management ratios for WestJet Airlines for 2015 and 2014: (1) times interest earned ratio, (2) debt-to-equity ratio, and (3) debt-to-total-assets ratio.

Why:

The calculation of debt management ratios indicates whether a company will be able to generate sufficient cash from operations to meet debt obligations.

Solution:

		2015	2014
1. Times interest earned $= \dfrac{\text{Earnings before income tax and interest expense}}{\text{Interest expense}}$		$\dfrac{(\$520{,}258 + \$53{,}655)}{\$53{,}655} = 10.70$	$\dfrac{(\$390{,}307 + \$51{,}838)}{\$51{,}838} = 8.53$

(Continued)

2. Debt-to-equity $= \dfrac{\text{Total liabilities}}{\text{Total equity}}$

CORNERSTONE

13.5

2015	**2014**
$\dfrac{(\$1,551,925 + \$1,617,106)}{\$1,959,993} = 1.62$	$\dfrac{(\$1,338,301 + \$1,530,630)}{\$1,777,502} = 1.61$

(Continued)

3. Debt-to-total-assets $= \dfrac{\text{Total liabilities}}{\text{Total assets}}$

	2015	**2014**
	$\dfrac{(\$1,551,925 + \$1,617,106)}{\$5,129,024} = .62$	$\dfrac{(\$1,338,301 + \$1,530,630)}{\$4,646,433} = .62$

YOUDECIDE Credit Analysis

You are a loan officer at the Bank of Montreal (BMO). Your assistant has prepared the following financial statement and debt management ratio information to help you evaluate Amherst Manufacturing's loan application:

				Industry
	2017	2016	2015	(2015–2017)
Sales	171.2%	131.9%	100%	183.2%
Gross margin	168.7%	129.4%	100%	184.6%
Operating expenses	180.3%	134.7%	100%	160.5%
Operating income	160.5%	124.3%	100%	202.4%
Net income	162.2%	125.7%	100%	201.7%

You also have the following data for the year ended December 31, 2017:

	Amherst	
For the Years 2015–2017	Manufacturing	Industry
Average current ratio	2.06	1.55
Average debt-to-equity ratio	19.47	80.14
Average times interest earned	9.55	3.87

Amherst has asked BMO for a long-term loan that will double its long-term debt.

Should you approve the loan for Amherst?

The data you have are somewhat mixed. The debt management ratios for the company are more outstanding than for the industry. Even after doubling the amount of long-term debt, it is apparent that Amherst will remain better than the industry averages for the debt-to-equity and times interest earned ratios. The operating results, however, are not as encouraging. Amherst's growth is somewhat below industry averages. Furthermore, the growth in operating expenses signals a problem—especially when you consider that many operating expenses are fixed (such as salaries).

Although you probably want to follow up with Amherst regarding their projected results of operations, given their low debt burden, BMO should probably grant the loan.

Asset Efficiency Ratios

Asset efficiency ratios (or operating ratios) are measures of how efficiently a company uses its assets. The principal asset efficiency ratios are measures of **turnover**, that is, the average length of time required for assets to be consumed or replaced. The faster an asset is turned over, the more efficiently it is being used. These ratios provide managers and other users of a corporation's financial statements with easily interpreted measures of the time required to turn receivables into cash, inventory into cost of goods sold, or total assets into sales.

But managers are not the only people interested in asset efficiency ratios. Since well-managed, efficiently operated companies are usually among the most profitable, and since profits are the sources of cash from which long-term creditors receive their interest and principal payments, creditors seek information about the corporation's profit prospects from asset efficiency ratios. Shareholders also find that larger profits are usually followed by increased dividends and higher share prices, so they, too, are concerned with indicators of efficiency.

Accounts Receivable Turnover Ratio The length of time required to collect the receivable from a credit sale is the time required to turn over accounts receivable. The accounts receivable turnover ratio indicates how many times accounts receivable is turned over each year. The more times accounts receivable turns over each year, the more efficient are the firm's credit-granting and credit-collection activities. The **accounts receivable turnover ratio** is expressed as follows:

$$\text{Accounts receivable turnover ratio} = \frac{\text{Net credit sales or net sales}}{\text{Average accounts receivable}}$$

In the equation above, "net credit sales" means credit sales less sales returns and allowances. While some firms make all their sales on credit, many also make a substantial proportion of their sales for cash (or on credit cards, which are essentially cash sales). It is unusual for a company making cash and credit sales to report the proportion that is credit sales. For that reason, the accounts receivable turnover ratio is often computed using the number the firm reports for sales. In addition, to find the average balance for any financial statement account, such as average accounts receivable, divide the sum of the beginning and ending accounts receivable balances by two.

Using net sales (or revenue), Canadian Tire's receivables turnover ratios were 15.6 and 15.2 for 2013 and 2014, respectively, so they are very efficient at collecting cash from their sales. This ratio probably means that a vast majority of their sales are for cash (or third-party credit cards that are collected very quickly). Canadian Tire also has an in-store credit card that increases receivables balances and reduces third-party credit card fees.

Careful analysts examine quarterly or monthly financial statements, when available, to determine whether the amount of receivables recorded in the annual statements represents the receivables carried during the year. For example, retailers like Canadian Tire often have much larger receivables after the Christmas selling season than during other parts of the year.

The accounts receivable turnover ratio can be converted to measure the number of days necessary to collect the average account receivable. The average age of accounts receivable is calculated as follows:

$$\text{Average age of accounts receivable} = \frac{365 \text{ days}}{\text{Accounts receivable turnover ratio}}$$

After this ratio is calculated, it must be analyzed to assess whether the resulting amount is an improvement in operations. Customer credit terms, business seasonality, trends in prior periods, and comparisons with competitors should all be considered in the assessment.

Inventory Turnover Ratio Inventory turnover is the length of time required to sell inventory to customers. The more efficient a firm, the more times inventory will be turned over. The **inventory turnover ratio** indicates the number of times inventory is sold during the year and is expressed as follows:

$$\text{Inventory turnover ratio} = \frac{\text{Cost of goods sold}}{\text{Average inventory}}$$

Average inventory is calculated by adding the beginning inventory to the ending inventory and dividing by two.

Canadian Tire's inventory turnover ratios were 5.4 and 5.4 for 2013 and 2014, respectively. This means that Canadian Tire turns over its inventory almost six times per year or once every two months. Remember that inventory sitting in the warehouse or on the shelf is not earning a return. A weakening inventory turnover deserves some attention. For example, a slower moving inventory may indicate weakening sales. Canadian Tire managed its inventory turnover well by maintaining turnover at 5.4 times, despite a sales increase in 2014 from 2013, which otherwise may have resulted in inventory increases experienced in other companies.

The inventory turnover ratio can be converted to measure the number of days that inventory is held before sale. The number of days inventory held ratio is calculated as follows:

$$\text{Days of inventory held} = \frac{365 \text{ days}}{\text{Inventory turnover}}$$

After this ratio is calculated, it must be analyzed to assess whether the resulting amount is an improvement in operations. The type of inventory held, business seasonality, trends in prior periods, and comparisons to competitors are all factors to consider in an assessment.

Now that we have examined both receivables and inventory turnover, let us combine these measurements to approximate the length of the operating cycle (the length of time required for an investment in inventory to produce cash). Canadian Tire's 2014 operating cycle can be estimated by adding the number of days needed to turn over both receivables and inventory. The inventory turns over in approximately 68 days (365 days ÷ 5.4 inventory turnover ratio) and the receivables turn over in approximately 24 days (365 days ÷ 15.2 receivables turnover ratio), which gives an operating cycle of approximately 92 days.

The longer the operating cycle, the larger the investment necessary in receivables and inventory. When assets are larger, more liabilities and equity are required to finance them. Large amounts of capital negatively affect net income and cash flows for dividends. Therefore, firms attempt to maintain as short an operating cycle as possible.

Accounts Payable Turnover Ratio The accounts payable turnover ratio measures the company's effectiveness at managing amounts owing to trade creditors. Paying too quickly results in the loss of "free" money, while paying too slowly results in lost discounts and interest charges. The accounts payable turnover ratio is calculated as follows:

$$\text{Accounts payable turnover} = \frac{\text{Net credit purchases}}{\text{Average accounts payable}}$$

A practical issue arises, since net credit purchases are not usually disclosed in the financial statements. However, purchases can be estimated by inverting the cost of goods sold equation as follows:

$$\text{Purchases} = \text{Cost of goods sold} - \text{Beginning inventory} + \text{Ending inventory}$$

For Canadian Tire for 2014, the accounts payable turnover ratio is 4.5, which means that Canadian Tire pays its suppliers every 81 days (365/4.5) on average. Given that the operating cycle from selling inventory to cash collection is 92 days, Canadian Tire should consider slowing down its payments to creditors, increasing its inventory turnover, or improving credit terms granted to customers to better match these two time periods.

As with the accounts receivable and inventory turnover ratios, we can convert the turnover ratio to a number of days to pay ratio. The number of days to pay ratio for accounts payable is calculated as follows:

$$\text{Number of days to pay} = \frac{365 \text{ days}}{\text{Accounts payable turnover ratio}}$$

The analysis of these ratios must consider factors such as creditor payment terms, past trends, and comparison to competitors.

Asset Turnover Ratio Another measure of the efficiency of a corporation's operations is the **asset turnover ratio**. This ratio measures the efficiency with which a corporation's assets are used to produce sales revenues. The more sales dollars produced by each dollar invested in assets, the more efficiently a firm is considered to be operating. The asset turnover ratio is expressed as follows:

$$\text{Asset turnover ratio} = \frac{\text{Net sales}}{\text{Average total assets}}$$

Average total assets is calculated by adding beginning total assets to ending total assets in the reporting period and dividing by two.

Canadian Tire's asset turnover ratios were .88 and .88 in 2013 and 2014, respectively, which means about every 415 days (365 ÷ 0.88) in 2014. Sales must be increased or the total assets employed decreased to improve this ratio.

Care must be exercised when evaluating the asset turnover ratio. Some industries (such as electric utilities and capital-intensive manufacturers) require a substantially larger investment in assets to produce a sales dollar than do other industries (such as fast-food restaurants or footwear and catalogue merchants). And obviously, a company's total assets turn over much more slowly than its inventories and receivables.

Fixed Asset Turnover Ratio A company's operating efficiency can be measure by the fixed asset (i.e., property, plant, and equipment) turnover ratio. For Canadian Tire for fiscal 2014, the **fixed asset turnover ratio** is calculated as follows:

$$\text{Fixed Asset Turnover Ratio} = \frac{\text{Net Sales}}{\text{Average Net Fixed Assets}}$$
$$= \frac{\$12,462.9}{\$3,629.6} = 3.43$$

This ratio means that the company was able to generate $3.43 of sales for every dollar invested in net property, plant, and equipment in fiscal 2014. This ratio was consistent with Canadian Tire's fixed asset turnover ratio in 2013 of 3.43.

The fixed asset turnover ratio is often used to evaluate capital-intensive businesses such as utilities, airlines, and telecom companies, where ratios are often substantially lower than for retailers such as Canadian Tire. For example, Telus Corporation's fiscal 2014 fixed asset turnover ratio was 1.36.[1]

Overview of Asset Efficiency Ratios Cornerstone 13.6 illustrates how to calculate and interpret asset efficiency ratios.

---

[1] Telus Corporation 2014 Annual Report

Calculating and Interpreting Asset Efficiency Ratios

CORNERSTONE 13.6

CORNERSTONE VIDEO

Information:

Refer to the information in Canadian Tire's statement of earnings and statement of financial position in Exhibit 13.2. Additionally, accounts receivable, inventory, total assets and fixed assets for 2012 were $750.6, $1,503.3, $13,228.6 and $3,343.5, respectively.

Required:

Calculate the following asset efficiency ratios for Canadian Tire for 2014 and 2013: (1) accounts receivable turnover ratio, (2) inventory turnover ratio, (3) accounts payable turnover ratio, (4) asset turnover ratio and (5) fixed asset turnover ratio.

Why:

The calculation of asset efficiency ratios indicates how efficiently a company is using its assets.

Solution:

		2014	2013

1. $\dfrac{\text{Accounts receivable}}{\text{turnover ratio}} = \dfrac{\text{Net sales}}{\text{Average accounts receivable}}$ $\dfrac{\$12,462.9}{(\$880.2 + \$758.5)/2} = 15.2$ $\dfrac{\$11,785.6}{(\$758.5 + \$750.6)/2} = 15.6$

2. $\dfrac{\text{Inventory}}{\text{turnover ratio}} = \dfrac{\text{Cost of goods sold}}{\text{Average inventories}}$ $\dfrac{\$8,416.9}{(\$1,623.2 + \$1,481.0)/2} = 5.4$ $\dfrac{\$8,063.3}{(\$1,481.0 + \$1,503.3)/2} = 5.4$

3. Accounts payable turnover ratio $= \dfrac{\text{Cost of goods sold } - \text{ Beginning inventory } + \text{ Ending inventory}}{\text{Average accounts payable}}$

$\dfrac{\$8,416.9 - \$1,481.0 + \$1,623.8}{(\$1,961.2 + \$1,817.4)/2} = 4.5$ $\dfrac{\$8,063.3 - \$1,503.3 + \$1,623.8}{(\$1,817.4 + \$1,631.3)/2} = 4.7$

Source: Canadian Tire Corporation Annual Reports.

4. $\dfrac{\text{Asset}}{\text{turnover ratio}} = \dfrac{\text{Net sales}}{\text{Average total assets}}$ $\dfrac{\$12,462.9}{[(\$14,553.2 + \$13,630.0) \div 2]} = 0.88$ $\dfrac{\$11,785.6}{[(\$13,630.0 + \$13,228.6) \div 2]} = 0.88$

5. $\dfrac{\text{Fixed asset}}{\text{turnover ratio}} = \dfrac{\text{Net sales}}{\text{Average fixed assets}}$ $\dfrac{\$12,462.9}{[(\$3,743.1 + \$3,516.1)/2]} = 3.43$ $\dfrac{\$11,785.6}{[(\$3,516.1 + \$3,343.5)/2]} = 3.44$

Turnover ratios must be interpreted carefully. A company's ability to increase its receivables turnover is limited by competitive considerations. If competitors allow customers a lengthy period before payment is expected, then the firm must offer similar credit terms or lose customer sales. In periods of high interest rates, the cost of carrying customers' receivables should not be underestimated. For example, a firm with credit sales of $10,000 per day that collects in 30 rather than 90 days would save $72,000 per year at a 12% interest rate (60 days × $10,000 × 12%).

However, a corporation's ability to increase its inventory turnover is also affected by its strategy and what the competition is doing. For example, if its strategy is to offer a wide selection or if its competitors stock large quantities of inventory, a corporation will be forced to keep more inventory on hand. This, of course, leads to lower inventory turnover.

If a company pays its accounts payable too slowly, this could result in poor supplier relationships, increased interest charges, and delayed shipments, all of which might negatively affect profitability. However, use of "free" credit positively contributes to operating results.

Asset efficiency ratios measure the efficiency of a corporation's operations—a factor ultimately related to the corporation's profits. Let us now closely examine some direct measures of a corporation's profitability.

Profitability Ratios

Profitability ratios measure two aspects of a corporation's profits:

- elements of operations that contribute to profit
- the relationship of profit to total investment and investment by shareholders

The first group of profitability ratios, which includes gross profit (or gross margin) percentage, operating margin percentage, and net profit margin percentage, expresses statement of earnings elements as percentages of net sales. The second group of profitability ratios, which includes return on assets and return on equity, divides measures of income by measures of investment.

Gross Profit (or Gross Margin) Percentage **Gross profit percentage** is a measurement of the proportion of each sales dollar that is available to pay other expenses and provide profit for owners. It indicates the effectiveness of pricing, marketing, purchasing, and production decisions. Gross profit percentage is expressed as follows:

$$\text{Gross profit percentage} = \frac{\text{Gross profit}}{\text{Net sales}}$$

Canadian Tire's gross profit percentage was 31.6% in 2013 and 32.5% in 2014. This means that for every dollar in sales the merchandise cost approximately 67 cents, which results in approximately 33 cents in gross profit. Based on 2013 sales, the increase in gross profit percentage in 2014 to 32.5% added $106 million to the gross profit.

Operating Margin Percentage The operating margin percentage measures the profitability of a company's operations in relation to its sales. All operating revenues and expenses are included in income from operations, but expenses, revenues, gains, and losses that are unrelated to operations are excluded. For example, a retailer would exclude interest revenues produced by its credit activities from income from operations. For Canadian Tire, operating margin consists of income before tax and net finance costs. The **operating margin percentage** is expressed as follows:

$$\text{Operating margin percentage} = \frac{\text{Income from operations}}{\text{Net sales}}$$

Canadian Tire's operating margin percentage was 7.6% in 2013 and 7.9% in 2014. The difference between the gross profit and operating margin percentage of approximately 25% in 2014 (32.5% gross margin percentage − 7.9% operating margin percentage) means that approximately 25 cents on every dollar of sales were spent on operating expenses in 2014. Although an operating margin of 7.9% may not sound very good, it was an increase from 7.6% in 2013 and added approximately $35,000,000 to operating margin in 2014 based on 2013 sales levels.

Net Profit Margin Percentage   The net profit margin percentage measures the proportion of each sales dollar that is profit. The **net profit margin percentage** is expressed as follows:

$$\text{Net profit margin percentage} = \frac{\text{Net income}}{\text{Net sales}}$$

Canadian Tire's net profit margin percentage was 4.8% in 2013 and 5.1% in 2014. Canadian Tire is producing an increasing net profit margin annually.

In evaluating the gross profit, operating margin, and net profit margin percentage, it is important to recognize that there is substantial variation in profit margins from industry to industry. For example, retail grocery stores earn a relatively small amount of gross profit, operating margin, and net income per sales dollar. Pharmaceutical manufacturers, on the other hand, earn much more per sales dollar. Since the magnitude of these percentages is affected by many factors, changes from period to period must be investigated to determine the cause.

Return on Assets   The return on assets ratio measures the profit earned by a corporation through use of all its capital, or the total of the investment by both creditors and shareholders. The **return on assets ratio** is expressed as:

$$\text{Return on assets} = \frac{\text{Net income} + [\text{Interest expense} \times (1 - \text{Tax rate})]}{\text{Average total assets}}$$

Profit, or return, is determined by adding interest expense net of tax to net income. Interest expense net of tax is expressed as follows:

$$\text{Interest expense net of tax} = \text{Interest expense} \times (1 - \text{Tax rate})$$

Interest expense is added to net income because it is a return to creditors for their capital contributions. Because the actual capital contribution made by creditors is included in the denominator (average total assets), the numerator must be computed on a comparable basis to shareholders.

Canadian Tire's return on assets was 4.8% in 2013 and 5.1% in 2014. As with the percentages discussed above, appropriate values for this ratio vary from industry to industry because of differences in risk. Over a several-year period, the average return on assets for an electric utility ought to be smaller than the average return on assets for a company that makes and sells home appliances. Companies in the home appliance industry, such as Whirlpool Corporation, have a much larger variability of net income because their operations are more sensitive to economic conditions.

Return on Equity   The return on equity ratio measures the profit earned by a firm through the use of capital supplied by shareholders. Return on equity is similar to return on assets, except that the payments to creditors are removed from the numerator and the creditors' capital contributions are removed from the denominator. The **return on equity ratio** is expressed as follows:

$$\text{Return on equity} = \frac{\text{Net income}}{\text{Average equity}}$$

One of the primary objectives of the management of a firm is to maximize returns for its shareholders. Although the link between a corporation's net income and increases in dividends and share price return is not perfect, the return on equity ratio is still an effective measure of management's performance for the shareholders. As is the case with return on assets, firms often differ in return on equity because of differences in risk. For example, the average several-year return on equity for a grocery store should be lower than the average return on equity for a retail department store because of the lower sensitivity to economic conditions.

The return on equity for Canadian Tire was 11.1% and 11.5% in 2013 and 2014, respectively.

Quality of Earnings Ratio Many financial statement users are concerned with the quality of a company's earnings because of the perceived ability of management to liberally interpret the meaning and application of generally accepted accounting principles. In order to evaluate the quality of earnings of a company, a comparison of net income to the cash flows from operating activities is performed. The **quality of earnings ratio** for Canadian Tire for fiscal 2014 is calculated as follows:

$$\text{Quality of Earnings Ratio} = \frac{\text{Cash Flows from Operating Activities}}{\text{Net Earnings}}$$
$$= \frac{\$578.8}{\$639.3^2} = .91$$

A quality of earnings ratio greater than 1 is generally considered to reflect a greater quality of earnings because at least one dollar of cash flow exists for each dollar of net earnings. A score of less than 1 in this ratio score calculation means that accruals of income and expense, being noncash items, are having a significant impact on the calculation of net earnings. In this latter case, as this ratio decreases further and further below 1, ever-increasing scrutiny of net earnings by financial statement users is prudent.

Overview of Profitability Ratios Cornerstone 13.7 demonstrates how to calculate and interpret profitability ratios.

CORNERSTONE 13.7   Calculating and Interpreting Profitability Ratios

Information:

Refer to the information in Canadian Tire's statement of earnings and statement of financial position in Exhibit 13.2. On Canadian Tire's income statement of earnings, assume that Canadian Tire's interest expense is $105.8 in 2013 and $108.9 in 2014. Note that Canadian Tire's total assets and equity for 2012 were $13,228.6 and $4,764.3, respectively.

Required:

Calculate the following profitability ratios for Canadian Tire for 2013 and 2014: (1) gross profit percentage, (2) operating margin percentage, (3) net profit margin percentage, (4) return on assets, and (5) return on equity.

(Continued)

---

[2] Canadian Tire 2014 Annual Report

Why:

The calculation of profitability ratios indicates how well a company is managing profit-ability, return on assets, and return on shareholders' equity.

CORNERSTONE

13.7

Solution:

(Continued)

	2014	2013
1. Gross profit percentage $= \dfrac{\text{Gross profit}}{\text{Net sales}}$	$\dfrac{\$4,046.0}{\$12,462.9} = 32.5\%$	$\dfrac{\$3,722.3}{\$11,785.6} = 31.6\%$

	2014	2013
2. Operating margin percentage $= \dfrac{\text{Income from operations}}{\text{Net sales}}$	$\dfrac{\$987.1}{\$12,462.9} = 7.9\%$	$\dfrac{\$890.4}{\$11,785.6} = 7.6\%$

	2014	2013
3. Net profit margin percentage $= \dfrac{\text{Net income}}{\text{Net sales}}$	$\dfrac{\$639.3}{\$12,462.9} = 5.1\%$	$\dfrac{\$564.4}{\$11,785.6} = 4.8\%$

4. Return on assets $= \dfrac{\text{Net income} + [\text{Interest expense} \times (1 - \text{Tax rate**})]}{\text{Average total assets*}}$

2014	2013
$\dfrac{\$639.3 + [108.9^{***} \times (1 - 27.20\%)]}{[(\$14,553.2 + \$13,630.0) \div 2]} = 5.1\%$	$\dfrac{\$564.4 + [105.8^{***} \times (1 - 28.07\%)]}{[(\$13,630.0 + \$13,228.6^{***}) \div 2]} = 4.8\%$

*Note: Average balance $= \dfrac{\text{Beginning balance} + \text{Ending balance}}{2}$

**Note: $\left(\text{Tax rate} = \dfrac{\text{Income taxes}}{\text{Income before taxes}}\right)$

***Provided in the *Information* section above.

5. Return on equity $= \dfrac{\text{Net income}}{\text{Average equity*}}$

2014	2013
$\dfrac{\$639.3}{[(\$5,630.8 + \$5,449.9) \div 2]} = 11.5\%$	$\dfrac{\$564.4}{[(\$5,449.9 + \$4,764.3^{***}) \div 2]} = 11.1\%$

Source: Canadian Tire Corporation Annual Reports.

Shareholder Ratios

Shareholders are primarily interested in two things:

- the creation of value
- the distribution of value

Shareholder ratios such as earnings per share and return on common equity provide information about the creation of value for shareholders. As discussed in Chapter 10, value is distributed to shareholders in one of two ways. Either the corporation issues dividends or it repurchases shares. Four key ratios are typically used by shareholders in addressing the return on their investment. These four ratios are earnings per share, dividend yield, dividend payout, and the price/earnings ratio. The price/earnings ratio is understood to represent the amount that a shareholder would pay for a dollar of future company earnings.

Earnings per Share (EPS) The earnings per share ratio (EPS) measures the income available for common shareholders on a per-share basis and is examined by nearly all statement users representing the controlling interest in a consolidated business entity. The **earnings per share ratio (EPS)** is expressed as follows:

$$\text{Earnings per share ratio} = \frac{\text{Net income attributable to controlling interests} - \text{Preferred dividends}}{\text{Weighted average number of common shares outstanding}}$$

Preferred dividends are subtracted from net income because those payments are a return to holders of shares other than common shares. In fact, the numerator, net income attributable to the controlling interest in a consolidated entity less preferred dividends, is often called *income available for common shareholders* who represent the controlling interest in a consolidated business entity.

Although this formula allows you to calculate EPS on your own, public corporations are also required to disclose EPS on the statement of earnings. For example, Canadian Tire's EPS attributable to the controlling interest of Canadian Tire was $6.96 in 2013 and $7.65 in 2014. Obviously, 2014 was a better year than 2013.

Return on Common Equity The return on common equity ratio is arguably the most important ratio for investors. It's similar to the return on equity discussed in the profitability ratio section, but it uses the return on *common* equity rather than equity. Common equity when noncontrolling interests and preferred shares exist is expressed as follows:

Common equity = Total equity − Equity attributable to noncontrolling interests − Preferred shares

The **return on common equity ratio** where noncontrolling interests exist and preferred shares do not exist is expressed as follows:

$$\text{Return on common equity} = \frac{\text{Net income} - \text{net income attributable to noncontrolling interests}}{\text{Average common equity attributable to the controlling interest}}$$

When there are no preferred shares or noncontrolling interests, return on common equity will equal traditional return on equity (ROE).

Dividend Yield Ratio The dividend yield ratio measures the rate at which dividends provide a return to shareholders by comparing dividends with the market price of a share. This ratio is conceptually similar to an interest rate on debt where the dividend is like the interest payment and the cost of the share is the principal. The **dividend yield ratio** is expressed as follows:

$$\text{Dividend yield ratio} = \frac{\text{Dividends per common share}}{\text{Closing market price per share for the year}}$$

For the year ended December 31, 2014, Canadian Tire paid dividends of $2.15 per common share and the closing market value of its common shares was $122.74. This gives a dividend yield ratio of 1.75%.

Dividend yield is affected by both the corporation's dividend policy and the behaviour of its share price. Because share prices often change by substantial amounts over short periods, the dividend yield ratio is not stable. In fact, when a share is traded regularly, the market price is likely to change many times each day. For this reason, some analysts compute dividend yield based on the average share price for a given period. Others use the highest and the lowest prices for a period and present the dividend yield as a range. For ease, dividend yield has been calculated in this text by using the closing market price for the year.

Dividend Payout Ratio   The dividend payout ratio measures the proportion of a corporation's profits that are returned to the shareholders immediately as dividends. The **dividend payout ratio** when noncontrolling interests exist is expressed as follows:

$$\text{Dividend payout ratio} = \frac{\text{Common share dividends}}{\text{Net income attributable to controlling interest}}$$

You could also calculate dividend payout using per-share amounts (dividends per share ÷ EPS). You can find the dividends declared in the retained earnings column of the statement of changes in equity and dividends paid in the statement of cash flow.

For Canadian Tire, the common dividends paid were $1.88 per share in 2013 and $2.15 per share in 2014. This produces dividend payout ratios of 27.01% and 28.10% in 2013 and 2014, respectively.

The dividend payout ratio varies from corporation to corporation, even within a given industry. Most corporations attempt to pay some stable proportion of earnings as dividends. Corporations are reluctant to reduce dividends unless absolutely necessary. The result of these two tendencies is that dividends per share are usually increased only when management is confident that higher earnings per share can be sustained. An increase in the dividend payout ratio is usually a signal that management expects future net income to be larger and sustainable.

Price/Earnings Ratio   This ratio compares the market price of a company's shares with the company's earnings per share. The price/earnings ratio is typically calculated by taking the market price of the company's common shares and dividing by the earnings per common share. While many factors affect the resulting "multiple" derived from this calculation, the multiple is considered by stock analysts to represent what a shareholder will pay for a dollar's worth of earnings. Canadian Tire had a price/earnings ratio of approximately 16 (market price of $122.74 divided by earnings per share of $7.65) at December 31, 2014. The price/earnings multiple is generally low for companies that have poor growth opportunities or where the perceived level of risk is high. Companies that have significant growth potential or low levels of perceived risk will generally have a higher price/earnings ratio.

Overview of Shareholder Ratios   Cornerstone 13.8 demonstrates how to calculate and interpret the shareholder ratios.

Calculating and Interpreting Shareholder Ratios

Information:

Refer to the information for Canadian Tire's statement of earnings and statement of financial position in Exhibit 13.2. Canadian Tire's average common share equivalents*** for 2014 and 2013 were 78.9 and 80.6, respectively. They paid dividends of $2.15 in 2014 and $1.88 in 2013. The price of Canadian Tire's shares was $122.74 and $99.49 at the end of 2014 and 2013, respectively.

Required:

Calculate the following shareholder ratios for Canadian Tire for 2013 and 2014: (1) earnings per share, (2) return on common equity (assume 2012 total equity and preferred shares, were $4,764.3, and $0, respectively), (3) dividend yield, (4) dividend payout, and (5) price/earnings ratios.

(Continued)

CORNERSTONE
VIDEO

CORNERSTONE
13.8

(Continued)

Why:
The calculation of shareholder ratios indicates how well a company is creating value for shareholders.

Solution:

1. $EPS = \dfrac{\text{Net income} - \text{Preferred dividends} - \text{earnings attributable to noncontrolling interests}}{\text{Average number of common share equivalents outstanding}}$

2014	**2013**
$\dfrac{(\$639.3 - \$0 - \$35.3)}{78.9} = \$7.65$	$\dfrac{(\$564.4 - \$0 - \$3.2)}{80.6} = \$6.96$

2. $\text{Return on common equity} = \dfrac{\text{Net income} - \text{preferred dividends} - \text{earnings attributable to noncontrolling interests}}{\text{Average common equity*}}$

2014	**2013**
$\dfrac{(\$639.3-\$0-\$35.3)}{[(\$5,630.0-\$0-\$775.3)+((\$5,449.2-\$0-\$282.6)/2)\div2]}$ $=12.1\%$	$\dfrac{(\$564.4-\$0-\$3.2)}{[(\$4,004.9-\$0)+(\$3,643.1-\$0)\div2]}$ $=11.62\%$

3. $\text{Dividend yield ratio} = \dfrac{\text{Dividends per common share**}}{\text{Closing market price per share for the year}}$

2014	2013
$\dfrac{\$2.15}{\$122.74} = 1.75\%$	$\dfrac{\$1.88}{\$99.49} = 1.89\%$

*Common equity = Total equity – Preferred shares – Equity attributable to noncontrolling interests

**Dividends per share are taken from the financial statement notes. Stock market price is given in the information section of this Cornerstone.

***Class A shares treated as common share equivalents

4. $\text{Dividend payout ratio} = \dfrac{\text{Common dividends paid per share}}{\text{Net income attributable to controlling interest per share}}$

2014	2013
$\dfrac{\$2.15}{\$7.65} = 28.10\%$	$\dfrac{\$1.88}{\$6.96} = 27.01\%$

5. $\text{Price/earnings ratio} = \dfrac{\text{Stock market price}}{\text{Earnings per share}}$

2014	2013
$\dfrac{\$122.74}{\$7.65} = 16.0$ times	$\dfrac{\$99.49}{\$6.96} = 14.3$ times

Source: Canadian Tire Corporation Annual Reports.

We will now discuss the DuPont analysis, which formalized the analysis of return on equity.

DuPont Analysis

Return on common equity (or return on equity, which is hereafter abbreviated as ROE) is the most important measure of profitability for investors. It represents the amount of income generated per dollar of book value of equity or common equity. In that way, it is conceptually similar to an interest rate. Recall that ROE is calculated as:

$$\text{ROE} = \frac{\text{Net income}}{\text{Average equity}}$$

DuPont analysis recognizes that ROE can be broken down into three important aspects of return—net profit margin, asset turnover, and leverage.

$$= \frac{\text{Net income}}{\text{Sales}} \times \frac{\text{Sales}}{\text{Average total assets}} \times \frac{\text{Average total assets}}{\text{Average equity}}$$

Net Profit Margin × Asset Turnover × Total Leverage

The logic of this breakdown is compelling. First, profitability requires that the corporation be able to earn an adequate gross profit margin. That is, Canadian Tire and other retailers must be able to sell their products for more than it costs to buy them. Net profit margin carries this idea down the statement of earnings from gross profit to net income. As we learned earlier in the chapter, the net profit margin represents how many cents of profit exist on every sales dollar.

Second, how efficient is the corporation with its net assets? The desire for asset efficiency is obvious. Everyone knows that you would rather earn $1,000,000 on an investment of $5,000,000 than on an investment of $50,000,000. Before discussing leverage, we will focus a little more closely on net profit margin and asset turnover, which taken together give us return on assets (Net income ÷ Average total assets), albeit ignoring the after-tax effect of interest expense in the numerator. To illustrate, consider Canadian Tire for 2014. The net profit margin, asset turnover, and return on assets ratios were:

	Net Profit Margin	**Asset Turnover**	**Return on Assets**
Canadian Tire	5.1%	0.88	4.5%*

*Difference from Cornerstone 13.7 arises due to DuPont analysis not adding back the after-tax effect of interest expense to net income.

Based on these figures, Canadian Tire's return on assets was calculated as 5.1% × 0.88 = 4.5%. However, this same asset return could have been achieved with a net profit margin of 4.5% and asset turnover of 1.00 since 4.5% × 1.00 = 4.5%. These calculations demonstrate that if a company were to pursue a strategy of having a low selling price in the industry in which it operates, return on equity need not suffer if a sufficient asset turnover can be generated to compensate for lower selling prices.

Product differentiators experience lower asset turnover. You can probably think of these distinctions within and between industries. For example, Walmart is a cost leader. It has very low margins but makes up for it by being extremely efficient with its assets. Nordstrom's, on the other hand, has much higher margins, but this is offset by lower turnover. Grocery stores have low margins and high turnover; auto dealers and jewellery stores have high margins and low turnover. Furthermore, the trade-off between margins and turnover is evident in a number of decisions. For example, if a store puts an item on sale, it sacrifices margins and hopes to make up for it with higher turnover.

Notice that the 2014 ROE of 10.1% for Canadian Tire is higher than its respective returns on assets. Return on *equity* can be made larger than return on *assets* by leveraging these assets through the use of debt. The idea of leverage is simple. For example, if you can borrow at 8% and earn 10% (assuming the same tax rates on the interest and return), then you win. If you could guarantee these two figures after taxes, you should borrow all you can because you are netting 2% on every dollar. That is, if you borrow $1,000,000 you will make $20,000 (a $100,000 return less $80,000 in interest). If you can borrow $1,000,000,000, then you will make $20,000,000.

This effect is captured by the total leverage component of the DuPont analysis. Recall that a company can obtain money to finance its business by either selling shares or borrowing. If they choose to sell shares, then shareholders are entitled to their share of the returns. If they borrow the money, on the other hand, the creditors do not share in the returns. So why don't all corporations use debt instead of equity? There are two reasons:

- They may not be able to find a low enough interest rate.
- While interest is guaranteed, returns are not. That is, while the returns may seem better than the interest right now, in a few years it may not be so. For evidence of this, consider stories of people who borrowed money at 15% on credit cards to invest in the stock market in the late 1990s.

Cornerstone 13.9 illustrates how to perform and interpret DuPont analysis.

CORNERSTONE 13.9

CORNERSTONE
VIDEO

Performing and Interpreting DuPont Analysis

Information:

Refer to the information from Canadian Tire's statement of earnings and statement of financial position in Exhibit 13.2. Assume that the company's total assets and equity for 2012 were $13,228.6 ($ million) and $4,764.3 ($ million), respectively.

Required:

Perform DuPont analysis for Canadian Tire for 2014 and 2013.

Why:

DuPont analysis analyzes a company's return on shareholders' equity in three components—net profit margin, asset turnover, and total leverage. The analysis can be used to increase return on shareholders' equity.

Solution:

Canadian Tire 2014

$$\text{DuPont analysis: ROE} = \left(\frac{\text{Net income}}{\text{Sales}}\right) \times \left(\frac{\text{Sales}}{\text{Average total assets}}\right) \times \left(\frac{\text{Average total assets}}{\text{Average equity}}\right)$$

$$= \left(\frac{\$639.3}{\$12,462.9}\right) \times \left\{\frac{\$12,462.9}{(\$14,553.2 + \$13,630.0) \div 2}\right\} \times \left\{\frac{(\$14,553.2 + \$12,630.0) \div 2}{(\$5,630.8 + \$5,449.9) \div 2}\right\}$$

$$= 5.1\% \times 0.88 \times 2.54$$

$$= 10.1\%$$

Canadian Tire 2013

$$= \left(\frac{\$564.4}{\$11,785.6}\right) \times \left\{\frac{\$11,785.6}{(\$13,630.0 + \$13,228.6) \div 2}\right\} \times \left\{\frac{(\$13,630.0 + \$13,228.6) \div 2}{(\$5,449.9 + \$4,764.3) \div 2}\right\}$$

$$= 4.8\% \times 0.88 \times 2.63$$

$$= 11.1\%$$

Source: Canadian Tire Corporation Annual Reports.

The DuPont analysis in Cornerstone 13.9 shows that Canadian Tire performed better in 2013 compared to 2014. An increase in net profit margin in 2014, due to a rising gross profit percentage in 2014 compared to 2013, was offset by a decrease in asset leverage due to the retention of a large amount of earnings in 2013. By the end of 2014, the company was leveraging its assets further in response to market opportunities and to enhance its return on equity. The interpretation of this ratio can inform the user in a substantial way about the company's future plans.

Summary of Financial Ratios

Exhibit 13.3 summarizes the financial ratios presented in this chapter. More advanced accounting texts may present additional ratios; however, the ratios introduced here are among the most widely used.

$$\left(\text{EXHIBIT 13.3}\right)$$

Summary of Financial Ratios

Short-Term Liquidity Ratios

1. $\text{Current ratio} = \dfrac{\text{Current assets}}{\text{Current liabilities}}$

2. $\text{Quick ratio} = \dfrac{\text{Cash} + \text{Short-term investments} + \text{Receivables}}{\text{Current liabilities}}$

3. $\text{Cash ratio} = \dfrac{\text{Cash} + \text{short-term investments}}{\text{Current liabilities}}$

4. $\text{Operating cash flow ratio} = \dfrac{\text{Cash flows from operating activities}}{\text{Current liabilities}}$

Debt Management Ratios

5. $\text{Times interest earned} = \dfrac{\text{Earnings before income tax and interest expense}}{\text{Interest expense}}$

6. $\text{Debt-to-equity ratio} = \dfrac{\text{Total liabilities}}{\text{Total equity}}$

7. $\text{Debt-to-total-assets ratio} = \dfrac{\text{Total liabilities}}{\text{Total assets}}$

Asset Efficiency Ratios

8. $\text{Accounts receivable turnover ratio} = \dfrac{\text{Net credit sales or net sales}}{\text{Average accounts receivable}}$

9. $\text{Inventory turnover ratio} = \dfrac{\text{Cost of goods sold}}{\text{Average inventory}}$

10. $\text{Accounts payable turnover} = \dfrac{\text{Credit purchases (or Cost of goods sold} - \text{Beginning inventory} + \text{Ending inventory)}}{\text{Average accounts payable}}$

11. $\text{Asset turnover ratio} = \dfrac{\text{Net sales}}{\text{Average total sssets}}$

12. $\text{Fixed asset turnover} = \dfrac{\text{Net sales}}{\text{Average net fixed assets}}$

Profitability Ratios

13. $\text{Gross profit percentage} = \dfrac{\text{Gross profit}}{\text{Net sales}}$

14. $\text{Operating margin percentage} = \dfrac{\text{Income from operations}}{\text{Net sales}}$

(Continued)

(EXHIBIT 13.3)

Summary of Financial Ratios (*Continued*)

15. Net profit margin percentage $= \dfrac{\text{Net income}}{\text{Net sales}}$

16. Return on assets $= \dfrac{\text{Net income} + [\text{Interest expense} \times (1 - \text{Tax rate})]}{\text{Average total assets}}$

17. Return on equity $= \dfrac{\text{Net income}}{\text{Average equity}}$

Shareholder Ratios

18. Quality of earnings $= \dfrac{\text{Cash flow from operating activities}}{\text{Net income}}$

19. Earnings per share (EPS) $= \dfrac{(\text{Net income} - \text{Preferred dividends})}{\text{Average number of common shares outstanding}}$

20. Return on common equity $= \dfrac{\text{Net income}}{\text{Average common equity}}$

21. Dividend yield ratio $= \dfrac{\text{Dividends per common share}}{\text{Closing market price per share for the year}}$

22. Dividend payout ratio $= \dfrac{\text{Common dividends paid}}{\text{Net income}}$

23. Price/earnings ratio $= \dfrac{\text{Stock market share price}}{\text{Earnings per share}}$

DuPont Analysis

24. Return on equity $= \left(\dfrac{\text{Net income}}{\text{Sales}}\right) \times \left(\dfrac{\text{Sales}}{\text{Average total assets}}\right) \times \left(\dfrac{\text{Average total assets}}{\text{Average equity}}\right)$

Data for Ratio Comparisons

As we pointed out earlier in the chapter, developing information from financial ratios requires that comparisons be made among the ratios of the following:

- the same corporation over time
- similar corporations over time
- similar corporations at the present time

Analysts rely on several sources to fulfill their need for a broad range of data for individual corporations as well as for industries and the economy.

We believe that the best source of information about a corporation starts with the investor relations section of its website. This part of the website should contain links to the corporation's regulatory filings, analyst conference calls, and press releases. However, you can also gain information through the financial press (such as *The Globe and Mail* and *The Wall Street Journal*) and investor discussion boards, although the latter must be evaluated with a critical eye.

Information on the industry can be obtained from industry guides such as Statistics Canada, Standard & Poor's, and IBISWorld. These are often available through your university library website or in hard copy at the library. We also like websites like Google Finance, Yahoo! Finance, BizStats, and MSN.

SIGNIFICANT DIFFERENCES BETWEEN IFRS AND ASPE

Throughout this text we have highlighted the significant differences between IFRS and ASPE in terms of how they measure and report various financial statement elements. Since public companies use IFRS, and most private companies use ASPE, the financial statement figures generated by these two sets of accounting standards can differ significantly in several areas. Those who analyze financial statements must ensure that they are knowledgeable regarding the financial reporting standards being used by the company being analyzed. This knowledge will be particularly important when a public company's financial statements are being compared to those of a private company.

SUMMARY OF LEARNING OBJECTIVES

LO1.   **Explain how creditors, investors, and others use financial statements in their decisions.**

- The role of financial statements is to provide information for
  - Creditors
  - Investors
  - Customers
  - Suppliers
  - Employees
- This information will help these groups form judgments, which will serve as the foundation for various decisions.

LO2.   **Explain the difference between cross-sectional and time series analysis.**

- Cross-sectional analysis entails comparing a corporation's financial statements to its primary competitors and industry averages.
- Time series (or trend) analysis involves comparisons of the current year to previous years.
- Differences may exist in the size of two corporations or even in the same corporation from year to year (perhaps due to the acquisition of another corporation). Analysts address this problem by restating the financial statements in percentage terms.

LO3.   **Analyze and interpret financial statements using horizontal and vertical analysis.**

- In horizontal analysis, each financial statement line item is expressed as a percentage of the base year (typically the least recent year shown).
- In vertical analysis, each financial statement line item is expressed as a percentage of the largest statement amount—net sales on the statement of earnings and total assets on the statement of financial position.

LO4.   **Calculate and interpret profitability, liquidity, solvency, and shareholder ratios to evaluate a company's financial position and business operations.**

- Ratios help remove the effects of size differences (as measured in dollars).
- Six categories of ratios are discussed:
  - short-term liquidity
  - debt management
  - profitability
  - asset efficiency (or operating)
  - shareholder
  - DuPont
- More advanced accounting and finance texts may present additional ratios; however, those introduced here are among the most widely used.

KEY TERMS

REVIEW PROBLEM

Ratio Analysis

Following are consolidated statements of financial position and statements of earnings for Kellman Company:

Kellman Company Consolidated Statements of Financial Position (in thousands)			
	December 31,		
	2017	2016	2015
ASSETS			
Current assets:			
Cash and cash equivalents	$ 40,588	$ 70,655	$ 62,977
Accounts receivable, net	93,515	71,867	53,132
Inventories	166,082	81,031	53,607
Income taxes receivable	614	4,310	—
Other current assets	11,028	8,944	5,252
Deferred income taxes	10,418	8,145	6,822
Total current assets	322,245	244,952	181,790
Property and equipment, net	52,332	29,923	20,865
Intangible assets, net	6,470	7,875	—
Deferred income taxes	8,173	5,180	—
Other noncurrent assets	1,393	1,438	1,032
Total assets	$390,613	$289,368	$203,687
LIABILITIES AND SHAREHOLDERS' EQUITY			
Current liabilities:			
Accounts payable	$ 55,012	$ 42,718	$ 31,699
Accrued expenses	36,111	25,403	11,449
Income taxes payable	–	–	716
Current maturities of long-term debt	4,111	2,648	1,967
Current maturities of capital lease obligations	465	794	1,841
Total current liabilities	95,699	71,563	47,672
Long-term debt, net of current maturities	9,298	1,893	2,868
Capital lease obligations, net of current maturities	458	922	1,715
Deferred income taxes	–	–	330
Other long-term liabilities	4,673	602	272
Total liabilities	110,128	74,980	52,857
Shareholders' equity:			
Class A common shares	12	12	10
Class B common shares	4	4	5
Contributed surplus—common shares	162,362	148,562	124,803
Retained earnings	117,782	66,376	28,067
Accumulated other comprehensive income	325	(566)	(2,055)
Total shareholders' equity	280,485	214,388	150,830
Total liabilities and shareholders' equity	$390,613	$289,368	$203,687

Kellman Company Consolidated Statements of Earnings (in thousands)			
	December 31,		
	2017	2016	2015
Net sales	$ 606,561	$ 430,689	$ 281,053
Cost of goods sold	301,517	215,089	145,203
Gross profit	**$305,044**	**$215,600**	**$135,850**
Operating expenses			
Selling, general and administrative expenses	218,779	158,682	100,040
Income from operations	**$ 86,265**	**$ 56,918**	**$ 35,810**
Interest income	1,549	2,231	273
Interest expense	(800)	(774)	(3,188)
Other income, net	2,029	712	79
Income before income taxes	**$ 89,043**	**$ 59,087**	**$ 32,974**
Income tax expense	36,485	20,108	13,255
Net income	**$ 52,558**	**$ 38,979**	**$ 19,719**
Cumulative preferred dividends on preferred shares	—	—	5,307
Net income available to common shareholders	**$ 52,558**	**$ 38,979**	**$ 14,412**

Additionally, you will need the following information:

Weighted average common shares outstanding	48,021	46,983	37,199
Cash flows from operating activities	$(14,628)	$10,701	$15,795
Dividends per share	$0	$0	$0
Dividends	$0	$0	$0
Market price per share at year-end	$43.67	$50.45	$38.31

Required:

1. Calculate the short-term liquidity ratios for Kellman Company for 2016 and 2017.
2. Calculate the debt management ratios for Kellman Company for 2016 and 2017.
3. Calculate the asset efficiency ratios for Kellman Company for 2016 and 2017.
4. Calculate the profitability ratios for Kellman Company for 2016 and 2017.
5. Calculate the shareholder ratios for Kellman Company for 2016 and 2017.
6. Perform DuPont analysis for Kellman Company for 2016 and 2017.

Solution:

1. Short-term liquidity ratios:

$$\text{Current ratio} = \frac{\text{Current assets}}{\text{Current liabilities}}$$

	2017	2016
Current assets	$322,245	$244,952
Current liabilities	95,699	71,563
Current ratio	**3.37**	**3.42**

$$\text{Quick ratio} = \frac{\text{Cash} + \text{Short-term investments} + \text{Accounts receivable}}{\text{Current liabilities}}$$

	2017	2016
Cash	$40,588	$70,655
Short-term investments	0	0
Accounts receivable	93,515	71,867
Current liabilities	95,699	71,563
Quick ratio	**1.40**	**1.99**

$$\text{Cash ratio} = \frac{\text{Cash} + \text{Short-term investments}}{\text{Current liabilities}}$$

	2017	2016
Cash	$40,588	$70,655
Short-term investments	0	0
Current liabilities	95,699	71,563
Cash ratio	**0.42**	**0.99**

$$\text{Operating cash flow ratio} = \frac{\text{Cash flows from operating activities}}{\text{Current liabilities}}$$

	2017	2016
Cash flows from operating activities	$(14,628)*	$10,701*
Current liabilities	95,699	71,563
Operating cash flow ratio	**(0.15)**	**0.15**

*Provided in the information section

2. Debt management ratios:

$$\text{Times interest earned} = \frac{\text{Earnings before income tax and interest expense}}{\text{Interest expense}}$$

	2017	2016
Earnings before income tax	$89,043	$59,087
Interest expense	800	774
Times interest earned	**112.30**	**77.34**

$$\text{Debt-to-equity ratio} = \frac{\text{Total liabilities}}{\text{Total equity}}$$

	2017	2016
Total liabilities	$110,128	$ 74,980
Total equity	280,485	214,388
Debt-to-equity	**0.39**	**0.35**

$$\text{Debt-to-total assets ratio} = \frac{\text{Total liabilities}}{\text{Total assets}}$$

	2017	2016
Total liabilities	$110,128	$ 74,980
Total assets	390,613	289,368
Debt-to-total assets	**0.28**	**0.26**

3. Asset efficiency ratios:

$$\text{Accounts receivable turnover ratio} = \frac{\text{Net sales}}{\text{Average accounts receivable*}}$$

$$\text{*Average balance} = \frac{(\text{Beginning balance} + \text{Ending balance})}{2}$$

	2017	2016	2015
Net sales	$606,561	$430,689	$281,053
Receivables	93,515	71,867	53,132
Accounts receivable turnover ratio	**7.34**	**6.89**	

$$\text{Inventory turnover ratio} = \frac{\text{Cost of goods sold}}{\text{Average inventories}}$$

	2017	2016	2015
Cost of goods sold	$301,517	$215,089	$145,203
Inventories	166,082	81,031	53,607
Inventory turnover ratio	**2.44**	**3.20**	

$$\text{Asset turnover ratio} = \frac{\text{Net sales}}{\text{Average total assets}}$$

	2017	2016	2015
Net sales	$606,561	$430,689	$281,053
Total assets	390,613	289,368	203,687
Asset turnover ratio	**1.78**	**1.75**	

$$\text{Fixed asset turnover ratio} = \frac{\text{Net sales}}{\text{Average net fixed assets}}$$

	2017	2016
Net sales	$606,561	$430,689
Average net fixed assets	41,128	25,394
Fixed asset turnover ratio	14.74	16.97

4. Profitability ratios:

$$\text{Gross profit percentage} = \frac{\text{Gross profit}}{\text{Net sales}}$$

	2017	2016
Net sales	$606,561	$430,689
Gross profit	305,044	215,600
Gross profit percentage	**50.29%**	**50.06%**

$$\text{Operating margin percentage} = \frac{\text{Income from operations}}{\text{Net sales}}$$

	2017	2016
Net sales	$606,561	$430,689
Income from operations	86,265	56,918
Operating margin percentage	**14.22%**	**13.22%**

$$\text{Net profit margin percentage} = \frac{\text{Net income}}{\text{Net sales}}$$

	2017	2016
Net sales	$606,561	$430,689
Net income	52,558	38,979
Net profit margin percentage	**8.66%**	**9.05%**

$$\text{Return on assets} = \frac{\text{Net income} + [\text{Interest expense} \times (1 - \text{Tax rate})]}{\text{Average total assets*}}$$

$$\text{*Average balance} = \frac{(\text{Beginning balance} + \text{Ending balance})}{2}$$

	2017	2016	2015
Total assets	$390,613	$289,368	$203,687
Income tax expense	36,485	20,108	
Net income	52,558	38,979	
Interest expense	800	774	
Income before taxes	89,043	59,087	
Tax rate*	40.97%	34.03%	
Return on assets	**15.60%**	**16.02%**	

*Income tax expense ÷ Income before taxes

$$\text{Return on equity} = \frac{\text{Net income}}{\text{Average equity*}}$$

*Average balance $= \frac{(\text{Beginning balance} + \text{Ending balance})}{2}$

	2017	2016	2015
Net income	$ 52,558	$ 38,979	
Shareholders' equity	280,485	214,388	$150,830
Return on equity	**21.24%**	**21.35%**	

$$\text{Quality of earnings ratio} = \frac{\text{Cash flow from operating activities}}{\text{Net income}}$$

	2017	2016
Cash flow from operating activities	$(14,628)	$10,701
Net income	52,558	38,979
Quality of earnings ratio	(.28)	.28

5. Shareholder ratios:

$$\text{Earnings per share ratio} = \frac{\text{Net income} - \text{Preferred dividends}}{\text{Average number of common shares outstanding}}$$

	2017	2016
Net income	$52,558	$38,979
Preferred dividends	0	0
Average common shares*	48,021	46,983
EPS	**$ 1.09**	**$ 0.83**

*Provided in the information section.

$$\text{Return on common equity} = \frac{\text{Net income}}{\text{Average common equity*}}$$

*Common equity = Total equity − Preferred shares

	2017	2016	2015
Net income	$ 52,558	$ 38,979	
Shareholders' equity	280,485	214,388	$150,830
Preferred shares	0	0	0
Return on common equity	**21.24%**	**21.35%**	

$$\text{Dividend yield ratio} = \frac{\text{Dividends per common share}}{\text{Closing market price per share for the year}}$$

	2017	2016
Dividends per share*	$ 0	$ 0
Closing market price for year*	43.67	50.45
Dividend yield ratio	**0.0%**	**0.0%**

*Provided in the information section.

$$\text{Dividend payout ratio} = \frac{\text{Common dividends}}{\text{Net income}}$$

	2014	2013
Common dividends*	$ 0	$ 0
Net income	52,558	38,979
Dividend payout ratio	**0.0%**	**0.0%**

*Provided in the information section.

6. DuPont analysis:

$$\text{ROE} = \frac{\text{Net income}}{\text{Sales}} \times \frac{\text{Sales}}{\text{Average total assets}} \times \frac{\text{Average total assets}}{\text{Average equity}}$$
$$= \text{Net profit margin} \times \text{Asset turnover} \times \text{Total leverage}$$

2017:

$$= \left(\frac{\$52,558}{\$606,561}\right) \times \left\{\frac{\$606,561}{(\$390,613 + \$289,368) \div 2)}\right\} \times \left\{\frac{(\$390,613 + \$289,368) \div 2}{(\$280,485 + \$214,388) \div 2}\right\}$$
$$= 8.66\% \times 1.78 \times 1.37$$
$$= 21.12\%*$$

*Does not equal ROE of 21.24% shown in parts 4 and 5 because of rounding in the individual components.

2016:

$$= \left(\frac{\$38,979}{\$430,689}\right) \times \left\{\frac{\$430,689}{(\$289,368 + \$203,687) \div 2}\right\} \times \left\{\frac{(\$289,368 + \$203,687) \div 2}{(\$214,388 + \$150,830) \div 2}\right\}$$
$$= 9.05\% \times 1.75 \times 1.35$$
$$= 21.38\%*$$

*Does not equal ROE of 21.35% shown in parts 4 and 5 because of rounding in the individual components.

DISCUSSION QUESTIONS

1. Describe how some of the primary groups of users use financial statements.
2. What is the difference between time series and cross-sectional analysis?
3. What is the difference between horizontal and vertical analysis?
4. How do the current and quick ratios differ? Which is a more conservative measure of short-term liquidity? Support your answer.
5. How does the operating cash flow ratio differ from the current, quick, and cash ratios?
6. What are you trying to learn by calculating debt management ratios?
7. Why are higher asset turnover ratios considered to be better than lower turnover ratios?
8. What two aspects of a company's profitability are measured by profitability ratios?
9. What are the two major categories of shareholder ratios?
10. DuPont analysis breaks down return on equity into what three components?
11. Why must you analyze the accounting policies of a company when performing financial statement analysis? Provide an example of how knowledge of accounting policies would affect your analysis of inventory.

MULTIPLE-CHOICE EXERCISES

13-1 Which of the following use financial statement data to make decisions?
a. customers
b. investors
c. suppliers
d. all of these

13-2 Which statement would best provide information about a company's current liquidity?
a. statement of financial position
b. statement of earnings
c. statement of cash flows
d. none of these

13-3 A banker is analyzing a company that operates in the petroleum industry. Which of the following might be a major consideration in determining whether the company should receive a loan?
a. The petroleum industry suffers from political pressures concerning the selling price of its products.
b. Inflation has been high for several years in a row.
c. All companies in the petroleum industry use the same accounting principles.
d. The company has a large amount of interest payments related to many outstanding loans.

13-4 Which type of analysis compares a single corporation across time?
a. Cross-sectional analysis
b. Time series analysis
c. Timetable analysis
d. Company analysis

13-5 Which of the following types of analysis compares one corporation to another corporation and to industry averages?
a. Cross-sectional analysis
b. Time series analysis
c. Timetable analysis
d. Company analysis

13-6 Which of the following types of analysis is particularly useful for trend analysis?
a. Vertical analysis
b. Timetable analysis
c. Trend-setting analysis
d. Horizontal analysis

13-7 Vertical analysis expresses each financial statement line item as a percentage of:
a. the average statement amount.
b. the smallest statement amount.
c. the largest statement amount.
d. the mean statement amount.

13-8 Horizontal analysis expresses each financial statement line item as a percentage of:
a. net income.
b. total assets.
c. base year.
d. shareholders' equity.

13-9 How is the current ratio calculated?
a. Current assets ÷ Current liabilities
b. (Cash + marketable securities + Accounts receivable) ÷ Current liabilities
c. (Cash + marketable securities) ÷ Current liabilities
d. Cash flows from operating activities ÷ Current liabilities

13-10 Partial information from Fabray Company's statement of financial position is as follows:

Current Assets:

Cash	$ 1,200,000
Marketable securities	3,750,000
Accounts receivable	28,800,000
Inventories	33,150,000
Prepaid expenses	600,000
Total current assets	$67,500,000

Current Liabilities:

Notes payable	$ 750,000
Accounts payable	9,750,000
Accrued expenses	6,250,000
Income tax payable	250,000
Total current liabilities	$17,000,000

What is Fabray's current ratio?
a. 0.25
b. 3.0
c. 1.8
d. 3.97

13-11 Hummel Inc. has $30,000 in current assets and $15,000 in current liabilities. What is Hummel's current ratio?
a. 0.5
b. 1
c. 2
d. 3

13-12 How is the cash ratio calculated?
   a. Current assets ÷ Current liabilities
   b. (Cash + marketable securities + Accounts receivable) ÷ Current liabilities
   c. (Cash + marketable securities) ÷ Current liabilities
   d. Cash flows from operating activities ÷ Current liabilities

13-13 A firm's quick ratio is typically computed as follows:
   a. Total liabilities ÷ Total assets
   b. (Cash + Short-term investments + Receivables) ÷ Current liabilities
   c. Current liabilities ÷ Current assets
   d. Current assets ÷ Current liabilities

13-14 Schuester Company has $40,000 in current liabilities, $20,000 in cash, and $25,000 in marketable securities. What is Schuester's cash ratio?
   a. 1.125
   b. 0.889
   c. 1.6
   d. 0.625

13-15 What ratio is used to measure a firm's liquidity?
   a. Debt ratio
   b. Asset turnover
   c. Current ratio
   d. Return on equity

13-16 Which of the following transactions could increase a firm's current ratio?
   a. Purchase of inventory for cash
   b. Payment of accounts payable
   c. Collection of accounts receivable
   d. Purchase of temporary investments for cash

13-17 Total liabilities ÷ Total equity equals:
   a. times interest earned ratio.
   b. accounts payable turnover ratio.
   c. debt-to-equity ratio.
   d. receivables turnover ratio.

13-18 Which of the following ratios is not a debt management ratio?
   a. Times interest earned
   b. Debt-to-equity ratio
   c. Debt-to-total-assets ratio
   d. Return on equity ratio

13-19 The statement of financial position for Sylvests Ltd. at the end of the first year of operations indicates the following:

	2018
Total current assets	$600,000
Total investments	85,000
Total property, plant, and equipment	900,000
Current portion of long-term debt	250,000
Total long-term liabilities	$350,000
Common shares	600,000
Contributed surplus—common shares	60,000
Retained earnings	325,000

What is the debt-to-total assets ratio for 2018 (rounded to one decimal place)?
   a. 37.9%
   b. 40.0%
   c. 22.1%
   d. 41.7%

13-20 When analyzing a company's debt-to-equity ratio, if the ratio has a value that is greater than one, then the company has:
   a. less debt than equity.
   b. more debt than equity.
   c. equal amounts of debt and equity.
   d. None of these are correct.

13-21 Cost of goods sold divided by average inventory is the formula to compute:
   a. accounts receivable turnover.
   b. inventory turnover.
   c. gross profit percentage.
   d. return on sales percentage.

13-22 A firm's asset turnover ratio is typically computed as follows:
   a. Net sales ÷ Average total assets
   b. Gross profit ÷ Net sales
   c. Operating income × Net sales
   d. Net income + [Interest expense × (1 − Tax rate)] × Average total assets

13-23 Which of the following ratios is used to measure a firm's efficiency at using its assets?
   a. Current ratio
   b. Asset turnover ratio
   c. Return on sales ratio
   d. Return on equity

13-24 Which of the following ratios is used to measure a firm's efficiency?
   a. Net income ÷ Equity
   b. Net sales ÷ Average total assets
   c. Assets ÷ Equity
   d. Net income ÷ Sales

13-25 Patna Corporation has $65,000 of cost of goods sold and average inventory of $30,000. What is Patna's inventory turnover ratio?
a. 0.46
b. 1.17
c. 1.46
d. 2.17

13-26 If Abrams Company has an inventory turnover of 7.3 and a receivables turnover of 9.6, approximately how long is its operating cycle?
a. 72 days
b. 88 days
c. 95 days
d. There is not enough information to calculate the operating cycle.

13-27 Which of the following ratios is used to measure the profit earned on each dollar invested in a firm?
a. Current ratio
b. Asset turnover ratio
c. Return on sales ratio
d. Return on equity

13-28 Which of the following is the formula to compute the net profit margin percentage?
a. Net income ÷ Net sales
b. Operating income ÷ Net sales
c. Net income ÷ Average equity
d. Net income + [Interest expense (1 − Tax rate)] ÷ Average total assets

13-29 Selected information for Berry Company is as follows:

Average common shares	$600,000
Average contributed surplus	250,000
Average retained earnings	370,000
Sales revenue for year	915,000
Net income for year	240,000

Berry's return on equity, rounded to the nearest percentage point, is:
a. 20%
b. 21%
c. 28%
d. 40%

13-30 Which of the following ratios is used to measure a firm's profitability?
a. Liabilities ÷ Equity
b. Sales ÷ Assets
c. Assets ÷ Equity
d. Net income ÷ Net sales

13-31 Why might an industry group have higher five-year average returns on equity than do other industries?
a. It is a higher-risk industry.
b. It is a lower-risk industry.
c. It is a high-growth industry.
d. None of these.

13-32 The dividend yield ratio measures:
a. the income available for common shareholders on a per-share basis.
b. the rate at which dividends provide a return to shareholders.
c. the proportion of a corporation's profits that are returned to the shareholders immediately as dividends.
d. the profit earned by a firm through the use of capital supplied by shareholders.

13-33 Corporations are required to disclose earnings per share on which of the following statements?
a. Statement of financial position
b. Statement of earnings
c. Statement of cash flows
d. All of these

13-34 Hudson Lake Company has preferred dividends of $15,000, a net income of $40,000, and average common shares outstanding of 8,000. What is Hudson's earnings per share?
a. $2.67
b. $5.00
c. $3.13
d. $2.13

13-35 Which of the following are not part of common equity?
a. Common shares
b. Contributed surplus—common shares
c. Retained earnings
d. Preferred shares

13-36 DuPont analysis recognizes that return on equity can be broken down into three important aspects of return, which are:
a. net profit margin, asset turnover, and leverage.
b. net profit margin, asset turnover, and average assets.
c. sales, income, and leverage.
d. sales, income, and equity.

13-37 If a company has a higher net profit margin than most of its competitors, this means that:
  a. the company is more efficient with its assets.
  b. the company has more loyal customers.
  c. the company has a lower proportion of debt financing.
  d. the company has a higher proportion of each sales dollar that is profit.

13-38 Which of the following ratios is decomposed using the DuPont framework?
  a. Return on equity
  b. Asset turnover
  c. Assets-to-equity ratio
  d. Return on sales

13-39 Which of the following is not included in the DuPont framework?
  a. A measure of profitability
  b. A measure of efficiency

  c. A measure of market share
  d. A measure of leverage

13-40 When DuPont analysis reveals that a company has much higher than average asset turnover and much lower than average profit margin, what can be concluded about the company's strategy?
  a. It is a product differentiator.
  b. It is a low-cost provider.
  c. It has no strategy.
  d. It needs to concentrate on improving its profit margins.

13-41 Which of the following questions would be appropriate for an analyst to investigate regarding a company's liabilities?
  a. Are all liabilities reported?
  b. Are the liabilities properly classified?
  c. Are estimated liabilities large enough?
  d. All of these.

CORNERSTONE EXERCISES

OBJECTIVE ❷
CORNERSTONE 13.1

Cornerstone Exercise 13-42   Cross-sectional Analysis

Cross-sectional analysis entails comparing a company to its competitors.

Required:

Indicate one of the biggest weaknesses of using cross-sectional analysis when analyzing a company.

OBJECTIVE ❷
CORNERSTONE 13.1

Cornerstone Exercise 13-43   Time Series Analysis

Time series analysis involves comparing a company's statement of earnings and statement of financial position for the current year to its previous years' statements of earnings and statements of financial position.

Required:

Explain whether it is always bad if a company's cost of goods sold is increasing from year to year.

OBJECTIVE ❸
CORNERSTONE 13.2
CORNERSTONE 13.3

Cornerstone Exercise 13-44   Horizontal and Vertical Analysis

Selected data from the financial statements of Beirut Hardware Company follows.

	2018	2017
Accounts receivable	$ 60,000	$ 38,000
Merchandise inventory	12,000	16,000
Total assets	450,000	380,000
Net sales	380,000	270,000
Cost of goods sold	160,000	210,000

Required:

1. Calculate by how much accounts receivable, merchandise inventory, total assets, net sales, and cost of goods sold increased or decreased in dollar terms from 2017 to 2018.
2. Indicate what happened from 2017 to 2018 to accounts receivable and merchandise inventory as a percentage of total assets (rounded to the nearest whole percent). Indicate what happened from 2017 to 2018 to cost of goods sold as a percentage of net sales (rounded to the nearest whole percent).

Cornerstone Exercise 13-45   Short-Term Liquidity Ratios

OBJECTIVE **2** **4**
CORNERSTONE 13.4

Three ratios calculated for Puckerman, Cohen, and Chang Companies for 2017 and 2018 follow.

(in millions)		Puckerman	Cohen	Chang
Current ratio	12/31/18	2.8 to 1	2.3 to 1	1.8 to 1
	12/31/17	2.0 to 1	1.5 to 1	2.2 to 1
Inventory turnover ratio	12/31/18	6.9 times	5.8 times	8.0 times
	12/31/17	7.6 times	5.8 times	9.6 times
Quick ratio	12/31/18	2.5 to 1	2.1 to 1	0.5 to 1
	12/31/17	1.0 to 1	1.4 to 1	1.2 to 1

Required:

Explain which company appears to be the most liquid.

Cornerstone Exercise 13-46   Debt Management Ratios

OBJECTIVE **4**
CORNERSTONE 13.5

Selected data from the financial statements of Lopez Company follow.

	2018	2017
Total liabilities	$1,205,000	$952,000
Common shares	250,000	225,000
Contributed surplus—common shares	150,000	135,000
Retained earnings	155,000	145,000

Required:

Determine whether the debt-to-equity ratio is increasing or decreasing and whether Lopez should be concerned.

Cornerstone Exercise 13-47   Debt Management and Short-Term Liquidity Ratios

OBJECTIVE **4**
CORNERSTONE 13.4
CORNERSTONE 13.5

The following items appear on the statement of financial position of Figgins Company at the end of 2017 and 2018:

	2018	2017
Current assets	$6,000	$3,000
Long-term assets	7,000	4,000
Current liabilities	2,000	3,000
Long-term liabilities	7,000	0
Shareholders' equity	4,000	4,000

Required:

Between 2017 and 2018, indicate whether Figgins's debt-to-equity ratio increased or decreased. Also, indicate whether Figgins's current ratio increased or decreased. Interpret these ratios.

Cornerstone Exercise 13-48   Asset Efficiency Ratios

Selected financial statement numbers for Hunan Company follow.

Net sales	$277,480	Average inventory	$ 4,145
Cost of goods sold	179,000	Average property, plant, and equipment	75,705
Average accounts receivable	20,730	Average total assets	126,127

Required:

1. Using this information, calculate Hunan's receivable turnover ratio (rounded to two decimal places).
2. Using this information, calculate Hunan's asset turnover ratio (rounded to two decimal places) and also convert the ratio into days (rounded to the nearest whole day).

Cornerstone Exercise 13-49   Profitability Ratios

The following data came from the financial statements of Maldives Company:

Revenue	$900,000	Assets	$600,000
Expenses	600,000	Liabilities	100,000
Net income	300,000	Average equity	500,000

Required:

Compute Maldives' return on equity (in percentage terms, rounded to two decimal places).

Cornerstone Exercise 13-50   Profitability Ratios

Tanaka Corporation's statement of financial position indicates the following balances as of December 31, 2018:

Cash	$ 70,000	Bonds payable (due in 2022)	$100,000
Accounts receivable	80,000	Common shares (12/31/2017)	275,000
Inventory	110,000	Common shares (12/31/2018)	325,000
Property, plant, and equipment	500,000	Retained earnings (12/31/2017)	200,000
Accounts payable	75,000	Retained earnings (12/31/2018)	260,000

Required:

If Tanaka's 2018 net income is $80,000, determine its return on equity (in percentage terms, rounded to two decimal places).

Cornerstone Exercise 13-51   Shareholder Ratios

The following data came from the financial statements of St. James Corp. for 2018 and 2017:

	2018	2017
Net income	$150,000	$120,000
Cash dividends paid on preferred shares	$ 15,000	$ 15,000
Cash dividends paid on common shares	$ 42,000	$ 38,000
Weighted average number of preferred shares outstanding	20,000	20,000
Weighted average number of common shares outstanding	105,000	95,000

Required:

Calculate St. James's earnings per share as it would be reported on the 2018 statement of earnings.

Cornerstone Exercise 13-52 Shareholder Ratios

The following data came from the financial statements of Ryerson Corp. for 2018 and 2017:

OBJECTIVE ④
CORNERSTONE 13.8

	2018	2017
Net income	$110,000	$123,000
Cash dividends paid on common shares	$ 42,000	$ 38,000
Market price per common share at the end of the year	$ 16.00	$ 13.00
Common shares outstanding	140,000	140,000

Required:

Calculate Ryerson's dividend payout ratio for 2018 (in percentage terms, rounded to two decimal places).

BRIEF EXERCISES

Brief Exercise 13-53 Cross-sectional Analysis

Cross-sectional analysis entails comparing a company to its competitors.

OBJECTIVE ②

Required:

Indicate one of the biggest strengths of using cross-sectional analysis when analyzing a company.

Brief Exercise 13-54 Time Series Analysis

Time series analysis involves comparing a company's statement of earnings and statement of financial position for the current year to its previous years' statements of earnings and statements of financial position.

OBJECTIVE ②

Required:

CONCEPTUAL CONNECTION Explain whether it is always good if a company's cost of goods sold is increasing from year to year.

Brief Exercise 13-55 Horizontal and Vertical Analysis

Venus Clothing Company specializes in selling apparel for special occasions. In 2017 and 2018, Venus's account balances were as follows:

OBJECTIVE ③

	2018	2017
Accounts receivable	$ 45,000	$ 32,000
Merchandise inventory	9,000	11,000
Total assets	375,000	340,000
Net sales	330,000	260,000
Cost of goods sold	145,000	185,000

Required:

1. Calculate the change in each of the Venus's accounts from 2017 to 2018.
2. Indicate what happened from 2017 to 2018 to accounts receivable and merchandise inventory as a percentage of total assets. Indicate what happened from 2017 to 2018 to cost of goods sold as a percentage of net sales.

Brief Exercise 13-56 Short-Term Liquidity Ratios

Larry, Curly, and Moe companies operate in the same industry. Each company provided financial information to the public containing three ratios for 2017 and 2018.

OBJECTIVE ④

(Continued)

(in millions)		Larry	Curly	Moe
Current ratio	12/31/18	2.3 to 1	1.9 to 1	1.8 to 1
	12/31/17	2.0 to 1	1.5 to 2	2 to 1
Inventory turnover ratio	12/31/18	5.6 times	4.6 times	6.0 times
	12/31/17	7.6 times	5.8 times	9.6 times
Quick ratio	12/31/18	2.2 to 1	1.9 to 1	0.7 to 1
	12/31/17	1.0 to 1	1.4 to 1	1.2 to 1

Required:

Explain which company appears to be the most liquid at December 31, 2018.

OBJECTIVE ④   **Brief Exercise 13-57   Debt Management Ratios**

Glow Corporation provides annual and quarterly financial data to the public. For the years of 2017 and 2018, Glow's financial data included the following account balances:

	2018	2017
Total liabilities	$1,390,000	$988,000
Common shares ($25 par)	270,000	235,000
Paid-in capital in excess of par—common shares	155,000	140,000
Retained earnings	167,000	152,000

Required:

Determine whether the debt-to-equity ratio is increasing or decreasing and whether Glow should be concerned.

OBJECTIVE ④   **Brief Exercise 13-58   Debt Management and Short-Term Liquidity Ratios**

Magellan Company is an international travel agency providing travel planning services to customers in over 20 countries. Recently, the travel industry has been experiencing volatility as a result of increases in oil prices. Magellan's investors have been following its financial information closely to determine its ability to continue as a going concern. Its investors have used the following information to determine financial ratios:

	2018	2017
Current assets	$5,000	$3,600
Long-term assets	6,000	3,900
Current liabilities	1,500	2,200
Long-term liabilities	5,000	0
Shareholders' equity	3,900	3,900

Required:

Between 2017 and 2018, indicate whether Magellan's debt-to-equity ratio increased or decreased. Also, indicate whether Magellan's current ratio increased or decreased. Interpret these ratios.

OBJECTIVE ④   **Brief Exercise 13-59   Asset Efficiency Ratios**

Rumsford Inc.'s financial statements for 2018 indicate the following account balances:

Net sales	$256,340
Cost of goods sold	162,000
Average accounts receivable	18,710
Average inventory	3,845
Average property, plant, and equipment	72,345
Average total assets	119,124

Required:

1. Using this information, calculate Rumsford's receivable turnover ratio. (*Note:* Round to two decimal places.)
2. Using this information, calculate Rumsford's asset turnover ratio and also convert the ratio into days.

Brief Exercise 13-60   Profitability Ratios

OBJECTIVE ❹

Meade Publications is a magazine publisher established in southern Ontario. Financial analysts are concerned about Meade's ability to generate positive returns as printed material becomes less popular than digital material. Financial analysts observe the following account balances from Meade to determine financial ratios:

Revenue	$1,100,000
Expenses	700,000
Net income	350,000
Assets	625,000
Liabilities	175,000
Average equity	600,000

Required:

Compute Meade's return on equity.

Brief Exercise 13-61   Profitability Ratios

OBJECTIVE ❹

Tinker Corporation operates in the highly competitive consulting industry. Tinker's statement of financial position indicates the following balances as of December 31, 2018:

Cash	$ 80,000
Accounts receivable	87,000
Inventory	52,000
Property, plant, and equipment	485,000
Accounts payable	73,000
Bonds payable (due in 2020)	110,000
Common shares (12/31/2017)	250,000
Common shares (12/31/2018)	275,000
Retained earnings (12/31/2017)	180,000
Retained earnings (12/31/2018)	220,000

Required:

Calculate Tinker's return on equity if Tinker's 2018 net income is $90,000.

Brief Exercise 13-62   Shareholder Ratios

OBJECTIVE ❹

Katrina Corp. is a publicly traded company on a large stock exchange. Katrina's financial statement for 2018 and 2017 included the following data:

	2018	2017
Net income	$140,000	$115,000
Cash dividends paid on preferred shares	11,000	11,000
Cash dividends paid on common shares	38,000	34,000
Weighted average number of preferred shares outstanding	18,000	18,000
Weighted average number of common shares outstanding	97,000	94,000

Required:

Calculate Katrina's earnings per share as it would be reported on the 2018 statement of earnings.

OBJECTIVE **4**   **Brief Exercise 13-63   Shareholder Ratios**

Orion Corp.'s financial data for 2018 and 2017 included the following:

	2018	2017
Net income	$120,000	$135,000
Cash dividends paid on common shares	49,000	42,000
Market price per share of common shares at the end of the year	19.00	17.00
Shares of common shares outstanding	150,000	150,000

Required:

Calculate Orion's dividend payout ratio for 2018.

EXERCISES

OBJECTIVE **2**   **Exercise 13-64   Financial Statement Decision Makers**

Many groups analyze financial statements to make decisions.

Required:

1. **CONCEPTUAL CONNECTION** Explain why a person who is selecting an employer should be sure to view and analyze the company's financial statements.
2. **CONCEPTUAL CONNECTION** Explain why a business that is considering selling goods or providing services to another business should review the company's financial statements.

OBJECTIVE **2** **3**   **Exercise 13-65   Horizontal Analysis of Statement of Earnings**

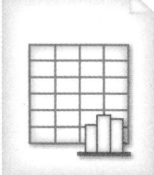

Consolidated statements of earnings for Karofsky Computer follow.

Karofsky Computer Inc. Consolidated Statements of Earnings (in thousands except per share amounts)			
	Three fiscal years ended December 31,		
	2018	2017	2016
Sales	$9,188,748	$7,976,954	$7,086,542
Costs and expenses:			
Cost of goods sold	6,844,915	5,248,834	3,991,337
Research and development	564,303	664,564	602,135
Selling, general, and administrative	1,384,111	1,632,362	1,687,262
Restructuring costs and other	(126,855)	320,856	0
	8,666,474	7,866,616	6,280,734
Operating income	522,274	110,338	805,808
Interest and other income, net	(21,988)	29,321	49,634
Income before income taxes	500,286	139,659	855,442
Provision for income taxes	190,108	53,070	325,069
Net income	$ 310,178	$ 86,589	$ 530,373
Earnings per common share	$ 2.61	$ 0.73	$ 4.33
Common shares used in the calculations of earnings per share	118,735	119,125	122,490

Required:

1.   Prepare common size statements of earnings for horizontal analysis (in percentage terms, rounded to two decimal places). You do not need to include the actual dollar amounts shown above.

2. **CONCEPTUAL CONNECTION** Explain why net income decreased in 2017 and increased in 2018.

Exercise 13-66 Vertical Analysis of Statements of Financial Position

Consolidated statements of financial position for Karofsky Computer follow.

OBJECTIVE 3

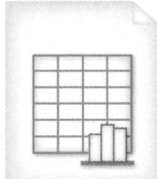

Karofsky Computer Inc. Consolidated Statements of Financial Position (dollars in thousands)		
	December 31,	
ASSETS	2018	2017
Current assets:		
Cash and cash equivalents	$1,203,488	$ 676,413
Short-term investments	54,368	215,890
Accounts receivable, net of allowance for doubtful accounts		
of $90,992 ($83,776 in 2017)	1,581,347	1,381,946
Inventories	1,088,434	1,506,638
Deferred tax assets	293,048	268,085
Other current assets	255,767	289,383
Total current assets	4,476,452	4,338,355
Property, plant, and equipment:		
Land and buildings	484,592	404,688
Machinery and equipment	572,728	578,272
Office furniture and equipment	158,160	167,905
Leasehold improvements	236,708	261,792
	1,452,188	1,412,657
Accumulated depreciation and amortization	(785,088)	(753,111)
Net property, plant, and equipment	667,100	659,546
Other assets	159,194	173,511
Total assets	$5,302,746	$5,171,412
LIABILITIES AND SHAREHOLDERS' EQUITY		
Current liabilities:		
Short-term borrowings	$ 292,200	$ 823,182
Accounts payable	881,717	742,622
Accrued compensation and employee benefits	136,895	144,779
Accrued marketing and distribution	178,294	174,547
Accrued restructuring costs	58,238	307,932
Other current liabilities	396,961	315,023
Total current liabilities	1,944,305	2,508,085
Long-term debt	304,472	7,117
Deferred tax liabilities	670,668	629,832
Total liabilities	2,919,445	3,145,034
Shareholders' equity:		
Common shares: 320,000,000 shares authorized; 119,542,527 shares		
issued and outstanding in 2018 (116,147,035 shares in 2017)	297,929	203,613
Retained earnings	2,096,206	1,842,600
Accumulated translation adjustment	(10,834)	(19,835)
Total shareholders' equity	2,383,301	2,026,378
Total liabilities and shareholders' equity	$5,302,746	$5,171,412

Required:

1. Prepare common size statements of financial position for vertical analysis (in percentage terms, rounded to two decimal places). You do not need to include the actual dollar amounts shown above.

2. Indicate from what sources Karofsky appears to have secured the resources for its asset increase.

OBJECTIVE    **Exercise 13-67   Horizontal Analysis Using Statement of Earnings**

The consolidated 2018, 2017, and 2016 statements of earnings for Corcoran Inc. follow.

Corcoran Inc. Consolidated Statements of Earnings (in millions except per share amounts)			
	December 31,		
	2018	**2017**	**2016**
Net sales	$ 25,020.7	$ 21,970.0	$19,292.2
Costs and expenses:			
Cost of goods sold	(11,946.1)	(10,611.7)	(9,366.2)
Selling, general, and administrative	(9,864.4)	(8,721.2)	(7,605.9)
Amortization of intangible assets	(303.7)	(265.9)	(208.3)
Operating profit	2,906.5	2,371.2	2,111.8
Interest expense	(572.7)	(586.1)	(613.7)
Interest income	88.7	113.7	161.6
Income before income taxes	2,422.5	1,898.8	1,659.7
Provision for income taxes	(834.6)	(597.1)	(597.5)
Net income	$ 1,587.9	$ 1,301.7	$ 1,062.2

Required:

1. Prepare common size statements of earnings for horizontal analysis (in percentage terms, rounded to two decimal places). You do not need to include the actual dollar amounts shown above.
2. Indicate what Corcoran's 2018, 2017, and 2016 tax rates were on its income before taxes (in percentage terms, rounded to two decimal places).
3. **CONCEPTUAL CONNECTION** Explain why net income increased by a larger percentage than sales in 2018 and 2017.

OBJECTIVE    **Exercise 13-68   Horizontal Analysis Using Statements of Financial Position**

The consolidated 2018 and 2017 statements of financial position for Corcoran Inc. follow.

Corcoran Inc. Consolidated Statements of Financial Position (in millions except per share amounts)		
	December 31,	
ASSETS	**2018**	**2017**
Current assets:		
Cash and cash equivalents	$ 226.9	$ 169.9
Short-term investments at cost which approximates market	1,629.3	1,888.5
Accounts and notes receivable, less allowance:	1,883.4	1,588.5
$128.3 in 2018 and $112.0 in 2017		
Inventories	924.7	768.8
Prepaid expenses, taxes, and other current assets	499.8	426.6
Total current assets	5,164.1	4,842.3
Investments in affiliates and other assets	1,756.6	1,707.9
Property, plant, and equipment, net	8,855.6	7,442.0
Intangible assets, net	7,929.5	6,959.0
Total assets	$23,705.8	$20,951.2

LIABILITIES AND SHAREHOLDERS' EQUITY		
Current liabilities:		
Short-term borrowings	$ 2,191.2	$ 706.8
Accounts payable	1,390.0	1,164.8
Income taxes payable	823.7	621.1
Accrued compensation and benefits	726.0	638.9
Accrued marketing	400.9	327.0
Other current liabilities	1,043.1	1,099.0
Total current liabilities	6,574.9	4,557.6
Long-term debt	7,442.6	7,964.8
Other liabilities	1,342.0	1,390.8
Deferred income taxes	2,007.6	1,682.3
Total liabilities	17,367.1	15,595.5
Shareholders' equity:		
Common shares, per share: authorized 1,800 million shares, 14.4 million and 7.4 million shares issued at December 31, 2018 and 2017, respectively	14.4	7.4
Contributed surplus—common shares	0	7.6
Retained earnings	6,508.2	5,439.7
Other comprehensive income (loss)	(183.9)	(99.0)
Total shareholders' equity	6,338.7	5,355.7
Total liabilities and shareholders' equity	$23,705.8	$20,951.2

Required:

1. Calculate the percentage that Corcoran's total assets increased by during 2018 (in percentage terms, rounded to one decimal place). You do not need to include the actual dollar amounts shown above.
2. Determine whether any of the asset categories experienced larger increases than others.
3. Indicate where Corcoran acquired the capital to finance its asset growth.
4. Indicate whether any of the individual liability or equity items increased at a rate different from the rate at which total liabilities and equity increased.

Exercise 13-69   Preparation of Common Size Statements for Vertical Analysis

OBJECTIVE ② ③

Financial statements for Gorky Inc. follow.

Gorky Inc. Consolidated Statements of Earnings (in thousands except per share amounts)			
	2018	2017	2016
Net sales	$ 7,245,088	$ 6,944,296	$ 6,149,218
Cost of goods sold	(5,286,253)	(4,953,556)	(4,355,675)
Gross margin	1,958,835	1,990,740	1,793,543
General and administrative expenses	(1,259,896)	(1,202,042)	(1,080,843)
Special and nonrecurring items	2,617	–	–
Operating income	701,556	788,698	712,700
Interest expense	(63,685)	(62,370)	(63,927)
Other income	7,308	10,080	11,529
Gain on sale of investments	–	9,117	–
Income before income taxes	645,179	745,497	660,302
Provision for income taxes	(254,000)	(290,000)	(257,000)
Net income	$ 391,179	$ 455,497	$ 403,302

(Continued)

Gorky Inc. Consolidated Statements of Financial Position (in thousands)		
ASSETS	Dec. 31, 2018	Dec. 31, 2017
Current assets:		
Cash and equivalents	$ 320,558	$ 41,235
Accounts receivable	1,056,911	837,377
Inventories	733,700	803,707
Other	109,456	101,811
Total current assets	2,220,625	1,784,130
Property and equipment, net	1,666,588	1,813,948
Other assets	247,892	248,372
Total assets	$4,135,105	$3,846,450
LIABILITIES AND SHAREHOLDERS' EQUITY		
Current liabilities:		
Accounts payable	$ 250,363	$ 309,092
Accrued expenses	347,892	274,220
Other current liabilities	15,700	–
Income taxes	93,489	137,466
Total current liabilities	707,444	720,778
Long-term debt	650,000	541,639
Deferred income taxes	275,101	274,844
Other long-term liabilities	61,267	41,572
Total liabilities	1,693,812	1,578,833
Shareholders' equity:		
Preferred shares	100,000	100,000
Common shares	89,727	89,727
Contributed surplus—common shares	128,906	127,776
Retained earnings	2,122,660	1,950,114
Total shareholders' equity	2,441,293	2,267,617
Total liabilities and shareholders' equity	$4,135,105	$3,846,450

Required:

1. Prepare common size statements of earnings and statements of financial position for Gorky to be used in vertical analysis (in percentage terms, rounded to two decimal places). You do not need to include the actual dollar amounts shown above (use the percentage of the largest amount on the statement. For the statement of earnings use net sales for the statement of financial position use total assets.

2. **CONCEPTUAL CONNECTION** Indicate whether gross margin grew as much as sales between 2016 and 2017 and between 2017 and 2018, and if so, why it grew.

3. **CONCEPTUAL CONNECTION** Indicate whether the relative proportion of Gorky's assets changed between 2017 and 2018, and if so, explain the change.

4. **CONCEPTUAL CONNECTION** Indicate whether the relative proportion of Gorky's liabilities and equity changed between 2017 and 2018, and if so, explain the change.

5. **CONCEPTUAL CONNECTION** Explain how Gorky appears to have financed the 7.5% increase in assets that occurred between 2017 and 2018.

Exercise 13-70 Common Size Statements for Vertical Analysis

OBJECTIVE  ❷ ❸

The following consolidated statements of earnings and statements of financial position are available for Azimio Products:

Azimio Products
Consolidated Statements of Earnings

	Year Ended December 31,					
	2018		2017		2016	
	Amount	%	Amount	%	Amount	%
Revenues	$901,170	100.0	$728,035	100.0	$661,850	100.0
Costs and expenses:						
Cost of goods sold	539,801	59.9	439,005	60.3	401,743	60.7
Selling and administrative	318,113	35.3	206,034	28.3	176,052	26.6
Interest	17,122	1.9	18,201	2.5	17,208	2.6
Other expenses (income)	9,913	1.1	2,912	0.4	(1,324)	(0.2)
Total costs and expenses	884,949	98.2	666,152	91.5	593,679	89.7
Income before provision for income taxes	16,221	1.8	61,883	8.5	68,171	10.3
Provision for income taxes	4,506	0.5	22,569	3.1	23,827	3.6
Net income	$ 11,715	1.3	$ 39,314	5.4	$ 44,344	6.7

Azimio Products
Consolidated Statements of Financial Position

	December 31,					
	2018		2017		2016	
ASSETS	Amount	%	Amount	%	Amount	%
Current assets	$147,129	31.4	$ 62,417	14.3	$ 66,927	16.1
Investment	30,925	6.6	95,589	21.9	91,453	22.0
Property, plant, and equipment (net)	270,831	57.8	261,015	59.8	241,519	58.1
Other assets	19,680	4.2	17,459	4.0	15,796	3.8
Total assets	$468,565	100.0	$436,480	100.0	$415,695	100.0
LIABILITIES AND SHAREHOLDERS' EQUITY						
Current liabilities	$ 68,410	14.6	$ 29,244	6.7	$ 28,683	6.9
Long-term debt	152,284	32.5	162,807	37.3	152,976	36.8
Total liabilities	220,694	47.1	192,051	44.0	181,659	43.7
Common shares	183,209	39.1	182,332	41.8	171,266	41.2
Retained earnings	64,662	13.8	62,097	14.2	62,770	15.1
Total shareholders' equity	247,871	52.9	244,429	56.0	234,036	56.3
Total liabilities and shareholders' equity	$468,565	100.0	$436,480	100.0	$415,695	100.0

Required:

1. **CONCEPTUAL CONNECTION** Explain why income from operations decreased in 2017 and 2018 while sales increased.
2. Determine whether the proportion of resources invested in the various asset categories changed from 2016 to 2018.
3. Determine whether the proportion of capital supplied by creditors changed.
4. Indicate from what sources Azimio secured the capital to finance its increase in current assets in 2018.

OBJECTIVE ❹

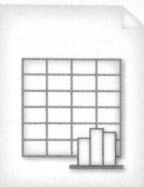

Exercise 13-71   Short-Term Liquidity Ratios

The financial statements for Proust Corporation, a retailer, follow.

Proust Corporation Consolidated Statements of Earnings (millions of dollars)			
	December 31,		
	2018	2017	2016
Revenues	$19,233	$17,927	$16,115
Costs and expenses:			
Cost of retail sales, buying, and occupancy	14,164	13,129	11,751
Selling, publicity, and administration	3,175	2,978	2,801
Depreciation	498	459	410
Interest expense, net	446	437	398
Taxes other than income taxes	343	313	283
Total costs and expenses	18,626	17,316	15,643
Earnings before income taxes	607	611	472
Provision for income taxes	232	228	171
Net earnings	$ 375	$ 383	$ 301

Proust Corporation Consolidated Statements of Financial Position (millions of dollars)		
	December 31,	
ASSETS	2018	2017
Current assets:		
Cash and cash equivalents	$ 321	$ 117
Accounts receivable	1,536	1,514
Merchandise inventories	2,497	2,618
Other	157	165
Total current assets	4,511	4,414
Property and equipment:		
Land	1,120	998
Buildings and improvements	4,753	4,342
Fixtures and equipment	2,162	2,197
Construction-in-progress	248	223
Accumulated depreciation	(2,336)	(2,197)
Net property and equipment	5,947	5,563
Other	320	360
Total assets	$10,778	$10,337

LIABILITIES AND SHAREHOLDERS' EQUITY		
Current liabilities:		
Notes payable	$ 200	$ 23
Accounts payable	1,654	1,596
Accrued liabilities	903	849
Income taxes payable	145	125
Current portion of long-term debt	173	371
Total current liabilities	3,075	2,964
Long-term debt	4,279	4,330
Deferred income taxes and other	536	450
Loan to employees	(217)	(267)
Total liabilities	7,673	7,477
Shareholders' equity:		
Preferred shares	368	374
Common shares	72	71
Contributed surplus—common shares	73	58
Retained earnings	2,592	2,357
Total shareholders' equity	3,105	2,860
Total liabilities and shareholders' equity	$10,778	$10,337

Required:

1. Compute the four short-term liquidity ratios (rounded to two decimal places) for 2017 and 2018, assuming operating cash flows are $281 million and $483 million, respectively.
2. **CONCEPTUAL CONNECTION** Indicate which ratios appear to be most appropriate for a retail organization. Indicate what other information you would like to know to comment on Proust's short-term liquidity.

Exercise 13-72 Debt Management Ratios

OBJECTIVE 4

Refer to Gorky's financial statements in Exercise 13-69.

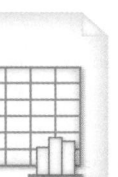

Required:

1. Compute the three debt management ratios for 2017 and 2018 (rounded to two decimal places).
2. **CONCEPTUAL CONNECTION** Indicate whether the ratios have changed and whether the ratios suggest that Gorky is more or less risky for long-term creditors at December 31, 2018, than at December 31, 2017.

Exercise 13-73 Asset Efficiency Ratios

OBJECTIVE 4

Refer to Gorky's financial statements in Exercise 13-69 and the information below.

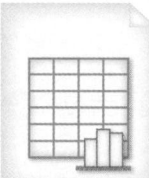

Statement Item	January 1, 2017 (in thousands)
Accounts receivable	$ 752,945
Inventories	698,604
Total assets	3,485,233

Required:

1. Compute the three asset efficiency ratios (rounded to two decimal places) for 2017 and 2018.
2. Indicate the length of Gorky's operating cycle in days (rounded to two decimal places) for the years ended December 31, 2018, and December 31, 2017.

OBJECTIVE 4

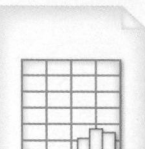

Exercise 13-74   Profitability Ratios

Refer to Gorky's financial statements in Exercise 13-69 and the information below.

Statement Item	January 1, 2017 (in thousands)
Total assets	$3,485,233
Total shareholders' equity	2,083,122

Required:

1. Compute the seven profitability ratios (in percentage terms, rounded to two decimal places) for both 2017 and 2018. *Note:* Assume cash flow from operating activities is $1,250,000.
2. **CONCEPTUAL CONNECTION** Explain what these ratios suggest about Gorky's profitability. Indicate what other information you would like to know to further assess Gorky's profitability.

OBJECTIVE 4

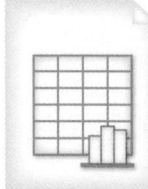

Exercise 13-75   Shareholder Ratios

Refer to Gorky's financial statements in Exercise 13-69 and the information below.

	Year Ended December 31,	
Item	2018	2017
Weighted average number of common shares outstanding (thousands)	362,202	364,398
Preferred dividends (thousands)	$ 24,000	$ 24,000
Dividends per common share	0.54	1.54
Common dividends (thousands)	194,633.00	561,172.30
Common share repurchases	0	0
Market price per share:		
High	$ 83.25	$ 79.10
Low	63.25	59.00
Close	78.42	66.36

At January 1, 2017, total shareholders' equity was $2,297,292 and there were no preferred shares outstanding.

Required:

1. Compute the five shareholder ratios (in percentage terms, rounded to two decimal places except for EPS, which should be rounded to nearest cent) for 2017 and 2018.
2. **CONCEPTUAL CONNECTION** Indicate whether there were significant changes in these ratios between the years ended December 31, 2018, and December 31, 2017. Determine whether the shareholder ratios suggest that Gorky was a better investment at December 31, 2018, or December 31, 2017.

OBJECTIVE 4

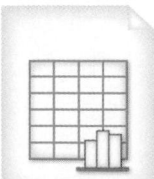

Exercise 13-76   DuPont Analysis

Refer to Gorky's financial statements in Exercise 13-69 and the information below.

Statement Item	January 1, 2017 (in millions)
Total assets	$3,485,233
Total shareholders' equity	2,083,122

	Year Ended December 31,	
Industry Averages	2018	2017
Return on equity	5.31%	12.54%
Profit margin	4.00	6.21
Asset turnover	0.83	1.96
Leverage	1.60	1.03

Required:

1. Perform DuPont analysis (in percentage terms, rounded to two decimal places) for 2017 and 2018.
2. **CONCEPTUAL CONNECTION** Explain what you learn about Gorky's trends from 2017 to 2018 by comparing its performance to the industry averages.

PROBLEM SET A

Problem 13-77A Using Common Size Data for Credit Analysis

OBJECTIVE

You are the credit manager for Carmichael Supply Company. One of your sales staff has made a $50,000 credit sale to Zizes Electronics, a manufacturer of small computers. Your responsibility is to decide whether to approve the sale. You have the following data for the computer industry and Zizes:

For the Years 2014–2018	Industry	Zizes Electronics
Average annual sales growth	13.4%	17.6%
Average annual operating income growth	10.8%	9.7%
Average annual net income growth	14.4%	9.9%
Average annual asset growth	10.3%	14.2%
Average debt-to-equity ratio	0.32	0.26
Average current ratio	4.04	3.71
Average inventory turnover ratio	2.53	2.06
Average accounts receivable turnover ratio	3.95	4.18

For Zizes, you have the following data for the year ended December 31, 2018:

Sales revenue	$3,908,000
Net income	$359,000
Total assets	$3,626,000
Current ratio	1.82
Debt-to-equity ratio	0.37
Inventory turnover ratio	1.79
Accounts receivable turnover ratio	3.62

The salesperson believes that Zizes would order about $200,000 per year of materials that would provide a gross margin of $35,000 to Carmichael if reasonable credit terms could be arranged.

Required:

State whether or not you would grant authorization for Zizes to purchase on credit and support your decision.

YOUDECIDE

Problem 13-78A Using Common Size Data for Investment Analysis

OBJECTIVE 2 3

Assume that you are a trust officer for Wu Bank. You are attempting to select a pharmaceutical manufacturer's stock for a client's portfolio. You have secured the following data:

	Five-Year Averages				
	Industry Average	Hitchens	Rhoades	Castle	Rumba
Sales growth	8.3%	9.8%	7.9%	7.2%	10.1%
Net income growth	13.0	12.0	10.7	4.2	16.1
Asset growth	5.0	6.1	4.6	4.4	6.2

(Continued)

	Current Year				
Return on equity	16.2%	17.5%	17.5%	19.4%	21.6%
Return on assets	8.5	7.8	12.7	8.4	11.4
Dividend payout	43.0	40.0	23.0	31.0	31.0

Required:

CONCEPTUAL CONNECTION Comment on the relative performance of these firms.

 OBJECTIVE ❷ ❸

Problem 13-79A   Using Common Size Statement of Earnings Data

The 2018, 2017, and 2016 statements of earnings for Argon Entertainment Enterprises follow.

Argon Entertainment Enterprises Consolidated Statements of Earnings			
	Year Ended December 31,		
	2018	2017	2016
Revenues			
Theme parks and resorts	$3,440.7	$3,306.9	$2,794.3
Filmed entertainment	3,673.4	3,115.2	2,593.7
Consumer products	1,415.1	1,081.9	724.0
	$8,529.2	$7,504.0	$6,112.0
Costs and Expenses			
Theme parks and resorts	$2,693.8	$2,662.9	$2,247.7
Filmed entertainment	3,051.2	2,606.9	2,275.6
Consumer products	1,059.7	798.9	494.2
	$6,804.7	$6,068.7	$5,017.5
Operating Income			
Theme parks and resorts	$ 746.9	$ 644.0	$ 546.6
Filmed entertainment	622.2	508.3	318.1
Consumer products	355.4	283.0	229.8
	$1,724.5	$1,435.3	$1,094.5
Corporate Activities			
General and administrative expenses	$ 164.2	$ 148.2	$ 160.8
Interest expense	157.7	126.8	105.0
Investment and interest income	(186.1)	(130.3)	(119.4)
	$ 135.8	$ 144.7	$ 146.4
Income (loss) on investment in Asian theme park	$ (514.7)	$ 11.2	$ 63.8
Income before income taxes	1,074.0	1,301.8	1,011.9
Income tax expense	402.7	485.1	375.3
Net income	$ 671.3	$ 816.7	$ 636.6

Required:

1. Calculate how much each of the revenues and expenses changed from 2016 through 2018 (in percentage terms, rounded to two decimal places). You do not need to include the actual dollar amounts shown above.
2. **CONCEPTUAL CONNECTION** Explain the primary causes of Argon's increase in net income in 2017 and the decrease in 2018.

Problem 13-80A   Using Common Size Statements

OBJECTIVE ❷ ❸

The following statement of earnings and vertical analysis data are available for Colfer Audio Products:

	Colfer Audio Products Consolidated Statement of Earnings					
	Year Ended June 30,					
	2018		2017		2016	
(in thousands)	Amount	%	Amount	%	Amount	%
Sales	$2,970.0	100.0	$3,465.0	100.0	$3,960.0	100.0
Other income, net	23.7	0.8	34.6	1.0	39.6	1.0
Total revenues	2,993.7	100.8	3,499.6	101.0	3,999.6	101.0
Costs and expenses:						
Cost of goods sold	1,303.8	43.9	1,566.2	45.2	1,920.6	48.5
Selling and administrative	1,571.1	52.9	1,593.9	46.0	1,564.2	39.5
Interest	62.4	2.1	65.8	1.9	59.4	1.5
Total costs and expenses	2,937.3	98.9	3,225.9	93.1	3,544.2	89.5
Income before income taxes	56.4	1.9	273.7	7.9	455.4	11.5
Income tax expense	14.8	0.5	107.4	3.1	182.2	4.6
Net income	$ 41.6	1.4	$ 166.3	4.8	$ 273.2	6.9

Required:

1. **CONCEPTUAL CONNECTION** Suggest why net income declined from $273,200 to $41,600 while the cost of goods sold percentage decreased each year and selling and administrative expenses remained nearly constant.
2. **CONCEPTUAL CONNECTION** Determine what could cause sales to decline while the gross margin percentage increases.

Problem 13-81A   Using Common Size Statements

OBJECTIVE ❷ ❸

ILLUSTRATING
RELATIONSHIPS

Gilsig Ltd. owns and operates a small chain of sportswear stores located near colleges and universities. Gilsig has experienced significant growth in recent years. The following data are available for Gilsig:

	Gilsig Ltd. Consolidated Statements of Earnings (in thousands)		
	Year Ended December 31,		
	2018	2017	2016
Sales	$51,638	$41,310	$34,425
Cost of goods sold	31,050	24,840	20,700
Gross margin	20,588	16,470	13,725
Other income, net	383	426	405
	20,971	16,896	14,130
Costs and expenses:			
Selling and administrative	16,570	13,465	11,350
Interest	1,237	765	554
Total costs and expenses	17,807	14,230	11,904
Income before income taxes	3,164	2,666	2,226
Provision for income taxes	885	746	623
Net income	$ 2,279	$ 1,920	$ 1,603

(Continued)

Gilsig Ltd. Consolidated Statements of Financial Position (in thousands)			
		December 31,	
ASSETS	2018	2017	2016
Current assets:			
Cash	$ 360	$ 293	$ 236
Accounts receivable	4,658	3,690	3,285
Inventories	6,064	4,478	3,442
Total current assets	11,082	8,461	6,963
Property, plant, and equipment (net)	4,860	3,600	2,756
Other assets	574	585	562
Total assets	$16,516	$12,646	$10,281
LIABILITIES AND SHAREHOLDERS' EQUITY			
Current liabilities:			
Short-term notes payable	$ 4,230	$ 1,620	$ 450
Accounts payable	1,147	1,013	720
Total current liabilities	5,377	2,633	1,170
Long-term debt	3,150	3,150	3,150
Total liabilities	8,527	5,783	4,320
Common shares and contributed surplus	4,725	4,725	4,725
Retained earnings	3,264	2,138	1,236
Total shareholders' equity	7,989	6,863	5,961
Total liabilities and shareholders' equity	$16,516	$12,646	$10,281

Required:

1. Determine how much Gilsig's sales, net income, and assets have grown during these three years.
2. Explain how Gilsig has financed the increase in assets.
3. Determine whether Gilsig's liquidity is adequate.
4. **CONCEPTUAL CONNECTION** Explain why interest expense is growing.
5. If Gilsig's sales grow by 25% in 2019, what would you expect net income to be?
6. If Gilsig's assets must grow by 25% to support the 25% sales increase and if 50% of net income is paid in dividends, how much capital must Gilsig raise in 2019?

OBJECTIVE

Problem 13-82A   Preparing Common Size Statements

The financial statements for Lynch Shoes Inc. follow:

Lynch Shoes Inc. Consolidated Statements of Earnings (in thousands, except per share data)			
		Year Ended December 31,	
	2018	2017	2016
Revenues	$3,930,984	$3,405,211	$3,003,610
Costs and expenses:			
Cost of goods sold	2,386,993	2,089,089	1,850,530
Selling and administrative	922,261	761,498	664,061
Interest	25,739	30,665	27,316
Other expenses (income)	1,475	2,141	(43)
Total costs and expenses	3,336,468	2,883,393	2,541,864
Income before income taxes	594,516	521,818	461,746
Income taxes	229,500	192,600	174,700
Net income	$ 365,016	$ 329,218	$ 287,046

Lynch Shoes Inc. Consolidated Statements of Financial Position (in thousands)		
	December 31,	
ASSETS	2018	2017
Current assets:		
Cash and equivalents	$ 291,284	$ 260,050
Accounts receivable, less allowance for doubtful accounts of $19,447 and $20,046	667,547	596,018
Inventories	592,986	471,202
Deferred income taxes	26,378	27,511
Prepaid expenses	42,452	32,977
Total current assets	1,620,647	1,387,758
Property, plant, and equipment	571,032	497,795
Less accumulated depreciation	(193,037)	(151,758)
Net property, plant, and equipment	377,995	346,037
Goodwill	157,894	110,363
Other assets	30,927	28,703
Total assets	$2,187,463	$1,872,861
LIABILITIES AND SHAREHOLDERS' EQUITY		
Current liabilities:		
Current portion of long-term debt	$ 52,985	$ 3,652
Notes payable	108,165	105,696
Accounts payable	135,701	134,729
Accrued liabilities	138,563	134,089
Income taxes payable	17,150	42,422
Total current liabilities	452,564	420,588
Long-term debt	15,033	77,022
Noncurrent deferred income taxes	29,965	27,074
Other noncurrent liabilities	43,575	23,728
Redeemable preferred share	300	300
Total liabilities	541,437	548,712
Shareholders' equity:		
Common shares at stated value:		
Class A convertible—26,691 and 26,919 shares outstanding	159	161
Class B—49,161 and 48,591 shares outstanding	2,720	2,716
Contributed surplus	100,661	86,939
Retained earnings	1,542,486	1,234,333
Total shareholders' equity	1,646,026	1,324,149
Total liabilities and shareholders' equity	$2,187,463	$1,872,861

Required:

1. Prepare common size statement of earnings to be used for horizontal analysis for Lynch for 2016 to 2018 (in percentage terms, rounded to two decimal places). You do not need to include the actual dollar amounts shown above.

2. **CONCEPTUAL CONNECTION** Indicate why Lynch's net income increased between 2016 and 2018.

3. Prepare common size statements of financial position to be used for vertical analysis for 2018 and 2017 (in percentage terms, rounded to two decimal places). You do not need to include the actual dollar amounts shown above.

4. Indicate whether the proportion of dollars invested in the various categories of assets has changed significantly between 2017 and 2018.

5. Indicate whether the proportion of capital raised from the various liability categories and common shareholders' equity has changed significantly between 2017 and 2018.

6. **CONCEPTUAL CONNECTION** Describe Lynch's performance and financial position.

OBJECTIVE **4**   **Problem 13-83A   Preparation of Ratios**

Refer to the financial statements for Gilsig Ltd. in Problem 13-81A.

Required:

1. **CONCEPTUAL CONNECTION** Compute the asset efficiency ratios (rounded to two decimal places) for Gilsig for 2018 and 2017 (in percentage terms, rounded to two decimal places). Indicate whether efficiency has changed.
2. **CONCEPTUAL CONNECTION** Compute the profitability ratios (rounded to two decimal places) for Gilsig for 2018 and 2017. Explain if profitability has increased or decreased from 2017 to 2018.
3. **CONCEPTUAL CONNECTION** Compute the debt management ratios (in percentage terms, rounded to two decimal places) for Gilsig for 2017 and 2018. Discuss whether creditors are as secure in 2018 as they were in 2017.

OBJECTIVE **4**   **Problem 13-84A   Comparing Financial Ratios**

Presented below are selected ratios for four firms. Mirbeau is a heavy equipment manufacturer, Rilke is a newspaper publisher, Cervantes is a food manufacturer, and Dickens is a grocery chain.

	Mirbeau	Rilke	Cervantes	Dickens
Short-term liquidity ratio				
Current ratio	1.3	1.7	1.0	1.6
Debt management ratio				
Debt-to-equity	1.81	0.45	0.30	0.25
Asset efficiency ratios				
Accounts receivable turnover	4.66	8.28	11.92	116.15
Inventory turnover	6.26	40.26	7.29	8.43
Profitability ratios				
Operating income	12.6%	25.4%	21.2%	3.8%
Net income	5.9	10.9	10.8	1.9
Return on assets	4.7	10.6	16.8	10.3
Return on equity	36.0	22.6	38.0	21.2

Required:

1. Which firm has the weakest current ratio?
2. **CONCEPTUAL CONNECTION** Explain why the turnover ratios vary so much among the four firms.
3. **CONCEPTUAL CONNECTION** Explain why the return on equity ratio is larger than the return on asset ratio for all four firms.
4. **CONCEPTUAL CONNECTION** Discuss whether the large differences in the return on equity ratios can exist over long periods of time.

OBJECTIVE **4**   **Problem 13-85A   Preparation of Ratios**

Refer to the financial statements for Lynch Shoes Inc. in Problem 13-82A and the following data.

Amounts in thousands, except for per share data	2018	2017	2016
Average number of common shares outstanding	77,063	76,602	76,067
Accounts receivable	$ 667,547	$ 596,018	$ 521,588
Inventories	592,986	471,202	586,594
Total assets	2,187,463	1,872,861	1,708,430
Shareholders' equity	1,646,026	1,324,149	1,032,789
Share repurchases	930,111	581,134	288,320
Cash flows from operating activities	190,000	150,000	137,000
Common dividends paid	57,797	45,195	39,555
Dividends per common share	0.75	0.59	0.52

Amounts in thousands, except for per share data	2018	2017	2016
Market price per share:			
High	90.25	77.45	54.50
Low	55.00	35.12	26.00
Close	86.33	71.65	43.22

	Year Ended December 31,	
Industry Averages	2018	2017
Return on equity	25.98%	23.04%
Net profit margin	5.0%	4.0%
Asset turnover	2.24x	2.56x
Leverage	2.32x	2.25x

Required:

1. Prepare all the financial ratios for Lynch for 2018 and 2017 (using percentage terms where appropriate and rounding all answers to two decimal places).
2. **CONCEPTUAL CONNECTION** Explain whether Lynch's short-term liquidity is adequate.
3. **CONCEPTUAL CONNECTION** Discuss whether Lynch uses its assets efficiently.
4. **CONCEPTUAL CONNECTION** Determine whether Lynch is profitable.
5. **CONCEPTUAL CONNECTION** Discuss whether long-term creditors should regard Lynch as a high-risk or a low-risk firm.
6. Perform DuPont analysis (rounding to two decimal places) for 2017 and 2018.

PROBLEM SET B

Problem 13-86B   Using Common Size Data for Credit Analysis

OBJECTIVE **2** **3**

You are the credit manager for Balzac Supply Inc. One of your sales staff has made a $60,000 credit sale to Monteith Technology, a manufacturer of small computers. Your responsibility is to decide whether to approve the sale. You have the following data for the computer industry and Monteith:

For the Years 2014–2018	Industry	Monteith
Average annual sales growth	12.6%	16.8%
Average annual operating income growth	11.2%	10.2%
Average annual net income growth	15.3%	10.6%
Average annual asset growth	9.9%	13.9%
Average debt-to-equity ratio	0.36	0.29
Average current ratio	4.12	3.88
Average inventory turnover ratio	2.61	2.19
Average accounts receivable turnover ratio	3.89	4.11

For Monteith, you have the following data for the year ended December 31, 2018:

Sales revenue	$4,120,000
Net income	$ 367,000
Total assets	$3,752,000
Current ratio	1.79
Debt-to-equity ratio	0.42
Inventory turnover ratio	1.83
Accounts receivable turnover ratio	3.71

The salesperson believes that Monteith would order about $240,000 per year of materials that would provide a gross margin of $40,000 to Balzac if reasonable credit terms could be arranged.

(Continued)

Required:

CONCEPTUAL CONNECTION State whether or not you would grant authorization for Monteith to purchase on credit and support your decision.

Problem 13-87B   Using Common Size Data for Investment Analysis

Assume that you are a trust officer for Bay Street Bank. You are attempting to select a pharmaceutical manufacturer's shares for a client's portfolio. You have secured the following data:

Five-Year Averages

	Industry Average	Morrison	Rivera	O'Malley	Theba
Sales growth	9.3%	8.8%	10.2%	10.0%	7.9%
Net income growth	6.0	15.3	1.9	1.4	1.6
Asset growth	7.0	6.6	8.3	8.9	6.3

Current Year

	Industry Average	Morrison	Rivera	O'Malley	Theba
Return on equity	19.5%	18.4%	22.7%	20.8%	17.3%
Return on assets	11.7	10.4	13.7	12.8	11.1
Dividend payout	31.0	30.0	39.0	37.0	29.0

Required:

CONCEPTUAL CONNECTION Comment on the relative performance of these firms.

Problem 13-88B   Using Common Size Statement of Earnings Data

The 2018, 2017, and 2016 statements of earnings for Talton Electronics Limited follow.

Talton Amusement Limited Consolidated Statements of Earnings			
	Year Ended December 31,		
	2018	2017	2016
Revenues			
Theme parks and resorts	$2,723.8	$3,299.9	$3,502.7
Filmed entertainment	2,601.4	3,127.3	3,682.4
Consumer products	752.3	1,121.6	1,493.5
	$6,077.5	$7,548.8	$8,678.6
Costs and expenses			
Theme parks and resorts	$2,263.9	$2,723.4	$2,703.7
Filmed entertainment	2,300.2	2,566.3	3,104.9
Consumer products	503.7	804.5	1,120.6
	$5,067.8	$6,094.2	$6,929.2
Operating income			
Theme parks and resorts	$ 459.9	$ 576.5	$ 799.0
Filmed entertainment	301.2	561.0	577.5
Consumer products	248.6	317.1	372.9
	$1,009.7	$1,454.6	$1,749.4
Corporate activities			
General and administrative expenses	$ 161.2	$ 150.2	$ 165.3
Interest expense	103.7	130.8	158.9
Investment and interest income	(121.1)	(127.4)	(193.6)
	$ 143.8	$ 153.6	$ 130.6
Income (loss) on investment in Asian theme park	$ 62.1	$ 13.6	$ (520.8)
Income before income taxes	928.0	1,314.6	1,098.0
Income taxes	376.2	492.3	410.4
Net income	$ 551.8	$ 822.3	$ 687.6

Required:

1. Calculate how much each of the revenues and expenses changed from 2016 through 2018 using horizontal analysis (in percentage terms, rounded to two decimal places). You do not need to include the actual dollar amounts shown above.
2. **CONCEPTUAL CONNECTION** Discuss the primary causes of Talton's increase in net income in 2017 and the decrease in 2018.

Problem 13-89B   Using Common Size Statements

OBJECTIVE  2 3

The following statements of earnings and vertical analysis data are available for Sussman Audio Products:

	Sussman Audio Products Consolidated Statements of Earnings (in thousands)					
	Year Ended June 30,					
	2018		2017		2016	
	Amount	%	Amount	%	Amount	%
Sales	$4,122.0	100.0	$3,566.0	100.0	$2,965.0	100.0
Other income, net	39.7	1.0	36.7	1.0	21.3	0.7
Total revenues	4,161.7	101.0	3,602.7	101.0	2,986.3	100.7
Costs and expenses:						
Cost of goods sold	1,893.6	45.9	1,610.3	45.2	1,310.8	44.2
Selling and administrative	1,610.3	39.1	1,603.6	45.0	1,505.3	50.8
Interest	61.4	1.5	69.7	2.0	63.2	2.1
Total costs and expenses	3,565.3	86.5	3,283.6	92.2	2,879.3	97.1
Income before income taxes	596.4	14.5	319.1	8.9*	107.0	3.6
Income tax expense	181.5	4.4	109.6	3.1	14.5	0.5
Net income	$ 414.9	10.1	$ 209.5	5.9*	$ 92.5	3.1

*Differences due to rounding

Required:

1. **CONCEPTUAL CONNECTION** Suggest why net income increased from $92,500 to $414,900.
2. **CONCEPTUAL CONNECTION** Explain what could cause sales to increase while the gross margin percentage decreases.

OBJECTIVE ❷ ❸

Problem 13-90B   Using Common Size Statements

Groff Graphics Company owns and operates a small chain of sportswear stores located near colleges and universities. Groff has experienced significant growth in recent years. The following data are available for Groff:

Groff Graphics Company
Consolidated Statements of Earnings
(in thousands)

| | Year Ended December 31, | | |
	2018	2017	2016
Sales	$54,922	$42,893	$35,526
Cost of goods sold	32,936	25,682	21,721
Gross margin	21,986	17,211	13,805
Other income, net	397	439	421
	22,383	17,650	14,226
Costs and expenses:			
Selling and administrative	17,857	14,665	12,754
Interest	1,356	863	622
	19,213	15,528	13,376
Income before income taxes	3,170	2,122	850
Provision for income taxes	885	746	623
Net income	$ 2,285	$ 1,376	$ 227

Groff Graphics Company
Consolidated Statements of Financial Position
(in thousands)

| | December 31, | | |
ASSETS	2018	2017	2016
Current assets:			
Cash	$ 372	$ 301	$ 245
Accounts receivable	4,798	3,546	3,369
Inventories	5,673	4,521	3,389
Total current assets	10,843	8,368	7,003
Property, plant, and equipment (net)	4,912	3,541	2,937
Other assets	592	592	552
Total assets	$16,347	$12,501	$10,492
LIABILITIES AND SHAREHOLDERS' EQUITY			
Current liabilities:			
Short-term notes payable	$ 4,314	$ 1,731	$ 463
Accounts payable	1,256	987	783
Total current liabilities	5,570	2,718	1,246
Long-term debt	3,241	3,234	3,266
Total liabilities	8,811	5,952	4,512
Common shares and contributed surplus	4,367	4,598	4,725
Retained earnings	3,169	1,951	1,255
Total shareholders' equity	7,536	6,549	5,980
Total liabilities and shareholders' equity	$16,347	$12,501	$10,492

Required:

1. Calculate how much Groff's sales, net income, and assets have grown during these three years.
2. Explain how Groff has financed the increase in assets.
3. **CONCEPTUAL CONNECTION** Discuss whether Groff's liquidity is adequate.
4. **CONCEPTUAL CONNECTION** Explain why interest expense is growing.
5. If Groff's sales grow by 25% in 2019, what would you expect net income to be?
6. If Groff's assets must grow by 25% to support the 25% sales increase and if 50% of net income is paid in dividends, how much capital must Groff raise in 2019?

Problem 13-91B   Preparing Common Size Statements

OBJECTIVE

The financial statements for Tobolowsky Hats Inc. follow.

Tobolowsky Hats Inc. Consolidated Statements of Earnings (in thousands except per share data)			
	Year Ended December 31,		
	2018	2017	2016
Revenues	$4,102,721	$3,652,412	$3,178,569
Costs and expenses:			
Cost of goods sold	2,256,236	2,234,985	1,952,123
Selling and administrative	927,412	653,986	598,236
Interest	23,974	32,596	31,853
Other expenses (income)	1,925	2,254	(102)
Total costs and expenses	3,209,547	2,923,821	2,582,110
Income before income taxes	893,174	728,591	596,459
Income taxes	247,692	183,456	163,524
Net income	$ 645,482	545,135	$ 432,935

Tobolowsky Hats Inc. Consolidated Statements of Financial Position (in thousands)		
	December 31,	
ASSETS	2018	2017
Current assets:		
Cash and equivalents	$ 301,695	$ 269,648
Accounts receivable, less allowance for doubtful accounts of $20,568 and $18,322	670,469	604,236
Inventories	601,396	469,582
Deferred income taxes	23,415	24,397
Prepaid expenses	43,624	36,478
Total current assets	1,640,599	1,404,341
Property, plant, and equipment	583,152	501,239
Less accumulated depreciation	(206,452)	(148,231)
Net property, plant, and equipment	376,700	353,008
Goodwill	162,325	127,695
Other assets	29,158	23,598
Total assets	$2,208,782	$1,908,642

(Continued)

LIABILITIES AND SHAREHOLDERS' EQUITY		
Current liabilities:		
Current portion of long-term debt	$ 63,169	$ 5,665
Notes payable	112,596	110,423
Accounts payable	128,696	139,364
Accrued liabilities	143,874	133,569
Income taxes payable	23,541	38,972
Total current liabilities	471,876	427,993
Long-term debt	16,254	83,456
Noncurrent deferred income taxes	33,489	31,238
Other noncurrent liabilities	46,685	27,434
Redeemable preferred shares	200	200
Total liabilities	568,504	570,321
Shareholders' equity:		
Common shares at stated value:		
Class A convertible—27,723 and 25,832 shares outstanding	164	175
Class B—49,756 and 47,652 shares outstanding	3,152	3,120
Contributed surplus	101,855	88,687
Retained earnings	1,535,107	1,246,339
Total shareholders' equity	1,640,278	1,338,321
Total liabilities and shareholders' equity	$2,208,782	$1,908,642

Required:

1. Prepare common size statement of earnings to be used for horizontal analysis for Tobolow-sky for 2016 and 2018 (in percentage terms, rounded to two decimal places). You do not need to include the actual dollar amounts shown above.
2. Indicate why Tobolowsky's net income increased between 2016 and 2018.
3. Prepare common size statements of financial position to be used for vertical analysis for 2018 and 2017 (in percentage terms, rounded to two decimal places). You do not need to include the actual dollar amounts shown above.
4. Determine whether the proportion of dollars invested in the various categories of assets has changed significantly between 2017 and 2018.
5. Determine whether the proportion of capital raised from the various liability categories and common shareholders' equity has changed significantly between 2017 and 2018.
6. **CONCEPTUAL CONNECTION** How would you describe Tobolowsky's performance and financial position?

OBJECTIVE ④   **Problem 13-92B   Preparation of Ratios**

Refer to the financial statements for Groff Graphics Company in Problem 13-90B.

Required:

1. **CONCEPTUAL CONNECTION** Compute the asset efficiency ratios for Groff for 2018 and 2017 (in percentage terms, rounded to two decimal places) and determine whether their asset efficiency has changed.
2. **CONCEPTUAL CONNECTION** Compute the profitability ratios (rounded to two decimal places) for Groff for 2018 and 2017. Explain if profitability has increased or decreased from 2017 to 2018.
3. **CONCEPTUAL CONNECTION** Compute the debt management ratios for 2017 and 2018. Discuss whether creditors are as secure in 2018 as they were in 2017.

OBJECTIVE ④   **Problem 13-93B   Comparing Financial Ratios**

Presented below are selected ratios for four firms. Rosemont is a distiller, Adler is a jewellery retailer, Menzel is an airline, and Gallagher is a hotel chain.

	Rosemont	Adler	Menzel	Gallagher
Short-term liquidity ratio				
Current ratio	1.5	3.5	0.9	1.4
Debt management ratio				
Debt-to-equity	0.24	0.20	2.62	1.09
Asset efficiency ratios				
Accounts receivable turnover	7.66	17.07	19.72	11.09
Inventory turnover	2.30	0.95	31.43	7.24
Profitability ratios				
Operating income	17.7%	15.5%	4.2%	9.2%
Net income	13.1	9.6	2.2	5.4
Return on assets	11.9	8.6	1.8	7.9
Return on equity	23.7	14.9	49.2	34.5

Required:

1. **CONCEPTUAL CONNECTION** Explain why the debt-to-equity ratio is so much higher for the airline and hotel chain than it is for the distiller and jewellery retailer.
2. **CONCEPTUAL CONNECTION** Explain why the turnover ratios vary so much among the four firms.
3. **CONCEPTUAL CONNECTION** Explain why the return on equity for the airline and hotel chain is higher than for the distiller and jewellery retailer when their operating income and net income percentages are considerably smaller.

Problem 13-94B Preparation of Ratios

OBJECTIVE **4**

Refer to the financial statements for Tobolowsky Hats Inc. in Problem 13-91B and the data below.

Amounts in thousands, except for per share data	2018	2017	2016
Average number of common shares outstanding	78,273	77,325	77,021
Accounts receivable	$ 670,469	$ 604,236	$ 545,556
Inventories	601,396	469,582	592,524
Total assets	2,208,782	1,908,642	1,699,432
Shareholders' equity	1,640,278	1,338,321	1,075,952

Amounts in thousands, except for per share data	2018	2017	2016
Share repurchases	990,521	623,259	310,132
Cash flows from operating activities	495,000	380,000	265,000
Common dividends paid	61,836	49,488	37,740
Dividends per common share	0.79	0.64	0.49
Market price per share:			
High	92.17	79.13	56.22
Low	56.59	37.23	27.10
Close	88.47	73.83	44.26

	Year Ended December 31,	
Industry Averages	**2018**	**2017**
Return on equity	32.71%	27.86%
Net profit margin	6%	5%
Asset turnover	2.31x	2.51x
Leverage	2.36x	2.22x

(Continued)

Required:

1. Prepare all the financial ratios for Tobolowsky for 2018 and 2017 (using percentage terms where appropriate and rounding all answers to two decimal places).
2. **CONCEPTUAL CONNECTION** Indicate whether Tobolowsky's short-term liquidity is adequate.
3. **CONCEPTUAL CONNECTION** Discuss whether Tobolowsky uses its assets efficiently.
4. **CONCEPTUAL CONNECTION** Determine whether Tobolowsky is profitable.
5. **CONCEPTUAL CONNECTION** Discuss whether long-term creditors should regard Tobolowsky as a high-risk or a low-risk firm.
6. Perform DuPont analysis (rounding to two decimal places) for 2018 and 2017.

CASES

Case 13-95   Ethics and Equity

Lauren Avenido is employed as a financial analyst at a large brokerage house. Her job is to follow companies in the computer hardware sector and issue reports that will be used by her firm's brokers in making recommendations to the brokerage house's clients. Her reports are summarized by her ratings of the company—strong buy, buy, hold, sell, or strong sell. She is in frequent contact with the top management of the companies she follows.

After a thorough investigation, she believes she should downgrade Dreamware from a "strong buy" to a "hold." However, when she informs Dreamware's CFO, the CFO threatens to call her boss. Later that week, her boss calls her to request that she reconsider her downgrade and states that her cooperation will be "greatly appreciated."

Required:

How should Lauren respond to her boss? Are there any other steps she should consider taking?

Case 13-96   Assessing the Effects of the "Clean Air" Legislation

Parliament is considering legislation that would require significant reductions over a several-year period in the quantity of emissions that electric utilities will be allowed to discharge into the air. Electric utilities that generate their electricity by burning inexpensive but relatively high-sulphur coal would be most affected by this legislation. Some utilities plan to comply with this legislation by burning coal with a lower sulphur content. Other utilities plan to comply with this legislation by installing devices on power plant smokestacks that would filter emissions before they are discharged into the air.

Required:

1. In what places on the financial statements of coal-dependent electric utilities do you expect to observe the effects of this legislation?
2. In what places on the financial statements of companies that mine coal do you expect to observe the effects of this legislation?

Case 13-97   Changes in the Price of Fuel for Aircraft

Fuel is reported to be about 20% of the total operating cost for a major airline. Events in the Middle East caused jet fuel costs to nearly double between 2013 and 2016.

Required:

1. If you were the CEO of a major airline, how would you suggest that the airline respond to the fuel price increase?
2. How would you expect the financial statements of major airlines to be affected by the fuel price increase and the actions that the airlines take in response?

Case 13-98 Analyzing Growth

Consolidated financial statements for Initech Corporation follow.

Initech Corporation Consolidated Statements of Earnings (in millions except per share amounts)			
	Three Years Ended December 31,		
	2018	2017	2016
Net revenues	$8,782	$5,844	$4,779
Cost of goods sold	3,252	2,557	2,316
Research and development	970	780	618
Marketing, general, and administrative expenses	1,168	1,017	765
Operating costs and expenses	5,390	4,354	3,699
Operating income	3,392	1,490	1,080
Interest expense	(50)	(54)	(82)
Interest income and other, net	188	133	197
Income before taxes	3,530	1,569	1,195
Provision for taxes	1,235	502	376
Net income	$2,295	$1,067	$ 819

Initech Corporation Consolidated Statements of Financial Position (in millions except per share amounts)		
	December 31,	
ASSETS	2018	2017
Current assets:		
Cash and cash equivalents	$ 1,659	$ 1,843
Short-term investments	1,477	993
Accounts and notes receivable, net of allowance for doubtful accounts		
of $22 ($26 in 2017)	1,448	1,069
Inventories	838	535
Deferred tax assets	310	205
Other current assets	70	46
Total current assets	5,802	4,691
Property, plant, and equipment:		
Land and buildings	1,848	1,463
Machinery and equipment	4,148	2,874
Construction in progress	317	311
	6,313	4,648
Less accumulated depreciation	(2,317)	(1,832)
Property, plant, and equipment, net	3,996	2,816
Long-term investments	1,116	496
Other assets	130	86
Total assets	$11,344	$ 8,089

(Continued)

LIABILITIES AND SHAREHOLDERS' EQUITY		
Current liabilities:		
Short-term debt	$ 399	$ 202
Long-term debt redeemable within one year	98	110
Accounts payable	427	281
Deferred income on shipments to distributors	200	149
Accrued compensation and benefits	544	435
Other accrued liabilities	374	306
Income tax payable	391	359
Total current liabilities	2,433	1,842
Long-term debt	426	249
Deferred tax liabilities	297	180
Other long-term liabilities	688	373
Total liabilities	3,844	2,644
Shareholders' equity:		
Common shares, $0.001 stated value, 1,400 shares authorized; and		
issued and outstanding in 2018 and 2017	1	1
Contributed surplus	2,193	1,775
Retained earnings	5,306	3,669
Total shareholders' equity	7,500	5,445
Total liabilities and shareholders' equity	$11,344	$8,089

Required:

1. Prepare common size statement of earnings to be used for both vertical and horizontal analysis for 2017–2018 (in percentage terms, rounded to two decimal places). You do not need to include the actual dollar amounts shown above.
2. Using the common size statement of earnings for both vertical and horizontal analysis prepared in part 1, indicate why Initech's profits increased more rapidly than sales for 2017 and 2018.
3. Prepare common size statements of financial position for vertical analysis for 2017 and 2018 (in percentage terms, rounded to two decimal places). You do not need to include the actual dollar amounts shown above.
4. Did the proportion of assets invested in the various classes of assets change significantly from 2017 to 2018?
5. How has Initech financed its growth in assets?
6. Did the statement of earnings change as much between 2017 and 2018 as the statement of financial position?

Case 13-99 Identifying the Causes of Profitability Changes

The consolidated financial statements for Dowsett Shipping Corporation follow.

Dowsett Shipping Corporation Consolidated Statements of Earnings (in thousands, except per share amounts)			
	Year Ended May 31,		
	2018	2017	2016
Revenues	$7,808,043	$7,550,060	$7,688,296
Operating expenses:			
Salaries and employee benefits	3,807,493	3,637,080	3,438,391
Rentals and landing fees	658,138	672,341	650,001
Depreciation and amortization	579,896	577,157	562,207
Fuel	495,384	508,386	663,327
Maintenance and repairs	404,639	404,311	449,394
Restructuring charges	(12,500)	254,000	121,000
Other	1,497,820	1,473,818	1,551,850
	7,430,870	7,527,093	7,436,170
Operating income	377,173	22,967	252,126
Other income (expenses):			
Interest, net	(160,923)	(164,315)	(181,880)
Gain on disposition of aircraft and related equipment	4,633	2,832	11,375
Other, net	(107,537)	(8,312)	(8,679)
Payroll tax loss	–	–	(32,000)
Other income (expenses), net	(263,827)	(169,795)	(211,184)
Income (loss) before income taxes	113,346	(146,828)	40,942
Provision (credit) for income taxes	59,480	(33,046)	35,044
Net income (loss)	$ 53,866	$ (113,782)	$ 5,898

Dowsett Shipping Corporation Consolidated Statements of Financial Position (in thousands)		
	May 31,	
ASSETS	2018	2017
Current assets:		
Cash and cash equivalents	$ 155,456	$ 78,177
Receivables, less allowance for doubtful accounts of $31,308 and $32,074	922,727	899,773
Spare parts, supplies, and fuel	164,087	158,062
Prepaid expenses and other	63,573	69,994
Deferred income taxes	133,875	0
Total current assets	1,439,718	1,206,006
Property and equipment, at cost		
Flight equipment	2,843,253	2,540,350
Package handling and ground support equipment	1,413,793	1,352,659
Computer and electronic equipment	947,913	851,686
Other	1,501,250	1,433,212
	6,706,209	6,177,907
Less accumulated depreciation and amortization	(3,229,941)	(2,766,610)
Net property and equipment	3,476,268	3,411,297
Other assets:		
Goodwill	432,215	487,780
Equipment deposits and other assets	444,863	358,103
Total other assets	877,078	845,883
Total assets	$ 5,793,064	$ 5,463,186

(Continued)

LIABILITIES AND SHAREHOLDERS' EQUITY		
Current liabilities:		
Current portion of long-term debt	$ 133,797	$ 155,257
Accounts payable	554,111	430,130
Accrued expenses	761,357	799,468
Total current liabilities	1,449,265	1,384,855
Long-term debt, less current portion	1,882,279	1,797,844
Deferred income taxes	72,479	123,715
Other liabilities	717,660	577,050
Total liabilities	4,121,683	3,883,464
Shareholders' equity:		
Common shares, 100,000 shares authorized, 54,743 and 54,100 shares issued	5,474	5,410
Contributed surplus—common shares	696,392	667,757
Retained earnings	969,515	906,555
Total shareholders' equity	1,671,381	1,579,722
Total liabilities and shareholders' equity	$5,793,064	$5,463,186

Required:

1. Evaluate Dowsett's performance in 2018.
2. What were the primary factors responsible for Dowsett's loss in 2017 and return to profitability in 2018?
3. How did Dowsett finance the $329,878,000 increase in assets in 2018?

Case 13-100   Continuing Problem: Front Row Entertainment

The statement of earnings and consolidated statements of financial position for Front Row Entertainment follow.

Front Row Entertainment Inc. Consolidated Statements of Financial Position		
	December 31,	
ASSETS	2018	2017
Current assets:		
Cash	$ 30,322	$ 9,005
Accounts receivable, net	98,250	17,000
Prepaid expenses	133,400	57,200
Supplies	2,200	3,700
Inventory	61,380	2,850
Total current assets	325,552	89,755
Property, plant, and equipment:		
Building	1,857,250	–
Equipment	27,350	7,000
Accumulated depreciation	(53,835)	(2,160)
Trademark	25,000	–
Total assets	$2,181,317	$94,595

LIABILITIES AND EQUITY		
Current liabilities:		
Accounts payable	$ 2,450	$12,240
Salaries payable	2,500	3,690
Interest payable	48,917	2,250
Unearned sales revenue	1,780	28,650
Income tax payable	550	2,180
Total current liabilities	56,197	49,010
Long-term liabilities:		
Notes payable	405,000	25,000
Bonds payable, net	1,500,000	–
Less: Discount on bond payable	(109,530)	–
Total long-term liabilities	1,795,470	25,000
Equity:		
Preferred shares	150,000	–
Common shares	17,300	16,000
Contributed surplus:		
Preferred shares	75,000	–
Common shares	34,100	–
Retained earnings	53,250	4,585
Total shareholders' equity	329,650	20,585
Total liabilities and equity	$2,181,317	$94,595

Front Row Entertainment Inc.
Statement of Earnings
For the Year Ended December 31, 2018

Revenues:	
Sales revenue	$3,142,800
Service revenue	636,000
Total revenues	3,778,800
Expenses:	
Artist fee expense	2,134,260
Rent expense	952,663
Cost of goods sold	74,800
Salaries and wages expense	345,100
Depreciation expense	51,675
Interest expense	98,087
Income tax expense	22,000
Other expenses	26,550
Total expenses	3,705,135
Net income	$ 73,665

Additional information:

- The market price of the common shares at the end of the year is $17.55 per share.
- The average number of common shares outstanding for 2018 is 16,400.
- The dividends for 2018 were $25,000, which is approximately $1.45 per share ($25,000/17,300 common shares). The 17,300 shares can be calculated from information in Chapter 10 (16,000 shares at Jan. 1, 2018 + 2,000 shares issued on June 15, 2018 – 700 shares repurchased on July 10, 2018).
- Common share repurchases for 2018 were $11,200. This is taken from Chapter 10 as 700 common shares were repurchased at a cost of $16 per share.
- Preferred dividends for 2018 were $0.
- "Cash flows from operating activities" was $(77,783) for 2018.

Note: Round all answers to two decimal places.

(Continued)

Required:

1. Calculate the short-term liquidity ratios for Front Row Entertainment for 2018.
2. Calculate the debt management ratios for Front Row Entertainment for 2018.
3. Calculate the asset efficiency ratios for Front Row Entertainment for 2018.
4. Calculate the profitability ratios for Front Row Entertainment for 2018.
5. Calculate the shareholder ratios for Front Row Entertainment for 2018.

Case 13-101   Professional and Ethical Behaviour

Nicky is the owner of Nicky Automotive Limited (NAL). NAL is a family business that has served southern Ontario for the last 40 years. With large chain stores now offering automotive services to consumers, the competition has been fierce and NAL has seen a significant decrease in sales over the last two years. NAL finds itself struggling to pay off current obligations and needs to obtain financing from the local bank to help the business through the summer months when customers normally don't need as many automotive repairs and hence cash flow is tight.

NAL has never needed a loan from the bank, and Nicky doesn't know where to begin. He contacts the bank to see what is required to obtain financing. The bank asks Nicky to bring in NAL's current-year draft financial statements. The bank says it wants to make sure the statement of financial position looks strong and will use the statements to assess the ability of NAL to pay back the loan. Showing strong ratios will help NAL's cause in getting the loan. Nicky says he'll get them together and be in on Friday.

Laura is a professional chartered accountant who takes care of all of NAL's accounting and preparation of financial statements. Nicky tells her about the call with the bank and requests that she have the financial statements ready by Friday. Nicky also tells Laura that the company's future depends on getting this loan. "We're either going to stay afloat or have to file for creditor protection." Nicky goes on to tell Laura, "Make sure that the statement they want looks good, especially those ratios they always look at. Even if you have to reclassify items to make the ratios look better, just do it and we'll deal with it later!"

Laura is a bit shocked at Nicky's comments but proceeds to put together the draft financial statements.

Required:

Comment on any professional behaviour issues.

1 Appendix

Time Value of Money

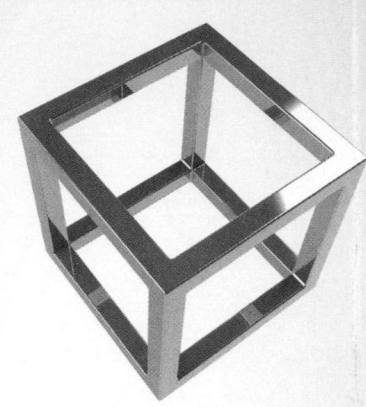

After studying Appendix 1, you should be able to:

1. Explain how compound interest works.
2. Use future value and present value tables to apply compound interest to accounting transactions.

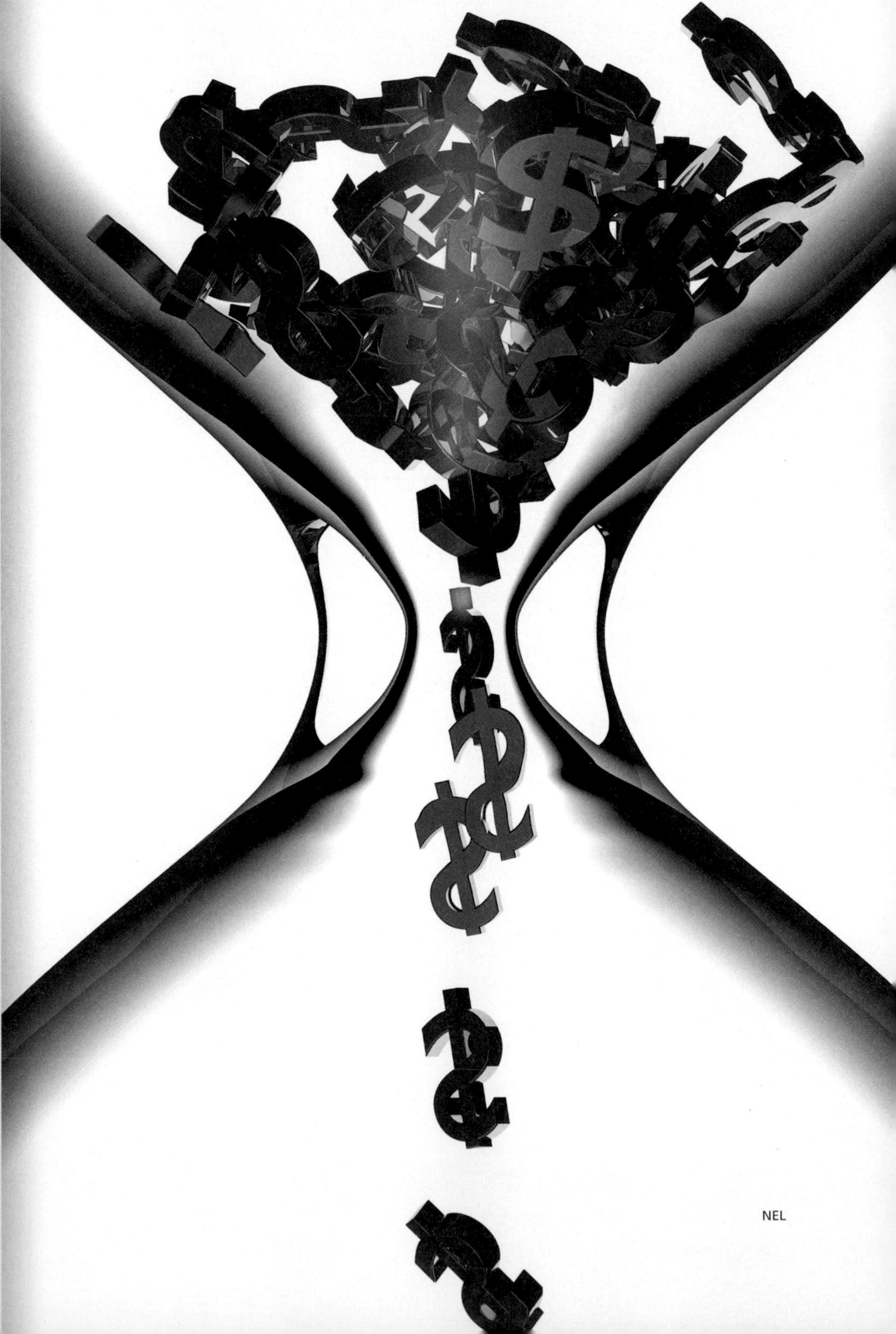

BrooksElliott/iStockphoto

Time value of money is widely used in business to measure today's value of future cash outflows or inflows and the amount to which liabilities (or assets) will grow when compound interest accumulates.

In transactions involving the borrowing and lending of money, the borrower usually pays *interest*. In effect, interest is the **time value of money**. The amount of interest paid is determined by the length of the loan and the interest rate.

However, interest is not restricted to loans made to borrowers by banks. Investments (particularly, investments in debt securities and savings accounts), installment sales, and a variety of other contractual arrangements all include interest. In all cases, the arrangement between the two parties—the note, security, or purchase agreement—creates an asset in the accounting records of one party and a corresponding liability in the accounting records of the other. All such assets and liabilities increase as interest is earned by the asset holder and decrease as payments are made by the liability holder.

COMPOUND INTEREST CALCULATIONS

Compound interest is a method of calculating the time value of money in which interest is earned on the previous periods' interest. That is, interest for the period is added to the account balance and interest is earned on this new balance in the next period. In computing compound interest, it's important to understand the difference between the *interest period* and the *interest rate*:

OBJECTIVE **1**

Explain how compound interest works.

- The **interest period** is the time interval between interest calculations.
- The **interest rate** is the percentage that is multiplied by the beginning-of-period balance to yield the amount of interest for that period.

The interest rate must agree with the interest period. For example, if the interest period is one month, then the interest rate used to calculate interest must be stated as a percentage "per month."

When an interest rate is stated in terms of a time period that differs from the interest period, the rate must be adjusted before interest can be calculated. For example, suppose that a bank advertises interest at a rate of 12% per year compounded monthly. Here, the interest period would be one month. Since there are 12 interest periods in one year, the interest rate for one month is one-twelfth the annual rate, or 1%. In other words, if the *rate statement period* differs from the *interest period*, the stated rate must be divided by the number of interest periods included in the rate statement period. A few examples of adjusted rates follow:

Stated Rate	Adjusted Rate for Computations
12% per year compounded semiannually	6% per six-month period (12%/2)
12% per year compounded quarterly	3% per quarter (12%/4)
12% per year compounded monthly	1% per month (12%/12)

If an interest rate is stated without reference to a rate statement period or an interest period, assume that the period is one year. For example, both "12%" and "12% per year" should be interpreted as 12% per year compounded annually.

Compound interest means that interest is computed on the original amount plus undistributed interest earned in previous periods. The simplest compound interest calculation involves putting a single amount into an account and adding interest to it at the end of each period. Cornerstone A1.1 shows how to compute future values using compound interest.

CORNERSTONE A1.1   Computing Future Values Using Compound Interest

Information:

An investor deposits $20,000 in a savings account on January 1, 2017. The bank pays interest of 6% per year compounded monthly.

Required:

Assuming that the only activity in the account is the deposit of interest at the end of each month, how much money will be in the account after the interest payment on March 31, 2017?

Why:

When deposits earn compound interest, interest is earned on the interest.

Solution:

Monthly interest will be $1/2$% (6% per year/12 months).

Account balance, 1/1/17	$20,000.00
January interest ($20,000.00 × $1/2$%)	100.00
Account balance, 1/31/17	20,100.00
February interest ($20,100.00 × $1/2$%)	100.50
Account balance, 2/28/17	20,200.50
March interest ($20,200.50 × $1/2$%)	101.00
Account balance, 3/31/17	$20,301.50

Note: Here, interest was the only factor that altered the account balance after the initial deposit. In more complex situations, the account balance is changed by subsequent deposits and withdrawals as well as by interest. Withdrawals reduce the balance and, therefore, the amount of interest in subsequent periods. Additional deposits have the opposite effect, increasing the balance and the amount of interest earned.

As you can see in Cornerstone A1.1, the balance in the account continues to grow each month by an increasing amount of interest. The amount of monthly interest increases because interest is *compounded*. In other words, interest is computed on accumulated interest as well as on principal. For example, February interest of $100.50 consists of $100 interest on the $20,000 principal and 50¢ interest on the $100 January interest ($100 × 0.005 = 50¢).

In Cornerstone A1.1, the compound interest only amounts to $1.50. That might seem relatively insignificant, but if the investment period is sufficiently long, the amount of compound interest grows large even at relatively small interest rates. For example, suppose your parents invested $1,000 at $1/2$% per month when you were born with the objective of giving you a university graduation present at age 21. How much would that investment be worth after 21 years? The answer is $3,514. In 21 years, the compound interest is $2,514—more than $2^1/_2$ times the original principal. Without compounding, interest over the same period would have been only $1,260.

The amount to which an account will grow when interest is compounded is the **future value** of the account. Compound interest calculations can assume two fundamentally different forms:

- calculations of future values
- calculations of present values

As shown, calculations of future values are projections of future balances based on *past and future* cash flows and interest payments. In contrast, calculations of present values are determinations of present amounts based on *expected* future cash flows.

PRESENT VALUE OF FUTURE CASH FLOWS

Whenever a contract establishes a relationship between an initial amount borrowed or loaned and one or more future cash flows, the initial amount borrowed or loaned is the **present value** of those future cash flows. The present value can be interpreted in two ways:

- From the borrower's viewpoint, it is the liability that will be exactly paid by the future payments.
- From the lender's viewpoint, it is the receivable balance that will be exactly satisfied by the future receipts.

For understanding cash flows, cash flow diagrams that display both the amounts and the times of the cash flows specified by a contract can be quite helpful. In these diagrams, a time line runs from left to right. Inflows are represented as arrows pointing upward and outflows as arrows pointing downward. For example, suppose that Hilliard Corporation borrows $100,000 from Citizens Bank of New Liskeard on January 1, 2017. The note requires three $38,803.35 payments, one each at the end of 2017, 2018, and 2019, and includes interest at 8% per year. The cash flows for Hilliard are shown in Exhibit A1.1.

The calculation that follows shows, from the borrower's perspective, the relationship between the amount borrowed (*the present value*) and the future payments (*future cash flows*) required by Hilliard's note.

Amount borrowed, 1/1/17	$100,000.00
Add: 2015 interest ($100,000.00 × 0.08)	8,000.00
Subtract payment on 12/31/17	(38,803.35)
Liability at 12/31/17	69,196.65
Add: 2016 interest ($69,196.65 × 0.08)	5,535.73
Subtract payment on 12/31/18	(38,803.35)
Liability at 12/31/18	35,929.03
Add: 2017 interest ($35,929.03 × 0.08)	2,874.32
Subtract payment on 12/31/19	(38,803.35)
Liability at 12/31/19	$ 0.00

Present value calculations like this one are future value calculations in reverse. Here, the three payments of $38,803.35 exactly pay off the liability created by the note. Because the reversal of future value calculations can present a burdensome and sometimes difficult algebraic problem, shortcut methods using tables have been developed (see Exhibits A1.7, A1.8, A1.9, and A1.10, at the end of this appendix).

Interest and the Frequency of Compounding

The number of interest periods into which a compound interest problem is divided can make a significant difference in the amount of compound interest. For example, assume

Cash Flow Diagram

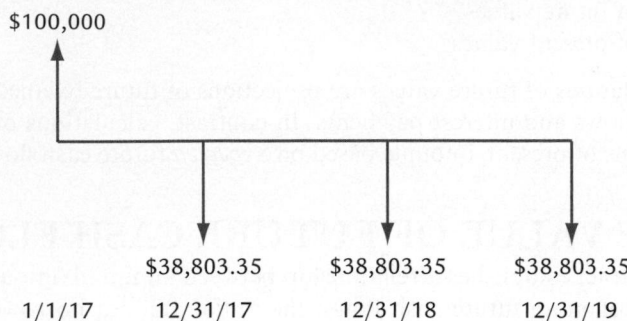

| | $38,803.35 | $38,803.35 | $38,803.35 |
| 1/1/17 | 12/31/17 | 12/31/18 | 12/31/19 |

that you are evaluating four 1-year investments, each of which requires an initial $10,000 deposit. All four investments earn interest at a rate of 12% per year, but they have different compounding periods. The data in Exhibit A1.2 show the impact of compounding frequency on future value. Investment D, which offers monthly compounding, accumulates $68 more interest by the end of the year than investment A, which offers only annual compounding.

FOUR BASIC COMPOUND INTEREST PROBLEMS

OBJECTIVE 2

Use future value and present value tables to apply compound interest to accounting transactions.

Any present value or future value problems can be broken down into one or more of the following four basic problems:

- computing the future value of a single amount
- computing the present value of a single amount
- computing the future value of an annuity
- computing the present value of an annuity

Computing the Future Value of a Single Amount

In computing the future value of a single amount, the following elements are used:

- f: the cash flow
- FV: the future value
- n: the number of periods between the cash flow and the future value
- i: the interest rate per period

Effect of Interest Periods on Compound Interest

Investment	Interest Period	I	N	Calculation of Future Amount in One Year*
A	1 year	12%	1	($10,000 × 1.12000) =$11,200
B	6 months	6%	2	($10,000 × 1.12360) = 11,236
C	1 quarter	3%	4	($10,000 × 1.12551) = 11,255
D	1 month	1%	12	($10,000 × 1.12683) = 11,268

*The multipliers (1.12 for Investment A, 1.12360 for investment B, etc.) are taken from the future value table in Exhibit A1.7.

To find the future value of a single amount, establish an account for f dollars and add compound interest at i percent to that account for n periods:

$$FV = (f)(1 + i)^n$$

The balance of the account after n periods is the future value.

Because people frequently need to compute the future value of a single amount, tables have been developed to make it easier. Therefore, instead of using the formula above, you could use the future value table in Exhibit A1.7, where M_1 is the multiple that corresponds to the appropriate values of n and i:

$$FV = (f)(M_1)$$

For example, suppose Allied Financial loans $200,000 at a rate of 6% per year compounded annually to an auto dealership dealer for four years. Exhibit A1.3 shows how to compute the future value (FV) at the end of the four years—the amount that will be repaid. Assuming Allied's viewpoint (the lender's), using a compound interest calculation, the unknown future value (FV) would be found as follows:

Amount loaned	$200,000.00
First year's interest ($200,000.00 × 0.06)	12,000.00
Loan receivable at end of first year	212,000.00
Second year's interest ($212,000.00 × 0.06)	12,720.00
Loan receivable at end of second year	224,720.00
Third year's interest ($224,720.00 × 0.06)	13,483.20
Loan receivable at end of third year	238,203.20
Fourth year's interest ($238,203.20 × 0.06)	14,292.19
Loan receivable at end of the fourth year	$252,495.39

As you can see, the amount of interest increases each year. This growth is the effect of computing interest for each year based on an amount that includes the interest earned in prior years.

The shortcut calculation, using the future value table (Exhibit A1.7), would be as follows:

$$\begin{aligned} FV &= (f)(M_1) \\ &= (\$200,000)(1.26248) \\ &= \$252,496 \end{aligned}$$

You can find M_1 at the intersection of the 6% column ($i = 6\%$) and the fourth row ($n = 4$) or by calculating 1.06^4. This multiple is the future value of the single amount

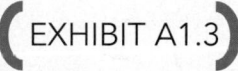

EXHIBIT A1.3

Future Value of a Single Amount: An Example

FV = ?

1   2   3   4

f = $200,000

$n = 4$
$i = 6\%$

after having been borrowed (or invested) for four years at 6% interest. The future value of $200,000 is 200,000 times the multiple.

Note that there is a difference between the answer ($252,495.39) developed in the compound interest calculation and the answer ($252,496) determined using the future value table. This is because the numbers in the table have been rounded to five decimal places. If they were taken to eight digits ($1.06^4 = 1.26247696$), the two answers would be equal. Cornerstone A1.2 shows how to compute the future value of a single amount.

CORNERSTONE A1.2   **Computing Future Value of a Single Amount**

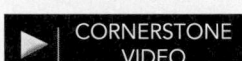
CORNERSTONE
VIDEO

Information:

Kitchener Company sells an unneeded factory site for $200,000 on July 1, 2017. Kitchener expects to purchase a different site in 18 months so that it can expand into a new market. Meanwhile, Kitchener decides to invest the $200,000 in a money market fund that is guaranteed to earn 6% per year compounded semiannually (3% per six-month period).

Required:

1. Draw a cash flow diagram for this investment from Kitchener's perspective.

2. Calculate the amount of money in the money market fund on December 31, 2017, and prepare the journal entry necessary to recognize interest income.

3. Calculate the amount of money in the money market fund on December 31, 2018, and prepare the journal entry necessary to recognize interest income.

Why:

The future value of a single amount is the original cash flow plus compound interest as of a specific future date.

Solution:

1.

FV = ?

n = 3
i = 3%

1   2   3

f = $200,000

7/1/17   12/31/17   7/1/18   12/31/18

2. Because we are calculating the value at 12/31/17, there is only one period:

$FV = (f)(FV \text{ of a Single Amount, 1 period, 3%})$
$= (\$200,000)(1.03)$
$= \$206,000$

(Continued)

The excess of the amount of money over the original deposit is the interest earned from July 1 through December 31, 2017.

CORNERSTONE

A1.2

(Continued)

Dec. 31, 2017	Cash	6,000	
	Interest Income		6,000
	(Record interest income)		

		Shareholders' Equity
Assets	= Liabilities +	(Interest Income)
+6,000		+6,000

3. $FV = (f)(FV \text{ of a Single Amount, 2 periods, 3\%})$

$\quad = (\$206,000)(1.03^2)$

$\quad = \$218,545.40$

The interest income for the year is the increase in the amount of money during 2018, which is \$12,545.40 (\$218,545.40 − \$206,000). The journal entry to record interest income would be as follows:

Dec. 31, 2018	Cash	12,545.40	
	Interest income		12,545.40
	(Record interest income)		

		Shareholders' Equity (Interest
Assets	= Liabilities +	Income)
+12,545.40		+12,545.40

Computing the Present Value of a Single Amount

In computing the present value of a single amount, the following elements are used:

- f: the future cash flow
- PV: the present value
- n: the number of periods between the present time and the future cash flow
- i: the interest rate per period

In present value problems, the interest rate is sometimes called the *discount rate*.

To find the present value of a single amount, use the following equation:

$$PV = \frac{f}{(1+i)^n}$$

You could use the present value table in Exhibit A1.8, where M_2 is the multiple from Exhibit A1.8 that corresponds to the appropriate values of n and i:

$$PV = (f)(M_2)$$

Suppose Marathon Oil has purchased property on which it plans to develop oil wells. The seller has agreed to accept a single \$150,000,000 payment three years from now, when Marathon expects to be selling oil from the field. Assuming an interest rate of 7% per year, the present value of the amount to be received in three years from the borrower's perspective can be calculated as shown in Exhibit A1.4.

The shortcut calculation, using the present value table (Exhibit A1.8), would be as follows:

$$PV = (f)(M_2)$$
$$= (\$150,000,000)(0.81630)$$
$$= \$122,445,000$$

EXHIBIT A1.4

Present Value of a Single Amount: An Example

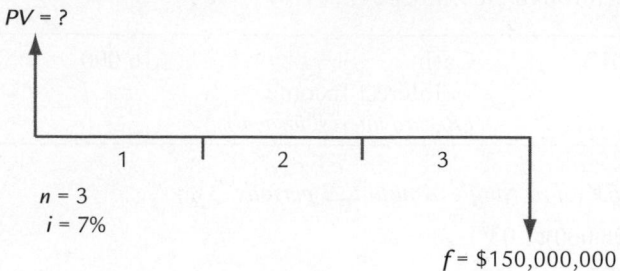

You can find M_2 at the intersection of the 7% column ($i = 7\%$) and the third row ($n = 3$) in Exhibit A1.8 or by calculating $[1/(1.07)^3]$. This multiple is the present value of a \$1 cash inflow or outflow in three years at 7%. Thus, the present value of \$150,000,000 is \$150,000,000 times the multiple.

Although the future value calculation cannot be used to determine the present value, it can be used to verify that the present value calculated by using the table is correct. The following calculation is proof for the present value problem:

Calculated present value *(PV)*	\$122,445,000
First year's interest (\$122,445,000 × 0.07)	8,571,150
Loan payable at end of first year	131,016,150
Second year's interest (\$131,016,150 × 0.07)	9,171,131
Loan payable at end of second year	140,187,281
Third year's interest (\$140,187,281 × 0.07)	9,813,110
Loan payable at end of the third year *(f)*	\$150,000,391

Again, the \$391 difference between the amount here and the assumed \$150,000,000 cash flow is due to rounding.

When interest is compounded on the calculated present value of \$122,445,000, then the present value calculation is reversed and we return to the future cash flow of \$150,000,000. This reversal proves that \$122,445,000 is the correct present value. Cornerstone A1.3 shows how to compute the present value of a single amount.

CORNERSTONE A1.3

Computing Present Value of a Single Amount

CORNERSTONE
VIDEO

Information:

On October 1, 2017, Adelsman Manufacturing Company sold a new machine to Raul Inc. The machine represented a new design that Raul was eager to place in service. Since Raul was unable to pay for the machine on the date of purchase, Adelsman agreed to defer the \$60,000 payment for 15 months. The appropriate rate of interest in such transactions is 8% per year compounded quarterly (2% per three-month period).

Required:

1. Draw the cash flow diagram for this deferred-payment purchase from Raul's (the borrower's) perspective.

(Continued)

2. Calculate the present value of this deferred-payment purchase.

3. Prepare the journal entry necessary to record the acquisition of the machine.

Why:

The present value of a single cash flow is the original cash flow that must be invested to produce a known value at a specific future date.

Solution:

1.

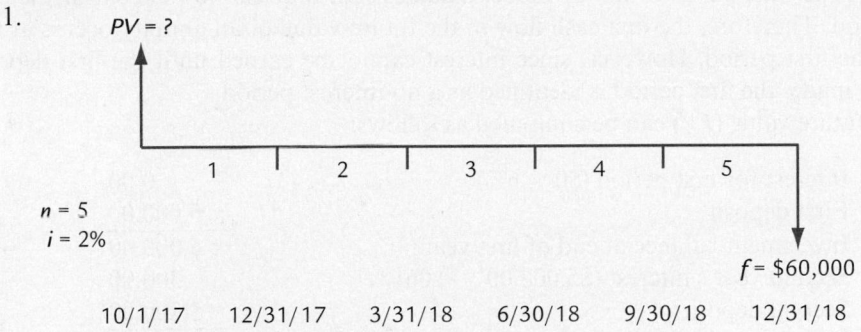

2. $FV = (f)(FV$ of a Single Amount, 5 periods, 2%)

    $= (\$60,000)(0.90573)$

    $= \$54,344$

3.

Oct. 1, 2017	Equipment	54,344	
	Note Payable		54,344
	(Record purchase of equipment)		

Assets	= Liabilities +	Shareholders' Equity
+54,344	+54,344	

Computing the Future Value of an Annuity

So far, we have been discussing problems that involve a single cash flow. However, there are also instances of multiple cash flows one period apart. An **annuity** is a number of equal cash flows: one to each interest period. For example, an investment in a security that pays $1,000 to an investor every December 31 for 10 consecutive years is an annuity. A loan repayment schedule that calls for a payment of $367.29 on the first day of each month can also be considered an annuity. (Although the number of days in a month varies from 28 to 31, the interest period is defined as one month without regard to the number of days in each month.)

In computing the future value of an annuity, the following elements are used:

- f: the amount of each repeating cash flow
- FV: the future value after the last (n^{th}) cash flow
- n: the number of cash flows
- i: the interest rate per period

To find the future value of an annuity, use the following equation:

$$FV = (f)\left[\frac{(1 + i)^n - 1}{i}\right]$$

Alternatively, you could use the future value table in Exhibit A1.9, where M_3 is the multiple from Exhibit A1.9 that corresponds to the appropriate values of n and i:

$$FV = (f)(M_3)$$

Assume that CIBC wants to advertise a new savings program to its customers. The savings program requires the customers to make four annual payments of $5,000 each, with the first payment due three years before the program ends. CIBC advertises a 6% interest rate compounded annually. The future value of this annuity immediately after the fourth cash payment from the investor's perspective is shown in Exhibit A1.5.

Note that the first period in Exhibit A1.5 is drawn with a dotted line. When using annuities, the time-value-of-money model assumes that all cash flows occur at the end of a period. Therefore, the first cash flow in the future value of an annuity occurs at the end of the first period. However, since interest cannot be earned until the first deposit has been made, the first period is identified as a no-interest period.

The future value (FV) can be computed as follows:

Interest for first period ($\$0 \times 6\%$)	$ 0.00
First deposit	5,000.00
Investment balance at end of first year	5,000.00
Second year's interest ($\$5,000.00 \times 0.06$)	300.00
Second deposit	5,000.00
Investment balance at end of second year	10,300.00
Third year's interest ($\$10,300.00 \times 0.06$)	618.00
Third deposit	5,000.00
Investment balance at end of third year	15,918.00
Fourth year's interest ($\$15,918.00 \times 0.06$)	955.08
Fourth deposit	5,000.00
Investment at end of fourth year	$21,873.08

This calculation shows that the lender has accumulated a future value (FV) of $21,873.08 by the end of the fourth period, immediately after the fourth cash investment.

The shortcut calculation, using the future value table (Exhibit A1.9), would be as follows:

$$FV = (f)(M_3)$$
$$= (\$5,000)(4.37462)$$
$$= \$21,873$$

You can find M_3 at the intersection of the 6% column ($i = 6\%$) and the fourth row ($n = 4$) in Exhibit A1.9 or by calculating $(1.06^4 - 1)/0.06$. This multiple is the future value

(EXHIBIT A1.5)

Future Value of an Annuity: An Example

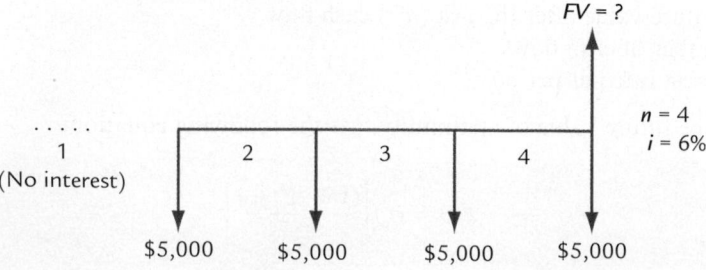

of an annuity of four cash flows of $1 each at 6%. The future value of an annuity of $5,000 cash flows is $5,000 times the multiple. Thus, the table allows us to calculate the future value of an annuity by a single multiplication, no matter how many cash flows are involved. Cornerstone A1.4 shows how to compute the future value of an annuity.

Computing Future Value of an Annuity

CORNERSTONE A1.4

Information:

Greg Smith is a lawyer and CA specializing in retirement and estate planning. One of Greg's clients, the owner of a large farm, wants to retire in five years. To provide funds to purchase a retirement annuity from London Life at the date of retirement, Greg asks the client to give him annual payments of $170,000, which Greg will deposit in a special fund that will earn 7% per year.

Required:

1. Draw the cash flow diagram for the fund from Greg's client's perspective.

2. Calculate the future value of the fund immediately after the fifth deposit.

3. If Greg's client needs $1,000,000 to purchase the annuity, how much must be deposited every year?

Why:

The future value of an annuity is the value of a series of equal cash flows made at regular intervals with compound interest at some specific future date.

Solution:

1.

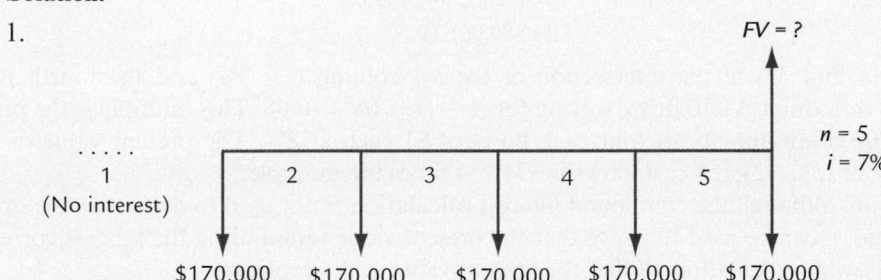

2. $FV = (f)(FV \text{ of an Annuity, 5 periods, 7\%})$

   $= (\$170,000)(5.75074)$

   $= \$977,626$

3. In this case, the future value is known, but the annuity amount (f) is not:

   $1,000,000 = (f)(FV \text{ of an Annuity, 5 periods, 7\%})$

   $1,000,000 = (f)(5.75074)$

   $\quad\quad f = 1,000,000/5.75074$

   $\quad\quad f = \$173,890.66$

Present Value of an Annuity

In computing the present value of an annuity, the following elements are used:

- f: the amount of each repeating cash flow
- PV: the present value of the n future cash flows
- n: the number of cash flows and periods
- i: the interest (or discount) rate per period

To find the present value of an annuity, use the following equation:

$$PV = (f)\frac{1 - \dfrac{1}{(1+i)^n}}{i}$$

You could also use the present value table in Exhibit A1.10, where M_4 is the multiple from Exhibit A1.10 that corresponds to the appropriate values of n and i:

$$PV = (f)(M_4)$$

For example, assume that Xerox Corporation purchased a new machine for its manufacturing operations. The purchase agreement requires Xerox to make four equally spaced payments of $24,154 each. The interest rate is 8% compounded annually and the first cash flow occurs one year after the purchase. Exhibit A1.6 shows how to determine the present value of this annuity from Xerox's (the borrower's) perspective. Note that the same concept applies to both the lender's and borrower's perspectives.

The shortcut calculation, using the present value table (Exhibit A1.10), would be as follows:

$$PV = (f)(M_4)$$
$$= (\$24,154)(3.31213)$$
$$= \$80,001.19$$

You can find M_4 at the intersection of the 8% column ($i = 8\%$) and the fourth row ($n = 4$) in Exhibit A1.10 or by solving for $[1 - (1/1.08^4)]/0.08$. This multiple is the present value of an annuity of four cash flows of $1 each at 8%. The present value of an annuity of four $24,154 cash flows is $24,154 times the multiple.

Again, although the compound interest calculation is not used to determine the present value, it can be used to prove that the present value found using the table is correct. The following calculation verifies the present value in the problem:

(EXHIBIT A1.6)

Present Value of an Annuity: An Example

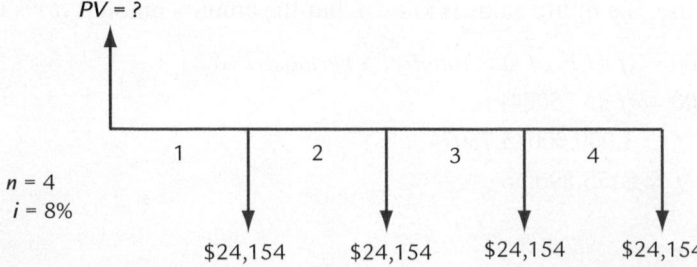

Calculated present value *(PV)*	$ 80,001.19
Interest for first year ($80,001.19 × 0.08)	6,400.10
Less: First cash flow	(24,154.00)
Balance at end of first year	62,247.29
Interest for second year ($62,247.29 × 0.08)	4,979.78
Less: Second cash flow	(24,154.00)
Balance at end of second year	43,073.07
Interest for third year ($43,073.07 × 0.08)	3,445.85
Less: Third cash flow	(24,154.00)
Balance at end of third year	22,364.92
Interest for fourth year ($22,364.92 × 0.08)	1,789.19
Less: Fourth cash flow	(24,154.00)
Balance at end of fourth year	$ 0.11

This proof uses a compound interest calculation that is the reverse of the present value formula. If the present value *(PV)* calculated with the formula is correct, then the proof should end with a balance of zero immediately after the last cash flow. This proof ends with a balance of $0.11 because of rounding in the proof itself and in the table in Exhibit A1.10.

Cornerstone A1.5 shows how to compute the present value of an annuity.

Computing Present Value of an Annuity

CORNERSTONE A1.5

CORNERSTONE VIDEO

Information:

Windsor Builders purchased a subdivision site from the Royal Bank on January 1, 2017. Windsor gave the bank an installment note. The note requires Windsor to make four annual payments of $600,000 each on December 31 of each year, beginning in 2017. Interest is computed at 9%.

Required:

1. Draw the cash flow diagram for this purchase from Windsor's perspective.

2. Calculate the cost of the land as recorded by Windsor on January 1, 2017.

3. Prepare the journal entry that Windsor will make to record the purchase of the land.

Why:

The present value of an annuity is the value of a series of equal future cash flows made at regular intervals with compound interest discounted back to today.

Solution:

1.

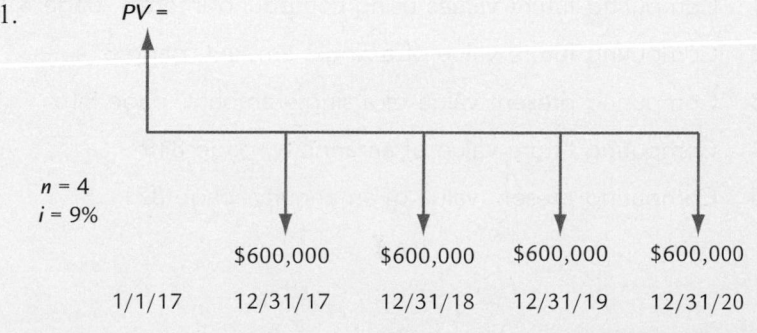

(Continued)

CORNERSTONE
A1.5

(Continued)

Assets	= Liabilities +	Shareholders' Equity
+1,943,832	+1,943,832	

2. $PV = (f)(PV\ of\ an\ Annuity,\ 4\ periods,\ 9\%)$
   $= (\$600,000)(3.23972)$
   $= \$1,943,832$

3.

Jan. 1, 2017	Land		1,943,832	
	Notes Payable			1,943,832
	(Record purchase of land)			

SUMMARY OF LEARNING OBJECTIVES

LO1.   Explain how compound interest works.

- In transactions involving the borrowing and lending of money, it is customary for the borrower to pay interest.
- With compound interest, interest for the period is added to the account and interest is earned on the total balance in the next period.
- Compound interest calculations require careful specification of the interest period and the interest rate.

LO2.   Use future value and present value tables to apply compound interest to accounting transactions.

- Cash flows are described as either
  - single cash flows, or
  - annuities.
- An annuity is a number of equal cash flows made at regular intervals.
- All other cash flows are a series of one or more single cash flows.
- Accounting for such cash flows may require
  - calculation of the amount to which a series of cash flows will grow when interest is compounded (i.e., the future value) or
  - the amount a series of future cash flows is worth today after taking into account compound interest (i.e., the present value).

CORNERSTONES

KEY TERMS

Annuity   (p. 817)
Compound interest   (p. 809)
Future value   (p. 811)
Interest period   (p. 809)

Interest rate   (p. 809)
Present value   (p. 811)
Time value of money   (p. 809)

DISCUSSION QUESTIONS

1. Why does money have a time value?
2. Describe the four basic time-value-of-money problems.
3. How is compound interest computed? What is a future value? What is a present value?
4. Define an annuity in general terms. Describe the cash flows related to an annuity from the viewpoint of the lender in terms of receipts and payments.
5. Explain how to use time-value-of-money calculations to measure an installment note liability.

CORNERSTONE EXERCISES

Cornerstone Exercise A1-1   Explain How Compound Interest Works

Jim Emig has $6,000.

OBJECTIVE ❶
CORNERSTONE A1.1

Required:

Calculate the future value of the $6,000 at 12% compounded quarterly for five years. (*Note:* Round answers to two decimal places.)

Cornerstone Exercise A1-2   Use Future Value and Present Value Tables to Apply Compound Interest

Cathy Lumbattis inherited $140,000 from an aunt.

OBJECTIVE ❷
CORNERSTONE A1.2

Required:

If Cathy decides not to spend her inheritance but to leave the money in her savings account until she retires in 15 years, how much money will she have, assuming an annual interest rate of 8%, compounded semiannually? (*Note:* Round answers to two decimal places.)

Cornerstone Exercise A1-3   Use Future Value and Present Value Tables to Apply Compound Interest

LuAnn Bean will receive $7,000 in seven years.

OBJECTIVE ❷
CORNERSTONE A1.3

Required:

What is the present value at 7% compounded annually? (*Note:* Round answers to two decimal places.)

Cornerstone Exercise A1-4   Use Future Value and Present Value Tables to Apply Compound Interest

A bank is willing to lend money at 6% interest, compounded annually.

OBJECTIVE ❷
CORNERSTONE A1.3

Required:

How much would the bank be willing to loan you in exchange for a payment of $600 four years from now? (*Note:* Round answers to two decimal places.)

OBJECTIVE ②
CORNERSTONE A1.4

Cornerstone Exercise A1-5   Use Future Value and Present Value Tables to Apply Compound Interest

Ed Flores wants to save some money so that he can make a down payment of $3,000 on a car when he graduates from university in four years.

Required:

If Ed opens a savings account and earns 3% on his money, compounded annually, how much will he have to invest now? (*Note:* Round answers to two decimal places.)

OBJECTIVE ②
CORNERSTONE A1.4

Cornerstone Exercise A1-6   Use Future Value and Present Value Tables to Apply Compound Interest

Kristen Lee makes equal deposits of $500 semiannually for four years. The first deposit is made at the end of the first six months.

Required:

What is the future value at 8%? (*Note:* Round answers to two decimal places.)

OBJECTIVE ②
CORNERSTONE A1.4

Cornerstone Exercise A1-7   Use Future Value and Present Value Tables to Apply Compound Interest

Chuck Russo, a high school math teacher, wants to set up an RRSP account into which he will deposit $2,000 per year. He plans to teach for 20 more years and then retire.

Required:

If the interest on his account is 7% compounded annually, how much will be in his account when he retires? (*Note*: Round answers to two decimal places.)

OBJECTIVE ②
CORNERSTONE A1.4

Cornerstone Exercise A1-8   Use Future Value Tables to Apply Compound Interest

Larson Lumber makes annual deposits of $500 at 6% compounded annually for three years.

Required:

What is the future value of these deposits? (*Note:* Round answers to two decimal places.)

OBJECTIVE ②
CORNERSTONE A1.5

Cornerstone Exercise A1-9   Use Future Value and Present Value Tables to Apply Compound Interest

Michelle Legrand can earn 6%.

Required:

How much would have to be deposited in a savings account today in order for Michelle to be able to make equal annual withdrawals of $200 at the end of each of the next 10 years? (*Note:* Round answers to two decimal places.) The balance at the end of the last year would be zero.

OBJECTIVE ②
CORNERSTONE A1.5

Cornerstone Exercise A1-10   Use Future Value and Present Value Tables to Apply Compound Interest

Barb Muller wins the lottery. She wins $20,000 per year to be paid for 10 years. The province offers her the choice of a cash settlement now instead of the annual payments for 10 years. Payments are at the end of each year.

Required:

If the interest rate is 6%, what is the amount the province will offer for a settlement today? (*Note*: Round answers to two decimal places.)

EXERCISES

Exercise A1-11   Practice with Tables

OBJECTIVE ②

Refer to the appropriate tables in the text.

Required:

Note: Round answers to two decimal places. Determine:

a.   the future value of a single cash flow of $5,000 that earns 7% interest compounded annually for 10 years.

b.   the future value of an annual annuity of 10 cash flows of $500 each that earns 7% compounded annually.

c.   the present value of $5,000 to be received 10 years from now, assuming that the interest (discount) rate is 7% per year.

d.   the present value of an annuity of $500 per year for 10 years for which the interest (discount) rate is 7% per year and the first cash flow occurs one year from now.

Exercise A1-12   Practice with Tables

OBJECTIVE ②

Refer to the appropriate tables in the text.

Required:

Note: Round answers to two decimal places. Determine:

a.   the present value of $1,200 to be received in seven years, assuming that the interest (discount) rate is 8% per year.

b.   the present value of an annuity of seven cash flows of $1,200 each (one at the end of each of the next seven years) for which the interest (discount) rate is 8% per year.

c.   the future value of a single cash flow of $1,200 that earns 8% per year for seven years.

d.   the future value of an annuity of seven cash flows of $1,200 each (one at the end of each of the next seven years), assuming that the interest rate is 8% per year.

Exercise A1-13   Future Values

OBJECTIVE ②

Refer to the appropriate tables in the text.

Required:

Note: Round answers to two decimal places. Determine:

a.   the future value of a single deposit of $15,000 that earns compound interest for four years at an interest rate of 10% per year.

b.   the annual interest rate that will produce a future value of $13,416.80 in six years from a single deposit of $8,000.

c.   the size of annual cash flows for an annuity of nine cash flows that will produce a future value of $79,428.10 at an interest rate of 9% per year.

d.   the number of periods required to produce a future value of $17,755.50 from an initial deposit of $7,500 if the annual interest rate is 9%.

Exercise A1-14   Future Values and Long-Term Investments

OBJECTIVE ②

Fired Up Pottery Inc. engaged in the following transactions during 2019:

a.   On January 1, 2019, Fired Up deposited $12,000 in a certificate of deposit paying 6% interest compounded semiannually (3% per six-month period). The certificate will mature on December 31, 2022.

b.   On January 1, 2019, Fired Up established an account with Rookwood Investment Management. Fired Up will make quarterly payments of $2,500 to Rookwood beginning on March 31, 2019, and ending on December 31, 2020. Rookwood guarantees an interest rate of 8% compounded quarterly (2% per three-month period).

(Continued)

Required:

1. Prepare the cash flow diagram for each of these two investments.
2. Calculate the amount to which each of these investments will accumulate at maturity. (*Note:* Round answers to two decimal places.)

Exercise A1-15   Future Values

On January 1, Beth Walid made a single deposit of $8,000 in an investment account that earns 8% interest.

Required:

Note: Round answers to two decimal places.

1. Calculate the balance in the account in five years assuming the interest is compounded annually.

2. Determine how much interest will be earned on the account in seven years if interest is compounded annually.

3. Calculate the balance in the account in five years assuming the 8% interest is compounded quarterly.

Exercise A1-16   Future Values

Kashmir Transit Company invested $70,000 in a corporate bond on June 30, 2019. The bond earns 12% interest compounded monthly (1% per month) and matures on March 31, 2020.

Required:

Note: Round answers to two decimal places.

1. Prepare the cash flow diagram for this investment.

2. Determine the amount Kashmir will receive when the bond matures.

3. Determine how much interest Kashmir will earn on this investment from June 30, 2019, through December 31, 2019.

Exercise A1-17   Present Values

Refer to the appropriate tables in the text.

Required:

Note: Round answers to two decimal places. Determine:

a. the present value of a single $14,000 cash flow in seven years if the interest (discount) rate is 8% per year.
b. the number of periods for which an initial investment of $5,820 must be invested at an annual interest (discount) rate of 7% to produce an investment balance of $10,000.
c. the size of the annual cash flow for a 25-year annuity with a present value of $49,113 and an annual interest rate of 9%. One payment is made at the end of each year.
d. the annual interest rate at which an investment of $2,542 will provide for a single $4,000 cash flow in four years.
e. the annual interest rate earned by an annuity that costs $17,119 and provides 15 payments of $2,000 each, one at the end of each of the next 15 years.

Exercise A1-18   Present Values

Weinstein Company signed notes to make the following two purchases on January 1, 2019:

a. a new piece of equipment for $60,000, with payment deferred until December 31, 2020. The appropriate interest rate is 9% compounded annually.

b. a small building from Johnston Builders. The terms of the purchase require a $75,000 payment at the end of each quarter, beginning March 31, 2019, and ending June 30, 2021. The appropriate interest rate is 2% per quarter.

Required:

Note: Round answers to two decimal places.

1. Prepare the cash flow diagrams for these two purchases.

2. Prepare the entries to record these purchases in Weinstein's journal.

3. Prepare the cash payment and interest expense entries for purchase *b* at March 31, 2019, and June 30, 2019.

4. Prepare the adjusting entry for purchase *a* at December 31, 2019.

Exercise A1-19   Present Values

OBJECTIVE **2**

Krista Kellman has an opportunity to purchase a government security that will pay $200,000 in five years.

Required:

Note: Round answers to two decimal places.

1. Calculate what Krista would pay for the security if the appropriate interest (discount) rate is 6% compounded annually.

2. Calculate what Krista would pay for the security if the appropriate interest (discount) rate is 10% compounded annually.

3. Calculate what Krista would pay for the security if the appropriate interest (discount) rate is 6% compounded semiannually.

Exercise A1-20   Future Values of an Annuity

OBJECTIVE **2**

On December 31, 2019, Natalie Livingston signs a contract to make annual deposits of $4,200 in an investment account that earns 10%. The first deposit is made on December 31, 2019.

Required:

Note: Round answers to two decimal places.

1. Calculate what the balance in this investment account will be just after the seventh deposit has been made if interest is compounded annually.

2. Determine how much interest will have been earned on this investment account just after the seventh deposit has been made if interest is compounded annually.

Exercise A1-21   Future Values of an Annuity

OBJECTIVE **2**

Essex Savings Bank pays 8% interest compounded weekly (0.154% per week) on savings accounts. The bank has asked your help in preparing a table to show potential customers the number of dollars that will be available at the end of 10-, 20-, 30-, and 40-week periods during which there are weekly deposits of $1, $5, $10, or $50. The following data are available:

Length of Annuity	Future Value of Annuity at an Interest Rate of 0.154% per Week
10 weeks	10.0696
20 weeks	20.2953
30 weeks	30.6796
40 weeks	41.2250

Required:

Complete a table similar to the one below. (*Note:* Round answers to two decimal places.)

(Continued)

Number of Deposits	Amount of Each Deposit			
	$1	$5	$10	$50
10				
20				
30				
40				

Exercise A1-22   Future Value of a Single Cash Flow

Jimenez Products has just been paid $25,000 by Shirley Enterprises, which has owed Jimenez this amount for 30 months but been unable to pay because of financial difficulties. Had it been able to invest this cash, Jimenez assumes that it would have earned an interest rate of 12% compounded monthly (1% per month).

Required:

Note: Round answers to two decimal places.
1. Prepare a cash flow diagram for the investment that could have been made if Shirley had paid 30 months ago.

2. Determine how much Jimenez has lost by not receiving the $25,000 when it was due 30 months ago.

3. **CONCEPTUAL CONNECTION** Indicate whether Jimenez would make an entry to account for this loss. Why, or why not?

Exercise A1-23   Installment Sale

Wilke Properties owns land on which natural gas wells are located. Windsor Gas Company signs a note to buy this land from Wilke on January 1, 2019. The note requires Windsor to pay Wilke $775,000 per year for 25 years. The first payment is to be made on December 31, 2019. The appropriate interest rate is 9% compounded annually.

Required:

Note: Round answers to two decimal places.
1. Prepare a diagram of the appropriate cash flows from Windsor Gas's perspective.

2. Determine the present value of the payments.

3. Indicate what entry Windsor Gas should make at January 1, 2019.

Exercise A1-24   Installment Sale

Bailey's Billiards sold a pool table to Sheri Sipka on October 31, 2019. The terms of the sale are no money down and payments of $50 per month for 30 months, with the first payment due on November 30, 2019. The table they sold to Sipka cost Bailey's $800, and Bailey uses a perpetual inventory system. Bailey's uses an interest rate of 12% compounded monthly (1% per month).

Required:

Note: Round answers to two decimal places.
1. Prepare the cash flow diagram for this sale.

2. Calculate the amount of revenue Bailey's should record on October 31, 2019.

3. Prepare the journal entries to record the sale on October 31. Assume that Bailey's records cost of goods sold at the time of the sale (perpetual inventory accounting).

4. Determine how much interest income Bailey's will record from October 31, 2019, through December 31, 2019.

5. Determine how much Bailey's 2019 income before taxes increased from this sale.

(**EXHIBIT A1.7**)

Future Value of a Single Amount

$FV = 1(1 + i)^n$

n/i	1%	2%	3%	4%	5%	6%	7%	8%	9%	10%	12%	14%	16%	18%	20%	25%	30%
1	1.01000	1.02000	1.03000	1.04000	1.05000	1.06000	1.07000	1.08000	1.09000	1.10000	1.12000	1.14000	1.16000	1.18000	1.20000	1.25000	1.30000
2	1.02010	1.04040	1.06090	1.08160	1.10250	1.12360	1.14490	1.16640	1.18810	1.21000	1.25440	1.29960	1.34560	1.39240	1.44000	1.56250	1.69000
3	1.03030	1.06121	1.09273	1.12486	1.15763	1.19102	1.22504	1.25971	1.29503	1.33100	1.40493	1.48154	1.56090	1.64303	1.72800	1.95313	2.19700
4	1.04060	1.08243	1.12551	1.16986	1.12551	1.26248	1.31080	1.36049	1.41159	1.46410	1.57352	1.68896	1.81064	1.93878	2.07360	2.44141	2.85610
5	1.05101	1.10408	1.15927	1.21665	1.27628	1.33823	1.40255	1.46933	1.53862	1.61051	1.76234	1.92541	2.10034	2.28776	2.48832	3.05176	3.71293
6	1.06152	1.12616	1.19405	1.26532	1.34010	1.41852	1.50073	1.58687	1.67710	1.77156	1.97382	2.19497	2.43640	2.69955	2.98598	3.81470	4.82681
7	1.07214	1.14869	1.22987	1.31593	1.40710	1.50363	1.60578	1.71382	1.82804	1.94872	2.21068	2.50227	2.82622	3.18547	3.58318	4.76837	6.27485
8	1.08286	1.17166	1.26677	1.36857	1.47746	1.59385	1.71819	1.85093	1.99256	2.14359	2.47596	2.85259	3.27841	3.75886	4.29982	5.96046	8.15731
9	1.09369	1.19509	1.30477	1.42331	1.55133	1.68948	1.83846	1.99900	2.17189	2.35795	2.77308	3.25195	3.80296	4.43545	5.15978	7.45058	10.60450
10	1.10462	1.21899	1.34392	1.48024	1.62889	1.79085	1.96715	2.15892	2.36736	2.59374	3.10585	3.70722	4.41144	5.23384	6.19174	9.31323	13.78585
11	1.11567	1.24337	1.38423	1.53945	1.71034	1.89830	2.10485	2.33164	2.58043	2.85312	3.47855	4.22623	5.11726	6.17593	7.43008	11.64153	17.92160
12	1.12683	1.26824	1.42576	1.60103	1.79586	2.01220	2.25219	2.51817	2.81266	3.13843	3.89598	4.81790	5.93603	7.28759	8.91610	14.55192	23.29809
13	1.13809	1.29361	1.46853	1.66507	1.88565	2.13293	2.40985	2.71962	3.06580	3.45227	4.36349	5.49241	6.88579	8.59936	10.69932	18.18989	30.28751
14	1.14947	1.31948	1.51259	1.73168	1.97993	2.26090	2.57853	2.93719	3.34173	3.79750	4.88711	6.26135	7.98752	10.14724	12.83918	22.73737	39.37376
15	1.16097	1.34587	1.55797	1.80094	2.07893	2.39656	2.75903	3.17217	3.64248	4.17725	5.47357	7.13794	9.26552	11.97375	15.40702	28.42171	51.18589
16	1.17258	1.37279	1.60471	1.87298	2.18287	2.54035	2.95216	3.42594	3.97031	4.59497	6.13039	8.13725	10.74800	14.12902	18.48843	35.52714	66.54166
17	1.18430	1.40024	1.65285	1.94790	2.29202	2.69277	3.15882	3.70002	4.32763	5.05447	6.86604	9.27646	12.46768	16.67225	22.18611	44.40892	86.50416
18	1.19615	1.42825	1.70243	2.02582	2.40662	2.85434	3.37993	3.99602	4.71712	5.55992	7.68997	10.57517	14.46251	19.67325	26.62333	55.51115	112.45541
19	1.20811	1.45681	1.75351	2.10685	2.52695	3.02560	3.61653	4.31570	5.14166	6.11591	8.61276	12.05569	16.77652	23.21444	31.94800	69.38894	146.19203
20	1.22019	1.48595	1.80611	2.19112	2.65330	3.20714	3.86968	4.66096	5.60441	6.72750	9.64629	13.74349	19.46076	27.39303	38.33760	86.73617	190.04946
21	1.23239	1.51567	1.86029	2.27877	2.78596	3.39956	4.14056	5.03383	6.10881	7.40025	10.80385	15.66758	22.57448	32.32378	46.00512	108.42022	247.06453
22	1.24472	1.54598	1.91610	2.36992	2.92526	3.60354	4.43040	5.43654	6.65860	8.14027	12.10031	17.86104	26.18640	38.14206	55.20614	135.52527	321.18389
23	1.25716	1.57690	1.97359	2.46472	3.07152	3.81975	4.74053	5.87146	7.25787	8.95430	13.55235	20.36158	30.37622	45.00763	66.24737	169.40659	417.53905
24	1.26973	1.60844	2.03279	2.56330	3.22510	4.04893	5.07237	6.34118	7.91108	9.84973	15.17863	23.21221	35.23642	53.10901	79.49685	211.75824	542.80077
25	1.28243	1.64061	2.09378	2.66584	3.38635	4.29187	5.42743	6.84848	8.62308	10.83471	17.00006	26.46192	40.87424	62.66863	95.39622	264.69780	705.64100
26	1.29526	1.67342	2.15659	2.77247	3.55567	4.54938	5.80735	7.39635	9.39916	11.91818	19.04007	30.16653	47.41412	73.94898	114.47546	330.87225	917.33330
27	1.30821	1.70689	2.22129	2.88337	3.73346	4.82235	6.21387	7.98806	10.24508	13.10999	21.32488	34.38991	55.00038	87.79880	137.37055	413.59031	1192.53329
28	1.32129	1.74102	2.28793	2.99870	3.92013	5.11169	6.64884	8.62711	11.16714	14.42099	23.88387	39.20449	63.80044	102.96656	164.84466	516.98788	1550.29328
29	1.33450	1.77584	2.35657	3.11865	4.11614	5.41839	7.11426	9.31727	12.17218	15.86309	26.74993	44.69312	74.00851	121.50054	197.81359	646.23485	2015.38126
30	1.34785	1.81136	2.42726	3.24340	4.32194	5.74349	7.61226	10.06266	13.26768	17.44940	29.95992	50.95016	85.84988	143.37064	237.37631	807.79357	2619.99564

EXHIBIT A1.8

Present Value of a Single Amount

$$PV = \frac{1}{(1+i)^n}$$

n/i	1%	2%	3%	4%	5%	6%	7%	8%	9%	10%	12%	14%	16%	18%	20%	25%	30%
1	0.99010	0.98039	0.97087	0.96154	0.95238	0.94340	0.93458	0.92593	0.91743	0.90909	0.89286	0.87719	0.86207	0.84746	0.83333	0.80000	0.76923
2	0.98030	0.96117	0.94260	0.92456	0.90703	0.89000	0.87344	0.85734	0.84168	0.82645	0.79719	0.76947	0.74316	0.71818	0.69444	0.64000	0.59172
3	0.97059	0.94232	0.91514	0.88900	0.86384	0.83962	0.81630	0.79383	0.77218	0.75131	0.71178	0.67497	0.64066	0.60863	0.57870	0.51200	0.45517
4	0.96098	0.92385	0.88849	0.85480	0.82270	0.79209	0.76290	0.73503	0.70843	0.68301	0.63552	0.59208	0.55229	0.51579	0.48225	0.40960	0.35013
5	0.95147	0.90573	0.86261	0.82193	0.78353	0.74726	0.71299	0.68058	0.64993	0.62092	0.56743	0.51937	0.47611	0.43711	0.40188	0.32768	0.26933
6	0.94205	0.88797	0.83748	0.79031	0.74622	0.70496	0.66634	0.63017	0.59627	0.56447	0.50663	0.45559	0.41044	0.37043	0.33490	0.26214	0.20718
7	0.93272	0.87056	0.81309	0.75992	0.71068	0.66506	0.62275	0.58349	0.54703	0.51316	0.45235	0.39964	0.35383	0.31393	0.27908	0.20972	0.15937
8	0.92348	0.85349	0.78941	0.73069	0.67684	0.62741	0.58201	0.54027	0.50187	0.46651	0.40388	0.35056	0.30503	0.26604	0.23257	0.16777	0.12259
9	0.91434	0.83676	0.76642	0.70259	0.64461	0.59190	0.54393	0.50025	0.46043	0.42410	0.36061	0.30751	0.26295	0.22546	0.19381	0.13422	0.09430
10	0.90529	0.82035	0.74409	0.67556	0.61391	0.55839	0.50835	0.46319	0.42241	0.38554	0.32197	0.26974	0.22668	0.19106	0.16151	0.10737	0.07254
11	0.89632	0.80426	0.72242	0.64958	0.58468	0.52679	0.47509	0.42888	0.38753	0.35049	0.28748	0.23662	0.19542	0.16192	0.13459	0.08590	0.05580
12	0.88745	0.78849	0.70138	0.62460	0.55684	0.49697	0.44401	0.39711	0.35553	0.31863	0.25668	0.20756	0.16846	0.13722	0.11216	0.06872	0.04292
13	0.87866	0.77303	0.68095	0.60057	0.53032	0.46884	0.41496	0.36770	0.32618	0.28966	0.22917	0.18207	0.14523	0.11629	0.09346	0.05498	0.03302
14	0.86996	0.75788	0.66112	0.57748	0.50507	0.44230	0.38782	0.34046	0.29925	0.26333	0.20462	0.15971	0.12520	0.09855	0.07789	0.04398	0.02540
15	0.86135	0.74301	0.64186	0.55526	0.48102	0.41727	0.36245	0.31524	0.27454	0.23939	0.18270	0.14010	0.10793	0.08352	0.06491	0.03518	0.01954
16	0.85282	0.72845	0.62317	0.53391	0.45811	0.39365	0.33873	0.29189	0.25187	0.21763	0.16312	0.12289	0.09304	0.07078	0.05409	0.02815	0.01503
17	0.84438	0.71416	0.60502	0.51337	0.43630	0.37136	0.31657	0.27027	0.23107	0.19784	0.14564	0.10780	0.08021	0.05998	0.04507	0.02252	0.01156
18	0.83602	0.70016	0.58739	0.49363	0.41552	0.35034	0.29586	0.25025	0.21199	0.17986	0.13004	0.09456	0.06914	0.05083	0.03756	0.01801	0.00889
19	0.82774	0.68643	0.57029	0.47464	0.39573	0.33051	0.27651	0.23171	0.19449	0.16351	0.11611	0.08295	0.05961	0.04308	0.03130	0.01441	0.00684
20	0.81954	0.67297	0.55368	0.45639	0.37689	0.31180	0.25842	0.21455	0.17843	0.14864	0.10367	0.07276	0.05139	0.03651	0.02608	0.01153	0.00526
21	0.81143	0.65978	0.53755	0.43883	0.35894	0.29416	0.24151	0.19866	0.16370	0.13513	0.09256	0.06383	0.04430	0.03094	0.02174	0.00922	0.00405
22	0.80340	0.64684	0.52189	0.42196	0.34185	0.27751	0.22751	0.18394	0.15018	0.12285	0.08264	0.05599	0.03819	0.02622	0.01811	0.00738	0.00311
23	0.79544	0.63416	0.50669	0.40573	0.32557	0.26180	0.21095	0.17032	0.13778	0.11168	0.07379	0.04911	0.03292	0.02222	0.01509	0.00590	0.00239
24	0.78757	0.62172	0.49193	0.39012	0.31007	0.24698	0.19715	0.15770	0.12640	0.10153	0.06588	0.04308	0.02838	0.01883	0.01258	0.00472	0.00184
25	0.77977	0.60953	0.47761	0.37512	0.29530	0.23300	0.18425	0.14602	0.11597	0.09230	0.05882	0.03779	0.02447	0.01596	0.01048	0.00378	0.00142
26	0.77205	0.59758	0.46369	0.36069	0.28124	0.21981	0.17220	0.13520	0.10639	0.08391	0.05252	0.03315	0.02109	0.01352	0.00874	0.00302	0.00109
27	0.76440	0.58586	0.45019	0.34682	0.26785	0.20737	0.16093	0.12519	0.09761	0.07628	0.04689	0.02908	0.01818	0.01146	0.00728	0.00242	0.00084
28	0.75684	0.57437	0.43708	0.33348	0.25509	0.19563	0.15040	0.11591	0.08955	0.06934	0.04187	0.02551	0.01567	0.00971	0.00607	0.00193	0.00065
29	0.74934	0.56311	0.42435	0.32065	0.24295	0.18456	0.14056	0.10733	0.08215	0.06304	0.03738	0.02237	0.01351	0.00823	0.00506	0.00155	0.00050
30	0.74192	0.55207	0.41199	0.30832	0.23138	0.17411	0.13137	0.09938	0.07537	0.05731	0.03338	0.01963	0.01165	0.00697	0.00421	0.00124	0.00038

(EXHIBIT A1.9)

Future Value of an Annuity

$$FVA = \left[\frac{(1+i)^n - 1}{i}\right]$$

n/i	1%	2%	3%	4%	5%	6%	7%	8%	9%	10%	12%	14%	16%	18%	20%	25%	30%
1	1.00000	1.00000	1.00000	1.00000	1.00000	1.00000	1.00000	1.00000	1.00000	1.00000	1.00000	1.00000	1.00000	1.00000	1.00000	1.00000	1.00000
2	2.01000	2.02000	2.03000	2.04000	2.05000	2.06000	2.07000	2.08000	2.09000	2.10000	2.12000	2.14000	2.16000	2.18000	2.20000	2.25000	2.30000
3	3.03010	3.06040	3.09090	3.12160	3.15250	3.18360	3.21490	3.24640	3.27810	3.31000	3.37440	3.43960	3.50560	3.57240	3.64000	3.81250	3.99000
4	4.06040	4.12161	4.18363	4.24646	4.31013	4.37462	4.43994	4.50611	4.57313	4.64100	4.77933	4.92114	5.06650	5.21543	5.36800	5.76563	6.18700
5	5.10101	5.20404	5.30914	5.41632	5.52563	5.63709	5.75074	5.86660	5.98471	6.10510	6.35285	6.61010	6.87714	7.15421	7.44160	8.20703	9.04310
6	6.15202	6.30812	6.46841	6.63298	6.80191	6.97532	7.15329	7.33593	7.52000	7.71561	8.11519	8.53552	8.97748	9.44197	9.92992	11.25879	12.75603
7	7.21354	7.43428	7.66246	7.89829	8.14201	8.39384	8.65402	8.92280	9.20043	9.48717	10.08901	10.73049	11.41387	12.14152	12.91590	15.07349	17.58284
8	8.28567	8.58297	8.85234	9.21423	9.54911	9.89747	10.25980	10.63663	11.02847	11.43589	12.29969	13.23276	14.24009	15.32700	16.49908	19.84186	23.85769
9	9.36853	9.75463	10.15911	10.58280	11.02656	11.49132	11.97799	12.48756	13.02104	13.57948	14.77566	16.08535	17.51851	19.08585	20.79890	25.80232	32.01500
10	10.46221	10.94972	11.46388	12.00611	12.57789	13.18079	13.81645	14.48656	15.19293	15.93742	17.54874	19.33730	21.32147	23.52131	25.95868	33.25290	42.61950
11	11.56683	12.16872	12.80780	13.48635	14.20679	14.97164	15.78360	16.64549	17.56029	18.53117	20.65458	23.04452	25.73290	28.75514	32.15042	42.56613	56.40535
12	12.68250	13.41209	14.19203	15.02581	15.91713	16.86994	17.88845	18.97713	20.14072	21.38428	24.13313	27.27075	30.85017	34.93107	39.58050	54.20766	74.32695
13	13.80933	14.68033	15.61779	16.62684	17.71298	18.88214	20.14064	21.49530	22.95338	24.52271	28.02911	32.08865	36.78620	42.21866	48.49660	68.75958	97.62504
14	14.94742	15.97394	17.08632	18.29191	19.59863	21.01507	22.55049	24.21492	26.01919	27.97498	32.39260	37.58107	43.67199	50.81802	59.19592	86.94947	127.91255
15	16.09690	17.29342	18.59891	20.02359	21.57856	23.27597	25.12902	27.15211	29.36092	31.77248	37.27971	43.84241	51.65951	60.96527	72.03511	109.68684	167.28631
16	17.25786	18.63929	20.15688	21.82453	23.65749	25.67253	27.88805	30.32428	33.00340	35.94973	42.75328	50.98035	60.92503	72.93901	87.44213	138.10855	218.47220
17	18.43044	20.01207	21.76159	23.69751	25.84037	28.21288	30.84022	33.75023	36.97370	40.54470	48.88367	59.11760	71.67303	87.06804	105.93056	173.63568	285.01386
18	19.61475	21.41231	23.41444	25.64541	28.13238	30.90565	33.99903	37.45024	41.30134	45.59917	55.74971	68.39407	84.14072	103.74028	128.11667	218.04460	371.51802
19	20.81090	22.84056	25.11687	27.67123	30.53900	33.75999	37.37896	41.44626	46.01846	51.15909	63.43968	78.96923	98.60323	123.41353	154.74000	273.55576	483.97343
20	22.01900	24.29737	26.87037	29.77808	33.06595	36.78559	40.99549	45.76196	51.16012	57.27500	72.05244	91.02493	115.37975	146.62797	186.68800	342.94470	630.16546
21	23.23919	25.78332	28.67649	31.96920	35.71925	39.99273	44.86518	50.42292	56.76453	64.00250	81.69874	104.76842	134.84051	174.02100	225.02560	429.68087	820.21510
22	24.47159	27.29898	30.53678	34.24797	38.50521	43.39229	49.00574	55.45676	62.87334	71.40275	92.50258	120.43600	157.41499	206.34479	271.03072	538.10109	1067.27963
23	25.71630	28.84496	32.45238	36.61789	41.43048	46.99583	53.43614	60.89330	66.17894	79.54302	104.60289	138.29704	183.60138	244.48685	326.23686	673.62636	1388.46351
24	26.97346	30.42186	34.42647	39.08260	44.50200	50.81558	58.17667	66.76476	76.78981	88.49733	118.15524	158.65862	213.97761	289.49448	392.48424	843.03295	1806.00257
25	28.24320	32.03030	36.45926	41.64591	47.72710	54.86451	63.24904	73.10594	84.70090	98.34706	133.33387	181.87083	249.21402	342.60349	471.98108	1054.79118	2348.80334
26	29.52563	33.67091	38.55304	44.31174	51.11345	59.15638	68.67647	79.95442	93.32398	109.18177	150.33393	208.33274	290.08827	405.27211	567.37730	1319.48898	3054.44434
27	30.82089	35.34432	40.70963	47.08421	54.66913	63.70577	74.48382	87.35077	102.72313	121.09994	169.37401	238.49933	337.50239	479.22109	681.85276	1650.36123	3971.77764
28	32.12910	37.05121	42.93092	49.96758	58.40258	68.52811	80.69769	95.33883	112.96822	134.20994	190.69889	272.88923	392.50277	566.48089	819.22331	2063.95153	5164.31093
29	33.45039	38.79223	45.21885	52.96629	62.32271	73.63980	87.34653	103.96594	124.13536	148.63093	214.58275	312.09373	456.30322	669.44745	984.06797	2580.93941	6714.60421
30	34.78489	40.56808	47.57542	56.08494	66.43885	79.05819	94.46079	113.28321	136.30754	164.49402	241.33268	356.78685	530.31173	790.94799	1181.88157	3227.17427	8729.98548

EXHIBIT A1.10

Present Value of an Annuity

$$PVA = \frac{1 - \frac{1}{(1+i)^n}}{i}$$

n/i	1%	2%	3%	4%	5%	6%	7%	8%	9%	10%	12%	14%	16%	18%	20%	25%	30%
1	0.99010	0.98039	0.97087	0.96154	0.95238	0.94340	0.93458	0.92593	0.91743	0.90909	0.89286	0.87719	0.86207	0.84746	0.83333	0.80000	0.76923
2	1.97040	1.94156	1.91347	1.88609	1.85941	1.83339	1.80802	1.78326	1.75911	1.73554	1.69005	1.64666	1.60523	1.56564	1.52778	1.44000	1.36095
3	2.94099	2.88388	2.82861	2.77509	2.72325	2.67301	2.62432	2.57710	2.53129	2.48685	2.40183	2.32163	2.24589	2.17427	2.10648	1.95200	1.81611
4	3.90197	3.80773	3.71710	3.62990	3.54595	3.46511	3.38721	3.31213	3.23972	3.16987	3.03735	2.91371	2.79818	2.69006	2.58873	2.36160	2.16624
5	4.85343	4.71346	4.57971	4.45182	4.32948	4.21236	4.10020	3.99271	3.88965	3.79079	3.60478	3.43308	3.27429	3.12717	2.99061	2.68928	2.43557
6	5.79548	5.60143	5.41719	5.24214	5.07569	4.91732	4.76654	4.62288	4.48592	4.35526	4.11141	3.88867	3.68474	3.49760	3.32551	2.95142	2.64275
7	6.72819	6.47199	6.23028	6.00205	5.78637	5.58238	5.38929	5.20637	5.03295	4.86842	4.56376	4.28830	4.03857	3.81153	3.60459	3.16114	2.80211
8	7.65168	7.32548	7.01969	6.73274	6.46321	6.20979	5.97130	5.74664	5.53482	5.33493	4.96764	4.63886	4.34359	4.07757	3.83716	3.32891	2.92470
9	8.56602	8.16224	7.78611	7.43533	7.10782	6.80169	6.51523	6.24689	5.99525	5.75902	5.32825	4.94637	4.60654	4.30302	4.03097	3.46313	3.01900
10	9.47130	8.98259	8.53020	8.11090	7.72173	7.36009	7.02358	6.71008	6.41766	6.14457	5.65022	5.21612	4.83323	4.49409	4.19247	3.57050	3.09154
11	10.36763	9.78685	9.25262	8.76048	8.30641	7.88687	7.49867	7.13896	6.80519	6.49506	5.93770	5.45273	5.02864	4.65601	4.32706	3.65640	3.14734
12	11.25508	10.57534	9.95400	9.38507	8.86325	8.38384	7.94269	7.53608	7.16073	6.81369	6.19437	5.66029	5.19711	4.79322	4.43922	3.72512	3.19026
13	12.13374	11.34837	10.63496	9.98565	9.39357	8.85268	8.35765	7.90378	7.48690	7.10336	6.42355	5.84236	5.34233	4.90951	4.53268	3.78010	3.22328
14	13.00370	12.10625	11.29607	10.56312	9.89864	9.29498	8.74547	8.24424	7.78615	7.36669	6.62817	6.00207	5.46753	5.00806	4.61057	3.82408	3.24867
15	13.86505	12.84926	11.93794	11.11839	10.37966	9.71225	9.10791	8.55948	8.06069	7.60608	6.81086	6.14217	5.57546	5.09158	4.67547	3.85926	3.26821
16	14.71787	13.57771	12.56110	11.65230	10.83777	10.10590	9.44665	8.85137	8.31256	7.82371	6.97399	6.26506	5.66850	5.16235	4.72956	3.88741	3.28324
17	15.56225	14.29187	13.16612	12.16567	11.27407	10.47726	9.76322	9.12164	8.54363	8.02155	7.11963	6.37286	5.74870	5.22233	4.77463	3.90993	3.29480
18	16.39827	14.99203	13.75351	12.65930	11.68959	10.82760	10.05909	9.37189	8.75563	8.20141	7.24967	6.46742	5.81785	5.27316	4.81219	3.92794	3.30369
19	17.22601	15.67846	14.32380	13.13394	12.08532	11.15812	10.33560	9.60360	8.95011	8.36492	7.36578	6.55037	5.87746	5.31624	4.84350	3.94235	3.31053
20	18.04555	16.35143	14.87747	13.59033	12.46221	11.46992	10.59401	9.81815	9.12855	8.51356	7.46944	6.62313	5.92884	5.35275	4.86958	3.95388	3.31579
21	18.85698	17.01121	15.41502	14.02916	12.82115	11.76408	10.83553	10.01680	9.29224	8.64869	7.56200	6.68696	5.97314	5.38368	4.89132	3.96311	3.31984
22	19.66038	17.65805	15.93692	14.45112	13.16300	12.04158	11.06124	10.20074	9.44243	8.77154	7.64465	6.74294	6.01133	5.40990	4.90943	3.97049	3.32296
23	20.45582	18.29220	16.44361	14.85684	13.48857	12.30338	11.27219	10.37106	9.58021	8.88322	7.71843	6.79206	6.04425	5.43212	4.92453	3.97639	3.32535
24	21.24339	18.91393	16.93554	15.24696	13.79864	12.55036	11.46933	10.52876	9.70661	8.98474	7.78432	6.83514	6.07263	5.45095	4.93710	3.98111	3.32719
25	22.02316	19.52346	17.41315	15.62208	14.09394	12.78336	11.65358	10.67478	9.82258	9.07704	7.84314	6.87293	6.09709	5.46691	4.94759	3.98489	3.32861
26	22.79520	20.12104	17.87684	15.98277	14.37519	13.00317	11.82578	10.80998	9.92897	9.16095	7.89566	6.90608	6.11818	5.48043	4.95632	3.98791	3.32970
27	23.55961	20.70690	18.32703	16.32959	14.64303	13.21053	11.98671	10.93516	10.02658	9.23722	7.94255	6.93515	6.13636	5.49189	4.96360	3.99033	3.33054
28	24.31644	21.28127	18.76411	16.66306	14.89813	13.40616	12.13711	11.05108	10.11613	9.30657	7.98442	6.96066	6.15204	5.50160	4.96967	3.99226	3.33118
29	25.06579	21.84438	19.18845	16.98371	15.14107	13.59072	12.27767	11.15841	10.19828	9.36961	8.02181	6.98304	6.16555	5.50983	4.97472	3.99381	3.33168
30	25.80771	22.39646	19.60044	17.29203	15.37245	13.76483	12.40904	11.25778	10.27365	9.42691	8.05518	7.00266	6.17720	5.51681	4.97894	3.99505	3.33206

GLOSSARY

A

account   a record of increases and decreases in each of the basic elements of the financial statements (each of the company's asset, liability, shareholders' equity, revenue, expense, gain, and loss items). (p. 81)

accounting   the process of identifying, measuring, recording, and communicating financial information about a company's activities so that decision makers can make informed decisions. (p. 4)

accounting cycle   the procedures a company uses to transform the results of its business activities into financial statements. (p. 66)

Accounting Standards for Private Enterprises (ASPE)   accounting standards that apply to private for-profit corporations. (p. 31)

accounting system   the methods and records used to identify, measure, record, and communicate financial information about a business. (p. 206)

account payable   an obligation that arises when a business purchases goods or services on credit. (p. 451)

accounts receivable   money due from another business or individual as payment for services performed or goods delivered. Payment is typically due in 30 to 60 days and does not involve a formal note between the parties nor does it include interest. (p. 256)

accounts receivable turnover ratio   net credit sales or net sales divided by average accounts receivable. (p. 746)

accrual-basis accounting   a method of accounting in which revenues are generally recorded when earned (rather than when cash is received) and expenses are matched to the periods in which they help produce revenues (rather than when cash is paid). (p. 132)

accrued expenses   previously unrecorded expenses that have been incurred, but not yet paid in cash. (p. 141)

accrued liabilities   liabilities that usually represent the completed portion of activities that are in process at the end of the period. (p. 452)

accrued revenues   previously unrecorded revenues that have been earned but for which no cash has yet been received. (p. 139)

accumulated depreciation   the total amount of depreciation expense that has been recorded for an asset since the asset was acquired. It is reported on the statement of financial position as a contra asset. (p. 388)

adjusted trial balance   an updated trial balance that reflects the changes to account balances as the result of adjusting entries. (p. 139)

adjusting entries   journal entries that are made at the end of an accounting period to record the completed portion of partially completed transactions. (p. 137)

aging method   a method in which bad debt expense is estimated indirectly by determining the ending balance desired in the allowance for doubtful accounts and then computing the necessary adjusting entry to achieve this balance; the amount of this adjusting entry is also the amount of bad debt expense. (p. 261)

allowance for doubtful accounts   a contra-asset account that is established to "store" the estimate of uncollectible accounts until specific accounts are identified as uncollectible. (p. 258)

amortization   the process whereby companies systematically allocate the cost of their intangible operating assets as an expense among the accounting periods in which the asset is used and the benefits are received. (p. 409)

amortized cost method   a method that amortizes bond investment premium or discount from the purchase date of the investment to the date of bond maturity. (p. 699)

annuity   a series of equal cash flows at regular intervals. (p. 817)

asset acquisition   the purchase by a company of one or more assets from a selling company. (p. 712)

asset efficiency ratios (operating ratios)   ratios that measure how efficiently a company uses its assets. (p. 745)

assets   economic resources representing expected future economic benefits controlled by the business (e.g., cash, accounts receivable, inventory, land, buildings, equipment, and intangible assets). (pp. 7, 69)

asset turnover ratio   a ratio that measures the efficiency with which a corporation's assets (usually accounts receivable or inventory) are used to produce sales revenues. (p. 748)

audit report   the auditor's opinion as to whether the company's financial statements are fairly stated in accordance with generally accepted accounting principles (GAAP). (p. 29)

authorization of transactions   transactions should be performed by or under the direction of a person who has the appropriate level of authority. (p. 203)

authorized shares   the maximum number of shares a company may issue in each share class. (p. 567)

average age of depreciable capital assets   the estimated average length of time that a depreciable asset has been in use. (p. 406)

average days to sell inventory   an estimate of the number of days it takes a company to sell its inventory. It is found by dividing 365 days by the inventory turnover ratio. (p. 337)

B

bad debt expense   the expense that results from receivables that are not paid. (p. 258)

balance sheet a financial statement that discloses the assets, liabilities, and equity of an entity at a point in time. (p. 9)

bank reconciliation the process of reconciling any differences between a company's accounting records and the bank's accounting records. (p. 208)

bond a type of note that requires the issuing entity to pay the face value of the bond to the holder when it matures and, usually, periodic interest at a specified rate. (p. 503)

book value (carrying value) the value of an asset or liability as it appears on the statement of financial position. Book value is calculated as the cost of the asset or liability minus the balance in its related contra account (e.g., cost of equipment less accumulated depreciation; notes payable less discount on notes payable). (p. 388)

business combination a transaction or series of transactions that brings together two or more previously separate entities to form a single accounting entity. (p. 712)

business process risks threats to the internal processes of a company. (p. 202)

C

callable bonds bonds that give the borrower the right to pay off (or call) the bonds prior to their due date. The borrower typically "calls" debt when the interest rate being paid is much higher than the current market conditions. (p. 504)

capital a company's assets less its liabilities. Capital is also known as shareholders' equity. (p. 15)

capital expenditures expenditures to acquire long-term assets or extend the life, expand the productive capacity, increase the efficiency, or improve the quality of existing long-term assets. (p. 401)

carrying value the amount at which a financial statement component is recorded in the entity's financial statements. (p. 388)

cash-basis accounting a method of accounting in which revenue is recorded when cash is received, regardless of when it is actually earned. Similarly, an expense is recorded. Cash-basis accounting does not tie recognition of revenues and expenses to the actual business activity but rather to the exchange of cash. (p. 132)

cash equivalents short-term, highly liquid investments that are readily convertible to cash and have original maturities of three months or less. (pp. 218, 253, 628)

cash flow adequacy ratio the cash flow adequacy ratio provides a measure of the company's ability to meet its debt obligations and is calculated as: Cash flow adequacy = Free cash flow ÷ Average amount of debt maturing over the next five years. (p. 652)

cash flows from financing activities any cash flow related to obtaining resources from creditors or owners, which includes the issuance and repayment of debt, common and preferred share transactions, and the payment of dividends. (pp. 27, 630)

cash flows from investing activities the cash inflows and outflows that relate to acquiring and disposing of operating assets, acquiring and selling investments (current and long-term), and lending money and collecting loans. (pp. 27, 629)

cash flows from operating activities any cash flows directly related to earning income, including cash sales and collections of accounts receivable, as well as cash payments for goods, services, salaries, and interest. (pp. 26, 628)

cash over and short an account that records the discrepancies between deposited amounts of actual cash received and the total of the cash register tape. (p. 215)

cash ratio a short-term liquidity ratio calculated as: (Cash + Short-term investments) – Current liabilities. (p. 738)

chart of accounts the list of accounts used by a company. (p. 81)

commitments contractual obligations to conduct transactions with specified parties in the future. (p. 464)

common shares the basic ownership interest in a corporation. Owners of common shares have the right to vote in the election of the Board of Directors, share in the profits and dividends of the company, keep the same percentage of ownership if new shares are issued (preemptive right), and share in the assets in liquidation in proportion to their holdings. (p. 568)

common-size statements financial statements that express each financial statement line item in percentage terms. (p. 731)

comparability one of the four qualitative characteristics that useful information should possess. Information has comparability if it allows comparisons to be made between companies. (p. 67)

compound interest a method of calculating the time value of money in which interest is earned on the previous periods' interest. (p. 809)

consignment an arrangement where goods owned by one party are held and offered for sale by another. (p. 319)

consistency one of the four qualitative characteristics that useful information should possess. Consistency refers to the application of the same accounting principles by a single company over time. (p. 67)

consolidated financial statements financial statements that reflect the combination of a parent company's financial statements with the financial statements of the parent company's subsidiaries. (p. 710)

consolidation worksheet an Excel-based worksheet that is used to efficiently prepare a parent company's consolidated financial statements. (p. 710)

contingent liability an obligation whose amount or timing is uncertain and depends on future events. For example, a firm may be contingently liable for damages under a lawsuit that has yet to be decided by the courts. (p. 449)

continuity (or going concern) assumption one of the four basic assumptions that underlie accounting that assumes a company will continue to operate long enough to carry out its existing commitments. (p. 68)

contra accounts accounts that have a balance that is opposite of the balance in the related account. (p. 147)

contract rate see *interest rate* (p. 503)

control activities the policies and procedures that top management establishes to help ensure that its objectives are met. (p. 203)

control environment the collection of environmental factors that influence the effectiveness of control procedures such as the philosophy and operating style of management, the personnel policies and practices of the business, and the overall integrity, attitude, awareness, and actions of everyone in the business concerning the importance of control. (p. 201)

convertible bonds bonds that allow the bondholder to convert the bond into another security—typically common shares. (p. 505)

copyright an intangible asset that grants the holder the right to publish, sell, or control a literary or artistic work. The legal life is the life of author plus 70 years. (p. 410)

corporation a company chartered by the government to conduct business as an "artificial person" and owned by one or more shareholders. (p. 6)

cost any expenditure necessary to acquire the asset and to prepare the asset for use. (p. 388)

cost constraint qualitative characteristic of useful information that states that the benefit received from accounting information should be greater than the cost of providing that information. (p. 68)

cost of goods available for sale the sum of the cost of beginning inventory and the cost of purchases. (p. 313)

cost of goods sold an expense that represents the outflow of resources caused by the sale of inventory. This is often computed as the cost of goods available for sale less the cost of ending inventory. (p. 310)

coupon rate see *interest rate*. (p. 503)

credit the right side of a T account; alternatively, credit may refer to the act of entering an amount on the right side of an account. (p. 82)

credit cards a card that authorizes the holder to make purchases up to some limit from specified retailers. Credit cards are a special form of factoring in which the issuer of the credit card pays the seller the amount of each sale less a service charge and then collects the full amount of the sale from the buyer at some later date. (p. 264)

creditor the person to whom money is owed. (p. 7)

cross-sectional analysis a type of analysis that compares one corporation to another corporation and to industry averages. (p. 729)

cumulative dividend preference a provision that requires the eventual payment of all preferred dividends—both dividends in arrears and current dividends—to preferred shareholders before any dividends are paid to common shareholders. (p. 582)

current assets cash and other assets that are reasonably expected to be converted into cash within one year or one operating cycle, whichever is longer. (p. 12)

current dividend preference a provision that requires that current dividends be paid to preferred shareholders before any dividends are paid to common shareholders. (p. 582)

current liabilities obligations that require a firm to pay cash or another current asset, create a new current liability, or provide goods or services within one year or one operating cycle, whichever is longer. (pp. 14, 450)

current ratio a measure of liquidity that is computed as: Current assets ÷ Current liabilities. (pp. 17, 737)

D

date of record the date on which a shareholder must own one or more shares in order to receive the dividend. (p. 578)

debenture bonds another name for unsecured bonds. (p. 504)

debit the left side of a T account; alternatively, debit may refer to the act of entering an amount on the left side of an account. (p. 82)

debit card a card that authorizes a bank to make an immediate electronic withdrawal (debit) from the holder's bank account and a corresponding deposit to another party's account. (p. 265)

debt management ratios a type of ratio that provides information on two aspects of debt: (1) the relative mix of debt and equity financing (often referred to as its capital structure) and (2) the corporation's ability to meet its debt obligations through operations because interest and principal payments must be made as scheduled, or a company can be declared bankrupt. (p. 742)

debt security a security that evidences the indebtedness of an entity to the security holder. (p. 698)

debt-to-equity ratio a measure of the proportion of capital provided by creditors relative to that provided by shareholders. This ratio is calculated as: Total liabilities ÷ Total equity. (p. 743)

debt-to-total assets ratio a measure of the proportion of capital provided by creditors. This ratio is calculated as: Total liabilities ÷ Total assets. (p. 743)

declaration date the date on which a corporation announces its intention to pay a dividend on common shares. (p. 577)

declining balance depreciation method an accelerated depreciation method that produces a declining amount of depreciation expense each period by multiplying the declining book value of an asset by a constant depreciation rate. Declining balance depreciation expense for each period of an asset's useful life equals the declining balance rate times the asset's book value (cost less accumulated depreciation) at the beginning of the period. (p. 392)

deficit the accumulated losses over the entire life of a corporation that have not been paid out in dividends. (p. 584)

depletion the process of allocating the cost of a natural resource to each period in which the resource is removed from the earth. (p. 413)

deposit in transit an amount received and recorded by a company, but that has not been recorded by the bank in time to appear on the current bank statement. (p. 211)

depreciable cost depreciable cost is calculated as the cost of the asset less its residual (or salvage) value. This amount will be depreciated (expensed) over the asset's useful life. (p. 390)

depreciation the process whereby companies systematically allocate the cost of their tangible operating assets (other than land) as an expense in each period in which the asset is used. (pp. 147, 387)

depreciation expense the amount of depreciation recorded on the statement of earnings. (p. 388)

direct method a method of computing net cash flow from operating activities by adjusting each item on the statement of earnings by the changes in the related current asset or liability accounts. Typical cash flow categories reported are cash collected from customers, cash paid to suppliers, cash paid to employees, cash paid for interest, and cash paid for taxes. (p. 637)

discount   when a bond sells at a price below face value, due to the yield being greater than the stated rate of interest. (p. 504)

discount period   the reduced payment period associated with purchase discounts. (p. 318)

dividend payout ratio   a ratio that measures the proportion of a corporation's profits that are returned to the shareholders immediately as dividends. It is calculated as: Common dividends ÷ Net income. (p. 755)

dividends   amounts paid periodically by a corporation to its shareholders as a return of their invested capital. Dividends represent a distribution of retained earnings, not an expense. (p. 568)

dividends in arrears   cumulative preferred stock dividends remaining unpaid for one or more years are considered to be in arrears. (p. 582)

dividend yield ratio   a ratio that measures the rate at which dividends provide a return to shareholders, by comparing dividends with the market price of a share. It is calculated as: Dividends per common share ÷ Closing market price per share for the year. (p. 754)

documentation adequacy   documentation that provides necessary information about transactions undertaken by the business. (p. 204)

double-entry accounting   a type of accounting in which the two-sided effect that every transaction has on the accounting equation is recorded in the accounting system. (p. 81)

DuPont analysis   a type of analysis that recognizes that ROE can be broken down into three important components—net profit margin, asset turnover, and leverage. (p. 757)

E

earned   one of two requirements for the recognition of revenue. Revenues are considered "earned" when the earnings process is substantially complete. This typically happens when the goods are delivered or the service is provided. (p. 252)

earnings per share (EPS) ratio   a ratio that measures the income available for common shareholders on a per-share basis. EPS is calculated as net income less preferred dividends divided by the average number of common shares outstanding. (pp. 587, 754)

effective interest rate method   a method of interest amortization that is based on compound interest calculations. (p. 509)

equity   see shareholders' equity (p. 71)

equity method   an accounting method for strategic investments that records the underlying periodic profit or loss of an investee. (p. 707)

equity security   a security that evidences an ownership interest in a corporation. (p. 698)

events   events make up the multitude of activities in which companies engage. External events result from exchange between the company and another outside entity, and internal events result from a company's own actions that do not involve other companies. (p. 72)

exercise (or strike) price   the price at which employees can buy shares when their employer grants stock options. (p. 573)

expenses   the cost of assets used, or the liabilities created, in the operation of the business. (p. 8)

external auditors   the professional firm engaged to express an opinion on an entity's financial statements. (p. 205)

F

face value   the amount of money that a borrower must repay at maturity; also called par value or principal. (p. 503)

factor   a method of handling receivables in which the seller receives an immediate cash payment reduced by the factor's fees. The factor, the buyer of the receivables, acquires the right to collect the receivables and the risk of uncollectibility. In a typical factoring arrangement, the sellers of the receivables have no continuing responsibility for their collection. (p. 264)

faithful representation   qualitative characteristic of information stipulating it should be complete, neutral, and free from error. (p. 67)

finance lease   a non-cancellable agreement that is in substance a purchase of the leased asset. (p. 526)

financial accounting   accounting and reporting to satisfy the outside demand (primarily investors and creditors) for accounting information. (p. 4)

financial leverage   the extent to which a company uses fixed-income securities to finance a company as opposed to common shares. (p. 524)

financial ratios   amounts that are calculated and used to compare the financial results of a company to itself or to similar firms over time. (p. 737)

financial statements   a set of standardized reports in which the detailed transactions of a company's activities are reported and summarized so that they can be communicated to decision makers. (p. 8)

finished goods inventory   the account in manufacturing firms that represents the cost of the final product that is available for sale. (p. 311)

first-in, first-out (FIFO) method   an inventory costing system in which the earliest (oldest) purchases (the first in) are assumed to be the first sold (the first out) and the more recent purchases are in ending inventory. (p. 327)

fiscal year   an accounting period that runs for one year. (p. 11)

fixed asset turnover ratio   the ratio of sales to the carrying amount of fixed assets. (p. 752)

FOB destination   a shipping arrangement in which ownership of inventory passes when the goods are delivered to the buyer. (p. 252)

FOB shipping point   a shipping arrangement in which ownership of inventory passes from the seller to the buyer at the shipping point. (p. 252)

footnotes   notes to the financial statements that help clarify and expand upon the information presented in those statements. (p. 29)

franchise   an exclusive right to conduct a certain type of business in some particular geographic area. (p. 410)

free cash flow   the cash flow that a company is able to generate after considering the maintenance or expansion of its assets (capital expenditures) and the payment of dividends. Free cash flow is calculated as: Net cash flow from operating activities – Capital expenditures – Cash dividends. (p. 652)

freight-in the transportation costs that are normally paid by the buyer under FOB shipping point terms. (p. 252)

freight-out the transportation costs that the seller is usually responsible for paying under FOB destination shipping terms. (p. 252)

full disclosure principle a policy that requires any information that would make a difference to financial statement users to be revealed. (p. 69)

fundamental accounting equation Assets = Liabilities + Shareholders' equity. The left side of the accounting equation shows the assets, or economic resources of a company. The right side of the accounting equation indicates who has a claim on the company's assets. (p. 10)

future value the value of a specified asset or liability at a specified date in the future. (p. 811)

G

general ledger a collection of all the individual financial statement accounts that a company uses in its financial statements. (p. 91)

Generally Accepted Accounting Principles (GAAP) the standardized accounting principles, policies, and procedures used in financial accounting to prepare financial statements. (p. 31)

goodwill an unidentifiable intangible asset that arises from factors such as customer satisfaction, quality products, skilled employees, and business location. (pp. 410, 713)

gross margin (gross profit) a key performance measure that is computed as sales revenue less cost of goods sold. (pp. 21, 310)

gross profit percentage a measurement of the proportion of each sales dollar that is available to pay other expenses and provide profit for owners. (p. 750)

gross profit ratio a measurement of the proportion of each sales dollar that is available to pay other expenses and provide profit for owners; it is computed by dividing gross margin by net sales. (p. 336)

H

historical cost principle a principle that requires the activities of a company to be initially measured at their cost—the exchange price at the time the activity occurs. (p. 69)

horizontal analysis a type of analysis in which each financial statement line item is expressed as a percentage of the base year (typically the first year shown). (p. 731)

human resource controls controls that provide protection to a company through proper recruiting activities, the rotation and segregation of duties among employees, and the obtaining of fidelity insurance on employees who work in sensitive areas of the business. (p. 205)

I

impairment a permanent decline in the future benefits or service potential of an asset. (p. 402)

income from operations gross margin less operating expenses. This represents the results of the core operations of the business. (p. 22)

independent checks the checking of recorded amounts for accuracy by a person who is independent of the preparation of the recorded information. (p. 205)

indirect method a method that computes operating cash flows by adjusting net income for items that do not affect cash flows. (p. 639)

installment debt a loan that is repaid by the borrower in regular installments. (p. 522)

intangible assets nonmonetary assets that are identifiable and without physical substance. (p. 14)

intangible capital assets assets that provide a benefit to a company over a number of years but lack physical substance. Examples of intangible assets include patents, copyrights, trademarks, and goodwill. (p. 409)

interest the excess of the total amount of money paid to a lender over the amount borrowed. (p. 266)

interest amortization the process used to determine the amount of interest to be recorded in each of the periods a liability is outstanding. (p. 509)

interest period the time interval between interest calculations. (p. 809)

interest rate a percentage of the principal that must be paid in order to have use of the principal. It is multiplied by the beginning-of-period balance to yield the amount of interest for the period. (pp. 454, 503, 809)

internal auditors employees of an organization who perform audit duties. (p. 205)

internal control system the policies and procedures established by top management and the board of directors to provide reasonable assurance that the company's objectives are being met in three areas: (1) effectiveness and efficiency of operations, (2) reliability of financial reporting, and (3) compliance with applicable laws and regulations. (p. 199)

International Financial Reporting Standards (IFRS) financial reporting standards that have been developed for use internationally by publicly accountable enterprises. (p. 31)

inventory products held for resale that are classified as current assets on the statement of financial position. (p. 310)

inventory turnover ratio a ratio that describes how quickly inventory is purchased (or produced) and sold. It is calculated as cost of goods sold divided by average inventory. (pp. 336, 746)

involuntary disposal a type of disposal that occurs when assets are lost or destroyed through theft, through acts of nature, or by accident. (p. 404)

issued shares the number of shares actually sold to shareholders. (p. 567)

J

journal a chronological record showing the debit and credit effects of transactions on a company. (p. 86)

journal entry a record of a transaction that is made in a journal so that the entire effect of the transaction is contained in one place. (p. 86)

junk bonds unsecured bonds where the risk of the borrower failing to make the payments is relatively high. (p. 504)

L

last-in, first-out (LIFO) method an inventory costing system that allocates the cost of goods available for sale between ending inventory and cost of goods sold based on the assumption that the most recent purchases (the last in) are the first to be sold (the first out). (p. 327)

lease an agreement that enables a company to use property without legally owning it. (p. 525)

leasehold improvements capital alterations made by a tenant to leased premises. (p. 410)

lessee one who uses an asset during the term of the lease. (p. 525)

lessor the legal owner of an asset who retains substantially all of the risks and obligations of ownership. (p. 525)

liabilities probable future sacrifices of economic benefits; liabilities usually require the payment of cash, the transfer of assets other than cash, or the performance of services. (pp. 7, 69, 448)

liquidity a company's ability to pay obligations as they become due. (p. 17)

long-term debt obligations that extend beyond one year. (p. 502)

long-term investments investments that the company expects to hold for longer than one year. This includes land or buildings that a company is not currently using in operations, as well as debt and equity securities. (p. 14)

long-term liabilities the obligations of the company that will require payment beyond one year or the operating cycle, whichever is longer. (p. 14)

lower of cost and net realizable value (LCNRV) rule a rule that requires a company to reduce the carrying value of its inventory to its market value if the market value is lower than its cost. (p. 334)

M

Management's Discussion and Analysis (MD&A) a section of the annual report that provides a discussion and explanation of various items reported in the financial statements. Management uses this section to highlight favourable and unfavourable trends and significant risks facing the company. (p. 29)

manufacturers companies that buy and transform raw materials into a finished product, which is then sold. (p. 311)

market rate the market rate of interest demanded by creditors. (p. 503)

maturity the date on which a borrower agrees to pay the creditor the face (or par) value. (p. 503)

merchandise inventory the inventory held by merchandisers. (p. 311)

merchandisers companies, either retailers or wholesalers, that purchase inventory in a finished condition and hold it for resale without further processing. (p. 311)

minority interest the portion of a subsidiary's common shares not owned by the parent corporation. (p. 712)

monetary unit assumption see *unit-of-measure (or monetary unit) assumption.*

mortgage bonds bonds that are secured by real estate. (p. 504)

N

natural resources resources, such as coal deposits, oil reserves, and mineral deposits, that are physically consumed as they are used by a company and that can generally be replaced or restored only by an act of nature. (p. 412)

net income the excess of a company's revenue over its expenses during a period of time. (p. 8)

net loss the excess of a company's expenses over its revenues during a period of time. (p. 8)

net profit margin percentage a measure of the proportion of each sales dollar that is profit, determined by dividing net income by net sales. (pp. 23, 750)

net sales revenue computed as gross sales revenue minus sales returns and allowances, as well as sales discounts. (p. 255)

noncash investing and financing activities investing and financing activities that take place without affecting cash. For example, a company may choose to acquire an operating asset (e.g., building) by issuing long-term debt. (p. 630)

noncontrolling interest the voting shares owned by shareholders in a corporation that are not owned by the parent company. (p. 712)

nonsufficient funds (NSF) cheque a cheque that has been returned to the depositor because funds in the issuer's account are not sufficient to pay the cheque (also called a "bounced" cheque). (p. 212)

nontrade receivables receivables that arise from transactions not involving inventory (e.g., interest receivable or cash advances to employees). (p. 256)

normal balance the type of balance expected of an account based on its effect on the fundamental accounting equation. Assets, expenses, and dividends have normal debit balances while liabilities, shareholders' equity, and revenues have normal credit balances. (p. 82)

note(s) payable a payable that arises when a business borrows money or purchases goods or services from a company that requires a formal agreement or contract. (pp. 453, 503)

notes receivable receivables that generally specify an interest rate and a maturity date at which any interest and principal must be repaid. (p. 266)

notes to the financial statements (or footnotes) notes that clarify and expand upon the information presented in the financial statements. (p. 29)

O

operating cash flow ratio a ratio that looks at the ability of operations to generate cash, which recognizes the more general concept that current obligations will be paid through operations (after all, selling inventory and collecting receivables is a big part of operations). This ratio is calculated as: Cash flows from operating activities ÷ Current liabilities. (p. 739)

operating cycle the average time that it takes a company to purchase goods, resell the goods, and collect the cash from customers. (pp. 12, 218)

operating lease the most common form of lease in which the lessor (the legal owner of the asset) retains the risks and obligations of ownership, while the lessee uses the asset during the term of the lease. (p. 525)

operating margin percentage a measure of the profitability of a company's operations in relation to its sales that is calculated as: Income from operations ÷ Net sales. (p. 750)

organizational costs significant costs such as legal fees, share issue costs, accounting fees, and promotional fees that a company may incur when it is formed. (p. 409)

outstanding cheque a cheque that has been issued and recorded by the business but that has not been "cashed" by the recipient. (p. 211)

outstanding shares the number of issued shares actually in the hands of shareholders. (p. 567)

P

parent a company that controls the operating and financial policies of a subsidiary. (p. 706)

participating dividend preference a provision that shareholders of participating preferred shares receive, in addition to the stated dividend, a share of amounts available for distribution as dividends to other classes of shares. (p. 583)

partnership a business owned jointly by two or more individuals. (p. 5)

par value for shares, it is an arbitrary monetary amount printed on each share that establishes a minimum price for the share when issued, but does not determine its market value. For debt, par value is the amount of money the borrower agrees to repay at maturity. (p. 503)

patent a type of intangible asset that grants the holder the right to manufacture, sell, or use a product. The legal life is 20 years from the date of the grant. (p. 410)

payment date the date on which the dividend will actually be paid. (p. 578)

payroll taxes taxes that businesses must pay based on employee payrolls; these amounts are not withheld from employee pay, but rather they are additional amounts that must be paid over and above gross pay. (p. 458)

percentage of credit sales method a method of determining bad debt expense whereby past experience and management's view of how the future may differ from the past are used to estimate the percentage of the current period's credit sales that will eventually become uncollectible. (p. 259)

periodic inventory system an inventory system that records the cost of purchases as they occur (in an account separate from the inventory account), takes a physical count of inventory at the end of the period, and applies the cost of goods sold model to determine the balances of ending inventory and cost of goods sold. The inventory account reflects the correct inventory balance only at the end of each accounting period. (p. 315)

periodicity (or time period) assumption the assumption that allows a company's life to be divided into artificial time periods to allow the measurement of net income. (pp. 69, 133)

permanent accounts accounts of asset, liability, and shareholders' equity items whose balances are carried forward from the current accounting period to future accounting periods. (p. 153)

perpetual inventory system an inventory system in which balances for inventory and cost of goods sold are continually (perpetually) updated with each sale or purchase of inventory. The accounts reflect the correct inventory and cost of goods sold balances throughout the period. (p. 314)

petty cash a fund used to pay for small dollar amounts. (p. 216)

physical controls controls that provide physical control over assets, including fireproof vaults, locked storage facilities, and keycard access to premises. (p. 204)

post-employment benefit a benefit provided by a company to a former employee after retirement. (p. 531)

posting the process of transferring information from journalized transactions to the general ledger. (p. 91)

preferred shares a class of shares that generally does not give voting rights, but grants specific guarantees and dividend preferences. (p. 568)

premium when a bond's selling price is above face value. (p. 504)

prepaid expenses asset arising from the payment of cash that has not been used or consumed by the end of the period. (p. 145)

present value determinations of present amounts based on expected future cash flows. (p. 811)

principal the amount of money borrowed and promised to be repaid (usually with interest). (pp. 266, 503)

prior period adjustment the correction of an error made in the financial statements of a prior period. The adjustment is entered as a direct adjustment to retained earnings. (p. 584)

profitability ratios ratios that measure two aspects of a corporation's profits: (1) those elements of operations that contribute to profit and (2) the relationship of profit to total investment and investment by shareholders. (pp. 270, 750)

property, plant, and equipment the tangible, long-lived, productive assets used by a company in its operations to produce revenue. This includes land, buildings, machinery, manufacturing equipment, office equipment, and furniture. (pp. 14, 383)

provisions liabilities of an uncertain amount or timing. (pp. 465, 530)

prudence (conservatism) constraint the principle in accounting that accountants should be careful to ensure that assets and revenues are not overstated (or deliberately understated) and that liabilities and expenses are not understated (or deliberately overstated). (p. 68)

purchase allowance   a situation in which the purchaser chooses to keep the merchandise if the seller is willing to grant a deduction (allowance) from the purchase price. (p. 319)

purchase discounts   price reductions (usually expressed as a percentage of the purchase price) that companies offer their customers to encourage prompt payment. (p. 318)

purchase returns   the cost of merchandise returned to suppliers. (p. 319)

purchases   the cost of merchandise acquired for resale during the accounting period. (p. 317)

Q

quality of earnings ratio   the ratio of cash flow from operating activities to net income. (pp. 629, 752)

quick ratio   a measure of a company's short-term liquidity that is calculated as follows: (Cash + short-term investments + Receivables) ÷ Current liabilities. (p. 738)

R

ratio analysis   an examination of financial statements conducted by preparing and evaluating a series of ratios. (p. 737)

ratios (financial ratios)   data that provide meaningful information only when compared with ratios from previous periods for the same firm or similar firms; they help by removing most of the effects of size differences. (p. 737)

raw materials inventory   the account in manufacturing firms that includes the basic ingredients to make a product. (p. 311)

realized/realizable   one of two requirements for revenue to be recognized. An item is realized, or realizable, if noncash resources (i.e., inventory) have been exchanged for cash or near cash (e.g., accounts receivable). (p. 252)

recoverable amount   the greater of an asset's value in use or its fair value less costs to sell. (p. 402)

relevance   one of the four qualitative characteristics that useful information should possess. Accounting information is said to be relevant if it is capable of making a difference in a business decision by helping users predict future events or by providing feedback about prior expectations. Relevant information must also be provided in a timely manner. (p. 66)

research and development (R&D) expense   the cost of internal development of intangible assets that is expensed as incurred. (p. 409)

residual value (salvage value)   the amount of cash or trade-in consideration that the company expects to receive when an asset is retired from service. (p. 390)

retailers   merchandisers that sell directly to consumers. (p. 311)

retained earnings (or deficit)   the accumulated earnings (or losses) over the entire life of the corporation that have not been paid out in dividends. (p. 584)

retractable bond   a bond where the bondholder has the option of demanding early repayment. (p. 505)

return on assets (ROA) ratio   a ratio that measures the profit earned by a corporation through use of all its capital, or the total of the investment by both creditors and owners. Return on assets is calculated as: [Net income + Interest (1 – Tax rate)]/Average total assets. (p. 751)

return on common equity ratio   a ratio that is basically the same as the return on equity ratio. It is calculated as: Net income/(Total equity + Preferred stock + Paid-in capital – Preferred shares). (pp. 587, 754)

return on equity ratio   a ratio that measures the profit earned by a firm through the use of capital supplied by shareholders. Return on equity is computed as net income divided by average equity. (p. 751)

revenue   the increase in assets that results from the sale of products or services. (p. 8)

revenue expenditures   expenditures that do not increase the future economic benefits of the asset. These expenditures are expensed as they are incurred. (p. 400)

revenue recognition principle   a principle that requires revenue to be recognized or recorded in the period in which it is earned and the collection of cash is reasonably assured. (pp. 69, 133)

S

safeguarding   the physical protection of assets through, for example, fireproof vaults, locked storage facilities, keycard access, and anti-theft tags on merchandise. (p. 204)

sales allowance   a price reduction offered by the seller to induce the buyer to keep the goods when the goods are only slightly defective, are shipped late, or in some other way are rendered less valuable. (p. 255)

sales discount   a price reduction (usually expressed as a percentage of the selling price) that companies may offer to encourage prompt payment. (p. 253)

sales returns   merchandise or goods returned by the customer to the seller. (p. 255)

sales taxes   money collected from the customer for the governmental unit levying the tax. (p. 457)

salvage value   the estimated resale value of an asset at the end of its useful life. (p. 390)

secured bond   a term used for a bond that has some collateral pledged against the corporation's ability to pay. (p. 504)

securitization   a process in which large businesses and financial institutions frequently package factored receivables as financial instruments or securities and sell them to investors. (p. 264)

segregation of duties   the idea that accounting and administrative duties should be performed by different individuals, so that no one person has access to the asset and prepares all the documents and records for an activity. (p. 203)

separate entity assumption   the assumption in accounting that the business activities of an entity can be accounted for separately from the activities of the entity's owners. (p. 68)

service charges   fees charged by the bank for chequing account services. (p. 211)

share acquisitions the purchase of shares by an investor as opposed to assets. (p. 712)

shareholder ratios ratios such as earnings per share and return on common equity that provide information about the creation of value for shareholders. (p. 753)

shareholders the owners of a corporation who own its shares in varying numbers. (p. 567)

shareholders' equity the owners' claims against the assets of a corporation after all liabilities have been deducted. (pp. 7, 567)

short-term liquidity ratios a type of ratio that compares some combination of current assets or operations to current liabilities. (p. 737)

sole proprietorship a business owned by one person. (p. 5)

specific identification method an inventory costing method that determines the cost of ending inventory and the cost of goods sold based on the identification of the actual units sold and in inventory. This method does not require an assumption about the flow of costs but actually assigns cost based on the specific flow of inventory. (p. 325)

stated rate see *interest rate*. (p. 503)

stated value the value assigned to issued shares by a company's Board of Directors. (p. 570)

statement of cash flows a financial statement that provides relevant information about a company's cash receipts (inflows of cash) and cash payments (outflows of cash) during an accounting period. (pp. 9, 626)

statement of changes in equity a statement that reports the changes in the components of a company's shareholders' equity over a period of time. (p. 9)

statement of comprehensive income a financial statement that begins with profit or loss (bottom line of the statement of earnings) and displays the items of other comprehensive income for the reporting period. (p. 9)

statement of earnings a financial statement that reports the profitability of a business over a specific period of time. (p. 31)

statement of financial position a statement that reports a company's assets, liabilities, and shareholders' equity at a point in time. (p. 8)

statement of retained earnings a financial statement that reports how much of the company's income was retained in the business and how much was distributed to owners for a period of time. (p. 9)

stock dividend a dividend paid to shareholders in the form of additional shares (instead of cash). (p. 579)

stock split a share issue that increases the number of outstanding shares of a corporation without changing the balances of its equity accounts. (p. 581)

stock warrant the right granted by a corporation to purchase a specified number of shares of a stated price and within a stated time period. (p. 572)

straight-line depreciation a depreciation method that allocates an equal amount of an asset's cost to depreciation expense for each year of the asset's useful life. Straight-line depreciation expense for each period is calculated by dividing the depreciable cost of an asset by the asset's useful life. (p. 390)

straight-line method a method that allocates (amortizes) an equal amount of bond discount or premium to each accounting period. (p. 509)

strategic risks possible threats to the organization's success in accomplishing its objectives that are external to the organization. (p. 202)

subsidiary a company that has its operating and financial policies controlled by another company. (p. 706)

T

T-account a graphical representation of an account that gets its name because it resembles the capital letter T. A T-account is a two-column record that consists of an account title and two sides divided by a vertical line—the left side is called the debit side and the right side is called the credit side. (p. 82)

tangible capital asset turnover ratio the ratio of revenue divided by the average of the carrying value of capital assets at the beginning and end of the reporting period. (p. 406)

temporary accounts the accounts of revenue, expense, and dividend items that are used to collect the activities of only one period. (p. 153)

timeliness quality of information where it is available to users before it loses its ability to influence decisions. (p. 67)

time series (or trend) analysis a type of analysis that compares a single corporation across time. (p. 729)

times interest earned ratio a ratio that measures the excess of net income over interest to gauge a firm's ability to repay its debt. It is calculated as: Income from operations ÷ Interest expense. (p. 742)

time value of money the idea that a cash flow in the future is less valuable than a cash flow at present. (pp. 454, 809)

trademark an intangible asset that grants the holder the right to the exclusive use of a distinctive name, phrase, or symbol. The legal life is 20 years but it can be renewed indefinitely. (p. 410)

trade receivable an account receivable that is due from a customer purchasing inventory in the ordinary course of business. (p. 256)

transaction any event, external or internal, that is recognized in the financial statements. (p. 72)

transaction analysis the process of determining the economic effects of a transaction on the elements of the accounting equation. (p. 74)

transportation-in see *freight-in*.

treasury shares previously issued shares that are repurchased by the issuing corporation. (p. 575)

trial balance a list of all active accounts and each account's debit or credit balance. (p. 92)

turnover the average length of time required for assets to be consumed or replaced. (p. 745)

U

understandability quality of information whereby users with a reasonable knowledge of accounting and business can comprehend the meaning of that information. (p. 67)

unearned revenue a liability that occurs when a company receives payment for goods that will be delivered or services that will be performed in the future. (pp. 143, 460)

unit-of-measure (or monetary unit) assumption the assumption in accounting that an entity can account for its business activities in monetary terms. (p. 69)

units-of-production method a depreciation method that allocates the cost of an asset over its expected life in direct proportion to the actual use of the asset; depreciation expense is computed by multiplying an asset's depreciable cost by a usage ratio. (p. 395)

unrealized gains the excess of fair market value over cost of a security that is still owned at the end of an accounting period. (p. 704)

unrealized losses the excess of cost over fair market value of a security that is still owned at the end of an accounting period. (p. 704)

unsecured a term used for bonds in which the lender is relying on the general credit of the borrowing corporation rather than on collateral. (p. 504)

useful life the period of time over which the company anticipates deriving benefit from the use of the asset. (p. 389)

V

verifiability quality of information indicating the information is verifiable when independent parties can reach a consensus on the measurement of the activity. (p. 67)

vertical analysis a type of analysis that expresses each financial statement line item as a percentage of the largest amount on the statement. (p. 733)

voluntary disposal a type of disposal that occurs when a company determines that the asset is no longer useful; the disposal may occur at the end of the asset's useful life or at some other time. (p. 403)

W

warranty a guarantee to repair or replace defective goods during a period (ranging from a few days to several years) following the sale. (p. 465)

weighted average cost method a generally accepted method to calculate the cost of inventory. (p. 329)

wholesalers merchandisers that sell to other retailers. (p. 311)

withholding businesses are required to withhold taxes from employees' earnings; standard withholdings include federal, provincial, and possibly municipal income taxes, as well as CPP/QPP and EI. (p. 458)

working capital a measure of liquidity computed as: Current assets – Current liabilities. (p. 17)

work-in-process inventory the account in manufacturing firms that consists of the raw materials that are used in production as well as other production costs such as labour and utilities. (p. 311)

Y

yield the market rate of interest demanded by creditors; yield may differ from stated rate because the underwriter disagrees with the borrower as to the correct yield or because of changes in the economy or creditworthiness of the borrower between the setting of the stated rate and the date of issue. (p. 503)

Z

zero coupon bond a bond with a zero coupon rate of interest. (p. 520)

CHECK FIGURES

Chapter 1

P 1-57A		2018 ending retained earnings = $93,450
P 1-58A	(b)	Equity at the beginning of the year = $52,600
	(d)	Expenses = $477,300
P 1-59A		Net income = $102,450
P 1-60A	(d)	Total liabilities = $1,165
	(e)	Total revenue = $72
P 1-61A		Net income = $30,100
		Retained earnings = $135,710
P 1-63A		2017 ending retained earnings = $41,850
P 1-64A	(d)	2017 dividends = $3,700
P 1-65A	1.	Net income = $36,000
		Ending retained earnings = $90,000
		Total current liabilities = $35,990
P 1-66A	(f)	Manning Company 2018 ending retained earnings = $7,500
	(m)	Perlman Company 2018 net income = $7,100
P 1-67A	2.	Net loss = $11,450
	4.	Net income = $9,550
P 1-68B		2018 ending retained earnings = $303,700
P 1-69B	(b)	Total liabilities at the end of the year = $426,630
	(d)	Net income for the year = $94,120
P 1-70B		Net income = $143,425
P 1-71B	(d)	Total liabilities = $860
	(e)	Total revenue = $503
P 1-72B		Net income = $12,250
		Retained earnings = $48,200
P 1-74B		2017 ending retained earnings = $93,500
P 1-75B	(c)	Net income = $12,400
P 1-76B		Net income = $76,500
		Ending retained earnings = $179,800
		Total current liabilities = $68,400
P 1-77B	(f)	Compton Company total equity = $60,600
	(m)	Merlotte Company total equity = $34,400
P 1-78B	2.	Net income = $63,250
	4.	Net income $71,250

Chapter 2

P 2-58A	1.	Cash column total = $31,410
		Retained Earnings column total = $8,940
	2.	Trial balance total = $58,790
P 2-59A	2.	Trial balance total = $8,200
P 2-62A	2.	Ending Cash balance = $10,290
P 2-63A	3.	Ending Cash balance = $9,820
	4.	Trial balance total = $168,850
P 2-64A	3.	Ending Cash balance = $520,400
		Ending Accounts Receivable balance = $11,000
	4.	Trial balance total = $1,372,100
P 2-66B	1.	Cash column total = $14,910
		Retained Earnings column total = $5,740
	2.	Trial balance total = $33,495
P 2-67B	2.	Trial balance total = $6,335
P 2-70B	2.	Ending Cash balance = $11,745
P 2-71B	3.	Ending Cash balance = $57,220
	4.	Trial balance total = $178,800
P 2-72B	3.	Ending Cash balance = $226,700
		Ending Accounts Receivable balance = $121,000
	4.	Trial balance total = $914,000

Chapter 3

P 3-67A	1. b.	Credit to Accounts Receivable = $2,332,028
	e.	Debit to Accounts Payable = $39,200
	h.	Debit to Interest Expense = $30,000
	2.	Ending Cash balance = $2,012,324
		Ending Interest Payable balance = $30,000
	3.	Net income = $1,125,948
	4.	Ending retained earnings = $1,563,323
	5.	Total current liabilities = $578,707
P 3-68B	1.	Cash-basis March income = $1,950
	2.	Accrual-basis March income = $1,560
P 3-69B	1 and 2.	2018 total expenses = $51,670
P 3-70B	2. b.	Credit to Service Revenue = $2,825
	d.	Credit to Prepaid Insurance = $750
	g.	Debit to Supplies Expense = $175
P 3-71B	1. b.	Debit to Accounts Receivable = $17,640
	c.	Debit to Supplies Expense = $661
	2.	Net understatement of income would be $32,734
P 3-73B	2.	Total operating expenses = $923,890
		Ending retained earnings = $67,730
		Total current liabilities = $69,130
P 3-74B	1. (a)	Adjusted Prepaid Insurance = $4,144
	(d)	Adjusted Service Revenue = $132,130
	(e)	Adjusted Depreciation Expense = $10,500
	2. (b)	Credit to Interest Payable = $4,175
	(c)	Credit to Wages Payable = $17,600

P 3-75B	1.	Credit to Retained Earnings = $49,250
	2.	Net income = $49,250
P 3-76B	1. b.	Credit to Accounts Receivable = $199,100
	g.	Debit to Accounts Payable = $73,000
	h.	Debit to Interest Expense = $2,700
	2.	Ending Cash balance = $12,300
		Ending Interest Payable balance = $2,700
	3.	Net income = $38,500
	4.	Ending retained earnings = $86,500
	5.	Total current liabilities = $36,800

Chapter 4

P4-60A	1.	Adjusted cash balance = $5,805
P 4-61A	1.	Adjusted cash balance = $7,806.81
P4-62A	1.	Adjusted cash balance = $7,550
P4-63A	f.	Credit to Cash = $320
P 4-67B	1.	Adjusted cash balance = $5,725
P 4-68B	1.	Adjusted cash balance = $8,100
P 4-69B	1.	Adjusted cash balance = $9,500
P 4-70B	f.	Credit to Cash = $675

Chapter 5

P5-81A	1.	Expected gross margin with discount policy = $196,000
P 5-82A	2.	Cash collected = $2,810,700
P 5-83A	2.	Debit to Cash = $84,150
	4.	Implied interest rate = 24% (approximate)
P 5-85A	1.	2018 loss rate = 0.082
	6.	Increase in income from operations = $49,034
P 5-86A	3.	Credit to Allowance for Doubtful Accounts = $16,179
P 5-87A	4.	Credit to Allowance for Doubtful Accounts = $17,438
P 5-88A		May 1, 2019, credit to Interest Income = $150
		Sept. 1, 2019, credit to Interest Receivable = $53.33
P 5-89A	1. b.	2017 operating margin = 37.04%
	d.	2017 accounts receivable turnover = 10.34
P 5-92B	1.	Expected gross margin with discount policy = $277,500
P 5-93B	2.	Cash collected = $1,452,250
P 5-94B	2.	Debit to Cash = $242,500
	4.	Implied interest rate = 36+% (approximate)
P 5-96B	1.	2018 loss rate = 0.087
	6.	Increase in income from operations = $4,824
P 5-97B	3.	Credit to Allowance for Doubtful Accounts = $16,993
P 5-98B	4.	Credit to Allowance for Doubtful Accounts = $20,161
P 5-99B	1.	May 1, 2019, credit to Interest Income = $267
		Sept. 1, 2019, credit to Interest Receivable = $120

P 5-100B	1. b.	2017 operating margin = 17.95%
	d.	2017 accounts receivable turnover = 5.38

Chapter 6

P 6-61A	(c)	2017 cost of goods sold = $243,170
	(f)	2018 ending inventory = $54,680
P 6-62A	2.	Gross margin = $12,444
P 6-63A	1.	FIFO cost of goods sold = $452.60
	2.	Weighted average cost method cost of goods sold = $455.90
P 6-64A	1.	FIFO 2017 cost of goods sold = $9,540
	2.	Weighted average cost 2018 cost of goods sold = $4,490
	5.	Weighted average 2018 inventory turnover = 1.73
P 6-65A	2.	Credit to inventory = $1,225
P 6-66A	1.	FIFO cost of goods sold = $36,700,000
		Weighted average cost method cost of goods sold = $36,753,500
	2.	FIFO final inventory valuation = $4,060,000
P 6-67A	2.	2017 gross margin = $2,035,400
P 6-68A	1.	FIFO ending inventory = $48
	2.	Weighted average cost per unit = $7.1514
P 6-69A	1.	FIFO 2017 gross margin = $12,210
	2.	Weighted average 2017 cost per unit = $11.3478
P 6-70B	(c)	2017 goods available for sale = $111,670
	(f)	2018 ending inventory = $11,670
P 6-71B	2.	Gross margin = $6,524
P 6-72B	1.	FIFO cost of goods sold = $4,066
	2.	Weighted average cost method cost of goods sold = $4,102.40
P 6-73B	1.	FIFO 2017 cost of goods sold = $63,300
	2.	Weighted average cost 2018 cost of goods sold = $72,155
	5.	Weighted average 2018 inventory turnover = 3.52
P 6-74B	2.	Credit to Inventory = $1,200
P 6-75B	1.	FIFO cost of goods sold = $32,180
		Weighted average cost method cost of goods sold = $32,256
	2.	FIFO final inventory valuation = $840
P 6-76B	2.	2017 gross margin = $372,750
P 6-77B	1.	FIFO ending inventory = $405
	2.	Weighted average cost per unit = $111.7750 / unit
P 6-78B	1.	FIFO 2017 gross margin = $44,700
	2.	Weighted average 2017 cost per unit $54.1765

Chapter 7

P 7-67A		Total property, plant, and equipment = $226,700
P 7-68A	1.	Acquisition cost = $38,218
	2.	Two items were expensed.

P 7-69A	3.	Straight-line year 2 book value = $99,000
		Double-declining year 2 book value = $73,125
		Units-of-production year 2 book value = $91,932
P 7-70A	2.	Year 3 ending book value = $11,750
P 7-71A	2.	Book value after renovation = $17,800
	3.	Revised yearly depreciation = $1,630
P 7-73A	1.	Gain on building = $30,000
		Loss on furniture = $32,500
P 7-74A	1.	Debit to Goodwill = $85,000
	3.	Credit to Accumulated Depletion = $225,000
P 7-75A	1.	Credit to Patent = $159,600
	2.	Debit to Patent = $122,500
	4.	Debit to Loss from Impairment = $478,800
P 7-76B		Total property, plant, and equipment = $303,155
P 7-77B	1.	Acquisition cost = $54,908
	2.	One item is expensed.
P 7-78B	3.	Straight-line year 2 book value = $76,680
		Double-declining year 2 book value = $60,480
		Units-of-production year 2 book value = $76,680
P 7-79B	2.	Year 3 ending book value = $29,160
P 7-80B	2.	Book value after renovation = $36,160
	3.	Revised yearly depreciation = $2,930
P 7-82B	1.	Gain on truck = $1,350
		Loss on furniture = $350
P 7-83B	1.	Debit to Goodwill = $1,250,000
	3.	Credit to Accumulated Depletion = $3,696,429
P 7-84B	2.	Credit to Copyright = $90,625

Chapter 8

P 8-75A	1. h.	Debit to Unearned Sales Revenue = $22,000
	2.	Debit to Interest Expense = $16,900
P 8-76A	1.	Credit to Cash = $222,159.80
P 8-77A	2.	Credit to Interest Payable = $12,000
	4.	Debit to Interest Expense = $16,000
P 8-78A	2.	No journal entry necessary.
	4.	Credit to Cash = $81,600
P 8-79A	1.	Total billing = $2,556,135
P 8-80A	1.	Reported as current liability = $50,000
	2.	Debit to Cash = $150,000
		Reported as noncurrent liability = $62,500
	3.	Debit to Unearned Sales Revenue = $75,000
P 8-81A	1.	2018 warranty expense = $57,300
	3.	Balance 12/31/18 = $44,300
P 8-82A	2.	2018 quick ratio = 0.81
	3.	2017 cash ratio = 0.29
	4.	2018 operating cash flow ratio = 0.33
P 8-83B	1. h.	Debit to Unearned Sales Revenue = $40,000
	2.	Debit to Interest Expense = $12,250

P 8-84B	1.	Credit to Cash = $1,018,050
	2.	Total cost = $105,994
P 8-85B	2.	Credit to Interest Payable = $2,750
	4.	Debit to Interest Expense = $6,875
P 8-86B	2.	No journal entry necessary.
	4.	Credit to Cash = $823,900
P 8-87B	1.	Total billing = $413,449.50
P 8-88B	1.	Reported as current liability = $91,000
	2.	Debit to Cash = $364,000
		Reported as noncurrent liability = $65,000
	3.	Debit to Unearned Sales Revenue = $104,000
P 8-89B	1.	2018 warranty expense = $101,250
	3.	Balance 12/31/18 = $16,250
P 8-90B	2.	2018 quick ratio = 0.81
	3.	2017 cash ratio = .29
	4.	2018 operating cash flows ratio = 0.33

Chapter 9

P 9-95A		Current liabilities = $158,100
P 9-96A	2.	Credit to Interest Payable = $5,850
	3.	Debit to Interest Expense = $1,950
P 9-97A		Carrying value 12/31/19 = $101,800
P 9-98A	2.	Credit to Discount on Notes Payable = $360
	4.	Carrying value = $796,400
P 9-99A	1.	Carrying value 12/31/21 = $710,400
	2.	Debit to Interest Expense = $30,650
P 9-100A	1.	Carrying value, 06/30/22 = $495,200
	2.	06/30/19 credit to Discount on Bonds Payable = $1,600
P 9-101A	1.	Carrying value, 12/31/20 = $5,100,000
P 9-102A	2.	Debit to Interest Expense = $12,900
P 9-103A		Carrying value, 12/31/20 = $2,590,000
P 9-104A	3.	Debit to Lease Liability = $30,322
P 9-105B		Current liabilities = $144,500
P 9-106B	2.	Credit to Interest Payable = $15,767
	3.	Debit to Interest Expense = $1,433
P 9-107B		Carrying value 12/31/21 = $250,000
P 9-108B	2.	Interest expense = $44,213
	4.	Carrying value 12/31/23 = $991,184
P 9-109B	2.	Interest expense 06/30/19 = $29,408
		Interest expense 12/31/19 = $29,273
P 9-110B	2.	Interest expense 06/30/19 = $31,715
		Interest expense 12/31/19 = $31,791
P 9-111B	2.	Interest expense 06/30/19 = $101,065
		Interest expense 12/31/19 = $100,968
P 9-112B	2.	Debit to Interest Expense = $10,150
P 9-113B		Carrying value, 12/31/20 = $3,160,000
P 9-114B	3.	Debit to Lease Liability = $26,068

Chapter 10

P 10-73A		Total shareholders' equity = $1,218,000
P 10-74A	c.	Contributed Surplus - Preferred Shares $60,000
P 10-75A	2.	Total shareholders' equity $2,690,000

P 10-76A	1.	d.	Credit to Dividends Payable $169,425
		f.	Debit to Retained Earnings (or Dividends) = $470,625
		g.	Credit to Dividends Payable $197,663
	2.		Total dividends for the year = $950,213
	3.		Cumulative effect on assets = $(479,588)
P 10-77A	2.		Retained earnings reported = $73,000
P 10-78A	1.		Total annual dividends = $174,200
	2.		Total dividends in arrears = $41,700
P 10-79A	1.		Share repurchase payout = 61.44%
	2.		Return on common equity = 43.13%
P 10-82B			Total shareholders' equity = $9,883,000
P 10-83B	c.		Contributed Surplus - Preferred Shares $10,000
P 10-84B	2.		Total shareholders' equity = $6,258,500
P 10-85B	1.	d.	Credit to Dividends Payable = $329,000
		f.	Debit to Retained Earnings (or Dividends) = $1,233,750
		g.	Credit to Dividends Payable = $407,138
	2.		Total dividends for the year = $2,133,888
	3.		Cumulative effect on assets = $(900,138)
P 10-86B	2.		Retained earnings reported = $197,500
P 10-87B	1.		Total annual dividends = $275,500
	2.		Total dividends in arrears = $157,500
P 10-88B	1.		Share repurchase payout = 53.66%
	2.		Return on common equity = 48.89%

Chapter 11

P 11-54A	1.	Financing = 4 items
	2.	No cash effect = 2 items
P 11-55A	1.	Total adjustments = $179,525
P 11-56A	1.	Total adjustments = $43,215
		Net cash used for investing activities = $(105,800)
P 11-57A		Gain on disposal of equipment = $(2,500)
		Gain on sale of investments = $(4,100)
		Net cash provided by operating activities = $27,100
		Net cash used for investing activities = $(5,250)
P 11-58A	1.	Total adjustments = $12,400
		Net cash used for investing activities = $(84,200)
P 11-59A	1.	Net cash provided by operating activities = $8,765
		Net cash provided by financing activities = $92,000
P 11-60A		Cash paid for operating expenses = $(887,700)
		Net cash provided by operating activities = $287,645
P 11-61A	1.	Total of Adjustments columns = $1,276,000
		Total adjustments to net income = $257,000
		Net cash used for investing activities = $(419,000)

P 11-62B	1.	Financing = 3 items
	2.	No cash effect = 3 items
P 11-63B	1.	Total adjustments = $313,945
P 11-64B	1.	Total adjustments = $151,900
		Net cash used for investing activities = $(102,060)
P 11-65B		Loss on disposal of PP&E = $4,200
		Loss on sale of investments = $1,500
		Net cash provided by operating activities = $58,125
		Net cash used for investing activities = $(45,725)
P 11-66B	1.	Total adjustments = $301,000
		Net cash used for investing activities = $(295,000)
P 11-67B	1.	Net cash provided by operating activities = $170,700
		Net cash used for financing activities = $(28,000)
P 11-68B		Cash paid for operating expenses = $(824,400)
		Net cash provided by operating activities = $359,245
P11-69B	1.	Purchase of investments = $15,000
		Total of Adjustments columns = $965,600
		Total adjustments to net income = $63,800
		Net cash used for investing activities = $(434,400)

Chapter 13

P 13-79A		2018 total revenues = 139.55%
		2017 total costs and expenses = 120.95%
		2018 total operating income = 157.56%
		2017 net income = 128.29%
P 13-81A	1.	Net income growth = 42%
	3.	Quick ratio = 0.93
	5.	2019 expected net income = $2,849
	6.	Capital to be raised = $2,704.50
P 13-82A	1.	2018 revenues = 130.88°%
		2018 total costs and expenses = 131.26%
		2018 net income = 127.16%
		2017 revenues = 113.37%
		2017 total costs and expenses = 113.44%
		2017 net income = 114.69%
	3.	2018 current assets = 74.09%
		2018 total liabilities = 24.75%
		2018 shareholders' equity = 75.25%
		2017 current assets = 74.10%
		2017 total liabilities = 29.30%
		2017 shareholders' equity = 70.70%
P 13-83A	1.	2018 average accounts receivable = $4,174
		2017 accounts receivable turnover ratio = 11.85
		2018 average inventories = $5,271
		2017 inventory turnover ratio = 6.27
		2018 average total assets = $14,581
		2017 asset turnover ratio = 3.60

2. 2017 gross profit percentage = 39.87%
2017 operating margin percentage = 8.31%
2017 net profit margin percentage = 4.65%
2018 interest expense net of tax = $890.64
2018 average total assets = $14,581
2017 return on assets = 21.55%
2018 average equity = $7,426
2017 return on equity = 29.94%

3. 2018 EBIT = $4,401
2017 EBIT = $3,431
2017 debt-to-equity ratio = 0.84
2017 debt-to-total assets ratio = 0.46

P 13-85A 1. 2018 quick assets = $958,831
2017 quick assets = $856,068
2017 cash ratio = 0.62
2017 operating cash flow ratio = 0.36
2018 EBIT / Operating income = $620,255
2017 times interest earned ratio = 18.02
2017 debt-to-equity ratio = 0.41
2017 debt-to-total assets ratio = 0.29
2018 average accounts receivable = $631,782.50
2017 accounts receivable turnover ratio = 6.09
2018 average inventory = $532,094
2017 inventory turnover ratio = 3.95
2018 average total assets = $2,030,162
2017 asset turnover ratio = 1.90
2018 income from operations = $620,258
2017 income from operations = $552,483
2018 net income + interest net of tax = $380,819.75
2017 average total assets = $1,790,645.50
2018 average common equity = $1,485,087.50
2017 return on common equity = 27.94%
2017 total payout ratio = 190.25%
2018 stock repurchase payout = 254.82%

P 13-88B 2018 total revenues = 70.03%
2017 total costs and expenses = 87.95%
2018 total operating income = 57.72%
2017 net income = 119.59%

P 13-90B 1. Net income growth = 907%
3. Quick ratio = 0.93
5. 2019 expected net income = $2,856
6. Capital to be raised = $2,658.75

P 13-91B 1. 2018 revenues = 129.07%
2018 total costs and expenses = 124.30%
2018 net income = 149.09%
2017 revenues = 114.91%
2017 total costs and expenses = 113.23%
2017 net income = 125.92%

3. 2018 current assets = 74.28%
2018 total liabilities = 25.74%
2018 shareholders' equity = 74.26%
2017 current assets = 73.58%
2017 total liabilities = 29.88%
2017 shareholders' equity = 70.12%

P 13-92B 1. 2018 average accounts receivable = $4,172
2017 accounts receivable turnover ratio = 12.41
2018 average inventories = $5,097
2017 inventory turnover ratio = 6.49
2018 average total assets = $14,424
2017 asset turnover ratio = 3.73

2. 2017 gross profit percentage = 40.13%
2017 operating margin percentage = 5.94%
2017 net profit margin percentage = 3.21%
2018 interest expense net of tax = $976.32
2018 average total assets = $14,424
2017 return on assets = 16.85%
2018 average equity = $7,042.50
2017 return on equity = 21.97%

3. 2018 EBIT = $4,526
2017 EBIT = $2,985
2017 debt-to-equity ratio = 0.91
2017 debt-to-total assets ratio = 0.48

P13-94B 1. 2018 quick assets = $972,164
2017 quick assets = $873,884
2017 cash ratio = 0.63
2017 operating cash flow ratio = 0.89
2018 EBIT = $917,148
2017 times interest earned ratio = 23.35
2017 debt-to-equity ratio = 0.43
2017 debt-to-total assets ratio = 0.30
2018 average accounts receivable = $637,352.50
2017 accounts receivable turnover ratio = 6.35
2018 average inventory = $535,489
2017 inventory turnover ratio = 4.21
2018 average total assets = $2,058,712
2017 asset turnover ratio = 2.02
2018 income from operations = $919,073
2017 income from operations = $763,441
2018 net income + interest net of tax = $662,815.20
2017 average total assets = $1,804,037
2018 average equity = $1,489,299.50
2017 return on equity = 45.16%
2017 total payout ratio = 123.41%
2018 stock repurchase payout = 153.45%

INDEX

A

Accountants, business need/career choices, 30
Accounting
  accrual accounting, cash basis of accounting (contrast), 130
  assumptions, 66–67, 93
  concepts, 64–69
  constraints, 93
  continuity assumption (going-concern assumption), 66–67
  cost constraint, 66
  cost method, 706–710
  double-entry accounting, 79–84
  equity method, 707–710
  errors, 212
  ethics/legal liability, 31
  full disclosure principle, 67
  gains/losses, 641–642, 657
  historical cost principle, 67
  IFRS/ASPE differences, 91–92
  information, qualitative characteristics, 64–66, 93
  manipulations, instances, 133e
  periodicity assumption (time period assumption), 67
  principles, 67, 93
  process, 4
  prudence constraint, 66
  records, reconciliation, 208–215
  revenue recognition principle, 67
  separate entity assumption, 66
  standards, conceptual framework, 64, 65e, 68–69
  system, control activities (relationship), 206–207
  unit of measure assumption (monetary unit assumption), 67
Accounting cycle, 64, 69–71, 155–156, 158
  completion, 130
Accounting information, communication, 8–11
Accounting Standards Board (AcSB), 30
Accounting Standards for Private Enterprises (ASPE), 30
  IFRS, differences, 32, 91–92, 156–157, 469, 531–532, 595, 654, 713–714, 761
Accounts, 79–80
  adjustment, 137–150
  analysis, 634–637
  balance, 80, 82, 212
  chart, 79
  closing, 151–155
  contra accounts, 145

contra-asset account, 14
contra-revenue account, sales returns and allowances, 255–256
impacts, determination, 84
permanent accounts, 151
role, 94
T-account, 80
temporary accounts, 151
types, 79e
Accounts payable, 8, 451, 643
  current liability type, 14
  turnover ratio, 747–748
Accounts receivable, 8, 256, 642
  average age, calculation, 746
  cash flow implications, 274
  collection, monitoring, 266
  contingent loss, 464
  control account, 257
  current asset type, 12
  management, 264–266
  turnover, calculation, 272–273
  turnover ratio, 746
  valuation, 257–263
Accrual accounting
  accounts, adjustment, 137–150
  adjusted trial balance, preparation, 137–150
  cash basis of accounting, contrast, 130, 157
  elements, 131–135
  entries, adjustment, 135–136
  ethical decisions, fraud (relationship), 132–133
  IFRS/ASPE differences, 156–157
  matching concept, 132–135
  periodicity assumption, 131
  revenue recognition principle, 131–135
Accrual-basis accounting, 130
  revenue recognition, 252
Accruals, adjusting entries, 137e, 157
Accrued expenses, 139–141
Accrued interest, recording, 454
Accrued liabilities, 452
Accrued revenues, 137–139
  adjustment, 146
  recording, 138–139
Accumulated depreciation, 14, 388
  financial statement presentation, 145e
Accumulated other comprehensive income, 567
  changes, 595–596
  public company reporting, 586
  reporting/analysis, 584–587
ACE Bakery, 63
Acid test ratio, 738
Activities (inference), T-accounts (usage), 83
Adjusted cash balances, production, 212
Adjusted trial balance, 137–150, 150e, 157–158

Adjusting entries, 135, 146–151, 146e
  impact, 137
  preparation, 157
  types, 137e
Administrative expenses, expenses type, 20
Aging method, 261–262
  conceptual/practical differences, 263
  percentage of credit sales method, contrast, 263
  usage, 262–263
Air Canada
  annual report, excerpt, 502e
  current liabilities, 527e
  debt structure, 527e
  financial accounting, 501
  financial statements (2014), excerpt, 526e
  long-term liabilities, 527e
  net minimum leases payments, present value, 525
  statement of financial position, current liabilities section, 450, 451e
Allowance for doubtful accounts, 258–259
Allowance method, 258–263
Alternative costing methods
  financial statement effects, 332
  income tax effects, 332
American Express, nonbank credit cards (receivables), 265
Amortization, 382, 409
  interest amortization methods, 509
  term, usage, 92
Amortized cost model, 699
Annual depreciation expense, decrease, 395e
Annual expense changes, 397e
Annual report
  components, 27–29
  independent auditor report, 29
  information, description, 33
  Management's Discussion and analysis, 29
  notes to the financial statements (footnotes), 29
Annual statement of earnings, money borrowing (effect), 455e
Annuity, future value, 818e, 831e
  computation, 817–819
Annuity, present value, 820–822, 820e, 832e
  computation, 821–822
Apple, product differentiation objective, 202
Asset retirement obligations (AROs), 530
Assets, 7
  acquisition, 384, 712
  book value (carrying value), 388, 393
  calculation, 10, 11
  company construction, 385

current assets, 12
decrease, credit (impact), 208
depreciation, 382
efficiency ratios (operating ratios), 737,
    745–750, 759
estimated residual value, 390
estimated useful life, 389
financial statement element, 67
future asset replacement, 406
impairment, 416
increase, debit (impact), 208
intangible assets, 14, 382
life (period), depreciation expense (recording),
    393
management ratios, calculation, 275
non-cash assets, shares (issuance), 570–572
noncurrent assets, 13–14
physical protection, 204
plant assets, 382
residual value (salvage value), 390
tangible assets, 382
turnover ratio, 748
use, extent, 397e
Audit report, 29
Authorized shares, 567
Average age of accounts receivable, calculation, 746
Average age of depreciable capital assets,
    calculation, 406
Average collection period ratios, calculation,
    272–273
Average days to sell inventory, calculation, 337

B

Bad debts, 257–263
    aging method, 261–262
    allowance method, 258–263
    contingent loss, 464
    direct write-off method, 258
    expense, 260–261, 274
    management perspective, 263
    seller avoidance, 265
Balances, financial measures, 634
Balance sheet, 9, 32
Balances, transfer, 151
Bank borrowing, notes payable, 454–455
Bank credit cards, factoring form, 264–265
Bank of Montreal (BMO), 745
Bank reconciliation, 208
    impact, 214–215
    performing, steps, 212–214
Bank statement, 210e
    accounting records reconciliation, 208–215
    balance, development sources, 209
    cash balance, 212
Barnes & Noble, bricks and mortar, 202
Basic Accounting equation, 10–11
    business transactions, effect, 94
    dual effect, 73
    expanded basic accounting equation, 71e
    usage, 10–11
    writing, 72
Basket purchases, 387
Beginning inventory, 313
BizStats, 760

BlackBerry, true value, 409
Black, Conrad, 198
Board of directors, integrity/attitude/awareness/
    actions, 201
Bond payable, 7, 14
Bonds, 503
    accounting, 506–507
    amortization, effective interest rate method,
        699–700
    callable bonds, 504
    carrying value, 509
    cash inflows (outflows), 506e
    convertible bonds, 505
    discount, 507–508, 511–512
    face value, 507–510
    foreign currency denominated bonds,
        505–506
    interest payments, premium/discount sale, 514–
        519
    issuance, discount level, 517e
    junk bonds, 504
    market value, 504, 532–533
    monthly installment payment schedule, 522e
    mortgage bonds, 504
    premium, 507–508, 512–513
    purchase, 701
    regular interest payments, par sale, 510–513
    sale (discount level), straight-line method
        (usage), 515–516
    secured bonds, 504
    types, 504–506
    unsecured bonds, 504
    value balance, straight-line/effective interest
        methods (usage), 514e
    zero coupon bonds, 520–521
Bonds at maturity, redeeming, 521
Bonds before maturity, redeeming, 521
Bonds payable, 503–506
    carrying value, 517e, 519e
    issuance, 533
    market price, calculation, 535
    premium/discount amortization, 534
    pricing, 531
    retirement, 521
Book value (carrying value), 388, 393, 509
Boston Pizza, financial accounting example,
    447
Bounced cheque, 212
Bre-X Minerals Ltd., 198
Bricks and mortar, 202
Bristol-Myers Squibb, channel stuffing
    allegations payments, 319
Buildings
    basket purchases, 387
    property, plant, and equipment asset, 383
Business
    activities, 626e, 631–632
    combinations, 712–713, 715
    commitments, 464–465
    financing activities, 7
    forms, 5–6
    investing activities, 7
    lawsuits, 463–464
    operating activities, 7–8

organization, forms, 5–6, 6e, 32
    personnel policies/practices, 201
    withholding/payroll taxes, 458–459
Business activities, 5, 6–8, 203
    identification, 32
    measurement, 69–71
    relationships, 7e
Business process risks, 202–203

C

Caesars Windsor, 197, 203, 207
Callable bonds, 504
Call provisions (redeemable), 569
Canada Business Corporations Act (CBCA), 566,
    570
Canada Pension Plan (CPP), 458
Canada Post Corporation, 129
Canadian Income Tax Act, 469
Canadian Institute of Chartered Accountants
    (CICA), 30
Canadian Securities Administration (CSA), 198
Canadian Tire Corporation, Limited
    accounts payable turnover ratio, 747–748
    annual report, excerpt, 324–325
    asset turnover ratio, 748
    cash reporting, statement of financial position,
        218e
    common dividends, payment, 755
    common size statement of earnings, 731
    comprehensive income statement, 28e
    consolidated financial statements, notes,
        453e
    consolidated statements of earnings, 725,
        732–733, 735
    consolidated statements of financial position,
        734, 735–736
    cost of sales, decrease, 736
    dividends, payment, 754
    earnings per share, 754
    financial accounting, 3, 725
    financial highlights, 725
    financial statements, 586e, 587e, 730, 737
    gross profit margin percentage, 729
    gross profit percentage, 750
    internal credit cards, usage, 265
    inventory, 310
    multiple-step statement of earnings, 22e
    net profit margin percentage, 751
    operating margin percentage, 751
    quality of earnings ratio, 752
    return on assets, 751, 757
    return on equity, 752
    statement of cash flows, 26e
    statement of changes in equity, 24e
    statement of earnings, 19e, 741e–742e
    statement of financial position, 11, 13e,
        741e–742e
Canadian Tire Petroleum, 3
Capital, 15
    expenditures, 401, 416
    requirements, 219
    share capital, balances, 82e
    stated capital, 572
    working capital, 17

TYPICAL CHART OF ACCOUNTS

ASSETS

Accounts Receivable
Accumulated Depletion
Accumulated Depreciation
Allowance for Doubtful Accounts
Allowance to Adjust Available-For-Sale Securities to Market
Allowance to Adjust Trading Securities to Market
Buildings
Cash
Copyright
Equipment
Finished Goods Inventory
Franchise
Furniture
Goodwill
Interest Receivable
Inventory
Investments
Investments—Available-For-Sale Securities
Investments—Equity Method
Investments—Trading Securities
Land
Leased Assets
Leasehold Improvements
Natural Resources
Notes Receivable
Other Assets
Patent
Petty Cash
Prepaid Advertising
Prepaid Insurance
Prepaid Rent
Prepaid Repairs & Maintenance
Prepaid Security Services
Raw Materials Inventory
Rent Receivable
Supplies
Tax Refund Receivable
Trademark
Trucks
Work-in-Process Inventory

LIABILITIES

Accounts Payable
Bonds Payable
Canada Pension and Employment Insurance Payable
Capital Lease Liability
Charitable Contributions Payable
Commissions Payable
Discount on Bonds Payable
Discount on Notes Payable
Dividends Payable
Employee Tax Payable
GST and HST Taxes Payable
Income Tax Payable
Interest Payable
Lawsuit Payable
Lease Liability
Notes Payable
Premium on Bonds Payable
Premium on Notes Payable
Property Tax Payable
Rent Payable
Repairs & Maintenance Payable
Royalties Payable
Salaries Payable
Sales Tax Payable
Unearned Rent Revenue
Unearned Sales Revenue
Unearned Service Revenue
Union Dues Payable
Utilities Payable
Wages Payable
Warranty Liability

SHAREHOLDERS' EQUITY

Accumulated Other Comprehensive Income
Common Shares
Contributed Surplus
Preferred Shares
Retained Earnings
Unrealized Gain (Loss) on Available-For-Sale Securities

EQUITY-RELATED ACCOUNTS

Dividends Declared
Income Summary

REVENUES/GAINS

Dividend Income
Interest Income
Investment Income—Equity Method
Rent Revenue
Sales Discounts
Sales Returns and Allowances
Sales Revenue
Service Revenue

Gain on Disposal of Property, Plant, & Equipment
Gain on Sale of Intangibles
Gain on Sale of Investments
Gain on Settlement of Lawsuit
Unrealized Gain (Loss) on Trading Securities

EXPENSES/LOSSES

Advertising Expense
Amortization Expense
Artist Fee Expense
Bad Debt Expense
Bank Service Charge Expense
Cash Over and Short
Commissions Expense
Cost of Goods Sold
Delivery Expense
Depreciation Expense
Employee Benefit Expense
Income Tax Expense
Insurance Expense
Interest Expense
Legal Expense
Miscellaneous Expense
Organizational Costs
Other Expense
Postage Expense
Property Tax Expense

Purchase Allowances
Purchase Discounts
Purchase Returns
Purchases
Rent Expense
Repairs & Maintenance Expense
Research and Development Expense
Royalties Expense
Salaries Expense
Security Services Expense
Service Charge Expense
Supplies Expense
Transportation-In
Unemployment Tax Expense
Utilities Expense
Wages Expense
Warranty Expense

Loss from Impairment
Loss on Disposal of Property, Plant, & Equipment
Loss on Sale of Intangibles
Loss on Sale of Investments

Note:

The Chart of Accounts for this edition of *Cornerstones of Financial Accounting* has been simplified and standardized throughout all hypothetical in-chapter examples and end-of-chapter assignments in order to strengthen the pedagogical structure of the book. Account titles for real company financial statements will vary. Common alternative account titles are given in the textbook where the account is introduced, as appropriate, and real financial statement excerpts are included to help familiarize readers with alternative account titles.

When additional information is needed for an account title, it will be shown in parentheses after the title [e.g., Accumulated Depreciation (Equipment) and Canada Pension Plan Payable (Employer)].

This Chart of Accounts is listed alphabetically by category for ease of reference. However, accounts in the textbook and in real financial statements are listed in order of liquidity.